Skepticism and American Faith

Skepticism and American Faith

From the Revolution to the Civil War

CHRISTOPHER GRASSO

OXFORD
UNIVERSITY PRESS

Oxford University Press is a department of the University of Oxford.
It furthers the University's objective of excellence in research, scholarship,
and education by publishing worldwide. Oxford is a registered trade mark of
Oxford University Press in the UK and certain other countries.

Published in the United States of America by Oxford University Press
198 Madison Avenue, New York, NY 10016, United States of America.

© Oxford University Press 2018

All rights reserved. No part of this publication may be reproduced,
stored in a retrieval system, or transmitted, in any form or by any means,
without the prior permission in writing of Oxford University Press,
or as expressly permitted by law, by license, or under terms agreed with
the appropriate reproduction rights organization. Inquiries concerning
reproduction outside the scope of the above should be sent to the
Rights Department, Oxford University Press, at the address above.

You must not circulate this work in any other form
and you must impose this same condition on any acquirer.

Library of Congress Cataloging-in-Publication Data
Names: Grasso, Christopher, author.
Title: Skepticism and American faith : from the Revolution to the Civil War /
Christopher Grasso.
Description: New York : Oxford University Press, 2018. |
Includes bibliographical references and index. |
Identifiers: LCCN 2017038186 (print) | LCCN 2017058966 (ebook) |
ISBN 9780190494384 (Updf) | ISBN 9780190494391 (Epub) |
ISBN 9780190494377 (hardcover : alk. paper)
Subjects: LCSH: United States—Church history—19th century. | United
States—Church history—18th century. | Skepticism—United States—19th
century. | Skepticism—United States—18th century. | United
States—Religion—19th century. | United States—Religion—18th century.
Classification: LCC BR525 (ebook) | LCC BR525 .G665 2018 (print) |
DDC 277.3/081—dc23
LC record available at https://lccn.loc.gov/2017038186

1 3 5 7 9 8 6 4 2
Printed by Sheridan Books, Inc., United States of America

For Karin

CONTENTS

Note on Sources   ix

Introduction   1

PART ONE   REVOLUTIONS, 1775–1815

1. Deist Hero, Deist Monster: On Religious Common Sense in the Wake of the American Revolution   25
2. Souls Rising: The Authority of the Inner Witness, and Its Limits   65
3. Instituting Skepticism: The Emergence of Organized Deism   97
4. Instituting Skepticism: Contention, Endurance, and Invisibility   118

PART TWO   ENLIGHTENMENTS, 1790–1840

5. Skeptical Enlightenment: An American Education in Jeffersonian Pennsylvania   159
6. Christian Enlightenment: Eastern Cities and the Great West   193
7. Christian Enlightenment: Faith into Practice in Marion, Missouri   227
8. Revelation and Reason: New Englanders in the Early Nineteenth Century   250

PART THREE   REFORMS, 1820–1850

9. Faith in Reform: Remaking Society, Body, and Soul   279

10. Infidels, Protestants, and Catholics: Religion and Reform in Boston   323
11. Converting Skeptics: Infidel and Protestant Economies   357

PART FOUR   SACRED CAUSES, 1830–1865

12. Political Hermeneutics: Nullifying the Bible and Consolidating Proslavery Christianity   397
13. Lived Experience and the Sacred Cause: Faith, Skepticism, and Civil War   441

Epilogue: Death and Politics   480

Appendix: Grounds of Faith and Modes of Skepticism   493
Acknowledgments   507
Notes   511
References   593
Index   633

NOTE ON SOURCES

I have preserved spelling, capitalization, and punctuation from the original sources. In a very few instances, I have supplied clarifications within brackets. Full citations of the primary sources appear in the notes. Citations of secondary sources are shortened in the notes, with full bibliographic information available in the references list.

Skepticism and American Faith

Introduction

The SCEPTIC and the CHRISTIAN, Robert Dale Owen and Origen Bacheler, argued for ten months in the pages of the *Free Enquirer*, a freethought newspaper, in 1831. Their discussion articulates many of the major issues marking the relationship of skepticism and faith from the era of the American Revolution to the Civil War, when these two terms were used to organize a field of thought and experience the way the poles of a magnet arrange metal shavings tossed onto a piece of paper. "I was brought up by a kind and strictly religious mother, in the very lap of orthodoxy," the SCEPTIC wrote. But the more he read and reflected, the more convinced he became that nature was "silent regarding the doings, the attributes, nay the existence of a God." Turning away from the "ghostly dreams and disquieting imaginations" of the churches, he felt freed from religious anxiety. He stepped forward publicly as the SCEPTIC to challenge religious dogmas so that others might be freed, too. The CHRISTIAN countered: "It was once my unhappy lot to be for a time a Sceptic." But then he became convinced that the Bible really was the Word of God, and that God's Spirit was at work in his soul and in the world. He thought it his duty to help others similarly free themselves from the "snare" of skepticism.

Each man knew that beneath the intellectual debate they were conducting about the existence of God, the nature of humanity, and the possibility of revelation ran a current of personal psychological experience. But each knew, too, how the concerns about religious skepticism and faith also flooded over and transformed a much broader social, economic, and political landscape. Religion was not just false, the SCEPTIC argued, but dangerous. "It excites fears that are without foundation; it consumes valuable time that can never be recalled, and valuable talents that ought to be better employed; it draws money from the layman to support a deception; it teaches the elect to look upon their less favored fellow creatures as heathen men and publicans, living in sin here and doomed to perdition hereafter; it awakens harassing doubts, gloomy despondency and fitful melancholy; it turns our thoughts from the things of this world, where alone true knowledge is to be found: worse than all, it chains us down to antiquated orthodoxy and forbids the free discussion of those very subjects which it most concerns us to discuss. If such a religion be a deception, its votaries are slaves."

The CHRISTIAN answered that the fears that religion excited were necessary to keep bad people in check. And religion had other crucial social benefits. "The time, talents, and money devoted to the subject, are vastly overbalanced by the good effects on society, to say nothing of futurity. Thus it is of immense advantage to the world in a temporal point of view. It does *not* turn our thoughts from social duties, but affords a most powerful incentive to vigilance therein. It does *not* forbid the discussion of *any* subject, or hold us back from following *truth*, lead where she may; but, on the contrary, it directs us to 'prove *all* things, and *hold fast* that which is good.' "

Time and money; power and persecution; freedom and obligation; blindness and insight: the stakes for a society, for a people, were high.[1]

The Personal and the Political

His family and friends thought he was dying, so a local minister came to ask the pale, sick young man questions about his faith. A divinity student, he gave orthodox answers to the pastor's questions about doctrine—orthodox for his mid-eighteenth-century New England town, where something like Puritan piety still passed for religious common sense. Even on what he thought might be his deathbed, though, he could not reveal his secret: he had long been wandering in what he would later call the "cloudy darksome valley" of religious skepticism. His skeptical turn had not been prompted by a public debate or even by private conversations with friends or acquaintances. He had internalized the dialogue of skepticism and faith from his reading. As an intellectually voracious college student and then a tutor he had read not just the standard Puritan divines but their liberal and deist critics, as well as the new enlightened philosophy and science. His studies had forced him to confront an awful, unspeakable idea: What if the Bible was not the revealed word of God after all? What if Christianity, like other religions, was merely "nothing but priestcraft and artificial error?"[2]

Ezra Stiles recovered from his illness, returned to his faith, and eventually became a clergyman. But after the American Revolution he watched with grave concern as other doubters came out of the closet and started to achieve positions of social prestige and political power. This development was especially worrisome at a time when states were reframing the relationship between religion and government. Few critics of Christianity were as outspoken as Ethan Allen, the Revolutionary War hero from Vermont who published *Reason, the Only Oracle of Man* in 1785, a book that urged readers to discard the warped theologies derived from ancient biblical fables. Yet Stiles saw dangerous trends in voters who were indifferent to a candidate's religious opinions and opposed to the state patronizing Christianity. From his own experience and from his observation of the broader national scene, he understood that the relationship of religious skepticism and faith was at once an intellectual concern and a matter of personal psychological struggle, a pressing social issue and a potentially explosive political problem for the new American republic.

On the eve of the Civil War, the relationship of skepticism and faith was still fraught—intellectually, psychologically, socially, and politically. A young teacher in Alabama wanted to believe but doubted the claims of the Bible and the Christian churches. She had read the new biblical criticism from Germany that seemed to expose the scriptural accounts as myths, the Romantics who tried to reenvision Christianity by reducing it to poetic truth, and the Transcendental philosophers who turned to worship a divinity in man and nature. But more fundamentally, she chafed at a Christian culture that cast women as particularly sinful and powerless. Mag Barclay—the alter ego of author Alice Hayes Mellen in the autobiographical novel *The Female Skeptic* (1859)—ultimately learns how to vanquish doubt and pride through submissive love. The romance, though, is also a parable about the Union during the sectional crisis. Mag the feisty Northerner realizes that she must channel her reformist energy into conservative patriarchal and proslavery forms, submitting to the biblical authority of her Southern husband and coming to terms with slavery as a necessary evil in God's plan for America.

As it was for Stiles, the triumph of faith in *The Female Skeptic* is the key to private, social, and national happiness. Ethan Allen in the 1780s and John R. Kelso, a Methodist minister in Missouri who renounced his faith in the 1850s and fought Confederate guerrillas during the Civil War, argued instead that Americans needed to use skeptical criticism to finally "break the bonds of superstition" in order to be free. These are just four voices in a cacophonous dialogue whose polarized extremes mask the fact that the experience even of those who stepped forward to debate was usually an oscillation between varieties of doubting and believing.[3]

For spiritual power and authority, Christians looked up to God through His Word, they looked to fellow followers of Christ as they built Christian communities, and they looked within themselves for the work of the Holy Spirit. But skepticism attacked the authenticity of the scriptures. It challenged the idea that either the special love that Christians shared or the historical success of the church attested to the truth of doctrine. It contested the notion that subjective experience could evidence contact with things supernatural and divine. This was the framework of experience, discussion, and debate for Stiles and Allen at the birth of the Republic; it remained the basic framework as Mellen and Kelso watched the Republic begin to unravel.

Only from a considerable distance, though, can Stiles's experiences in the Yale college library, the quasi-fictional Mag's on an Alabama plantation, Allen's in a Vermont tavern, and Kelso's at a revival campsite in backwoods Missouri be called similar. The problem of skepticism and faith in the United States from the 1770s to the 1860s needs to be seen not just as a contest of opposing ideas but as lived experiences: lived religion, and lived irreligion, too. This book examines how individual people moved back and forth on the continuum of skepticism and faith, as well as between engagement and indifference. It attends to what they said and asks how their faithful or skeptical attitudes played out in the daily practices of their complicated personal, social, and political lives in their specific communities.

To consider skepticism and faith on the ground and in the lives of eighteenth- and nineteenth-century Americans goes beyond the confines of traditional intellectual history.[4] The struggles of skepticism and faith can be found even where they are least expected: in the diaries of a Freewill Baptist preacher in Vermont during the first years of the nineteenth century, for example, or hidden in plain sight among the prolific publications of a health reformer in the 1840s. The accumulation of such stories—not just as religious biographies but as tiles in a larger mosaic of American cultural politics—suggests that the skeptical habits that converted believers struggled with lingered in the broader society as well. By the time Abraham Lincoln had turned from his earlier skepticism to see himself as an instrument of Providence, and Christian soldiers in North and South marched off to war, the triumph of American faith over deists, infidels, and doubters might seem complete. But the nature of that faith, the manner of its apparent triumph, and the character of the skepticism that had only been temporarily quieted by the noise of war had all been shaped by the preceding decades of dialogue.[5]

The tense dialogue of skepticism and faith did evolve, however much the closet dramas of Ezra Stiles the eighteenth-century clergyman and Mag Barclay the antebellum female skeptic might seem to share the same basic plot. In Mag's America, though a *female* skeptic was considered a "monster," a violation of feminine nature, skeptical arguments against traditional religious claims about God, humanity, and revealed truth were considerably more common in the masculine world than they were in Stiles's day. The American faith that Mag hoped would reunify North and South was necessarily much vaguer than the Trinitarian Protestantism that Stiles had hoped would unite the country after the Revolution. It was a faith stripped of nearly all doctrinal content save love for a divine Father and a trust that fellow Christians could quietly, privately work out their own salvation on their own terms. It was a faith that manifested a sentimental reverence for biblical authority while at the same time trying to keep scripturally grounded disputes from curdling social relations or poisoning political debate. It was a faith, in other words, however emotionally satisfying in private life, that as a public ideology seems to have been hollowed out by the very skeptical critiques it claimed to have vanquished.[6]

Hiding Doubt and Silencing Skepticism

Both the CHRISTIAN and the SCEPTIC assumed that religious skepticism was far more pervasive than the number of uncloseted, vocal "infidels" would suggest. The SCEPTIC attributed the silence of most skeptics to the power of Christian persecution. Because a Christian majority shamed, shunned, and punished doubters, the "progress of orthodoxy is ostentatiously announced; the progress of heterodoxy is rapid but silent. A conversion to Christianity is trumpeted all over Christendom; a conversion to scepticism is hardly whispered to one's next door neighbor." The CHRISTIAN instead thought that so many skeptics kept their doubts hidden because they lacked moral courage.[7]

Readers of the standard religious histories of the period, however, might wonder if there was even much religious skepticism for Owen and Bacheler to be arguing about. At about the same time that the SCEPTIC and the CHRISTIAN published their *Discussion*, Alexis de Tocqueville wrote in *Democracy in America* that Americans were skeptical about everything *but* religion. Many commentators in the years since have echoed Tocqueville. The United States, where churches thrive, supernaturalism sells, and spirituality can trump other issues at the ballot box, has long been considered the Western world's exception to the secularization and disenchantment that was commonly thought to attend modernity. Historical explanations during the Cold War looked to the nation's supposed Puritan heritage. Interpretations at the end of the twentieth century focused instead on the decades after 1776. In the early Republic, according to one prominent account, American Christianity was democratized, its surge of religious revivals revealing a religious movement that absorbed and redirected the radical, egalitarian, populist, individualistic energies of the Revolution. In the early nineteenth century, according to another, as proselytizers vigorously competed for adherents in a denominational free market, a higher proportion of Americans formed closer associations with Christian institutions, ideas, and practices than ever before. According to a third, Americans created a powerful intellectual synthesis fusing republican political ideology, Common Sense moral reasoning, and evangelical Protestantism. A rich and deep literature shows us how the evangelicalism that emerged from what is mislabeled the "Second Great Awakening" shaped the politics of the second party system; how activist Protestantism fueled the great movements for social reform; how religious faith and scriptural argument underpinned proslavery, antislavery, and every conceivable moral argument; how Christian views of Providence and Creation dictated understandings of nature, history, and progress; and how pious sentimentalism was the beating heart of family life. Christianity refined the genteel, rocked the cradle of the middle class, and provided both comfort and a language of resistance for the poor, the oppressed, and the enslaved.[8]

But in the early twenty-first century the tangle of American commitments to democracy, capitalism, and religious faith emerging out of the first fourscore and seven years of the nation's existence deserves another look. If the United States had long troubled the theoretical distinctions between the "religious" and the "secular" that seemed to fit Western Europe, now these categories seem dubious not just for America but in general, not just for the postmodern present but for the past, too. Rather than categories helping to describe the development of modern society, the "religious" and the "secular" are labels that risk distorting the meaning of historical evidence. Paying more attention to what people in the past actually said and the relationship between how they talked and how they lived may reveal different conclusions about broader transformations—and continuities—in American society and culture.[9]

Religious skepticism has been rendered nearly invisible by histories that stress the era's overbearing "evangelicalism," or the "secularization" happening behind people's backs, or the assumption that skepticism was for intellectuals, while ordinary people who stayed away from church were merely indifferent. The standard historical accounts might give a nod to heterodox Enlightenment ideas in the late eighteenth century that would soon be swept away by the evangelical tsunami, and perhaps glance at a few fringe figures who continued to bob for air in its wake. Some of the Founding Fathers—notably Benjamin Franklin and Thomas Jefferson—were deists who believed in a Creator and in morals derived from nature but not in the divinity of either the Bible or Jesus. While these gentlemen tried to keep their heterodox views to themselves, small groups of other deists, inspired by Thomas Paine's *Age of Reason* (1794), organized a few deistical societies and published newspapers in the late eighteenth and early nineteenth centuries. The socioeconomic transformations wrought by new markets and new modes of industrial production after 1815 launched a new generation of social and religious radicalism. From the mid-1820s to about 1840, some social reformers identified themselves as religious skeptics and freethinkers—or "free enquirers"—who doubted or denied most of Christianity's claims about God, man, and salvation. As with the deists, the free enquirers' energies were divided between criticizing traditional (supernatural) religion and trying to offer an alternate vision. By the mid-nineteenth century, though, even that fringe threat of organized freethought had faded.[10]

Christians called the skeptical deists, free inquirers, and doubting seekers "infidels," a pejorative term that some would proudly adopt. Certainly the efforts of these small groups of infidels were dwarfed by the legions conducting religious revivals, creating missions and moral reform societies, distributing Bibles and Christian tracts, and building churches across the land. Just as certainly, though, the experiences and beliefs that these infidels embraced and that many other people wrestled with have been overshadowed by the dominant narratives of the nation's religious past. Even if few Americans publicly challenged Christian truth claims, the reasons why and how the skeptical critique continued to haunt American Christianity need to be explained.[11]

More significantly, many observers in the early Republic looked beyond the strident infidels to note the entanglement of skepticism and faith as a central issue in American culture. In 1840, Orestes Brownson, sounding like the SCEP-TIC a decade earlier or Ezra Stiles in the 1780s, argued that "there is not much open scepticism, not much avowed infidelity, but there is a vast amount" that "[is] concealed" and "untold." Other commentators came to similar conclusions. One in the 1820s believed that "the number of decided infidels, is probably much more limited than that of a sort of skeptic who are content to remain suspended in doubt whether the Christian revelation is true or false," but who for the time being continued to respect Christianity as the custom of the country and an amiable superstition. A decade later, the *Christian Secretary* prepared a series of articles attacking skepticism and infidelity because the editors agreed with that central point. A long essay in the *Spirit of the Pilgrims* focused not on outspoken freethinkers or closeted skeptics but on the way that doubt could hollow out Christianity from within. Newfangled ideas encouraged Christians to doubt one traditional doctrine, qualify a second, and throw out a third, until believers had "been gradually and unconsciously drawn away from their old belief.... They begin with doubting; they next give up, and are finally in danger of ending in the disbelief of almost everything but that they are themselves very exemplary believers." In the 1850s and early 1860s, commentators worried about English translations popularizing German biblical criticism and philosophy; they also began to be anxious that the skeptical habits of scientific inquiry were "impinging on the religious beliefs of the Christian public."[12]

Because of the entanglement of skepticism and faith, then, seasoning the narrative of American religious history with the stories of a few vocal freethinkers is not enough. Self-proclaimed deists, skeptics, and freethinkers were so threatening because they gave voice to the doubts Christians had about their own faith or about the fidelity of the fellow in the next pew. Putting skepticism back into the story of American religious history in this period involves attending to both the "not much" skepticism that was open and avowed and the "vast amount" that observers insisted was hidden and silenced. Certainly the specter of the dangerous infidel threatening the religious foundations of society was conjured by paranoid Christians and put to work by cynical politicians. Some did anxiously exaggerate the threat, such as the Calvinist apologists who blamed Universalists for destroying the grounds of faith, and the Universalists who blamed Calvinists for the same. Others exploited popular fears of anti-Christian subversives, such as the Federalists who tried to link Jefferson's deism and the horrors of the French Revolution to Republicanism, or the Whigs who later tried to tar the Workingmen's movement with religious infidelity. But the story of the relationship of skepticism and faith is more than the tale of a few marginalized freethinkers and artificially induced moral panics. Religious skepticism touched—and in some cases transformed—many more lives than we might expect in the early American republic.

Framing the Discussion

What is "religion?" What is "skepticism?" Robert Dale Owen, writing in the early 1830s as the SCEPTIC, argued that theological terms like "religion" and "God" were often ambiguous or meaningless, and he tried to clarify what he, at least, was talking about. "I speak here of *Revealed Religion*; that is, of *a belief in supernatural beings, one or many, to whom worship and obedience is rendered*; and not of ethical codes or moral precepts.... I speak not of other religions than our own [Christianity], because I am, in a measure, unacquainted with the details of their history." The CHRISTIAN, Origen Bacheler, argued that the "skeptical" position actually collapsed into either deism or atheism despite the so-called skeptic's attempt to sit on the fence, or, even more often, the term signified nothing at all: "No doubt if the truth were known, many of those converts who pass under the name of Sceptics, would... be found to have 'no fixed opinions of any kind.'" The two positions—skeptical inquirer and religious believer—were easier to recognize socially and colloquially than to sharply define in formal debate.[13]

"I am an unfortunate being called a sceptic," wrote a correspondent to Robert Dale Owen's *Free Enquirer* in 1830, "...which word, I learn from the dictionary, to mean *one who doubts*. 'Doubts what?' said I, and my church going neighbors replied, 'what is taught in the churches.'" Learning from natural history that whales had small gullets, he had concluded that the biblical story of Jonah being swallowed by a whale must be a fable akin to Jack and the Beanstalk. Perhaps the other biblical stories, and Christianity itself, were fables, too? It makes little sense to try to root this writer, who was "young in both years and learning," too carefully in a specific philosophical tradition. In such lower-altitude discussions, the term "skeptic" was applied to those who doubted the primary grounds of Christian faith—the Bible, the church, or personal spiritual experience—and were persistently unpersuaded by the foundational claims of their churchgoing neighbors.[14]

The passive voice—how skepticism "was applied" or "was discussed"—reflects a generalization about how language operated and concepts were formed. But it masks who had more power in such dialogues and was usually able to set the terms of discussion and debate. The writer signed his letter as "Sceptic," which was "the name pinned to me by my neighbors." They did not pin the label upon him as someone who questioned the abstract category of "religion" but specifically as a person who doubted "what is taught in the churches." Still, calling him a skeptic meant something different than calling him unorthodox or a heretic. He was not challenging mainstream belief with an alternate religious vision, as a Jew, a Muslim, a Mormon, or a pagan. Using a simple fact about the natural world to wonder if the biblical stories were fables and to doubt "what is taught in the churches" put him outside "religion" entirely—not just from the perspective of the churchgoing neighbors but for the Young Sceptic himself, who recognized that he was being labeled as something "sinful" and "dangerous."

Then as now, "religion" was a contested term, but some of the players in this contest had considerably more power and authority than others. If the Young Sceptic had also consulted his dictionary for an authoritative definition of religion, he would have found it described from the perspective of Christian theology: religion "in its most comprehensive sense" included "a belief in the being and perfections of God, in the revelations of his will to man, of man's obligation to obey his commands, in a state of rewards and punishments, and in man's accountableness to God; and also true godliness or piety of life, with the practice of all moral duties."[15] Had he turned to an encyclopedia as well, he might have found a newer, less explicitly Christian, comparative definition, though it was built from the scaffolding of theism: it explained that the term signified duties performed for "one or more superior beings" who were believed to "govern the world," and upon whom, the religious person believed, "the happiness or misery of mankind ultimately rests."[16] By the time the Young Sceptic wrote to the newspaper in 1830, some who were called or called themselves "liberals" began to chafe against such parochial understandings of religion and what it meant to be religious. They tried to cast off the references to superhuman beings and broaden the definition of religion to mean, for example, "'the tendency of human nature to the Infinite'...manifested in the pursuit of perfection in any direction whatever." Such transcendent ideals could be marked as "sacred" and thought to create dispositions in people that oriented them in the world and offered a meaningful path through life—intensifying joy, perhaps, or helping them confront suffering. If religion could be defined so broadly as to include any such orienting ultimate concerns, then even those pinned as skeptics by their churchgoing neighbors could be legitimately called "religious," too.[17]

Most Christians would have none of this. If merely the tendency of human beings to try to perfect themselves was "religion," one wrote, then "the 'pursuit of perfection' in the art of rope-dancing is religion."[18] Christians argued among themselves about how religion connected knowledge, belief, sentiment, and practice. But they insisted that it primarily and fundamentally invoked man's relationship to God. "Natural" religion—what human beings could discern about this relationship using only their natural faculties, without the Bible or Christian teaching—was at best incomplete and more often dangerously confused. Other attempts to worship and obey the Divine Being (or, mistakenly, beings) were actual religions but false ones, they argued. Nontheistic ways of finding allegedly meaningful paths through life did not deserve to be dignified by the label "religion" at all. True religion, these dominant voices in eighteenth- and nineteenth-century American discussion contended, was recognizably Christian: God and the Bible, souls and the church. One needed not just ideals to motivate ethical action but an all-powerful being who would reward and punish and a savior who could pardon the sins of flawed creatures; not just forces to admire in nature but a Father to love and obey as a child loves and obeys his parent. Only such a religion could connect cosmic order and the depths of an individual soul, and could link even the lives of the poorest and meekest to the grand meaning of human existence and history.

Yet when discussing the importance of Christianity to American society at large, most commentators focused less on the term "religion" than on "faith." A deist writer in 1804 complained that "religion," as commonly understood, was "a complex idea compounded of three things totally distinct from each other": rituals, metaphysical propositions, and moral codes. Perhaps champions of a Christian America preferred to speak of "faith" rather than "religion" because the latter suggested instituted modes of worship and other practices—precisely those things that the First Amendment seemed to say that the government could not establish. Defenders of a faith-based society wanted to confirm the link between metaphysical propositions and morality without getting tangled in denominational and political debates about proper forms of worship. One writer in 1837 noted that "to mention the word religion in connection with politics" stigmatized one "as the enemy of free institutions, of the rights of man, and, of course, of the rights of conscience" and conjured "all the horrors of the Inquisition." The primary line of defense against skeptical critique, therefore, was usually a vague invocation of religious *faith*—a trust and confidence in divine direction—that was said to undergird not just particular denominational affiliations but basic morality and virtuous American citizenship. This basic American faith, often hailed as the bedrock of American society, usually resembled a kind of lowest-common-denominator Protestantism, as Catholics and others liked to point out.[19]

The relationship of skepticism and faith framed the discussion—and the experience—of the Young Sceptic and his churchgoing neighbors. People argued about the different grounds of faith and distinguished different modes of skepticism (topics treated at further length in the appendix). In general, skepticism was more than fleeting doubt; it was doubt highly reflective, intellectually elaborated, perhaps regularized as a default attitude, and directed specifically toward the claims of religious faith. But if more than doubt, skepticism was less than "secularism," at least not the explicitly nonreligious cultural program promoted under that name after 1851 in Britain by George Jacob Holyoake. As a modern scholar has recently written, "Skepticism (of the nonepistemological variety, epistemological skeptics positing that knowledge is impossible) is merely another name for agnosticism"—"agnosticism" being a term coined by Thomas Henry Huxley in 1869. The Young Sceptic in 1830 may have doubted the authenticity of the Bible, the reliability of his neighbors' allegedly spiritual experiences, or even the existence of God without necessarily being able to envision or articulate an alternate way of being in the world. Religious commentators answered this skepticism with appeals to faith. The faith they invoked was more than mere belief in a set of ideas about God and humanity, the world and history; it was also a personal attitude of trust or confidence associated with those ideas. Faith was more than belief but less than religion, the latter including the elaboration of "practical duties" such as worship and other obligated behaviors proceeding from the relationship to God.[20]

Debate, Dialogue, and American History

The CHRISTIAN and the SCEPTIC, Bacheler and Owen, described their early 1830s *Discussion* as a debate, a contest between two champions of opposing positions. "No subject is thoroughly investigated, and settled on an immoveable basis," the CHRISTIAN wrote, "till it has been assailed at every point, and has met and repelled its assailant at full strength; till on it the belligerents have met, and measured swords, and done their mightiest." The SCEPTIC used similar terms. But the two also described their exchange as a dialogue, a more open-ended inquiry. "Let us therefore, like rational creatures," the CHRISTIAN urged, "calmly approach these subjects, not to *overthrow* or *upbuild* this, that, or the other, but to examine, to investigate, to *see how things are*." The SCEPTIC assured his interlocutor that he wanted to seek truth wherever it could be found, "within the pale of orthodoxy or without it; in religion or in skepticism; under the form of popular virtue or of moral heresy; in the histories of all ranks as of all countries. My single object is, not to find truth in this creed or in that system, not in the code of one country or the customs of another, but, wherever it be, to find it."[21]

Debaters expect a decisive outcome, as with two gladiators battling in an arena. The CHRISTIAN in particular imagined his readers as an audience of judges, each of whom would determine a winner and a loser. He believed that the debate, as with advocates in a courtroom or legislators in Congress, ought to produce an outcome. Actual debates between skeptics and believers were sometimes staged as public performances, as when Robert Dale Owen's father, the freethinking Scottish industrialist and reformer Robert Owen, debated the Rev. Alexander Campbell (Disciples of Christ) for eight days in Cincinnati in 1829, or when Dr. William Sleigh defended Christianity against a tag-team of infidels in a six-evening New York City debate in 1835. In both cases, the audience at the conclusion was asked to choose a winner (the public show of support for Christianity was unanimous in the second debate and nearly so in the first).[22]

Yet the SCEPTIC's and the CHRISTIAN's adherence to the principles of free inquiry, and the give-and-take of the discussion as it progressed, nudged their exchanges more toward an open-ended dialogue. They did not strictly adhere to the fiction that a discussion has two, rather than many, sides. The performance did not simply rehearse arguments leading to a predictable conclusion: the triumph of one position over the other, as Truth over Falsehood. Nor was the dialogue a dialectic that produced a neat synthesis of the preceding thesis and antithesis. A dialogue could be a process of inquiry that was itself, as the SCEPTIC wrote, a worthy voyage of discovery "beyond the inland sea of our own sect or party," where we become "citizens of the world of opinion" by making acquaintance "with other beliefs besides our own" and being "introduced to more doctrines than we have been cradled in."[23]

Similarly, the broader discussion of skepticism and faith in American culture from the nation's founding to its great crisis in the 1860s had the character of both debate and dialogue, with partisans squaring off in contests that tried to simplify a set of more complex conversations and experiences. These public debates and dialogues, too, were, in part, representations of personal psychological experiences that were projected into the social realm or public sphere. Once there, they could also be internalized, creating, as the theorists of the dialogical self like to say, voices and positions in the landscape of individual minds.[24]

What provoked such discussions about skepticism and faith in the first place—whether in formally staged debates, dialogues in print, fireside conversations, or even in the minds of Americans who quietly pondered these questions? The CHRISTIAN thought that they arose from both natural inclination and moral obligation. Rational beings like to think, and social beings like to share their thoughts. And about the most vital of all topics—the meaning of life and the fate of the soul—they ought to articulate their reasons for belief or disbelief to each other, he argued. Moral beings, in addition, ought to support the cause of truth, and discussion and debate strengthened their own grasp of truth while helping to enlighten the ignorant, rouse the indifferent, and persuade the skeptical. Because the CHRISTIAN thought that religious belief and faith were so crucial to moral practice, he believed that the discussion ultimately served to better lives both in this world and in the next.

The SCEPTIC also celebrated the natural human inclinations to reason and converse. But he argued that religious beliefs ought to be sharply distinguished from moral practice. A person could not be forced to believe what he or she found unbelievable and should not be punished for failing to assent to a neighbor's hopes and fantasies about a supernatural realm. A dialogue or debate about skepticism and faith might enlighten the deluded and embolden the doubter, but more importantly it could protest against the unjust political and social power of the Christian majority, which in subtle and not so subtle ways punished people for disbelieving, doubting, or believing differently.

The SCEPTIC did not think that formal debates were a venue in which doubters in the audience would likely be inspired to rise to publicly challenge the Christian majority. Even debates in print might not change many minds. Public discussions were less tools to sway public opinion than signs that private opinions were already quietly changing. As much as any reasoned arguments, the insolence of the Christian clergy and the scandalous behavior of so many professing Christians were fueling doubts about the doctrines they professed. The movement of history in France, Germany, Great Britain, and the United States, the SCEPTIC believed, was the halting yet ultimately hopeful progress of reason and common sense over superstition and Christian hegemony. The CHRISTIAN, on the other hand, was confident that Christianity would only strengthen as America's faith spread throughout the world.[25]

Ezra Stiles in the eighteenth century thought that because the modern age had so rigorously challenged all the grounds of faith, Christians in every subsequent generation would have to return to articulate and defend first principles and win the arguments again. In some periods, belief in the authenticity of the Bible, in the reality of Christian spiritual experience, and in Christianity's historic mission to redeem the world might be so broadly accepted and professed as to become a kind of unquestioned common sense. But in other periods, when intellectual, political, or economic turmoil encouraged fallible and fickle human beings to doubt religious truth, Christians would need to return to the ramparts. Christian common sense and the debate with skeptics, then, would alternate from one historical moment to the next, like the diastole and systole, the pause and heartbeat, of the nation.

A mid-nineteenth-century writer, in contrast, thought that the tension between skepticism and faith had more to do with a fragile balance in the split personality of American character. "Skepticism or Superstition," an article appearing in an 1858 issue of the Episcopal *American Quarterly Church Review*, argued that Americans had a "national proclivity to Skepticism." This inclination was due to the population's predominantly Anglo-Saxon lineage and was especially prevalent in New England. "From all this, it follows that our American mind is northern, active, and decidedly subjective, so it is, from its very nature, opposed to all authoritative dogmatism, the excess of which is superstition. It questions all dogmas until it has proved them true. It is fond of the subtleties of analysis, and prefers to establish its own dogmas, and call them conclusions, rather than receive them, authoritatively, from man, or from God." There was, however, also an American inclination toward faith or credulity, or even superstition. This characteristic the author attributed to Norman blood, which was especially potent in the upper-class white South. A healthy nation, like a healthy individual mind, requires a balance of skepticism and faith—or at least a Southern counterweight to the dominant Northern inclination, the author advised. The article therefore argued both for a healthy religious attitude and the preservation of the Union.[26]

Christians and skeptics alike perceived that the nature of the skeptical threat evolved over time. In the last quarter of the eighteenth century, Christians worried about the foreign contagion of British deism and French infidel philosophy. The number of Americans who had imbibed such notions was probably small, most observers thought. By the presidential election of 1800 Federalist conspiracy theorists were warning of secret cabals of anti-Christian radicals who were taking over Masonic societies and republican clubs to subvert religion and good government. One pamphleteer in 1802 wrote that because "the constitution of the United States...has been erected on the fundamental principles of christianity...the standard of infidelity" should "only be regarded as the signal of vice, treason, and rebellion." But the Jefferson administration did not end up toppling churches and ripping the Bibles from the hands of Christian patriots. Radical deism receded from public view, although the effects of Paine's *Age of Reason* lingered. Defenders of the faith continued arguing with Paine's ghost at least through the 1840s. For Christians, the nightmare images of France's atheistic Reign of Terror also lingered.[27]

As the pace of religious revivals and reform societies quickened in the 1820s, a new kind of skeptic emerged. No longer working in secret, they presented themselves as philanthropists. Their subversive ideas about God and man, instead of being confined to treatises and histories, were printed in cheap newspapers and tracts and targeted the urban working class. They had moved from the comparatively genteel deism of the age of powdered wigs to a frank pantheistic or atheistic materialism. An observer in 1834 was shocked to discover that there were five freethought newspapers circulating to thousands of readers in the United States. The economic collapse of 1837 dealt a severe blow to the free enquirers and the labor movement they tried to court, but a Methodist paper reporting an infidel convention in 1845 still warned readers about these "snakes in the grass." When an essayist in a magazine devoted to politics, society, and the economy worried in 1853 that "the very foundations of religious belief are rotten and shaking," however, he was referring to yet another form of "Modern Skepticism." This was not the skepticism of coarse radicals or rabble-rousing fanatics, the author insisted. "It is not an Unbelief to be laughed, or hooted at, or hunted down. It is calm, abiding, earnest, sorrowful."[28]

Théodore Jouffroy, a French philosopher admired by American religious liberals, had anticipated the form of skepticism that writers described taking hold in America at midcentury. Earlier skepticism, he had written, was content to criticize and tear down the old monuments of religion. The new generation shared the criticism of the old faith but also hungered for a new one. It had cast aside atheism, materialism, and the simplistic political panaceas of the Revolutionary generation and once again tried to cultivate the life of the spirit. Christian apologists attacked what they saw as the old skepticism masquerading as a new religion. But like critics of skeptical deists and freethinkers in decades past, they were ultimately less concerned about the heterodoxy in plain sight than about the strong hints of a vast subterranean reservoir of doubt. "Whether preachers know it or not," the *Christian Inquirer* lamented in 1853, "there is now a great deal of secret or lurking skepticism in all assemblies. Some are doubting about the very existence of God while listening to his Word or standing or bowing in his worship. Others, with the leaves of the Bible open before them, are skeptics as to its divinity." In the same year, the author of "Modern Skepticism" argued that "a great Change is preparing in religious opinion, of which [scholars and preachers] and many of our best men know nothing.... Among all earnest-minded young men who are at this moment leading in thought and action in America, we venture to say that four-fifths are skeptical even of the great historical facts of Christianity."[29]

Some of these hyperventilating assessments, no doubt, came from believers who read about provocative new ideas, noticed parishioners dozing in their pews, and, connecting the two, thought they were diagnosing a dangerous cultural crisis. In retrospect, the anxious commentators of the 1850s—like those a generation earlier who were spooked by freethinkers or those a generation before that who were troubled by radical deists—were wrong to tremble for the future of American Christianity. Nevertheless, they understood that the skeptical response to their faith was a live option that had broad implications that were "felt individually, socially, and politically." And they were right when they suspected that complacent churchgoers and religiously indifferent citizens alike were liable to underestimate the effects of skepticism upon American faith.[30]

The prevalence of skepticism ensured that what believers wanted to cast as religious common sense continued to be a matter of public debate. No matter how much or how often Christians asserted that basic beliefs in the existence of God, the divine inspiration of the Bible, the ameliorative social effects of

Christianity, or the witness of conscience to Christian truth should be beyond dispute, they were not. The circulation of skeptical arguments against the grounds of faith made intramural squabbles much more contentious, inflating sectarian disagreements into angry battles over fundamentals. Because there seemed to be so few card-carrying infidels, Christians blamed the persistence of skepticism upon each other. Catholics blamed Protestant private judgment; Protestants thought it an overreaction to Catholic superstition. The cool-headed and reasonable blamed evangelical enthusiasm; evangelicals blamed the dead hand of High Church formalism. Many argued that bad theology drove people to doubt. Freewill Baptists and Methodists thought skepticism was a response to the perverse theology of Calvinism, which dangerously overemphasized the helplessness of sinners. Calvinists charged that preachers pandering to the sinner's free will were granting permission to doubt God's essential truths. Trinitarianism and Unitarianism, Universalism and partialism, Millerism, Spiritualism, and perfectionism—debaters on every side of major disputes tried to damn their opponents by holding them responsible for the skepticism of the age. They threw the charge of "skeptic" or "infidel" in each other's faces; they had frequent recourse to the slippery-slope argument, showing how an opposing position encouraged radical doubt and skidded quickly down to the atheist's hell. They were not merely trying to score rhetorical points, for the survival of their churches and the fate of their nation were at stake. So they continued to argue, even while realizing that sectarian contention itself was often said to be a major cause of religious skepticism.

Skepticism held the believer's feet to the fire; the popularity of faith pressured the skeptic to trust the transcendent. The Episcopalian focusing on so-called Anglo-Saxon and Norman characteristics in 1858, however, was wrong: Americans had a "national proclivity" toward faith rather than skepticism, even if religious faith for some had expanded beyond the bounds of traditional Christianity. Christianity itself continued to offer a way of life, an interpretive key to everything from the slightest flicker of consciousness to the deep connections of family and friendship to the rise and fall of nations and the direction of human history. It offered guidance, challenge, and comfort in the face of a harsh and otherwise unpredictable world. It promised nothing less than a blissful immortality. Skepticism was not merely a casual attitude, a style of thinking, or at best an intellectual habit. It too could powerfully shape a person's place in and sense of the world. But without the accumulating force of Christian institutions, there were still few psychological and social resources to sustain skeptical inquiry as part of an alternative way of being—one that was agnostic about spiritual claims, secular in orientation, humanist in its ethical concerns, and merely pragmatic in its approach to social and political problems. Comparatively few Americans would have agreed with the SCEPTIC, Robert Dale Owen, who suggested that it was easy to enjoy life, seek truth, live virtuously, and work for a better world without supernatural props and promises of a blissful hereafter. It was, ultimately, not so easy even for Owen himself, who in later years became a Spiritualist.

From the era of democratic revolutions and the age of enlightenment through the decades of reform and sectional crisis, American society was fertile ground for the religious institutions that cultivated faith. The numerous contentious Christian churches competing for adherents could make religion seem like a matter of personal choice, but it was a choice conditioned if not overdetermined by social pressures. In the new nation, Christianity was called upon to do much of the work to create a virtuous citizenry necessary to the survival of the Republic. In the fluid, industrializing North, outward signs of an inward faith were signals that a stranger could be trusted. In the South, churches were mechanisms of solidarity and social reproduction both for whites eager to perpetuate slavery and for the enslaved trying to survive and resist it. In the frontier West, organizing churches was a reassuring sign that civilization was being reestablished. But in what so many called a Christian nation, was there enough content to the common faith? There was no national church, no instituted national creed, no developed rituals in any "civil religion" that could prevent disunion. One could swear an oath on the Bible but could not go into too much detail about what that Bible said and still keep all the Christian patriots in the politician's big tent. The mystic cords tying Americans together in a sacred Union were revealed to be a collection of vaporous sentiments about the virtues of a Christian citizenry and God's love for America. When tested by the greatest moral challenge of the age—slavery—Christians interpreted their Bibles differently, snapped the bonds of fellowship, and conscientiously marched off to slaughter one another.

Americans were inclined toward faith, but this inclination was not some manifestation of European character. It was not primarily an inheritance from a Puritan past or a tradition of English religious dissent. It was not the simple product of the democratization of Christianity or of a free market of religious competition ushered in by the separation of church and state. It was not, so far as we can tell, because God shed his special grace upon the United States or because American styles of Christianity are best suited to the natural yearnings of the human spirit. It was a proclivity made and remade, year after year, forged in the foundry of culture. To investigate the relationship of skepticism and faith by examining the lives and times of particular people and communities is to get a better sense of how that work was done.

"The Providential Detection" (Philadelphia, [1800]). A Federalist cartoon: God's eye watches an American eagle prevent Thomas Jefferson from sacrificing the U.S. Constitution on the altar of French despotism. Courtesy of the Library Company of Philadelphia.

PART ONE

REVOLUTIONS, 1775–1815

> The CHRISTIAN and the SCEPTIC debated the character of the American and French Revolutions, and the relation of both to religious skepticism and faith:
>
> SCEPTIC: "That Sceptics were the most active in that great struggle for liberty, is true. And in what democratic struggle have they not been conspicuous?... If the French revolution was 'infidel throughout,' far more the American. If skepticism is to be abused for the ultimate failure of the one, let her at least have credit for the glorious success of the other."
>
> CHRISTIAN: "The French Revolution, Sir, will stand as a beacon to all future ages, to warn mankind to beware of war with Heaven—and with Heaven's sacred Book...."
>
> "But the lame attempt of my opponent to prove those petty infidel tyrants [of the French Revolution] to have been republican patriots, is not so *flagrantly outrageous*, as his statement that Washington and the master spirits of *our* Revolution were *Sceptics*."[1]

The American Revolution, it is not controversial to say, was a critical event in the history of American religion. And the American reaction to the French Revolution made a deep and lasting impression on religious culture. But the devil is in the details.

Gauging the relationship of religion and the Revolutionary era depends at the outset, of course, on how we define each term. We might consider the Revolutionary era as a period encompassing the battle of the thirteen British North American colonies for independence from Great Britain through the establishment of the United States on its new constitutional foundations. We could extend this to see how things played out in the generation that followed by moving through the reaction to the French Revolution and the development of the first two-party system in the 1790s, the Jeffersonian "Revolution" of 1800, and the upsurge of nationalism in what was considered by some to be a second war of independence from Great Britain (the War of 1812), bringing the era to a close at about 1815.[2]

Religion is defined variously, and sometimes very broadly; confining it to "what [was] taught in the churches" allows us at least to mark some institutional changes and shifts in doctrine as well as style. Of the four leading denominations in 1775 (Congregationalists, Presbyterians, Baptists, and the Church of England), the two that had benefited from state establishment—the Congregationalists in New England and the Church of England (later, Episcopalians) in New York, Virginia, Maryland, North and South Carolina, and Georgia—grew most slowly. This is true even though Congregationalists remained quasi-established, receiving state money, until 1818 in Connecticut, 1819 in New Hampshire, and 1833 in Massachusetts. The Episcopalians and the Baptists had roughly the same number of congregations (just shy of 500) at the beginning of the war. In 1820, after the U. S. population had grown from 4 million to about 10 million, the Episcopalians had only about a hundred more congregations while the Baptists had 2,700. The Congregationalists, with nearly 700 congregations in 1775 and 1,100 in 1820, were also dwarfed by the astonishing expansion of Methodism, which surged from a mere 65 to 2,700 in the same time period. The growth of Methodists and Free Will Baptists also illustrates a movement by many away from Calvinism, which taught that souls were predestined to be saved or damned, and toward theologies stressing an individual's ability to choose. The popularity of these evangelical churches, too, signals the increased prominence of revivals featuring emotional preaching and powerful conversion experiences.[3]

Although the surge of religion after 1800 demonstrates neither the "democratization" of American Christianity nor a nostalgic Christianization of American culture to replace the lost monarchy, Americans did wonder and worry about the relations of their religious and political lives, and they did question (or try to reinforce) traditional authority, including religious authority, in the "new order for the ages" they were creating. The first two chapters in this book's first section, "Revolutions, 1775–1815," examine the two dimensions of religion so briefly mentioned in the First Amendment with its establishment and free-exercise clauses: the relationship of religion and government, and the ways that religion could be practiced in a "free" environment.[4]

Chapter 1 looks at the struggle to define what counted as legitimate religious faith and the efforts to insist upon its crucial social and political importance in the new climate of debate in the early 1780s. Patriot religious writers during the war knew that they had to put aside the sectarian differences that had so often bitterly divided colonial Christians in order to forge an interdenominational and intercolonial alliance against the British. But as states rewrote their constitutions and united under the Articles of Confederation, Christians wondered how far the boundaries of toleration ought to be stretched. Should officeholders be required to swear an oath professing belief in God, or that belief and faith in the scriptures, too? Belief in a future state of rewards and punishments or also in Christ? Should deists, who professed belief in a Creator but were skeptical about most of the other tenets of Christianity, be considered legitimately "religious" and encouraged in the free exercise of their faith alongside their Christian neighbors, or should they be shunned as akin to atheists, dangerous to the community? The deist treatise *Reason the Only Oracle of Man* by the Revolutionary War hero Ethan Allen in 1785 tried to connect deism to patriotism. But when William Beadle, a self-proclaimed deist, murdered his family and then committed suicide, his beliefs, taken as the cause of his acts, were condemned along with his crimes, allowing commentators to mark the dangers of both deism and skepticism and to try to define the acceptable parameters of American faith.

As deism was castigated and further marginalized in the late eighteenth century, Methodism, the focus of chapter 2, faced challenges even as it began its spectacular rise. While deists attacked the Christian grounds of faith in the scriptures, Methodists and other evangelicals professed another religious authority: the inner witness of the Holy Spirit. Christianity was validated by their personal religious experiences. The demonstrable effects of the Gospel message upon their minds, hearts, and bodies testified to its truth. Sarah Jones and Jeremiah Minter were devout Methodists in Virginia witnessing the rapid expansion of the American church. Yet even within their faith community they faced restrictions on the free exercise of their religious belief and practice—restrictions on the testimony of the Spirit imposed not by the state or by biblical mandate but by the power and authority of their church.

Events in France only exacerbated the religious and political concerns and struggles of Americans in the 1790s. The French Revolution (1789–99), too, had a profound ideological impact upon American religion.

Early on, it inspired some Americans to see the battle against ecclesiastical tyranny and Christian superstition as an extension of the fight for liberty and equality. Many others, after the French dechristianization campaign (begun in 1792), the Festival of Reason (November 1793), and Robespierre's proclamation of his deistic Cult of the Supreme Being (May 1794) in the midst of the Reign of Terror, pointed to the blood in the streets as a stark warning: this would happen in America, too, if the nation turned away from Christianity.

It was in this climate that Thomas Paine's deistic *Age of Reason* (1794–95) sold well and was repeatedly pilloried in the American press, and the deist lecturer Elihu Palmer attracted supporters while being mocked and condemned by conservatives. Anglophile Federalists called Francophile Republicans Jacobins and atheists, while Republicans called their opponents crypto-monarchists intent on religious persecution in the spirit of the Inquisition. The battle was more than a mere war of words. Partisans formed clubs and societies, too, living their religion and politics in communities created through the new impetus for voluntary association. Some of these were the allegedly dangerous self-created societies that George Washington warned about; others were networks and organizations created by or affiliated with the churches. As small deist groups sprang up and tried to fan the fires of radical religion and politics, Bible societies and missionary efforts organized to douse the flames of religious infidelity by spreading the Word.

Organized deism—attempts to institutionalize a skeptical critique of Christianity and an alternative natural religion—rose and fell in this period. Chapters 3 and 4 compare Palmer's deists to other groups similarly trying to achieve some sort of institutional stability in these years: the Universalists, the Freemasons, the New Jerusalem (Swedenborgian) Church, and the African Methodist Episcopal Church. When organized deism is juxtaposed to these other groups, it becomes clear that its fate rested in part on its continued skeptical provocations but was also determined by the role of the state, the constraints of the law, and the fraught politics of religious and political association. Republican politicians, even if sympathetic to deism or skepticism, quickly realized that they needed to distance themselves from radical critiques of Christianity to win votes, just as they realized they needed to mute Northern Republican antislavery rhetoric if they wanted to sustain a national coalition. The growing legions of Methodist and Baptist voters might respond to anticlerical rhetoric aimed at elitist and overbearing Congregationalists, Presbyterians, and Episcopalians, but they would not stand for attacks on the faith itself. Christian Republicans could vote for a reputed deist like Jefferson if those views were kept quiet and they could focus on Jefferson the champion of liberty and the prime mover behind the Virginia Statute for Religious Freedom (1786). Organized deism was already fading by the deaths of Palmer (1806) and Paine (1809). Religious skepticism had mostly retreated from partisan political debate by 1815 but had certainly not disappeared.

1

Deist Hero, Deist Monster

On Religious Common Sense in the Wake of the American Revolution

Familiar as a leader of the Green Mountain Boys, celebrated as a hero of the capture of Fort Ticonderoga, and well-known as the author of a vivid account of his experience as a British prisoner of war, Ethan Allen had some reason to hope that his Hartford printers would agree to publish his treatise on deism. Allen's political letters had long run in the *Connecticut Courant*, and the Hartford press had produced six political pamphlets by Ethan and his brother Ira by the spring of 1783. Although Allen would curse their moral cowardice and have to borrow money to eventually get the book published in Vermont, Barzillai Hudson and George Goodwin had good reasons to turn him down. A thick philosophical tome by a hotheaded backwoodsman would hardly produce the sales of his wartime captivity narrative. But the timing of Allen's proposal was especially bad. A deist tract was the last thing that Hudson and Goodwin would have wanted to advertise for sale in the spring of 1783. The shock of the Beadle murder and suicide in neighboring Wethersfield on December 11, 1782, had not yet faded. Why had William Beadle, a respected merchant, known as a doting father and husband, cut the throats of his wife and four young children and then fired two pistols into his head? It was neither a crime of passion nor a fit of delirium, the article in the *Courant* had explained: in the previous years, Beadle "betook himself more to books than usual, and was unhappily fond of those esteemed Deistical; of late he rejected all Revelation as imposition, and (as he expresses himself), 'renouncing all the popular religions of the world, intended to die a proper Deist.'" "What a monster of a man was this!" exclaimed Pastor John Marsh at the funeral for Mrs. Beadle and the children.[1]

When Allen's *Reason the Only Oracle of Man* (also known as *Oracles of Reason* and *Ethan Allen's Bible*) was finally published in the fall of 1785, it was read more than its paltry sales might indicate, discussed more than it was read, and treated with clerical contempt more than it was refuted. The major published attack, *Sermon to Swine* by "Common Sense" (Josiah Sherman), could not simply try to draw a straight line between deistic principles and monstrous practices, as the commentary on Beadle had attempted. Allen was both deist and hero; to attack his reputation was to assault the character of the man who had taken Ticonderoga and defied British tyranny even while in chains. Deism tested Americans' commitment to religious freedom and complicated the connection between religious doctrines and republican virtue. These encounters with deism in the 1780s uncover contests over the place of religion in emerging conceptions of American citizenship and connect everyday concerns and the cultural imperatives of the Revolutionary moment to longer-standing theological and philosophical debate. They at once provide a revealing glimpse of people struggling to understand their religious and political lives in the years immediately following the war and sketch an episode in the formation of American religious common sense—a stance assuming that virtuous citizenship presupposed Christianity and that skepticism about the divine inspiration of the Bible was therefore un-American and, perhaps, lunacy.[2]

"Deism" is usually associated with belief in a noninterventionist Creator, reliance upon what reason can discern in the natural world, and skepticism about miracles, mysticism, the divine inspiration of the scriptures, and the divinity of Christ.[3] One of the fullest discussions of deism published in America in the 1780s was John Murray's *Bath Kol* (1783), a book that assessed colonial religious history and America's spiritual condition at the end of the war. Part historical review, part jeremiad, and part polemic, *Bath Kol* insisted that public bodies, both civil and ecclesiastical, and not just individuals, had a duty to testify for Christ and against suddenly prominent forms of infidelity. Closing an impassioned peroration with a reference to the Beadle murder, Murray concluded that deism was "the grand patron of wickedness and debauchery of the present time." In the same year, Yale president Ezra Stiles, in his well-known election sermon, *The United States Elevated to Glory and Honor*, looked forward to the American future and addressed the personal, intellectual, and ideological dimensions of the deist threat. He called for Christian scholars to engage deism in open debate. Yet the 1783 sermon as a whole argued that the Christian character of the United States would continue in future generations because of demographic realities, support from the state, and control of important public institutions like colleges, learned societies, and the press. In the wake of the American Revolution, as citizens argued about foundational principles, questioned basic presuppositions of society, and debated the proper relations of church and state, deism had become a threatening ideological problem that needed to be answered by assertions of power and authority.[4]

After deism—once a secret sin, then a topic of scholarly debate—progressed to become a brazen threat to post-Revolutionary political and moral order, antideist writers, like those responding to Beadle and Allen, sometimes invoked "common sense" to battle against it. Doing so was less a call for rational public inquiry into the claims of deism than an attempt to delegitimize it as a defensible position for a virtuous citizen in a land of religious liberty. To mention common sense was to gesture toward a natural capacity for judgment about the practical concerns of daily life or to a fund of basic beliefs and self-evident truths that were too obvious to require reasoned argument. Whatever resemblance such references might have to prominent strands of British philosophy, rhetorical appeals to common sense were usually attempts to claim uncontestable authority and forestall critical debate—or at least to set the terms of that debate. They were efforts to spread the blanket of argumentative immunity from normally unproblematic epistemic assumptions (I have a body; there is an external world; two plus two make four) to claims that a significant minority, at least, would more readily recognize as ideological (whites are superior to blacks; no island should rule a continent; the Bible is God's revelation). In late eighteenth-century America, nervous Christians appealed to common sense to try to shove foundational beliefs back outside the arena of public dispute. North Carolina Presbyterian Henry Pattillo noted in his "Address to Deists" that most common folks understood no real distinction between denying the Bible and denying God and morality. The success of the American experiment, most Christians believed, depended upon perpetuating such religious common sense.[5]

Damnnation Murray and the Religious History of the American Revolution

John Murray, crusader against deism and Universalism, was a pastor of the Presbyterian Church in Newburyport, Massachusetts. Local wags called him "Damnation Murray," to distinguish him from the Universalist John ("Salvation") Murray, who preached twenty-five miles away in Gloucester. Born in Ireland and educated at Edinburgh, "Damnation" Murray had emigrated in 1763 and served parishes in Philadelphia and Maine before settling in this port town forty miles north of Boston in 1781. *Bath Kol*, unlike his other published works, did not bear his name. The text was not meant to be seen as the product of one man; it was the testimony of "the First Presbytery of the Eastward," approved by committee and signed by the presbytery's clerk and moderator.[6]

Murray's concern about the fate of Christianity in American public life was a common theme for the post-Revolutionary ministry. Comparing the new nation to ancient Israel had become a pulpit commonplace, and most preachers argued that the nation, like all corporate bodies under God's Providence, was rewarded and punished according to its behavior. Yet, as *Bath Kol* lamented, public officials and civil institutions—grand juries, magistrates, courts, legislative assemblies—were nearly mute. The Declaration of Independence castigated Britain's king but made no mention of the King of Kings, Murray complained, and "every following step" in governmental affairs—from the new state constitutions to the confederation of states to treaties with other nations—"spoke the same language." Murray did not explain the advent of this de-Christianized public language as the result of efforts to insulate the state from sectarian disputes, protect the churches from state interference, or create an inclusive model of citizenship that transcended particular regional, ethnic, and religious identities. In *Bath Kol*, the cause was the general moral declension of the times and, more specifically, the inroads made by deism and Universalism. People seemed to blame eight years of war on the sins of Britain and the Tories alone; they excused their own moral lapses by pointing to the extreme conditions created by "war times." More significantly, as Murray put it, a disease in the head had been communicated to the body. Important governmental posts in some provinces had been filled by deists. Officers in some of the forts bragged of having read Thomas Chubb's deistic tract and found it unanswerable. In principal towns, Murray claimed, many leading lawyers were deists, and physicians brought the contagion to the sickbeds of their patients. In polite society, a false gentility reigned, with the better sort scoffing at revelation, joking about Christianity, and passing around Lord Chesterfield's *Letters to His Son* as a perverse guide to moral life.[7]

Bath Kol, then, was an attempt to counter the decay of piety and the rise of deism by asserting a religious interpretation of the American Revolution. As such, it followed other notable publications from Murray's Newburyport. Nathaniel Whitaker, for example, blasted Tories from the pulpit in 1777 and 1783, arguing that those who did not actively support the sacred cause of liberty had blood on their hands and deserved to be stripped of their property and banished. Murray himself, who had raised volunteers for the Continental Army and helped effect prisoner exchanges, discussed the "near and necessary connection" between civil and religious liberty. He also reminded citizens who were framing new state constitutions "that some line of distinction should appear to be drawn between the duties of a body considered merely as a *civil society*—and those of a *civil society of christians*: if men are christians while in a state of nature, they will not cease to be such when they enter into the connections of members of society—their religion is a portable thing—they must carry it with them into every relation they sustain in the world."[8]

Murray and his Newburyport brethren were members of the "black regiment" of Whig clergymen—predominantly Calvinistic New Englanders and Middle Colony Presbyterians—who preached and published in support of the patriot cause. If they did not lead the charge toward independence, they helped give the cause moral legitimacy by placing Revolutionary events within the narrative of sacred history and exhorting the faithful to righteous action. Looking backward to the scriptural history of Israel and forward to the prophesied millennial age, and employing Puritan tropes and arguments from a tradition of

Dissent against Anglican domination, they linked spiritual, ecclesiastical, and political liberty and fused republican civic virtue to Christian morality. Not all American Christians were Whigs, not all Whigs embraced the views espoused from the pulpit, and not all Whig preachers followed the same script. But throughout the war, these religio-political doctrines had been frequently and forcefully proclaimed.[9]

Murray's *Bath Kol* placed the Revolution in moral and historical context. It reviewed the story of English colonial settlement, hailing the Puritans as champions of liberty, gliding past their persecution of dissenting Quakers and Baptists. Murray did not trumpet the revivals of 1739–44 as an epochal "Great Awakening" but described them merely as the most prominent in a long string of periodic seasons of grace—a surprisingly muted description, since his own church was formed out of the revivals, and the Grand Itinerant, George Whitefield, had preached his last sermon in Newburyport in 1770 and was buried beneath Murray's pulpit in a crypt that Revolutionary soldiers visited for relics to take into battle. *Bath Kol* devoted much more attention to the wars with France beginning in 1744 and the backsliding of an ungrateful people. The celebrations of the fall of New France in 1760, which Murray likened to "heathen orgies," marked the beginning of twenty years of ungodliness. Despite the threats to liberty signaled by Anglican schemes to impose bishops on the colonies and by the Quebec Act's embrace of Catholicism, most were preoccupied by land fever and were busy aping English fashions, while colonial legislatures fought over boundary disputes. Wallowing in worldliness, most people failed to confront the "leprosy" of heterodoxy and heresy, infecting even colleges and pulpits, that paved the way for deism.[10]

Focusing on his own region, Murray pointed a finger at the Universalist John Murray, who first came to Newburyport in early November 1773 and preached in the Presbyterian and North Congregational meetinghouses until his tenets became known. "The increase of deism and infidelity at this time was generally promoted by the preachments of a young gentleman, who called himself Murray, who had lately been imported from England: This man... insinuated himself into many families, and intruded into many pulpits, zealously retailing, at first under deep disguise, but at last with avowed boldness... UNIVERSAL SALVATION: This scheme was pleasing to the libertine heart; and his manners being found easy enough for the loosest company, he soon became the idol of rakes and the oracle of deists." For Calvinists, the Universalist's argument that all people, and not just the elect, eventually would be saved was not just a different interpretation of the New Testament's message of salvation; it undercut entirely the authority of the Bible and destroyed Christ's plan of redemption; it emasculated God the Father, attributing to him "a feminine sort of goodness" that "constrains him... to keep all sinners from pain," so "we must turn and caress the offender" instead. Though adopting the name of Christianity and preaching from the scripture, Universalists, "Damnation" Murray argued, were in fact on a very slippery slope to deism and eventually atheism.[11]

Deism, in turn, was not in *Bath Kol* an attempt to understand God's will and man's duty through reason and an investigation of the natural world; it was atheism in thin disguise. Murray did nod toward a tradition of philosophical skepticism, but the true beginnings of the modern movement, he claimed, were in Italy and France in the mid-sixteenth century, when libertine atheists simply adopted a new name to avoid "popular odium." Herbert of Cherbury, "the Father of English Deism," gave their tenets systematic form in 1624, and he was followed by a parade of thinkers including Hobbes, Toland, Shaftesbury, Bolingbroke, and David Hume. After being decisively refuted, according to Murray, by Christian luminaries including John Locke, deists changed tactics. After 1750 they adopted a "strategy of secret ambuscades": satiric sneers, low puns, and malicious innuendos dropped casually in private clubs while they conformed publicly to the Christian forms of their society. There were differences among them: some believed in God's providential intervention, while others did not; some argued for the immortality of the soul, while others denied it. Yet they all united behind the goal of toppling Christianity. Because deists did not gather in meetinghouses like Universalists, it was hard for Christians to scout out the enemy. Like the secret Tories Nathaniel Whitaker described in 1783, who were still plotting in dark corners, Murray's private deists were dangerous subversives.[12]

Deism and the Revolution, in different ways, disturbed the relations among faith, belief, and morality, on one hand, and among the individual, the corporate community, and God, on the other. In Reformed thought, faith is a gift of sovereign grace; it is the disposition of the elect soul after regeneration by the Holy Spirit. True belief—right thinking about essential theological matters—is a necessary but not sufficient condition for salvation. Good works do not earn the sinner any points with God; a habit of benevolence, however, may be a sign of election. Yet when Calvinistic Protestants went to church, they did not just hear about faith and the salvation of souls. Especially on fast and thanksgiving days, they heard about the community—congregation, colony, state, nation—and its relation to God. When preachers shifted their focus from the individual soul to the corporate body, the interconnections of faith, belief, and morality were altered.[13]

Social entities were not just convenient groupings of individuals, established by social contracts among themselves. Their members were collectively responsible, and God rewarded and punished them accordingly. Because corporate bodies, unlike souls, were not immortal, communities and nations were rewarded and punished in this world, rather than the afterlife. So while personal misfortune might be a test of the truly righteous (like Job) rather than punishment for sin, the afflictions of the community—drought, earthquakes, fires, epidemics, war—were much less ambiguously signs of public sin that had provoked God's wrath. (Peace, health, and prosperity, however, were officially interpreted as undeserved blessings from a loving Father.) God might spare a whole sinful community for the sake of a few of the truly faithful, but usually he rendered judgments according to the public acts of the community or the prevalence of sinful behavior by its members. Proper belief, it was thought, even if unconnected to saving faith in individuals, was essential to maintaining moral order in a social body. Those who argued in favor of continued tax support for the churches in the last quarter of the eighteenth century stressed that inculcating Christian ethics was essential to the public virtue needed to sustain a republic. If faith was the concern of individuals and churches, morality and the beliefs thought to be essential to it were also the concern of the state.

The Revolution further complicated and confused the already battered notion of the individual as a member of a series of covenant communities, from congregation to colony to nation to Christendom.[14] Evangelical "New Lights" since the revivals of the 1740s in New England and the incursions of Separates and Baptists into the South in the 1750s and 1760s had turned away from moral communities defined by political jurisdiction to create communities of shared religious affection that could be at once intensely local and linked to translocal networks of the faithful. Their petitions for toleration as dissenters became demands for religious freedom when liberty became the byword in the 1760s and 1770s. Murray's predecessor Jonathan Parsons acknowledged theological fissures, too, and could only speak of "occasional" communions between Calvinist and non-Calvinist Christians in 1774. As war approached, Whig and Tory neighbors severed bonds and formed separate political communions. Nathaniel Whitaker's sermons against Tories insisted upon it and described the distinguishing marks that could reveal a neighbor's "tory heart." The war itself weakened the link between personal responsibility and corporate suffering. When pastors like Murray decried selfishness, monopolizing, Sabbath-breaking, and profanity, parishioners blamed war times rather than seeing the prolongation of the war as punishment for their sins. "Community" did not collapse into "individualism," but the moral relation between individual actors and the amorphous public body that politicians and ministers were calling "the people" had become blurred.[15]

The resistance movement and then the Confederation required new affiliations among religiously and ethnically diverse colonial regions, but it was not immediately clear how the new United States would be defined in moral and religious terms. In 1783, Murray hoped that someday the states would "grow together, as one living body, animated by one living soul...demolish all divisioned lines between state and state—and reduce all... into ONE GREAT REPUBLIC," just as he hoped that someday the different Christian churches would form some plan of union. But these were only hopes. Rhetorically, the states were often compared to the tribes of Israel. Theologically, however, most ministers distinguished between the special and peculiar covenant Israel had with Jehovah and the status of the United States, which played by the same rules as other corporate bodies under God's universal moral law. Even those fervent millennialists who thought that the Revolution might augur the advent of Christ's second coming usually considered the nation, at best, as compost to prepare the ground for the final flowering of the True Church. In the era before romantic nationalism, America was not yet the redeemer nation. Christians did not yet see revivalism as a tool that could replace the outmoded invocations of a national covenant as a ritual of public solidarity. By the 1780s, in sum, the new nation's religious identity was as yet inchoate, and the means by which its Christian character would be defined remained uncertain.[16]

Deism, Christian opponents believed, was an effect and would be a further cause of this uncertainty and moral disorder. Christian writers like "Damnation" Murray considered Thomas Jefferson's famous defense of religious liberty in *Notes on the State of Virginia* anathema: "It does me no injury for my neighbour to say there are twenty gods, or no god. It neither picks my pocket nor breaks my leg." Monstrous principles, the preachers believed, would sooner or later lead to monstrous practices, like pocket picking, leg breaking, or worse. Even before such a neighbor reached that point, his subtler sins would corrupt the commonwealth. The neighbor merely professing such heterodox beliefs, too, had its dangers, aside from the divine punishments that unchecked blasphemies might bring down upon the whole. The communities that preachers like Murray had in mind were, at some basic level, rooted in a communion of sentiment and a consensus of basic beliefs; they were not merely pragmatic organizations designed to protect person and property. The open profession of unchristian beliefs, therefore, weakened the bonds of union. Liberty of conscience might have to be stretched far to contain the sectarian diversity of America, but not beyond the bounds of what many considered to be common sense: morality rested in a belief in a God who would punish bad behavior even where the state could not; this belief, in turn, relied on the recognition that the Bible was God's revealed Word and that its warnings were true. Religion and morality were divinely connected, Murray argued. Atheists and polytheists, without the Word to hold them accountable, could not be trusted to be accountable when they gave their own word. Despite a deist's insistence that he *did* believe in God, and in an immortal soul that was rewarded and punished, by this Christian common sense he was the equivalent of Jefferson's atheist. The deist, by denying the Bible, and the Universalist, by grossly distorting its teaching on future punishment, were not only sinners on the road to hell; they were dangerous neighbors and a threat to society.[17]

William Beadle, Murray concluded, made this logic clear to any who had eyes to see. He did not even have to mention Beadle by name; in 1783, his readers would have caught the reference. Deism, Murray wrote, was

> the arch-murderer that, having made its votaries the pests of society, while they lived, hurries them on to be their own butchers at last. To the spreading of this principle we may ascribe the overgrown wickedness of AMERICA at this unhappy period. This is the monster that threatens to extirpate all the remains of virtue and piety from among us: And has already hardened so great a part of this generation at once, to cast off the fear of God and the regard of man; that we are now habituated to the news of self-murders, committed in the shade of these principles, yea, of the husband and the father imbruing his hands in the blood of the beloved wife and all the tender offspring, to give a sanction to their scheme.[18]

Deist Hero: Ethan Allen

Ethan Allen grew up in "Damnation" Murray's New England. Kicked out of Salisbury, Connecticut, for brawling and warned out of Northampton, Massachusetts, for debating religion in the taverns, Allen moved to the Green Mountains in 1770 and became a leader of the settlers resisting—by legal argument, propaganda, and violence—New York's claims to the vast tracts of land west of the Connecticut River. Allen's role in the capture of Fort Ticonderoga in the early days of the war with Britain led to two and a half years as a prisoner of war, recounted in his *Narrative*. Allen wrote *Reason the Only Oracle of Man* in the early 1780s, after he had withdrawn from the battles of war and politics, developing the treatise from notes begun two decades earlier during discussions with his deist friend Thomas Young. He presumed the book would "turn to money," as he wrote one correspondent early in 1785, but his primary goal was to rescue "the human species" from "Priestcraft." The Protestant clergy were "trafficking" in pernicious doctrines that gave them great power and income. *Reason*, he hoped, would be "fatal to the ministerial Damnation Salvation, and their merchandise thereof."[19]

Allen accepted being "denominated a Deist," though he claimed not to have read any deistical books, writing the text with only the Bible and a dictionary by his side and relying upon what he described to his friend Hector St. John de Crèvecoeur as "untutored logic, and Sallies of a mind nursed principally, in the

Larkin G. Mead, "Ethan Allen" (1876), National Statuary Hall Collection, U.S. Capitol. No image of Allen made during his lifetime exists; this statue of the heroic general was commissioned by the state of Vermont.

Mountanous wilds of America." Over nearly five hundred pages, Allen constructed a philosophy (or a theology—he used both terms to describe it) and then measured Christianity against it. He established the being and attributes of God, argued for the eternity of creation, and then discussed human agency, reason, sensation, the soul, immortality, and the nature of faith and morality. From this foundation, he then criticized idolatry, the Mosaic account of creation, and the Christian notions of Providence, original sin, prophecies, miracles, spiritual experiences, the Trinity, Jesus as the Son of God, the atonement, and revelation. The book is a treatise, not a personal narrative, except when he tells of his own enlightenment after a conversation with a minister. The work makes little reference to Allen's immediate social, political, or historical context, aside from a few references to the current enlightened age or the Calvinistic customs in his part of the country. Yet his prominent name, boldly printed in large type on the title page and at the end of a pugnacious preface, clearly linked the text to the public image of the Green Mountain hero.[20]

Allen's *Narrative*, as a whole, was not explicitly deistic. On the contrary, it used religious language for rhetorical effect—language that nevertheless might suggest a conventionally Christian author. But after reading *Reason the Only Oracle*, a reader of the *Narrative* would know that the Allen who took Ticonderoga "in the name of the great Jehovah and the Continental Congress" did not believe in a Supreme Being that resembled the Old Testament God; the Allen who referred to the book of fate did not believe in fate; the Allen who described devils ready to receive General Howe thought them chimera; and the Allen who invoked "Heaven's vengeance" did not think God's Providence worked that way. *Reason the Only Oracle* can be read as the philosophical system undergirding the virtuous character on display in the earlier book, a theory of moral agency already illustrated by a heroic struggle for liberty.[21]

Both the *Narrative* and *Reason the Only Oracle* are meditations on liberty and the abuse of sovereign power. "Ever since I arrived to a state of manhood, and acquainted myself with the general history of mankind," the *Narrative* begins, "I have felt a sincere passion for liberty. The history of nations doomed to perpetual slavery, in consequence of yielding up to tyrants their natural born liberties, I read with a sort of philosophical horror; so that the first systematical and bloody attempt at Lexington, to enslave America, thoroughly electrified my mind, and fully determined me to take part with my country." In *Reason*, different tyrants are decried: "When I was a boy, by one means or another, I had conceived a very bad opinion of Pharaoh, he seem'd to me to be a cruel despotic Prince... but after a few years of maturity, and examination of the history of that monarch given by Moses... I conceived a more favorable opinion of him, in asmuch [*sic*] as we are told that God raised him up, and hardened his heart, and predestinated his reign, his wickedness and overthrow." Allen's political response to George III's tyranny was to answer the call to arms; his philosophical response to the Tyrant God was to rescue the true character of the deity from this scriptural misrepresentation.[22]

We can only understand God's character, Allen argued, through reason, for God does not reveal himself to us in any other way. We learn through our senses; language communicates by signs apprehended by the ear or the eye. God, an immaterial being outside of time, cannot communicate to us through human discourse because of our natural limitations. Allen dismissed the Pietist's spiritual discernment of supernatural things as a fantasy conjured up by fevered imaginations. He criticized the faith in scripture as a misplaced reliance on fables from an earlier, more superstitious age, tales that had been further garbled by their transmission through different and evolving languages and through "all the vicissitudes and alterations of human learning, prejudices, superstitions, enthusiasms and diversities of interests and manners, to our time." In building his own system, Allen returned to the epistemological (rather than the purportedly historical or supernatural) foundations of true belief.[23]

The reasoning of *Reason* presupposed our sense of our independence (free will) and, concurrently, of our dependence (upon God), topics Allen would treat at greater length in his appendix to his treatise. Human beings, Allen argued, are intuitively certain of their own free agency. This consciousness of our liberty is implanted within us, universally impressed upon human minds by God. It is not the product of reason or experience in the world but is bundled with consciousness itself, it seemed to Allen. We have a double consciousness, he wrote: we know that we act, and we know that we act freely. Further, we understand the moral consequences of our actions, and our accountability for them.[24]

Our knowledge of the nature of humanity, therefore, is rooted in an intuitively certain and immediately apprehended consciousness of liberty. But we come to our knowledge of God differently. Our experience in the world and our reflections upon our mental lives produce in us a "feeling" that we are dependent upon a ruling power. Though we are free to act, the world we act in, the laws that seem to shape the natural world, the rules stamped upon our consciences, and our very existence all point to a higher source. We have no idea of God immediately apprehended in consciousness; nor does God, an incorporeal being, come before our senses. We have only this feeling of dependence, and from it we infer the existence of a God. This is the uniform conclusion of all rational beings, and Allen called it "certain knowledge." It is merely a first hint, though, of God; to discern his character, we must reason carefully from the facts of the moral and empirical worlds as we apprehend them. Such reasoning should lead us to an appreciation of God's wisdom, power, and goodness. But in connecting and compounding ideas, men are apt to stumble into error, deviating from sound logic and the facts at hand, which is why the understanding of God and humankind in most religions had become so distorted.[25]

A belief in immortality joins free agency and dependence upon God as the third pillar of Allen's philosophy. Without it, our conception of God's moral government would be "low, unjust, and improper," for it is clear that justice does not always reign in this world; without it, too, "our motives to the practice of virtue would be exceeding weak and deficient." Allen argued that immortality could be inferred from God's justice and goodness and was "as clearly demonstrable as any proposition that respects the moral sciences." Without a belief in a future world of rewards and punishments meted out for behavior in this one, society would be "nothing but deceit, oppression fraud and injustice of every kind." So here he would agree with ministers like Damnation Murray, though relying on reason rather than revelation. He conceded, however, that the chain of logical deductions demonstrating the immortality of the human self or soul was "not so readily conceived by such minds as are but little accustomed to reasoning, as other moral truths which may be investigated by a less number of propositions and inferences." This is a difficult admission for one claiming that the ethical foundations of society could be built upon reason. Indeed, the relationship between grasping truth and acting virtuously seems rather tenuous for Allen in any case. "Those who are wicked and abandoned to wickedness, may, and often do, possess more knowledge, and consequently a more extensive faith than those who are ignorant and virtuous." Such was the case with the "scientific barbarity" of the British, which he castigated in the *Narrative*.[26]

If Murray and his clerical brethren spoke as the conscience of the saints, cudgeling sinners with divine law for the sake of the moral community, Allen in *Reason* is the reflective free agent, addressing the reader, as it were, from the solitude of his study and over the heads of most of his neighbors—those New Englanders, he lamented, still imagining themselves subjects of a "sacerdotal empire" ruled by the Bible's tyrannical sovereign and unable to "break the fetters of education," tradition, and imagination. All people had the common sense—if they would only use it—to discern their true liberty, and the capacity to reason and discover God's basic laws: it is not required "that we should become philosophers... to know that we are (free) agents," he wrote. But there was a great gap between natural capacity and actual practice. The backwoods philosopher was himself proof of that natural capacity, publishing a treatise and undaunted by the admission that he lacked a liberal education and was not well read. He did not celebrate the common wisdom of the common man, though, but thought that good sense was only found in the enlightened few—not necessarily in polished intellectuals, but in the few who had the courage to follow the "painful" road of ratiocination, to face down the "squibbing hell fire" of the superstitious, and to willfully expose themselves to the severe chastisement of "philosophers, divines or Critics" in the cause of truth and humanity. The heroic philosopher of *Reason the Only Oracle of Man*, therefore, resembles the heroic patriot of the *Narrative* who wore England's "heavy irons, and bore [its] bitter revilings and reproaches," and who, with a "smattering of philosophy" and an understanding of human nature, could clearly see England's crimes and "exhibit a good sample of American fortitude."[27]

Allen the detached deist philosopher put a premium on self-interest: "All finite beings are under greater obligations to themselves than to any other creature or race of creatures whatever." In the *Narrative*, the Vermonter—not yet a citizen of the confederated states of America—warned against the narrow prejudices of nationalism and suggested that individuals could learn to see beyond their selfish interests and parochial attachments through social exchange. Commerce can be an engine of benevolence. "Commercial intercourse" tends to "erase the superstition of the mind" by assuring people "that human nature, policy and interest are the same in all nations, and at the same time they are bartering commodities... they may reciprocally exchange such part of their customs and manners as may be beneficial, and learn to extend charity and good-will to the whole world of mankind." The *Narrative* repeatedly demonstrates how social bonds that might normally emerge through noncommercial intercourse, too, become severed in a society that extinguishes liberty.[28]

National power, Allen argued, is always the offspring of national virtue and wisdom. But when a nation begins to exercise power without virtue, when state policy creates a system of tyrannous exploitation, it warps people, numbing moral sense and encouraging them to think only of their narrow material interests, like the bitter Tories who licked their lips and rubbed their hands in anticipation of the estates they could confiscate once the rebel leaders were dangling from the gallows. They are allowed to turn the exercise of power to the twisted pleasures of domination, like the imperious Sergeant Keef, in charge of the provost-jail in New York. They become like the idolaters Allen condemned in *Reason*, worshipping powerful men instead of the Creator; referencing Romans 1:16–32 in the *Narrative*, Allen described "haughty Britons" who "forgot the Lord their God" and toasted General Burgoyne as a "demigod" after his victory at Ticonderoga, when "their faith was raised to assurance." A tyrannous and corrupt state empowers not virtuous men but monsters, like Joshua Loring, commissary of prisoners in the British army: "This Loring is a monster!—There is not his like in human shape. He exhibits a smiling countenance, and on a superficial acquaintance, seems to wear a phiz of humanity, but has been instrumentally capable of the most consummate acts of wickedness, (which were first projected by an abandoned British council, cloathed with the authority of a Howe) murdering premeditatively (in cool blood) near or quite two thousand helpless prisoners, and that in the most clandestine, mean and shameful manner, (at New York)." Although such crimes call out for "Heaven's vengeance," there is no need to imagine a wrathful God who providentially intervened to rebuke a wayward people, for when "power is not directed by wisdom, virtue, and policy, [it] never fails to destroy itself as yours [England's] had done,—it is so in the nature of things, and unfit it should be otherwise; for if it was not so, vanity, injustice, and oppression might reign triumphant forever."[29]

Allen pitied the individual Britons who remained virtuous, honorable, and humane but who nevertheless would suffer when their nation was plunged headlong into calamity. Even as a prisoner charged with treason and moved from ship to ship and prison to prison, he had met many such Englishmen, and he took pains to give them "full and ample credit" in the *Narrative*: the generous officers Bradley and Hamilton, the friendly Captain Littlejohn, the obliging Captain M'Cloud, a humane surgeon and doctor's mate, the kind midshipman Putrass, the gentlemanly Captains Smith and Craig, and others. The "good usage" he received, however, was "but little, in comparison of the bad."[30]

The challenges of his captivity summoned forth all his fortitude as a "philosopher or soldier." He had to both compose himself "inwardly" and determine how he would act toward the people around him. How could there be virtue without liberty? That is, how could he act virtuously and serve the American cause when, as a prisoner, shackled in the hull of a ship, he had so little freedom to act at all? Early in his captivity, he realized that he "could conceive of nothing more in my power but to keep up my spirits, [and] behave in a daring soldier-like manner." He would conceal his anxiety from fellow prisoners, demand proper treatment from his captors, and face death with philosophical equanimity and military courage. But this was a survival tactic: "Such a conduct (I judged) would have a more probable tendency to my preservation than concession and timidity." Late in the narrative, the primary exempla of both "internal" and "public virtue" were two brothers, common soldiers who were ready to die of starvation and disease in their fetid prison rather than swear an oath of allegiance to King George. Allen and the other paroled officers in New York were powerless to do anything to alleviate the horrible conditions of their suffering men. They were afraid to offend General Howe by petitioning him on the matter, fearing that he would simply throw them back into prison, too. Considerations of "self-preservation" deterred them; while not dishonorable, there was little public virtue in this. The hero appearing on the scene was George Washington, whose victories at Princeton and Trenton led to the prisoners' release through an exchange. Allen's only moral victory was his rejection of General Howe's offer to make him a colonel, pay him in "hard guineas," introduce him at court, and give him "a large tract of land" in Connecticut or New Hampshire if he would switch sides. Allen told the officer making the proposal that he viewed the offer "to be similar to that which the devil offered Jesus Christ."[31]

Beyond basic survival and maintaining his inward resolve, Allen's main challenge during his captivity was to navigate a social world where he seemed to be denied any basis of legitimate exchange and to negotiate with reigning powers that were morally bankrupt. He repeatedly tried to find morally acceptable grounds on which to appeal to his captors. His most frequent claim was to insist that he be treated as an officer and a gentleman, though he did not actually have a commission as an officer and did not bear the marks—education, wealth, or manners—that the British would normally recognize as gentlemanly. On board the frigate *Solebay*, he enraged Captain Thomas Symonds by demanding the gentleman's privilege of walking on the leeward side of the deck. He persistently complained whenever he was herded into the same prison cells with the common privates, "without regard to rank, education, or any other accomplishment." When one of his captors acknowledged his claim to gentlemanly status, it moved him to tears of gratitude. When that claim failed, he appealed to his captors' sense of honor. Or he tried to reason with them, arguing that their mistreatment of prisoners violated basic fairness, or that hanging him as a traitor was not in their self-interest, since he was worth more to them if used in a prisoner exchange. He appealed to their basic humanity, to a common moral sense of repulsion at the needless suffering of a fellow creature. On a couple of occasions, he turned to simple commerce, offering to buy needed provisions with his own money.[32]

All these attempts usually failed. Captain Symonds showed Allen that "a captain of a man of war was more arbitrary than a king, as he could view his territory with a look of his eye, and a movement of his finger commanded obedience." Symonds merely answered Allen's arguments by saying that a rebel's life "was of no consequence in the scale of their policy." But Symonds, Allen discovered, could at least "be diverted by good sense, humour or bravery." The next captain he had to deal with, James Montague of the frigate *Mercury*, was worse. Allen "tried to reason the matter with him, but found him proof against reason; I also held up his honour to view... but found his honour impenetrable. I then endeavored to touch his humanity, but found he had none; for his prepossession of bigotry to his own party, had confirmed him in an opinion, that no humanity was due to unroyalists, but seemed to think that heaven and earth were made merely to gratify the king." The captain thought Allen should be executed as a traitor as soon as they arrived at Halifax. He "uttered considerable unintelligible and groveling ideas, a little tinctured with monarchy, but stood well to his text of hanging me." Montague resembled the dogmatic sectarians denounced in *Reason*, who stuck to their biblical text, clung to absurd metaphysical notions, and remained irrationally committed to arbitrary sovereign power.[33]

Allen therefore reasoned that "humanity and moral suasion would not be consulted in the determining of my fate... [and] that moral virtue would not influence my destiny." Instead, he "had recourse to stratagem." He concealed his true thoughts, feelings, and intentions and attempted to manipulate his jailers into doing his bidding. He was inwardly delighted (though he "concealed it with pretended resentment") when he tricked a British officer into showing one of his letters to Lord North. With the satisfaction of a shrewd—or devious—New England merchant, he found that he had "come Yankee over him." He even determined that, "in extreme circumstances at certain times," it was "political to act in some measure the madman." Suffering insults on board the *Gaspee*, he flew into a fit of rage and with his teeth twisted out the tenpenny nail securing his handcuffs, prompting his spectators to wonder if this wild man could "eat iron." In New York City, he convinced the enemy that he was "crazy" and "wholly unmanned."[34]

Moralists would say that playing the manipulative Yankee, the self-interested dissimulator, was not merely a stratagem employed in the extreme situation of wartime captivity but a sign of a society that had lost its moral compass. But Allen's critics, like the conservative Connecticut Wits who mocked him in verse, took a different tack. Timothy Dwight's *Triumph of Infidelity* derided the "great Clodhopping oracle of man." Lemuel Hopkins, in a Hartford newspaper, began a twenty-four-line poem entitled "On Allen's Oracles of Reason": "Allen escap'd from British jails, / His tushes broke by biting nails, / Descends from hyperborean skies, / To tell the world, *the bible lies*." With class disdain, and aghast at what he perceived as democratic lawlessness in the era of Shays's Rebellion, Hopkins concluded by picturing the frontier fighter, "One hand clench'd to batter noses; / While tother other scrawls 'gainst Paul and Moses." Another writer "corrected" Hopkins's poem a month later: "Allen, who burst the tyrant's Bands, / Gnaw'd iron fetters, from his hands, / Descends from Hyperborean skies, / By Reason shews, tradition lies." The verses linked Allen's courage as fighter and writer: "His Oracle, draws bigots scowles, / And shews Priest-ridden they are fools; / When right, or reason, they may sink, / He sheds his blood, or sheds his ink."

Newspapers in Vermont and Connecticut printed a fuller attack on him in 1788. Purporting to be a letter from "Mr. Woolston, of London," the commentary seemed to focus more on the bold signature in *Reason the Only Oracle*'s preface—the assertion of self—than on the contents of the argument. The letter castigated Allen for his overweening ambition and vanity. It jabbed at his reputation as a hot-tempered brawler: the desire to "appear to know more than other men" was identical to the need "of being thought to have more courage than others" and being "ready to quarrel with every man he meets." But there was a broader point: this ambition for singularity was the root of all skepticism—religious skepticism particularly. Turning the tables on Allen's politics, the author connected the deist's vanity to the impulse for tyranny. Trying to appear different from—and more knowledgeable than—the rest of the world was a braggart's attempt to triumph as a kind of "universal monarch" in the empire of wisdom. Only this could explain why deists like Allen were "ready to contradict the reason and sense of all men."[35]

Allen concluded in *Reason the Only Oracle* "that if the human race in general, could be prevailed upon to exercise common sense in religious concerns, those spiritual fictions would cease, and be succeeded by reason and truth." A writer signing as "Common Sense, A. M." (New England clergyman Josiah Sherman) answered in *A Sermon to Swine*. Sherman admitted that he "once" gave *Reason* a "cursory reading" but did not have the book by his side as he wrote his reply. No matter: the book was patently absurd and deserved a response only because it might "strengthen the prejudices of *weak* and *wicked* minds" against the Bible. Despite the promise of a "demonstrative argument" for the divine inspiration of the scriptures, no such argument appeared in the sermon, because none was needed: their divinity was "self evident."[36]

"Common Sense" took particular aim at Allen's critique of the doctrine of atonement, the belief that Christ made reparations for man's sins by suffering and dying on the cross. Allen had found the notion that Christ could serve as the substitute for all mankind "repugnant to the first perceptions of common-sense." A person's virtues and vices were his or hers alone. Considered as a question of law, the comparison of Christ to a person who could "pay, satisfy and discharge a cash debt for another" could not work, Allen argued, because sins against God, "being of a criminal nature[,] could not be discharged or satisfied by cash or produce, as debts of a civil contract." Sherman answered that Allen had utterly misunderstood the scriptural doctrine of atonement, which was perfectly consonant with "reason, justice, common sense, or the usages of nations."[37]

Sherman's discussion of atonement, however, not only silently agreed with Allen that commercial exchange was no proper model for the forgiveness of sins but also departed from what had been the orthodox Christian position since at least the eleventh century. Sherman summarized an innovative understanding of the atonement that had been developed by the "New Divinity" followers of Jonathan Edwards, especially Sherman's mentor, Joseph Bellamy. Christ could not have sins imputed to him, and he like any innocent person could not serve as a substitute, suffering a penalty for someone else's crime. Nor could Christ "purchase" forgiveness; as one of Sherman's New Divinity colleagues put it, the language of buying and selling, of debt and credit, was appropriate for commerce but not for maxims of sin, duty, and justice. Like his fellow Edwardsean innovators, Sherman swept away Calvin's and the Puritans' understanding of the atonement; he instead described the crucifixion as an occasion allowing the Moral Governor to pardon undeserving sinners even while enforcing his laws against sin, demonstrating both his hatred of sin and his benevolence at the same time. This was a controversial view, and Sherman admitted that it was unorthodox. So much for the principal truths of the Bible being unproblematically transparent to common sense.[38]

Although Sherman, who had been a chaplain at Valley Forge, was utterly contemptuous of Allen, his discussion of atonement conceded Allen's reputation as a virtuous Revolutionary hero. To explain how Christ's suffering could atone for unworthy sinners, Sherman created a hypothetical example in which a patriotic General Allen, who had sacrificed everything for the sake of his country, could justly ask Congress to pardon traitorous sons. "For instance, we will suppose, in the time of the late contest, that Gen. Allen was a great and worthy friend of his country," Sherman began. He imagined Allen's sons joining Britain to conquer and destroy the United States. In Sherman's extended analogy, Allen is appointed by Congress to engage the enemy at his own expense. The general is captured, and the British "sacrifice, for a time, his liberty, his ease and honour, and all his wealth, and he faces death in all its formidable shapes—and his sufferings are extremely great." After the war, Allen's sons still deserve to be executed for treason. But the old general appears before Congress as their mediator and advocate. He "shews his wounds that he hath received in the cause of his country, and pleads his expense of honour, blood, and treasure," as well as the honor he brought to his country. He asks that his penitent sons be pardoned, and Congress grants his request "freely of their own grace, on account of the merit that is in their father." The story was fictitious, but the reference to Allen's wartime experience and public character was not. To admit, however grudgingly, that a deist could be a patriotic leader or a virtuous republican citizen contradicted the axiom that many like "Common Sense" continued to hold: that there was a necessary connection between deism and depravity.[39]

Deist Monster: William Beadle

William Beadle, the Wethersfield merchant, seemed to demonstrate that connection. On Tuesday, December 10, 1782, he passed a pleasant evening with family and friends. He awoke before sunrise the next morning, sent his maid on an errand, and then murdered his family. He took an axe to the heads of his wife and four young children, whom he had probably drugged with an opiate the night before, and then slit their throats from ear to ear. The horrified neighbors found the bloody footprints on the stairs leading to a Windsor chair by the kitchen fireplace, where Beadle had sat, placed the carving knife on the table in front of him, and fired two pistols into his head.

"So awful and terrible a disaster wrought wonderfully on the minds of the neighborhood," Beadle's friend Stephen Mix Mitchell would write. "The very inmost souls of the beholders were wounded at the sight." Mitchell himself had been one of the first to enter the house; a servant girl who discovered the scene with him fainted, and he had to rush back out into the cold December air and steady himself against a garden fence. All the townspeople—men and women, young and old—were drawn together and "torn by contending passions": astonishment, grief, and furious indignation. Few in town slept much that night, Mitchell wrote. Near the end of the following day, December 12, a crowd gathered in front of Beadle's house and "grew almost frantic with rage," demanding the body of the murderer. Some insisted that it be dragged to a place where four roads met and "perforated by a stake." But none wanted Beadle's corpse buried near his or her property. Finally, they stuffed the body out a window, tied the bloody knife to Beadle's chest with cords, took the corpse to the banks of the Connecticut River by a horse-drawn sled, and dumped it into a hole by the water's edge, "like the carcass of a beast." The funeral for Lydia Beadle and the children—Ansell, Elizabeth, Lydia, and Mary—was held the next day. Pastor John Marsh addressed the congregation and tried to make sense of "an event so extraordinary, surprising, and unheard of, that we can scarcely believe it a reality, though the corpses of the unhappy woman and children, with the most affecting marks of violence upon them, are here present before our eyes." Nine days later, in his Wallingford pulpit, James Dana was still so overwhelmed by the tragedy that he found it difficult to speak.[40]

The first newspaper article, printed in both the *Connecticut Courant* and *Connecticut Journal*, appeared on December 17. The opening paragraph described Beadle as a native of South Britain who had lived in Wethersfield for about ten years and in America for about twenty. He had an "amiable" wife and "four lovely and promising children" and had seemed to be a doting father and affectionate husband. A merchant whose business had been in decline for some years, he had immersed himself in "Deistical books." Papers he left behind, the article explained, showed that he had discarded common ideas of morality and came to consider human beings as "mere Machines." Letters written shortly before his death contained his declaration that he "intended to die a proper Deist" and that he believed he had the right to take his family with him. He acted "with all imaginable deliberation & composure of mind," the article reported. "The Jury of inquest were of the opinion, that he was of sound mind, and returned their verdict accordingly. 'Tis very difficult to determine where distraction begins. 'Tis evident he was rational on every other subject; on this no one conversed with him." Beadle had been alone in his closet with his thoughts and his deistical books. He developed a "new theoretic system" that on December 11 he "put in practice." The article closed by encouraging readers to weep for the victims and "detest the direful principles productive of such effects."[41]

By early January that initial article had been reprinted in newspapers in Massachusetts, Rhode Island, New York, Pennsylvania, and New Jersey. By the middle of that month, it had reached Virginia. In Boston, a broadside was published, pairing the article with eight stanzas of verse and two illustrations: a crude woodcut of three men apparently butchering babies with swords, and a skull and crossbones beneath six black coffins. The poem urged readers to "Detest the errors" that led Beadle to the deed, though it did not specify what those errors were, and also introduced the idea of the devil's influence, praying that "Satan may be bound, / Since to deceive so many he is found." One of

Beadle's letters that the initial news report mentioned found its way into print and quickly spread from newspaper to newspaper as well. It was an extract from Beadle's will, dated November 1782 and addressed to his friend Colonel John Chester. In it Beadle asked that he and his family be placed in a single coffin of natural wood—not painted black, "for the hearts it contains will be pure and white"—and buried in the grass near his garden, since he realized that "it will not do for one of my principles to approach holy ground." In the newspaper article Beadle's last requests were followed by a short account of his actual burial and the funeral service for his family at the Wethersfield church. The document and commentary were accompanied in some newspapers by "a letter from a Gentleman in Wethersfield," dated December 14, giving another account of the murder, and again mentioning the "very lengthy writings" designed "to justify his principles, which are, he says, truly deistical." The letter Beadle had his maid take to his friend Dr. Joseph Farnsworth on the morning of the murder was also published and reprinted; in it Beadle advised Farnsworth to "alarm the neighbors gently" and urge them "to be as much collected in their reason as I am now, when I and mine are going to visit our God."[42]

Letters to the editor and essays by moralists and polemicists began appearing early in the new year. Some writers expected, and others demanded, the publication of more of Beadle's writings. A correspondent signing as "A humble Professor of Christianity" linked the public exposure of Beadle's literary remains to the public display of his corpse, arguing that his papers should be published to reinforce the "fatal tendency" of his false doctrines, and his body should be exhumed and left to rot on a public gibbet to be devoured by birds of prey, as "an example for all atheists and deists." Calling upon the town, the state, or Congress to act, he declared that no authority had "a right in this case to retain the body from this just resentment of the public, nor to suppress or conceal his writings." "A Friend to Justice" also called for Beadle's body to be exhumed and hung on a gibbet to "make him a spectacle of horror to infidels." He argued that "thousands are uneasy in this State; our sister States hear of the execrable deed with horror, and are amazed that such a wretch should be suffered to be put in a grave." While no more of Beadle's letters appeared in print, his body kept reappearing like the return of the repressed. The land chosen for Beadle's grave happened to belong to the neighboring town of Glastonbury, whose townspeople, according to one account, felt themselves "insulted by the burying of such a monster" within their town limits and asked the Wethersfield selectmen to move the body. It was dug up and reburied at night in a secret spot nearby, but the second grave was soon discovered by some children. The spring waters exposed Beadle's skeleton, but before it could be moved and reburied again, the curious came, and some of "the bones were broken off and scattered through the country."[43]

As readers clamored for more information about Beadle's "character and abilities," the best that printer Isaiah Thomas in Worcester, Massachusetts, could do was reprint a verse advertisement Beadle had published in 1775, "at which time he was a considerable trader at Weathersfield." The forty-six lines "Addressed to the Ladies" revealed something of the merchant's wit and his politics as he tried to sell his stock of tea before the nonimportation agreement went into effect:

> Sweet fair ones, though I tell this Story,
> Upon my word, I am no tory;
> In spight of all tyrannick tools,
> I mean to follow virtue's rules.
> And now I pledge my word, and say
> The noble Congress I'll obey.[44]

Clergymen had been among the first to draw larger lessons from the tragedy when they attacked Beadle's principles from the pulpit. When published, their sermons joined the larger swirl of public discussion about him. James Dana's late-December sermon on Beadle, published in March, reinforced the sense of astonishment at the apparent motive for the crime. We know despotic ambition can lead to bloody war, Dana wrote to readers who had just endured the long struggle for American independence. We've heard of "murder perpetrated in the heat of passion, or through deliberate malice, or in vindication of supposed honor," and of "suicide proceeding from insanity, remorse, or discontent. But when did we hear! Where have we read of such deliberate and dispassionate murder! Murder upon principle!" John Marsh, in his funeral sermon for Lydia Beadle and the children, worried like Dana that "there are so many in this land, a land greatly distinguished in respect of religious light and liberty," who, like the deist monster Beadle, had become skeptical about the Bible as God's revealed Word.[45]

Yet there are important differences even among the New England clergymen who responded to the Beadle affair. Wethersfield's Marsh, a moderate and genteel Calvinist with a crippled hand, a large salary, and a meticulous white wig, argued that none should find it so astonishing that a man of Beadle's principles would slaughter his family. Anyone who could reject the "infallible evidences" of Christian truth could as easily reject the conscious mind's awareness of its own free agency, pervert the natural affection for his family, and extinguish natural conscience and reason. Without revelation to guide him, like religious enthusiasts he mistook the sinful impulses of his own heart for divine directives. It was obvious that men of such principles were unfit "to be intrusted either with private or public important affairs, whatever their accomplishments may be in other respects." Lyme, Connecticut's Old Calvinist George Beckwith, nearly eighty, mounted the pulpit and, like the New Light Presbyterian Damnation Murray in Newburyport, tarred the Universalists with Beadle's brush, insisting upon the crucial doctrine of the sinner's eternal punishment. James Dana, the Wallingford "heretick" who was too theologically liberal for Calvinists and too conservative for Harvard Arminians, discerned a rather different set of intellectual affinities. He had long condemned a counterintuitive though dangerous link between the teachings of certain hyper-Calvinist New England divines and the fatalism of European deists. He therefore suggested that Beadle represented a pernicious theological malady: the arguments propagated by Jonathan Edwards and his New Divinity followers denying a true freedom of the will.[46]

Pastor and poet Timothy Dwight, a grandson of Jonathan Edwards, agreed with Dana in considering what Dwight called "infidel philosophy" to be a dangerous social and political threat. However, not only did he think it was absurd to see any resemblance between deism and Edwardsean theology, he also believed it a waste of time to try to take deists seriously intellectually. Infidel philosophy, he believed, was an incoherent jumble. Deism was just another pathetically thin rationalization for sin. Years later, Dwight also confessed, as Ezra Stiles had, that as a young man he had been "strongly tempted" by deism and skepticism. But such temptation was irrational, Dwight insisted; it was the product not of cool deliberation but of sinful inclinations and prejudices, the natural bias of an unregenerate heart. The writings of deists, skeptics, and atheists merited attention only from "novelty, fashion, . . . ingenuity and celebrity," not "truth and evidence" or "serious and permanent conviction." These views enabled him to blithely gather thinkers as diverse as Voltaire, Ethan Allen, and liberal clergyman like Charles Chauncy and James Dana under Satan's banner in his 1787 poem *The Triumph of Infidelity*.[47]

Dwight's *Triumph* references Beadle several times in an eighteen-line passage. These allusions would surely have been understood by readers at the time, since the verses refer to details about the Beadle tragedy that had become part of the public record and had circulated widely. Dwight describes, for example, the deist monster pondering murder:

> In the deep midnight of his guilty mind
> Where not one solitary virtue shin'd,
> Hardly, at times, his struggling conscience wrought
> A few strange intervals of lucid thought,
> Holding her clear and dreadful mirror nigher,
> Where villain glow'd, in characters of fire. (593–98)

This refers to a passage from Beadle's letters, published in Marsh's *Great Sin and Danger*: "On the morning of the sixth of December I rose before the sun, felt calm, and left my wife between sleep and wake, went into the room where my infants lay, found them all asleep; the means of death where [were] with me, but I had not before determined whether to strike or not, but yet thought it a good opportunity. I stood over them and asked my God whether it was right or not, now to strike; but no answer came: nor I believe ever does to man while on earth. I then examined myself, there was neither fear, trembling nor horror about me. I then went into the chamber next to that to look at myself in the glass; but I could discover no alteration in my countenance or feelings: this is true as God reigns, but for further trial I yet postponed it." The final lines in this section of Dwight's poem reference Beadle being "Fix'd in cold death" (603).[48]

Later in his life, writing *Travels in New England and New York*, Dwight again reflected on the Beadle affair. He claimed that he had known the family "intimately" and concluded that "pride was unquestionably the ruin of Beadle." It was Beadle's prideful "passion"—not, in Dwight's view, a set of philosophical principles—that induced the merchant to "sit down in a sullen hostility against God and man." Seeing Beadle's deism as an effect rather than a cause, and blaming the tragedy on unreasoning passion rather than perverse philosophical principle, also seems to be the sentiment expressed by the inscription on the tombstone Wethersfield erected for Lydia and the children, "Who... fell by the hands of William Beadle, An Infatuated Man."[49]

Writers in the newspapers also pondered the relation between Beadle's beliefs and his monstrous acts. While some mentioned natural depravity, the passions of the heart, and pride, and four were sure that the devil had his hand in the tragedy, all decried Beadle's principles, though they differed in their assessment of what those principles were, the role they played in the murder/suicide, and how the public should respond to them. One writer simply blamed Beadle's turn away from the Bible; another indicated that the slaughter was the "natural fruit" of Beadle's alternative philosophy. One correspondent focused on Beadle's fatalism; another defined his speculative malady as atheism; a third insisted that his tenets had nothing to do with Universalism.[50]

In trying to assess the relation of principle to practice and determine what the public's response to either should be, two writers battled over the meaning of "common sense." A writer calling himself "A Friend to Common Sense" argued that all men were naturally sinful, but by denying eternal punishment they parted company with common sense. He himself appealed to common sense as a gesture to a commonly shared prudence, to presuppositions that should not need to be argued. Aiming not just at deists but at Universalists as well, he contended that they all ought to be "punished for entertaining and publishing [their] sentiments." Indeed, though some would call it religious persecution, he asked rhetorically, should those who deny the reality of hell be imprisoned for adhering to "this stupid, this detestable doctrine, which annihilates all restraints, insults common sense, and introduces a kind of insanity?... Common sense says yes." A newspaper essayist signing as "A Friend to Moderation and Free Inquiry" responded and, while also appealing to "common sense," charged that the first writer had blended ideas and schemes together—universalism, deism, atheism, skepticism—into a "strange jumble." The first writer had presupposed an extreme Calvinism that declared man naturally inclined to every evil and thus made God the author of sin—a warped version of Christianity that itself encouraged people to renounce the scriptures entirely and drove many to a dangerous spiritual despair. But, the "Friend to Moderation" continued, this effort of modern inquisitors to castigate and punish heterodox religious opinion was only the most recent that he had seen in his nearly sixty years. Arminians, Antinomians, Sandimanians—each in turn was denounced as a threat to religion, morality, and social order. Common sense dictated, however, that civil authority stay out of such disputes.[51]

The fullest account of Beadle's life and death was appended to Marsh's funeral sermon as "A Letter from a Gentleman in Wethersfield, to his Friend, containing a Narrative of the Life of William Beadle (so far as it is known) and the particulars of the Massacre of Himself and Family." The anonymous author was Stephen Mix Mitchell, a county court judge, representative to the General Assembly, and delegate to the Continental Congress. The letter was republished in July 1783 as *A Narrative of the Life of William Beadle*; its cover had a crude woodcut illustration bearing black coffins with hearts on them, for Lydia and the children, and Beadle's corpse lying next to his knife, hatchet, and pistols. The *Narrative* would be republished in 1794, 1795, and 1805, with more details of the murder scene added by another hand, and a German edition appeared in Ephrata, Pennsylvania, in 1796.

Much of the *Narrative* described the tragedy itself and the town's reaction to it, but since Beadle's death Mitchell had also been able to fill in some of the details of the merchant's biography. Beadle had been born the natural son of an English gentleman (Mitchell admitted that he was speculating on this point) in a village in Essex, not far from London, around 1730. After establishing a reputation as a man of honesty and integrity, Beadle went with Governor Charles Pinfold to Barbados, where he stayed for six years. In 1763 he became a merchant in New York, subsequently trading in three other Connecticut towns before settling in Wethersfield in the early 1770s. Mitchell was the first commentator to pay much attention to the trader's business troubles. Since coming to Wethersfield, he explained, Beadle had refused to sell on credit. When the war began, he had accumulated "a very handsome assortment of goods for a country store," which he sold for cash at the Continental currency's face value. Rather than investing in real estate, he kept the money, "intending to keep his property within his own reach; believing it always secure while his eye was upon it." But

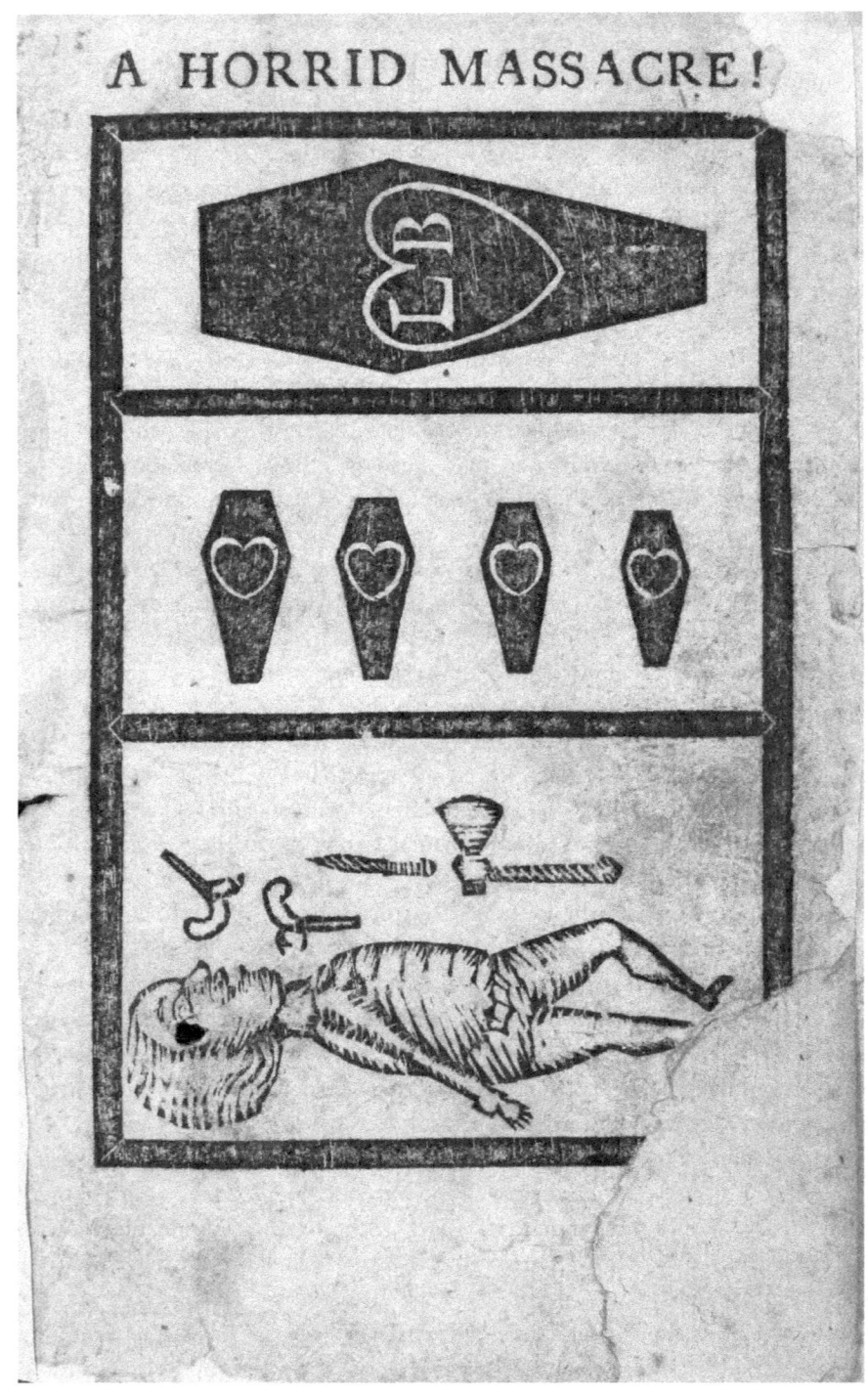

Stephen Mix Mitchell, *A Narrative of the Life of William Beadle* (Hartford, Conn., 1783), cover. In this crude woodcut, the coffins with hearts represent Beadle's wife, Lydia, and their children; below, his corpse is beside the weapons he used to slay his family and himself. Courtesy of the American Antiquarian Society.

the paper currency dropped in value through the war and was officially depreciated by the legislature. "Continental currency taught him that wealth could take itself wings and fly away; Notwithstanding his vigilance." As for the merchant's religious opinions, Mitchell learned that Beadle had made an offhand remark to a neighbor once indicating that "he very early became acquainted with a club in London who were Deists." Yet in Wethersfield, at least, "he claimed to be a Christian, and offered two of his children for baptism."[52]

As the printer of both the *Narrative* and extracts from Marsh's funeral sermon noted, Mitchell's view differed from the pastor's on at least one important question. Both men discussed the nightmares Lydia Beadle had endured the weeks before her murder. She had mentioned them to neighbors, and Beadle himself wrote about them in papers he left behind. In one she was threatened with a great punishment; in another, on Thanksgiving, she dreamed that she saw her three daughters lying dead and frozen; in a third, she saw blood spattering her husband's papers and was haunted by the sight of a man wounding himself "beyond recovery," causing blood to "guggle" from different parts of his body. Reverend Marsh mocked a man who would deny that the scriptures were God's revelation and yet superstitiously look for portents in dreams. Mitchell was more circumspect, perhaps revealing some of the popular religious beliefs that informed interpretations of the Beadle affair in the pews if not the pulpits. No one could tell where these dreams came from, Mitchell wrote. Perhaps, he began naturalistically, the fact that Beadle had started carrying his weapons to their bedside had simply alarmed his wife and troubled her sleep. And perhaps "in these modern days" the "learned world" would consider it fanaticism to even hazard a conjecture that there might be more to the dreams than that. No one could "pronounce with satisfactory certainty" on this question, he cautioned, and "every man must think for himself." Yet "some great and good characters have thought such intimations were at times given from on high, to convince mankind of the reality of the invisible world." Lydia Beadle's dreams, after all, had been almost literally fulfilled. The weather had been clear and pleasant on December 10, but both the sun and the moon were blotted from the sky during the terrible deed the next morning. It remained overcast until Beadle's corpse was dumped into its hole. Then suddenly the air cleared and grew cold, and the faces of the victims in their open coffins at the church stiffened with frost, just as Lydia had foreseen.[53]

Mitchell also told a story that would be referenced by the inscription on the gravestone that the town would erect for the murdered family, a story illustrating the Revolutionary virtue and manly sentiment that Beadle himself mistakenly thought he exemplified. Some old soldiers happened to be passing through town on the day of the murder. Seeing the bodies of Mrs. Beadle and the children, "notwithstanding all their firmness, the tender sympathetic tear stealing gently down their furrowed cheeks, betrayed the anguish of their hearts." Viewing Beadle's body, they muttered "an oath or two of execration" but were powerless to do anything except walk away in "silent sorrow." The story became elaborated. The soldiers, it was said, when first encountering the body of the perpetrator, "instinctively placed their hands on their swords, [and] half withdrew them from their scabbards." The last of four lines of verse concluding the victims' epitaph reads "And Indignation half unsheathe their swords." Too late to act, the soldiers could at least feel appropriately. There was no such sympathy, of course, expressed over William's remains. Tradition has it that Beadle's grave was marked, too; on a nearby tree, someone supposedly carved the following: "William Beadle! Here he lies, / Nobody laughs, nobody cries,— / Where he's gone, or how he fares, / Nobody knows, nobody cares."[54]

Stephen Mix Mitchell quoted from Beadle's papers for his narrative, but he supported the decision not to publish the papers themselves. "Much has been said in favour of publishing his writings by those who have not seen them; those who have seen them have doubted the propriety of such a measure." The decision was made by a committee of three clergymen: James Dana, Chauncy Whittelsey of New Haven's First Church, and Ezra Stiles. Stiles received copies of the papers from Beadle's former friend Colonel John Chester on Christmas Day 1782. The bundle contained four letters to Chester, two to Mitchell, and Beadle's will, all written between the first week of November 1782 and the evening before his death, the total amounting to about twenty-six folio pages. Stiles made long extracts in his Literary Diary.[55]

In his letters, Beadle tried to explain his beliefs to his friends. He utterly denied the common canard that deism could be equated with atheism. "That there is some wonderful Power or Powers that makes me and all," he wrote, "I have no doubt. But whether there is one Being only or one Million of Beings no man can judge." Yet human beings remained ignorant of the specific nature and intentions of God because no credible evidence demonstrated that there had ever been any direct communication between Creator and creature: "I believe in the Power that formed me, but I also believe that he never personated Man, nor ever condescended to talk to him." There was no reason to think that Moses, Mohammed, and Jesus (a truly sublime moral character, Beadle acknowledged) had not lived flawed lives and died like everyone else. Beadle had studied the scriptures and found much to admire there; clearly they were written by wise and good men who meant well, "but that there is any more real Inspiration in them than in any man that thinks and speaks as he passes along the street, I rather deny than doubt." The moral elements of Christianity would be a benevolent system if they were ever actually put into practice, but the religion as a whole was filled with inconsistencies, impenetrable mysteries, and absurd claims to the miraculous. Like the other religions of the world it was "foisted on ignorant mortals," and it took "a real reasonable Creature" to discover the "Trick." Reason—critical discernment—he argued, expressing the standard sentiment of radical Enlightenment demystification, allows the scales of fantasy and superstition to drop from our eyes. Only the "Deist truly sees God through that Book of Nature and is contented for Himself and rejoices that he can discover the springs of all other Religions which the Populace tumble about just as Babies do their play things." He believed that there was a future state of existence after death, or "perhaps a thousand different future states for man (and it may be for Brutes)."[56]

But he had no confidence that reason could press much beyond these bare suppositions of a creative power and an afterlife. He did not proceed, like Allen, and build a philosophical theology by following the necessities of logical implication. Nor did he look to the heavens and the earth and find God's character and intentions in the regular laws of the natural world. Although the critical rationality of the discerning deist could see through the foolishness of traditional religions, it could not fill the void left by the loss of faith. Beadle professed a profound epistemological skepticism: "I choose to leave this World as I found it, honestly confessing that I know not what to make of it nor never did, nor never will any man that thinks, know what to make of it while he stays in it."[57]

Terse statements Beadle left behind echoed skeptical sentiments in his favorite books. In his will, he left prized volumes to friends. To Thaddeus Burr, Esq., of Fairfield, Connecticut, he bequeathed the *Miscellanies* by Sir William Temple, "an author I dearly love." Temple acknowledged that reason gave man a great advantage over the rest of creation, but it also subjected him to trouble and misery. The skepticism ran deeper in the two volumes of Montaigne's *Essays* that Beadle willed to his friend John Chester. Although Michel de Montaigne was "the greatest Egotist on Earth," Beadle thought that "the whole town of Weathersfield is not worth half the Wisdom in that book." Montaigne famously criticized the limitations of human reason when it was not aided by supernatural grace. The early pages of Montaigne's longest essay, where he humbles human pretensions to knowledge and likens them in dozens of ways to animals, might be aptly, if crudely, summarized by Beadle's conclusion: "The Wisdom of Philosophers, the Trophies of Conquerors and the Squabbles of Divines, appear in reality more ridiculous than the droll faces and tricks of Baboons and Monkeys."[58]

To work out the relation of skepticism and faith, and to discover a way to live and die well, Beadle drew selectively from authors like Montaigne and Temple, but even more seemed to sacralize the process of sympathetic reading. Montaigne concluded that "philosophy in general agrees that there is an ultimate remedy to be prescribed for every kind of trouble: namely, ending our life if we find it intolerable." He was not championing this position, as Beadle would, but criticizing the ultimate powerlessness of philosophy. Yet Montaigne himself was drawn to classical tales of noble suicide and the Stoic virtues of dying well. Beadle assured

Colonel Chester that no one needs to "kill himself that reads him [Montaigne], for he is a merry old Wag and speaks as much of living as dying." Montaigne had the consoling guidance of his Catholic faith, which he believed offered truths about both morality and eternal salvation that were above reason and beyond nature. His curiosity and desire, his hope and his suffering, could finally come to rest on "the changeless foundation of [God's] holy Word." Beadle "discovered ten thousand Beauties" in the Bible and claimed to honor the men who wrote it and "delight in their thoughts," but ultimately it was a text like any other, an amalgam of human wisdom and foolishness. From those texts—the Bible as well as the works of writers like Montaigne, Shakespeare, Alexander Pope, and Temple— he gathered "opinions," if not divine truths, and made them his own: that the Creative Power in the universe was God, "my father and not my Enemy"; that there was no devil; that to fear death was cowardice.

Yet just as Christians claimed that reading the Word not only provided knowledge but could transform the soul, Beadle felt that his reading had molded the essence of who he was: "The Wisdom and Discernment of many noble fools that have tho't and wrote in almost every age and nation I have incorporated into my very frame and almost adore them." His private reading was important not just for what he read but for how he read. "Men in general read the best of Writers, as Clowns eat a delicate Dish, swallow it quick but never taste it nor think of it more." Beadle tasted good writing and became a man of good taste; he chewed things over and gave ideas due deliberation; he experienced books and felt such a profound admiration for some of what he read that his reaction bordered on reverence for the divine.[59]

The sympathetic correspondence between Beadle's "frame" and the "noble fools" who had thought and felt more deeply than most was a key to his quest for a higher truth. In the dead of winter he read James Thomson's "Summer," a hymn to the bounteous pleasures of a green and pleasant land, and he felt his spirits lift: "Serene and even joyful have I passed this pleasant day," he wrote. He recommended that Colonel Chester read the "exalted" passages in Thomson or "in a thousand other Books and when you find the highest strains, then you will find the Soul of Wm. Beadle." He reflected on the power of language and art to cross time and space to create "kindred Spirits" from "Sons of Science" with similar sensibilities. "When a fine voice, man or Woman, judiciously turn their strains to you, do you not cleave to and love them? Or if you hum a fine piece of Music to y[our]self, composed by one you never saw or heard, is there not a force of sympathy that binds your soul to his[?]" Beadle's imagined community of kindred spirits was composed mostly of personalities he encountered in books, since "there are but few men capable of Deism. They are when found like a Diamond among a million pebbles." Although "my circumstances were always rather narrow, which were great disadvantages in this world," Beadle wrote, "... I have great reason to think that my soul is above the common mould." On earth, or certainly in late eighteenth-century Christian America, such a soul could commune with like-minded men only when alone with his books; in heaven, as he tried to imagine it, "what then must be the Glee when every Discord is removed, and men that lived a thousand years ago shall hand us to our seats?"[60]

Beadle found few kindred spirits in the community of Wethersfield. He had a circle of friends and was a member of the highest society in that prosperous river town. But the façade that the respected merchant showed to neighbors was not the inner man. Mitchell, who claimed to know him best, said that he could never get Beadle "to mention a single syllable relating to his age, parentage, or early occupation." He conversed with Mitchell about some of his opinions—including his philosophy of suicide—and his letters to Colonel Chester indicate a friendship of some warmth, but Beadle masked his deism from everyone, including, apparently, the wife he professed to dearly love.

His philosophical alienation had a parallel in his failed economic strategy. It is impossible to know if his final disillusionment with Christianity preceded or followed his economic troubles; perhaps his despair merely strengthened long-held convictions. In his mind, though, the two were intertwined. In his 1775 verse advertisement, Beadle had invoked the values of the moral economy and had rooted marketplace exchanges in the relations of virtuous citizens and neighborly families. He asked "Fair Ladies" to buy his stock of tea before the boycott took effect; he had a wife, after all, he noted, who might find the "noxious Herb," like Eve's apple, too hard to resist. So to "help us keep our virtue sound," he urged his readers to "quickly purchase 'tother pound." However, by demanding cash and denying credit to the customers who came into his shop, Beadle placed his trust in a "Continental" cash economy over day-to-day commercial exchanges with his neighbors. He felt that he had done the lawful, patriotic, and honorable thing by selling goods for Continental currency according to its legal value; others cheated, speculated, abused credit, and then benefited when Congress devalued the currency, ruining honest fools like Beadle who had taken the government at its word. He had not been undone by abstract market forces; wealth, in his view, did not merely "take to itself wings and fly away," as Mitchell would phrase it. It was the fault of bad men in a corrupt society. Beadle was "greatly incensed with the public for Depreciation," Stiles wrote, summarizing passages of Beadle's will that Stiles chose not to transcribe. The merchant obsessed over the "parcel of Continental trash" that had cost him twelve hundred pounds and cursed the legislators who voted for depreciation. He condemned the "monstrous Conduct" of almost all who called themselves Christ's disciples and yet by their actions stabbed their supposed savior in the heart every day.[61]

The lesson was clear: the world did not reward virtue; it crushed the good along with the naïve, the weak, and the poor. Inferior wretches "laughed at and despised and trampled on" noble souls who had been thrown down by bad luck. For Beadle, this cruel turn of the marketplace and the upside-down social world it created had a broader philosophical and theological resonance. Christianity described human beings as "free agents," Beadle thought, and Christians claimed to perceive God's will in his acts of Providence, which at least to some extent were supposed to reward virtue and punish sin in this world as well as the next. But Beadle saw no moral logic to experience. Thomson taught as much in "Summer," in a dark passage telling the tale of blameless Amelia, inexplicably struck down by a lightning bolt in an afternoon storm (lines 894–944). The heartless realities of Revolutionary commerce had become Beadle's deadly storm. He used words like "fate," "fortune," "accident," and "luck." The result was a "desperate Disease" that required "a desperate Cure." Though he seems to have only fallen from the ranks of the wealthiest in Wethersfield to the middling sort, he felt he was enduring a hell on earth, claiming that "I am in such a situation that I cannot procure food, raim't nor fuel for myself and family." It made no sense that he should suffer so. He pointed to his "sincere prayers and desires both to know and do the will of the great creator." He mentioned his "continued efforts to promote the Happiness of my fellow men, even to the Emancipation of every slave on Earth" and his "Charity [that] has extended even to the Brutes and to the Insects." He stressed all his "strenuous Exertions for that system of Government I thought best for mankind." Benevolence, patriotism, and even piety of a sort: he had "lived well, meant well, and done well." And yet the world had crushed him. Where was the moral logic in that?[62]

Still, he insisted that only a creature puffed up with his own pride and vanity would conclude that there was no logic just because human beings were unable to actually see it—just because "the great Creator has not thought proper to let him know for what Purpose he conducts matters as he does on Earth." Shunning the atheist's universe of blind chance, Beadle determined that all of creation must be "directed by the Hand of Heaven" and that therefore man was "a perfect Machine who can do nothing but as he is operated upon by Some Superior Power." If this were the case, he reasoned, "we are all impelled to say and act all that we Say and act," and therefore "there is no Such Thing as Sin."[63]

Such convictions, however, did not free him to do whatever he wanted; they impelled him to somehow find out what God intended. Referring to Jesus in the Garden of Gethsemane, he agreed "that the Will of God should only be done and nothing of mine." It was a surrender of self, a surrender of agency, an attempt to become a more perfect machine for the frictionless enactment of divine intentions. The question, in the face of God's continuing silence, remained: What to do? The Stoic logic of suicide was persuasive; he had been convinced, and had even contemplated killing himself, twenty years before. But what of his children? He seems to be at once a caricature of eighteenth-century patriarchal power and of paternal sentimentalism. Because he had a "hand in bringing [them] into the World," he felt that his responsibility for his children, and his power over them, were absolute. As it is "a father's duty to provide well for his Flock, I chose to consign them over to better hands," he wrote, at once acknowledging his failure and asserting his right to transfer his proprietorship. His family was an extension of self. "For years back I have thought it no Crime to deprive myself of Life," he wrote. "But how to divide myself from myself that is my family, has been my only Disturbance." It was not his right, however, but his compassion that finally compelled him to act. He planned "to close the Eyes" of his children "thro' perfect Humanity, and the most endearing fondness and Friendship. For never did mortal father feel more of these tender Ties than myself." Deciding about his wife was more difficult. In her case, he acknowledged, he had no right to take her life. But she would be financially destitute without a husband, socially stigmatized after the "Shocking Disaster" that was about to take place, and psychologically broken after the loss of her beloved children. "I concluded it would be unmerciful in me to leave her behind." Beadle was indeed a man of feeling.[64]

He did not come to his final solution quickly. He deliberated about the murders, he wrote, for three years. "Any Man that undertakes any great affair... ought to be very deliberate indeed; and think and reflect again and again." But reason was not—and never could be—enough. So he sought for signs of divine intention in daily life. "I was determined not to hasten the matter, but kept hoping that still providence would turn up something to prevent it if the Intent was wrong." Mitchell would later report that Beadle had uncovered a well on his property: Would God choose to have one of his children fall in? During the previous summer, the merchant had encouraged his son to swim out into the deep waters of the Connecticut River: Would God use the currents to claim the boy? Beadle sent his wife to her relatives in Fairfield in November, but God returned her to Wethersfield ten days sooner than Beadle expected: Was this a sign that she should come with Beadle and the children to heaven? God, as always, was silent. On the morning of December 6, Beadle went into the bedroom where his children lay sound asleep. He had his weapons with him. "I stood over them, and asked my God, whether it was right or not now to strike, but no answer came. Nor I believe ever does to man while on earth."[65]

Perhaps Beadle's inner experience itself might allow him to sense God's inclinations. Perhaps the answer could be found not by trying to discern divine truths by reason or by close observation of daily life but by establishing a sympathetic connection to the Author of the Book of Nature. To read that Book, Beadle looked to his own heart rather than to the world. Perhaps his own sentiments, his own sensibilities, his own refined moral sense, could serve as a sensorium of the divine will. Hearing no answer from God as he stood over his sleeping children, "I then examined myself." He did not tremble; he felt neither fear nor horror. Walking into the next room, he looked at his face in the mirror, "but I could discover no Alteration in my Countenance or feelings." Who but God "has power to give a Mortal strength like this?" The experience of writing his final letters seemed to be another test, and another confirmation: "I really believe that the true God supports me! For while I am writing these very words, and meditating this intended Deed, no singular Anguish of Mind affects me, and why sh[oul]d it? For my Intentions are of the purest kind." When his wife told him her dream about his blood-spotted papers and the bleeding, dying man, he felt "unappalled," and that feeling helped support his conviction that "the hand of Heaven is really with us." When she dreamed of her daughters lying dead and frozen, "even yet I am little affected," he wrote. "O my God! Wonderful indeed are thy Works." His reaction to the dreams, rather than the dreams themselves, seemed to him to be the surest disclosure of divine will. In a letter to Mitchell, he wondered if he was actually becoming superstitious. He alluded to "Sundry Intimations," which he did not describe but which he thought came from God to convince him that he was right. "I seem to be convinced in a steady calm and reasonable way, that it is appointed for me to do it, that it is my duty and that it must be done. That it is God himself that prompts and directs me in all my Reflexions and Circumspection, I really believe." Aside from the valorization of calmness and reason, this was not Enlightenment rationality. Like those called Antinomians in the seventeenth century, he was searching for immediate revelations in experience; like those labeled enthusiasts in the so-called Great Awakening, he was trying to read God's will in the sensations of his body.[66]

He had, it was true, some lingering doubts. Like Descartes, who considered the possibility that an evil spirit rather than God was leading him out of the labyrinth of skepticism, Beadle sometimes wondered if the power that moved him was the devil's after all. But his intentions felt too pure, his inner light too clear, the elevation of his soul too sublime for that to be the case. "I and my family shall go off this stage Martyrs to that Cause that I fondly believed to be the Cause of Justice, Virtue & freedom." On December 10 he felt "serene and even joyful" reading Thomson's "Summer." "Thank Heaven," he wrote to Colonel Chester, "for I believe the day is now come, this a glorious one, and Providence seems to smile on the deed." The next morning the neighbors found the bodies.[67]

American Religious Common Sense in the New Republic

When Ezra Stiles delivered his election sermon on May 8, 1783, his main purpose was to celebrate America's rising glory at the end of the Revolutionary War and the beginning of what he hoped would be a new era of peace and prosperity. But he also discussed deism—as personal experience, intellectual problem, and political threat. Stiles knew that deism could not be dismissed as merely madness. He confessed that as a younger man he, too, had "passed thro the cloudy darksome valley of skepticism, and stood on the precipice...of deism." He pitied those caught in the "vortex" of deistical arguments, tempted by the hope to "ascend aloft above the clouds of prejudices" to "a superior discernment in morals, with high sensibility, sentimental and liberal ideas." Stiles suggested that there was considerable intellectual pride and juvenile self-delusion at work here, but there had been far more to his own struggle with deism decades before: he had wrestled with Hume, Bolingbroke, and the implications of Newtonian science for eight years and did not become settled in his Christian convictions until he was nearly thirty. By 1783, though, he could still tremble at the danger that dabblers in deism exposed themselves to; he could "almost bleed at every pore" for those captivated by "the deficient reasonings of deism."[68]

Stiles then conducted an elaborate thought experiment, imagining the establishment of three polities—one idolatrous, the second deistic, and the third Christian. The Yale College president began as if he were merely about to go through the paces of a familiar academic exercise in eighteenth-century Christian apologetics. Let us imagine, Stiles began, three contiguous empires beginning with the same "social virtues, laws of justice, benevolence and morals of civil

(Left) Nathaniel Smibert, "Ezra Stiles" (1756) and (right) Reuben Moulthrop, "Ezra Stiles" (1794). As a young man, Stiles was drawn to deism and skepticism; as an old one, he worried about their political implications. Both courtesy of the Yale Art Gallery, Yale University.

society." Nations rooted in either idolatry or deism would never be able to sustain virtue and morality. Idolaters, who transfer worship from the Creator to the creature, would, like those who kissed the golden calf, quickly descend into "the most impure obscenities and libidinous revellings." The deists would be able to say nothing about "pardoning mercy" for sins, holding as they do such an exorbitantly high opinion of the "excellency and dignity of man." But there was no need to stay with these hypothetical polities. Much of the globe was still populated by idolaters, Stiles wrote, pointing to the lewd temples and pagodas of the East Indies. As for the morality of modern deism, his American audience did not need to imagine a nation "full of *Rochesters* and *Chesterfields*" (the first remembered as an utterly debauched Restoration courtier and the second as a tutor in the aristocratic arts of social masquerade and manipulation) to conceive of its flaws. The development of modern deism could be represented by a figure much closer to home: "that sublime genius, that deistical madman," William Beadle.[69]

Stiles's comparison of polities was no mere intellectual exercise. His aim was to focus on the relations of church and state in the new United States. The country, he admitted, was "in no danger of idolatry." But although avowed deists were "very thinly sown," the early 1780s could nonetheless be called a "period of deism and skeptical indifferentism in religion." As the states formed new constitutions, he lamented, there was a general political sentiment against even "the most liberal" establishment of Christianity. Government, many Americans in various states were beginning to say, ought to have no more to do with religion beyond "keep[ing] the civil peace among contending sects." Moreover, the idea was gaining ground that a political candidate's religious convictions were irrelevant to an assessment of his suitability for office, or, even worse, that deists or men indifferent to religion were actually the most suited for government because they would not favor their own denomination. The political danger was obvious, and the solution equally so: government needed to patronize the "principles of our common Christianity."[70]

Legislatures struggled to affirm a Christian culture but safeguard religious liberty; politicians wanted to inculcate civic virtue but differed over its relation to sectarian forms of piety. In Massachusetts, the 1778 constitution guaranteed religious liberty to Protestants only; the 1780 constitution continued tax support for the Protestant churches (which they would receive until 1833). Connecticut's 1784 revision of laws also perpetuated state funding for churches, only liberalizing the previous legal preference for Saybrook Platform Congregationalism by extending, technically at least, equal treatment to all Protestant denominations. New Hampshire's constitution in 1784 continued to limit civil rights and restrict officeholding to Protestants. Ethan Allen's Vermont in 1786 extended rights to non-Protestants but still insisted that officeholders swear to a belief in God and the divine inspiration of the Old and New Testaments. Other states also limited officeholding to Protestants (North Carolina and Georgia), to Christians (Maryland and Pennsylvania), or to Trinitarian Christians (Delaware). Georgia, however, dropped its restriction in 1789, and Pennsylvania broadened its requirement to include all believers in God and a future state of reward and punishment. There were other countervailing trends, too. Supporters of a 1784 bill for a tax to support the Christian churches in Virginia were motivated in part by their perception of a worrisome spread of deism; petitioners against the measure shared this worry (most were evangelicals) but agreed with Jefferson and Madison that the proposed cure would be worse than the disease. Instead, the Act for Establishing Religious Freedom passed in 1786, and Virginia joined Rhode Island in its prohibition of religious taxes and religious tests for civil service. The double declaration of the First Amendment to the United States Constitution prohibiting the establishment of religion and protecting its free exercise applied only to the federal level, of course, leaving the states to continue to work out the meaning of religious liberty and the relationship of Christianity and public virtue on their own. When the maverick itinerant Baptist John Leland called in 1791 for religious liberty to be extended to "heathens, deists, jews and papists," his was a voice crying nearly alone in the wilderness in many states but articulating an increasingly common opinion in others: when Tennessee formed its constitution in 1796, it required officeholders to declare a belief in God and a future state of rewards and punishments—bringing deists like Allen or Beadle within the pale of state-sanctioned religiosity.[71]

Surprisingly, no one—not even Ezra Stiles—commenting on the Beadle affair mentioned that deism was not only outside the boundaries of constitutional toleration but also illegal in Connecticut. Colonial statutes often defined blasphemy and profanity specifically to include the disparagement of the Trinity or the scriptures, and these laws continued into the early national era and beyond. Since 1750 Connecticut had made merely denying ("by Writing, Printing, Teaching, or advised Speaking") that the scriptures were divine and Jesus was God a felony; the denial need not be made with "contumaciously reproaching" language or connected to any charge of malicious intent. The statute named the crime "Deism." Connecticut jurist Zephaniah Swift in 1795 explained that "to prohibit the open, public, and explicit denial of the popular religion of a country, is a necessary measure to preserve the tranquility of a government." Not even infidels who lived in a Christian country ought to complain of this, since they, too, benefited from the moral society that Christianity created.[72]

Stiles focused upon the character of American leadership rather than on specific legislation. In his own state he saw "deistical or dubious characters" who were "intriguing themselves into political popularity": of the eighty-five men who led the state ballot in 1794, he counted only thirty "religious characters"; of the forty lawyers in the group, there were "about one third decided Revelationists, one third said to be decided Deists, [and] the other third doubtful." He still had faith that the clergy could persuade voters to elect Christian magistrates. But his national scorecard was less precise, and less optimistic. By the early 1790s he felt that the cause might already be lost "in Congress and the Legislatures of the Southern States." He grudgingly admitted that deism and civic virtue were not always impossible to combine, writing admiringly of Governor Stephen Hopkins of Rhode Island, who, though a deist, was "a glorious Patriot!" When he heard of Ethan Allen's death in Feburary 1789, though, he could only think of the "scurrilous Reflexions on Revelation" in *Reason the Only Oracle of Man* and imagine Allen suffering torments in hell. After reading George Washington's reference to the "providential Agency" that had been "conspicuous in establishing these United States as an Independent nation," Stiles could happily conclude that Washington was "a Revelationist."[73]

The response of his old friend Benjamin Franklin to Stiles's 1790 inquiry about religious opinions was less cheering, although it illustrated the important distinction between private disbelief and public denial. Franklin, asking that his opinions be kept confidential, said he believed in God, Providence, and immortality but doubted the divinity of Christ. But because that last belief helped promote morality—because the supernatural warrant of the scriptures seemed to enforce, for most people, the excellent moral precepts they contained—skeptics in a Christian society ought to keep their doubts to themselves. William Beadle, in contrast to Ethan Allen, had agreed. The merchant had believed that the religions of the world, however warped by superstition and falsehood, tried to promote the honor of the Deity. (Purity of intention, for Beadle, could redeem the misguided act.) Christianity seemed suited to the people who embraced it, and they ought not to be disturbed in their faith. Beadle had no urge to demystify the masses; unlike Allen, he seemed not to have had a fantasy about entering the republic of letters and debating the learned, either, except perhaps when alone with his thoughts and his books. Colonel Chester, the merchant wrote, could share the literary remains of William Beadle with as few or as many people as he wished. Although he hoped that there might be some sympathetic reader out there for him—his writing might "someday give some new Ideas to a new Speculative Genius like myself that may prove beneficial to him, though it appears like the worst of poison to others"—Beadle did not ask that his letters be published. Stiles and the other ministers prevented publication because they worried about those other sympathetic readers. Stephen Mix Mitchell explained that Beadle's writings remained unpublished "not because his reasonings against revelation were in any degree unanswerable, but lest they might have some effect on weak and melancholy minds." This was the flipside of Franklinian prudence. The cautious deist was content to enjoy his beliefs and doubts privately. The cautious Christian would rather that deists stayed in the closet—not because

Christian apologists in the early American republic lacked confidence in the reasonableness of Christianity but because they lacked confidence in the reasonableness of the American people.[74]

Some Christians were not so cautious. Henry Pattillo, writing in 1788, expected Christian apologists in America, unlike their more genteel European brethren, to go after infidels with hammer and tongs. But others found trying to argue with deists exasperating. "It is very difficult to converse with men of this description with any prospect of advantage," complained a Massachusetts writer who summoned the "horrid memory" of William Beadle against a deistical opponent in 1791. "They directly deny most of those fundamental propositions, that are self-evident, and which admit not of demonstration, and upon which all argumentation is founded." The essential presupposition this writer had in mind was the divine inspiration of the scriptures. There were others: that conscience, or any natural moral sense, was a frail thing, unable to be the foundation of an ethical society; that those untouched by grace were so corrupted by sin that to keep their destructive passions in check they needed divine law as guidance and the fear of eternal punishment as a motive. Just as true liberty meant obedience to divine law and not licentiousness, the only commonsensical position, many Christian writers believed, was to realize that common sense alone was not enough to keep men and women from madness and society from chaos.[75]

The boundaries of acceptable religious belief were marked by scorn and policed by ridicule more than they were defined by argument. A newspaper anecdote in 1785 noted that the term "deist" had recently changed its meaning: whereas once it had signified believers in God (Christian and non-Christian alike) as opposed to atheists, now it stood for those who opposed and rejected Christianity. Another article in the same year contended that "deism" was the common term for indifference to all religion. A short essay attributed to Governor William Livingston of New Jersey that mocked deists as blockheads ran in five newspapers in the 1780s. Not every discussion of deism in the press labeled deists as fools and pariahs, however. A list of religious definitions by the British reformer John Jebb appeared in four newspapers in 1788, including presses from Beadle's Connecticut and Allen's Vermont. Jebb regretted that some lingering doctrinal absurdities in Protestantism drove some otherwise reasonable people to reject the scriptures. Yet Jebb, "a believer in Christ," still thought "that deism and sound morality are not incompatible."[76]

Allen and Beadle had raised troubling questions that could not be easily brushed aside, shouted down, or answered simply with a "thus saith the Lord." Without the guidance of the scriptures, did deism collapse the relation between God and man into fatalism—turning a moral agent into merely God's machine? That may have been true for Beadle, but the same was being said of Calvinism. Then did deism encourage man, on the other hand, to overemphasize his free will, divinize the self, and supplant God? Yet even those who derided Allen's arrogance did not misread him to this extent. Without the Bible, was sanity itself threatened? Yet Beadle seemed to his neighbors to be a reasonable and virtuous man until that final morning, and though Allen played the madman for his British captors, the *Narrative* portrayed him as crazy like a fox in the cause of liberty. What, then, was the relation between religious belief and public virtue?

The deist provocations of Ethan Allen and William Beadle expose the making of American religious common sense as a cultural process. Public champions of Christianity realized that because of the social, cultural, and economic disruptions caused by the Revolutionary War, and in the new political environment the Revolution had ushered into being, becoming a Christian nation would not simply be the easy perpetuation of a religious heritage. To maintain Christianity as the foundation of a nation that had rejected traditional authority by appealing to self-evident truths, many American Protestants felt compelled to link defenses of the Bible and appeals to "common sense"—a fund of sensible truisms derived from universal human experience. Yet before the last years of the eighteenth century, ethical reasoning grounded upon universal moral instinct or upon the epistemologically trustworthy faculties of normal human perception was rejected by most orthodox Christians and evangelicals because it flattered sinful human nature and seemed to render God's revelation in the scriptures unnecessary. In short, politics and ethics based upon common sense seemed more deistic than Christian. Scottish Common Sense philosophy would allow American theologians and educators to Christianize common sense, handing them arguments they would use against the faith's cultured despisers from the 1790s through the Civil War. But the references to common sense by antideist writers in the 1780s were not gestures toward the logical edifice of Scottish philosophy; they were rhetorical attempts to claim that the divine inspiration of the scriptures was a fact that could not be contested by reasonable American citizens. The dominance of Common Sense philosophy in American intellectual history grew out of the broader cultural strains and conflicts laid bare in the 1780s. Both the deist hero and the deist monster brought to the surface fundamental concerns about the moral nature of the new American citizen and about how the newly united states could secure religious liberty and yet create a society still beholden not just to Nature's God but to the God of the Old and New Testaments.

2

Souls Rising

The Authority of the Inner Witness, and Its Limits

How do we know, skeptics asked, that the Bible is true and the Gospel's offer of salvation real? Methodism, which grew from a tiny, despised branch of the Church of England in the 1770s to the largest religious denomination in the country by the middle of the nineteenth century, offered deceptively simple answers to these questions. The movement's founder, John Wesley, taught that anyone who had not willfully turned his conscience to stone would have an inner witness to the scriptures' moral truths and the reality of his own sinfulness; if he earnestly sought divine mercy, he would recognize the truth of salvation when he felt the Holy Spirit wash those sins away. Methodists and other evangelical Protestants considered faith to be a self-validating personal experience. The inner witness, though, was coached to follow scripts written by the believing community. Methodists built an elaborate social apparatus—small band and weekly class meetings, love feasts, watch nights, covenant renewals, quarterly and annual conferences, public worship services, and camp meetings—to encourage particular kinds of emotional states and reinforce the proper interpretation of them. Witnessing faith meant both listening to the inner voices of conscience and the Holy Spirit and then testifying—bearing witness—to and with other people. The genius of Methodism, in particular, was to cultivate impassioned and deeply personal experiences and then to channel those energies in vital and organized (if not always orderly) communities. It is in the dynamic relation between individual experience and communal life that the success of Methodism in late eighteenth- and early nineteenth-century America is visible. Sometimes, however, the inner witness could not be so easily disciplined by the church's established forms and practices.[1]

In 1809, a writer in a religious magazine called the *Observer* traced the rise of scoffing skepticism and enthusiastic Methodism to the same source. The "languid" and "lifeless" preaching of the modern clergy, the short piece claimed, caused many people to "stray in search of more animated pastors; while others forsake all ecclesiastical guidance whatever, and laugh at religion as a ceremony at once political and stupid. Those who are endowed with strong feelings become methodists; others, possessed of more firmness, prove infidels and sceptics." Itinerant preacher and bookseller Jeremiah Minter also saw a link between the growth of Methodism and skepticism. He argued that the arch-infidel Thomas Paine and the Methodist bishop Francis Asbury, though using different methods, were both in league with the devil. Paine and other skeptics appealed to false reason, attacked belief in the Bible, warped conscience, and promoted anarchy; Asbury and other religious imposters, from behind a mask of false piety, drowned out the inner voice of the Holy Spirit and misled believers into supporting religious tyranny.[2]

The Christianity that Minter defended against both of these threats was grounded in a passionate, life-altering experience of God's grace. He had been a circuit-riding preacher in Asbury's church in late eighteenth-century Virginia—the time and place of Methodism's first great expansion in America. There he had met Sarah Jones, a devout plantation mistress who, for Minter, exemplified Christian faith and life. But his intense spiritual friendship with the married Mrs. Jones caused a scandal—especially after Minter took the extraordinary step of having himself castrated so that desires of the flesh would not corrupt his spiritual life. For both Jones and Minter, the power and authority of their personal religious experiences came to clash with the authoritative demands of their families and their church. Jones died, still a Methodist, in 1794. Minter, who published a biography of Jones (no copies of which have survived), a volume of her letters, and the story of his own religious experiences as a testament to their shared faith, left the church but continued his itinerant preaching. Addressing not just like-minded evangelicals but all his fellow American citizens, however, Minter found that he had to argue not just that his spiritual experiences were scriptural but that the scriptures were divine. His last known publication in 1820 combined an attack on church leaders who perverted the authority of faith with a defense of the Bible against skeptics who destroyed its foundation.[3]

Jeremiah Minter and Sarah Jones were not "typical" early American Methodists—no more so than the obsessively itinerating Bishop Asbury or the demon-haunted William Glendinning, another Virginia preacher whose religious experiences transgressed the acceptable limits of Asbury's Methodism. What Jones and Minter described as being "born again" and then living life in communion with God followed a basic evangelical pattern, but they pushed their daily practices of piety to further extremes than most of their religious brothers and sisters. Other converts fasted and devoted themselves to prayer, but Jones at times seemed to aspire to something like the sainthood of a medieval mystic. Other passionate born-again Christians struggled with unregenerate family members who thought the converts had lost their minds, but few had a spouse like Jones's, who threatened to shoot her, or a father like Minter's, who chained him to a wall as a madman. Many young celibate itinerants struggled with sexual desire, but only one was known to become a eunuch. Nonetheless, the faith Jones and Minter professed—like the tensions they experienced between the inner witness and communal religious practice—illuminates the Methodist strain of the evangelicalism that, despite the cavils of the skeptics, rose to prominence after the American Revolution.[4]

Soul Exercises and Religious Community

In his *Statistical History of the First Century of American Methodism* (1866), Charles Chaucer Goss chronicled the astonishing success of Methodism in the United States during the century that stretched from the eve of the Revolution through the Civil War. About 1,100 members were on the rolls at the first annual conference in 1773. In 1776, although stigmatized as Tories and disrupted by the war, Methodists claimed nearly 5,000. A decade later, membership had leapt to over 20,000. The first General Conference in 1792 tallied almost 66,000. After a schism and other troubles flattened the growth curve for the rest of the eighteenth century, membership jumped to over 113,000 in 1804, 195,000 in 1812, and over 250,000 by 1820. In addition, observers estimated that throughout this period, several times the number of official members attended Methodist services and meetings. From a small offshoot of evangelical Anglicanism on the eve of the Revolution, Methodism had quickly become a powerful cultural force.[5]

Modern histories have puzzled over the nature of this force and the source of its power. Methodism, it has been argued, was simply a good fit for the competitive, more egalitarian, market-oriented democracy that emerged after the Revolution. It offered a religious agenda that supposedly "resonated with the logic of capitalism and individualism" that dominated the early American republic. If appealing to entrepreneurial white men "on the make," it was even more attractive to white women, who, it has been said, "found in Methodism a definition of self that was as individualistic as that found by men in politics." Yet others have pointed out that interpretively aligning Methodism and democracy stumbles over the actual Wesleyans who thrived within a decidedly undemocratic church run by powerful bishops and a clerical hierarchy. The intensely communal character of early Methodism, too, suggests that its attention to personal experience has been too easily misread as a sign of American individualism. Methodism from the 1770s to the early years of the nineteenth century has been cast as both a radical counterculture subverting the norms of society and a religious style well suited to the ambitions of post-Revolutionary middling Americans. Democratic and autocratic, egalitarian and patriarchal, culturally subversive and hegemonic, individualistic and communal—the early American Methodism of the history books is puzzlingly contradictory. Perhaps it is a little less surprising, then, that Minter ultimately attributed Methodist success to "sorcery."[6]

Wesleyan Methodism in America began with two small pockets of immigrants in the 1760s, one in New York City and the other in Maryland. Methodism entered northern Virginia by the middle of that decade and the southern part of the colony by 1771. The colony's first major Methodist revival, beginning in late 1775 and continuing into the summer of 1776, was vividly described by the Anglican rector of Bath in Dinwiddie County, Devereux Jarratt. The religious excitement eventually spread through fourteen counties south of Petersburg, including Sarah Jones's Mecklenburg County, and into northern North Carolina. The colonies were at war with Britain, and the Continental Congress was moving toward a declaration of independence, but in this part of Virginia, according to Jarrat, many turned their attention to religion.[7]

Prayer meetings lasted until dawn. Men, women, and children, blacks and whites alike, were affected. Jarratt was concerned about some of the enthusiastic displays he observed: the afflicted loudly groaning, crying, and shouting, or falling to the ground as if dead, or twitching with convulsions. He disliked chaotic prayer meetings where several laypeople prayed or exhorted all at once, in different parts of the room, making the assembly sound more like a raucous tavern with "a drunken rabble" than a church with "worshippers of God." Nonetheless, Jarrat had no doubt that he was witnessing "a blessed outpouring of the Spirit." Membership surged, giving the region more Methodist adherents—over 1,600—than any other district in America. By 1777, half of the Methodist preachers in the newly declared United States were riding circuits in Virginia.[8]

Sarah Anderson Jones, who lived in Mecklenburg County near Taylor's Ferry on the Roanoke River, almost certainly converted during this revival. Born around midcentury to a prominent planter family, Sarah married Tignal Jones in 1767, a man who would own over 1,300 acres and seventy or eighty slaves by the time she wrote her extant journal and published letters in the early 1790s. According to Thomas Ware, an itinerant preacher who heard the story from the couple sometime after 1784, Tignal was at first violently opposed to her interest in Methodism. He "cherished the most bitter and inveterate prejudice against the Methodists; and being naturally a man of violent passions, and most ungovernable temper, he, by his threats, deterred her for a time from joining them. Nor did he stop there, but positively forbade her going to hear them." When one of her favorite preachers came to the neighborhood, Sarah begged Tignal's permission to go to the meeting. Her husband refused, so she informed him that she felt compelled to attend by a higher power. "At this time he became enraged, and in his fury swore if she did, he would charge his gun and shoot her when she returned; but this tremendous threat did not deter her." She went to hear the sermon, "and on her return met her infuriated husband at the door, with his gun in his hand. She accosted him mildly, and said, 'My dear, if you take my life, you must obtain leave of my heavenly Spouse'; and thus saying, approached him, and took the deadly weapon out of his hand, without making any resistance."[9]

Published in the middle of the nineteenth century, this story rehearsed a familiar scene in Methodist literature: the angry patriarch trying to keep his pious wife from Methodism. Another enraged Virginia gentleman, Dr. Thomas Hinde of Hanover County, Patrick Henry's physician, also tried to keep his wife, Mary, from Methodist meetings. "I will stop you from going to hear these Methodists," Hinde told her, according to their son; "they are turning the world upside down, and setting people crazy. You shall not go to hear them;—you do not look like the same woman;—your very looks are changed!" A deist who thought religious enthusiasm was a mental illness, Dr. Hinde tried to "cure" her by applying "a blistering plaster to the whole length of the spine, which he left on for several days." Mrs. Hinde went the next day to the Methodist meeting anyway, bearing this painful treatment and a fall from her horse with "christian fortitude and meekness." Thomas Hinde and Tignal Jones can easily be taken as symbols of everything that, by some readings, early American Methodism opposed: the gentry's honor culture, patriarchal oppression, and slaveholding. Both wives went on to become leading Methodist "Mothers in Israel," and both husbands ended up repenting their actions and following their wives into the church. According to the preacher who heard the Joneses tell their story, Tignal's "virulent temper God in due time softened and subdued, so that the tiger became a lamb," and the couple seemed "united with one heart in the service of God."[10]

Sarah Jones was not trying to "turn the world upside down" and subvert patriarchal authority, only mark its limits. Being able to hear the Word preached was an essential matter of religious conscience, crucial to the relationship between her own soul and God. On other issues, even where Tignal's judgments seemed to her to obviously conflict with the Methodist way, she deferred to her husband's worldly authority. In an undated letter to her friend Susannah Williams, she grieved that "many of the dear people of God" complained about the way her children dressed. The Methodist *Discipline* discouraged "Superfluity of Apparel" and "Superfluous Ornaments" like "High Heads, enormous Bonnets, Ruffles or Rings." Sarah herself abhorred "dress and fashion, more than necessary decency." But she had "talked it over" with Tignal, "and Mr. Jones is my head, my dear, and he positively commands my children to dress as others do." To Susannah, Sarah portrayed this as a great trial and asked for her prayers. "I can witness it by my class and neighbours," she wrote, referring to testimonies in her Methodist class meetings and declarations to her friends, but "I cannot help it."[11]

Tignal and Sarah's disagreement about slavery was another of her trials. John Wesley had denounced slavery in 1774. Francis Asbury and the Methodist Connection's Baltimore Conference went on record against it in 1780. The

Methodist Episcopal Church's first *Discipline* in 1785 condemned it, and the church's two superintendents, Asbury and Dr. Thomas Coke, circulated a petition calling for the Virginia state legislature to abolish it. The Rev. James O'Kelly, a close friend of the Joneses, would publish an emancipationist tract, *Essay on Negro-Slavery*, in 1789. In a December 1788 letter, Sarah mentioned returning from a Quarterly Meeting with O'Kelly and his wife, apparently conversing about the subject. Convinced that slavery was a sin, Jones wrote with apocalyptic foreboding: "My mind is as solemn almost as death, my soul is cloathed with a profound sense of a present, awful, blazing Deity, pointing in glittering streams of keen justice, blood, blood, I will revenge, mine arm shall get victory—bend O nations, bow O Virginia, loose the captives, let the mangled objects go, or my sword shall wreak your bowels and be drunk with my fury." On March 24, 1792, she wrote in her journal that she had long agreed with the sentiment expressed in that day's sermon, which denounced slavery as "the grand Evil that kept Blessings from proffesers." She lamented that she had to "live with the heavy burden" of slaveholding even though she did "Not consent to it." A week later she noted a "Stiff debate upon slavery" at home, probably with Tignal, in which she felt "zeal and power," but although she took care to argue "gently" she afterward felt "miserable." A scene the following week provided a potent example of "the Miserys of Slavery" to the slaves themselves rather than to the troubled consciences of reluctant slaveholders. Near sunset she watched an enslaved woman parting from her crying baby. The woman had to walk two miles and cross a swollen creek each night and each morning before dawn to be with her baby and also had to do a full day's work for her master "or be cut in gasshes." Watching the mother leave and the baby cry made Jones's heart "[feel] as breaking," she wrote. "Oh God of Gods my heart melts at the inhuman Christians."[12]

But many—most?—white Southerners and many Methodists disagreed with the church's antislavery stance, and Tignal Jones was among them. Proslavery counterpetitions circulated in eight counties and were submitted along with the Methodists' call for emancipation to the Virginia legislature's fall 1785 session. The Mecklenburg County petition, bearing 223 signatures, opened by arguing that the antislavery proposal was yet another assault upon property rights by tools of the British administration. The petition from bordering Lunenburg County named names, castigating "a proscribed Coke an imperious Asb[ur]y and contemptible Emissaries and Hirelings of Britain." This rash strike against slavery, the petitions argued, violated the ideals of the American Revolution and the teachings of the Bible. "Slavery was permitted by the Deity himself," the petition signed in Mecklenburg declared, quoting from Leviticus 25:44–46. The petition from Brunswick, the adjacent county to the east, added five citations from Genesis and one from Ecclesiastes to make the point. Both documents noted in addition that Jesus and the Apostles in the New Testament never abridged the right to buy and sell slaves. Moreover, the proslavery advocates insisted, emancipation would wreak havoc on Virginia, plunging the state into poverty and unleashing a population of revengeful robbers, rapists, and murderers upon the citizenry. The legislature unanimously defeated the emancipation proposal (though a proslavery bill to repeal the 1782 act permitting private manumissions also failed, 52–35). The Methodist leadership, reacting to a storm of popular animosity and realizing that antislavery agitation would hamper their primary goal of saving souls, began to retreat. They suspended the slavery rules in the *Discipline* after six months. In 1796, the church reiterated that preachers and class leaders had to emancipate their human property (at least according to some gradual timetable), and the *Discipline* banned ordinary members from selling (but not owning) slaves—but these rules were inconsistently applied.[13]

Tignal and Sarah's disagreement over slavery reflected differences not between pious Christians and secular "worldlings" but within the Christian community and within Methodism itself. Their different positions did not mean that within her marriage Sarah was alienated from a Southern patriarch who could not share her faith. In a 1790 letter she wrote of feeling the eyes of her slaves upon her but was consoled that God knew she bore witness against the sinful institution: "Although the oppressed stare me through, I will try to be clear of their blood. My witness is in Heaven, my record is on high; and I will try to live in everlasting fire." In the same letter she described rejoicing when she found Tignal and two friends in the midst of religious devotions and "all on fire." Sarah joined them. "A storm of glory poured and we spent some hours in reading, praising and adoring the God of love, mixing much prayer, and frequent retirement for more Religion."[14]

Sarah Jones has been called "the embodiment" of early American Methodist spirituality. Faith not exercised is dead, she wrote in her journal in the fall of 1792. If "to trust God is the Total Sum of Faith," it was a trust that had to be demonstrated and rewarded every day, every hour, practically with every breath. Faith was a flame from God, a burning passion in the believer, and the "vigour" that fueled the essential devotional work of the embodied soul. Jones experienced faith-in-action most powerfully in daily meditative practices that she and other Methodists called their exercises. Exercising her faith was a kind of research into sacred truths, she wrote; it was also how she lived, day to day, in love with God.[15]

The Sarah Jones of the letters and journal entries from the late 1780s and early 1790s was a woman who had grown in faith past mere conviction of sin and conversion to Christ; she was assured of her salvation, believed she had been sanctified by the second blessing of the Spirit, and was devoted to the quest for perfect holiness. She yearned for more knowledge of God, "panted" for more

> *Journal Continued*
>
> *March 5th 1792*
> *to August 19th 1793.*
>
> *Faith! is the Substance of things hoped for, the Evidence of things Not Seen*
>
> *Bright day. as I arose I stopt to Look right at Jesus whose Sweet and Rosy voice dropt the above words*
>
> *I Clung about his lilly Neck*
> *And from his Smiling Glory Caut*
> *The living flame*
> *Which kindling Glow filled Every Power*
> *And in the Consecrated hour*
> *I Learnt his Name*
>
> *Was Love twas Love, twas Love indeed my Spirit found and Learned my Soul to fly fare from this world of Noise and Care. I Mount to dwell with angels there. This day from ten oclock my habitation was Silent heaven 6 hours undisturbed Repose gathering Sweets from Sharons rose New heights New depths of Consolations Fool and ——— Eternal Pour Upon my Soul joy breaks heaven Shines I triumph as I meet the Grave (true Taste of Life) Eternity's my Prize. oh what awfulness Seize my agitated breast at beginning this New Book indeed it is Striking oh how my heart flutter. Who can tell me what Shall be the Subject thro what joy or woe will Croud the Page*

Sarah Jones, Journal, 1792–93, first page. Jones recorded her spiritual experiences—the grounds of her faith—and shared her journal with close friends like Jeremiah Minter. Courtesy of the Special Collections Research Center, Swem Library, College of William and Mary.

intimacy with Jesus, prayed for "more Faith more Love...more Vital fire." Yet for all her rapturous confidence in her union with Christ, doubt and unbelief still lingered in the shadows. Unbelief was a "pest" that could work its mischief even among believers. She found it amazing that "all flesh"—including the earthly part of her own being—found it "So hard to beleive God" despite his immutable promises. Some verses she wrote asked for "a Stronger Faith...that cannot doubt what Jesus Saith." Other lines mentioned the struggle to completely conquer unbelief, prompting Minter to remark that "temptations to unbelief will haunt, at times, the purest embodied mind, during life; but the faithful shall only be more established, as she was."[16]

Religious skepticism may not have been a central concern for Jones in her daily practice, but she knew that doubt could be a threat to even the most devotedly pious. Another leading figure of early Virginia Methodism, the itinerant preacher William Glendinning, had been increasingly troubled by what he described as deistic and atheistic inquiries, which contributed to his breakdown after the famous Christmas Conference in 1784, the meeting that organized the American Methodist Episcopal Church. As he traveled to preach the Gospel in the 1770s and early 1780s, he read treatises and commentaries attacking the notion of original sin, challenging the sinless character of Christ, struggling to make sense of the Trinity, and questioning the state of angels and saints in heaven. Internalizing these debates and thinking philosophically about his religion led him "to question, *Whether the scriptures were the truths of God or not?*" Confused and increasingly desperate, he tried to understand his temptation "to disbelieve the Christian religion" as a trial of his faith thrown in his way by the devil. "*Deism* and Atheism were sorely thrust at me," he later wrote. He clung to the hope that his religious exercises would keep him from sin. "But my atheistical inquiries had then got such deep root in me, that my mind got more and more darkened, and I lost sight of my reconciled God, and all spiritual comforts departed from me. Thus darkened in my understanding, I became wretched in my soul."[17]

At the Christmas Conference in Baltimore, he chaffed at the authority being claimed by Coke and Asbury and resented the judgment that he lacked the "*gifts*" to be an elder. As Asbury led the assembled ministers in prayer, Glendinning "felt all light of Divine mercy, as in a moment, take its flight from me, and I felt as if I had been rent in two, and drove out, like an outcast, from the face of the Lord. My soul then sunk into the depths of misery and despair." His doubts had finally vanished—he knew that there was a God and that Christ's promises were true, but he was just as convinced that he was doomed to suffer in hell, and had already begun that suffering while still on earth. He retreated to live alone in a cabin on a friend's plantation, shoeless, sleep-deprived, and suicidal, claiming to be frequently visited by Lucifer himself. It took him five years to recover and begin preaching again.[18]

Faith was not necessarily a permanent possession, Methodists believed: even a saint could slide back into unbelief, sin, and apostasy. Christians were called to the discipline of daily practice. Faith called Jones to her work, to "prayer and Study," which she described as reading "the four Volumes": the Bible, creation, the heart, and the "deep Book" of her experiences with God in which she "read deep things." Her letters and journal entries regularly mention reading the Bible and brim with scriptural images and metaphors. For Jones, Bible study was not a matter of putting a particular verse in the context of a broader story, theological doctrine, or narrative of sacred history. Bible verses were gems, plucked from a treasure box, polished against the sleeve, and held up to the light. Most mornings upon rising she would apply the nugget of truth contained in a scriptural verse to her life or to the mood of the moment—or, rather, she would feel the text applied to her. When she awakened, phrases from the Bible seemed to drop from heaven into her soul; Jesus, she thought, was giving her a theme for her morning prayer. When she opened the Bible later in the day, particular words could strike her like "Bullets." On April 19, 1792, she turned to Psalms (39:7) and read "and Now, Lord, what wait I for? my hope is in thee"; she immediately "dropt with trembling nerves my book[,] intranced in a Secret view of the harmony I found in Jesus['s] promises." Bible reading was a spur to the holy experience of meditative prayer, faith in exercise.[19]

Jones's second volume, the book of God's creation, was a similar prompt to a contemplative practice that quickly left the things of the world behind. She would often walk or ride alone, away from her house, or sit by herself in a chair beneath a tree in her garden. An April stroll among the morning glories melted her heart and brought thoughts of Christ's "royal cross." A moonlit walk in the springtime was a paradise of lay locks, rose buds, and sweet honeysuckle. "The Soft air fan[ned] gently the Bosom of the peas which Leaned on their regular props[;] they apeard to Stand in rank to Suport their charge while Jesus veiwed my dancing heart." On a June day she took a volume of Wesley's sermons, sat in "a distant Shade," and admired "the lively Beauties of creation where Every herb and plant and bird was Enough to inspire Meditation and raise My Smoking thought to a burning flame." In her garden, nature, soul, and heaven aligned: "All around was Sacred beauty [and] all within a paradise [of] wisdom & Love." A "Delightful transport" allowed her to feel "an indearing corispondence between heaven and my waiting Soul." Singing birds called forth prayer; tall poplars drew her eyes to heaven.[20]

In darker moods, nature provided other correspondences. A mighty storm reinforced her feelings of helplessness. After one particularly difficult evening, when she left the house feeling like a worm in the dust, she could only attend to the solemn buzzing of flies. Insects crawling on the ground also put her in mind of her own insignificance. Her heart seemed most receptive to the beauties of springtime, though the "Blazing rays" of an August noon helped her experience God's flaming love with "Boiling tears," and a December moon glimpsed from beneath a pine's snowy boughs on a "piercingly cold" night helped her ponder eternity. But even on a pleasant day in June, reading the volume of creation in order to feel the presence of the Creator was not always easy. "Near Sun down I felt heavy. But [I] resolved Not to give way to flesh and Blood [and] I walked to a Mulbery tree at a distance where I Seated in great Solemnity. I had hard work to get ingaged altho Nattures beautiful Landscape Strove to help me[.] [I]t apeared to me as if the Blessing would come in reach almost and my Eager Soul would reach hard after but could Not fully touch it." Experiencing the divine was not just a reflexive response to a pretty sunset. It took work.[21]

Reading Jones's third book required an inward turn to examine her own heart. She wanted a deep "Experimental knowledge" of herself. In her journal she vowed to "Examine and Search and watch Every thought and action" in her soul. But she counted herself among the sanctified. She rejoiced that grace could help her avoid the snares of self-deception, in which vivacity and industry could mask covetousness, moderation conceal sloth, and religious routine camouflage a soul not actually Christ's bride but able only to "keep company and trade with Self." The self-inspection of a sanctified Christian, however, was not always sweetness and light. "I Looked on my Self," she wrote, and found "a weary Sore Sorowful afflicted mournful Loansome traveler. I Looked as one over a grave.... I Looked at my Soul and it was all Melted. I Searched for my heart & it was broke." Yet she was not a sinner asking repeatedly what she must do to be saved, or a convert seeking the assurance of salvation by trying to determine if the Holy Spirit had indeed regenerated her heart, inclined her will toward God, and given her a true taste and affection for divine things. She knew who she was and what she was. I am solid, she assured friends in the troubled years of the early 1790s; I am the same now as I was before; I stand on the rock of Christ. Her journal records not an agonized concern over the state of her soul but a tortured desire for more faith and more of God's love.[22]

Jones's fourth volume of Christian knowledge, and the primary ground of her faith, was her felt relationship with God, experienced most regularly and intensely in her hours of daily meditation and nearly constant prayer. She usually rose before dawn, before others in the house had stirred, and eagerly began her daily devotions. She prayed secretly while tending to her family and household chores. "I *pray without ceasing.* Walking, standing, sitting, lying down, rising up, eating, drinking I pray." She stole away every chance she could for a walk in the countryside, to her chair in the garden, or to the room over the front hall that she had "furnished entirely for prayer." Her hours set aside for solitary prayer—usually after lunch and then late into the night after the rest of the household had gone to bed—began with a resolution to fix her eye on God. If outdoors, she might walk slowly, look at the ground, and breathe. If in her room, she might kneel on the carpet. She would then work to command her passions and focus her entire attention on her task, without letting her thoughts wander for a moment— an effort she frequently described as agonizing. The next step, Jones wrote, was to "Beleive without doubting [that] God will come." Finally, she had to cultivate patience, maintaining this frame of mind and waiting as long as it took. When she felt God draw near, she was flooded with joy. Then the conversation began. "I am trying to learn to talk to God in faith, believing he is here," she wrote to a friend in an undated letter. By the spring of 1792 she could "talk as plain to God as if he was a man." Another journal entry described a similar encounter: "I tied up my head Stood up on my feet and adresst my Self to God as if he was in the flesh before me[.] I told him of the Simple truths that concerned my Soul & Shewed him my temptations. I Stood as a Servant before his Master and beged his favour with Streaming tears untill he arose and really give me Such Blesings I could just live."[23]

God did not usually come as a Master, however. In the spring of 1792, as Jones's heart danced in her flower garden, she continued a long Christian tradition of reading the Song of Songs and imagining—or experiencing—Jesus coming as a bridegroom. She wrote of Christ's melting glances and "spicy" smiles; of entering his chamber aflame and trembling with desire; of his kiss upon her lips, and his "Skilful touch" igniting her "Impassioned heart to a mighty flame." "I Love oh yess I I Love Love my darling Jesus with a Love Stronger than death." On July 5 she rose from her bed "to open the door to my beloved.... I opened to my beloved and he was not gone but smiled with Beauty.... I felt my body made his temple and springing wonders rooll anew." Whether her intimate encounters with the divine felt like lovers meeting, a servant before a master, or a child with a parent, she usually described them in language that mentioned copious tears and struggled to convey the qualities of her "Exstasies." At times, bliss seemed to lift her away from the world and the flesh; in other moments, her experience was powerfully physical. "I realy got far out of the body," she wrote in one journal entry, but then "I found my position had Leaned forward reaching as if Jesus was corporaly there looking and Speaking."[24]

All her senses were alive when she drew herself near to the Son or his Father, but she most often employed visual language to represent her experiences. Using biblical phrasing popular among Methodists, she described her exercises as acts of watching or looking, her hope on a given evening to get "a full view of Jesus" even "if it is thro a glass," and her ultimate desire "to See God face to face without a veil." She marked her progress in holiness by noting how "Faiths Eager gaze" was providing her with ever clearer views of heaven. She cited John Wesley on practical holiness as a supernatural sight of God and seemed to distinguish between seeing by faith and mundane visual perception. Some of the imagery in her writing may derive from her struggle to find words to describe experiences that were ultimately ineffable—she does, after all, remark on the inadequacy of language at least nineteen times in her journal. She may have borrowed visual tropes and painted word pictures to try to express and communicate the essence of encounters that were not actually experienced as visual. The language of seeing, and the images of things seen, may just have been a convenient verbal form for Jones and other Methodists, akin to the way they tended to shift into rhyming couplets within their narratives or move completely from prose to the verse quatrains of a hymnal. Some entries seem like set pieces, rhetorical performances crafted for an imagined future reader. Yet others have the immediacy of records of perception. "He Laid the Hand of My Faith upon his Heart Sealing me an assurance of my imidiate acess unto him.... [J]oy as a Noble casscade Tumbling from the anttient <u>Font</u> continued to Extend its roling Bilows with talls trees of life in regular roows of Divine Beauties Blossoming with Bliss more Flourishing than the orangery of the Fruitful Islands[.] [T]he rooling calmn rivers the green walks the Neat Stone Bridge well cornered admited Early Earnest Travelers into the citty of God.... I feasted & lived adored till Lost my Eye[. I] was caried to Veiws that have No Bounds and my acount got too deep to relate."[25]

Was this image of a heavenly city self-consciously visualized as a meditative technique, as when she practiced talking to Christ *as if* he were corporeally present? She did write of the imagination as the first wheel of the soul. But she also wrote that she had no need to search her "memory for images or my Fancy for ornament to dress my theme" because her heart was flaming with God's love. So, once she had achieved her ecstatic state, were these images experienced almost like perceptions of the material world, feeling as if they appeared spontaneously from outside her mind? These questions would make little sense to Jones. Grace was already "inside," working within the sanctified imagination; faith was already "outside," streaming upward, against nature, to God. From her perspective, the experiences were neither in her consciousness nor outside her subjectivity and located in the Divine Other; they were the product of a relationship occurring in the space between. God let down "chains of light to draw up my affections to himself"; her love and praise soared upward; this "Sweet interchange of rays" of "Enlightening and Enlightned[,] attracting and attracted[,] affords an Emblem of the Etternal *world*."[26]

Jones had to be careful about how she characterized her experiences in her letters and her journal entries (which she expected would be read by others eventually). Outsiders could take descriptions of visions inspired by God as claims to miraculous visual revelations and decry them as religious enthusiasm or even madness. While reports of visions among Methodist converts were not uncommon, within the society of believers Methodists had to be careful not to appear to be puffing themselves up with extravagant claims to divine blessings. In a letter to Minter, Jones intimated that there was more that could be said. "I have not told you all I have seen. A few minutes past as I sat writing, I heard some voice at my window, I arose to answer, and if God has not wrought a miracle for me, I know nothing: I fear to tell you it is so great; yet when I see you I may, possibly." Her letters to others, however, and even most of her journal entries that discussed having seen Christ usually carried the ambiguous qualification that she had seen with the "eye of renewed faith," or the suggestion that seeing was merely an analogy for feeling: "What I there felt," she wrote to William Heath in 1791, "as in the open vision of an uncovered deity, is past my expression."[27]

Jones's caution may have been shaped in part by the Methodists' reaction to William Glendinning. As he recovered from what he called his "Sodom of Misery" in 1790, he, too, had "views" of heavenly mansions opened to him. He "saw" prophets, Apostles, martyrs, and Christians from the history of the church blissfully united—he saw them, that is, "not with my bodily eyes" but with "the eye of my mind." But in the depths of his torment he had witnessed, on several occasions, when wide-awake and with his bodily eyes, Lucifer. Glendinning described his tormentor with empirical precision. The devil was about five feet tall, with a bulky body, four very short legs, wings, and chains that rattled when he moved. He was "as black as any coal" and had eyes and a mouth "as red as blood." Balls of fire could erupt from his eyes, and he could shoot out a horn, six to eight inches long, from the ridge on the top of his head. Glendinning would sometimes run in terror from his cabin to the house "where the white family was." Eventually he regained God's grace, mastered his fear, and in the name of Jehovah banished Lucifer back to hell. The agonies that the preacher suffered during those five years and the spiritual impressions he enjoyed in his remarkable recovery—ecstasies far surpassing anything he had experienced in his initial conversion years before—were powerful testimonies of faith that he witnessed from the pulpit when he returned to preaching. But his visions and views were controversial.[28]

The Methodists received him warmly at first. But at a conference in 1791 Dr. Coke, speaking for Asbury and the other ministers, told Glendinning that to be reinstated he would have to restrict what he said about his religious experiences. The preachers, Coke said, thought that Glendinning in some cases confused the work of his imagination with reality. Coke then added that he believed all accounts of people "having any intercourse with beings from eternity, were imaginary." Glendinning was stunned. All accounts of Christians making contact not just with devils but with angels or departed spirits were imaginary? The respected Methodist preacher Freeborn Garrettson had just published an account of encountering a devil in the shape of a cat. John Wesley himself had published a long account of Elizabeth Hobson's many meetings with ghosts, including the departed spirit of her wicked grandfather who, smelling of brimstone, came to advise her on a lawsuit. Wesley understood, as Glendinning did, that people who dismissed testimonies about witches, ghosts, devils, and angels as merely old wives' tales were "in effect giving up the bible." On the other hand, Wesley argued, "if one account of the intercourse of men with separate spirits be admitted, their [the skeptics'] whole castle in the air (Deism, Atheism, &c.) falls to the ground." Glendinning's testimony about his experiences was so important, he believed, because it was a compelling support for the Christianity the Methodists preached and because it demolished the skeptical inquiries that had originally driven him to distraction. Francis Asbury and other prominent Methodists like Garrettson did not join Coke in dismissing contact with spiritual beings. The delicate question was about what the church should allow Methodists to say about their experiences in public.[29]

Jones was no mystic recluse. Despite her several hours a day in solitary prayer, she ran a plantation household, visited with friends, neighbors, and her extended family, and was an active participant in the social life of early Virginia Methodism. She was embedded in what has been called a fictive kin network of brothers and sisters in Christ. Not only did she gather with others for prayer and go to outdoor meetings and Sabbath services, but she also held meetings (including at least one Quarterly Meeting) in her own home and helped establish a "preaching place" that Tignal had built on one of his quarters. She led congregations in public prayer, visited the sick, testified before sinners, counseled the convicted, advised the awakened, and exhorted the sanctified. Circuit-riding preachers (including Bishop Francis Asbury) stayed in her house, and on at least one occasion she even substituted for a minister when none was on hand to preach. These public religious practices, these experiences of communal piety, especially when she could amplify them afterward through solitary meditation, could lift her soul to God. As her journal and letters show, however, there were tensions between the demands of Christian fellowship and the desires of her private devotions—tensions that only increased as Jones (and early American Methodism) endured the trials of the early 1790s.[30]

In her journal entries, other people—even her husband and children—seem to be shadowy figures on the periphery of her relationship with God. Nonetheless, her journal-keeping was itself linked to a social network of kindred souls practicing a similar faith. Journals and journal-like letters describing soul exercises were passed around and read aloud by the faithful, a practice encouraged by John and Charles Wesley. "I can never tell how great the blessing I find in reading Journals," Jones wrote to the preacher William Spencer, her cousin, on December 5, 1791. "I thank you for the loan of yours. And I thank my dear Jesus Christ that I ever saw a Journal, or kept one. It is a great mean of grace." Journals were testaments of pious zeal that could inspire others to a similar diligence. Reading them could spark exercises of faith in the reader that were similar to those recorded by the writer. For Jones, writing her own journal was first and foremost a witness before God. It was also a record of her faith-in-exercise, allowing her to measure her progress. She could review old entries and ask, "Do I pray as much this night as I did this night twelve months [ago]? Am I as much engaged now as then? Do I love Jesus as well?" Sharing her journals with others, or "journalizing" in letters, as she put it, opened the book of her religious practice and experience, testified about the mysterious divine "reality" that could be found there, and exhorted her brothers and sisters in the church to go forth an do likewise. The response to her writing was also comforting. Thanking Susannah Williams for her "testimony," Jones was clearly gratified that it was "plain to my friends that God is with me." As much as Methodists and other evangelical Christians claimed that their experiences were self-validating, they treasured confirmation by communities of the like-minded.[31]

Private religious exercises also became markers of spiritual status in the community of believers. Journals and letters circulated like currency in a spiritual economy, accruing capital to the adepts. Early Southern Methodism is often described as an egalitarian counterculture to the patriarchal world the slaveholders made. Jones wrote disparagingly about members of her own class—including those in her own family—as "the great ones of the Earth" with "that harsh Sounded Title of gentlemen and Ladies." She did not condemn having wealth so much as pursuing or displaying it: she admired her daughter's country seat but worried about the state of her soul, and a splendid neighbor who drove a horse and carriage worth two hundred pounds prompted a prayer about seeking true riches. She did not necessarily dismiss politeness—there was, after all, that nice Mrs. Munford, educated in England, "who took such pains with me in my youth to instruct me in things of high life." But the idle chitchat of "Effeminite Ladies" and their grasping husbands nearly drove her to distraction. Jones corresponded with ministers as "brothers," spiritual equals on the same "adventure of Faith," and praised the piety of "a dear Negro woman." Still, some Christians were clearly more advanced in faith than others. Status was assigned and hierarchies reinscribed according to the rigors of devotion and self-denial: on top were the indefatigable circuit riders, who rode hundreds of miles and preached at every stop, and the fasting women on their knees like Jones, who "pray near one hundred times a day frequently."[32]

Sarah Jones, paragon of pious devotion, met her match when she encountered the Rev. Jeremiah Minter. Born in 1766, Minter was the youngest son of a prosperous planter. His parents were Calvinists, he later said, but they had not seemed to experience what he considered to be real religion. Having imbibed the values of the Virginia gentry, he attended balls, horse races, and other amusements, and he even fought a duel at eighteen (no one got hurt because the seconds loaded the pistols with powder but no lead). He decided to devote himself to religion and prayed intensely for four months. Working as a bookkeeper and training to become a merchant, he was so happy when he first thought he had experienced conversion while he prayed alone in the store's back room that he filled a tumbler of wine and solemnly drank to Christ's health—and then worried that he had committed the unforgivable sin by being so presumptuous. He chose the Methodists over the Baptists or the Presbyterians because of their stricter discipline. Encouraged to preach, by the age of twenty-one he was riding circuits in southern Virginia and counting himself among the sanctified. In 1789 he was ordained a deacon, and in 1790 the twenty-four-year-old Minter was promoted to elder.[33]

Jones, in a letter to a friend, described Minter as a zealous "champion for God." To another correspondent, Jones wrote that Minter, as an exemplary Christian, "stirs my soul every day and hour I live." His journal made her soul tremble; his letters melted her heart. On January 25, 1790, she wrote to Minter that his "letters on the one hand, and journal on the other" were like "blazing torches" threatening to keep her up all night. Jones would come to describe herself and Minter as "twin born minds" and "kindred souls." God seemed to anoint their friendship. When they were apart, she took long walks and talked with Minter as if he were present. Teasing him in one exchange of letters, she imagined him pouting, and then was forced to drop her pen "and fall on the bed" in "rapture." They agreed to join in covenant prayer every night at ten o'clock, and she was happiest, she wrote, when she imagined the two of them together with Christ, even envisioning them both suckling "streams of love" at Jesus's breast. She loved Minter's soul, she declared, and desired its prosperity above all others. He told her that he would willingly take all her sorrows upon himself; she told him, with her "lap...wet with tears" as she wrote, that she would willingly open a vein, would willingly die, for his sake. She told him she thought he was "sacred." "Surely our union, in Jesus, is more like paradise than earth."[34]

With Minter she wanted to share the most intimate thing about herself: how—and how much—she loved Jesus. Minter's writing thrilled her, cheered her, roused all her faculties to action; she was sure she got twice as much "exercise" from reading him as he did from reading her. She sometimes added a postscript noting that "Mr. Jones sends his love," and early on read at least some of Minter's letters aloud to others, including Tignal, who on one occasion gave a triumphant shout in response. In an undated letter, however, she told Minter that while she "once was fond to shew your letters," she was now "afraid, because they cannot bear it.—Your letters are for my own peculiar treasure." She also encouraged him not to share her letters and journals because some Christians less advanced in faith "can't bear *strong meat*." She thought the problem was envy and jealousy: "Those who are not sanctified can't bear the greatest Saints to be esteemed more than they." She knew that the nature of their correspondence might be misconstrued by carnal minds and that they had to keep it full of nothing but "holiness and purity." She recognized sinful temptations that had to be guarded against, although she insisted that the danger was not lust but "idol-worship." She had never felt the "daggars of emulation" so strongly from another human being before, she wrote. "I am so jealous for fear you will be holiest," she told Minter bluntly. She felt like a spring gnat next to his industrious bee. Having finished reading his journal, she wrote, "I am jealous of you, because I am afraid to my heart you have a greater taste in heaven than I have.... How can I bear you to love my dear Jesus best." Some "provoking lines" in a letter from him, though, fired a "holy ambition" within her, and she rose to his challenge. If he would be her "overseer," driving her to work harder at her faith, he would have to step lively himself to keep her in sight. He had an advantage because he could preach. But could he pray as often as she did?[35]

Minter apparently struggled with his own temptations. Perhaps he relished performing a bold, dramatic act of self-denial that would help him become the sort of heroic saint Jones thought she saw in him. For whatever combination of motives, some that were clear to Minter and others that surely were less so, he read Matthew 19:12, about men who had "made themselves eunuchs for the kingdom of heaven's sake," and he took the text literally. Sometime in 1790, Minter went to a surgeon and was castrated. When word got out, Methodists had a scandal on their hands. The leadership wished he could change his name, he later wrote, because "Minter" had become as notorious in Virginia as the name of a horse thief. Rumors flew about his relationship with Jones. Conference meetings led by Asbury, O'Kelly, and Coke stripped Minter of his standing as an itinerant minister and sent him packing to the West Indies. Minter later heard that Asbury had said he thought Minter had himself castrated so he could have relations with women without being discovered by pregnancy; to Minter this comment displayed an astonishing lack of Christian charity and a gross inversion of the facts of the case, as well as a surprising ignorance about the nature of castration. O'Kelly, still a close friend of Jones's, interrogated her about Minter for five days. The ordeal, Jones wrote with uncharacteristic understatement, "made me cry." The sanctified had turned "traitors," and her "once precious brethren" passed around the story that she and Minter had secretly planned to marry as soon as Tignal died. Jones sent a declaration of unshaken confidence and friendship to Minter, and then retreated to her garden with Jesus.[36]

Jones—and Methodism—faced two other trials as she bore the cross of the Minter affair. Even before the scandal broke, a backlash had been brewing against the pious elite as, in Jones's view, a small Methodist network with "one unanimous sentiment" grew quickly into "very large congregations" marked by discord. On January 1, 1790, she wrote to the Rev. William Spencer that "some say we are proud of so much praying and fasting, and setting up late, and rising early to wait on God, and that we boast of works." She argued in response that it was only halfhearted professors of Christianity "who cannot endure [the] sound doctrine of self denial, and earnest constant wrestling" for faith who cried out, "This woman is going too far." Two and a half years later her bitterness had increased. "In this Evil day to become rich in faith... to walk close to God and

Suppose [oneself to] have any Supereminences of gifts is a Loud drum to beat up for Enemies," marking the devout for persecution. "All our Heroic or Noble acts of charity or Self denial are immediately Suspected condemned without good judgment or mercy." One was expected, she wrote in exasperation, "to live at Ease in Idleness ignorance and Stupidity," make "Not much Noise about you as Long as you live upon Earth," and then slide quietly off to hell. The pious became afraid to circulate accounts of their spiritual exercises, for fear of censure. On October 25, 1792, she wrote again to Spencer: "These times are so difficult there is not two in fifty that dare to pen their real exercise, no not to each other. I see the wise and prudent must be careful how they order their conversation.... Watch, O, watch; professors persecute, I know it."[37]

Jones also suffered through the first major schism in American Methodism. It began as a dispute among the faithful over fundamental principles of government. Minter later claimed that he had first earned Asbury's hatred not when he became a eunuch but when in 1790 he strongly opposed the bishop's attempt to gain veto power over the decisions of the elders. At the conference in 1791, after news of the castration had become public, Asbury and O'Kelly raged at Minter "as tho they were kings and I a rebel subject." Minter likened a later Asbury speech to Caesar paying lip service to the Republic: the bishop "expressed his high approbation of the Constitution and Laws of the United States" even as he denied his own people basic liberties. Minter would come to think of both Asbury and O'Kelly as despots. But O'Kelly shared Minter's criticism of Asbury's authoritarianism, and the November 1792 General Conference in Baltimore, called to resolve grievances, erupted in discord and dissention. O'Kelly withdrew from the church, taking as many as twenty thousand members in Virginia and North Carolina with him. He formed the Republican Methodist Church, championed Christian liberty against monarchical tyranny, and denounced Asbury's ecclesiastical politics as, he later explained, "a son of America, and a Christian."[38]

William Glendinning, too, had grave concerns about the emerging Methodist autocracy, although he petitioned again for reinstatement at the 1792 Conference. Preserving Asbury's power, he came to discern, was the real reason why he had been asked to hide his extraordinary experiences under a bushel basket. In a letter to the Conference, he said he was willing to be accountable to them for the doctrines he preached and for his moral behavior. But he could not in good conscience be confined to a single preaching station or circuit, and he asked to be endorsed as an itinerant at large. Nor could he stop bearing witness to his admittedly extraordinary spiritual experiences. "None of you," he wrote to the Conference's ministers, "ever passing through any thing similar to what I passed through, so, I view you cannot be judges of what is laid on my mind, by the Lord, to speak of my past exercises. And you cannot stand betwixt the Lord and me, so that I cannot be accountable to you." The Conference responded in a letter signed by Asbury and twenty-one other preachers. "You consider yourself as having an *extraordinary mission*, and therefore do not choose to submit, as another preacher, to our government." Glendinning would therefore not be a member of their body, would not be allowed to use their preaching houses, and should not expect help in scheduling preaching appointments. He tried one last time and was granted an interview at the annual conference in 1793. His private experiences with the Lord, he pleaded, "required that liberty (if it might be called a liberty)" of free travel and expression. But Asbury and the conference would not budge. Glendinning had spoken disrespectfully of Asbury, the clergymen charged, and Glendinning admitted that he "thought the power he [Asbury] possessed, was too great for any human being." After insulting Glendinning by suggesting that he wanted to travel freely only to better peddle (unauthorized) religious books and leech off Methodist charity, they sent him on his way. He did not join the O'Kelly Republican Methodists but remained an unaffiliated itinerant preacher and bookseller.[39]

The case pitted the authority of the church against the authority of personal experience. Both sides agreed that personal spiritual experience motivated men and women to freely choose to submit to the church's government and discipline. Life in the church, then, like the conversion experience itself, was a mixture of free choice and submission to authority. Critics like Glendinning, O'Kelly, and Minter argued that church members should not have to leave so much of their liberty at the door when they entered the church. Wesley and Asbury countered that if all members were to plead for exemptions or modifications of church practices based on the dictates of their private spiritual experiences, it would be the end of any sort of church government and discipline. One side decried episcopal and clerical tyranny, the other the anarchy of individual judgment.[40]

Sarah Jones deeply mourned the contentions in her church. Her friendship with O'Kelly had survived the Minter interrogation, and she visited with him pleasantly eight times in as many months following it. At the same time, many were saying "Exceeding hard things" about her "Dear Mr Asbury," and she sympathized with him. On January 4, 1793, she received a letter from Asbury, who seemed humble, patient, and headed for heaven; three weeks later, the O'Kellys were staying in her home. Listening to the arguments about church government amid fearful rumors of schism in February, she confessed that she could not tell which side was right. By May she had come out in support of Asbury. She "Suffred thro dreadful opposition" for doing so, including a bitter letter from "a once dear Christian" now "divided from me in judgment"—perhaps a reference to O'Kelly himself. When O'Kelly announced his formal separation from the Methodist Church in late 1793, Jones reported that many doors in her neighborhood were shut to him—including, apparently, her own.[41]

The disputes that roiled Jones's church shook the foundations of Christian fellowship. The Minter episode exposed the difficulties of intense spiritual friendship between men and women; censures of ostentatious piety or unusual spiritual experiences tried to regulate the economy of religious expression; the O'Kelly schism played out what was to post-Revolutionary Americans a familiar struggle between liberty and power. This turmoil, too, only exacerbated the tension in Jones's religious practice between private devotion and communal Christian life. Her only extant journal contains daily entries from March 5, 1792 (about eleven months after Minter was first humiliated at a conference) to August 19, 1793 (a few weeks after the bitter letter from the once-dear Christian). In the early months of the journal she reveled in the beauties of spring and tried to describe the ecstasies of her daily relations with Christ. She longed for solitude, resenting the way that social and family obligations stole time from her hours of solitary prayer. The idle conversation of her polite relations abraded her pious sensibilities, but even godly friends could be a trial: they criticized the worldly clothing of her children, gently reproved her own overly plain and severe attire, and tried to tone down her exhortations when she visited the sick. She was happiest when she could be alone with Jesus. She had advised Minter before he left to confide in no one but God, and for the most part she took her own advice.

This emotional distance from her social world could lead to a kind of spiritual solipsism. In March 1792, she wondered if God was delaying a revival to the whole community as a trial of *her* faith. She valued a visit to "the afflicted" in May mostly for the "Soul cheering" meditation she had afterward. In June, dutifully riding a horse out to visit "the poor and Miserable," she shrugged that most of them were also "as wicked as Sodom," and she seemed more concerned with her own mood than with any good her charity might have done. In July, after she "administered means to a poor woman with a violent cancer," she prayed about Jesus administering grace to Sarah Jones. She shared the antislavery sentiments that flickered briefly in white Southern Methodism and her heart could break as she watched the slave mother and her baby, but the seventy or eighty slaves who worked on the Jones plantation were nearly invisible in the daily record of her spiritual concerns. Hearing the bells calling her "dear servants" to the fields, she worried briefly that the sound might interrupt her early morning prayers. When she was the only white person in the house, she described herself as being alone. She once mentioned bringing "a boy" with her to a church meeting, but with no further comment—the way one might mention bringing a handbag.[42]

By late July 1792, she began to turn outward again. On the twenty-second of that month her eldest brother arrived at the house, almost beside himself with sorrow: his only child, a young daughter, had died. Jones wept and prayed with him, and with her "poor backsliding young Brother," too. Six days later, she had expected to meet with her brethren and a preacher, but a hard rain kept them away. She went alone in the rain to a small chapel built next to an orchard. She hesitated before going into the "silent house" and was more uncomfortable still when "an amazing Large Spider" crawled next to her. She tried to pray "but found it hard to be happy." Returning home, she found only another "Lonesome house." On that "rainy day" it was "work to keep up the living fire," in both her hearth and her heart. "Still times about religion," she wrote. "Christians absent." Always so eager to be alone, now she was lonely. The next day she marveled at how "yesterdays Lonesome dull Scene" had so quickly changed. Two preachers arrived for an early breakfast, bearing twelve letters from "Eminent Divines" with "wondrous" news of a revival in a neighboring circuit. Fifty new converts! Many "groaning for redemption!" In two days she was trying to answer nearly twenty letters. Happily busy with her correspondence, sweetly doing charity work, and still attending to her private devotions, her journal entries began to shorten, but a balance to her religious practice seemed to have been restored.[43]

She noted, though, that she had become "lean and weak." She had not been sick for a day in 1791, but fasting, insufficient sleep, and the trials she had endured had done their work. In early fall, the "Violent Bilious cholic" that first struck her in mid-July was becoming a chronic condition. The vivid nature imagery faded from her journal, though on a cold and rainy November day she tried to imagine a green landscape, and she could still enjoy an occasional sunset from her bedroom window. Her metaphors became martial: soldiers girded for holy battle, and God's armies were on the march. Rather than the Song of Solomon, she read the book of Job, and focused on persevering through affliction. Rather than meeting Jesus as a lover, she approached God "as a child under the rod" of a stern but ultimately indulgent father. Her prayers in her sickbed could still lead to ecstasies, but these were mentioned rather than described. In March 1793, she tried to take a carriage out to view the springtime scenes she had once so enjoyed on her walks. She delighted in the warm breezes and singing birds flying from grove to grove, but she suffered "Violent Cholick" at night. In mid-May she tried riding out again but could report only "Exquisite pain." As she filled up the last pages of her journal, she reviewed what she had written and was convinced that from the first page it had showed that God had been leading her into the knowledge of something great. She ended the book with hope: "In prayer and in praises I Still upward rise."[44]

When Jeremiah Minter returned from the West Indies, he was partially restored to the good graces of the Methodist Church, demoted to local preacher (rather than circuit-riding elder). Tignal allowed Sarah to write to him. In a letter written as journal entries over several days, she declared her unshaken faith in Minter's piety and his honor. Reexamining her own heart in a second letter, she again declared that there had not been "one carnal wish" on her side of the relationship, and she had glimpsed no hint of anything "savage" on his. Theirs was a union of Christian friendship, intended to help each other grow in faith. Her last letter to him, written about a fortnight before her death in 1794, reasserted her faith. "My faith is strong: I stand as a mountain against Hell. My conscience is clear: I love God—I glow with burning love!" Her last lines asked for his prayers "that my faith fail not. Death's passage is all I dread. But Oh, my children!"[45]

Squinting to see Methodists and liberal individualists as fellow travelers blurs their different understandings of the self. Methodists insisted that individuals were free moral agents when they chose or rejected Christ, but they were not anointing the individual as sovereign. They wanted to be directed by God, not the self, running the Lord's errands, not their own. Surely, then, imagining self-empowered individualists imbibing the heady wine of democracy and creating voluntary associations is not the best way to understand the Methodist dialectic of personal spiritual experience and communal religious practice. Not for black Methodists who understood themselves as individually bearing their heavy crosses and collectively suffering as Israel under Pharaoh; not for white women like Jones; not even for middling white men who stood to benefit the most from the new American social order. A study of early Southern Methodist conversion relations and devotional texts notes some gendered differences. White women, for example, more than white men, seemed to use sensual and even eroticized imagery. Jones (an exemplar here) did write about Christ's lily-white hands, loving touch, and scented robes, though Glendinning just as vividly described Lucifer's phallic horn, black skin, acrid smoke, and rattling chains. Nevertheless, while the generalization about differently gendered styles may hold, early Methodist men's and women's experiences of themselves as souls empowered by grace are more alike than not. And both differ from notions of individualism linked to secular society, democratic politics, or the market economy.[46]

It is a mistake to see Methodists exalting the powers of the self—of human nature—when they were actually paying homage to the power of the Holy Spirit within the supernaturally regenerated soul. "No real Christian is *self-willed*," Minter wrote, "but willing to be taught and governed by the revealed will and word of God." Jones's asceticism was not consciously a quest for self-dominion but an attempt to empty her life of self-interested motives in order to intensify her relationship with God. The power Jones felt on the day she deeply affected her "wicked relations" as she fervently prayed before them arose because, she wrote, "God stept in me." On the other hand, her spiritual exercises did not extinguish the self in some mystical orgasm but tried to connect to divine power—often figured as flames or water—and channel it to do God's work (charity, worship, evangelizing) in the world. To read devout Methodists' repeated references to God's will as merely a smoke screen concealing their own self-assertions is to misconstrue how they understood their lives within God's spiritual economy.[47]

Glendinning's face-off with Lucifer may have been unusual, but his reconversion afterward followed the standard Wesleyan pattern of balancing human and divine power. On a beautiful April day he was suddenly filled with a sense of God's holiness, and then "these words were strongly impressed upon me, *That it yet lay in my power to do much for the LORD OF HOSTS*. This impression, at once, roused me. I began to think, how it was possible for me to do any thing for the Most High." For nearly five years "I could discover no way, in which it seemed possible for me *to do any thing*." If given the opportunity again to serve the Lord, "I would exert every power, and leave no stone unturned." The Spirit was reminding him what Wesleyans had long taught about human ability. Unlike Calvinists, who held that human beings had been utterly disabled by sin, or Pelagians, who thought that they had a natural capacity to contribute to their own salvation, Arminians like Wesley and Glendinning believed that God gave prevenient grace to all people, enabling them to choose and act, giving them the power to accept or reject Christ. Glendinning, following Methodist form, then received further spiritual impressions—that God was love, that Glendinning's sins were forgiven, that he was adopted by the Father. He both "felt these words applied with power to my heart" and experienced the realities that the words signified. Now it was God's power—regenerating and sanctifying grace—rather than Glendinning's own that captured his attention: "I was then so affected with the power and love of God, that my strength failed me.—I lay upon the ground and wept before the *Most High*." When he resumed preaching, his language reflected the interplay of human and divine agency: "I attempted to preach twice to them, and we were favoured with a solemn powerful season. The hearts of some *deists* were then reached.... I was sensible that the Lord had raised me out of the *Sodom of Misery*... and that I enjoyed his gracious favour.... [T]he Lord had raised me, and opened my mouth to speak again for him." The man senses God's actions, feels his favor, and speaks his Word, but God is the one who raises the man out of his misery, allows him to preach, and through the preached words reaches even the hearts of deists.[48]

The Methodists' relentless pursuit of personal transformation through faith in God shaped their relationship to society outside of "Zion," their biblical name for the true (evangelical) Christian community in the world. Some interpretations argue that the American Methodist movement surged in popularity in the late eighteenth century because it absorbed and directed populist discontent with the old elite. Others contend that it took off only after it smoothed its radical edges, accommodating to slavery and confining boisterous women like Sarah Jones to the domestic sphere. Both perspectives misperceive the nature of Methodist radicalism. Committed Methodists were intent on living lives immersed in God's gracious love. This orientation—in private, in church, and out in the world—dwarfed other motives. Moral effects, they thought, followed from spiritual regeneration and sanctification and changed the way people related to one another. But despite all their strictures against dancing, drinking, gambling, horse racing, swearing, Sabbath-breaking, slavery, and so on, they were not primarily social reformers. They did not aim to overturn the power of the patriarch in his household or of the rich man in society. The domestication of Methodism and the church's quick retreat from antislavery by the beginning of the nineteenth century were not the movement's fall from early Edenic purity but rather a shift in style and tactics. Giving up his antislavery agitation, Bishop Asbury reminded himself and his flock that spreading the Gospel to slaves was far more important than freeing them.

In her last years Sarah Jones tried to take comfort that her antislavery witness was recorded in heaven because it had failed to free any slaves on earth. Her husband, Tignal, once threatened to shoot her for disobeying him and attending a Methodist meeting. He continued to allow his children to dress as Southern ladies and gentlemen rather than Methodist ascetics and refused to manumit his slaves. But he did more than merely drop his opposition to Sarah's faith—he became a Methodist himself. He regularly welcomed itinerant preachers into his home, held Quarterly Meetings on his plantation, built a preaching house on his property, listened to Sarah read her religious correspondence aloud, supported her spiritual friendship with Minter, and could become "all on fire" in his own religious exercises. In the ways he chose to live his faith, Tignal was at least as representative of Southern white Methodism as Sarah was in hers. No journal survives recording Tignal's private religious devotions. Sarah's ended with her sights set on heaven: "In prayer and in praises I Still upward rise." To her admirers, that was what most mattered about her—it was what most mattered about anyone. Minter believed that she bore witness to a faith that even skeptics and infidels should not dare to doubt. And yet they did.

Religious Imposture and Skeptical Infidelity

If Sarah Jones managed to negotiate the tensions between the inner witness and social religious practice within the structures of the Methodist Episcopal Church, Minter did not. He left the church a few years after Jones's death. Like Glendinning he became an unaffiliated itinerant preacher, writing and selling his books as he traveled. For a time, Minter called himself an Independent Methodist because he continued to love the Wesleyan doctrines. But he became increasingly critical of what he came to see as Asbury's despotism and the church's corruption. Minter enjoyed the freedom to write and publish whatever he liked and preach wherever he chose without the "tyrannical" bishop's permission. But severed from Methodist social connections he was also exposed to persecutions by scoffers and other opponents hostile to his faith.[49]

A
BRIEF ACCOUNT

OF THE

RELIGIOUS EXPERIENCE, TRAVELS, PREACHING, PERSECUTIONS FROM EVIL MEN, AND GOD'S SPECIAL HELPS IN THE FAITH AND LIFE, &c.

OF

JEREM. MINTER,

MINISTER OF THE GOSPEL OF CHRIST,
Written by himself, in his 51st year of age. 1817.

In four parts, in one volume.

To which is added two Scriptural Tracts,
BY THE SAME.

He that is our God is the God of salvation: and unto God the Lord, belong the issues from death. Ps. 68. 20.
Not having mine own righteousness, which is of the law, but that which is thro' the faith of Christ. Phil. 3. 9.
This is the victory that overcometh the world, even our faith.
Who is he that overcometh the world, but he that believeth that Jesus is the Son of God. 1 John 5. 4. 5.

WASHINGTON CITY:
PRINTED FOR THE AUTHOR IN THE YEAR 1817.

Jeremiah Minter, *A Brief Account of the Religious Experience*... (Washington, D.C., 1817), title page. Three years later Minter published *A Brief Defence of the Bible... against Infidelity.*

In publicly testifying to that faith, Minter was less reticent than Sarah Jones in describing supernatural signs, voices, and visions. He wrote in his published autobiography that his initial conversion was marked by "a small circular place in the sky more luminous than the rest." He reported hearing God speak to him several times over the years, assuring him that he was on the right path. A divine "vision of faith" affirmed his decision to have himself castrated. One night, when chained in his room by his father, "there shone a light from heaven thro' my window, fully as bright as noon day, and I felt it was sent to help me." On another day of trials and tribulations, a vision of Christ comforted him: "I saw him as I would see any other man, in point of demonstration, for a short moment, and close before me. He said nothing. But his loveliness filled me with such love, that I was all peace and joy." During a low moment some years later, "Jesus Christ came to me and showed me one of his hands... and now my Soul rose anew." On a difficult journey through South Carolina in 1812, he caught a glimpse of God Himself: "This view of God, (God is a Spirit,) was not in full, only in part, thro' faith and the Holy Ghost: yet my bodily eyes had a glimpse of him." Methodists testified to similar experiences.[50]

Supernatural signs also helped convince Minter that Bishop Francis Asbury's success in building up Methodism was due to witchcraft. It took seven years after the castration scandal for Minter to finally declare his complete independence from the Methodist Church. Like Glendinning and the Republican Methodists, Minter had objected to the "despotic" powers Asbury had claimed for himself as bishop, which included deciding who were and who were not ministers in the church, annually determining where all preachers would travel and preach, and controlling what the faithful could print and publish. Minter came to feel that Asbury also had a personal vendetta against him, and by the close of the eighteenth century the independent itinerant was also publicly charging the Methodist bishop with bigotry, lying, and fraud. Asbury was a hypocrite, Minter declared, who seduced and deceived members of his flock, subverting what had begun as a glorious revival of religion to promote his own fame and power. In the spring of 1804, Minter claimed, he finally got definitive proof of the "secret" to Asbury's worldly success. Two days after observing what he considered to be false preachers manipulating people at a Methodist camp meeting in Pennsylvania, Minter happened to encounter Asbury on a trail in the Allegheny Mountains. Surprised, the bishop "cried out," then "*muttered* and *peeped* strangely." Asbury next stooped forward on his horse, "and giving a loud cry, which was to false or devil gods, he raised the fallen angel or devil, in the exact form of a pale grey horse, and I saw him as plain as eyes could see for a moment." The devil horse vanished as suddenly as it had appeared. "Thus was F. Asbury dealing with and bowing down to and worshipping devils." The secret to Methodism's remarkable rise was the same sort of sorcery that had allowed "Popery" and "Mohamedanism" to flourish.[51]

No sooner had Minter severed his connection to one tyrant than he fell into the clutches of another: his own father. Anthony Minter, a planter in Powhatan County, Virginia, with "a pretty good share of property in land and negroes," had Calvinist beliefs but "no vital Religion," according to his son. All Jeremiah's efforts "to lead him to true grace, faith, and holiness, seemed only to have hardened him." His father saw his youngest son get castrated for Christ and cast off by the Methodists. Then young Minter drew further attention by publishing that a miracle had preserved a local boy without food or drink for a year. Jeremiah felt that Anthony finally snapped after an argument in which the son proclaimed that the father was not a real Christian and was headed for hell. The father countered that his son was a fool and a madman. After hitting him with a cane and siccing the dogs on him, the elder Minter gathered a "mob" and with the permission of the local magistrate had Jeremiah chained to a wall in his room.[52]

So began two months of what the father called treatments for a distracted son and the son experienced as tortures by an enraged father under the sway of the devil. Father Minter and his Methodist accomplices first forcibly bled Jeremiah. Then they tried two variations of a water cure: stripping him and slowly pouring cold water over his head, and then forcing him through the ice to take morning plunges in a pond. Men came to talk with him while he was chained to the wall— "evil and carnal minded men, ignorant of God and true godliness"—and he felt like Paul debating the Stoics and Epicureans at Mars Hill (Acts 17:18–34), conquering with reason and scripture. His father, after threatening a hot water cure, whipping, and a trip to the madhouse, finally gave up and had his son unchained. Jeremiah Minter quickly got on his horse, renounced his patrimony, praised God as his only Father, and left home for good.[53]

Once freed from Asbury's "galling yoke" and his father's chain, Minter rejoiced at being able to use the talents God had given him and answer the call to spread the Gospel through preaching and print. His first publication was his "account of the Life and Death of that exemplarily pious Christian, and Mother in Israel, *Mrs. Sarah Jones*." He also wrote and published several sermons, the volume of Jones's letters, and a book of hymns and spiritual songs. By the time he published his autobiography in 1817 he had spent seventeen years traveling thousands of miles on horseback, journeying south to Georgia, north into Canada, and west into "the great Wilderness" beyond Tennessee, selling the books he carried in his saddlebags and portmanteau. Minter preached where he was able and counseled sinners in private conversation when they would listen.[54]

His life, in short, resembled that of his nemesis, the relentlessly itinerating bishop Francis Asbury. But unlike Asbury or Methodist preachers traveling smaller circuits, Minter did not have companions on the trail or a network of Methodists to sustain him. There were no conferences, meetings, and camp revivals; no Mothers in Israel to provide cornbread, a warm bed, and fervent prayers. Minter "stood alone with Christ." He "travelled so largely and lonely, thro' many difficulties," and even when passing through familiar towns he usually slept in unfamiliar houses. The benefit of doing so, he told himself, was to give him "greater openings to speak to thousands of different persons, for Christ and his Gospel, in set conversation"; it also made him "more entirely dependent on *God* and his *providence, to direct, protect, comfort,* and be *with me.*"[55]

After Sarah Jones's death, Minter had no friend but God. He might have formed an alliance with William Hammet, another preacher who had seceded from Asbury, tried to launch a rival denomination in South Carolina, and approved of Minter's ministry. But Hammet died in 1803. Minter's experience during one seven-month, three-thousand-mile journey was typical: "I was alone, but God was with me. And were he not with me...I should be miserable: for many are my trials through the diabolical lies, misrepresentations, and envious conduct of false professors who begrudge me, it seems, a friend on earth, as I will stand fast, though alone, and join no party." It was no better when he was back at his home base in Richmond. Methodists and other Christians there harassed him, limited his preaching, and forced him to continually change his lodgings. "I have no real Christian friend there to aid me in any thing." Yet such suffering could be endured, he reminded himself, with the prospect of the "enjoyment of God as a friend, in heaven forever."[56]

Asbury often won people over—as he had won over Sarah Jones—as a man showing them the way to heaven. Minter alienated them with his righteousness, warning them of hell. He felt it was his duty to denounce Asbury and the failings of the Methodist Episcopal Church to practicing Methodists, yet was surprised when they were hostile in return. The large number of Methodists living in Baltimore seemed to Minter to be "*Earthly, sensual,* and *devilish*—leading them to lie, defraud, and manifold sinning." Minter told them so. "They seemed much enraged at me, for warning them that they are a fallen society, and for telling them the plain truth, even as though they could tear me to pieces." In Philadelphia, John McClaskey, the Methodists' presiding elder, "with bitter words abused me as a stroller." Church people spread "false reports" about him through the exchange of letters and manuscripts in the Methodist Connection, and in various locales "sought hard to suppress" him or hinder his preaching.[57]

Minter had to deal with far more than just Methodists as he traveled. Encounters with worldly men often provoked trials of the "*Christian philosophy*" of turning the other cheek. The argument that had pushed his father over the edge had been on this very subject. Discussing fighting to defend one's honor, which Jeremiah himself had done before his conversion, the elder Minter insisted that if an opponent gouged his eye out (not an uncommon practice in Southern fights) he would kill him. Jeremiah countered that such retaliation was unchristian, a damning sin. His later travels gave him several opportunities to put his faith into practice. A "drunken reprobate" on the streets of Richmond once seized him by the lapels and threatened him. Minter calmly told the man that "if he did not repent of his sins he would go to hell." The man then gave Minter a few kicks. The preacher was tempted to strike back, but "grace and forgiveness prevailed" over that natural inclination. Someone else he angered struck him and knocked him down merely "for a small but just reproof" delivered in his sermon. "I must still love him," Minter wrote, "not as a friend, but with compassion and pity as a human being that Christ died for." Another man he offended threatened to kill him and severely punched him "on the bur of the ear," nearly knocking him off his feet. But Minter just walked away. In Maryland, a man who felt that Minter had snubbed and insulted him went to get his dueling pistols and threatened to send the preacher to hell. Minter refused to take a gun. His antagonist aimed and fired at the preacher's head, but the gunpowder flashed harmlessly. A young man from Tennessee also challenged Minter to a duel after feeling insulted; he pointed a pistol at the preacher and three times demanded an apology, which Minter refused to give. "Some may possibly think me a coward for bearing such treatment, without revenge," Minter wrote. "But if Christianity is a true religion, and I verily think it is, it is courage of the best and truest kind."[58]

In 1807 Minter finally gave up trying to reach backsliding Methodists, but he had long been trying to bear witness to his faith to Americans of every religious and irreligious persuasion. As he traveled he studied human beings "in both nature and grace; without religion, and with religion; both real, and hypocritical; both sincere, and under deception for carnal and earthly motives." His writings were "intended for no particular persons, or denominations of professing people; but for the use and benefit, in spiritual matters, of my fellow citizens at large." When he and Sarah Jones circulated descriptions of their soul exercises among fellow believers, their manuscript letters and journals sometimes strengthened and sometimes weakened the bonds of their local Methodist community. In the world of print that he had entered as both author and bookseller, the community of readers—at least as he imagined it as he traveled through nearly every state in the nation—was much broader, the opinions expressed within it more various, and the status of true Christianity far more tenuous. He knew booksellers who would refuse to sell his tracts yet sold Paine's *Age of Reason*. And he knew that Americans were not only reading Paine, Rousseau, Voltaire, Volney, and Hume but writing and publishing attacks on Christianity themselves.[59]

Just as he considered it his duty to proclaim the gospel and denounce Asbury, he felt called to defend Christianity against its skeptical critics. Minter no longer believed that he belonged to an actual community of Christians: "I feel real christians are exceeding scarce thro' the land. I seem sometimes as tho' I am left alone!" But he was still part of the American nation. Like the Methodists he denounced, by the second decade of the nineteenth century Minter began to think more deeply about the nation as well as the church, pondering the moral and theological significance of the United States. Visiting the President's House in 1815 after it had been burned by the British, he reflected on how God would punish the nation as a whole for its sins. In his *Brief Defence of the Bible ... against Infidelity* (1820), he worried that the nation, misled by skeptical infidels, would follow Revolutionary France's path toward atheism and anarchy.[60]

He knew, however, that he could not simply appeal to the inner witness to vouch for the truth of the Bible, showing how scriptural teaching had been brought to life in his own experience. He himself, he wrote, had "experimental, and internal evidence that the Scriptures of the Old and New Testament are the revealed will of God." This "inward witness of the certain truth of the Scriptures," though, could only be obtained with the aid of the Holy Spirit, aid given only to those who asked sincerely, "humbly, and perserveringly in prayer." For everyone else, the truth of the Bible needed to be established through "*reason* and calm reflection" upon "historic and common evidence," and the meaning of particular passages could be clarified by seeing them in light of the harmonious message conveyed by the whole. Though not providing the certainty of the inner witness, this reasoned approach would demonstrate that there had to be an afterlife of rewards and punishments, and that of all the religions in the world, Christianity had "the greatest probability of being the true and heaven-born religion." In an America where most people had not yet been awakened to their sins and born again, the inner witness of the Spirit could not be the foundation of a common faith. Reason and conscience, however, could lead Americans to the light, as long they were not corrupted by religious imposture and skeptical infidelity.[61]

Minter contrasted his use of "calm, reflective, and impartial reason" to the false appeals to reason by Paine and his ilk. The target in the first part of Minter's *Defence* was the anonymous author of a deistic work called *A Blow at Priestcraft, and a Stab at the Devil; or, A Set of Theological Queries for the Consideration and Solution of Believers*. Minter made an attempt to address some of the author's queries. Minter's central point was that while the apparent contradictions in the Bible could be resolved, most infidel objections were based on no more than wicked wit, misquotation, and unfounded assertion, all of which amounted, for Minter, to willful lying. The lies, in turn, convicted infidel authors of a "satanical" desire to annihilate Christianity. The adjective "satanical" for Minter was no mere figure of speech. As in his condemnation of Asbury, he was convinced that the author of *A Blow at Priestcraft* had "much of the evil cunning of the Serpent, or fallen angel in him, by which he labours to confuse and confound the minds of believers, and draw them into infidelity with himself." The second part of Minter's *Defence* set aside any real attempt at argument to blast other skeptical writers, such as the "evil and lying genius" Voltaire, the "egregious liar" Volney, and the lover of lies David Hume. Minter's chief villain, however, was Thomas Paine: "Lucifer...was surely in this man, as it were in full; and inspired him beyond the common state of corrupt nature, with hatred of holy Christianity."[62]

Minter sold his *Brief Defence of the Bible...against Infidelity* bound with his *Warning against Imposture in Religion: In a Concise Account of the Evil Life and Conduct of Francis Asbury*, which he labeled as another "Defence of True Christianity." Just as his autobiography and his volumes devoted to Sarah Jones testified to God's gracious work upon the souls of ardent believers, the *Defence* and the *Warning* testified against the two diabolic threats to that heart-felt religion: religious skepticism and religious imposture. The experience of the Holy Spirit's inner work, powerful as it was, could be misinterpreted and manipulated by self-seeking church leaders, corrupting religion. The rise of a corrupted Methodist Episcopal Church could interfere with an individual soul's "rise in faith and union with Christ." Even worse, though, would be to conclude with the skeptics that the fraudulent "priestcraft" of some church leaders was a sign that Christianity itself was false. "The abuses of religion are lamentable!" Minter wrote. "But far the greatest evils, even earthly and nationally, would be on the grounds of no religion tolerated, or encouraged, at all, in a nation." Following the skeptical infidel's critique in this direction could only lead to practical atheism. "The effect of abolishing religion would be utter confusion and national anarchy; with individual dread and fear on every side."[63]

An infidel nation might be an even greater evil than a corrupted church, Minter concluded in his last known publication, but false prophets like Asbury were more dangerous than infidel writers like Paine because imposter Christians actually ended up producing more religious skepticism. In a poem at the end of the booklet containing the *Defence...against Infidelity* and the *Warning against Imposture*, Minter wrote that corrupt Christians caused more harm and created more stumbling blocks to faith than did "downright infidels." False prophets made "the doubtful more and more to doubt: / Till oft they ripen into downright foes / to all religion." This connection explained to Minter why, along with the phenomenal growth of Methodism in the United States during the late eighteenth and early nineteenth centuries, it sometimes seemed that religious infidelity was "becoming common," too.[64]

When Jeremiah Minter died in 1829, a brief notice in a newspaper simply marked the passing of a minister "remarkable for his eccentricity of character." Despite Minter's eccentricities, though, he and his one true earthly friend, Sarah Jones, bore powerful witness to spiritual experiences that both fueled and fractured religious communities. But as some souls rose, as they believed, to commune with God and their fellow believers, others doubted whether the enthusiasm generated by fervent itinerant preachers, devout Mothers in Israel, and camp revivals amounted to much more than overheated imaginations and the contagious madness of crowds. An impassioned convert might feel that personal spiritual experience confirmed the Bible as certain truth, but the convert's neighbors—the churched and the unchurched, believers and skeptics—could just as passionately disagree.[65]

3

Instituting Skepticism

The Emergence of Organized Deism

In 1797, the deist orator and writer Elihu Palmer celebrated the American and French Revolutions for having dealt a mortal wound to the "double despotism of church and state." For centuries, these "unnatural institutions" had blinded people to their natural capacities and rights. Then British tyranny roused Americans "by a sudden impulse, the effects of which circulated with the rapidity of electrical fire." This was more than just a reflexive response of "suffering sensibility" to a bully's fist; it was an awakening of the oppressed to their true selves. The American Revolution was the most important event in recorded history, Palmer argued, because it had effects in "the operation of the human mind," and it changed "the moral, scientific and political condition of the human species." It magnified intellectual power and eroded superstition and fanaticism; it spurred the cultivation of science, the diffusion of knowledge, and the reform of society. The astonishing French Revolution, too, though in its later phases marred by excesses, had carried this project to the heart of corrupt old Europe. Writing a few years later, Palmer concluded that "the pernicious effects of such cruel institutions"—the despotic state and superstitious church—"have been constantly diminishing since the commencement of the American revolution, and their decrease and final destruction will be essentially accelerated by the revolution in France, and by many other revolutions, which will probably be consequential upon that important event."[1]

The American and French Revolutions, however, extended but did not yet complete what Palmer described as a kind of intellectual and political regeneration that had begun centuries earlier. There were many complex causes of man's awakening to his natural capacities and rights, he recognized, but in *Principles of Nature* (1801) he focused upon three epochal historical transformations that had preceded the late eighteenth-century revolutions: the invention of the printing press, the Reformation, and the seventeenth- and eighteenth-century philosophy that historians would later dub "the Enlightenment." Nothing was more important in his account than the invention of the printing press. The spread of

Portrait of Elihu Palmer. Frontispiece to the *Prospect*, vol. 1, 1803–4. The white cane and verses below the image reference the deist leader's blindness: "Though shades and darkness cloud his visual ray, / The mind, unclouded feels no loss of day."

print technology, and the diffusion of knowledge it enabled, ensured, Palmer believed, that republicanism was not vulnerable to the collapse and erasure it had suffered in ancient times. Republican ideas of liberty and equality had been "deposited in the archives of every school and college, and in the mind of every cultivated and enlightened man of all countries."[2]

The role of the Reformation in the emancipation of mankind, Palmer wrote, had been ironic. Luther and Calvin and their followers were at least as superstitious, fanatical, and narrow-minded as the Catholic Church from which they had separated. But their attacks against the church had dealt powerful blows to its authority. In the subsequent splitting and splintering of Protestant sectarianism, doctrines once taken for granted were critically examined and debated. Some groups—the more rationally inclined sects—began to toss out the old absurdities, one by one. Arminians cast off Calvinism and restored respect for human agency; Arians and Socinians moved toward a more realistic understanding of Jesus; and Universalists abandoned limited atonement and endless punishment. Together they applied "a purifying hand of reason, pruning and lopping off the decayed branches of the old theological tree, approaching still nearer to the source and principles of nature, till at length, by regular progression, the human mind discovered, that moral principle was placed upon a more solid foundation than the reveries of sectarian fanaticism." At the same time, "the philosophical investigations of French, English, and German philanthropists" helped produce "a new era in the intellectual history of man." Newton, Locke, d'Holbach, Rousseau, Voltaire, Hume, Bolingbroke, Paine, and many others "swept away the rubbish of ancient superstition."[3]

Writing at the commencement of the nineteenth century, Palmer knew that much work remained to be done. The virtuous needed to continue to spread enlightened philosophy through print, encouraging people to use their reason, become skeptical about the claims of revealed religion, and place faith, politics, and knowledge on natural, rational foundations. They needed to continue to fight for republican liberty and equality, at the ballot box or with a sword if necessary. And they needed to associate, organize, and institutionalize, replacing the old systems and institutions with new ones. Palmer and his fellow deistic reformers fought their political battles and spread their good news about the dawning Age of Reason with their printing presses. They made considerable efforts, but devoted less systematic thinking to shaping new religious institutions that could replace the old churches. Palmer called for scrutinizing and analyzing "the complicated association and application of the ideas of former institutions," and of "disorganizing the system" of antiquated religious, political, literary, and moral establishments. But he seemed to think that once oppression, ignorance, and error were removed, new cultural institutions would emerge naturally, and then inevitably "harmonize and form one grand system."[4]

Deist reformers in the age of the American and French Revolutions like Palmer and his friend Thomas Paine tried to combine a skeptical critique of revealed religion (especially Christianity) with a program for a simplified, liberated religion of reason and nature. Their ideas had a lasting legacy, but their institutions—their deist clubs, periodicals, and proposals for Temples of Reason—had a short life. Explanations for the fate of organized deism have tended to emphasize the limited popular appeal of reasoned religion in an era of evangelical enthusiasm. Organized deism, however, like other voluntary associations that sprouted up in the early republic, was a complex cultural formation with its own particular social makeup, political profile, internal structure, and precarious place in the evolving relations of early national cultural power. These facets can best be seen by comparing it to other groups that also worked to perpetuate themselves in stable institutions outside the Christian mainstream—in particular, the Universalists, the Freemasons, the New Jerusalem (Swedenborgian) Church, and the African Methodist Episcopal Church. Organized deism, like these other groups, was fashioned by the ideas, attitudes, and desires of its leaders and members but also by the power of the state, the constraints and authorizations of the law, and the bitterly contested politics of religious and political association in the 1790s.

Deism as Skepticism and Faith

Thomas Paine's *The Age of Reason* (1794, 1795), which was published in twenty editions and provoked at least as many printed rebuttals by the end of the century, aimed at a broad audience. Fusing religious reform to radical republican politics and revolutionary idealism, it blasted Christianity as the author had previously pitched into the pretensions of monarchy and aristocracy. If Paine shoved deism out of the gentleman's salon and into taverns frequented by artisans and laborers, it was Elihu Palmer who did the most to try to institutionalize deism in America to actually do the work of religious and political reform. Born in 1764, educated at Dartmouth College, and briefly a liberal Presbyterian who chafed at the theology in which he had been trained, Palmer publicly rejected the divinity of Christ in Philadelphia in 1791 during a failed attempt to organize a deist society. He lost his wife and his eyesight to that city's yellow fever epidemic in the summer of 1793. After delivering a successful series of deist lectures in Atlanta, in the winter of 1795–96 he helped found the Deistical Society of New York City, which soon became linked to similar societies in Philadelphia, Baltimore, and Newburgh, New York. He published his treatise *Principles of Nature* in 1801; a revised and expanded edition appeared the following year, and a third edition was published in the last year of Palmer's life, 1806. The deist movement's weekly journal, the *Temple of Reason*, edited by the former Catholic priest Denis Driscoll ran from November 1800 to February 1803; it was followed by Palmer's weekly journal, the *Prospect* (December 1803 to March 1805).[5]

Palmer tried to offer a balance between a skeptical critique of Christianity (and of all allegedly "revealed" religion) and a constructive program for a rational faith grounded in the observation of nature, though the balance tipped toward criticism. He argued that systems of education, politics, and religion had cultivated prejudices for centuries and that no prejudices were more deeply rooted than religious ones. Getting people to think critically about their faith, therefore, was no easy task. "No hopes of reform can be obtained relative to such obstinate minds, until you can render them susceptible to the impressions of doubt or uncertainty." About three-quarters of *Principles*, therefore, focused on the effort to "annihilate" Christianity. Chapters attacked the Bible as an authority; the reliance on wonders, miracles, and prophecies; the major Christian doctrines; and the moral characters of Moses and Jesus (as well as Mohammed). His efforts to articulate an alternative rational religion culminated in the penultimate chapter, a description of "pure and simple Deism."[6]

Critics howled that he had pushed beyond standard deism and was in fact advocating atheistic materialism. Modern readers, too, have claimed that "Palmer's thought evolved beyond the critique of revealed religion to philosophical naturalism," or, most recently, that Palmer stepped beyond deism or theism (the terms were synonymous, or nearly so, for Palmer) to a "radical alternative" that would come to be called "vitalism," leaving behind a God who was an intelligent, moral being to celebrate a "life force" in all matter. But Palmer's early nineteenth-century critics, as the author himself noted, measured his belief in God only against their own narrow, anthropomorphic, Bible-based theism. More recent readers who want to see Palmer the pragmatic naturalist or radical vitalist butterfly emerging from the dry chrysalis of eighteenth-century deism are confusing his arguments in one register for a substitute philosophical program.[7]

Palmer did move past most deists in important ways. Unlike Jefferson and many others, he criticized Jesus's moral character and Christian ethics. For Palmer, too, in contrast to Ethan Allen, for example, there is no survival of self or soul in an afterlife: death is the dissolution of consciousness and the reconstitution of matter in other forms. Significantly, Palmer proposed an entirely naturalistic ethics: if there were a thousand gods or no god, he wrote, "the moral relation between man and man would remain exactly the same." Morality was independent of any kind of theism, even his own pure, natural, rational version. Unlike some other deists, Palmer was not a dualist, separating matter and spirit. He thought that motion is an essential property of matter—that all matter is indeed animated by a life force. This "opinion," he wrote, is useful in helping to surmount humanity's alienation from the natural world. But animated matter organized in a particular way produces animals that can feel and, configured in another way, human beings who can feel and think. Each of these ontological categories in which humans exist—the material, the sensitive, and the intellectual (or what we have in common with rocks, dogs, and each other), and not just the first (matter-in-motion, or the vital force), has important implications for how people ought to understand their place in the world. "Vitalism" is folded into, and informs, Palmer's larger deist project.[8]

How did he get from his "theism," which, as he argued against the Christians who called him an atheist, postulates "only a mighty power by which the universe is sustained," a power whose "shape or form" is unknown, to the deist's God, an intelligent being with a moral character? Perhaps, he speculated, the material universe itself is analogous to the human brain, producing a supreme intelligence, a Mind that thinks and acts. Palmer did not erase his God for an atheistic materialism or reduce him to merely a vital force shared by all matter. God as an intelligent, moral being remained an important element of his stated beliefs. He revered "the God of nature, the intelligent organizer of the universe; possessed of all possible perfection and excellence, and directing the vast concerns of nature with the greatest harmony, and the most divine benevolence... [a being] incapable of any infraction of moral law." This notion of God, too, was an essential component of his continuing critique of Christianity.[9]

After *Principles of Nature*, Palmer sustained and developed his critique of Christian faith in his periodical, the *Prospect*, by targeting the religion's biblical foundations. His "Comments on the Sacred Writings" ran in fifty-five of the sixty-five issues. The series began with a discussion of the first chapter of Genesis in January 1804 and worked sequentially through the first four books of the Old Testament, concluding with his remarks on the Book of Numbers at the end of March 1805, when the journal ceased publication. In every installment Palmer relentlessly assailed the scriptures as a jumble of "unpardonable blunders" about the physical world and distortions of natural law, together with burlesques upon historical truth, "inextricable mysteries," fanciful fictions, and a false moral philosophy. "These sacred writings as they are called," he argued, "are nothing more than the ignorant effusions of scribbling and foolish fanatics."[10]

PROSPECT,
OR
View of the Moral World,
BY ELIHU PALMER.

VOL. I.   SATURDAY, *December 10th, 1803.*   No. I.

TO THE PUBLIC.

THE period has at length arrived in which the civilized world has recognized the necessity of moral principles to regulate the conduct of intelligent beings. If the principles be necessary, there also exists an equal necessity of diffusing through the mass of society a clear knowledge of their nature and character. Ignorance is the parent of vice, and vice the destruction of social order and happiness. In marching retrogressively over the historic page of man, the mind perceives with extreme regret, the immoral copartnership existing between superstition, vice, and ignorance; the testimony of past ages rises up in judgment against the flagrant crimes, the horrid murders, and the wide spreading devastations which have resulted from superstition,

Elihu Palmer's *Prospect* 1, 1 (Dec. 10, 1803), 1. In the periodical's opening address, Palmer hailed a new era in which enlightenment would dispel ignorance and superstition.

Palmer found it "one of the unaccountable facts of modern times" that even in "an enlightened age" so many could give credence to this farrago of ancient "folly, falsehood, and wickedness." Whereas *Christianity Unveiled*, a work serialized in Driscoll's *Temple of Reason* a few years earlier, had blamed unthinking habit, handed down from parent to child, for perpetuating superstitious Christian mythology, Palmer indicted public institutions: churches empowered by the state, Sabbath-day preaching, faulty education. To free their minds from the dogmas of official authority, which shrouded the ancient texts in a reverent haze and cultivated a fear preventing frank appraisal, he did not ask his readers to follow long strings of logic but merely to read the words on the Bible's pages with skeptical common sense. He adhered to the literalism of much of the Protestant tradition and happily took up the evangelical assumption, increasingly popular in the early American republic, that the Bible was intelligible to the simple common sense of ordinary people.[11]

Unlike those learned Christian interpreters who tried to peer beneath or explain away the Old Testament's extravagant imagery and apparently fantastical stories to find their golden nuggets of divine truth, Palmer held to the principle that any evidence of falsehood, folly, or injustice invalidated the entire text as a product of the divine mind. In any case, this was not a matter of a few corruptions introduced to divinely inspired words as they passed through human hands: there were inconsistencies, incoherencies, and absurdities in every chapter, practically in every verse. From the talking snake in the Garden of Eden to the impossible Flood covering every mountaintop, from the wild tale of the Tower of Babel to the silly stories of Jacob wrestling an angel, of Balaam's talking ass, or of the "childish" game of hide-and-seek that Moses and God played among the rocks, the "fiction, extravagance, and absurdity are visible upon the very face of the record." The stories, too, were often inconsistent or incoherent. In Exodus 33:11, for example, Palmer pointed out, "the Lord spake unto Moses face to face, as a man speaketh unto his friend," but nine verses later it says that no man could see God's face and live, so Moses, ridiculously, was only able to glimpse God's "back parts." Add to that the verses stuffed with useless historical or pseudo-historical anecdotes, such as details about the number of cattle Abraham and Lot possessed, and indecent stories, such as the one about a drunken Lot impregnating his daughters, and the result is hardly enlightening.[12]

More significantly, this so-called holy writ, Palmer contended, violated essential principles of morality and justice. Unblinkered reason recognized, and the American constitutions written in the flush of Revolutionary enlightenment proclaimed, that all men were born free and equal. But the God of the Old Testament played favorites, anointing one group as his "chosen people." A verse in Exodus, too—"Neither shalt thou countenance a poor man in his cause" (Ex. 23:3)—suggested that the poor ought not to be treated as equals to the rich before the law. Far worse, Jehovah endorsed—indeed, commanded—slavery. Reading the twenty-fifth chapter of Leviticus, in which God instructed Israel to make slaves of the surrounding peoples—slaves that could be bought, sold, inherited, and held "forever" (Lev. 25:44-46)—Palmer noted with disgust that "this single passage is of itself sufficient to stamp on the book the mark of infamy." Even the much-vaunted Ten Commandments were deeply flawed. The first two commandments, for example—"I am the Lord thy God, which have brought thee out of the land of Egypt" and "Thou shalt have no other gods before me" (Ex. 20:2-3)—seem to have more to do with the jealousies of a tribal chieftain than the Creator of the universe; the sixth, against killing, is too vague; and the tenth, on coveting, seems to outlaw a state of mind rather than an action. But by promising in the Decalogue to punish the descendants of sinners "unto the third and fourth generation" (Ex. 20:5), the Old Testament God destroys his own moral character by violating the basis of distributive justice.[13]

Palmer's most important and repeated point throughout the series of commentaries was that the God portrayed in the Old Testament was far different from and grossly inferior to the deist's God, established by reason's reading of nature. Palmer did not in these essays (or himself elsewhere in the *Prospect*) give the deist's argument for Nature's God. (This is in contrast to his colleague Denis Driscoll's *Temple of Reason*, which began with the design argument for the existence of an intelligent Creator, followed by a standard argument for the immortality of the soul, as two essential planks in the deistic platform.) Palmer simply presupposed Nature's God (an omnipotent, omniscient, eternal being who would not violate his own natural laws or the rules of universal morality and justice) to condemn the character of the Bible's Jehovah. Unlike the magnificent if distant God of deism, Jehovah was jealous, capricious, passionate, forgetful, profane, barbarous, and bloody. Violating both nature's laws and justice, he turns Lot's wife into a pillar of salt for merely glancing back at her former home. He commands Abraham to murder his son Isaac and institutes bloody ritual sacrifices that destroy the Jews' moral sympathies and prepare them to slaughter their neighbors in His name. He hardens Pharaoh's heart, making him do something wicked, and then kills him for doing it. He threatens to make his chosen people cannibalize their own children if they disobey him. The ignorance and superstition of this ancient theology, Palmer concluded, destroy "all rational confidence in the book by burdening the character of their god with a mass of detestable attributes that would disgrace" any human being, let alone the Creator of the universe. In sum, wrote Palmer, "this book is a distortion of every thing that is just.... [I]t is a reproach to virtue, a dishonor to the character of God, hostile to the immutable principles of justice and essentially destructive to the true interests of intellectual life."[14]

Most of the other articles printed in the *Prospect* extended this critique to the New Testament and criticized Christianity, both in doctrine and historical practice, or "revealed" religion more generally, or, even more broadly, supernatural superstitions. Palmer published short essays or comments on the sorry history of the Christian church, lingering over episodes like the persecution of Galileo and the witch hysteria in colonial New England. Articles railed against predestination, original sin, immaculate conception, atonement, and the notion that Jesus was God's son; they attacked belief in oracles, prophecies, miracles, and hell. A couple pondered the psychology of religious faith, with an extract from Locke on enthusiasm and another from Hume noting that it is the darker passions—melancholy, anxiety, and dread—rather than speculative curiosity that drives most people to ponder the existence of invisible intelligent powers. Palmer published reports from evangelical revivals that detailed the phenomena believers described as "religious exercises" caused by a "work of grace": shrieking, screaming, groaning, crying out, falling down as if struck dead, jerking with convulsive fits, and having visions of Christ. For Palmer and, presumably, his readers, these were manifestations of religious fanaticism, caused by nervous disease or the imagination pushed to the point of insanity.[15]

After a brief "Explanation of the Principles of Deism" in the *Prospect*'s second issue, most of the work of setting out deism as a positive philosophy was not a repetition of the arguments he had published in *Principles of Nature* but was left to Jean-Jacques Rousseau's Savoyard curate, whose creed from book 4 of *Émile* was serialized in twenty-seven issues. Palmer warned his readers that some might find Rousseau's Cartesian arguments for the being and nature of God too "metaphysical," and that they might disagree with the author, as Palmer himself did, about the dualistic separation of matter and spirit. Still, he wrote, Rousseau's work ought to be esteemed by the country's "virtuous and Philosophic" readers.[16]

Rousseau's Savoyard curate offered American deists a way to work out a balance between skepticism and faith. "I was in that state of doubt and uncertainty," the curate begins, "in which Descartes requires the mind to be involved in order to enable it to investigate truth." His skepticism, that is, was at once epistemological and methodological—it questioned all claims to knowledge and truth and therefore allowed him, like Descartes, to strip away all assumptions and try to build his philosophy from the ground up. Further, the curate was psychologically impelled to move in a positive direction. The completely skeptical "disposition of mind ... is too disquieting to last long," Rousseau wrote, and only "vice or indolence" would allow a person to remain in that state: "I cannot comprehend how any man can be sincerely a sceptic, on principle. Such philosophers either do not exist, or are certainly the most miserable of men. To be in doubt about things which it is important for us to know, is a situation too perplexing for the human mind." Reflecting upon his own sensations, the curate soon establishes that he exists and that other beings do, too. He feels that he has a soul that probably could survive the death of the body, and reasons that there must be a good and just God responsible for the astonishing works of creation. He reasons that human beings have free will and that they, and not God, are responsible for the moral evils that so often blight human life. For his moral code, the curate consults his conscience, the natural voice of the soul. Such are the elements of the curate's creed; his pupil recognizes that the sentiments closely resemble "that theism, or natural religion, which Christians affect to confound with atheism and impiety, though in fact diametrically opposite."[17]

When asked to move from "natural" to "revealed" religion and comment on the competing scriptures, contending claims to revelation, and mysterious doctrines of religions as they existed in the world, however, the curate can offer no path out of "perplexity," no resolution to "rational doubts." How, the curate asks his student, could you possibly sift through all the various claims of prophecies, revelations, and miracles, in all the countries of the world, from antiquity to the present? Even if you could master all the languages and read through all the world's libraries, how could you correct for the biases of the archive, which skewed what was published and preserved according to the tastes of the powerful? Besides, much popular religious belief and practice never makes it into books. Even if you could find other ways to immerse yourself in the customs and cultures of the world, how could you correct for your own parochial prejudices and biases? No, the curate concludes, about the claims of Christianity, Judaism, Islam, and all other "artificial" religions, he will remain a skeptic. "This scepticism, however," he added, "is not painful to me." Disquieting radical skepticism had initially driven him to establish, in his own mind, his rational, natural faith; that faith, in turn, allowed him to remain comfortable with a more limited religious skepticism. This was the relationship between skepticism and faith that Palmer and his coadjutors tried to institutionalize.[18]

Emergence: Deism and Universalism

Palmer spoke and wrote about an "impulse" to fight for liberty that circulated, as if by electricity, through revolutionary society, and about the "diffusion" of enlightened ideas through print. Institutions, however, as the sociologists put it, are what make practices and ideas not just flow but stick. A group of people sharing ideas and practices becomes institutionalized—becomes, say, a club or a church or a political party—when self-sustaining mechanisms are adopted to perpetuate the association without activists having to gin up support at every turn: rules of membership, structures of authority, stated norms of behavior, regularized forms of communication, and so on. Such a body can become a successful means of social and cultural reproduction only if it has a stable supply of social and material resources (people to do the work, money to pay the bills). In addition, it needs enough autonomy from other organizations to establish a separate identity, yet benefits by also demonstrating connections to broader, commonly shared cultural values, which gives the group legitimacy in the eyes of a wider world. Organized deism, like other new voluntary associations emerging in the early national period, had to confront these challenges.

Institutionalized organizations need to be seen relationally within larger organizational or institutional fields: environments of similar organizations along with all the resources, people, and entities that sustain them. Organizations within these fields take the shapes they do for several reasons. State regulations force or induce them to do certain things or exist in particular ways. The people within the different groups can tend to act according to generally accepted (though not state-enforced) norms. Often, organizations end up copying strategies from one another as they compete for resources and public support even as they try to distinguish themselves from their competitors by stressing differences through opposition. Organizations, however, do not compete in some "free market" (a standard metaphor) for material, social, and cultural capital as equals. Power asymmetries are a fact of institutional life.[19]

Organized deism in the United States emerged in the overlap of the religious and political fields that developed in the fraught political climate of the 1790s. The environment shaping deistic societies was defined by evolving and sharply contested norms of voluntary association, by the shifting laws refiguring the relationship of church and state, and by competition with other churches, political organizations, and clubs.

Although Alexis de Tocqueville in *Democracy in America* described a vibrant civil society created through voluntary association as a defining characteristic of American life, this civic voluntarism did not simply spring forth from notions of virtuous citizenship in the Revolutionary era. British American colonists had organized and participated in public life in various ways—as in Benjamin Franklin's Library Company and Union Fire Company in colonial Philadelphia, for example, or the Defense Association (an extralegal militia) or the Friendly Association (a Quaker society promoting peace with the Indians). During the imperial crisis, "patriots" formed associations, committees, and congresses outside of, opposing, and eventually replacing the normal institutions of government. As independence was declared and won, they built new governmental institutions according to their new political science: in the new order, no longer a relationship between a sovereign ruler and his ruled subjects, "the people" were sovereign, ruling themselves through representatives of their own choosing. In this new polity, however, what was the role of political associations or societies or clubs outside of government? The answer to that question remained unclear as George Washington took the oath of office in April 1789 and began his first administration under the new constitution.[20]

Two answers emerged in the early 1790s as a political cleavage developed over domestic and foreign policies and the Federalist and Republican Parties coalesced, even as partisans on both sides continued to decry partisanship and condemn political parties as dangerous factions. In the spring of 1793, Democratic-Republican societies began to form in most major cities and in some rural areas as well. They opposed the Anglophilia and yearning for aristocracy they saw becoming increasingly prominent in the Washington administration and condemned the Hamiltonian fiscal policies that fostered both; they toasted liberty, equality, and the French Revolution. With aggressive publicity and unconcealed electioneering, they described themselves as mediating institutions between the state and the people, circulating information about government to the citizenry and representing the will or the opinion of the people to the government. Supporters of the Washington administration (the Federalists) condemned the Democratic-Republican societies as dangerous factions: they were illegitimate political associations using strategies that were subversive of good government—strategies that had been fine against a tyrannical monarch but were not in a polity where the people's voices were already heard and their will exercised in the legislatures elected to represent them. The Federalists linked the societies to the French Jacobin Clubs and the Reign of Terror in France (September 1793 to July 1794) and then, more plausibly, to the Whiskey Rebellion in Western Pennsylvania, the militant tax-resistance movement put down by troops in the summer of 1794. President Washington condemned these "self-created societies" in his annual message to Congress in November, and they collapsed by 1795, only to be replaced by more circumspect groups like the Tammany Society, a fraternal organization that was quickly becoming a partisan club in the mid-1790s. The Federalists, meanwhile, commandeered public celebrations of national holidays for their partisan purposes, had their own politicized clubs and militias, and would, after the Jeffersonian victory in 1800, turn to voluntary associations with a vengeance. Still, the relationship between the ideals of patriotism and the pragmatic necessities of partisanship remained unclear into the early nineteenth century. Institutionalizing organizations for explicitly political purposes still emitted a suspicious stink.[21]

In the same period, Americans recast the relationship of religion and government. On the eve of the Revolution, nine of the thirteen colonies had collected taxes to support a state church. By 1790, only three states did. However, of the state constitutions ratified before 1787, eleven of fourteen required officeholders to swear to a belief in God and the divine inspiration of the Old and New

Testaments, and seven of those further excluded Catholics as well. Five state constitutions limited civil rights to Protestants, three to Christians, and one to theists. In Pennsylvania, which had never had an established church, the constitution of 1776 maintained the freedom of worship for everyone but also restricted officeholding to those who believed in God and the Bible. Even in states that no longer showed official preference to one Christian sect over another or used public funds to support religion, laws continued to maintain the Christian Sabbath, endorse public fast and thanksgiving days, and prosecute blasphemy. Churches, too, remained entangled with civil government even in those states that had formally disestablished. The privilege of incorporation, which allowed churches to own property and sue in the courts, was often tied to legislative controls over and judicial decisions about the church's wealth and even internal governance (though such legislative and judicial involvement could occur even where the state denied churches the ability to incorporate, as in Virginia). In disestablished states, as a legal historian has summarized, "religious societies became the quintessential private associations, simultaneously supported and disciplined by the states."[22]

For Palmer, organized deism would be a blend of voluntary religious association and political club, and he took his first steps toward trying to institutionalize it in Philadelphia in the early 1790s. After preaching moral discourses as a (very) liberal Presbyterian in various city pulpits, he became associated with a group who had broken away from the Baptist church and had reorganized as Universalists in 1790. By February 1792, however, the former Baptists in the Universal Church refused to allow Palmer to preach to them any longer, for "altho he had gained great applause amongst all ranks of people while he spoke there," apparently his sermons had veered into outright deism. This was "great news" to John Fitch. Fitch, a steamboat inventor who was then struggling (and failing) to profit from his invention, was also the founder of a deist club in Philadelphia called the Universal Society. The club had about forty members, although Fitch was convinced that many more in the city were skeptical about Christianity and held deist beliefs but were afraid to say so publicly. Philadelphia—indeed, the world—was ripe for "a revolution in Religion," Fitch believed, and needed only the right man to lead it. Believing himself too ugly and too poor a speaker for that role, he had been looking for "a person of real abilities and of Good address" to step forward. He thought he found that person in Elihu Palmer. The inventor immediately went to see the preacher, and as they spoke it became clear that they did indeed have similar religious views. Excitedly, Fitch signaled that he was ready to play John the Baptist to Palmer's deist Messiah: "I told him that I had been preparing the Way in the Wilderness for him thro' unbeaten Paths."[23]

Fitch had prepared the way with his Universal Society, which he and some friends had organized two years before. Modest though it was, Fitch had grand plans. The club met to discuss and debate scientific, philosophical, moral, and religious questions. Members talked about such topics as the nature of matter and the sandiness of the soil east of the Alleghenies, considered questions about dueling and capital punishment, and pondered Providence, conscience, prayer, and the afterlife. They had framed a constitution and took minutes at their meetings, which they dated, following the example of the French Revolutionary Republic, by discarding the Christian calendar (e.g., "AD 1790") and marking history with their own and their nation's founding ("in the first year of the Universal Society and of the Independence of America fifteen"). Fitch imagined that the society could develop by borrowing from existing religious and fraternal organizations. He would take the executive and legislative structures and strategies of publicity from Quakerism, the practices for cultivating friendly sociability from the Freemasons, and the model of small instructional class meetings from the Methodists. Finances would flow from admission fees (one-eighth of a dollar) charged to nonmembers who would flock to hear the charismatic deist speakers, eventually funding a deist academy, poor relief, and loans to entrepreneurial members who needed capital to start businesses. As local societies multiplied and linked, men of genius and ability in the society could make regional and even national connections, which could be parlayed into powerful political careers.[24]

All of this, Fitch thought, was in the future. In the short term, he believed that the Universal Society needed to move beyond being a private deist club by first throwing its doors open to "Christian Deists"—that is, liberal Christians in many denominations who were leaning toward Unitarianism: considering Jesus as having had a divine mission, perhaps, but not worshipping Christ as God. He imagined the society then quickly evolving further into a public forum where deists and Christians of all types (perhaps wearing identifying badges) could amicably debate all sorts of religious and moral issues, including foundational ones, with the questions advertised ahead of time in the weekly newspapers. Lectures given to the society, too, could be published and circulated for those who could not attend in person and "for the benefit of Mankind."[25]

Fitch was eager to join Palmer and use the opportunity of the preacher's popularity "to make a nois in the world" and take the next stride in the "revolution of Religion," but both men thought that it would be prudent for Palmer's Christian admirers to take the lead. So Palmer got them to secure permission to use the large "Long-Room" in Church Alley, a building owned by a deist. Palmer, still identifying himself as a "Preacher of Universal Salvation," posted an ad in the newspaper calling all "Friends of liberal Sentiments" to hear him preach. He did preach—from Micah 6:8 ("What doth the LORD require of thee, but to do justly, and to love mercy, and to walk humbly with thy God?")—and he "publicly denied the divinity of Jesus Christ before a Crowded audience." Perhaps too confident that Universal Society deists were as willing to openly support the bold preacher as Fitch himself was, Palmer published an ad promoting his next discourse "against the divinity of Jesus Christ." But when the Episcopal bishop at Christ Church down the street pressured the owner of the Long-Room, that man, though a member of Fitch's club, "fearing a temporal injury," locked the doors and would not let Palmer use the space. Writing a biographical sketch of Palmer three decades later, John Fellows concluded the episode dramatically: "In consequence of this advertisement, the society of Universalists were in an uproar; and being joined by people of other denominations, instigated probably by their priests, an immense mob assembled at an early hour before the Universalist Church, which Mr. Palmer was unable to enter. In fact, it is stated, that he was in personal danger, and was induced to quit the city, somewhat in the stile of the ancient Apostles upon similar occasions."[26]

Fellows's narrative is garbled but still revealing. First, Fellows, like later historical accounts that follow him too closely, seems to conflate Fitch's club—the Universal Society—and the Universal Church of former Baptists. Fellows may also be confusing this episode with one in 1801 when Palmer was first promised the chance, and then forbidden, to preach in Philadelphia's Universal Church. Second, the advertisement probably was more significant in angering the Christian Universalists because a clergyman associated with them and calling himself "a preacher of Universal Salvation" was denying Christ's divinity rather than just because it imprudently publicized the sorts of conversations that Fitch's deists had enjoyed privately in their club. Third, there is no other evidence of an "immense mob" involved in the dispute. In a published complaint written the day after the alleged "uproar," Palmer mentioned only the landlord reneging on their agreement. A sarcastic letter from an anonymous opponent published a few days later gave no hint of any unruly crowd, nor did John Fitch, who wrote his account within the next few months. Even if more than a few people gathered and caused some sort of a ruckus when Palmer tried to get into the building on Church Alley, which Fellows inflated into an "immense mob" putting Palmer in danger, there is no evidence that it was "instigated" by clergymen; nor, however, should it be taken to signify underlying, consensual religious sensibilities, a communal action to enforce an agreement among diverse Philadelphians about the proper limits of religious expression. For his part, Fitch was ready to press the issue publicly and set all Christendom at war if he could only find a way to support Palmer financially. Palmer, to Fitch's disappointment, merely backed down and left town. Fitch's club, already "dwindling" before this incident, would fade from view long before his death in 1798.[27]

Palmer's link to Universalism, however, still helps illuminate the later development of organized deism. Like deists, Universalists stressed a reasoned analysis of scripture, though they employed it for pietistic ends. Palmer himself saw

Universalism as a step in the sectarianism-as-rationalization process that helped the enlightened break free from Christianity altogether and embrace a rational religion of nature—so here Palmer was reading Western religious history as parallel to his own intellectual biography. In the 1790s, too, as Fellows recognized, Universalism itself "was then hardly tolerated in this country" and "had just begun modestly to bring forward its claims to indulgence." Universalists had already learned what Palmer said the Philadelphia episode had driven home to him: "that notwithstanding the legal and nominal freedom that obtains in this country, the law of opinion, and the internal spirit of persecution, bear hard upon the rights of conscience." Universalism's journey to legitimacy as a religious denomination, however, provides a telling contrast to the trajectory of organized deism.[28]

Universalism—the idea that all souls would eventually be saved—was an ancient doctrine that had had a few scattered and mostly quiet admirers in eighteenth-century Anglo-America, though more among the German sects in the mid-Atlantic region. In England groups began organizing around the middle of the century. John Murray was a leader of the movement that led to the institutionalization of Universalism as a separate denomination in the United States. After arriving in America in 1770, he traveled and preached universal salvation, though cautiously at first. He quickly found himself having to defend the Bible against deists and to defend himself against the charge of deism by other Christians. The first Universalist societies were organized in Massachusetts in the 1770s. In Pennsylvania, Elhanan Winchester, the minister of the Philadelphia Baptist Church, publicly admitted in 1781 that he had been preaching universal salvation from his pulpit; he and about a hundred followers were ousted and created the Society of Universal Baptists in 1785. Meanwhile, in Massachusetts, the established Congregationalists in Gloucester were calling Murray's Universalist society an irregularly constituted body of troublemakers who refused to pay their religious taxes: they were heretical and pernicious "strolling mendicants" who obstructed business, corrupted morals, and destroyed peace and harmony. The issue went to the courts, where it dragged on from 1783 to 1786. The final decision extended the tax exemption (previously granted to Quakers and Anabaptists) to the Universalists and to all Protestant denominations, incorporated or not. After having been fined for performing marriages, Murray also successfully petitioned the state to recognize his ordination, his status as a public teacher of religion and morality. State power, therefore, granted Universalism legitimacy.[29]

Universalists also tried to establish a denominational identity by building structures that could link local societies that were embedded in the polities of the separate states. In 1790, Murray, Winchester, and fifteen other Universalist preachers and laymen met in Philadelphia for a first attempt at a national convention. At the time, what it meant to be called a "Universalist" was still very fluid. People who put the idea of universal salvation at the center of their faith lacked uniform doctrines, reasoning, practices, or even nomenclature, calling themselves Universalians, Universelers, Restorationists, Redemptionists, Restitutionists, and so on. Murray, in a pamphlet entitled *Some Hints Relative to the Forming of a Christian Church. . . . Concluding with a Character of a Consistent Universalist* (1791), described seven different theological variations of Universalism, deriding one as "Pharisaical" and another as "scum." Even in Murray's New England, Universalists in the rural hill country had almost no contact with the Murrayite churches along the coast, and they resisted any attempt to standardize theology or practice. While Murray and other leaders tried to define the denomination in print, the 1790 Philadelphia convention attempted to establish it institutionally by codifying articles of faith and framing a plan of church government, though it would be at least another decade before Universalists would effectively create a unifying ecclesiastical organization and clerical bureaucracy.[30]

Together, state power and translocal association helped shape the emergence of Universalism. The laws in various states for licensing clergymen, incorporating religious societies, and, in the three states continuing some sort of religious establishment, collecting ecclesiastical taxes helped define Universalism as a legitimate denomination distinctive in its theology and practice and yet structurally similar to other Protestant groups. In 1801, the New Hampshire Supreme Court ruled that Universalists were not a recognized sect, and members therefore still had to pay taxes to support their local established Congregational churches. The court reasoned that Universalists differed from Congregationalists only theologically, not in their congregational structure and internal discipline. The theological differences among Protestants not being a matter that the state, constitutionally, was allowed to meddle with, the Universalists did not qualify as a distinctively different sect. The moves made by the Universalists' New England General Convention in 1803 to create a more robust regional organization were, in part, a response. The Convention regularized the rules for representation at its meeting and constituted itself as a supervisory body, especially in regard to ordination and the discipline of clergy. The Universalists in New Hampshire then applied for and received recognition as a distinct denomination by the legislature in 1805.[31]

Universalists were able to establish their legitimacy as a Christian denomination and grow (counting twenty-two ministers in 1800 and forty by 1813) despite the bitter opposition of other Christians. Like vocal deists, Universalists faced social opprobrium and physical intimidation. In the early years, for example, Murray had been barred from public meetinghouses and had been pelted with eggs and stones as he preached. Even as courts and legislatures recognized Universalists, self-described "orthodox" Christians continued to attack them in the press. This "deceptive [Universalist] idea of going to heaven without holiness," the critical chorus chanted year after year, was a "doctrine of devils" that opened "every floodgate of iniquity." Universalism, they said, was advocated "by every artifice that can warp the understanding or interest the passions." It was "the next step to Deism," or perhaps even worse than atheism.[32]

Deists, who always burned near Universalists in the orthodox image of hell, lacked the latter's path toward state-sanctioned (if not broader cultural) legitimacy. It is also true that Paine and Palmer chose a sharply adversarial stance—it was not just foisted upon them. Their understanding of the religious field mirrored the binary opposition of late eighteenth-century politics (democrats versus aristocrats) rather than John Fitch's fantasy of a sociable club. Paine's Paris Society of Theophilanthropists actually offered a different way to position deism: alongside Christianity as believers in God, supporters of religion, defenders of religiously sanctioned morality, and staunch opponents of atheism. But it was his combative *Age of Reason* that set the terms of the debate. The book assailed Christian power by firing directly at the biblical foundations of the faith. When New York City deists offered to build a society around Palmer in the winter of 1795–96, some suggested the name "Theophilanthropist" because it would have been "less frightful to [Christian] fanatics," John Fellows remembered. Palmer, however, whose first major publication had been an eighty-four-page defense of *The Age of Reason*, insisted on the name "Deistical Society." This name would be "without disguise": it announced the intention to institutionalize not just an alternate religion but also a tenacious, politically inflected, Paineite critique of supernaturalism.[33]

New York City was Palmer's home base, where his Deistical Society was guided by an approved list of eleven "Principles" and a set of regulations. But he also regularly traveled and lectured to deist societies that formed in Philadelphia, Baltimore, and Newburgh, New York, which financially supported his work. Palmer and the weekly circulation of the *Temple of Reason* and then the *Prospect* tied the local societies together into a broader movement. By late December in 1800, the societies in New York City and Philadelphia were trying to gather funds to build their own "Temples of Reason," which would serve as meeting places and also as schools and eventually, they hoped, as centers of art, science, and moral philosophy.[34]

The deists in Philadelphia did choose to be called Theophilanthropists, and their publication of a translation of the French Theophilanthropic Society's *Manual* in 1800 might suggest that they were opting for a less confrontational form of organized deism. The *Manual* presented natural religion not as a separate sect but as the essence of all religions and therefore friendly to all of them. Theophilanthropy avoided rational argumentation and professed a few sentimental truths that the French group contended were written on every heart: the existence of God, the immortality of the soul, the duty to cherish other people, and the obligation to serve one's country. It outlined a daily religious practice of simple prayers of gratitude and reflections for self-improvement; its public worship consisted of a recitation of its brief doctrines, some hymns, and moral instruction. Theophilanthropists, according to the *Manual*, were to shun controversy, abstain from religious debates and disputes, and go out of their way to avoid making their religious neighbors uncomfortable. The Philadelphia edition had a somewhat sharper edge, though, than the London version published three years earlier: it dropped the chiding of "Cold and mistaken reasoners" who foolishly demanded rational demonstrations to the mind rather than appeals to the heart, and its preface complained about being stigmatized as infidels and atheists and grumbled about supernaturalism as a disgrace to God and man. "A Discourse Delivered to the Philadelphia Theophilanthropic Society" in 1801 was more Palmerian still. It urged deists to come forward and publicly avow the truth, form more societies, provide a "rallying point to doubting Christians," and slay the "monster superstition" once and for all. When Palmer himself came to Philadelphia, he advertised "public discourses on Theological subjects," a bland title that did not prepare an unwitting Christian who attended and was shocked to hear what he considered to be "the most malignant aspersions" against Christianity imaginable.[35]

Palmer visited Philadelphia in 1801 and arranged with some of his old Universalist friends to deliver a lecture on morality in their church on a Sunday evening. Others in the church caught wind of this plan, held a vote, and got the invitation withdrawn. A year later, the Universal Church sponsored a series of lectures that contrasted the ethical excellence of the scriptures to the inferior and dangerous morality of modern unbelievers, as if attempting to dig a deeper moat between the skeptical deists and the pious Universalists. The editors of the *Temple of Reason* wondered why Universalists, many of whom now denied the divinity of Christ, too, and had given up most of the other distinguishing doctrines of Christianity, still "so tenaciously wish to retain the name of Christians." But then they answered their own question: "Christians, it seems, are still a privileged order, and there are certain loaves and fishes to which they only are entitled to a share in the distribution." As an example, the *Temple* pointed to a recent act of the Pennsylvania legislature that had established a college and restricted the board of trustees to clergymen of any Christian denomination.[36]

Yet deists and Universalists still shared more than just the animosity of the orthodox. Both could face the same serious legal disabilities. Most states had adopted the requirement from English common law that competent witnesses in courts had to swear to a belief in God and to a future state of rewards and punishments. Without the faith that God would punish a lie even if the state could not, the reasoning went, how could a person's word be trusted? Some Universalists (like some deists) did believe that God meted out punishment in the afterlife—just not endless punishment. And some courts looked to precedents allowing them to ignore the requirement for future (postmortem) punishment as long as the person believed that God punished in this life. Still, many judges invoked the requirement and deprived Universalists, deists, and other freethinkers of their civil rights in court.[37]

The issue remained very much alive in 1828 when a series of articles in the *Trumpet and Universalist Magazine* reviewed several cases. One of the earliest that the author had found occurred in the Connecticut Supreme Court of Errors in June 1809. In *Curtiss v. Strong*, an appeal had been made from a decree of probate, challenging the competency of one of the witnesses to a will because the witness did not believe in a future state of rewards and punishments. Another writer was still arguing in 1836 that in Massachusetts not a year passed without testimony being rejected for the same reason. While claiming to uphold their state constitutions by not infringing upon the rights of conscience, the writer complained, courts thus privileged one class of citizens (believers in God and the future state), took away the inalienable rights of everyone else, and subverted justice by excluding testimony.[38]

Deists could face the same legal obstacles. David Denniston, a leader of the Newburgh, New York deists, an associate of Elihu Palmer's, and the editor of a newspaper called the *Rights of Man*, had been feuding with a rival Republican paper, Dennis Coles's *Recorder of the Times*. On July 16, 1803, Denniston took Coles to court, suing him for $480 for breach of agreement. Before taking the oath to testify, Denniston was asked by Judge George Gardner if he believed in a Supreme Being and a future state of rewards and punishments. The plaintiff reportedly answered yes to the first question and quipped that he did not know anything about the second, but protested that the questions were inappropriate and unconstitutional. The judge nevertheless refused to have Denniston sworn in and dismissed the case.[39]

Denniston had been denied access to the courts because he lacked a particular religious belief. The appeal was heard by the Orange County Court of Common Pleas on September 6 before three judges (including Gardner) and two assistant justices. Coles's attorneys argued from precedent in British common law. They also apparently blamed deism for the blood in the streets of France, equated deism and atheism, and warned that Christianity in America was being threatened by civil procedures that took the notion of liberty of conscience too far. Denniston's lawyers attacked on several fronts. They referred the court to Sir William Blackstone's *Commentaries on the Laws of England*, which showed how even Muslims and Hindus could be sworn in as witnesses, but then quickly declared that the common law argument was nonetheless moot because those portions of the British common law connected to an establishment of religion had been abrogated by the New York constitution. They contended that the question rested on American law and institutions, pointing to the inalienable rights enshrined in the Declaration of Independence, the religious freedom protected by the First Amendment to the U.S. Constitution, and even the Virginia Statute for Religious Freedom (1786), which was authored, they reminded the court, by the man who now led the nation despite being bitterly attacked for his own religious beliefs. A New York statute gave them a bit more trouble: it allowed that potential witnesses who (like the Quakers) had scruples against taking an oath could be sworn in by mere affirmation or declaration as long as they affirmed or declared their belief in a Supreme Being and a future state of rewards and punishments. This statute seemed to open the door to the kinds of questions Judge Gardner had asked about Denniston's beliefs, but the attorneys insisted that it only reaffirmed the principle that witnesses could not be quizzed about their beliefs unless they first refused to take the standard oath. A final decision in the case was postponed until the next session, but observers thought the justices seemed to be leaning 3–2 against Denniston. The plaintiff, age thirty-six, died suddenly three months later, before the wheels of justice could produce a final verdict.[40]

Witness competency was a legal manifestation of the way that orthodox opponents lumped Universalists together with deists, atheists, and other dangerous deviants. Like deists of the Palmer and Paine persuasion, Universalists defended religious liberty, called for a stark separation of church and state, and attacked the pretensions to cultural authority of the mainline Protestant clergy, often employing sarcasm and ridicule. Universalists, however, were trying to purify, not tear down, Christianity. Legal recognition as a Christian denomination, along with institutional stability, continuous growth, and consistent demonstrations that they adhered to most of the norms of Christian worship and practice gradually removed much of the stigma from the denomination. But even before their rise to quasi-respectability, Universalists, like the orthodox Christians they debated, loathed and feared the deists for the latter's destructive skeptical attack upon the grounds of Christian faith. Deists were hobbled by all the handicaps imposed upon the Universalists but had none of the latter's advantages.

4

Instituting Skepticism

Contention, Endurance, and Invisibility

John Fellows anonymously published *Some Doubts Respecting the Death, Resurrection, and Ascension of Jesus Christ* in 1797. His authorship of the forty-two-page pamphlet may have remained concealed outside his circle of deist friends. No matter: he already had established a reputation as, in the words of the hostile *Connecticut Courant*, the bookseller who had probably "published more atheistical, impious, and seditious works, than all the other booksellers and printers in the United States." His New York City bookshop sold works by Thomas Paine, Elihu Palmer, Joel Barlow, and Volney (all personal friends), along with titles by Joseph Priestley, Voltaire, and Condorcet, among others. Decades later, Walt Whitman befriended Fellows, a tall, clean-shaven man of military bearing, with hair "white as snow," a relic from the Age of Reason. Still working as a city court constable in his late seventies, Fellows met with the poet and over "a social glass of toddy" talked of the days of Paine and Palmer. In his old age, Fellows published his reminiscence of Palmer and the end of organized deism, and a long book on Freemasonry—fitting, since around the turn of the nineteenth century the deist societies and the Masonic lodges had been linked and condemned as fronts for a vast, dark, dangerous political and religious conspiracy.[1]

A second group—the New Jerusalem (Swedenborgian) Church—was linked to the deists in a different way. The *Temple of Reason*, the flagship journal of the deist societies, connecting the New York City organization of Palmer and Fellows, the Theophilanthropists in Philadelphia and Baltimore, and other groups, was answered by a rival journal, the *Temple of Truth*. This second *Temple* tried to be the defender of the Bible and Christianity against the skeptical critiques of Palmer's lectures, of the books sold in Fellows's shop, and of the weekly provocations published in the *Temple of Reason*. The *Temple of Truth*, however, was also the mouthpiece of a tiny new church, outside the Christian mainstream and struggling to achieve institutional stability just as the deists were. The New

Jerusalem Church endured, but organized deism did not. The failure of the latter has often been explained in intellectual or psychological terms: deism's God was too austere and aloof, it is said; its Newtonian universe too mechanistic and sterile; its view of the moral world too focused on sunny benevolence; its skeptical demolition of mystery and its low opinion of elaborate ritual too dismissive of deep emotional needs. Perhaps. But a comparison to the New Church suggests that organized deism's failure may have been as much about the structural conditions and political developments that worked against it.[2]

Another institution emerging alongside the deist societies, the independent black church, seems a world apart, even if the African Methodist Episcopal Church met only blocks away from the Theophilanthropists in Philadelphia. The formation of independent black churches out of white-dominated institutions was not part of the sectarianism-as-rationalization process that Palmer celebrated. The AME Church perpetuated the central doctrines and practices of Methodism, which Palmer and the deists derided as rank enthusiasm and superstition. In 1797, John Fellows published an edition of James Lackington's *Memoirs*, a lively rags-to-riches account of a shoemaker's apprentice who, by reading voraciously, gradually freed himself from what he came to see as Methodist ignorance and superstition to become a wealthy London bookseller. The book had large print, accessible prose, amusing anecdotes, and a sympathetic portrait of life inside Methodism—and of a far happier, rational, and fulfilling life outside it. Fellows clearly hoped that he might attract some literate but poorly educated American Methodists who, like the British Methodists Lackington described, tended to read little besides the Bible and books by John Wesley, "so that they shut themselves up in darkness, and excluded every ray of intellectual light." Did Fellows imagine that some African American Methodists might be readers, too? Elihu Palmer taught that racial differences were superficial and that slavery was immoral: "That whites have a right to enslave blacks, is a complete abandonment of the principal of reciprocal justice." The liberation of the enslaved was a main goal of political revolution, he argued, and "the emancipated slave must be raised by the power of science into the character of an enlightened citizen." But when he lectured to deist societies in New York, Philadelphia, or Baltimore, were there any black faces in the crowd? The only reference connecting African Americans and organized deism is an opponent's mocking mention of a deist society member, a music teacher who taught "negroes to fiddle." Closer to Palmer than to most white Christians on the issues of slavery and race, black Methodists and other black Christians would have nonetheless stood with their white brethren against the skeptical infidels.[3]

A broader question remains, however: Was there religious skepticism among free and enslaved African Americans? This question returns to the relationship of religious skepticism to formally instituted voluntary associations. The organized deism that Elihu Palmer and John Fellows promoted made the skeptical critique of revealed religion more visible—and therefore, to its opponents, more worrisome and dangerous. The Freemasons, tied to the deists in the paranoid Christian imagination, tried to rule skepticism out of bounds by professing only generic theistic beliefs, and then tried to distance themselves further by asserting a more recognizably Christian character. The confrontation with the skeptical dimension of deism also left its imprint on the enduring institutional identity of the New Jerusalem Church, which had worked to co-opt and redirect the Paineite appeal to reason while trying to avoid skeptically undermining the basis of faith. Other forms of Christianity, however, like the AME Church and African American Christianity more generally, which seemed to have little direct contact with organized deism, could render religious skepticism all but invisible.

Contention: Deism and the Freemasons

In 1798, the Rev. Jedidiah Morse, defender of Calvinism and Federalism in Massachusetts, saw the dots connected: religious infidelity, radical democratic politics, Masonic secrecy, and political conspiracy. France was belligerent and dangerous; Americans were venomously divided; newspapers teemed with slander and abuse; Christianity and the venerable institutions of good government were under attack. The secret plot explaining it all, Morse argued in a sermon preached for the national fast day on May 9, had been revealed in a shocking book by Edinburgh professor John Robison called *Proofs of a Conspiracy against all the Religions and Governments of Europe*. A secret society, the Illuminati, intending to destroy Christianity and overturn all existing governments, had formed in Bavaria in 1776, spread through societies of Freemasons, kindled the French Revolution, and set up covert operations in the United States. The Democratic-Republican societies and the circulation of Paine's *Age of Reason* in America were all part of the Illuminati's master plan. Republican writers dismissed Robison as a crackpot and charged that frothing clergymen like Morse and other Federalist Party hacks were trying to ignite a fake religious panic for their own political ends. The contention did not end with Jefferson's victory in early 1801, however. The next phase of Illuminati conspiracy theories emerged on the Republican side. As the New York Republican coalition of factions led by the Livingstons, the Clintons, and Aaron Burr quickly broke apart, the Burrite writer John Wood published an exposé detailing links between the Clintonian faction and a secret deist society led by Elihu Palmer and explicitly modeled after the Bavarian Illuminati. Unlike the dark insinuations that Morse and his allies had cribbed from European conspiracy theorists, which smeared the Freemasons by association, Wood revealed his sources, printed what he claimed were secret documents, and named names.[4]

Samuel F. B. Morse, "Jedidiah Morse" (1820–22). Morse warned that Masonic lodges were being infected by deism, skepticism, and other forms of religious infidelity. Courtesy of the Yale Art Gallery, Yale University.

The vague charges by Morse, Robison, and other writers only temporarily wounded Freemasonry, a respected fraternal organization with many worthies as members and the revered George Washington as its head. A popular uprising against Freemasonry as a devious nest of political conspirators would wait another generation, when suspicions fueled the rise of the Anti-Masonic Party in the late 1820s. Wood's more specific charges against Palmer's deists, with a Jacobinical, atheistical, drunken caricature of Tom Paine nailed to them as a figurehead, helped bury organize deism. The relationship of religion, politics, secret societies, and conspiracy was similar in both episodes. And in both, notions of religious "infidelity" intersected with commitments to religious "toleration" and fears of political treason.

Morse in the first of his three Illuminati sermons tried to steer Robison's explosive charges away from Freemasonry and toward the Democratic-Republican societies. The Massachusetts minister clarified in his footnotes that Robison was describing the corruption of some Masonic lodges, not of all Freemasonry. Although Robison claimed that "illuminated" (infected) lodges had spread not just throughout Europe but to the United States as well, where there were allegedly "several," Morse suggested, again in a footnote, that most American lodges, at least "in the Eastern States," had probably avoided the contagion. After the predictably outraged response by Freemasons, Morse tried to make amends by addressing the Massachusetts Grand Lodge and affirming his respect for true Masonry and its values. Even this occasion, though, was shadowed by the Illuminati. The public principles of the society, Morse said, were admirable: uphold morality, patriotism, and good manners. As for the character of Masonic secrets, he, not being a member, could not say. Any institution could be corrupted, and secrecy, which could shield that corruption from the public, was bound to arouse suspicion even where nothing was amiss. By their actions Freemasons needed to show their fellow countrymen, Morse intimated, that their secret principles had not been perverted by the Illuminati. Yale president Timothy Dwight, another leading clerical Federalist who had been warning about the link of radical politics and religious infidelity for several years, threw his support behind Morse and Robison and made the point even more sharply in his 1798 July Fourth sermon, *The Duty of Americans at the Present Crisis*.[5]

The public rhetoric of Freemasonry could suggest links to deism. Like the deistical Theophilanthropists, the Masons proscribed atheism, claimed to cultivate reverence for the Grand Architect of the Universe by admiring His works, and promoted an enlightened cosmopolitanism that looked beyond religious, national, and class differences. As a collection of Masonic constitutions published in 1798 put it, whereas in ancient times Masons "were charged to comply with the religious opinions and usages of the country or nation where they sojourned or worked, yet it is now thought expedient that the Brethren in general should only be charged to adhere to the essentials of religion, in which all men agree; leaving each brother to his own judgment as to particular forms." These bare, inoffensive "essentials of religion" could sound a lot like deism. Robison, Morse, Dwight, and other critics, however, were more concerned with what Masons did in private. Screened from public view and censure within their Masonic lodges, men of "the Deistical sects" were free to enter debates about religion, morality, and government. "In the secured and unrestrained debates of the lodge," Dwight imagined, "every novel, licentious, and alarming opinion was resolutely advanced. Minds, already tinged with ['Deistical'] philosophism, were here blackened with a deep and deadly die; and those, who came fresh and innocent to the scene of contamination, became early and irremediably corrupted." The Illuminati, "grafted" onto Masonic institutions as "professedly a higher order," was able to exploit the society's oath-bound privacy to inculcate evil doctrines, highjack its "solemn and mystic rites and symbols" to "make and fix the deepest impressions" on the minds of members, and spread through Masonry's extensive correspondence network, which crossed national borders to link "most civilized countries." Dwight, too, in a footnote, tried to absolve American Freemasonry in general of any blame, yet asserted as fact that "Illuminatism exists in this country."[6]

The Federalist case for an Illuminati conspiracy in the United States, which reached its heights during the furor over the Alien and Sedition Acts, collapsed even before the fall elections of 1800. Robison's claims, amplified by the American edition of Abbé Augustin Barruel's *Memoirs Illustrating the History of Jacobinism* (1799), were doubted even by many conservative reviewers in Europe. Adam Weishaupt had indeed founded a secret fraternal society called the Order of the Illuminati in Bavaria in 1776, which tried to promote enlightened free inquiry in a society cramped by Catholicism and in an intellectual culture controlled by former Jesuits. The Illuminati had borrowed some Masonic techniques and structures, became allied with some German lodges in 1780, and by 1784 had two thousand to three thousand members. In the next three years, however, the Bavarian authorities outlawed the group and arrested its leaders, threatening banishment to any who subsequently tried to join it and the death penalty to any who tried to recruit. Neither Robison nor Barruel could persuasively demonstrate that the Illuminati had, in fact, survived to cause the French Revolution. As for evidence of the Illuminati in the United States, Morse could eventually only produce a vague letter from a French Masonic lodge in Virginia and a mention of a similarly suspect lodge in New York. Masonic clergymen rushed to the society's defense, and some lodges began stressing the order's Christian character. Republican newspapermen laughed at the charges as ridiculous. The prominence of Masons and Masonic symbolism at George Washington's funeral and memorial services reaffirmed the brotherhood's patriotic credentials. A pamphleteer turned the accusation against the New England Federalist clergy, calling them the real "Illuminati": a private group conspiring to pervert religion and politics and control all cultural institutions.[7]

John Fellows wrote his treatise on Freemasonry many years later, after the next wave of Anti-Masonic paranoia, and he included in it a belated defense of the Bavarian Illuminati. Fellows, who was not a Mason himself, intended to demystify Masonry and demonstrate that it was, in fact, harmless. In over four hundred pages he argued that Masonry's strange and secretive practices were rooted in ancient mythology. The religious sources had masked their true meaning through allegory and mystical obscurantism. Secrecy and disguise had originally been necessary because the grand truth, the secret knowledge to be protected both from outsiders and common practitioners—monotheism—was dangerously different from the reigning polytheism of ancient state cults. That the notion of one Supreme Being remained the great "mystery" revealed to higher orders of Masons was, in the modern age, absurd, Fellows wrote, since that belief was now the commonly accepted one. As for the mythological details perpetuated by Masonic practice, most modern Masons had not a clue about their religious origins or allegorical meanings. Practice had for the most part become disconnected from meaning. If Freemasonry was like a religion, its ritual practices lacked the backing of real faith. Masonic ritual merely facilitated fraternal revelry or, at its best, inculcated good morals, polite manners, and friendly sociability. Masonic ritual functioned, that is, the way the "mummery" of the Latin mass performed before illiterate peasants created an atmosphere of sacred awe and reverence useful for enforcing moral behavior and obedience. Fellows argued, though, that such a method of impressing manners and morality was utterly out of step with the modern world. People in the nineteenth century did not—or should not—need to be excited and awe-stricken by mysterious symbols and solemnly performed rites. The morals that the Masons professed, however, were unimpeachable. Freemasonry was silly, perhaps, but not dangerous.[8]

Organized deism, deist activists like Fellows and Palmer had thought, was not silly, but unlike Freemasonry it did have explicitly political and not just moral aims. They believed that deistic principles had logical political correlatives, though they were not the catalogue of horrors listed by Morse and Dwight. As Denis Driscoll wrote, "Deism and Liberty should go hand in hand." To "renounce *king-craft*," as Americans did in their revolution, "and still remain *enchanted* by superstition and Priest-craft" was "a contradiction in terms." But Palmer understood that the link between deistic religion and democratic politics had to be argued, not assumed. Deism, he wrote back in 1794, was not "a sure sign of a democrat." Many Federalists, he knew, were (closeted) deists, and many democrats still clutched their bibles and thought that deists had cloven hooves. Palmer in all his subsequent work endeavored to show that the same styles of thinking, the same stance toward authority, and the same commitment to liberty, equality, and self-determination, finally awakened by the American and French Revolutions, equally applied in the religious and political realms.[9]

The political project of activist deism put free inquiry and debate at the center of public life. Print, public lectures, and open meetings, not private clubs with secret signs and rituals, would be the engine of progress. Deists advocated not just the freedom of private conscience but the freedom of public religious and political expression and association. They did not reduce all claims made in a religious context to mere opinions and certainly did not think them equally valid and beneficial. Deism, they thought, made people better thinkers, better independent actors, better friends, better citizens. But they wanted to make their case through discussion, debate, and the demonstration of accumulated lived experience—through persuasion, not coercion. They were militantly opposed not to Christians, or to Christianity as a privately held opinion, or even to Christianity as a publicly professed faith, but to the unfair exercise of social, political, and legal power by Christians who infringed upon their rights in a society where all were supposed to be equal.[10]

The democratic deists had a different understanding of religious freedom than many of their Christian opponents, just as they had a different conception of virtuous citizenship than their Federalist adversaries. In 1798, a pamphlet by a member of the Newburgh, New York, deistical club responded to an attack printed in a local paper. The newspaper essayist's denunciation of deism had begged two questions, the pamphleteer wrote: first, "Is the gospel or any principle of religion incorporated in our federal or state constitutions?" and, second, "Are deism and patriotism irreconcilable?" The Newburgh deist answered no to both. Citizens, he argued, were "doubly shielded" in the United States by laws guaranteeing religious liberty and by a spirit of independent opinion and mutual forbearance of differences, a spirit essential in a republican society. The problem was often improperly defined as how a society committed to religious "toleration" should deal with religious "infidelity." "Infidelity" and "toleration" are relative terms defined by subordination to governmental power and cultural authority. A confessional state, one that has privileged and empowered a particular religious group, may deign to "tolerate" dissenters; believers in a dominant religious faith denigrate those who disbelieve or oppose it as "infidels." The Newburgh deist joined others—including some enlightened Christians—who called not for mere toleration but for religious liberty, and who hoped for less bigotry and more tolerance.[11]

For some commentators, disestablishment seemed to move the nation, for better or worse, from mere toleration (a Christian state condescending to grant rights to dissenters) toward complete religious liberty (a secular state with citizens free to express themselves on religious matters however they wished). Sometimes writers used "toleration" and "liberty of conscience" almost interchangeably. Some who continued to talk about toleration still tended to think about religious freedom less in terms of an individual's rights of conscience than of parity among Christian sects. In 1797 an article entitled "Toleration" assumed that having all Christian sects on an equal footing would secure the rights of conscience to individuals. In a 1799 tract, Mason Locke Weems was one of the few writers to include deists among the "band of brothers" created by the "universal toleration" or nonpreferential treatment of religious groups. A writer in 1820 supporting the Massachusetts constitution's tax support of Protestant churches perpetuated a tradition of construing toleration much more narrowly. Neither state support of Protestantism nor a requirement that officeholders be Christians, the writer argued, violated the notion of toleration. These provisions merely balanced the individual's reasonable liberties with the rights and duties of a Christian society to worship God as it should.[12]

For other commentators, however, religious liberty had to be reimagined for a revolutionary age. Some of these writers acknowledged that toleration had to mean something new and began using the phrase "*universal* toleration" as a synonym for a capacious religious freedom. Others, though, made a sharp distinction between toleration and the rights of conscience. The English Dissenter Richard Price had argued in 1784 that the ideal of liberty of conscience emerging from the American Revolution meant much more than toleration: "Not only all *Christians*, but all *men* of all religions ought to be considered by a State as equally intitled to its protection as far as they demean themselves honestly and peaceably." Thomas Paine in *The Rights of Man* (1791) applauded the announcement that "the French constitution hath abolished or renounced Toleration, and Intolerance also, and hath established Universal Right of Conscience. Toleration is not the opposite of Intolerance, but is the Counterfeit of it. Both are despotisms. The one assumes to itself the right of with-holding Liberty of Conscience, and the other of granting it." In the mid-1790s, Democratic-Republicans at patriotic events answered Federalist toasts to toleration by raising their glasses to "Universal Freedom of Religion, and no Toleration." Freedom of religious belief and expression was a prepolitical right, not a gift bestowed by the state; religious opinion and practice were matters of personal judgment, not to be meddled with by a state legitimating some religious groups and not others.[13]

Religious liberals and radicals writing from abroad and republican political clubs were not the only ones to make this distinction between toleration and liberty. In his 1790 letter to the Hebrew congregation in Newport, Rhode Island, George Washington wrote that "all possess a like liberty of conscience, and immunities of citizenship. It is now no more that toleration is spoken of, as if it was by the indulgence of one class of people, that another enjoyed the exercise of their inherent natural rights." William Linn, a minister of the Dutch Reformed Church in New York City, argued that the idea of toleration was a remnant from an age of "ignorance and superstition": "Let the word be forever blotted from the vocabulary of Christians." William Findley, a Pennsylvania Presbyterian, answering another Pennsylvania Presbyterian's 1803 criticism of the irreligious character of state and federal constitutions, argued that toleration made sense only in conjunction with a political establishment of religion; neither Pennsylvania nor the United States, thankfully, tried to interfere with an individual's rights of conscience, he wrote. Findley conceded that this meant that even the kind of deist who did not believe in an immortal soul—though not an atheist—could hold political office. His opponent, Samuel B. Wylie, warned that the state and federal constitutions threw the door open to atheists, too.[14]

The debate continued into the nineteenth century. A Massachusetts Presbyterian in an 1812 fast sermon plagiarized Paine on toleration, merely substituting the U.S. Constitution for the French. In 1821, an article in an evangelical magazine noted that despite its continued use in discussions of religious freedom, "the word *Toleration*, is not suited to the present state of the American Churches" because it implied the political establishment of religion. A year before Massachusetts became the last state to drop its support of Protestant churches in 1833, an article in the *Christian Watchman* supporting complete religious liberty quoted from a dictionary to show that toleration, in the strict sense of the word, only existed where government usurped the inalienable right of people to adopt their own religious opinions and forms of worship. "Infidels, and boasting free-thinkers will [also] contend for this liberty of thinking and judging for themselves," the author admitted. Although God could hold them accountable, government should not.[15]

This notion horrified other Christians. It was precisely the perspective that Jefferson had articulated in *Notes on the State of Virginia* (1788) when he famously remarked that "it does me no injury for my neighbour to say there are twenty gods, or no god. It neither picks my pocket nor breaks my leg." Federalists went back to this proof text repeatedly in the election of 1800. It purportedly revealed Jefferson's deism for all who had eyes to see, and since deism was but a step away from atheism, the argument went, America might very well repeat the horrors of Revolutionary France if Jefferson ascended to the presidency. Even after Jefferson's inauguration failed to usher in the apocalypse, critics warned of dangers brewing. For the Presbyterian Samuel Wylie in 1803, the election of a deist by a Christian people was "shameful": "Is it to be expected that the man, who is not a brother in the profession of the religion of Jesus, but an obstinate *Infidel*, will make his administration bend to the interests of Immanuel, whose existence he denies, whose religion he mocks, and whose kingdom he believes to be fictitious!" Yet for Wylie, Jefferson's victory was just a sign of a deeper rot. A government that did not protect Christ's church was anti-Christian; a state that did not acknowledge its power emanating from God was atheistic; a constitution that made no distinction between Christians and deists, atheists, Muslims, and Egyptians worshipping crocodiles "gives a legal security and establishment to gross heresy, blasphemy, and idolatry, under the notion of liberty of conscience." The United States did have an established religion, Wylie insisted, just not one that drew from God's Word. Instead, the Constitution established a free-for-all of individual conscience.[16]

Organized deism publicly crusaded against such attitudes. But did deism, like Masonry, also have a private face? David Denniston's deistic club in Newburgh, New York, had in fact evolved out of a Masonic lodge. The group, calling itself the Druid Society, adopted some Masonic ceremonies and was rumored to have mocked Christianity by baptizing a cat and giving communion to a dog—scandalous revelry that suggested to some outsiders that an Illuminati-like libertinism was hiding behind closed doors in Newburgh. More damaging, though, to the democratic deists was John Wood's *Full Exposition of the Clintonian Faction, and the Society of the Columbian Illuminati*, published in the first week of

September 1802. Wood had already produced a vicious denunciation of the Adams administration. When the New York Republican coalition fell apart shortly after his patron Aaron Burr became vice president, Wood turned his poison pen against the faction led by New York governor George Clinton and his nephew DeWitt, then a state senator. Wood's pamphlet aimed to expose the behind-the-scenes perfidy of the Clintonians, reveal the existence of New York's own dangerous society of Illuminati, and demonstrate the intimate links between the two groups. The author was already on record as doubting the charges of Robison and Barruel. But then, he wrote, he came upon solid evidence of a secret society in New York, led by Elihu Palmer, that directly borrowed from the founding documents of the Bavarian Illuminati. Palmer's group, Wood argued, was "erected in rebellion" against state law; "it was a society fraught with the blackest intentions, to overturn the divine revelation, and to raise the hand of opposition against the opinion of every Christian."[17]

Wood likened "the propagation of deism" to treason, a premise that shaped everything he said about the activities of the "blind preacher" and his associates. He wrote that "it is an idea too generally held among deistical republicans of the present day, that the constitution of America has granted to all its citizens an enjoyment of opinion in religious matters, unfettered either by the precepts of the Old Testament, or the superior mandates of the Son of God." This notion, however, was a mistake, Wood argued. The state legislatures had wisely regarded the First Amendment "in its proper light," understood the true "spirit" behind the broad language, and knew that the Constitution's "framers" had "never dreamt that a species of beings, would spring up in America, like the savage brute, that would acknowledge no divine superior, but only aim at glutting the appetites of hunger and lust." State laws privileging and protecting the Christian Sabbath, therefore, were perfectly consistent with religious liberty (properly understood), and propagating deism, which unfettered citizens from the Bible, should be considered a "heinous crime."[18]

Wood based his charges upon what he alleged was a copy of the society's constitution, the text of the oaths it used, and interviews with two members: George Baron, a mathematics teacher, and William Carver, the society's treasurer. The first article of the "Constitution of the Theistical Society of New York" announced the objective of the society, which was "to promote the cause of moral science, in opposition to all schemes of *religious* and *political imposture*." The remaining nine articles briefly set out the rules for membership, voting, and dues; established the terms for the president, treasurer, and secretary; formed a committee of correspondence; and expressed the desire to preserve decorum and "cultivate a spirit of friendly and philosophical intercourse." The group, with an estimated ninety-five members, met to discuss philosophical questions usually posed by Palmer, used Palmer's *Principles of Nature* as its textbook, considered the *Temple of Reason* its grand literary journal, and followed DeWitt Clinton as its political chief.[19]

If it all seemed quite benign, Wood assured his readers that it was not. The members were sworn to secrecy and exchanged secret signs, like the Freemasons. Suspiciously, the Theistical Society, just like the Bavarian Illuminati, was divided into three grades, with the lower grades having no knowledge of the higher ones and the higher ones having their own secret constitutions and oaths. New members supposedly took a loyalty oath that had been lifted nearly verbatim from the Bavarian Illuminati, as reported by Robison—though this, too, seemed innocuous: it included the promise that the society's secrets contained nothing "contrary to *religion*, the state, or good manners." The oath for members of the highest grade, also taken directly from Robison, included a more troubling pledge to submit to the order, in the person of the president (Palmer), "making a faithful and complete surrender of my private judgment, my own will, and every narrow minded employment of my power and influence." The initiation ceremony also included a moment when President Palmer whispered something in the new member's ear. Wood's informants did not say so, but Wood was certain that the whisper must have revealed "the real intentions of the society" and the directive that the member "was to consider himself as the perpetual enemy not only of christianity but of every christian; [and] that he was forever to renounce all form[s] of government but what was strictly democratical." Thus instituted, the society, committed to "the whimsical jacobinism of Paine, and the wild philosophy of his disciple blind Palmer," was plotting dark designs behind its veil of secrecy.[20]

Had Palmer's Deistical Society of 1797 been reconstituted as a secret fraternal Theistical Society in 1802, modeled on the Bavarian Illuminati? Or was Wood merely dumping material from Robison's *Proofs of a Conspiracy* upon the New York deists, like the contents of a chamber pot tossed from a second-story window, in the hope that the nearby Clintonian politicians would get splashed as well? Opposition newspapers gleefully printed long excerpts from Wood's *Full Exposition* and evasive replies by some of those directly named as members, such as David Denniston, or strongly implicated, such as the Republican editor James Cheetham. Libel suits were threatened on both sides, and Wood left town. In a short, misspelled letter to the editor of the New York *Evening Post*, treasurer William Carver admitted that Wood's copy of the Theistical Society's constitution was legitimate but contended that nearly everything else in Wood's pamphlet was false: there were no oaths of secrecy, and the meetings, rather than clandestine and suspicious, were often publicly advertised. But Carver's denials were lost in a blizzard of charges and countercharges. Rumors spread that Denniston had tried to bribe the publisher to suppress Wood's pamphlet, and that after it appeared, Palmer put the word out that all society documents should be destroyed; other accounts discredited Baron as an untrustworthy bigamist and Wood as a liar for hire.[21]

The real issue was not whether a deist society existed (it did), or whether it, like the Masons, employed oaths and elements of secrecy (which remains unclear), but whether its activities constituted, in the words of one hostile editor, "the zealous propagation of those disorganizing principles which are injurious to society, pernicious to morals, and destructive of all regular government." The Republican press, aside from some brief ridicule, tried to ignore the controversy. The *Temple of Reason* proudly reprinted the "Theistical Constitution" and the earlier "Principles of the Deistical Society." It dismissed George Baron, Wood's primary informant, as "a silly kind of fellow" and attacked the author of the *Full Exposition* as a "wooden headed bigoted Presbyterian." DeWitt Clinton's connection to the society had not been proved, but such patronage, the *Temple* thought, would do Clinton credit. Clinton, however, kept his distance from the deists, and other Republicans followed suit. New York City mayor Edward Livingston was tight-lipped about the issue when he visited Virginia in November, but he admitted that his city had a society of "infidels" who "no doubt would injure materially the cause of republicanism." Tiny, maligned, organized deism, unlike powerful, pervasive, and prestigious Freemasonry, could not easily weather a storm conjured by conspiracy theorists.[22]

Endurance: Deism and the New Jerusalem (Swedenborgian) Church

The *Temple of Reason*, edited by the former Catholic priest Denis Driscoll, was the first attempt of Elihu Palmer's New York Deistical Society to enter the lists with its own periodical. The first issue came off the presses on November 8, 1800. At the beginning of August 1801, the *Temple of Reason* was answered by the *Temple of Truth*, published in Baltimore and edited by the Rev. John Hargrove. This weekly paper was advertised as promising "to embrace every department of liberal science" but stated that its primary intention was to investigate and defend "*True Christian Theology*." Conspiracy theorist John Wood had claimed that the deists themselves had finagled to get a Christian paper launched to oppose them in order to stir up publicity, even picking out the title *Temple of Truth*, but Hargrove seems to have begun the publication because he was angry that Driscoll would not publish critiques of deism in the deist paper. The two *Temples* faced off against each other each week for the next three months. The *Temple of Truth*, however, was not "an orthodox antidote" to Elihu Palmer, as it has been described. Hargrove was the pastor of a small, heterodox New Jerusalem Church in Baltimore. This group, which was built upon the principles of the Swedish mystic Emanuel Swedenborg, had appeared less than a decade earlier. It was, in other words, an institution that had emerged alongside organized deism and provides another illuminating counterpoint to it. Unlike Palmer's deist societies, Hargrove's New Church, though similarly small and stigmatized, endured.[23]

Hargrove tried to position his *Temple of Truth* carefully in the multidimensional field of early national religious discussion and debate. He introduced his first issue by addressing "all candid and enlightened Christians" and declaring that "*Scepticism* and *superstition*" were the "hoary headed enemies of genuine truth and brotherly love." Assuming the stance of a moderate Christian between the extremes of doubt and enthusiasm, he also tried to co-opt the ground upon which Palmer and Driscoll stood by calling himself "a good deist." He could be labeled a deist, he explained, because he believed in a single God (not three, like the Trinitarians) and because he championed the use of reason. However, he was

Portrait of John Hargrove. From Sanfrid E. Odhner, *Toward a New Church University: ANC Centennial Album 1976* (Bryn Athyn, Pa., 1976). Hargrove countered the deists' periodical, *The Temple of Reason*, with his own, *The Temple of Truth*. Photo courtesy of Archives/Special Collections, Bryn Athyn Historic Landmark District, Glencairn Museum.

not a "mere deist" who relied on "mere reason," he hastened to add, but a "Christian deist" who endorsed the divinity of the Bible as well as the rationality of nature. "I believe with Tom Paine," Hargrove wrote, "that creation is the *word of God*; but not the *only word*." Human reason might be the best guide to truth, but it could not be the final judge on religious matters because it was always "adulterated" by prejudices and passions. While pleading with Christian clergymen and other "influential characters" in Baltimore to support his periodical as a defender of the Bible against deistic infidelity, Hargrove agreed with Palmer that the Bible, as it was commonly read and interpreted by most Christians, was shot through with inconsistencies and contradictions. Once rational readers had shaken off the "blind reverence" for the scriptures that they had learned at their mothers' knees, Hargrove realized, these problems were enough to drive them to skepticism. The solution, he argued, was not to remain skeptical about Christianity and try to prop up a bogus religion of nature in its place but to discover the "spiritual or allegorical" sense beneath the literal meanings of scriptural passages—to discern the patterns of meaning that did indeed reveal a wonderfully harmonious and rational theological system. Without directly mentioning the seer whose visions had revealed that system, Hargrove pointed toward Swedenborg's theology—which mainstream Christian commentators considered to be as delusional as deism. As one sarcastic writer wrote in 1796, to pervert or mutilate religion worse than "a *Paine* or a *Swedenborg*" was quite an accomplishment.[24]

Hargrove and Palmer each tried to recast the relationship between skepticism and faith. Palmer argued that the "skeptical confidence" most people had about the world was upside down: they doubted that mere matter could think and act yet trusted the fantastic claims of supernatural religion. They lived by warped fictions, therefore, rather than by real truths. And he did not understand why "faith" was considered to be such a great virtue in Christendom. Faith was just "an assent of the mind to the truth of a proposition supported by evidence." Why, then, was acknowledging the truth when it stared you in the face a virtue? Hargrove prayed at the beginning of the *Temple of Truth* that "all superstition and christian skepticism may come to an end"—but the passage was ambiguous about whether he meant skepticism about Christianity generally or the skepticism that Christians had about the peculiar new doctrines of the New Jerusalem Church. Similarly, when he answered a lecture Palmer had given in Baltimore by arguing that "faith" was more than simply "a *bare assent* of the *rational faculty* to a certain proposition," Hargrove was doing more than repeating the usual Christian insistence that faith was a matter of the heart as well as the head. In describing faith as including the faithful performance of good works, he was also following the New Church's repudiation of a central doctrine of Protestantism: *sola fide*—justification by faith alone.[25]

Hargrove's strategy was to insinuate some surreptitious Swedenborgianism into what on its face might appear to be an orthodox Christian attack against deism, and he had learned it with his first exposure to the new ideas. He had been a Methodist preacher in and around Baltimore when in 1793 he first heard the Rev. James J. Wilmer, an Episcopalian, preach some of the doctrines of the New Jerusalem Church. Wilmer touted himself as the first preacher of New Church doctrine in the United States. When Wilmer's next publication—*Consolation: Being a Replication to Thomas Paine, and Others, on Theologics*—appeared in 1794, Hargrove studied it carefully. He thought Wilmer's answer to deism was flawed because it seemed to rely on dubious Swedenborgian principles, so Hargrove borrowed some of the seer's works to better make his case. The more he read, though, and the more he spoke with Swedenborgians like the maverick Virginian Robert Carter and the British New Jerusalem Church missionary Ralph Mather, the more he was persuaded.[26]

It was the New Church doctrine of the Trinity that stopped Hargrove in his tracks, and as his Methodist faith began to crumble, but before he was quite willing to take the Swedenborgian plunge, he began to worry that he himself "was on the verge of deism." More than an arcane theological quibble about how Christians could speak of Father, Son, and Holy Ghost and yet still wave the flag of monotheism, the New Jerusalem critique of the Trinity nullified nearly all the doctrines of the "Old Church." In particular, the doctrine of the atonement—central in Old Church Christianity—collapsed. Jesus simply was Jehovah, the New Jerusalem Church taught: there was no bloody sacrifice of an innocent Son to appease the angry Father. The crucifixion had to have a very different meaning. So too, within the Swedenborgian interpretive system of spiritual correspondences, did most things in the Bible—passages that the Methodist Hargrove, like most of his Christian neighbors and the skeptical deist scoffers alike, read far too literally. Hargrove, a forty-seven-year-old man who had preached from Methodist pulpits for twenty years, came to see the scriptures "in a new, and striking light." He felt, he said, "as a man newly awakened out of sleep." He withdrew from the Methodists on June 5, 1798, even though it cost him his job teaching at a Methodist academy and he had eight children at home to feed. The small group of Baltimore Swedenborgians organized as a more formal church society a few weeks later, and Hargrove was ordained in early July.[27]

When Hargrove took the field as Christianity's champion against the deists with his *Temple of Truth* in August 1801, the New Jerusalem Church was still, from the perspective of most of the "influential characters" in his society, almost as suspicious a fringe group as the deists. John Wesley's condemnations of Swedenborg had run for six months in 1797 in the *Methodist Magazine*, where he described the seer's work as "errant nonsense" that was "silly and childish to the last degree," as a "jumble of dissonant notions" that was "as contrary to scripture as to common sense," and as a "deadly poison" that was "dangerous" to morality and faith. The first American edition of Abbé Barruel's *Memoirs Illustrating the History of Jacobinism*, published in 1799, had a fourteen-page section arguing that Swedenborg's system, while appearing "to reform Christianity on the reveries of Deism," was actually trying to overthrow the Bible in favor of atheism. In 1799, too, a pamphlet by an anonymous Baltimore resident aiming directly at Hargrove and the New Jerusalem Church derided Swedenborg's tales of "fantastical and ridiculous apparitions" and his "sophistical arguments" that perverted the scriptures. Hargrove and his flock had their work cut out for them.[28]

The institutional trajectory of the New Church in Baltimore, and in America, in many ways paralleled its development in London and Great Britain. Swedenborg had died in London in 1772, leaving behind voluminous writings in Latin that described the visions and revelations the former scientist and philosopher started experiencing in 1743, and the new doctrines that proceeded from those revelations. In Manchester and London, small groups formed in the early 1780s to translate and promote Swedenborg's works, including the London Theosophical Society. A box of books published by the British society quickly found its way to Philadelphia, and soon three people formed their own Swedenborgian club. The seer's admirers were publicly careful to stress the rationality of the new doctrines rather than their supernatural source—Swedenborg's visits to heaven and hell and his conversations with the angels, devils, and spirits he met in the spirit world. Advocates recognized that the seer's visions were often "stumbling blocks" for outsiders. They were initially obstacles for John Hargrove, too, who worried "that Swedenborg might have been indulging an enthusiastic imagination."[29]

British and American promoters of the new doctrines both developed innovative ways to spread Swedenborgianism. The London group, in an effort to reach "the higher classes of the community," handed out printed cards at Westminster Abbey during a Handel festival. Some years later in Washington, D.C., a Swedenborgian arranged to have a New Church sermon on the Trinity printed on the mailing envelope for the *National Intelligencer*, the most widely distributed newspaper in the United States. Even more unusual in the early nineteenth century was the work of the "very extraordinary missionary" John Chapman ("Johnny Appleseed"), who disseminated New Church doctrine with his apple seedlings on the American frontier.[30]

Early on in England, though, a difference of opinion arose over whether it was best to spread the new doctrines within the old churches or to create a separate church, something that Swedenborg himself had never done. A group in the London Theosophical Society broke off to form the New Jerusalem Church in the spring of 1787 and immediately took steps to institutionalize their beliefs and practices. They declared their general principles and published a list of rules and regulations. They defined church officers (president, treasurer, secretary), membership procedures (unanimous election), and a funding method (voluntary subscription). Fourteen men and two women met on July 31, 1787, determined by lot who should officiate as priest, celebrated the Lord's Supper, and baptized the first members into the New Jerusalem Church. A circular letter called all Swedenborgians to a General Conference at the end of 1788, and representatives came from all over England (and one each from Sweden, America, and Jamaica) to discuss and unanimously approve forty-two theological propositions. The church organized congregationally, with the General Conference recommending, not dictating, policies and procedures. That Conference standardized hymns, prayers, a catechism, a liturgy, and the requirements for baptism in 1790; approved a form of temple consecration, ministerial garments, and ordination procedures in 1791; and chose an episcopal rather than a presbyterian form of church government in 1793.[31]

The tiny Baltimore group that had clustered around Reverend Wilmer in 1792 immediately opened a correspondence with the London society. Forming a standing committee of "four worthy and respectable characters" and with twenty-two members, the Baltimore society secured a three-month lease on an old theater to use as a chapel and tried to raise money to build their own church. Christian Kramer, a member of the Baltimore group, wrote to Robert Hindmarsh, one of the founders of the church in London, to describe his experience. Although brought up as a Calvinist, Kramer wrote, he had always found the scriptures to be confusing and inconsistent. "I could not reconcile with the Word and sound reason," he told Hindmarsh, and he had determined that it would be better to believe nothing at all than the imaginary heaven preached in the old churches. "Thus I separated myself from all societies," and only the deep impression that Creation required a First Cause prevented him from becoming "a perfect Atheist." He might have been primed for deism, but Paine's *Age of Reason* had not yet been published; he happened upon Swedenborg's *True Christian Religion* and became a "receiver" of the new doctrines (as the New Church called converts). Maligned by his neighbors, Kramer was also denounced from the pulpit by local Methodists, until the Wesleyans realized that their campaign was only drawing more attention to Swedenborgian writings. The Methodists then changed their tactics, deciding to keep publicly quiet about the New Church but forbidding "their people to read the Writings of the Baron." Kramer, though, said that the members of the New Church in Baltimore were "determined to stand our ground," and they already felt a "communion" with the other societies in the world by reading the *New Jerusalem Magazine*, which had begun publication in London in 1790.[32]

Just as they were to Elihu Palmer and the organizing deists, financial resources were a challenge for the New Church societies in both the Old World and the New. The *New Jerusalem Magazine* quickly folded, as did two successors in the early 1790s. In 1794, London members were unable to launch a Bible and tract society that would have distributed free reading material to the poor "to guard them against the prevailing infidelity." In that year, too, the French Revolution began to "check the progress" of the New Church in Europe, and during the wars with France over the next two decades the church in Britain entered a fallow period: General Conferences were discontinued between 1794 and 1815 (with the exception of 1808), and the church failed to ordain more than a single new minister in any given year until 1818. Like the deists, who aimed their periodical at "the middling and industrious class of citizens," the Baltimore church at its inception had no poverty-stricken members, "but none of the rich, the great, or the noble" either. When Hargrove became the pastor in 1800, he served without a salary and tried to make ends meet by teaching a day school and a night school, and offering to tutor young ladies in their homes during the spare two hours he had each afternoon. In 1814, he reported to his British brethren that Church growth in Baltimore was still "limited and slow." In a city where clerical salaries ranged from $3,000 per year for the Presbyterian and Episcopal nabobs to the $100 annual stipend for Methodist preachers, Hargrove was still complaining that he was destitute "of any *external* support from glebes, patronage, or salary, or from membership of any of the *noble*, the *wise*, or the *wealthy* of this world." Since 1808, however, Hargrove had been able to work six days a week as the Baltimore city registrar to support his family.[33]

Church leaders in London and Baltimore took different approaches to shoring up the legal foundations of their institutions. In 1791, the General Conference in Great Britain drew up a petition to Parliament to be protected under the Toleration Acts, in which they pledged allegiance to the king, subscribed against popery, and asked to enjoy all the privileges of Protestant Dissenters without having to describe themselves as such. But the church never followed up on the petition, the law being "considered so obnoxious" by many of the members. Similarly, in 1793 the Conference discussed hiring lawyers to help constitute a lay board of trustees, to be established by a deed enrolled at the High Court of Chancery, which would allow the church to safely receive and manage bequests from donors as well as, when necessary, sue in court. As church founder Robert Hindmarsh later wrote, this would "form the *civil basis*, upon which the New Church stands in this country." For reasons that are not clear, however, the church waited twenty-eight years before it acted on this proposal.[34]

The Baltimore New Jerusalem Church, by contrast, moved quickly to secure legal standing. Maryland's 1776 constitution had effectively ended the establishment of the Church of England in the state, so there was no need to apply for "toleration." On January 8, 1803, during the session begun the previous November, the legislature passed "An act to incorporate certain persons in every christian church or congregation in this State," which allowed "all quiet and inoffensive christian societies" to "have perpetual succession in law, fact, and name" through a "body politic" of trustees that could own property and make use of the courts. Thirteen months later, seven trustees appeared before two Baltimore County justices of the peace and filed the papers for incorporating the New Jerusalem Church. The published *Incorporated Constitution* set out the church's rules for admission, voting, and church discipline, its procedures for changing church by-laws and constitutional articles, and the rights and responsibilities of the minister and the trustees. Incorporation was a sign of legitimacy. When a critic challenged Hargrove's bona fides as a real clergyman, a New Church member responded by referring the critic to the county clerk's office, where he would find a copy of the official document where Hargrove was "legally recognized" as the minister of the duly incorporated New Jerusalem Church.[35]

The Baltimore deist society that hosted Elihu Palmer and paid for his public lectures could not have reaped the institutional benefits of the 1802 incorporation law because, of course, it was not a "Christian society." Civil government, instead of facilitating organized deism, tended to obstruct its public expression. In New York City, for example, the Common Council refused to allow Palmer to give a July Fourth oration in City Hall's large courtroom because, as a marginal note in the council minutes explains, Palmer was "An Infidel."[36]

The political stances taken by the leaders of the New Jerusalem Church in both Britain and the United States also helped protect and aid their fledgling institutions. When the Fourth General Conference met in London in April 1792, Robert Hindmarsh recalled, "the whole country, from one end to the other, was agitated by contending political opinions, in consequence of the licentious and deistical principles, which followed in the train of the French Revolution, and which were then propagated with much zeal on this side of the water, particularly by the democratical Mr. THOMAS PAINE. By him it was urged that the people at large had the undoubted right to call to account all who were in authority over them, whether in the Church or in the State, and, if necessary, to cashier and depose them at pleasure, not excepting the Chief Magistrate of the realm, even the King himself." The Conference was eager "to guard against the introduction of sentiments of this description, and to convince the world that the Writings of Swedenborg gave no countenance whatever to them." As late as 1817, Hindmarsh refused to preach in a Unitarian chapel to avoid the taint of political radicalism still associated with the memory of Dr. Joseph Priestley from twenty years earlier. The New Church in America was also careful to distance itself from political radicalism. In 1812, a minister in central New York State founded the Halcyon or Free Church, which combined a modified Swedenborgianism with the notion that it was unlawful and sinful "for saints to acknowledge any other visible political Head" besides Christ. The New Church earnestly warned "every receiver" to avoid associating with such pernicious tenets.[37]

Just as the General Conference in London had been eager to demonstrate that New Jerusalem principles made people "the most loyal and peaceable subjects of His Majesty," the American New Church tried to signal its stalwart citizenship from the start. The "small in number, yet sincere" Baltimore church, "in the dawn of their institution," paid public tribute to President Washington in early 1793. The New Church's "Address" and the president's response were printed in the newspapers of several states along with a summary of New Church doctrines from one of its circulars. The exchange illustrates how Bible-based Christian patriotism and moderately deistic civil religious language could overlap in the climate of political and rhetorical compromise that could still prevail in the early 1790s. The members of the New Church declared their belief "that a new and glorious dispensation, or fresh manifestation of divine love, hath commenced in our land." Light was triumphing over darkness, and "all the corruptions in Church and State" were being corrected. The president's formal reply noted that Americans had reason to rejoice that in their country "the light of truth and reason has triumphed over the power of bigotry and superstition; and that every person here may worship God according to the dictates of his own heart. In this enlightened age, and in this land of equal liberty, it is our boast that a man's religious tenets will not forfeit the protection of the laws." Washington acknowledged "the manifest interposition of an over-ruling Providence" in America's success, if not the New Church's notion that "the Word" had been spiritually fulfilled, the "gospel state" inaugurated, and the love of the "One Lord" poured down from on high.[38]

When the Baltimore church's March 4, 1801, "Address" congratulating Thomas Jefferson upon his inauguration was published, it appeared in a much more contentious and polarized political climate and could not have been seen as anything but a partisan declaration. After the vicious election of 1800, when Federalist clergymen had attacked the Virginian as a deistic infidel and cast the contest as a referendum on Christianity, Hargrove, on behalf of his church, welcomed Jefferson's election "with singular pleasure and profound respect." Declaring that "the heavenly doctrines of the New Jerusalem Church" confirmed that God directed human history, the "Address" looked forward to the approaching day "when *reason* and *religion*, shall unite their sacred and all powerful influence" to promote peace on earth. It closed with a prayer that the "*Lord God of Hosts*" would "richly replenish" the president's will, understanding, affections, and perceptions as he began his term in office. Jefferson's "Answer" quoted the language in the New Church "Address" that promoted "genuine charity, liberality, and brotherly-kindness toward those who differ from us in opinion." The president did not use this opportunity, as he would in his famous reply to the Danbury, Connecticut, Baptists on January 1, 1802, to comment on the "wall of separation between Church & State." He merely closed by commending Hargrove "to the Being in whose hand we are."[39]

The deist editor of the *Temple of Reason* either did not know or did not put much stock in the New Church "Address" when he questioned Hargrove's political character seven months later. It was impossible to discern whether Hargrove was "Republican or Tory," Denis Driscoll wrote. By contrast, "Mr. Palmer's principles are well known, and tried as democratic, and consequently a friend to all republican institutions." Elihu Palmer "is no trimming priest, or temporizing patriot." Hargrove responded in the *Temple of Truth* that religion and politics, at least in the United States, were and should be "two distinct things." He said that he did not "ever bring politics into the pulpit," had no interest in partisanship, and knew from experience that "men may be good republicans, and good Christians at the same time."[40]

Six weeks later, Hargrove wrote to Baltimore's *Federal Gazette* to defend Jefferson against the charge of religious infidelity (and to make a Swedenborgian point about reading the scriptures allegorically to boot). An anonymous writer had called Jefferson an infidel because a geological passage in *Notes on the State of Virginia* denied that there could have been a worldwide flood, despite what Genesis said about Noah and the ark. Hargrove countered that belief in the Bible's divinity did not rest upon a literal reading of the Flood story. He implied that Jefferson, like any pious member of the New Church, could embrace scientific reasoning and still be a good Bible-believing Christian. To his British New Church brethren, however, Hargrove struck a different note: "It is said that Mr. Jefferson is a Deist: be it so (though it was never yet proved): I would hope for a better state of the Lord's New Church under an enlightened, calm, liberal Deist, than under a contracted bigot of any sect in Christendom." Although he had spent months as a Christian soldier on the ramparts of his *Temple of Truth*, pouring hot oil down upon the attacking deistic infidels, he here confided that the deists' skeptical critique of traditional Christianity was actually a good thing: "The Old Church must and will be vastated by some means, and, in my opinion, very considerably by Deistical men and arguments. I know we are the antipodes of the men; but there is a point where opposites unite."[41]

Just as the political conservatism of the London New Church probably was not unrelated to Robert Hindmarsh's appointment as Printer Extraordinary to the Prince of Wales, Hargrove's public defense of Jefferson might have had something to do with the invitation he received to preach in the Capitol to the president and some members of Congress on December 26, 1802. He had a return engagement on Christmas Day 1804. Hargrove, the pastor of this odd little church of a few dozen people, also managed to address a joint meeting of both houses of the Maryland General Assembly in 1806. But his most important political ties were local. He first got his job as city registrar in 1808. He had to be reelected to the position annually by both branches of the city council, a requirement that put a premium on his ability to stay in the good graces of Baltimore politicians. When an opponent warned him in 1818 that a shift in the political winds could cause him to lose his $1,700 annual salary, Hargrove hoisted the banner of nonpartisanship: "I have never written or caused to be written, or printed, either directly or indirectly, one line of a political nature these ten years—except my Thanksgiving Sermon for the providential deliverance of this city from the attack of the British." That War of 1812 sermon, too, he suggested, had been full-throated patriotism, not partisanship: it had coupled a rousing call for the defense of American freedom against their old British oppressors with a bitter lament for his son who had died at sea after being cruelly impressed into the British navy. He held his job as city registrar until he chose to retire in 1824. Social ties no doubt help explain his longevity: he was, for example, also grand chaplain of the Maryland Society of Freemasons and a manager of the interdenominational Bible Society of Baltimore, and "always kept an open house for ministers of every denomination visiting the city," many of whom "accepted his ever-ready hospitality."[42]

The Jeffersonian victory, one would have thought, ought to have helped the deists, too. But Jefferson and other moderate Jeffersonian nationalists distanced themselves from political and religious radicalism in what one study calls a "process of triangulation and demonization": "The respectable and electable Jeffersonian Democrats [a.k.a. Republicans] of 1800 defined themselves not only against aristocratic Federalists but also against the supposedly Jacobinical, atheistic, and foreign principles of those American Paineite democrats who had once been so influential." Denis Driscoll's *Temple of Reason* in Philadelphia was still linked to the Republican publishing network in the first half of Jefferson's first term, but because Federalists exaggerated Driscoll's influence to taint the whole party with infidelity, pragmatic Jeffersonians, especially after the Illuminati controversy, ran in the opposite direction. Driscoll, in any case, moved on to edit other Republican (but not deist) papers in April 1802, and the *Temple* ceased publication the following February. In New York, James Cheetham, editor of the Republican *American Citizen* and long connected to the deists through his brother and David Denniston, his former coeditor, fell out with the Clintonian faction and took revenge in a scurrilous biography of Paine in 1809. In a portrait as vicious as any ever painted by a Federalist, Cheetham lambasted Paine as a vain, drunken scribbler and the deists as a group of wretched, licentious bigots trying to hatch a "rebellion against heaven." When Jefferson received a copy of *Principles of Nature* from Palmer, he shelved it without replying. Although Palmer's religious beliefs were similar to Jefferson's, friendly Christians like Hargrove were far more useful to the president politically.[43]

In its first two decades, the New Jerusalem Church in America did not thrive, but it endured. The Baltimore church, with its unsalaried pastor, limped along. The progress Hargrove and others reported to London referred more to the continued circulation of Swedenborgian ideas, and of individuals and small groups of admirers popping up throughout the country, rather than new institutions. With the return of peace and prosperity after the War of 1812, however, the American church was able to build upon the foundations laid in the previous years: the correspondence network connecting Swedenborgians in the United States and across the Atlantic; the regular printing and distribution of New Church texts; the legal incorporation of the Baltimore church society, which built its own "temple"; and Hargrove's reputation as a trusted citizen and legitimate religious leader. In 1816, Philadelphians organized a church and founded the American Society for the Dissemination of the Doctrines of the New Jerusalem Church, which distributed circulars and urged receivers to form their own linked local societies. In the same year, a church formed in New York City, and in 1817, others opened in New Jersey, New York State, and Ohio, with New Church ministers soon active in Maryland and Virginia as well. The first annual National Convention met in Philadelphia that year and unanimously chose Hargrove as its president. As prospects brightened in the Old World, too, the New Church, it seemed, was entering a new era.[44]

As old founders like Hargrove in Baltimore and Hindmarsh in London aged, the New church looked backward as well as forward. A British member compared the institutional development of the New Jerusalem movement to the

The Baltimore Temple, New Jerusalem Church. From Sanfrid E. Odhner, *Toward a New Church University: ANC Centennial Album 1976* (Bryn Athyn, Pa., 1976). Hargrove and the Swedenborgians were able to institutionalize; Palmer and the deists were not. Photo courtesy of Archives/Special Collections, Bryn Athyn Historic Landmark District, Glencairn Museum.

evolution of modern government: just as individuals, "advancing from the state of solitary and uncivilized nature" unified to become "one body, forming a powerful State," so too scattered Swedenborgians had unified and were becoming "one great society" in an international church. A New Churchman from Philadelphia in 1817, however, had a somewhat different interpretation of the church's progress. William Schlatter wrote to London that "the rising empire of America" was "destined by Divine Providence for the grand centre or seat of the New Church." In the United States, he claimed, all religious denominations were perfectly equal and every person got to judge religious questions and make religious choices for him- or herself. One-half or even two-thirds of the inhabitants were unconnected to any religious society, and, Schlatter claimed, they hungered for "rational doctrines" rather than the incomprehensible "common jargon that is preached to them." An American New Church editor writing in 1818 agreed. In the United States, with its vast territory and rapidly multiplying population, where people devoured the publications churned out by the busy printing presses and publicly debated all the day's social and political concerns, "where religious prejudices are vanishing like the morning clouds, and neither political institutions nor religious establishments oppose the slightest impediment to the truth," and where even slavery—"the transportation of numerous hordes of degraded Africans"—seemed part of God's "great plan," he asked, "may we not see...the effectual and permanent establishment of the Church?" Receivers liked to think New Jerusalem doctrines were the "'age of reason' and revelation uniting." Hargrove's younger colleagues began to think that these beliefs were poised to become the American faith.[45]

By the second decade of the nineteenth century, few deists were under a similar illusion about the future of deism in the United States. While the Universalists, the Freemasons, and the New Church endured, external political pressures had contributed to the internal fragmentation of the deist movement. Wealthy deists, a piece in the *Temple of Reason* had charged, disliked the movement's link to democratic politics and, rather than support religious and political emancipation, were content to let their servants remain docile Christians. Republican deists, worried that organized deism remained too controversial and would hurt the party, wrote letters to the *Temple*, urging it to cease publication. The editors of that paper, by the end of its run, started castigating these cowardly "prudent Deists," who, they said, outnumbered avowed deists ten to one. The editors also began to suspect that many subscribers—many among even the avowed deists— were not real deists at all. Skeptical about Christianity, these people also remained skeptical that one could find God by observing the works of nature. They were, then, not deists but universal skeptics or atheists; the editors considered them "maggots" sheltering "under the wing of Deism" and wanted to purge them from the ranks. The *Temple*, though, ceased publication in 1803, and its successor, Palmer's *Prospect*, ended in 1805. Organized deism lost its leaders, too. David Denniston, the strongest link to the Clintonian political machine, had died in late 1803. Elihu Palmer had died suddenly of pleurisy in 1806, at the age of forty-one. Thomas Paine—vilified by Christians and never much of an organizer, but an inspiration to deists—died in 1809. John Fellows, who had been friends with all these men, later wrote that the New York Deistical Society had carried on for a few more years and then "was discontinued for want of zeal." In a last gasp, the *Theophilanthropist*, another deist periodical in New York City, launched by Fellows and other former society members, failed after nine issues in late 1811.[46]

The demise of organized deism, however, was due to more than a lack of zeal. Or, to put it another way, zeal for the cause was hard to maintain with so many obstacles blocking its success. Like Universalists, deists could be discriminated against in courts of law. Like the New Church, they were never able to attract either rich patrons or large numbers of small donations from the poor. Like the Unitarians, they privileged reason and intellect in an era of surging religious sentimentalism. Like many Freemasons, they bowed their head to Nature's God as Protestant revivalists were proclaiming Jehovah and Christ with more success than ever before. But unlike these enduring groups, Palmer's deists hitched their religious and political faith to a relentless skeptical critique of Christianity. This exposed them to partisan attacks that, in the era of the French Revolution, inflated political and theological disagreement into moral panic and spiritual crisis. Pilloried by the pious as moral degenerates, castigated by their political enemies as dangerous subversives, kept at arm's length even by their political friends and other religious progressives, and denied privileges afforded to Christian groups by the government, they were unable to cobble together an institutional infrastructure. Their ideas diffused, but their organizations did not stick.

Looking back at his old New York Deistical Society from the 1820s, John Fellows noted ruefully that some former members had eventually "returned to the slough of superstition." A decade later, his treatise on Freemasonry tried to show how ancient mythologies had been refashioned in Christianity, too, and still endured in the modern world, against all reason, as mumbo jumbo to soothe anxieties about the unpredictability of life and the fear of death. Christianity, though, unlike Masonry, was not merely a silly but harmless mechanism for maintaining moral order. The difference was power. In Masonry, Fellows wrote, there were a few "deluded members impelled by a fanatical zeal for their supposed secrets," and a few "political demagogues" who had tried to manipulate the order for their own benefit. In Christianity, there were many deluded fanatics, and they were powerful, and the superstitions of the faith were the common currency of political demagoguery. Protected by the law, coddled by the government, enforced by notions of respectability, Christianity in its many separate institutionalized forms was a de facto establishment, a hegemonic cultural power that made booksellers afraid to publish Paine's works on religion as late as the 1820s. If some former deists slunk back to the churches, Fellows wrote, others, including Fellows himself, even without formal institutions to sustain them, continued to adhere to a Paineite or Palmerian blend of religion and politics, of skepticism and faith.[47]

On the Invisibility of Black Skepticism

In 1819, Jarena Lee, a free black woman in Philadelphia, prayed at the bedside of a young black man dying of consumption. Lee had felt God's call to preach eight years earlier, but her pastor at the Bethel African Methodist Episcopal Church, the Rev. Richard Allen, had told her that the Methodist *Discipline* did not allow for female preaching. Lee's experience at the young man's bedside, however, would help renew her determination and launch her extraordinary career as a black female itinerant preacher. Before his illness the young man had attended Methodist meetings, but only to disturb and ridicule them. "He openly and uniformly declared that he neither believed in religion, nor wanted anything to do with it," Lee wrote in her autobiography. When the man became sick, his sister summoned Lee. As Lee prayed for him in his dying moments, she saw Christ on the cross appear above the man's head. "Brother, look up, the Savior is come, he will pardon you," she said. He did look up, and, as he held Lee's hand, he died, with an expression of ecstatic joy on his face. Lee was sure he was headed for heaven and felt herself filled with the Holy Ghost. Soon afterward, during a worship service at her church, she sprang to her feet "as by [an] altogether supernatural impulse" and began exhorting from the scriptural text the minister had chosen. Impressed, Reverend Allen decided that she had been called to be a preacher after all.[48]

Despite Allen's support, Lee would continue to struggle for recognition as a black female preacher even as her denomination, the African Methodist Episcopal Church, was completing its struggle to secure its autonomy. Allen and a large number of black Methodists had famously walked out of St. George's Methodist Church in 1792 after white trustees had tried to force all the black congregants to a segregated balcony. It was another insult in a long history in which white Christians, even those speaking about spiritual equality, denied their black brethren social equality. A quarter century after becoming a separate congregation, Allen and the black Methodists of Bethel Church secured their legal rights to their church property, formally separated from the Methodist Episcopal Church, and created a new denomination, the African Methodist Episcopal Church. The process was part of a broader movement in the early national period as free black

Portrait of Mrs. Jarena Lee. Frontispiece, *Religious Experience and Journal of Mrs. Jarena Lee* (Philadelphia, 1849). Lee described her encounter with a young black religious skeptic. Photo courtesy of the Library Company of Philadelphia.

Christians declared their independence and built new institutions that would have a profound impact upon African American life.[49]

Jarena Lee and the other members of the African Methodist Episcopal Church are examples of African Americans who took the doctrines and institutional forms of Christianity, so often used to oppress their people, and made them their own. But what of that young black man, before his apparent deathbed conversion? He had declared that "he neither believed in religion, nor wanted anything to do with it," yet he had attended black Methodist meetings as a leader "among young people of colour," Lee wrote. Such a determined and vocal opponent of evangelical Christianity, challenging the believers' claims to social and cultural authority with ridicule and disruption, would in a white community have been called a skeptical infidel. But the conceptual categories used to describe the religious character of blacks in Lee's day, and in much of the subsequent scholarship on African American religion, have rendered black skeptics like Lee's young man nearly invisible.[50]

The surviving commentary on religion in the lives of free and enslaved blacks in the United States between the Revolution and the Civil War—much of it authored by whites who observed from the outside and projected their biases onto what they saw—emphasizes ignorance, superstition, and emotionalism. Black leaders themselves described most of Philadelphia's nearly three thousand free blacks in 1792 as totally "ignorant" of religion. An eighteenth-century Episcopal sermon reprinted in 1815 and 1835 asserted that slaves were "poor ignorant creatures, who have little or no care taken for their principles; little or no notion of an all-seeing God, or a future judgment; nothing but sense and appetite to guide them; nothing but the present object to allure or terrify them." J. A. Jacobs, reporting from Kentucky in 1835, described the state's black population as "semi-heathen": a Christian black minority had a zealous faith, but Jacobs feared it was "a zeal without knowledge," and the unchurched black majority did not, he believed, even comprehend the Christian message. Henry Bibb, a former slave, wrote that many slaves were ignorant of Christianity because the slave South lacked the institutions (such as Sabbath schools) to sustain the faith. Another former slave, Henry "Box" Brown, remembered being "deplorably ignorant on religious subjects" when young, even thinking that his master was God and his master's son was Jesus Christ. A third former slave, James W. C. Pennington, reached the age of twenty-one without having seen an entire bible or having heard of Christ.[51]

If Bibles were few and reliable preaching rare, "superstition" was rife among the slaves, according to Bibb: "Many of them believe in what they call conjuration, tricking, and witchcraft, and some of them pretend to understand the art." The white writer Charles A. Raymond, after spending years in the slave South, concluded that "a leading trait in the American negro, reared under the influences of Southern slavery, is, that he is *intensely religious*. All the superstitious tendencies of his native constitution seem compressed into this channel." Raymond found that superstition and African fetishism blended with Christianity to define the worldviews of most of the blacks he met in Mississippi, Louisiana, Alabama, Georgia, South Carolina, and Virginia. Ignorant unchurched semiheathens, superstitious conjurors, or enthusiastic Afro-Christians: the options seem to preclude black skepticism—the intellectual engagement with, rational critique of, and irreligious response to Christian truth claims.[52]

Scholars of early African American life have long argued for the central importance of religion—of Christianity and the perpetuation of (modified) African religious beliefs and practices. Religion, writes the author of the premier study of Philadelphia's black community, was the center of black educational, associational, and political activities, and the organizing principle of all life. The black church in particular "was the primary instrument for forming black consciousness." The black church, writes another scholar, performed statelike functions: it "helped organize the resources of the community through [its] institutional mechanisms and administration," and it gave African Americans both "vocabularies of agency" and a lens through which to see the world. Although there were some black congregations in the South, slavery prevented the church proper from being the same sort of unifying force there. Still, most historians have seen Afro-Christianity as "the cultural center" of the slave community, stressing the "invisible institution" of slave religious practice and belief outside the formal church and away from the slaveholders' gaze.[53]

A few revisionists have lately suggested that historians have exaggerated the power and pervasiveness of Christianity among antebellum slaves. Rather than consider the possibility of black skepticism, however, these scholars have argued for the importance of non-Christian religious beliefs and practices. They have found evidence among some slaves, or in some populations, of Islam, and have turned more attention to syncretic religions like voodoo (vodun). One critique of the Christianity-centered interpretation of slave life argues that "most slaves simply did not become Christians." But, the argument continues, Africans are deeply religious people maintaining that "to live is to believe in and interact with things spiritual or supernatural." Therefore, it is not surprising to find evidence suggesting that "various forms of African religious practice, particularly the spiritually informed practice of conjure, may have served to organize the slaves' world view in many ways far more than Christianity did." Scholarly attention to the Northern free black population, too, has turned to evidence of conjure and other folk religious practices. Only a few scholars have explored the possibility of nonreligious perspectives (such as secular humanism or freethinking) among blacks before the Civil War.[54]

On second glance, however, the nineteenth-century sources do offer evidence of black skepticism, a position that existed without institutional structures to nurture and sustain it or cultural categories making it easily recognizable to most observers. Charles Colcock Jones, a Presbyterian clergyman, slaveholder, and missionary to slaves in Liberty County, Georgia, wrote that a preacher to slaves faced not only African ignorance and superstition but other prejudicial attitudes, too, including religious skepticism. "He who carries the gospel to them, encounters depravity entrenched in ignorance, both real and pretended. He discovers deism, skepticism, universalism. He meets all the various perversions of the gospel." Jones contended that the missionary to slaves would need to answer "all the strong objections against the truth of God; objections which he may have considered peculiar only to cultivated minds, the ripe scholarship, and profound intelligence of *critics and philosophers!*"[55]

Enslaved and free blacks could deplore proslavery Christianity without rejecting what they thought of as "true" Christianity. The testimonies of former slaves are filled with condemnations of Christian slaveholder hypocrisy and the abominations of proslavery Christianity, most famously in Frederick Douglass's writings. Condemnation of the slave master's religion is not the same as a skeptical critique of theistic religion as such. But Daniel Payne, a former slave and Lutheran convert who became a bishop in the AME Church, thought that many slaves were driven to doubt not just the white man's version of Christianity but religion in general. Slaves "scoff at religion itself," Payne wrote; they "mock their masters, and distrust both the goodness and justice of God. Yes, I have known them to question even his existence. I speak not of what others have told me but what *I have both seen and heard from the slaves themselves.*" Payne himself, after the legislature closed his Charleston, South Carolina, school for black children in 1834, "began to question the existence of the Almighty and to say, if indeed there is a God, does he deal justly?"[56]

Payne was not alone with such thoughts. John Jea, born in Calabar and brought to New York as a slave in the late eighteenth century, doubted there was a God for black people. Before his conversion at the age of fifteen, he hated professing Christians as lying oppressors. A slave in Kentucky, according to an account of his later conversion in 1826, made fun of religious people, "not believing that there was any such thing as religion." Former slave Henry Bibb believed that proslavery preaching had "driven thousands into infidelity." Frederick Douglass agreed. John Dixon Long, a white Philadelphia Methodist who had spent time in the South, thought that many slaves were "secret infidels" who doubted the promises of the Bible.[57]

"The wonder is," William W. Patton argued in *Slavery and Infidelity*, "that the slaves are not all *Atheists*." Patton, a white Congregationalist from Connecticut who began writing about the link between slavery and skeptical infidelity in the 1840s, noted that philosophers speculating about evil in the world were not infrequently driven to religious doubt and disbelief. Was it surprising, then, that a person "who has fallen into humanity's lowest condition, and is condemned to drink its bitterest cup," should come to the same conclusion? Patton pointed to an example of such slave skepticism in Harriet Beecher Stowe's *Uncle Tom's Cabin*. But Patton assured his readers that black skeptics could be found in real life and not just in abolitionist fiction. He presented a series of anecdotes, such as the account of the enslaved woman on the island of Mauritius who believed that God, if there was one, was absent from slave territory. Patton's point was that proslavery doctrine drove slaves from Christianity, and the horrors of slavery itself caused slaves to doubt God and reject religion.[58]

Among free blacks in the North, Patton argued, white Christian oppression drove many African Americans not to form their own churches but to reject religion altogether. The Rev. Theodore S. Wright, pastor of the First Colored Presbyterian Church in New York City, reported to Patton that "I have often heard my brethren say that they would have nothing to do with such a religion. They are driven away and go to infidelity." Other free black clergymen told Patton the same thing. By the early 1840s, the ten thousand African Americans in Philadelphia had sixteen black congregations to choose from. After white mobs tore down a black church, sacked the First African Presbyterian Church, and destroyed more than thirty black homes in 1834 and torched the Second African Presbyterian Church in 1842, a black minister in that city said that many former black Christians "now attend no church, and have become skeptical in their opinions."[59]

African Americans, free and enslaved, struggled to build their own institutions—the black church preeminent among them—to protect themselves from and uplift themselves within a racist society. The African Methodist Episcopal Church, founded in Philadelphia by Richard Allen and a group of committed black Christians like Jarena Lee, exemplifies black expression and agency in a culture that tried to deny both. Lee found her voice within that church, which celebrated Afro-Christianity as the foundation of African American culture though it only begrudgingly tolerated Lee's vocation as a female preacher. Within these stories of faith, one nested within another—Lee's, the AME Church's, Afro-Christianity's, African American culture's—skepticism can barely be glimpsed, but its presence should not be ignored.

The deathbed conversion of the young consumptive man on the eve of Lee's emergence as a preacher marked a triumph of faith in the story but also an erasure of skepticism—a perspective difficult to recover from the few lines Lee devoted to it:

> I cannot but relate in this place, before I proceed further with the above subject, the singular conversion of a very wicked young man. He was a coloured man, who had generally attended our meetings, but not for any good purpose; but rather to disturb and ridicule our denomination. He openly and uniformly declared that he neither believed in religion, nor wanted anything to do with it. He was of a Gallio disposition, and took the lead among young people of colour. But after a while he fell sick, and lay about three months in a state of ill health; his disease was consumption. Toward the close of his days, his sister who was a member of the society, came and desired me to go and see her brother, as she had no hopes of his recovery; perhaps the Lord might break into his mind.[60]

Lee described the young man as "wicked," but of what his wickedness consisted is unclear. Evangelicals reflexively linked skeptical opinions to immoral behaviors, but whether or not the young man was guilty of licentiousness or intemperance or some other sins cannot, of course, be known. Perhaps he had been like the Kentucky slave who, after conversion, described his former life as "wicked" because, "not even believing that there was any such thing as religion," he spent what little spare time he had "dancing, carousing, fighting, &c." Perhaps Lee's young man did not carouse, dance, or enjoy the secular African American music (the precursor to the blues) that sometimes poked fun at piety, and maybe his only "wickedness" consisted in his declared lack of faith and his habit of ridiculing and disturbing believers. The former slave John Jea described his younger skeptical self as "wicked" not for any immoral behavior but because "my own heart suggested to me that there was no God."[61]

On two other occasions in her autobiography Lee described encountering what she considered to be irreligious attitudes, one linked to blasphemy and the other to cruelty. On a trip to Hagerstown, Maryland, Lee met a seventy-three-year-old deist "who would reproach Religion" until she told him "that Solomon spoke of a man 70 years of age, and called him a fool,—and exhorted him to get religion; for God's name is worthy to be praised by all intelligent beings." At a meeting at her uncle's house in Cape May, New Jersey, she met another old deist, a slaveholder who came "from curiosity to hear the woman preacher." The old deist "said he did not believe that coloured people had souls" and was known to be a cruel master, "thinking nothing of knocking down a slave with a fence stake, or whatever came to hand." After hearing her preach, he changed his mind, became very friendly to her, and, although she was not sure if he ever "became a converted man or not," "became greatly altered in his ways for the better." The connection between infidel attitudes and sinful behavior was clear. Lee might have placed the young black skeptic in the same category as the old white deists.[62]

Lee wrote that the young man "was of a Gallio disposition," a reference to Acts 18:12–17. Gallio, the brother of the philosopher Seneca, was the Roman proconsul of Achaia when Paul was establishing a church in Corinth. Jewish leaders, trying to stop Paul, brought him before the tribunal, complaining that he was attempting to persuade people to worship God contrary to the law. But Gallio stopped the proceedings, telling them that "if it were a matter of wrong or wicked lewdness, O ye Jews, reason would that I should bear with you: But if it be a question of words and names, and of your law, look ye to it; for I will be no judge of such matters." When the Greeks subsequently beat up the chief ruler of the synagogue, "Gallio cared for none of those things."

In Jarena Lee's era, writers sometimes mentioned Gallio to suggest religious indifference. Some, thinking of Gallio shrugging as the Greeks beat the Jewish leader right in front of the tribunal, invoked Gallio to point out irresponsible neglect in the exercise of public moral authority, whatever Gallio's private character may have been. One writer in the early nineteenth century connected public indifference to "the spirit of deism and modern latitudinarianism" and argued that it deserved contempt. The author of an 1832 article entitled "I Don't Care" asserted that "every one will condemn Gallio, and say he *ought* to have cared for these things." Such indifference, the writer charged, "looks badly beside true piety." Other commentators lifted Gallio's indifference out of its political context and applied it to "thoughtless youths" who failed to ponder the state of their souls and to the "unbeliever" who failed to pay attention to God's lessons until death drew near. David Simpson's *Plea for Religion* in 1807 linked this Gallio-like attitude explicitly to "disciples of Thomas Paine." Jarena Lee was probably signaling the young skeptic's personal indifference to warnings about hell but might have thought, too, that someone intent on disrupting religious meetings was also indifferent to the necessary role of religion in maintaining moral order.[63]

Other writers, however, praised Gallio for preventing the Jews from using the state to do their dirty work in persecuting Paul and the Christians. As an 1829 election sermon put it, Gallio was unlike Pontius Pilate, who washed his hands but crucified Christ. "*Gallio* the wise," as Richard Price had earlier called him in *Observations on the Importance of the American Revolution*, separated church and state. If it were a matter of public wrongdoing or a vicious crime, Gallio would have had a reason to listen and act. But over theological disputes about "words and names" or a group's particular ecclesiastical laws, he would not judge. Gallio—like President James Madison, some commentators said—refused to act not because he was irresponsible or stupidly indifferent but out of philosophical principle. It was the correct principle, these writers, including many clergymen, argued.[64]

In any case, Lee's young skeptic hardly seems indifferent. If he did not care, why would he regularly attend black Methodist meetings, criticize their doctrines through ridicule, and try to disrupt their religious practice? Why did he openly declare his religious unbelief and position himself as a leader among young people of color? It is not unreasonable to suggest that his skepticism was a reasoned, principled opposition to the evangelical Christianity that he saw becoming a powerful force in the black community. Whether or not in his dying moments he saw Christ on the cross floating in the air over his head, whether or not at the end he changed his mind about skepticism and faith or merely died appreciating Lee's human kindness and the touch of her hand, his earlier doubts, and the doubts of other free and enslaved African Americans, need not be completely lost in the shadow of the rising black church.

Dresden Printing Press. The engine of enlightenment. Photo courtesy of the Vermont Historical Society.

PART TWO

ENLIGHTENMENTS, 1790–1840

What did it mean, the CHRISTIAN and the SCEPTIC asked, to be "enlightened?" What was the relationship of enlightenment to religious faith?

CHRISTIAN: "It is conceded, I perceive, that we are, in *some* respects, *considerably* in advance of the nations of antiquity in point of wisdom and improvement.... Now, Sir, please to explain the cause of the *continuance* of those nations that have not the Bible, in a state of heathen barbarism down to this day. *They* have *not* made improvements. *They* are *not* in advance of ancient heathen nations in these respects. Look at the most enlightened of them.... So much for the light of nature, and the progress of moral improvement without revelation."

SCEPTIC: "[I leave readers to judge] whether the spirit of progressive improvement, based on accumulating experience, be, or be not, adequate explanation of the world's progress since days of old.

"All over the world, the seeds which traduced philosophers have sowed, are rapidly springing up. All over the world, the Church is in danger. In every civilized country, men begin to ask whether the belief in the infallibility of any Book be not mischievous and immoral. In either hemisphere the reign of reason and light is approaching; the era when all actions shall be judged by their permanent utility, and all men esteemed according to their moral worth."[1]

Enlightenment linked knowledge to freedom. "Dare to know," Immanuel Kant famously wrote: enlightenment is man's emergence from the darkness of dogma and prejudice as he grasps the freedom to think for himself. It involves critical reflection upon and skeptical critique of received traditions. As literacy rates rose and knowledge circulated through print, enlightenment could become a social and political force as common people dared to think and act for themselves and rise up against the old tyrants who had long oppressed them. Or so the story goes.[2]

Americans in the late eighteenth and early nineteenth centuries did not think of themselves as living in "the Enlightenment," but they did talk about enlightened values and their enlightened age. Enlightenment was less an epoch than a process, a development linked both to the perceived progress of Western civilization and to the age of democratic revolutions. Stephen Cullen Carpenter, writing a two-volume assessment of Jeffersonianism in 1809, described an "enlightened" cultural politics. Visionary theorists, Jefferson chief among them, Carpenter wrote, believed "that the mind of every man, enlightened at once and fortified by learning and philosophy, would become at last the impregnable fortress of his own rights and freedom." Enlightenment was the engine of liberty. What was true for "every man" was also true for a community or a nation, because the diffusion of knowledge was said to lead to the betterment of society as a whole. Modern history had taught as much, the champions of enlightenment believed, and they celebrated the social practices that produced and circulated emancipatory knowledge through bodies politic. "According to those eulogists, the augmented circulation of letters, and the unrestrained liberty of the press, had already nearly constituted so strong and durable a security for the happiness and above all, for the freedom of the human race." These mechanisms of open discussion and debate "would soon erect so lasting and insuperable a barrier between nations and tyranny, and cast such a clear and intense light upon the frauds and artifices by which, in times of darkness and ignorance, men had been cheated and enslaved," that "despotism [would] shrink from the perpetration of its designs."[3]

But in the shadow of the French guillotine and the rise of Napoleon, and in the wake of the republican demagoguery that had put a man like Jefferson in power, Carpenter could only say all this with a sneer. The "boasted enlightenment of the world," it turned out, seemed merely a tool for ambitious men pursuing their own nefarious interests. "That very boasted liberty of the press...has been found the most convenient and operative instrument in the hands of despots," and the "diffusion of knowledge" had merely increased "the capacities of the people for embracing error." Jefferson's false philosophy stood in place of a Christian faith, grounded in the Bible, which, Carpenter contended, was the true foundation of virtuous politics and the pursuit of happiness: Jefferson "denied that faith which the people who were to elect him deemed necessary to future happiness, and to the right use of those powers which God has intrusted for useful purposes to man—he was destitute of faith in that fundamental law upon which alone virtue and integrity can stand unshaken. He was the avowed enemy of those sacred principles which give force and harmony to morals—which inspire men with zeal in the cause of human happiness, and furnish at once the motives and means to individual and national felicity." Most officeholders in Jefferson's reign were "deists, atheists, and infidels," Carpenter claimed. There were not enough of such people to form electoral majorities, but, to his dismay, many Christians had been duped into voting for Jefferson, the "infidel enemy of Christ."[4]

Christian Jeffersonians—and many Christian Federalists, too, for that matter—would not have so starkly separated enlightenment and Christianity into Carpenter's opposing categories. That is, they, too, could value natural knowledge, the crucial role of a free press, and the contributions of a busy republic of letters to the progress of learning and liberty. More frequently speakers and writers called Americans "an enlightened and Christian" people. This became a stock phrase in occasional sermons, political speeches, and other commentaries through at least the 1840s—a quarter century or so after most histories of "the Enlightenment" have marked the end of the period. American Protestants in particular, especially as they defined themselves as American and against Catholics, continued to anoint themselves as the vanguard of social and political progress and continued to claim all the "enlightened" values and practices as their own: free inquiry, open debate, the broad dissemination of print, the triumph over superstition.[5]

Just as Carpenter's stark opposition of Christianity versus enlightenment is an overly simplistic description of the way things were, the happy harmonies of the "enlightened and Christian" rhetoric papered over tensions and contradictions that repeatedly surfaced. While the efforts to promote enlightenment and Protestant Christianity overlapped considerably in the early American republic, the difference was that for the faithful, worldly learning was always to be supplemented and corrected by revelation; the progress of science and the struggle for freedom were thought to be directed by providential grace; and public scholarly and political debate were always to be informed and bounded by the truths of the Bible.[6]

Jefferson—deist, admirer of Christian morality, and wily politician—emphasized what he and his Christian Republican supporters had in common and tried to keep his controversial religious views to himself. His friend Thomas Cooper (1759–1839), however, the focus of chapter 5, brought the difference between enlightened and biblically grounded politics, as Carpenter had described it, to heightened public attention. An

English radical who emigrated to the United States in the early 1790s at the high point of American enlightened radicalism, he became a Jeffersonian agitator in Pennsylvania who was prosecuted by Federalists under the Sedition Act in 1801 and was persecuted by Pennsylvania democrats a decade later. Cooper was also a religious skeptic who believed that religion, just like all other topics, needed to be openly investigated, discussed, and debated in what he called the "public arena." His view of an enlightened society, centered on relentless skeptical inquiry and vigorous public debate, presents an alternate model to a culture that placed biblical teaching at its foundation.[7]

The Rev. Ezra Stiles Ely, discussed in chapters 6 and 7, was a leading Presbyterian clergyman, author, and editor in Philadelphia, who by 1830 had come to epitomize everything skeptical critics like Cooper loathed and feared about the public power of Christianity. Although Cooper helped sound the alarm at Ely's controversial call for "a Christian party in politics," the two men had more in common than either would have acknowledged. Like Cooper, Ely published prolifically in a variety of genres, welcomed debate with his opponents, edited periodicals, and became a college professor. Like Cooper, Ely also celebrated education and the broad dissemination of print as foundations for republican politics and social progress. But at the center of all Ely's activities were the divine truths revealed in the scriptures. Hardly afraid of a challenge like Cooper's, he believed that Christianity had repeatedly faced skeptical, deist, and atheist critics and had triumphed every time, demonstrating its superior reasonableness. Thomas Cooper warned that the danger of this metaphysical imperative became clear with Ely's talk of a Christian political party and hopes for the eventual evangelical domination of American society.[8]

Ely promoted a Christian cultural politics that laid claim to enlightened appeals to reasonableness, the dissemination of knowledge, and the emancipation of the human intellect. Ely's colleague Dr. David Nelson (chapters 6 and 7) was a Presbyterian clergyman who earlier in his life had been a Kentucky physician and a religious skeptic. Nelson's popular *Cause and Cure of Infidelity* (1837) inverted the skeptic's critique of religion and denounced infidels as the ones being deluded by ignorance and emotion. Ely and Nelson would have their biggest chance to put their enlightened faith into practice when they founded an experimental college and a new city on the banks of the Mississippi River in the 1830s.

In the first decades of the nineteenth century, the descendants of the Puritans also worked to reconcile faith in revealed religion with the dictates of enlightened reason. The "rational" or "liberal" wing of New England Congregationalism, concentrated in eastern Massachusetts, had drifted away from Calvinism to preach an enlightened Christianity. These New Englanders prayed to a benevolent God, preached an intellectualized faith, had confidence in man's natural faculties, and celebrated the progress of civilization. The theological liberals took control of Harvard in 1805–6, prompting much outcry and gnashing of teeth by Calvinist Congregationalists, conservatives who rightly predicted that their opponents would soon openly leave the Trinity behind altogether, demoting Christ from the Godhead and professing Unitarianism. In the midst of this controversy, a prizewinning divinity student emerged from the Harvard library and in the name of reason and free inquiry published *The Grounds of Christianity Examined* in 1813. George Bethune English, discussed in chapter 8, pushed far beyond Unitarianism and challenged the reliability of the New Testament. The liberals had their own heretic, whom they promptly flogged in the press and quickly excommunicated. When English later "turned Turk" by joining the Ottoman army, his bizarre transformation into a religious and cultural alien became an object lesson in the dangers of heterodoxy.

A generation later in New England, the Unitarians were the Old Guard on the Christian left, and the young Turks challenging them were the Transcendentalists. The Unitarians still relied on Lockean philosophy and eighteenth-century British empiricism. The Transcendentalists had imbibed German idealism; they brushed past Enlightenment "reason" as merely the flat-footed ploddings of the human faculty of understanding—the calculation of the countinghouse, the dry logic of books, the creaking gears of the machine—for the Romantics' intuitive "Reason," throbbing with the vital juices of spiritual and organic life. The "Pope of Unitarianism," Andrews Norton, who had helped swat down George Bethune English a quarter century earlier, denounced the Transcendentalists (Ralph Waldo Emerson, George Ripley, and others) as infidels, and the Transcendentalists responded in kind. The debate initially centered on whether or not the foundation of faith could be based on a reasoned reading of scriptures that established the miracles described there as historical facts.

Into this debate waded a Boston lawyer, journalist, and politician with a very different perspective. Richard Hildreth, also a focus of chapter 8, translated Jeremy Bentham and would publish his own books of utilitarian philosophy; he challenged the authority of claims to "revelation" (whether made by Unitarians or Transcendentalists, evangelicals or Catholics) and wanted to give morals a naturalistic and pragmatic foundation. As the Transcendentalists tried to transcend the Enlightenment's faith in reason, and the Unitarians sought the reason in faith, Hildreth imagined a future in which Christianity and other superstitions would no longer hinder social, political, and moral progress.

5

Skeptical Enlightenment

An American Education in Jeffersonian Pennsylvania

Thomas Cooper was never far from controversy. As a young English radical in 1792, he spent four months in Revolutionary Paris at the Jacobin Club and publicly quarreled with Robespierre. Upon his return to England, he was denounced by Edmund Burke in the House of Commons. Fleeing a reactionary political crackdown and bankruptcy, Cooper emigrated to America, became an outspoken Jeffersonian lawyer in Pennsylvania, and was fined and imprisoned under the Sedition Act for criticizing the Adams administration. Accustomed to being attacked from the right, he was then assaulted from the left, as the Pennsylvania Republican Party drove Judge Cooper from his district court bench in 1811.

Cooper's professional reputation rested on his vast erudition. Trained in medicine as well as the law, he published books and essays on political philosophy, political economy, banking, bankruptcy, Roman law, jurisprudence, theology, biblical criticism, mental illness, geology, mineralogy, chemistry, medicine, textile manufacturing, gas lighting, cooking, and other topics. He rarely claimed to be an original thinker, and when he did so he was wrong. But he read voraciously and had an extraordinary memory. "Cooper is acknowledged by every enlightened man who knows him," Thomas Jefferson wrote in 1819, "to be the greatest man in America in the powers of mind & in acquired information, & that, without a single exception." Throughout his career, Cooper argued that for all topics, including religion and politics, "experience has settled the rule, WHERE THERE IS DOUBT, LET THERE BE DISCUSSION." And the place for that discussion was "the TRIBUNAL OF THE PUBLIC," through the medium of a free press, where the mustering of facts and the collision of arguments would produce truth. A religious skeptic, he not only denied biblical authority but resented—especially after becoming president of South Carolina College in 1820—the ways that clergymen, spinning their exegetical webs from a musty and discredited old text, warped intellectual practice, political action, and social life. Such open debate was essential, in his view, to an enlightened society.[1]

He should not be dismissed as just an extremist in a landscape of opinion where most thoughtful people fancied themselves as both enlightened *and* Christian. His blunt language stripped away popular evasions and obfuscations to reveal the logic of a principle to which so many paid lip service. A serious commitment to enlightened inquiry would not exempt Christianity from skeptical critique, Cooper argued, and it was not an argument easily dismissed by a people who applauded their own reasonableness and claimed to value free inquiry.

A learned man, Cooper throughout his long career tirelessly advocated for public education, defended republican liberty, and crusaded for open discussion on all topics. Reflecting a central dynamic of the political thought of late eighteenth- and early nineteenth-century Europe and America, he wrestled with the tension between the impetus toward a more egalitarian society and the acknowledgment that "natural" human differences and the hierarchies they inevitably created would always exist. Yet Cooper the young English antislavery radical became Cooper the proslavery South Carolina conservative—and it was in Pennsylvania, not in the slave South, that he learned that quintessentially

Portrait of Thomas Cooper, ca. 1810. Cooper argued that all ideas, including religious ones, needed to be debated in the public arena. University Archives, University of Pennsylvania.

American form of political doublespeak, championing civil liberty and republican progress while supporting patriarchy and white supremacy. He shows how an enlightened cultural politics, like the Christian version of his opponents, could endorse both freedom and slavery, and lead to both blindness and insight.[2]

Free Discussion and the Public Arena

Throughout his career Cooper championed free and unlimited discussion. Born in Westminster in 1759, after studying at Oxford and the Inner Temple he became a partner in a firm of calico printers and threw himself into the work of the Manchester Literary and Philosophical Society. His *Tracts Ethical, Theological, and Political* (1789), a volume of papers delivered to the society, defended the publication of unpopular opinions. Conventional opinions needed to be held up to scrutiny, to stand or fall upon the basis of good evidence and sound reasoning. New ideas, too, needed to be tried in the fire of public debate so the dross of error could be burned away. In his *Reply to Mr. Burke's Invective* (1792), Cooper defended the public communication between political societies like his own Manchester Constitutional Society (which he cofounded) and the French Jacobin Club as grounded in the right of the people to political information and in the salutary benefits of exposing the operations of government "to public Observation." As he planned his move to America, Cooper imagined the United States as an asylum where one "might be permitted to enjoy a perfect freedom of *speech* as well as of sentiment, on the two most important subjects of human enquiry," religion and politics. At the close of the eighteenth century, living in Northumberland, Pennsylvania, with the philosopher Joseph Priestley and his family, Cooper published an essay, "On the Propriety and Expediency of Unlimited Enquiry," with Priestley's daughter-in-law Elizabeth. The essay reviewed and countered the standard arguments against allowing free discussion—including criticism of government—among what Burke had called the swinish multitude. Unrestrained popular political debate was still a touchy subject even in the United States, Cooper had quickly learned, especially in a region that had recently experienced the Whiskey Rebellion.[3]

Cooper insisted that free inquiry and debate were epistemological and social necessities. Sound thinking arose not from solitary attention to intuition or to some mystical inner witness but from the exchange—even the violent collision—of ideas in society. Man was a sociable creature, and the urge to communicate stimulated an individual's mental labors, Cooper believed. He was not, however, just championing freedom of expression. Relentless public examination and criticism of those freely expressed ideas were necessary for conjectures to be verified as useful public knowledge and for opinions to be bent toward truth. "Prove all things; hold fast that which is good"—on this maxim, at least, he could agree with the Apostle Paul (1 Thess. 5:21). There was no way to arrive at truth, Cooper wrote, except by unlimited discussion. Still, proving the true and the good was one thing, but holding them fast—setting "truth on a firm basis"—was another. Falsehood was often institutionalized, error was perpetuated by social habit, and prejudices rattled along in the ruts of tradition. Modernity's trend lines since the invention of the printing press were encouraging, but progress was slow.[4]

The political philosophy supporting Cooper's commitment to what he called "the republican principle of publicity" was clear from the start of his public career. In one of his Manchester essays from the 1780s, which he republished in Philadelphia in 1798 and again in South Carolina in 1826, he set out his political principles. He argued that political power could only derive from the consent of the people. The "people," he was careful to point out, is merely an aggregate of individuals who form a community to promote mutual happiness. They surrender only those rights necessary to pursue this aim, and they live in the community on equal terms. Governors remain accountable to the governed, and the people reserve the right to rise against any who usurp legitimate authority. All of these truths, Cooper believed, if not self-evident were logically demonstrable. But it was a logic that rulers throughout history had tried to deny. Instead, they worked to keep people ignorant of their civil rights, and they silenced dissenters with the point of a sword or with the more civilized muzzle of a sedition trial. Yet the "structure of political oppression begins now to totter," Cooper wrote in the late eighteenth century and repeated in the third decade of the nineteenth. And it tottered because "the extension of knowledge has undermined its foundations"—a spread of political knowledge, he added in 1826, that was "the necessary consequence of untrammeled discussion."[5]

Cooper supported a citizen's right not just to speak truth to power but to speak so that truth could be discovered and "the people" could be empowered. This was more than the philosophical conviction of a theorist in his armchair. Targeting members of the Constitutional Society that Cooper and Priestley had formed, and angered at the society's plan to celebrate Bastille Day in 1791, mobs in Birmingham rioted on July 14–17, destroying two Unitarian meetinghouses and fourteen other buildings, including Priestley's home and laboratory. In England in 1792, as the repression of Francophile radicalism intensified, Cooper was warned by the attorney general about the seditious implications of his *Reply* to Edmund Burke. The following year a Manchester man was arrested for distributing an antiwar address Cooper had written. Rioters attacked the print shop that produced the Manchester *Herald*, the reformist newspaper he wrote for and helped edit, and broke the windows of his friend Thomas Walker's house, where the Constitutional Society met—actions that were endorsed by conservatives in Parliament. Walker was tried for sedition and high treason in 1794, and Cooper helped secure his acquittal. Publishing a paean to the U.S. Constitution later that year as he prepared to emigrate, Cooper thought such a trial would not be possible in America. He soon learned otherwise.[6]

By the fall of 1799, the Federalist press had targeted Cooper as one of the most dangerous political writers serving the Republican Party after political essays originally published in the *Northumberland Gazette* were reprinted and widely distributed in pamphlet form. A correspondent to the Reading, Pennsylvania, *Weekly Advertiser* on October 26, 1799, charged that Cooper's "cunning and insidious" criticism of President John Adams derived from a base desire to seek revenge after the president had denied Cooper's application for a government post. Cooper replied on November 2 that at the beginning of the Adams administration he had indeed sought a position. He had frankly admitted in the application letter that he and Adams had different political philosophies. Still, he explained in his newspaper defense, at the time Adams "had just entered into office; he was hardly in the infancy of political mistake: even those who doubted his capacity, thought well of his intentions." Adams had not yet, Cooper went on, demonstrated that he would only favor members of his own party. The president had not yet signed the Alien and Sedition Acts, saddled the country with the expense of a permanent navy and threatened the creation of a standing army, reduced the country's credit, nearly provoked an unnecessary war, and interfered in a court case in order to allow an American citizen to be wrongfully court-martialed and executed by the British. Cooper would not have applied for a job back in August 1797, he wrote in late 1799, if had had known that Adams would go on to do such things. For these criticisms of Adams he was indicted for seditious libel on April 9, 1800, and tried in the U.S. Circuit Court in Philadelphia on April 11, 15, and 19.[7]

Cooper, acting as his own counsel, argued that he was not spreading falsehoods about John Adams but merely expressing his political opinion about the administration by listing well-known facts about its policies. The prosecution—and the presiding judge, Supreme Court Justice Samuel Chase, in his instructions to the jury—denied both that Cooper had proved his "facts" and that he had a right to disseminate such opinions. The court discounted Cooper's reliance on press accounts describing administration policies (such as Adams's support for a navy, or the government borrowing money at 8 percent interest), and the government did not respond to the defendant's request for copies of official documents. Cooper appealed to the jury that the evidence of the truth behind his remarks should not have to rest on such documents: Adams's actions and positions were "certain facts of public politics sufficiently notorious to obviate the necessity of legal proof, and whose notoriety, is itself a matter of fact, which may in all cases be safely left to a Jury to judge of." And how were jurors to determine political facts? Not by the all-but-impossible standard imposed by legal technicalities, Cooper contended, but by the same standards for evidence and the same kind of reasoning men applied when outside the jury box, acting as citizens and deciding for whom they should vote. But Judge Chase insisted that the defendant himself "must prove every charge he has made to be true; he must prove it to the marrow." That requirement, Cooper believed, would stifle the free exchange of ideas: "If such strictness of testimony is required, there is an end at once of all political conversation in promiscuous society."[8]

His opponents in the courtroom were less concerned with safeguarding the freedom of the press than with striking at what they argued was the abuse of that freedom. The dangers of misinformation in a volatile society were clear, prosecuting attorney William Rawle told the jury, with a nod toward the Whiskey and Fries Rebellions. (As U.S. district attorney for Pennsylvania, Rawle had prosecuted the Whiskey rebels in 1794; Justice Chase had presided over Pennsylvania tax rebel John Fries's treason trial earlier in 1800.) "Error leads to discontent, discontent to a fancied idea of oppression, and that to insurrection," Rawle argued. Criticism of an elected leader was, by definition, an error. "It was much to be lamented," Rawle said, "that every person who had a tolerable facility at writing should think he had a right to attack and overset those authorities and officers whom the people of this country had thought fit to appoint." Chase's instructions to the jury reinforced this point: no man should try to undermine the confidence the people have in their elected representatives; if a law was bad, legislators would change it, and if they did not, voters could remove them from office at the next election. Citizens should cast their votes and then be quiet. Cooper believed, on the contrary, that "if the Supreme magistrate adopts measures inconsistent with the public interest, it is... the duty of every good citizen to expose him to the public." There should be no penalties, he said, imposed on those who "boldly express the truth," or even on those "who may honestly and innocently err in their political sentiments." How could the people "exercise on rational grounds their elective franchise, if perfect freedom of discussion of public characters be not allowed"? he asked. The jury found Cooper guilty. On May 1, he was given a $400 fine and sentenced to six months in prison.[9]

From jail Cooper immediately published a sixty-four-page account of the trial "not merely to vindicate my own character, but to open the eyes of the public to the tendency of measures countenanced by Mr. Adams, and to the strange doctrines advanced by his adherents." He had to be careful that this exercise in republican publicity did not expose him to additional prosecution. The facts of the trial would have to make the case. "Reader, when you have perused this trial, shut the book, and reflect. *I dare not* state the conclusions with which it is pregnant, but which must force themselves with melancholy conviction on your mind: ask yourself, however, is this a fair specimen of the freedom you expected to derive, from the adoption of the Federal Constitution?"[10]

Still, he could not resist commenting upon Judge Chase's management of the trial and address to the jury, which highlighted how the court's interpretation of

Cooper's newspaper comments had been nothing more than a political inquisition and the whole trial a "disgrace." Cooper was held to a nearly impossible standard to prove political "facts," while Rawle and Chase made claims that were allowed to stand as self-evident truths (such as the assertion that Adams had honorably filled his high station and was a "benefit to his country"). Cooper had directly asked the jury to acknowledge the political nature of the trial. We all know, he said, that the country is divided into two great parties: "the one wishes to increase, the other to diminish the powers of the Executive; the one thinks that the people, (the Democracy of the country) has too much, the other, too little influence on the measures of government." The Federalists supported a standing army and a permanent navy, and their opponents thought a militia sufficient for defense and a navy dangerous and expensive. The first party "thinks the liberties of our country endangered by the licentiousness, the other, by the restrictions on the Press." These divisions were the obvious feature of contemporary politics, and "there cannot but be a bias among the partisans of the one side, against the principles and doctrines inculcated by the other." How could this reality not affect his trial, which was as much about the president as it was about Cooper—the very president who had nominated the judges, the marshal who summoned the jury, and the jury that judged the evidence? Judge Chase, according to Cooper, did not even try to conceal his bias. Cooper complained that the judge distorted the rules of evidence, insulted Cooper's legal abilities, and even intimated that it was a crime merely to doubt that Adams had the capacity to be a good president.[11]

Because there was only so much he could say in Chase's court, Cooper appended to his account of the trial a letter to the judge, which also served as an "appeal to the public on the points wheron we differ." In court Chase had the authority of his bench and an audience of friendly Federalists to smile and nod as he did his work, but the public would not be so admiring of his judicial behavior, Cooper wrote. At the trial, Cooper had to be silently deferential, but now he offered the judge "an opportunity, if you please, of descending into the arena of the public," to meet him without the shield of governmental authority. "We are now before the public—let them judge whether you or I more deserve the professional sarcasms you thought fit to aim at me."[12]

Cooper's public arena was not, however, some borderless, unregulated imagined community of free speech conjured by the magic of publication: it had its rules, and its geography. Cooper's crimes were aggravated, Rawle had argued at the sedition trial, by the particular relation he had to the local or regional public he addressed in the newspaper, and by that public's access—or lack of access—to political information. "Mischiefs of this kind were to be dreaded in proportion as the country around is less informed," Rawle said, stating the general rule, "and a man of sense and education has it more in his power to extend the mischief which he is inclined to propagate." Cooper had made a reputation for himself, at least in some parts of Pennsylvania, as a lawyer and "a man of education and literature," and he had used that status to gain "influence" in this "remote part of the country." Cooper denied that western Pennsylvanians were politically misinformed because of their remoteness. But in later years he made a similar argument about how a different set of standards for public writing—in this case, about plagiarism—had to be adapted to the geography of early American publication. In an anonymously published attack on Calvinism, he admitted that he was not writing anything that had not already been written by others. "But so imperfect and so slow is the propagation of knowledge in this country, by any other means than newspapers, that no book or pamphlet, however meritorious on a serious subject, has any chance of sale beyond the immediate neighborhood of the place of its publication. It is allowable, therefore, for a writer in Georgia to repeat what has already been said by a writer in Vermont or Maine, and *vice versa*; for there is about as much literary intercourse between either of those places and Japan, as with each other." In his South Carolina religious controversies, too, he thought he was safe as long as he published his heterodoxies outside of the state. Even if his neighbors knew that he published scandalous ideas elsewhere, he could not be accused of broadcasting such opinions to the public at home.[13]

Throughout his career Cooper argued that financial interests corrupted the process of public discussion and debate, and he repeatedly excoriated the clergy on this point. A man paid to publicize a certain set of opinions should immediately be held in suspicion by the public tribunal, he insisted. At the sentencing phase of the sedition trial, Judge Chase asked Cooper if he was "indemnified against pecuniary loss" by his political party. Cooper did not pretend that he lacked "party opinions," but he reacted indignantly to the suggestion that he was paid for them: he declared that he had never and would never "prostitute" his pen. The clerical scribblers who attacked him in subsequent decades could not make the same claim, Cooper contended. Those who peddled divinity as a trade diminished their authority in public debates over religious questions. Their status as paid proselytizers "render[ed] them biased and incompetent witnesses according to the rules of every court of justice in every civilized community," he argued. A jury would not believe a witness in court if it discovered he had been paid to deliver his opinions. The rules of the courtroom, at least in this matter, Cooper believed, ought to be applied to the arena of public discussion. And if the pronouncements of the paid clergy should, at the very least, be heard with suspicion, the obverse was also true, as Cooper argued in his *Treatise on the Law of Libel and the Liberty of the Press*. Who were raising skeptical questions about Christianity's truth claims? "Men who risk their reputation, their comfort, their consideration in society, their persons, their properties, the well-being of themselves, the prospects of their families, in opposition to all the power, all the wealth, all the rank and consideration prevalent in the community. And for what? Can any other reasonable motive be assigned, except that they feel desirous at all hazards, and without the possibility of recompense, to speak what appears to them the truth, on the most important of all human investigations?"[14]

Clergymen, too, were in Cooper's mind the prime carriers of one of the worst contagions infecting public discussion: "metaphysical logomachia," the habit of treating abstract terms as if they were actual things in the world and then arguing endlessly about them, while mistaking this process for the possession or pursuit of real knowledge. Dr. Cooper diagnosed this prevalent propensity as a serious ailment in the body politic. It was a deplorable mistake, he wrote in his *Lectures on Political Economy*, that "the grammatical being called a NATION, has been clothed in attributes that have no real existence except in the imagination of those who metamorphose a word into a thing; and convert a mere grammatical contrivance, into an existing and intelligent being," a being "distinct from the individuals who compose it; and possessing properties belonging to no individual who is a member of it." The same malady enfeebled contemporary Anglo-American moral philosophy. Cooper had no patience with the Scottish Common Sense school, so popular in America, a "tribe of metaphysical logomachists, who never dream that the phenomena of the body, are of any use in explaining the phenomena of the mind." Catering to clerical dogmas and popular prejudices, the Scots and their epigone clothed words like "thought," "reason," "memory," "will," and "understanding" "with a separate existence, and personified them. But this poetry of metaphysics—this prosopopeia of orthodoxy, is not reasoning." As for the clergy themselves, this verbal prestidigitation was their stock-in-trade. Protestant divines, even as they regularly denounced Catholic manipulations of mystery and paid lip service to biblical transparency, were masters of mystification. The complex metaphysical fictions they spun from the words of scripture required the expensive maintenance of the learned professional guild to which they belonged. That they often refused to meet their skeptical critics on the open ground of public debate was just one more indication that they had something to hide.[15]

Honest seekers of knowledge and truth should embrace open public debate, Cooper insisted. "The times," he continued to write in the early 1830s, "call for full and unlimited freedom of examination in every department of knowledge without exception; nor ought any opinion, of any kind or description, pass current as truth, unless it be founded on such facts and such arguments as will stand the test of minute and accurate investigation before the tribunal of the public." Religious creeds, too, must undergo "the searching ordeal of free discussion."[16]

Diffusing Enlightenment

Party politics would continue to teach Cooper bitter lessons through the early nineteenth century. But in 1811, he had an opportunity to engage a different sort of public. Becoming professor of chemistry at Carlisle (later Dickinson) College, he also took over as the editor of a scientific periodical in 1813, the *Emporium of the Arts and Sciences*. The *Emporium* appeared at a time when American printers and publishers were trying to extend their social reach and deepen their cultural significance. In the first quarter of the nineteenth century, five or six hundred periodicals other than newspapers were launched, the number of American magazines rising from a dozen in 1800 to nearly a hundred by 1825, though titles were often short-lived and circulation usually limited to a few thousand copies for any issue. Publishing entrepreneurs often justified their work with bold claims to public service: they were diffusing knowledge to the nation. Publications that sought to enlighten as well as (or rather than) entertain, though, not only had diverse textual forms and marketing strategies but also asserted different and sometimes incompatible relations between authors or editors and their readers. Thomas Dobson's *Encyclopedia* (1789–1803) republished the *Britannica* with American additions, offering an alphabetical organization of all knowledge. Periodical miscellanies, like Charles Brockden Brown's *American Register; or, General Repository of History, Politics, and Science* (1807–10), treated a wide variety of topics less systematically but still assumed its readers would and should range across all fields of inquiry. Yet more specialized periodicals also appeared, such as the *Philadelphia Medical Museum* (1804–11), the *American Law Journal* (1808–17), and the *American Minerological Journal* (1810–14). The *Emporium* shared the encyclopedia's idealism about the general diffusion of knowledge in an enlightened age, the miscellany's topicality and sense of knowledge production as more of an open-ended work in progress inviting discussion and debate, and the specialized learned journal's demand for expertise. These were rather different notions of how knowledge was or ought to be produced and circulated in a free country, complicating not just a particular publishing project like the *Emporium* but the entire notion of American enlightenment.[17]

The *Emporium* began in the spring of 1812, initially edited by Dr. John Redman Coxe, professor of chemistry at the University of Pennsylvania. The original prospectus, which Cooper would endorse a year later when he took over from Coxe, laid out the journal's grand purpose. The connection between the diffusion of knowledge and human happiness was obvious, the prospectus began. The new journal would be "a source of *practical information in the various branches of scientific research,* and is intended to convey the rich harvest of *facts* contained in foreign valuable papers on *Chemistry, Mineralogy, Natural Philosophy, Arts, Sciences,* and *Agriculture*." It would allow Americans to benefit from and build upon European discoveries, technological developments, and manufacturing innovations. Europe was continually producing such "treasures," but they remained hidden from most Americans, concealed between the covers of a few copies of imported books. "To be extensively useful, they must be widely disseminated.... Our own presses must diffuse their contents, or they will continue

Thomas Cooper, ed., *Emporium of Arts and Sciences*, n.s., vol. 3, title page. As editor of the *Emporium*, Cooper modeled critical thinking and tried to provoke discussion and debate.

to perish upon the shelves of individuals, or in public libraries!" This practical knowledge would enable American artisans and manufacturers to find new ways to save labor and produce wealth, serving both their private interests and the public good. The *Emporium* would be a "*text book* to our citizens." It would be nonpartisan, since Science "is of no party," and would be useful "to every class of society," since Science "will equally distribute her favours to all." The prospectus even hinted at a favorite fantasy of some enlightened philosophers, the perfectibility of man: "Standing, as it were upon the shoulders of our transatlantic rivals, we may hope to catch new views of the prospect before us, which will enable us to shorten the road to ultimate perfection."[18]

Published monthly and then bimonthly after June 1813, producing semiannual volumes of over five hundred letterpress pages each, including engravings (mostly of machinery), and costing an expensive seven dollars per year, the *Emporium* attracted a limited but influential patronage that marked it as a success after its first year. The subscriber list included Thomas Jefferson, James Madison, and James Monroe. Over 250 copies went to readers in Philadelphia, nearly 230 to New York, and 400 to Boston. New Jersey received 42 copies, Connecticut 33, and Virginia and Maryland 25 each. The *Emporium*'s practical knowledge was diffused less readily to other parts of the country, however. Only 4 subscribers lived in Delaware; Ohio, North Carolina, and Kentucky had 2 each; and single copies made their way to lone subscribers in Tennessee, Georgia, South Carolina, and the Michigan Territory.[19]

When Cooper started a new series in 1813, he hoped to continue and extend the publication's useful work but did not merely follow in Coxe's editorial footsteps. Cooper reconceived the role of the journal's editor, adding his own commentary and stepping forward to provide a single unifying intelligence to help give coherence to the various articles. He also fused the journal's original purpose—disseminating practical knowledge—to a vigorously articulated philosophy of political economy. And he ended up criticizing the nation that the *Emporium*'s diffusion of knowledge was intended to enlighten.[20]

Coxe thought that the "principal intention of an editor in such a work [was] to select" the best available articles on topics such as making wine, manufacturing steel wire, and dying cotton. He apologized to readers who were disappointed that the journal did not publish more original essays by American authors, but quality trumped patriotism, even during a war against Britain. Cooper made the same point, but he had no intention of limiting his role to mere selection. He would lift good articles from wherever he could find them; "still, the work shall bear evident marks of my own labour upon it." He curtly dismissed the desire of some readers for more variety and the expectation that he select a "medley" of twenty different topics for each issue. Such might be the "common method" among journal editors, and it would produce the sort of periodical that would be popular with "the generality of readers," but "it would neither be useful to the public, nor creditable to myself," Cooper insisted. "To make a medley of this kind, I have nothing to do but mark with my pencil the essays I choose to pillage from British compilations, and give the books to the printer. I will not do this." Cooper instead would connect a series of essays to treat a topic in depth, arranging them to best effect, abridging where necessary, and composing as coherent a discussion as possible from many disparate parts. He wanted "connected information" producing "a collection worth preserving." In his second volume, for example, he presented a series on the development of the steam engine: thirty-one essays, patents, mathematical papers, accounts of experiments, reports of accidents, comparisons of competing innovations, and engraved illustrations, the whole amounting to a kind of documentary history of steam power. Cooper followed this with his own short essay summarizing the main points.[21]

In and around the essays, documents, and statistical tables the *Emporium* republished on its various topics were Cooper's interpolations, notations, and extended commentaries, expressing the perspective of a critic who had both practical experience and scholarly erudition. He applauded progress, added facts, corrected errors, offered conjectures, voiced opinions, admitted (on occasion) ignorance, and tried to provoke discussion and debate. He modeled critical thinking. Following Cooper as a guide, the reader could learn to use an epistemological scale, weighing the reliability of various claims. At the beginning of his synthetic essay on geology, to take one example, he notified readers that he would be blending in his own views with his summaries from authorities and would clearly distinguish "the best acknowledged facts we possess" from "fair deductions from known phenomena" and "probable opinions." He alerted the reader when he shifted from knowledge to informed speculation: "I tread upon new ground; but I use the aids which wise men have furnished; I have none of my own." Concluding with confidence in the general system he had sketched, he nonetheless added a reminder about the "doubts and uncertainties" hanging over many of the particulars and about the provisional character of some geological claims.[22]

Public discussion and debate were essential to the progress of knowledge as long as talk was grounded in natural facts and verifiable experiences: the social dialectic of informed conjecture and refutation exposed error and added to the fund of fact. Editorial intervention in the *Emporium* could turn an essayist's monologue into a dialogue. In Dr. E. Bollman's "Vindication of Foreign Commerce," Cooper's footnotes offered a running critique of nearly all of Bollman's main points. He then told readers: "I shall be glad to receive condensed and well-considered replies to my own opinions." Similarly, after offering a few remarks on patent law in the United States, he noted that they were only his "present opinions, which I throw out for public consideration." In an essay on statistics, he expressed confidence in his calculations but added that "when I am further instructed, I shall be glad to correct my suppositions." Through more than fifteen hundred pages, he tried to keep the *Emporium* anchored to empirical demonstration and practical utility. He kept his promise to supplement extracts from books and periodicals with letters "from persons actually engaged in the manufactures" and his "own actual observation of manufacturing processes." He reported examining a clever improvement to a water wheel in Germantown, for example; he did not claim it was new, but it was new to him. From his own experience, he estimated the amount of land needed to maintain a horse, offering the discussion as an exercise in political arithmetic applied to common circumstances of everyday life rather than to great matters of national policy.[23]

Yet those great matters of national policy were always a visible horizon to the Cooper *Emporium*'s close-to-the-ground discussions of topics such as bleaching paper, manuring fields, or smelting copper. When he took over the journal in 1813, Cooper announced that he would explicitly link Coxe's enlightenment project to a philosophy of American political economy. Political economy was, he explained, the search for "the principles of public action... that lead most directly and permanently, to national wealth and national power—and are most consistent with national security and national prosperity." Diffusing practical knowledge about various manufacturing processes would only have real public value if that public could come to understand the importance of developing American manufacturing—of diverting some capital away from foreign commerce and toward the production of American-made goods.[24]

Especially during the War of 1812—"manifestly a mercantile war" on both sides—the profound national importance of the questions of political economy could not have been clearer, Cooper argued. But in the United States, those questions were little discussed and less understood. No "public sentiment" had yet been formed about the best relationship of agriculture, commerce, and manufacturing in the country, although "the popular opinions—prevalent among those who have not read or thought much on the subject, are greatly adverse here, to what I think a correct system." Shaping public sentiment and popular opinion were crucial to the fate of the nation, Cooper believed, especially since the issues were not a matter for government action but for the arena of public debate. A devotee of Adam Smith's "luminous" *Wealth of Nations* and a firm believer that the motto "*Laissez nous faire*" should be the standard response to government interference with economic activity, Cooper argued that decisions about where to invest capital and employ labor should be left up to individuals. These individuals worked together in a society, though, and could make informed choices that better served the public interest as well as their own. Public discussion of political economy could enlighten the citizenry if it sprang from careful study of treatises like Smith's and was grounded in as much reliable economic data as possible.[25]

In particular, Cooper contended, the question of the comparative value of foreign commerce had "not been sufficiently agitated." He was keen to do some agitating, since the few who had written on the question had argued from faulty premises and reached disastrously wrong conclusions, yet they seemed to be framing the "general reasoning on the topic" and forming "the fashionable creed." Against the powerful proponents of Atlantic commerce, who had dragged the United States into war, required expensive navies to protect them even in peacetime, and lobbied the government for protectionist policies that unfairly taxed the rest of the nation, Cooper argued for the development of domestic manufacturing and home markets. Agriculture and domestic manufacturing would support each other: farmers needed tools, and craftsmen needed to eat and wear clothes. The home trade, too, was a far more productive place to invest surplus capital, he wrote, because the capital would continue to circulate among the producers and consumers of agricultural products and finished goods, stimulating tillers of the soil and craftsmen in their shops alike to greater industry. Domestic commerce was a far safer investment than sending capital great distances to uncertain foreign jurisdictions; it was also far less expensive and dangerous to the country as a whole because, unlike international trade, it did not embroil the nation in warfare. Finally, the domestic trade was simply more profitable than many people thought, a point Cooper tried to back up with pages of countinghouse statistics.[26]

Far from being confined to a tally sheet of profits and losses, however, Cooper's discussion also mustered arguments on the broader field of cultural politics. International commerce encouraged the wrong sorts of character traits among merchants. The large windfall profits that occasionally enriched the lucky few encouraged the rest of the traders to engage in speculation and excessive risk taking. Maneuvering for profit around multiple foreign legal regimes encouraged them to cut ethical corners. These merchants then wielded far more political power than their numbers would merit because of their importance to banking and finance. Naturally pursuing their own interests, they bent government to serve those interests at the expense of everyone else, even as they waved the flag of patriotism. But Atlantic merchants were actually less patriotic than businessmen and workers devoted to the domestic market, he argued. Local merchants, farmers, and mechanics were bound "by all the ties of habit and interest, to their own country; while foreign trade tends to denationalize the affections." An investor with property dispersed in foreign countries, shifting his capital around the Atlantic world according to market conditions, would inevitably have his sentiments drawn away from his own country.[27]

The dominance of foreign trade in the American economy, though, did not just corrode the character of the merchants themselves, or of the politicians they influenced. The oppressive debts that American consumers owed British merchants for manufactured goods thrust the whole nation back into an enervating dependency: "We are almost again become colonists.... We are not an independent people." Most of the population, too, devoted to the production of raw materials, was scattered over too vast a territory. The nation was weakened; "the communication of society, and of course of knowledge, is greatly retarded; many of our citizens are tempted to live in a half savage state." A commitment to manufacturing could change all that in time. Domestic manufacturing would draw people closer together—physically, socially, and economically—into a more occupationally diverse but more fully integrated society. Hand in hand with agriculture, it would encourage Americans to "improve your roads, clear your rivers, cut your canals, build your bridges, establish schools and colleges, facilitate intercourse, and diffuse all kinds of knowledge." Domestic manufacturing could radically improve American culture: "But as a mean of national defence, and national independence—as a mean of propagating among our citizens the most useful and practical kinds of knowledge—as a mean of giving that energetic, frugal, calculating and forseeing character to every branch of our national industry, that does not exist but among a manufacturing people—as a mean of multiplying our social enjoyments by condensing our population—and as a mean of fixing the consumers and producers in the immediate neighborhood of each other—I would encourage the commencement at least of home manufacture."[28]

In painting a picture of the nation the United States could become if Americans shifted more of their energies toward domestic manufacturing and commerce, therefore, Cooper also criticized society as it existed in the early nineteenth century. John Redman Coxe in the original prospectus for the *Emporium*, while acknowledging the challenges facing a people starved for practical information and scattered over a vast territory, nonetheless declared that "our citizens are better informed and have fewer prejudices than any people on the globe." Like so many political orators, he celebrated axiomatic connections between freedom and the progress of knowledge: "Liberty, the surest pledge of free inquiry, is one prime source of the advantages we enjoy. Unfettered in our press—unshackled in our conscience, man here possesses means of happiness as perfect as is consistent with his nature. From the same cause, no doubt, in part arises that ingenuity which is so conspicuous in the American character. Few nations can boast of more improvements in labour-saving machinery, than have been discovered in the progress of the mechanical arts among us." In Cooper's hands, such encomiums fizzled like a soggy July Fourth firecracker: "I fear it is not true, that we are the most enlightened people upon the face of the earth; unless the facility of political declamation be the sole criterion of decision, and the universal test of talent." Neither did he think that ingenuity and industriousness were yet such marked features of the American character. The country did not yet have the forms of social organization that put a premium on such character traits. A "general spirit of energy and exertion...no where exists in so high degree as in a manufacturing country," and the United States was still far from being one. Great Britain, by contrast, had already progressed so far that a new profession was emerging, one that was well paid and socially respected: the "*civil-engineer.*" Civil engineering required a deep knowledge of math and chemistry, a facility in applying mathematical principles and calculations to mechanics and machinery, and a habit of closely studying machines in actual use. Cooper's *Emporium* almost seems directed at an ideal readership of American civil engineers who, for the most part, did not yet exist. Or perhaps he hoped that this publication project would help call them into being.[29]

Cooper had taken on the *Emporium* thinking that he could bridge the gap between the scholar and the mechanic. The armchair literati, the sort of men who usually became editors of learned periodicals, too often assumed that pages of theory would influence practice. Manufacturers, on the other hand, tended to be "secret-mongers, who live by their processes and who do not choose to expose them to the world." The *Emporium*'s public demonstrations of theories being put into practice and practices analyzed to generate new useful methods would help rationalize and improve manufacturing processes. Knowledgeable and experienced readers, moreover, would no doubt find useful hints and suggestions in the periodical's mass of information that neither the original authors nor Cooper had recognized. The community of readers would also enrich the sum of knowledge by a kind of cross-fertilization among areas of expertise that might seem, on their face, quite different: watchmakers had helped perfect cotton machines, Cooper noted, and men who understood barometers had helped improve the steam engine.[30]

But his actual readers complained. Some disliked the way he was mixing politics into the journal's practical science. Cooper thought it ridiculous that any subscriber was "incapable of distinguishing between the petty discussions of party politics, and the great questions of political economy!" He denied that he was being political: "Whatever my politics may be, *I have none in this work.*" He suspected that the complaint about "politics" was really a screen for those devoted to foreign trade who had no interest in developing home manufacturing in the first place. Cooper refused to back down from his arguments on political economy, even if they alienated readers and forced him to lose a segment of his paying subscribers. By his third volume, his publishers were receiving complaints for which Cooper had even less patience: that his articles were too long. "I will not condescend to skim over my subjects with the appearance of knowledge, but with useless or shallow information," he responded testily. If the public would not support the *Emporium*'s effort to diffuse important knowledge, "I will give it up: but I will not swerve from my own ideas of propriety in conducting it." Cooper's third volume in 1814 was his last.[31]

The *Emporium* under Cooper collapsed under the weight of the effort to enlighten a public without making the concessions to popular tastes that were necessary to sustain that effort. Like the engines its pages described, the *Emporium* itself was initially intended as a kind of machine, a technology that improved

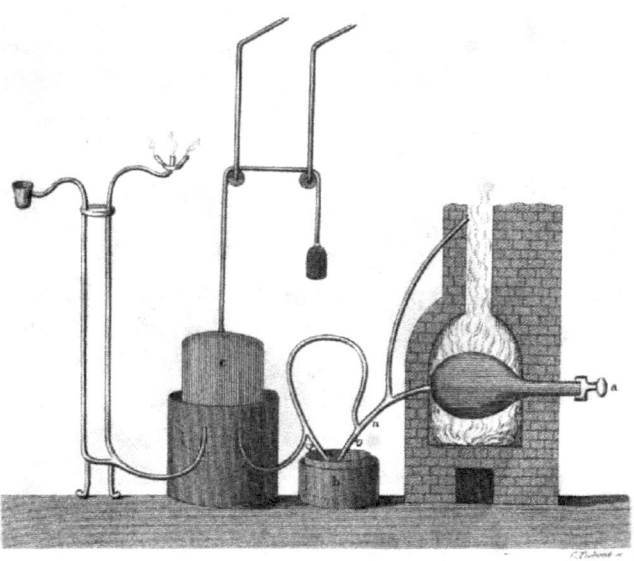

Coal Gas Apparatus.

Coal Gas Apparatus. From Thomas Cooper, ed., *Emporium of Arts and Sciences*, n.s., vol. 1, 472. Like the engines its pages described, the *Emporium* itself was initially intended as a kind of machine, a technology that improved upon the production and distribution of practical knowledge.

upon the production and distribution of practical knowledge. But like other machines, it could only be socially useful if adopted by the public and put to work. The periodical had to compete for attention against other commodities in the marketplace, creating and sustaining a stable body of consumers. It could not just disseminate knowledge to readers eager to be enlightened; it needed to cultivate readers and teach them to think like civil engineers. In the end it became not like a machine at all but an extension of an effort at cultural and political persuasion. If not so dramatically embittering as Cooper's experiences with the democratic degradations of republican politics, the cultural politics of diffusing enlightenment had also proved disappointing.

Soul, Self, and Citizen

By 1811, after seventeen years in Pennsylvania, a state that had been dominated by different factions of Jeffersonian Democratic Republicans since the election of 1799, Cooper admitted that democracy "was not quite so perfect in practice as it is beautiful in theory, and that the speculations of my youth do not receive the full sanction of my mature age." But if experience moderated some of his youthful idealism it did not, he thought, alter his basic beliefs. He continued to argue that doubt and debate were the solvents of despotism. He demonstrated the steadfastness of his political philosophy and commitment to republican principles by republishing in America (with what he characterized as merely "slight additions") his 1787 "Propositions respecting the Foundation of Civil Government" in 1798 and 1826. He showed that he stood by the moral philosophy that he had professed in the 1780s by incorporating his key argument about moral obligation into his 1812 edition of *The Institutes of Justinian*. In 1836, the self-proclaimed South Carolina conservative wrote to his friend and former student James Henry Hammond that if he were to move back to England he would still be considered a radical there, and for the same reasons that had marked him as one in the 1780s. Rather than seeing significant change in himself over time, Cooper believed that the apparent alteration was more due to the dissimilar social and political contexts, which called forth different facets of the same fundamental convictions.[32]

Others have had different interpretations. On the question of race and slavery in particular, Cooper was accused of conveniently changing his attitude with his latitude when he moved from Pennsylvania to South Carolina. Other critics claimed that Cooper illustrated the moral bankruptcy of Enlightenment skepticism. Maximilian LaBorde, a student under Cooper and then a professor in South Carolina College's later, more explicitly Christian regime, remembered Cooper's staunch practicality. LaBorde did not mean this as a compliment. Cooper, LaBorde wrote, "looked upon man very much as an animal, and believed that the frame-work of society was designed to provide for his physical wants and necessities.... Of man in his higher nature, as a being of immortal powers, with aspirations reaching into a never-ending futurity, he had no just conception.... [Cooper's philosophy] was partial, incomplete, contracted. It was not co-extensive with the nature of the soul, and was therefore wanting in humanity.... It was cold and forbidding, and could not touch the heart." Cooper's Christian critics in South Carolina, though, for all their veneration of soul, heart, and humanity, were also champions of slavery and white supremacy. Cooper the enlightened republican became a leading political voice in the slave South not because he adapted to Southern racism, or because of the inherent shallowness of the Enlightenment, but because he allowed the desire to preserve political and social power for men like himself to distort his interpretation of the kind of evidence he claimed to value above all others: the empirical facts on the ground.[33]

Cooper's late eighteenth-century progressive politics and hopes for social reform were rooted in his understanding of people as creatures of circumstance, as products of webs of associated causes and effects. Like his friend Joseph Priestley, Cooper was a materialist, but this was no barrier to religious belief, no slippery slope toward atheism. In the 1780s Cooper still professed to be a "rational Christian"—a Unitarian. He indicated belief in God, the Bible, and Jesus Christ as Savior (though not as God himself). He rejected the "standard account" of human nature still held by orthodox Protestants who spoke of a dualism of material and immaterial substances: an active and immortal mind or soul was housed while on earth in a passive and corruptible body. David Hartley in 1739, in a work later abridged and republished by Priestley, "proved" (or so Cooper believed) that mind could arise from matter—it was a function of matter, not a separate substance. Arguing from an associational psychology and philosophy, Cooper recognized a "self" not as a thing but as a perception formed by living in the material world and interacting with other people: "The idea of *self* always arises at first from circumstances referred to the body." The self not only arises "at first" but is reproduced in different circumstances, and as the circumstances and sensations change, as the ideas and feelings associated with this self change, so too does the self. It is a fluid, shifting, contingent effect of consciousness, just as consciousness itself is a dynamic construct arising from physiological processes. Conscience, too, was a social construct. People usually made the kinds of choices that philosophers called moral "without stopping to ask why." When they did pause to reflect and tried to act according to ethical ideas or a moral sense of things, they simply drew from what been impressed upon them by parents, teachers, friends, and books. Cooper argued that "these complex associations give rise at length to that feeling we call conscience, and to the idea of obligation and duty." Different societies built different moralities—witness, Cooper wrote, Eastern polygamy, Athenian pederasty, and Spartan infanticide. But human beings could learn and reflect and reason; they could see that some moral orders were better than others and then engineer societies encouraging people to act as they ought to act.[34]

In his pamphlets against the slave trade (1787–91), written in Manchester when he was a committee member of the Society for the Purpose of Effecting the Abolition of the Slave Trade, he dismissed the notion that blacks and whites were separate species because their union produced not "a mule" but progeny who could reproduce. The main difference between the two groups of human stock—skin color—was simply the effect of the body's reaction to different climates. The character traits that slavery's apologists attributed to Africans were the results of their natural, social, and political environments. Did Africans appear lazy? That was because "the necessaries of life in Africa [were] almost spontaneously produced": having only to reach up to a nearby tree for a piece of fruit instead of tilling the land for their daily bread, Africans "from their infancy [were] accustomed to perpetual indolence." Did not slaves' excessive devotion to music, dancing, and drink in their leisure hours suggest that they were happily suited to a sensual life rather than one of rational reflection? "It is notorious," Cooper answered, "... that in every despotic country, in proportion as the subjects feel the weight of the hand of tyranny, ... men fly from their own reflections, and enter more heartily into those enjoyments that bring on the momentary contrast." Did free blacks such as the Maroons, who lived by themselves and subsisted by "hunting and plunder," demonstrate that emancipated slaves will never be suited to free labor in civilized society? No, Cooper answered, the Maroons live this way because "they have been educated to this mode of life, and it is a known fact, that either white or black thus brought up from infancy, will never voluntarily settle to regular labor." Free blacks living in a slave society, too, avoided plantation labor only because they had learned that working alongside slaves would be a "disgrace."[35]

Englishmen also had their sensibilities shaped by their circumstances. Daily exposure to the brutality of the slave trade rendered many slave merchants and owners "insensible to the misery of their fellow-creatures." Moral ideas (such as the golden rule) and moral feelings (such as the ability to empathize with another person's pain) failed to produce moral actions. It was the failure of the socially constructed conscience. Others who condoned the trade did so not because their moral sense had been numbed but because they did not yet perceive the truth about slavery. "A worthy man may be ignorant of the question; he may be mistaken; he may be deceived by his own sophisms, or those of his friends; he may be led away by example, by authority, by long custom, by habitual inattention." Cooper did not think that his pamphlets would regenerate the hardened hearts of slave traders, but he was confident that publishing facts illustrating the horrific cruelties of the trade would focus attention and elicit the appropriate moral response among the public at large.[36]

Virtue, Cooper believed, was built upon enlightened self-interest—self-interest that was enlightened and not merely selfish because in civilized society people can learn to see that their own good is bound up with the greater good of their community. Obeying God and focusing on the afterlife were still ways of pursuing self-interested happiness. Future rewards and punishments motivated present behavior and encouraged believers to delay the short-term gratifications of worldly things for the far greater bliss (or to avoid worse punishments) in the hereafter. Belief in a future state, therefore, was useful for enforcing moral codes but not essential. Parents, through sheer repetition and the association of ideas, could implant their society's ideas of right and wrong and the accompanying feelings of obligation in their children. Magistrates could do the same with their subjects. The moral regime that family and state authorities instilled need not be merely the arbitrary enforcement of obedience to their own power, however. Natural laws could be deduced without divine revelation and enforced without the inducements of heaven and hell, Cooper contended. But reason alone could not prove the existence of a future state of rewards and punishments. On this point, he declared in the 1780s, he parted company with deists like Shaftesbury and Hume. Only Christianity guaranteed such an afterlife, and it was a guarantee that had to be taken on faith. In the 1780s Cooper indicated that he, like Priestley, shared that faith and thought it made a difference to moral behavior on earth. Without hopes for heaven, the unbeliever lacks some of the motives to moral action that the believer has. The enlightened unbeliever would still be able to set aside the pleasures of the moment for his or her own good in the long run, but that long run would be confined to life in the world and not extended eternally after death. The religious skeptic might avoid drinking to excess, but only for health and social reasons, and not because he was motivated by the more powerful belief that God bars drunkards from the gates of paradise. In social relations, Cooper conceded in the 1789 *Tracts*, the Christian with his faith in Judgment Day was more dependable than the skeptic who lacked it.

Besides appealing to "the common feelings of humanity, and the common principles of morality," Cooper invoked this Christian morality in his pamphlets against the slave trade in the late 1780s and early 1790s. But he also addressed members of the different "religious characters" in Manchester individually—Quakers, Methodists, Presbyterians, and Anglicans—and then insisted that the issue transcended theological and denominational differences: slave-trade abolition was "not the cause of Arianism or of Calvinism" but of "Christianity" itself. Cooper applauded the few clergymen who recognized this fact and criticized the majority who remained silent. Writing in support of the campaign to boycott the consumption of West Indian sugar in 1791, he reminded his readers that they would be held accountable before God in the next life: "Remember, friends, there is another tribunal, before which sooner or later we must all appear." The charge was grave: "Every person who habitually consumes one article of West Indian produce, raised by Slaves, *is guilty of the crime of murder.*" Although British law would not punish people for wanting to stir some sugar into their tea, in the afterlife they would not evade justice: "The best of us will tremble when that awful day approaches; but let it not be said, in addition to our other crimes, that we encouraged a traffic fatal to the happiness of our brethren—of the children of that great Being, before whom we then shall stand." Christian belief in future retribution, Cooper recognized in 1791, was a potent motive to moral reform.[37]

Soon Cooper was no longer tipping his hat politely to the superior moral utility of Christianity. Priestley noted Cooper's growing religious skepticism as early as 1794. In 1806, two years after Priestley's death, Cooper indicated in his published review of Priestley's metaphysical and political ideas that he had moved beyond some of the opinions that he had once shared with his departed friend. He had grown more contemptuous of how the doctrines of the immaterial immortal soul and eternal punishment for sinners had for centuries been the bit and bridle of priests and kings riding on the backs of the people. "The doctrine of a future state, and that of an immaterial and immortal soul, became therefore mutual supports to each other; and herein the civil power willingly joined in aid of the dogmas of metaphysical theology, from observing the convenience that might arise in the government of civil societies, from inculcating a more complete sanction of rewards and punishments for action in this life, by means of the dispensations to come.... Indeed, in every age, and in every country, the priesthood have found it so powerful an engine of influence over the minds of the people, and in too many cases, so fruitful a source of lucrative imposture, that its prevalence is not to be wondered at."[38]

Christianity, Cooper believed by the beginning of the nineteenth century, was simply not essential to the moral progress of either self or society. Discussing religious liberty, he elaborated upon Jefferson's famous remark in *Notes on the State of Virginia*: "Whether a man believes in one God with the Unitarians," Cooper wrote, "or in one God and two thirds with the Arians, or in three Gods with Dr. Horseley and the Trinitarians, or in thirty or thirty thousand Gods as Varro tells us the heathens of his day could reckon up, or in no God at all like the Atheists, under any of these modes of belief a man *may* be a good member of society, and under all of them men *have been* good members of society; such a man's course of life may be just and benevolent; he may pay full obedience to the laws; he may be a good father, a good husband, a dutiful son: his *actions*, his *conduct* may be kind, generous and upright: what more has society to require?" The doctor did not recoil, as Priestley had, at Erasmus Darwin's suggestion that life could have evolved from "unorganized matter" without divine intervention. Science at the turn of the nineteenth century did not yet know enough to either prove or disprove such a theory, Cooper thought, and even if true he was not sure that the idea necessarily led to atheism. "But if it do lead to Atheism, what then? There can be no crime in following truth wherever it lead, and I think we have sufficient reason upon the whole to believe, that the result of truth must be more beneficial to mankind than error." Nor could he see how religious skepticism "can be more detrimental to society or render a man less fit as a citizen than" familiar forms of religious faith. The pursuit of truth and the spread of knowledge, after all, he argued, had been the source of all of Europe's progress in the previous four or five centuries, and he was still optimistic about the future. Humankind would not attain perfection, but the horizon of social improvement through knowledge had still not yet been glimpsed. The "dispositions" and "manners" of the masses were increasingly being tamed, and "the sources of pleasurable intercourse, and mutual improvement" were becoming increasingly common.[39]

Cooper may have dismissed the soul as an unnecessary hypothesis and demoted the self to a fluctuating perception of consciousness, but he still needed individuals to be citizens. His twice-reprinted essay on the foundation of civil government first established the "grand maxim" that political power was derived from the consent of the people, and then derived thirty-three "principal deductions." Lines added in 1826 mark less a sudden rejection of the philosophy of Jefferson's Declaration than further evidence of his long struggle with the idea of natural individual rights and powers. One addition clings to the notion of an equal distribution of political power among individuals: "All communities are formed for the promotion of the mutual happiness of the members composing it: this implies equality in its origin." Other added sentences, though, made explicit why Cooper, even in the original composition of the essay in the 1780s, did not build his argument from a foundation of equal rights: "It is easy to say that all men are born equal; or that they are born with equal rights: but it is difficult to prove it, for this plain reason, that it is not true, when asserted in this vague and unlimited extent.... I fear it will be found that men are born equal in no respect; or with equal rights any where; either by the laws of nature, or of nations. Civil Liberty must be placed on another basis."[40]

The original essay, too, had no sooner granted rights to an abstract "individual" than it stripped them from specific classes of people. Cooper's first deduction from his "grand maxim" was that "no power, authority, or dominion can justly be exercised over any individual which has not been precedently derived from his own consent." This principle, however, was immediately undercut by a list of exceptions: "infancy, idiocy, lunacy" and "such persons also being either naturally or by compact, *sui incompotes*, incapable of self-direction." Who were the persons incapable of self-direction and liable to be dominated without their consent? As the years went by, Cooper's list grew as his humanitarian vision narrowed by class, gender, and race.[41]

Should the right to vote, Cooper asked, be limited to the class of (substantial) property holders? Arguing for parliamentary reform in 1783, Cooper had supported universal suffrage. By 1790, he had changed his mind. It did not make sense for people who lacked property and did not pay taxes, he argued, to elect representatives who mostly dealt with property issues. More ominously, he reasoned that landowners owned the very territory that was "essentially necessary to the existence of a political community," and that therefore they could "admit or reject as members of the community on their own terms" those who had no rights to the land. The poor, too, usually lacked sufficient wisdom and self-direction to be voters: Cooper pointed to "the probable suspicion of want of knowledge and independence in this class of people." In the United States, as property requirements for adult white males to vote were gradually dropped in the early nineteenth century, Cooper's position only hardened. By 1812, he could say from bitter experience that in a republic without sufficient property requirements for the franchise, "the ignorance of the community is almost exclusively represented, and wisdom and wealth, are held in distrust."[42]

In 1826, Cooper also added paragraphs to "Propositions" defending his position and showing how the public good could trump claims to individual rights: "Government is not merely a thing of theory, and of abstract right. It is founded on public expedience, guided by past experience. We are not required to shut our eyes to notorious facts. The great object of all laws is the general welfare—public utility. There can be no rights inconsistent with this. If a right may be safely exercised under some circumstances and not under others, it ought not to be allowed in the latter cases.... So if experience shews us, that under the present circumstances of a political community, the privilege of suffrage is always liable to be abused by a certain class of people, there is no injustice of depriving that class of the privilege." He was even blunter in his *Lectures on the Elements of Political Economy* in 1829. There were no political rights apart from civil society, he told his South Carolina students. The propertied and the propertyless have different interests, and society should be directed by the former. Dependent persons like factory workers should not be allowed to vote, and the great mass of people in America's democracy was still too uneducated to make wise political choices.[43]

Cooper's ouster from his circuit-court judgeship in 1811 had driven home the point that popular ignorance dominated his political community. In January of that year, a petition printed in Lancaster charged that Judge Cooper "exhibited the manners of a tyrant, and treated like slaves a people determined to be free." Pennsylvania Republicans, he soon saw, could do their political dirty work with populist rhetoric, public petitions, and legislative hearings as efficiently as Federalists had with sedition laws and libel trials. Cooper's *Narrative* of his experience, published immediately upon his dismissal from the bench in April 1811, argued that he had merely tried to bring order and decorum to what had been a raucous courtroom and reprimanded some "ignorant" young country lawyers. Seeking revenge, these young men combed through the records of Cooper's eight years as presiding judge and developed a list of over fifty charges of alleged misconduct. Then for several weeks they rode throughout the district, going door to door to collect signatures. When that strategy did not yield enough names, they circulated a "gull-trap petition," asking people to sign if they believed that the rumors of misconduct at least deserved a legislative inquiry. When the issue came before the legislature on February 21, it became clear that Cooper's young persecutors were allied with politicians who disliked him for other reasons—Samuel Satterlee of Lycoming, for example, the chair of the investigating committee who acted as "a public prosecutor," resented Cooper for thwarting a land speculation scheme. The case against Cooper "was taken up as a party business by the political description of citizens usually termed democrats, on two grounds: 1st That I was a foreigner; 2d. That I had gone over to the federalists." His imperious manner, along with the fact that he socialized with

Federalist gentlemen, was enough for his accusers to raise suspicions that he was a political turncoat.[44]

The legislature, Cooper charged, ignored the state constitution by denying him a formal impeachment trial. Instead, his opponents read the charges against him in the chamber of the House of Representatives in front of many public spectators, shunted him off to a small committee room for his rebuttal, denied him time to gather evidence, and left his fate up to a biased committee. The House and Senate voted in favor of the committee's recommendation to dismiss him, even though nearly all of the charges had been thrown out; Cooper, though he argued "that every kind of publicity should be given to the defence as well as to the accusation preferred against the president judge of a district, for the sake of public information as well as public justice," was denied the opportunity to address either chamber. Governor Simon Snyder, leader of the rural radicals and Cooper's Northumberland neighbor, signed the dismissal on April 3, 1811.[45]

Cooper saw what he believed to be a partisan majority of the ignorant and self-interested manipulate popular sentiment and republican institutions to execrate an educated and talented man. None of this was particularly unusual in the political gamesmanship of early nineteenth-century Pennsylvania, where judicial appointments were frequently attacked to score political points in factional contests or settle personal scores as men competed for money and power. A year after what he called "the tragicomedy of my accusation, trial, condemnation and dismissal," Cooper was diagnosing ailments of democratic political culture that went back to the ancient Greeks. In fifth-century Athens as in nineteenth-century America, men of superior station, wealth, or abilities were held up to vicious public calumny because the people were cruel, ambitious, and morbidly jealous of them. "Almost every where among us, the antient hatred, not merely to the aristocracy of rank, and the aristocracy of wealth, but to the aristocracy of talent also, strongly prevails." He backed away from his support of popular political clubs like his own Constitutional Society in Manchester or the republican societies that had formed in America in the 1790s: such "self-created societies" were "were violent, turbulent, and perhaps mischievous.... Where great oppression and usurpation of popular rights takes place, they may be instruments of much good, and convey much political information to the people; but they are so liable to be perverted into factions, and employed for factious purposes." He even began to wonder "whether the Freedom of the Press itself, may not be purchased at too high a price."[46]

His dampened enthusiasm for democratic practice, inflected by class disdain, joined a dimmer view of the common man. He explained his views to friends in 1815—fittingly, in a privately printed pamphlet circulated to an elite circle including Jefferson and Madison, and written in the form of a letter about the education of a young gentleman. Cooper wrote that previously, like other republican theorists, he had "considered man, not indeed guided by virtuous motives, but as guided by those motives of public and private *self-interest* which ought reasonably to guide him. We all took for granted, that where his interest as a member of the community in common with others, was plain and obvious, and did not clash with his private interest, he would follow it." But experience in Pennsylvania had taught Cooper "that there is a perpetual and almost irresistible inclination among the people to cheat themselves, and to be cajoled and cheated by others. That temporary and short sighted motives are always more powerful, than those that look to a great but distant benefit." Popular opinion was "rash and violent, as well as unreflecting: prone to sacrifice its friends to its flatterers, and to commit injustice in the wantonness of power, as well as through mistake or resentment." It was no wonder that he concluded after his dismissal that "justice and disinterestedness, wisdom and tolerance" were not "the necessary fruits of universal suffrage, as it is exercised in Pennsylvania." Most voters were narrow-minded, impetuous, and ill informed, and they chose men like themselves on Election Day. Yet however much Cooper came to disparage the ignorant multitude, he still held out hope that proper education could correct the problem. Property requirements for voting, he wrote in 1826, would be unnecessary if a decent public education system were in place. Individuals—white male individuals, at least— might be redeemable after all.[47]

What about women? In the 1790 version of his "Propositions," he immediately listed "coverture"—the legal subordination of a wife to her husband—as one of the exceptions, along with "infancy, idiocy, [and] lunacy," to his proposition about the individual's necessary consent to authority. He did note, however, that the common practice limiting the rights of unmarried adult women "appears to be inequitable," adding that perhaps the treatment of married women was as well. In a 1792 revision of the essay, republished in the first American edition of 1798, Cooper pushed the implications raised in this passage toward a declaration of women's equal rights. Written when he was in the vanguard of British feminism and republished in late eighteenth-century Pennsylvania, a long footnote explained that he had "repeatedly considered" this question and had become convinced that the political subordination of women was simply another "system of despotism." If women seemed to lack the capacity for serious (male) occupations it was because (male-dominated) society had made them so. "We educate women from infancy to marriage, in such a way as to debilitate both their corporeal and mental powers." After encouraging them to cultivate the "petty passions" instead of their minds, "we [men] say they are not fit to govern themselves, and arrogate the right of making them our slaves through life." He had read the leading progressive women writers in England and had conversed with the great female *salonistes* in Revolutionary Paris. He "felt his own inferiority" in the presence of these brilliant women, and the dogma of male superiority seemed blatantly "iniquitous and most absurd." "I have seldom met with views more enlarged, more just, more truly patriotic; or with political reasonings more acute, or arguments more forcible, than in the conversation of Theroigne [Anne-Josèphe Théroigne de Méricourt], and the writings of Miss [Mary] Wolstonecroft [sic]." He challenged "the defenders of male despotism" to try to answer Wollstonecraft's *A Vindication of the Rights of Woman* (1792) if they could.[48]

However, by 1812, the year he remarried (his first wife had died while he was in prison for sedition in 1800), he was arguing that the subordination of women conformed to the law of nature: "For generally speaking, there is a natural prevalence of mental energy, as well as of corporeal force in favour of the man, independent of the means of acquiring knowledge." In the 1826 edition of "Propositions," the long footnote on women's rights is gone. He glossed the original text's suggestion that the treatment of women might be inequitable with a single sentence: "But the question must be determined by an impartial consideration of what practice is most likely to produce the greatest sum of good to the whole community, male and female." "Nature" now justified male despotism, and utilitarian calculation now determined that female subordination served the public good.[49]

This shift from malleable, relational selves to fixed orders of human nature also marked his thinking about race and slavery. Some of his writings suggest that he jumped from Enlightenment environmentalism to biological racism by adopting phrenology, the "science" that decoded intellectual character by mapping the shapes of skulls. An unsigned 1835 article entitled "Slavery" attributed to him cited phrenological analysis as definitive proof of black inferiority. But this essay also argues from scripture (which for Cooper personally was not authoritative in the least); the article drew rhetorical support for a proslavery position wherever it could. A signed article published three months later sketched a more nuanced take on phrenology. The debates over it, Cooper began, resembled the arguments he participated in about materialism and the relation of mind and brain at meetings of the Manchester Literary and Philosophical Society forty-five years earlier. He resented the way that these new investigations of crania and the mental organs beneath were being dismissed out of hand because of theological and ideological biases. He still, though, acknowledged serious objections to the new theories: they seemed to be based on unsupported assumptions about the meaning of the size and shape of parts of the brain. Perhaps the most serious objection was that the theories ignored the development of the brain "by education and the effects of social intercourse on the mind after the skull has acquired its adult thickness." Phrenologists who were flummoxed by an Oxford don who had the skull shape of murderers they had measured failed to appreciate how education and social environment could counteract physiological propensities. His objections seemed to undercut the phrenological support for the racism in the "Slavery" article.[50]

Yet throughout the 1820s and '30s, Cooper privately and publicly maintained that he had "not the slightest doubt of [blacks] being an inferior variety of the human species." In 1823, three years after coming to South Carolina and a year after the Denmark Vesey slave-conspiracy executions in Charleston, Cooper published an article on "mixed marriages" in the state's leading newspapers. Mocking a decision by Supreme Court Justice William Johnson, a prominent South Carolinian critic of the Vesey court proceedings who declared a subsequent law restricting free blacks unconstitutional, Cooper surveyed the place of black people in the country. "In all and every state from Maine to New Orleans, he is of degraded caste; of an inferior rank, condition, or status in society. This feeling and the conduct in conformity to it, and the laws implying it, are universal throughout the United States." White society had strong "practical prejudices against the negro race," and the laws reflected those sentiments: nowhere in the country did blacks enjoy full civil rights. Their status resulted, however, not from ignorant bias and a system of despotism but was "dependant on the differences which nature ordained." These differences were discerned, Cooper contended, not so much by reading skulls as by interpreting the social facts of historical experience.[51]

Cooper had spent much of his nearly three decades in Pennsylvania studying chemistry and mineralogy and acting as a consulting physician. Frustrated by the philosophers' and theologians' empty battles over words, and wary of how lawyers and politicians twisted language for their own purposes, he championed the study of empirical facts as the surest road to truth. His antislavery tracts had in the 1780s and '90s explained behaviors and characteristics (why Africans seemed lazy, Maroons plundered, and slaves danced) by examining social conditions. By the 1820s and '30s he had persuaded himself that the social facts instead supported black inferiority: free blacks in Haiti, he claimed, would "not labor voluntarily," and the blacks living in the mud huts of Africa were hardly "superior to the beasts of the field." His late eighteenth-century defense of African intellectual capacity had pointed to empirical evidence: "They are men; susceptible of the same cultivation with ourselves.... As to their capacity, let the Poems of Phillis Wheatley, and the letters of Ignatius Sancho be perused, and the question is decided." A quarter century later he cited empirical "facts" to make the opposite point: "In the northern and middle states they have black teachers, black preachers, black physicians—they have had access to all the means of improving their condition, and their inferiority remains manifest and undeniable. They are not superior in one thing to the slave of the south. They are not capable of much mental improvement, or of literary or scientific acquirement." He claimed to have observed the free blacks of Philadelphia for forty years, but he ignored all their accomplishments: stabilizing families and communities; building churches, schools, and fraternal orders; struggling against economic discrimination and militant racism to become independent laborers, artisans, shopkeepers, and professionals. He chose to stop seeing their deprivation as an effect of tyranny and instead cast it as evidence of natural inferiority.[52]

Cooper had needed to persuade himself of black deficiencies to justify slavery, and he needed slavery to support his vision of a society directed by learned, propertied gentlemen like himself. The utility of slavery for the good of the community as a whole—or at least for its aristocracy of talent—was a lesson he began to learn not in South Carolina but in Pennsylvania. He had originally settled there in part because he could not imagine a man of his philosophical principles and political convictions suited to the slave societies in the South. He tried to clear some wooded acres in Northumberland, living in a rough two-room dwelling that his wife did not even want to enter, but after a season agricultural labor lost its charms. He realized that he needed to begin practicing law, and that his growing family needed servants. Good help being hard to find, he sought, as he wrote to an English friend in the spring of 1796, "a set of negroes.... They are purchasable here till they are 28 years old." This was precisely the time, too, when democratic newspapers north of Baltimore stopped printing antislavery essays in order to join forces with slaveholding Southerners, an oppositional political coalition that would win the presidency for Jefferson in 1800. Self-interest and political affiliation combined to encourage Cooper to rethink slavery.[53]

By 1812, while teaching chemistry at Carlisle College, he argued in print that slavery, though regrettable, was still an open question. Since slave labor was not as productive as free labor, and slave societies lacked "any permanent feeling, either of individual or of public security," he continued to approve, on pragmatic grounds, the prohibition of the transatlantic slave trade and the hope for the gradual abolition of slavery itself. Slavery, however, was no longer the obvious moral outrage he had once condemned. Such power in the hands of the master had a "*tendency*" to corrupt, he admitted, but slave owning did not necessarily dull one's sensibility "to the sufferings of a fellow creature, because these dispositions are very frequently indeed counteracted by the natural good qualities of the master, and by the general manners of civilized society, at a period when kindness and humanity are fostered and respected by public opinion." He was more than ready to move to Virginia when Jefferson tried to have him join the faculty of the new university. When Cooper instead accepted a position at South Carolina College, he was, his daughter later remembered, eager to purchase slaves as soon as he entered the state.[54]

The Night of Superstition

Education was, for Cooper, a realm that demonstrated the limitations of his laissez-faire political economy as a model of enlightened politics. A man did not devote himself to the acquisition of knowledge in literary and scientific pursuits to further his economic interests, he argued, for such pursuits rarely paid well. The "ardor" for learning itself, and perhaps the hope for "honorable fame," were the only motives. Seeing few pecuniary benefits, however, most families would not pay to send their sons to college. But if the pursuit of knowledge was not the way to wealth for individuals, it certainly did enrich the nation as a whole. New inventions and ideas fueled progress. Therefore, Cooper concluded, the state, through an income tax upon the wealthy, should support free universal education through the age of twenty-one. And the professors who taught in the free public colleges and universities should be paid salaries equivalent to those earned by other learned professionals, such as lawyers and physicians, to ensure that the professoriate was filled by men of talent and accomplishment. The advancement of learning through governmental support of an aristocracy of intellect and the enlightenment of the broader public would be served by the same state institutions. Even as Cooper railed against the clergy as a class of theological professionals who were always plotting to divert public funds toward their efforts to Christianize the nation, he sought similar ways to institutionalize skeptical inquiry and secular enlightenment.[55]

He thought he might have a chance to advance this agenda by joining his friend Jefferson's new University of Virginia. In March 1819, Cooper was formally elected professor of chemistry, mineralogy, and natural philosophy, and was expected to also temporarily serve as professor of law. The school's opening, planned for the fall of 1819, was delayed, and as everyone waited for construction to be completed, Presbyterian critics in Virginia vigorously opposed Cooper's appointment. In February 1820, the *Virginia Evangelical and Literary Magazine*, edited by the Presbyterian pastor John Holt Rice, otherwise a strong supporter of the new university, published a long review of Cooper's remarks in the *Memoirs of Dr. Joseph Priestley*. The reviewer was stunned that a man elected to teach the future leaders of the state had scoffed at the doctrines of the Trinity, freedom of the will, eternal future punishment, and even the existence of the soul. "But we are principally struck with horror," Rice continued, at the way Cooper cavalierly and impiously dismissed worries that materialistic science could lead to atheism. " '*But if it do lead to Atheism, what then?*' " the review quoted Cooper. "*What then? Why then*, farewel [sic] to the dearest hopes and best consolations of man!" If heaven were but a dream, Rice warned, human beings would be left helpless and hopeless. Publicly combating such ideas was the duty not just of clergymen but of all American patriots. A single "speculative infidel" in a Christian nation might bow to the pressures of public opinion and act with "general decorum and propriety," Rice admitted. "But let the faith of a nation be undermined; let the control of religion be removed, let the whole community be without the fear of God before their eyes," and disaster would ensue. A speculative infidel like Cooper being allowed to train the rising generation would only accelerate the irreligious character of the age and further remove the restraints on its "peculiarly violent" passions. Published within weeks of the Missouri Compromise, with the nation wakened to the slavery question as to "a fire bell in the night," as Jefferson famously wrote, the review suggested that nothing less than the fate of the Union was at stake: "Should the bonds which now unite us as a people be dissolved, and civil war arise—which may God in his great mercy forbid—we believe that the contest would be marked by deeds of ferocity, and works of desolation, of which the history of the world has exhibited few examples."[56]

This critique, apparently, was echoed from other Presbyterian pulpits in the state. Because of the delay, Cooper had sought temporary employment at the College of South Carolina, and since by the spring of 1820 that school was eager to make his appointment permanent, Cooper offered to resign from the Virginia university. Jefferson, bitter about the sectarian campaign against his friend, reluctantly accepted the resignation.[57]

Within a few months of his arrival in South Carolina, the college's president died, and Cooper was named his replacement. He and Jefferson continued their correspondence. In an exchange of letters in the early 1820s, they pondered the state of religion in America. Cooper and Jefferson lamented the "fanaticism" that swept up so many Americans in an emotional religious fervor and warily eyed the "holy alliance" of evangelicals that was increasingly dominating the cultural politics of the Republic.[58]

Both men had a particular scorn for Presbyterianism. In an October 1822 letter Cooper fumed about this denomination's role in the "progress of fanaticism." He had taken a trip back to Pennsylvania, and the scourge of sectarian bigotry was evident wherever he went. When he had lived in Northumberland with Priestly, he remembered, "the harmony of private society was hardly interrupted by politics, and not at all by religion." But now "the bitterness and intolerance of theological hatred reigns in full force." This change he ascribed to "the predominant influence of the Presbyterian preachers, over the women particularly, whom they tempt out to nightly sermons and prayer meetings" while their husbands crowded into the taverns and grumbled into their cups. In Columbia, South Carolina, Cooper told Jefferson, the college faculty had different religious sentiments yet tolerated one another happily, but because the school did not host revivals and prayer meetings the Presbyterians denounced it as a bastion of infidelity. Cooper was convinced that Presbyterian clergymen throughout the Union were trying to infiltrate families "by making the females...the engines of their influence over the male part"; they were trying to dominate intellectual life by scheming to gain control of colleges; they were duping the public with their "missionary societies, Bible societies, and theological seminaries"; and they ultimately hoped to pervert government and "establish a system of tythes," tax support that would create "a *Church establishment*."⁵⁹

Jefferson agreed with Cooper that "the atmosphere of our country is unquestionably charged with a threatening cloud of fanaticism, lighter in some parts, denser in others, but too heavy in all." He also blamed the problems in Pennsylvania, once renowned for "toleration and freedom of religion," on "the growth of Presbyterianism," the "haughtiest of all religious sects." Turning his attention to Richmond, Virginia, Jefferson seconded Cooper's notion that "fanaticism" operated chiefly among and through women: "They have their night meetings and praying parties, where attended by their priests, and sometimes a hen-pecked husband, they pour fourth their effusions of their love to jesus in terms as amatory and carnal as their modesty would permit them to use to a mere earthly lover." Presbyterians warped public discussion in other ways besides encouraging the panting effusions of evangelical women, however. The logical absurdities of the Calvinist theology they felt compelled to defend, Jefferson suggested, made them "irritable & prone to denunciation" in preaching and public discussion. They were also "systematical in grasping at an ascendancy over all other sects"; they had a tyrannical ambition that "would tolerate no rivalry if they had power." Further, like Jesuits elsewhere, "they aim...at engrossing the education of the country [and] are hostile to every institution which they do not direct."⁶⁰

Jefferson offered three remedies to the situation. Using his own village of Charlottesville as an example, he wrote that in the short term a balance of power among the contending Protestant sects would tend to neutralize their prejudices. Lacking churches or meetinghouses, the four denominations in Charlottesville—Episcopalian, Presbyterian, Methodist, and Baptist—all had to take turns leading worship in the courthouse, each getting one Sunday a month. They all "listen with attention and devotion to each other's preachers and all mix in society with perfect harmony," Jefferson observed. Boston offered a different lesson: it illustrated how the "blasphemy and absurdity" of Calvinism could be checked by the rising influence of Unitarianism, which had already humbled the haughty Calvinists there. But the ultimate solution to Presbyterian fanaticism and tyranny would be the progress of education, which would in the not-too-distant future, Jefferson believed, tip the American balance toward a liberal and rational faith. These reflections prompted his famously wrong prediction that enlightened Unitarianism would "ere long be the religion of the majority [of Americans] from North to South." Perhaps he even hoped that most Americans would someday press beyond Unitarianism and do as he had privately done some years before: cut out the myths, miracles, and superstitions from their New Testaments and paste together a new Bible from the sensible moral teachings of Jesus.⁶¹

Cooper, too, was optimistic about the progress of knowledge and education: "Within fifty years the march of mind has been more rapid than for 500 previous," and it was possible that the trend would continue to accelerate, he wrote to Monticello in 1825. This was, perhaps, Cooper's only leap of faith: "I *think* it will be so, induced by the hope that it will be so." Still, Cooper did not endorse Jefferson's prediction. The doctor thought that Unitarianism might prevail "among the better informed people" by the middle of the nineteenth century, but evangelicals—most notably the Methodists—"addressing the passions, will keep fast hold of the multitude; more especially from the erotic language of their devotional poetry.... I am persuaded this class of associations has its full effect on the female part of the sectarians, who are not affected by mere argument or sound reasoning." And where women went with the affairs of the heart, husbands and sons often followed. Cooper was far less sanguine, too, about the Unitarians. "Even the Unitarians are sectarian, with the sectarian spirit about them," he wrote. He might have added that the New England Unitarians in the 1820s, still clinging to biblical miracles, would have been unfriendly to Jefferson's radical redactions of scriptural superstition and hostile to Cooper's skeptical critique of biblical faith. Neither would a balance of power among mainstream Protestant groups, while it might frustrate Presbyterian schemes for sectarian hegemony, do much to reduce the number of stones thrown at the humanistic skeptics and scientific atheists Cooper insisted could be good citizens. A Christian balance of power would prevent the tyranny of a single sect but did nothing to address the "holy alliance" of interdenominational associations that was consolidating power on a national scale and silencing inquiry, doubt, and dissent.[62]

Jefferson could observe with detachment from his mountaintop retirement; Cooper was plunged into the conflict. "I foresee another night of superstition, not far behind the Inquisition," Cooper wrote to Jefferson, "for so rancorously is every opponent calumniated that the persecution becomes gradually irresistible, and the men who hate these [clerical] imposters & their frauds are actually compelled to bow down to them." Among educated gentlemen, Cooper hardly felt alone at being forced to bow to the reigning dogmas of a Bible-thumping majority. "I look around me, and knowing, as I do, the general prevalence of liberal opinions on religious subjects among well educated men, I regard with absolute horror the system of simulation and dissimulation which they are compelled to adopt." He had to dissimulate himself: he regularly attended Episcopal services in Columbia, led daily prayers at the college, sounded more Christian in his public statements than his actual beliefs would warrant, and strenuously insisted that he avoided discussing religion with any of his students. But some of his religious opinions were known, and his deeper skepticism was surmised; his critics claimed to see through his charade. In South Carolina in the 1820s and '30s, Cooper's struggles to promote his version of enlightenment would enter a new chapter—a struggle further complicated by the cultural politics of slavery.[63]

6

Christian Enlightenment

Eastern Cities and the Great West

Religious skeptics often placed the Church next to Monarchy, and Christianity alongside folk superstition, as the foes of enlightenment. Yet skeptics confronted not just religious enthusiasts swept away by emotion but a powerful phalanx of religious believers who insisted that they were Christian *and* enlightened. These were people of faith who valorized learning and reason, committed themselves to mass education and publication, and asserted that they, and not the skeptics, scoffers, and infidels, knew the true connection between knowledge and freedom. They staked their claim in two major ways. They simply corralled enlightenment appeals to reason and nature and kept them bounded by Christianity. Or they inverted the skeptical enlightenment critique of religion, arguing that Christians were actually the ones devoted to reason, common sense, empirical evidence, historical fact, and rigorous critical inquiry, whereas religious doubters were blinded by self-interest, swayed by emotion, and willfully ignorant of simple truths.

The Rev. Ezra Stiles Ely was a master of the first strategy. A prominent Presbyterian clergyman, author, and editor in Philadelphia, Ely became particularly well known by calling for "a Christian party in politics." Like Thomas Cooper, he championed education and public enlightenment through mass publication and a public sphere of discussion and debate. Still, Christianity, he contended, could not be treated merely as an opinion or a conjecture. Its claims were not just notions developed by practical reason, tested by doubt, and established by public opinion. The Gospel was divine truth, and as such it compelled obedience, enkindled faith, and created particular forms of life. Christianity had to be the prerequisite to any public tribunal, the originating ground and ultimate end of intellectual work and political practice. Ely worked at the heart of the evangelicals' "benevolent empire," extending the reach of his church and promoting Sabbatarian, temperance, Bible, and tract societies. He could in one breath celebrate American democracy's frank and free discussion of diverse opinions and its religious liberty, and in another insist that America was a

Christian nation, its Constitution rooted in the Gospel and its government intended to privilege Christian institutions.[1]

The second strategy, the inversion of the skeptic's critique of religion, was employed by Ely, too, but it was most prominently illustrated by the work of a man who would become his colleague at Marion College in Missouri in the 1830s: Dr. David Nelson. Nelson was a Presbyterian clergyman who earlier in life had been a physician and a religious skeptic. He had mingled with admirers of French philosophy while studying medicine in Danville, Kentucky. Serving as a surgeon in the militia during the War of 1812 and traveling from the Great Lakes to Mobile, he commonly heard scoffers and wits mock Christianity by tavern fireplaces. He read Voltaire, Volney, and Paine. His doubts finally fell away while reading *Scott's Family Bible* (with Protestant annotations) in the forests of Tennessee. Licensed to preach in 1825, he was convinced that the religious infidelity that had ensnared him was on the march—not just in Europe or in the cities back east but in the American West. Religious infidelity might sprout from sin, Nelson believed, but it was cultivated and fertilized by ignorance. The answer was Christian enlightenment through education. In 1837, he published his major work, *The Cause and Cure of Infidelity*, a 350-page book discussing doubt and faith in a common vernacular and promoted especially to "the vigorous minds of the West"; said to have quickly sold a hundred thousand copies, the work was republished several times and later translated into German, Spanish, Dutch, Armenian, and Bulgarian. Examining his own passage from skepticism to faith and reporting on nearly two decades of trying to convert other infidels, Nelson in *Cause and Cure* argued that while allegedly enlightened scoffers might bluster about reason, stamp their feet as they demanded free inquiry, and try to make a show of higher learning, they were actually willfully ignorant about what the Bible really said and nearly as uninformed about the basic facts of history. Though called "skeptics," they were in fact overly credulous, eagerly swallowing baseless cavils against faith; though they praised rationality, their reaction to religion was really driven by pride and anger. By pretending to think for themselves, they gave themselves license to ignore facts established by careful scholarship. Their skeptical critiques of Christianity actually rested on ignorance, distortion, and falsehood, and their only weapon was privately snickered sarcasm rather than informed public debate. The diffusion of knowledge, on the other hand, could only advance the cause of Christ as it promoted human freedom.[2]

Ely and Nelson articulated and demonstrated in daily practice aspects of a philosophical theology not only of Christian enlightenment but of Christian agency. How did the notion of knowledge as an engine of liberty—of social, political, intellectual, and spiritual freedom—jibe with the Calvinist understanding of human depravity and of a God who had predetermined who would be virtuous and who vicious, who saved and who damned? How, among evangelicals, could Calvinists compete against the explosive growth of Arminian Methodists and Free Will Baptists who argued that knowledge could be transformed into the power of benevolent action through free human choice? As Calvinist social reformers, Ely and Nelson felt that they needed to define a position between the fatalists who reduced human beings to cogs in God's (or Nature's) machine and the freewill philosophers who thumbed their noses at God's sovereignty.

Reflecting a central tension in Christianity that became especially acute in eighteenth- and nineteenth-century American Protestantism, therefore, Ely and Nelson tried to find—and live—the proper balance of God's will and human agency. This was not merely a matter for abstract theological or philosophical debate. Ely and Nelson, like vast numbers of their fellow Christians, struggled to come to some coherent conception of enlightened Christian agency in order to understand and shape their individual and collective lives as followers of Christ. The practical applications of philosophical questions about enlightenment, agency, and faith became especially pronounced as benevolent reformers sought to transform American society and convert the world. Ely and Nelson would have their biggest chance to put enlightened faith into practice when they founded an experimental college and a new city on the banks of the Mississippi River. This bold project in Christian enlightenment at Marion College and Marion City, Missouri, would lay bare competing moral economies of benevolent reform and expose tensions between Christian ethics and the values of the marketplace. Both men would become embroiled in the conflict over slavery. Nelson would be driven out of the state by a proslavery lynch mob, and Ely would find himself a slaveholder accused of fraud and embezzlement. Ely and Nelson demonstrate once again how, in the alchemy of real life, ideas about skepticism and faith, exposed to the flames of power and self-interest, are transmuted in practice and experience.

Skeptical Maniacs, Moral Agents, Evangelical Print, and the Christian Party in Politics

Since childhood, Ezra Stiles Ely had hoped to become a minister like his father, Zebulon. Converted at age nine and officially admitted to his father's church in Lebanon, Connecticut, at fourteen, Ezra was sent to study at his father's alma mater, Yale College. After graduation, he was briefly tutored in divinity by Zebulon and was licensed to preach as an eighteen-year-old in 1804. Two years later he was installed as pastor to a tiny congregation in the neighboring town of Colchester. His first appearance in print, a conventional sermon preached the Sabbath after his ordination, matched the one his father had delivered on the occasion itself.[3]

But when he turned twenty-four, the son stopped following quite so closely in his father's footsteps. Zebulon, pious but socially awkward, had chosen an undistinguished and poorly paying parish because he thought it was God's will. He lived his life as a country parson who had to farm as well as preach. He published a handful of sermons, mostly for funerals, and could have fit his entire library, it was said, in a wheelbarrow. Ezra, handsome, smoothly sociable, and ambitious, left Colchester for New York City in the spring of 1810. There he became a preacher to the New York City Almshouse and Hospital, an urban mission funded by charitable donations, and began experimenting with various forms of publication in the burgeoning evangelical print culture of the early nineteenth century. A flurry of unusual publications quickly earned him a public reputation both for polemics and piety: a book of poems sold for charity, a spirited fund-raising sermon criticized the wealthy, a quirky volume of theological criticism ignited controversy, and two popular journals graphically described his experiences with the poor, the sick, the debauched, and the insane. After becoming embroiled in bitter ecclesiastical wrangling in both New York and Philadelphia, he accepted a call to a prosperous Presbyterian church in the latter city and married a wealthy merchant's daughter. The country parson's son would rise to the top post in the Presbyterian Church. In his book-lined gatehouse study at the entrance to his Philadelphia mansion on Second Street, he would write books and edit religious periodicals when not composing the Sunday sermons he would deliver from his red-velvet-trimmed pulpit. Zebulon's rather tormented spiritual experiences, preserved in a journal edited and published by his son, reflected central theological tensions within late eighteenth- and early nineteenth-century American Calvinism. Ezra believed that he had untied those theological knots. He contrasted an enlightened Christian faith with fatalistic infidelity, and he promoted a notion of Christian agency well suited, he thought, to an era effervescing with optimistic schemes for moral and social reform.[4]

Ely's *Journal of the Stated Preacher to the Hospital and Almshouse in the City of New-York* (1812) framed tales of pious suffering of the sick and the poor against what he described as the madness of skeptical infidelity. New York City's population had grown rapidly after 1790 to over ninety-six thousand people by 1810, but its economy had soured after the Embargo Act in 1807, and the suffering of the urban poor was especially acute. In June 1810, Ely had begun preaching Christ and counseling sinners amid the "poverty, misery, and madness" in the crowded, filthy wards. He started keeping a journal on New Year's Day in 1811, describing how he catechized the poor and the blind, prayed with prostitutes wracked with venereal disease, and sang hymns in the sickrooms where patients were bloated with dropsy, crippled by rheumatism, and suffering from consumption, typhus, and spotted fever. Of the twenty-four hundred people who passed

Portrait of Ezra Stiles Ely. From R. H. Allen, ed., *Leaves from a Century Plant: Report of the Centennial Celebration of Old Pine Street Church (Third Presbyterian), Philadelphia, Pa.* (Philadelphia, 1870), 126. A prominent Presbyterian clergyman, author, and editor in Philadelphia, Ely championed education and Christian enlightenment through mass publication, and he called for "a Christian party in politics."

through the doors of the two institutions in the year he kept his first journal, more than two hundred would die, and Ely's special task was to prepare the dying to meet their Maker. His address to one woman dying of consumption was typical: "Well, then, I think you are a poor wretch, covered with sin, shame, and guilt. You are unholy, and unclean. You deserve hell. You are soon to die; and if you die without union to the Lord Jesus Christ, I think, I know, that you will sink into perdition." Many ignored him. Catholics insisted on confessing their sins to a priest, and some Methodists seemed too confident of their own righteousness. But skeptical infidels earned his harshest rebukes. His confrontations with infidels in the early journal entries, and the book's concluding character sketch and appended sermon—both of which equated skeptical infidelity with madness—helped delineate all the stories of pious suffering as "a practical application of scriptural doctrine."[5]

Ely recorded that he had verbally "attacked" a deistic infidel in the Almshouse who had ridiculed a lady's hope for salvation. The deist had traveled to Judea, he claimed, and he assured the woman that the story of Jesus was a fiction. The "boaster" had also been "retailing that knowledge, which is contained in that primer of infidelity, 'The Age of Reason.'" No man is a friend, Ely declared, who would try to shake a Christian's faith and deprive her of its consolations under affliction. The lady herself related an anecdote about David Hume's mother, who on her sickbed supposedly begged her son to help her recover her faith, "the consolations of which he had deprived her, by making her a sceptic." Ely silenced the "bold and ferocious" deist by pointing precisely to what the rest of the book intended to demonstrate: the power of Christianity to console people crushed by poverty, tortured by illness, and drawing near to the threshold of death. "The religion of Jesus can injure no one," he proclaimed, "and were it a delusion, I would gladly cherish it in preference to despair; I would support it merely for the advantages it affords in the hour of dissolution, until a better source of consolation should be substituted in its place."[6]

Ely in his *Journal* then related another occasion when, in a very different setting, he again rose to "cut and thrust with the sword of the Spirit" in defense of Christianity against its skeptical enemies. At a private dinner, he found himself at a table with two men who were "avowed Deists." Raised in religious families in New England, they "had removed to one of the Southern States, and were now men of consequence, because they possessed five or six hundred slaves. Their dignity is commensurate with their plantations, and their honors have been multiplied at the birth of every negro or mulatto child." They adopted vices that would have appalled them in their youth. "To quiet their consciences, they have concluded, very philosophically, to believe nothing." In conversation after dessert, they openly denied the divine institution of the Sabbath and the divine inspiration of the Bible. Then "one of these mighty men of the plantation turned to me, and said, 'Christianity has made more damned rascals, than all other religions under heaven.' With indignation, I arose to leave the room, and said, 'It is false! it is false, Sir!' He arose too, in terrible wrath, exclaiming, 'I demand explanation, Sir, or satisfaction!'" Ely repeated that the statement was "utterly false" and "a base aspersion on Christianity." The deist then "swore, with the oath of a bully, that I was a fellow of low breeding." The plantation owner demanded that Ely meet him on the dueling ground, and his "brother infidel" volunteered to be his friend's second, "to carry the powder-horn and bullet-bag." Ely answered that he was ready to meet his challenger immediately, but only with the weapons "of truth and conscience."[7]

No shots were fired. Ely clarified that he was asserting that the statement about Christianity producing rascals was false, not calling the deist a liar. The deist "made his retreat" by alleging that he had intended to say only that more rascals hid behind the cloak of Christianity than behind any other religion. As with Ely's encounter with the Almshouse Paineite, challenging the truth of

Christianity was bad enough, but denying or interfering with the salutary practical effects of Christian faith was too much for Ely to bear.[8]

Ely's argument about Christian faith and skeptical infidelity did not fully emerge until the end of the volume. When attacking the Almshouse deist, he had proclaimed that Christianity would have therapeutic value even if it were a delusion. But of course he emphatically believed the Gospel true and salvation real. Deism—skepticism—unbelief: these were the delusions. The volume's appended sermon, entitled "The Maniac," addressed "self-styled friends of reason" and traced "an analogy between natural maniacs, and those who renounce the Lord Jesus Christ." These deluded thinkers imagine a God, if they imagine one at all, to be a being much like themselves, Ely wrote. In their warped view of reality, Jesus is just a man, the Bible is just a book, humanity is not depraved, and regeneration is an idle dream. With their distorted sense of value, unbelievers grasp at worldly trifles like madmen in their cells clutching pebbles and shells: "They love dress, houses, gardens, equipages, entertainments, and the fashionable amusements of the metropolis, more than the immortal soul." They waste their lives looking for meaning and consequence in all the wrong places: "You retire to rest with a novel for your prayer-book, or awake and consult your ledger as the oracle of God."[9]

The book's final character sketch, subtitled "The Punishment of Infidelity," showed how skeptical infidelity could quite literally drive a person insane. Here Ely told the story of a man named John from Long Island who had grown up in a reputable Presbyterian family. But in his youth "he read the productions of Voltaire and other infidel writers," which taught him to dismiss the claims of Christianity. His new philosophy was not, however, in this case accompanied by moral dissipation: John remained prudent and hardworking and was respected by his neighbors. He became a successful export merchant to the West Indies. Even an agonized, deathbed repentance by one of his infidel friends did not immediately shake him. Then one summer, while at sea, he had a powerful premonition that his mother was dying. He rushed home to find that she had indeed choked on a piece of food and died. This experience turned him back toward Presbyterian orthodoxy but also unhinged his mind. He once again came to believe in an angry God, who would eternally punish sin, and in the saving blood of Christ. But he also became convinced that it was his duty to suffer eternal torment: Christ's blood had not been shed for him. Confined in the maniacs' ward, he thought his black attendant was the devil. John's brother Ben, who was still an unbeliever, urged him to cheer up and stop making a fool of himself. John answered that he had been a fool when years before he had taken to heart the philosophy of those infidel books. Now he saw the truth, and it was too late. Not long after his brother's visit, John strangled himself by tying his cravat to his window grate. Ely believed that John, though a madman, had had in many ways a better grasp of reality than did his skeptical brother Ben.[10]

Ely's *Journal*, published in 1812, was both acclaimed as a portrait of piety and benevolence and criticized for its indiscreet references to prostitution. It was republished in London the following year, and friends urged him to write a second volume, which appeared in 1815. During the three years the young minister was making his exhausting rounds of the Almshouse and Hospital, he also published his volume of poetry, a fund-raising sermon, and the *Contrast*, a theological tome that would become notorious. *William and Ellen... with Other Poetical Works of an American* was published anonymously, but Ely's authorship was known. Ely wrote that he was willing to risk having literary critics call him "a miserable poetaster" if sales of the book would help raise money for charity: "The intention of the writer will certainly be commended by those who may not applaud his verses." Readers did not applaud. An extravagantly sarcastic sixteen-page pamphlet hailed Ely as an "exalted genius [who] could immortalize the memory of a toad." An opponent in the later church controversies included *William and Ellen* in his brief against Ely's character, condemning the "lascivious tendency" of the verse. This antagonist also disparaged Ely's *Sermon for the Rich to Buy, That They May Benefit Themselves and the Poor*. The sermon, sold to help support the Almshouse mission and featuring the deathbed conversion of a deist in the city hospital, argued that it was every Christian's duty to share "the burden of diffusing the knowledge of Jesus" through preaching and print, but the publication was censured for its "bold, biting, and imprudent" criticism of "Physicians, Lawyers, and Rich men."[11]

Ely's *Contrast*, however, was his "original sin" according to his opponents. It was a strange work of theological criticism through textual collage, a manifesto blamed for bitterly dividing whole presbyteries in New York and Philadelphia. Even more than his Almshouse *Journal* it made him a "public man" and probably helped secure him his honorary doctorate. The book is not a contrast of Christian faith and skeptical infidelity but an exercise of heresy-hunting and boundary-drawing within Calvinism. Still, it not only blamed prominent theologians for gross heterodoxy but said that they had (inadvertently) imbibed styles of argument from deists and other infidels that could undermine the theological foundations of faith. The debate concerned fundamental questions about moral agency that were directly relevant to the work of revivalism and reform.[12]

Ely believed that popular philosophical attitudes in America were being pulled in opposite directions. On one side were those who overemphasized human free will. On the other were those who overstressed either God's sovereignty or a natural deterministic universe to such an extent that a person was reduced to a mere object being moved by forces beyond his or her control. Within Protestantism, this spectrum placed Arminians (New England Unitarians and other Liberals, Methodists, and Free Will Baptists) on the left, giving too much leash to the self, and the New Divinity followers of Jonathan Edwards and other hyper-Calvinists on the right, inclining too far toward fatalism. Throughout his career, Ely believed that the drift toward fatalism was the greater danger—both for its kinship to mechanistic, atheistic philosophies and because it made people passive as they faced moral challenges and considered their spiritual lives. The New Divinity—especially the branch following Edwards's student Samuel Hopkins (the Hopkinsians)—claimed to be reforming Calvinism and making it more philosophically consistent. In the *Contrast* and later writings, Ely argued that Calvinism properly understood was the sensible and scriptural mean between the Arminian and fatalist extremes. But the increasingly influential Hopkinsians were, under the sign of Calvinism, he believed, in fact destroying it.[13]

The idea for Ely's *Contrast between Calvinism and Hopkinsianism* emerged shortly after the Rev. Gardiner Spring, a former Yale roommate of Ely's and the son of the New Divinity theologian Samuel Spring, was called to the pulpit of the Brick Presbyterian Church in New York City in the summer of 1810. Old Calvinist members of the presbytery were concerned with what sounded like Hopkinsian sentiments in Spring's preaching and encouraged Ely to write some articles comparing standard Calvinism to Hopkinsian innovations that might be placed in the *Christian Magazine*. They continued to support the project as it grew instead into a 280-page book. To damn the Hopkinsians out of their own mouths, Ely set out, in parallel columns, excerpts from Calvin and other orthodox statements and creeds on various theological topics alongside excerpts from Hopkins and other New Divinity writers. The twelfth chapter put columns of Calvinist and Hopkinsian quotations in a broader theological context by placing them next to columns of texts summarizing other "heresies": Universalism, Arminianism, Arianism, Sabellianism, Socinianism and Deism. Long footnotes and chapter endnotes gave the author the opportunity to write mini-essays of critical commentary. Ely wrote one of the essays as a Hopkinsian sermon, asking the reader to imagine the footnotes as expressing the reactions that a "sensible Scotchman" whispers to himself during the sermon's delivery. Two other chapter appendices were written as dialogues between an Arminian, a Hopkinsian, and a Calvinist—characters who pause to dine, smoke, and sometimes nap. The multiplication of characters and voices, along with the formal and typographical complexity, bewildered some readers, but the overall point was clear: the Hopkinsian system was "repugnant" to the Presbyterian confession of faith.[14]

Gardiner Spring, who read the *Contrast* in manuscript, was furious, and he warned Ely that if he published it he would "get a *drubbing*," adding that "if no body else gives it to you, I will." Spring was as good as his word. Two churches—the Third Presbyterian (Pine Street) Church in Philadelphia and the Rutgers Street Church in New York City—were interested in having Ely as their pastor, but a few ministers and elders in each presbytery, apparently egged on and aided by Spring, blocked the process, causing bitter battles that dragged on for over a year. Ely's opponents filed complaints about his writings (indiscreet! polemical! divisive!) while supporters offered testimonials to his character (pious! benevolent! orthodox!). Rumors spread suggesting that Ely visited prostitutes to do more than evangelize. His enemies instead latched onto claims that he had lied in letters to the Philadelphia church, and they filed charges in the New York Presbytery. Ely's trial, where he felt that he was fighting for his ministerial life, was held on January 26–29, 1814, with a bitter Gardiner Spring acting as chief prosecutor. The case against Ely collapsed, and he was acquitted. He was finally installed over his Philadelphia congregation in September, but the theological divisions and personal animosities that the *Contrast* helped to enflame would remain. He had in fact brought to the surface disputes between what would come to be called the Old School conservatives and the New School that had been influenced by New England Congregationalism, disputes that would be a primary cause of the schism of the national Presbyterian Church in 1837–38.[15]

Ely knew very well that the challenge of Hopkinsianism was not merely a matter of petty ecclesiastical politics or of philosophical abstractions being batted back and forth like badminton birdies among theologians. Voiced from dozens of pulpits throughout the Northeast, New Divinity innovations were shaping churchgoers' language and thus Christian practice and experience. Presbyterians and Congregationalists calling themselves Calvinist and inspired by Jonathan Edwards had unwittingly adopted arguments from deists and materialists that stripped human beings of their moral agency and confused thinking about how willful acts were sinful or virtuous, he believed. Ely himself had nearly been led astray by the heady philosophizing of the Edwardsean epigoni while he was in college, but paternal advice from Yale president Timothy Dwight (a grandson of the great Edwards) set him straight. Ely had also seen aspects of the dangerous theology translated into practice by his own father, a stark example of the experiential effects of theological convictions. Although Zebulon had held his own Yale president, Ezra Stiles, in very high regard (hence the name of Zebulon's firstborn son), and Stiles had been an even sharper critic of the Hopkinsians than Dwight, important New Divinity ideas inflected Zebulon's theology and religious experience. The main reason Ezra published extracts from his father's private spiritual journals in 1825, a year after Zebulon's death, was as a testimonial to his piety. Yet the *Memoirs of the Rev. Zebulon Ely* also usefully displayed an unnecessarily fraught religious psychology shaped by Hopkinsian teaching. The disputes within Calvinism over the nature of free agency and authentic religious affections that had helped launch Ezra's career and would contribute to schism in his church had been internalized by his father, producing psychological turmoil and physical pain that had lasted for decades.[16]

Born in 1759, Zebulon had attended Yale during the American Revolution. Having almost drowned while swimming in the summer of 1778, and then seeing friends and relatives die of "contagious distemper" in early 1779, he began seriously reflecting on the state of his soul. Another near-drowning during a riding accident, and getting shot at in a skirmish with the British when they marched on New Haven on July 5, 1779, only deepened his convictions. He decided that the real "glorious freedom," the true "cause worth fighting for, [and] a liberty worth defending" was to "live above the world" in devotion to Christ. He vowed to turn away from the vanity and vices of polite company. His despair at being separated from God and his remorse for enjoying pleasures such as a frivolous sleigh ride with friends were replaced by intense joy as he experienced conversion. His gendered language of spiritual ravishment by his lover, Jesus, "the Bridegroom of souls," is indistinguishable from the effusions of a mystical Methodist like Sarah Jones. Although Ezra never used such heated language to describe his own spiritual experiences, he approved of such a heart-felt faith.[17]

In 1780, Zebulon was licensed to preach, but within a few months he began to experience an affliction that would trouble him the rest of his life—what his son Ezra would describe as nervous headaches brought on by too much study. Zebulon, however, seems to have interpreted the crippling pain as God's punishment for his pride. Year after year, he strove to preach with the right "temper"—not seeking applause, not with thoughts of his own reputation, but feeling God's love and conveying it to his congregation. He repeatedly resolved to "preach only when I annihilate myself and am swallowed up in my subject. But I too often hide my subject behind myself; I desire to hide myself behind my subject." He agonized over the duty to set aside the "amazing love of that idol self." He prodded and probed his true motives. Was he preaching primarily for the money to support his family? If so, it was his duty to resign. Was he softening God's message to sinners to avoid offending people? If so, he deserved damnation. He relentlessly critiqued his pulpit performances. On December 18, 1782, for example, he thanked God for giving him the power "to speak with pertinency, freedom, and enlargement" but blamed himself for his lack of enough "humility and heart-melting compassion toward sinners." Thirty-eight years later, he was still feeling unqualified for ministerial work and wondering whether he should quit.[18]

Ezra described his father as a Calvinist who rejected the major doctrines of Samuel Hopkins but nonetheless moved back and forth in his studies between the Old and the New Divinity. Zebulon seemed to illustrate what Ezra in the *Contrast* and later works described as spiritual and psychological impediments created by flawed modes of religious conception. Hopkins, developing ideas from his mentor Edwards, taught that true holiness was disinterested love to "being in general"—which sounded to critics like an impossibly pure, self-annihilating affection toward an abstraction. Self-interest was sin, Hopkins taught, and all sin was rooted in self-love. Hopkins notoriously wrote that the truly holy person should even be willing to suffer eternal damnation if doing so would serve the glory of God. Ezra had seen such a warped desire in the New York City Hospital's insanity ward, with John the former infidel. Hopkins's critics, the younger Ely among them, answered that self-interest need not be opposed to holy affections and equated to sinful selfishness. And even when self-interest did dip toward selfishness, it did not necessarily destroy everything positive in a moral act taken as a whole. A preacher could do God's work and still appreciate that his salary put food on his table. True Calvinists, Ely insisted, understood that humans were complex beings and that their motives for action were almost always mixed. Selfishness mingled with self-denial, and affections rarely resembled "the pure stream." A Christian could recognize his imperfections but still be confident that he was growing in grace. Zebulon's relentless quest to annihilate self in the pulpit was misguided perfectionism.[19]

In a variety of publications, Ely elaborated his Old Calvinist notions of an enlightened Christian agency that was neither a self-annihilating disinterested benevolence nor a godless self-determination. His *Ten Sermons on Faith* (1816), essays in his *Quarterly Theological Review* (1818–19), *Conversations on the Science of the Human Mind* (1819), and *Synopsis of Didactic Theology* (1822) featured enlightened Christian agency in a variety of formats. So did his curious *Retrospective Theology* (1825), a fantasy in which Ely imagines himself visiting heaven and hell and chatting with theologians and thinkers—including Samuel Hopkins—who now see the truth clearly and admit the mistakes they made when alive on earth. As Ely explained to a correspondent to his religious newspaper in 1830, both of these propositions are true: "*that man is a free agent* and *that God foreordains every event.*" Difficulties arise when we try to logically reconcile the two. That a man is an agent—a doer of his own deeds, the efficient cause of his own actions—is confirmed by his own consciousness, the response of other people, and the Bible. That he is a free agent, with no physical constraints on his will (with some limitations) is similarly confirmed. Materialist infidels—and Ely mentioned Robert Owen and Abner Kneeland specifically—denied this, turning man into a mere piece of nature's machinery. All too similarly, Hopkinsians made God the only real agent in the universe. Arminians and other Liberals went to the other extreme and thought that a person could freely choose to save him- or herself without the influences of the Holy Spirit. The true way to reconcile human free will and God's predetermination, Ely argued, was to understand that some of the events God preordained were the free acts of human agents. More important to how people lived and made sense of their lives, though, was to understand that God dealt with humans not as passive objects but as intelligent agents—not as a physical force causing them to act but as a moral governor.[20]

Properly discerning the character of human free agency and God's moral action led, Ely contended, to clearer conceptions of both Christian conversion and rational enlightenment. As a good Calvinist, Ely argued—with an arresting image—that a person without first being regenerated by the Holy Spirit could no more perform a truly holy act and please God than a dead body floating in the Niagara River could prevent itself from being washed over the falls. But unlike New Divinity and other enthusiastic evangelicals, he taught that the new birth of conversion did not supply any new bias to the soul, essence to the heart, or disposition to the will, or bestow new faculties of perception. Following an intellectualist tradition with a long lineage in theology and moral philosophy, Ely held that the Holy Spirit first enlightened the understanding, convincing the mind by offering clear views of the truth; this apprehension of truth then kindled holy emotions, and both together motivated virtuous volitions. Real faith was true belief, which excited holy feelings and directed moral practice. Sounding like many other moderate Calvinists, including his mentor Timothy Dwight, Ely wrote that the Holy Spirit usually did this illuminating work by employing the normal "means of grace"—public worship, education, conversation, preaching, and, in recent centuries, the diffusion of Christian knowledge through print. Could an unconverted person, then, come to right views of God and of her own spiritual predicament simply by studying the Bible, reading religious tracts, and listening to sermons, but without a divine and supernatural lightning strike by the Spirit? She could not convert herself, Ely answered, tapping another long tradition in Protestantism, but she could enlighten herself through study and prepare herself for conversion through worship and prayer. Moreover, in a Christian culture, the Holy Spirit was already at work in all the ordinary means of enlightenment—in every sermon, religious meeting, and Christian pamphlet or book.[21]

Such conceptions, Ely believed, motivated and energized Christian action. They empowered the new voluntary associations for moral reform and evangelical outreach. Ely's perspective was similar to that of Jedidiah Morse and Lyman Beecher (two other Dwight allies) and the leaders of the Massachusetts Society for Promoting Christian Knowledge, whose institutional innovations would be copied by national organizations. The New England Congregationalist proponents of benevolent association and interdenominational activism, however, tried to mute differences between Old Calvinism and Hopkinsianism to maintain a united front against the Liberals who were drifting toward Unitarianism. Ely, in an effort to promote moral reform projects and shore up Calvinist orthodoxy within the Presbyterian Church, exacerbated divisions. New Divinity men would deny that their teaching inclined toward fatalism and impeded Christian social activism—Hopkins had been a noted antislavery agitator, after all. But Ely articulated a brand of Calvinism that was on the ascendant in mid-Atlantic Presbyterianism: it stayed close to the formulas of the Westminster Confession of Faith, sidestepped the philosophical tangles of Edwardsean metaphysics, and preferred the plain language of Scottish Common Sense Realism. In Philadelphia Ely would become a member of a society supporting indigent widows, an agent for Sunday schools, a preacher in the state prison, and a major benefactor to a medical college, among other philanthropic activities. More broadly, both the "center-left" philosophical positioning of Presbyterian activists like Ely and their participation in interdenominational reform societies placed them in a quickening American Protestant reform movement with Arminians, quasi-Arminians, crypto-Arminians, and softening Calvinists who all valorized the free-agent American citizen under God the Moral Governor.[22]

Ely's broadly shared notion that Christianity was grounded in a person's intellectual faculties, which were enlightened through the ordinary means of disseminating the Word, put a premium on the diffusion of print. And in the years of his ministry, the exponential growth and transformation of religious publishing was a wonder to behold. New national organizations such as the American Bible Society (founded in 1816) and the American Tract Society (1825) pioneered new modes of centralized production, used new technologies (stereotyped plates, papermaking machines, and steam-powered presses), and partnered with local auxiliaries for distribution. The American Bible Society was publishing a hundred thousand Bibles annually by 1819. The American Tract Society produced more than thirty-two million tracts in its first decade; in 1827 it also started publishing religious books, and between 1829 and 1831 its publications were reaching five million Americans annually. Between 1815 and 1830, too, seventy-six weekly religious newspapers were established, and by the latter date four hundred thousand circulated weekly in the United States. Sixty-two journals in 1830 also promoted the work of various voluntary societies for social and moral reform.[23]

Ely's participation in this dynamic evangelical print cultural reached new heights when in 1829 he became the editor of the *Philadelphian*, a weekly religious newspaper. The *Philadelphian*, he explained proudly to his readers, was a direct descendant of the first religious weekly in the United States, John W. Scott's *Religious Remembrancer*, begun in 1813. The notion of a weekly religious newspaper had seemed laughable at first, but the *Remembrancer* "practically demonstrated that religious intelligence may be diffused through the instrumentality of the mail, at a cheap rate, and as extensively as political news." By the time Ely took over as editor, the *Philadelphian* was part of a rapidly growing national network. On its own it had only a regional distribution: Ely listed eighty-eight agents in thirteen states and territories, but well over half of them were in Pennsylvania. The paper had a less extensive circulation than a competing

Philadelphia Presbyterian weekly, the *Presbyterian*, edited by the Rev. John Burtt, which had over two hundred agents in twenty-two states, territories, and Canadian provinces (three-quarters of them in Pennsylvania, New Jersey, New York, or Ohio). Ely's paper had about the same geographical reach but probably fewer readers than David Nelson's monthly *Calvinist Magazine*, published out of little Rogersville, Tennessee, which had 146 agents in thirteen states and territories, half of them in Kentucky and Tennessee. But all of these evangelical periodicals participated in networks where editors exchanged papers and reprinted each other's stories. Ely listed thirty-eight papers in his evangelical network stretching from Upper Canada to Georgia and as far west as Indiana. The list included the Rochester, New York, *Observer*, a champion of the Sabbatarian movement; Richmond, Virginia's *Southern Religious Telegraph*, a scourge of infidelity in the Old Dominion; the *Cherokee Phoenix and Indian's Advocate*, published in English and Cherokee; and the *Columbian Star and Christian Index*, which was published by the Baptist Church in Philadelphia but circulated more extensively among Southern Baptists than any other paper. Two of the most important papers were published in New York City: the Methodists' *Christian Advocate*, which printed twenty thousand copies weekly, and the *New York Observer*, a paper that provided "a large portion of the religious intelligence which is circulated through our country." The *Philadelphian*, Ely wrote, joined with these other evangelical newspapers "in diffusing the light of divine truth, and promoting the reformation and salvation of our fallen race." The editor knew, too, that divine truth would not be diffused unless the papers appealed to popular tastes and did not just have pages filled with sermons: "We must have a little life; a little sprightliness; some anecdotes; some news; some controversy about important doctrinal differences; something about all world's, and every man's concerns, or we cannot cause our sheet to circulate."[24]

The dissemination of Christian enlightenment through print was part of a larger project: the Christianization of America and the conversion of the world, a mission fueled by millennialist fervor to hasten the coming of the Kingdom of God on earth. The *Philadelphian*'s reports from Bible, tract, African colonization, domestic and foreign mission, education, temperance, prison reform, Sunday school, and Magdalen societies; the accounts of church revivals and camp meetings; the discussions of free agency and God's power; the satires of skeptical infidelity and anecdotes of Christian piety; even the regular "Annals of Human Depravity" column, noting sensational crimes—all were dedicated to this end. An article published in 1830 entitled "The Future Destinies of America, as Affected by the Doings of the Present Generation" argued that the first three decades of the nineteenth century had been unlike any preceding era because Christians, convinced that the prophesied millennial age was rapidly approaching, had labored to convert the world. The global challenge was not a small one:

a few weeks before, the paper had run a piece on the "Obstacles to the Diffusion of Christianity," estimating that only 388 million of the world's 737 million people lived under "wholesome Christian laws," and merely 194 million of those were in Protestant nations. Furthermore, living under Christian laws or even being nominal members of a church, the author of "Future Destinies" pointed out, did not make people truly Christian: of the 5 million adults in the United States (of a total population of 12 million), probably only a million were truly pious. The writer estimated that in the year 2000, the U.S. population could reach 1 billion, and if current trends continued, the number of real Christians would be overwhelmed by the teeming masses of American sinners. Despite the explosion of evangelical energy evident by 1830 in the diffusion of Christian knowledge and the proliferation of reform societies, the church, facing the powerful enemies of infidelity ("undisguised blasphemy") and popery ("abject superstition"), remained divided and weak, the writer lamented. There was work to be done.[25]

In his own statistical breakdowns of American church affiliation, Ely was more content to glide over the distinction between real and nominal Christians. He diplomatically divided over half the population equally among the largest Protestant denominations, assigning 2,194,620 people each to the Baptists, Presbyterians, and Methodists. Other Americans were sorted into twenty-two other denominations, from Orthodox Congregational (800,000) through Lutheran and Roman Catholic (700,000 each) to the smaller sects (Shakers, New Jerusalem, and Six Principle Baptists, each at or a bit under 6,000). Ely's estimates, which assumed a thousand hearers for every minister when no better information was available, left only 542,740 citizens in the "Deists, Atheists, Nothingarians" category. He noted that some would find his estimate of infidels far too low, but he argued that few people were willing to state openly that they were not affiliated in some sense to one religious society or another. He certainly recognized infidelity to be a bigger problem than such numbers would indicate. Yet where others would condemn the hypocrisy of the merely nominal Christians and crypto-skeptics, Ely saw the opportunity for full conversion. Aside from the militant infidels, who were probably hopeless cases, the rest acknowledged the benefits of living in a Christian culture and were still open to the work of the Holy Spirit, which operated through the activities and experiences of everyday life and especially through the printed means of Christian enlightenment. "Infidelity in this region of our country has revived of late, and it exerts itself with astonishing malignity and power," Ely wrote in 1832. "It is now very prevalent among the ignorant, young apprentices, mechanics, and laboring people of our cities, and the dissolute sons of rich men. Infidelity has availed itself of the periodical press, and by that same powerful agent it must be exterminated. Next to the preaching of the gospel, prayer, and the religious government of families, I apprehend that religious newspapers are the most extensive and effective means of doing good.... If political newspapers can revolutionize governments, pull down systems of tyranny, and defend and establish the cause of liberty; weekly papers, well edited, devoted to the best interests of the Redeemer's kingdom may defeat infidelity, destroy popery and prelacy, prevent encroachments upon Christian liberty, expose to merited disapprobation heretics and schismatics, encourage the feebleminded, awaken the slumbering energies of the saints, and prove the means of illumination, conversion, and edification in holiness to millions of sinners. It is by these papers, pre-eminently, that knowledge is to run to and fro, until it shall fill the earth."[26]

Ely was a Christian soldier on the battleground of American enlightenment. In the late 1820s, however, his battle spilled over into the territory of electoral politics as well, and he became a notable—or notorious—national figure both within and outside evangelical circles with his call for "a Christian party in politics." The central idea—that Christian voters should elect men of good Christian character—had been preached by New England Election Day ministers like his father for nearly two centuries. But while other prominent Protestant ministers in the first quarter of the nineteenth century, such as Lyman Beecher or the Rhode Island Baptist Francis Wayland, preached a vaguer Christian political morality because they worried about ministers appearing too partisan, Ely, characteristically, did not mince words. He had published complaints about the muted role of religion in national politics as early as 1818. "Surely, our Presidents might have intimated their knowledge of the person and authority of the Son of God; and might have spoken respectfully, in some of their proclamations and messages to Congress, without picking the pocket of a Jew, or breaking the neck of a Socinian, or invading the conscience of an infidel," he wrote. Every monument to representative institutions in the United States, he declared, should be carved with an inscription: "THE RELIGION OF THE REDEEMER IS THE ONLY STEDFAST BASIS OF THAT MORALITY ON WHICH REPUBLICS ARE FOUNDED." On Election Day, he continued, anticipating the statements that would become so controversial, Christians should vote exclusively for Christians, Jews could vote for Jews, and infidels for infidels, and then the majority would rule. These remarks in 1818, however, appeared in his *Quarterly Theological Review*, which could not have had a very extensive circulation. Ely's *Duty of Christian Freemen to Elect Christian Rulers*, a sermon delivered on the Fourth of July, 1827, was published in the *Philadelphian*, then excerpted by other papers in the evangelical network, and quickly drew notice and commentary in the secular press.[27]

It was the duty of every member of "this Christian nation," Ely argued in that sermon, to honor Jesus Christ. He tried to make it clear that he was not calling for a religious test oath to be added to the U.S. Constitution, or for the state officially to establish "any one religious sect" by civil law. However, although the constitution would allow "Pagans, Socinians, Mussulmen, Deists, the opponents of Christianity" to hold office, God would not approve. "God, my hearers, requires a Christian faith, a Christian profession, and a Christian practice of all our public men; and we as Christian citizens ought, by the publication of our opinions, to require the same." Christian voters had the constitutional right to vote for Christians and the religious duty to do so. Therefore, Ely proposed "a new sort of union, or, if you please, *a Christian party in politics.*" As he would repeatedly try to clarify in the years ahead, he did not mean an actual political organization. His Christian "party" would have no leader but Christ, no platform but the Bible, and no structure beyond an "association of kindred minds." When in the spring of 1829 there was a call for a meeting in New York State to discuss the formation of an actual organization, Ely declined to attend and discouraged the idea.[28]

His sermon called instead for the members of the four largest Christian denominations in the United States—the Presbyterians, Baptists, Methodists, and Congregationalists—to resolve only to vote for professing Christians. If they did so, "our country would never be dishonored with an *avowed infidel* in her national cabinet or capitol." He boasted of the strength of his own church: "The Presbyterians alone could bring *half a million of electors* into the field, in opposition to any known advocate of Deism, Socinianism, or any species of avowed hostility to the truth of Christianity." Ely's interdenominational coalition, which he thought would also include members of the German churches, the Dutch Reformed Church, and Episcopalians, would be an imagined national community of Protestants acting as a moral majority whenever they were asked to cast their votes. Denominational attachments would not be erased; Ely freely confessed that he would prefer to elect a fellow Presbyterian rather than a Baptist, and he expected Baptists to have the opposite preference. But the important point was that together they would always support a candidate "of any one of the truly Christian sects, to any man destitute of religious principle and morality." The category of the "truly Christian" pointedly excluded Unitarians and Universalists, who were classed with the skeptical infidels, and, of course, the Catholics.[29]

Because Ely's sermon circulated at the same time that his comments in favor of Andrew Jackson appeared in the press, Ely was denounced as having crossed the line into blatant partisanship. His *Duty of Christian Freeman* did not mention Jackson, but he had assured readers of the *Philadelphian* that the general was a friend and supporter of Christianity, and lauded his character from the pulpit in the summer of 1827. When challenged, Ely published excerpts from some private letters he had received from Jackson, whom he had known personally for several years, containing the general's praise for religious liberty in America and indicating his personal preference for his mother's Presbyterianism. In an appendix to the republication of the July Fourth sermon in 1828, Ely testified to the Baptist piety of Mrs. Jackson as well. In September of that year, Ely preached a sermon that lashed President John Quincy Adams for flagrantly violating the Sabbath: after worshipping in his "Socinian temple," the president had mounted his horse and had ridden forty miles. A year later, with Jackson in the White House, Ely was still at center stage: the Presbyterian minister conveyed the rumors about the sexual immorality of Margaret Eaton, the wife of Secretary of War John Henry Eaton who was being shunned by Washington society, to the president; Mrs. Eaton visited Ely's church and confronted the minister directly; and Ely was present at the dramatic cabinet meeting where a furious Jackson defended Eaton's honor. The scandal helped confirm the fears of Jackson's critics that the general would try to rule the nation like a Turkish "Grand Seignor" and that Ely would be his "Chief Mufti."[30]

Much more disturbing than Ely's personal ties to Jackson, however, were the worries that Ely's call for a Christian party in politics revealed the plans of Presbyterians and other like-minded reformist evangelicals to unite the powers of church and state. Alarmed writers in the press were convinced—or wanted to score points by convincing their readers—that Ely had revealed a much broader conspiracy. A "Rhode-Islander" wrote to his local paper to warn other freemen of this threat to liberty. An angry citizen sent a letter to Ely at the *Philadelphian*, subsequently reprinted in other papers, charging him with planning a "conspiracy on the liberties" of Americans and threatening "avenging steel" to such a "vile traitor of thy God and country." The *Universalist Magazine* argued that Ely's indiscreet comments unmasked all the reformers' mission, Bible, Sunday school, and other societies as nothing more than "instruments of their ambitious purposes." The writer went on to expose what he said were the real desires of Ely and his brethren: destroy existing political parties, take over the government, use the sale of western lands to fund the clergy, impose a national creed, and prevent the expression of contrary religious opinions.[31]

Ely defended himself by insisting that he was a champion of both religious liberty and an unfettered public sphere of open discussion and debate. He claimed nothing more for Christians than what the Constitution secured for believers and nonbelievers alike: "the liberty of thinking for themselves, of publishing their opinions, and of acting in conformity with them, in any such manner as will not interfere with the rights of others." But to relegate Christianity to a private opinion that had to be kept out of politics and public life was, in effect, to make an establishment of skeptical infidelity. In fact, he contended, Christians were already being discriminated against. Christian ministers were not allowed to hold public office in New York, for example, or be regents of its university. A conscientious Christian could not work for the post office, even as a stage driver, because he would be forced to work on the Sabbath and violate the Fourth Commandment. Rather than the union of church and state, have we not reason to fear, Ely asked, "the *union of the State and Infidelity*, and the proscription of all pious people of the Christian order?" Yet in addition to arguing that the civil government could neither prohibit nor enjoin any religion, Ely contended that the United States was a Christian nation, and not just because Christians could sustain majorities at the polls. The Constitution, including the First Amendment's prohibition of religious establishment, according to this line of thinking, presupposed Christianity as already existing in the hearts and habits of the people. Article 1, Section 7 closed the government on the Christian Sabbath, and nine of the thirteen states in 1789 had publicly recognized Christianity in their state constitutions. Although the U.S. Constitution did not explicitly acknowledge the authority of Jesus Christ, which was a flaw in the document, it did so implicitly—or so argued a Presbyterian sermon that Ely published in the *Philadelphian* and endorsed.[32]

Ely's language about a Christian party in politics came to symbolize concerns that many had about the growing power of national, interdenominational associations for benevolent reform. These concerns were voiced not just by cantankerous old skeptics like Thomas Cooper, who was dragged before a tribunal for allegedly weakening the religious faith of South Carolina College students, or a bitter anticlerical writer like Anne Royall, who was prosecuted as a common scold, or vocal freethinkers like Frances Wright, Robert Dale Owen, and Abner Kneeland, who were pilloried repeatedly in the press, or the Unitarians and Universalists that Ely castigated as "anti-Christians" and the equivalent of infidels. Hicksite Quakers, too, who divided Philadelphia Quakerism in 1827, denounced the benevolent reform associations. But even believers that Ely would have considered orthodox enough for his "Christian party" protested. Antimission Baptists and Methodists bristled at Presbyterian elitism; hyper-Calvinists and Campbellites distrusted the resort to human means, political or institutional. Lutheran and German Reformed rallies in the late 1820s and early 1830s condemned the political involvement of clerical activists along with the worldly spirit displayed by evangelical reformers in their relentless fund-raising, publication, institution-building, and overheated revivalism. German publications warned of a clerical aristocracy, particularly Presbyterian, threatening religious liberty, and a Berks County, Pennsylvania, rally mentioned Ely in particular. Ely was not just a symbol of clerical despotism in his own state: resolutions by a Baptist society in New Hampshire decrying the threatened calamity of church and state union quoted him at length. Ely's Presbyterians gave him a rousing vote of confidence when the General Assembly elected him as moderator, its highest office, in 1828. But his neighbors were less enthusiastic: Philadelphians at an Anti-Sabbatarian public meeting on February 15, 1830, in the courthouse nine blocks from Ely's mansion hooted against Presbyterian ministers, with one speaker "bending a brawny arm" and shouting, "If Dr. Ely is among ye, turn him out!"[33]

In the backlash against the aggressive benevolent reforms that were beginning to smell like a Christian political party dangerously threatening the separation of church and state, two causes that Ely and other reformers championed went down to defeat: the effort of the interdenominational American Sunday School Union to be incorporated in Pennsylvania and the campaign to stop the federal government from moving the mail on Sundays. In February 1828, when the bill to incorporate the Sunday School Union was pending before the Pennsylvania State Senate, a handbill entitled "Sunday School Union, or Union of Church and State" was placed on all the senators' desks. The handbill contained excerpts from the ASSU's annual report, which spoke of being "dictators to the consciences" of their students, of organizing a "disciplined army" of churches, and of looking forward to a time when "the political power of our country will be in the hands of men whose characters have been formed under the influence of Sabbath schools." The handbill also presented excerpts from Ely's July Fourth sermon, with inflammatory phrases italicized. When the Senate debated the bill, Senator Stephen Duncan made a long speech that dismissed worries about Ely's "indiscreet zeal" and regarded the threat of ecclesiastical tyranny as a "phantom" while praising the ASSU's efforts to "enlighten the minds of thousands" through "the diffusion of knowledge." The successful opponents to the memorial, however, led by Senator John Hare Powel, condemned the "machinations" of blind zealots of orthodoxy who were scheming for political power. Powel's long speech contained more excerpts from the notorious sermon by that "Machiavellian politician" Ely to underline the point.[34]

The battle lines between those who feared a union of church and state and those who, like Ely, condemned the state's de facto endorsement of infidelity were similarly drawn in the nationwide furor over the Sunday mails. The General Union for Promoting the Observance of the Christian Sabbath was formed in May 1828, with auxiliary chapters quickly springing up throughout the states (Ely preached in support of chapters in Pennsylvania). The General Union was careful to declare itself to be a nonpartisan, nonecclesiastical, noncoercive reform organization, and it tried to mask the prominent role of clergymen such as Lyman Beecher within it. In the petitions that flooded Congress to stop the mail and close post offices on Sundays, Sabbatarians argued on both religious and political grounds. The Christian Sabbath was a divine institution, and every nation was obliged to keep it holy, they contended. Moreover, a virtuous citizenry was essential to a republic, and Sabbath institutions—church services and Sunday schools—were necessary to inculcate that civic morality, whatever other spiritual functions they performed. Even if the U.S. government could not explicitly promote Christian worship, it should not actively trample the people's religious obligation to avoid unnecessary Sabbath labor, nor should it disturb the free exercise of religion by the majority of its citizens by keeping post offices—popular gathering places of worldly men—open and having noisy stagecoaches rattling through town during church services. By campaigning and petitioning Congress, reformers maintained, they were asserting their political rights and religious duties. But Anti-Sabbatarian petitions and the blisteringly anticlerical reports by Senator Richard M. Johnson in 1829 and 1830 vehemently decried government interference in religion (the state deciding which day of the week should be the Sabbath and how it should be observed) and religious interference with government (despotic religious parties bending civil institutions to their will). After a Senate debate in May 1830, the bill to stop the Sunday mail was tabled. The petition movement had failed, but the debate continued in the press, including Ely's *Philadelphian*, which published an article placing Senator Johnson in league with Robert Owen, Frances Wright, and Thomas Paine. Both sides distorted their opponent's position. Sabbatarians were not conspiring to establish a national church and Anti-Sabbatarians were not doing the work of skeptical infidels in trying to create a godless nation. Yet these caricatures did convey the central terms of debate over the public and political role of American faith.[35]

In the early 1830s, the tectonic plates of American politics began to shift beneath Ely's feet. The mass publicity campaigns and petition drives that the Sabbatarians had pioneered would be taken up by the more radical abolitionists, while Ely maintained a conservative antislavery position as an advocate of African colonization. Many Sabbatarians and other politically engaged reformers joined the Whig Party, while Anti-Sabbatarians tended to become Jacksonian Democrats. Ely himself was deeply troubled when his old friend President Jackson vetoed the Bank Bill, and in the fall of 1832 the press reported that Old Hickory's former Mufti was quietly supporting Henry Clay. The clergyman subsequently told his readers in the *Philadelphian* that he was too busy with religious revivals to even bother to vote in the presidential election of 1832. By 1834, he was offering full-throated denunciations of Jackson's ruinous economic policies and apparent drift toward something like absolute monarchy. Ely was also at the epicenter of an earthquake in ecclesiastical politics. Once again a young minister bearing philosophical-theological innovations from New England arrived to upset the peace of conservative Presbyterianism. That, at least, is how the conservatives saw the problem. This time, however, Ely thought that the new ideas—from the New Haven Theology of Nathaniel William Taylor, brought to the Philadelphia Presbytery by the Rev. Albert Barnes—were philosophical errors but not theological heresies. Moreover, emphasizing the free choice of moral agents, Taylorites tipped Calvinism in an activist Arminian direction rather than toward what Ely still considered to be the paralyzing fatalism of Hopkinsianism and hyper-Calvinism. So when the Philadelphia Presbytery split apart, Ely cast his lot with Barnes and what was emerging as New School Presbyterianism in a schism that anticipated the division of the national church a few years later.[36]

Both church and state seemed blighted. Ely grew restless trying to sow the seeds of Christian enlightenment in the same old well-plowed fields. As his colleague in Calvinist reform Lyman Beecher published broadly circulated lectures against what he called "political atheism" and called for redoubled efforts to Christianize the West, Ely began looking west, too, for the regeneration of American society.[37]

The Cause and Cure of Infidelity

Both Ezra Stiles Ely and Dr. David Nelson believed that a major challenge for Calvinist evangelicals in nineteenth-century America was to articulate a robust conception of enlightened Christian agency that could undergird revivalism and reform. For Ely, this meant getting American Calvinism on the right course by slapping down those theologies that would steer it toward fatalism and the dangerous shoals of religious infidelity. Nelson targeted infidelity itself. Infidelity in the form of the organized and vocal freethought movement that was disseminating skeptical critiques of Christianity was "growing and spreading to an extent the blindness of the Church does not suspect," Nelson observed in the 1820s and '30s. In much of Catholic Europe, the masses were becoming atheist; in Great Britain, "multitudes" were renouncing the Bible. "Is not our own nation walking down the same track?" Furthermore, "in almost every congregation, there are some, more or less imbued with Infidelity, who do not avow it. They are not confirmed skeptics," Nelson conceded, but Satan had suggested "unbelieving doubts" to them. Having once been a skeptical deist himself, Nelson after his conversion felt called to combat this scourge.[38]

David Nelson was born in 1793 near Jonesborough in East Tennessee. His parents were Presbyterians, his father read the Bible aloud for the family twice a day, and an elder brother became a minister. But Nelson drifted away from the faith when, after graduating from Washington College, he went to study medicine with Dr. Ephraim McDowell in Danville, Kentucky. He did not begin what he later described as his descent into infidelity by reading deist tracts, skeptical critiques of religion, or satires of Christianity. He became a "deist" with "moments of doubt whether or not God existed" through the influence of his fellow medical students and other leading men in town. Religious skepticism was part of a genteel masculine style that impressed him in casual conversation. The men he socialized with were "admirers of the French philosophy." There was nothing really deeply philosophical about their discussions, but when they mentioned religion, "their feelings were always awake. They seemed to believe that in disregarding inspiration there was something peculiarly original and lofty. The sparkle of the eye, the curl of the lip, and the tone of the voice, if interpreted, seemed to say that the rest of mankind were contemptible fools, but 'we are not.'" This pose spoke to a quiet yearning that young Nelson recognized in himself, a "longing after the character of *singular intellectual independence*." He came to identify even more closely with such men when he served as a surgeon's mate in the Kentucky militia and then as a surgeon in the Tennessee militia during the War of 1812. Older officers approved of him, praised him, welcomed him to their wine clubs and card parties, and stroked his "self-esteem." He mirrored their attitudes about religion and was content, for a while, to believe, without investigating the matter himself, that great philosophers supported his skeptical creed.[39]

Portrait of the Rev. David Nelson, M.D. A former skeptic, Nelson wrote *The Cause and Cure of Infidelity* in 1837, describing his own conversion and prescribing antidotes he had used with other doubters. Courtesy of the U.S. National Library of Medicine, Digital Collections.

Nelson's disillusionment with infidelity began when he finally sat down to read some deist and skeptical books. In a sense, he would reverse the experience of Benjamin Franklin, who had become a deist after reading—and seeing the weaknesses of—Christian arguments against deism. The man Nelson boarded with had bought at a book auction a copy of Voltaire's *Philosophical Dictionary*, which Nelson, who knew of Voltaire as the "leader of the army of skeptics," began to read. His blood quickly ran cold. The young physician still retained enough biblical literacy to see that the great philosopher's witty criticisms of the scriptures were based on misrepresentations and falsehoods. Voltaire, for example, pointed with a laugh at a verse in Proverbs (23:31) referring to a "glass" of wine as proof that the text had been written much later than claimed because there had been no glass in the age of Solomon. Nelson knew from his reading of history that this was not true, and then confirmed with a little research his suspicion that in any case "glass" was just a poor translation of the original Hebrew word, which meant "cup." Worse, Nelson realized, was that Voltaire himself must have known these facts and was merely trying to manipulate his reader's presumed ignorance. His suspicions aroused, Nelson proceeded to read through the *Philosophical Dictionary* carefully and critically, and discovered that the entire masterwork was built upon such errors and distortions. The next book he read, Thomas Paine's famous *Age of Reason*, was just as bad.[40]

A third volume Nelson tried, Volney's *Ruins of Empires*, was not like Voltaire's *Dictionary* or Paine's screed—it was not a "constant stream of malignant untruth." Nelson found its style "excellent," its manner "captivating," and its two central arguments worth taking seriously. The first was that religions were simply perpetuated through the ordinary means of cultural reproduction: children became Christians, Jews, Muslims, or Pagans if their parents were Christians, Jews, Muslims, or Pagans. This seemed true enough—like father, like son. But the fact that true and false religious doctrines alike could be handed down from generation to generation did not make them all false.[41]

Volney's second argument was that all religions had their sacred texts, prophets, martyrs, and miracles. How, Volney asked, could one be "*expected to decide between various and plausible claims, zealously and tumultuously attested?*" This question had some weight, but Nelson eventually reasoned that in other realms of life we were always having to judge between the real and the counterfeit—when accepting a banknote, for example, or assessing the character of a potential business partner or mate. We are called upon to make such critical judgments in daily life "as our interest is threatened, and in accordance with the thing presented." Why should it be different in religion? In *The Cause and Cure of Infidelity*, Nelson would later tell the story of "a swearing, Sabbath-hating man from New England" whom he had met on the bank of the Illinois River. When Nelson asked the man about Bible precepts, the latter grinned and asked, which Bible?

For the Mormons had one and the Christians another, and how was he to judge between them? Although this man was a sharp horse trader, could detect a counterfeit silver dollar as quickly as a chemist, and was a keen judge of complicated business deals, when it came to making critical judgments in religion he was content to plead ignorance. Nelson insisted, too, that there were ways to test competing religious claims—to evaluate alleged miracles, measure practice against universal ethical standards, and compare the quality of adherents' religious experiences. Volney and the Sabbath-hating man, Nelson would conclude after his conversion, were merely rationalizing their sinful disinclination to accept Christian truth.[42]

Nelson had been put on the road to that conversion when he read *Scott's Family Bible* with "Christian" (i.e., Protestant) commentary in the margins. In the Rev. Thomas Scott's long exegetical footnotes Nelson first observed a dramatic difference in style. The contrast to Voltaire and Paine was jarring. Nelson found in Scott's commentary no "smutty" remarks, "no self-complaisant ridicule, no coxcomical jeerings," no purposeful misrepresentations, no arguments built on falsehoods. "The difference between the two styles and the two modes, is only known to those who have felt the sudden transition from one to the other." More importantly, Scott gave Nelson the interpretive key to unlock the meaning of biblical prophecy. When Scott persuaded him that the beast in the Book of Revelation referred not just to pagan Rome but also to the later Roman Catholic Church, and then he lined up the text's coded predictions against events that had occurred over the subsequent centuries, passages previously obscure suddenly began to make sense within a coherent narrative. Historical facts demonstrated that many of the prophecies had been fulfilled and that, therefore, the text had recorded a foreknowledge that could only be divine. Moreover, the scriptures gave providential meaning to the historical events, placing them within God's larger plan of redemption. History confirmed the truth of the Bible, and the Bible gave meaning to history—to all human history, from the rise and fall of civilizations to the life course of a single young man reading the words in the forests of Tennessee in the second decade of the nineteenth century.[43]

Giving up his lucrative medical practice, Nelson was licensed to preach in 1825. He became something of an eccentric figure, a shabbily dressed revivalist with the fervor of an ancient prophet, too absorbed in the spirit to pay much regard to "earthly interests." He devoted himself especially to seeking out "all sceptics who might be prevailed on to read, and to induce them faithfully to investigate the subject of Christianity." *The Cause and Cure of Infidelity*, first published in 1837 and revised and republished by the American Tract Society in 1841, contains the story of his own journey from skepticism to faith but is even more focused on the lessons he had learned from eighteen years of trying to enlighten other deists, doubters, and scoffers. He wrote it for young people, he said, and for older readers who lacked a higher education, using a "plain every day dialect." Dr. John C. Young, president of Centre College in Kentucky, noted in a preface to the 1841 edition that the book successfully translated "abstruse argument" for a general audience and strikingly presented facts "to arrest the attention of the indifferent and the sceptics." These facts, too, "drawn from history, science and observation," were infused with "an earnestness—a personality—a warm life's blood of reality." The book, Young wrote, seemed particularly well "adapted to the peculiar tastes and condition of our community (especially to many vigorous minds of the West, where the author's life has been chiefly spent)."[44]

The infidelity that Nelson discussed was not an apparition in European books but a malady infecting his neighbors. He met men on the western plains who dismissed the Bible because the geological strata they could see with their own eyes seemed to contradict the scriptural account of Creation. He knew a rich old man in Kentucky who said that the Bible was filled with meaningless jargon, and a tavernkeeper's wife in Tennessee who had picked up the same idea from the smart scoffers who sat at her table. Nelson's own father-in-law, David Deaderick, a deist merchant in East Tennessee, refused to acknowledge that the moral laws he lived by came from Christianity and not from reason. Nelson spoke with a Kentucky businessman who could wield skeptical argument skillfully but was woefully deficient in historical knowledge, and a disbelieving western farmer who resisted the spiritual testimony of his own experience. Dr. Nelson the former physician diagnosed the disease, explained its etiology, and prescribed cures that had been empirically field tested for nearly two decades.[45]

"Infidelity is produced by two causes, acting conjointly," Nelson wrote in the opening lines of the book's first chapter. "The primary or remote cause is man's depravity; the second, or proximate cause, is man's want of knowledge." Dr. Nelson prescribed two cures. A powerful remedy for the ignorance that led to skepticism about Christianity was knowledge—specifically, biblical literacy and historical information that corroborated the text's prophetic claims. But being enlightened by knowledge, being enabled to see the truth, did not always lead to faith. The "*all-powerful*" remedy for the lack of faith was the "*experimental evidence of Christianity*." That is, one not only had to acknowledge the Gospel truth but had to try to live a life of Christian love and obedience. The infidel's skepticism could be overpowered by knowledge, but it would be completely obliterated by the lived experience of faith.[46]

Religious skepticism did not proceed from informed criticism, Nelson argued, but rather from the absence of knowledge and a lack of critical inquiry. Skeptics often remained in ignorance because they deferred to the opinions of people they thought were wiser, not realizing that the learned men who rolled their eyes at Christianity were just as ignorant about religious questions.

In college, young men read Virgil and Horace, Longinus and Cicero, but they neglected serious Bible study and the history of the ancient Near East. Lawyers were especially good at "weighing proof and appreciating argument," but they "float along on the surface of secular schemes and political turmoil, [and] they have little time, they think, for any thing but business." One skeptical lawyer he knew, for example, a respected man who had been elected to Congress, rested his unbelief on a flimsy objection he had picked up from reading Gibbon's *Decline and Fall of the Roman Empire*, which noted that the pagan philosopher Pliny in a discussion of eclipses had failed to corroborate the Gospel account of a dark day at the time of the crucifixion. Physicians, too, were trained to reason from evidence. But Nelson knew several who, on faulty reasoning about the constituent particles of a living organism, considered the resurrection of the body impossible. People who were well educated or even brilliant in other fields often knew or understood little of the Bible. A sharp old Kentuckian Nelson knew might not have complained that many scriptural passages were "unmeaning jargon" if "he had read one fiftieth part as much Bible history, as he had read of political disputes in his newspapers."[47]

Infidels liked to praise reason, but in Nelson's view they failed to see its limitations. Reason was a better tool for explaining truths than for discovering them. A person could immediately understand how gunpowder worked after hearing about the properties of sulfur, charcoal, and potassium nitrate, but it had taken many centuries before it had been discovered. Similarly, "reason assents to the first principles of astronomy, as soon as they are presented. Nothing appears plainer. But reason was long in finding out these truths." Deists like his father-in-law thought of reason as the "*celestial lamp*" that could reveal a good and rational God as well as the path of moral virtue. They failed to realize, Nelson argued, that they had absorbed all these ideas by living in a Christian culture. No one in a Protestant country believed that human sacrifice or self-mutilation or bacchanalian festivals would please God. But in lands without the Bible, where people were left with only the lamp of reason to guide them, such abominable practices were precisely what came to define moral and religious life. Just look at ancient Greece, or contemporary Asia or Africa, Nelson wrote. Furthermore, true enlightenment did not just depend on high literacy rates and the broad circulation of print generally but on the circulation and informed reading of the Bible. It was no coincidence that in those countries "where the Bible had been in the longest and most plentiful circulation, where every class, high and low, are able to read, and do read the volume most commonly, and with most ease, such as England, Scotland, and the United States of America, *there* you will find men most enlightened, and most amiable in demeanor."[48]

Other doubters placed too much reliance on their own common sense. What appeared implausible at first glance or felt counterintuitive at first blush might in fact be demonstrated to be true with more persistent inquiry. A skeptic who doubted the historical narratives in the scriptures because they seemed to defy common sense might as easily doubt that thirteen colonies could defeat the world's greatest power in the American Revolution. In each case, Nelson wrote, the doubter needed to consult historical evidence rather than his common sense. But the turn to common sense as a defense for religious skepticism was often just an excuse for avoiding informing onself of the facts. Nelson told the story of a skeptical merchant he had met: "I have (said he) heard these things spoken of all my life; I have looked through the Bible; I have thought on these things as I rode my horse, as I lay on my bed, as I stood behind my counter, and I cannot believe, because I am unable to understand the subject. Many things in religion seem to contradict my plainest reason." But suppose, Nelson offered, that a plowman had a similar dislike of chemistry. The chemist's recipe for making black ink directs the plowman to mingle "several clear white liquids together," but this "contradict[s] his plainest common sense." How can white liquids make black ink? The chemist's explanation—"alkalis, caloric, affinities, &c"—strikes the plowman as "a mass of confusion, and a jargon of nonsense." The plowman, like the merchant, rejects the claims not after investigating the matter but after merely thinking it over and consulting his common sense.[49]

The cure for this ignorance was knowledge. It might seem odd, Nelson admitted, to speak of vast ignorance blighting a nation where the population was more literate and generally more educated than perhaps any other on the face of the earth, and where newspapers and periodicals and, yes, even Bibles and religious tracts circulated in ever-increasing numbers. There were several reasons why this was so. First, most church members did not recognize the problem. They thought of their unchurched neighbors as "almost Christians," but if they knew of their neighbors' private doubts they would have considered them almost infidels. Moreover, few of the many books that had been published on the evidences of Christianity were in circulation. In an ordinary village such books were hard to find. One or two might be on the local minister's shelf, but they were rarely read. When Christian friends tried to get a skeptic to read one of these books, the unbeliever might read it, but he would then usually report that the subject remained as perplexing as ever. The book might not have addressed the skeptic's particular concerns and in treating others may have just given him more reasons to doubt. The Christians could try again with another book. "The [skeptical] man, perhaps, looks at the book occasionally, and lays it down, takes it up again, and thinks it hard to comprehend—thinks it does not touch the points which perplex him. He lays it down again, the world presses, his business harasses, amusements divert; and after some months, they find he has not read, and they lose all hope in the case." After a few such experiments, Christians, even ministers, would lose confidence that reading such arguments is an effective means of pointing unbelievers toward conversion. But Dr. Nelson argued that these physicians of the soul had administered too small a dose of the remedy. The skeptic needs to be persuaded to read at least six or eight different volumes from a list of twenty-nine titles, a selection presenting a variety of arguments and a broad spectrum of antidotes against the many different poisons of doubt.[50]

Nelson tried to make a strong case for the use of scriptural commentaries, which had been so instrumental in his own conversion. He noted that many people had an aversion to reading the Bible with scholarly annotation, saying they wanted to judge for themselves. They worried that notes attached to Bible passages were written by commentators with their own theological axes to grind; they suspected that any particular scriptural exegesis was not a disinterested aid to comprehension but rather an argument doing battle in a contentious arena of doctrinal dispute. The idea of every person as his or her own Bible interpreter became very powerful in the United States in the first half of the nineteenth century. Interdenominational Bible societies reinforced the principle, in part to avoid sectarian disagreements over the meaning of words like "baptism" or "bishop" but also to signal their confidence in *sola scriptura*. But Nelson declared that this fetishizing of the individual reader with only the Bible in his or her hands was an excuse and a subterfuge disguising the natural tendency toward religious falsehood. Unlike other believers who argued for a kind of epistemological exceptionalism, holding that Christianity offered not only a special kind of knowledge but also a unique way of knowing, Nelson stressed epistemological equivalency. The intellectual aspect of Christianity, he argued, was no different than any other branch of knowledge. "Men do not refuse to read the notes of others on chemistry, astronomy, or philosophy, because writers have disputed here," he wrote. Why not benefit from the labor of others on religious questions, as inquirers did in every other field of inquiry? "An author on geography will tell you more in an hour, than you could explore or measure for a week, should the pride of originality make you decline the assistance of others in this case." The same practice should hold for religion.[51]

Benefiting from the work of a commentator, Nelson was quick to add, did not mean passively accepting all his judgments, no matter how eminent a scholar he might be. Nelson's model was Sir Isaac Newton. It was well known that "Newton would not indulge in wild speculations, and vain conjecture. It is stated in all his astronomical and philosophical researches, every doctrine he advanced was built on fact, and that further than this he would not proceed. He seems to have preserved this feature of his mind whilst writing on prophecy." But even Newton should not be blindly followed. Even the best exegete could offer unsatisfactory explanations of passages. Still, a reader could make use of the commentator's linguistic skills and historical research without automatically accepting the commentary's conclusions. If not the final word on a scriptural verse, a commentary could draw the reader's attention to many things he would not have seen on his own, inspiring more attentive reading and perhaps more research. Biblical commentaries did not replace the reader's own close reading and critical thinking, Nelson argued. They nourished it.[52]

The knowledge remedy worked almost every time, Nelson assured his readers. He claimed that in eighteen years, only two of his many skeptical patients who had persisted through the full course of treatment had not been cured. Though powerful, however, his study regimen could not be a foolproof cure. Even with all the evidence staring them in the face, people could still choose to disbelieve. Because a man had "free agency" and was not "a piece of thinking, necessary mechanism," he could "judge wrong, and choose to his own hurt." And many did so. The problem, after all, was not just ignorance but *willful* ignorance. Although religious inquiry ought to proceed in the same manner as investigations in chemistry, astronomy, or geography, in practice, for most people, there was a crucial difference: the natural inclinations and biases of unconverted men and women actively worked against the reception of divine truth. This resistance—which appeared in ancient times in the Israelites' desire to worship idols, in Christ's time as the inclination to explain away miracles as demonic magic, and in later centuries as a superstitious belief in Catholic priestcraft, and in the modern era was manifested in skeptical infidelity—"exhibits the *fall of man.*" In matters of religion—and only in religion—human beings naturally prefer darkness to enlightenment.[53]

Nelson saw this willful avoidance of facts and passionate antipathy to divine truth in himself and in his skeptical friends. Even when still a skeptical deist, he noticed the strange emotional charge that Christianity produced in skeptics. "If you will sit down by the side of that [skeptical] man who is near the Hotel fire, or at the dining table, or in the stage-coach, and exhort him to be a worshipper of Vishnu, or Siva, or implore him to become a Mohamedan, (being sincere and in earnest we mean,) he will laugh at you." The man will be happy to talk "with more scientific interest"—though with personal "indifference"—on "the different religions of the earth." Yet on the subject of Christianity he responds very differently. His brow will darken, and his eyes will flash with anger. Why this reaction? Skeptics and scoffers who "hissed at the Bible" also seemed impatient if anyone tried to challenge them in an argument. They took on a "lordly look" when the subject came up. "They put on the consequential air of high authority, and with the tone of emphatic decision, they pronounced others more than idiots," even as they revealed that they actually knew very little about either the Bible or ancient history. Nelson, even before he converted, began to suspect that men opposed Christianity not because they had been enlightened by long hours of study but from "a spontaneous and special dislike." Nelson later came to understand that the unconverted man hates God. He is not conscious of this enmity, because he does not hate his own idea of God, which is usually an idealized version of himself. But he hates the actual God, the God of the Bible. "*Men (without knowing it) love darkness rather than light.*"[54]

Some skeptics called themselves free inquirers and imagined themselves on a heroic quest for religious truth, but even those who were sharp thinkers and diligent scholars in other fields of knowledge were afflicted by an intellectual lethargy that prevented any real inquiry into the topic. Their depraved natures weakened any effort to search after the facts that would persuade them. "Many unbelievers desire knowledge on the great subject, but they never undergo the labour of research." This disinclination even seemed to be manifested in their bodies: "Their hands hang down, and their nerves are all unstrung as soon as vigorous and industrious research is proposed." There was another class of people who were inclined to unbelief but did not call themselves infidels or skeptics. They did not bitterly and publicly denounce the Bible and had never bothered to read infidel writers such as Hume, Gibbon, Voltaire, or Paine. But their doubts were "enough to paralyze their energies in seeking conversion," and they were much closer to such infamous Christ-haters than they thought. For Nelson, the doubts themselves seemed less troubling than the paralysis that prevented doubters from doing anything to improve their condition.[55]

The natural bias against Christianity also affected an unconverted person's attention, memory, taste, and judgment. Nelson had experienced some of this himself. He had failed to work hard enough to grasp the meaning of difficult Bible passages as his eyes passed over the words. He had failed to make what later seemed like obvious connections between statements in the text and historical facts he had already learned. Unbelievers also had trouble retaining important biblical facts in memory; they read the verses, but the words just slipped away. Their taste perverted, they found little pleasure in reading the scriptures. Nelson knew literary types who could praise a Greek poem while ignoring the fact that the poet sang of sodomizing young boys, overlook the disgusting habits revealed in Plutarch's *Lives*, and turn a blind eye to Roman cruelty and obscenity, but they sneered at Hebrew literature and grossly exaggerated the failings of the Israelites. The infidels' anti-Christian bias also warped how they weighed evidence. They latched onto any geological observation, for example, that might support the idea of an earth much older than what was described in the Old Testament but dismissed much more powerful facts that, Nelson insisted, supported the Mosaic account. Because of their biased judgment, "the skeptical...will swallow the greatest *absurdities*, they will take down the *wildest incredibilities* on the side of darkness, rather than believe any one plain, simple gospel fact, as related in the New Testament. And of all men on earth, unbelievers have to be the most credulous."[56]

Nelson, however, had a second cure for the malady of infidelity—an "*all-powerful*" one. The best way to convince the plowman who doubted that white liquids could be combined to produce black ink, after all, was not to explain the chemistry but to have him mix the liquids and see for himself. The skeptical merchant needed to stop turning Christian doctrine over and over in his mind as he lay in bed, rode his horse, or stood behind his counter; he needed to "*investigate in reality*" by putting Christian teachings into practice. "Experimental knowledge is the safest and the best in the world," Nelson argued. "The doctrines of the Bible may be known, and their usefulness tested practically." He described "the *experimental* evidence of Christianity" as infallible. "This remedy is indeed invincible. Millions have used it with success, and no one has ever used it in vain." The only reason why there were unbelievers in the world at all was because some people simply chose not to use it. Even those who continued to doubt the truth of the Gospel message should try to live by Christian teachings. "Every man *may become* a Christian. Many will not. Every Christian may have the most satisfactory evidence of *experience*. Many do not try.... No matter who you are, atheist or double atheist, if you bend to each order there written, you will be cured, and your life will be everlasting."[57]

Such passages in *The Cause and Cure of Infidelity* might seem to be reviving old heresies and suggesting that any person could convert him- or herself and earn salvation through the good work of obedience. But there was a Calvinist catch. The person had to obey God in the right way—with the proper feelings in his or her heart. How would those feelings get there? A person cannot move his or her affections at will, cannot choose to love. "*Man cannot feel by simple effort, and by mere resolve.*" The Holy Spirit had to change the carnal heart and implant new feelings there. Still, Nelson makes this act of the Spirit less like a divine and supernatural light that strikes like a lightning bolt and regenerates the heart of the elect and more like a sort of potential energy already dwelling inside almost everyone. The Holy Spirit is there to help even the "confirmed unwavering Bible hater," the deist who still clings to the one truth that the universe had a Creator. The Holy Spirit abandons only committed atheists, but all is not lost even for them if that commitment wavers a bit and they sincerely try to live a life of Christian obedience despite at first still believing in their heart that there is no God. Conversion, Nelson implied, seemed to follow sincere effort as a matter of course. He did not include any discussion of seekers who yearned for grace but lacked any assurance that they had received it, or of self-deluded nominal Christians who thought they loved God and lived pious lives but actually displayed counterfeit religious affections and virtues. If one tried to live a Christian life, Nelson's exhortations suggest, the Holy Spirit would take care of the rest, and regeneration would follow. The important distinction among professing Christians in his view was not between hypocrites and actual saints but between "infant" and "full-grown" Christians. The latter experience God's love and love for God as a nearly continuous "*sensation*"; the former experience divine communion only faintly and sporadically, and in their lives still struggle against the lingering effects of natural depravity—what Nelson called "*Christian stupidity*."[58]

The first part of Nelson's book, on the powerful cure of knowledge and biblical literacy, resembled, in a looser and more colloquial form, the intellectualist morphology of conversion that Ely took pains to delineate theologically and philosophically: a properly enlightened understanding was the necessary (but not sufficient) foundation for true faith; we can only act virtuously if our actions are infused with love, and we can only love properly if we have an accurate conception of what we are loving. Nelson's discussion of the second cure for infidelity—Christian experience—in the second part of the book, however, indicated that virtuous practice could prepare the sinner's heart for saving grace even in the absence of belief. Nelson realized from his own experience that the sinful habits of natural man continued even after the mind had been enlightened. "Physicians say of the body of man, that it may be formed into habits," he wrote. "They say of some intermittent fevers long continued, that the chill returns in accordance with the habits of the system. Many habits of the flesh run on, even when opposed by our enlightened wishes. Habits of infidelity often exist when wishes militate; and after an instructed judgment tells us better!" From his observations of other skeptics turned Christians, though, he thought the inverse could also be true: Christian practice could help turn the mind toward truth despite lingering skepticism.[59]

Nelson's *Cause and Cure* was aimed at persuading an individual reader who had doubts about Christianity. But it recognized infidelity as a broader social problem. The church needed to be awakened to the issue; Christians in local communities needed to encourage their skeptical acquaintances to read the right books; tracts on the evidences of Christianity and Bibles with commentaries to aid comprehension needed to be much more widely distributed than they were. When republished by the American Tract Society, *Cause and Cure* itself became part of a massive collective effort to promote biblical literacy and Christian knowledge by flooding the nation with evangelical print. Evangelical publication, in turn, was part of a larger educational project that, along with revivalism and social reform, aimed to transform the nation and the world. In the 1830s, David Nelson and Ezra Stiles Ely would get to advance that project with more than preaching and publishing as they founded a college of the saints and a Christian metropolis of the West.

7

Christian Enlightenment

Faith into Practice in Marion, Missouri

The uproar over the Christian party in politics had not yet faded by the mid-1830s. But by this time Ezra Stiles Ely had turned his attention to an extraordinary opportunity to advance both his own interests and the interest of the Redeemer's Kingdom. As he put it in an April 25, 1835, letter to the moderator of the Presbyterian General Assembly resigning all his church positions—as clerk and trustee of the Assembly, vice president of the Board of Education, and member of the Board of Missions and of two lesser committees—Providence had opened a door for him to the great West. He was packing up his family and investing his whole heart, soul, and fortune in a benevolent project that could vastly outshine all his other efforts to put enlightened faith into practice.[1]

He would help build up a new Presbyterian college and a new city on the banks of the Mississippi River in Missouri. The vision for Marion College and Marion City began with two men who together seemed to combine inspired benevolent theory and ingenious practical know-how: Dr. David Nelson and William Muldrow. Nelson, revival preacher, coeditor of the *Calvinist Magazine*, and self-appointed missionary to skeptical infidels, would publish *The Cause and Cure of Infidelity* in 1837. At the beginning of the 1830s he was focused on a different educational project: establishing a great western Presbyterian college on the manual labor system, where students would pay tuition as part-time farmers on college property. Marion College was chartered by the state of Missouri in January 1831.[2]

William Muldrow, a Presbyterian layman, was a man of action. Other men moving into Missouri in the late 1820s farmed timbered land because the thick sod on the prairie was too much for their small bar-shear plows; Muldrow invented a large plow, pulled by several yoke of oxen, and was able to cultivate a stunning six hundred acres (some accounts stretched it to a thousand acres) in just a year. A farmer would need thirty years to clear and get all the stumps out of that much wooded land, Ely would write admiringly. A former "infidel" himself, Muldrow was converted when Nelson moved to Marion County in 1829.

The prairie farmer then asked himself, "Why should I not do for Christ what I have done for myself?" He formed a partnership with Nelson and a third man, David Clark. In April 1833, they borrowed $20,000 at seven percent interest against their own property and purchased five thousand acres to endow the college. The three then made separate tours to the South and East to raise more money and recruit faculty.[3]

The Marion experiment, like Ely's and Nelson's evangelical publications, was a project in enlightened Christian moral economy: it took up and modified the ordinary means of commerce and communication, repurposing social and discursive forms for religious ends. The Marion plan to have a cluster of new cities sprouting from the rich soil of America's heartland, with their churches and religious schools, their Sabbatarian steamboats and temperance hotels, cities linked by river and rail to the rest of the continent, would have given flesh and material form to the virtual communities created by the networks of evangelical print that sustained religious newspapers like Ely's *Philadelphian* and tracts like Nelson's *Cause and Cure of Infidelity*. Religious newspapers borrowed the form of the political press, adopted the ethic of not-for-profit charitable organizations even as they competed in the print marketplace, and made use of the state-sponsored postal system to diffuse knowledge and spread the Gospel. Marion's dreamers and schemers combined charitable fund-raising and commercial agriculture with a creative use of the financial instruments available to them in the capitalist economy supported by the state. The point of it all, they said, was to fund the colleges, schools, and churches that would enlighten and evangelize not just the nation but the globe.

Skeptical infidelity threatened the operation of these Christian moral economies in two ways, the Presbyterian reformers thought. On the systemic level, the de facto union of state and infidelity (or political atheism)—that is, a strict church-and-state separationism that walled off Christian commitment in the realm of private opinion and gave an antireligious bias to civil society and public life—would, it was feared, put Christians at an economic disadvantage. That was Ely's conclusion when, for example, Pennsylvania denied the American Sunday School Union the financial benefits of incorporation and the Sabbath-breaking post office effectively barred pious men from seeking employment. Skeptical infidelity, too, also threatened to warp the motives of the individual economic actors—the capitalists and laborers who were expected to behave as Christian moral agents. That was why Nelson began writing *The Cause and Cure of Infidelity* as soon as he was driven out of Missouri by the proslavery mob. Slavery was the product of the economic selfishness of natural (sinful) man; skepticism was the self-conscious rationalization, and infidelity the settled practice, of a subset of such selfish sinners. That, at least, was the evangelical antislavery position that Nelson came to adopt. His New School Presbyterian colleague Ely would calibrate the relation of slavery, self-interest, and enlightened Christian moral agency somewhat differently.

The Marion Dream

William Muldrow, who left Missouri for Boston on October 11, 1834, on his first fund-raising tour, stopping at other cities along the way, was especially successful in promoting the Marion cause. Forceful and earnest, a man of business and practical experience, he had facts and figures at his command to support his supreme confidence. As a Marion County resident later remembered, with "characteristic shrewdness and foresight, [Muldrow] had connected his own with the interests of the college. As he said himself, he wanted to *do* good and *get* good." His pitch to potential investors had the same combination of piety and self-interest, because many of them imagined themselves to be, in varied degrees, both philanthropists eager to promote the faith and speculative capitalists interested in substantial profits. Initially, too, the college needed not just money but prominent professors to join Nelson and establish the school's academic reputation. So Muldrow had to persuade some eminent Presbyterian divines to set aside their obligations to their congregations in eastern cities and show them that God had a higher calling for them on the western frontier. But this need not be a call to a martyrdom of virtuous poverty. Muldrow explained that the soil was so rich, and agriculture so flourishing, that excess profits, after the student-farmers' board and tuition had been paid, would fund very generous salaries for the professors. Ely, an early convert to the cause, thought that simple mathematics demonstrated the certainty of the plan's success. It only cost $130 for a mile of fence, $2 per acre to plow prairie land, and $1.50 per acre to harrow and sow timothy grass seed. Each acre with minimal labor would produce two tons of hay. Fifty students selling the hay from five hundred acres would yield $12,000. One-third of the profit would pay the students' room, board, and tuition, another third would be divided among the students, and the final $4,000 would go to the professor. That similar profits would flow by raising cattle, Indian corn, hemp, wheat, or onions, Ely was sure beyond "a shadow of a doubt."[4]

Money poured in. Cyrus Nicholas, who became an agent for the college in New York City, published fulsome praise for the project and linked it to the need to combat the growing influence of Roman Catholicism in the West. The Rev. James Gallaher, an old friend of Nelson's and coeditor of the *Calvinist Magazine*, visited the college in 1834 and had a testimonial printed in the *New York Evangelist*: "I have been born and brought up and labored all my life in the great west: I surely understand the country and its wants as well as any man alive. I tell you that this education enterprise is the *great object*. I see nothing else before the church, that, if sustained by the Christian public, promises so much for the *church* and for the *world.*" Twelve miles south of the college in Palmyra, however, Edwin G. Pratt, editor of the *Missouri Courier,* an observer no doubt worried that development around the new school would draw people and money from his own town, began to attack the project as a fraudulent scheme, charges that were reprinted in eastern newspapers. Muldrow, Nelson, and Clark responded by transferring the deed to eleven trustees and circulating newspaper articles and handbills testifying that the finances were sound, that construction proceeded apace, and that the founders had certainly not, as Pratt's *Courier* had charged, directly profited from the project.[5]

Muldrow had not skimmed profits from the college enterprise. Of course, the development of the institution would make all the land in the area more valuable. In partnership with Gallaher, he developed a plan for the creation of Marion City. This metropolis of the West would rise on muddy bottom land six miles east of Palmyra on a bend of the Mississippi. In 1834, the three-mile tract contained little more than a riverboat dock and was occupied only by frogs, turtles, and mosquitoes, but Muldrow had plats drawn up and a colored lithographed map made that showed where another branch of the college would be, and a female seminary, and a grand hotel, and an opera house. The slough that drained flood waters three miles in from the riverbank, marking the back side of the city, would be deepened into a canal, allowing riverboats to circle the metropolis. And that was not all. Another city, a new "New York," would rise forty miles to the west in Shelby County; a city adjoining the main branch of Marion College would be called "Philadelphia"; and a fourth city, twelve miles southeast of the "Upper College," where a "Lower College" was already being established, would be named for the prominent easterner who had become a leading investor in the entire project: "Ely." Muldrow had a railroad route surveyed and a bill to charter it introduced into the state legislature, a rail line that would connect his cities, run through the state capital, and then head west. In an 1835 letter, Muldrow predicted that in twenty years his railway would stretch across the continent, all the way to the Pacific. He wrote that a man "must be blind" who could not see that Marion City, situated on the mighty Mississippi and linked by rail to the East and West Coasts, would rival any city in the West. A county resident described Muldrow tracing his railroad route with his finger on a map as he prophesied: "He is in the habit of using the words 'just exactly' very frequently; he pronounces them in a peculiar way, slowly and with much emphasis. Marion City was j-u-s-t e-x-a-c-t-l-y, in the center of the United States territory, and would just exactly be the seat of the General Government, in time when the Pacific railroad should be built."[6]

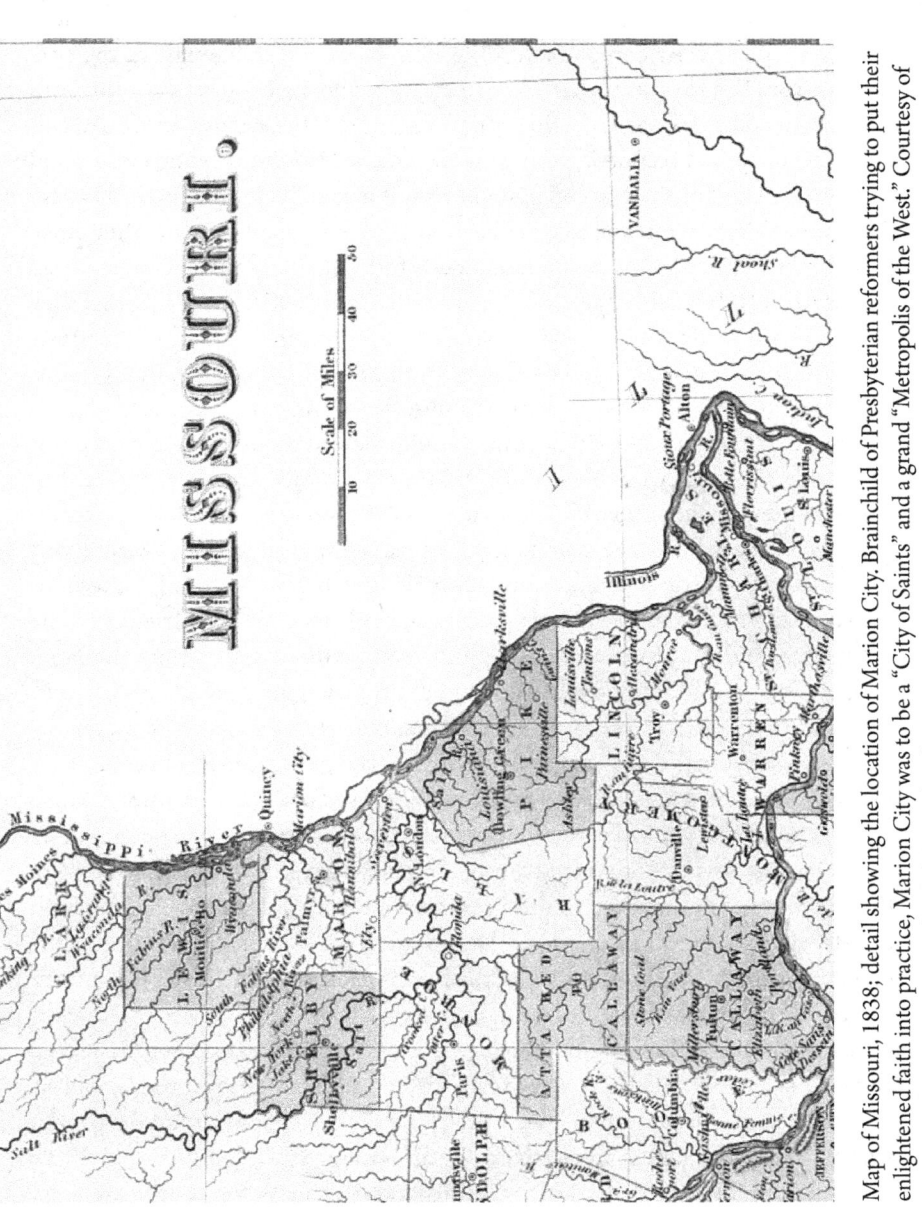

Map of Missouri, 1838; detail showing the location of Marion City. Brainchild of Presbyterian reformers trying to put their enlightened faith into practice, Marion City was to be a "City of Saints" and a grand "Metropolis of the West." Courtesy of the State Historical Society of Missouri, Columbia.

Ely had gone to Missouri to see for himself and sent back glowing descriptions. Although a letter from David Nelson describing a cholera epidemic in 1833 had been published in the evangelical press, Ely found an Eden. He had never seen such land before—even the fertile meadows of the Connecticut River Valley paled by comparison. "The rich, black, vegetable part of the soil, here, is from *two* to *eight*, and even *ten* feet deep; and for centuries to come, can have no need of lime or any other kind of manure." The beauty of the prairies could scarcely be imagined. "The general diffusion of the blessings of a good education and of piety," Ely concluded, "would make this the glory of all lands." Reckoning his own fortune as worth at least $100,000 thanks to an inheritance from his late father-in-law, he took out loans from the Bank of the United States and in April 1835 made large investments in Missouri lands, "believing that they would be productive of great gain." He became professor of "Biblical Literature, Polemic Theology, and Sacred Criticism" at Marion's Lower College and built a fine residence on the site of what he was sure was destined to become the city of Ely. In the winter of 1835–36 he joined Muldrow and six others as a proprietor of Marion City. After traveling with Muldrow on another fund-raising tour of eastern cities, Ely became nearly intoxicated with land speculation. An observer later remembered that the two men "completely monopolized the business at the land office for some time, continually making vast entries of land, sometimes by whole townships at once. Ely, in particular, made most of his entries by whole townships, and that too, as we were informed, without ever seeing the land, taking good, bad and indifferent altogether." Ely's own memoranda of Missouri real estate list nearly 250 separate transactions over the next several years.[7]

Dr. Nelson and the divines Ely joined at the college were just as ambitious for evangelical progress as Muldrow and the other investors were in worldly affairs. What should the young men who graduated from Marion College and all its satellites do? Nelson announced a mission plan. He estimated that there were thirty thousand young men in the Presbyterian Church. If half of them would devote themselves to mission work (and if many would come to Marion) they could convert the world. He divided the heathen lands on the globe into fifteen thousand sections of forty thousand people each, assigning one section to each future missionary. Thirty current college students had already committed to the work by late 1835, and three were ready to set sail for Madagascar. Nelson expected to be able to recruit at least a thousand more that winter and have them studying and farming the college lands by the spring.[8]

As Nelson, Ely, and the rest of the faculty and students at the college dreamed of converting the world, new settlers began to arrive at Marion City. In early April 1836, the steamboat *Caledonia* approached the small cluster of whitewashed buildings sprouting like the first seedlings from the low, flat, "naked prairie," markers of the western metropolis that was to blossom. Freshly painted on the steamboat's wheelhouse were the words MARION CITY PACKET. Owned by Muldrow, Ely, and the other city proprietors, the *Caledonia* was one of two vessels planned to make regular runs from Marion to Wheeling and Pittsburgh— Sabbatarian steamboats that would be idle on the Lord's Day and would deliver visitors to the new city to a promised temperance hotel. On board for this first trip were nearly two hundred settlers, including forty-seven children. "Among the passengers were house builders, and mechanics of all kinds," according to a newspaper account; there were "brick makers, brick layers, masons, carpenters, blacksmiths, shoemakers, &c." They brought with them "their effects, of every description, from the humble spinning wheel to the splendid piano, and from the plow and wheel-barrow to the steam engine." The boat also carried the frames of twenty-five houses, ready to be assembled, as well as roofing shingles and glass for 150 windows. Some of the passengers already owned a number of the 33' × 140' city lots, which had sold initially for $200 each, though it was said that the best sites had gone to "gentlemen of fortune" paying as much as $1,000. An extensive fishery was to be established "immediately," a large steam flour mill and four steam sawmills were to be operating in a few months, and the hotel, the schoolhouse, and, of course, the church would be finished by the end of the year. With its perch on the Mississippi, Marion City was closer than Louisville to "the great market of the West," New Orleans; with a rail line stretching west, it would absorb the Missouri River trade; with rail connections to Baltimore and Philadelphia, travel to the East Coast would drop from twelve days to four. Marion City promised to become, the newspaper correspondent concluded, "the great thoroughfare" for travel and commerce.[9]

Then the Four Horsemen of the Marion Apocalypse came and in rapid succession destroyed the dream: the floodwaters of the Mississippi, the blight of slavery, the Panic of 1837, and the torture of interminable litigation.

The snow fell heavily in the winter of 1835–36, and when it melted in the spring, the rivers and streams rose. Marion City flooded, though to what extent is hard to discern from the existing commentary. In early May, the St. Louis *Missouri Republican* reported that "a great portion of Marion City is submerged." The *Daily Commercial Bulletin*, also in St. Louis, printed various reports denying this, arguing that the city was still three feet above the watermark, or two feet, or at least sixteen inches, and that the water covering the surrounding land was no more than three and a half feet deep and could be forded on horseback. A cartoon circulated, showing Ely and Muldrow floating on the floodwaters in a canoe, sounding the water with long poles to try to find the houses of Marion City. A dialogue bubble emerged from the caricatured Ely's mouth: "I declare, Muldrow, I believe I have found the top of one of the chimneys!" The drawing was labeled "Marion City—the Metropolis of the West." Ely, Muldrow, and the other proprietors printed a handbill at the end of June, insisting that the water never reached half of the land laid out for the city; they also promised refunds to any purchasers, announced the construction of a five-foot levee that would protect the entire city in the future, and restated their unimpaired "confidence in the suitableness of the plat of Marion City for the site of a great and important river town." A visitor in September did not share this optimism. "An Impartial Spectator" found "the famous City" better described as a "prairie swamp" or a "frog pond," with four shabby framed houses, a log building being called a hotel, and a warehouse standing on the only spot that the few remaining locals would claim had not been flooded, and housing three men suffering from the malaria that had swept through the area after the flood. Marion City, the visitor concluded, "can never be made a town, with all the railroads and improvements that can be put upon it."[10]

Even before the floodwaters had receded from Marion City in the spring of 1836, the conflict over slavery and abolition had erupted at Marion College. The reformist press in the East had first caught wind of trouble the previous fall when a story circulated about Ely himself. Ely had sent back to his old religious weekly the *Philadelphian* a "short story, most pleasantly told," which was published under the title "Case of Conscience." A female slave, Ely wrote, carrying her youngest child, had appeared at Ely's door, distraught and "trembling." Her husband, Ambrose, she cried, had been grabbed at his plow and put in irons—his owner had sold him to a slave dealer. Ambrose had escaped and was thought to be hiding nearby. The next morning, after a troubled night's sleep, Ely visited the slave trader. " 'It's a pity to separate the man,' said I, 'from his wife and children.' " The slaver agreed and said he was willing to sell Ambrose for what he had paid for him because before the slave had escaped he had done nothing but moan about missing his family. Ely paid the man $700. "I felt, that in so doing, I was doing as I would be done by. I could not have obeyed the Savior's golden rule, had I not redeemed him." Hearing the news, Ambrose came out of hiding and went to Ely's house. " 'Well, Ambrose,' said I, shaking hands with him, 'are you willing to be my servant while you live?' 'O, yes, sir,' he exclaimed, 'not only willing, but glad to be your servant for life, but I am ten thousand times obliged to you for buying me.' "[11]

That was how the Rev. Dr. Ezra Stiles Ely, champion of philanthropic reform, became a slaveholder—but only in a "nominal" sense, the clergyman argued, only according to "the laws of the land." Ely preferred to think of Ambrose as his hired man, for the benevolent master would allow his slave to work off the debt of purchase and additional expenses, eventually buying his freedom. "In this I think myself free from all unrighteousness in enslaving a fellow man," Ely wrote, noting that he slept very well after the decision. "In this way, thousands, who hate slavery, could free men from slavery. And in this way, a nominal slaveholder may be no oppressor of a brother in the human family. Most heartily do I wish that our land had never known slavery; but since it exists here, let us mitigate its evils until it can be wholly abolished."[12]

The story was quickly picked up by other papers and reprinted not as "Case of Conscience" but under the headline "DR. ELY A SLAVEHOLDER!" His friends in the benevolent empire, his former colleagues in reform, were shocked. Joshua Leavitt in the *New York Evangelist* did not doubt Ely's generous heart or his "noble and *characteristic* philanthropy." But why hold Ambrose as a slave at all? Why not free him immediately and let him sign a note for the $700 as a loan? What if Ely died before Ambrose paid off the debt—would not Ambrose have to be inventoried and disposed of as part of Ely's estate? Or what if Ely became insolvent—his philanthropic intentions might have to be nudged aside if he faced financial difficulties. As another clergyman noted, "There are few men so humane as not to sell their *property*, when pressed for money." Leavitt closed, too, by encouraging Ely to think about how his actions would shape the character of Marion College. What would the mission of that grand educational experiment be in regard to slavery?[13]

Ely answered Leavitt coolly in November 1835, and his reply shows how his understanding of free agency and Christian ethics shaped his lived experience—and the lives of people like Ambrose, too. Ambrose, Ely claimed, "came to me of his own accord, with his full consent, and cheerfully agreed to serve me, as my slave, while he should live." Like the allegedly "free agent" in the Calvinists' predetermined universe, Ambrose was free to do what he willed to do. Freedom consisted in being able to act according to one's will; we should not look too hard at the external conditions that might in fact be limiting choices in the first place. "It may be true," Ely conceded, that Ambrose "would not have chosen to have entered into the relation in which he now stands to me, had he been born free, and had the circumstances of his life been more favorable." But Ely was not responsible for those circumstances; he did not initially enslave Ambrose. "I had no agency in procuring the evils of his state, and could not be answerable for them." By taking those "circumstances" as a given, Ambrose could be seen as freely choosing to be Ely's slave, and Ely could be seen as morally blameless for keeping him in slavery. Why not emancipate Ambrose immediately? Ely, who initially had expected Ambrose to be his one experiment in slaveholding, decided that he could be more philanthropic—and serve his own interests at the same time—by buying more slaves: "I have a lawful claim to his services for the refunding of the money, with interest, which I paid for him, and my plans for benevolent operation render it undesirable that I should forgive him the debt. I wish to purchase more slaves in the same way, for my advantage and their own, for I can thereby increase my means of doing good."[14]

Leavitt responded in early 1836 that Ely, the temperance advocate, would never think of holding a mortgage on a distillery; so why did this reformer who had always denounced slavery as evil not see that he was participating in that evil by holding a man in slavery as a financial security? Ambrose, Leavitt argued, was not acting freely when he made his choice. But Ely was. And Ely had chosen to identify himself—and Marion College?—with the slaveholder's interest.[15]

The position of Marion College on the subject of slavery was not yet clear before the spring of 1836. In Missouri, heavily settled by Southerners, antislavery sentiment of any sort was suspect. A small colonization society was formed in St. Louis in 1833, but even when the motive to deport troublesome free blacks to Africa was emphasized and the vague hope that American slavery would someday wither away was uttered with mumbled asides, most white Missourians worried about abolitionist conspiracies. Marion County, established in 1826, had been populated mostly by proslavery families from Kentucky, and these settlers were suspicious of the new immigrants being drawn from northeastern states by Marion City and College. The Presbyterian Synod of Missouri, meeting at the college in the fall of 1835, had passed resolutions that endorsed antislavery in principle but condemned abolitionism. The body declared that slavery was "a great evil" and expressed its pious hope that it be "removed as soon as the interests of all concerned will permit." While asserting that they were prepared to support "any safe and practicable method" to end slavery, the Presbyterians recorded their conviction that immediate abolition would be "ruinous" for everyone involved, including the enslaved. Marion College president David Nelson had been a slaveholder when he came to Missouri in 1829, though it was said that he had converted to some form of antislavery in 1831, influenced in part by Elijah P. Lovejoy, who agitated the question in the pages of the *St. Louis Observer*. At the Presbyterian General Assembly in Pittsburgh in 1835 he joined abolition revivalist Theodore Dwight Weld in the antislavery cause and published a powerful "Address" that called for individual slaveholders to immediately emancipate their bondspeople. William Muldrow owned slaves—according to a later account, he was said to have been Ambrose's original owner—but he was nonetheless suspected "of a leaning toward anti-slavery sentiments." When the newspapers started printing excited reports about lynch mobs, murder, and Marion College at the end of May 1836, Muldrow and Nelson—and Ezra Stiles Ely— were at the center of the stories.[16]

As Marion City was flooding, rumors spread that two students at the college twelve miles away were trying to enroll blacks and smuggle a trunk of abolitionist literature into the county. On Monday, May 17, 1836, a group of fifty to seventy armed men rode on horseback and in carriages to the college, looking for the suspects. They were directed to the nearby farm of a man named Williams, who was away, but they found A. C. Garratt plowing in the fields. Garratt had only been in Missouri since the beginning of the month. He had come with other young men, planning to enter the college, and had brought two free blacks with him: a boy, who was to be bound to Dr. Nelson until he was twenty-one, and a man who expected to be trained as a missionary by Garratt or some other student and then journey to Africa to preach the Gospel. Realizing that trouble was brewing, Garratt had already sent the two away, but the question of the box of books and pamphlets remained. The posse, led by Uriel Wright, who was a militia captain, a lawyer, and a Marion City proprietor, citing the authority of "Lynch law," searched Williams's house and threatened to burn it to the ground. Then they marched Garratt through the college campus to Nelson's house. After the president made a short, angry speech to the posse, Garratt reluctantly led his captors to the antislavery publications, which were in an outbuilding within a box marked GLASS and hidden under a pile of corn husks. Taking two other students prisoner, the posse began driving the three out into the prairie. Nelson followed, pleading with Captain Wright and the others to release Garratt and the students; when the old man could walk no further, he sat down and wept bitterly. After marching five miles across the prairie to a grove on the banks of the North River, they stopped under a large tree with spreading limbs. They let the two students go and then pondered Garratt's fate. Tarring and feathering was proposed, but Wright said that they would give Garratt 150 lashes if he refused to leave the state, and if he survived that and they found him in Missouri after Saturday, they would hang him from the tree until he was dead. Garratt and Williams paddled across the river to Quincy, Illinois, two days later, and the abolitionist literature was ceremonially burned on a Palmyra street.[17]

The following Sunday, Nelson preached a sermon on 2 Corinthians 4:17–18 (temporal afflictions serving eternal glory) to his congregation gathered at the Presbyterians' camp meeting site halfway between Palmyra and the college. After the sermon, Muldrow handed him a paper to read. Nelson hesitated, but Muldrow encouraged him to proceed. Accounts differ as to precisely what was said: some claimed that it was an appeal to raise money to emancipate slaves, and others that it was a call to start a fund to indemnify slaveholders if the government should abolish slavery. Nelson later explained that it outlined a large-scale effort to colonize free blacks in Africa. The plan, which Muldrow was ready to support with $20,000, was not much different from what Henry Clay was advocating in Kentucky or what Nelson himself had mentioned at a Palmyra meeting only a few years before. But the mere mention of slavery was enough to enrage Dr. John Bosley, who started cursing Nelson and rushed the pulpit. Muldrow, a massive man known for his physical strength and courage, stepped between them and took the blows from a sword cane that Bosley had intended for Nelson. The sheath broke; the sword came out; some accounts say Bosley aimed and snapped a pistol, too, that did not fire. Muldrow then stabbed Bosley with a long pocketknife, plunging the blade into his right side under his arm. Bosley collapsed, his mouth spurting blood, and the Sabbath camp meeting turned to chaos. Muldrow and Nelson left the scene on horseback.[18]

The news spread quickly that Bosley had been killed. Nelson went into hiding, resigned the college presidency, crossed the Mississippi into Illinois, and was warned never to return. His wife and young daughters followed shortly afterward: "A man in his field," Nelson wrote, describing the scene, "bawled out to my trembling family as they passed, 'if Nelson does not quit his *abbylution* he'll be burnt.'" Muldrow waited calmly on his front porch for the inevitable lynch mob, and when they arrived, he told them he would turn himself in to the authorities in Palmyra in the morning, and, resting a rifle on his left arm, he warned them that he would kill the first man who stepped across his property line. The next day he made his way serenely through an angry crowd, accompanied, according to one account, by his friend Ely. Though reported dead by the press, Bosley survived his wound, and Muldrow, pleading self-defense, was eventually acquitted on all charges and returned to his home. Nelson did return briefly to Marion County to care for his sixteen-year-old son, sick at the college with what was thought might be typhus. The "Palmyra mob" threatened him again. He told them he would meet them alone in the town square and they could do what they wanted with him, but only after his son recovered. Instead, ninety-two of his neighbors signed a note demanding that he leave the state forever as soon as his son was well enough to travel. One of them, a lawyer with political ambitions—probably Uriel Wright—admitted that "mobocracy is the order of the day." Fearing to try to raise his family in a place "where the dregs of society have risen to the top, and are permitted by the civil authorities to remain there," Nelson left for good. He immediately began writing *The Cause and Cure of Infidelity*.[19]

For Ely and the rest of the faculty in the days and weeks following the lynch mobbing, book burning, and Sabbath stabbing, the primary challenge was to save Marion College. The main purpose of the public meeting held on Saturday, May 21, was to procure a popular endorsement of the posse's actions, but the assembly also demanded a statement from the college. Ely rose and addressed the meeting. He said that he considered slavery an evil but that he thought abolitionists "deficient in philanthropy and piety" and denied any connection to them "either in opinion or action." The professor added that "he was the absolute owner of one slave, and was at present contracting for others." The resolutions of a Marion College faculty meeting held the previous day were then read to the assembly. The faculty formally disapproved of the circulation of any literature that might "render the slave population of this state discontented," condemned any interference with slaveholding, and announced that they would "forbid all discussions and public meetings amongst the students, upon the subject of domestic slavery." With proslavery Presbyterian clergyman William S. Potts of

St. Louis being quickly named the new president, the college's supporters had hope that the institution could survive the crisis.[20]

Marion City investors tried to be hopeful, too. A puff piece in the *National Intelligencer* in the summer of 1837 responded to critics who called the project a disaster and painted a rosy picture of the future. The city had not been "wholly inundated" by the spring floods of 1836, the writer contended: three to four thousand acres had been left "high and dry." Only a quarter to a third of the buyers had taken the proprietors' offer of a refund after the flood, and construction was continuing. A commodious hotel was being built, the church and the school would be done by January, and within a year, the writer predicted, as many as three hundred houses would stand in Marion City. The correspondent argued that the proprietors were not swindlers, having already spent over $100,000 on improvements, and the plan was no wild, visionary scheme, for the city must rise to greatness "in the nature of things." But the author of "Scenes and Incidents in the Far West" in the same newspaper said that of the long list of profligate land schemes that had recently gone bust in the Mississippi Valley, it was universally agreed that Marion City was the worst. Planned for a floodplain that would be underwater whenever the river rose, lots were dangled before the credulous by smooth talkers with fanciful lithographed maps that grossly misrepresented what was being sold and bought. Worse, "It was to be a *City of the Saints*," and a certain "Rev. Dr. ____" had even sold lots to a Pittsburgh congregation after a sermon. "The bubble has now burst; the whole place would not sell for one thousand dollars," the writer argued. "Various frame buildings have been run up by the victims of this project," he admitted, but, punning on Ely's name and Christ's lament on the cross, he quipped that "the poor dupes who have raised them have good reason to call out, '*Eli, Eli, lama sabacthani.*'" If the floods had not convinced the dupes that the real estate bubble had burst, then surely, the writer suggested, the "Treasury Circular"—which had made dollars scarce, caused credit to collapse, and paralyzed the entire region—would. The Treasury Department's Specie Circular put a stop to the acceptance of land-office paper money (speculators' notes) in payment for public lands. It was one of the triggers of the Panic of 1837 and the economic depression of 1837–43.[21]

Ely's finances collapsed. As a member of the Marion City Company of investors, in May 1837 he had endorsed their note for $50,000 and given his bonded warrant to the Bank of the United States for $100,000. The bank's director, Nicholas Biddle, would not have allowed the loan to the Marion City investors, who were strangers to him, without the endorsement of the prominent Philadelphia clergyman. But Ely defaulted on the loan. Scrambling to protect himself from creditors, especially William Muldrow, in November 1837 Ely conveyed in deeds of trust a good portion of his estate to his mother-in-law, Mrs. Margaret Carswell, and his friend Dr. Samuel McClellan, both members of his household. They authorized him to act as a trustee to pay off his debts, but his creditors suspected him of trying to escape his obligations. "Dr. Ely lodges deed after deed in the office till his friends are shields over all liabilities," one later complained. In December 1837, as he resigned his professorship at the college, he tried to sign over all his Marion City property to one of his creditors. Learning that the local lawyers doubted the validity of this move, he deeded this property as well to his mother-in-law and McClellan, hoping it would become profitable so he could pay debts he owed his niece and ward Mary Ann Ely Carswell, whose trust fund he had invested and lost. Trying to get $20,000 to pay some of his debts in April 1840, he worked out an arrangement with Abram Barnes of Maryland, who moved to Missouri with sixty of his slaves to farm the land and run a sawmill. Barnes quickly went bankrupt; Ely made no money from the deal but wound up with some of Barnes's slaves.[22]

In 1843 Ely learned that his young niece Mary Ann, whom he had raised with his children in his home, was going to marry Thomas J. Miles; Ely feared that Miles would sue him for Mary Ann's trust fund. Ely's wife had died in 1842, but by 1843 he had formed an attachment to Caroline Thompson Holmes of Philadelphia. In order to try to shield the remainder of his personal property, in June Ely deeded it all to a trust for Caroline before their wedding, stipulating that she would have sole control over it after they married just as if she had remained a single woman. This property included about 320 acres, six houses (including a two-story brick house and a structure known as the West Ely Hotel), several barns and outbuildings, about four hundred books, silver, cut glass, a chaise, three carts, two wagons, sixty head of cattle, eighteen horses, "one negro woman slave named Matilda and her two negro children, named Jane and Margaret, one negro woman slave named Eliza the wife of Jesse Spencer, and her child named Matilda, one negro girl slave named Jane Bowman, [and] one negro man slave named George Buonaparte." (Ely's first slave, Ambrose, was not listed, and accounts differ as to what happened to him, with one claiming that he was sold to pay Ely's debts and another that he had purchased his freedom with profits made from selling liquor to Marion College students.) Ely's prenuptial contract also made sure to stipulate that Caroline would "have all the use and benefit... of such children as may hereafter be born of her female slaves."[23]

"Litigation with its thousand evils poured into our Courts," the recorder for the Marion County Circuit Court later recalled. "The docket was crowded; all saw ruin staring them in the face, save the hyena-like lawyer, who enjoyed a rich harvest with peculiar zest." William Muldrow had moved more quickly than nearly everyone when the panic hit in 1837, deeding property to his creditors but mixing into the long list of tracts some land that still belonged to the U.S. government. At the sale, potential buyers were afraid to bid, not knowing which tracts were actually Muldrow's. His friends were able to purchase his land for a penny per acre, his agent was able to buy up many of his debts at a small fraction of what he owed, and his attorney pressured buyers of his Marion City lots to pay up. "The other important personages connected with the college, not possessing as much cunning as Muldrow, became victims to the difficulties environing them. They fell out amongst themselves. Brother went to law with brother, and Presbyterian minister with Presbyterian minister." One list in Ely's financial records shows that he lost twelve lawsuits in Marion County for debts ranging from $161 to nearly $12,000. The college itself was sued, and shut its doors in 1842. In the arbitration over the dissolution of the Marion City Company, it was determined that Ely owed nearly $40,000 to the other investors, about half of it to Muldrow. "Although Dr. Ely knew more about *gospel* than Muldrow, at the *law* he was completely foiled by his adversary, and it became to him a *schoolmaster* to bring him to a knowledge of the ways of the world." A sharp conversation between the two was overheard. Ely upbraided Muldrow, "observing that when he came to this country, he was worth one hundred thousand dollars, and that now he was worth nothing, and that he [Muldrow] was the cause of it. To which Muldrow very coolly and with the utmost sang-froid replied: Do I understand you to say, Dr. Ely, that you are now worth nothing? On the Doctor answering in the affirmative, Muldrow replied in his peculiar style: Well, sir, you may just exactly, sir, return to Philadelphia, just as soon as you please, sir, for we have no further use for you at all, sir."[24]

Ely did limp back to Philadelphia, hoping he could find a congregation and start over. He sent a pro forma request for a dismissal from the Presbytery of Northern Missouri so he could join the Third Presbytery of Philadelphia and start earning a "scanty salary" as pastor of the First Presbyterian Church in the Northern Liberties section of the city. But the Rev. Henry H. Hayes and the Rev. James Gallaher, who had been Ely's neighbors, friends, business partners, and faculty colleagues in Missouri, objected. Hayes led the charge. A friendly letter in May 1844 casually mentioned that Ely still owed Hayes $125; a harsher note from Hayes a few months later described that small debt as "but the vertical point of the pyramid that you have built upon me and its weight is crushing me to death." By October, a committee of the Missouri presbytery was investigating formal charges against Ely, which included dishonesty (in his dealings with the Bank of the United States), fraud (for shielding property from his creditors by conveying it to family members), and lying (to friends he had involved in the Barnes bankruptcy). Ely tried to defend all his actions, explaining his financial dealings in considerable detail and declaring that he had never "knowingly and intentionally deceived or injured" anyone. He concluded his response to the initial charges with pathos and a dash of self-righteousness: "By Marion College I have been robbed of about $18,000; by Marion City operations I have been beguiled into a loss of $15,000; by an unforeseen change of times and business

Marker, site of Marion City, Missouri (2017). Photos courtesy of Mary Lou Montgomery.

I have been compelled to part with all my property to pay my debts, except my wearing apparel; and now if the presbytery of Northern Missouri, or any member of it, can take away my good ministerial character—what have I left? Nothing but a quiet conscience, a good wife, and a reconciled God in Christ."[25]

Hayes pressed the case before the presbytery, formally challenging twenty-one of the claims that Ely had made in his defense. The dispute dragged on into the spring of 1845, the charges ballooning to nine counts of fraud, two counts of violations of good faith, two counts of "violation of Christian Duty to his Securities," and three counts of misrepresentation. A trial was scheduled, with sixteen witnesses listed and public records as well as Ely's letters entered as evidence. Ely had to return to Missouri to defend himself; congregants of his old Pine Street Church chipped in $51 to pay the cost of his travel. Thirty years before, when he had first come to Philadelphia, he had had to assure the elders of the presbytery of his moral character: "Before any suitable tribunal I am also ready to meet all the charges which can be brought against me for while I confess I am a sinner against God and depend entirely upon the righteousness of Jesus Christ yet I know not a single immoral action which could be proved against me since in the fourteenth year of my age I made profession of the Christian religion." He probably had to give similar assurances to the Northern Liberties church as it waited for him to clear his name.[26]

The Presbytery of Northern Missouri's indictment cited not Hayes but "Common Fame" as the source of the accusations, although Ely concluded that Hayes had joined forces with Muldrow and the two were "striving to prove all my dealings in Missouri frauds, that they may seize on all the lands which I mortgaged to pay my debts." The trial began on June 11, 1845, and as it waded into Ely's financial morass the sloppiness of the financial transactions in the speculative frenzy of the mid-1830s became evident: the gentleman theologians were signing each other's bonds and even signing each other's names to bonds in a flurry of complicated and overlapping deals. The ownership of slave property was especially tangled legally—but not, apparently, morally problematic. Who owned the "sundry slaves" that had once belonged to Abram Barnes when Muldrow had the marshal come to take them away and have them sold for debt? "It is hard to tell whose slaves they were at this time," Hayes testified. "Dr. Ely had a mortgage on them, and I had a bill of sale on them. The mortgage was recorded in Ralls County before the bill of sale, and I never knew of this mortgage on them until this week." Hayes said he did not know "of any incumberances except the attachment levied by the Marshall of the State." Hayes himself had a mortgage on the slaves written by Ely but not signed by him. Hayes said that Ely then pressured him to cosign another bond on the slaves, but that document was lost. Didn't you promise me, Hayes asked Ely at the trial, that I was not running any financial risk for cosigning on the Barnes slaves? "Dr. Ely answered, that there were many promises made in good faith, which men found themselves unable to perform."[27]

Hayes and others had gotten involved with the Barnes slaves because Ely had called them in to cosign his security bond in order to keep the slaves out of jail until the case was heard. According to Hayes, Ely had reasoned that having the slaves sit in a jail in St. Louis "would be attended with entire loss of their time—a great expense—and the great hazard of their lives." When the law sided with Muldrow, Ely tried to prevent the slaves from being taken and auctioned by confining them in a brick house with armed guards, but Muldrow came and seized them when Ely was away from home, and Ely's son-in-law, left in charge, declined to offer any resistance. Muldrow even sent Ely the subsequent bill from the jailer. When, in a later trial, Ely was asked about the fate of the slaves in his own household—Matilda, Jane, Margaret, Eliza Spencer, Matilda Spencer, Jane Bowman, and George Buonaparte—Ely testified that they, too, had been seized and sold for his debts. So he did not know—they were no longer in his "possession or control." Whatever had happened to his first slave, Ambrose, the subsequent ones did not get the chance to benefit from their master's philanthropy.[28]

Ely's trial before the Presbytery of Northern Missouri came to focus on his intentions—whether or not he knowingly committed fraud in his financial dealings and willfully misrepresented facts. Ely had reminded them that "ignorantly a man may perpetuate what is denominated a *fraud in law*, without having any criminal intention, and without violating any moral, law of God." Hayes testified that all the leading lawyers of Palmyra had considered Ely an intentional fraud for at least five years, "and it was generally thought that [Ely] meant to cheat me." Ely laid document after document on the table—bank account records, deeds of trust, mortgages, affidavits, bonds, bills of sale, notes—and tried to explain his transactions and place them well within the boundaries of ethical business practice. At the end of the trial's third day, the eight presiding ministers and elders of the Presbytery of Northern Missouri, perhaps in confused exhaustion rather than from firm conviction, acquitted Ely and gave him his letter of dismissal, even as they affirmed that Hayes had not brought the charges with any "motives of an unworthy character."[29]

Ely got back to Philadelphia on July 4, 1845, "much emaciated with a fever and a long continued bilious affliction." Sickness and worry had wasted the flesh from his frame: the pastor finally installed at the First Presbyterian Church in Northern Liberties was nearly thirty-five pounds lighter than the philanthropist who had first set off for Missouri, eager to do God's work and his own, a decade before. He had barely been home a month when he received notice that he was going to be sued by his niece. The auditor of the Philadelphia County Orphans' Court thoroughly reviewed the relevant records and reported to the court that Ely owed his niece and former ward Mary Ann Miles $57,409.55. Ely's first mistake was when, many years before, he had transferred the three hundred shares of Bank of the United States stock that he held in trust for her into his own account. His second mistake was to use it as his own money, as collateral for the Marion City loan in 1835. He took the risk, and he, not the trust, was responsible for the loss. When the bank suspended specie payments, currency depreciated, the speculative bubble burst, and the price of land cratered, Ely lost about $100,000, the auditor estimated. (Ely's own calculations show him about $120,000 in debt.) But the auditor concluded that Ely "had acted without fraud, and to the best of his judgment." The court confirmed the auditor's report, though it adjusted the amount Ely owed his niece to slightly less than $50,000. When Mary Ann and her husband, Thomas, next went after stock Ely owned in Jefferson Medical College, the judge in the Philadelphia Court of Common Pleas, sympathetic to the plaintiffs, removed Ely as a trustee of that institution, which he more than anyone else had founded, and then lectured the reverend doctor, complimenting his "skill in theology" but deploring "his want of legal knowledge in the management of money."[30]

Because Ely could not pay his niece as the court had ordered, on Saturday, March 20, 1847, the sheriff came to arrest him. After a gentlemanly conversation conducted over a long walk in the streets, the sheriff agreed to let Ely preach to his congregation the next day and turn himself in on Monday, at which time friends were able to pay his bail and keep him out of jail. In June, Ely filed a petition of insolvency at the county court. Miles's attorneys argued to have the petition dismissed, and if the court had agreed Ely probably would have gone to prison. "I rode past the Eastern Penitentiary," Ely wrote in the midst of this crisis, "and reflected on the pain it would give my friends, should I, in the course of a few weeks, be confined there, at hard labour; but I was enabled calmly to hope in God, and say 'the will of the Lord be done.'... I think I am willing to work and even die in one of the cells." He was still waiting for a final judgment in early November. "The worst I have to dread, so far as I know, must be the Eastern

Penitentiary for a work-shop, a bed-chamber, a place for prayer, & a house of death. I can find God there; & if he sends me to that gloomy abode, it may soon prove the gate to heaven." He got a glimmer of hope when one of the judges said that he did not think the statute on embezzlement on the part of trustees applied to Ely's case, since it had been passed after Ely had transferred the trust fund to his own account. The other judges agreed, and on January 27, 1847, they ruled that Ely had not committed any penal offence. He would be bankrupt, but he would "not saw stone nor die in a State's prison." He took great satisfaction that "not a word was uttered implicating my moral character" and believed the judgment confirmed that he had "done my ward all the justice in my power."[31]

Ely was ready to put the entire Marion experiment in Christian philanthropy behind him. "Surely, my confidence in God has not been misplaced, & my earnest prayer is, that henceforth I may have little to do with worldly business, and may be more unreservedly devoted to the ministry of reconciliation than in any former part of my life." His prayer went unanswered. Through the following year, 1848, he was still trapped in the mire of litigation as his niece's husband, Thomas Miles, went after the property that Ely had deeded in trust and then mortgaged to Mrs. Carswell (Mary Ann's grandmother) and Dr. McClellan. Ely suffered a debilitating stroke in August 1851: "The fatal blow seemed to fall upon his intellectual powers, upon the delicate and mysterious organism of the mind, laying it in ruins,—but it did not reach his heart, or destroy his hope and confidence in God." With this simpler faith he lingered on, dying in 1861.[32]

Moral Economies

Years before the Marion experiment, Ely had learned some important lessons about the economics of social reform during his years at the New York City Almshouse and Hospital, particularly the value of formal association and the systematic organization of benevolent work. Sympathy was cheap and easy, he quickly saw, but benevolence was more difficult to sustain. Any man or woman of feeling could be persuaded to toss coins to a beggar in the street, just as they could be brought to tears in a theater. But benevolence—which is what God required and the social and moral problems demanded—was more than a tender heart; it was "a rational regard for the welfare of others, which is manifested by corresponding actions." Benevolent action to be successful had to be sustained, and to be sustained it needed the regular support of material resources. But Ely's initial funding plan at the Almshouse had been "radically deficient," as a friend noted. Ely tried to support himself by charitable subscriptions, but to an already difficult ministry this added the burdens of attempting to solicit and collect his own funds and manage his own accounts. Never able to raise even half the money he needed to cover basic living expenses, he quickly went into debt. He was rescued by the formation of a voluntary association—the Society for Supporting the Gospel among the Poor in the City of New York—with a nine-member board of trustees, a secretary, and a treasurer, which raised and managed funds and paid him a salary of $800 per year. This was a lesson Ely's whole generation learned as they raced to formalize and institutionalize a host of new organizations to do good works in a rapidly developing society, writing bylaws, electing officers, seeking incorporation, investing funds, and rationally managing beneficent labor. The role of the state in all of this was to provide the legal and commercial structures to make voluntary benevolent action possible, but then to get out of the way—just as New York City was right, Ely believed, to build a chapel with its new Almshouse but not to fund the preaching that would occur there because doing so would favor one denomination over another and interfere with the free market of religious opinion.[33]

Ely also came to understand the double relation of evangelical print in the public marketplace. Christian reformers prized tracts and newspapers because they disseminated religious knowledge and served as a means of grace. The problem was that a primary audience—the unconverted—could not recognize this value and would therefore not pay to cover the costs of production. Unconverted readers had to be taught to appreciate the value of religious publications, like the children in the Almshouse who were paid a penny for every hymn they memorized. The production of evangelical print, therefore, had to be subsidized by a second audience: Christian converts. Pious Christians could read and personally benefit from religious newspapers, tracts, and books, too, of course. But they also needed to be persuaded to contribute additional funds that would allow the production and distribution of print to innumerable others—the reluctant mass audience who would only be enticed if the publications were cheap, if not free. So besides being textual means of knowledge and grace, evangelical publications were also tokens of faith: objects given as gifts, commodities sold to raise further funds for religious enterprises, copies to be tallied and publicized as tangible expressions of faithful benevolence. The astounding growth of the evangelical press in the early nineteenth century was not just the result of a mastery of innovative means of production (economies of scale, steam presses) and distribution (local tract societies and newspaper exchange networks). Nor was evangelical publication wholly "anticommercial" in its inversion of the law of supply and demand by responding to initially low consumer desire with a flood of product to the market. As with any new commodity, religious marketers had to create desire. Religious publishers combined commercial savvy and appeals to benevolence, as Ely did when he published *A Sermon for the Rich to Buy* and catered to popular tastes in the *Philadelphian*. These, like other evangelical publications, circulated as texts bearing knowledge and grace and as tokens of benevolent outreach.[34]

The Marion project similarly tried to merge experimentation in the capitalist marketplace with bold moral activism. Nelson promoted his new experiment in educational funding by chiding those who feared innovation. Such people probably thought Robert Fulton had taken leave of his senses when he first described his steam engine, Nelson wrote. "Why should not the economy of education be susceptible of improvement, resembling those witnessed in the progress of other arts?" But he also tried to raise capital the old-fashioned way, by asking for donations after sermons and lectures. When Nelson swung through Boston on a fund-raising tour in 1835 and preached against infidelity, the local free inquirers expected him to reason from his own premises (that God exists, Jesus is His son, and the Bible His revelation), "attacking the flimsy philosophy of his own mind, instead of the philosophy and arguments of the Sceptic," but they were also not surprised that the meeting ended with the sound of coins clinking into collection boxes. The repeated appeals for money led to charity fatigue in the churches and dark suspicions outside of them. Ely decried the lack of generosity among the rich in Philadelphia in 1833 and noted that even ruling elders in the Presbyterian Church complained of the repeated cries from charitable organizations for more money. Scoffers and skeptics argued that Nelson and other clerical fund-raisers begged for money to Christianize mankind but often appropriated the funds "in fattening and pampering *their own selfish carcasses.*" But even some religious writers criticized the incessant fund-raising and financial schemes of the benevolent reformers. In a debate with a Vermont clergyman, Ely argued that Bible and tract societies were not moneymaking operations, but even if they were, America was a land of liberty, and citizens could spend money on whatever they chose. He dismissed the claims that such incorporated benevolent societies denied funds to the public treasury (they could be taxed), took money out of the economy (print production infused capital, and their distribution networks circulated cash), or that they monopolized the printing trade (they competed in the free market). Marion City and College, too, he had thought, would harness the tools of the capitalist economy to do moral work.[35]

In Missouri, however entangled with land speculation and slavery Ely became, he was confident that benevolent intentions could sanctify commercial actions in a morally ambiguous marketplace. His heart was in the right place when he bought his first slave, Ambrose, he said, and his philanthropic calculus determined that he could do more good by keeping the man enslaved and purchasing others like him. He argued that a man might technically commit fraud or embezzlement according to the law but still remain blameless before God as long as his intentions were good. He did teach that a person's motives— even a person reborn in Christ—were almost always mixed. But the morality of an act was determined by the agent's overriding conscious intention, measured against God's law. So there was nothing necessarily sinful about also serving his own economic self-interest as he worked to build Marion City and College for the greater good.

Dr. David Nelson, however, who shared Ely's commitments to education, revivalism, reform, and New School Presbyterian Calvinism, did not think that self-interest and Christian benevolence could be so cozily intertwined. He felt that virtuous acts usually involved some personal sacrifice. Before he died in 1844, he had written a treatise on "Wealth and Honor," urging that Christian wealth be devoted to the redemption of souls, but the manuscript was lost before the work could be published. His widow, though, remembered that he had already grown disillusioned with Marion College even before the crisis over slavery brought a sudden end to his presidency. He had planned to deed nearly all his property to the college but had retracted the offer when the trustees started spending extravagantly. It had been Muldrow, after all, who had been the one to promise that the students' agricultural labor would not just pay for room, board, and books but would also enrich the faculty. Nelson's rejection of this model is evident in the plan of the school he established after he was driven across the river into Illinois. There he bought land five miles from Quincy and established his Mission Institute in the fall of 1836, where students would build their own cabins, which avoided the expense of constructing a college building and dormitories. More advanced students would teach underclassmen, negating the need for a faculty other than the head of the institute—Nelson himself. Students were expected to labor eight to nine hours a day on their farms rather than the promised three at Marion, but the instruction and books would be free. Having donated the land and a library for the institute, Nelson exhausted his own financial resources and had to make fund-raising tours to the East again. He lectured and preached, shabbily dressed in his ill-fitting pantaloons and "old linsey-woolsey coat," his notes tucked in the crown of his wool hat, even as his epilepsy got worse and his health declined.[36]

Yet the treatise Nelson wrote immediately upon being forced out of Missouri by the mob—*The Cause and Cure of Infidelity*, begun two days after the Sabbath stabbing while Nelson hid out in a hazel thicket with pen, ink, and paper, according to one account—was not on the surface an attack on mammon-serving money changers or selfish slave drivers. And the skeptics and infidels he described in the book do not seem obviously related to the "dregs of society" that formed the "mobocracy" driving him away. Nor does he suggest that the ninety-two townspeople who signed the petition demanding that he leave, or the neighbor who warned that he would be burnt for his "*abbylution*," were skeptical infidels. Dr. Bosley, too, who would have tried to shoot Nelson at the Sabbath meeting if Muldrow had not intervened with his long pocketknife, was a Presbyterian and not a freethinker. Why Nelson wrote a book about curing skeptical infidels right after his Marion experience only becomes clear if a reader maps the author's coordinates of skepticism, faith, enlightenment, and economic success.[37]

Although in *Cause and Cure* Nelson at one point referred to young urban male apprentices and laborers as a threatening population of infidels, most of the skeptics he discussed in the book were rich or at least economically comfortable. They were professional men—military officers and doctors, lawyers and merchants, a congressman and a governor's son. They were shrewd businessmen and successful commercial farmers. Others—like a tavernkeeper's wife—imbibed their skepticism from such characters, as young Nelson himself had. The doubters and scoffers were sharp and successful and fancied themselves as enlightened. Like their Christian neighbors, they were sinners, and their sin came from their natural enmity toward God. Christians who believed the truth, who even had saving grace working in their hearts and minds, still struggled against the sinful inclinations of natural man—against a selfish worldliness that pursues temporal riches even to the point of enslaving other human beings. In the skeptic, however, the enmity toward God becomes fully conscious, though rationalized, Nelson thought, as an allegedly enlightened critique of the Gospel message. The delusions of skeptical infidelity and the immoral economy of slavery, if not necessarily the acts of a benevolent slaveholder like Ely, are therefore different symptoms of the same cause. In the evangelical reformers' cultural politics of enlightened Christianity, to doubt Christianity was to pledge allegiance to all the baser instincts of sinful human nature.[38]

8

Revelation and Reason

New Englanders in the Early Nineteenth Century

In 1813, a young clergyman named George Bethune English, fresh from divinity school, walked out of the Harvard library and published *The Grounds of Christianity Examined*. Addressing everyone "willing to listen to every opinion that is supported by reason," hailing "the good sense of this enlightened age," invoking the American guarantees to the rights of free inquiry and expression, and reminding his readers that religious "skepticism" was not "criminal," English offered a book that sought to demolish the scriptural foundations of Christianity. Working as a college librarian, he had reviewed the seventeenth- and eighteenth-century debate between deists and Christians. He had been pleased to find that the Christians had the stronger arguments. But then he found some little-known Jewish critiques of Christianity that had been translated into Latin, including a text written in the late sixteenth century by a Lithuanian rabbi, and his faith in the New Testament as a revelation from God crumbled.[1]

Theologically liberal New England Congregationalists had for two decades stood with their conservative colleagues to denounce deism, skepticism, and other forms of religious infidelity. The liberals' leading biblical scholar, for example, the young Joseph Buckminster, pastor at the prestigious Brattle Street Church in Boston, made it clear that the age of reason dawning in enlightened New England was not that of Tom Paine. Christian faith, rather than being opposed to reason, was "the most reasonable thing in the world," he preached. The erudite Buckminster responded to the hyperrationalist with the higher truths of revelation, to the skeptic with the fact of the resurrection, and to the infidel with the meaning Christianity bestowed upon history. But when the liberals captured Harvard in 1805–6 it opened a rift between them and the "orthodox" (Trinitarian Calvinist) party that would only widen. The conservatives, anchored at Yale and strongest in the Connecticut River Valley, founded Andover Theology Seminary in 1808 to combat Cambridge heresies at closer range. By 1813, the year English published *Grounds*, orthodox clergymen were already beginning to lump liberal Congregationalists in with the skeptics and deists. A conservative critic of

Andrews Norton's "Defence of Liberal Christianity" in the early spring of that year refused to make any distinction between "sober deists," "profligate revilers of Christianity," and corrupted (liberal) versions of Christianity at the root of infidelity. The conservatives would be able to tut that a book like English's *Grounds*, flushed from the bowels of Harvard's divinity school, was proof that the "reasonable" and "enlightened" religion that the liberals preached would only lead away from scriptural truth to skepticism and atheism.[2]

Skepticism would haunt the Unitarian controversy and the Transcendentalist controversy that followed it. As the parties fought over the meaning of scripture, they also debated the nature of faith and doubt, the character of reason, and the politics of enlightenment. After the leading orthodox provocateur in Massachusetts, the Yale-trained Jedidiah Morse, called for an open break from the liberals in 1815, and liberals rallied to William Ellery Channing's manifesto, "Unitarian Christianity," in 1819, the party division hardened. Andrews Norton, whom wags dubbed the "Unitarian Pope," would try to use the latest biblical scholarship to secure the scriptural grounds of Unitarian Christianity. Norton, who had helped defend the liberal faith against George Bethune English's skeptical critique in 1813, rose again to battle Transcendentalism, which he considered to be the latest form of infidelity, in the 1830s. Against Norton, both the Transcendentalist Theodore Parker, who tried to reform Christianity while abandoning the old arguments for the Bible as a special divine revelation, and the skeptical utilitarian philosopher Richard Hildreth, who wanted to move past religion to better enlighten and reform society, offered very different ways to read the Bible and very different visions of the relationship of reason and faith.[3]

Doubting Scripture

Christians from the beginning had taught that Jesus fulfilled the Old Testament prophecies of the Messiah. But did he? A close examination of all those prophecies, George Bethune English argued, showed that the Jews were right to be skeptical of Christian claims. The scriptures by any reasonable reading had taught them to expect that the Messiah would be a king of Israel, in the line of King David, who would reign on the throne in Jerusalem and bring peace. Jesus of Nazareth was the opposite of such a figure. Rather than a triumphant political leader who reestablished the kingdom of Israel, he preached about a kingdom that was not of this world, he was rejected by most of his people, and he was executed alongside common criminals. The genealogical attempts in two of the Gospels to try to connect this Galilean carpenter to the House of David were contradictory and nonsensical. Moreover, the New Testament writers, when they described Jesus fulfilling different scriptures, seemed blatantly to distort the

Old Testament, misquoting, misinterpreting, and wrenching words out of context. Therefore, English concluded, if the Old Testament was divinely inspired, the New Testament could not be; if, on the other hand, the Jewish scriptures were not a revelation from God, neither were the Christian scriptures, which tried to rest on that Old Testament foundation.[4]

The major line of argument in *Grounds* concerned the prophecies, but English also criticized the authenticity of the Gospels and the moral character of Christianity. He borrowed from scholars who argued that internal evidence in the texts indicated that the Gospels had been composed not by eyewitnesses but by writers sometime in the mid-second century. The early Church Fathers who formed the canon that became the New Testament were merely a victorious party that declared its views to be orthodox, suppressed competing texts and beliefs, accepted gross superstitions, and admitted to lying to promote its cause. Even many deists, however, who had similarly argued that Christianity was a jumble of fiction, fantasy, and forgery had praised the religion's moral system. Not English. The Golden Rule about doing unto others was excellent, but it had not originated with Jesus, he argued. As for the Nazarene's other teachings—loving your enemy; giving all your possessions to the poor; taking no thought for the morrow; hating parents, spouse, children, and even your own life to become a disciple: these were impossible to perform and the attempt to follow them was destructive to the individual and to society.

English also addressed a subject that would loom large in subsequent New England debate: miracles. Christ and the Apostles, Christians had long argued, had verified their fulfillment of the scriptures and their divine mission by performing miraculous acts. But every religion, English countered, claimed miracles. The accounts in these flawed New Testament texts were worth no more than other ancient fables or modern ghost stories. Jesus seems to have been a well-intentioned but mistaken enthusiast who probably experienced hallucinations, English concluded. The testimonies of his deluded and credulous followers resembled similar accounts of supernatural wonders and transforming faith by subsequent Catholics, Baptists, Quakers, Methodists, and Shakers—accounts that the purportedly rational Unitarians readily dismissed even as they affirmed biblical supernaturalism. Christians generally accepted the New Testament miracles because of "the dogma of *implicit faith*," the conviction "that *Faith* is every thing; that doubt is *damnable* and a *proof* of an *unregenerated* mind.'" It was no wonder, English argued, "that the most enlightened men are commonly bad Christians."[5]

Boston Unitarians, already being accused of promoting skepticism and infidelity by Trinitarians, responded quickly and forcefully to this startling defection from their own ranks. English had first privately circulated a manuscript of abstracts from his reading on the prophecies among clergymen and divinity students around Cambridge. Channing and others urged him not to publish but failed to offer persuasive counterarguments. When false rumors spread claiming that English had become an atheist, he added twelve more chapters to the seven of abstracts and published *Grounds* in late September 1813. He did so, he wrote, to defend his reputation, speak up for the despised Jews, and support the cause of Truth. Channing responded from the pulpit on October 24, a performance quickly published as *Two Sermons on Infidelity*. Other ministers, according to English, preached and spoke against him, too. The Rev. Samuel Cary scrambled to produce a 136-page response in four weeks, which was published in November. Edward Everett, newly installed at the Brattle Street Church, labored for over ten months and published a scholarly refutation of nearly five hundred pages in August 1814.

Channing's *Two Sermons*, as English noted in a respectful reply, was more of an appeal to pious sentiment than an argument. Channing did not mention English directly, but he touched upon the major points in *Grounds*. Infidels attacked Christianity out of vice, vanity, or ignorance, Channing preached. The reader of scriptures merely needed to distinguish fact from metaphorical expression and discern moral character behind figurative language. It was true that Jesus did not meet Jews' expectations for their Messiah, but the bold metaphors of the Old Testament were easily misinterpreted. Christ's moral teaching, Channing reassured his congregation, was not extravagant if his figurative language was read with the "obvious rules of common sense." The New Testament writers, too, were hardly wild enthusiasts: "You see in every page a love of virtue, a love of mankind, [and] a sincere desire of enlightening and reforming the world." They may have, at times, erred on minor points, and reasoned incorrectly or expressed themselves in ways that struck the modern eye as awkward, but the *"facts"* that were "presented to all their senses"—in particular, the miracles— were reliably recorded. The religion they proclaimed should not have to answer for all the blood spilled and atrocities committed in its name over the centuries. Christianity itself, the historical record by Channing's reading attested, was the most powerful force elevating the human character morally and intellectually. "For centuries it has been the only religion of the most enlightened nations," and in those nations "its warmest patrons have been found in the most enlightened classes of society."[6]

Cary, a young pastor at the Boston Chapel and a kinsman and former friend of English's, produced a more pointed (English would say "violent") critique in his longer *Review*. He offered an important caveat to English's appeal to free inquiry and open debate. Unrestricted discussion about biblical interpretation was fine among Christians, Cary argued: although it often stirred up animosity, it ultimately refined faith and practice. But skeptics, who wanted to challenge the very grounds of Christianity by attacking the reliability of the scriptures, were pernicious because they threatened the virtue and happiness of the community. And what was their motive for doing so? In English's case, Cary suggested, it was to puff up his own pride rather than to pursue truth. Cary then challenged the interpretation of prophecy in the first seven chapters of *Grounds*; more importantly, he turned the discussion back to miracles. The ancient language of prophecy was often ambiguous, and it generated different interpretations, Cary conceded. But surely the interpreters who performed miracles showing that they were sent by God made a strong case that their interpretations were the right ones. English, in a bitter reply to Cary, expressed his exasperation with this argument. The conviction that those miracles had occurred rested on the belief that the New Testament was an accurate historical record and that the miracles were empirical facts verified by reliable testimony. Modern biblical scholarship, English protested, was demolishing precisely this point.[7]

The third response to *Grounds*, however, tried to bring the full weight of modern scholarship down upon English to crush him. The Rev. Edward Everett, the Harvard valedictorian who had just been installed as Buckminster's successor at Boston's most prestigious church, did not publish his *Defence of Christianity, against the Work of George B. English* to reignite public controversy. Clearly, though, he was reaching for Buckminster's mantle and seeking to make a name for himself in the top rank of American biblical scholarship. He began by convicting English of scholarly malpractice. Cary had accused English of hiding behind his claim of Jewish texts "discovered" in the archives while actually plagiarizing most of *Grounds* from the eighteenth-century English deist Anthony Collins—a charge English denied. Everett demonstrated that 94 of English's 182 pages were copied from other sources, 74 of them without acknowledgment. (English took 26 pages from Collins, 28 from Jewish writers, and the rest from a variety of other authors.) Everett then proceeded to methodically dismantle every single argument in *Grounds*—whether by English or his cited or uncited sources. Against every claim Everett marshaled numerous authorities. He exposed mistranslations, interpolations, contradictions, and carelessness. He compared variants in the ancient texts. He quoted the Hebrew, plunging into arcane discussions of accents and vowel points. He sifted through prophetic images and examined competing genealogies and chronologies. Even as he did so, though, he warned the reader not to be distracted by scholarly subtleties, not to lose sight of the actual meaning of a passage and the basic "facts" being presented in it. For "enlightened Christians" in an "enlightened age," he endorsed scriptural interpretation guided by reason, common sense, and "manliness."[8]

Everett distinguished between what Theodore Parker, a quarter century later, would call the transient and the permanent in Christianity—between those things that could be sloughed off as the accidents of particular historical contexts and the transhistorical essence of the faith. Modern enlightened

Christians, Everett contended, did not expect the New Testament authors to be verbally inspired—that is, infallible, word for word. The authors made mistakes in grammar, logic, and interpretation. They wrote in the peculiar style of their age and tradition. But none of this detracted from their religious message and the basic facts of Christ's life, death, and resurrection. Jesus, too, "did not address himself to a philosophical skeptick, who was to live eighteen hundred years after," but to people accustomed to the language and images of the Hebrew scriptures. His message now had to be applied in a very different modern context where "a philosophy both of nature and the mind ... has undergone incalculable improvements since the era of [early] Christianity." In any case, the books of the New Testament should not be read as a "forensick defense and exposition of Christianity": "The evangelists do not *rest the proof* of Christianity upon these fulfilled prophesies, nor upon anything else. Their writings were not meant to contain what we mean by a defence of the religion, or an examination of its evidences." The truth of Christianity was instead evidenced by morality, testimony, and history. It shone forth in the sublimity of Jesus's moral character and of the moral system he preached. (Like Cary, Everett believed that it should not "be necessary to prove to an enlightened public that Jesus was not a deceived and insane enthusiast.") Christian truth was sustained by the reliable reports of miracles by contemporaries. It was verified by the prophecies that were gradually being fulfilled by the Christian enlightenment of the world.[9]

Everett's defense of liberal Christianity was lauded by those who already agreed with its conclusions. The Unitarian *Christian Disciple* responded to the "truly and deeply" learned book with "wonder and delight." The reviewer described Everett on the New Testament's alleged misquotations of the Old as "the best survey of the subject with which we are acquainted in any language," and Everett's two main chapters on the prophecies, he said, "display[ed] an extent and accuracy of critical learning, of which we have had no example in any work, which has appeared in our country." The performance as a whole was "full and satisfactory on every point." Within six months of the book's publication, Everett was inaugurated as Harvard's new professor of Greek literature, an endowed chair that also funded two years of study with the finest biblical scholars in Germany.[10]

Everett and English had shared Harvard's Bowdoin dissertation prize in 1812, but their career paths by 1814 could hardly have been more different. The *Christian Disciple*'s review praising Everett had assured readers that English's book had not deserved such a magnificent response, since *Grounds* had been greeted with universal disgust and indignation in pious and enlightened New England anyway. Andrews Norton in the *General Repository and Review* had already catalogued English's "remarkable deficiencies" of mind. English's *Grounds of Christianity Examined* had been effective only in "destroying his own reputation, blasting his prospects, putting an end to his usefulness, [and] cutting himself off from the society of the wise and good," Norton wrote. In his published reply to Cary, English complained about former friends and colleagues stabbing him in the back from the pulpit, or whispering among themselves that he should be ignored because his arguments were unoriginal, his thinking immature, or his mind deranged. English realized that he stood alone against public opinion. He left town before Everett's book appeared and before his church voted to excommunicate him. He joined the marines as a second lieutenant and shipped to the Mediterranean; in Constantinople he resigned his commission to become the commander of the artillery corps for the Ottoman army in Egypt, joining an expedition up the Nile to conquer Abyssinia.[11]

That this child of Boston and Harvard, this once-promising young divinity student who had preached from Unitarian pulpits, had then abandoned Christianity to nearly become "a Jew!" (as the reviewer in the *Christian Disciple* had exclaimed) was shocking enough. But newspaper stories about English in the decade following the publication of *Grounds* only reinforced the idea that straying from the faith had pushed his alienation to bizarre extremes, erasing his very identity. Articles in New England newspapers began to report in 1819 that English had "turned Turk" and converted to Islam. A description of him by a British traveler in 1822 only seemed to confirm this. English now called himself Mahomed Effendi, according to the traveler's account: he wore a turban and Turkish dress "and ha[d] been successful in acquiring the calm look of the Turks, and the slow motion of the head, and roll of the eyes." It was true that he passed as a Turk when he worked as a secret agent for John Quincy Adams but not that he had converted to Islam. Yet the publication of English's *Narrative of the Expedition to Dongola and Sennar* in 1822 did not settle the matter, and the story was not put to rest until his obituary circulated in 1828. Even without the conversion to Islam, English's life story was a cautionary tale, as one New England editor put it, for any who "involve themselves in the mazes of skepticism."[12]

Edward Everett went on to a long and distinguished career, but not the one that was expected for him. The *Christian Disciple* considered his *Defence of Christianity* "as the first fruits of a mind destined to be an illustrious ornament to the church of God." But modern biblical criticism, Everett discovered in Germany, could not vanquish skepticism and ground a liberal faith after all. He studied with the leading Old Testament scholar J. G. Eichhorn, translated Eichhorn's *Introduction to the Old Testament,* and earned a doctoral degree from Göttingen University in 1817, the first awarded to an American. Meticulous historical, linguistic, and textual analysis, however, only pushed the historical facts that were said to warrant faith in Christianity further out of reach. Already in January 1816, he had confided in a letter to his brother that his opinions had shifted dramatically since he had written against George Bethune English a year and a half earlier. He still found much of what English wrote to be "exaggerated or false." But he nevertheless looked back "with nearly as much disapprobation on many parts of my book [and] on Cary's." He wished there was a way "to separate the public worship of God and the public teaching of duty, from all connection from arbitrary facts, supposed to have happened in distant ages and nations... and of which generally he believes most, who knows least." Everett had lost his faith, which he had so confidently argued against English, that Christian revelation was authenticated by history. He still believed in God and Christian morality, but he had come to see that the ancient texts did not, it turned out, sustain a systematic theology, the very terms of which had become "loathsome" to him.[13]

Everett had discovered that pursuing truth through critical and historical scholarship had made him unfit to be a minister and also that the requirements of the clerical profession worked against being able "to study the subject of Religion fairly." Simple self-interest tended to bend a clergyman's opinions toward the congregation that paid his salary. The demand to preach persuasively twice each week tended to harden opinions into certainties and stifle doubts that could lead to productive inquiries. Everett even wondered if his study of divinity had been a waste of time. He decided that he would have developed doubts about the faith in any case, but mastering the "modern historical and critical enquiries" into Christianity allowed him to feel less troubled by those doubts—his scholarship had probably, he said, made him "feel easy in scruples." Everett was happy, he told his brother, to leave it to others "to fight out the cause of Religion." When he returned to Harvard, he taught only classical Greek. George Bethune English, in a belated reply to Everett published in 1824, correctly guessed Everett's private reasons for leaving divinity behind. In 1825, Everett left the university to begin his political career (becoming a congressman, governor, secretary of state, senator, and noted orator).[14]

Other New England divinity students who followed Everett's path to Germany were also discomfited by modern biblical criticism. George Bancroft went to Göttingen to study biblical criticism, earning his doctorate in 1820, but was repulsed by the irreverent way that German scholars treated the scriptures, as if the sacred narratives were little more, he complained, than old wives' tales. Like Everett, Bancroft abandoned biblical scholarship and left Harvard for a different career (the first volume of his *History of the United States* appeared in 1834). Ralph Waldo Emerson's older brother William was diverted from the ministry by a revolution of mind and faith that he experienced at Göttingen, most of which he attributed to studying with Eichhorn.[15]

Two New England scholars continued to engage and battle German biblical criticism: the Trinitarian Calvinist Moses Stuart at Andover Theological

Seminary and Andrews Norton at Harvard's divinity school. Stuart learned German to read Eichhorn and the other leading scholarship, but though he admitted some textual problems in the Bible (conceding, for example, that several chapters in the Books of Jeremiah and Ezra could not have been written by those prophets), he argued that every biblical text (if not every word) was divinely inspired: Christ himself, after all, had vouched for the Old Testament. There were therefore strict limits to what a biblical exegete could discount as merely rhetorical embellishments or historical peculiarities of the ancient Near East. Norton, as editor of the *General Repository*, as Harvard's Dexter Professor of Sacred Literature, and later as an independent scholar, was liberal New England Congregationalism's leading polemicist—the "Unitarian Pope." He dismissed the Old Testament as too corrupted by mythology to be considered a reliable revelation of God. He explained away the New Testament's invocations of Hebrew scripture with the theory of accommodation: Jesus and the Apostles had merely clothed their truths in the peculiar styles and idioms of their original audience. Thus Norton dismissed, too, the problem of prophetic fulfillment that had so concerned George Bethune English. Against German critics like David Strauss, whose *Life of Jesus* (1837) also read the New Testament mythologically, however, Norton held to the Lockean argument about the reliable historical testimony of miracles. Read reasonably, Norton argued in his three-volume *Evidences of the Genuineness of the Gospels* (1837, 1844), the New Testament offered essential divine truths; following German criticism on the Christian scriptures would only lead to skepticism and atheism.[16]

Andrews Norton had helped discredit George Bethune English's *Grounds of Christianity Examined* because he thought it demonstrated how an allegedly rationalist but misguided biblical criticism could lead to skeptical infidelity. More than two decades later the Unitarian leader had to battle a much broader internal revolt against the scriptural grounds of a liberal faith. By that point, Norton had conceded English's central argument: that the Old Testament prophets' predictions of a messiah could not have been referring to Jesus. This made the argument from miracles, Norton believed, even more important. And so he found the new movement that arose within New England Unitarianism in the late 1830s—Transcendentalism, which brushed the miracles aside—particularly dangerous. It was, he believed, a direct attack on the historical authenticity of the scriptures and thus "the latest form of infidelity," as he put it in the title of his biting 1839 critique. This time, from Norton's perspective, young Harvard-trained divines were being led astray not by biblical criticism but by German philosophy; in this case they attacked the historicity of the faith not by analyzing the scriptures but by leaving them behind.[17]

Transcending Scripture

In September 1836, the first gathering of what was later named the Transcendental Club met at George Ripley's house. Emerson's *Nature* was published that month, too, but it was an article by Ripley two months later in the *Christian Examiner* that provoked the first public response from Norton. There were several leading combatants in the controversy between the Unitarians and the Transcendentalists, with Emerson, particularly in *The American Scholar* (1837) and the *Divinity School Address* (1838), emerging as a singular voice. The breach first opened in public, though, with the exchange between Norton and Ripley. Their subsequent publications through 1840, totaling several hundred pages, illuminate how both sides were struggling not just over the meaning of liberal Protestantism but also to avoid the abyss of religious skepticism.

Reviewing *The Rationale of Religious Enquiry* by the English Unitarian James Martineau, Ripley, a former student of Norton's and a pastor at Boston's Purchase Street Church, began his *Christian Examiner* essay by bemoaning the "degraded" state of English (and American) theology. The "idea of infusing any fresh life into its aged veins has been deemed chimerical," he complained; it remained "encrusted with ancient errors," bearing a "withered form and rigid features of the past," with hardly a new idea since the Reformation. Ripley found it "hard to imagine a study more dry, more repulsive, more perplexing, and more totally unsatisfactory

Christopher Pearse Cranch, "Illustrations of the New Philosophy," ca. 1837–39. In Cranch's cartoon, Andrews Norton denounces Transcendentalism as the latest form of religious infidelity before a group of Harvard alumni. MS Am 1506, Houghton Library, Harvard University. Photo courtesy of the Houghton Library, Harvard University.

to a scientific mind than theology.... It is no wonder that the heart is pulverized, that the freshness of life is exhausted, under its influence." Ripley, however, went on to agree with much of what Martineau had to say, and one can imagine Norton nodding in agreement at the major points: that the New Testament was a collection of human books written by authors who were divinely inspired but not infallible; that the scriptures needed to be brought before the "supreme tribunal" of reason; and that reason could also distinguish between true religion and "the fancies of enthusiasm, or the reveries of superstition." But then in the final eight pages Ripley turned to the issue that would drive a wedge between the young Transcendentalists and the Unitarian establishment. It was a "fallacy," he argued, that faith in Christianity required belief in miracles; it was an "error, under any circumstances, to rest a system of spiritual truth addressed to the soul, upon the evidence of miracles addressed to the senses."[18]

Ripley decisively pivoted away from the Gospels as historical testimony and toward intuition, away from Locke and toward Kant and Schleiermacher, away from Andrews Norton and toward Ralph Waldo Emerson. Man's intuitive perception of spiritual truth was the real foundation of all religion and morality, Ripley wrote; man's "primitive and universal dictates of the absolute reason" were the true measure of the divine. The moral beauty of Jesus's character corresponded with "our most exalted ideas of divine perfection," and this correspondence was "a better demonstration that he was of God and from God, than if we heard it thundered forth from the flames of Sinai, or saw it written by an angel's hand on the noon-day sky." The scriptures themselves, Ripley continued (making an argument that George Bethune English had also made) warned against being persuaded by apparent miracles—by signs and wonders. Ripley argued that the first Christians were not converted because they believed the miracles authenticated Jesus; they believed his message, and their faith led them to see that his marvelous acts were divine. In the nineteenth century there was even less reason to rest faith on stories of wondrous acts performed eighteen hundred years before. A Christian could truly believe "without connecting his faith with historical events that are uncertain in their meaning, and difficult of proof." Whether the miracles even occurred or not became merely an academic question. We do not need the historical testimony in ancient texts, Ripley concluded, for once our inward eye of intuitive reason is unsealed, we shall experience miracles enough in our own souls.[19]

Norton first responded in the pages of the *Boston Daily Advertiser* that such ideas dangerously fanned the flames of religious doubt. His initial jab acknowledged the "rights of free discussion" but challenged the propriety of rashly publishing opinions that controverted those doctrines that the wise and the many considered to be "of the highest importance to the happiness of man." It was the same argument that Samuel Cary had raised against George Bethune English:

just as the right of free speech did not allow someone to falsely yell "fire" in a crowded church, so the commitment to free religious inquiry did not extend to a skeptical critique of the very grounds of a community's religious faith. The man yelling "fire" endangered public safety, and the writer challenging the New Testament endangered public morals. Ripley's opinions, Norton argued, were "vitally injurious to the cause of religion, because tending to destroy faith in the only evidence on which the truth of Christianity *as a revelation* must ultimately rest." This new form of infidelity, Norton explained in his later *Discourse*, cribbed from Germany (or taken secondhand through Germanized English and French writers), was more insidious than that of the deists and freethinkers who attacked the faith in the previous century. This latest form assumed the name of Christianity even as it attacked the religion's very root by denying the New Testament miracles.[20]

Ripley agreed that they lived in an unfortunate "age of skepticism" but attributed that fact to a very different cause. The source of the problem was bad philosophy. Ripley placed Norton's hero Locke in a genealogy that identified him with atheistic, materialistic, and skeptical infidelity: "Locke—the successor of Hobbes and the precursor of Condillac and Voltaire." And this was not just a problem of the scholar's study. Many New England laymen and -women, Ripley argued, had become "unable to rest their religious faith on the foundation of a material philosophy." They were not themselves reading Locke's *Essay concerning Human Understanding* or his *Reasonableness of Christianity*, but they had absorbed basic principles from generations of teachers and pastors who had been "led by the philosophy of Locke to attach an extravagant value to external evidence." The mind at birth was like a blank piece of paper, they had been misinformed, and all a person's knowledge came from sensations of the material world. A miracle, a direct display of supernatural power before one's very eyes, was weighty evidence of divine power in this scheme. But the age of miracles, said Protestants, was long over. There were accounts of miracles in the scriptures, but even the common folks had caught wind of the textual and historical problems involved with admitting biblical miracles as valid evidence. Even you, Ripley wrote to Norton, doubt the literal truth of Old Testament miracles and, in your *Evidences of the Genuineness of the Gospels*, discount some passages in the New Testament, such as the nativity story in Luke. One did not have to be a scholar to perceive that some biblical accounts of miracles seemed false on their face, reading more like legends than histories. In any case, the argument from miracles was the wrong place to begin when trying to persuade someone who doubted Christianity, because the "evidence of miracles depends on a previous belief in Christianity, rather than evidence of Christianity on a previous belief in miracles."[21]

There was a better way, Ripley argued, pushing for a Transcendentalist revision of religious knowledge in his *Discourses on the Philosophy of Religion*,

Addressed to Doubters Who Wish to Believe (1836) and other publications. Man had "Reason," by which Ripley meant not "the power of reasoning, of evolving derivative truth from admitted premises; but in its highest philosophical sense, as the faculty of perceiving primitive, spiritual truth." This faculty "enables him not merely to count, to weigh, and to measure, to estimate probabilities and draw inferences from visible facts, but to ascertain and determine certain principles of original truth." Rather than reading his Bible to assess miracle stories as historical testimony (which requires considerable scholarly expertise), he could compare its doctrines against his intuitive grasp of higher truth.[22]

As they fought for their versions of faith against skepticism, the Unitarians and the Transcendentalists also battled over the character and politics of enlightenment. They debated the rules of public discussion, the power and authority shaping the production of knowledge, and the nature of "enlightenment" itself.

Norton clearly wanted some "controlling power of intellect" to establish a baseline for what did and did not count as "Christianity"—even though two

Mathew B. Brady, photograph of George Ripley (detail of "The Editorial Staff of the *New York Tribune*," ca. 1844–60). Ripley's *Discourses . . . Addressed to Doubters Who Wish to Believe* (1836) redefined faith, reason, and enlightenment from a Transcendentalist perspective. Photo courtesy of the Library of Congress.

decades earlier he had bitterly objected when the orthodox party had done the same thing and excluded the Unitarians from the fellowship of faith. Ripley and his friends were stunned that Norton and his allies—Unitarians! The "very Protestants of the Protestants"! The champions of free inquiry!—had become heresy hunters. Norton's first response to Ripley argued that he should have consulted privately with senior colleagues rather than simply foisting his dangerous opinions upon the public. Private criticism could filter and purify. Once published, bad ideas were difficult to debunk, sometimes requiring twenty pages to correct the errors in one. Ripley objected to this on principle and also bristled at the condescension of his former teacher, who apparently thought that the public sphere should operate like his classroom.[23]

Norton argued that religious knowledge was no different than other kinds of knowledge. The quest for certainty and the other side of that coin, "metaphysical skepticism," he wrote, are as absurd in religion as in other areas of inquiry, or in the affairs of common life, such as building a factory or a railroad. We "must use the same faculties, and adopt the same rules in judging" facts about the invisible world as for those concerning the visible one. We apply the "common and established principles of reasoning." There are no special intuitions, no direct perceptions—the gross religious ignorance in human societies before the time of Christ or among savage peoples currently should be enough to demonstrate that fact. As with other kinds of knowledge, Norton insisted, we believe and act in religion according to probabilities (not the intuitionist's fantasy of certainty). Religious knowledge, like all forms of higher knowledge, "requires labor, thought, and learning to attain it." Like other forms of higher knowledge—like astronomy, Norton argued—religious knowledge is progressive, with society as a whole benefiting from the long labor of experts: "The mass of knowledge which enlightened men are continually bringing into the treasury of human improvement, are soon converted into common currency."[24]

Ripley objected that this template of enlightenment, this model of the production of the knowledge necessary for faith, was elitist and false. It elevated "artificial culture" over "the healthy, religious soul, when enlightened by the spirit of God." It deprived "unlettered" people "of all religious knowledge whatever... because they have not besieged the libraries of the learned." It established their dependence on the learned class for the foundation of their faith. But such people, Ripley contended, have the potential for "a faith, no less rational, no less enlightened, no less fervent, than that of the most profound antiquary." Christ himself "saw that the parade of wisdom, which books impart, was nothing before 'the light that enlighteneth every human mind.'" Ripley shifted the understanding of "enlightenment" from the acquisition of knowledge through research and study to the activation and continued cultivation of primal intuitions. He stressed "a higher light than that which comes from the printed page."[25]

Norton dismissed Transcendentalist intuition and their critique of scholarly enlightenment. Crucial religious ideas such as the Providence of God or the immortality of the soul, he argued, were learned, not generated from within. The feelings that Ripley, Emerson, and their ilk identified as primal intuitions actually came from their imaginations, their childhood experiences, or their responses to the material world. There was "no other mode of establishing religious belief, but by the exercise of reason, by investigation, by forming a probable judgment upon facts." It was also true, Norton acknowledged, that the informed criticism of the Bible essential to an enlightened faith required deep learning, advanced skill in ancient languages, and proficiencies in other areas of scholarly research and analysis. Most people had neither the time nor the ability to do this research on their own and decide for themselves. But we are not isolated individuals, Norton contended. We share in the collective wisdom of our communities, of the republic of letters, and of the accumulated knowledge of the human race. As with other kinds of knowledge, we accept the testimony of others when we cannot develop an expertise ourselves. We trust the neighbor who has such expertise unless he gives us reason not to. In this way, religious knowledge—faith itself—rested on trust in one's community. The rash publication of dangerous ideas on such an important topic by men like George Bethune English or George Ripley, men who by their education and position claimed expertise or authority, violated this communal trust.[26]

Two notable responses to the Norton-Ripley debate emerged in the pamphlet literature. The Rev. Theodore Parker would restate the Transcendentalist argument, and then in subsequent publications push it even further amid cries of heresy and skeptical infidelity. Richard Hildreth's work met a similar, if more muted, response. Hildreth, a former lawyer, journalist, and politician turned philosopher and historian, was an outsider to the three-cornered debate among Trinitarians, Unitarians, and Transcendentalists over the character of religious faith. He was a religious skeptic and a secular utilitarian who sought to privatize and marginalize religion and put ethics, politics, and intellectual life on a naturalistic foundation. Parker tried to give old terms, like "Christianity," and old forms, like the Protestant ministry, new meaning and life, and much of New England was shocked by his radicalism. Hildreth tried to move past the old language and forms of faith, and New England could hardly hear him.

Theodore Parker had been a poor farmer's son who earned degrees from Harvard and the Cambridge Theological School before becoming the pastor of a tiny church in West Roxbury, near Boston, in 1837. As a voracious young scholar with an extraordinary talent for languages, he was already steeped in German biblical criticism and theology when he befriended Ripley in 1836 and became part of the Transcendentalists' club the following year. He first joined the Norton-Ripley debate behind the pseudonym "Levi Blodgett," who was supposed to be a farmer without higher learning, in a pamphlet entitled *The Previous Question between Mr. Andrews Norton and His Alumni Moved and Handled* (1840). Ripley and Norton had drifted into an argument about the proper translation and interpretation of Spinoza and Schleiermacher; "Blodgett" returned the discussion to the central questions and again made the case for intuition over the testimonies of miracles. Parker's *Discourse on the Transient and the Permanent in Christianity* the following year, however, was the publication that caused a firestorm. Ripley had argued that the testimony of miracles was not the surest foundation of faith, though he still claimed to believe that the New Testament miracles had occurred. Parker tossed out the miracles completely, and with them, the entire Bible as an authoritative text.[27]

Parker went further than any other liberal Protestant minister in New England in the effort to clear away the transient historical dross from Christianity's permanent essence. Emerson had followed a similar evolution and had called miracles monstrous in his *Divinity School Address* in 1838—a major provocation for Norton to write his *Discourse on the Latest Form of Infidelity* the following year. But Emerson had left his pastorate in 1832. Parker, a Christian minister delivering an ordination sermon, proclaimed that Christianity as popularly understood had grossly distorted the faith by making an idol or fetish of the Bible. This collection of diverse books had been declared the certain rule of faith and practice. "On the authority of the written Word, man was taught to believe impossible legends, conflicting assertions; to take fiction for fact." To disbelieve any of the Bible's statements "was held to be infidelity if not atheism." Modern biblical criticism had shown, however, that the Old Testament authors had made many factual and logical mistakes and had uttered predictions never fulfilled; they were certainly not infallible and were no more inspired than other wise men. Christians, moreover, had been expected when reading the New Testament "to believe, on the smallest evidence, accounts which shock the moral sense and revolt the reason" and tended to portray Jesus as a fabulous figure like Hercules. They were expected to close their eyes to the obvious differences between the Gospels of Luke and John and to the "serous disagreement" between Peter and Paul. Yet modern biblical criticism was smashing the New Testament idol, too. Scholars were finding mistakes and problems from the beginning to end of the canon and doubting the genuineness of whole chapters and epistles. It was fortunate, Parker argued, that Christianity—real Christianity—did not, despite all that had been said to the contrary, rest on the authority of the New Testament. Nor did it rest on the personal authority of Jesus, despite his being imagined as mankind's Savior and even as God Himself. Even if the books of the New Testament had been lost, even if "Jesus of Nazareth had never lived, still Christianity would stand firm, and fear no evil."[28]

Both scriptural authority and historical testimony could drop away because, Parker believed, Christianity was merely an articulation of a couple of simple

Photograph of Theodore Parker, ca. 1855. Parker's Transcendentalist Christianity dismissed the Bible as a reliable authority. Courtesy of the Boston Public Library, Print Department.

ideas: There is a God, and we should try to imitate his divine perfections. These truths "are perceived intuitively, and by instinct"; these intuitions can be cultivated and developed by the teachings of wise men, Jesus preeminent among them.[29]

Parker had preached the sermon on May 19, 1841. Rumors spread quickly. In early June, several newspapers printed a testimony signed by three Trinitarian minsters who had heard it delivered—a Congregationalist, a Baptist, and a Methodist; they denounced Parker's ideas as unchristian and challenged the Unitarians to disown him. In mid-June, the first edition of *A Discourse of the Transient and the Permanent in Christianity* appeared in print and sold out quickly. The Unitarian *Monthly Miscellany* had to agree that Parker's views promoted irreligion by destroying the authority of the Bible and of Christ. By the fall, the Unitarian *Christian Examiner* was marveling that in fewer than fifty pages Parker had managed to insert "almost every objection to authoritative or historical Christianity and its evidences that can be found in the works of earlier or later *unbelievers*, as they used to be called." The review compared Parker to skeptical deists (Hume, Gibbon, and Paine) and complained that there was little left to

Parker's "Christianity" besides the name. A review in a nondenominational magazine was astonished to find such a piece written by a purportedly Christian minister, rather than "some infidel writer" borrowing doctrines from the deists, and scoffed that the "internal evidence" Parker was left with was no better than that claimed by Muslims or Mormons. The Baptist *Christian Review* compared, in parallel columns over three pages, passages from Parker's sermon to quotations from Paine's *Age of Reason*. A year later (after Parker had published his *Discourse of Matters pertaining to Religion* to further explain his opinions) the Unitarian *Monthly Miscellany* reported that most Unitarians had disowned him, rejecting his infidelity and leaving the "Strauss of our American theology" to stand "almost alone."[30]

Unitarians needed to quickly distance themselves from Parker because he illustrated the very dangers the orthodox party had long associated with religious liberalism generally: the skeptical turn away from biblical authority and the concomitant embrace of man-made ideologies. In 1839, a Unitarian tract by the Rev. James Walker had lamented the "latent and passive skepticism [that was] much more widely diffused in the community than is generally supposed." Walker's *Unitarianism Vindicated against the Charge of Skeptical Tendencies*, as the title indicates, insisted that his own denomination was not responsible. In all educated and enlightened communities, he argued, traditional Christianity was losing ground. But a skeptical critique of traditional religious authority could revivify, rather than extinguish, true faith. Walker concluded that if freedom of inquiry produced some cases of intellectual licentiousness, such was the price of progress. Another James Walker, this one a Trinitarian, would later argue that Parker exemplified the dangerous liberal combination of religious skepticism and philosophical arrogance. In his *Philosophy of Skepticism and Ultraism*, Walker contended that in Parker we see "the audacity of the skeptic who sets his own reason above the reason of the Bible, and rejects or modifies it when it does not accord with his own conceptions."[31]

Richard Hildreth, standing outside this battle of Christians over the essence of their faith, joined the debate to challenge the place of religion in society more generally. Like Andrews Norton, he ranked Bacon, Newton, and Locke high above the modish Germans. But he found the Unitarian attempt to use Lockean philosophy to establish miracles as historical facts to be fatally flawed. He was happy to let the Transcendentalists win the debate and have religion established as subjective intuition. For Hildreth, though, this relegated religion to a matter of personal taste and destroyed any pretentions it might have to being regarded as "knowledge," any claims to public authority, or any legitimate exercise of political power. In his anonymously published *Letter to Andrews Norton, on Miracles as the Foundation of Religious Faith* (1840) he presented himself not "as a dogmatist, or a mystic, a naturalist, or a pietist, a believer, or an unbeliever" but "simply in the character of a rational man." He was someone who had devoted all his "time and thoughts either to practical affairs, or to the moral sciences" and who did "not profess to be versed in spiritual knowledge." His *Letter* denied what all the other participants in the controversy simply presupposed: that true religion was the taproot of human happiness and enlightened progress. History had shown, he argued, that it was not the theologians who had banished superstition and fought for human rights but philosophers like Bayle, Locke, Leibniz, and Voltaire. The art of advancing human happiness depended not on interpreting sacred texts but on the work of the physical and moral sciences. Religion properly understood, he contended, was a personal matter: it concerned feelings and intuitions about the infinite and the eternal, feelings that could calm passions, console suffering, and cheer those who tired of worldly pleasures and interests. It was idiosyncratic and incommunicable and should renounce "all pretentions to regulate opinion, or to interfere with morals, politics, or any of the practical business of life."[32]

Robert M. Pratt, "Richard Hildreth" (1858). The skeptical utilitarian philosopher and historian Richard Hildreth joined the debate over Transcendentalism but wanted to move past religion entirely to better enlighten and reform society. Courtesy of the New-York Historical Society.

Hildreth had graduated from Harvard in 1826. After studying law and opening a law office in Boston, he had thrown himself into political journalism, becoming a leading correspondent and editorial writer for the Whig *Boston Daily Atlas*. He was also a prominent figure in local politics as a leader of the temperance wing of the Whig Party. The year 1836 has been described as Transcendentalism's annus mirabilis because of the publication of Emerson's *Nature*, important statements by Orestes Brownson and Bronson Alcott, the organization of the Transcendentalists' club, and the beginning of the Norton-Ripley debate, but it was also an important year for Richard Hildreth. He returned that spring after eighteen months spent in Florida for his health. In his luggage he had two antislavery manuscripts and ambitions for philosophical as well as social and political reform. The philosophical project bore its first fruits that summer as he completed the translation of Jeremy Bentham's *Theory of Legislation*, which would be published in two volumes in 1840.[33]

Hildreth considered Jeremy Bentham, the founder of British Utilitarianism, to be "an original genius of the first order." Bentham's works were little read but "sneered at" in America by critics who had never actually seen his work, Hildreth wrote in his preface to the volume. Yet Bentham, in Hildreth's view, developed the best insights of the enlightened philosophy of the previous two centuries and applied them to practical reforms. Like Bacon, he championed the observation and analysis of observed facts, and the inductive method; like Newton, he wanted to discover laws, but for the human sciences. He followed Locke in trying to demystify knowledge, dismissing the notion of innate ideas and the metaphysical confusions of words and things. He considered himself to be continuing the project of the French philosophes to produce knowledge useful for human progress. The *Theory of Legislation* had originally been published in French by Etienne Dumont, who had distilled as much as translated from Bentham's manuscripts. In Hildreth's text, Dumont's Bentham, and Hildreth's Dumont, did not blast religion as directly as Bentham did in other writings. Still, the *Theory* assessed the appeal to the will of God in moral (and other) matters as useless. To look for it in conscience or intuitive feeling is to fall into a "circle of sophistry": "For if we judge everything by feeling, there is no means left to distinguish the dictates of an enlightened conscience from those of a blinded one. All persecutors will have the same pretence; all fanatics the same right." To look for God's will in the Bible is to assume that the scriptures are easily interpreted, yet the history of Christianity shows that this is certainly not the case. "Unless God explains himself to each individual by immediate acts and particular revelations, what is called his will can only be what we presume to be such," Bentham argued.[34]

Hildreth had finished drafts of his own "Theory of Morals" and "Theory of Politics" by the spring of 1841. His health failing again, he had stepped away from the rigors of political journalism and the frustrations of party politics in the fall of 1840 and left Boston for Demerara (British Guiana) on the coast of South America. He returned with an ambitious plan for a career as a philosopher and historian, imagining a series of ten theoretical volumes, a half-dozen histories (including a "History of the Christian Religion," a "History of the United States," and a "History and Refutation of the Mystical Philosophy"), four novels, some biographies (including studies of Jesus, Voltaire, Rousseau, and the English freethinkers), and other works. The philosophical project was most pressing. He wrote to a friend in January 1841, "The object at which I aim is neither more nor less than a total revolution in the whole system of philosophy relative to man considered as an intellectual and active being. My principle is, to apply to the philosophy of man's nature the same inductive method which has proved so successful in advancing what is called natural philosophy. Man is a part of nature; the philosophy of man is part of natural philosophy; and it ought to be investigated by the same methods."[35]

Hildreth's *Theory of Morals*, like Bentham, argued that "Platonic" theories positing an innate faculty (conscience, moral sense, intuition) that could distinguish right from wrong were utterly untenable. Hildreth also, though, criticized "Selfish" theories, including Stoicism, Epicureanism, and a strand of Bentham's Utilitarianism, which called an act good or bad according to the pleasure or pain derived by the actor. (Morally good acts for Hildreth were those intending pleasure to someone other than the actor). A more important distinction for how the book would be received in mid-nineteenth-century New England, however, had to do with the difference between "Forensic" and "Mystical" theories. Forensic theories, like his own, concerned human relationships; Mystical theories involved God. The latter derived from the "Mystical Hypothesis": human beings, trying to explain the unknown operations of nature, imagined an invisible, immortal, supernatural being who nonetheless acted something like a man. Instead of realizing that morality grew out of the natural constitution of humanity, "mystics" (religious believers) imagined its origin in this God. The moral character of a human act in this scheme was determined by measuring it against the pain or pleasure it gave the Almighty. In historical experience, Hildreth wrote, mystical systems of morality had often been "turned into engines of universal despotism."[36]

The Mystical Hypothesis, Hildreth argued, had for centuries plunged ethical thinking into a tangle of contradictions from which its adherents could not escape. It had produced "unnumbered volumes of abstruse, but barren and inconclusive controversy" about a "fruitless" metaphysics. In recent years, however, liberalizing Christians had been turning away from the logic that had rendered man a mere puppet on God's hand. They placed more value on man's natural actions. Their God "gradually etherealized into a personification of Benevolence," pleased only by those who promoted happiness in their fellow human beings. In the writings of a few on the radical edge of progress, God was "openly declared to be, what, in all systems of theology he covertly is, Man, individualized, glorified, deified." It was happening in Europe, Hildreth wrote, mentioning David Strauss. It was happening in New England theology, too, which resembled European theology in miniature. This was "the secret of that recent alarming outbreak, even in the very bosom of the orthodox sects, of what is called just now in New England, Transcendentalism."[37]

Hildreth's book sold poorly and received scathing reviews from a Catholic and from a Unitarian of the Andrews Norton party—critics that Hildreth in his pamphlet response dubbed "Parson Thwackum" and "Mr. Square" after characters in Henry Fielding's novel *Tom Jones*. The Catholic Thwackum had written that Hildreth's book was "an exaggeration, in morals, of what Mr. Parker's 'Discourse on Matters Pertaining to Religion' is in theology"; it was "as absurd as Bentham's Utility, as skeptical as Hume, and as positively atheistic as D'Holbach." The Unitarian Mr. Square in the *North American Review* had also condemned the "bald, blank atheism" in Hildreth's book, shuddering at how the author described standards of moral obligation varying among (and within) communities rather than measuring all against divine, immutable laws. Both critics, Hildreth observed, demanded that the study of morals in societies be grounded in the Bible's divine revelation. Both demanded "implicit faith and unquestioning obedience" to the moral laws in the Old and New Testaments. But, Hildreth asked, how were these texts to be interpreted? "To say nothing of older commentaries, since the art of printing came into use, not less than a hundred thousand volumes of disquisitions have been written on the Scriptures; and what they really mean, or whether or not they have any positive precise and definite meaning, becomes every day more doubtful." And even the clearest verses in scripture shed little light upon moral questions. "'Thou shalt not kill.' This seems plain,—but does it really mean so? Shall I never kill? Are capital punishments forbidden? Is war forbidden? Is self-defence forbidden?" The appeal to scripture failed.[38]

Yet the Catholic's and the Unitarian's appeal to scripture and to divine authority was merely empty rhetoric in any case, Hildreth argued. Thwackum of Rome settled the interpretation problem by holding up his church as the one true and authorized interpreter of the Bible. Thus one was supposed to have faith in and obey the church, a corrupt, self-perpetuating corporation of bishops and a pope (as Hildreth described it) who proclaimed themselves the sovereign law-giver. Mr. Square of Unitarian Boston pointed to moral laws as being built into the structure of the universe and argued that every intelligent being acts according to inherent laws in his own nature, which he ought to measure against the divine standard in the Bible as he understands it. So if the Catholic's God is really the church, the Unitarian's God is really himself. Both were actually more atheistic than Hildreth, he argued: he believed in God as an uncaused Cause of nature, but he did not make this Cause into a person to be idolized or a power to be manipulated from behind the mask of piety. Against conservative Catholic and liberal Protestant calls for faith and obedience, Hildreth championed reason, free inquiry, progress, and the people's liberation from the heavy hand of religious institutions.

Most galling for Hildreth was how his pious critics seemed oblivious to the central argument in his book. The "aim of the enlightened moralist," he argued, was to raise the general standard of morals in his society—promoting civilization and human happiness by advancing knowledge and education and by cultivating and increasing the sentiment of benevolence in the population. The latter was achieved by reducing the pains and difficulties that tended to dampen benevolent feelings: hunger, disease, insecurity, exploitation. Moral reform rested in large measure, therefore, on social reform. And here was another failure of the religious moralists. They declaimed to the point of "nauseousness" on minor issues, and yet when faced with the greatest moral evil, slavery, they were either feckless foot-draggers and moral cowards or, reciting the proslavery sentiments in both the Old and New Testaments, were on the wrong side entirely. The proof of moral theory, after all, was in the practice.[39]

Hildreth had seen plantation slavery firsthand during his time in Florida, and he responded with a scalding inversion of Tocqueville's *Democracy in America* in a treatise he called *Despotism in America*. He also wrote a didactic novel, *The Slave; or, Memoirs of Archy Moore* (1836), which he expanded and reissued after the success of Harriet Beecher Stowe's *Uncle Tom's Cabin*. Political opponents were already condemning him for being a "*Snapping Turtle Abolitionist*" as well as a "thorough infidel" by 1839. In the 1840s, as he was writing the first volumes of his *History of the United States*, he was active in the New England Antislavery Association and the Vigilance Committee protecting fugitive slaves.[40]

Abolitionism was the cause where the skeptical humanitarian Richard Hildreth, accused of atheism, and the radical Christian Theodore Parker, accused of heretical skepticism, could link arms. Parker, though shunned by most Unitarians, had a Boston congregation formed to support him in 1846 and was still popular on the speaking circuit. Unlike Hildreth, Parker wanted to modernize rather than move beyond religious faith and to reform rather than neuter the Christian churches and ministry. But his criticism of churches and clergymen as they existed matched Hildreth's. Timid pastors, bowing to the interests of their wealthy congregants, preached against small vices but not great social evils, he argued. So concerned to prop up American faith, they turned a blind eye to American injustice. And to judge by the church publications of the previous twenty years, Parker wrote in his *Sermons of Theism, Atheism, and the Popular Theology* (1853), a stranger would think that the greatest sin in America was religious skepticism—"doubt of theological doctrines." From this flood of writing the stranger "would not suppose that there were as many slaves in America today as there are church members." Parker had not become an ardent and outspoken abolitionist until 1845–46, but he quickly emerged as a leader of the movement in New England (eventually becoming a member of the secret committee supporting John Brown's plan to ignite a slave insurrection). Parker started an antislavery journal, the *Massachusetts Quarterly Review*, in 1848, and Hildreth contributed articles to it. In the 1850s, the two men led petition drives against the Fugitive Slave Act. Both traveled to Italy in failing health at the beginning of the next decade. Parker died in the spring of 1860. Hildreth died in the summer of 1865 and was buried in the Protestant cemetery in Florence, not far from Parker's gravesite.[41]

In one of his first publications, a young Richard Hildreth had written a series of humorous newspaper pieces as "the Limping Philosopher"; in the second installment he sketched the intellectual culture of enlightened New England in the second quarter of the eighteenth century—and, unwittingly, prophesied the place he would achieve within it. It was an age where "we are all philosophers": one fellow lectured at the lyceum like a second Plato, and another played the sage in published essays and reviews; young ladies could both dance and "talk metaphysics," while "shop-boys read behind the counter, the profound treatises for the society for the diffusion of useful knowledge." The philosophers of this philosophizing age could be divided into three groups. Croakers, austere and stoical, and inclining toward Calvinism in religion, always found flaws and fault. Once this class had contained nearly all New Englanders, but lately the Croakers had been overtaken by the Perfectionists. Members of this second group were ardent and enthusiastic, feeling much but reasoning little. They nonetheless considered themselves the wisest people who ever existed, and had the recipe to cure all evil. The third, much smaller sect was the Skeptics. "Men hate to doubt; and to doubt is the philosophy of the Skeptics. They are held too in very bad repute, and both the other sects have a great dread of their cool-headed logic." Since there were so few of them, and because they were temperamentally incapable of "playing upon the imaginations of men, they commonly make but little figure in the world, and never become conspicuous but as an ally of one of the other sects." The Limping Philosopher said that he tended to be a Croaker before dinner and a Perfectionist after a good meal and a bottle of claret. But in truth Hildreth was a Skeptic. His *History of the United States* got a tepid reception until years after his death because he avoided playing upon the imaginations of readers with the grand rhetorical flourishes and paeans to democratic nationalism that marked George Bancroft's popular histories. His philosophy was dismissed as religious infidelity hidden behind cool-headed logic, and he learned early on that someone who challenged popular religious ideas could be "spit upon or knocked down in the name of the Prince of Peace." Yet Hildreth never became quite the pariah that George Bethune English had been. Hildreth, in alliance with ardent men of faith like Parker, and at the intersection of enlightened progress and religiously motivated moral reform, was able to help increase the force of benevolence in his community after all.[42]

F. Bate, "A Bird's Eye View of a Community, as Proposed by Robert Owen" (1838), a painting based on an earlier architectural sketch by Stedman Whitwell, "A Bird's Eye View of One of the New Communities at Harmony, in the State of Indiana" (1825). A reformer's vision of a better society. Photo courtesy of the Mary Evans Picture Library.

PART THREE

REFORMS, 1820–1850

> The SCEPTIC and the CHRISTIAN agreed that America in the second quarter of the nineteenth century, which was experiencing dramatic social, economic, and political changes, cried out for reform. But they disagreed about what reform was and how it should proceed:
>
> SCEPTIC: "Democracy and Scepticism do go hand in hand.... Reform is opposed to Religion.... Cite to me one solitary instance in which a church party ever supported political reform, or one in which a skeptical party ever opposed it."
>
> CHRISTIAN: "[Christianity is] the world's only hope. In vain have they looked to philosophy, in vain to their own inventions.... Nor have mankind more to expect from infidelity. What has *she* ever done for them?... What vice has she eradicated? What suffering has she alleviated?... No, Sir, Christianity must reform the world, or it will not be reformed at all."[1]

"Reform! reform!" The word rang like an alarm bell, wrote a woman working in the Lowell, Massachusetts, textile mills in 1845. "The world is changing; and all who are not making it worse, are striving to amend the badness of its ways." Religious skepticism and faith framed how Americans in this period thought about and experienced economic and social life—work and wealth, buying and selling, getting ahead or just scraping by through seasons of boom and bust. From the economic depression following the Panic of 1819 through the California Gold Rush at midcentury, the dialogue shaped how they understood the moral effects of socioeconomic change—a society of local farms and handicrafts being transformed by the rapid expansion of national and international markets, the concentration of capital in cities, the increased mobility of wage-earning workers, the development of industrial mass production, and the expansion of the slave-based Cotton Kingdom. Americans responded to this social and economic transformation by making "'Reform'... the characteristic motto of the nineteenth century."[2]

Reform, however, had many faces. An 1847 advertisement for yet another periodical devoted to reform promised to cover many of the movements that vigorously worked to mend the flaws of a changed and changing world. The *Christian Reformer* would devote space to antislavery, pacifism, temperance, and prison reform; to the labor movement, the women's movement, and to innovators who focused on health and the body. But it also promised to criticize the Bible, Christianity, and the clergy. This went too far for a Universalist observer who generally supported social and moral reforms but suspected that, despite the proposed publication's title, religious skepticism was the main engine of the new publication.[3]

Christian enthusiasm was a wellspring for many nineteenth-century reforms. But sometimes the new movements could come to compete with forms of traditional religious faith and practice. "It is only in our own generation that Reform has been distinguished by itself into one separate theme, profession, or object of human interest," an essayist in the *Christian Register* wrote in 1848. Previously reform was seen as a part of religion. "Now Reform advances a rivalry with Religion, and in some shapes stands in apparent opposition to Religion, or claims to be the whole of it." Christian social and moral reformers continued to insist that the Gospel was the only legitimate source of "Reform Power," as one put it. But for those who doubted that the old church doctrines made sense in a modern age, reform itself could become a new faith.[4]

"The skepticism of the present age," the French philosopher Théodore Jouffroy wrote, was different from that in the preceding ages of Enlightenment and Revolution. Jouffroy's lecture of that title was translated by William Henry Channing and published in the *Christian Examiner* in 1838, a time when the philosopher's works were being enthusiastically received by religious liberals in America. The skepticism of the eighteenth and early nineteenth centuries, Jouffroy argued, was not an absolute skepticism that lacked confidence in attaining knowledge or truth; it was a critical dissatisfaction with Christianity, a faith once taken for granted but now failing to adequately address fundamental human concerns. This "actual skepticism," as he called it, was not confined to "the philosophic class," but penetrated "all classes... to the base of society." "The people do not trouble themselves with asking, 'what is the authority of the human faculties,' or 'what is the nature of the object of knowledge, or the nature of knowledge itself.'" They did recognize, however, that the "errors and imperfections" of Christianity had been exposed, most aggressively in the eighteenth century. The best and brightest had lost the power of religious conviction. The public at large had lost a set of common principles and a set of shared criteria for judgment. The consequence was a de facto "intellectual democracy": "Each individual will feel that he is free to believe as he chooses, and will declare with authority his chosen faith. By what test shall it be condemned?" With religious truth claims rendered generally dubious by skeptical critique, faith was left to the whims of private opinion. Individuals could hold these opinions dogmatically, and if challenged by the skeptic they could merely shout louder and revel in an anti-intellectual contempt for serious reflection or historical fact. Furthermore, without a common religious vocabulary people came to perceive their collective social problems only in political terms. The late eighteenth-century struggle for civil liberty was certainly beneficial, Jouffroy argued, but liberty was only a means to an end and not an end in itself. The current skeptical age needed a new foundation, a new common religious and moral faith. Jouffroy's comments were originally about France, but observers of the United States in the second quarter of the nineteenth century such as the reformer Orestes Brownson, a central figure in chapter 10, were coming to similar conclusions.[5]

Chapters 9 and 10 look at how religious skepticism or faith inflected various projects for social and moral reform. The first focuses on "free enquirers" Frances Wright and Robert Dale Owen, who, after the failure of reform communities founded at New Harmony, Indiana, and Nashoba, Tennessee, in the 1820s, established a freethought society and press in New York City and tried to appeal to the urban working class. The skeptic turned Christian health reformer and self-help author William Alcott rejected his earlier support of Wright and Owen, turning his attention from the social to the individual, and from labor reform to body cures. At midcentury, women's rights advocate Ernestine Rose blasted the biblical foundations of patriarchal society.

Chapter 10 concentrates on the efforts of three reformers in Boston in the 1830s and '40s: Abner Kneeland, a freethought lecturer and editor who endured a series of blasphemy trials for indicating that he did not believe in God; the education reformer Horace Mann, who led the public school movement as he struggled privately with religious doubt; and especially

Orestes Brownson, who for a time was a skeptical "infidel" trying to envision a new society and a new way to be religious, and then moved through different versions of Christianity (Presbyterianism, Universalism, Unitarianism) before converting to Roman Catholicism. It also looks at William Miller, a skeptical deist who converted and began a movement that would lead to the founding of Adventism, a prophetic voice whose warnings of the imminent end of the world made social reforms irrelevant.

Political conservatives argued that the reformers' grand schemes to remake American society were misguided. Perhaps old Europe needed such reforms, "but to call out for reform, as if our republic should be materially changed, or society likely to be improved by new moral or conventional maxims," the *American Magazine* declared, "is quite mal-apropos in this country." Religious conservatives contended that no reform denying that the "principal agency" of improvement was Christianity's salvation of souls would be successful. While reformers sought to change the world, others simply tried to make moral sense of nineteenth-century American social and economic life as they found it. Chapter 11 analyzes the spiritual autobiographies of three religious skeptics who became Methodist ministers: Charles R. Baldwin, a western Virginia lawyer; John Scarlett, a New Jersey shoemaker; and John Bayley, a journeyman printer who had emigrated from Manchester, England. Arguing only for spiritual reform through Christian conversion, these narratives illustrate socially conservative evangelicalism's fraught response to middle-class values and antebellum socioeconomic change.[6]

9

Faith in Reform

Remaking Society, Body, and Soul

The work of three reformers—Frances Wright, William Alcott, and Ernestine Rose—illuminates the ways that the dialogue of skepticism and faith informed important projects to transform American society in the second quarter of the nineteenth century. Wright tried to channel working-class radicalism away from self-defeating Christian pieties. Alcott developed a program of health reform that spoke to middle-class anxieties by overcoming religious skepticism. Rose advanced the cause of women's rights by hacking at the religious roots of patriarchy.

On a mid-January evening in 1828, as Frances Wright delivered her lecture on the nature of knowledge to a crowded Masonic Hall in New York City, someone set a barrel of turpentine ablaze by the back door. The fire spread to the first floor and sent billows of smoke up the stairs and into the hall. Some people panicked and jammed the stairs in an effort to escape, but Wright called for calm, and no one was hurt. The New York *Evening Post* blamed the speaker and the sort of people willing to listen to her for the near-catastrophe. It was not surprising, the *Post* editorialized, that "the singular spectacle of a female, publicly and ostentatiously proclaiming doctrines of an atheistical fanaticism, and even the most abandoned lewdness, should draw a crowd from prurient curiosity." Even though disaster had been avoided in this instance, such circumstances made it likely that "a riot should ensue, which should end in the demolition of the building or even in the burning it down." When Wright next spoke at the Masonic Hall, someone tried to disrupt the meeting by turning the stopcock to the main gas pipe, extinguishing all the lights and "leaving some 2000 people in complete darkness." Candles were brought out, however, and when Wright finished her talk, the "long and loud hurras of applause" followed her out into the street.[1]

Frances Wright was a phenomenon. Known as the author of *Views of Society and Manners in America* (1821) and infamous as a promoter of failed Utopian communities at New Harmony, Indiana, and Nashoba, Tennessee, Wright became a sensation as a female lecturer on a tour begun the previous summer in Cincinnati. She had a powerful personality, a sharp mind, and broad reading, but she was also a skilled orator whose mere appearance on the stage defied gender conventions and drew attention. She and her partner, the skeptical editor and writer Robert Dale Owen, moved their base of operations to New York City in 1829 and launched a new reform project. Chastened by the failures of their experiments with alternative communities, they hoped to achieve radical reform gradually, working within existing American social and political structures. Their two means of persuasion would be public lectures and a journal, the *Free Enquirer*. Their singular goal would be the passage of legislation creating a national, rational, republican educational system. The social and political vehicle to achieve this end would be an awakened working class. And their primary obstacle, the freethinkers knew, would be the clergy, in league with moneyed interests.

In the late 1820s, in a village in the rocky hills of central Connecticut, a schoolteacher with a medical license in his pocket and dreams of reform read Frances Wright's published lectures aloud, and wept. William Andrus Alcott would in a few years leave his native Wolcott for Boston and become a prolific and popular health and education reformer, publishing over a hundred volumes and a thousand articles before his death in 1859. Central to his self-help books for young middle-class men and women, his guides for teachers and parents, his vegetarian manifestos, and practical health advice was the conviction that intellectual and moral reform had to be joined to a relentless focus on the body and the daily demands of physical life. He has been called a leader of the "body reform" or "Christian physiology" movement that combined science and religion: on the one hand, it stressed that from empirical observation of natural facts one could discover physical laws to guide a rational pursuit of happiness; on the other, it sacralized daily practices (ways of eating, drinking, washing, dressing, and exercising) as rituals of obedience to these divine laws. Enlightenment optimism for improvement through the study of nature fused with a missionary fervor for building a New Eden on earth for the coming millennium. Missing from accounts of Alcott's reform project, however, is how he brought Christianity and physiology together. He did so by first overcoming religious skepticism and turning away from Wright's freethought reform movement, which he had almost joined.[2]

Ernestine L. Rose arrived in New York City from England in May 1836 and within months, as she later put it, "took up the work" that Frances Wright had left off. Born in Poland, Ernestine Louise Susmond Potowski had rebelled against her father, a rabbi, rejected the marriage he had arranged for her, and, as a sixteen-year-old, successfully sued in civil court to get her dowry money returned. After studying in Berlin, she went to London, embraced the socialism of industrialist and reformer Robert Owen, married William E. Rose, and emigrated to America, initially intending to join an Owenite community not unlike the one that Frances Wright and Owen's son Robert Dale had seen fail at New Harmony. Instead, the Roses settled in New York City, and Ernestine began petition drives urging passage of legislation for married women's property rights. In the

1840s she became a well-known lecturer for women's rights, serving as a featured speaker at the movement's national conventions. She was also a leading voice in the freethought and abolition movements. At the height of her fame in 1853, she became the focal point of the Bible Convention convened in Hartford, Connecticut, by other radical reformers such as the abolitionist William Lloyd Garrison and the Spiritualist Andrew Jackson Davis. The convention was called to debate the question of the origins and authority of the Bible and thus of the relationship of Christianity to reform. Rose's bold denunciation of the Bible as American culture's major obstacle to securing women's rights as human rights answered the question with rare clarity and power. And it nearly provoked a riot.[3]

Frances Wright, Infidel Politics, and the Working Class

Frances Wright and Robert Dale Owen moved from Tennessee and Indiana to New York City in 1829 to publish their *Free Enquirer*, open their Hall of Science, and promote their new campaign for national reform. The metropolis was "the centre of the civilized world," Wright wrote; the state "forms the head of the Union"; and the people were "already engaged in the battle of truth against error." If it was a leader "in the work of reform," she would note a year later, the city was also "deepest in corruption." The "Lords of Wall street" had made the city "the prime seat of dishonest speculation, fraudulent bankruptcy, monopoly, extravagance, and every evil that overstrained commerce." A corrupt and secret caucus at Tammany Hall controlled politics. As the site of national Bible, tract, and mission societies, New York City had become the "chosen throne of church power and church influence," flooding "the whole country with superstition." It was the perfect place for the free inquirers to speak truth to power.[4]

Skeptical attitudes toward traditional religion also seemed to be reviving in the city in the 1820s. Benjamin Offen, a self-educated deist shoemaker who had arrived from England in 1824, helped organize the first of what would be annual celebrations of Thomas Paine's birthday in January 1825. Forty deists and freethinkers attended that first dinner; the numbers rose at subsequent celebrations and the custom spread to other cities. Another English émigré toasting Paine at those dinners was George Houston, a deist who had moved to the United States after spending two years in Newgate prison for publishing d'Holbach's satirical history of Jesus, *Ecce Homo*. Houston started a deist paper, the *Correspondent*, in 1827, which would publish Thomas Cooper's critical examination of the scriptures. In the same year, New York City deists and freethinkers also formed the Free Press Association, which sponsored lectures by Offen or visiting speakers and soon began holding debates. In 1828, a group calling themselves free inquirers began meeting in a different part of the city. Although Robert Dale Owen

J. Gorbitz (artist) and J. C. Buttre (engraver), "Frances Wright." From Elizabeth Cady Stanton, Susan B. Anthony, and Matilda Joslyn Gage, eds., *History of Woman Suffrage*, vol. 1 (New York, 1881), frontispiece. Reformer Frances Wright tried to channel working-class radicalism away from self-defeating Christian pieties. Photo courtesy of the Library of Congress.

would later say that he and Wright "pitched our tents in this city, chiefly because here the clerical profession was the most numerous, its resources the most concentrated, [and] its influence most overruling," it was also true that groups of freethinkers who might be receptive to their message were already gathering and organizing before they arrived.[5]

Wright and Owen had learned important lessons from the failures at New Harmony and Nashoba. Robert Dale Owen had grown up in New Lanark, a Scottish mill town his father, Robert, had made famous through his educational and industrial reforms. The elder Owen's ambitious experiment in Indiana had begun in 1825. Owen had purchased thirty thousand acres and the buildings of Harmonie, Indiana, a prosperous village built by a tight-knit group of hardworking, water-drinking, hymn-singing, celibate German Christian communalists led by George Rapp. Owen thought that with his cooperative labor plan (each member with an equal stake and an equal voice), a polyglot group of American social pioneers might thrive in the same mills, farms, and shops that had been staffed by the disciplined Rappites. Robert Dale arrived in New Harmony in the fall of 1825, only to watch it fall apart by the spring of 1827 because the new community members lacked the skills to labor profitably and bickered constantly over governance. New Harmony had shown, Robert Dale later wrote in New York, "that to form a successful cooperative society, there needs precaution, prudence, forethought, and a degree of experience which, in the present state of society, is not easily acquired." "I have learnt," he wrote on another occasion, "that it is not enough to know *what* should be done; we must also know *how* to do it: and that, suddenly to attempt a radical change in the situation and habits of the present generation, may be, to begin at the wrong end."[6]

Wright had planned Nashoba as something of a colony of New Harmony. She had met Robert Owen when he arrived in Washington, D.C., in February 1825 to much acclaim and had been inspired by his vision. Wright and her younger sister, Camilla, traveled to Indiana in the spring to see New Harmony at its creation, as the Rappites finished moving out and Owen and the first group of community members approved their new constitution. By the summer she had formed the plan for an experimental community of her own. Owen's socialist cooperative in Indiana had been an attempt to develop an alternative to the selfish rapacity of capitalism; Wright's commune in Tennessee would offer a solution to the problem of slavery.

Wright's remarkable life seemed to have led her to some great purpose in the cause of human improvement. Born in 1795 to a well-to-do linen merchant of radical Paineite principles, she had been orphaned at two and educated in the library of her great-uncle, a moral philosopher at the University of Glasgow. At sixteen she read a book about the United States and fell in love with the idea of this new land of liberty and equality. In her early twenties she toured the northeastern states and, as she later wrote, "seemed to hear and see the declaration of independence everywhere." The book she published in 1821, *Views of Society and Manners in America*, brought her to the attention of reformers in Europe. She became friends with old Jeremy Bentham, the utilitarian philosopher. The marquis de Lafayette, the aging hero of the American and French Revolutions, became a heroic father figure to her, and she and Camilla were following him around on his triumphant tour of America when she first met Robert Owen.[7]

As she traveled the United States this second time, she became much more aware how far American society in practice was from the noble ideals of her beloved Declaration of Independence. This time, she saw slavery firsthand—slave ships in Virginia, slave marts in New Orleans, slave catchers in the woods of Illinois. A cooperative community might be designed, she thought, that could demonstrate a practical path toward emancipation. Slaves in the community she imagined would be trained in an Owenite industrial school alongside whites. The enslaved would labor diligently to pay off the price of their purchase and achieve their freedom, and would then be colonized in Haiti. Free members of the community would contribute equal shares of labor or money for equally distributed benefits as well. With a more motivated and efficient labor force, the community would show the rest of the South an economically profitable way to end slavery and remove worrisome free blacks.

Wright, therefore, tried to harness self-interest and accommodate white racial prejudice in the cause of humanitarian reform. Former presidents Jefferson, Madison, and Monroe either approved the plan or at least applauded Wright for proposing the idea. Andrew Jackson pointed her toward some decent woodland that his agents could sell her along the Wolf River in Tennessee, fifteen miles from Memphis. In late fall 1825, she bought 320 acres for $480 and ten slaves at $400–$500 each. These acquisitions were followed by her purchase of 800 more acres and a donation of six more slaves (a pregnant enslaved woman and her five daughters). Joined by her sister, a Scottish former medical student named James Richardson, and the reform-minded farmer George Flower and his family, Wright named the community Nashoba, a word left behind by the Chickasaw who had been driven off the land not many years before.[8]

Robert Dale Owen, who became a Nashoba trustee, saw the community at its height in the spring of 1827: four leaky log houses and a few slave cabins; meals of cornbread, hunks of pork, and bad water. After being deathly ill for months with dengue fever, Wright left Nashoba in June of that year to go to Europe to recover her health, and Owen left with her. In their absence, the remaining resident trustees, Camilla Wright and James Richardson, tightened the discipline on the slaves, apparently with Frances's approval. They separated the enslaved parents and children and refused to let any of them eat except at the communal meals. For some unknown infraction, Richardson tied up two female slaves, stripped their backs, and flogged them while Camilla watched. An enslaved woman named Isabel, complaining that an enslaved man, Redrick, had tried to rape her in her bedroom, asked the philanthropists for a lock on her door. They denied her a lock but gave all the slaves a lecture: "We consider the proper basis of sexual intercourse to be the unconstrained and unrestrained choice of both parties." Richardson started having unconstrained intercourse with a free woman of color, Josephine Lolotte, and Camilla was soon doing the same with Nashoba's farm manager, Richeson Whitby. Richardson, as he recorded in Nashoba's daily log, informed the slaves that he and Josephine would be living together, "repeating to them our views of color and the sexual relation." He then sent a copy of the Nashoba log for publication in the reformist newspaper *Genius of Universal Emancipation*, and word quickly spread that Wright's communal experiment had become a cesspool of sexual promiscuity and miscegenation.[9]

Frances Wright heard the news while in Europe and drafted her defense of Nashoba as she sailed back across the Atlantic in November 1827. Published in a few newspapers and excerpted in others in early 1828, Wright's "Explanatory Notes, respecting the Nature and Objects of the Institution of Nashoba" only made things worse. In it, she criticized the baleful effects of the division of labor, the pernicious class divisions, and the rampant selfishness of capitalist society. But an experiment that had begun as an economic cooperative of whites aiming at the gradual emancipation and eventual colonization of black slaves had become something else. Encouraged by Robert Owen's 1826 July Fourth address at New Harmony, "The Declaration of Mental Independence," Wright railed at the "tyranny" of matrimonial law and declared that American marriage practices and sexual customs had no force at Nashoba because they had "perverted the best source of human happiness—the intercourse of the sexes—into the deepest source of human misery." Unlike Robert Owen, who had not wanted blacks at New Harmony, Wright encouraged free blacks to come to Nashoba and thought that the community could be a model for "the amalgamation of races" in America. She also proclaimed "that religion occupies no place in the creed of the institution" and that "no religious doctrines shall be taught in the schools," holding instead to a single rule of moral practice, encouraging virtue as the pursuit of human happiness.[10]

The response to this was predictable. Nashoba's sentiments and practices, a correspondent to the *Western Luminary* wrote, "are at war with all civil and moral government, and are calculated to subvert, demolish, and utterly destroy piety, virtue, and good order in society, and entirely banish every thing like religion, or a belief in the Bible as the word of God from our world." By the time this outrage had flared in the press, however, the Nashoba experiment had collapsed. With poor management, resistant laborers, plunging cotton prices, and a complete lack of public support beyond the good wishes of some other starry-eyed reformers and the grandees who had been nudged by Lafayette, Nashoba had had little chance even before the revelations about sex, race, and religion.[11]

Wright and Robert Dale Owen retreated to New Harmony and quickly formulated a new reform project. It was not long before they fixed their gaze upon New York. From the failure at Nashoba, Wright learned, as she later wrote, that she had tried to do too much, too quickly. She had also trusted too much in the power of individuals to effect change when the principles of society worked against them. She had underestimated the immense distance between the American ideal of liberty and equality "and its development in practice." The Nashoba experiment had more "righteous intent" than "practical wisdom."[12]

A better way would be to persuade the masses—the sovereign American people—to transform themselves. She and Robert Dale would try to mobilize public opinion—she primarily on the lecture stage and he primarily in the pages of the *Free Enquirer*—and work within American political institutions rather than by forming an experimental alternative community outside of them. They would, Wright lectured, pursue reform "by firmly adhering to the constitutional principle, of effecting wholesale changes, *peacefully through their legislatures*...not by hastily subverting the existing *forms* of society." They would continue to decry economic inequality and slavery but postpone attacking either directly, instead leaving those problems to a future, wiser generation. The key to peaceful, gradual, but ultimately radical social transformation was to make that rising generation wiser through a rational, egalitarian, national education system. Going forward, Wright would try to avoid the dangerous topics of marriage and miscegenation and focus on education as the foundation of reform. She wished she could have avoided religion, too, but that topic instead loomed larger in 1828—a year, as she noted, of Sabbatarian campaigns, intensified religious revivalism, and Ezra Stiles Ely's "Christian Party in Politics." Religious notions and the clergy that promoted them were the biggest obstacles to the sort of rational learning and human improvement that she envisioned.[13]

Frances Wright's lecture series, repeated several times in various cities and published both in the *Free Enquirer* and in a separate volume, focused on a distinction between knowledge, on one hand, and opinion or belief, on the other. Knowledge, she argued, was the accumulation of facts derived from sense impressions of the material world. "MATTER AND ITS PHENOMENA are the real objects of human investigation and real subjects of human inquiry." The clergy who spoke of knowledge by faith or of faith as the knowledge of things unseen spoke nonsense. Beliefs and opinions ought to be based on facts. They needed to be tested against the available facts, a test that could show the belief or opinion to be either true, doubtful, or false. There were different grades of intellectual assent, "from the matter-of-fact certainty supplied by knowledge, down to the lowest stage of probability, supplied by belief." Religion was at best, though, a false belief, a mistaken judgment of facts. More often, however, religious beliefs arose with very little reference to facts at all: they derived from the imagination rather than from the nobler intellectual faculty of judgment. Or they were merely embedded in the mind by rote, the way a parrot learns words.[14]

Religion, then, had nothing to do with knowledge. Religion was "a belief in, and homage rendered to, existences unseen and causes unknown." Morality, a code of practice, had no necessary connection to "the stony ground of religious faith." The code derived from our natural ability to see the good and bad consequences of actions; the practice was powered by a natural, cultivatable moral sense allowing us to sympathize with others and to desire to be generous toward them. What, then, was religion's value? Her materialist epistemology rendered it nonsensical, and her naturalist, utilitarian ethics rendered it useless: "What is unreal in its nature, vague and ever varying in its lessons, could afford no safe guide to human reason, no just rule to human conduct."[15]

Wright's epistemological argument was wedded to her political strategy. Like many others in a tradition of political liberalism, she wanted to privatize religion in order to sequester it from public debate. She did so for at least three reasons. First, she denied that religion offered any viable intellectual resources for public deliberation. Public reason needed to operate on established facts—on knowledge—not on imagined speculations. Second, religion, historically, had damaged society. Its danger lay not just in its false beliefs and its cultivation of the wrong mental faculties, emotions, and behaviors (fancy, fear, and slavish obedience). It was more dangerous in its institutional development as a "trade" in which a body of men (the clergy), "set apart from the people," get wealthy by exploiting the ignorant. It was more dangerous, too, in its political mutation into a weapon of (or manipulator of) oppressive state power. Third, in a pluralistic society, religious arguments in a political forum were necessarily sectarian, serving the partial and parochial aims of a narrow interest group and enflaming passionate divisiveness for no legitimate public purpose.[16]

Both Wright and Robert Dale Owen wanted political deliberation to be uninfected by religious concerns—or even by the dialogue of skepticism and faith—but they differed over where discussion about religion did belong. Wright's ideal would have been a radical privatization. Ideas and feelings about God and the afterlife were so ungrounded by any factual evidence and so guided by personal peculiarities that they were not even worth discussing at all. She had strictly laid down a rule for herself, she said, a rule she recommended to others: "If beyond the horizon of things seen... any speculations should force themselves on my fancy, I keep them to myself, even as I do the dreams of my nightly sleep, well satisfied that my neighbor will have his own speculations and his dreams also, and that his, whatever they may be, will not coincide precisely with mine." People would best attend to their religious notions "by entering their closet and shutting the door." When on April 26, 1829, she opened the Hall of Science, an old Baptist church in a working-class neighborhood near the Bowery that she had purchased and converted for use as a forum for free inquiry she added the proviso that the free inquirers should "curb that futile curiosity" that encouraged the imagination to fly beyond the world of the five senses. They should "lay aside dreaming, and apply to observing." She hoped they would "preserve our popular meetings in this place uncontaminated and undistracted by religious discussions and opinionative dissensions."[17]

Robert Dale Owen agreed that specifically political deliberations (framing the platform of the Workingmen's Party, for example) should exclude religious (or irreligious) opinions and bracket sectarian identities. But the critical evaluation of religious truth claims remained a vital topic for nonpolitical public discussion. Perhaps in a lecture series or an essay one could clear the ground of religious detritus and then argue for reform by reasoning from empirical facts alone. But day to day in America in the 1820s, he knew, the progressive political, intellectual, and social struggle had several fronts, battles that had to be fought simultaneously rather than in sequence. Reformers, Owen believed, had to argue continually for the value of free inquiry and against the presumptions of religion even as they contended for specific reforms in public policy. The dialogue of skepticism and faith was crucial to the hearts-and-minds campaign in the arenas of public opinion, and it dominated the pages of the *Free Enquirer*. Rather than wishing to set aside debates with believers to focus on pressing social problems, Owen encouraged those debates. After Alexander Campbell had debated Owen's father in Cincinnati in April 1829, Robert Dale challenged, even taunted, Christians in New York City to step up and do likewise. The skeptics, he said, were more than ready to debate; the clergymen needed only to "name their own hour and place." Wright, too, whatever her ideal about religion-free public debate, was constantly drawn into questions about God and faith in the pages of the *Enquirer*. And in the New York Hall of Science a year after it opened, the free inquirers were busily debating Christianity.[18]

The free inquirers' singular political aim—to get legislation passed to establish their national, rational, republican educational system—was another matter. After Robert Dale Owen attended a public Mechanics Meeting in late October 1829 and was chosen as its secretary, his name became attached to the approved resolutions printed in the newspapers, allowing opponents to stamp the Workingmen's Party as a tool of religious infidelity, even dubbing it the "Fanny Wright Party." Owen argued strenuously that he was participating as a citizen and not as an infidel, free inquirer, or religious skeptic. His participation was "totally without reference to my speculative opinions," he wrote, and the Workingmen's Party ought not "be associated with *any* speculative opinions," either orthodox or heterodox. Wright and Owen both agreed that the issue was "national and not sectarian; political and not religious." That is, it was "national" in that the legislation would reflect the will of the people, as voiced in public assemblies; it was "political" in the narrow or formal sense of being about elections, legislation, and government. As such, religious issues were to be quarantined. Wright wrote that "the real object of such reform is *practical*, not *speculative*; it is not to convert men to Christianity, or to anti-Christianity, to Religion, nor to Irreligion, but to lead them to truth and virtue, by the paths of sound knowledge, fearless enquiry, and above all, by the national education of youth." In praising the stance of another newspaper, Wright defined what she considered to be appropriate political discussion: "We cannot detect to what sect our new editors belong. They may be Jews, Christians or Mahomedans for aught that appears in their columns; of only this we are satisfied,—*they are Americans*."[19]

Daguerreotype portrait of Robert Dale Owen (ca. 1840s). The son of industrial reformer Robert Owen, and a fellow free inquirer with Frances Wright, Owen published his debate with Origen Bacheler as the *Discussion on the Existence of God and the Authenticity of the Bible between the Christian and the Sceptic* (1832). Photo courtesy of the National Portrait Gallery, Smithsonian Institution; gift of Andrew Oliver.

Was free inquiry a sectarian position, and were the free inquirers an interest group, defined by their relation to religion, alongside Baptists, Presbyterians, Jews, Catholics, and other groups in a pluralistic society? No, Wright answered, free inquirers supported the human rights of free thought, speech, and assembly that had been built into the American experiment, and on the basis of these rights celebrated the ability to investigate and discuss all topics, including religious ones, and the opportunity for individuals to decide for themselves. In common parlance, however, free inquirers or freethinkers were not just those championing the freedom to think but those who had also come to particular conclusions critical of traditional religion. Owen called himself a "sceptic." He admitted that his skepticism was an opinion, a reasoned judgment he had come to about religious questions. He dismissed "infidel" as a bigot's label. He denied the charge of "atheism" because, he explained, he did not say that there was no God, only that he did not see enough evidence to decide the question either way. Skepticism for Owen was a position that after the 1860s would come to be known as agnosticism, which Owen combined with a habit of thinking: a fallibilist orientation toward all truth claims and a resistance to dogmatism of all sorts. Owen argued, though, that his opinions about religion, however labeled, just like his fellow citizens' Episcopalianism or Catholicism, ought to be screened from political debate.[20]

Wright, who liked to lecture with a copy of the Declaration of Independence on the desk in front of her, argued that she was reasoning not from a narrow, sectarian philosophy but from the self-evident principles of liberty and equality that were the foundation of the American republic. Whatever she or anyone else thought about God or religious faith was irrelevant; American political deliberation had to be religiously neutral, which meant agnostic about religious truth claims. The public educational system the nation needed to create also had to be neutrally indifferent to religion. As Owen and Wright portrayed it, they, equally with other citizens, would leave their religious or irreligious philosophies at the door of the public political forum. As their opponents saw it, by leaving God out of politics and the schoolroom Wright, Owen, and their ilk were in fact modeling American politics and education in their own (narrow, sectarian, atheistic) image.

Owen and Wright failed to see that if an education bill had gone forward, their religious opponents could easily have turned the tables on them. After petitions, politicians, and public opinion had beaten back the attempt to stop Sunday mail delivery and had raised alarm bells over Ezra Stiles Ely's loose talk about a Christian party in politics, the free inquirers were confident that powerful Protestant groups would be prevented from taking over public education and shaping it to their purposes. Probably too confident, a friendly correspondent to the *Free Enquirer* suggested. Christian beliefs and practices could have been smuggled into the national educational system under the names of common sense, reasonable consensus, or American moral traditions. Perhaps that outcome was too horrible to contemplate. Owen wrote that if the clergy did manage to take control of a national educational system, it would be fatal to reform; he would consider all his efforts to have failed, and he would leave the country in despair.[21]

Just like their Christian opponents, Wright and Owen saw their own ideological positions, through a disguised sort of metonymic inflation and abstraction, as the procedural framework for democratic politics and education. Religious skepticism was in their perspective at once the foundation of a comprehensive philosophy of a small minority of citizens and the default constraint of public reasoning and public schooling in a pluralistic society. Similarly, but in a less disguised way, they conceived of the social and political vehicle for achieving their goals—the working class—as both part and whole. In her opening address to the Hall of Science, Wright said that the eyes of the American "*people*" were opening, and then clarified that she meant "that large, and, happily, sounder part of the population who draw their subsistence from the sweat of the brow and whose industry constitutes at once the physical strength and moral prop of the nation." In an "Address to Young Mechanics" in the Hall of Science, she called the working class "the first[,] the largest, and the soundest fraction" of an artificially fragmented community, but one "whose immediate interests are most in unison with those real and natural interests of man." Even as she said she was not addressing manual laborers "as a class" but "as citizens," she argued that their "habits of industry," and the talents and good sense they developed in their occupations, made them ideally suited for the work of reform needed for "the salvation of the country." In an editorial in late December 1829, however, she simply wrote that the "industrious classes have been called the bone and marrow of the nation, but they are in fact the nation itself.... Here the people govern; and *you* are the people."[22]

Wright was a Wollstonecraftian feminist who had earlier championed the intellectual equality of women. Her very presence on the public stage as a lecturer on moral and political topics was a bold challenge to gender conventions. Moreover, when the *Free Enquirer* first started drawing serious attention to the plight of the working class, it did so by reprinting and commenting on Mathew Carey's shocking report on the exploitation of female workers—seamstresses—in Philadelphia. But the working class that Wright and Owen rallied to the cause of state-funded education was male. Free white male suffrage had just come to New York in 1827 as the last of the property requirements for voting were removed. The free inquirers courted this new enlarged voting bloc as the popular base for their plan of rational reform. Later in the same editorial where Wright had referred to "the industrious classes" as "the people," she further clarified that "men of industry" were "*the people*," and since in the United States "*the people govern*," she urged them to "govern as fathers as well as citizens, as citizens as well as fathers."[23]

Owen and Wright saw the nation approaching a crisis. Owen recalled the miseries he had seen in the dark satanic mills of Manchester and London's Spitalfield district, pondered the wretchedness, famine, and riots that the industrial system naturally produced, and worried that he had glimpsed the American future. Wright argued that in America the "improvements in machinery, in navigation, roads, canals, &c., and yet more, by the principle of competition" had already given an "excessive impetus" to commerce and manufacturing, ruining small businesses and oppressing the entire laboring class. A corrupt banking system had bent the scheme of internal improvements to "the advantage of speculators and capitalists," further depressing the wages of manual laborers. The "professional aristocracy, compounded of priests, lawyers, and college-educated aspirants" to commerce and politics had curtailed the rights of the many to benefit themselves. Finally, "as the roots of all these many abuses, we find a false system of education, stolen from aristocratic Europe" that "places the public mind under the dominion of priests, the legislatures at the mercy of lawyers, the industrious classes at the mercy of speculators, and, generally, all honest men and simple women at the mercy of rogues."[24]

In New York City by the end of the 1820s, the industrial revolution was already well under way, driven less by machinery in large factories than by a social reorganization of craft labor. In five years, since 1825, the city's population had grown from 166,000 to over 197,000 as young men and women from the hinterland and from New England came there looking for work. The jobs they often found were old crafts—shoemaking, tailoring, furniture manufacture—that had been subdivided into tasks for semiskilled and poorly paid piece workers. An economic depression in 1829 only made things worse, and neither the Jacksonians who had come to power in Washington nor the local political bosses at Tammany Hall had any policies aimed at helping urban laborers. In late April of that year, a rumor that shop owners were going to push for a change from a ten- to an eleven-hour workday led to public meetings of thousands of mechanics who threatened to strike. They created a standing Committee of 50, the first organizational step in a Workingmen's movement.

By October, the movement was becoming a political party pushing its own slate of candidates, a party with three factions emerging and struggling to control it. One group, led by Thomas Skidmore, who would publish *The Rights of Man to Property*, argued that the gross inequalities in society could only be addressed by an appropriation and redistribution of wealth. Owen and Wright thought that Skidmore and his followers were impractical extremists and that this plank in a Workingmen's Party platform would doom it to failure. They acknowledged the problem of economic inequality but thought that it could only be addressed by a generation that had been educated in an egalitarian school system. So the free inquirers allied with another group of more moderate political activists, entrepreneurial master craftsmen and shopkeepers who had once supported the party of John Quincy Adams and were now looking to Henry Clay. After the Workingmen's Party demonstrated surprising strength by taking a third of the vote at the November elections, the Adams-Clay men who said they supported a political voice for laborers and the free inquirers who lobbied for national education successfully outmaneuvered and marginalized the Skidmore men.[25]

But the free inquirers' education plan, which Wright outlined in public lectures and Owen developed in newspaper essays and editorials, had radical elements as well. They proposed a state guardianship system—state-run boarding schools for all children, who would be separated from their parents and educated equally according to rational (nonsectarian, fact-based) principles. When in the spring of 1830 the entrepreneurial Adams-Clay men in the Workingmen's Party then turned to purge the followers of Wright and Owen, they denounced the free inquirers' education plan as a "doctrine of *infidelity*," arguing that "skepticism was at the bottom of the proposal." The Jacksonians at Tammany Hall gleefully co-opted some of the more moderate pro-worker positions and stigmatized the entire Workingmen's Party ticket as a Skidmorian attack on private property and a Fanny Wright assault on God and morality. Tammany Hall won big in the November 1830 election. The Workingmen's Party only received 11 percent of the vote, barely a third of the number of votes it had gotten the previous year.[26]

The defeat dealt a mortal blow to the now-fractured "Workies" and to the free inquirers' dreams of a working-class movement that would produce gradual but radical reform by reinventing American education. Wright had already left the country the previous June, and had hoped that her absence would prevent political opponents from using her name as an infidel "scarecrow" (in this hope, as in much else, she would be disappointed). When she heard the news about the fall defeat at the polls, she sighed and turned her attention to what she thought might be signs of reform in France. By the time she returned to America in 1835, her moment of peak celebrity and influence had passed. Robert Dale Owen continued editing the *Free Enquirer* long enough to debate Origen Bacheler in its pages in 1831, exchanges that would produce the *Discussion on the Existence of God and the Authenticity of the Bible between the Christian and the Sceptic* (1832). Before leaving New York City, he delivered a farewell address in the Hall of Science in late October 1831, on the influence of the clergy. He followed this up with an early-November editorial, "Inroads of Superstition, Calling for Continual Exertions from Freedom's Friends." In it, he still expressed confidence "in man's *ultimate* redemption from superstition," but lamented "partial ebbings" in the rising tide of rational human improvement. He saw the clergy gaining more influence through clever ways to manipulate "that sovereign in a republic, Public Opinion": emotional revivals aimed at women, schemes to dominate colleges, and domestic missions to catechize families.[27]

The free inquirers had tried to shape public opinion by contesting religion's claims to knowledge and arguing for a politics that set those claims aside. The opening of the Hall of Science in New York City in 1829, and the crowds that regularly filled it, had seemed a sign that they were having some success. Although organized freethought in New York City would continue through the 1830s with Benjamin Offen's Society of Moral Philanthropists and other groups (which had no direct ties to working-class radicalism), the free inquirers' Hall of Science closed in the spring of 1832 and was sold in November. It was purchased by a congregation of Methodists.[28]

Health Reform and the Three Confessions of William Alcott

By the time William Alcott's publishing career began in the early 1830s, he was turning away from the reforms advocated by Frances Wright. Reflecting his conviction that reform needed to address all three dimensions of human beings—the intellectual, physical, and moral—the books and booklets listed on the bibliography published a year before his death in 1859 can be divided into three categories: works on education (nineteen volumes); works on physiology and health (thirty-one volumes); and moral conduct guidebooks and books written for the Sabbath School Library (fifty-eight volumes). His efforts in education reform had some influence: his focus on the construction of schoolhouses and calls for attention to physiology and health, for example, had an impact on the common school movement. His self-help books were the most popular, with *The Young Man's Guide* (1833) reaching twenty-two editions and *The Young Mother* (1836) twenty-one before 1858. Although overshadowed by Sylvester Graham, who was both mocked and celebrated for his gospel of bran-bread vegetarianism and sexual restraint, Alcott probably reached more people on the topic of health reform than any other antebellum writer. His didactic Sunday school books had a steady readership in his day but have been mostly ignored since his death.[29]

Portrait of William Alcott. From William A. Alcott, *Lectures for the Fireside: Founded on the Ten Commandments* (Rochester, N.Y., 1850), frontispiece. Alcott's turn away from religious skepticism marked his work as a health reformer.

Similarly, he published three volumes of "confessions," corresponding to the domains of mind, body, and spirit: *Confessions of a School Master* (1839); *Forty Years in the Wilderness of Pills and Powders; or, The Cogitations and Confessions of an Aged Physician* (1859); and *My Progress in Error, and Recovery to Truth: or, A Tour through Universalism, Unitarianism, and Skepticism* (1842). Each book, published without his name on the title page and masking many of the details of his personal life, illustrates knowledge gained through experience—self-reform through a bruising process of trial and much error—in education, medicine, and spiritual life. Each book, too, argued for a dynamic and progressive balance among the forces of intellectual, physical, and moral or spiritual development. Alcott only came to his mature understanding of the harmonious relationship of the three domains after a protracted struggle with religious skepticism and his ultimate rejection of religious liberalism—or, as he put in in the subtitle to his neglected spiritual confessions, his *Tour through Universalism, Unitarianism, and Skepticism*.[30]

Alcott and other "conservative," "nonpolitical" reformers—Sylvester Graham, insane-asylum director S. B. Woodward, and phrenologists O. S. and L. N. Fowler, among others—have been described as anxiously addressing the turbulence of Jacksonian America, particularly the corrosive effects of the market revolution upon traditional agricultural families and communities. Many of the leading advocates of health reform had, like Alcott, left their fathers' farms for the city and were frightened by the hordes of other rootless young men. The reformers then "condensed their sociosexual anxieties into a symbol system"—one that fantasized about the purity of the precapitalist order and imagined bodies needing to be carefully balanced with the energies of their material and moral environments. They urged individuals to take control of every aspect of their physical and sexual lives by recognizing and then adapting themselves to the natural and moral laws of health that had been obscured by the transformations wrought by modern commercial society. In the void left by the passing of the old patriarchy, they worked to restore order through the management (and some have called it the obsessive or neurotic management) of the body and daily behavior.[31]

Alcott's reform project in particular has been seen as emerging from his extended adolescence and tensions with his own father. But by the time he started publishing, he was in his early thirties, had been exercising "parental" governance in the classroom for well over a decade, and had earned status as a physician. Even before he married in 1836 and started his own family, he wrote to similar young men who were both fathers and sons, and he wrote from a religious perspective that worshipped God as a loving but commanding father and Christ as a selfless, obedient son. Reform for Alcott began with the individual but one who was embedded in his—and her—intergenerational family. The family—like the body itself—was in Alcott's work an inherited, natural form that nonetheless could be improved by informed, intentional acts. More often looking eagerly forward than anxiously backward, Alcott would see individuals and families, especially in the middle class emerging from the new market forces, as the agents of progress. He had discovered through painful personal experience that the avenues for self-determination within the constraints of obedience to divine law were both more effective and more comforting than the fretful, skeptical uncertainties underlying the Promethean arrogance of merely materialistic reform.[32]

William Andrus Alcott was born to a farming family in Wolcott, Connecticut, in 1798. A bookish boy in a town with few books, the teenaged Alcott tried to start a subscription library, but with little success. He practiced the prose style of a scholarly gentleman in letters exchanged with his cousin down the road, Amos Bronson Alcott, the future Transcendentalist, visionary education reformer, and Brook Farm communitarian. From a friend of the family, a garrulous veteran from the Revolutionary War, young Billy learned to venerate Benjamin Franklin, and soon his "heart throbbed" at the thought of someday becoming a printer, philanthropist, and philosopher like his hero. From this old veteran, "Sergeant K.," too, Alcott got his first taste of religious skepticism. The sergeant had drunk "deeply of the spirit and sentiments of Thomas Paine and Ethan Allen" and "had also become familiar with what has usually been called the 'French Philosophy.'" The main church in the town of about two hundred families was Congregationalist, another was Episcopal, and there were some Universalists. Most of the townspeople, Alcott remembered, "also knew something of the dream-book and of palmistry, and of the influence of the moon...on the world of humanity.... Many of them knew how to tell fortunes in connection with a cup of tea," and "not a few of them were skilled in astrology." To young Alcott, Christian beliefs seemed as fanciful as these popular superstitions. "Though I was unwilling boldly to deny, I could not believe. All sacred things appeared to me either visionary or doubtful."[33]

Around the age of seventeen, he read in a schoolbook the idea that in an hour of danger or distress the mind naturally seeks a Deity just as a hungry body seeks food or a tired one craves sleep. This made sense, he thought. Why would such desires be implanted in human beings if there were not objective realities to answer them? So there must be a God. On the basis of this natural theology, he became "a confirmed Theist." As a baby he had been baptized by an Episcopal minister, and as he approached adulthood his godfather urged him to be confirmed in the Episcopal Church. So he went through the ceremony, but for him it was an empty ritual. "The skepticism" of Sergeant K. "had made too deep an impression on my youthful mind to be very soon eradicated." Nonetheless, he "became nominally attached to the Episcopal church," even reading sermons to the small congregation, which often lacked a minister. So began his career as a

"Pharisee," as he later described it: going through the motions and attending to the external forms and rituals of religion without really believing any of it, other than the bare claim that there was a God.[34]

In 1816, just past his eighteenth birthday, Alcott began teaching school. He found the work exhausting, challenging, and crucial to any hope of reforming society. Thrown into a small, drafty room with forty students ranging in age from three to twenty, teachers were thought to be successful if they could, first and foremost, govern the classroom well. The townspeople expected strict discipline (at least if meted out to someone else's obstinate child), and Alcott gave it to them. He became known for his silent classroom and was not afraid to whack students with a rod or a ruler (as was the custom) to keep them in line. During ten school terms over a fourteen-year period, however, he came to see that his discipline had been too harsh and tyrannical. He learned to punish philosophically, continuing to think it wrong to spare the rod entirely but regretting having boxed ears and banged heads with a book. He came to allow more noise and movement in his classroom and strove to be kind without coddling. Two other lessons were equally important. First, he tried to develop a student's ability to think and reason rather than just recite well from memory and with proper elocution, and he invented creative exercises based on practical experience to engage a pupil's interest. Second, he realized that the classroom had to address the student as a whole person—as a physical and moral being and not just an intellectual one. He encouraged physical exercise, gave lessons in hygiene, and developed guidelines for building schoolhouses that would be more healthful physical spaces. He thought about the ways the schoolteacher had to set a moral example during school hours and in the community.[35]

But education reform was just a part of a much larger reform project. Improve a village school, he thought, and you can begin to improve a whole village—an idea he would develop, in fictionalized form, in *Charles Hartland, the Village Missionary* (1839). Unlike schoolmaster Hartland in the late 1830s, however, schoolmaster Alcott in the 1820s was not yet a missionary for Christian piety. He was, though, passionately dedicated to reform. "My mind was prone to dwell, with great pleasure," he later wrote in *Confessions of a School Master*, "on the idea that I was born for the purpose of improving the condition of my fellow men." His spiritual confessions, *My Progress in Error*, give a better sense of the nature of his reform project. He saw infants as pure rather than contaminated by original sin and thought human beings had the potential to either rise toward the angels or sink toward the beasts as their domestic and social institutions shaped them. The notion of the perfectibility of man, of civilization's improvement toward a future golden age, was inspiring. As for the traditional beliefs of his Christian neighbors, he thought that faith in God's "supernatural interference" was misguided and that the evangelical teachings about a work of divine grace in conversion destroyed human agency, making a person "wholly passive like a mere machine." The "disinterested benevolence" some preachers talked about was a fantasy; a person's every act was connected to self-interest of some sort, and the aim should be to enlighten that self-interest and to connect it to the greater good. The doctrine of the Trinity was incomprehensible, and the thought of sinners suffering in an eternal hell was repulsive. It was clear that true reform had to rest on modern, enlightened, post-Christian ideas, and that these were the ideas he had to introduce to his village. Carefully.[36]

Based on views that would have been decried as "infidelity" if openly expressed in a rural village in once-Puritan Connecticut, still called the "land of steady habits," the work of reform had to involve, Alcott determined, considerable efforts to publicly pass as a Christian and conceal his real beliefs from nearly everyone. He attended church every Sunday, though he felt a much stronger attachment to his Masonic lodge and did little more, as he listened to weekly sermons, than sit in his pew and imagine counterarguments. As a teacher required to board with different families through the school term, he made sure that he participated in the morning and evening family prayers. In 1827, Alcott joined the Congregational society in town and volunteered to be taxed for its support. In this he was not unlike his old skeptical friend, Sergeant K., who at times throughout his life had affiliated with different sects "for the sake of appearances" and for social reasons, even though he thought the Bible was a pack of falsehoods. Alcott even started teaching Sunday school and began a Sunday school library—for which, however, he made sure he selected several titles expressing "liberal" sentiments.[37]

His critical habits of mind and ability to analyze all sides of a question helped him talk some of his neighbors toward more enlightened ideas without directly advocating them. "I was peculiarly fond of hearing discourses and reading books, which supported sentiments wholly contrary to my own; for it afforded me much gratification to refute them, mentally—sometimes in notes with my pencil. I always fancied that I could prove my own sentiments from the very sermons and books which contained the strongest arguments against them. Hearing a sermon, one day, on the eternity of future punishment, I could not help thinking and remarking that I could prove the contrary doctrine from the minister's own concessions." In conversation, he would argue a heterodox position held by the Unitarians, Universalists, or Quakers, not as his own view but merely, ostensibly, to demonstrate that popular prejudices against those groups did not do them justice. "Perhaps," he would say, a member of the sect you are criticizing "might meet your argument thus...." He made great efforts, he later wrote, "in endeavouring to convert my friends and neighbors to the true 'faith,' as I regarded it; though in general, rather by the Socratic mode of argument, and by throwing difficulties in the way of their former beliefs, than by openly avowing, and boldly and honestly inculcating my own sentiments." When pressed on his own beliefs, he made great use of paradox. "There is no such thing as self-denial," he might say; "the whole business of life is pleasure." If someone challenged this, he could backtrack to define "pleasure" in such a way as to remove the objection. When sometimes he went too far, and drew accusations of infidelity, he found refuge in ambiguous definition. Did he or did he not believe in the Fall? Yes, he could say publicly, though among his intimate friends and "disciples," he could confess that he "believed" in the Garden of Eden story allegorically, as a story referring to the general tendency of people, as they matured, to fall away from the purity they had as infants. Did he believe that Jesus Christ is our Savior? Yes, he could say, though privately reserving the right to construe the term "Savior" in a very particular way: Jesus was a good man with a moral message that could save us from vice.[38]

He told himself and he told his friends that they could redefine traditional religious language according to the terms of modern enlightened moralism: "We hear much said about God. Now God means *good*, and good is *God*. Devil means *evil*, and all evil is *devil*. Just in proportion as you can get rid of evil, by forming good habits, just in the same proportion, you are delivered from the bondage of the devil; and 'God dwells in you, and you in God.' Again: hell is bad feeling; heaven is good feeling, or mental and moral pleasure. Your great business is to get rid of the devil, and make your way to God as fast as possible.... As to seeking Divine aid, the truth is about thus. When you have any good or proper feeling, that is Holy Spirit, or Holy Ghost. The more you are actuated by proper feelings and dispositions, the more you will improve in this respect, or in other words, the more you will be influenced by the Holy Spirit."[39]

For Alcott, "forming good habits" was as much a physical as a moral practice. He had always been relatively sickly, suffering from a bad case of the measles, dropsy, erysipelas (a skin condition), and consumptive tendencies that augured an early death. When his health broke down from overwork in 1825, he decided that he might not have the physical stamina for schoolteaching. So he studied with a local physician, took courses at Yale, earned his medical degree, and began practicing medicine in his hometown. Through experience at his patients' bedsides and experiments on himself, richly illustrated in the pages of *Forty Years in the Wilderness*, he came to the conviction that most of what passed for medical knowledge was guesswork and quackery. Physicians prescribed poisonous pills and potions that usually did more harm than good. If people could only be taught basic lessons in anatomy, physiology, and hygiene, they would see that there was much they could do, by reforming their daily habits, to avoid becoming sick in the first place. Natural laws determined how bodies worked and best interacted with their material environments. Violating those laws produced illness and disease; adopting habits that accorded with them promoted health and well-being. Alcott prescribed fresh air, moderate exercise, adequate sleep, daily bathing, and a bland vegetarian diet consisting mostly of whole-grain bread and root vegetables. Tobacco, alcohol, coffee, and tea were all poisons to be completely avoided, he insisted; people should drink only water (but not too much of it). He denounced feather beds, hot food, condiments, spices, and constrictive clothing. The sweet shop could lead to the brothel's bed and the barroom gutter, and masturbation produced epilepsy, palsy, apoplexy, blindness, idiocy, and insanity. People needed to keep their minds calm, their bodies cool, and their appetites controlled.[40]

In *Forty Years in the Wilderness*, Alcott described the dramatic moment in 1826 when he fully embraced the principles behind these new ideas—a conversion experience of sorts. He was twenty-eight years old and "in one of the darkest periods" of his life, "driven to desperation, nay almost to insanity and madness." His health had broken down again, and, suffering from "cough, night-sweats, purulent expectoration, and hectic fever," he thought he might be beginning his slide toward death from consumption. He had tried all sorts of medicines but had worsened. He was tired of being "dependent on the physician and the apothecary's shop." It was July Fourth, and he imagined his own declaration: "Why can I not declare independence of all external remedial agents, and throw myself wholly on nature and nature's God? I know, full well, the laws of my being. If trust in these, and faithful and persevering obedience will not save me, nothing will." The following day, though he could not walk more than a short distance without succumbing to a coughing fit or breaking out in a cold sweat, he took a long carriage ride to a mountain he had always wanted to visit. Atop the mountain "was a tower some sixty or seventy feet high, which commanded a view of the surrounding country." He was determined, despite his illness, to climb to the top, and after a night's rest he did so. Reaching the observation deck, "I took a survey of what seemed to me a new world. Here I renewed my declaration of independence with regard to those earthly props on which I had so long been wont to lean, and of dependence on God, and on his natural and moral enactments."[41]

The God he depended on was Nature's God, who had framed the physical laws suggesting that proper diet, exercise, and Alcott's own willpower might allow him to overcome his ailments. He did gradually get better and began planning for his medical career—an optimistic focus on life, he thought, rather than a depressive fear of impending death, also serving as a powerfully restorative tonic. After this experience, he claimed, he was "emancipated from slavery to external forms, especially to medicated forms. But I had not only declared and found myself able to maintain independence from medicine, but I had acquired much confidence in nature and nature's laws. And this faith in the recuperative power of nature was worth more to me than worlds would have been without it."[42]

The reform of bodies, then, as well as the reform of minds and morals was part of Alcott's plan for village enlightenment and reform in the late 1820s. Through reading and writing, though, he also began to connect his hopes for little Wolcott to the progress of larger reform movements. Writing short articles and reviews for the newspapers brought him to the attention of other reformers in New England, and he opened a correspondence with one who happened to be a Unitarian. The gentleman was "a zealous friend of every measure which had for its object the improvement of our race." Gradually religious topics came up, and this "fellow worker in the common cause of humanity" began sending books, tracts, and papers on various reform movements, which Alcott "read with great pleasure." He also began reading in Unitarianism more broadly and found many of the ideas and sentiments easy to accept. He started corresponding with other "distant 'liberal' brethren" and learned that his efforts were applauded by still more. He asked them how he might best enlighten and reform his neighbors, and they cautioned him to go slowly and improve by degrees.[43]

Alcott began secretly circulating liberal books and tracts but found more success through conversation. Political suspicions about consolidating evangelical institutions (national missionary, Bible, temperance, and Sunday school societies) were "an entering wedge" for his ideas. Alcott related his discussion with a Mr. H., a man of a particularly anticlerical bent, who rested on his hoe and listened as Alcott portrayed the American Bible Society as a step toward a publishing monopoly and therefore toward the curtailment of freedom of thought and expression. This was part of the "orthodox" clergy's scheme, Alcott continued, to finally secure something like a union of church and state, and it was time for an "*enlightened* moral influence" to oppose it and save the nation. Mr. H. listened for half an hour and nodded in agreement. Alcott had similar successes as a village "apostle of free inquiry," swaying small groups with tavern and tippling-house harangues about the evils of bigotry, superstition, religious mystery, and sectarianism. He made lists of his "converts" for his correspondents, with some labeled as "*certain*" and others as "*thinking*."[44]

Alcott broadened his reading: he read all the Unitarian publications he could get his hands on, and those of Universalists, Swedenborgians, and even Catholics. He read classics from the previous century by Godwin, Voltaire, Mirabeau, d'Holbach, Wollstonecraft, Roland, Paine, Cooper, and Jefferson. He explored the writing of contemporary freethinkers in both the United States and England: Frances Wright, Robert and Robert Dale Owen, Robert L. Jennings, Abner Kneeland, Orestes Brownson, Robert Taylor, Richard Carlile. "With the *enlightened deists*, as they were sometimes called, of New Harmony, New York, and Philadelphia, and subsequently with those of Boston, perhaps few men in the country kept up a better acquaintance." As he expanded his correspondence network, he began "to dwell on Utopian projects," studying the communal experiments of Ballou, Owen, St. Simon, Fourier, and the Shakers, and dreaming of transforming the world. "I procured the lectures which Frances Wright delivered in some of the principal cities of the United States, and read some portions of them to my friend's family. They interested me so much, that I sometimes read with tears in my eyes; at others, I read and wept alternately."[45]

Despite these tears, Alcott's head, as he put it, may have been full of "the *enlightened deists* or *free-thinkers*," but his "*heart* was with the *Unitarians*." In Wolcott it was murmured that he had, in fact, gone over to the Unitarians, which Alcott denied. Few in Wolcott had ever glimpsed a living, breathing Unitarian in town, and Alcott did not want to be the first. Privately, his skepticism had already driven him "*beyond Unitarianism*" to "the confines of Rationalism or Deism"— he had concluded, for example, that the scriptures did not offer any moral insights beyond what could be gleaned from everyday experience. But if he were outed as a Unitarian, and driven out of town as a liberal prophet without honor in his own country, he could at least run away to Boston and be welcomed by a community that already claimed him as a convert. He knew that if instead he "became suspected of Deism, or Skepticism," finding a community of refuge, "a safe resting place," would be considerably more difficult. There were, he knew, small groups of freethinkers in the major northern cities, but they were far less stable and reliable than the polished and respectable Unitarians of eastern Massachusetts. So sometime probably in early 1830 he set out on a journey to meet with Unitarians, and then on another to visit free inquirers, in both cases meeting people he had known to that point only on paper.[46]

These trips would change the direction of Alcott's religious life. The dialogue of skepticism and faith that continually played in his mind would shift dramatically. The change came initially less from any decisive intellectual breakthrough or upwelling of religious sentiment than from a recognition of his social affinities.

He also visited Universalists but never seems to have seriously considered joining them. He was already familiar with Universalists, since there were a few in town, and he had even boarded with a Universalist family while teaching school. He found them to be, in general, a moral and quite open-minded people, some even, "though ostensibly opposed to skepticism," secretly approving of Frances Wright. He thought that when they finished shaking off the doctrines of the Trinity and of the plenary inspiration of the scriptures, they would "be on the high road to Robert Owen's and Fanny Wright's land of mental and moral 'independence.'" For the time being, though, they were just not that intellectually or socially interesting.[47]

The Unitarians were a different, more exotic species. Alcott was eager to enter their social circles, talk with them, and hear them preach. He did so and felt welcomed. But he was struck by their fondness for fashion, luxury, and extravagance. They had little interest in proselytizing for what they claimed was the truth and were too fond of feasting at elaborate dinners, enjoying evening parties, dancing at balls, attending the theater, and playing whist. Their religion began to seem like an unstable amalgam of skepticism and faith merely pasted together by social custom. A Unitarian preacher Alcott heard seemed to waffle on the nature of Christ. (Was Jesus just a man? More than a man? It was never clear.) Another, chatting with Alcott, was so evasive on the same topic that Alcott left their meeting sure that the man was actually "a skeptic." In a private conversation with Alcott, a candidate for the Unitarian ministry revealed his knowledge of Hume and Godwin and conceded that St. Paul's reasoning was "sometimes quite *inconclusive*," though with a knowing look and tone he admitted that he would not be so frank publicly. A Unitarian layman felt freer to declare his conviction that the Bible was "an obstacle in the way of human improvement." Alcott secretly agreed but still found it shocking to hear someone calling himself a Christian but arguing like a disciple of Voltaire.[48]

Unitarianism, Alcott decided after seeing it firsthand as a living practice rather than just on the page, was a weak-willed, inconsistent, halfway system. It seemed clearer after his tour that there was "no defensible middle ground between orthodoxy and downright skepticism." He could not believe in what he considered to be "orthodox" Christianity, but "skepticism I was a little afraid of." So he "stood on the verge of skepticism, not knowing whether to go backward or forward."[49]

Alcott then traveled to meet the free inquirers and tried to imagine joining them. "I found that they had greatly overrated their numbers, talents, and respectability; though not their zeal or disposition to make proselytes." He was not pleased when, after a Sabbath lecture on chemistry, they amused themselves with nitrous oxide (laughing gas). The Unitarians were too polished, worldly, and complacent; the freethinkers were too crude, abrasive, and vulgar. The skeptics seemed more honestly to pursue the logic of liberal principle to its rational end, but joining them would be an "apostacy" more painful to his friends and family back in Wolcott. "I returned to my home, and for some time continued in a state of painful suspense." He had tiptoed to the edge of apostasy, peered over at radically different possible futures, and then stepped back. His liberal correspondents would later suggest that there were financial considerations behind his turn toward orthodox Christianity, which Alcott denied. But there were other costs—personal and social ones—that made him draw back from a life dedicated to a radical reform project rooted in a skeptical critique of Christianity.[50]

He spoke with two orthodox friends on other topics and clutched at the fact that their sentiments on issues he cared about other than religion—medicine and health, or education—seemed so sensible. Then someone, perhaps one of these orthodox friends, handed him a book by the Scottish Presbyterian moral philosopher and theologian Thomas Chalmers (probably *The Evidence and Authority of the Christian Revelation* [1814]). He next reread William Paley's famous

View of the Evidences of Christianity (1794). Both books, Alcott wrote, "made some impression," perhaps because Alcott was ready to be impressed. "I began to think that religion, after all, *might be true.*" The more he worked through the arguments, the more he saw the balance tipping in favor of Christianity. On any other subject, he thought, if he found nineteen arguments against a proposition but twenty for it, it was his duty to "yield at once to the preponderating evidence." With religion it should be no different. So he became a Bible believer, but it was hardly a eureka moment: "As a choice of difficulties, then, Revelation was received."[51]

Belief in the Bible as God's revelation still left him, however, with all the perplexing doctrines of "orthodoxy." The Trinity—and therefore the questions of Christ's true nature and of the operations of a Holy Spirit—still remained a major sticking point. Though later Alcott would come to accept that some doctrines had to be considered mysteries beyond the grasp of human rationality, in the early 1830s he still found this notion philosophically repugnant. A friend talking with him on a walk one day then offered an analogy that provided a way out of the impasse. Dr. Alcott, the friend said, "you are fond of making man a kind of *triune*, composed of body, mind, and heart; but do you contemplate the nature of this triple union? If you do not, why do you speak of them so frequently, as if they were in some measure independent of each other, when they really constitute but one individual?" Alcott had no answer. He was utterly committed to this way of understanding the "wonderful and wonderfully complicated" human character, speaking of the three aspects as analytically distinct but completely integrated in an individual human being. The parallel, as imperfect as it was, allowed him to return to troublesome passages in the New Testament and find support for Trinitarian belief.[52]

His turn toward orthodoxy helped him change his efforts at reform, not abandon them. He had just recently begun a "grand experiment" in education reform in his schoolhouse. Significantly, he had decided he would not "attack or even slight old usages. My object was to change the spirit of the school, rather than innovate largely upon its forms." This would become his defining strategy in the next phase of his career: change the spirit within old institutions rather than create new ones. It would align with the evangelical's emphasis on individual conversion and church revival rather than the social engineering of Wright and Owen; with the conservative's call to strengthen "traditional" families and communities rather than the radical's effort to revise gender roles and reinvent communal structures. It would create a reformer who would acknowledge slavery as a "great national evil" but devote himself to combating the "still more shocking... slavery of bad physical habits."[53]

As he was reorienting his spiritual and intellectual life and recovering once again from an illness that had driven him from the classroom, Alcott met William

C. Woodbridge, who had just returned from Europe with dreams of educational reform. Alcott started sending out articles to newspapers and magazines, published his prizewinning essay on schoolhouse construction, and, in 1832, followed Woodbridge to Boston to help edit the *Journal of Education* and other periodicals. The next year, he published *The Young Man's Guide*, a manual offering advice on health and hygiene, character formation, and navigating the social world. The chapter on business management included a guide to the six sorts of unsympathetic people; the one on intellectual improvement offered six rules for reading newspapers; and the chapter on marriage featured eleven qualifications to consider when choosing a wife. The book was a best seller, and suddenly Alcott, who had always skated on the edge of poverty, was free from debt and could see a new way to maintain his financial security. He had found his audience, and he found his voice as a health advocate, education reformer, and life coach to the young, aspiring, Christian middle class. He started churning out books and articles at a remarkable pace, which he kept up for the next quarter century.[54]

The industrialization of the northeastern economy and the commercialization of the countryside enabled Alcott's new career. The Boston book trade had developed and expanded in the 1820s as major firms stabilized their financial foundations and improved their distribution networks. In the 1830s, exploiting new technologies (stereotyped plates and new papermaking machinery), publishers began lowering prices to spur sales. With better roads, new canals, expanding postal routes, and more rural printers and booksellers, reading became "a necessity of life" for all but the very poorest inhabitants of the rural northeast, too. Driving demand in the new book market was a new middle class—a class more distinctive in its ways of working and styles of living than previous generations of middling artisans and farmers had been, and more powerful as producers and consumers of the commodities sustaining those lifestyles.[55]

Alcott intended *The Young Man's Guide,* he wrote, for "persons in the middle rank of life." It was a book-buying public that, as he later noted, "most imperiously demanded" books that were written "in the right style and spirit." The middle class certainly needed reform, though perhaps less so than the classes on either side of it: in *The Young Husband* (1839), he noted that while the prostitution of marriage did exist in "the industrious middling class," it was found "most among the two extremes of luxury and abject poverty." Alcott's reform project was less a reactionary's recoil from the disorder of the modern city than an effort to bring a hybrid provincial sociability—neither country-bumpkin rusticity nor overly refined urban gentility—to it. The members of the American Physiological Society that Alcott helped found in 1837, and who shared his vision, were either skilled artisans or tradesmen (neither unskilled laborers nor elite professional men), all with middling incomes. Alcott wrote to and for men like them and their wives. He offered them neither elegant prose nor cheap sensationalism but straight talk for earnest self-improvers. He would come to imagine that this "class of citizens," this group of readers with such tastes, numbered in the "many millions."[56]

In Boston, Alcott joined Lyman Beecher's former church, and much of Alcott's writing for women, such as *The Young Mother* (1836), *The Mother in Her Family* (1838), and *The Young House-Keeper* (1838), shares the philosophy of domesticity of Beecher's daughter Catharine, whose *Treatise on Domestic Economy* appeared in 1842. Married in 1836, the man who had once (secretly) admired Frances Wright now wanted women in the home as wives, mothers, and housekeepers. A woman loses her great influence, he wrote in *The Young Woman's Guide to Excellence* (1840), "the moment she departs widely from the province which God in nature seems to have allotted her; when, like a Wollstonecraft, or a Wright, or others still of less painful notoriety, she mounts the rostrum and becomes the center of gaping, perhaps admiring thousands of the other sex, as well as of her own." He sought to elevate the importance of women's work in the domestic sphere as an intellectually challenging "profession" and hailed women as society's essential early moral, physical, and intellectual educators.[57]

Alcott's animus against institutional innovation sharpened when he focused on the family. God had authorized two institutions, the family and the church, he wrote, and we should be content with those (though in truth he concentrated on the family and the school). He would become so disenchanted with political innovation as an engine of social reform that in an 1836 essay he would denounce the American Revolution as an unchristian act of rebellion against "parental care." Even setting the extreme case of revolution aside, Alcott would come to believe that the idea of human happiness depending on "the modes and forms of government," the "influence of rulers," or "the efficacy of free institutions" was misguided. No civil government could bring liberty and happiness to a nation unless the whole physical, moral, and intellectual characters of the individuals who composed it were brought under the influence of a holistic Christian education, which was most importantly provided in the home. With a proper control of the nursery, Alcott wrote in *The Young House-Keeper*, it mattered little "whether the government be that of a monarchy, an aristocracy, or a democracy."[58]

Alcott's most enthusiastic and optimistic testimonials for the power of health reform to change the world came in a late publication, *The Laws of Health* (1856). As a general rule, he argued, obedience to God's physical laws would be rewarded with good health and long life. This led to some tantalizing questions. With enough knowledge of the physical laws, was it possible even to purge the body of inherited diseases? Since we can pass on our improved physical health to our progeny, might not the human life span, after generations where obedience to the laws approached ever closer to perfection, reach, if not immortality, then a length measured in centuries, as in the age of the patriarchs? Such speculations can seem like some sort of perverted postmillennialism, a heresy of works-righteousness, a fantasy of human perfectibility in which flawed creatures recover Eden through their own efforts. This view of Alcott the self-help author and body reformer links him to strains of American individualism, optimism, and bootstrap-tugging progressivism, but it misses the character of the faith he found after his years of skepticism.[59]

God gave man two sets of laws, Alcott believed. The Decalogue, or moral law, was given to Moses on Mount Sinai. God's physical laws, the second set, are learned only through studying the human body and its interactions with its environment. God requires obedience to both sets of laws, but the analogy between the two goes only so far. Violation of both moral and physical laws entails punishment, and obedience to them is rewarded. But human beings, flawed as they are, cannot—or will not—adequately obey the moral law. To be restored to God's good favor, they must be redeemed from sin by Christ. Obedience or disobedience to the physical laws works differently. Rewards and punishments are meted out in this world rather than the next. They are built into the very fabric of the material world: obeying the law requiring moderate exercise produces health and happiness; violating the law against consuming poisons causes illness or death. Good works—healthful habits—will earn people blessings (though not a ticket to heaven); bad habits—sins against the body—will not, however, be redeemed by Christ.[60]

As much as Alcott promoted the idea that human beings held, in their own hands, the power to improve their physical lives, he recognized the limitations of that project. It was, after all, merely polishing the temporary vessel of the soul. Satan might fill his own mind with knowledge and buff up a healthy physical body, but he was still Satan. Without a renewed heart, intellectual power and physical health meant little. That was the lesson Alcott learned when he turned toward Christianity in the early 1830s. He found faith not when he decided that the Bible might be true after all but when he subsequently experienced "a striking change of feeling. From a habit of regarding myself as the centre of the universe, the point at which all my efforts ought to turn, I began to regard God as the centre of the moral world." As subjects of the double set of divine laws, human beings needed to recognize both their power and their impotence, their ability to improve their lives through self-determination and their abject need for God's grace.[61]

Alcott's experience was also a testimony to the lingering power of doubt. His interior dialogue of skepticism and faith was never entirely silenced by these new beliefs and feelings. Even after he accepted the Bible, he constantly found himself falling back into former mental patterns, "so thoroughly were all my habits of thinking, and feeling, and reasoning, and acting, formed in the school of skepticism." At the end of *My Progress in Error*, he described this continuing conflict—no longer speaking metaphorically—as a battle with the devil: "But alas! You know not how I have destroyed myself. You know not how strangely my former skepticism has insinuated itself into all my feelings, thoughts and habits. You know not what worlds the devil is permitted to hold out to me; to what an extent he is permitted to assail me; and how feeble my unhappy and unholy habits of thinking render me, in conflict with him."[62]

To see Alcott in his medical "confession," *Forty Years in the Wilderness of Pills and Powders*, marching down from the mountaintop like a Mosaic lawgiver with his Laws of Health and as a prophet of American renewal with his new Declaration of Independence, is to miss some of the ironies undercutting that scene. First, he deflates his own self-dramatization a bit by admitting that he actually missed making the trip to the mountain on the Fourth of July and had to strain to retain the symbolism by reminding himself that "one of the South American provinces" (Venezuela) declared its independence on July 5. Second, his declaration is as much one of dependence (on God's laws) as of independence (beginning a journey of self-determination). And the emphasis on dependence—on obedience to authority—would only deepen in the next decade after he embraced Christianity. He would come to describe the "fancied independence and strength of fallen humanity" as a satanic delusion. He would no longer see, as he once had, the human subject—the pupil at his desk or the American citizen at the polls—as needing only to be informed and then freed to make his own choices; he needed instead to learn the law and obey. Finally, Alcott's bold claim that he had emancipated himself from artificial aids (like medicine) is more than a little qualified by the admission, several chapters later, that after the mountaintop epiphany, Alcott, dosing himself to get through the school day, was briefly an opium addict.[63]

The mountaintop scene in his medical confession resembles two others in his spiritual confession, *My Progress in Error*. After reading about the ritual of church covenant renewal, Alcott resolved to perform something similar for himself. So on a beautiful October day in the mid-1820s he hiked up to a high hilltop with pen, ink, and paper, and at sunset, "overlooking a humble parish church," "with the 'ghosts of departed' *skepticism* hovering about" him, he signed his own confession of Christian faith. But he would set that creed aside and not return to it for another half-dozen years, for those skeptical voices had not yet departed, were not mere ghosts. When he did return to Christianity, he described another mountaintop view. This one was not from an actual mountain but in his imagination, after he had paced alone in his locked room where, he wrote, again "the ghosts of former skepticism appeared and beset me." He likened himself not to Moses on Sinai receiving the commandments but to Moses on Mount Pisgah at the end of his life, gazing into but not being able to enter the promised land: "When from Pisgah's top, to which I had climbed to catch a glimpse at the promised Canaan, I first saw the fair fields which a feeble but kindling faith anticipated as mine... how could I help rejoicing in Divine Goodness?" However: "Here I stand on the very confines of the land of promise, but am not permitted to go over and take full possession." He feared his faith was not strong enough, his skeptical habits too ingrained, the damage done by years of error not fully reparable, like the harm to the body done by years of smoking tobacco. Then there was the fear of relapse: "Sometimes I find myself falling back even into the very wilderness from which I have just emerged; indeed I sometimes stray so far away, that it appears quite doubtful for the moment, whether I ever find my way out again."[64]

Alcott wrote books encouraging young middle-class men and women to wash behind their ears, eat their vegetables, be nice to their neighbors, and enjoy marital congress no more than once a month, not because he thought such things alone made up a Christian life but because he felt that he could not speak authoritatively about the experience of faith—about being selfless like Christ, constantly walking in God's presence, and loving God with all his heart. His Sunday school books retold Bible stories and taught moral lessons but did not try to portray the inner life of saving faith. In *Travels of Our Savior* (1840), he paused to describe himself as having once been "as destitute of spirituality as these apostatizing Jews" who rejected Jesus, but he may have found some solace in the fact that even the Apostles Peter and John "half relapsed into their former skepticism" during times of trial. Alcott could better relate to the skeptical sinners than to the selfless saints.[65]

Skepticism was dangerous, he thought, because he worried that it could permanently warp a person's character. He wrote *My Progress in Error*, after all, to warn others not to follow the path he took, though many others seemed to be doing so. He believed that the current educational system, dominated in Massachusetts, at least, by religious liberals and closeted skeptics, focused only on enlightening the intellect, ignoring the student's physical and moral character and thereby creating an intellectual "monster," a creature with only a head. Such monsters tended to speculate, criticize, and rely on their own reason. "Hence... our Universalism, Unitarianism, Rationalism, and in fact our Skepticism."[66]

It is true that, after writing that "the *modern school* of 'free inquiry'... is the way to death and hell" in 1840, he was more sanguine by 1849: freethinking did not necessarily lead to skepticism, he wrote in *Familiar Letters to Young Men*, but even if it did it was worth the risk. Freethinking or free inquiry really just meant inquisitiveness, and that was a good thing: "Greatly do I rejoice when I find a young man who *thinks*, even if his road should chance to lead through skepticism." What explains the difference? Semantics, in part. In the first instance, he was referring to free inquiry as a synonym for the skepticism or infidelity of a Wright or an Owen. In the second, he was referring to how free inquiry ought to be understood. Still, while the older Alcott did not think the poison of skepticism less potent, he seems to have acquired more confidence in the antidote. There were "two classes of men," he believed, who were "the principal persons who became infidels or skeptics in this country." One class was composed of "our intellectual, speculative, superficial men," the intellectual monsters. The other was made up of "physical monsters," people who lived as if they were all body, born to do nothing but gratify their sensual appetites. Together, these formed "the two extremes of society... the *scum* and the *dregs*," one rising to the top, the other sinking to the bottom (genteel Unitarians playing whist; coarse freethinkers playing with laughing gas). Few skeptics or infidels, Alcott thought, inhabited "the middling class—the plain, the honest, the sensible, and the moral." Perhaps Alcott became less afraid of skepticism as he aged because he came to have more faith in the good sense of the aspiring American middle class—the sorts of people who bought his books.[67]

Ernestine Rose and the Religious Roots of Patriarchy

What were Americans to make of the Hartford Bible Convention, held from June 2–4, 1853? *Harper's New Monthly Magazine* had an answer. Begun in 1850 by the nation's most powerful publisher, *Harper's* by 1853 had already achieved an unprecedented national circulation, and its editors took seriously the ambition for the literary periodical to produce and promote American nationalism. In the "Editor's Table," a several-page editorial that opened every issue, they tried to guide readers toward what was appropriate to read—and to think—in a unified, advancing national culture. "Error must develop itself," the article on the Hartford Convention in the August 1853 issue began. The convention, the editors explained, was itself "utterly undeserving of notice," but it "becomes significant as one of the signs of the times." The Hartford assembly of "reformers of every grade" demonstrated how error had progressed within the reform movement. Many of the leading reformers had been, some years before, "sincere professors of evangelical truth," but after finding that biblical teaching did not fit the social "machinery" they wanted to create, they tried to reinterpret the sacred text. Then they dropped the Old Testament and wrote off parts of the New Testament that they decided had to be the mistakes of fallible human authors. Finally, the reformers had to face the facts and give up the whole Bible because it "does teach and will teach conservative doctrine. It does uphold government, it does consecrate the domestic relations; it does establish the family; it does say, Children obey your parents, Wives be subject to your husbands; it does acknowledge the relation of master and servant, of ruler and subject. It enjoins obedience to laws we may not have made, submission to authority we may not have created. It is in all respects conservative." Error must develop itself, the editors repeated: the reformers then turned to try to find God in Nature. But they eventually had to admit that everywhere they looked in the natural world they found not purity and order but "pain, disease, pestilence, death." They inevitably docked in their final port, denying a personal God in a "cheerless, hopeless, soulless atheism." Wise conservatives—wise Americans—followed a far more reasonable route: they realized "that in these latter days of the world, faith is more rational than ever before," that reason's highest exercise was in "discern[ing] the limits of its own powers," and that scriptural revelation was their safest harbor.[68]

"Prejudice must develop itself," the *New York Reformer* answered. "It may take the form of fashionable piety." The *Reformer* was not surprised at the "groaning" that was heard after the Hartford Convention from publications trying to be popular and profitable—from the nexus of religion, commerce, and cultural power. "So long as commercial religion possesses the power to promote men to worldly distinctions, to honor and emoluments, so long may we expect certain institutions and money-making periodicals to unfurl the flag of popular superstition, and under it to fight each and every Reform." The *Reformer* did not blame the *Harper's* editors personally, for their criticisms merely emanated from "existing social arrangements. Society is a combination of mutual antagonisms. We blame and condemn not individuals, but the institutions which make them what they are. Men first form constitutions and laws; then the constitutions and laws form them." Real reform could not occur unless people reconstituted fundamental social institutions.[69]

What had actually happened at the Hartford Convention may have been difficult for readers to discern from the newspapers that reported—or, rather, condemned—the event (the convention *Proceedings* would not be published until the following year). News accounts mocked the participants. It was a "gathering of brain-cracked odds and ends of both sexes," the Universalist *Gospel Banner* reported. The *New York Tribune* described a "motley" concourse, "there being a sprinkling of blacks, persons with unshorn beards, women of a very quarter-of-a-dollarish air, and men of longing and enthusiastic aspects. There were those who seemed to be ambitious of playing the Christ of the movement, in so far as it could be done by parting their hair on their foreheads, and leaving it uncut behind, and wearing beards to match." The *New York Herald* noted that many of the convention men "were remarkable for the length of their beards, and their general appearance indicated that their washerwomen were deceased. The ladies bore upon their countenances that rigid, inflexible and stern gravity, which has characterized strong-minded lady philosophers of every age. The sable portion of our population was but feebly represented by two ladies of color, who, if we may judge from the frequent exhibition of their 'ivories,' thought the whole matter the best joke in the world." A New York correspondent for the New Orleans *Daily Picayune* thought cold contempt rather than chuckling ridicule was the appropriate response: "There is not a person prominent in the convention who is not known as an infidel and a traitor to his country, and notoriously polluted from top to toe." What such people had to say was, many reports insisted, not worth serious attention. The convention produced only the "wildest rant" and "declaration without substance," the *New York Times* sputtered; nothing more than "ignorance, presumption, folly, nonsense" and "twaddle" suited only for "idiots and lunatics."[70]

The call for participants, circulated in the spring of 1853, had been signed by 168 men and women mostly from Connecticut, Massachusetts, New York, New Jersey, Pennsylvania, and Ohio—itself a sign, according to the *New York Herald*, "of the spread of infidelity, if not insanity, in this latitude." The call was addressed "To the Friends of Free Discussion" and it proposed a full and open dialogue on the "Origin, Authority, and Influence of the Jewish and Christian Scriptures." Although the sponsoring committee imagined debate divided equally between speakers arguing "pro and con" in regard to the plenary inspiration of the scriptures, it recognized, and welcomed, a diversity of opinion. "There are many who believe that a supernatural Revelation has been given to man; many others who deny this, and a large number who are afflicted with perplexing doubts—trembling between the silent skepticism of their reason and the fear of absolute denial." Some believed the Bible to be a perfect record of God's will. Others thought it an incomplete revelation that had served man well in the past but needed to be superseded by a new dispensation for the modern age. A third group thought it "a curse rather than a blessing to mankind." The convention invited "all who feel an interest in this question, without distinction of sex, color, sect, or party, to come together, that we may sit down like brethren in a communion before the altar of intellectual and spiritual freedom." Press accounts dismissed this language about free inquiry and discussion as mere façade for what was to be a platform for infidels to revile God's Word. The *New York Times* called the convention "a mere sink of skepticism fed from the impurest sources." The *New York Observer* identified those sources: the "leading spirits" of the convention, the paper reported, were the Spiritualist Andrew Jackson Davis, the abolitionist William Lloyd Garrison, and the women's rights advocate Ernestine Rose.[71]

Davis had in fact been a main organizer of the event. The "Poughkeepsie Seer" had caused a stir in 1846 with the publication of *The Principles of Nature, Her Divine Revelations, and a Voice to Mankind*, eight hundred pages reminiscent of Emanuel Swedenborg that Davis said had been revealed to him in a trance state. With the sensation caused by sisters Catherine, Margaret, and Ann Fox, who claimed to have made contact with the world of the departed through "spirit rappings" in Hydesville, New York, in 1848, Davis emerged as a leading philosopher of the rapidly expanding Spiritualist movement. He had moved to Hartford in the winter of 1850–51, joined a group of "spiritual investigators," and worked on his "Harmonial" philosophy, which he hoped would move beyond Christianity and unify progressive reform movements.[72]

Davis was the first speaker at the Hartford Convention, which may have led some press accounts to misinterpret the whole four-day event as an affair run by "Spirit Rappers" and devoted to their "strange mania." But Davis did not use his time to talk about mesmerism, clairvoyance, trance visions, or messages from the spirit world. His address was a paean to free inquiry and public discussion. He denied that the organizers of the convention were motivated, as critics charged, by a "desire to spread skepticism on religious subjects." On the contrary, he said, "we design to do all we can to prevent skepticism in those principles which God declares to be *the true religion!*" The purpose was to find God, to find out what that true religion actually was, and then cultivate not skepticism but a rational faith. He was not, he insisted, anti-Christ. But he was antibigotry, antislavery, and antisuperstition. He was against anything either within the covers of the Bible or outside of them that prevented the growth of true religion and the progress of true reform.[73]

When Davis concluded, a "burly fellow" who was "much excited"—a man identified in the press as "one Dr. West, a notorious theological pugilist and a strolling adventurer"—rose in the back of the hall and denounced what had just been said. He castigated "Davis and the Davisites" for trying "to seduce the affections of the people from their government, and to introduce anarchy and confusion." Davis's "hellish stuff," West charged, was "an attack upon all our institutions that are worth living for—it is blasphemy." This outburst caused a "boisterous uproar." After order had been restored, an old antislavery reformer named William Stillman tottered forward. "'I know,' said he, 'that the Bible is true and that it is the Word of God, and you cannot shake that.... it is all I've got left in this world, and I mean to stick to it.... I agree with you on the rum question, and the slavery question, and upon many other questions—[but] upon this *I pity your delusion.*'" The convention was off to a rocky start.[74]

The Spiritualist perspective was not voiced on the floor until two days later when Samuel B. Brittan spoke. Discussion until then had focused on exchanges between reformers Joseph Barker, Henry C. Wright, and Parker Pillsbury on one side, and Adventists George Storrs and Elisha M. Turner on the other. Barker sometimes sounded like deist Elihu Palmer, criticizing the contradictions and absurdities of the scriptures, and he took a few shots at Dr. David Nelson's *Cause and Cure of Infidelity* along the way. Wright sometimes sounded like William Alcott in his liberal phase, urging obedience to God's natural laws for life, health, and happiness. Pillsbury, a former Congregationalist, confessed that he had become convinced six years before "that neither slavery, war, nor intemperance could be abolished until the faith of mankind was shaken in the divine authority of written, re-written, transcribed, re-transcribed, translated, and re-translated Scriptures. A people blindly bowing before such divinities never will, never can, advance." The Adventists argued that critics of the Bible used Nature's God or Nature, an imagined natural theology or natural moral sense, to expose the flaws of the text, but that "nature" in any of these guises was even more ambiguous, opaque, and ethically dubious than what they charged the scriptures with being. Brittan, the Spiritualist, argued that both the naturalists, who confined their gaze to the visible, material world, and the biblicists, who confined inspiration to the authors of the Testaments, missed the fact that "Inspiration," the influx of the spiritual world into the physical, was universal and perpetual. With "illuminated vision," men and women now, in the middle of the nineteenth century, could draw back the "vail [sic] that separates man from the invisible world." Brittan offered a resolution to that effect, and Davis spoke again to reinforce the point. But none of the other speakers who were skeptical of the Bible addressed the Spiritualists' claims. Storrs, the Adventist, noted that the desperate and misguided turn toward Spiritualism was simply a result of the poverty of the old, deistic religion, which could establish a God as a First Cause but say nothing of his moral character, and offer people advice for life in the world but say nothing about immortality: "The very resort to rapping spirits is an acknowledgment that the God of Nature reveals nothing in regard to man's future life."[75]

Garrison did not give a full address to the convention until late Friday evening, but press accounts, and the brawlers who broke up the meeting on Sunday, singled him out. His notoriety helped give the gathering its radical political character. When the Portsmouth, New Hampshire, *Journal* described the Hartford meeting as a gathering of "infidels and fanatics," it named abolitionists, with Garrison leading the list. The Hartford *Courant* placed Garrison at the head of the "ultra Anti Slavery men," fanatics who would rather abolish slavery than save souls through Jesus Christ. The "ruffians"—many of whom were identified as theology students at Hartford's Trinity College—who had thrown the convention into turmoil whenever Ernestine Rose spoke gathered after the last session around the stairway and doors to the convention hall, hurling insults and curses at the people who filed out. But they chanted one name: "'Garrison! Garrison!'... 'Where is Garrison? 'Bring him out!' 'Put a halter around his neck!'" Somehow, though, Garrison, who had been mobbed before, was able to slip through the crowd unnoticed.[76]

When Garrison began his famous antislavery paper, the *Liberator*, in 1831 on the uncompromising platform of immediate abolitionism, he had been an orthodox Baptist. But by the mid-1840s, after years of facing hostility to his cause by clergymen and the institutional mouthpieces of the major Protestant denominations, he had abandoned many of his former beliefs, including the notion that all of the Bible was divinely inspired. In his convention speech, he made it clear that he still valued much that was in the Bible. He summed up his position with resolutions he proposed on the convention's final day. The Bible, he argued, "embodies a large amount of truth—vital, precious, eternal; ... some of its requirements are just and obligatory; some of its warnings are salutary and instructive; some of its promises soul-searching and glorious; some of its commands and precepts rational and righteous; some of its views of God and Nature elevating and inspiring." But "it also contains many fallacious contradictions, misconceptions, misrepresentations, fabulous stories, incredible assertions, and hurtful errors." Every individual had to use his or her reason and conscience to separate the wheat from the chaff. For resolving social and political questions, the Bible was nearly useless: on vital issues such as slavery, capital punishment, and war, one could find biblical verses to support either side of the question. It could not be a rule of faith and practice. As history had shown, adopting it as such had turned it into a tool of religious and political despotism.[77]

Garrison aimed his bitter censure not at the Bible but at the American "educated, popular, 'evangelical' clergy": the cowards who had refused to come to the convention, and had left the defense of their sacred volume to two self-taught Adventists—men they despised as heretics; the Pharisees who had urged the press to treat the convention with contemptuous silence; the dogmatists who insisted that their faith had already triumphed over the skepticism of Bolingbroke, Voltaire, and Paine, so there was nothing left to say; the hypocritical, corrupt men of the cloth who retreated from moral principle for the sake of their salaries, winking at the Fugitive Slave Act and deaf to the crack of the slave driver's lash.[78]

As much as Davis rankled and Garrison antagonized the guardians of American faith, it was Ernestine Rose's addresses that most provoked both the crowd in the hall and the commentators in the press afterward. Davis and Garrison did more than touch nerves: the Spiritualist threatened the boundaries of reason, and the abolitionist challenged the privileges of race. But Rose slashed at the deep sources of patriarchal rage.

Rose, according to the Middletown, Connecticut, *Constitution*, "made herself conspicuous by her blasphemy." The Bridgeport, Connecticut, *Republican Farmer* reported that she "was sarcastic and aggravating in her remarks and seemed disposed to exasperate those who differed with her." The Hartford *Courant*, having already described the convention as "a miniature Hell," turned to Rose's performance in high dudgeon: "The most revolting scene was when a specimen of the 'fair sex' pronounced her tirades against the Deity and the Scriptures—said to be the most blasphemous stuff uttered in the Convention." Christianity alone, the *Courant* declared, had rescued woman from the degradation she suffered in

Photograph of Ernestine Rose. From Elizabeth Cady Stanton, Susan B. Anthony, and Matilda Joslyn Gage, eds., *History of Woman Suffrage*, vol. 1 (New York, 1881), opp. 97. At the Hartford Bible Convention in 1853, Rose advanced the cause of women's rights by hacking at the religious roots of patriarchy.

savage nations; it alone had softened and dignified her condition, purified and ennobled her character. "Shame then to the woman, who will so far unsex herself as to be engaged, amid an assembly of male Infidels and scoffers, in attacking that institution which has rescued her from her bondage." This woman, the *Courant* continued, avoiding the use of Rose's name, "boldly impugns the Almighty for the station in which he has placed her, and belches out blasphemies against Him for her physical inferiority, and for His declaration in His holy Word that He has given woman to man as his 'help-meet.'... God so ordered—the Bible so proclaims—nature so ordains—and shame to that woman who loudly asserts in a public assembly that such a God is unfit for her worship and is not hers. Shame to the piebald assemblage of Atheists and Abolitionists and misguided fanatics that would encourage the declaration."[79]

Rose began her address on Saturday evening by calling the movement against the authority of the Bible "one of the highest and greatest importance" of the age. It was even more important than the cause that, she said, had so long "lain at my heart," the crusade for women's rights, because biblical faith was at the root of the oppression of women. Because women were, with scriptural warrant, condemned to inferior education and experience, they were more vulnerable to the pernicious effects of superstition. Thus, "the errors of the Bible which have been palmed off upon society as emanations from some superior wisdom and power," Rose argued, had "enslaved her far more than man."[80]

At this point, the hall was filled with some applause, as well as loud hisses and cries of "Shame, shame." Rose paused and surveyed the audience. The hall—a former church, with the pulpit removed—was full, with little standing room left on the floor or up in the galleries. She estimated that at least 1,600 people were present. Some of them, especially in the galleries, were angry. The convention to this point had had its pro and con speeches, its various resolutions, its less formal exchanges among the speakers, and an occasional outburst from the audience. But far more than in any previous session, here the presentation from the stage was becoming a dialogue between the speaker and a volatile crowd. Rose said something about pitying rather than scorning people who behaved irrationally, and then continued.[81]

Behind the convention's central question of the origin, influence, and authority of the Bible, Rose said, was the idea of "God." Where did the idea come from? In any age, she argued, it was simply the embodiment of a people's conceptions of greatness, wisdom, virtue, and perfection.

The hisses began again to rain down from the galleries. "I will wait till I can be heard," Rose said. There was more commotion. "This confusion is an evidence of the influence of the Bible," Rose said, because that book taught that women should not speak in public. "Oh, no, she must not raise her voice in behalf of truth and humanity, and if she does, she is met with confusion and riot by the believers of that doctrine." Scripture at once created the conditions that tried to silence women and in doing so invalidated its claim to be a font of knowledge and a rule for justice. In the deep past, she continued, men admired great hunters, warriors, and conquerors, and they shaped their gods of wood and stone in those images. In more civilized times, they closed their eyes and imagined more refined perfections. "It has been a great mistake to say that God has made man in his own image, for man in all ages and times has made his god in his image."[82]

Here Rose moved past the high-water mark reached by other speakers. Davis, Pillsbury, Garrison, and the rest distrusted parts of the Bible but still sought after God—in nature, conscience, or new inspirations from the spirit world. Rose was arguing that the quest itself was just a projection of the human imagination, the effect of the human propensity to fashion ideas and ideals into idols and then come to believe that they had independent life and power. Her comments brought another round of applause, hissing, and hooting. "Hiss on, if it does you any good," she said defiantly. "I know but too well what it is to go against the long-cherished and time-honored prejudices and superstitions." Persecution, often in more potent forms than hissing and hooting, she said, was the price of mental freedom.[83]

Rose then returned to the ground previous speakers had covered, arguing that the "inconsistencies, vices, and cruelties" found in the scriptures were impossible to ascribe "to a wise or kind and benevolent power or being." Her repetition of this point, however, prompted "hissing, stamping of feet, and whistling in the gallery," while other voices urged her to continue. "My friends," she said, "there once was a time when I had a voice strong enough to speak against all opposition and be heard, but that time is past." Someone shouted: "Go [to] it, mother." Rose continued: "My constitution has been somewhat broken, and mainly broken in the great conflict against error." This provoked laughter and hisses. Rose said that she hoped that people who opposed her opinions could at least behave like gentlemen ("Hear, hear," some shouted). A "Strong Minded Lady, very much excited" in the audience called out, "If you have a heart to speak, speak on." This prompted laughter and someone shouting, "Bravo, old 'un." Rose thanked her, to great applause, and said that she had long wished for this moment, hisses and all. Twenty-five years ago, she noted, she had started speaking out on this topic but had then felt completely alone. A small boy called out from the gallery, to much laughter, "Where was that, old gal?"[84]

Rose returned to her topic. The Bible was a "two-edged sword" to man but a "millstone" around the neck of woman: "it subjected her to the entire control and arbitrary will of man." Its libel against human nature began in its first verses. Genesis described God creating man and calling him good. But then he created woman—"not for the same aims and objects of life that he created man—oh, no!"—but to be "a mere plaything or a drudge" for man. Ridiculous, Rose said. "And yet, do you know, my sisters, that most of the subjugation of woman, the tyranny and insult heaped upon her sprung directly from that absurd and false assumption."[85]

There were many more such false assumptions in the Bible, the speaker continued, for it was an artifact of a different age, written by people—by men—who had less light. It held up "a blind faith in things unseen and unknown" as "the greatest virtue." This irrational faith, coupled with a call for obedience to irrational commands, was easily passed on from parent to child. It burrowed so deeply into the childish mind and heart that people would grow up willing to kill or die to defend it.[86]

Rose was then interrupted again by "hissing, hooting, and stamping." The convention chairman tried to restore order, to "ironical cheers," but then decided to have a collection plate passed while the audience resettled, which only caused further uproar. A woman shouted disapprovingly toward the galleries that "George Washington had more respect for a woman," a comment that was answered by clapping and hisses. Then someone turned off the gas for the lights, and the hall was plunged into darkness. For "some minutes a continual hissing, shrieking, stamping, drumming of canes, and whistling" was kept up. Men in the galleries in particular seemed to be making noise "to the utmost extent of their lungs." When the lights were restored, the chairman called on a Miss Murdoch for a song, in an attempt to calm the crowd, but she was drowned out by the gallery, where singers sang several songs at once, including "Yankee Doodle" and "I Once Knew a Nigger."[87]

As things quieted, Rose returned to the stage. When the lights went out, she began, it reminded her of one of the true things we find in the Bible: that there are some "'who love darkness better than light' (Laughter and applause)." She returned to her discussion of how religious faith, across cultures, was inculcated in the young; even so, she said, she remained hopeful that despite the cultural power of superstition, more rational and humane notions were still deeply "engrafted" in human beings. She then turned to the nature of belief, which was simply an automatic response to the evidence presented. It was a basic error of Christianity, she argued, to reward those who believed and to damn those who did not. When the crowd hissed at this comment, she noted that their hissing was perfectly consistent with their (mistaken) beliefs.[88]

Rose then turned to the influence of the Jewish and Christian scriptures and mentioned how Czar Nicholas in his subjugation of Hungary had justified his bloody atrocities with the Bible. When the crowd hissed loudly, she asked them, were they hissing Nicholas or the Bible? This produced "confusion and groaning," and more calls from the chairman for order. Rose said that her "friends" in the galleries "kept as good order as they were capable of," but she had "charity" for them, which was answered by "ferocious groans." A man in the gallery who was rudely dangling his legs over the railing called out what seemed to be a vague warning: "Don't, now, mother." Noticing him, Rose said that she had not heard of exhibiting one's boots over a railing as a way to defend the Bible, but that in the United States he was free to do it as long as he did not interfere with the rights of others. "I guess, mother," he answered, "that I have as good a right to show my boots as you have to discuss the Bible."[89]

She tried to return to her address, and her language grew more heated: "My friends, ... there never has been a heart broken, a tear drawn from the eye, a drop of blood from the human heart, nor a sigh of agony from the expiring victim, but the perpetrators of these horrid inhumanities have found authorities for it in the Bible." It was a "terrible outrage," she declared, and "a sad reflection" on humanity, that people "could be so enslaved by the authority of a book." When these remarks caused a further disturbance in the crowd, she noted that the confusion in the hall proceeded from a confusion in the mind, which itself was a "consequence of the confusion of the ideas taught by the Bible." The "Protestant republic" of the United States claimed to guarantee free speech, but "look at the conduct of the believers and defenders of the Bible.... Their disorder and riot is the best argument they can bring in support of it." She mentioned that Luther received the same reception from the pope, and when that remark earned more loud hisses, she asked who they were hissing—Luther or the pope? Someone yelled, "Good night. Time's up.... Sit down, old lady." In a tradition inherited from Protestantism, she said, we, too, "protest against the right to shackle the mind and prevent private judgment and freedom of speech; our protest here is in consequence of the protest of Luther; do you dislike it?" The crowd answered her question with applause, but also "hissing, and drumming of feet and canes."[90]

Rose went on. The Bible had kept humanity ignorant and vicious (more hisses, and shouts of "Time's up"). The Bible had done more to produce war, slavery, and intemperance than any other book ("Time's up, Mother!"). Then someone yelled, "You ain't a woman." "I have stood more than that," Rose responded, "but it does not ruffle my temper." There was "renewed hissing, indecent expressions, and disturbance." So Rose concluded. "To you my sisters," she said with passion, pointing to the women in the audience, "I would but say, that the defenders of the Bible have given you a most practical evidence of the rights and liberties Christianity has conferred upon you. The Bible has enslaved you, the churches have been built on your subjugated necks; do you wish to be free? The you must trample the Bible, the church, and the priests under your feet." Rose stepped down from the stage, and amid shouting and confusion that went on for "at least five minutes," the meeting was adjourned for the evening.[91]

The convention reconvened on Sunday morning. One of the Adventists, the Rev. Mr. Turner, responded to some of Rose's remarks. He denied that the Bible subjugated women. God's Word, he said, also required husbands to love their wives. Yes, wives had to obey their husbands—their loving husbands. Was there anything so wretched in the obedience Sarah rendered unto Abraham? Ernestine Rose stood to respond with another question. She asked if Turner would like to be placed in Sarah's position when she had to obey Abraham as he took a second wife. Turner said he could only answer that question if he were a woman. He explained that he was a friend of "*woman's rights,*" but women's rights were different from men's rights. "I go for the rights of woman and the Bible goes for the rights of woman. The Bible has assigned woman her place in the most tender department of human life." And, he added, "are there not those here who know that the very physiology of the female puts her sphere of action where the Bible places her? We know this as well as we know any other fact in the science of physiology. We know that the woman has had to be, of necessity, a woman, and not a man." Besides, Turner said, "when a woman becomes a man she will have no charms for me."[92]

Rose addressed the convention again in the afternoon. She clearly had not been cowed by the disturbances the night before. She pointed at the Rev. Mr. Turner "with much feeling and vehemence." What a "farce," she declared, "for him to stand here and talk about women's position and women's sphere, when he is incapable of placing himself for one moment in her position, to judge how she should feel under certain circumstances." The Bible writers, too, were men. How can man prescribe woman's proper sphere, define and interpret for her, enact laws to govern her, judge and condemn her, if he cannot understand her nature, motives, and feelings? "No! woman must speak for herself, she must help enact the laws by which she is governed, she must plead her cause, she must judge for woman." Turner had spoken about the "happy condition" of women in Christian society, as compared to their condition among Indians or Turks. "But," Rose countered, "if we compare her present position with what she ought, what she might, and would be, had she her full rights, as a human being, to education and position, then we find a difference almost too great to realize it, but of which Mr. Turner, not being a woman, can know nothing whatever [Laughter]."[93]

What do women want? She pointed again to Turner: "Our friend there," she said, "insinuated that we desire to become men. Do you, my sisters, wish to become men?" A voice from the crowd answered no. "We claim our rights irrespective of sex. We claim them, not only in accordance with the laws of humanity, but also in accordance with the Declaration of Independence." As she went on in this vein, her remarks were punctuated by applause. We want our inalienable rights, she said. Without them, I suffer; all women suffer; and men suffer, too. "We ask for knowledge, for knowledge is power." Eve should have eaten more of the fruit from the tree of knowledge, not less. "We want to be independent, for dependence is degrading," unless it is mutual and reciprocal, among equals. We do not want Turner's version, the Bible's version, of "women's rights"; we want equal "human rights, without distinction of sex, color, or country." We claim these rights, "not as a grant, or charity, but as our birthright."[94]

As she went on, she turned from the flaws of the Bible to the injustices in the common law, continuing to take occasional pokes at Turner and getting laughs and applause as she did so. Then it was back to the Bible, which she portrayed as anything but a promoter of civilization, progress, and happiness. When she criticized God in the Eden story for the harsh penalties he laid on Adam, Eve, and all their descendants, someone in the gallery cried out, "Hear, blasphemy." "Blasphemy!" Rose replied, "oh yes, blasphemy has ever been the cry against progress, and opposition to superstition." When she criticized the saints in heaven, as portrayed in the Book of Revelation, happily smelling the smoke of sinners roasting in hell, there was another disturbance in the gallery. But she was able to conclude her address without further disruptions. She closed by saying that the "simple law" of kindness was the only law, the only Gospel, that human beings needed to join together. "This is my faith!" It was a faith motivated by love. "Humanity! ... I feel a gushing of love within me beyond the power of utterance, not only for mankind but for all that are capable of feeling pleasure and pain." She sat down to "great applause."[95]

At the beginning of the convention's last session on Sunday evening, the chairman announced that the mayor of Hartford was present, and he had requested that there be no clapping or hissing in response to the speakers, especially in consideration of the Sabbath. Rose got into a brief exchange with the Rev. Mr. Storrs over various comments she had made about the scriptures. After Storrs professed his love for the Bible, to loud applause, Rose again got up to speak, but "the storm which had been brewing burst like an avalanche upon her head." She was immediately interrupted by "stamping of feet, clapping of hands, drumming of canes, whistling, and ribald speeches in the gallery." There was also "groaning, hissing... barking, crowing," and cries of "down, down," and "Go home." The exasperated chairman called the scene "the most infamous proceeding I ever knew," to "ironical cheers" and "ferocious yells." "I was told today," Rose tried to say above the noise, "that the cause of disturbance last evening was owing to some very irritating language I used." The commotion in the gallery continued. She asked if anyone could point out any such language she had used toward any person, a question that provoked more furious yells. She said a few more words about her honest convictions, commitment to truth, and hopes that her comments might do some good, and then she sat down. The chairman, Joseph Barker, tried to present a closing address, but stopped when "bursts of indignation" poured down upon him from the gallery. Then a fight broke out. Someone pulled out a short dagger. Others swung canes. Town officials tried to make some arrests but were pulled into the brawl. Men crowded around the steps and the doors, calling for Garrison, but all the convention's speakers, including Ernestine Rose, were able to exit the building safely.[96]

The radical reformers had been heard and mocked, condemned and ignored, shouted down, applauded, and threatened with violence, but were left standing to talk and argue another day. And so the Hartford Bible Convention ended, a fitting emblem of the dialogue of skepticism and faith that occurred in the antebellum American public sphere.

10

Infidels, Protestants, and Catholics

Religion and Reform in Boston

In the mid-1830s, an exposé of Boston politics by the disaffected Jacksonian John Barton Derby had marveled how "infatuated" Protestants had wound up pushing religious life in the city to extremes. One of the most infatuated, the Rev. Lyman Beecher, delivered "Lectures on Catholicism" in Boston over four evenings in December 1830. Just as he would denounce freethinking infidels in his *Lectures on Scepticism* a few months later, he argued that Catholics could not be faithful citizens in a republican government. As Beecher spoke, the city's Catholic population was surging: from five thousand in 1825, it would exceed twenty thousand by the time Derby published in 1835 and would surpass thirty thousand (one-quarter of Boston's population) by 1845, the eve of the Irish potato famine. The new and more confrontational leadership of this rapidly growing church did not let Beecher's insults go unanswered. Bishop Joseph Fenwick and Father Thomas J. O'Flaherty responded with lectures of their own. O'Flaherty was particularly pugnacious in his reply to the "rank aspersions" that had been "wantonly and wickedly flung against Catholics" by the Calvinist minister. As the press reported at the time and Derby recalled later, "thousands of good Protestants went to hear what the Catholics had to say for themselves." Derby contended that many of these Protestants "found Dr. O'Flaherty more than a match for Dr. Beecher. And as they could not believe the absurdities of Catholicism, they became sceptics." This was a rather fanciful explanation for how the "formidable infidel party in Boston" led by Abner Kneeland was founded—a faction that Derby claimed constituted "at least a third of the Jackson party of the City." Still, Derby's account captures the sudden widening of religious and irreligious possibilities in Boston, as well as their political potency and perceived cultural threat.[1]

In the spring of 1839, the infamous freethinking reformer Abner Kneeland left Boston for good. A former Baptist and then Universalist minister who had renounced Christianity and had joined with Frances Wright and Robert Dale Owen, Kneeland had spent sixty days in jail for blasphemy the previous summer.

In that same year William Miller, a skeptical deist turned Baptist preacher, gave his first Boston lecture, arguing that Christ would return to earth in 1843—and so, presumably, progressive reform was beside the point. As Kneeland shook the dust of Boston from his shoes and Miller proclaimed that the end was near, Boston lawyer and politician Horace Mann extended his public crusade for education reform and struggled privately with religious doubt. By 1839, another Boston reformer, Orestes Brownson, had already been a Presbyterian, a Universalist, and a socialistic free inquirer. The thirty-six-year-old editor of the *Boston Quarterly Review* was by then a staunch Democrat in a Whig city and a Unitarian in the orbit of New England Transcendentalism. Few writers of the period wrote with more sustained attention to the problem that concerned all four men: the challenge of religious skepticism to the grounds of American faith and the relation of both to social and moral reform. Brownson, however, in a few years would convert to Catholicism and condemn infidel and Protestant reform alike.[2]

Orestes Brownson's religious experience stretched right across the range of extremes that Beecher had condemned and Derby had described, from skeptical infidelity to Catholicism. His examination of philosophical, theological, social, and political problems in the pages of the *Boston Quarterly Review* and its successor, *Brownson's Quarterly Review*, earned him a reputation for vigorous prose and probing criticism. His knack for acquiring a new religious identity more often than some men put on a new suit, and his habit of dismantling arguments he himself had published a few years before, also earned him a reputation as a gadfly, especially after his turn away from Protestantism and radical reform and toward Rome and political conservatism by 1844. Together with his essays and reviews, three of his books tie questions about skepticism, faith, and reform to personal and historical experience: *Charles Elwood; or, The Infidel Converted* (1840), *The Spirit-Rapper* (1854), and *The Convert* (1857).[3]

The books might be called epistemological narratives because they combine personal narrative and epistemological argument. Each book depicts the progress of a narrator as he thinks his way through his involvement in events such as the rise of the Workingmen's movement in the 1820s, the interest in mesmerism in the 1830s, the presidential election of 1840, and the European crises of 1848. Each story concentrates on the way that its central figure encounters different dogmas and philosophies, and his eventual enlightenment analyzes the spirit of the age. Brownson specifically engages philosophical arguments about the relations of subject and object, and the nature of knowledge, belief, and opinion. The books construct what can be described more specifically as a social epistemology because Brownson examines the ways that social practices allowed individuals, communities, or whole nations to form true beliefs—or how society's well-worn ruts prevented people from gaining real knowledge and grasping the

A. L. Dick and A. Morand, "O[restes]. A. Brownson," ca. 1843. Brownson, who was a Presbyterian, a Universalist, a skeptical free inquirer, and a Unitarian before becoming a Catholic, thought in 1840 that there was not much open religious skepticism in America, but there was a "vast amount" that was hidden and untold. Courtesy of the Library of Congress.

truth. Brownson's narrators are not Cartesian subjects alone in their rooms, or Emersonian eyeballs gazing at the truth of Nature (and the nature of Truth). They are young New England and New York men searching for knowledge amid the social and political turmoil of their era.[4]

The years when Brownson, Miller, Kneeland, and Mann made their way to Boston and made names for themselves can be considered a transitional period in American religious history. The early Republic's revivalism, with its appeals to *sola scriptura* and individual conscience, had led to a confusion of competing voices proclaiming different religious truths. The swell of Catholic immigration from Germany and Ireland challenged the hegemony of Reformed Protestantism. Presbyterians, Methodists, and Baptists split along sectional lines as the morality of slavery became an inescapably public moral issue. In the seminaries, German Idealism began to transform a Protestant theology that had been wedded to Common Sense Realism, and in some wealthier parishes, the growing appeal of High Church sacramentalism further diversified religious practice.

The economic depression of 1837–43 dealt a blow to the reform impulse and prompted desperate people to seek new religious and social answers. Especially in New England and New York, a region being rapidly remade by industrialization and the expansion of commercial markets, these changes could sometimes open the door to more than just a reorientation of existing forms of Protestantism. Some people became profoundly alienated from the religious culture they inherited and embraced radical departures such as Mormonism. Others, instead of looking for new ways to fulfill their religious desires, were prompted to reflect upon the ways those desires themselves might be, as we would say, socially constructed: produced by time, place, and circumstance rather than a reliable guide to transcendent truth. Pondering life and death, God and the soul, the state of the world and the direction of history, they asked fundamental questions and were no longer easily satisfied by their preachers' practiced answers.[5]

Brownson's epistemological narratives offer a useful way to explore not only his experiences but those of infidels and converts like Miller, Kneeland, and Mann as well. Brownson's three books dramatized, contextualized, and gave narrative form to the philosophical argument, social criticism, and historical reflections found in his periodical essays. The books addressed problems that the other men, in quite different ways, worked through as well. Like Brownson, the others confronted religious skepticism and sought for new grounds of reliable knowledge. Like him, they criticized aspects of American society that impeded progress, and thought their own life stories reflected larger historical patterns. Highlighting these similarities is not meant to suggest that the three other writers connected personal narrative and socio-epistemological critique in the same way that Brownson did. None of them wrote quasi-novels or fictionalized autobiographies. Yet together the stories of these four very different characters recovers the increasingly open religious skepticism and the "vast" reservoir of concealed religious doubt that, as Brownson argued, inflected several varieties of American faith flourishing in the second quarter of the nineteenth century. Miller's answer to doubt was to return to the Bible; Kneeland's was to ground reform in free inquiry; Mann's was to preach the gospel of education. Brownson's Catholic answer was to submit to the authority of Rome and see progressive reforms—including those that after 1848 became attached to the new Spiritualist movement—as the work of the devil.[6]

Doubt and Calvinist Orthodoxy

Brownson, Miller, Kneeland, and Mann came of age during the first four decades after the American Revolution. Each rejected an inheritance of New England Calvinism and struggled with religious doubt. Brownson and Miller returned to

Protestantism after their bouts with skepticism. In doing so they had to come to terms with the Bible as an authoritative source. They had to make sense of the relationships between their own acts of scriptural interpretation, the norms established by their faith communities, and the challenges made to their truth claims by others in the larger society who believed differently, or not at all. Skepticism helped mold Miller's Adventism, for the arguments he had used to persuade himself that the scriptures were divine were also the key to persuading doubters of Christ's imminent return. For Brownson, by contrast, a steady course of Bible reading did not quiet his doubts. Nagging questions about the logic of Protestant biblical interpretation and his resistance to Presbyterian efforts at social control led him to slough off Calvinism once and for all.

Brownson was born in Stockbridge, Vermont, in 1803. After his father died, six-year-old Orestes was sent to live with foster grandparents on a small sheep farm in the adjoining township of Royalton. In *The Convert*, Brownson described these plain country people as nominal Congregationalists who taught him the Calvinist catechism without requiring him to believe it. With few books in the house beside the Bible, Brownson spent a lonely childhood in imagined spiritual conversation with Jesus, Mary, and the angel Gabriel. He sampled the local Protestant denominations and usually attended the meetings of the Methodists and "Christian" sect because they made the most noise and painted the most vivid images of hellfire. Evangelical preaching, however, made him fear hell more and love God less. At fourteen, he was thrown into a very different world when he moved back with his mother to the bustling resort town of Ballston Spa, New York. "I fell in with new sectaries, universalists, deists, atheists, and nothingarians," he wrote. Confused by the turbulent religious pluralism of early nineteenth-century New York and confronted for the first time by people who challenged not only evangelical doctrines but the divine inspiration of the Bible and the existence of God, Brownson found himself "in a labyrinth of doubt, with no Ariadne's thread to guide me out to the light of day." Brownson's fictional Charles Elwood described the author's own feelings of alienation as a village infidel: the pious regarded him with righteous horror, and Christian friends shunned him in public, fearing their own orthodoxy would be questioned.[7]

Like Brownson, William Miller grew up with a thirst for knowledge in a small farmhouse that contained few books beside the Bible.[8] Born in Pittsfield, Massachusetts, in 1782, Miller moved with his family to Low Hampton, New York, in 1786. Whereas Orestes Brownson looked back upon his youth and saw an aimless boy needing a father's authoritative guidance, Miller recalled the tension with a father who once threatened to whip him for reading rather than resting at night. Miller turned instead to local gentlemen like Jeffersonian congressman Matthew Lyon, who lent him books and encouraged his studies. Miller's mother was a Baptist, and his grandfather and uncle were Baptist ministers, and young William brooded over the eternal destiny of his soul. But he drifted away from Baptist concerns about sin and damnation through his association with religious liberals like Lyon, and made a decisive break when he married in 1803 and moved to his wife's hometown of Poultney, Vermont. There he found a public library where he read Voltaire, David Hume, Thomas Paine, and Ethan Allen; he found fellowship in a Masonic temple, where he rose to the highest rank; and he found that the leading citizens, men who would become valuable friends and patrons, were deists. Miller continued to believe in God but considered the Bible to be a work of priestcraft. He amused his deist friends by mimicking and mocking the pulpit mannerisms of his grandfather and uncle. For Brownson (and his fictional Charles Elwood), religious skepticism was coupled with social ostracism and alienation, but for Miller, doubting the old family dogmas was the sensible orthodoxy for a young man on the rise in Poultney.[9]

William Miller's deist phase lasted from 1804, when he established himself in Vermont, to 1816, when he moved back to Low Hampton, New York, after

Lithograph of William Miller (1851). Converting from skeptical deism, Miller decoded biblical prophecies and became convinced that Christ's Second Coming would occur in 1843. Photo courtesy of the National Portrait Gallery, Smithsonian Institution.

fighting in the War of 1812. By the later years of his deism, however, while coming no closer to a biblical faith, he had soured on the deists' platitudes about the nobility of man. His study of history had demonstrated the corruption of human character, and his social experience had persuaded him that self-interest and dependence always marred friendships. The vices of military life convinced him that the patriotism he had praised in July Fourth verse was a sham. In the fall of 1812, a conversation with a friend showed him that the logic of deism led to a belief in personal annihilation at death, not to hopes for heaven, despite what writers like Paine maintained. "I began to think," he recalled years later, "that man was no more than a brute, and the idea of hereafter was a dream; annihilation was a cold and chilling thought." In the war, he saw men around him killed on the battlefield and swept away by a fever that also claimed his father, sister, and grandfather in the winter of 1812–13. In letters home to his wife, he brooded about mortality, horrified at the thought of his life going out "like an extinguished taper." His despair increased after the war: "The more I reasoned, the further I was from demonstration. The more I thought, the more scattered were my conclusions. I tried to stop thinking, but my thoughts would not be controlled." Though still an unbeliever, he began attending Baptist meetings in Low Hampton with his mother and uncle.[10]

Miller concluded that the astonishing victory of the Americans over superior British forces at the battle of Plattsburg in 1814 belied the notion of the deists' distant, watchmaker God, for he could only explain the victory he had witnessed by ascribing it to the interposing hand of Providence. As he prepared to celebrate the anniversary of the battle in 1816, he heard a sermon that deeply moved him. A week later, he was overcome with emotion while trying to read aloud a sermon on parental duties to his mother's Baptist congregation. Miller then decided that he needed a savior like the Jesus the Baptists spoke about, but he was still not sure he could trust the Bible. His old deist friends repeated the questions and criticisms that he himself had once aimed at Christians: How do you know the Bible is true? Why would God cloak his truth in such complexity, contradiction, and ambiguous mysticism? Miller decided that if the Bible really was God's Word to humanity, then it must be consistent, harmonious, and intelligible. He began his intensive Bible study, declaring that he would "harmonize all those apparent contradictions to my own satisfaction, or I will be a Deist still." Miller found what he was looking for: an intelligible revelation, a savior that washed away human corruption, a key to understanding the meaning of human history, and a reason to hope for a blissful hereafter.[11]

Miller answered doubts about the divine inspiration of the Bible by adopting the prevalent "common sense" method of biblical interpretation. Arguing that divinity schools produced sectarian bigots and intellectual slaves, Miller presupposed that a common person, armed with no more than English literacy, could interpret all parts of the Bible. He liked to portray himself as a simple farmer "with the *Bible alone*" in his hand. He set aside teachers, creeds, and scriptural commentaries to study the Bible for a dozen years with only the aid of a concordance. Once a voracious reader, especially of history books borrowed from friends or the local library, he found that he had little desire to read anything but the scriptures after his conversion in 1816. Miller fell in love with the Bible. When addressing an audience that was "not well indoctrinated," he told a Baptist elder in 1832, "you must preach *Bible*; you must prove all things by *Bible*; you must talk *Bible*; you must exhort *Bible*; you must pray *Bible*, and love *Bible*; and do all in your power to make others love *Bible* too." In another letter, he looked forward to when he and a friend could "sit down and have a good dish of BIBLE together." A third letter began with a prayer—"O may the Bible be to us as a rock, a pillar, a compass . . ."—and went on to list seventy-four other terms that completed the simile. Miller's interpretative method did more than reveal the Bible's intelligibility and harmony. It also verified Reformed doctrine. God as a trinity of Father, Son, and Spirit; the fact of sin and the plan of salvation; the eternal punishment of the wicked and the glory of the faithful—all, Miller discovered, were clearly presented in a text that offered proof of its own divine origin and contained all the knowledge that human beings would ever need.[12]

But Miller did not become famous because he responded to Christianity's critics with the excesses of what some, like Orestes Brownson, would call bibliolatry. Miller's fame rested on his conviction that he had cracked the code of the scriptures' prophetic imagery. He argued that if a word or passage "makes good sense as it stands, and does no violence to the simple laws of nature, then it must be understood literally." If the literal interpretation did not make "good sense," then the words had to be understood figuratively by noting how they were used in other parts of the Bible. Once Miller had decoded the prophets' figures ("mountains" means governments, "water" means people, "lamp" means the Word of God), he could then turn to history to see how the prophecy had been fulfilled in a past event or awaited fulfillment in the future. The prophecies gave meaning to the history that had unfolded since the last biblical book had been written; the historical fulfillment of scriptural prophecy, in turn, provided the skeptic with the strongest evidence that the Bible was divine.[13]

Miller thought his method was a sure way to answer unbelievers on the grounds of reason alone, and he devoted special attention to converting rationalistic skeptics. "The more I read," he wrote to a Baptist elder in 1832, half a year after beginning his public lecturing, "the more I see the folly of the infidel in rejecting this word." He wrote gleefully to a friend in 1836 that infidels and deists as well as Universalists and Christians of every stripe "were all chained to their seats, in perfect silence, for hours—yes, days,—to hear the old stammering man talk about the second coming of Christ." A gentleman in Waterford, New York, stood up after a lecture and testified that Miller had convinced him that the Bible was God's Word by showing how the history of Napoleon was a fulfillment of prophecy. The man confessed that he and four friends had been infidels for years; by the end of the week, the former skeptics and several others in town like them had converted. Miller no doubt took pleasure from a report from a letter in the *Boston Investigator* asserting that a hundred of Abner Kneeland's freethinking followers had embraced the scriptures thanks to Miller. A pastor from a church in Portland, Maine, concluded that with the rise of Millerism, "infidelity falls and Universalism withers."[14]

If Miller's method of argument seemed to persuade those who were skeptical about the divine inspiration of the Bible, he believed that the standard modes of biblical interpretation practiced by the learned clergy had the opposite effect. "I am sick of all this continual harping on words," he wrote about the ministers who challenged his interpretation. "Our learned critics... have made more infidels in our world than all the heathen mythology in existence. What word in revelation has not been turned, twisted, racked, wrested, distorted, demolished, and annihilated by these voracious harpies in human shape, until the public have become so bewildered they know not what to believe?" After his own lecturing, by contrast, he estimated that he had seen seven hundred former infidels convert, and perhaps twice that number.[15]

When William Miller accepted the call to spread the word about the Second Advent, he thought he was confirming and revitalizing Protestantism, but he ended up creating a new sect. Initially, he was invited to lecture to established congregations and was, in effect, incorporated into revival machinery in use since George Whitefield's tours a century before. Local pastors brought the itinerant evangelist in to rouse the flock, even if the ministers themselves were not fully persuaded by Miller's interpretation of the Second Coming. "They like to have me preach, and build up their churches; and there it ends, with most of the ministers," he complained in 1839. The turning point for Miller was not joining the revival circuit but meeting the activist clergyman Joshua Himes of Boston in 1839 and joining the message about Christ's return to the engines of nineteenth-century reform: associational activity and the printing press. While Brownson was wondering how new religious ideas could not just be uttered but produce new institutions, Miller was demonstrating the answer.[16]

Ironically, the old farmer who had prided himself on having only a concordance and a Bible in his library became the leader of a movement that sold Adventist newspapers, tracts, and books by the tens of thousands; the reader who had vowed to determine the Bible's meaning by himself in the silence of his study promoted Bible classes and Sabbath schools; the evangelist who tried to avoid creating a new sect helped organize Adventist conventions and then withdrew from the Baptists to create a separate fellowship and creed in 1845. Finally,

Miller, who had tried to convince Christians and skeptics alike by guiding them through his scriptural calculus and aligning biblical predictions to historical facts, became convinced of his last date for the end of the world—October 22, 1844—not because he did any recalculation but because the blissful sentiments of his expectant followers seemed to be a new sort of evidence that Christ was about to return. His calculations failed, he later explained, "not by the word of God, nor by the established principles of the interpretation I adopted, but by the authorities I adopted in history and chronology, which have been generally considered worthy of the fullest confidence." If the historians were wrong, "then no human knowledge is sufficient in this age to rectify it with any degree of certainty." The skeptical deist who had once loved reading history and doubted the Bible had become an Adventist clinging to his scriptural faith and doubting the reliability of historical knowledge.[17]

Orestes Brownson, like William Miller, returned from religious skepticism to Protestantism. Brownson was an Old Calvinist Presbyterian only briefly, but the memory lingered and sharpened the barbs of his later criticism. At the age of nineteen, after five years in his New York "labyrinth of doubt," he became a Presbyterian. His conversion in 1822 was an attempt, he later explained in *The Convert*, to silence the unsettling speculations of reason by following his heart. Just as his fictional Charles Elwood was tempted to embrace Jesus for the sake of his born-again fiancée, Brownson himself succumbed to the sentimental seductions of a Presbyterian church on a beautiful October day when the hymn singing seemed to lift his soul. He soon regretted it. Within three years, he was studying to be a Universalist minister, and after four more, he became a skeptical socialist. The later Catholic Brownson, however, regretted only his decision to become a Presbyterian. In his other spiritual and intellectual incarnations, he felt that he had honestly pursued truth wherever it led him. Looking back, he concluded that sacrificing his reason to become a Presbyterian was a cowardly act, an attempt to escape rather than confront his doubts, and he described renouncing Presbyterianism as nothing less than the reclamation of his manhood.[18]

Brownson, even before his conversion to Catholicism, criticized the Protestant reliance upon the Bible. First, he argued, "orthodox" (Trinitarian Calvinist) Protestants reasoned in a circle. The harmony they claimed to discover as evidence of the divine authorship of the Bible was the harmony they presupposed when interpreting individual scriptural passages. Second, rationalistic interpreters like Miller who said that natural reason was sufficient to determine the truth actually made reason the test of scripture. Third, the orthodox Protestant church held the Bible and the individual interpreter's conscience as sacrosanct and yet still presumed to dictate what communicants were supposed to believe. Lacking interpretive authority, the churches claimed social authority over church members. Read the Bible and decide for yourself, the Presbyterians told the young Brownson, but if you do not come to profess the tenets of our confession and live a godly life as we define it, you cannot be a good Christian. The Presbyterians, Brownson claimed, maintained church discipline through a covenant watchfulness that amounted to a "system of espionage." Church members kept a sharp eye on each other's conduct. They were also encouraged to treat neighbors who were outside the church as pariahs, "and thus, by appeals to their business interests, their social feelings, and their desire to stand well in the community, to compel them to join the Presbyterian Church."[19]

Orthodox Protestantism, Brownson came to see, was a tangle of contradictions. It both celebrated reason and feared its free exercise; it empowered individuals as interpreters of their own Bibles, but it established authoritarian covenant communities; it could foster a stifling conservatism yet carried the logic of radical dissent like a dormant virus. When passions were aroused, or other social forces weakened the control of the covenant community, the Protestant appeal to private judgment would splinter the old church and create new ones—a process that occurred repeatedly in Protestant America. Brownson could do little more than sigh and shake his head at the apocalyptic predictions of the Millerites, but he knew that the transition from Millerism as an interdenominational movement to Adventism as an independent sect was hardly unique.[20]

Universalism and Free Inquiry

In the early nineteenth century, many apostates denounced their former sects, and many converts castigated their old beliefs for the sake of the new. Yet more people than ever before were taking more radical positions—doubting that the Bible was God's Word, that Jesus was the Christ, or that a Heavenly Father watched over human affairs—and increasing numbers were even doing so publicly. The notion that religious skepticism might be a public problem was not new, for clerics had howled in the 1790s about the contagion of infidel philosophy. What was new was that rapid social change encouraged more people to question what had once passed for common sense, that alternate ways of thinking were disseminated broadly with the spread of cheap print, and that in urban areas in particular opportunities arose for self-proclaimed freethinkers to form communities and institutions of their own. Religious skepticism was being fused to radical social reform movements, and it threatened to become prominent among the urban working class.

Brownson did not move from Calvinism to freethought in a single leap. After his brief dalliance with Presbyterianism, he became a Universalist preacher and editor after being ordained in the summer of 1826. Although Universalists defined themselves against Protestant "Orthodoxy" by arguing over passages in the scriptures, for Brownson Universalism became a congenial moral and natural philosophy that happened to use scriptural language to communicate truths—truths, however, that did not need to be tethered to supernaturalism. Although convinced that the Calvinists were wrong, and that a just God could not punish sinners eternally, he was not really persuaded that the Universalists were right when they claimed that the Bible taught that everyone would eventually be saved. Being a Universalist preacher, therefore, involved some pragmatic concealment of his actual beliefs. He thought that most of his fellow Universalist clergymen were actually deists or skeptics, too, who spoke the language of nominal Christianity because few Americans were ready to listen to avowed infidels. But in later years he revised his assessment. Universalists, he concluded, had not followed the logic of their beliefs; they were defined wholly within the dialectic of opposition to Orthodoxy. The parameters of their religious knowledge were shaped by neither reason nor scripture but by polemical debate.[21]

Combating Orthodoxy was especially important in New York and New England in the late 1820s, when aggressive Christian activists tried to enact temperance and sabbatarian reforms through legislation rather than persuasion. Brownson joined the battle as editor of the *Gospel Advocate and Impartial Investigator* in Auburn, New York. Like other ambitious young clerics awakening to the uses of cheap print in the early nineteenth century, he found that becoming an editor of a religious periodical not only supplemented his income from preaching but also offered a new professional identity. Yet as he embraced the role of religious journalist, he became less and less comfortable as a Universalist. On July 29, 1829, Brownson published his personal creed, which mentioned honesty, benevolence, self-improvement, and social service, but nothing about Jesus or heaven. The *Gospel Advocate's* publisher, Ulysses F. Doubleday, announced four months later that Brownson had given up religion altogether to become an advocate of the godless socialism of Robert Dale Owen and Frances Wright. A man could only be "*as honest as the times would admit*," Brownson supposedly said to a fellow Universalist editor shortly before leaving the flock. A public speaker and writer on moral issues had to have an audience who would hear him and pay to support his family. Owen and Wright's freethought movement seemed to allow Brownson the practical opportunity to be more honest about his doubts and his beliefs.[22]

Abner Kneeland also left Universalism in the summer of 1829, and he, too, became associated with Wright and Owen.[23] But Kneeland was a generation older than Brownson, and it had taken him longer to doubt his biblical faith. Born in Gardner, Massachusetts in 1774, he learned carpentry from his father but then had become a Vermont schoolmaster (and a Baptist) by the turn of the century. When he joined the Universalists in 1803, he began teaching himself Latin, Greek, and Hebrew and was ordained two years later. Historical and linguistic biblical criticism not only confirmed his antipathy to Calvinism but also started to undermine his faith in the scriptures as the revealed Word of God. In 1814, he left the ministry to run a dry-goods store in Salem, Massachusetts, and opened a correspondence with Universalist leader Hosea Ballou on the evidences of Christianity. Published in 1820, these letters gave Kneeland the opportunity to challenge the prevailing psychology that characterized religious doubt as a mental malady. He and Ballou agreed that contemplating the Calvinist doctrine of eternal torment produced anguish and despair. But against Ballou's assumption that religious doubters were tortured by existential anxiety because they had no hope for an afterlife, Kneeland argued that unbelievers could be perfectly calm and cheerful. Considering death an eternal sleep, the happy religious skeptic lives in the present and enjoys the good things of this world. Kneeland even suggested that the Universalist's impassioned hope for eternal bliss with a benevolent God could be as psychologically dangerous as the Calvinist's fear and trembling. Echoing the words of a Universalist who committed suicide so he could run into the arms of his loving Maker, Kneeland described doubt as a helpful, moderating influence upon a Christian's religious affections: "The moment I begin to think about the certainty of immortality and eternal life, I am all on fire! I hardly know how to contain myself! And were it not for the special obligations, which I feel to my family, and to the world, ... I should long to 'depart, and be with Christ, which is far better.' Thus my doubts, whatever they are, may be needful for me."[24]

In his exchange with Ballou, Kneeland questioned the Christian's reliance upon testimony. The alleged facts—Christ's miracles and resurrection—were unlike anything that could count as positive knowledge, he argued, and the scriptural testimonies could be explained by mankind's superstitious nature. On their face, Christianity's truth claims seemed no more plausible than those of Mother Ann Lee and the Shakers. They, too, had well-attested miracles and healings that were difficult to disprove; they, too, had sincere converts whose lives had been completely transformed and who suffered persecution for their faith. Epistemologically equivalent, Shakerism and Christianity differed only in their relationship to the rest of society. Let the Shakers be persecuted for a couple of centuries, Kneeland wrote, and then let them be adopted by a powerful state like Rome under Constantine. Would Ann Lee then seem any less believable than Jesus? Despite this critique, which Ballou never adequately addressed, Kneeland announced that he had regained enough hope that Ballou's form of Christianity was true to resume preaching and editing Universalist periodicals. Perhaps not coincidentally, he had also failed as a dry-goods merchant.[25]

Yet his efforts to defend Christianity always seemed to develop stronger arguments against the faith. Joseph Priestley's *Disquisitions relating to Matter and Spirit* (1777) allowed him to embrace philosophical materialism, and Frances

Portrait of Abner Kneeland. From Abner Kneeland, *A Series of Lectures on the Doctrine of Universal Benevolence* (Philadelphia, 1818), frontispiece. Kneeland was fined and imprisoned for blasphemy for writing that he did not believe in the Universalists' god.

Wright and Robert Dale Owen introduced him to their non-Christian community of freethinking reformers in New York City. When his Prince Street congregation objected to the radical ideas he preached—what he described in 1826 as his Bible deism and his materialistic theories about the nature of God—he argued that his church had no right to silence his honest inquiries into the truth and pushed those inquiries even further. The research that this "persecution" prompted finally severed his ties to Christianity. On September 23, 1829, he publicly renounced the faith in Owen and Wright's *Free Enquirer*, having determined that the existence of God and life after death were improbable, and that the so-called evidence for Christ's resurrection would be tossed out of any decent court or history book. He had been persuaded by the historical scholarship and courtroom analogies of Dr. Thomas Cooper, whose essays as "Philo-Veritas" had been printed from May to July in the freethought *Correspondent*. Kneeland read and commented upon Cooper's essays in a series of six lectures delivered in August 1829, and by the time he printed those lectures three months later as his *Review of the Evidences of Christianity*, he felt liberated: "If people only knew what it is to be free, they would be no longer slaves—slaves to the opinions of others, the worst kind of slavery."[26]

Kneeland arrived in Boston in December 1830, on the heels of some successful lectures by Frances Wright, and tried to extend the New York–based freethought movement to the old bastion of Puritanism. While the Standing Order of tax-supported churches in Massachusetts was fracturing from within as Unitarian and Trinitarian Congregationalists fought over church property, an increasing number of religious sects competed for adherents in Boston and rural areas alike. In 1830, Boston was a rapidly growing city, the nation's fourth largest. Its population of over sixty-one thousand in that year would grow by twenty-three thousand by 1840 and would almost double by 1845. In those years, the foreign-born population—only 5.6 percent in 1830—would increase sevenfold, but before the 1840s many of the migrants streaming into the city were young men from farming villages in Massachusetts and northern New England. They came to a city where strong international maritime trade and packet lines to other coastal cities and to the industrializing hinterland offered work in commerce and manufacturing. Many left—annual population turnover in the 1830s was 30 percent—but more replaced them. To the rich and powerful, and to the clergymen who spoke for them, these new workers, and the new, more class-conscious urban culture they helped create, threatened social and moral order. When workers tried to unionize, strike, and run their own candidates for office in the Workingmen's Party, merchants, professionals, and capitalists decried the rhetoric of class warfare and worried about the rule of law. The mob that burned the Ursuline convent in 1834 and the Broad Street riot of Protestants and Catholics in 1837 only underlined that threat.[27] Kneeland combined anticlericalism and reform politics, and did his best to ally himself with the Workingmen's movement. He helped organize Boston's Society of Free Enquirers, lectured twice weekly, and edited the *Boston Investigator*, which would be sold by 243 agents and circulate to 2,500 subscribers in twenty-seven states and territories by the end of Kneeland's tenure. The Free Enquirers sponsored dances and published cheap new editions of skeptical books, including Kneeland's edition of Voltaire's dictionary, which Kneeland suggested might replace the family Bible as a repository of sound thinking on a variety of topics.[28]

Christian writers were not sure how to respond to infidels like Kneeland. Some urged public silence about infidelity, hoping to avoid fanning the flames with more publicity. Others tried to defend Christianity without directly stating— and thereby aiding the circulation of—the critics' objections. Religious tracts often dismissed skeptical arguments out of hand and considered freethinking a shallow attempt to rationalize vice. Christian writers assigned a variety of other reasons for the rise of religious skepticism as well. John Barton Derby blamed the exchange between Lyman Beecher and the Catholics, but others mentioned the inexpensive publications and higher literacy rates that had allowed texts once confined to the literati to circulate among all ranks of society. An "Old Man" in a pamphlet confession and exhortation called *The Conversion of an Infidel* described infidelity as a reaction to the clergy's hypocrisy and aristocratic pretensions. One Unitarian tract blamed hyper-Calvinism for driving people to doubt all religion; another indicted the commercial spirit. Cyrus Pitt Grosvenor, pastor of Boston's First Baptist Church, believed in 1829 that young men had simply been bewitched by the charms of Frances Wright.[29]

Lyman Beecher's *Lectures on Scepticism*, first delivered at the Park Street Congregational Church, marked Kneeland's first year in Boston. Religious skepticism, Beecher declared, was "now the epidemic of the world, as superstition was in the dark ages." The primary cause was humanity's sinful nature, which always and everywhere tempted people to deny religious truths and try to rationalize immorality. Beecher also pointed to intellectual errors that were peculiar to the nineteenth century. His contemporaries tended to demand too much evidence in religious matters, and they overestimated the powers of their own reason; they put too much stock in the opinions of philosophers and the misguided German critics who raised questions about the divine inspiration of biblical texts. In America, with the rise of literacy and the broad dissemination of print, too many insisted upon being self-taught. Many Americans devoured all sorts of books, impatiently hunting for knowledge and trying to tackle profound questions without being properly tutored in first principles. The result was the skeptic's mental desolation and despair; the antidote, Beecher advised, was to break the habit of philosophical speculation and substitute daily Bible reading.[30]

According to Beecher, there were social explanations for the rise of religious skepticism as well. The union of church and state, which lingered in Massachusetts until 1833, had filled the pews with nominal Christians who came there for the sake of social status or political power. Naturally inclined toward a loose religious liberalism, they gradually purged the evangelical doctrines from the church, doubting everything but their comforting—and false—moralism. More dangerous were the freethought societies that had sprouted like mushrooms on the darker streets of Boston, Philadelphia, New York, and Baltimore and were spreading throughout New England and the mid-Atlantic states. Led by men (like Kneeland) who seemed outwardly "mild, polite, well-meaning" and honest, these organizations of what Beecher called "political atheists" conspired to abolish marriage, the family, private property, civil government, moral accountability, and religious worship. The associations did not yet contain large numbers, but "the power of small organized bodies acting systematically and perseveringly upon improvident and unorganized masses" should not be underestimated, Beecher warned. Skeptical demagogues were haranguing the working class in the grog shops of the nation. They were inciting the poor to resent the rich, even though social inequality was necessary for a healthy society; this could gradually poison public opinion in an already fractious republic and "undermine the faith and moral principle of the nation." Judicious men, Beecher urged, had to launch a counteroffensive with sermons and speeches, lyceums and lending libraries.[31]

When Kneeland began drawing crowds in Boston, especially among the city's working class, Unitarians as well as orthodox Trinitarians like Beecher worried that he was successfully luring laborers away from Christianity. By the middle of the decade, when Kneeland's society had a thousand dues-paying members and his lectures were sometimes heard, opponents claimed, by at least twice that number, Unitarian leaders George Ripley and William Ellery Channing thought they had found an antidote: create a Unitarian urban mission to the working class. For this they needed an energetic Unitarian pastor who was devoted to the cause of the laborer and who could refute Kneeland in ways that common people could understand. They thought they had their man in a minister currently in Canton, Massachusetts, who had recently converted from skeptical freethought himself: Orestes Brownson.[32]

Brownson arrived in Boston in early 1836. By June he was organizing an urban congregation called the Society for Christian Union and Progress and editing the *Boston Reformer*, which had previously been a Workingmen's paper. Convinced that class warfare would only make things worse for workers, he announced that he supported laborers but not the Workingmen's Party. To those workers who were drifting toward religious skepticism as well as political and social radicalism, he offered gentle counsel. When a young man wrote to the *Reformer* to question the Bible's miracles and describe himself as an unbeliever, Brownson sympathized. Respect honest doubt, Brownson urged; don't be alarmed or discouraged by your inquiries; look beneath the Bible's symbolic stories to the doctrines it teaches; look within to the cravings and aspirations of your own soul. In his *Discourse on the Wants of the Times*, Brownson argued that Kneeland's popularity had more to do with politics than with religion: "Why has this society [of Free Enquirers] been collected? Not, I venture to say, because their leader is an infidel. People do not go to him because he advocates atheistical or pantheistical doctrines; not because he denies Christianity, rejects the Bible, and indulges in various witticism at the expense of members of the clerical profession; but because he opposes the aristocracy of our churches, and vindicates the rights of the mind. He succeeds, not because he is an infidel, but because he has hitherto shown himself a democrat." Kneeland countered that he thought his philosophical and political principles were all of a piece. At the end of March 1837, Brownson challenged Kneeland to a debate that would run in both their publications. The question to be debated, chosen by Brownson, was this: "Can all the phenomena of consciousness be traced back to sensation?" Kneeland, the materialist, was expected to answer yes. Brownson was clearly planning to develop the argument he had used to reason his way back from religious skepticism to liberal Christianity. Drawing from the philosophy of Victor Cousin and Benjamin Constant, Brownson would argue that when a human subject confronts any object in the world, his understanding is already shaped by the power of spontaneous reason. That power also manifests itself as an aspiration toward God, an aspiration that is inherent in the human race and needs to be cultivated.[33]

Yet that is not how the discussion proceeded. For seven weeks they jousted over the definition of terms. Brownson insisted that Kneeland be philosophically precise when he used a word like "feeling," which could refer to touching, sensation, sensibility, or consciousness; Kneeland countered that all of these processes relied on the nervous system and were more alike than not. Brownson argued that epistemological analysis required that one distinguish between subject, object, and concept; Kneeland stoutly refused to "go into these verbal criticisms" because all three terms were embraced in the act of perception itself. Frustrated that he could not get Kneeland to admit his presuppositions and argue philosophically, Brownson withdrew. Kneeland declared that the exchange had proven, as he knew it would, how useless such dialogues were. It underlined the criticism he often leveled at liberal Protestant discourse: it strung together words, especially abstract nouns like the Invisible, the Infinite, the Absolute, the Eternal, and the True, which had no meaning whatsoever. His complaints about Brownson's unintelligibility (though Brownson insisted that a nine-year-old boy understood him) supported Kneeland's insistence that his friend Orestes, as well as Transcendentalists like Ralph Waldo Emerson, were just blowing metaphysical smoke. Since Brownson's politics were in the right place, Kneeland dismissed the philosophy as harmless nonsense rather than more dangerous clerical mystification. A reader calling himself "A Man of the People," however, distrusted the political implications of Brownson's rhetoric, reminding him that "Republicans have but five senses," and that the "extra consciousness, and mysterious sensations, and incomprehensible language" were more suited to European courtiers than Americans. Kneeland's contrast of "self-evident" and "common sense" principles to philosophical inquiry ("bombast") was more than a bit disingenuous, however. His paper not only told workingmen that sense experience was the only path to reliable knowledge, but he also published and recommended essays on Hume and Reid's notions of causation, the very arguments that Brownson had tried to engage. "Common sense" was both a label Kneeland gave to his philosophical presuppositions and a shield against philosophical arguments that tried to attack them.[34]

Brownson, however, was convinced that a philosophical redescription of Christianity was essential to the survival of the faith in nineteenth-century America, and that a reinvigorated Christianity was essential to social and moral reform.³⁵ He would try to make his argument more accessible three years later in his quasi-novel, *Charles Elwood; or, The Infidel Converted*, an attempt to convince religious skeptics like Kneeland through sympathetic understanding as well as philosophical demonstration. The book was not the first dramatic narrative and work of fiction published in Boston to address religious skepticism and infidelity. Like Lucius M. Sargent's temperance tract, *I Am Afraid There Is a God!*, these other tales linked infidelity to liquor, debt, and whoremongering, to which Sargent added an appearance by Kneeland himself as the leader of the Boston infidels, a "hoary-headed scoundrel" who throws a Bible across a lecture hall in disgust. In these stories, religious skepticism is merely the first step on a very slippery slope toward depravity and damnation.³⁶

Charles Elwood was different. Brownson stressed that religious doubt itself was not sinful but arose from the philosophic element of human nature—the desire to comprehend, account for, and verify one's beliefs. The problem was not with doubt itself, a friendly religious liberal taught Elwood, but with the intellectual, social, and institutional barriers that in the nineteenth century prevented an honest reconciliation of reason and faith and hardened one's doubts into unbelief and infidelity. Another religious liberal who helped rescue Elwood late in the book argued that "infidelity indicates an inquiring mind, an honest mind, not a depraved heart," and contended that Christians should treat their skeptical neighbors as lost sheep, not social lepers. The book's enlightened Christians charged that institutional Christianity often stands in the way of both rational inquiry and efforts at social and political reform, creating more infidels than an army of Voltaires—or Kneelands—ever could.³⁷

Brownson's *Charles Elwood*, therefore, posited a natural process that begins in unreflective faith, moves through doubt and inquiry, and arrives at a rational faith—a process that was being impeded for people like Kneeland and the Free Enquirers by institutional, social, and intellectual obstacles. Elwood concluded that the answer was reform: Americans needed to reinvent their churches, schools, and voluntary associations; Christians needed to embrace their skeptical neighbors; and the religious press needed to address contemporary modes of thought and not just rehash outmoded arguments. These were, of course, the positions that Brownson himself had been articulating through the 1830s in his periodical essays and publications such as *New Views of Christianity, Society, and the Church* and *A Discourse on the Wants of the Times*.³⁸

Brownson and Kneeland at least agreed on the value of free religious expression and debate. Other forces in Boston, however, mobilized to silence Kneeland as a dangerous subversive. On December 20, 1833, less than six weeks after the people of Massachusetts had voted by a ten-to-one margin to finally end the state's legal establishment of Protestantism, Lucius Sargent forwarded a copy of Kneeland's *Boston Investigator* to the county attorney's office, with a note urging that Kneeland be indicted by a grand jury for blasphemy. So began a series of four well-publicized trials and a final appeal that would eventually lead to Kneeland's sixty-day jail sentence in the summer of 1838. The trials brought up several issues, including charges that the Free Enquirers were spreading filth about birth control and nonsense about racial and sexual equality; that their cheap dances encouraged illicit sex; that the use of the word "testicle" in connection with a discussion of the Immaculate Conception was obscene; and that a comparison of God hearing prayers to President Jackson being besieged by petitions was blasphemous. The prosecution, however, came to focus upon a single sentence of Kneeland's: "Universalists believe in a god which I do not," he wrote. Kneeland argued that he was speaking about the Universalists' particular conception of God, and not all conceptions of God. He explained that he was a pantheist, not an atheist, so he did actually believe in God, at least as he defined the term (as a synonym for an unintelligent, material nature). But, he taunted Boston's theologically liberal Unitarians and conservative Trinitarians, whose understanding of God, and whose reading of the Bible, was the 1782 blasphemy statute supposed to protect? Even if he had been trying to articulate a general disbelief in God, disbelief—which he described as a probable and provisional judgment based on the best currently available evidence—was not the same as the outright denial mentioned in the statute. At any rate, Kneeland contended, the statute was an unconstitutional infringement of his right to free religious expression. On this last point, his opponents countered that the state constitution protected religious, and not irreligious, expression.[39]

Although infrequent, blasphemy prosecution could define and stigmatize infidelity both in the courtroom and in the court of public opinion. Two earlier cases show how blasphemy statutes could be a legal snare for infidels. The first sketches the sort of legal argument that could make a defendant's appeal to constitutional rights irrelevant. In November 1818, Robert C. Murray was indicted at the Philadelphia Mayor's Court. Friends gathered at the Rialto tavern to protest what they considered to be the persecution of a man merely for expressing religious opinions similar to those "of *Franklin* and *Jefferson*, two of the greatest and best men." But in court the prosecutor quickly convinced a jury that the case had nothing to do with religious persecution. Two witnesses testified that the defendant had been heard "at various times and places" saying "That *Christ was a bastard—his mother a w——and the Bible a pack of lies.*" An unrepealed act of 1700 made it a crime to "willfully, premeditatedly, and despitefully, blaspheme, or speak loosely and profanely of *Almighty God, Christ Jesus, the Holy Spirit or Scriptures of Truth.*" Defense counsel presented evidence of Murray's good character and argued against the constitutionality of the act, pointing to sections of the Pennsylvania constitution on religious liberty and free speech. However, as the prosecution argued and the court explained in greater length at sentencing,

Murray was free to express whatever religious opinions he wished as long as he used "decent language." "While one man exercises his rights, let him not offend against the rights of others." Not only did Murray use obscene language, he appeared to do so with malicious intent, accosting people in the streets as they made their way to church. He seemed intent on trying "to destroy the happiness of another, by depriving him in his confidence in revealed religion, and rendering him prey to doubt and despair." Government had a duty to protect a citizen's peace of mind from wanton attack just as it protected private property. Murray needed to "be taught that respect even to the prejudices of others on so important a topic as that of religion, is due to the humblest individual in society." Although the court adopted a Christian perspective when the judge warned Murray that he would ultimately have to face the truth of revealed religion, the conviction was based on the argument that he had used what a later generation would call hate speech, maliciously and publicly, that threatened to disturb the peace, and the religious content of those words seemed almost as beside the point as Murray's deism.[40]

The legal logic in a much more famous case, *The People of New York v. Ruggles* (1811), resembled that of the Murray case, but the broader arguments by Chief Justice James Kent articulated assumptions that would continue to bolster Christian hegemony and help position deists, skeptics, and freethinkers as pariahs. Ruggles, too, called Jesus a bastard and Mary a whore. Lacking a statute, the prosecution contended that Ruggles could be convicted under common law. The defense countered that the New York constitution's provisions separating church and state and protecting religious liberty had abrogated those portions of British common law relating to religious establishment—like the precedents shielding the notion of Jesus's divinity from attack. Kent reiterated a lower court jury's conclusion that Ruggles's utterance did not arise from a dispute among learned men but was simply obscene language proclaimed loudly in public with malicious intent, wicked words that were an offense against public peace and safety. Such a verbal assault was not covered by constitutional protections of free speech and religion; it was considered an attack not on an established church but on civil society.

Kent, however, did not merely say that the blasphemer's words attacked beliefs that, whether truths or just "prejudices," were important to the neighbor's pursuit of happiness. Such words for Kent also struck "at the root of moral obligation and weaken[ed] the security of social ties." Christianity deserved special protection, and not only because it was the religion of the majority and therefore defined the community's cultural norms, including those norms determining what words might give so much offense as to disturb the public peace and lead to violence. Christianity was special because it was the essential foundation of a morally refined society, and because it was true. (Kent also declared that one could maliciously insult Jesus but not Mohammed because the former spoke the truth and the latter was an "imposter.") The chief justice argued that Christianity was part of the common law that New York had incorporated. Other states (Pennsylvania in 1824 and Delaware in 1837) would make similar affirmations. Although common-law arguments would not be decisive in blasphemy trials or other church-and-state cases, the assertion by one of America's leading jurists that "we are a christian people and the morality of the country is deeply ingrafted upon christianity" affirmed that courts could maintain Christianity's privileged position in American society no matter what constitutions seemed to say about religious establishments and the rights of conscience.[41]

Kneeland's case was the most widely publicized blasphemy prosecution in the nineteenth century. His opponents ultimately seemed less interested in what he believed, or even what he said or wrote, than in how he disseminated his opinions, and to whom. Prosecuting attorney Samuel Parker argued the following at one of the trials: "There have been other infidels—Hume, Gibbon, Voltaire, Volney, etc.—but the works of those persons were read only by men of literary habits—necessarily a few—and to men of sound understanding they carried their antidote with them. But here is a Journal, a Newspaper, cheap—and sent to a thousand families.... Where *one* man would be injured by Hume, Gibbon, or Volney, a thousand may be injured by this Newspaper so widely circulated, so easily read—so coarsely expressed—so industriously spread abroad." A newspaper, he continued, "finding its way to the poor and unlearned, to those who have not learning nor leisure enough to consider and refute its falsehoods—an offence also aggravated by his pampering that depraved appetite which vulgar and illiterate minds are apt to have for obscenity and gross scurrilousness." Judge Peter Thacher reminded the court that "the poor stand in most need of the consolations of religion," and that no state could uphold its own authority without condemning a revolt "against the government of God." Judge Samuel Wilde at the third trial reportedly said that even if Kneeland were right and Christianity was merely a superstitious fable, he should keep that discovery to himself, for Christian doctrines were essential to the happiness and virtue of the community.[42]

In the summer of 1838, Kneeland watched the construction of the Bunker Hill Monument from the window of his jail cell and cast himself as a martyr for liberty. He listed fifty-eight newspapers from across the nation that denounced the court decision. He left Boston for a fresh start in Iowa the following year, escaping financial problems resulting in part from the Panic of 1837—an economic depression that had also broken the back of the Workingmen's movement. Liberal and conservative Christians alike, refusing to let go of the vestigial forms of civil religion as a means of social control, were not sorry to see him go.[43]

Kneeland's freethought movement, however, had not been hampered only by external social, legal, and financial obstacles. He had struggled to articulate a coherent ideological position that was more than merely a critique of Christianity. Doubt was a powerful tool, Kneeland believed. It was the beginning of intelligent inquiry, the first step toward acquiring reliable knowledge. He and his likeminded friends were skeptical only about theological claims; they were not philosophical skeptics who persistently rejected other kinds of knowledge claims. The twelve "Principles of Free Enquirers" he published in 1837 combined materialism, empiricism, utilitarianism, and a condemnation of superstition. Kneeland had to explain, therefore, why statements about the material world could be accorded the status of truth or knowledge whereas metaphysical notions were ruled out of court by definition and, in practice, derided as foolish superstition. He had to show that he paid more than lip service to methodological doubt and free inquiry and expression, and was not just replacing religious dogmas with secular materialist dogmas.[44]

Moreover, "free enquiry" in practice, like "lived religion," was no simple enactment of a set of principles in daily life; it was shaped by its particular social and political environment.[45] Readers tested the relationship between principle and practice when they challenged Kneeland's claim that the *Boston Investigator* was a forum of free and open discussion. Why was religion always criticized and never defended? There were plenty of publications, Kneeland explained, written from a Christian point of view. But why did the paper venture into politics, and then present only Democratic and not Whig opinions? Kneeland's paper advocated universal education, equal rights for women, liberal divorce laws, and electoral, tax, and legal reforms; it supported the laboring and producing class, condemned monopolies, and—initially—called for the abolition of slavery. Political writer John Barton Derby claimed that "nineteen-twentieths of the followers of Abner Kneeland" were Jacksonians. Kneeland's lawyer at his first trial, Andrew Dunlap, was a former Democratic state attorney general; David Henshaw, leader of the "Statesmen" wing of the Boston Jacksonians, wrote as the "Cosmopolite" against Kneeland's prosecution. Some readers complained that Kneeland's political bias not only alienated Whig freethinkers but betrayed the core values of the movement.[46]

Kneeland's political commitments did sharply limit the reach of his professed egalitarianism; or perhaps his inability to transcend racial prejudice led him to a politics content to struggle for the liberty and equality of whites only. In 1826, when still a Universalist, Kneeland denounced slavery as a national sin, and the prospectus for the *Boston Investigator* committed the freethought paper to abolition. But slavery became for him a parenthetical aberration rather than a cancer on the body politic. For a time his Boston office was next door to William Lloyd Garrison's *Liberator*, and while Garrison argued that abolitionists were not infidels, Kneeland began to argue that freethinkers need not be abolitionists. When Kneeland's candidate for vice president, Richard M. Johnson, was criticized for fathering children with his slaves, Kneeland joked that "if Col. J. prefers color to white, we may be allowed to *smile* at his taste, being so different from ours, without wishing to deprive him of the privilege of enjoying it." By the spring of 1837, a year and a half after his neighbor Garrison had been attacked by an antiabolitionist mob, Kneeland could argue that he was "not prepared to admit that slavery in our southern states is an evil until we can see better proof that the slaves of the South are less happy than the free negroes of the North. We believe there is a chain from the vegetable organic matter upwards, even to the most polished man; and we are not disposed to alter the size of the links." Although still opposed to slavery in principle, he was not convinced that blacks would be better off with freedom than they were as slaves to his Democratic allies in the South. Kneeland's social radicalism and commitment to freedom allowed him to see beyond the gender stereotypes of his day but stopped at the color line.[47]

Protestant Liberalism, Catholicism, and Spiritualism

Orestes Brownson had believed since the early 1830s that some sort of religion was an essential foundation for social reform and had told Kneeland that an antireligious reform agenda was doomed to fail. Horace Mann agreed, and as he labored tirelessly for education reform he tried to accommodate a vague, nondenominational Protestant piety in his plan for public education—something all but skeptical Kneelandites could agree to, he hoped. Nevertheless, his own religious doubts and the philosophy that he had privately substituted for the Christianity he had learned in his youth shaped his plan. Critics of Protestant liberalism liked to jump to the conclusion that this sort of substitution was in fact the heart of all forms of liberalism. Whether seen as a secularization of religious ideals or a sacralization of worldly ambitions, the result was the same, they argued. After his conversion to Catholicism, Brownson became one of the sharpest of these critics, broadening this social and philosophical critique to condemn evangelical Calvinists, reforming liberals, and the new Spiritualists alike. By the 1850s, he concluded, militant religious skepticism had nearly disappeared, and fewer wrestled privately with doubt. Yet skepticism had not been defeated; it had done its work, and Protestant Americans, lulled back to sleep under the sign of Christianity, had learned to have faith in only themselves.

Mann's doubts about God and the reliability of the scriptures were never as public as his rejection of Calvinism. He remembered an unhappy childhood in Franklin, Massachusetts, marred by poverty, toil, and fear.[48] A good share of his youthful distress seems to have stemmed from the fear cultivated by the local minister, the Calvinist Congregationalist Nathanael Emmons. Like his Edwardsean mentors, Emmons preached that sinners were in the hands of an angry God.

In 1808, at the age of twelve, Mann witnessed a revival in the congregation. With the awakened he felt the torments of conscience, and like them was driven to a psychological crisis and a sudden turn in a new direction. For Mann, however, the "agony of despair" was broken not by surrendering his will to Emmons's God but by rejecting the faith that Emmons preached and constructing different theories about God and man, ethics and eternity. Mann looked to his own consciousness rather than to the Bible for religious insight, and privately professed a naturalistic faith in a benevolent deity and a universe run by moral as well as natural laws. But this faith, too, was shaken when his wife of two years died in 1832. Mann, in despair, doubted divine Providence and even the existence of God.[49]

After becoming a lawyer and rising within state politics to become president of the state senate, Mann was named director of the newly established Massachusetts Board of Education in 1837. The position gave him something he had needed since the death of his wife: a cause to live for. Education reform became his sacred mission, and he worked himself to exhaustion traveling,

Joseph Edward Baker, "Horace Mann" (1860). Mann privately struggled with religious doubt as he publicly crusaded for education reform. Photo courtesy of the National Portrait Gallery, Smithsonian Institution.

lecturing, publishing, organizing county conventions, and evangelizing local communities. He edited the semimonthly *Common School Journal* for ten years and produced twelve elaborate annual reports, becoming nationally and even internationally known as a pioneer in education reform. Brownson, who heard about Mann's religious beliefs through a mutual friend when Mann first became secretary of the board, declared privately that Mann was not fit for the position because he was an infidel. The philosophy and sentiments that Mann poured out into his private journal in these years, however, might be better described as post-traumatic Stoicism rather than a radical opposition to Christianity that resembled Kneeland's. He later blamed Calvinism for depriving him of any "filial love for God," but in the 1830s it was the painful loss of his wife that prevented him from contemplating God as anything more than an intellectually necessary First Cause. All that was left was duty—duty to work for human progress in this world. He also idealized his late wife into a perfect being, the Christ figure in his private religion, and redefined central Christian terms for his own purposes. His essential "faith" was in human progress; he redefined "regeneration" as the moment moral sentiments prevailed over animal nature; he called "skeptics" all those who doubted humanity's natural potential and the role that universal education played in progress.[50]

Fortunately, the keys to the improvement of the human race were right at hand. Mann believed that the moral world, like the natural, was ruled by fixed laws of cause and effect. This truth, he wrote, discoverable through personal reflection, was a species of revelation far superior to any ancient text requiring historical corroboration, or to any traditional wisdom relying upon uncertain transmission from generation to generation. He wrote in his journal that "I know it is [seen] by many—perhaps most professing Christians as a fatal heresy, and worthy of being purged by fire, but for myself Natural Religion stands as preeminent over Revealed religion as the deepest experience over the lightest hearsay." Furthermore, he thought, the day was coming when "the light of Natural Religion will be to that of Revealed as the rising sun is to the day star that preceded it." Experience and reflection taught him that the essence of true religion was ethics, that noble motives produced good effects, and that education was the root of personal improvement and the perfectibility of the race.[51]

These ideas took on a more systematic form when Mann met the Scottish phrenologist George Combe, a thinker Mann would come to see as his closest friend and as a genius on the order of Francis Bacon. Combe, Mann believed, was able to "understand far better than any other man I ever saw, the principles on which the human race have been formed, and by following [those principles] their most rapid advancement would be secured." Combe's popular book *The Constitution of Man Considered in Relation to External Objects* argued that human character could be divided into thirty-three different faculties, each corresponding to a different area of the brain and a different set of objects in the world. Like muscles, these faculties enlarged and strengthened with proper use and atrophied through neglect. Some individuals—and, indeed, some races—had larger capacities for intellectual, moral, or physical development than others. Such a system could obviously provide a warrant for racism, sexism, class exploitation, and the domination of all sorts of phrenologically superior individuals over the inferior. Mann saw in it not only a physiological index to human character but also a handbook for both personal growth and the progress of humanity. Combe acknowledged the diversity of the human species and the multidimensionality of the human personality; he urged that individuals would be happiest if allowed to develop their natural capacities to the fullest; he argued, furthermore, that the highest level of moral or intellectual achievement was passed on from parent to child. In other words, he believed in the inheritance of acquired characteristics—not the parents' moral or intellectual knowledge but the enlarged capacity of their developed moral and intellectual organs. Combe's phrenological philosophy, in short, gave Mann a pseudo-scientific basis for his gradualist progressivism. If Combe's phrenology could help support the status quo—that is, rule by a certain set of phrenologically superior white Anglo-Saxon Protestant males—it also held out hope for the perfectibility of the whole species.[52]

Mann, however, knew phrenology was controversial, and he knew that his position as secretary of the Board of Education was politically sensitive and precarious. "I must be a fluid sort of man," he wrote in his journal on June 29, 1837, "adapting myself to tastes, opinions, habits, manners, so far as this can be done without hypocrisy or insincerity, or a compromise of principle." He told himself that he needed to embrace the spirit of "self-abandonment—the spirit of martyrdom" and say nothing to offend or alarm anyone. Although he recommended Combe's book for older students, Mann's plan for public education included not phrenological analysis but Bible reading and heavy doses of Christian ethics. Yet because of the way he interpreted the legislation against teaching "sectarian doctrine" in the public schools, he angered religious conservatives anyway. In the *Common School Journal*, he argued that the public schools could teach only what the various Protestant sects held in common—the Ten Commandments, the Golden Rule, natural theology—and leave particular theological instruction to the churches. But his opponents countered, as an editorial in the *New York Observer* put it, that this public religion was in fact merely "the lowest, and least religious form of Unitarianism."[53]

He also provoked criticism from the left. Brownson criticized Combe's phrenology as well as Mann's religious infidelity, arguing that by fracturing human personality into thirty-three faculties Combe destroyed the unity of the self and any sense of moral accountability.[54] Mann's educational reform project, however, did not publicly root itself in his fondness for phrenology or his doubts about revealed religion. Brownson in the 1830s shared Mann's conviction that humanity had an enormous capacity for progress and awaited only the right vision, and the right institutions, to lead the way. Brownson and Mann differed initially over means. Brownson, then a Democrat, attacked Mann's Whiggish assumptions about a state-directed educational bureaucracy, managed by elite professionals who told local communities what books their students should read, what methods their teachers ought to use, and even how the local schoolhouse should be designed. Insisting that Mann's program imitated absolutist Prussia, Brownson argued that knowledge ought to be allowed to emerge from organic local communities, in churches, lyceums, and a free press. Brownson also complained that the vague civil religion Mann promoted bled the life out of religious faith for the sake of political compromise. Mann wrote to Samuel Gridley Howe in 1839 that Brownson had declared war on him because he was a Whig and "in favor, as he has heard, of Kneeland's prosecution."[55]

A couple of years after publishing his critique of Mann on education, however, Brownson started backing away from the liberal assumptions the two men had shared. The publication of "The Laboring Classes" in July 1840, where Brownson called for the elimination of the clergy, the banking system, and the inheritance of property, had been the high-water mark of his radicalism. The logic propping up liberal Protestant philosophy and reform was flawed, he decided, and he developed this argument in a series of philosophical works beginning in the early 1840s, including a long critical review of his own book, *Charles Elwood*. With the word "Reason," he argued, philosophers like Kant and Cousin had yoked the objective impersonal world of abstract ideas to the subjective power by which we recognize those ideas. Cousin's "spontaneous and impersonal reason" was at the same time divine and a faculty of the human soul, and the American Transcendentalists had followed suit. In so much modern philosophy, the subject (me) determined its object (the not-me); the sentimentalist philosopher's twist on the Cartesian formula was "I feel, therefore it—or God—is." This, Brownson determined, put things epistemologically backwards. Objects in the world exist not because we think or feel them but because they present themselves to our intelligence: "In all human life the action of the object precedes and renders possible the action of the subject," he wrote in *The Convert*. Human beings learn and grow not by developing the seed implanted within but by assimilating what is outside of them. Humanity, he decided in the early 1840s, did not have an inherent capacity to reform and progress after all; it needs an external power to lift it up. What he had previously understood as humanity's natural power had really been the work of society and history, infused by providential grace.[56]

Brownson now sharpened the distinction between humanity in a savage state and people raised "in the bosom of Christian civilization." As Brownson was moving ever closer politically to John C. Calhoun, and worrying about the minority rights of slaveholders more than the minority rights of workers, his socio-epistemological analysis also revealed the influence of racialism upon his thought: "The African Negro, as a race," Brownson wrote to illustrate his point, "does not aspire, or at least only to a feeble degree. He can therefore be made contented and apparently happy in a condition from which the proud Caucasian, under the influence of Christianity, recoils with horror." Disillusionment with politics after the slogan-filled campaign of 1840 also helped him realize the folly of placing one's faith in human institutions. Human beings needed to be acted upon by an external source—by God's grace—and the only authoritative source of that grace in the world, he concluded, was the Catholic Church, the only church that Jesus himself had founded.[57]

The later, Catholic Brownson described the relationship between skepticism and faith differently than had the liberal Protestant Brownson who had published *Charles Elwood* in 1840. He still preferred the honest, intelligent infidel to the canting religious hypocrite, and he still scoffed at the idea that doubt was the devil's instrument. But he insisted that belief, not doubt, was man's normal state. The intellectual obstacle to faith was not merely that old arguments like Paley's *Natural Theology* no longer convinced readers who had gone on to Hume and Kant but that the entire project of modern philosophy since Descartes, which included Hume and Kant as well as Paley and Reid, was fundamentally misguided. Modern philosophy had mistakenly focused on an epistemological question ("What can I know?") rather than an ontological one ("What is?"). Concentrating on the problem of knowledge, modern philosophy inflated the methodological importance of doubt while forgetting that all knowledge was grounded in faith of some kind—a presupposed assent to basic, unquestioned beliefs, like the confidence in reason itself. Beginning in the wrong place—with subjectivity—and reasoning from faulty premises, modern philosophy, Brownson argued, struggled with intractable problems that it had created for itself: how to reconcile reason and faith, subject and object. These patterns of thought were not just speculative games played by philosophers; they permeated Protestant culture. Modern philosophy arose at the time of the Reformation and supplied a new authority to those rebelling against the church: individual consciousness. The logic of Protestant individualism had been tempered in Europe and colonial America by state authoritarianism but was fully manifest in America by Brownson's time after the country's religious pluralism had led to the politically expedient separation of church and state. By midcentury, the proliferation of schisms and sects and the political deification of the democratic individual transformed the lives of even simple farm folk as much as canals and the coming of the railroad. Thoughtful people like Brownson, Miller, Kneeland, and Mann struggled with religious doubt not because they were naturally exercising their reflective reason, the later Brownson would have said, but because they had imbibed styles of Protestant philosophical and scientific thought without understanding their limitations.[58]

Brownson illustrated other dangerous implications of Protestant culture—and another dimension of skepticism—in *The Spirit-Rapper*. The narrator is a descendent of Connecticut Puritans who grew up, like Brownson, in a small New York town. Unlike Brownson, the narrator has no interest in metaphysics and focuses instead upon mathematics, physics, chemistry, and medicine. Drawn to Auguste Comte's scientific "positivism" and intrigued by phrenology until he heard a laughable lecture by George Combe, the narrator considers himself a modern scientist freed from old-fashioned superstitions about spiritual forces and God's Providence. With a circle of acquaintances in late 1830s Boston that includes a jocular lawyer, a rationalist doctor, a left-wing Unitarian minister, a Universalist clergyman, and a rigid Orthodox Congregationalist named Increase Cotton Mather, the narrator begins dabbling in mesmerism. While his associates try to explain hypnotic trances on naturalistic principles or assess their theological implications, the narrator burns with desire to control the deep forces of nature. While they debate the reliability of testimony and the experimental conditions necessary to produce knowledge, he has a will to power. After he discerns an intelligence operating behind some of the effects of his experiments in animal magnetism, he begins communicating with the spirit world by rapping on a table. The mesmerist becomes the Spirit-Rapper; Dr. Frankenstein becomes Dr. Faustus.[59]

The Spirit-Rapper claims to have launched modern American Spiritualism by mesmerizing the Fox sisters, neighbors of his in upper New York State who would hear their famous ghostly rappings shortly after meeting him. He is more interested, however, in joining his powers to visionary reform movements. He journeys to Philadelphia in the winter of 1841–42 and finds a reform community composed of "Hicksite Quakers, Unitarians, Swedenborgians, Universalists, and open unbelievers in all religion." At the salon of young Priscilla, a disciple of William Godwin and Mary Wollstonecraft modeled after Frances Wright, the narrator mingles with abolitionists, women's rights advocates, communitarians, and radical individualists. He listens to an Italian democratic nationalist and a French socialist. A thin, large-nosed New England Transcendentalist utters prophetic sayings about Nature and individuality. Another Transcendentalist calls for a return to the simplicity of childhood. In a corner of the room, a Jewish woman resembling Ernestine Rose attacks the Bible. The narrator hears a midwestern physician argue the merits of dietary reform, an Englishman hold forth about eugenics, and an unwashed radical named Thomas Jefferson Andrew Jackson Hobbs insist that all government should be abolished. "The majority were from the middle and upper classes," the narrator observes. "All were of course abolitionists, or friends of the blacks, and therefore excluded studiously the negroes from their social gatherings." Some were in petticoats, others in trousers, and "the majority appear[ed] to be of what grammarians call the epicene gender."[60]

Despite contradictory proposals and vastly different visions of the future, the philanthropic reformers are united by a passion for radical change. The Spirit-Rapper hopes that, joined to the powers he wields, these reformers can remake the world. With a growing sense of his own messianic destiny, he sails for Europe and helps stir up the troubles of 1848. A year later his revolutionary dreams are thwarted and his connection to Priscilla severed when she converts to Christianity and her formerly emasculated Quaker husband stabs the narrator in the chest. The Spirit-Rapper then returns home to die; the continued arguments of his old acquaintances help him find the true meaning of Spiritualism and the progressive spirit of the age.

Brownson's narrative sets out two interconnected arguments. The first is an interpretation of Spiritualism. Not all the wonders being reported in the 1840s and 1850s, he believed, could be dismissed as fraud or trickery. Physicians who automatically labeled spirit possession as hallucination or insanity merely begged the question. Other naturalistic explanations were also inadequate: the Spirit-Rapper detected an electric or fluid substance at work in mesmeric phenomena, but mesmerism could only account for a fraction of the reported marvels. Spiritualists were right, Brownson contended, when they claimed that they had contacted the spirit world, but wrong when they thought those spirits were departed souls. Whether they knew it or not, Spiritualists were dabbling in the black arts, and the voices they listened to had a Satanic source. That scholars and scientists scoffed at such a conclusion only showed the inroads skepticism had made upon the modern mind. Christianity had not been toppled by freethinking infidels; it had been hollowed out from within. Nominal Christians explained away demonic phenomena by the same process that "explained away the miracles and supernatural character of Christianity."[61]

Brownson's second argument showed the essential links between Spiritualism and liberal or radical reform, thereby demonizing what he called "modern philanthropy." Disparate as they were, he claimed, progressive reform movements shared a commitment to the divinization of humanity. "At the bottom of this idea of progress, which our modern reformers prate about, is the foolish notion that man is born inchoate, an incipient God, and that his destiny is to grow into or become the infinite God." It was not merely this common principle, however, that created solidarity. Ideas did not build institutions or launch social movements and revolutions on their own. An external, spiritual power had to be at work. Enlightenment philosophes like Voltaire, Rousseau, d'Alembert, Diderot, and Mirabeau had but a feeble effect upon the masses in the eighteenth century,

Brownson argued. The revolutionary madness of 1789—and of 1848—came from a different source. "There was at work...a power that the wits ridiculed, that science denied, philosophy disproved, and the clergy hardly dared assert.... There was a mighty power...which all ages have called Satan." Mid-nineteenth-century reformers had learned to exploit that power more effectively than their Enlightenment predecessors. They had understood that Christianity could not be overturned by the cool negations of religious skepticism, so they set out to fight it with an alternate religion. This revolutionary religion of world reform would spread and grow by a system of demonically charged spiritual communication. That, Brownson had decided, was the only explanation for the growth of radical social movements and anti-Christian ideologies. Infidelity did not require the power of rational persuasion to metastasize in the social body; it did not require the spread of literacy, the dissemination of print, or even the full awareness of the people involved. It required only a few conspirators who sought not truth but power, and a world full of sinners easily mesmerized.[62]

The Catholic Brownson liked to see religious skepticism in its various public and private forms as intimately connected to the heterodoxy, sectarian zeal, institution building, and impetus toward reform that were so prominent in nineteenth-century America. All proceeded from the Protestant Reformation's turn away from the Catholic Church, he argued, and were different facets of modernity's attempt to put Man on God's throne. Brownson the author of epistemological narratives, however, as opposed to Brownson the philosopher, knew that the relationship between skepticism and faith in America was more complicated than that. His fusion of epistemological analysis, social criticism, and personal narrative showed that real lives and the larger movements of history were not explained as the working out of a simple cultural logic. There is no such thing as an "a priori autobiography," he wrote in a review of a book with that title: a life is not merely the playing out of a given set of principles. Neither is history. To the biographer and the historian alike, the story "is never a series of logical sequences.... To him much must always appear anomalous, arbitrary, inexplicable, the result of chance." Brownson's case studies of individuals—Charles Elwood, the Convert, and the Spirit-Rapper—allowed him to describe religion and philosophy as dynamic experiences. This is true even though the stories unfold according to a particular point of view—Brownson's understanding of truth— that the characters themselves achieve only at the stories' end. Each character's alienation from what others were still trying to hold on to as American religious common sense in the 1820s, '30s, and '40s becomes an occasion for an epistemological critique of American institutions. The skeptical questions the stories raise are at least as powerful as Brownson's ultimate assertions of faith.[63]

Brownson's work contended that religious skepticism was an important force through the first half of the nineteenth century. *Charles Elwood* showed that it was too simplistic to see it merely as Christianity's adversary (the view of the Protestant clergyman who attacked the "Infidel"). Despite Brownson's later Catholic arguments, however, it is also too simplistic to see skepticism as the natural fruit of Protestantism. For individuals and the larger culture alike, too, skepticism was more than just a way station on the road to religious commitment; it exerted an intellectual pull even if the doubts themselves got left behind. Some Christians concluded that the rise of freethought was rooted in anticlericalism and ignorance about what the Bible actually said. Their solution was to close their ears to clerical chatter and philosophical speculation and return to the text itself. Millerites argued that doubting God and the Bible was a mistake that could be corrected by rational demonstration. By matching biblical predictions to historical facts, they addressed skeptics with the forms of evidence and argumentation the doubters already claimed to value. Spiritualists also met those who were skeptical of metaphysical truth claims on their own ground, offering empirical evidence rather than testimonies of mystical rapture. Many liberal Protestants, however, sought not to vanquish doubt by argument or evidence but to use skeptical inquiry to hone a progressive and rational Christianity. Others accepted the critiques of the old faith and substituted romantic redescriptions of Christianity based on individual experience. Some reformers, like the young Brownson, acknowledging that skeptics' arguments had corroded the authority of the church and the Bible, called for new visions that would connect a vague spirituality or religious sentimentality to communal efforts toward moral and intellectual progress. For others, like Mann, doubts about Christian revelation and the popular beliefs of the day helped inspire a desire to define doctrinal commitments as personal and private, topics unsuitable for polite conversation and public discussion.

Freethinkers' experiences with religious doubt, however, called for a more complicated response than the evangelical's return to the Bible, the romantic's redescription of religious terms, or the liberal's privatization of faith. Religious skepticism was not a sin, a mistake, or an embarrassment, they argued, and it was more than an intellectual mechanism that would distill a purer form of faith. Doubt was a psychological declaration of independence and a weapon to wield against the tyranny of organized religion. It was also the wedge that opened up the possibilities of free inquiry; free inquiry, in turn, led to the establishment of rational knowledge, which was the foundation of human progress. Metaphysical and supernatural truth claims could be discarded because they did not pass the test of reasonable doubt, they shut down rather than opened up free discussion, and they had, historically, inhibited rather than accelerated progress. Free inquirers called themselves theological but not philosophical skeptics because they thought other kinds of knowledge claims had passed those tests. Yet unlike the religionist's dogmatic conviction, they argued, the freethinker's assent was always to some degree provisional, always open (at least theoretically) to further curious questioning, testing, and doubting. The freethinkers were radical not just in what beliefs they discarded but in how they changed what it meant to "believe."

Many Americans before the second quarter of the nineteenth century had questioned their faith. But never before had so many doubters thought they might have the intellectual, social, and institutional resources to sustain a critique of Christian hegemony and construct an identity outside of it. Religious skepticism became a viable possibility because a poor farm boy like Brownson could get his hands on books by Paine or Hume; a young skeptic like Miller could find a circle of deistic Masons who scoffed at Christianity as so much superstition; and a preacher and editor like Kneeland could become a freethought lecturer and publicist and still earn a living. Yet despite the flowering of heterodoxies in an age of religious innovation, the cultural resources available to sustain a public religious skepticism could only go so far against such powerful and yet diffuse opposition. Religious skepticism did not secularize America, as the free inquirers of the 1830s had hoped, or produce armies of militant atheists, as some Christians had feared. But to rest with that conclusion is to miss the more complicated effects that skepticism did have—effects best seen in the stories of individual lives and in the complex connections of ideas to social and political practices. Religious doubt shaped Miller's crusade for the Bible, Kneeland's challenge to the limits of religious freedom, the young Brownson's social radicalism, and Mann's campaign for education reform. Coming to terms with skepticism and faith was profoundly important to infidels and converts alike—people who knew what it meant to both doubt and believe.

11

Converting Skeptics

Infidel and Protestant Economies

On February 14, 1833, at a little after five o'clock in the afternoon, a thirty-year-old lawyer named Charles R. Baldwin, sitting alone in his office in Charleston, in western Virginia, turned the back of his chair to the door and began to pray. He was a leading light of the Kanawha County bar, an admired orator, a rising star. Twenty days earlier his young wife, Elizabeth, had died. She had been declining since the previous November and had struggled to surrender herself completely to Christ. She found peace a week before her death. In a cot next to her bed on the night of her conversion, Charles was relieved for her but was still tormented by the idea that her impending death was a punishment for his sins. He promised her that he would seek real religion just as she had. As he sat in his office at the end of that busy February day, he vowed that he would do anything to experience the assurance of salvation. He would give up all he had—his books, his office, his career, even his baby daughter—for Christ's sake. The prosperous lawyer would turn his back on all the honors and pleasures of the world and become a Methodist preacher. With that conviction, he wrote, "I experienced a feeling which I had never known before.... I had peace, and love, and joy. My heart rose up in my throat, and I was filled with delight and surprise."[1]

About five months later, John Scarlett, a thirty-year-old New Jersey shoemaker, sat alone on a decaying log in the woods and remembered the sharp knife in his pocket. He had been attending his first Methodist revival meeting. Friends and strangers alike had prayed and wept for him. But when an old woman publicly prayed for his conversion at the meeting he felt like slinking home in disgrace. He had tried to read the Bible, but the words that thrilled and comforted so many others only seemed strange to him. He vowed not to work, eat, or drink until the question of his conversion was settled, but as he sat on the log he could only feel a crushing despair. He took the knife out of his pocket, and with the other hand felt his chest where the blade would have to penetrate to pierce his heart. A large stone nearby had a concave surface, like a shallow bowl; he imagined it filling with a suicide's blood. Suddenly he heard "an intelligible voice, not of audible sound," asking him why he thought killing himself—merely separating his soul from his body—would give any relief to his spiritual anguish. He knew it was the voice of God. He hurried back to the meeting, asked the preacher to say a prayer for him, and felt Christ remove his burden of sin. Later he had a vision: a high mountain, a bright cloud, an amber light, the lovely face of a man smiling with no earthly smile. He shouted God's glories until sunset, then walked home, supported by two Methodist brethren, the three of them praising God the whole way.[2]

John Bayley's spiritual transformation occurred while he was alone in his room with a "small negro boy," the slave who had been assigned to wait on him. It was early January 1838. Bayley was a twenty-four-year-old journeyman printer, an immigrant from England who had traveled much of the eastern seaboard before ending up in Farmville, Virginia. He had been confined to bed with a violent attack of dyspepsia and thought he might be dying. No stranger to thoughts of suicide, he was friendless and homesick, sobbing and "suffering all the day long without speaking to any one except this little ignorant boy." A letter arrived from his sister in England, and he suddenly wished he could be a Christian so he might see her again in heaven if not on earth. This thought was a turning point: he had made up his mind to become a Christian. In a few days he recovered from his illness, but he was still unable to speak with anyone about his spiritual struggles. He wandered the woods and wept. When he visited a Methodist meeting, the preacher walked from the pulpit directly up to Bayley and told him to pray. Bayley fell to the floor, crying for mercy, and prayed on his knees until after the congregation was dismissed. For the next few days, he attended prayer meetings, and the preacher and other brethren went to his room to pray with him afterward, "but still there was a mountain of unbelief on my heart and I could not trust God for salvation." When the Methodists left, Bayley was again alone with the young slave. Bayley sat by the fire, deep in thought. "The little negro boy who sat in one corner of the room looked very earnestly at me, and inquired, 'What was the matter with you when you hallooed so?' 'God was punishing me for my sins,' I replied. 'What did the little man [the preacher] do for you?' 'He prayed to God for me.' 'Would God hear him?'" Bayley did not know how to answer, so he was silent. "With a sigh the little boy exclaimed, 'I wish I could pray.... Won't you teach me to pray, sir?'" Bayley spoke a line he remembered from an old hymn: "Lord, teach a child to pray." The boy "instantly knelt down at my feet, put his face to the floor, and whispered, 'Lord, teach a little child to pray.' The thought instantly flashed into my mind, if that little boy can believe in me, why cannot I believe in God." At that moment he began looking "at the Savior with the eye of Faith."[3]

These stories of men coming of age in the 1820s and converting to Christianity in the 1830s were all published in the 1850s. All three conversion narratives are ostensibly less concerned with the particularities of their nineteenth-century moment or calls for social reform than with playing variations on a familiar evangelical theme: an individual's agonizing and then joyous journey from awakening to God's call, being convicted of sin, converting to Christ, and finally being sanctified by the Holy Spirit. The twist is that the sinful lives being renounced in *The Conversion of a Skeptic*, *The Life and Experience of a Converted Infidel*, and *Confessions of a Converted Infidel* are marked not by obvious moral failings but by doubt about the truth of Christianity. Charles Baldwin, John Scarlett, and John Bayley were religious skeptics who became Methodist preachers. Their passages from skepticism to faith are seen through the tinted glass of their postconversion perspectives. In each case, their experiences of doubt and belief are also colored by signature motifs that run through their narratives and take symbolic form even within their accounts of their central moments of conversion crisis. Baldwin the prosperous lawyer performs his crucial turn away from his "worldly prospects" and toward God by literally turning his back to his law office door. Scarlett the New Jersey shoemaker had from childhood wrestled with the problem of interpreting purportedly supernatural signs until the intelligible voice settled the truth of the Gospel beyond any reasonable doubt. Once mocking the idea that God would intervene in a man's economic affairs, he came to learn that money for one's daily bread came not just from virtuous labor but from the invisible hand of Providence. In Bayley's story, black slaves, like the "ignorant boy" in his room, are figures of redemptive piety in America; they replace the symbol of his earlier infidel resentment, the worker toiling in the dark mills of Manchester who was beaten down by an industrial capitalism that was propped up by the Christian church.[4]

Each man converted from skepticism to faith at a time of profound economic transformation and intense questioning about the moral and religious implications of those changes. While social reformers responded to economic disruption by trying to adjust or replace American institutions, socially conservative evangelicals argued that real reform, real progress, could only come about by converting more souls to Christ. Baldwin, Scarlett, and Bayley, after their conversions, would have agreed that true reform was a work done on individual hearts by God's grace, and that economic developments and the vagaries of material life paled in importance to a soul's ultimate destiny. Still, their stories show them struggling to make moral sense of economic life as skeptical infidels and as faithful Christians.

Infidel and Protestant Economies

It has been said that there was "no one Protestant approach to money" in this period, no singular Protestant ethic informing the spirit of capitalism. But most were dedicated to living in the world without being worldly, rejecting, as they saw it, both the Catholic's monastic withdrawal and the infidel's blinkered materialism. Protestants struggled to find the right relationship between the material and spiritual economies—between the system of the production, exchange, and consumption of material things creating the wealth of a nation, on one hand, and the system through which human sin is overcome by divine grace in the work of redemption, on the other. They criticized covetousness and materialism, and blamed infidel philosophy for promoting both, but they wanted to benefit from economic prosperity, and they stoked the furnaces of the entrepreneurialism that produced it. One midcentury tract, for example, made the case for charitable giving by arguing that such beneficence would promote "*prosperity... industry, energy, and enterprise,*" as well as the habit of "judicious management of business," in the giver himself. Here the hope is that Christian benevolence could produce, not just coexist with, savvy capitalism.[5]

American Protestants adopted and adapted many of the concepts the British had developed to explain, defend, or attack the new capitalist order. In England, the Rev. Thomas Malthus, recoiling from the infidel utopianism of Revolutionary France and its radical English incarnation in William Godwin's *Political Justice* (1793), published his famous *Essay on the Principle of Population* in 1798. Against Condorcet's enlightened fantasies about the perfectibility of man and Godwin's contention that a secular millennium could be ushered in by replacing the wicked institutions that had sanctified private property, Malthus argued that property was the foundation of civilization, inequality was an essential part of society, and the divine laws of supply and demand must be left alone to create the best of all possible worlds. Trying artificially to lift the poor above a bare subsistence level, Malthus wrote, would only encourage them to breed more. Population would then quickly outstrip the food supply, leading to starvation and other miseries. In the early nineteenth century, British writers developed a Protestant laissez-faire political economy, combining Malthus's strictures on population with Adam Smith's invisible hand of the marketplace (*Wealth of Nations*, 1776) and William Paley's *Natural Theology* (1802). This Protestant laissez-faire, promoted by the prolific Scottish Presbyterian clergyman Thomas Chalmers, combated other forms of godless economic theory such as the utilitarianism of Jeremy Bentham, the socialism of Robert Owen, and the liberalism of John Stuart Mill. In the United States, views similar to Chalmers's were disseminated by the Rev. Francis Wayland, Baptist president of Brown University, whose *Elements of Political Economy* (1837) went through twenty-three American editions and was summarized in encyclopedias and schoolbooks.[6]

Protestant and "infidel" political economists could sometimes come to the same policy recommendations—arguing against social welfare programs or the government's interference in the economy, for example—but they had different ends in mind. The godless philosophers sought the greatest good for the greatest number; the Christian advocates of laissez-faire saw the economy as an arena for providential rewards and punishments. Chalmers, Wayland, and other laissez-faire evangelicals combined economic individualism with moral paternalism: individuals should be able to rise or fall on their own in the marketplace, but their moral lives should be tutored and guided by religion. Many American Protestant commentators, without being students of political economy, came to similar conclusions about the relation of economic and religious life (though in the United States, which lacked an established church and had citizens who celebrated the ability to choose the church within which they could submit to divine authority, the paternalism was more muted).[7]

Critics decried both the new economic order and the theories of political economy that justified it. In Britain, ultra-Tory old-money conservatives found competitive economic individualism vulgar and socially corrosive; in America, slave-holding planters voiced analogous paeans to an organic patriarchal order. British Romantic poets loathed the narrow, grasping materialism of Economic Man. New England Transcendentalists did, too, though Ralph Waldo Emerson's doctrine of self-reliance ended up making the marketplace spiritually palatable more than his hymns to the Over-Soul criticized it. In 1834, the French Catholic Alban de Villeneuve-Bargemont called for a different sort of Christian political economy, arguing that Christianity would need to save the masses impoverished by mechanization and the concentration of capital. A decade later, John Hughes, the Catholic bishop of New York, contended that Protestant political economies—whether in Democratic laissez-faire or Whig interventionist dress—fostered selfishness and greed.[8]

In 1851, a book published anonymously in Philadelphia called *New Themes for the Protestant Clergy* blasted the churches for sanctioning the cruelties of the capitalist marketplace and was in turn attacked as an enemy of true religion. The tension between moral values and the pursuit of wealth was a familiar theme in high-circulation newspapers such as Horace Greeley's *New York Tribune*, popular magazines from *Godey's Lady's Book* to *Hunt's Merchant Magazine*, and best-selling fiction, but *New Themes* put a sharper point on the discussion. The author argued that although the Catholic Church had for centuries robbed and blinded the people, Protestants had created, as the book's subtitle put it, *Creeds without Charity, Theology without Humanity, and Protestantism without Christianity*. Protestantism, stressing faith rather than good works, had encouraged a "new race of men" to spring up in the modern age, men channeling "intense selfishness in the pursuit of wealth and power." The systematic benevolence touted by moral reformers created bureaucratic mechanisms, not real Christian charity. The free market had accelerated "a devotion to mammon never before equaled; a grinding competition in all pursuits of life." Labor was reduced to a mere marketplace commodity, and people were considered little more than machines for making money. Not only did the churches approve of all this, the author charged, but Malthus's pitiless strictures against giving food to the poor (because starvation would cull the surplus population) had become a doctrine of the Church of England and was echoed in American pulpits and religious publications.[9]

Writers in that American religious press, especially Episcopalians, were outraged. Despite the book's many pages of scriptural quotations, one critic called it "the splenetic raving of an avowed unbeliever," and another worried that *New Themes* would do more harm than Paine's *Age of Reason*. "The miscreant Paine has uttered nothing more reckless, nor more guilty," a third fumed. When the author was revealed to be the industrialist Stephen Colwell, a devout Presbyterian, his opponents were astonished but continued to insist that his doctrines aided and abetted the cause of religious infidelity, whatever his confused intentions. Colwell himself had said the same about Reverend Malthus and subsequent champions of Protestant laissez-faire political economy. The author of *New Themes* blamed the rise and persistence of religious skepticism and infidel socialism upon the intransigent conservatism of the churches and cheered when he read Godwin's indignant response to Malthus and saw the infidel crush the clergyman "as a venomous reptile."[10]

Both sides in the debate over *New Themes* claimed true Christianity for themselves and saw religious infidelity in the "spirit and tendencies" of their opponents' views. The argument was particularly bitter but not new. Americans had long contested the ethical and religious dimensions of economic theory and practice. Nor were the arguments about the morality of modern economic life confined to the world of print. Middle-class shopkeepers turned entrepreneurs expressed attitudes about the sacrosanctity of a free marketplace and the inviolate rights of property in their daily business practices. Wage-earning workers in the early labor movement countered that the brutal logic of capitalist exploitation was incompatible with either republican virtue or Christian love. Businessmen who quietly doubted the truth of Christianity could nonetheless appreciate how it could help legitimate capitalism in society at large. Freethinkers were more vocal on the side of labor, struggling against the hegemony of the Christian churches and the capitalist regime as twin oppressors.[11]

Labor leaders such as Thomas Skidmore in New York City usually tried to distance themselves from freethinking labor reformers like Frances Wright and Robert Dale Owen and also tried to silence distracting radical critiques of Christianity within their ranks. But while many (though not most) labor activists were church members, and Christian ideas and language often inflected labor protests, there was a broad spectrum of religious opinion among working men and women, a range that included religious skepticism and indifference. Labor activists who editorialized in working-class newspapers, moreover, did not express the opinions of the "mind of antebellum labor" as a whole. Labor spokesmen were sometimes a step or two removed from the workers they claimed to represent and even further away from the unskilled toilers at the bottom of the "free" labor market. A similar range of opinion and practice probably also characterized the most cruelly exploited workers in the American economy: the slaves.[12]

Unsurprisingly, therefore, the three narratives of Charles R. Baldwin, John Scarlett, and John Bayley, which detail their conversions from skeptical infidelity to Christian faith, also present conversions from infidel to Christian economies. Each in different ways intends to show how people lacking religious faith fail to perceive the true relations of spiritual and material life.

The Prosperous Professional

The Conversion of a Skeptic: A Member of the Bar is a biography of Charles Baldwin written by another clergymen, Maxwell Pierson Gaddis, and it includes long extracts from Baldwin's speeches, letters, and journals. Baldwin was the twelfth child of a once-affluent farmer. He demonstrated precocious abilities in classical learning, accomplishments that fired his political ambitions while he was still in his teens: after finishing Virgil's *Aeneid*, he recalled, "I now felt a NEW FIRE BURNING WITHIN ME—I was no longer content to be an humble farmer. Prompted by ambition, I looked forward to a period when I might fill the highest office of State." He read Greek and Hebrew as well as Latin, and before he turned twenty he was asked to deliver a public oration on George Washington's birthday. Passing the bar exam with ease, he quickly built a lucrative practice in Kanawha County, Virginia, and earned a reputation as a sharp debater and skilled orator.[13]

Gaddis included excerpts from some of Baldwin's July Fourth orations in the book to demonstrate the young lawyer's eloquence and establish his credentials as a patriotic American "defender of freedom." The speeches were ideological performances, just as, in another vein, his later sermons would be. They invoked foundational principles (liberty and equality) from founding texts (the Declaration of Independence and the Constitution). They declared that these principles had molded a collective identity, directed a shared history, and pointed toward a glorious future. The United States was a moral engine revolutionizing the world, Baldwin proclaimed. As Europe flailed, Americans were undermining the foundations of tyranny, having created a government based on compromise and a society where men rose according to their talents, integrity, and industry. Here political freedom and economic opportunity meshed like gears in the mighty machine of progress. The "spirit of enterprise" was at work "conquering *space* and *time*, removing the *barriers* which nature has opposed to friendly and commercial intercourse," and happily creating "a rapid increase of wealth." In the mid-1820s he prophesied that one day soon, with the thickening social connections advanced by science and civilization, citizens on the eastern seaboard and the banks of the Mississippi would feel like neighbors.[14]

Political values and social bonds kept the pursuit of individual economic self-interest within ethical bounds. Baldwin tossed a bouquet of clichés to the memory of George Washington, "the immortal savior and deliverer of his country." He said that the Republic had been "redeemed by [the] blood" of patriots in the past and called those in the present to "sacrifice upon the altar of our country's good all party animosities" and narrow self-interests. Tugging on the cords of mutual sympathy, Baldwin also called for individuals to pledge their lives to preserving "the principles of the constitution...the fabric of the social order...[and] the prosperity of the state." Wretches concerned only with wealth and self would forfeit all renown and go down to the dust "unwept, unhonored, and unsung."[15]

How much these flag-saluting phrases actually made Baldwin's own pulse race is hard to say. Rehearsals of political dogma and calls to shed blood for country can, especially in peacetime, be ritually spoken and routinely cheered like rhetorical balloons set to the breeze. Similarly, assurances about the compatibility of self-interested commerce and the public good are uttered easily in times of plenty. There is no reason, though, to doubt whether his patriotic nationalism and sunny view of material progress were sincere. Surely, too, when he appreciated a political and economic system that allowed men to rise according to their talents, he was thinking of men like himself. But was prosperity and worldly renown enough? Few could achieve the secular immortality of a Washington. Baldwin reflected privately that after "an honourable burial—a handsome monument—a paragraph in the columns of a fleeting newspaper," even good men are soon forgotten.[16]

Until his thirtieth year he was "a SKEPTIC...an unbeliever in the truth of divine revelation." At eighteen he had been confirmed in the Episcopal Church, but only to honor the wishes of his late father. His orations made a few vague references to a distant deity who stood behind "the natural operation" of the political principles and economic enterprise that were shaping the course of American history.[17] But reading David Hume's essay on miracles confirmed the drift of his own thinking about religious matters. Baldwin disbelieved the Bible and doubted that there was an afterlife. "To me the 'preaching of the Cross was foolishness.' If there was any such a thing as *religion*, I supposed it to consist in *mere amendment of life*—a rigid adherence to moral duties coupled with the observance of the mere external forms of devotion. I could not comprehend *how* the *heart of man* could be changed, even if such a change was necessary. I therefore disbelieved in the agency of a Holy Ghost.... What [evangelicals] called 'conversion,' I supposed was nothing but an undue excitement, produced ordinarily by powerful and well directed appeals to the passions, and the noise and excitement of their meetings operating simply on weak nerves. And what they termed 'conversion' or a 'change of heart' as they professed to receive it, I thought was simply the *change* experienced by the *dying away* of that excitement—the calm that usually succeeds the storm—or the removal of the cause." Prudently keeping these opinions to himself, however, he "attended fashionable places of public worship whenever it was convenient" and "endeavored to keep on good terms with the christian part of the community."[18]

Mixed with his skepticism about fundamental Christian doctrines was a class disdain for a church that still drew much of its membership from the lower sort. Occasionally attending a fashionable Episcopal church and being friendly with respectable Christians was prudent for a gentleman of the bar who needed clients. But while Baldwin privately "opposed and denounced all orthodox churches," he had a special contempt for the church he eventually joined: "The Methodist Church I despised above all others. I regarded her members as the very 'filth and offscouring of the world.'"[19]

Baldwin saw Methodism in western Virginia in the early 1830s as a church still predominantly composed of poorer whites and blacks. But American Methodism more generally had by that time become a firmly established institution in cities and towns of long-settled areas. Its members had grown wealthier, and as they did so they absorbed (and helped shape) middle-class values. They built elegant churches, founded colleges, and demanded an educated ministry. Complainers called "croakers" insisted that the church continue to be defined by its army of threadbare itinerants constantly on horseback and its fervent "mothers in Israel" like Sarah Jones. Even in places where it had not yet earned middling respectability, Methodism had for many become less a radical spiritual movement than a religion of mainstream routine. Even when not stiffened by the stays of refinement, a Methodist meeting could be more of a social event than a devotional ritual. John Bayley's depiction of an ordinary Methodist service in Virginia echoed the critical descriptions that evangelicals in the same region had leveled at complacent Anglicans a century before. Groups of gentlemen chatted earnestly about crop prices and politics, and then ostentatiously walked in to take their seats after the service had already begun. Women continued to whisper and gossip through the opening prayers. Some in the congregation ate fruit and candies, others picked their teeth or filed their nails, and many spat tobacco juice on the floor. With the closing prayer barely finished, the congregants stampeded out the door, eager to get back to their worldly pleasures—as if they had ever left them.[20]

Looking back on his skeptical infidelity after his conversion, Baldwin claimed that he had never been completely satisfied and secure in his own worldly philosophy. "We may be skeptics here, but death will soon put an end to our skepticism," he wrote to a doubting nephew in 1833. He had brooded about death for years, and even before his wife's illness his heart had been prepared to receive the Gospel. One Sunday he happened to hear a sermon on Matthew 16:26: "For what is a man profited, if he shall gain the whole world, and lose his own soul?" "If the sermon demolished my skepticism, the prayer which followed it *completely* melted down my proud and obdurate heart," he later wrote. But the warm feelings faded, and he attributed the experience to merely being roused by an effective speaker. On another occasion he met a man after church, a Unitarian and Universalist, who criticized the day's sermon. Baldwin found himself jumping into a debate, defending the Trinity and limited salvation as the true scriptural doctrines. Wanting to be better prepared for a future contest, he went home and started reading the Bible closely. Instead of gathering debater's points, though, he found himself choking up as he read the stories of Abraham and Joseph. When he read aloud to his wife the account of Christ's sufferings, he felt his skeptical opinions vanish.[21]

It was the suffering and death of Elizabeth Baldwin, however, that finally drove him to his knees. Charles had become a believer by the time he buried his wife, but he had still not experienced faith as others described it. He attended a Friday night Methodist meeting in the Charleston schoolroom and heard an acquaintance relate his conversion experience, but to Baldwin it seemed an "idle tale." Reading John Wesley's sermons on the witness of the spirit, Baldwin almost set the book down as the work of "a great enthusiast," but became convinced that either Wesley and the Bible were wrong or Baldwin himself still lacked saving faith. "I continued to pray for the witness of the Spirit—an evidence that would *banish all doubt*. What that inward testimony was I had no conception of, but I believed it was a divine and glorious reality, and I longed to experience it." Shortly after that February day when he turned his chair to the door to pray, he shuttered his office and sold his law books, and in a few months he delivered his first sermon to astonished friends and neighbors.[22]

Describing the practical consequences of his conversion, Baldwin stressed his turn from material prosperity to pious poverty as he crossed class lines to join the world's filthy offscouring. "Nothing short of a perfect assurance of the truth of divine revelation and an experimental knowledge of Christ, would have induced me to forego my worldly prospects and become a houseless wanderer," he explained to his nephew. "*I know* that the Bible *is* true. I have felt—I have experimentally proved its truth."[23]

He also had to explain, especially to his high-toned Episcopal relatives, why he had chosen Methodism. It had been an eventful year, he admitted to his sister in a letter written on New Year's Eve 1833. He had lost his wife, converted to Christianity, given up his profession, become an itinerant Methodist preacher, and remarried. He was preaching nine sermons a week and visiting twenty congregations a month on his circuit in Ohio. His choice of Methodism over Episcopalianism, he explained, was based on a practical assessment of rhetorical and liturgical effectiveness rather than on any theological difference. Both churches shared the same basic doctrines. But the staid forms of worship in his sister's church, though fine for those accustomed to them, were not well suited to draw in strangers or appeal to those who read poorly or not at all. Extempore prayers guided by the Spirit rather than fixed language read from a prayer book, too, were far better at awakening feelings and exciting reflection. To his brother Cyrus a few weeks later he argued for the benefits of the Methodist's circuit system, where preachers were shifted to a different preaching field every year or two. Congregations got shaken out of familiar routines with new arguments and preaching styles; ministers faced new challenges with renewed energy, determined to be at least as successful as their predecessors. "The only question with me was, how could I win most souls to Christ," he told his sister. The answer seemed clear: "The system and economy" of Methodism seemed "far better adapted for extensive and general usefulness."[24]

The goal was numbers—winning as many souls for Christ as he could—and the Methodist "system and economy" could simply win more than other forms of Christianity. Baldwin had become a peddler in divinity, as was said of the itinerant evangelist George Whitefield a century before. In four weeks, he told his sister to underline his point about general usefulness, he had preached thirty-two sermons in twenty different places. His circuit required twenty-five sermons each month throughout the year, he explained in a letter to his niece, but he hoped to average thirty. Baldwin experienced the pleasures of spiritual bookkeeping common among nineteenth-century Methodists, measuring devotion in miles ridden, sermons preached, and prayers uttered, calculating (spiritual) profits as avidly as a merchant at his ledger books. He did not, though, estimate converts made. He would wait to meet his hearers again "at the bar of the Almighty" to answer for his efforts in preaching as they answered for theirs in listening and applying what he said to their own lives. Baldwin the peddler neither made what he sold nor was responsible for how the consumer made use of it.[25]

Just as when he had argued cases in court or had given patriotic speeches, Baldwin continued to define himself through rhetorical performance. He was known for clear and argumentative sermons delivered with faultless elocution. Never reading from the pulpit, he preached from outlines prepared in advance to avoid repeating phrases and illustrations. Gaddis thought Baldwin's previous experience as a public speaker had been helpful. But the charismatic—Spirit-filled—evangelist was no longer the July Fourth Cicero: one person who had seen Baldwin's debut sermon in Charleston remembered that "at times he seemed so filled with the Holy Ghost that his face was radiant like that of Stephen when he saw 'heaven opened.' "[26]

God called Baldwin, the former lawyer believed, to proclaim the Gospel from the pulpit and to testify about the work of the Spirit on his own heart. There is little sense in Baldwin's writings (or Gaddis's commentary) of Baldwin himself learning through dialogue with fellow believers, of the call and response of a pastor and his flock, of God's grace as social grace. An 1834 letter urged his sister-in-law to seek the Lord not just alone in her closet but with fellow seekers, and through singing, conversation, and prayer the group would be "mutually edified, comforted, and strengthened in the faith." *The Conversion of a Skeptic*, however, depicts Baldwin in the pulpit and alone with his thoughts but rarely experiencing the joys (and the tensions) of Christian fellowship. A journal entry described a Sunday love feast as a "communion season," but it was a communion between Baldwin and God. The clergyman witnessed before his brethren about his spiritual experiences and was rewarded not by the congregation's response but by a vision of Christ nailed to the cross, blood and water streaming from his side.[27]

Baldwin counseled his skeptical nephew to follow the path that he himself had taken. Cornelius did not believe that the Bible was true. Was he a deist or an atheist, Baldwin asked? Did he believe that men were moral agents? That they had immortal souls? Did he follow Hume, Voltaire, Rousseau, or Tom Paine? "Or are you undecided, resting upon your skepticism—satisfied to doubt?" Without the Bible, Baldwin warned, we are like weather-beaten ships on a boundless sea, without chart or compass, "our passions sometimes blowing to a tempest, and reason standing motionless at the helm," driven relentlessly forward toward death. "Such are the happy results of skepticism, the boasted triumphs, the glorious uncertainties to which reason brings us, when we get loose from the moorings of Christianity, and launch upon the broad sea of doubt and infidelity." We can only build our hopes upon the Bible, he told his nephew. But the scriptures could not be mastered like other branches of learning. They could only be truly understood if the reader's heart was first illuminated by a divine and supernatural light.[28]

A journal entry from January 4, 1839, illustrated how Baldwin thought this process worked. Alone in his room, he prayed for help in understanding Romans 8:32 ("He that spared not his own Son, but delivered him up for us all, how shall he not with him also freely give us all things?"). "I found my mind led along by the Holy Spirit, farther and farther and farther into the intricate and amazing subject—and stretching my feeble understanding wider and wider—and in the effort to grasp it, I really feared I would loose my intellect, but the Lord gave me *strength* as I proceeded, binding up the faculties of my soul, and at the last, apparently from *every point* of the Heavens, light and glory poured in upon me, streaming into my soul, until I was let into the immeasurable expanse of the boundless 'fullness of God.' ... The earth was far below, and quite too small for me ... and for some time I lay not like my Redeemer, in an 'agony on the cold earth' covered with sweat and blood—but on the floor of my study, in *inexpressible joy*, shouting the high praises of God." Being freely given "all things" from God was a different sort of prosperity.[29]

Pressing on after his conversion, Baldwin sought the further blessing of sanctification, believing that it was a Christian's duty to be perfected—to be freed from sin—while still on earth. The Methodists' *"severe, self-denying rules of living,"* strictly applied, and the rigorous life of an itinerant preacher, provided the purifying discipline that he felt he needed to reach his goal. It was another way that Methodism's "system and economy" produced spiritual profit. Affections and desires had to be nailed to the cross; even the little indulgences people allowed themselves needed to be watched. "'Whatever is not faith is sin,' and there is harm in everything that is not done expressly with reference to the glory of God. No action of our lives is indifferent." The presiding elder of one of Baldwin's preaching circuits remembered him as a man who never wasted a moment. He struggled in prayer for months and then finally "felt the *cleansing* operation of the blood of Christ, the sanctifying influence of the Holy Spirit removing every guilty stain, *destroying all sin*, emptying the heart of everything evil, and causing me to feel that I was clean." He became a refined spiritual instrument, detecting the slightest touch of the Holy Spirit, recoiling in horror at the mildest sinful thought. A journal entry recorded his spiritual sensations on a spring day as he crossed the Ohio River and rode toward Gallipolis: "I felt *perfect love* and a clear witness of the mighty work wrought by the Holy Spirit, of which I retained an abiding sense during the remainder of the day. I felt no inward 'motions of sin,' and the worth of souls never lay so near my heart. I felt an almost constant *direction* of the Holy Spirit dwelling within me, and the least omission or backwardness in duty and obedience caused an uneasy, painful sensation at my heart.... To-day I have been unspeakably happy; my soul filled with pure seraphic fire, the witness of the Holy Spirit constant, and *so clear as to leave no manner of doubt.*"[30]

Baldwin's perfect love of God and constant sense of His presence cast out all his remaining fears. "I have no fear of death, let it come at what hour or in what form it may," he told his niece, noting in the same letter that his brother George had just died of typhus a day after burying his wife and thirteen-year-old daughter. In the spring of 1835, a little more than two years after the death of Charles Baldwin's first wife, he watched his second wife, Mary Jane, pass away. Her deathbed scene, he wrote in his journal, was more like a vision of glory than the groaning strife of a mere mortal. He wished, however, that her last breaths had been spent praising God rather than praying. This deviation from pious protocol was not his only concern. When he married a third time two years later, he prayed that his new wife would survive him, so he that would not be asked to endure the loss of a spouse yet again. His prayer was answered. On November 9, 1839, after being stricken by what he described as bronchitis, he ensured by his own last words that the observers at his bedside would record a triumphant Christian death: "Victory! Victory!! Glory! Glory!!"[31]

When Maxwell Gaddis published the memoir of Baldwin as *The Conversion of a Skeptic: A Member of the Bar* in 1858, he subtly addressed both the "croakers" who admired the pious poverty of the old itinerants and the midcentury evangelicals who felt that religion could fit hand in glove with middle-class respectability. Baldwin the successful lawyer and eloquent speaker had admirable talents and accomplishments even before his conversion. His spiritual transformation represented not a rejection of his worldly success but a redirection of his energy and ambition away from winning court cases and toward winning souls for Christ. The Methodist "economy" systematically expanded its market and tailored its product to meet the needs of consumers. It used methods and means that any middle-class entrepreneur could admire but turned them toward spiritual ends. Baldwin's conversion, then, was not an alteration of character or even, at a deep level, a change in how he worked in the world to achieve his goals. It was a removal of the religious skepticism that had kept his infidel gaze locked on lower but not necessarily sinful or evil things: material prosperity, social renown, and political ambition.

The Urban Artisan

The New Jersey shoemaker John Scarlett could mark the downward turn of his economic fortunes to a particular day and a specific hour during the fall of 1832. Scarlett, who had learned his craft during a four-year apprenticeship, owned his own shoemaking shop in Newark. Urban New Jersey had participated in the brief but significant confluence of labor radicalism and freethinking centered in New York City's Workingmen's movement, and Scarlett had joined other Newark artisans to oppose "aristocratic" power in either church or state. The shoemaker in the shop next door, however, was an evangelical who espoused precisely the sort of superstitions, Scarlett believed, that kept the working class in a kind of mental slavery. One day during a thunderstorm, he found his pious neighbor cowering at every thunderclap and muttering about divine judgments. Laughing, Scarlett took the knife he had been using to cut leather and stuck his arm out an open window, daring the heavens to take a crack at it. The next lightning bolt did indeed sound like it struck very close by, as if God intended a rebuke. On that fall day in 1832, however, Scarlett was among some Christians who were talking about "temporal prosperity" being affected by "the superintendence of divine Providence." This superstitious notion struck right at Scarlett's core sense of himself: he was a proud artisan who believed in the dignity of his labor and that his own and his family's livelihood depended upon the skilled work he did each day at his bench. So he declared that his shoemaking business would be a success "in spite of" their ideas about Providence and that he would "show them there was no truth in such things." So began what Scarlett later called the gloomiest period of his life. "I dated the rapid decline of my temporal affairs from that very hour."[32]

The life that the nearly thirty-year-old shoemaker had made for himself since he had completed his apprenticeship and entered adulthood was about to unravel. He had decisively turned away from Christianity eight years earlier. The sudden and unexpected death of his father in 1824 had helped harden him against religion. John recalled that he loved his "father with filial affection and placed unbounded confidence in his ability." He described himself as having been a puny, timid boy, running to his father for comfort and relief, hanging on the man's words as though he were an oracle. When he was sick, his father was his physician; when he was terrified of soldiers in the War of 1812, his father soothed his jangled nerves. If his father had one flaw as a parent, John reflected, it was that he did not do much to help the boy distinguish between fact and fiction, authentic spirituality and foolish superstition. It was a problem that would linger.[33]

An immigrant from Ireland in the 1790s, the elder Scarlett liked to sit under a tree, smoke his pipe, and spin stories that filled his children's heads with thoughts of ghosts, witches, and hobgoblins. Young John had believed in all these things, and also thought that some hills were monuments left by a race of giants, that a whippoorwill call was a message from the land of spirits, and that watches and guns could think. When a self-proclaimed prophet named Hughes said that the world would soon end in a great conflagration, the father set the boy's mind at ease by confidently telling him that the prediction was nonsense. The boy's fears of sin and hell, picked up from some Sunday school tracts, could not be so easily soothed. So he prayed for a sign from God concerning his salvation when he went fishing one day: catching a bass would mean he was saved, and any other fish would mean he was damned (he got a bass on the line, but it slipped from the hook before he could grab it). In 1824, John was just finishing his apprenticeship and had set aside what he understood to be both superstition and Christianity. He stood in a drenching rain at his father's funeral with a handful of other mourners, unable to weep and feeling "a kind of misanthropy." Writing three decades later, he concluded that at the funeral his "sympathies for mankind" were already "frost-bitten by infidelity, and benumbed by what I had suffered." He did not say in the 1850s—but did he feel in the 1820s?—that as he stood over the grave he became convinced that a personal God, a loving Father, would not have taken his own father from him.[34]

Scarlett's drift away from his parents' casual Episcopalianism had been intellectual and social as well as emotional. His "mind was active and restless." He read Volney's deistic *Travels in Assyria* and *Ruins of Empire* and Paine's famous *Age of Reason*. The book that made the deepest impression was Elihu Palmer's *Principles of Nature*. He read poetry by Alexander Pope and was charmed by the daring Romantic atheism of Percy Bysshe Shelley and especially Lord Byron. In Newark's Mechanics' Library he devoured fiction (though in later years he would condemn the "insinuating vein of infidelity" that ran through the work of popular novelists like Charles Dickens). He studied popular astronomy and doubted that the Creator of such a vast universe would sacrifice his son on our tiny insignificant world. But skeptical sentiments, expressed in offhand remarks by older men whom he respected, affected him as much as his reading. So did the attitudes of his fellow apprentices and young mechanics, his fun-loving companions at taverns, dances, and the theater. He himself did not dance, but he stayed and watched others do so late into the night; he did not gamble or brawl, but he saw plenty of both; he was never drunk, but he did raise a social glass or two. Sampling sermons at the various churches in town, he could sometimes be quite moved, but those feelings evaporated as quickly as the morning dew. Why would not a deity allow a man harmlessly to indulge some of his natural appetites, he reasoned? Even through the fog of the older Scarlett's stern disapproval, the younger man's delight in the social life of Newark flashes between the lines of the narrative.[35]

He worked out his religious identity amid the pushes and pulls of personal friendships, artisanal camaraderie, and ideological conviction. Democratic politics came to engross his energies and attention. The deists and other infidels who met regularly in Old Cadet Hall shared his abhorrence of aristocratic political and religious power, so he began attending their meetings. He published a few newspaper articles on religious intolerance (which the older Scarlett described as veiled attacks upon Christianity itself). Yet he still had Christian friends who lent him books such as James Beattie's *Essay on the Nature and Immutability of Truth* (1770), an answer to David Hume's skepticism, and Edmund Burke's *A Philosophical Enquiry into the Origin of Our Ideas of the Sublime and Beautiful* (1757). One evening Scarlett watched with distaste as a deist orator visiting from New York had a glass of strong liquor with his wife, and he had heard that some of the leading Newark deists had rather loose notions of the marriage compact. He began to wonder if Christians were right when they claimed that deism lead to drunkenness and licentiousness. He visited a friend dying of consumption to see how an infidel faced death. Lying on his deathbed, a well-worn copy of *The Age of Reason* on his mantelpiece, the man appeared unafraid of anything he might face in the next world, if there was one. But he also seemed consumed by bitterness about petty slights in this world, turning to face the wall and grumbling about another friend, a "Presbyterian hypocrite," who failed to visit him. Scarlett then joined a "Young Men's Society" and met Christians who seemed smart, open-minded, and honest. His infidel friends started to wonder if he secretly wanted to become a Christian himself. To prove otherwise, he visited some of them as they worked to finish building the new Methodist church on Franklin Street. He mounted the pulpit, buttoned his coat up to his chin, combed his hair down over his forehead, and mimicked a Methodist preacher. They laughed, but his conscience stung him afterward.[36]

Still believing that God could only be discerned through reason and nature, and that the Bible was fiction and Christianity false, in 1829 Scarlett wrote to his uncle David in Ireland defending these positions. Uncle David slapped down his arguments as vigorously as Charles Baldwin had dismissed the doubts of his nephew Cornelius. But Scarlett continued to denounce the foolish superstitions of the religious. In the summer of 1832, as Biela's comet became visible in the night sky, rumors spread associating its appearance with an outbreak of cholera. A cheap pamphlet predicted that the comet would collide with the earth, and the author urged sinners to fly to Christ. Scarlett was disgusted. This sort of emotional manipulation was even worse than the pulpit theatrics that had made his brother break down and cry at a Methodist sermon that same summer. At a meeting of the Newark infidels, and after a glass of brandy to steady his nerves before his first-ever speech, Scarlett rose with the offending pamphlet in his hand and ridiculed the fear-mongering evangelicals who were trying to scare people into their pews. "Does Christianity rest on *such grounds*, that motives to influence in its favor must be derived from *such sources*?" Scarlett answered his own rhetorical question by denouncing both the interpretation of the comet and the claims of Christianity. But when a drunken deist with a red nose stood to second the opinion with an oath, Scarlett decided that he was done associating with such people.[37]

In the fall of 1832, not long after his comet speech, Scarlett made his declaration about his business success and temporal prosperity being the result of his own hard work and not "the superintendence of divine Providence." Soon thereafter he fell into debt and had to sell his business for much less than it was worth. He and his wife, Mary, and their children suddenly faced poverty. Approaching his thirtieth year, he thought again of his father's funeral in the drenching rain and began to wonder if he had wasted his life on frivolous things. He joined a temperance society as a sign of his new seriousness. In January 1833, his Methodist neighbor dragged him along to a meeting. Scarlett slunk into the church and sat in the gallery, next to the wall. There in the pulpit was the Rev. Charles Pitman, the preacher who had made Scarlett's brother David sob like a weakling six months earlier, an episode that had prompted John to write a harshly critical, but ultimately unpublished, letter about Pitman to the newspaper. This time as Pitman preached Scarlett listened in a very different frame of mind. Scarlett began to tremble and broke into a sweat; he tried to pray, found doing so difficult, and left the church before the service had concluded. On the walk home that January night, he worried that he would fall into a Methodist trance, collapse on the cold ground, and freeze to death. For the next five months, as his economic prospects continued to dim, mental anguish destroyed his health. "My way on every hand seemed to be hedged up.... My suffering was great."[38]

In his house Scarlett had a battered old Bible that he had used for waste paper. One night he grabbed it and tried to read its torn pages. "The Scriptures had long appeared to me as an immense mass of ponderous lumber, which I could not measure nor define." How could such a book be the grounds of faith? "How could I determine that the Bible was a printed copy of God's own thoughts?" Must he simply take the word of Christians who said that it was? There did seem to be something peculiar in the Bible that distinguished it from other books, but Scarlett did not know what that something was. He repeated the name "Jesus" to himself and, almost like a magical incantation, it seemed to have a power in it, "a supernatural sound." He tried other names—Moses, David, Isaiah, Socrates, Seneca, Washington—but none of these produced the same feeling. Yet was this "peculiar something the only evidence by which [the Bible's] divine inspiration is made to appear? Was the strongest proof of its supernatural claim, at best, but favourable conjecture" based on a peculiar feeling? It suddenly occurred to him that if the Resurrection could be established as a historical fact, then Jesus was God, and therefore the New Testament was true. Scarlett turned to a tract called "The Conversion of a Deist," drawn from the works of the eighteenth-century Genevan writer Charles Bonnet, which the shoemaker had read and dismissed some years before. Bonnet argued, now to Scarlett's satisfaction, that the historical testimony in the Gospels could be trusted, that the evidence presented outweighed any counterevidence, and that therefore the Resurrection passed the test of reasonable doubt. To Scarlett's surprise and delight, he now believed in the Bible—though he knew that intellectual assent was not saving faith.[39]

Scarlett soon found himself defending his new belief in a conversation with an infidel friend. The two men met in a store. Since Scarlett's temperance pledge, Christians in town had begun to treat him more warmly, and his former infidel companions had grown cold. So he could not have been too surprised when his friend began chiding him for becoming yet another superstitious dupe of Reverend Pitman. Scarlett's friend pointed to a portrait that had just been painted of the storekeeper. "That is the work of a skilful artist; it is calculated to deceive," he said. "It puts me in mind of your Bible and your religion. Like this deceptive picture, they have the appearance of *substance* and *life*, when they are nothing but *illusive* representations, through an ingenious arrangement of light and shade. That picture professes to be a *reality*, when it is nothing but a pleasant deception; and so it is with them." Scarlett replied: "'The portrait claims to be nothing more than a *faithful and true picture* of the original, and *not the original himself*; and the Bible, and the religion of Christ, claim to be the work of God with design, as much so as the portrait does the work of the artist with design; but no *real* deception is intended in either case, nor will it ever be experienced from them."[40]

The two men were talking past one another. Scarlett argued that neither the portrait nor the Bible tried to disguise its status as representation. The painting, he contended, is not a trompe l'oeil attempting to trick the observer into thinking that the flesh-and-blood storekeeper is actually peering out from the wall. The portrait does the artist's work (representing the storekeeper) with design (the techniques of painting), just as the Bible does God's work (representing His thought) with design (language). In both cases, the representation is the artist's or Author's vehicle. Implicitly, the lack of deception might even suggest that those intentions, and the products of those intentions, are good—like the quality of a shoe measured by the trustworthiness of the shoemaker rather than by how it fits the foot. For Scarlett's friend, however, the deception of the portrait is in the way it presents the "appearance of substance and life" while having neither. The painting seems to show us a human face, but it is just a flat canvas dabbed with paint, an illusion created by human artifice; the Bible seems to reveal divine truths, but that is just an illusion created by the artful arrangement of language. The real issue for skeptics, however, is not that we understand picture and text as representations but that we assess their claims to be "faithful" to what we otherwise know to be true. Doing so asks us to hold the portrait up to the actual shopkeeper to see if it is a good likeness and to hold the biblical God up to the moral values and scientific facts. Deists and skeptics measured the seven-day Creator and jealous Jehovah of the Old Testament and the son-sacrificing Father of the New Testament in this way and saw the Bible's claims to truth vanish.

On Wednesday, June 26, 1833, Scarlett accompanied his pious shoemaker neighbor to a Methodist camp meeting. When he heard the praying and singing he began to have second thoughts, but his neighbor, weeping, grabbed him by the coat collar and shoved him toward the mourners' bench, where unconverted sinners received the prayers of the assembled worshippers. Scarlett knelt down in the straw and tried to pray but could not. A horn blew to summon people to a sermon, but Scarlett remained where he was until dusk. On the second day, he returned to the straw in front of the mourners' bench. More than prayers or preaching, he craved conversation. He recognized an acquaintance named Aaron, a sincere Christian "without much talent or learning." Scarlett pleaded with Aaron to describe his own conversion and tell him what else he ought to do. Aaron offered to find someone more suited to be a teacher, but Scarlett insisted that he just wanted the testimony of an "honest, simple-hearted man." Aaron agreed but said that Scarlett should confess everything that was in his heart before all the brethren.[41]

So with great difficulty, Scarlett bared his soul to the Methodists. He described his stubbornness, his hardness of heart, and the "bad thoughts" that continued to race through his mind, and expected them to tell him to take his hat and go home. But they encouraged him and prayed for him. During the evening sermon, troublemakers from town crept to the edge of the camp and pelted the worshippers with stones. Scarlett felt glad that he "was not among the rabble, but with those who were on the Lord's side." On the third day he awoke disheartened and felt nothing but despair as the Methodists prayed for him. He retreated to the log in the woods, took out his knife, heard the intelligible voice, and rejoined the meeting. He marched to the altar before the preaching stand and requested a prayer. Feeling his sins and troubles lift away and then "an inconceivable ecstasy of soul," he rose from his knees praising Jesus at the top of his lungs. "The world itself seemed more beautiful": the sun shone brighter, the green leaves were more vibrant, the camp's tents were white and clean.[42]

Even as he proceeded from his initial conversion to receive the blessing of sanctification, Scarlett lacked a full command of Wesleyan terminology to make sense of his experience. But after reading some basic Methodist theology and consulting with a clergyman, he more fully understood that faith—at least saving faith—was not merely an automatic response to evidence proving that a proposition was true. If the Bible contained doctrines as easily demonstrated as the sum of two plus two equaling four, what possible credit could be attached to believers? If spontaneous intellectual assent to evidence was all that was required—if one merely concluded after being presented with overwhelming evidence that Jesus rose from the dead the way one concluded that George Washington had fought in the American Revolution—how could such a "faith" purify the heart? "Faith," Scarlett argued, "while it begins by resting on evidence of divinely-revealed truth, rises into its finishing work, by also giving evidence of its author and finisher, to the saved believer." In the exercise of saving faith there was no room for doubt. Not just skepticism about religious propositions but critical distance from one's own experience drops away as the soul is acted upon by the Spirit. Those seeking after conversion or sanctification should not, he wrote, be asking, "'Am I now believing?—or, am I doubting?' 'Have I the blessing I seek?—or, is it a delusion?' 'Will I have any other witness than consciousness?—or, will some supernatural appearance convince me?'" They need what Scarlett in another context called learning "to be *sick of rotten-hearted self*, and the GREAT I, in which it always figures." They must seek saving faith and sanctifying grace "without reasoning, and without philosophizing," and yield to the influence of the Holy Spirit. Saving faith is "too simple for the wise of the world to understand; and too sublime for the speculations of metaphysics. To know *what* it is, is to enjoy the blessings connected with it."[43]

These experiences, Scarlett knew, were not ones he could keep to himself. He had a duty to publicly and repeatedly bear witness to the work God had done and was doing in his soul. His first lesson had been at the camp meeting, and his first instruction from a minister after his conversion was to go home, relate his experiences to his family, and lead them in prayer. For several days after his conversion Scarlett felt physically exhausted from being "sin-sick" for so long, and his mind was "wholly taken up with things of religion." Concerned friends thought that taking him to a political meeting would do him some good. Scarlett went but could not pay attention to the speeches. Sitting with his eyes closed and thinking about "the hope of glory," he heard a speaker say the word "banner," pictured the "glorious banner of the cross" waving overhead, and shouted out, "Glory to Jesus!" before remembering where he was, apologizing, and retiring from the scene of "political fooleries."[44]

For health reasons he gave up shoemaking and became a letter carrier in Newark. Delivering mail gave him a good opportunity to meet, talk with, and testify before a wide variety of people, conveying a message that cut across class differences. With "a desire to profit, and be profited," he visited "the cellar, the garret, the poor-house, and the prison, as well as the splendid dwellings of the rich.... I was as happy while praying with a criminal in the cell, as I was with the *élite* kneeling on a Brussels carpet, amid rich furniture and glittering splendour. Jesus gave me an introduction to all classes and all conditions." On Sabbath afternoons he started going down to the wharf to exhort sinners. One day he was threatened by a "brawny Irishman" raising a "*huge fist.*" Feeling especially "*light and feeble,*" and preparing to go home "*mangled* and *bloody,*" Scarlett was saved by the "providential interference" of a "*pugilistic*" Yankee sailor.[45]

Scarlett felt a special call to relate his experience and bear witness to the Gospel, "at every opportunity," before infidels in particular. While fasting and praying one day he received a special "impression" from the Spirit to go and visit one of his "old infidel associates," describe his conversion, and try to persuade the man to become a Christian. The infidel threw him out of the house, but Scarlett's heart was light—he felt happy to be doing the Lord's work. With a Methodist friend he journeyed northward to Connecticut as a lay exhorter, conversing with people during the day, organizing prayer meetings in the evenings, and introducing himself as a "converted infidel." In *The Life and Experience of a Converted Infidel*, Scarlett described various encounters and conversations with skeptical infidels back in New Jersey: with the doubting "Mr. A——" on a steamboat; with a deistical tavernkeeper in a barroom; with a pedantic young man of skeptical pretensions; with a tall infidel who challenged him to a debate on a moonlit evening after a sermon; with a magistrate who was "an influential skeptic" and had a Methodist wife; and with "an ingenious mechanic," fond of making experiments in chemistry and filing patent applications for new machines, "who was then a skeptic."[46]

The shoemaker turned letter carrier was convinced that infidels were more likely to be converted by former infidels, and that they needed "a sin-killing shock of spiritual power" rather than reasoned argument. "Experience, related in the demonstration of the Spirit, will do more than all the ethical argumentation in the world." He had heard "that the infidels of New York City—especially the Deists—assembled every Sabbath in Tammany Hall, as 'philanthropists' to discuss questions on 'true, and fabulous theology.'" Scarlett was determined, as he put it, to hurl a stone into that hornet's nest. [47]

The Moral Philanthropists of New York City's Tammany Hall had been organized in 1829 and through much of the 1830s drew hundreds of people to their weekly meetings. An outgrowth of the Free Press Association that had formed in the late 1820s, and spurred on by the popularity of Frances Wright and the activism of associated free inquirers like Robert Dale Owen, the Philanthropists met three times each Sunday for morning readings and lectures, afternoon debates with Christians, and evening lectures and music. The list of regular speakers included deist editor George Houston, Paineite writer and mathmatician Gilbert Vale, a freethinking apothecary clerk named George Purser, feminist and social reformer Ernestine Rose, and an enlightened dry-goods merchant named John Ditchett. The society of reformers stressed rationality, morality, sobriety, education, and progress and was led by Benjamin Offen, a self-taught shoemaker from England who was in his late fifties by the time of Scarlett's visit.[48]

Scarlett climbed the stairs of Tammany Hall and gave his three cents to the "Cerberus" at the door. Despite the usual Christian assumptions and his own doubts about the moral consequences of deism, Scarlett knew that often infidels "in their secular dealings, were more correct" than many of their Christian neighbors. This was true of Offen, who throughout his life "bore a character for honesty and fair dealing." The old man himself rose to give an address. He criticized the Bible as "solely the work of priestcraft"; Christianity "was a system of *nonsense*, that was calculated to operate on the fears of the ignorant and superstitious, and afforded, also, means for the cunning and ambitious to acquire power and unrighteous gain."[49]

After Offen finished, Scarlett took a glass of water (not brandy this time) and went to the rostrum to speak. Newark infidels who were there expected him to endorse Offen's sentiments; when Scarlett began by saying that he had recently been to a camp meeting, they winked and smiled at one another, expecting him to mock the Methodists again. But then in serious tones he related his experience:

"While I saw all around me engaged in what they called the worship of God, I *felt* there *was* heart in this matter, and *truth,* and *life,* and *power.* I was entreated by the Methodists to go forward, and kneel at the bench, and join them in prayer for my salvation. I *went,* and prayed, and struggled, and agonized. I found peace in believing. That Jesus you revile here, Sabbath after Sabbath—that *very same blessed Jesus, by the efficacy of his own most precious blood, blotted out my sins*!! I can now testify in the Holy Ghost, to *the truth* of what you pronounce *a lie.* I know you are altogether deceived, and will be lost, unless you flee to the same almighty Jesus for life and salvation." In this version of Scarlett's conversion experience, there was no mention of his suicidal thoughts while sitting alone in the woods, no intelligible voice, and no vision in amber light. It was simply a person's discovery of spiritual truth in the midst of a believing community. Offen waved off Scarlett's remarks, confident that the warm fellow's feelings would evaporate soon, and the old infidel then "cheered his companions in their unbelief."[50]

At Scarlett's second visit to Tammany Hall, a young man "of some talents and learning" addressed the assembly. He argued that nature, not the Bible, taught morality, virtue, and justice. The natural world in the "unbroken harmony, as unfolded by geography, geology, and astronomy" inspired benevolence and had "a perfect response in all the *natural inclinations* of man." The audience, both men and women, seemed respectable and intelligent, Scarlett admitted, and they listened with eagerness and understanding to everything the young man said. When he was through, audience members looked to Scarlett for a rebuttal, and the former infidel trembled and suddenly wished he had "scientific knowledge, as well as spiritual." He had once admitted dreading the "sophistry" by which infidels "entangle their victims, by inducing them to answer questions of their asking," and wanted to stick to his plan of testifying with spiritual power rather than engaging in debate. Scarlett tried to rise to the challenge, but in attempting to argue for the asymmetries, diversity, and variety in nature and the Bible, he started to get tangled in his own logic.[51]

After Offen challenged him on one point, Scarlett changed strategy. "I now thought best to pursue the subject no further, and began again to relate my experience." He then went on to say that Christianity did not need to be corroborated by historical evidence or facts about the natural world. It surrounded their souls, right there in that room, the way the atmosphere surrounded their bodies, and it carried its self-authenticating evidence with it. "I know, said I, its existence in my heart, the way I know that I have eyes, and bones, and blood." He next appealed to the sentiments of listeners who, he knew, had been raised as at least nominal Christians. Did not any of them remember praying? Did not they ever have a prayer answered, feeling comfort, love, or forgiveness? When a woman in the audience wept aloud, the moderator reminded Scarlett that he was "*not* in a *Methodist* meeting."[52]

For his third (and, it would turn out, his final) visit to Tammany Hall, the Philanthropists invited Scarlett to speak first. Standing before the crowded room, trembling again, he did not know exactly how to proceed. He declared "that a thousand experimentalists on the subject," that is, a thousand people experiencing real Christianity, "shut up in different apartments, to prevent consultation among themselves, like a thousand separate mathematicians working at one of Euclid's problems, would give the *same answer*." Just as history and nature were irrelevant to determining Christian truth, so too was social context. The thousand isolated experimentalists that he conjured erased the camp meeting community, the "consultation," that had shaped his own experience. Instead he posited a group of independent souls like so many spiritual atoms responding with mathematical uniformity to the gravitational field of grace. Then Scarlett turned his discussion in a different direction. We can know the essence of something by examining the character of its origin or founder, he said, and Christianity flows directly from its faultless Author, Jesus Christ. The Bible is Christ's narrative testimony, uttered with self-evident sincerity.[53]

Benjamin Offen told Scarlett that he " 'would not give a bladder of wind (!) for your arguments, or your feelings, either.' " After Scarlett's appeal to prayer, Offen dismissed providential intervention just as the infidel Scarlet had once done. And like the skeptical Scarlett who dared a lightning strike from heaven, Offen proposed a test, saying that if Scarlett would "pray that God will fling down a cent before us all, and that prayer is answered, it will be satisfactory."[54]

Scarlett, in a reversal of his preconversion views about Providence and economic life, now did believe that for the faithful pennies almost literally could fall from heaven. At the first Methodist class meeting he attended, the class leader reminded the assembled of their duty to contribute money to the church. A brother stood up, saying that times were hard and that he could not afford to give his three cents per week. Scarlett, not sure how he was going to afford the loaf of bread his family needed the next day, nevertheless paid his shilling, and thereafter paid six cents each week on behalf of himself and his wife. He never went without bread, but the brother who held back went bankrupt. Clearly, Scarlett believed, it was not superstitious to think that divine Providence intervened in temporal prosperity after all. On another occasion, after praying and fasting on the question, he gave his last few dollars to the poor and came up twenty dollars short on a debt. But then he met a Methodist brother on the road who handed him twenty dollars after being directed in a dream to do so. Scarlett had other stories, too, of money coming unexpectedly into his hands at opportune moments. God's divine economy of rewards to the faithful here intersected with the worldly economy of money and material goods.

The way God's purposes worked through the human activities of labor and commerce, through a society's modes of producing and consuming material things, and within the ebbs and flows of a nation's poverty and wealth, however, were not always so clear. In the depression following the Panic of 1837, Scarlett was stunned at the depth of the poverty and distress that he witnessed in Newark. Men and women were "cold and shivering, with a look of hunger," and "families of half-clad children, pale and sickly," huddled in the poorer sections of town. But there was, Scarlett decided, a moral logic at work here, too. Often, he thought, destitution could be traced to intemperance—to the failings of the poor themselves. He admitted, though, that some suffered not from their own mistakes but from the greed of financial speculators whose failed bets had ruined the lives of thousands. Yet the power of Christian benevolence could be more than a match for the sins of the speculators. Even better than delivering bread, Christian charity could bring the Gospel to the worthy poor. Christ's work of redemption, after all, was the larger purpose not just of charity but of all economic exchange. Understanding that the material economy was a means of grace for the spiritual economy brought hope even in the depths of the depression. "No doubt God intends that money shall be used in carrying out the Gospel plans in the redemption and salvation of the world," Scarlett wrote, optimistic about the wealth of the nation in the long run. Scarlett, who would become a preacher in 1841 and serve the church for the next forty-eight years, remained confident that God's invisible hand guided the marketplace, as it guided everything else.[55]

On Factory Workers and Plantation Slaves

John Bayley learned very different lessons from the economic life he witnessed while walking the streets of Manchester, England. He agreed with a man he knew who said that "there is not a hell-hole in the world equal to a cotton factory." Bayley could see the fruits of industrial capitalism for himself. "Indeed, the whole factory system, as it was presented to my mind, seemed to be in plain, palpable violation of the principles of truth and justice. My heart sickened within me when I walked through the crowded thoroughfares of this immense Babylon of bricks and mortar—this mart of the world—this hive of industry—this rendezvous of all that is beautiful, great and good, and all that is uncomely, little and mean, as far as English society is concerned." He saw the mansions of the nobility, with well-groomed grounds containing beautiful cemeteries, with elaborately carved headstones, for their pets. He walked by the estates of the cotton lords, whose well-fed servants made the hungry artisans look like walking cadavers. Spinners and weavers were thrown out of work to starve in dirty alleys and narrow streets. He knew a sallow, sickly man who had watched his baby suck blood from his mother's breast. Bayley saw families go begging from door to door for a piece of bread or a cold potato. "I saw the operatives at work, at their homes, at their pleasures, in their sorrows and their joys, and when I looked upon the immense mass of sin, ignorance and misery, and contrasted it with what appeared to me to be the happy lot of a favored few, I thought that a religion which sustained such a state of things could not be from God who is the father of all."[56]

Bayley had grown up in Newcastle-under-Lyme. His mother died when he was four; his father, an admirer of Voltaire, Volney, and Paine, had troubles with drink after she died. John did not become an infidel because he was following his father's example—he had suffered too much at the old man's hands. On his own from a young age and working as a printer's compositor in Manchester, he associated with many working-class skeptics, deists, and atheists. His reading list resembled John Scarlett's: there was Paine, Palmer, and Volney, Pope, Byron, and Shelley—but also works by Robert Taylor, the Anglican turned radical freethinker known as "the Devil's Chaplain." "I had the daring impiety," Bayley wrote, "to carry Paine's Age of Reason with me to church, and use it instead of a prayer-book during the tedious morning service." He marked the infidel publisher Richard Carlile's release from jail after serving his term for blasphemy and seditious libel, and argued on the side of the socialists at the Debating Society of Salford.[57]

He also read books and sermons in favor of Christianity, like William Paley's *Natural Theology* (1802) and Richard Watson's belated response to Paine, *An Apology for the Bible* (1828), and discussed them with his friends. But he resented the way that the church blithely supported the tyranny of capital over labor. After sitting for twelve hours a day, six days a week in the printing office, he liked to take open-air walks on the Sabbath, rambling around Manchester, Salford, and their surrounding villages, and sometimes taking rail or steamboat excursions to Liverpool for a stroll on the beach. Especially on a nice day, being stuck in church felt like a prison sentence, and in any case he thought a higher law granted him a day of healthful exercise and rest. On one of his rambles, he met the rector of Newcastle, who rebuked him for abusing the Lord's Day. "It may be very well for preachers, I thought, who have the privilege of riding and walking out every day, and who once every year, if not more frequently, can leave home and dwell in a pleasant cottage by the sea-side, religiously to abstain from such pleasures on the Lord's day, but if they were placed in the situation of the poor working man, they would tell a different story." A local tragedy that occurred at about this time illustrated for Bayley how Christianity seemed to blind people to the suffering of the working class. "A poor little factory girl, whose parents were pious, obstinately refused to go to the Sabbath school, preferring to spend the time" the way Bayley did, getting some fresh air and exercise. "One day, after having received a severe whipping from her father, under mingled emotions of rage and despair, she threw herself into the canal and was drowned. This afforded me quite a triumph over the people, who, as I thought, by violating the laws of nature thus drove oppressed and innocent childhood to suicide."[58]

Blaming the intertwined tentacles of church and state in England, Bayley became "more and more an infidel." Sometime in the mid-1830s, he "determined to visit the United States of North America, where I thought I should see the operations of Deism, on the system of nature, to a much greater extent than I could see them in a land in which religion was established by law." He assumed that the constitutional ban on religious establishment and guarantee of religious liberty meant that America was nature's nation. With the priesthood stripped of political power and misguided traditions no longer enforced by law, Americans, he imagined, could live according to the higher laws of enlightened conscience. "My impression had been that in a country like this, free from the depressing influences of tyranny and priestcraft, a state of happiness such as I had never seen would be found." In England, freethinking—or, rather, the public expression of skepticism about Christianity or irreligious dissent—landed radical reformers like Taylor and Carlile in jail. But their movement was a powerful one, with significant support among the working class. Religious infidelity in the United States had a different character.[59]

Bayley found "most of the infidelity in the United States" to be "a poor sneaking thing, that will scarcely show its head in the company of the virtuous and the intelligent, but worked in secret." Landing in New York City, he found his way to the Moral Philanthropists' meetings at Tammany Hall. He listened there "to lectures on moral and theological topics, and heard orators declaim against the Bible and the religion of Jesus." The Philanthropists also sang "National Hymns," like Abner Kneeland's adaptation of a familiar Christian doxology:

> Praise life to which all blessings flow,
> Praise life, all creatures, high and low,
> Praise life alone, ye rich and poor,
> Praise life till life shall be no more.

Bayley then moved on to Baltimore, Philadelphia, and the District of Columbia. Apart from a few relatively small groups of organized freethinkers, public expression of religious skepticism was rare. He heard that an editor of one of the leading daily newspapers in the country was an infidel who pretended to be a Christian because it was better for business. A lecturer who gave addresses on temperance, peace, socialism, antislavery, and moral reform, though he drew his foundational principles from materialist treatises like George Combe's *The Constitution of Man* (1828) rather than theism, admitted that he prudently avoided discussing religious infidelity itself. This "dimes and dollars" practicality seemed pervasive in the United States, Bayley observed, and hypocrisy followed as a matter of course. He noted that "in this free country, in which public opinion is the source of wealth, and power, and honor, and, in many instances, above all laws, divine and human, almost everything depends upon popularity." Criticizing Christian beliefs and practices was not an avenue to popularity.[60]

In the cities he visited, Bayley "became acquainted with infidels and skeptics" but "found little to interest me, less to admire, and nothing to love." Often sick with dyspepsia and homesick for England, he kept aloof from his coworkers in the print shops, too. A boy he worked with once called Bayley the strangest man he had ever met—an odd English fellow who always seemed angry, spoke very little, and claimed not to be religious even though he never swore, drank, or joked like the other men. Bayley remarked on his own diffidence, awkwardness around American manners, and miserable sadness.[61]

A journey to the Blue Ridge Mountains in Virginia, however, would change his life. He stayed with a devout old Methodist woman and her daughters. They read the Bible, sang hymns together, and prayed fervently for the stranger at their table, asking the Lord to make him "a good and holy man." Bayley's "heart was deeply affected," and he felt as though he were "treading on holy ground." In Farmville, Virginia, he witnessed his first Methodist revival, watching as about a hundred people converted. He became fascinated by the *"unearthly-looking"* preacher, the Rev. John Wesley Childs, who would become instrumental in Bayley's later conversion and call to the ministry. Someone slipped Bayley a tract called "Conversations with a Traveler," which led him to reexamine his infidel philosophy by reading Joseph Butler's famous answer to deism, *The Analogy of Religion* (1736), and Jacob Abbott's *The Young Christian* (1832), which had chapters reviewing the difficulties of believing and the historical, textual, and experiential evidences of Christianity. Bayley felt most of his intellectual opposition to the Bible "scattered to the winds."[62]

He started going to church on Sundays but still found the notion of prayer absurd. Why would an all-knowing God need to be informed of our needs and desires? Why would an infinitely wise and good God need our direction, an unchangeable God our supplications to change some state of affairs or course of events? As he pondered these questions while walking alone in the woods one day, he heard "a plaintive and earnestly supplicating voice." He walked toward it. "I saw a negro man on his knees, under a tree, with hands clasped together and uplifted to heaven, while he cried out with great earnestness, 'Jesus, master, have mercy on me a poor sinner!' And this he continued to repeat. The poor fellow did not observe me, so intently was he in prayer." Puzzling over the logic of prayer seemed ridiculous in the face of this display of religion's emotional power. "An awful feeling came over my soul," Bayley wrote. These feelings faded, however, until he was confined to his sickbed with no one to talk to except "a small negro boy." When he left that room on that mid-January day in 1838, feeling convinced that he was "a child of God, and an heir to everlasting life," he took a walk along the banks of the Appomattox River, and even the bare trees seemed bright and beautiful. "I felt then disposed to shake hands with every one that I met, and thought it strange when any one did not sympathize with me in my joy."[63]

The praying man in the woods, the "ignorant" boy in his room: black slaves became for Bayley exemplary figures of Christian piety. Not long after his conversion, Bayley got permission from a local slaveholder, James Jackson, to read the Bible and pray with the slaves on Jackson's plantation. "Every night and every morning, as many of them as could be induced to attend were collected together for the worship of God." On Sunday mornings before church, too, Bayley would try to explain the Bible to slaves who worked in tobacco factories, and he became known as a preacher even before he "was clothed with authority from the church to minister in holy things." Yet he resisted the entreaties of local Methodist clergymen to become a minister himself and start preaching on one of the understaffed Virginia circuits. "How could I, so young in the cause, with so little knowledge of sacred things, and of America and its institutions, go out among the sons and daughters of the Old Dominion as an ambassador of the Most High!" He had been immediately comfortable teaching and preaching to black slaves, but bringing the Gospel to their white owners was too awesome a responsibility. Yet even after years as an itinerant, Bayley looked at Christian slaves as icons of exemplary faith. The best examples of the Gospel's power to elevate the believer above the world's suffering, he wrote, were "furnished among the lower classes of society." He would frequently become perplexed or discouraged by a "gentleman or lady" blinded by carnal reasoning, distracted by the pursuit of wealth, or bogged down with worldly complaints. But then his soul would be "abundantly refreshed by the pious conversation of some poor slave with whom I have met in the cornfield, in a steamboat, or upon the highway."[64]

A chapter in *Confessions of a Converted Infidel* entitled "The Pious Slave" related the story of "a colored man, bowed down with the infirmities of age," visiting a young plantation mistress. Realizing that the old "uncle" had walked several miles without breakfast, she offered him buttered biscuits, a slice of ham, and a glass of milk, but he would accept only a single biscuit. How can you live without eating more than that, she asked? " 'O,' he replied, 'I live by faith in Jesus Christ.' " He came to warn the young woman about the danger of riches. Once, he said, his master had allowed him to work a piece of ground for himself. He harvested a good tobacco crop from the land and sold it for almost fifty dollars, proud of the work he had done. He then lent the money to a merchant in order to earn some interest as well. "I felt right down independent, and did not feel as humble as I used to feel." But the merchant went bankrupt, and the pious slave lost all his money. God, he was sure, was teaching him a lesson about independence and pride. Then the old man told a second story, about visiting his master, who thought he was dying. "Master," the slave reported having said, "you have a fine house, fine carpets, white walls, so much land, so many black people, and money piled upon your desk; but, master, you have no place prepared for your soul." The master's problem, it seems, was not money itself, or independence and pride, but allowing riches to distract him from also pursuing salvation. The master asked his slave to pray for him, and the old man did, every day, fervently, on his knees. The "uncle" received such an assurance from God that the "*poor master*" would be spared and have one more chance to repent and seek the Lord that he relayed his confidence to the sick plantation owner, who did indeed get better and convert. Bayley considered this story a good illustration of how God uses the foolish, weak, and base things of the world to confound the mighty and the wise.[65]

How far Bayley the American minister of the Methodist Episcopal Church, South had come from the freethinking British socialist he once had been is shown in a chapter describing a return visit to England in 1845. He visited London for the first time and was impressed by its size, power, and vitality. Its success seemed threatened only by "impieties" and an "increasing prevalence of Popery," which might anger God. He also saw, only a few blocks from the beautiful parks, splendid mansions, and magnificent churches, filthy streets choked by poverty, disease, and crime. Thirty thousand people in the city, he learned, did not know where their next meal would be coming from. Some politicians in Parliament argued to repeal the Corn Laws, and others to reduce the expenses of government. Bayley, admitting that he was no politician, nonetheless gave his opinion: "Government may do all that it can,—and it certainly may do more than it does,—but all it can do will never permanently ameliorate the condition of the working classes, until these classes shall learn to fear God and keep his commandments—to frequent the haunts of dissipation less and the abodes of science and religion more. Even now, it rarely happens that an industrious sober man suffers." The problem was primarily moral rather than socioeconomic; the solution would be found not in changing the industrial system that he had once decried but in the moral transformation of individual sinners. To critics like Horace Greeley of the *New York Tribune* who challenged the vast sums of money going to churches while people starved in the shadows of their steeples, Bayley also defended the institutional church. God's people Israel in the Bible also suffered from pauperism and crime. The reason was not unwise laws and flawed institutions, since these had been devised by God Himself. The cause, then as now, was the people's "rebelliousness and wickedness." And as Jesus said, Bayley noted, "The poor ye have always with you" (Matt. 26:11).⁶⁶

Sentimental appeals for compassion and charity toward the poor and the oppressed were not always what they appeared to be, Bayley warned. At his breakfast table in London one morning, Bayley heard the "pitiful cries" of a poor man in the street: " 'For God's sake, kind people, buy a skein of thread.... I want to get an honest penny to buy my children some bread, they have had no breakfast this morning.... I have applied again and again for work; most gladly would I do it.... For God's sake, dear people, buy a skein of thread.' " Out of compassion, Bayley bought some thread. But an acquaintance standing by told him that the thread seller was an imposter, a scam artist, like thousands of others begging in the streets who could do honest work but chose not to and actually had more money at home than Bayley himself. A few days later, while sitting in his room writing a letter to a friend in Virginia, Bayley again heard mournful cries out in the street, only this time the voice strangely sounded like that of a black slave from back home. "I ran to the door, and lo! A genuine runaway slave, from Virginia, stood before me." His clothes were ragged, his feet bare and sore from walking the hard streets of London. To Bayley and the others in the crowd that had gathered, he "told a sad tale" of his life as a slave first in Charleston, South Carolina, and then in Richmond. Traveling with his master, a Mr. Dandridge, as a body servant, he had made his escape to England three years before and had only been able to survive as a beggar. But a beggar's life in London was better than a slave's in Virginia, where whites treated blacks worse than they treated their horses, he said. Slaves received only a peck of corn and a little salt fish to eat each week. They labored from sunrise to sunset, through the heat of the day. They labored, sweating beneath the gaze of the overseer who sat in the shade of a tree or under an umbrella held by a slave. They labored, and if "they were a little slack in their work, they were tied up and whipped." The escaped slave repeated a refrain as he told his story: "And I am sure, you good Christian people here would not like any of your children to be treated this way."⁶⁷

Bayley approached the barefoot man, and others gathered around as they talked. The minister asked if slaves in Virginia ever ate corn bread. Yes, the man admitted, they did. Bacon? Yes, he said, sometimes offal bacon that no one else would eat. Biscuits? Yes—town slaves got biscuits sometimes, but not country ones. Did he ever see anyone begging for bread from door to door in Virginia, as he did in London, Bayley asked? No, the former slave said. "Why don't they beg in Virginia?" Bayley inquired. "O they has plenty to eat there," the man said, and the bystanders began to laugh. Bayley then revealed that he had recently left Virginia himself and had never seen anything like the hard treatment the beggar had described. "It's God's truth," observed the negro, "but if you has been there, you knows all about it." Bayley asked the man why he didn't get a job in London, perhaps down at the docks. When the former slave answered that they would not "let colored men work there," one of the bystanders called him a liar, "and then the poor mendicant slunk away, to endeavor, perhaps, to excite the sympathies of the people in another part of the city."[68]

Bayley shook his head at the idea of someone preferring to beg rather than work. As for the "honest and industrious poor," they ought to "always bear in mind that there is another world, in which God's suffering saints will be amply compensated for all their privations here." That was an assurance that the religious skeptics and infidel socialists that Bayley had once consorted with could never provide.[69]

In the second quarter of the nineteenth century, Methodists and other evangelicals, like other Americans, had to try to come to terms with the transforming hand of the market economy, including the relentless expansion of cotton plantations and the domestic slave trade. Protestants always felt called to live in the world but not of it, but the pace of change in the first half of the nineteenth century made that challenge especially acute. The lawyer in western Virginia, with his enthusiasm for American progress, saw these changes. So did the preacher calling to devotees of Mammon in the small towns along the Ohio River. The shoemaker stitching his leather and the letter carrier walking the avenues and alleys of Newark felt the economy expand and contract in its inexplicable rhythms. The itinerant print compositor, moving from Manchester and Liverpool to New York City, Philadelphia, and Washington, D.C., before landing in central Virginia, could see, at the junctures of commercial power, lives shaped by the larger Atlantic system: the factory girl and the textile baron, the export merchant and the dockworker, the plantation mistress and the field slave. Conservative evangelical Christians had several responses to the pressures and temptations of this new world, but the central one was not a call for economic reform but the insistence that people needed to experience an inner spiritual transformation and then live their faith in Christ.

The narratives of skeptical infidels who converted to Methodism were intended to depict the triumph of that spiritual transformation over a particular kind of modern worldliness. Within the church, Methodists could be losing the battle against the temptations of wealth and prosperity and torn apart by arguments about slavery. But they could still rally to external challenges: to convert the heathen in foreign lands, to contain the growing influence of Catholics in American politics and culture, and to defeat the menace of skeptical infidels in their midst. Skeptics claimed to express modern thinking for a modern world. They urged Americans to slough off old superstitions and ecclesiastical tyranny the way that the Revolutionary Fathers had shed monarchical rule and the slavish deference to aristocrats. They contended that supernaturalist creeds inhibited rather than promoted virtuous lives. Conversion narratives answered the infidels not with biblical exegesis, historical analysis, or arguments for the necessity of religion as the glue of social order but by witnessing the power of personal religious experience.

The narratives of Charles Baldwin, John Scarlett, and John Bayley in different ways try to represent religious skepticism as blindness rather than critical insight, as an evasion of moral and spiritual reality. For Baldwin the lawyer, skepticism was the private rationalization of an outwardly moral and prosperous professional man. Baldwin and his editor/biographer Gaddis did not denigrate the work of lawyers and courts, the ambitions of commerce, or the political sentiments proclaimed on public occasions. These worldly pursuits were not in themselves sinful or even misguided—but compared to Baldwin's later calling they were merely business, merely politics. Success at the bar and public applause

Portrait of John Bayley. From Bayley, *Confessions of a Converted Infidel*, 3rd ed. (New York, 1856), frontispiece. A former skeptic and socialist, the Methodist Bayley came to see hierarchal structures (capital over labor, master over slave) not as man-made injustices but as givens in a fallen but transient world.

were no more comfort in the face of death than the cool intellectual negations that Baldwin had once privately used to parry the claims of religion. He could not find evidence of Christianity that would banish all his doubts until he turned inward. And he could not fully turn inward until he had turned his back on his worldly pursuits. Skepticism, the born-again Baldwin came to believe, was just an intellectual and psychological camouflage for a willful avoidance of the facts of mortality and the truths of the Gospel.

For the shoemaker John Scarlett, skepticism was an admission ticket to a community of young urban artisans and political radicals. As he came of age after his father's death, he first found himself and his adult voice within this web of social relations. The skepticism he picked up from his reading and conversation had swept away his childish credulity and allowed him to perform his manhood by denouncing superstitious religion and elitist politics. Economic hardship encouraged him to switch affiliations, turning him from the frolics of his "wild companions" and the boisterous dissent of the organized infidels to the emotional catharsis and communal discipline of Methodism. Throughout his long life he would continue to identify himself as a "converted infidel"—the phrase is even carved on his gravestone. He would not have admitted that either the skeptical infidel he had once been or the evangelical Christian he became had merely been creatures of different social circumstances. Religious doubt is not only a bad habit picked up from the wrong crowd, he believed, but the inclination of a dishonest heart—just as true faith is not primarily a set of words and practices learned in church but arises from a heart transformed by God's Spirit. The argument of Scarlett's book, in other words, running against the grain of his own narrative detail, is that skepticism and faith are not socially constructed but derive from essential facts about human nature and saving grace.

John Bayley's religious skepticism first emerged as a corollary to his socialist critique of the heartless industrial capitalist order that the Christian church seemed to support. Religious faith was less an opiate to dull the exploited workers' pain than a false consciousness making their oppression worse. Personally alienated from Christians and infidels alike, it was not until he stayed with the mother and daughters in the Blue Ridge Mountains that he felt the power of religious sentiment to make people happy. His own conversion did not just bear fruit in an inversion of values (suffering is redemptive; true riches are in heaven). It encouraged him to see hierarchal structures (capital over labor, master over slave) not as man-made injustices but as givens in a fallen but transient world. For Bayley the Christian convert, socialism and skepticism at once promised too much and too little. Socialism was a reformer's utopian fantasy to remake the social order, and yet it conceived of individuals as powerless victims of vast socioeconomic forces. Religious skepticism, even in its negations, presupposed that men could reason their way to an understanding of the cosmos and yet denied that individuals could be morally regenerated by supernatural grace. Converts from skepticism insisted that their own experience proved that human beings were not condemned to struggle alone to earn their daily bread in a cold, godless world.

"Warrior amidst a Battle" (1860). Joshua 10:13: "And the sun stood still, and the moon stayed, until the people had avenged themselves upon their enemies." Photo courtesy of the American Antiquarian Society, Worcester, Massachusetts.

PART FOUR

SACRED CAUSES, 1830–1865

> The alliance of religion and political power, the SCEPTIC argued, had stained history with blood. There were such things as sacred causes, the CHRISTIAN answered, and armies could march to serve the Lord. That did not mean that every political crusade that invoked God's name did God's work:
>
> SCEPTIC: "But supernatural imaginations have ever been, and now are, far worse than superfluous—mischievous, frightfully mischievous.... Religion's bitter jarrings have brought, not peace on earth but a sword. Its schisms have drenched the world with innocent blood, and raised to the honor of its God thousands of human hetacombs."
>
> CHRISTIAN: "But admitting all he says to be true; admitting that eighteen millions of human beings have been sacrificed in contentions denominated religious; it does not hence follow that religion itself has been the cause."[1]

Nothing clarifies a people's sense of itself as a people quite like an appeal to shared moral values and to a sacred authority backing them up. And nothing focuses a people's sense of purpose quite like an enemy that is said to threaten those values and deny that authority. As American nationalism broke in half during the sectional crisis, Northerners and Southerners alike rallied around God and country. Potent ideological compounds—sacred causes or "civil religions"—drawn from American republican political values and Protestant traditions helped unify the Union, consolidate the Confederacy, and define the bitter, bloody antagonism between the two.

"Civil religion" is an ancient concept but an ambiguous one. The term can refer to the sacralization of the state as well as to the extension of traditional faith into politics. It has been used to describe what political speakers are doing when they make nationalistic patriotism a substitute religion, even as they appropriate some of the symbols and narrative forms from (in this case) Christianity. But it has also designated the attempt of believers "to absorb the political community at large into a wider theological destiny" as they stamp the nation's political rituals and rhetoric with their religion's character. In practice, in its articulation of a sacred cause, civil religion derives its power from a confluence of political and theological appeals to ultimate moral authority, a convergence that can accommodate different motives even as it promotes similar behaviors. In different hands, (traditional) religion "may drive politics or become a tool of politics." Yet even if that difference is sometimes clear to those in the pulpits of civil religion, it may be less evident to those listening in the pews.[2]

This is not to suggest that civil religious language invoking a sacred cause always expresses deep convictions and rallies people to decisive action. Political speeches and July Fourth sermons repeated nationalistic pieties that, over the years, became tired clichés. Yet in times of crisis, and in the face of existential threats, appeals to a fusion of political and religious principles could take on an ideological charge—could translate mere words into power.

The swords of Confederate civil religion had been hammered into shape by years of antebellum conflict—not only conflict with the North but also within the South. Conservative Protestantism ultimately strengthened the alloy of proslavery, white supremacy, and states'-rights constitutionalism and then sharpened the blade. Religion sanctified the civil order, and the civil order empowered religion. This relationship, however, did not sprout naturally from the old colonial church establishment or even from the popularity of religious revivals in the early nineteenth century. Church leaders seeking cultural power and social authority initially faced opposition from many in the Southern political elite—worldly men, merely nominal Christians, strict church-state separatists, and skeptical freethinkers—who wanted to keep religion out of politics. Many in the clergy, too, were committed to keeping church and state at arm's length, even as they hoped to Christianize every aspect of their society, including political life. But slavery was at the center of Southern white identity, and with heightened abolitionist agitation in the North after 1830 the debate was increasingly engaged on moral and religious as well as political, constitutional, and economic grounds. Clergymen had moral and religious answers—not just for Northern critics but for their Southern neighbors as well.

Chapter 12 explores the Christianization of proslavery politics by focusing on Presbyterians in South Carolina. They first battled Thomas Cooper—religious skeptic, political provocateur, and president of South Carolina College. In the 1820s and '30s, intertwined debates demonstrated the political power struggles in play when reading both the Bible and the U.S. Constitution. Cooper, a leader of the Nullification Party, provided arguments from political economy and constitutional law that helped shape South Carolina's and ultimately the white South's defense of slavery. At the same time, he attacked the grounds of religion's public authority. But the Presbyterians and their allies from other Christian denominations were able to form and institutionalize a public theology in the 1830s, '40s, and '50s that solidified, far more comprehensively, proslavery thought and white Southern identity. The ascension of a Christian public theology melded to proslavery ideology shows the process by which religious skepticism came to be, if not unthinkable, at least unutterable in a region that would come to be called the Bible Belt.

Chapter 13 moves north and shows how personal religious experience—in this case, one Methodist's quest for sanctification, and another's turn from faith to skepticism—was interwoven with daily life and could be recast as civil religious ideology. The journals, preaching, and letters of George Shane Phillips and his fiancée (then wife), Elizabeth Kauffman, in Ohio (1840s), in California (1850s), and during the Civil War, when Phillips served as a chaplain in the Union army, provide an experiential context for the civil religion proclaimed in his wartime book, *The American Republic and Human Liberty Foreshadowed in Scripture*. John R. Kelso was a schoolteacher and Methodist preacher in Missouri who left his faith behind and, motivated in part by an ardent secular nationalism, became a guerilla-fighting Union army hero in the Ozarks. The manuscript autobiography he left for his children illustrates the reconstitution of self and community involved in this transformation. Phillips and Kelso professed faith in different versions of Northern civil religion: one man was convinced that the Union armies were doing God's work, and the other, doubting that any such God existed, killed in devotion to the American promise of Freedom and Equality.

12

Political Hermeneutics

Nullifying the Bible and Consolidating Proslavery Christianity

On December 4, 1832, in the crowded hall of the South Carolina State House of Representatives, Dr. Thomas Cooper, president of South Carolina College, rose to face the college's Board of Trustees and answer the charges against him. Cooper was poisoning the minds of the students, his opponents said, by disavowing the Holy Scriptures and scoffing at Christianity. The president, still vigorous at seventy-three years old, was a stooped, plump little man well under five feet tall with an enormous bald head that one observer said resembled a pumpkin. A popular teacher affectionately called "Old Coot" by his students (a reference to a "cooter," or turtle), he was known to his friends as an devoted family man, a genial companion, a witty conversationalist, and a polemicist irresistibly drawn to religious as well as political controversy. Presbyterians complained about his suspected infidelity when he taught at Carlisle (later Dickinson) College, publicly opposed his election to the faculty of the new University of Virginia, and petitioned grand juries for his removal early in his tenure at South Carolina College. By 1832, he had become one of the most prominent political figures in the state: he was a leading states' rights theorist for the Nullification Party and had been ahead of most in suggesting the possibility of secession. Political opponents wanted to strike him down, and they joined the Presbyterians in a renewed attack. He spoke for two hours on that December day, and then for another two the next evening. This was "a court of ecclesiastical inquisition," Cooper said in his defense; it was trying to ruin a man because of how he understood the scriptures. He argued that the text being dangerously misinterpreted in this controversy was not the Bible but the Constitution.[1]

James Henley Thornwell, the top student of South Carolina College's senior class in 1831, had been among the students called to testify about Cooper for his hearing. A small, sickly boy when he had arrived on campus three years earlier, Thornwell, the son of a plantation overseer in the Marlborough district, had had his religious beliefs shaken by his college studies. For a time Cooper had been his intellectual idol, but by 1831, buffeted by spiritual longing and skeptical argument, Thornwell was in a state of religious turmoil. He said nothing damaging about Cooper in his testimony, recalling the president's geology lecture against the Old Testament chronology but no particular attacks upon Christianity. The young student did, however, defeat an effort by his classmates to submit a petition in Cooper's favor. As Cooper waited for his hearing in the spring of 1832, Thornwell bought a copy of the Westminster Confession of Faith at a local bookstore and fell in love with the intellectual edifice of Presbyterianism. He experienced conversion somewhat later, studied divinity, and entered the ministry. In 1837, he was called back to the college to teach, soon occupying the Chair of Sacred Literature and the Evidences of Christianity, a professorship created to scrub the school clean of Cooperian infidelity. Long before becoming president of the college in 1851 and then professor of theology at the Presbyterian Theological Seminary in Columbia in 1857, Thornwell was one of the leading voices in Southern Presbyterianism and one of the important architects of proslavery Christianity. The victories of the faith proclaimed by Thornwell, his colleague Thomas Smyth of Charleston, and other proslavery Christians over the skepticism of Cooper and his intellectual heirs in the next generation would help define the antebellum white South.[2]

"On Political Hermeneutics" is the title of an article published in 1837 not by Cooper or Thornwell but by Francis Lieber, who joined the faculty of South Carolina College in 1835, a year after Cooper resigned. Lieber called for systematic attention to the interpretation of legal terms and political language, the kind of scholarly care that European critics were devoting to the Old and New Testaments, a field where "hermeneutics" referred to theories of interpretation. But Cooper's South Carolina career, his conflicts with his Christian antagonists, and the following generation of Presbyterians who continued the argument for slavery and against religious infidelity illustrate "political hermeneutics" in a deeper sense, as the recognition that the interpretation of public language—either religious or secular—always occurred in a political context. Interpreting foundational texts (creeds and scriptures, statutes and constitutions) can rarely be abstracted from relations of power—from the formal politics of electioneering and governance or the informal, and related, politics of social and family life. Cooper and the Southern Presbyterians he opposed dramatized political hermeneutics; the climax of his career at South Carolina College was merely the opening chapter in the consolidation of proslavery ideology and Christian faith.[3]

Cooper and his Presbyterian opponents had distinct visions of the relation between interpretation and power. Cooper entered what he understood as the public arena armed with encyclopedic knowledge and ready for intellectual battle. The Presbyterian leadership in South Carolina could be just as combative. They began, however, with the divine Word, which set the limits and possibilities for political authority and public debate. Cooper's arguments from political economy and constitutional law defended slavery for the South. Yet his Christian opponents, especially after the 1830s, fused proslavery thought and conservative

Protestantism as a much broader basis for Southern white identity, even if they did not quite become the mouthpieces of Christian consensus that they hoped and sometimes imagined themselves to be.[4]

Forgetting their own history and failing to recognize how the Christianization of public life had intensified in the 1830s, some white South Carolinians by the 1850s would find it hard to understand how Southerners could have tolerated an infidel like Cooper at all. A religious skeptic leading South Carolina College was by that time about as conceivable as an abolitionist as governor. Cooper and his Presbyterian opponents shared the same practical political aim: defend the slave plantocracy. But the strategies they used to achieve that goal were in tension: Cooper's notion of the public arena clashed with the Presbyterians' methods of disseminating doctrine. And the foundational commitments informing those practices were miles apart: Cooper's devotion to the skeptical demystification of metaphysical claims was as uncompromising as the Presbyterians' faithful profession of what they understood to be biblical truths. In his struggles with his religious opponents, Cooper was only temporarily successful. In the generation after his death, the consolidation of a Christian proslavery theology (which would become the basis of Confederate civil religion) would effectively silence religious skepticism in the South.

Religion and Politics

The plan for South Carolina College had originally been proposed by lowcountry planters at the turn of the nineteenth century. Even after the capital was moved to Columbia, in the center of the state, in 1786, and the new constitution of 1790 gave somewhat more power to upcountry elites, lowcountry planters still dominated politics (with only a quarter of the white population, the lowcountry still had twenty of thirty-seven state senators). But the grandees along the coast saw how population and power were shifting; the college could be an institution where the sons of rich tidewater rice planters and wealthy upcountry cotton growers who still spoke of the virtues of the yeoman farm could be educated and cultivated as a consolidated slaveholding class. This project seemed to be a success by the time Cooper assumed the presidency in 1820. The religious question was another matter. The college was a public institution in a state where Anglicanism had been disestablished and religious liberty celebrated since 1778. Yet sectarian jealousies were never far from the surface. There were twice as many Baptists and four times as many Methodists as Presbyterians in the state, though perhaps only one in ten adult whites was a church member of any sort. Still, Presbyterians made up a large proportion of the tuition-paying parents sending their sons to the college. They criticized Cooper almost from the start.[5]

A. B. Durand and C. Ingraham, "Thomas Cooper" (1829). The climax of Cooper's career at South Carolina College was the opening chapter in the consolidation of proslavery ideology and Christian faith. Photo courtesy of National Library of Medicine.

Cooper had three strategies when his opponents attacked. He could insist that religious opinions were a person's constitutionally protected private property. Invoking privacy, however, suggested a retreat from his conviction that citizens had a right to freely discuss and debate all ideas—even the Christian grounds of faith—in the public arena. He could instead try to argue that some of his opinions, mistakenly construed as dangerous infidelity, were in fact supported by the Bible itself. This was, in effect, to play the politics of scriptural hermeneutics, trying to broaden the range of what counted as acceptably "Christian." It was to argue for a different variety of scriptural faith, not for the legitimacy of religious skepticism. Finally, he could engage his opponents' claims head-on with a skeptical critique of their central doctrines and even of their ground of faith, the Old and New Testaments. Cooper pursued all three strategies in his South Carolina years, becoming bolder as his political star rose in the States' Rights Party.

The doctor's published address to the senior class in 1821 tried to quiet his critics. Outlining the moral and civic uses of religion, he tried to sound as if he were still the "rational Christian" of the 1780s. He encouraged his students to cultivate the religious dimension of their education by doing their duty to God. Every Christian denomination, he said, had faith in the moral government of God and in a future state of rewards and punishments. He told his students that these beliefs made better men and better citizens. Prudently conceding that these basic elements of religious belief had social value, he quickly consigned the rest of Christian faith to the realm of private opinion. Civil society and public education, he argued, should only be concerned with religion to the extent that it shaped virtuous behavior, and not meddle with a person's private religious beliefs.[6]

He subtly tweaked the noses of his Christian critics in another part of the address, too. After reviewing the uses of the liberal arts for various professions, Cooper then discussed the relation of the clergy to higher learning. From another speaker the words could have been taken as high praise for the rigors of training in divinity, but from Cooper they were a challenge to clergymen to step up to their intellectual responsibilities, enter the public arena, and defend their beliefs. Every religious leader who presumed to expound upon the meaning of the Bible had better have the necessary linguistic, historical, and philosophical knowledge required for biblical exegesis, he said. A Christian minister should be able not just to read Greek and Hebrew but to understand how meaning was embedded in and shaped by the manners and customs of particular peoples in the ancient Near East. He needed to know how metaphysics and theology had changed over the centuries. He had to measure all his denominational dogmas against the texts themselves and "be able to prove beyond doubt that the tenets he insists on as articles of faith, are absolutely essential to the christianity propounded by Christ himself." The clergyman had to be able to defend his faith rationally—after all, Cooper reminded his audience, the Bible calls upon the believer "to be able to give a reason for the hope that is in him" (1 Pet. 3:15). A Christian pastor, charged with leading his flock to the truth, ought to be able to answer all the doubts that the scriptures were really the revelation of God; he must command all the relevant historical facts and internal textual evidence and be able to expose the fallacies of skepticism. It was a minister's solemn duty, Cooper said, "to clear up the doubts and fears that may oppress the weak consciences under his pastoral care." Cooper confided privately to Thomas Jefferson in 1818 his belief that "if the evidences of Christianity are fairly given on both sides, it is impossible to avoid very strong doubts as to the validity of the evidences in its favor." He had come to that conclusion after he consulted "nearly all the antient fathers, and studied the question with great labor and anxiety." So he did not think that clergymen could actually clear up a learned skeptic's reasonable doubts, but he wanted to see them try.[7]

In the fall of 1822, Cooper's religious opponents in South Carolina saw an opening when enrollments dipped and some disciplinary problems disturbed the peace of Columbia. Grand jury presentments from two upcountry counties with significant Presbyterian populations, York and Chester, blaming the college problems on the religious attitudes of the president, prompted the legislature to create a special committee to investigate the situation at the school. The committee vindicated Cooper's administration and reported that he was being persecuted by sectarian zeal. Even before the committee's report, Governor Thomas Bennett voiced strong support for Cooper in his annual message. Cooper in the spring of 1823 "exasperated" the Presbyterians, he admitted to Jefferson, by submitting two letters to the Columbia *Telescope* detailing the ways that the churches drained money from the public, signing, in a reference to Proverbs 27:27, as "One of the Goats" being milked by the clergy. William K. Clowney, the college's mathematics tutor, published a pamphlet that challenged the "Goat's" financial figures and indignantly defended the churches.[8]

A second, simultaneous controversy drew even more attention to Cooper's views about religion. It began with the unintended publication of a letter by Supreme Court Justice William Johnson that criticized a pamphlet on public schools he mistakenly thought Cooper had written. Cooper denied having anything to do with the pamphlet and used this example of Johnson's carelessness in interpreting textual evidence to make sarcastic comments about Johnson's history books. (He had published a two-volume biography of Revolutionary War general Nathanael Greene.) Most inflammatory, though, was Cooper's jab at the judicial ineptitude and "want of common sense and common decency" the justice displayed when he criticized the Charleston court that tried and executed thirty-five blacks in the alleged Denmark Vesey slave conspiracy. Justice Johnson's vitriolic rejoinder filled more than a five-column page of the newspaper. The justice blasted Cooper's snide attack as a vulgar, malicious, contemptuous product of "a low, groveling mind" and threatened a libel suit. Much of the letter was devoted to character assassination through an exegesis of some of Cooper's writings on religion. Johnson, a member of Charleston's Circular Congregational Church, set out some of the notorious statements in the *Memoirs of Priestley* and showed how the comparatively pious exhortations from Cooper's 1821 *Address to the Senior Class* flatly contradicted the doctor's avowed positions. The justice reminded his readers that South Carolina's constitution and judicial process—the very fabric of civil society—rested on the sanctity of oaths, and oaths "imply a Searcher of Hearts, and a future state of rewards and punishments." While a private citizen might doubt or deny the existence of God, the soul, and a future state, the opinions of the president of a public college were indeed a legitimate public concern.[9]

Taken aback, Cooper tried to reposition himself as merely a Christian who was privately and harmlessly interpreting his Bible as best he could. "I hold no opinions that I have not carefully and anxiously deduced, with a sincere desire at arriving at truth, from the christian scriptures," he wrote in a letter published in Columbia and Charleston newspapers. He explained that materialism was not inconsistent with the Christian belief in future retribution, and that he had not written "a syllable" on this subject in nearly seventeen years, but he would defend his scriptural argument if necessary. In any case, he asked, in America was not a man's conduct more important than his opinions? Was not freedom of conscience and discussion guaranteed to every citizen? Yet "is it in the United States that I am to be thus pelted on all hands, because my sincere and unbiased interpretation of Christ's gospel, is not quite fashionable?" Later in 1823 he wrote *The Scripture Doctrine of Materialism*, which defended materialism not as a scientific doctrine for atheistic infidels but as a more accurate Christian interpretation of the scriptures. It was an attempt to shift the ground from a contest between skeptical infidelity and religious faith to a difference over biblical hermeneutics. Although he strained to write with "all circumspection and moderation" on this subject, and he told Jefferson that he doubted there was a printer or bookseller in America who would touch it, he found a publisher in Philadelphia for his four-hundred-page book.[10]

Grand juries from York and Chester, this time joined by one from Greenville County, repeated their complaints against the college president in 1823. A new governor, John Lyde Wilson, was even more forceful in Cooper's defense. Wilson praised the president's "unrivalled" abilities and denounced the "spirit of hostility" that had "been kept alive and inflamed by a limited number of sectarians." Cooper was not merely being protected by political friends. The doctor had been in the state for only two years when the presentiments were first considered. He had as yet published little on South Carolina politics. Although he had published an important essay against the tariff in 1823, he was not yet the partisan lightning rod he would be later in the decade during the Nullification controversy and was not yet worth a politician's expenditure of much political capital. Cooper was triumphant in this first battle because many in the ruling class did not share the Presbyterians' vision of a Christian society. Governor Wilson's annual message stated the view of the proper relation of church, state, and college that had strong support in the legislature: "If his [Cooper's] religious tenets be in accordance with none of those that would remove him from his present situation, it is a matter of little consequence to the student. Our constitution tolerates all religions, and legalizes none." The state had no business creating "a situation where any particular creed or belief should be instilled into the minds of the rising generation."[11]

This view—that government should not meddle with religion and that religion was an individual's private concern—was debated in the press as commentators considered the Cooper affair. The editor of the *National Gazette* examined Governor Wilson's defense of Cooper and wondered: If no particular creeds were to be taught in state colleges, "were Americans to be made Christians *in the abstract*?" The *Religious Intelligencer* supported the citizens who protested rather than the legislature that dismissed their petitions. The *Columbian Star* criticized the committee's report: the complaints about Cooper derived not from the "narrow bigotry" of "some religious societies" but from the sensible conviction that "no college can or ought to flourish, unless it be managed and governed by Christians." New England newspapers took sides too. The *New Hampshire Observer* quoted the atheism passage in Cooper's *Memoirs of Priestley* and proclaimed that Cooper's appointment as a college president was "an open insult" to Christians. The *Boston Recorder* saw the conflict as a struggle between infidelity or atheism and Christianity. The *Vermont Gazette* responded by asserting that Cooper was no infidel but a Unitarian standing up to Calvinist clergymen who thought they could topple colleges they disliked at their pleasure. An article reprinted from the *National Advocate* in the *New England Galaxy* did not have to assume that Cooper was a Unitarian battling Calvinists to defend him. Let his sentiments be what his opponents claimed—infidelity or even atheism: "It has pleased the Almighty Sovereign of the universe to shed his blessings on the great family of mankind without distinction," the article intoned, in a rare statement of tolerance for the unreligious. Even infidels and atheists enjoyed the warmth of the sun and the dews of the evening. "How dare men pro-scribe what God tolerates?" The *Boston Commercial Gazette* noted that the Cooper affair was not an isolated case. A Presbyterian-influenced grand jury in Kentucky was similarly overstepping its authority and trying to oust Unitarian Horace Holley from the presidency of Transylvania University.[12]

Cooper reported the legislative committee's exoneration to Jefferson, but he knew that while his Presbyterian enemies might retreat, they would not give up: "I have scotched the snake, not killed it." He had made his stand against the "holy alliance" in South Carolina and wanted to keep fighting the good fight. However, publishers and booksellers in the United States—"according to our own account the most enlightened nation on earth!"—were paralyzed by the frowns of the Christian clergy. He realized, too, that he had "gone to the limits of prudence, and I should certainly be compelled to retire if I were to push opposition to the Clergy any further." He privately lamented how "a prudent dread of public ignorance and priestly rancor" made otherwise honest men hide their skepticism. "One is compelled to act here as I should act in Turkey: if an honest Mussleman were to say to me, 'Christian Dog, take your choice, become a follower of the prophet or be impaled,' I should not put him to the trouble of the latter operation.... When will the American people acknowledge that Truth is the offspring of unfettered discussion!"[13]

In the 1820s, Cooper also turned his prodigious energies to debates over interpreting the federal Constitution. He had, in fact, sent Jefferson his pamphlet on the national tariff along with his work on materialism in late 1823. Cooper's searing criticism of the tariff as a disastrous economic policy for the South not only drew on his free trade principles but insisted that the tariff was unconstitutional: a northern majority in Congress was distorting the language of the Constitution to pick the pockets of Southern planters. His critique of national politics extended the analysis he had developed in the previous decade. "Constitutional and legal forms, especially when they are ill devised and constructed, are always part of the instruments of political warfare," he had written. The ambiguities of the "necessary and proper" clause offered just such a weapon. Cooper championed a strict construction of the Constitution as a check on federal power, and this became a central plank of states'-rights doctrine in South Carolina. Yet for Cooper, simply to search for the original intent of the Founders to set the boundaries of interpretation for the written text was to misunderstand how the words on the page became meaningful and authoritative. The framing of the U.S. Constitution was only the latest and best effort in an ongoing republican experiment in an era when political science was—as it still remained in the 1820s—in its infancy, he believed. The document was the result not of timeless genius but of political compromise, and it contained ambiguities that papered over disagreements. Its greatest flaw was in not instituting a mechanism whereby a new convention could meet every thirty years to make adjustments and revise the Constitution in light of accumulated practical experience. The document that Americans revered and argued about, Cooper wrote in "On the Constitution of the United States" (1826), had been crafted in 1787 by a group of men who had very different opinions about the proper relation of state and national power. As soon as the new government began to function, two parties emerged, one seeking to enhance and the other to restrict the power of the federal government. Yet in the ongoing political contests about issues large and small, as party leaders on both sides scrambled for prestige, influence, and profit, and voters adhered to personalities and empty campaign slogans, parties could lose sight of the principles that had created them in the first place. That was precisely what happened to Republicans after the War of 1812. What had once been the ultranationalist views of a small group of Hamiltonian Federalists, Cooper wrote in *Consolidation* (1824), was now the fashionable dogma in Congress as members found license in the Constitution to fund their pet projects in the name of the national good.[14]

The dangers of an unconstitutional consolidation of national power went beyond the tariff: it opened the door for Northerners to interfere with slavery. South Carolina's recourse, Cooper believed, was for the state to resist the tyranny of the national majority by nullifying federal laws it deemed unconstitutional. The Virginia and Kentucky Resolutions of 1798, written by Madison and Jefferson to oppose the Alien and Sedition Acts, had suggested this line of argument. But Cooper and other Nullifiers in South Carolina would go further than those resolutions. Cooper read the Constitution, despite its "We the people" opening, as a compact of the states, and just as states had power to nullify, they also had the power to secede from the compact they had originally ratified. In a famous—or infamous—speech on July 2, 1827, Cooper suggested that South Carolina might do just that. He delivered a line that would be repeated in subsequent congressional and newspaper debates: "We shall before long, be compelled to calculate the value of our union; and to inquire of what use to us is this most unequal alliance?"[15]

When Cooper began making these arguments in the early 1820s he felt like a lone prophet, ignored when he was not vilified. But many upcountry farmers would come to blame their economic woes on the tariff, and tidewater planters, nervous about abolitionist agitation, would join them in worrying about Northern consolidation. Other political theorists and propagandists, especially the former nationalist John C. Calhoun, would elaborate and systematize what came to be called the South Carolina doctrines. As the states'-rights radicals (though they would have called themselves conservatives) gained power in the state, climaxing in the Nullification Convention and Ordinance of November 1832, Cooper was viciously attacked by political opponents as a dangerous fomenter of treason—the "chief of the Southern Nullifiers" and the "Father of Disunion"—but toasted by the ascendant states' rights party as a patriot. Fighting, as he thought, for political liberty, he also reopened his campaign for religious liberty.[16]

The politics of textual interpretation was again central. Teaching geology, Cooper felt compelled to "take up the gauntlet" that the textbook author, Yale's Benjamin Silliman, "had thrown down on my table" by drawing from the Old Testament for scientific evidence. Silliman's geological assumptions, Cooper charged, came not from what the Yale professor saw in the ground but from Bible stories such as Noah's Flood. Although Cooper felt that he continued to abide by his pledge to avoid religion, per se, in his classroom, for purely scientific reasons he had to show his geology students that the Pentateuch was not written by Moses and was not divinely inspired. Later expanding this lecture into a short book, *On the Connection between Geology and the Pentateuch* (1833), Cooper chided Silliman for not keeping up to date with scholarship and realizing that sound principles of criticism and interpretation were now being applied to all ancient texts—the scriptures included. The doctor referenced Johann Gottfried Eichhorn's analysis of Genesis, showing the Creation narrative to be a fusion of two different accounts with different names for and notions of God (Jehovah and Elohim, the latter being plural). Considering all the anachronisms, contradictions, absurdities, and uncorroborated claims he found in the text, Cooper could only conclude that Genesis was "a fugitive, anonymous collection of uncertain and popular traditions, collected or compiled no one knows by whom, concerning a supposed history of the earth and its population, [that] carries with it no authority because it is founded on no evidence as to its date, as to its authorship, or its facts." Invoking supernatural explanations, as the clergy often did to try to wash all the difficulties away, merely begged the question; to dismiss serious doubts as just "the unreasonable cavils of men who are skeptically inclined" was merely to hide behind name-calling and inflame popular prejudices against "Infidelity." Cooper looked past Silliman and challenged the clergy directly: "The clerical craft is in danger.... The glove has been thrown down before them: let those who choose take it up."[17]

Cooper also struck at the "very foundation" of Christianity by applying the same critical techniques to the Gospels. Writing a series of essays under the pseudonym "Philo-Veritas" in the New York *Correspondent* in the spring and summer of 1829, Cooper drew from law books, literary and historical criticism, and the commonsensical habits of daily life to examine the credibility of the New Testament. Legal treatises gave good guidance for evaluating the competence and credibility of witnesses and for drawing reasonable conclusions from collateral facts and circumstantial evidence. A recent article in the *North American Review* conveniently summarized the historian's rules of source criticism and methods for evaluating the plausibility of a particular group's traditions with corroborating evidence from contemporary outsiders. Beyond the courtroom and the scholar's study, too, people had reliable strategies for determining credibility. Was a neighbor's extraordinary account true? Well, was he generally an honest fellow? Does he have any motive to deceive us? Might he be deceived, mistaken, or deluded? From the common interactions of social life arose the sensible notion that a proportional strength of testimony was needed to overcome skepticism about stories that claimed to be true but seemed, based on previous experience, highly improbable.[18]

The Gospels fail every test, Cooper argued. The texts as we have them, contradictory in themselves, date much later than the events they describe and come to us from the hands of the early Church Fathers (Origen, Jerome, Eusebius), who admitted to the practice of *economia*—"forging and lying for the purpose of promoting a common cause." Little corroborating evidence comes from non-Christian sources (Pliny, Tacitus, Suetonius), which were silent even on alleged events that would have been public and notorious, such as the rending of the veil in the temple and the rising of the dead from their graves at the crucifixion.[19]

"To rest our faith" on the Bible, therefore, "is leaning our weight on a broken reed," Cooper wrote. Yet if the scriptural grounds of faith were so weak, why were there so many Christians? To answer, Cooper once again summoned the lessons of associational psychology: "Because man is a creature of circumstances. Because they were bred from infancy to manhood among Christians; because every body around them, their mothers, their nurses, their fathers, their teachers, their older and revered friends, their companions, were Christians: they were taught that it would be criminal to doubt the truth of Christianity: infidelity was held out to them to be an unpardonable crime." More was at work here, though, than just the inertia of cultural tradition and social reproduction. Who benefited from this perpetuation of falsehood? The men who gained wealth and power from preaching Christianity as a trade; the men who held up the Bible, proclaimed it the Word of God with necessary truths for eternal salvation, and positioned themselves as a divinely appointed order to explain and enforce those truths.[20]

Returning again to one of his favorite themes—the pernicious influence of clerical self-interest—Cooper in the *Correspondent* essays offered some of his most bitter denunciations of the Christian clergy. To the Massachusetts Unitarians who "labored honestly and diligently" to understand the theological implications of higher biblical criticism (even if they remained "riveted" to Christian faith in some form out of habit or professional calculation), Cooper was "throwing down not the gauntlet, but the glove of courteous controversy." But "against the ignorant, the insolent, the intolerant among the calvinistic professors particularly; and against the idle and comparatively illiterate episcopalians," he directed deservedly "harsh tirades." He blamed the clergy as a whole, though, for working to suppress skeptical critiques of religion, for keeping "the multitude in mental bondage," and for repeatedly trying to persuade the civil government to aid their cause. America, though a land of "*theoretical* toleration," had "much *practical* bigotry" that was continually stoked by the pulpit and religious press. Bible, tract, missionary, and clerical societies hunted and hounded infidels. Unless a man joined the lowing herd, they attacked his moral character, poisoned his family and social life, and tried to "prevent his success in the world." If, when skeptical critiques publicly exposed the problems with the clergy's doctrines, ministers merely cleared their throats, thumbed their Bibles, and passed the collection plate, they were "either impudent and unprincipled swindlers" or "careless, hired, prostituted advocates of an indefensible imposture." Yet Americans—especially weak-minded women—imbibed their Christianity "on trust" from their parsons, "nine-tenths of whom in these United States never took the trouble of investigating the grounds and foundations of their own faith."[21]

Philo-Veritas revealed the depths of Cooper's religious skepticism. After consulting, he claimed, a hundred books, including thirty folio volumes of the ancient fathers, Cooper could find "nothing but doubt and darkness, fraud and forgery, on all sides." At best, one could concede "that some seditious fanatic may have been put to death under the procuratorship of Pontius Pilate is possible; and that he may have had disciples, like Johanna Southcote, or Jemima Wilkinson, is possible also; and that the Gentile followers of this Jew malefactor may have named him *Christos*, anointed, is possible also." None of the superstitions and dogmas built up around this character over the centuries, however, and certainly not the claim developed in the second century that Jesus was God, deserved any credence or respect. What is more, the doctor added in the last essay of the series, the entire monotheistic system upon which Christianity was grafted was philosophically dubious. If God is wise and good, why "is he moved from his purpose by prayers and entreaties like a silly woman" influenced by flattery? Why does he shroud his revelation in darkness and doubt, and why does he promote his church through falsehood and fraud? If there was an eternal God who acted as the moral governor of the universe, Cooper contended, he was a miserable governor for permitting horrors such as war, pestilence, famine, and earthquakes. There was no need even to posit a Creator: "I know of no creator extraneous to, and different from the universe I behold." Such statements surely would have caused an uproar in South Carolina if his opponents—and perhaps even if his friends—had discovered that he had written them. But in this case Cooper had covered his tracks well.[22]

Cooper's critics, though, had other evidence of his dangerous opinions. In 1829 he anonymously published *To Any Member of Congress*, a scathing address responding to the Christian reformers who were petitioning Congress to stop the Sunday mail because it violated the Sabbath. He argued that the United States was not, as was so often claimed, a Christian country in any constitutional or legal sense. He defended the motives of "the persons called skeptics and infidels" and dismissed the Sabbath itself as nonsense invented by "those avaricious, ambitious, fraudulent and impudent imposters, the Christian priests." A published letter by South Carolina congressman James Blair, an anti-Nullifier, named Cooper as the author of the offending pamphlet. Blair, who wrote that he hoped to die a Christian "without *doubt* or *wavering*," insisted that any man who tried to "shake our faith in the Divine authenticity of Christianity" was neither a patriot nor a good citizen. He hammered Cooper for meddling in politics, corrupting his students, and trying to lead South Carolina to the "immorality and atheism" of Revolutionary France. In a subsequent letter he called Cooper an "old political prostitute" and an "Anti-Christ." Blair was a wealthy slaveholder from Kershaw; he was a horseman, a dualist, and a brawler (well over six feet tall and three hundred pounds), known for his fondness for ruffled shirts, a gold-tipped cane, brandy, and opium. Cooper replied "with some astonishment" at Blair's "new character as a defender of the faith" and dismissed the congressman's religious posturing as "manifestly a *political* attack."[23]

Two more provocative publications led to renewed calls for Cooper's removal. *An Exposition of the Doctrine of Calvinism* (1830) was also anonymously published outside the state, but Cooper's South Carolina opponents caught wind of it. The pamphlet denounced the basic tenets of Calvinism as more satanic than divine and doubted that anyone using the Westminster Confession of

Faith as a guide to moral conduct could ever be a virtuous citizen. Cooper signed his name to his translation of F. J. V Broussais's *On Irritation and Insanity* (1831), a materialist theory of the mind and mental illness. In this volume he also included older essays of his own on materialism and the association of ideas, and added a preface and an appendix marked by his customarily caustic anticlericalism. All of this was too much for a writer who identified himself only as "Censor." In his *Appeal to the State*, Censor argued that Cooper should be fired. South Carolina was a Christian country, he wrote, where the Bible was the foundation of society, legislation, manners, and customs. Agreeing with Censor, the Presbyterian *Observer* in Charleston ran a series of eight anti-Cooper articles in the summer of 1831, followed by eight more the next spring by Presbyterian minister Samuel P. Pressley. Pressley's letters to Cooper tried to counter the doctor's biblical hermeneutics and defend the faith. But for Censor, whether Christianity was true or false was almost beside the point: 90 percent of the (white) population, if asked, would want Christianity to remain the rock upon which the state rested. To criticize the faith under the guise of "free discussion," therefore, was to mock the sovereign will of the people.[24]

One of the pamphleteers who rallied to Cooper's defense surmised that the state's Unionists were simply trying to use religion to divide the states' rights party. Another suggested that bigoted Christians who called themselves orthodox were exploiting the turmoil over Nullification to achieve sectarian ends. What was the cloak, and what was the dagger? Though it is not inaccurate to refer to a coalition of Cooper's religious and political enemies, as the doctor himself did, for many of them religion and politics, means and motives, were thoroughly entangled. Some of his opponents, too, saw a deep connection of religion and politics in Cooper himself, especially in what they saw as Cooper's willful misreading of authoritative texts: as one wrote, "Atheist as well as Traitor, he would nullify the Bible as well as the Laws."[25]

In the December 1831 session of the state house, Representative John S. Pressly from Abbeville rose and introduced a resolution to remove Cooper from the presidency of the college. Pressly was both a Unionist and an Associate Reformed Presbyterian; after his political defeat three years later, he would enter the ministry and help found the Clarke and Erskine Theological Seminary. Most of the argument supporting Pressly's resolution was delivered by the Unionist lawyer and orator James L. Petigru, who "portrayed in vivid colors the evils which have arisen from the publications of Dr. Cooper... a man who openly and zealously sought to overthrow the fabrics of Religion." The vote followed party lines, and the measure was defeated 71–67. A compromise measure, which recommended an inquiry by the Board of Trustees, passed almost unanimously. Quickly formed in the week following the vote, a five-man committee charged that Cooper had endangered public support of the college by attacking religion and that he taught his students to sneer at the Sabbath, prayer, and particular religious sects. Though quick to report the charges, the board postponed the hearing until May and then again to the following December (1832).[26]

Not waiting for his day in court, Cooper immediately took his case to the public. His forty-four-page pamphlet *The Case of Thomas Cooper, M.D.*, appeared before the end of 1831. In it Cooper drew insistent parallels to the Nullification controversy, beginning with an epigraph from John C. Calhoun contrasting philosophies of government (benignly laissez-faire versus intrusive). Cooper argued that just as inattention to what the U.S. Constitution actually said had allowed people to be duped and deceived by the "Tariff Monopolists" controlling the federal government, disregard for the state constitution was allowing clergymen to use state power to monopolize religious discussion, gag the press, and extinguish religious liberty. Articles V and VIII in the South Carolina Constitution very plainly guaranteed freedom of the press and religion. Unless the constitution was "waste paper," it was the paramount law of the land, not to be modified by loose interpretation and the whims of legislative discretion. The constitution certainly did not establish Christianity or define "infidelity," but in the case against him the legislature was being called to act as if it did.[27]

Cooper glanced back at his long career on the "liberal" side of this even longer "transatlantic" argument: he had celebrated the U.S. Constitution while still in England, suffered a sedition trial in Pennsylvania, and endured attacks by Presbyterians from almost the moment he arrived in South Carolina. Yet there had been progress. For the most part, Americans in general and South Carolinians in particular now understood the essential role of open political debate in a free society. They expected citizens to publicly criticize and cast doubt upon laws and political policies. Why, then, did the clergy claim to be exempt from the same sort of skeptical critical inquiry? As for the specific charges against him, Cooper denied that he was making the college unpopular, pointing to high enrollments despite the difficult economic times. He denied mocking religion in front of his students and claimed that he only criticized clerical pay in the context of a lecture on political economy and only challenged the Mosaic authorship of the Pentateuch as the question pertained to geology. He closed by praising open discussion and universal education. A second edition of the pamphlet added an appendix reprinting press clippings from across the country that purported to reveal Presbyterians (such as Ezra Stiles Ely) scheming to consolidate political power, breach the constitutional separation of church and state, and violate the liberties of the people.[28]

Cooper's hearing before the Board of Trustees in Columbia's crowded statehouse on the evenings of December 4 and 5, 1832, was the culmination of his long career in the public arena. Such a "court of ecclesiastical inquisition" was "a new scene in Republican America," he proclaimed, and it "would furnish a new page in the history of South Carolina." He spoke as the Nullification controversy neared its climax: the Ordinance of Nullification had been adopted by the convention meeting in Columbia on November 24; the Unionist Convention met in the city on December 1; President Jackson's Nullification Proclamation would be issued on December 10. The old man whom opponents dubbed the High Priest of Nullification stood up and answered the charges against him. The thriving state of the college and the sworn testimony of his students proved that he had not interfered with their religious opinions or damaged the school's reputation. But there were more than enrollment numbers and student affidavits to assess. Fundamental principles were at stake. The proceedings, he insisted again, violated the state constitution and represented a tyrannical usurpation of power not unlike what the federal government was trying to do to South Carolina. The complaints against him referred to offending passages in his various publications, but he swatted those charges away with his familiar defense of republican principles, individual liberty, and the importance of a free press. The crowd interrupted his speech at several points with applause. Two days later, the board dismissed the charges. Old Coot went back to his library in triumph.[29]

Although Cooper's enemies had lost the Board of Trustees battle in 1832, they soon won the larger war. They refused to send their sons to the college. Enrollments plummeted, and Cooper finally agreed to step down in November 1833. He continued as professor of chemistry and mineralogy for another year, but the boycott continued, and the board felt compelled to ask the entire faculty to resign at the end of 1834. Cooper was awarded a Doctor of Laws degree, and his friends at first proposed to create a law school around him, but instead the legislature hired him to publish a revision of the state's laws. If he took the time to pause and contemplate his legacy, Cooper could have claimed to have effectively tutored the South on political economy and to have helped frame the South Carolina doctrines on states' rights. But in the last years of his life he was disappointed that his adopted state had backed down in the face of President Jackson's belligerence and had accepted a compromise on the tariff. A visitor described a conversation on the topic:

> Upon my congratulating him upon that measure [the Compromise Act]... he rose from his easy chair, and although almost bent double like a hook, he seized the hearth-brush, and with his eyes full of fire, and wielding the brush as if it were a broadsword, denounced the Compromise Act as if it were an ignoble measure which he never could approve of; declared that Nullifiers were quite wrong to make peace with the Union men (their opponents in South Carolina), and that it would have been a much better course for them to have taken the field against General Jackson, and have fought all the power he could have brought against

them. "We have lost a fine opportunity, sir, of carrying this State to the highest renown," said this little crooked octogenarian; and then giving General Jackson a desperate cut with the hearth-brush, he went back to his easy chair again.[30]

Cooper remained as irascible as ever. Working on the revision of the state laws during the day, in the evenings he took up his pen as Philo-Veritas, revising his *Correspondent* essays and drafting an additional work intended to detail the bloody abominations inflicted by Christianity throughout history. A few months before his death in May 1839, in a letter to a fellow freethinker, he reaffirmed his skepticism about religious promises of an afterlife: "Of a future state, I have no evidence. Knowing therefore nothing about it, I shall die believing nothing, hoping nothing, fearing nothing, caring nothing."[31]

Presbyterians continued their campaign for the Christianization of the college even after Cooper had departed from the scene. The institution was important in its own right but was also symbolic of the place Christianity, they believed, ought to have in public life. The new faculty brought in to replace Cooper and his colleagues did not satisfy critics of the college. Letters and editorials in the Charleston *Observer*, a Presbyterian weekly with an extensive circulation in South Carolina and Georgia, contributed to the broader battle being conducted in newspapers and pamphlets in the summer and fall of 1835. The critics argued that the new professors were not religious men: one was said to scorn belief in the Bible, two others made no profession of personal piety, and even the two who were church members were thought lukewarm at best—one of them, Francis Lieber, was suspected of believing little more than the newfangled deism of the German schools.[32]

The Board of Trustees was a body composed of thirty-three of the leading public men in the state, and five of them stepped forward to defend themselves against what they thought were groundless prejudices left over from the Cooper era. How, they asked, was the board supposed to define what a suitably "religious" man was? Would not such a demand transform this civil body into an ecclesiastical tribunal? The Rev. Dr. Benjamin Gildersleeve, the Presbyterian editor of the *Observer*, answered: a "religious" person was not merely a moral one, for even Cooper, all acknowledged, was a moral man; neither should "religious" designate someone paying only a casual respect to the church, nor even someone who signaled mere belief in the Bible. The adjective "religious" should properly signify "*Vital, evangelical piety*," "the *faith* which the Bible requires," and the board should hire only college professors who could demonstrate to the major evangelical denominations in the state that they possessed it. Gildersleeve called for a total purge of infidelity at South Carolina College, wanting to "purify even the

Library of the infidel notes with which infidel instructors have interlarded its pages."[33]

Other commentators parsed the religious and political commitments of the board itself, which stood as a proxy for the state's political leadership. One analysis described the party in power as being composed of a small but powerful antireligious faction, enemies of the Gospel like Cooper. These were allied with— and manipulated—a larger nonreligious group, men who thought religion was well and good as a private matter but wanted to keep denominational disputes away from politics and the college, and therefore concluded that quiet skeptics were better than loud and obnoxious sectarians. A third group, better reflecting broader public opinion (or so it was argued), wanted the college to be decisively Christian. Complicated as well by divisions between Nullifiers and anti-Nullifiers, the board had cobbled together the new faculty through a series of political compromises. Gildersleeve's analysis was even less generous: only three or four of the thirty-three trustees were known church members, a fact demonstrating that even if most were not closet skeptics, they certainly did not live the faith that the Bible required.[34]

Opinion pieces in other newspapers in the state urged that the new faculty be given a chance, and although a state senate committee was formed to investigate whether the board was indeed still under the influence of religious infidelity, the controversy quieted with an endorsement of the new faculty by the house and the appointment of a respected Episcopal minister as professor of sacred literature. But the dispute had again showed Presbyterian leaders appealing to biblical faith in an attempt to destroy what they perceived to be the political power of skepticism.[35]

The Southern Presbyterian leadership sometimes, like Cooper's critic Censor, claimed to speak for a Christian majority. Censor had contended that ninety out of a hundred white South Carolinians were Christians, even if not church members. Cooper had argued that 995 out of a thousand, no matter what they called themselves, never bothered to think seriously about religion at all. They did not investigate whether the religion they had inherited from their parents was true or false; their profession "is mere matter of accident," they "comply with the usual forms," and they "have no other faith but the *fides carbonaria*," a blind acceptance of whatever their church professed. Presbyterian leaders, too, could sometimes criticize what popularly passed as religious faith. When they did so they set committed, orthodox, Bible-based Christians like themselves apart from a nominally "Christian" public that had been corrupted by worldliness or corroded by infidelity, especially in its leadership class. And church leaders could switch from being majority spokesmen to minority critics in the blink of an eye. In an essay published in the *Southern Presbyterian Review*, for example, Abner A. Porter argued that "the Christian people of the South, *are the South*," yet a page later suggested that Christians could be alienated from the Southern cause if popular prejudices against slave missions continued to hold sway. This tension between wanting to serve as mouthpieces for Southern white Christianity as it was and the desire to speak as Bible prophets envisioning a Christian South as it ought to be would define not only Presbyterian efforts to capture the college for Christ but their attempts to articulate the proper relation of religion and politics, support slavery and white supremacy, and, ultimately, sacralize the Confederacy.[36]

Presbyterians and the Southern Cross

The Presbyterians, the denomination that had led the fight against Cooper, were not politically powerful because of sheer numbers. The total South Carolina population in 1830 was about 580,000, with nearly 55 percent enslaved. In the upcountry, evangelical revivals beginning in 1802 pushed church membership, according to one estimate, from 8 to 23 percent of the adult white population by 1810. Though the people who joined the Methodist, Baptist, and Presbyterian churches "included a broad cross-section of the region's population," the "preponderance" were the middling sort, especially young white families eager to cultivate more land and own more slaves. But a Presbyterian periodical in 1830 counted only 42 ministers, 75 churches, and 5,813 communicants in the entire state. Clergymen sometimes liked to claim that three, four, or even as many as six adherents filled their pews for every one communicant or full church member. But A. W. Leland, assessing South Carolina Presbyterianism in 1839, did not try to inflate the numbers. He bemoaned the "feeble, declining condition" of the church, which had lost twenty-five congregations in the upcountry since 1805. While the Baptists and the Methodists had doubled and tripled in size, even with all the out-migration, the Presbyterians' increase had been deplorably small. Perhaps not coincidentally, the Presbyterians had stopped participating with their fellow evangelicals at interdenominational camp meetings after 1805, fearing theological impurity and excessive emotionalism. In the lowcountry, Methodists, Baptists, and Presbyterians remained marginal and Episcopalianism genteel and tepid until a series of revivals coinciding with the Nullification Crisis in 1831–32 made evangelicalism a dominant cultural force. Although the revivals were led by a Presbyterian minister from Georgia, Daniel Baker, only a handful of the hundreds of converts he made joined a Presbyterian church.[37]

By 1860, the state's population had grown to over 700,000, and about 57 percent were enslaved. Two-fifths of the native-born white population had moved out of the state by midcentury, many taking their slaves with them as the cotton kingdom expanded west. Planters had brought cotton and plantation slavery to many parts of the upcountry, too, leading to black majority districts even there, while lowcountry rice-growing districts along the coast were still above 70 percent black by 1860. The South Carolina synod in 1861 reported 97 ministers, 128 churches, and 13,746 communicants. Denominational comparisons can give a better sense of relative size and wealth. Throughout the slave South at the birth of the Confederacy, Presbyterians had seating accommodations in their churches for about 729,000 people; Cumberland Presbyterian churches could hold nearly 215,000. Southern Methodists, however, could seat over 2,788,000, and Southern Baptists nearly 2,414,000. Considering the value of church property reported in the 1860 census, each Baptist seat was worth a penny shy of three dollars, and each Methodist one $3.60, but Presbyterians, with their whiter and wealthier membership, had seats representing $8.62. The Episcopal Church, the one still favored by the planter elite, had seating for only 287,500 throughout the South, yet each seat represented $17.92. Rough as they are, these numbers give some sense of the Presbyterian Church's relative affluence and popular appeal.[38]

Statistics, however, cannot convey intellectual leadership and political influence. Presbyterians prided themselves on their learned ministry and theological rigor. They championed education, agitated for moral reform, and avidly employed the printing press. Cooper targeted them in part because they claimed to be willing to fight him in the public arena with his own weapons: they appealed to reason, science, and empirical facts. They also worked to ensure that South Carolina's political and cultural institutions were grounded in biblical teaching. When the state's Presbyterians first drafted the constitution for a seminary in 1824, they envisioned a "Classical, Scientific and Theological Seminary of the South," not only stressing its particularly sectional character with the last word in the title but also suggesting with the first two terms that it would directly compete with Cooper's South Carolina College. When the school was actually founded in 1828, its declared intention had narrowed: it would not be an alternative Christian college but a seminary to train Southerners to fill Southern Presbyterian pulpits. Yet when they moved the seminary to Columbia in 1830 and erected their building a seven-minute walk from Cooper's campus, they explicitly did so "to provide an institution free from the skeptical influences" they believed were pervading the college and the state.[39]

The Southern Presbyterians repeatedly claimed that they grounded their faith and religious practice in the Bible. They were, they liked to say, children of the Reformation's turn back to *sola scriptura*; they were a people of the Word. As one of Cooper's old tormentors, Virginia's John Holt Rice, proclaimed in 1828, "We will know no *isms*... but *Bibleism*." The leadership's theories of biblical interpretation were vital to everything they did. The Rev. George Howe, who began as professor of biblical literature at the Presbyterian Theological Seminary in Columbia in 1832 and continued teaching there for fifty-two years, asked the key question: "By what laws shall the Bible be interpreted?" His answer was the "common sense" principles normally used to interpret "the language of daily discourse" and the strategies historians employed to "ascertain the meaning of any ancient author." This meant stripping away the multiple mystical or allegorical interpretations first introduced by Jewish commentators and passed on to the early Church Fathers, for only the "literal or grammatical sense" of a passage could reliably said to be divinely inspired. Much remained to be done, Howe noted, to free the science of biblical interpretation from such perverting errors. Modern hermeneutics for Howe meant continuing the work of the Protestant Reformation, not adopting the faddish approach of German Rationalists who, like David Hume before them, excluded the possibility of the miraculous. In his inaugural 1832 address to the seminary, Howe paused to answer the "modern skeptics" who challenged the Mosaic authorship of the Pentateuch. Defending biblical truth against such attacks was an essential task of the learned clergy, he wrote. He claimed that any ignorant man could easily discern the central doctrines of the Gospel. But when those doctrines were assailed, the common layperson often could give only "a lame and stumbling defence of his belief." The common Christian "either shrinks abashed from the contest; or exclaims against the piety of his opponent," not because (as Cooper asserted) he does not actually understand the faith he professes but because he lacks the conceptual and rhetorical tools to argue for the truth against its cultured despisers. The Presbyterian clergy had the training to demonstrate the reasonableness of biblical faith.[40]

A quarter century later, Southern Presbyterian writers differed over how the clergy ought to defend scriptural doctrine and answer skepticism. In an address delivered to the Columbia seminary, the Rev. W. C. Dana implied that Howe's strategy was not adequate in "a skeptical and luxurious age." The divine inspiration of the Bible, instead of being assumed, was the very thing to be proved. To provide "A Reasonable Answer to the Skeptic," the exegete needed to attend to the ways that human and divine elements were braided throughout the scriptures. The Holy Spirit who inspired the ancient authors had accommodated the divine message to the human modes of thought prevalent in ancient times. Colloquial language referring to the natural world—for example, references to the sun "rising"—need not be taken as contradictions of facts established by modern science. Careful interpretive distinctions between human form and divine content were needed at a time when the "poison" of skeptical infidelity was contaminating nearly all fields of artistic and scientific endeavor. But the Presbyterian layman E. A. Nisbet argued that the place for learned disquisitions defending the Bible against "the infidel, and the metaphysics of semi-infidel philosophers" was the press, not the pulpit—especially not the Southern pulpit. Because public challenges to the authority of the Bible had become so rare in the South by 1860, Nisbet claimed, Presbyterian clergymen should continue to battle skeptics in the pages of learned periodicals but should ignore them in the pulpit, where they ought to preach to touch hearts and reach the masses, as the Methodists did.[41]

In the lead article of the first issue of the *Southern Presbyterian Review* in 1847, James Henley Thornwell took aim at the hermeneutic of skeptical infidels like his former teacher Cooper. How—and how much—one could criticize the Bible is a question, Thornwell wrote, that is a hotly contested issue among "infidels and believers in Christianity." Christianity is a system that claimed to be not just psychologically useful or socially popular but *true*. The Bible, then, as a text asserting that it is the true Word of God, invites full discussion and criticism just like other texts making such claims, such as the Koran and the Book of Mormon. At the same time, professing to be God's Word, the Bible "speaks with authority" and "demands implicit submission." How, then, can we judge the scriptures? Allowing reason to determine what is and is not revelation, Thornwell realized, is very dangerous, "particularly in modern times, with the rise of philosophical infidelity."[42]

Portrait of James Henley Thornwell. From John B. Adger, ed., *The Collected Writings of James Henley Thornwell*, vol. 1 (Richmond, Va., 1871), frontispiece. Thornwell was one of the leading voices in antebellum Southern Presbyterianism and one of the important architects of proslavery Christianity.

To resolve this interpretive dilemma, Thornwell distinguished two different kinds of purported facts presented by the text: natural and supernatural. He also differentiated two kinds of readers: the person with only natural reason unaided by grace, and the Christian perceiving through faith instilled by grace. The Bible contained statements claiming to be revelations of supernatural facts (like the mysteries of election, the Trinity, and redemption) and others offering natural knowledge (historical narratives, geographical references, and sometimes obscure allusions to events, manners, and customs in the distant past). The natural reader would be able to examine natural facts claimed or referenced in the Koran or the Book of Mormon and could demonstrate that those books could not be divine because they contain "contradictions, palpable falsehoods or gross absurdities." Thornwell believed that the Bible, however, could pass this test. The natural reader, he also argued, should be able to at least dimly perceive the supernatural—the stamp of divine character upon scriptural words when he read them, "the traces of power, wisdom, goodness and glory which produce a divine original." When reading about supernatural things in the Bible, and seeing the scheme of redemption offered there, the natural reader should be able to recognize that such a system, "in its majesty and grandeur, its harmony, beneficence, and purity," was so clearly authored by God "as to render skepticism little less than madness." But natural reason and common sense were powerless to judge in the realm of the supernatural and refute supernatural mysteries. The skeptical critiques of philosophers such as Herbert, Bolingbroke, and Hume collapsed, Thornwell contended, because they failed to see that supernatural things did not obey the cramped logic of the natural world; they failed to acknowledge that God through the gift of faith could grant a new sense to a believing reader, opening his mind and heart to this new reality.[43]

Theories of biblical interpretation also influenced how these Presbyterian writers understood denominational identity and broader Christian union in the United States. Thomas Smyth advocated a three-tiered system of public Christian discussion: one mode for denominations to speak and write among themselves, the second for a denomination's champions to appear before the broader public to defend their church's particular principles, and the third to form the basis for interdenominational cooperation. For the first he supported a Presbyterian Board of Publications that would authorize books and tracts like a mint stamping a seal on "sterling coin," creating an official "currency" among the members of the church. As Presbyterians turned outward to face competing claims in America's crowded religious marketplace, they were also called to defend the truths of their confession. Theological controversies were important and necessary, Smyth believed, and he shocked his Episcopal neighbors in Charleston when in the late 1830s he had the bad form to publish vigorous scriptural defenses of Presbyterianism and criticisms of prelacy. But when he read his Bible, he found that the guidance offered there was not all of the same nature or consequence. Some doctrines (such as the Trinity and the atonement) he considered fundamental to Christianity and individual salvation. Other teachings about church government, discipline, and worship were more general guidelines that left some space for differences of opinion. This distinction allowed Smyth to support participation in interdenominational mission, Bible, tract, and education societies in which members of the various Christian denominations set aside their differences and worked toward common goals on the basis of their common faith.[44]

Thornwell read the Bible differently, and he and Smyth ended up replaying the constitutional arguments between strict and loose construction that Cooper and his political opponents had voiced in the 1820s. Old School Presbyterians severed their entanglements with interdenominational associations after the great national Old School–New School schism of 1837–38, creating their own boards for missions, education, and publication. But in the early 1840s Thornwell pressed the case further, arguing that even the Old School Presbyterian boards had become dangerous distractions. They had become quasi-independent hierarchical corporations drawing money, energy, and power from the church itself. Worst of all, the boards were unscriptural. Thornwell debated Smyth in the synod, and then the two traded lengthy articles in the press. "We lay it down as an universal principle," Smyth wrote, "that the imposition of any duty implies the correspondent right to use such means as are necessary to its discharge." This was true, he argued, of "any Constitution, civil or sacred." The Bible obliged the faithful to preach the Gospel throughout the world, for example, but left men to prudently devise means to accomplish that goal. Since the Bible did not forbid the creation of organizations like the boards, the church could create them. Although Smyth insisted that even "the most strict constructionists" among constitutional scholars agreed with this principle, he must have known that in South Carolina especially he would have sounded like the nationalists who had cited the "necessary and proper" clause in the U.S. Constitution as a warrant to consolidate power.[45]

Thornwell's premise was that "the Word of God is a perfect rule of practice as well as of faith." He therefore erased Smyth's distinction between essential doctrines of faith and less important rules of discipline and worship. The Presbyterian system as it had existed before the creation of benevolent associations and church boards had been dictated by the scriptures, Thornwell contended: all other "inventions" were condemned by "the *silence* of the Word of God." Where in the U.S. Constitution, strict constructionists had asked, was the language authorizing the creation of a national bank or road or canal? Where in the Bible, Thornwell asked, was the language authorizing the church to join or create quasi-independent bureaucracies for benevolent purposes? The answer was the same: nowhere.[46]

Smyth's interpretive principle was useful for harnessing the church to the strategies and energy of antebellum reform, including proslavery reform. Thornwell's principle, which would come to be called "the spirituality of the church," could function as a useful prophylactic against abolitionist agitation. Resisting Northern Christian reformers' attempts to interfere with Southern institutions, Christian conservatives could protest that the church had no biblical authorization to meddle with such social reforms and political questions: its scripturally sanctioned work was purely spiritual. In the late 1850s in the Old School Presbyterian General Assembly, Thornwell would reignite this debate over biblical warrant and the nature of the church, this time contending not with his South Carolina colleague Smyth but with the redoubtable Dr. Charles Hodge of Princeton. In the General Assembly of 1859, another opponent looked back to the Presbyterians' stalwart defense of liberty during the American Revolution and called the notion that the church must avoid "interfering" with politics and other temporal concerns "preposterous." These debates helped fan the flames as the Old School Presbyterian Church approached sectional schism and Civil War.[47]

The Southern Presbyterian leadership's conceptions of social and political power sprang from the way they read the Bible. While church leaders such as Smyth and Thornwell could disagree over the biblical license for social activism, they and their colleagues all argued that any commonsense reader of the scriptures could see that the Old Testament endorsed slavery and the New Testament enjoined slaves to obey their masters. Proslavery theologians had little patience for the casuistical contortions of the antislavery exegesis that tried to explain away scriptural support of slavery by confining those passages narrowly to the circumstances of ancient Israel or to the Roman Empire at the time of the Apostles. Such an interpretive move opened the door to questioning the premise that there was a single divine moral intelligence unifying all the books of the Bible from Genesis through Revelation, or went even further to the godless, historically contingent ethics that Thornwell had glimpsed in Thomas Cooper: "Dr. Cooper was an avowed materialist," Thornwell wrote, who "looked upon utility as the criterion of right.... Moral rules, according to Dr. Cooper, were flexible and variable." When Northern Christian abolitionists tried to dodge behind appeals to the general "spirit" of the faith rather than attending to the actual words in the text, they seemed to Southern white Christians after the 1830s less like loose constructionists misreading the scriptures than like infidels as bad as Cooper, trying to wage war on the Bible itself. When in 1845 abolitionist William Lloyd Garrison gave a polite bow to Thomas Paine for enabling him to see that not everything in the Bible was divinely inspired and that therefore morally objectionable passages could be discarded, he merely confirmed what the proslavery South had long suspected.[48]

Cooper had been so focused on Presbyterian scheming that he was unable to see that within the church itself some critics also attacked the fatuousness of the faith endorsed by public opinion, offering critiques from the other side of the theological spectrum that were not so different from his own. In 1839, J. C. Coit, pastor of the Presbyterian Church in Cheraw, pitched into what he called "the established Religion in the united States." In America's democracy, omnipotent public opinion, through "an active power of consolidation," had created a national church and subtly forced the citizenry to accept a vague, interdenominational American faith. This faith, however, was Christian in name only; it was not wrought by supernatural grace. It was the product of mere common sense and sentimentality, intuition and conformity. Despite all the cant about *sola scriptura*, Coit declared, "the popular zeal for circulating the printed Bible is a mere sham." All the tract societies, Sunday schools, and benevolent reform associations endowed the individual's own conscientious opinions, and not the scriptures, with sovereign authority. Self-love was the approved biblical hermeneutic, "the oracle within *every breast* being *the law* of *republican exposition*." This American faith worshipped the idol of human benevolence. It exalted "the sovereign self-determination of the human will" rather than the will of God. It looked to statistics about church membership rather than biblical miracles as sacred signs. Like Cooper (though for very different reasons), Coit believed that republican virtue and Christian piety were very different things, that secular education should not be confused with Christian indoctrination, and that one "cannot be too anxious to keep the lines of demarcation *distinct* and *well defined*, that separate the *Church* and the *State*."[49]

Yet there were other views of the proper relation of religion and politics even among other leading South Carolina Presbyterians. Benjamin M. Palmer, at the dedication of a new Presbyterian church in Columbia, noted that religion functioned "as a great instrument of conservation of bodies politic." Religion was about more than the individual's relation to God. It was also a "ligature of souls" to one another. Public worship was a kind of gravity that brought people together, drawing them out of the seclusion of the self and allowing them to exercise their social natures even as—for those few hours on Sunday, at least—the artificial distinctions of rank, wealth, and education were ignored. Christian public worship moderated the "spirit of unlicensed speculation" that could lead a person to doubt or error, and it muted individual differences in the pursuit of a common goal. Going to church was more than receiving instruction from the pulpit. Public worship blended the attainment of knowledge with ritual devotion; wisdom flowed from biblical truth, but it also echoed back from a community of souls. Church was not a lyceum, Palmer wrote. Nor was it Cooper's public arena, a forum for arriving at knowledge through a contest of reasoned argument and the presentation of empirical fact—a forum that left the cultivation of sensibility and sociability to private life. Public worship at once cultivated knowledge and acted as a social cohesive, laying the foundations for both Christian communion and political community.[50]

Other Presbyterian clergymen in the state were more specific about the connections between their religious practice and republican society. In published tracts and then in a book-length treatise in 1843, the Rev. Thomas Smyth of Charleston argued that Presbyterianism and the American political system were remarkably similar structures and that both were founded on republican principles. In both, "*the people*, under certain restrictions, [were] possessed of the supreme power." Republicanism, as Smyth defined it, was the sensible middle way between the extremes of true democracy (mob rule) and monarchical or aristocratic tyranny. In ecclesiastical terms, presbyterial republicanism was the mean between strict congregational autonomy and the hierarchical control of bishops and popes. Republicanism in church and state was government with liberty, and liberty without anarchy. Presbyterians elected ministers and lay elders who served in deliberative bodies that functioned according to a written constitution. Therefore, the Presbyterian form of church organization, Smyth offered, should seem familiar and attractive to every American citizen. This happy homology was hardly a coincidence. Republican principles, which included for Smyth those essential tenets that had so exercised Cooper—liberty of conscience, freedom of expression, and the separation of church and state—were developed first by Presbyterian and Puritan church reformers, long before the framers of the U.S. Constitution had been born. Looking to models of the Jewish church in the Old Testament and early Christianity before popish corruptions, he wrote, Protestant Reformers—especially Scottish Presbyterians in the seventeenth century—had rediscovered the form of government most conducive to ordered liberty in both religious and political life.[51]

In Smyth's political demonology, papists played the role that Presbyterians had for Cooper: they adhered to principles that were antithetical to republican equality and liberty—principles that were, Smyth argued (betraying no sense of irony), more like the relation of "Master and slave." Just as Cooper had suspected that Presbyterian clergymen were plotting to subvert the Constitution and establish Christianity, Smyth surmised that Catholic priests had "an *ulterior political design*, and that no less than the *entire subversion* of our *republican government*." Cooper's binary system, born of eighteenth-century enlightenment and revolution, imagined the (white, male, property-holding) individual in a struggle against tyrannical civil or ecclesiastical power. Smyth's mean-between-extremes republicanism put the pope on one side and anarchic, skeptical individualism on the other. A person should neither passively obey a despotic religious authority, the Charleston pastor argued, nor indulge in "free thinking, by which the mind is thrown loose upon its own vagrant notions," with the danger of being "brought to the verge of universal skepticism." The way to sail safely between these two dangers was in part to create a privileged class, an elected aristocracy of elders who, like senators in Congress, could function as "a check to the unreflecting passions and revolutionary spirit of the multitude." But republican institutions could only do so much. The Presbyterian synod or General Assembly, unlike a secular legislature, could not merely be a public arena for the contest of individual arguments and opinions—and here was where the similarity between the civil and the ecclesiastical broke down: "On all subjects in which man may be regarded as the author, the speaker, and the inquirer, there is ample room for discussion, and for unlimited diversity of sentiment. But in religion, where God is the Author...—where there can be but one right standard, and one right interpretation, we are limited by that word, and to be indifferent to it, is either blasphemy or presumption."[52]

The difference between Presbyterianism and civil republicanism was even wider for James Henley Thornwell. The representative government in the church, he argued, did not rest, as it did in the state, on the sovereignty of the people. Elders were elected but did not represent "the caprices of the people." They did not listen to "authoritative instructions" from their constituents. They were to "study and administer the laws of the Savior" in the Bible; they were to obey the dictates of Christ their king, found in the sacred text. [53]

But for Thornwell and other Presbyterians, acknowledging the difference between church and state, and supporting the institutional separation of church and state, were not the same as building a wall between religion and politics. Before midcentury, few South Carolina Presbyterian preachers went as far as the Rev. Richard B. Cater did in his saber-rattling 1833 fast sermon in support of Nullfication, a performance that was unusual for two reasons. First, many if not most of the state's Presbyterian clergymen were opposed to the Nullification radicals. Even though the revivals of 1831–32 in some areas of the lowcountry seemed to fuse evangelicalism to the new political movement, converting notable Nullifiers such as Robert Barnwell Rhett and Charles Cotesworth Pinckney, some Presbyterian revival promoters in the field saw the political frenzy draw energy away from, rather than catalyze, God's work. Other Presbyterian observers such as Smyth were sure that the partisan excitement was the vile product of Columbia, "the hotbed of nullification, infidelity, & every other evil," where "old Dr. Cooper sits like a spider in his web watching & ready to dart, although *secretly*, upon everyone who opposes these." Second, most clergymen considered that speaking directly on policy matters like Nullification was inappropriate in the pulpit. Benjamin Gildersleeve in the Charleston *Observer* warned that such worldly controversies unsettled the peace of mind and religious devotion not just of ministers but of any Christians. Yet a week later Gildersleeve was enthusiastically endorsing *The Relation of Christianity to Civil Government in the United*

States by the Rev. Dr. Jasper Adams, Episcopal president of the College of Charleston, a sermon that argued against the "infidel" (and Jeffersonian) notion that "Christianity has no connection with the law of the land, or with our civil and political institutions." Bible truths had to inform politics even if politics had to be kept at arm's length from religion.[54]

Thornwell, Smyth, and other Presbyterian writers helped white Southerners recognize racial slavery as their era's central test of a biblical faith. An 1847 visit to the Charleston Literary and Philosophical Society (informally known as the Conversation Club) by the renowned Harvard naturalist Louis Agassiz, who discussed the possibility of the multiple origins of the different human races, prompted Smyth to write articles about race that circulated in a half-dozen periodicals throughout the South. Smyth joined with John Bachman, a Charleston naturalist (and pastor of St. John's Lutheran Church), to combat the pluralist view that was finding favor among the Southern intelligentsia, especially physicians and other naturalists. The balder polygenetic claims of the freethinking physician Josiah Nott, a former protégé of Thomas Cooper's, goaded Smyth to expand his articles into a four-hundred-page treatise. While Bachman attacked the new ethnology as bad science, Smyth argued that the new theories trying to explain racial difference by positing multiple creations or suggesting that blacks and whites were not the same species were a direct challenge to the Bible. Undermining the authority of the scriptures and promoting religious skepticism, he suspected darkly, were the real motives behind this supposedly scientific ethnology. Not only did the Old Testament give an account of human creation, but the New Testament explicitly proclaimed that all nations were of one blood (Acts 17:26). Moreover, the unity of mankind was essential to the Bible's central message: all sinned with Adam, and all were eligible to be redeemed by Christ. Smyth mined his nine-thousand-volume personal library and spent hundreds of pages showing how the best historical evidence, linguistic analysis, and natural science also supported the "unity of the human races." Even if all the scholarship failed to persuade, the doctrine of human unity was ultimately an essential matter of religious "faith," determined by "the same rules of historical criticism which decide every other doctrine of the Bible."[55]

Thornwell agreed that polygenesis was skeptical infidelity's latest weapon against the Bible. He argued from the Scottish Common Sense principles that had shaped his thinking since he had memorized long passages of Dugald Stewart as a young teenager. All human beings were naturally religious, he asserted. The existence of God was "nearly a self-evident truth," and man's "mind craves a God even more intensely than his heart craves society." (Religious skepticism was the unnatural result of when we "mystify ourselves with vain deceit" in the form of long chains of speculation.) All human races and nations—even, Thornwell believed, the rudest savages in Africa—shared this religious character. The Bible was meant for all of them. "No Christian man, therefore, can give any countenance to speculations which trace the negro to any other parent than Adam," Thornwell wrote. "Those who defend slavery upon the plea that the African is not of the same stock with ourselves are... [in] conflict with the dearest doctrine of the Gospel."[56]

The *Southern Presbyterian Review*, too, pounded away at the new ethnography and its challenge to the unity of the human species. The editors' main concern was to "forestall that skepticism, which we apprehend was about to be revived among us." Josiah Nott's *Two Lectures on the Connection between the Biblical and Physical History of Man* (1849) in particular made it clear that these new men of science were aiming at "denial of the plenary inspiration and present integrity of the scriptures, of the genuineness of the Pentateuch, and indeed of the credibility of any and every portion of the word of God which the advocates of the Unity have supposed to bear on the question." Two reviewers of Nott's book were equally aghast; one felt when reading it as if he were "in the society of Thomas Paine, Rosseau [sic], and Voltaire." The reviewer found Nott's argument against the reliability of the Pentateuch quite familiar: "It used to greet us some twenty years ago from the walls of our State College." But one could use the same arguments that denied Mosaic authorship—"the absurdity of this whole method of higher criticism"—to "prove that Dr. Cooper did not write the treatise on political economy, once issued in his name." George Howe contributed articles reviewing Samuel George Morton's *Crania Americana* (1839), among other books. Abner A. Porter did not blanch when confronting the great Agassiz of Harvard, for, the Presbyterian wrote, a truth-loving man who finds an error running loose through the world will try to strangle it "as he would a mad-dog, no matter whose name is written on the collar."[57]

The writers thought they were encountering a new form of skeptical infidelity even when their opponents professed to be Christians who revered the Bible. The "skeptical doubts" about the scriptures voiced by d'Alembert, Condorcet, and Voltaire in the previous century, complained one essay, were "anew thrust forth." "The generation of Deists and skeptics is not yet extinct," warned John B. Adger. Eighteenth-century infidelity, they argued, had tried but failed to reject the scriptures with arguments based on philological and historical evidence. The new higher critics and Rationalist theologians, to whom the ethnologists often turned when trying to discount scriptural evidence for the unity of the species, now looked inward, found the divine spark in human genius, and proclaimed the Bible inspired the way Shakespeare's plays were inspired. The new infidelity the Presbyterians combatted, then, combined the "self-complacent skepticism" of authors such as Nott, Agassiz, and Morton with the misplaced faith in human reason of critics such as Johann Gottfried Eichhorn, Wilhelm Gesenius, Henrich

Ewald, Wilhelm de Wette, and David Strauss, who turned the Bible into "a thing of wax to be shaped at will by any Philosopher" who devises a new theory.[58]

If the Bible established the unity of the human "race" (species) with infallible certainty, it was admittedly less clear on the origins of "racial" difference (varieties within the species). Proslavery Christians had their proof texts to plainly show that God endorsed slavery; why and how God made Africans a degraded branch of humanity best suited to that condition remained more mysterious. The proslavery Southern Presbyterians were not, contrary to what some commentators have said, confusing the biblical justification of color-blind slavery as such with the biblical support for African slavery as it existed in the South. Nor did they fail to appreciate that their scriptural arguments for modern African enslavement had to be supplemented by what they considered to be historical and empirical evidence confirming that Providence in the current epoch had suited Africans to servitude. Smyth thought that the best racial science confirmed three basic varieties of mankind, which corresponded to Noah's three sons: Ham, Shem, and Japeth. But he concluded that it was relatively unimportant whether God impressed different branches of the human family with different intellectual and physical characteristics at the time of Cain, after the Flood, with the dispersion at Babel, or at the Exodus from Egypt, or produced those differences more gradually over generations in which the separate stocks reproduced in different providentially orchestrated social, political, and environmental circumstances. The facts of "racial" (varietal) difference were obvious. A stable of prancing Thoroughbreds and a field of sway-backed plow horses were all clearly horses, though their distinguishing characteristics were just as apparent. In the mid-nineteenth century, blacks were manifestly a corrupted and depraved branch of the human tree, Smyth asserted, voicing the virulent white prejudice of his time; he assumed that on average their intellectual abilities were considerably below those of whites, not because they were created with deficient brains but because God had providentially suited them to different tasks and a lower social station. Just as, in His plentitude, God seemed to devise diverse forms of life to fit every ecological niche, just so had He suited some nations to extract material wealth from the abundant world and privileged others to intellectually organize and direct that extraction, for the greater good of humanity as a whole. God, therefore, and not the visionary philosophers who tried to outthink Him, was a utilitarian social engineer. Society, as Thornwell put it, was not the machinery of man but the ordinance of God.[59]

As human beings, then, even black slaves had certain inalienable rights—though the list was short. Slaves had the right to obey God, wrote the Rev. John B. Adger, Smyth's brother-in-law, in *The Christian Doctrine of Human Rights and of Slavery* (1849); they had the moral freedom, Thornwell preached the following year, to show reverence to God by serving their masters. The fatal mistake that abolitionists made, both men argued, was in abstracting other rights from their necessary and particular social, political, and providential circumstances, and then using these abstracted and fanciful "human rights" to deny biblical truth. The rights of fatherhood only apply to actual fathers; the rights of property only pertain to those who own property; the right to vote in an American election is held only by duly qualified citizens of the United States. Most rights are not universal but are contingent upon specific social relations or political institutions. The conservative Southern Presbyterians came to the same conclusion about equality, too, that Cooper had, but by a different route. Few things were clearer in the Bible, they argued, than the fact that spiritual and moral equality did *not* entail social and political equality. When the Apostle wrote that "there is neither Jew nor Greek, there is neither bond nor free, there is neither male nor female: for ye are all one in Christ Jesus" (Gal. 3:28), he meant that Christianity was apart from and superior to those identities, not that it destroyed them while Christians lived in the world. The Christian life was lived within the social relations in which one found oneself. The Golden Rule, both Thornwell and Smyth argued, did not mean doing unto others as if particular asymmetric social relations (parent to child, husband to wife, rich to poor) did not exist, but treating the other person as you would wish to be treated if the roles and circumstances were reversed.[60]

Christianity bound master and slave in a moral relation; it embedded the basic fact of the master's ownership of the slave's labor in a set of divinely sanctioned reciprocal duties. The Christian master, the South Carolina Presbyterian clergymen argued, acknowledged the humanity of his slave. He understood the slave's natural yearning for God and his need for the Gospel. When Southern whites, out of fear provoked by rumored or actual slave uprisings like Denmark Vesey's in Charleston in 1822 or Nat Turner's in Virginia in 1831, tried to prevent slave literacy (to avoid liberationist misinterpretations of scripture) or slaves' religious assemblies, they were neglecting their Christian duties. If not taught how to read, slaves would misread on their own; if not permitted to worship in controlled circumstances, they would gather in secret; if not assigned white preachers, they would choose spiritual leaders from among themselves. Both Smyth and Thornwell, therefore, supported the reformist mission to slaves.

The Rev. Charles Colcock Jones, the Presbyterian "Apostle to the Negro Slaves" in Georgia who also taught at the Columbia Theological Seminary, had been writing for years in the Charleston *Observer* and elsewhere, complaining of white apathy—or outright resistance—to slave Christianization. Not only was it the ruling race's Christian duty to preach the Gospel to the enslaved, he argued, but doing so was also sound policy. "Let [religious] infidelity prevail among the negroes and a foundation is laid broad and deep for confusion and every evil work," Jones wrote in 1835; Christianizing the slave population was the key to the security and prosperity of the South. Jones himself owned three plantations and held over a hundred slaves. "Physical force may be resorted to," he warned in another publication, "but the growing population of our slaves, and their restless discontentment, will soon prove the utter insufficiency of all coercive measures." The Gospel, by contrast, would "extinguish the flame of discontentment."[61]

Yet preaching to slaves remained controversial in South Carolina. In Columbia in 1833, it was rumored that a visiting Presbyterian missionary might have said something inappropriate to slaves—a mention of Liberia. A mob attacked a stagecoach about to cross the Columbia Bridge, looking for the minister and threatening to cut out his tongue and cast it "upon a dunghill." The Presbyterian press blamed Cooper and his friends because the outrage must have been "the result of principles that have been industriously instilled into this community, viz. that religion is a cheat, and a Clergyman a knave, and the Bible a tale." In 1847, when Charleston's Episcopalians started erecting a building to house a black congregation, a white crowd in this "city full of churches" threatened to tear it down. A similar plan proposed by Thomas Smyth's brother-in-law John B. Adger of Smyth's Second Presbyterian Church in Charleston faced resistance even from within Presbyterianism. A. G. McGrath of Charleston's First Presbyterian Church, soon to be a U.S. district court judge, denounced Adger's plan in the pages of the Charleston *Mercury* and was supported by his pastor and the newspaper's editor, along with white mechanics (roused to resent the city's blacks) and other white Charlestonians who were still haunted by memories of Denmark Vesey (who had, indeed, been a member of Charleston's Second Presbyterian Church). With assurances that the black Presbyterians would remain entirely under the supervision of whites, and that the Gospel made obedient slaves and not dangerous rebels, other city leaders endorsed the idea, and the Anson Street Church was erected in 1850. Reverend Thornwell preached "The Christian Doctrine of Slavery" at its dedication, the congregation that day being entirely white.[62]

Christian leaders such as Jones, Smyth, Adger, and Thornwell answered the increasingly vitriolic moral critique of slavery emanating from the North. They wrapped the South's domestic and political institutions in a holy embrace, and they justified slavery and the structure of Southern society with the transcendent authority of Holy Writ. They tried to speak to and for slave masters—and slave mistresses as well. By giving religious and moral legitimacy to white supremacy, they also spoke to nonslaveholding whites. Cooper had addressed slavery as an economic and political matter but left its personal relations to the realm of private life. He merely offered the vague hope that the manners of the "natural" aristocracy, smoothed and softened by the progress of knowledge and sociability in the modern age, would indirectly mitigate the cruelties and abuses that could attend a slave system. The Presbyterians argued, in contrast, that without the biblical bonds binding master and servant—with no "common standard of truth and duty"—the masters would indeed come to resemble the abolitionists' caricature and consider their slaves as merely brutes or things. Slaveholders would be driven only by profit, self-interest, and the whims of public opinion; slaves would have no motive to work peacefully and industriously other than the whip. The result for the South, Smyth wrote, would be "suicidal."[63]

Proslavery Christianity spoke clearly and directly to the intimate relations of family life and the psychological needs of a white minority desperate to maintain social control. Even as slaveholders resisted clerical calls for the state to mandate that slaves be catechized, they could fashion themselves as "good" masters under the penumbra of Christian legitimation. "Paternalism," though, is not quite the right term to convey even the ideal that Presbyterian leaders prescribed for the South in the pulpit and the press, much less the reality of Southern slavery. Charleston Baptist Richard Furman, in an important address to the governor of South Carolina in 1823, wrote about the familial bonds of slavery, and Presbyterians, too, could sometimes describe master-slave relations as an extension of the sentiments of family life. George Howe, in an article called "The Baptism of Servants," for example, described the affectionate obligations of the Christian master: "As the husband is to shelter and provide for the wife of his bosom, as the parent is to care for the children God has given him, so, with those just modifications the relation supposes, is the master to care for, protect and cherish the bond-servants." More frequently, however, Southern Presbyterians recognized the limitations of the family analogy. One writer was careful to distinguish between family government (parents over children) and household government (masters over slaves). Another drew distinctions even as he likened masters to parents: if "the responsibilities of the master are analogous to those of the parent," E. T. Baird wrote, mentioning parents training their children and providing for basic needs, in other "respects they are more fearful and abiding," masters being more like magistrates who control, restrain, and punish. Presbyterians sometimes admitted that sentiment could not transcend the barrier of race. A report by the Charleston Presbytery in 1854, "The Organization, Instruction, and Discipline of the Colored People," acknowledged the "want of social sympathy between the two races" and their *moral and spiritual uncongeniality.*"[64]

Sometimes the language of family government—of slavery as a domestic institution—was merely a shield against any interference by church or state with a master's property rights. Outside institutions had no right to intrude upon the "household estate," an anonymous writer argued, and they had no reason to intrude because "the softening influence and social intercourse of the family relation" would naturally prevent any abuses. This position, though published in the *Southern Presbyterian Review* and later championed by a Baptist newspaper in

Columbia, differed little from Thomas Cooper's: paternalist sentiment merely sugarcoated what was in essence an ideology grounded in property rights.⁶⁵

James Henley Thornwell's Christian slavery, by contrast, neither surrendered the institution to the brutal dictates of the laissez-faire marketplace nor bedewed it with sentimental paternalism. He did hope that one day "every Christian master will feel, that he is somewhat in the same sense responsible for the religious education of his slaves as for the religious education of his children." A key word in this passage, however, is "somewhat." The theologian likened slaves to children again in the same essay on the following page, arguing that it would make as much sense to allow slaves to preach as it would to ordain children. Rather than getting entangled by misleading paternal analogies, Thornwell taught that the master-slave relationship was based upon labor and was bound by reciprocal moral duties: "As the labour of the slave is expended for their [the masters'] benefit, they are bound, by the double consideration of justice and mercy, to care for his soul." Slaves were less extensions of the family under the authority of the great white parent than a providentially subordinate laboring class. Southern slaves, as both Thornwell and Adger preached and wrote in support of the Anson Street black congregation in Charleston, were less like children than like the dependent urban poor in Britain and Northern cities. Adger expressed the tortuous blend of intimate relation yet insurmountable difference: "Nowhere are the poor more distinctly marked out than our poor; and yet, strange to say, nowhere are the poor so closely and intimately connected with the higher classes as our poor with us. They belong to us. We also belong to them. They are divided out among us and mingled up with us. They live with us...forming parts of the same families." Yet despite all this, "they are a class separated from ourselves by their color, their position in society, their relation to our families, their natural origin, and their moral, intellectual and physical condition." Slaveholders had one main moral obligation to them. As Thornwell put it, voicing a sentiment that had been officially endorsed by the Synod of South Carolina and Georgia, "Our design in giving them the Gospel, is not to civilize them—not to change their social condition—not to exalt them into citizens or freemen—it is to save them."⁶⁶

The rhetoric of sentimental paternalism seems even more distant from the realities of South Carolina slaveholding. Proslavery reformers in the presbyteries wrung their hands over the problem of slave marriages—unrecognized by the state and frequently dissolved by slave sales. This embarrassment did not prevent the Christian owners of the enslaved men and women who attended the Presbyterian church from selling off husbands or wives when economic concerns so dictated. On the very day in 1845 that Jones, Adger, and the interdenominational elite of Charleston met in the Depository on Chalmers Street to discuss slave missions, Thomas Ryan's slave market down the street was auctioning off over thirty enslaved people, from six years of age to "elderly." The roll book of the Zion church (the black Presbyterian successor to Anson Street) is filled with the names of enslaved members dismissed because they were "sold away." Thornwell nodded in passing to proposed reforms that would encourage masters to try to keep slave families intact, but his overwhelming focus was on religious instruction.[67]

In other ways, too, Presbyterian leaders such as Thornwell and Smyth demonstrated little sense that they thought of their slaves as family. For someone so committed to Calvinist theology and the Presbyterian way, Thornwell was surprisingly content to have a white Methodist preach to his own plantation slaves, which at least one South Carolina presbytery condemned as a "very objectionable" practice. (In setting aside his own particular theological commitments and acknowledging the utility of Methodism for the enslaved, he was not so different from his former teacher Cooper, the religious skeptic who gave his slave Sancho a Bible and encouraged him to attend Methodist class meetings on Tuesday evenings.) Thomas Smyth's wife, Margaret, whined about "impudent" slaves, wishing she could be rid of them; Smyth's father, the devout Samuel, not only bitterly opposed abolition but preferred to have slaves stay in the fields rather "than have one of them Dirty lazy Animals about the house." Reverend Smyth himself would not let his children play with the black children in his household, and when one of his young "body servants," Edward, who had to attend to the feeble pastor's needs around the clock, ran off, Smyth did not hesitate to send the slave to Charleston's public workhouse to be whipped. When another body servant, Burt, was captured after running away, Smyth simply sold him.[68]

Perhaps these households were families in a sense rather different from those celebrated by bourgeois sentiment in the North, even if slaveholders could employ that sentimental rhetoric when it suited their purposes. One study of antebellum South Carolina has argued that the Nullification revivals of 1831–32 fused evangelicalism and proslavery politics by sacralizing the patriarchal family, giving divine sanction to the authority of white male heads of households as the foundation of social and moral order. This view may very well explain much of the appeal of Christianity to the large numbers of white men who followed their wives into the churches in the 1830s, '40s, and '50s. The appeal for the white women, who made up about 60 percent of the communicants in any given congregation, was less straightforward: the message of Christian salvation may have "offered them hope, self-respect, [and] a means of self-assertion," but the model of passive and submissive evangelical womanhood made them "agents of their own subordination" to their domestic masters. Yet this notion of a broad, evangelical, patriarchal "familialism" (Baptist, Methodist, or Presbyterian) can mask how the Presbyterians, in particular, by articulating the biblical grounds and Christian character of Southern slavery, were trying to do more than sanctify the mastery of white men over their households. White patriarchs, the Presbyterians insisted, derived their power from but also had to bow to the dictates of the Bible.[69]

The leading Presbyterian proslavery reformers did not think that individual masters—either tenderly paternal or sternly patriarchal—were the answer to the problem of slave Christianization either, however much preachers and writers harped on the moral duties demanded of the Christian slaveholder. Many slaveholders, the reformers knew, were not themselves connected to a church. Even those masters who were would not have had the best information about the moral behavior and spiritual development of their slaves. Increasingly, too, slaveholders—church members and nonadherents alike—were moving to cities and towns as they sent their slaves to work on distant plantations under the supervision of overseers who were instructed to put profits above all else. In such circumstances, a Southern Presbyterian pastoral address to the General Assembly was still admitting as late as 1863, there was no chance for "domestic ties" to develop between master and slave, and therefore Southern slavery still did not function as the patriarchal institution described in the Bible.

Practically speaking, then, the responsibility for slave Christianization shifted from families to churches and whole communities. Yet Presbyterians were unsure about how to proceed with the work. Episcopalians, they thought, stressed catechetical instruction and religious exercises that might hinder blacks' religious development, but the Baptists, who allowed black churches and preachers, fostered too much dangerous independence. The Presbyterian model established with the Anson Street Church had a separate black congregation under the supervision of a white minister who was chosen and continually supervised by the presbytery. Rural missionaries had an even greater challenge. Imagine, one country pastor said at a meeting in Barnwell in 1847, a parish with forty to fifty plantations, 2,000 to 2,500 people, and four hundred black church members scattered over six hundred square miles. A missionary might be able to visit a plantation once a month, but he would need the help of enslaved church members—"watchmen"—to enforce Christian discipline and perpetuate worship in his absence. In both the rural and urban models, however, the Presbyterian Church assigned the responsibility of Christian discipline and the education of slaves to itself, working through clergymen specifically devoted to the task, though in practice enslaved and free black class leaders such as Thomas Catto and John Mathews of Charleston's Second Presbyterian Church provided much of the pastoral care to black Presbyterians.[70]

Charles Colcock Jones, the leading Presbyterian missionary to the slaves, argued that the work was intellectually as well as physically and emotionally demanding. The missionary to slaves battled depravity, ignorance, and superstition but also universalism, deism, and skepticism. That Jones had to face thoroughgoing skepticism as well as competing forms of spiritual belief should have made Thornwell rethink his view that skepticism only arose among bookish young men who were too fond, as he himself had been, of philosophical speculation. John Adger, who became the first pastor at Anson Street, was not particularly successful at facing these challenges, though the popular preacher who replaced him built the black Presbyterian congregation in Charleston to over five hundred by 1860, with three times that number attending services every Sunday (the nonwhite population of Charleston and its suburbs at the time, however, was over twenty thousand). In general, Southern whites were never very enthusiastic about funding such missionary efforts. Into the 1860s, proponents of slave missions were still blaming that lack of popular support on a reaction to the meddling of Northern abolitionists. The haughty disdain that whites showed for even the most pious of their black brothers and sisters in Christ in all of Charleston's churches, recalled by an anonymous black Presbyterian in a letter to Smyth after the war, was no doubt a more valid reason for the missions' muted success.[71]

By midcentury, Presbyterian writers seemed convinced that they had defeated if not extinguished religious skepticism among the white population in the South, even as they saw the madness of religious infidelity dominate the North. The Episcopal theologian James Warley Miles in Charleston was "perhaps alone among Southern theologians of his time" in taking the "psychological reality" of skepticism seriously and understanding "that widespread atheism was about to become a historical possibility, perhaps a probability"; the Presbyterian E. A. Nisbet expressed a more widely held satisfaction among Southern churchgoers "that there is less infidelity, and less of what might be called perverted Christianity at the South, than at any part of the world." Nisbet happily noted that "open repudiation of the Scriptures is rare," and "not one hearer in fifty needs to be convinced of any essential truth of Christianity." The commitment to Christian proslavery as the central tenet of Southern white identity was a key. In 1850, Smyth voiced the increasingly common idea that the South had "a high and holy mission" sanctioned by God's Word. It was "the duty of the South to perpetuate the present relations of master and servant, for the mutual and best interests of both parties, [and] she must do it as to the Lord." Religion, morality, and politics all aligned. Thornwell wrote in the same year that the slavery issue was really a battle between "atheists, socialists, communists, red republicans, Jacobins on the one side, and the friends of order and regulated freedom on the other." In sum, "Christianity and Atheism [were] the combatants." Yet if resistance to slave missions in the white Christian South could nonetheless make the devout sometimes doubt the depth of the professedly Christian public's biblical faith, the South Carolina movement to reopen the slave trade in the 1850s was even more of a shock.[72]

The cotton boom of the 1850s had fueled visions of slavery's expansion, and large slaveholders in the lowcountry had begun agitating to reverse the half-century-old constitutional ban on the transatlantic trade. In November 1856, South Carolina governor James H. Adams endorsed the idea. Committees in the state house and senate published reports supporting it the following year. Debate exploded in 1858 when the navy brought the *Echo*, an illegal slaver captured off Cuba, into Charleston's port and unloaded the human cargo: the 144 (of the original 314) enslaved Africans who had survived the voyage. Articles in the Charleston *Mercury* argued for a legal and "reformed" transatlantic trade. John B. Adger joined writers in the *Southern Episcopalian* to cautiously condemn the idea. In an essay in the *Southern Presbyterian Review* that was also published as a pamphlet, Adger criticized the recommendations in the committee reports as bad policy but found the greatest fault in their seemingly casual assumption that a proslavery citizenry would not have serious moral and religious objections to a revived trade. "In the name of the Southern people, especially of the religious class at the South, and still more especially of Southern Presbyterians, we raise our voice of protest against the re-opening amongst us of the African slave trade, whether openly or in disguise."[73]

The chairman of the senate committee and author of its report, Edward B. Bryan, quickly answered Adger in an anonymous pamphlet that challenged Adger's claim to speak for the Southern people, for the "religious class," or even for Presbyterians. Only a synod, declaring its interpretation of the scriptures, Bryan wrote, could speak for the Presbyterian Church. As for public opinion, Bryan argued that nearly all the opposition to a reopened trade was on policy and not moral grounds, and this was true for "many excellent Presbyterians" as well. And that, he scolded Adger, was the proper ground for political dispute. In a polity where church was separated from state, bills and laws needed to be measured against the Constitution, and policy decisions against a calculation of dollars and cents—and little else. Citizens were allowed to worship God in their own way and could even be immoral as long as they paid their taxes and followed the laws. "If pork is not to be taxed to please the Jew, nor fish to hurt the Catholic, why should government exclude the African to please the Presbyterian?" Bryan did not apologize for his tone: Adger had left his own "sphere," where he was "clothed with the prestige of an ambassador of Christ," and had "entered the political arena" where men revered nothing but the truth. In that arena, the clergyman might be surprised to learn, statesmen were as skilled in hermeneutics as he was in his: "Legislators, in their temporal sphere, consult Calhoun, Puffendorf, Aristotle, Moses, and other great lawgivers and philosophers, with the same care and with equal intelligence and success, that the reverend reviewer, in his spiritual sphere, consults the Gospel and its inspired commentators." Further, simple logic, Bryan contended, destroyed the distinction that Adger tried to make between slaveholding (which was virtuous) and slave trading (allegedly immoral), and simple facts belied his assertion that New Englanders and the British but not South Carolinians had been responsible for the slave trade that existed before the 1808 ban.[74]

But Bryan's critique was most devastating when it first attacked the Presbyterian clergyman with an appeal to the Bible and then undercut the reliability of any such appeal. Like the writer who answered the *Southern Episcopalian* in the Charleston *Mercury*, Bryan demanded that Adger cite biblical "chapter and verse" to prove his doctrine. Adger's vague condemnations of "man-stealing," Bryan warned, sounded suspiciously similar to the rhetoric of abolitionists. Yet abolitionists, though wrong about the Bible, were at least consistent in treating slavery and the slave trade as one. Bryan seconded what the Southern Presbyterians and other proslavery Christians had repeated for decades: the Bible was clear about slavery; Moses endorsed it, and Christ did not abrogate it. Bryan simply followed the same logic, quoting the sacred text to show that God's chosen people were allowed to buy and sell heathen bondservants. "Time cannot alter the edicts of Sinai," Bryan wrote—or was Adger one of those "modernizing" Christians who posited that "some great convulsion in the moral world" had subsequently rewritten the Bible's moral law? But perhaps, Bryan admitted disingenuously, he himself was wrong about what the plain words of the scripture actually said. He was no theologian. Of course, "learned theologians sometimes put their own interpretation upon the facts as well as the precepts of the Bible: in which cases, we will not positively deny that the wish is father to the thought. A very large and very intelligent portion of the Northern and British clergy, for example, piously contend that slavery is prohibited in the Bible, and do not hesitate to claim Christ for an abolitionist." The Bible might be a useful guide to public policy, but the refined sophistry of professional exegetes was not. Adger could only respond weakly in the *Southern Presbyterian Review* by restating his opinion and worrying about a providential punishment of the South. He did not comment about what the slave trade debate revealed about the biblical grounds of political power.[75]

By the birth of the Confederacy, many Southern Presbyterians, including the great proponent of the spirituality of the church, James Henley Thornwell, would recast the relationship of religion and the state, and the role of the Bible in informing the constitution of each. In a sermon marking the death of John C. Calhoun in 1850, preached in the chapel of South Carolina College, Thornwell had addressed the "present crisis" in the country. After noting that atheists and skeptics were as foolish to deny the hand of Providence in such a death as they were to reject the scriptures as divinely inspired, he argued that although the church must remain separate from the state—meaning that no particular denomination or religious "species" could be established by the government—religious concerns remained central to the fate of the nation and to the proper functioning of the state. The religious responsibility to fear God, revere the Gospel, and believe in Jesus Christ did not fall on the nation as "an organic whole" but on "the *individuals* who collectively compose it." Governmental officials and citizens alike had to meet these obligations as they performed their public functions; they personally shared in the nation's corporate sins and would be punished for them in the afterlife. A decade later, however, what some Presbyterians liked to call the separate "orbits" of religion and politics had become much more closely aligned, even for Thornwell.[76]

In November 1860, on the South Carolina fast day declared after Lincoln's election, as Thornwell opened the Book of Isaiah, he did more than merely apply general biblical principles to a day of trouble and rebuke. He preached politics, though he squirmed a little as he did so. He was "anxious," he confessed, that he might be crossing the line of propriety. He explained that for twenty-five years he had "never introduced secular politics into the instructions of the pulpit." A minister had "no authority to expound to senators of the Constitution of the State, nor to interpret for judges the law of the land." The "angry disputes of the forum" had no place in "the house of the Lord." Yet a preacher, he continued, in applying divine teachings by inculcating civil obedience and chastising public sins, could not help but allude to his own human political theories and opinions. So between biblical principles (which were the minister's duty to preach) and specific policy recommendations (which would be improper for him to offer) was the realm where the moral logic of biblical doctrine intersected with reasoning from "the nature and structure of Government" and "the common grounds of historical knowledge." It was precisely here, at the meeting of biblical exegesis and political ideology—the sweet spot of political hermeneutics—that this champion of the spirituality of the church articulated the Christian character of the state.[77]

A political state ought to be grounded in Christian faith, Thornwell argued: "As the subjects of a State must have religion in order to be truly obedient, and as it is the true religion alone which converts obedience into a living principle, it is obvious that a Commonwealth can no more be organized, which shall recognize all religions, than one which shall recognize none. The sanctions of its laws must have a centre of unity some where. To combine in the same government contradictory systems of faith, is as hopelessly impossible as to constitute into one State men of different races and languages." And South Carolina was such a Christian state: "We accept the Bible as the great moral charter by which our laws must be measured." The United States was another matter. Though not God's New Israel in a special covenant with the Lord and not even, in the strictest sense, a single nation at all, it had been "a city set upon a hill" with a manifest destiny "to redeem this continent, to spread freedom, civilization, and religion through the whole length of the land." But the North had broken the constitutional compact with the South, and the once-great Union was about to dissolve.[78]

In 1861, with the beginning of the Confederacy, Thornwell saw the opportunity to correct what he now considered to be the flaws in the former religio-political system and the moral economy it set in motion. Our forefathers had erred, Thornwell now argued: the American way had flattered the democratic will of the people but had dishonored the revealed will of God. No longer so squeamish about the church dictating constitutional principles to the state, he penned a petition on behalf of the Southern Presbyterian General Assembly to the Congress of the Confederate States of America. It praised the new Confederate Constitution's explicit invocation of the favor and guidance of God. But Thornwell and his twelve cosigners wanted to go further. Now he argued that religious obligations did fall upon the nation "considered in its organic capacity as a person." In his vision of Confederate Christianity there would still be no establishment of a particular church, but "the separation of Church and State is a very different thing from the separation of religion and the State." He proposed that Christianity be formally proclaimed as the state religion of the C.S.A.[79]

The religious establishment he had in mind would not, he insisted, infringe upon the individual's rights of conscience: "He may be Atheist, Deist, Infidel, Turk or Pagan: it is no concern of the State, so long as he walks orderly." Even government officials would not have to profess the faith personally—a Jew could be a governor—as long as they swore to defend Christianity as "the religion of the State" and the rule of "public conscience." But the Confederate Constitution's guarantee of religious liberty required a fifty-eight-word addendum beginning with "Nevertheless," Thornwell and his fellow petitioners argued: "Nevertheless, we, the people of these Confederate States, distinctly acknowledge our responsibility to God, and the supremacy of His Son, Jesus Christ, as King of kings and Lord of lords; and hereby ordain that no law shall be passed by the Congress of these Confederate States inconsistent with the will of God, as revealed in the Holy Scriptures." The Bible would then be the higher law regulating the state as it already regulated the church, but with a difference. For the church, Thornwell explained, the Bible served as a positive prescription: "Nothing shall be done but what they [the scriptures] enjoin"; for the state, the scriptures would be a negative check on power: "Nothing shall be done which they forbid."[80]

The petition was debated (and ultimately tabled) in the General Assembly, and debated further in the press. One delegate insisted that the time was ripe: even worldly politicians and the secular press were speaking of Stonewall Jackson as an exemplar of Southern piety, and "the mind of our whole people was become Christian." Others raised theological, political, and practical questions: If we should acknowledge the Son as well as the Father, why not the Holy Spirit, too? Does the political empowerment of divine law interfere with the sovereignty of the people? Would this establishment of Trinitarian Protestantism drive Catholics, Unitarians, deists, and Jews away from the Southern cause? Professor Thomas E. Peck of Union Theological Seminary in Virginia argued that there was "no magic in the name of Christ emblazoned in our Constitution and on our banners to transform us into a Christian people." How could the Confederacy call itself a Christian nation? Not even half of its adult white citizens professed to believe in Christ, and far fewer had felt the transforming power of grace. The church was a supernatural institution, derived from the authority of God as savior and restorer, and directed by the Bible, but the state was a natural institution, instituted by God the creator and moral governor, and directed by the light of nature and man's reason. The best model of the relation between the two, Peck insisted, was the Virginia one articulated by Jefferson's "Bill for Establishing Religious Freedom" and supported by Virginia Presbyterians during the Revolutionary War. It was the best way to steer a path between fanatics who wanted none but born-again saints to guide the ship of state and "tender-conscienced atheists, also, who are shocked at the recognition of a God at all in the administration of government."[81]

Their biblical faith was so bound up with their commitment to slavery and the white Southern way of life, it was no wonder that when they felt threatened by Northern aggression the leadership of Southern white Presbyterianism—like official Southern white Christianity generally—responded with a holy crusade. On the South Carolina fast day observed after Lincoln's election in 1860, Thornwell called on the state to persevere through what might be "a baptism in blood." Smyth echoed the sentiment in a letter on New Year's Eve 1860, two weeks after the state had seceded from the Union: "Blood must be shed! In an awful sense, without the shedding of blood there can be no peace, no at-one-ment." A quarter century earlier, Thomas Cooper, taking his hearth-brush in hand, had performed an old man's pathetic pantomime of South Carolinians settling their argument over constitutional interpretation on the battlefield. Blood would, indeed, be shed, but not just over the Constitution. On June 13, 1861, the Rev. Thomas Smyth celebrated the Battle of Fort Sumter: "We have crossed swords with the Northern Confederacy over the Bible," he exulted. It was a triumph over "despotism and infidelity." The war had begun, and as they banged their war drums, Southern clergymen like Smyth loudly proclaimed in the pulpit and in print what the struggle was really about. "Now, the whole movement in the South is based upon God's Word, simply and sincerely interpreted, believed, and obeyed."[82]

In South Carolina, as in other states throughout the Confederacy, the formerly "secular" press—and not just clergymen in pulpits and religious periodicals—preached the sacred cause of Southern independence. Newspapers taught biblical lessons about the divine purposes behind battlefield defeats and wartime afflictions while assuring readers that God was on their side. Articles rehearsed the North's religious infidelity—its false interpretation of the Bible, fanatical attacks on Christianity, and even turn toward atheism. Others celebrated the Confederate nation as God's special people, chosen from among all the world to maintain the true principles and institutions of the Gospel. Letters from soldiers begged for Bibles; letters from ladies prayed for Carolina soil to drink Yankee blood. Poetry urged Southerners to "Stand and conquer! / In the name of the mighty God" beneath the Confederate flag, "Our Southern cross" and "Sacred Sign."[83]

Biblical warrants, political preaching, and the enthusiastic support of the major Southern white Christian churches were essential components in the construction of Confederate nationalism. The public theology articulated by conservative evangelicals and Christian ideologues since the 1830s took a new turn and sacralized the state at the bloody baptism of the C.S.A. But the Confederate Christianity proclaimed in the pulpit, broadcast by the press, and invoked by the Jefferson Davis administration's ten fast and two thanksgiving days was less a monolithic consensus than a public silencing of the religiously indifferent, of the skeptical, and of those who still preferred a wall of separation not just between church and state but between religion and politics. Secular proslavery arguments, nonreligious fashioning of Southern white identity, and merely pragmatic justifications for Confederate independence continued to inform the slaveholders' republic. In Richmond, Virginia, the Confederate capital, the prominent newspaper editor John Moncure Daniel had by May 1862 already grown tired of what he considered to be President Davis's ostentatious and unmanly piety and the sanctimonious breast-beating of the Southern clergy. In August 1863, reeling from the news of Gettysburg and Vicksburg, Daniel bluntly stated in an editorial that "there is neither Christianity nor religion of any kind in this war. We prosecute it in self-defense, for the preservation of our liberty, our homes and our Negroes." But Daniel's was a rare public voice making such a claim. Southern honor, social conservatism, and states'-rights constitutionalism did not have to be—as they had not been for Thomas Cooper—linked to a Christian public theology rooted in the Bible. But neither could the holy sanction offered by God's Word to the South be directly challenged.[84]

13

Lived Experience and the Sacred Cause

Faith, Skepticism, and Civil War

John R. Kelso had been a Missouri schoolteacher when the shots were fired on Fort Sumter in April 1861. "Religion," he wrote in his autobiography two decades later, "that greatest of all fomenters of discord and bloodshed, rushed, like a hungry vulture, into the conflict." The iron tongues of church bells seemed to call for blood as clergymen raged from their pulpits. Secessionist preachers were supremely confident that God would destroy the abolitionist Union, and Unionist preachers were just as certain that He would smite the proslavery rebels. Kelso, who fought for the Union and earned fame that would carry him to Congress, had been a Methodist preacher himself in the 1850s, so he was well versed in the religious arguments on both sides.[1]

George Shane Phillips, chaplain to the 49th Regiment of Ohio, was one of those clergymen proclaiming the larger meaning of the conflict. In lectures he delivered that were published as *The American Republic and Human Liberty Foreshadowed in Scripture* (1864), the United States of America is the redeemer nation prophesied in the Bible. Its divine purpose is to spread Christianity and liberty throughout the world. The proslavery South, dominated by raving madmen, had risen in rebellion against God's will. Slavery, though, was a national and not a regional sin, and it needed to be purged from the nation's soul.[2]

At the very beginning of the war, Kelso had heard a similar prophetic argument from the Confederate side. At a secessionist rally in his hometown of Buffalo, Missouri, a speaker named Peter Wilkes argued that prophetic images in the Books of Genesis and Revelation showed God's approval of the seven seceding states. But when Wilkes finished speaking, Kelso leapt in front of the speaker's platform and addressed the crowd. He countered the secessionist's scriptural arguments, and then made a very different appeal by quoting from Washington's Farewell Address and rhetorically waving the "Star-Spangled Banner." Kelso could cite scriptural chapter and verse against Wilkes, and he could argue like Wilkes when he became a Union spy in Confederate territory and preached proslavery to ingratiate himself with the enemy. But his real convictions were rooted in a fervent patriotism that had nothing to do with Christianity, a faith he had left behind.[3]

George Shane Phillips and John R. Kelso represent two sides of the spectrum of patriotic American nationalism that motivated supporters of the Union to fight the Civil War. Many Northerners, in varying degrees, drew on both Christianity and romantic political idealism to articulate their cause. But the arguments for liberty and republican government, on one hand, or for God's chosen nation ushering in the millennial age, on the other, can seem "abstract and intangible," as a prominent historian has noted. Could such ideas really motivate men to kill and risk their lives in battle, as Kelso did, or sacralize bloody killing fields, as Phillips did? The link between the personal and the political for the Missouri guerrilla fighter and the chaplain at the Battle of Chickamauga is not only in the ideas themselves but in how during the crisis of war those ideas resonated with Kelso's and Phillips's previous experiences.[4]

The ardent Christian nationalism that Phillips expressed in *The American Republic* is not a prevalent theme in his sermons, journals, letters, and commonplace books from the 1840s and 1850s. Yet the roots of the ideological convictions that burst forth in the Civil War can be glimpsed in unlikely places: in an exchange of letters twenty years earlier with his future wife, Elizabeth Kauffman, discussing marriage and personal holiness, and in his work as a missionary in post–Gold Rush California. For Kelso, the war offered a chance to reconstitute the community he had lost when he walked away from his church. He would remake himself as an admired leader and at the same time devote himself to a transcendent cause—an American faith that a religious skeptic could live and die for.[5]

Sanctifying Union

Phillips's Civil War book was not a best seller, but in most ways it voiced the prevailing religious interpretation of the war that emerged in the North. A nation, the Methodist minister argued, is not merely a collection of self-interested individuals joined as if by a business contract and perpetuated by stump speeches and votes stuffed into ballot boxes. A nation is organized by a great idea that becomes the "germ of national life and civilization, *its soul*." The central organizing idea of the United States is expressed in the preamble to the Declaration of Independence: all men are created equal, with rights to protect their lives, enjoy liberty, and pursue happiness. Equality and liberty, moreover, were not principles primarily drawn from Athenian democracy or the Roman republic; they sprang from the Bible and from the Christian faith of the Founding Fathers. According to Phillips, God had designed the United States of America for a redemptive purpose.[6]

The organic sense of nationality, notably developed by Connecticut theologian Horace Bushnell, had become a commonplace in Northern preaching. Countering Southern claims that the United States was a confederation of sovereign states and not a consolidated nation, Northern religious writers argued that the Union, which Daniel Webster had revered a generation before in soaring rhetoric that Northern schoolchildren had subsequently memorized, was the political form of a deeper, singular national identity—a nation with a divine vocation. Bushnell, a New Englander, thought that the Puritans had understood the true basis of nationality with their covenant theology, in which individuals were morally and spiritually bound together and with God. Bushnell argued that the Revolutionary Fathers' Enlightenment notions of government as being created by voluntary contracts and deriving its power from the consent of the governed (rather than from God's Higher Law) did not create a covenant and did not adequately express nationality. The blood and vicarious sacrifice of the Civil War itself, for Bushnell, enabled the true birth of the American nation. Phillips, in contrast, but more like most Northern commentators during the war, tried to connect his Christian patriotism to the values of 1776.[7]

After the Preliminary Emancipation Proclamation in 1862 was seen to expand the purpose of the war beyond merely preserving the Union as it had existed in 1860, religious commentators in the North could sharpen, as Phillips did, the emphasis on political equality. Southerners dismissed the fuzzy philosophy of Thomas Jefferson's preamble to the Declaration of Independence and defended slavery as a Christian institution that served as the foundation for a free and enlightened white society. Most of Phillips's fellow Northerners, too, if they had not discarded the preamble completely before the war, had confined the full application of liberty and equality to white males. By the time Phillips delivered the lectures that became *The American Republic and Human Liberty Foreshadowed in Scripture* in 1863, however, most antislavery religious moderates in the churches had come to Lincoln's conclusion that the battle for freedom, the battle for America's soul, had to include the destruction of slavery.

Many Northerners might have balked at Phillips's vision of multiethnic nationality, but they would come to endorse, especially after the war, his Christianized American imperialism. The Methodist preacher had spent ten years in California and was inspired by the mixture of Europeans, Chinese, Mexicans, Indians, and other groups he saw there. He was also confident that a benevolent American empire would one day cover the globe (a dream other patriots could have shared), incorporating all foreign peoples as citizens (a consequence far less appealing to the many who thought republican institutions suited only to Anglo-Saxons). Reviving and extending American manifest destiny from the continent to the globe, though, fit the growing Northern optimism at the time of the book's publication in 1864.[8]

Phillips's Christianized interpretation of American history went even beyond the usual distortions of evangelical sentimentality. He supplemented the standard dewy-eyed Christian myth of Washington fighting the Revolution on his knees in prayer to insist that almost all the Founding Fathers were pious Christians. He dodged Benjamin Franklin's well-known deism by emphasizing that the patriot had been raised in Puritan Boston and by applauding Franklin's call for prayer at the Constitutional Convention. Phillips even rehabilitated Jefferson by praising his Christian sentiments and claiming that the Virginian's false reputation as an unbeliever had been spread by slaveholders in the South who hated the equal liberty proclaimed by the Declaration. *The American Republic*, in short, simply erased deism and religious skepticism in the Revolutionary era from the nation's religious history. Quoting various Founders' mentions of divine Providence, Phillips concluded that the American republic was established by the direct intervention of God.

Phillips's combination of American nationalism and Christianity was unusual only in the specificity of its prophetic interpretation. He held that the Jewish theocracy was not a divinely instituted type of the later Christian church, as most Christian exegetes had taught, but prefigured the American republic. The Methodist preacher thought that the similarities between the two polities were striking. The tribes of Israel were like the American states, the rulers of each government were elected, and both the ancient and modern judiciaries were independent. But the two were not just analogous, as in the staple comparisons of much Revolutionary-era civic preaching, or rhetorically (but vaguely) linked, as in much of the religio-political effusions about manifest destiny in the earlier nineteenth century. For Phillips Israel was a model polity anticipating and historically fulfilled by the United States of America; they were God's chosen nations in their respective historical epochs, ordained to do divine work. [9]

Further, Phillips contended, scriptural prophecies predicted the rise, rapid progress, and ultimate dominion of the United States. Previous interpreters had misread key scriptural passages as referring to the future restoration of the Jews to Palestine, he wrote. Phillips tried to demonstrate that God clearly meant that Zion (the Christian church) would thrive in a *new* Israel—a Christian nation in a spacious, previously uncultivated land between two seas (Ezek. 38:8 and 47:18–20). The new Israel would be a people gathered out of many nations, including China (Isa. 49:12), Phillips wrote knowingly, pointing to the Chinese immigration he had witnessed during his decade in California. The woman escaping to the wilderness in the seventh chapter of the Book of Revelation foretold the Pilgrims' flight to America, and the man-child she bore was the (American) nation born of the church. Isaiah 33:21 predicted the Boston Tea Party. The nation born in a day mentioned in Isaiah 66 was the United States, and the day was July 4, 1776. Indeed, even that particular day was prophesied:

through a complex calculation of "Sabbitic time" Phillips translated the seventy weeks mentioned in the text as indicating 3:00 p.m., at the meridian of Philadelphia, on the fourth day of July, 1,776 years after the birth of Christ. "The calculation being purely mathematical, and being guided by astronomy, has been rigidly made to the decimal fraction of a second, and must be reliable." Verses in Daniel showed that the United States would ultimately destroy all other political governments, and the American flag would "wave over every land and encircle the world in its majestic folds."[10]

The United States, therefore, was the redeemer nation prophesied in the Bible, created by the direct intervention of God, and born of the church. Other students of scripture in the North made similar prophetic claims, but proponents of this sort of interpretive calculus were in the minority. Most Northern Protestants who commented on the deeper religious and historical meanings of the war avoided trying to read the fulfillment of specific biblical prophecies in current events. But they joined Phillips in celebrating the world-historical importance of the war and thought the rise of the United States connected, somehow, to the coming millennial age.[11]

One Christian denomination, Phillips contended, was particularly crucial to the emergence of this perfected form of human government: Methodism. Just as Bushnell and other New Englanders tried to ground American nationalism in the New England Puritan past, Phillips and other Methodists connected America's rise to the formation of their own denomination. The central ideas articulated in the Declaration and institutionalized, if imperfectly, by the Constitution had first been recognized by John Wesley and woven into the fabric of Methodism thirty-seven years before Thomas Jefferson picked up his pen in 1776, Phillips wrote. Such a claim was not simply Phillips's tip of the hat to a happy analogy. It was an argument about the epochal importance of two linked events in the history of divinely inspired human progress: the founding of Methodism and the American Revolution.[12]

Yet Methodists were latecomers to this sort of American Protestant nationalism. Like the Baptists, they had had an ambivalent reaction to party politics as it had developed in the second quarter of the nineteenth century. Good citizenship was an important duty, but democratic politics as it was actually practiced was considered a worldly distraction at best and a sewer of sin and corruption at its frequent worst. Still, Methodists, pushed or pulled to try to morally reform the rapidly changing society in which they had an increasing stake, became more politically engaged. Although regional variations mattered mightily, the Methodist rank and file tended to lean Democratic, while their clergy was considerably more Whiggish. The frenzied politicking of the presidential election of 1840, it has often been noted, both borrowed techniques from evangelical revivalism (stump speakers in the role of itinerant preachers) and bore the marks of a modern image-laden campaign to mobilize the masses. Methodists, like other Americans, paid attention. In Phillips's Ohio the old war hero William Henry Harrison was called out of retirement in North Bend to lead the ticket for the Whigs. Harrison, an Episcopalian, attended a weeklong Methodist revival meeting in Cincinnati's Wesley Chapel. The Rev. Maxwell P. Gaddis watched "Old Tippecanoe" warmly shake the lead revivalist's hand and described the moment as "electrical."[13]

In 1840, George Shane Phillips had been a twenty-one-year-old divinity student still keeping his distance from national politics. A June 12 letter to his father from school in Norwalk, Ohio, described a scene unlike anything he had previously witnessed: a grand Whig celebration of "Old Tip" Harrison, with a parade including horse-drawn floats; hundreds of marching mechanics, merchants, and farmers; bands playing; women waving flags and handkerchiefs; and plenty of hard cider. Although he boarded with the town's Whig mayor, Phillips remained an observer, not a participant. Electoral politics along with the temperance and antislavery crusades captivated public attention in town, he noted, but he regretted that religion among the citizens of the place remained "rather dull." Among his fellow students, however, "the fire of God's love appears to burn with great rapidity." They, at least, had their priorities in order. Phillips himself focused on striving to serve God.[14]

As a young itinerant preacher riding the Richwood Circuit of the North Ohio Conference, he recognized the problem of skeptical infidelity as a threat to Christian faith. On a list of twenty-six books and pamphlets he read while traveling in 1841, for example, two focused on religious infidelity. He preached a sermon on the "cause and cure of unbelief." Another of Phillips's sermons outlined in his journal from the early 1840s cast infidels as the first of five categories of sinners who neglected the work of salvation. A third sermon, delivered in Kenton, Ohio, on December 21, 1843, was written as a direct address to an infidel. A fourth, preached in the same place a month later, focused on atheism. He did not think that any of his listeners were so degraded as to doubt the existence of God: even the ignorant Indian, he preached, "sees God in clouds and hears him in the wind" (though a footnote acknowledged "the Hottentots of Africa & Aborigines of [New] South Wales" as exceptions to the rule of universal belief). Nevertheless, rehearsing the arguments for God's existence, he thought, might help give believers more "exalted views" of their Creator. When a self-professed skeptical infidel came forward at a meeting in December 1842, it was a cause of great rejoicing.[15]

But more immediate threats to the success of Christianity in America, Phillips believed from his vantage in Ohio, came from Catholicism, misguided strains of Protestantism, and the political radicalism that was tearing apart national church bodies like his own Methodist Episcopal Church. Catholicism was a superstitious idolatry that led people away from Christian truth and whose papal tyranny was incompatible with republican institutions. "Campbellites," the restorationist followers of Alexander Campbell also known as Disciples of Christ, competed directly with Methodists for adherents: two of Elizabeth's aunts, she wrote to Phillips in February 1843, had been baptized by the Campbellites, and she worried that they were not—and might never be—truly converted Christians. In another letter she reported that a mutual friend was preparing to leave the Methodist Episcopal Church for an abolitionist splinter group. On his preaching circuit, Phillips wrote of having to combat both Campbellism and radicalism. In the midst of the sectional division of the MEC, he argued in a lecture called "Knowledge is Power" that the perpetuation of the Union depended on a united Protestantism. He was calling not for the erasure of denominational distinctions but for the preservation of national churches that knit together North and South, and for the friendly cooperation of Protestants in all churches and regions. In 1845, a year after the schism, Phillips was lamenting the division between pro- and antislavery Christianity as a threat to the nation, and blamed extremist demagogues on both sides.[16]

George, Elizabeth, and their children journeyed to California in 1851 to do the Lord's work. In New York City, before beginning the first ocean leg of the trip, George, neither an ascetic nor a croaker, visited a "gorgeous" Methodist church and admired its organ, which cost fifteen hundred dollars. While crossing Panama, he observed a mass being celebrated in a crumbling Catholic cathedral, a building that, with its altar overlaid with silver and its walls crowded with painted saints, reinforced his sense of Catholic corruption. On the steamship to San Francisco, when not miserably seasick, Phillips enjoyed the company of three Southern Methodists. The division of the church was still a matter of intense dispute—itinerants and church members from the Northern and Southern branches competed bitterly on either side of an uncertain border, and the courts would not settle the legal issues until 1854—but for Phillips, relations on a personal level could still be congenial. (Once in California, Phillips would find that some of his Northern Methodist clerical brethren welcomed their Southern Methodist counterparts with open arms; other Northerners eyed the Southerners warily.) The family finally reached San Francisco in late January 1852. As a minister in the Oregon-California Mission Conference of the MEC, for the next decade he would preach and teach in San Francisco, Stockton, Sacramento, San Jose, and Santa Clara. He also lectured on temperance and education reform, and wrote for and helped edit the new state's first Methodist newspaper, the *California Christian Advocate*.[17]

The first authorized attempt to organize Methodism in California had begun less than five years before the Phillips family's arrival when the missionary William

Roberts sailed into San Francisco Bay from Oregon in the spring of 1847. He described the town as a small settlement of sixty to a hundred wooden houses. Roberts preached his first sermon in a dining hall where the sailors and the locals agreed to stop gambling and eating while he spoke. The minister then organized a group of six Methodists into a class and returned to Oregon.[18]

Vivid accounts by another Methodist missionary, William Taylor, describe how San Francisco and the surrounding region were utterly transformed by the Gold Rush of 1849. When Taylor arrived in September of that year, the small port town had swollen to a tent city of over twenty thousand people composed mostly of young men eager to strike it rich and go back home. And home could have been any number of places: in a journal entry dated February 3, 1850, Taylor remarked on a class meeting with people "from almost all parts of the United States, from Maine to Texas; and from Buenos Ayres in South America, from Costa Rica in Central America; from Prince Edward's Island; from England, Scotland, and Ireland; from Germany, Sweden, and Denmark; from North Wales, New South Wales, and New Zealand." He lived near a group from Malta and another from Manila, and addressed crowds that included Frenchmen, Spaniards, Prussians, Hawaiians, and Chinese. Taylor began his regular street preaching by standing on a bench in Portsmouth Square near the most elaborately appointed gambling house. Accompanied by his wife and another woman, he sang a hymn to draw the crowd's attention away from the band trying to lure people into the saloon and the cart men hawking their produce and wares. He made it his practice to preach from porches, atop woodpiles, or standing on casks of whiskey or rum, these last being especially good props for his temperance sermons. In early 1850, he traveled the 125 miles to Sacramento to visit his fellow missionary Isaac Owen, Phillips's predecessor there, who preached in a tent and a blacksmith's shop. In a "city" Taylor described as a "vast mud-hole" with sodden gold diggers' tents and hastily constructed shacks, the two men began planning for a Methodist book depository, academy, and university.[19]

Missionaries like Taylor, Owen, Roberts, and Phillips competed not just with other denominations on Sundays but with the main attractions in California: horse racing, bull fighting, bear baiting, and drunken boating excursions. The Methodists also rode huge preaching circuits over rough mountain trails known to be frequented by bandits and grizzly bears. Taylor and Phillips rode horses, and Roberts, the superintendant of the California Conference, rode a mule and, according to Taylor, carried his Bible in one hand and his Colt revolver in the other. The traveling preachers visited the mining camps, where they competed with "itinerant theatricals, minstrels, circuses, performers in legerdemain, dog and monkey shows, etc., constantly travelling to and fro, entertaining the miners at a dollar per head."[20]

Elizabeth Phillips entered a California culture dominated by young, mobile, single males: women made up 4 percent of the Euro-American population aged twenty to thirty-nine in 1850; this figure rose to 30 percent by 1860, but in mining regions there were still twenty-three men for every woman. Taylor found California in the 1850s to be a peculiar place that exposed both the brighter and darker sides of manly individualism. Migrants "soon learned that to succeed in California, every man must be self-reliant and independent, a *brave* on his own account." In a land where inscrutable chance was thought to rule every endeavor, a man was not supposed to flinch in the face of sudden and drastic turns of fortune (it was no wonder that gambling was considered an honorable pursuit). Californians, too, seemed as committed to their own individual opinions as they were extraordinarily tolerant of those who differed from them. But the "social element of their souls seemed to be absorbed by raging thirst for gain, an excitement that burned with quenchless glow." The facts of their social lives, as well as the inclinations of their souls, made building communities—especially religious communities—difficult. "Social ties and relationships, and ties of blood," Taylor wrote, "are very important 'conductors' for Gospel electricity." Preachers were used to reaching a person through his bonds to "his parents, his wife, and children, brothers, sisters, and intimate acquaintances." California had the Gospel "battery" but too few social conductors; in Taylor's view, it was "the hardest country in the world in which to get sinners converted to God."[21]

For George Shane Phillips, California was both a rough-hewn, half-formed society and a golden land of opportunity for the advance of Christian civilization. He visited Chinese camps and Indian villages, and from a summit marveled at the ships from all nations in San Francisco Bay, just as he pondered the many nationalities gathered for worship on the Lord's Day or represented in the city's cemetery, resting alongside one another and waiting for Judgment Day. He was shocked the first time he heard of one man murdering another in broad daylight and in front of witnesses, and noted a friend who longed for the day in California when knife and pistol would not be common tools of social interaction. But Phillips's main moral concerns were drinking, gambling, and greed. In his journal, the people who worried him the most were not Catholics, Campbellites, radicals, skeptical infidels, or Southerners but backsliders among his own people. Pious Methodists who came from the East could change once they settled in the golden land. He saw formerly religious men first begin avoiding church, then selling liquor and gambling. He was saddened when one day riding his circuit he stopped at the house of an old friend from Ohio, only to find the man offering alcohol for sale. Traveling with the state temperance agent a few months later, he stopped at a tavern owned by people who had been Methodist church members back home but here operated a bar. Taylor, too, preached against backsliders and told similar stories, quoting one migrant who self-consciously left his religious character, along with his cloak, back east: "I knew I couldn't carry my religion with me through California, so when I left home in Missouri I hung my religious cloak on my gate-post until I should return." Phillips's own brother, a former Methodist and minister, had come west and had forgotten his God. He worked on the Sabbath, sold liquor, and prospered at first, being elected county treasurer and nominated to serve in the legislature. But then God struck him down, and George buried him in the fall of 1852.[22]

The *California Christian Advocate* shared Phillips's optimism about California's important role in the future of American Christianity but portrayed the state's moral and political climate somewhat differently. "There is a more rapid movement of mind in California than on any spot of the globe," an editorial declared on May 18, 1853. "California is the great social experiment of Protestant society in the 19th century.... California is an important link in the experiment to demonstrate truth as truth." With few of the traditional authorities in either church or state to provide moral restraints, people were able to choose to live as they pleased. And because by nature "all hearts are more or less infidel," people tended to "doubt if there is really any absolute right, and a spiritual might to enforce it." The state would be a test, then, between the natural forces of skepticism and sin on one side and Christians armed only with the Word of God on the other, a test that would show more clearly than ever before, too, the *Advocate* argued, that American liberty need not produce licentiousness and anarchy. Already Christianity was on the march. Where were the Gold Rush gamblers of 1849, the corrupt judges who winked at crime, the whoremongers and drunks in political office? On the defensive, the editorial answered, and they were realizing that political parties could not shelter them. Christian sentiment was strengthening in the state and demanding that the moral conduct of politicians be called to account.[23]

Rather than concentrating on Christian backsliders, the *Advocate* aligned belief and behavior. Despite the May 18 editorial's admission that all hearts were more or less infidel, the *Advocate* generally conveyed the sense that Christianity was competing for the soul of California—and, by extension, of America—against a single party comprised interchangeably of drunks, political "liberals," gamblers, religious skeptics, and plotting slaveholders. A notice in the February 17, 1853, issue exposed a meeting of so-called liberals, reported in another newspaper, as nothing more than six men getting drunk and making resolutions that slandered Christian churches as fanatic sects. An article in the May 18, 1853, issue pondered the question, "What are the chief hindrances to the reception of Christianity, by the skeptical portion of the community, and how can they best be removed?" Address the skeptic's heart rather than his intellect, the editor answered, because skepticism originated not in reasoning but in the alienation of a sinner's affections from God. "The Confession of a Deist," an essay also published in the spring of 1853, argued that "infidel sentiments in their various forms and channels are the great danger of the age." Infidels "unsettle everything, but settle nothing. To them mystery and doubt surround everything. The state of their minds is epitomized in these grand questions: 'But who knows?' 'How do I know?' It is all uncertain. The work of demolition is theirs; to pull down; not to build up; to uproot Christianity, and establish nothing in its stead."[24]

The connection of infidel sentiments to political theory, with an immediate application to political practice, was made in a Washington's Birthday address to the Sons of Temperance by Phillips's colleague and the former editor of the *Advocate*, the Rev. Martin Clock Briggs. The address, summarized in the *Advocate*, included a description of the speaker's fanciful dream of a "Men's Rights Convention" with delegates drawn from the prominent thinkers and lawmakers in history. Settling the fundamental difference between Christian legislators who measured their laws against God's Word and a long train of misguided political writers from Hobbes to Paine was the majestic Washington, who pointed to the Bible and upward to the throne of heaven. The lesson, Briggs said, was clear: legislation must "embody the principles of social justice which God reveals," and therefore he urged the state legislature to pass temperance laws. Drunkenness, infidelity, and political liberalism could all be slain with the same sword.[25]

Thus the children of light struggled against the party of darkness. But to name slaveholders as members of that party was to aim at a more dangerous target. In a January 21, 1852, editorial, Briggs exposed plans by proslavery politicians who had met in Wilmington, North Carolina, to recast California as a slave state. Briggs received death threats, and on one occasion was threatened by a mob. On December 22, 1854, Phillips wrote in his journal about the "unjust" and "shameful" libel suit that was brought against the editors of the *Advocate* for taking a firm stand against the introduction of slavery into the state. The plaintiffs were awarded $3,000, and a San Francisco newspaper denounced the *Advocate* for mixing religion and politics. A conference of the MEC South held in Sacramento when Phillips was also stationed there resolved "in favor of non-intervention and non-agitation" about slavery, and Northern Methodists were expected to do the same. The *Advocate*, and Phillips, remained more involved with the temperance movement than with antislavery. In 1855, the paper was renamed the *California Christian Advocate and Temperance Journal*; Phillips lectured against strong drink but like most clergymen in the state stayed away from the topic of slavery.[26]

That George Shane Phillips became more radicalized on the slavery question through the later 1850s is hardly surprising: he had a lot of company among Christians in both North and South. The same can be said of the Christian nationalism he articulated in the midst of the Civil War. *The American Republic and*

Human Liberty Foreshadowed in Scripture heralded the United States, rather than the church, as God's central instrument for redeeming the world. Phillips himself would probably have considered such sentiments extravagant in 1853 and dangerous demagoguery in 1843, but by 1863 sectional animosity and then a horrific war had driven many people to extremes their younger selves would not have imagined. Yet from another perspective the young Methodist itinerant and the Civil War chaplain hardly seem different at all. Beneath Phillips's explicit translation of religious principles into political theories, or his self-conscious ideological development from moderate antislavery to radical abolitionism, there is his particular way of being Methodist—of being Christian. The young man and the older one similarly converted the potential energy of personal religious experience into kinetic Christian practice.

A revealing exchange of letters through the first half of 1843 between Phillips and his future wife, Elizabeth Kauffman, illuminate the ways that George—and Elizabeth—lived Methodism. George's letter of January 6 established a pattern that Elizabeth also followed: it opened with an account of God's work on the circuit, then provided a status report on his own spiritual experiences, and finally turned to discuss their relationship. The news from his Richwood Circuit's Quarterly Meeting was cheering, he wrote: seventy-nine were added to the church, including some men of prominence and influence. After a nearly constant outpouring of the Spirit, another 120 were on probation, seeking salvation. Martial imagery conveyed George's enthusiasm: Gideon marching, God raising his sword and striking fire, arrows sticking fast into sinners' hearts, flags of peace waving. He then noted that many on the circuit professed sanctification and enjoyed the perfect love of God, a topic that provided a transition to a discussion of his own spiritual progress. He was still seeking sanctifying grace, he confessed, and although he had made some advances he did not yet have evidence that his heart had been completely cleansed and made holy. But he was eager, as he put it, to scale the summit of perfect holiness. George closed the letter with a topic that he said he had been praying over for two years, seeking the guidance of the Holy Spirit because he was afraid of being led by passion. That was how George asked Elizabeth to marry him and join him in the work of the ministry.[27]

Elizabeth's response on January 25 began by rejoicing at good news from the Wooster circuit: a two-week protracted meeting yielded 114 new church members. She made no mention of swords striking fire and arrows piercing hearts, however. She wrote that she had made some progress in divine life but lamented that much remained in her heart that was still unholy. She desired to be entirely consecrated in the service of God, "to be prepared for his will and have my will entirely lost in his." Then she responded to George's proposal: "I at present have no objection to becoming your companion for life, and doing what I can to aid you in your arduous task in which you are engaged. But while I say this I am fully aware that unless this is my duty, unless God joins us together we cannot be happy to each other or useful to each other. Let us still commit our cause into the hands of the Lord."[28]

George's February 4 reply was buoyant. He was "fully persuaded" that God approved their union and that together they could be more useful bringing souls to Christ. He continued to seek sanctification, though apparently he was not seeking in the proper way. But he was "resolved never to stop importuning with God" until love filled his soul. He proposed that the two of them "meet at the throne of grace" by praying each day at 8:30, 12:00, and 5:00. Doing so would help them achieve holiness, strengthen their attachment to each other, and seek the Spirit's guidance in all things. Elizabeth, too, continued to interweave revival news, spiritual introspection, and the discussion of marriage. She told George that God enabled her, though she was unworthy, to renew her covenant and give herself completely to him. She prayed that He would finish the work He had begun in her heart. She counseled George to be resigned to whatever God decided about their marriage—to be willing to be denied in temporal things without disappointment just as they were being denied in things spiritual. She added that she had not yet told her parents about his proposal and was not sure how they would react.[29]

As their epistolary conversation progressed, his eagerness and certitude intensified, while her passive sense of resignation deepened. One hundred fourteen new converts, he wrote on March 19: "May the great God of battles continue to fire us to victory." He had not the "least shade of doubt" that they should marry—and soon (for one thing, he needed her help counseling women at the protracted meetings). They could defer their wedding for another year, but a "whole year" would seem "quite long," he wrote, double-underlining these phrases. He had prayed that God would remove every obstacle (including, presumably, parental obstacles) and was confident his prayers would be answered. He did not apologize for his warmth—husbands, after all, were commanded to love their wives the way Christ loves the church, "and that's not a little." He thought he detected some evidence of cleansing holiness in his blood. The happiness he felt in his studies and work as he contemplated their future together seemed to be evidence of God's love and approval. "Do not love inordinately," Elizabeth reminded George a week later, worried that she was not worthy of his high esteem. She was ready to marry in the fall and begin work as an itinerant preacher's wife, but she prayed that God would prepare her for whatever the future held. If George were called away on a mission for a year before they could marry, she was resigned to God's will. She had finally told her mother about his proposal, and she had no objections, but Elizabeth did not think her father would respond so favorably.[30]

The greater goal, Elizabeth reminded George at the beginning of June, is that we are both sanctified, whatever else happens in our lives. Though the work of grace continues to deepen in my heart (she wrote), I continue to ask and do not yet receive holiness. I know it is my fault, know I must not be complying with God's conditions, but I do not know how else to ask. I still have not spoken to Father. George responded: I have been striving, and my efforts have not been in vain. Sometimes I am almost ready to say that I have taken hold of the blessing. Prospects brighten. Talk to your father—I could write to him if you want. "I have no doubt that you will soon obtain the desire of your heart." Elizabeth at the end of June: "Dear George our experience of seeking the blessing of perfect love seems similar[;] frequently have I been in sight [of] the blessing and ready to grasp it when the recollection of my unworthiness or of the unfavorableness of the circumstances in which I was placed has arisen and I have again lost sight of it. Such a state of feeling has always (in me) been followed by a degree of apathy. Sometimes when earnestly praying I have been powerfully blessed[;] the greatest blessings I have ever received were while praying for sanctification, yet I did not believe it to be that for which I had been seeking. I have sometimes thought such unbelief to be wrong." The scripture says that when we ask our earthly parents for bread, they will not give us a stone, so when we ask our Heavenly Father for perfect love and He blesses us, what shall we call the blessing? I have been away teaching school and only visited home briefly—I did not get the opportunity to have a private conversation with Father.[31]

So continued the interweaving of religious devotion and courtship. George bought a book nearly five hundred pages long, George Peck's *Scripture Doctrine of Christian Perfection, Stated and Defended* (1842), and summarized its wisdom for Elizabeth. Seekers of sanctification, Peck advised, needed to focus on a specific object—just as a politician needed to work toward winning a particular election and not just hope for the general success of his party, and a businessman had to have discrete projects and investments and not just vaguely wish for wealth. Sanctification had to be more precisely understood than it often was: it was distinct both from regeneration (in conversion) and restoration (in heaven). The difficulty, though, was that, like regeneration, it could not be fully grasped until experienced. Christians needed to move forward by trust and faith in Christ without stopping to reason. They needed to *feel*—apathy was a great obstacle. They needed to hunger and thirst for grace and, especially, exercise feelings of self-renunciation, self-abasement, and self-loathing. If Elizabeth's problem was occasional apathy, a resigned numbness, George's was the inability to surrender all to Christ. As George was writing all this, he began running out of space on his sheet of paper. His words became smaller and smaller, but his emotions became more forcefully expressed as his desires for the consummations of matrimony and holiness fused. He had been powerfully blessed since she had accepted his proposal, he wrote. When they met at the throne of grace three times a day, when he thought of her encouraging him as he preached, his spirits soared and the Spirit drew near. The combination of the "precious" spiritual happiness he experienced and the "ardor" of his love for her had utterly convinced him that their union was God's will.[32]

George's tone had changed by the middle of July. He wrote of being "depressed in spirit," having endured "some of the darkest seasons that I have realized for years and I do not know that I ever before experienced in all my christian pilgrimage a combination of such gloomy hours." He was still striving to be holy, and the blessing still eluded him. "I often have an anxiety to spend a season in your society," he confessed, and added that he, too, worried that he would not live up to her expectations as a spouse. He adopted her tone of resignation about their marriage: even if they could not marry, he wrote, he had the consolation that their correspondence had been a spiritual benefit to him. What happened in the future was up to God. Then he pondered Elizabeth's comments about sanctification. If we ask God for perfect love, and then feel His blessing, should we then doubt that what we receive is just what we have asked for? Doubt might be the problem, George agreed. A Methodist brother once told him that he had experienced perfect love and holiness until the moment he doubted his experience.[33]

Reviewing the scriptural texts that had grounded John Wesley's teaching on the Witness of the Spirit—Romans 8:10 and 1 John 5:12—George reminded Elizabeth and himself about what they were seeking. Being sanctified meant being able to love God above all other people and things: "True[,] objects there may be which will be dear to our hearts but they will be placed in subordination to God." How would they know they were sanctified? The Holy Spirit would witness inwardly, banishing all doubt, followed by their own inward witness or consciousness of victory over sin. Then love would flow out of the soul toward God and all mankind. In a state of holiness, there would still be sinful "temptations" and inner "infirmities" but no "movements" in the soul, no "unholy elements" within that opposed God's will and would rise in "rebellion." It would be a perfect faith—"Our confidence in God will be unwavering"—and an uninterrupted communion with the Lord. "Again when made perfect we will have no will of our own[.] God's will will be both our *Rule* and *Delight*." Despite his depressed state, George was still confident that both of them would receive the blessing of sanctification before they saw each other again at the end of the summer.[34]

George had mentioned in an earlier letter that he might be able to get assigned to the circuit near Elizabeth's parents' home. She told him not to seek such an appointment for her sake. "I think a Methodist preacher's wife has no right to choose where she will live," she wrote at the end of July, and added that even if she did have that choice she would surrender it into God's hands. She said that her chief desire was to love God perfectly and regretted only that other things tended to divert her from that primary goal. She added, almost as an aside, that her mother had spoken to her father about the marriage, and he said he would not oppose it.³⁵

George experienced sanctification five days later on August 1, at about six o'clock in the evening as he prayed alone in a manger. The letter is dated August 10; he would have written sooner, he explained, but he had been struck by a "Bilious fever" on the way to a camp meeting, followed by "Influenzy or cold plague" that left him unable even to sit up in a chair to write. He did not try to describe what it felt like to be sanctified, except to say that the evidence was clear: "The Spirit bore witness with my spirit that it was perfect love." He did not feel great ecstasy but rather a peaceful, unshaken confidence in God. When the blessing washed over him, he thought of his discussion with Elizabeth about the dangers of doubt and set all questioning aside. He did not explicitly say that he had also learned to subordinate a chief object of his affections—her—to his love for God. But in the same letter he did report being "so very ill I felt willing to bid adieu to Earth. I thought of you and other kindred dear but O! the joys of heaven[,] the thought of being with Jesus and the redeemed kindled my soul." Elizabeth's sanctification is not described in the couple's existing correspondence. Only in the fall, after she and George were married, could she let her affection for him share a sentence with her submission to God: mentioning how hard it would be to leave her family, she wrote, "But my trust is in God, and the society of my dear husband will be compensation."³⁶

George Shane Phillips's personal experience of faith would be the taproot of his later religious nationalism. Elizabeth, displaying characteristics often coded "feminine" in nineteenth-century America, was not always passive, but she was certainly reactive—resigning herself to adapt to circumstances as they arose as deference to God's will, preferring to accept duty rather than make choices. Like Sarah Jones, she would not have followed the dictates of male authority if they directly conflicted with obedience to God. But she strove to avoid disapproval—her father's, George's, or God's. Utterly surrendering her will to God was less a challenge than not being affectionately reciprocated for doing so. She was closer than George was to the ideal of self-renunciation recommended by his sanctification textbook. For George, regeneration and sanctification were calls to action. He was not just asking and waiting to receive but banging on the door of grace until it was opened for him, the certainty of his convictions measured by the intensity of his passions. For all his manly bluster about scaling summits and marching off to battle, however, his was not a willful, sovereign self that was so enamored of its own sense of agency that it would not brook any interference from a higher authority. If he could not consistently feel that his will was lost in

God's will, he at least wanted his choices always to be guided by the Spirit; he strove to be not an individual conquering life's adversities but an instrument of God's work in the world—a sword striking fire, an arrow piercing hearts. Piety fueled his moral activism—as an education reformer, a temperance advocate, and, eventually, as a Christian chaplain serving the Union.[37]

This was also the kind of Christian citizen that Phillips imagined in *The American Republic and Human Liberty Foreshadowed in Scripture* as best capable of "self-government" in a republic. "Republican government is that civil form, which a people who have felt the changing power of the Gospel, will always take to themselves, because of its perfect adaptation to their high state of intelligence." The outcast and oppressed subjects of other nations were called together to subdue nature on the continent's "work-field" and were lifted up to enjoy divinely directed political self-determination.[38]

In these passages Phillips casts the citizens of the American republic as converted if not yet sanctified Christians—they "have felt the changing power of the Gospel." Perhaps it was easier back in Ohio, and in the midst of war, than it had been in the mission field of California in the 1850s to imagine the nation as so thoroughly Christian. Ohio in 1860 had 1 church for every 449 inhabitants, the lowest ratio in the country. California had 1 for every 1,297—a ratio that more clearly suggests the missionaries' lack of success compared to other recently settled areas like Iowa, which had a church for every 711 people. Californians were much better at donating money to build churches than they were at personally joining church societies. A historian examining Protestant missions in the state's first decade has concluded that despite the missionaries' optimism, "the goal of personal conversion through revivalism was an unabashed failure."[39]

William Taylor, Phillips's fellow laborer in the California vineyard, offers a telling contrast to the Phillips of *The American Republic and Human Liberty*. Taylor, standing on the corner of Sacramento and Liedesdorff Streets in San Francisco in the summer of 1856, preached a series of sermons responding to desperate cries for political reform. The Vigilance Committee had recently mustered six thousand men to seek vigilante justice if state authorities were too weak or too corrupt to punish a state supreme court judge who had stabbed another man. Taylor argued that real reform was not achieved by hanging a few rogues and chasing corrupt politicians out of town. He appealed to Protestants, Catholics, Jews, Muslims, and even infidels who were skeptical about the divine authority of the Bible to look inward and examine their own consciences in order to begin the needed change within. Rather than preach to persuade Christians to be patriotic, he delivered a sermon called "Patriotic Persuasives to Be a Christian." "The health of a people," he argued, "consists of the health of the individual members composing society. If, therefore, we sincerely desire to see a reformation in this city, and to see society elevated and established on a permanent moral basis, we must earnestly apply ourselves to the work of *personal* reformation." Here the individual is more than just the site of God's gift of reforming grace. Listeners could easily have understood Taylor as saying that the graceless individual was the source of the righteousness that would redeem society. The individual, it seems, through his own agency, applies to himself the work of personal reformation. Toward the end of the sermon a passage acknowledges Christ's work and indicates that human efforts must be accomplished by God-given faith: "Jesus Christ is here in the street to-day. He is bending in sympathy over your guilty, blood-bought spirits, *now*. O, speak to him! Reach out the hand of faith and touch the hem of his garment." Nonetheless, the main argument of the sermon appears to turn the forgiveness of sins, the regeneration of the soul, and the moral reformation of a person and then of his or her community into effects flowing from the individual's sovereign act. Go home and pray, Taylor told San Franciscans, whether or not you have the right feelings in your heart. "Make an honest effort upon the decision of your judgment, with or without feeling; the feeling will come in due time." Men and women could decide to reform themselves, and their resulting righteousness would exalt their nation. This is not Phillips's sense of Christian agents as God's instruments.[40]

If Taylor's "Patriotic Persuasives" edged dangerously close to secular individualism, another of his street sermons from the summer of 1856 suggested the hope that such attitudes would not be prevalent in California for much longer. California, Taylor preached, was like a young giant who was growing up "without parental restraint or the refining influence of female society." He is smart and generous, "but he thinks as he pleases, acts as he thinks, and does not feel that he needs instruction." But gradually the young giant "is becoming domesticated, and is beginning to attend church regularly, and we expect to see him converted to God yet." Once Californians were rerooted in more normal family and social relationships, Taylor believed, and settled in more stable communities, the work of Christianization could proceed.[41]

The United States in Phillips's Civil War book resembled not an unregenerate individualist but a converted (though not yet sanctified) Christian. A nation was simply a larger form of humanity, he wrote, a larger receptacle than a single person for divine presence in the world. Imagining the political realm as a magnified mirror image of personal experience is a psychologically powerful conceptual move that is as least as old as the Old Testament. Likening the nation to a single human being had become commonplace in the Northern pulpit, though preachers described the spiritual status of America's soul somewhat differently. The German Reformed theologian Philip Schaff, for example, spoke in 1865 about the nation's baptism (in blood) and hopes for regeneration. Phillips argued that in America's constitutional heart dwelled the Christian principles of civic liberty and equality. This was the great "regenerative idea," already implanted by God, that defined America's "*soul.*" At the level of foundational principles there was no conflict between contraries yoked together—equal liberty and slavery, Christian faith and skeptical infidelity. America's soul hungered for freedom and for Christ. But it had not yet been cleansed of all sin. There were still unholy elements that could be—that had been—roused to rebellion. Slavery was its central evil; quoting John Wesley, Phillips declared that slavery was the sum of all villainies, promoting other wrongs like intemperance, profanity, and licentiousness. Unlike these subordinate sins, though, slavery until the election of Lincoln had the full power of the government behind it, perverting the national will away from its true Christian inclinations. Phillips joined other Northern clergymen who belatedly embraced emancipation as a war aim in 1862. The Union struggled to do right in the eyes of the Lord, he argued, after the attack on Fort Sumter, but like a Christian yearning for holiness but not knowing how to obtain it, the nation did not have a clear enough sense of the specific objective it needed to pursue. Aiming at restoring the Union with Southern slavery still intact, Phillips wrote, led to a string of battlefield defeats, showing God's displeasure. The Emancipation Proclamation changed all that. Not only did God grant victories in the field, he allowed the proclamation to work a moral revolution in the national mind. As the sin of slavery was being purged, the Lord was calling America to its great and holy task: the universal dominion of republican government and Christianity.[42]

God dealt with a nation the way he dealt with an individual soul—Phillips's own soul, for example. This was not merely a rhetorical figure like Taylor's California giant but, Phillips believed, the way that God actually worked. Furthermore, the spiritual parts (individual souls) were connected to the national whole they resembled. Just as Phillips's courtship of Elizabeth was bound up with his quest for sanctifying grace, so too each citizen's daily efforts to protect American liberty and equality were part of the cosmic battle against sin. For Phillips, the triumph of the Union was a vindication of Methodist principles and a victory for Christ. The inner witness of the Spirit, the divine directives of the scriptures, and the historical progress of the nation all testified to the truth of Protestant Christianity, America's faith. In this triumphalist vision, there was no place for doubts about America's destiny and no room for religious skeptics.

Freed from the Bonds of Superstition

"Born of strict Methodist parents, and naturally of a religious turn of mind, the Author was early bound in those strong mental chains, in which ignorance and superstition, under the name of religion, are wont to bind the masses of mankind." The Author was John Russell Kelso, former preacher, schoolteacher, and

Civil War guerrilla fighter, writing, in the third person, an autobiographical preface to a verse critique of the Bible. "He was told that without *faith* he would certainly be *damned*," the preface continued, referring to events that had occurred in the 1840s and '50s. "At the same time he was taught that this faith, so essential to salvation, '*is the gift of God*,' and that he could not exercise it unless God gave it to him. With all the earnestness of a hungry and despairing soul, he then prayed daily and almost hourly to God for faith, but none was given him." Kelso became a Methodist exhorter and then a preacher in Missouri, but for years his private spiritual misery continued. "At last... the instincts of his nature began to revolt against such a system of religion, and he finally determined to weigh all its doctrines in the balances of *reason*, of *science*, and of *common sense*, and ascertained for himself, whether they were, or were not, founded on *truth*.... In the strength of despair, therefore, he went boldly forward and having once dared to use his reason, he soon emerged from the darkness of ignorance and superstition, and into the light and gladness of truth. His fetters were broken and he became a free man."[43]

John R. Kelso (ca. 1861–65). A former preacher who lost his faith, Kelso became a Union hero fighting Confederate guerrillas in Missouri. Carte de visite, folder 25, Charles Lanham Collection, State Historical Society of Missouri, Columbia. Photo courtesy of the State Historical Society of Missouri.

What Kelso meant by weighing Christian doctrines in the balances of reason, science, and common sense is clear from a series of freethought lectures he delivered after the war in which he invoked this trinity several times. Doubt was the beginning of the process. "Primitive men had no idea of any kind of agency except that of a will or a mind like their own," so they imagined gods as the cause of all sorts of phenomena. Modern people who inherited ancient religious beliefs often did not think to doubt that God was the grand cause operating behind the screen of the observable world. Questioning this presupposition allowed for a rigorous examination of the available evidence on, for example, whether the order found in nature really did reveal an intelligent designer. The preponderance of available evidence one way or another produced belief or disbelief. Doctrines also stood or fell by the test of logic. Kelso dismantled key Christian tenets concerning God's creation of the world, His incarnation as Christ, and Christ's atonement on the cross. Kelso did so by moving from "premises no sane man will deny" through "a series of logical arguments and deductions," ultimately revealing Christianity to be absurd. He also exposed key notions like ascending into heaven or suffering in an underground hell as being based on an ancient cosmology that had long been exploded by modern astronomy and physics. A personal God like the one carried over from ignorant paganism into the Bible, he concluded, could not be the creator of the infinite universe known to modern science. Yet the God of some modern theology, stripped of all individuality and locality, becomes "an intangible, invisible, imponderable, incomprehensible, negation equivalent to empty space," no more able to be worshipped as a person than electricity or gravity. Taking the universe to be self-existent and self-sustaining, he argued, made more sense than imagining an antecedent God of any sort.[44]

Religious faith was perpetuated, Kelso argued, because people were born into belief systems the way they were born into race and nationality. Most never paused to doubt and investigate, and their societies, with "vast armies of priests," tried to ensure that they did not. Absurd stories like the virgin birth or the resurrection were believed because they were *"shrouded in mystery,"* having occurred in a dim and distant past. To combat this, Kelso tried to collapse the distance between the ancient world of wonders and the commonsensical present. The Christians' God in the Old Testament encouraged polygamy, so why not condemn Him for it just as we condemn the Mormons? Would nineteenth-century Americans believe Mary's story about being impregnated by the Holy Ghost if she had been Mary Smith or Mary Brown, a pregnant girl in the neighborhood? Jesus in the Gospels is an itinerant enthusiast with dirty hands and soiled clothes who wanders about encouraging his followers neither to sow nor to reap nor to show concern for their families. Is this really supposed to be an exemplary life? And Christians were taught to constantly praise Christ for his remarkable sacrifice on the cross. But who would not endure a painful death if they were certain that everlasting bliss in heaven awaited, and that by this relatively brief suffering they could rescue even one of their children (to say nothing of all of humanity) from eternal torment in hell? Such appeals to common sense joined reason and science in Kelso's freethought lectures. He suggested that his employment of the three, together with a natural history of religion and a close textual analysis of the scriptures, recapitulated and elaborated the "long and thorough *investigation*" that initially freed him from religious superstition in the 1850s.[45]

The autobiographical story in the preface sketches a standard Enlightenment counternarrative to the formula of Christian conversion. A young man, alone in his study, dares to use his reason and questions the sacred dogmas that have been bequeathed to him—suppositions upon which, up until that point, his understanding of life had rested. Doubt opens a space for rational inquiry, and he is able to hold beliefs at a critical distance for examination, rather than unconsciously drawing inspiration from a pervasive atmosphere of faith. Solitude, too, opens up a space, a critical distance from family, friends, and community. The secluded and self-aware thinker sees the idols of his tribe for what they are. The result is a passage from ignorance and superstition to truth, from darkness to light, from mental slavery to freedom.

Kelso's preface and poem, "The Devil's Defense," were published. But his much longer unpublished autobiography retells the story of his life, showing a journey from faith to skepticism less as the product of a solitary thinker reasoning in his study (though it was that, too) than as a spirit distilled from a mash of psychological turmoil and social experience.

The preface to "The Devil's Defense" says that his religious conversion occurred when he was twelve. "Frightened almost out of his wits by the horrible descriptions of hellfire and damnation which he heard at Methodist revivals, he became at the age of twelve years a devoted member of that church. He experienced that magnetic condition called '*getting religion*,' and believing that this ecstatic feeling was a direct evidence of God's love, he was, for a time, inexpressibly happy, as all are when under the same influence." The autobiography expanded the interpretive gloss. "All I will say here is that, in itself, the phenomenon is a reality, and is attended with feelings of an indescribable rapturous nature." The mature Kelso understood that what Christians called regeneration, the second birth, and a change of heart was an experience familiar to people in all nations and religions, and those who had such experiences tended to attribute them to the god they happened to worship and took them as a sign of their god's approval. "So far from being any thing of the kind, I now know it to be a psychological or magnetic excitation which... is not at all dependent upon any god or any religion." The priests of various religions, who are usually cunning imposters, he wrote, know how to produce these psychological effects, and are thereby able to hold "the people in subjection to themselves."[46]

The young Kelso, however, did not doubt that his heart had been touched by God. His problem was that the ecstatic joy soon evaporated. And if the joy had been a sign of God's gracious favor, then just as surely the departure of those feelings must be a mark of His displeasure. What had Kelso done, or even thought, that had offended God? He did not know, but he prayed several times a day for an answer. "He was so fearful of doing wrong that he rarely ever laughed, and when he did he would go all alone and spend hours in weeping and praying God to forgive him for having so far forgotten heavenly things as to give way to laughter." He was terrified that he had somehow unwittingly committed the unpardonable sin against the Holy Ghost "and that he was already doomed to writhe forever and ever in flames of fire and brimstone."[47]

Although the preface is silent about the matter, the autobiography insists that during the very months Kelso felt God's caress and then mourned the Spirit's withdrawal, he fell in love with Sina, a Methodist preacher's daughter. She was three years his senior; for the next five years he desperately yearned for her and subsequently, agonizingly, tried to avoid her, ashamed of the poverty so evident in his dirty bare feet and ragged clothes. Religious despair—and sexual longing—tormented him. In 1848, at the age of seventeen, he finally confided in his minister about the religious problem, and the clergyman decided that Kelso was being tested and called to be a preacher. Kelso had become so distraught that on the day before he was licensed by the Methodists he left his work, planning to kill himself, and was only prevented by a chance meeting with a neighbor. Instead, he became an exhorter and a schoolteacher, and started studying for the ministry. "My dark sky began to brighten a little."[48]

On Wednesday evenings after his teaching and chores around the house and farm, Kelso led a youth prayer meeting. It was held about eight miles away, and he usually had to run there to make it in time. Piety alone would have gotten him to those meetings, he asserted in the autobiography. But there was also a girl. Finally having mastered his affections for his first love, he found himself falling for another preacher's daughter, Adelia Moore, who at the time was fourteen years old. The feelings he had for Adelia were quite different from the desires he had for Sina, though if anything they were even more intertwined with his religious faith. In many ways, he realized, he and Adelia were not suited to each other. "There was but little magnetic attraction between us. I never felt any strong desire to caress her, as I would have unavoidably felt had my love for her been founded upon nature. On the religious plane we met, and on that plane I loved her. I loved her because she seemed so full of religion,—because God seemed to love her and to be always with her. I felt that if my lot were cast with a being so little human,—so nearly angelic, I could live a better Christian. I felt that God would be present in my house every day on her account, and that, on her account, he would probably bless me, too." He outmaneuvered a rival for Adelia's affections, the sort of man whom Kelso would come to loathe: a conceited, overbearing slaveholder whose position in society, and in the marriage market, rested on wealth derived from the exploitation of others rather than his own hard work and talent. Kelso married Adelia a few years later, when he turned twenty.[49]

From the start the marriage was an unhappy one. His new bride "seemed oppressed with some great sorrow" that he did not understand. Kelso was successful with everything but his domestic life. He remained a popular exhorter; he was publishing poems in the newspaper that received a good deal of praise; he worked his way through textbooks on natural philosophy and astronomy and was teaching himself higher mathematics. The town of Ridgely, Missouri, called him in to try to take control of a large school that had been terrorized by a gang of over twenty teenagers. Aged sixteen to nineteen years, allied with older brothers who were noted "rough characters" in the area, and coming to school armed with bowie knives, the band had already chased off several previous teachers. As expected, the gang challenged his authority. He calmly explained the need for order and laid out his just and reasonable rules for maintaining it, and described his desire to treat all his pupils with kindness. He also explained that a teacher attacked by a student with a deadly weapon was justified in defending himself, killing his assailant if need be. Then he pulled out a five-and-a-half-foot whip fashioned from tough swamp dogwood and called the gang leader forward to take his twenty lashes. The leader put his hand to his knife, pulled it partially out of its scabbard, and gave Kelso a murderous look. "I then thought that I would have to kill him, and I confess that all at once I *felt* like killing him," Kelso remembered. The "ruffian" backed down and took his twenty lashes, and so did the rest of the gang members. The principal leader got forty lashes the next day for trying to reignite the "wholly unprovoked and unjustifiable rebellion," and Kelso added further humiliation to the punishment by putting a split lathe on his nose and mocking him as "my elephant on exhibition" before expelling him from the school. No more punishments were required for the rest of the term, and Kelso was hailed as a success.[50]

But at home he was still miserable. He often found Adelia weeping, and she would not explain why. She seemed interested in nothing but religion, but that, too, failed to make her happy. "Home" for her still meant her parents' house, not where she lived with Kelso. "She became irritable and often treated me very unkindly. Indeed, it seemed only from a sense of duty and not for any love for me that she even treated me with any wifely consideration at all." It became painfully obvious that she did not love him, and perhaps never had. He prayed to God to be able to win her affections and did all he could to be a compassionate and devoted husband. He also had a "great desire" for children and was saddened that two years of marriage had not yet borne any fruit. "It was but natural, then, for me to feel deeply hurt and shocked when I learned, as by chance I did, that she was using effectual means to prevent conception. Besides its unkindness to me, I then regarded this act as criminal.... I told her that I regarded her as a kind of murderess, and that I could not live with a woman that would destroy, in her own womb, the life germ of her own child." Wringing her hands in agony, Adelia begged Kelso's forgiveness, promised never to do it again, and worried that even if her husband could forgive her, God might not.[51]

In the autumn of 1853, the Kelsos tried to make a fresh start. John taught at a "remarkably pleasant" school in Buchanan County and was promoted from exhorter to minister in the Methodist Episcopal Church, South. "I preached every Sunday to good congregations and soon became a first class revivalist." In what little spare time he had, Kelso studied a college curriculum, sleeping only five or six hours each night. "Every thing succeeded that I touched, and every body was loud in my praise." In April 1854, their daughter, Florella, was born in the crude little log cabin they rented. Kelso in his autobiography remembered himself turning twenty-three and feeling, despite his melancholy disposition, "quite happy."[52]

A year later that happiness was already just a memory. The family was living in Platte County, seven miles from the city of Weston, where Kelso had landed a teaching job paying the "very high" salary of forty dollars a month. His Christian neighbors were predominantly followers of Alexander Campbell, and they feuded bitterly with Methodists in that part of Missouri. As a result they were "very clannish" and did not befriend the Kelsos. "Besides this, they were nearly all of that class of haughty slave owners who looked with contempt on anyone who did not own slaves and who had to earn his own livelihood. This haughty disposition on their part was greatly intensified, too, at this time, by the general excitement that prevailed on the subject of slavery. Kansas was just across the river and there actual war was going on to determine whether slavery should or should not exist in that territory when it became a state. Every body on our side of the river was suspected and ostracized who was not wont to loudly hurrah for slavery, and to just as loudly curse the abolitionists and the 'Black Republicans.'" Kelso kept his mouth shut about slavery. He had enough problems at home. Adelia, alone most of the time with the baby, grew more unhappy than ever. At times Kelso feared for her sanity. When she spoke, sometimes her memory would seem to become paralyzed, and she would drift off, at a loss for even common words. Kelso was feeling "worn out by her fretful temper and almost constant but unexplained tears." Feeling his love for her slowly dying, he daily prayed to God for the ability to love her as a good Christian husband.[53]

Mima Snyder came to live with them for a few months. Twenty years old, she had once been one of Kelso's best students. She was no beauty, but she was an intellectual equal who could share "in the most lofty flights" that his own mind was capable of taking. Sweet and cheerful Mima was also the most charming woman he had ever met. Quickly she became a true and deeply sympathetic friend. He worked to conceal his domestic unhappiness from everyone, but Mima could see it all and "was able to read my secret and my sorrow." He could not admit to himself that he was falling in love with her, because such feelings would have been a terrible sin. In the fall of 1855, Mima returned to her parents' house, leaving Kelso alone with his wife, his child, and his despair. By the spring of 1856, with a second baby in the house, Adelia was more unkind to Kelso than ever, and the last embers of his affections for her finally flickered and died.[54]

Then Adelia confessed the cause of her great sorrow. "She said that in marrying me she had done me a great and irreparable wrong which she feared God could never forgive." She had always respected him but had never loved him. Deeply in love with another man, she nevertheless had obeyed her father's command that she marry Kelso instead since he seemed a better bet to "attain honor and distinction in the world." She had hoped that she could overcome her love for the other man and grow to love Kelso, which her father assured her would happen in due course. Instead her desire for the lost suitor had increased with her anguish at having made the wrong choice, "till it had become a species of madness." Desperately hoping to still have the man she loved, she tried to make Kelso "so intolerably wretched" that he would leave her. Kelso, in turn, confessed that he realized he loved Mima and was sure she loved him. Adelia and John agreed to an amicable divorce; she took the children back to her parents' house, and he engaged counsel, began a divorce suit, and professed his love to Mima, who gave him a lock of her hair.[55]

The Sunday following Adelia's departure, Kelso went for the last time to preach to his congregation. In his pocket he had a letter written by Adelia absolving him from any blame for their separation. "My congregation here was very large, and was composed in large part of fine shouters" who, next to Jesus and the chapel's owner, seemed to idolize Kelso himself. "As yet, they knew nothing of my domestic infelicities. They welcomed me as usual with demonstrations of delight." The meeting began with hymns and an opening prayer, as it always had. Instead of preaching a sermon from the pulpit, Kelso addressed his flock and told them he could not preach to them that day or ever again. He told them he was separating from his wife, which Methodist preachers were not supposed to do. He then read Adelia's letter, dismissed the meeting, and walked out of the chapel. "No one spoke to me as I departed. All seemed speechless with amazement."[56]

"The storm soon burst forth in all its fury," Kelso remembered. "The storm which I had been dreading but which I knew was bound to come." But the impact of the scandal was far worse than he had imagined. Adelia's father, the Rev. L. W. Moore, "raved like a fiend" and "vowed the direst vengeance." He brought countercharges against Kelso, all of them false, according to the autobiographer, except the one true and damaging claim that Kelso had fallen in love with another woman. Mima was summoned to testify; Mima's father, in language taken by Missouri's culture of endemic violence to be a declaration of intent to commit justifiable homicide, said that if his daughter were dragged into this scandal, he and Kelso "could not both live." Kelso quickly wrote to Mima, "requesting her to regard my words of love as recalled—as never having been uttered." He had hoped that she would see this as a tactical, temporary move and not an expression of his real affections. He was also concerned that professing his love to her before he was divorced was a sin. Apparently taking Kelso to be a cad, a coward, or both, Mima never contacted him again and quickly married someone else. As his hopes for a future with Mima crumbled, Kelso watched as "Old Moore," his fellow minister in the Methodist church, continually worked to destroy his reputation. "A thousand conjectures, generally more or less unfavorable to myself, soon grew into positive assertions. Moore's version of the affair, black with malicious falsehoods, was soon obtained and duly magnified. Indeed, for many weeks, in several counties in which I had been very popular, unleashed almost warlike excitement. Several fights in regard to the matter did actually occur. The church, led by Moore, almost unanimously took sides against me." On the Sunday following his resignation, he returned to the chapel to sit among the members of his congregation as another man preached from Kelso's pulpit. "Most of my former flock shunned me as if I had been a ferocious beast." Only one man, a friend he loved as a brother, would shake his hand, and even he would turn against Kelso soon afterward.[57]

Why had his community so quickly and completely forsaken him? Had he abused his power as a minister, they would have forgiven him, he reflected bitterly. Had he seduced some young woman in the church, they would have pardoned him. "They always do forgive a beloved shepherd for such little peccadillos. Many of them seem to think that these are almost the proper things for a popular preacher to do. But I had been guilty of nothing of this kind. My offense was, in their eyes, a far greater one. My offense was that of being crushed under a *great misfortune*; and this is an offense which the public, and especially the religionists thereof, seldom forgive. With them, it is far better to be *fortunate* in *sin* than to be *unfortunate* in *innocence*." Power, even when abused, is respected. Weakness is not. Or perhaps the faithful suspected that Kelso was not an innocent man suffering from the bad luck to have married a woman who could not love him; perhaps, instead, they thought that his domestic infelicities were God's judgments upon a secret sinner.[58]

As Kelso was building his reputation as a teacher and preacher, and agonizing about his failing marriage, he was also, it seems, weighing Methodist doctrines in the balances of reason, science, and common sense. A short time after his Sabbath shunning, a conference of ministers in his circuit of the Methodist Episcopal Church, South met in Plattsburg. "I attended this conference," Kelso wrote, "intending then and there to sever my connection with the ministry and with the church. I had come to be an unbeliever in an endless hell of fire and brimstone, and in many other things which my church required me to preach." He no longer believed in the central doctrines of Methodism. He had not yet come to doubt everything in the Bible, but his skepticism had started him down the path toward freethinking infidelity. "Indeed, I was just in process of bursting the bonds of superstitious slavery and becoming free. Besides this, I knew that, according to the laws of the M. E. Church, a minister is not permitted to separate from his wife for any cause except that of adultery; and, in my case, that cause did not exist." The braided bonds of dogma, dismal matrimony, and his connection to a Christian community would be cut with the same knife. But he would not slink away quietly into the night: "I wished to burst a bomb in the camp of the Lord and to leave all in consternation. This I did, with better success than I anticipated."[59]

Few of the ministers at the conference had yet heard anything about the scandal. The presiding elder of his district, the Rev. William Goss Caples, who would be remembered as the greatest preacher in the first century of Missouri Methodism, even gave a little speech in praise of Kelso. "Grateful for this favor, I concluded now to throw in my bomb." Kelso stood up and proceeded to attack "the doctrine of hell and several others of the doctrines that constituted our priestly stock in trade." The uproar was immediate. He had expected to stand alone, but to his surprise about half a dozen other clergymen rose and argued, not in support of his heretical opinions, but for a Methodist preacher's right to freedom of thought and expression. The majority vehemently argued against such freedoms. Reverend Caples, who had earlier praised Kelso so highly, "finally threw himself into the breach and came to the help of the Lord against the mighty. He declared me a very powerful and dangerous enemy, and warned his hearers that if my heresies were not nipped in the bud and my influence with the people destroyed, I would, within ten years, ruin the church and demoralize society." Someone quickly produced the damning fact of his separation from Adelia, and the brethren lunged, making great use of it, "in order to break me down." The battle raged into the night. Methodist conferences usually combined a short business meeting with long hours of preaching, praying, and hymn singing. This one came to focus on the destruction of John R. Kelso. Eventually, a letter purportedly written by Adelia and attacking his character was read aloud to the assembly. He knew the letter to be a forgery and promptly said so. He suspected that the forgers were Adelia's father and the Rev. Daniel H. Root, who in Kelso's eyes was "one of the Roots of evil." Kelso withdrew from the conference and the church "and armed myself to shoot those two Godly forgers," but his father and some friends "prevented the shooting."[60]

At the end of that year, 1856, Kelso, age twenty-six, set off on foot through the snow in a southerly direction, with a book in hand, twenty-five dollars in his pocket, a change of linen wrapped in a handkerchief, and no particular destination. "I was now a wifeless, homeless, churchless, and almost friendless and moneyless wanderer upon the earth. I was free, however, and the world was before me. But whither should I go and what should I do?" He was as self-directed as any Emersonian individualist, as free as any California forty-niner. He came to the banks of the Missouri River. The ferry had stopped running because of the ice, but that ice was not yet safe enough, the people on shore told him, to be crossed on foot. He walked out boldly anyway, proud of his own daring. Spectators watched him stride out without even testing the ice near the riverbank. They saw him disappear through a snow-covered hole, struggle to thrust his arms, and then his head, and then the rest of his body back out onto the ice, and as he made his way stiffly to the opposite bank they cheered and waved their hats in the air. Exhausted, his clothes frozen, Kelso could barely wave his arm and croak a reply. With freedom had come a certain recklessness.[61]

By the spring of 1861, Kelso had rebuilt his life. He had earned a degree at Pleasant Ridge College and then had established a successful school in Buffalo, Missouri, the Dallas County seat. He had married one of his students, Suzie Barnes, and they lived with the two children from his first marriage and a child the couple had together on a "beautiful little farm" about a mile and a half from town. But circumstances would again prompt him to stand up alone and declare heretical principles before a hostile community, throwing another bomb into another congregation as he asserted his independence.[62]

He had to close his school a few weeks early that spring. The intense and fearful excitement that had followed the firing on Fort Sumter by secessionists in South Carolina had swept up the schoolteacher and his pupils alike. His schoolroom opened right onto the Buffalo town square, and "whenever any news arrived favorable to the South, there was loud cheering right at our door." The enthusiasm that electrified Missouri seemed to Kelso to pervert human nature itself. Children wished they could trade their toys for guns. Women wished they could march off to battlefields. Farmers left their fields, merchants their shops, and artisans their tools to crowd the streets and public squares of the state's cities and towns. "At every corner, fiery orators, with burning words and wild gesticulations, heightened still the already morbidly inflamed passions of the multitude." No public speakers could enflame passions quite like the preachers.[63]

Kelso had, up until this time, kept quiet about slavery and politics. He had seen what could happen to people who dissented from local opinion. In Weston, Missouri, in the 1850s, he had watched "a well-dressed, well-educated, and well-behaved stranger," rumored to be an abolitionist spy, be "taken by a mob composed of nearly the whole city, tarred and feathered, ridden on a rail, and then sold for ten cents at a mock auction." Kelso's parents were strongly in favor of slavery and the South, and so were the rest of the members of his extended family save one wayward cousin. When he told his mother and father and other near relatives that he was against slavery and would stand by the Union, "they had expressed their indignation and had ceased to correspond with me at all." He knew that declaring his sentiments and principles in Buffalo would cut the bonds of sympathy with his students and friends, too, nearly all of whom were secessionists. Since it did not seem that there were any other stalwart Union men in the entire town, he also knew that a public declaration would be extremely dangerous. "I felt that I was again standing alone and was about to take the most critical step of my life."[64]

The day he closed his school, "there was an unusually large crowd upon the public square, and the excitement was intense. The news had just reached us of the seceding of several more states. The speakers were jubilant, and represented the united States as virtually destroyed, the confederate States as virtually established." When the last speaker finished yet another secessionist harangue, Kelso climbed the courthouse steps, called the attention of the crowd, and read a series of pro-Union resolutions that he had prepared. He declared to the stunned townspeople that secession was treason, and that he and other loyal citizens would fight to the death against the rebellion and in support of the United States. He realized, he said, that prosecession Missouri governor Claiborne F. Jackson had just issued a proclamation stating that everything Kelso was now saying constituted treason against the state of Missouri and was a capital offense. But it was Jackson and the prosecessionist legislators, Kelso charged, who were the traitors deserving death. To underline the point that this was not just a political dispute but a question of personal honor, he called out the governor and declared that he and Jackson "could not both live." Then Kelso walked down the steps and stood silently in the crowd.[65]

At first there was only "a general indistinct murmur of low voices." Taken "utterly by surprise," the crowd "seemed thunderstruck" by Kelso's "audacity." Then he began to hear some louder voices denouncing him as a "traitor to the South" who "ought to be shot down like a wolf or a sheep-killing dog." As the crowd's fury began to build, Kelso suddenly felt a child's fingers clutching one of his hands. "Looking down, I saw the anxious face of one of my pupils, a bright little boy of eight years." The boy tugged at him, pulling him away from the crowd. "The little boy led me around some store buildings and into an old ware house, the doors and windows of which were all closed." Four men sat in the darkness of the warehouse. We believe everything you just said out there, they told Kelso. But by publicly declaring your principles like that, you are just recklessly throwing your life away, practically begging the crowd to tear you to pieces. They offered to help hide him until tempers cooled. Kelso refused to hide or keep quiet, and asked to borrow a revolver.[66]

A great meeting was held in the town a week later. Peter Wilkes and other noted secessionist speakers arrived from Springfield with a Confederate flag to be flown from the courthouse roof, and they processed into a town square crowded with people from throughout the county. A band was ready to play "Dixie" and secession songs after the speeches, and men were ready to fire their guns into the air. Kelso stood near the speakers' stand as Wilkes delivered his address. But Kelso also saw a young Buffalo merchant named John McConnell and about half a dozen other secret Union sympathizers that he had met over the previous week. They knew what Kelso planned to do and had tried, unsuccessfully, to dissuade him. Now here they were, as if by chance, heavily armed and stationed near him and the speaker's stand. The orator's remarks were cheered and loudly applauded. As Kelso scanned the crowd, though, knowing that Union sentiment was stronger in the county than in Buffalo itself, he also saw "many men with pale earnest faces who did not join in the applause." He next observed "a rough looking set of customers," about thirty hunters from the Niangua hills, dressed in buckskin, carrying long rifles, and belted with revolvers and bowie knives. Their hard faces did not betray their intentions. "They had heard I was to be killed on that occasion if I attempted to speak," they told Kelso afterward, "and they had come to see who killed me and how the killing was done."[67]

Wilkes concluded his powerful and eloquent speech urging the people to stand as one for secession and the South. The Christian scriptures showed secession from Northern tyranny to be a sacred cause. More particularly, Wilkes cited images from Genesis and the Book of Revelation to argue that current events could be plotted according to the arc of sacred history—or at least that biblical analogies could reveal God's political sentiments in 1861. "He said that the seven states which had then seceded were typified by the seven stars, the seven churches, the seven candlesticks, the seven years of plenty, the seven angels, and other sevens of the scripture, all of a glorious, a heaven-approved character." As the crowd applauded Wilkes and before the next speaker could be introduced, Kelso leaped in front of the stand and waved his hand for attention. "Instantly a dead silence prevailed. No one in the audience seemed even to breathe. The very audacity of my act seemed to hold them all fixed with a kind of fascination." Kelso the former Methodist preacher knew how to play Wilkes's language game. He parried Wilkes's reference to Genesis 41:29 (years of plenty) by drawing from the verse following it, which supplied an opposite image (years of famine); he turned the prosecessionist speaker's invocation of the first three chapters of Revelation upside down by drawing contrary images from later chapters in the same book. "I showed that the seven seceding states were typified by the seven lean kine, the seven years of famine, the seven vials of wrath, the seven heads of the dragon, the seven devils, and many other sevens of the scriptures, all of a damnable, a heaven abominated character. I showed that, as Satan had drawn away one third of the hosts of heaven, so the arch fiend of secession had drawn away one third of the hosts of our Union, our heaven on earth."[68]

When Kelso had read his pro-Union resolutions a week earlier, he was defiantly expressing heretical political sentiments and severing his connection to the community, contemptuously tossing a rhetorical bomb in the face of a hostile crowd. This speech was different. He still thought he stood alone and knew that he was again risking his life to speak out for his unpopular principles. But this time he seemed motivated by something grander than defiant self-assertion. Inspired not by God's grace but by what he portrayed as a self-sacrificing patriotic spirit, he spoke—he preached—not just to damn the rebels but to embolden timid Unionists and to convert the undecided. "My whole soul aglow with a kind of inspiration, I seemed to see in great letters of flame the very words I should speak. I forgot myself and my danger. I thought only of the cause I was defending and of victory." After neutralizing Wilkes's biblical rhetoric he turned to a different prooftext: "the inimitable words of our immortal Washington's Farewell Address." He invoked the history of the Revolutionary "forefathers" and prophesied the carnage and desolation that would follow from the Southern rebellion. His words, at least according to the recollections in his autobiography, had their effect, like a revival sermon making sinners weep and saints shout. "Tears—loyal tears rolled down the rough cheeks of many a brave and honest man who came there believing himself to be a secessionist.... A change was wrought in that great assembly. A tidal wave was rising that could not now be turned back, or resisted. When I closed, the pent up feelings of hundreds found vent in loud and hearty hurrahs for the Union and our brave old flag." After Kelso had finished, W. B. Edwards, one of the closet Unionists he had met in the darkened warehouse a week before, an old soldier lame from a war wound, hobbled on his crutches into Kelso's place and "poured forth a torrent of patriotic eloquence" that turned "the loyal fire" Kelso had kindled "into a flame."[69]

Then Kelso decided it was time to separate the sheep from the goats. He asked Edwards to go to one side of the town square and encouraged those who supported "Washington, the Union, and the Star-spangled Banner" to go with him. Wilkes, Kelso said, could walk to the other side to represent "Benedict Arnold, treason, and the Confederate flag." As Edwards "hobbled to his place, several hundred men waved their hats, hurrahed for the Union, and formed in a long line by his side." Wilkes, the other Springfield secessionists, and their local supporters, "thunder-struck and alarmed" at this completely unexpected transformation of their secession rally, conferred quickly, grabbed their flag, and hurriedly withdrew in their wagons as the Union men cheered. "We had won a great, though a bloodless victory."[70]

Few victories for Kelso over the next four years would be bloodless, but the political infidel previously standing alone had reconstituted a community of shared sentiment. The Union sympathizers quickly organized into military companies called Home Guards. Kelso was elected captain and then major of the Dallas County Battalion. He later was a lieutenant and then a captain in Missouri infantry and cavalry regiments, serving as a scout and a spy and gaining renown as a fearless fighter in the brutal guerrilla battles of the Missouri Ozarks.[71]

A nineteenth-century history based upon postwar interviews with soldiers on both sides of the conflict recorded some of the stories that earned Kelso a reputation for reckless heroism. He refused any promotion that might prevent him from having "personal conflicts with the enemy, which appears to have been almost a burning desire with him." On one occasion, as he alone charged a farmhouse occupied by armed men who knew he was coming, he was attacked by a big black dog that seized him by the calf. Without dropping his eyes from the front door or lowering the shotgun he had aimed there, he removed his revolver with his other hand, shot the dog in the head, and kept running. Astonished by his daring, the men in the house, according to the story, turned and ran out the back door without firing a shot. He had the "eccentric" habit of entering small camps of Confederate raiders or bandits alone, by stealth or in disguise, catching the enemy off guard, and then gunning them down. Once, feigning friendliness with two rebels he had found hiding out in the almost inaccessible bluffs above the Elk River, he asked them to inspect a thorn he had stuck in his finger, and when they dropped their gun barrels slightly to do so, he shot them both. In the White River Mountains near the Arkansas line, Kelso, scouting alone, found six tethered horses and three bandits sleeping by a fire. Gently removing a fine quilt that covered them so as not to stain it with blood, he shot them all and then took the quilt and the horses before the other three men, wherever they were, could capture or kill him. In a political speech after the end of the war, Kelso spoke of feeling "a strange, wild pleasure while beholding my foes fall before my own fatal shots."[72]

Perhaps it was as easy to shoot the "thieves and murderers" he chased through the Ozarks as it had been to kill squirrels that attacked the family corn when he was a child. Perhaps standing up to secessionists trying to destroy the United States felt no different than taking a stand against a band of knife-wielding rebels in the classroom. Surely, as he took aim and pulled the trigger he felt more than just resentment for the depredations pro-Confederate forces had inflicted upon Missouri since 1861—there was also his long-smoldering resentment against haughty slaveholders who looked down their noses at plain laboring men. Whatever mix of personal inclinations and grievances motivated him, Kelso also tried to articulate a larger ideological purpose during his brief political career (he delivered his first formal political speech in the spring of 1864 and served one term in Congress, 1865 to 1867).[73]

"We are in the midst of a revolution, the most fearful, the most gigantic the world ever knew," Kelso declared in a speech delivered at Mount Vernon, Missouri, on April 23, 1864. They were not just fighting for themselves and

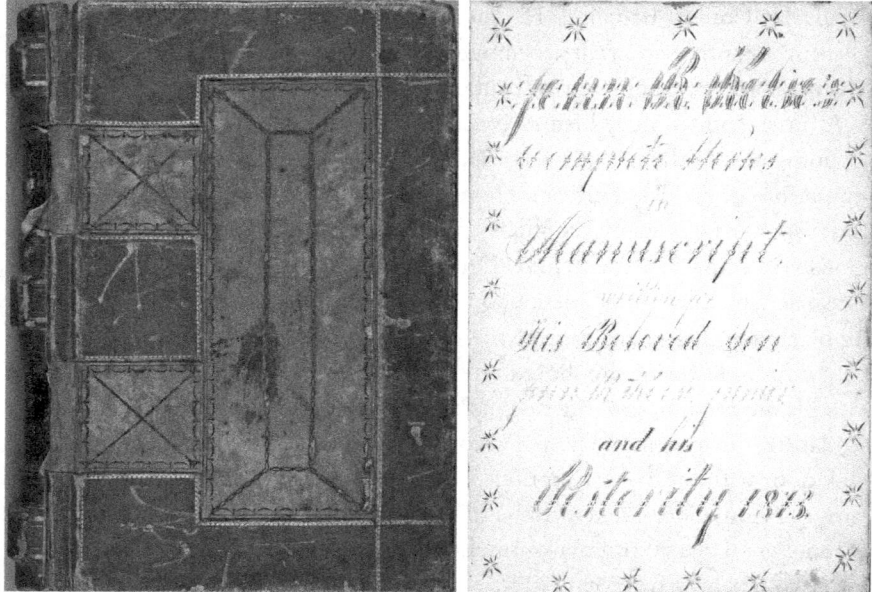

"The Works of John R. Kelso," cover and title page. Kelso preserved his poems, speeches, lectures, and partial autobiography in an 800-page ledger book. Photos courtesy of the Huntington Library, San Marino, California.

their own nation. The effects of the American Civil War, he believed, were "destined to extend to all future ages, and to be felt by every individual, by every nation, and by every race." Victory would bring freedom and joy to millions; it would "give the zenith of glory to our republican institutions, to usher in the great political millennium." Defeat would extinguish the world's beacon of liberty and hope and plunge civilization back into the dark ages. Nothing less than this, Kelso told his audience, was "the grand drama in which we are all actors." He supported the abolition of slavery and a vigorous prosecution of the war until the Confederacy was crushed. He argued for a hard line against rebels (disfranchise the disloyal and confiscate their property) and pondered the problem of free blacks (wondering if it would be possible to force a regime change in Mexico and colonize them there). He developed these ideas further in a speech at Walnut Grove, Missouri, on September 18, 1865, five months after the surrender at Appomattox but, Kelso insisted, as the battle continued in political form. More than merely stump speeches by a radical Republican, these addresses were meditations on the meaning of the war and the nature of equality.[74]

It was a war of antagonistic principles that had been coiled together in the Constitution at the nation's founding, an "*irrepressible conflict*" between "the Spirit of Slavery, that foulest monster of the dark ages," and "the Spirit of Liberty."

Great statesmen—Washington, Jefferson, and Jackson; Clay, Webster, and Benton; Douglas and Lincoln—had all seen the battle coming. Treasonous Southern aristocrats, corrupted by African slavery, disdainful of honest labor, unable any longer to manipulate the national government to serve their own selfish interests, appealed to the "low passions of bad men," blinded the masses of poor and ignorant whites, and "resolved to *ruin* what they could no longer *rule*." After the war, like Satan and the fallen angels of *Paradise Lost*, but without a hell to contain them, the traitors plotted their revenge. They did more than plot, Kelso warned in 1865. They were already reshackling blacks in a form of serfdom that was "*worse* than *slavery*," and with their conservative Northern friends they were again reaching for the levers of political power.[75]

The fundamental doctrine at stake was political equality, and Kelso's central text in both speeches was the second sentence of the Declaration of Independence. The principle worth fighting and dying for was that all men were created equal and had the same inalienable rights to life, liberty, and the pursuit of happiness. He quickly assured his audience that he considered blacks the equal to whites in no other way, and called Africans "kinky heads" as if to confirm that he shared his listeners' racism. Even as he did so, however, he acknowledged that his strong antipathy to blacks came from being "reared up in a Slave state by ultra proslavery parents" where he "unconsciously imbibed many of their prejudices." By 1865, he had given up his fantasies about colonization, praised black bravery in battle and loyalty to the Union, and insisted that freedmen be given all the rights of citizens. The crucial task for Americans was to finally incorporate the sublime sentiment of the Declaration into the Constitution and the laws of the land, securing political equality once and for all.[76]

All men were endowed "by their Creator" with inalienable rights, Kelso kept quoting, and the quotations were not the only place God appeared in the speeches. A recollection of a prosperous and contented country before the war included mention of churches where "happy congregations sang praises to God." His 1865 speech opened by thanking the Almighty, as well as the army, for the salvation of the United States. "O God!" he paused to exclaim while arguing for black citizenship, "if it be so great a *crime* to be *black* why hast thou made them thus?" One passage, too, even referenced God's dreadful judgments upon a Christian nation. If it was true, he asked, that we should do unto others as we would have them do unto us, "how dare we, a Christian people, do these things unto [blacks]? Can we hope for God's blessing if we continue to violate this His solemn commandment? Have not the judgments of the last five years been sufficient to teach us wisdom? Have not these judgments come upon us as the direct consequences of the crime of slavery?"[77]

Such language might suggest that Kelso's move from Methodism in the 1850s to the atheism he publicly proclaimed in the 1870s took longer than his reminiscences indicate. But it is unlikely that in the mid-1860s he could still have been counted among the faithful. In the midst of the bitter and brutal war he watched a poor young woman, forced out from her home into a snowstorm by her rebel neighbors, crying to God as she died in childbirth. Kelso decided then that he had "no use, no love, no respect for any such god," who, if he existed, only seemed to answer the prayers of the wealthy. His political speeches suggest instead that Kelso was a prudent politician, knowing his audience and using religious tropes just as he used quotations from Milton, phrases from "The Star-Spangled Banner," and racist slang for his rhetorical purposes. The speeches as delivered, too, despite these few lines of God talk, seem conceptually closer to his freethought lectures in the next decade than to anything he would have preached from a Methodist pulpit in the previous one.[78]

Appeals to reason, science, and common sense drive most of the arguments in the political speeches. In the freethought lectures, Kelso interrogated Christian speculations about how God might have created the universe by infusing matter in a chaotic state (Gen. 1:2: "the earth was without form") with the force of gravity or attraction. Kelso argued that attraction was an essential property of matter in the first place, so any talk of force being applied or infused was false by definition. Similarly, Southerners talked about the Confederate states reentering the Union as if they were indestructible political atoms. But a state, Kelso reasoned in his 1865 speech, by definition had a fixed territory and a people coherently organized in a government—without both characteristics it ceases to exist as a state, just as without both hydrogen and oxygen "water ceases to exist *as such.*" The science that Kelso hailed in the lectures was the disciplined investigation of natural causes and effects, processes playing out in time and originating not from some supernatural first cause but from properties inherent in matter itself. Similarly, the political science in the speeches examined how natural laws (like "that first great law of nature,—*self defense*") shaped particular historical circumstances. The Civil War was "the natural result of a well known cause," the unstable compound of liberty and slavery in the Constitution. Blacks and whites had a "natural" repulsion to one another and would separate "as do oil and water" if they had not been unnaturally bound together in a slave society. Kelso also appealed to common sense in the speeches as he tried, in a "plain way" to "communicate plain truths to plain people." He presented some of his conclusions as if they would be self-evident to any reasonable person without extended logical deduction or scientific analysis of causes and effects. On treason as a capital offense: Don't nations, just like the individuals of which they are composed, have a right to defend themselves, killing murderous assailants if they have to? On the confiscation of rebel property to pay the national debt incurred by the war: Don't plaintiffs who lose an unjust lawsuit have to pay court costs? On blacks and political rights: Shouldn't men who cast bullets in the war to defend the country be able to cast ballots in peacetime?[79]

Still, Kelso's sermonic political speeches opened a foundational text (the Declaration) and extracted a fundamental doctrine (political equality) to orient moral action. He appealed to his audience's deepest convictions and ultimate concerns, animating hearts as well as minds. He did not just try to motivate them to fight or vote but encouraged them to embrace a shared identity and purpose in their daily lives. Was not this patriotic nationalism a "religion" to replace his Methodism?

Not as Kelso of the freethought lectures understood the term. In those later lectures, the irrepressible conflict was between religion, another vestige from the dark ages, and freethinking science, the engine of progress and freedom. "Religion" referred to outmoded systems of belief and practice positing a deity or deities as an ultimate reality existing behind the veil of the material world. Playing off of the etymological root (*religare*, to bind), he even turned religion into a verb: "In order, then, to still cling to these antiquated embodiments of ignorance, men must be *religioned—tied back*, as the word means, from the light and the knowledge of the bright present, to the impenetrable gloom of the dark past." "Religionists," as he called them, believed that their sacred texts were unique revelations of divine truth, not just particularly pleasing expressions of truths already evident from nature or historical experience. They valued mystical trances and rapturous moods, which Kelso came to see as psychological effects of natural causes, rather than respecting reason, science, and common sense. They bowed to the collective wisdom and traditions of fellow believers in their churches, whereas Kelso found that truth often lay on the opposite side of a community's majority opinion, even when he had to stand alone. They chided him for skeptical criticism that tore down Christianity without building up anything in its place, failing to see that skepticism, and not their credulity, was the handmaiden to truth. A Christian's faith, Kelso had once taught, was a gift of divine grace; his new beliefs, he claimed, were a reasonable person's response to empirical evidence and logical analysis. A Christian's faith persisted despite evidence against its truth claims; Kelso's beliefs were always open to refutation or correction: show me where my reasoning or information is faulty, he said at the end of his lectures, and I will change my positions.[80]

If the Kelso who threw himself into war and politics in the 1860s could be said to have any "faith" at all—a deep trust and commitment based more in a hopeful heart than in hardheaded analysis—it was a faith in America itself. This American faith was not that of George Shane Phillips, who by the Civil War had come to see Christianity manifested by and perfected in American institutions. Kelso's America did not need God to underwrite the laws of nature, the Spirit to work supernaturally to form a more perfect Union, or churches and preachers to tell people what to think. His faith was in America as a place and a polity that allowed ambitious young men like John R. Kelso to still upward rise.

The Creative Ambiguity of Civil Religion

Phillips's Civil War book and Kelso's political speeches can be seen through the lens of "civil religion," even though Kelso at the time would have denied the term "religion" and Phillips would have rejected the modifier "civil." As chaplain to the 49th Ohio Regiment, Phillips preached to soldiers; as a political candidate, Captain John R. Kelso addressed voters, many of whom were members of his own regiment in the 8th Missouri State Militia Calvary. Surviving letters and diaries suggest that perhaps as many as a quarter of the soldiers in the Union army were devout Christians, some of them converting in army camp revivals like the one that occurred after the defeat at Chickamauga. For some of these men, Phillips's depiction of the war as a holy crusade would have struck a chord. Other believing soldiers shared his broader notion that the war was being directed by divine Providence, though they (like Abraham Lincoln) thought that God's purposes might be more mysterious, a response to events that could tip them toward fatalism. A larger group—active church members and merely nominal Christians alike—held the conviction that they were fighting in a just (and therefore divinely sanctioned) cause and turned to faith for comfort in the shadow of suffering and death. Large numbers of men fighting for the North (and for the South, too, for that matter) were indifferent to religion, and a smaller percentage were, like Kelso, skeptical or hostile to it. Yet many of these, too, expressed ideological convictions and did not just enlist for pay or adventure, or fight only to defend themselves and their comrades. They fought, as Kelso did, to preserve what they understood to be a government that was the world's best hope for freedom. Kelso's civil religion made liberty a sacred cause; Phillips's showed how the cause of liberty served a sacred purpose.[81]

Much later in life, a quarter century after the war, John R. Kelso had come to see that his patriotic nationalism, even emptied of all theological content, had functioned—psychologically and socially—as something very much like a religion. Although as a younger man he had "discovered the utterly mythical nature of all the gods," he had "unfortunately failed to discover, at the same time, the equally mythical nature of all governments." Writing during his final illness in 1891, he saw that during the war he had been as "ignorant and superstitious" as any other patriotic defender of the Union. He had responded to the call to "butcher" his Southern brothers as a "sacred duty," a call that "was sanctified by the commandment of my *government*; and to me, this was the commandment of my *god.*" He and his fellow patriots, he now thought, had deified a superstitious idea—the Union—which was really just a myth covering the crimes of a plutocratic oligarchy. After all the death and destruction and heartache, this Union had been preserved. But blacks freed from one form of slavery were merely reenslaved under a worse form as the plutocrats continued to use the machinery of government to exploit them and everyone else. Hoping for a revolution that would create a "New Nation" on the bedrock of individualism, where "every sane individual will be a sovereign, and *self*, his kingdom," Kelso decided that during the Civil War he had had too much faith and not enough skepticism: "How blindly, how piously, how patriotically inhuman even the best of us are capable of being made by superstition, whether with regard to those mythical monsters, called gods, or those equally mythical monsters called governments."[82]

Epilogue

Death and Politics

In Columbus, Mississippi, in early April of 1841, the townspeople who crowded into the Cumberland Presbyterian Church for eighteen consecutive evenings witnessed their own dialogue of skepticism and faith. Charles G. Olmsted, a Yale graduate and an attorney in his early fifties, was the author of a deistic critique called *The Bible, Its Own Refutation*. James Smith, a decade younger, was a Presbyterian preacher and editor who had been touring the South the winter before when he encountered Olmsted as the leader of a group of infidels. Olmsted's "easy manners and gentlemanly bearing, had so ingratiated himself with many of the citizens of the place," Smith wrote, "especially with the young men, as to exercise a most pernicious influence, by the dissemination of his Infidel principles." As a younger man, Smith himself had been "a Deist," having concluded after reading Paine and Volney "that Religion was a fraud contrived to govern mankind." Smith felt that he personally knew the danger of religious skepticism better than some—better, perhaps, than the clergymen in Columbus who seemed cowed by the lawyer's eloquence and erudition. So when Olmsted challenged Smith to a debate, Smith, giving himself over a year to prepare, accepted. Smith published his version of the argument in 1843 as *The Christian's Defence*. It was, as an otherwise sympathetic review noted, a "ponderous volume" of over 670 pages.[1]

A decade later, Smith was the pastor of a Presbyterian church in Illinois preaching a funeral sermon for the four-year-old son of a local couple. Neither parent was a member of Smith's church. The dead boy's mother had been casually connected to the Episcopalians. The father, Smith had heard, was "a deist inclined to skepticism." The mother, almost undone by grief, turned to Smith for comfort and joined his congregation two years later. The father, a lawyer, "very much depressed and downcast by the death of his son" and "perplexed and unsettled on the fundamentals of religion," paid the pew rental but did not the join the church. Still, he befriended Smith, gratefully received a copy of the pastor's defense against religious skepticism, and seemed, at least to Smith, to move toward Christianity. For Smith, the former skeptic, it was not surprising that

"Washington and Lincoln (Apotheosis)." (Philadelphia, ca. 1865). Photo courtesy of the Library Company of Philadelphia.

death would prompt the grieving couple—Abraham and Mary Todd Lincoln—to seek "the consolation of the gospel."[2]

In this world, the old deist Ben Franklin could have quipped, nothing can be said to be certain except death and politics. Politics—writ both large and small—had changed between Franklin's day and Lincoln's. A cluster of British colonies declaring themselves an independent, confederated Republic had become a mighty continental Union torn apart by slavery and then reborn on bloody battlefields as a modern nation-state. Religion did a fair amount of the work to secure allegiance to this political experiment in both North and South—the cultivation of sentiment, the assurance that the political project was tied to foundational moral values and transcendent authority. Religious and political faith for many were tightly intertwined. A vocal Christian majority, empowered by aggressive institutions, fervent revivalism, and an ideology often linking American progress to millennial expectations, was unable to imagine any ideals that could properly motivate patriotic commitment without a God in heaven to set the rules or a Redeemer to make up for human failings. They condemned the faithlessness, the untrustworthy shallowness, of any who doubted their fundamental doctrines.

Death, believers said, was the ultimate test—the existential crisis revealing the pathetic inadequacy of skeptical philosophy. The Civil War, where thousands were routinely cut down in cornfields and on country roads on a given afternoon, merely magnified the brute physical fact awaiting everyone.

Death

Death was the test, Christians continually argued, that skeptics always failed. In 1864, as the war ground on, the lists of casualties lengthened, and tens of thousands of families mourned their dead, William Rounseville Alger published *A Critical History of the Doctrine of a Future Life*. A treatise in comparative religion and mythology as well as a philosophical analysis, the *Critical History* argued that the belief that the soul survived the death of the body was the "cardinal tenet of religion"—it was the "common faith of mankind" professed by most people in all civilized nations from ancient to modern times. Among every people, however, there were "persons with less credulous hearts and more skeptical faculties" who doubted it. Freethinkers resisted the tyranny of the authorities who demanded such faith. Satirists mocked the dogmas and superstitions that in every culture inevitably enveloped religious notions of the afterlife. Pantheists ancient and modern imagined that their consciousness, rather than continuing after death, would be swallowed up by the great All. "Worldlings" focused on this life rather than wonder or worry about the next: one type did so by philosophical choice and intentional practice, chasing away thoughts of death with the pleasures and beauties of the present; another, the gross sensualists, did so because they could not conceive of anything past the gratification of their animal appetites. The largest group of dissenters to the common faith in a future life, however, were the skeptics who refused to accept it because their neighbors made the case for it with bad arguments and fanciful dreams that seemed to contradict what they saw as the hard facts of experience.[3]

After hundreds of pages of learned analysis and discussion, Alger agreed that neither science nor philosophy could provide positive proof of a future life. What should we do, then, in the face of death? Across cultures and throughout history, we see a predominant hope for life after death, Alger wrote. Beneath the arguments, speculations, fanciful dreams, and dogmas handed down from authority, that hope seemed to arise from a basic human instinct—an instinct that had to have been implanted in the human soul for a reason. As we lie down to die, Alger counseled, we need to fling out our loving hope, like a spider casting its silken thread into space, and leap after it, trusting that rather than sinking into an abyss of nothingness we will land "safe in some elysium better than we know, to find ourselves still in God."[4]

The "good death" of the pious was a staple of Christian literature. Nearly every issue of the *Experienced Christian's Magazine* (1796–97), for example, had deathbed narratives. While health reformer and physician William A. Alcott did not think deathbeds were particularly revelatory about skepticism and faith, Dr. David Nelson in *The Cause and Cure of Infidelity* (1841) argued that near-death experiences offered important evidence supporting Christian doctrines of the afterlife. William Taylor's *Seven Years' Street Preaching in San Francisco* (1857) concluded with nearly fifty pages of "triumphant death scenes." The Christian press never tired of printing stories of infidels quavering or converting in the face of death. Christian readers read again and again about Tom Paine's besotted and miserable death, Voltaire's cowardly call for a priest, Ethan Allen's supposed recommendation of Christianity to his dying daughter, and the claim that Abner Kneeland asked for a Bible as he succumbed to his final illness. Writers criticized or mocked the despairing doubt of the historian Edward Gibbon, the weak-kneed Romantic atheism of Percy Shelley, and even the philosophic serenity of a dying David Hume. Anonymous local infidels received the same treatment. Freethinkers rolled their eyes at the stories of triumphant Christian deaths, noting that many diseases, such as consumption, had tranquilizing effects upon the mind in its final moments, and they challenged the stories of recanting infidels as distortions or outright lies. Robert Dale Owen, in his debate with Origen Bacheler, considered the alleged recantations as reliable as Cotton Mather's reports of witchcraft. Other skeptics responded with accounts of infidels, such as Dr. Thomas Cooper, dying calmly with their convictions intact.[5]

Skeptics had nothing to offer in the hour of crisis, believers contended. A discussion of George Bethune English's *Grounds of Christianity Examined* (1813) noted that nothing in English's critical perspective would help a reader prepare for death. An attack on Frances Wright and Robert Owen included a long section describing how Christians, unlike the free inquirers of the 1820s, did not fear death. A discussion of Abner Kneeland's blasphemy case in the following decade dismissed any counternarrative of infidels calmly accepting death as a lie. American reviewers warmly received *The Eclipse of Faith; or, A Visit to a Religious Sceptic* (1852), by the British Congregationalist Henry Rogers, the story of a dying skeptic who wades through several schools of modern thought to make his way back to Christianity. *The Female Skeptic; or, Faith Triumphant* (1859), anonymously published and little noticed, was a similar tale from a woman's perspective. The protagonist's final submission to God, connected to her sexual and intellectual submission to her male suitor, is also shadowed by death, for her skeptical despair had driven her to contemplate suicide with a pistol.[6]

Spiritualism enabled some skeptics, however, to affirm a belief in life after death while still criticizing traditional religious faith. Robert Hare, MD, professor emeritus of chemistry at the University of Pennsylvania, had been a religious skeptic for over half a century when he was invited to investigate Spiritualist phenomena in 1853. As a scientist Hare had adhered to the Newtonian postulate of a Divine Mind behind the observable properties of matter rather than the atheistic scientific positivism of August Comte. Newton's postulate, however, was as far as Hare could go. He found the claims of religion—Christianity as much as Judaism, Islam, Buddhism or Mormonism—to be utterly unpersuasive. His reason rebelled against the idea of a God who would create human life as a probation, manufacture miracles as an (inadequate) mode of persuasion, and devise a hell as punishment. Hare's historical studies exposed the scriptures as collections of ancient myths. His moral sense recoiled at Christ's call to love evildoers, embrace poverty, and focus on glory in heaven. Unlike Thomas Paine and Elihu Palmer, Hare thought the attempt of "a set of skeptics" to come together to profess an alternative natural religion and debunk popular beliefs was a fool's errand. He did wish, though, that religion's central claims about life after death could come under the purview of scientific scrutiny. So when invited to a Spiritualist circle to see for himself, he devised experimental methods and an apparatus (his "spiritoscope"), expecting to refute the notion that departed spirits were rapping tables and spelling out messages from the beyond. Instead, Hare was persuaded.[7]

Soon Hare had become a medium himself. Like Lincoln, he had lost two young sons, and the professor was comforted to learn that their spirits still hovered about him lovingly as he went for his afternoon walks. From his father's spirit, he learned much more about the afterlife than could ever be gleaned from the vague and contradictory scriptures. Six concentric spheres, invisible to the human eye, existed from 60 to 120 miles above the earth. Each sphere or plane of existence contained progressively more wonderful "picturesque landscapes" of "lofty mountain ranges, valleys, rivers, lakes, forests" and "trees and shrubbery, crowned with exquisitely beautiful foliage and flowers." Each also contained six separate societies of spirits, all of which were confederated, beneath the authority of the Supreme Intelligence, as a republic. Assigned initially to a society and a sphere according to their merit (not their creeds), spirits gradually progressed as they gained knowledge and virtue. Hare learned all this from the spirit of Robert Hare Sr. but was careful to have the description authenticated by a convocation of spirit worthies that included Newton, Franklin, Lord Byron, Andrew Jackson, and Hare's personal hero, George Washington. (Washington lived in the highest sphere with Confucius, Socrates, and Jesus—and the latter, it turned out, had been misquoted in the Bible.) Converted to his new faith, Hare remained just as critical of traditional religion. He was not surprised when Episcopalians ignored his letter about his discoveries. He was more disappointed when his former colleagues in the American Association for the Advancement of Science did likewise. But he was especially hurt when his old friend the Yale scientist Benjamin Silliman put more faith in what Hare still maintained was the hearsay of ancient bigots recorded in the Bible than in a respected colleague's careful scientific experiments.[8]

Robert Dale Owen, who freely inquired with Frances Wright in the 1820s and debated Origen Bacheler's CHRISTIAN as the SCEPTIC in the 1830s, converted to Spiritualism in the late 1850s. In the later 1830s and 1840s in Indiana, Owen had distanced himself from his earlier radicalism to become a cautious politician dutifully serving the Democratic Party, but he lost his congressional seat when his Methodist opponent effectively painted him as an infidel by reading passages from the old *Free Enquirer* on the stump. Owen still considered Spiritualism a delusion when he heard that his elderly father had converted to the new faith in 1853. As a diplomat in Naples in 1856, however, he began investigating spiritual phenomena, and curiosity gradually turned to hope and then to conviction. Critics in the freethought press savaged Owen's best seller, *Footfalls on the Boundary of Another World* (1860), by quoting the skeptical Owen of 1831 against the credulity of the older man.[9]

Owen answered in his sequel to *Footfalls* that Spiritualism was the antidote to modern skepticism. There were no longer "many open scoffers at religion among us," he acknowledged. Still, "scepticism is silently, but surely, undermining once-popular doctrines: the old ground is giving way under our feet." The "better class of sceptics" in the latter nineteenth century, he wrote, regretted the loss of their faith and only reluctantly settled for a stunted secularism. Finding no emotional sustenance in cold materialism when they pondered the grave, some were even seeking shelter in Catholicism. Modern men and women who kept their eyes open, however, who continued to prize reason and the scientific investigation of natural laws, needed better evidence of life after death than the flawed accounts in old books or the dogmatic claims of old churches. The séance table was providing exactly that, Owen argued. Spiritualism promised both to purify Christianity and to make it a progressive science for modern civilization. It offered not miracles—violations of natural law—but a new dimension of nature that had previously been misunderstood. After he used his reason and conscience to evaluate hundreds of spirit communications, Owen found tenets that matched precisely what he thought Jesus—if not Paul or Calvin or the pope—actually taught: Jesus the Greatest Man, not the Son of God; a wonder-working ethical teacher, not the redeeming Christ. Jesus taught, and the spirits testified to, a religion of love, not fear, and of God as a Father, not a wrathful Sovereign. There was no perfectly inspired Bible or infallible church, no justification by faith alone, no salvation through sacraments. After death we encounter not a fiery hell or blissful heaven but a better world, though with the same "duties, occupations, and enjoyments" as this one—a new opportunity to make moral progress.[10]

Illustrating different blends of skepticism and faith within the Spiritualist movement, Robert Hare converted to deistic Spiritualism, Robert Dale Owen to a "Christian" Spiritualism of a sort, and John R. Kelso, the Civil War guerrilla fighter in Missouri, to Spiritualistic atheism. In the midst of war and in the face of death, suffering in the snow, Kelso had lost his faith in God, and he never recovered it. A few years after the war, having lost two young sons within the span of a week—a five-year-old to tetanus and a fourteen-year-old to suicide—a distraught Kelso found some hope and comfort at a séance table with some "professed communications" from them. He was not fully convinced, however: he wrote to his daughter that he was "not very strong in the Spiritualist faith." When his "extreme skepticism" was finally conquered at a Spiritualist camp meeting years later, in the spring of 1885, and he became convinced that the spirits of his departed loved ones hovered about him, he wept tears of joy for the first time in forty years. Like Hare and Owen, he argued that there was nothing "supernatural in what are known as Spiritual Manifestations. To me they appear to be just as strictly in accordance with the laws of nature as are any of the phenomena with which we are acquainted." The persistence of conscious spirits after the death of the body was a wonderful natural discovery, not a signal of the return of God to Kelso's cosmos. Finite spirits did not imply an Infinite Spirit. "I am a thorough atheist myself," he wrote in *Spiritualism Sustained in Five Lectures*. He stood by his earlier conclusion that the Christian's God "like all other gods is simply an invention with which priests manage to keep the ignorant and superstitious masses in subjection."[11]

For most believers in life after death, however, that belief, as William Rounseville Alger had argued in his *Critical History*, was bound up with faith in a God who gave purpose and meaning within a larger plan for human history and for all Creation. Such a faith had implications here and not just for the hereafter—social and political implications as well as psychological ones as a personal comfort and inspiration. Faith in an afterlife that had a moral relation to our lives lived on earth because it was superintended by a just Supreme Being had long been seen as "the moral cement of the social fabric," a doctrine "necessary to order this world." Such a faith, like nothing else, Alger contended, could motivate men to give their lives to a sacred cause, to rush enthusiastically at the cannon's mouth. Alger recognized that civil and ecclesiastical powers had long abused this doctrine to tyrannize over the consciences of the men and women they tried to control. Because life after death could not be established as a fact, however, doubt in it should not be considered a sin or crime. Rather, such skepticism was a "misfortune." Skeptics could be blamed not for being skeptical but for how they were skeptical. One should not, Alger argued, be like Thomas in the New Testament, demanding empirical proof that the crucified Jesus had risen from the dead: "I will not believe unless I see the prints of the nails and lay my fingers in the marks on the wounds." One should instead have the attitude and mood of the man in the Gospels who approached Jesus for help: "Lord, I believe: help thou mine unbelief." Sorrowful, humble doubt could be justified, but public skepticism—setting oneself up "as a propagandist of disbelief"—was socially offensive, politically corrosive, and morally contemptible.[12]

Politics

Since his death, commentators have argued over the nature of Abraham Lincoln's religion. They have parsed the often wildly contradictory assessments of the people who knew him and sifted his own often ambiguous statements. He thought long and deeply about moral and religious questions, but his reticence about his personal beliefs, his talent as a public writer, and the contradictions in the existing evidence make him rewarding to investigate but difficult to categorize. Lincoln's faith seems to flutter just out of reach, escaping the lepidopterist's pin. However, his language, especially in his Gettysburg and Second Inaugural Addresses, is so remarkable and culturally resonant that historians still chase him, waving their nets.[13]

In one of the first biographies published after the assassination, Josiah Holland described Lincoln as a committed Christian whose faith had deepened under the scourge of death—the loss of two young sons (Eddie in 1850 and Willie in 1862) and of the many thousands on the battlefield and in the disease-ridden camps. Lincoln's former law partner and close friend William Herndon countered that Lincoln had remained a religious skeptic, or at best a fatalistic deist, until the end. Various groups tried to claim him. Lincoln was an evangelical, some said. Or, like his wife, he had become a Spiritualist trying to contact his dead sons at the séance table. There was even the suggestion that he had been a crypto-Catholic.[14]

Lincoln had been raised in a Calvinist Baptist household. He was steeped in the Bible but never joined his father's church. The evidence persuasively indicates that in the 1830s and 1840s he was a religious skeptic of some sort, and may have even written a short "infidel" book, the manuscript of which a friend tossed into the fire to protect Lincoln's public reputation. Running for Congress in 1846 against a popular Methodist preacher, Lincoln published a handbill to confront the charges of infidelity being whispered by his opponents. In two paragraphs—a little more than three hundred words—he admitted that he was not a member of any Christian church but denied that he was "an open scoffer at Christianity." Adhering, no doubt, to his reputation for honesty, but also, perhaps, drafting the handbill with a lawyer's precision, he added that he had "never denied the truth of the Scriptures" and had "never spoken with intentional disrespect of religion in general, or of any denomination of Christians in particular." Of course, one could poke fun at religion privately, as Lincoln's friends said he did, without being an "open scoffer," and one could sincerely doubt the truth of the scriptures without flatly denying it.[15]

In the 1846 handbill, Lincoln also offered a brief glimpse of what observers have called his "fatalism" or "providentialism." He admitted that he had, on occasion, in his "early life," argued before a few friends in support of what he called "the 'Doctrine of Necessity'—that is, that the human mind is impelled to action, or held in rest by some power, over which the mind itself has no control." He was quick to note, however, that such a philosophical position did not necessarily make him a freethinking fatalist, since that opinion was held by "several of the Christian denominations," too (including his parents' predestinarian Baptist church and the Rev. James Smith's Old School Presbyterianism).

Scholars have long pondered Lincoln's Doctrine of Necessity and how it might have shaped the Whig moralism of his politics in the 1850s and his interpretation of the Civil War as president. Less attention has been paid to the second paragraph of the handbill, where Lincoln spelled out what he considered to be the expected and proper relationship of skepticism and faith in mid-nineteenth-century American politics:

> I do not think I could myself, be brought to support a man for office, whom I knew to be an open enemy of, and scoffer at, religion. Leaving the higher matter of eternal consequences, between him and his Maker, I still do not think any man has the right thus to insult the feelings, and injure the morals, of the community in which he may live. If, then, I was

guilty of such conduct, I should blame no man who should condemn me for it; but I do blame those, whoever they may be, who falsely put such a charge in circulation against me.

Here Lincoln acknowledges freedom of conscience with the notion that the state of a man's soul was a question best left to him and his Maker. However, he condemns any "open enemy of, and scoffer at, religion" who would try to run for public office. In other words, anyone who shared Elihu Palmer's or Ernestine Rose's conviction that sharply worded criticism of what they considered to be superstition—criticism they considered to be a moral and patriotic duty—could not serve the public even in a democracy supposedly committed to freedom of religion and expression. Doing so would "insult the feelings" of the community. Further, Lincoln's restrictions on public religious skepticism seem to reach far beyond the specific case of political candidacy. He seems to suggest more broadly that he did not think that anyone, in any context, had the right to insult the feelings of the community by publicly denying the truth of the scriptures. However a person might doubt religion privately, religious skepticism was to have no political or public role at all. A political vision of a nation's history, identity, and destiny, however expressed, therefore, had to respect—and not criticize—the grounds of the majority's religious faith: the Bible, their feelings, and their churches.

Lincoln thus recognized and endorsed a narrow view of the religious boundaries of public discussion. This is not to say that he employed providential language as a secret skeptic working with the only rhetorical tools available, the way that Thomas Paine used biblical tropes in *Common Sense*. Through the personal and national crises of 1850 to 1865, Lincoln seems to have been working out what his Doctrine of Necessity, coupled with his sense of moral responsibility, really meant. He wrestled with both the brighter and the darker angels of his experience to determine what it meant to be an instrument in the hands of Providence, compelled to act and suffer consequences. In some of his antebellum speeches, Providence could seem like merely a pious word for the Enlightenment's Nature, the natural laws and concatenation of causes and effects propelling history forward. By 1862, however, he was praying to a personal God, a God who granted victory at the Battle of Antietam as a signal to Abraham to go forward with the Emancipation Proclamation—a notion that the younger Lincoln would have called "superstition."[16]

The president seemed to preach a Calvinism without Christ. All things are predetermined, and our wills are not free, but we must struggle to discern and then follow God's will—the moral logic of Providence—or suffer the consequences. It is the blood of soldiers, not of Jesus, that advances the work of the "new birth" of freedom at Gettysburg. Lincoln sacralized death not by promising an afterlife but by arguing that "under God" it had gained profound political meaning, helping to ensure "that government of the people, by the people, for the people, shall not perish from the earth."[17]

Christian hearts have long been warmed by the humility of the Second Inaugural. Both Northerners and Southerners, Lincoln said, "read the same Bible, and pray to the same God; and each invokes his aid against the other. . . . The prayers of both could not be answered; neither has been answered fully." God seems to have willed that the South would suffer for slavery. Lincoln found it "strange"—to say the least—"that any men should dare to ask a just God's assistance in wringing their bread from the sweat of other men's faces." But the North, even in victory, had suffered greatly, too. So he urged his countrymen to "judge not" and to have malice toward none and charity for all as they "finish the work" and achieve a "lasting peace." Nonetheless, Lincoln's God, here and elsewhere, seems less like the Christian Father than the voice speaking from the whirlwind in the Book of Job. This God may be "just," but He also "has His own purposes," which are often unclear. He allowed slavery to continue for two and a half centuries, "through His appointed time," and then to remove it He gave "to both North and South, this terrible war" for the offense. If the present generation—even those fighting to end slavery—had to pay with their own blood for the sins of past generations as well as their own, could they complain about injustice? That would be like complaining about original sin. No, they must say with the Psalmist that "the judgments of the Lord, are true and righteous altogether." Lincoln died neither as a skeptic nor as a "technical Christian," as his wife put it, but as an almost Christian president for an almost chosen people.[18]

If the relationship of doubting and believing was complicated in Lincoln, it was more complicated still in the nation he left behind. The institutional power of the churches in the political realm reached a high-water mark and then receded. Church leaders from eleven denominations in the North, at what appeared to be the height of their public influence, began pressing in 1863 for a constitutional amendment that would recognize God, the authority of the Bible, and "the Lord Jesus Christ as the Governor among the nations." The proposal never came to a vote in Congress, but the phrase "In God We Trust" was added to the two-cent coin in 1864. Such a symbolic gesture may not have meant much to the practice of piety among the faithful. For many who had faced death in battle, suffered the loss of loved ones, and tried to bind up the wounds of the nation after 1865, religious faith and practice would return to familiar channels after the war, receding from the maelstrom of political crisis, historical rupture, and personal trauma to the mundane, winding course of normal life. For a smaller number, however, the war had swept away what they would see as the dangerously naïve pieties of American faith. Moral and intellectual dissent to religion would bubble up from the bloody ground. Freethinkers would again agitate and organize in what has been called a golden age of late nineteenth-century freethought. These dissenters took a principled turn away from religious belief to various forms of agnosticism, secularism, humanism, and naturalism, and the resurgence of religious skepticism once again drew popular attention. There was no simple arc toward a more religious or more secular American future. In our world, the continued dialogue of skepticism and faith, like death and politics, may be a certainty, too.[19]

Appendix

GROUNDS OF FAITH AND MODES OF SKEPTICISM

How did Americans in this period talk about skepticism and faith? Surveying essays and articles published between 1775 and 1865 in both scholarly journals and popular magazines can begin—but only begin—to answer that question. These are not the writings of canonical philosophers and theologians but public commentary about philosophical and theological ideas, along with anecdotes, stories, letters, and reports featuring skepticism and faith as everyday experiences. This body of periodical literature cannot support an analysis that could claim to be anything as grandiose as a contextualized history of the concepts "skepticism" and "faith" in this period of American history. While nets can be cast considerably beyond the usual sources of intellectual history, they do not reach much further than the magazines' and newspapers' middling literate readerships and cannot claim to have captured anything that might confidently be called folk beliefs. Still, these essays and articles reveal important patterns of discussion; they sketch prominent features of the cultural landscape through which the skeptics and believers discussed in this book made their way.[1]

Grounds of Faith

> The CHRISTIAN argued that belief in God and in Christianity were rational positions. A commonsense assessment of nature and the voice of conscience testified to the existence of God; logic declared that such a God would reveal himself to intelligent creatures; and evidence in scripture and history proved that Christianity was that revelation. But intellectual assent—mere reasonable belief—was but a step toward a living faith, a faith grounded in personal spiritual experience, the daily practice of living according to scriptural teaching, and an ongoing relationship with God within the historical community of believers (the church).

SCEPTIC: "Whereupon rests the superstructure of the believer's faith?"

CHRISTIAN: "I would say in the language of scripture, 'Seek, and ye shall find:'—'Do his will, and thou shalt know.'"[2]

"Faith" is belief, trust, or confidence. Derived from the Latin *fides* and linked to the Greek *pistis*, it originally connoted trusting surmise or conjecture rather than definitive knowing or perceiving. The New Testament refers to faith as this sort of personal attitude or orientation, but also as that which is (or should be) believed in. Faith in a Christian context, therefore, has both a subjective and an objective character—the Christian's believing and trusting, and the content of the Christianity that he trusts and believes. To explain themselves Christians liked to quote an enigmatic verse from Paul's Letter to the Hebrews, which describes faith as "the substance of things hoped for, the evidence of things not seen." Here we have a subject hoping and perhaps trying to see, as well as the object of that hope: the substance of things, invisible but evidenced. But how, skeptics asked, could one grasp the "substance" of something merely hoped for? In what way did "things not seen" provide evidence of their reality?[3]

A Christian's subjective experience of faith was said to be bound up with the objective contents of *the* faith—the doctrines and practices of the religion. In 1834, William R. Williams, a Baptist pastor in New York City, noted that the scriptures used the same word—"faith"—for "both the truth received, and the temper or habit of mind receiving it." For Williams, inward faith was more than mere belief: it was not just the assent of the intellect to a proposition. It was "a submission of the entire soul, not of the intellect only, but also of the affections and the imagination." This "submission" involved an acknowledgment of human fallibility, ignorance, and sin, and a reverence for God's perfections. It entailed a subjection to divine authority, a "surrender" of the will to God's standard for human conduct. In such a state, a person is able to fully receive truths about God, humanity, life, death, and salvation. Williams described the truths in God's testimony (the Bible) as the necessary nutrients for a spiritual life. They pour into the mind and change the soul. Faith then "suddenly widen[s] the mental horizon, letting in the vision of realities before present, but hitherto unseen." Through faith, the Christian sees by a new light; by faith, she judges by a new standard; in faith, restored to communion with God, she lives a new life.[4]

Christians of other denominational and theological persuasions would agree that faith was more than mere belief but would challenge almost everything else in Williams's descriptive definition: his emphasis on the individual's subjective experience over creeds, rituals, or communal worship, for example, or his insistence that the work of faith was due to the supernatural action of the Holy Spirit rather than, say, the development of humanity's God-given spiritual potential. They would also contend with Williams over the list of essential truths contained in God's testimony and experienced by the believer. As Christians argued among themselves, skeptical outsiders asked why we should trust any of these things—the temper of mind, the allegedly revealed doctrines, or the Christian practices they were said to entail.

Christian apologists answered by exploring the authoritative grounds of their faith. A series of articles in the early 1860s examined what the author, George Park Fisher, called the foundations of the Christian faith and "the conflict with skepticism." The central principle of Protestantism, he argued, was to rest with the objective authority of the Bible. Roman Catholics also claimed an objective authority: the tradition of the Catholic Church, handed down from generation to generation and interpreted by the pope. A third ground of faith was subjectivity or consciousness: the Rationalist rejects any authority in matters of religion beyond what he can establish in his own mind through Reason, and the Mystic takes his own feelings rather than any external rule as the source and criterion for the truth of faith. Fisher's essay also illustrates, however, how proponents for one of the grounds of Christian faith—the Bible, experience, or community—would often shift to one of the others, like someone sitting on a wobbly three-legged stool, shifting his or her weight to rest first on one leg and then another.[5]

Other writers, too, invoked the three grounds of faith. An article in a Methodist journal published a year before Fisher's series pointed to a "center and citadel" of Christian evidence, which could stand firm against the rising threat of natural science: the testimonies in the Bible about supernatural events, and "the witnessing experience of Christians, conscious of a new life within them by the Spirit of God." Corroboration for the inner witness, and reasons to trust the scriptural testimonies, could be found in the social world. Trusting the evangelists was consistent with the "candid and open-minded intelligence" that people use in daily life. "I know men," the doubter needs to remind himself; "I can weigh the force of their words.... I can know, also, what is truth and what is falsehood when I meet the one or the other." The effort to shore up the foundations of Christian faith by turning to the Bible, Christian community, and personal experience was certainly not confined to high-toned theological and philosophical discussions. A religious newspaper happily reported the conversion of a sixty-six-year-old Ohio physician and his son from skeptical infidelity to Christianity in 1833. "The Bible is now their choicest book... Christians are now their chosen companions... and celestial treasures are, apparently, the only riches on which their affections are placed." An 1842 "Letter from a Believer to a Skeptic" printed in a monthly magazine encouraged the doubter to read the Bible and "listen to the voice of reason and of God as it speaks through others." The Believer also hoped that "the felt presence of an infinite Power and Love" would solve the Skeptic's doubts and comfort his soul.[6]

What were three pillars of faith for some, however, were three stumbling blocks for others. A wealthy lawyer in New York State recalled his life as a skeptic in the *Weekly Messenger*. He read his Bible diligently but found "contradictions, absurdities, and inconsistencies." He looked to the Christian community but was struck by the hypocrisy of those professing the faith. He tried to turn inward and to pray but only became more confused.[7]

Each of the three grounds of faith had problems. Scholarship critically examining the Bible, pursued in earnest since the Renaissance, popularized in the eighteenth century, and further developed and extended by German critics in the nineteenth century, exposed what seemed to be very human modes of composition, poking holes in the notion of a divinely inspired and infallible text. American Protestants responded with reassuring treatises, sermons, and tracts about "the genuineness and authenticity" of the Bible, as Timothy Dwight put it in 1793, and they pointed to what they called internal and external evidence. A prominent feature of the internal defense was the assertion that the Bible offered such a sublime moral system, so obviously superior to anything fashioned by heathen philosophers or the prophets and seers of other world religions, that it had to have divine origins. This argument assumed, though, a natural and universal aesthetic and moral standard that would confirm such a conclusion. As a Catholic writer observed, no doubt a Muslim would make the same claim for the Koran.[8]

Pursuing the external line of defense, authors repeatedly argued that the Bible could be authenticated as a reliable historical document. William C. Brownlee in an 1835 sermon contended that it passed the test as easily as the Declaration of Independence. The perpetuation of Jewish traditions like Passover, for example, ensures that the Bible stories they commemorate are not merely fables, just as annual July Fourth celebrations help support the claim that American independence was in fact declared in 1776. Recognizing that a similar argument could be made for Islam, Brownlee changed his tack. Christ's miracles and his spotless moral character, Brownlee insisted, put the New Testament in a wholly different category from the pretenses of Mohammed and fictions of the Koran. The author of a dialogue between a Universalist and a skeptic a decade later also used the miracles-and-moral-character argument to denounce any analogy between Christ's Gospel and Joseph Smith's *Book of Mormon*.[9]

The argument between Catholics and Protestants about the Bible and the church as rules of faith, begun in the Reformation, continued to echo through the eighteenth and nineteenth centuries. Catholics claimed that their church was a communion of the faithful, begun by Christ himself, perpetuated through the centuries by apostolic succession, sustained by God's grace, and maintaining a unity of belief and practice through divinely directed authority. Protestants saw instead worldly corruption and papal despotism. The Reformers' slogan of a priesthood of all believers interpreting the Bible for themselves, as a Vermont lecturer explained, was a means to an end. Martin Luther and John Calvin were not championing individual free inquiry for its own sake; they were convinced that readers would find a singular truth in the scriptures: that sinners were justified by faith alone, and not by doing good works or partaking of the Catholic Church's sacraments. But, Catholics pointed out, the Bible did not turn out to be so transparently clear once put into the hands of a literate laity. Allowing the sacred texts to be interpreted by the private judgment of every reader only multiplied interpretations and splintered Christianity into an ever-increasing number of competing sects. Catholic convert Gardner Jones in the 1830s repeated the common Catholic argument that the Protestant's *sola scriptura* actually made every individual's private judgment, and not the Bible, the ground of faith, replacing coherent belief and practice with a Babel of confusion.[10]

When arguing against Catholics rather than each other, Protestants insisted that their interpretive differences were being exaggerated. Even within Protestantism, however, there were blistering critiques of the majority's infatuation with *sola scriptura*. A Lutheran complained how "the holy Bible itself is violently sundered from its living connection with the Church of Christ, and its contents measured by the contracted judgment of the single individual, without any regard to the united wisdom of the pious of past ages, or of the present time; the great doctrines of our holy religion are separated from the pillar and ground upon which alone they can safely rest, and every man is to be the infallible interpreter of them for himself, not being accountable to any power for his belief and practice, excepting the invisible authority of God alone."[11]

From this Lutheran's High Church perspective, the other side of the excessive bibliolatry of so much American Protestantism was an attenuated ecclesiology that misperceived the social and historical grounds of faith. Most American Protestants, the writer argued, seemed to consider the church as merely a convenient voluntary association of individuals, a social organization that was at best an aid to private devotion. Even in the primary social ritual of evangelicalism, the revival meeting, a shouting enthusiast, "though he may be in the midst of a dense crowd, is as effectually separated from his fellow men as" a monk in a monastery: "There is no actual communion between him and his fellow worshippers." Their temper of mind was stunted by excessive subjectivity; their ability to receive, understand, and live by objective Christian truths was maimed by mistaken notions of community. Claiming to be guided by the Bible alone, they failed to recognize the church as a grace-bearing communion of believers that continued in the world as generations of individuals were baptized, lived in the faith, and passed on to their eternal reward.[12]

Protestants who caught the stench of popery in such High Church attitudes were not as blind to the social and historical grounds of faith as these criticisms—and sometimes their own pronouncements of "Bible alone"—would suggest. Christians commonly asserted that their faith improved the manners and morals of societies that adopted it, and they marveled at the historical success of a religion that had grown from a handful of poor fishermen to envelop the globe.

Many would have agreed with a Baptist writer who argued that the moral and historical successes of Christianity were facts testifying that the religion was not just useful but true. These facts could reinforce the trustworthiness of the scriptures and the assurance of personal belief. "Clericus," a character in a dialogue printed in a Quaker magazine, stated the case baldly: "I have never permitted a doubt to enter my mind concerning the authenticity of the Bible. It has been the source of so much consolation to millions of pious Christians, it has had so great influence in civilizing and enlightening the world, and it has received the sanction of so many learned men in different ages and countries, that I cannot for a moment suppose it to be a fabrication." History and society could also be seen as not just corroborating Christianity's truth claims but also shaping the character of faith. A Calvinist Congregationalist was not saying anything controversial when he recognized that men and women were social beings drawing from each other strength for their faith and "an excitement to holy affections." As another writer affirmed, a healthy piety needed to be disciplined and purified "in the generous charities which bind neighbors and fellow citizens in one wide community of interest and endeavor." Some would join the Unitarian who professed to be glad to "exchange the paths of solitary research for the communion of Christ's followers... [and] willingly part with the absolute privacy of a mind trusting its own exclusive judgments, for the united faith and sympathy of the Church."[13]

Yet the "absolute privacy" of a single mind remained a more common site for exploring the grounds of faith. Philosophers focused on the thinking and perceiving subject; theologians scrutinized the effect of grace upon, and the volitions stemming from, the soul; and popular writers drew from both, if indirectly. Revivalists emphasized that faith was a personal experience. You can feel the Holy Spirit working upon your heart, they said. The guilt of sin is like a gnawing pain. The truths of the Gospel dawn in the mind as obviously as light at sunrise. The desire to follow God's law is like a parching thirst. When converted you will know you love Christ the way a wife knows her love for her husband or a mother knows her love for her child. When you attain an assured faith, you will feel the same deep conviction that Christ loves you and has saved your soul. Evangelicals themselves, however, worried about being misled by blind emotional impulses and excited passions. A Methodist in 1824 warned his brethren about people who took "their own vain conceits and unwarrantable imaginations for the immediate influence of the Holy Spirit," allowing emotional states and bodily sensations to be their religious guide. Critics had claimed that Methodism had been based on just this sort of religious enthusiasm since its beginnings in the eighteenth century. An essay in the *Quarterly Christian Spectator* called Methodism's claim to apprehend spiritual truths by a self-validating inner witness a species of mysticism. We can believe the Methodist sincere when she reports that she has had such experiences and thinks they derive from God's Spirit, the author wrote.

But we are not obliged to acknowledge her claims to an authoritative inner witness any more than we should acknowledge the pope's claim to infallibility.[14]

Modern philosophers had long examined the contents of consciousness as they tried to explain and defend Christian faith. Laurens P. Hickok, president of Union College in the mid-nineteenth century and the author of a book on religious psychology, praised the effort but criticized the lack of success. One branch of eighteenth-century philosophy, derived from an analysis of our sensations of material things and assuming, like John Locke, a mind with no innate ideas, had no way to discern an absolute, personal God, Hickok argued. Another branch, most prominently the Scottish school after Francis Hutcheson, focused on the sensibilities and appetites of the perceiving subject who is drawn toward some objects in the world and repulsed by others. Theological versions of this, as in the revamped Calvinism of Jonathan Edwards, described the Holy Spirit implanting a "new sense" of divine things as it regenerated the soul. But if these "new sense" theologians could explain the new perceptions and inclinations of the converted soul, they were stumped, according to Hickok, when it came to understanding God; their whole system collapsed into pantheism, a god-in-nature who can only grow like a vegetable rather than act like a person. Ultimately the Lockeans, the Scots, and the Edwardseans, he argued, remained locked in the prison house of subjectivity.[15]

In the nineteenth century other thinkers looking for the ground of faith in their own minds rather than in the Bible or the church turned from the mechanics of matter and the impulses of sensibility to focus upon the logical laws of thinking. The Transcendentalist Theodore Parker held that drawing from the intuitive facts of consciousness built a surer foundation for faith than trying to generalize from historical facts or scriptural texts. Other writers, like a Unitarian book reviewer in 1835, simply declared without any fancy philosophizing that humans were essentially religious beings. Although there were some freakish exceptions to the general rule, the reviewer contended, people universally recognized God as their creator, felt a sense of reliance and dependence upon him, felt accountable to him as moral agents, and sensed his relation to a higher state of being. Most who considered themselves to be traditional or "orthodox" Christians, however, were deeply critical of this notion of a natural religious consciousness. One commentator was willing to concede the existence of a natural religious instinct, a craving like a baby's initial thirst for the breast milk it has not yet tasted. But this natural desire needs to be satisfied by divine revelation; man cannot spin religious truths out of his own intuitions the way a spider spins a web out of its own body. The human mind alone, another essayist insisted, could not discover fundamental religious truths such as God's perfect love, the forgiveness of sins, and the immortality of the soul. Those like Parker who thought they could do so "mistake the spontaneous consent of the human mind to the leading truths of Christianity for the native power to discover those truths," argued a writer in the *North American*

Review. They think they have declared independence from Christian beliefs and traditions, but what they misperceive as intuitive reason and natural moral taste were instead absorbed from the society in which they were raised, itself the product of a deep history shaped by Christianity as well as less benign forces. "Our moral intuitions (so called) are a motley mixture of conscience, prejudice, and passion." Consciousness needed the truths revealed only in the Bible.[16]

And so the arguments moved, weight shifting on the three-legged stool, as Christians in the American republic repeatedly insisted that there were reasonable grounds for their faith. They maintained that faith was more than assent to a system of truths. It was an inclination of the soul, an affirmation of a relationship with the divine, and a way of living in this world and confidently hoping for a better one. But it was a reasonable faith. They continued to look to the Bible to find God as a Father, within themselves for the work of the Spirit, and to their communities for ways to understand and follow Christ. And as they argued about how to understand these three grounds of faith—self, text, and historical community—and how to gauge the relation between them, skeptical arguments threatened all three.

Modes of Skepticism

The SCEPTIC argued that it was reasonable to suspend one's judgment about claims that lacked reliable evidence. Doubting the foundational pieties of one's own culture was not easy, but skepticism, he contended, was an honest response to the facts at hand. The CHRISTIAN doubted the honesty of those who would deny what he considered to be overwhelming evidence for God and Christ:

SCEPTIC: "I perceive no evidence whereby to affirm, or deny, that one or a million beings superior to man, exist, throughout space. One may, or a million may, so exist. They may take cognizance of man's actions. They may influence his destiny. I deny it not; I affirm it not."

CHRISTIAN: "I believe there are evidences sufficient within reach of every man, to convince him of Divine Existence: and that if he is unconvinced thereof, it is either because he has not fully examined those evidences, or has not fully examined them with a becoming spirit."

SCEPTIC: "'It is easy and agreeable to trust and believe; to doubt requires an unpleasant effort.' Every Sceptic, who has once been a believer, knows this. From the time our infant ears first drink in the nurse's ghost story, we *wish* to believe, and *do* believe, without the trouble of suspicion, or the anxiety of suspense and examination. Youth learns to doubt and mistrust slowly and painfully, after many a bitter lesson in the school of experience."

CHRISTIAN: "I can conceive both of sincere Sceptics and insincere ones—of those who doubt from want of conviction, and of those who, rather than believe in future retribution, would forego 'riches, honour, a good name,' or almost any thing else."[17]

The English word "skepticism" comes from the Greek *skeptikos*, meaning to consider and examine, and is akin to *skepsis*, meaning inquiry and doubt. People can be skeptical about (just as they can have faith in) many different kinds of things. A man could be said to have faith in his trusted hunting dog and be skeptical about the abilities of an aging horse. In both cases, the objects of the faithful or skeptical attitudes are quite different from those broad existential concerns intended in a religious context. The subjective experience of confidence or doubt, too, has a different depth and intensity when we turn from everyday things to confront the meanings of life, death, and salvation. In eighteenth- and nineteenth-century America, to call someone a skeptic or to mention skepticism as a significant attitude, method, or position was usually a reference to religion. A 1791 article in the *Christian's, Scholar's, and Farmer's Magazine* defined modern skeptics as those who introduced doubts that weakened the subordination to Christian authority. "I am a sceptic," wrote the author of an article entitled "Of Religion" in the *New Harmony Gazette* in 1828. "I doubt the accuracy of all predictions regarding our fate beyond the grave: I do not think we yet know, and doubt whether we shall ever know, any thing about it." An author in 1860 simply and emphatically defined the "Scepticism of the Times" as "*unbelief*, or the WANT OF FAITH in the history and doctrines of the Bible, as the INFALLIBLE WORD OF GOD."[18]

Some commentators objected to this popular usage. "If a person is said to be a sceptic without any further qualification, it is generally understood that he is a disbeliever in the Christian religion," wrote one. We already have a word—infidel—to denote such an unbeliever, the author complained, so why stigmatize a term that also means an often useful (and not necessarily anti-Christian) style of thinking? The linkage of skeptic and infidel, however, was hardly accidental. Christian polemicists often used the two words synonymously and believed that a skeptical attitude or style of thinking usually led to or accompanied the infidel's rejection of Christianity. As an 1835 article in the *New-England Magazine* suggested, this equation of skepticism with antireligious critique grossly distorted the place and meaning of skepticism in the history of philosophy. Indeed, the skeptical Pyrrhonists of ancient Greece doubted all truth claims in any category, not just religious ones. Their radical doubt was supposed to be a kind of therapy, freeing the individual from any dogma, and it did not prevent Pyrrhonists from upholding the religious traditions of their communities. Early modern European skeptics like Montaigne wielded skepticism to undercut excessive claims to religious rationality as they championed a Christianity with all its mysteries intact. René Descartes used skepticism as a tool to strip away false assumptions before attempting to rebuild Christian philosophy on foundations of certainty.[19]

There could be no question, however, that by the eighteenth century skeptical inquiry had become a critical weapon to attack Christian faith. Skepticism about religious matters was no longer merely an aspect of a broader epistemological distrust of any and every claim to knowledge, the sort of skepticism that could make philosophers at their desks doubt the existence of their bodies and the external world but that could trouble few other people. Neither were skeptical arguments any longer primarily thought of as tools in the service of piety, recollecting the fallibility of human intellect and chastening philosophical pretensions to knowledge.

Yet commentators across the decades from the 1780s to the 1860s described the cause, character, and cure of skepticism in quite various and sometimes contradictory ways. This confusion arose, some writers suggested, because critics were blindly groping different parts of the same elephant. One mode of skepticism might be termed an initial "attitude of intellectual hesitation"—a suspension of judgment until one could gather more facts and think more carefully. Christian apologists often attacked even this doubting pause as a sign of a sinful heart rejecting Gospel truth. But other writers argued that this "intellectual hesitation, far from being a bad thing, is very often, so far as it goes, a good thing, for it arises from the appreciation of the complexity of the phenomena submitted to investigation, and from a determination not to cheat the mind itself and external observers by pretending to greater certainty than is really possessed." An essayist agreed that this kind of skeptical hesitation was "legitimate and praiseworthy." Another in the *Methodist Quarterly Review* also conceded that such skeptical doubting, "in which a man does not, and *for the time being* cannot, see his way clear to a well-grounded Christian faith," was not "a product of depravity." It could be, other writers agreed, a healthy sign of an inquiring mind and a thirsting soul, the beginning of a process that could eventually lead to a mature and well-tested faith.[20]

A common problem with this initial posture of skeptical doubting according to Christian critics, however, was that the doubter did not press forward and pursue the necessary inquiry. He would not take the trouble to study the Bible, evaluate historical testimonies, or ponder the laws of his own mind, a Universalist wrote. "The languid mind will hardly make such an exertion, but will prefer for the hour to remain in incertitude, rather than to perform the requisite toil." The hesitating skeptic did not inquire too much, but too little. After all, an article in the *Christian Secretary* noted, self-complacent doubting was easier than investigation. "The skeptic cannot undergo a long process of rational deduction," an essay argued in 1849. "He prefers to halt and criticize, to speculate and cavil; to raise objections and chase phantoms; to disbelieve what he cannot comprehend, and reject whatever appears improbable." The lazy doubter, therefore, could harden into the decided infidel: "He becomes familiar with doubts, and yearns after them, and hugs them, till he is insensible to proof, troubled and bewildered, and full of disorder and contention."[21]

Others recognized skepticism as an extended intellectual process. It was an important "habit of analysis, of separation and distinction among things that differ, in the sphere especially of religion and morals." The skeptical inquirer delays conclusions, diligently tests assumptions and presuppositions, clearly ascertains facts, takes stock of multiple perspectives, and refuses to oversimplify complexity. According to an 1843 article in the *Knickerbocker*, skeptical inquiry in religious matters was the duty of every thinking person; it was slavish to accept faith merely on the authority of parents, teachers, and ministers. The danger here, critics charged, was that the inquirer might begin "to prefer the workings of thought in a search without end, in which there is no wish to discover anything." In contrast to this portrait of the complacently fruitless researcher was the caricature of the skeptical inquirer as indecisive hand wringer. An 1802 sketch described the skeptic as confused and perplexed by everything he read and afraid of having convictions: "His whole life is a question." An alleged "Confession of a Sceptic" in a Methodist journal published in Cincinnati in 1835 moaned about the meaninglessness of life and lamented having no compass by which to steer. A former skeptic confessed in the *New York Evangelist* in 1849, "[I have] been acquainted with many skeptics; and have waded through the sea of infidelity myself," he wrote, "and yet I can truly say, I never knew any piece of mind.... [A] life of skepticism...is a perturbed and unhappy life." An article entitled "Skepticism: Its Causes; Its Cure" in 1856 described skeptical inquirers as longing for faith and eager for certainty about immortality but perplexed by doubt. "They revolve the subject, ask if there can be any possibility of mistake, and straightaway are involved in a cloud of difficulties." What if Christianity, like Islam, is an imposture? What if the scriptures are forgeries, or the disciples—and subsequent Christians—are victims of their own fond dreams? "Vague misgivings overspread their mental horizon. Thus they live, often exulting in transports, often sunk in hopelessness."[22]

Christian writers eagerly diagnosed what they considered to be flaws in the process of skeptical inquiry. They argued that skeptics assumed the posture of a critic from the beginning of investigation, always and immediately trying to find fault. A converted skeptic remembered reading the Bible that way in his former life. William Alcott, when attending church as a secret skeptic, would sit in his pew imagining counterarguments to everything the minister preached. Skeptics were also accused of refusing to apply the normal rules of establishing historical facts, rules holding that if an event—such as, say, the raising of Lazarus from the dead—was perceptible, public, and reliably recorded, it passed the test. Other critics charged that skeptics placed too much reliance on sense perception and ignored spiritual evidence. Listing infidelity's erroneous principles of reasoning in 1854, the *New Englander* groused that skeptics expected a level of certainty in religion that they did not ask for anywhere else. Popular magazines urged that reverent Bible study and humble self-examination replace the skeptical inquirer's critical distance and methodical "wade through all the subtleties of theology."[23]

Any analysis of skepticism's methods and moods was never far from moral evaluation. The skeptical freethinker Abner Kneeland in the 1830s was not alone in arguing that credulity or incredulity in the face of evidence was an involuntary mental reflex, and therefore a person should not be blamed for not being persuaded. A Universalist pondering Kneeland noted how phrenologists claimed that there were particular parts of the brain for reverence and the appreciation of the marvelous, so perhaps these religious portions of a skeptic's brain had become diseased even though other faculties remained unimpaired. Other writers spoke more generally about infidelity resulting from a disease of the mind or from an undeveloped moral nature, and of religious skepticism being produced when doubting became a reflex habit and then hardened into a psychological weakness. Such conceptions of infidelity as infirmity rather than willful depravity suggested that Christians should pity rather than despise. Other commentators normalized the diversity of religious opinion. The author of "Are Great Minds Prone to Skepticism?" argued in 1835 that religious skepticism was a natural phase as a person moved from childhood credulity through the doubts produced by rational inquiry before arriving at a mature and reasonable faith; Orestes Brownson in his autobiographical novel described how outmoded religious ideas and practices in the early decades of the nineteenth century were causing many thoughtful people to stall in that middle phase. Calls for tolerance and compassion rooted in such points of view, however, were overwhelmed by repetitions of the venerable Christian argument that infidels were merely sinners rationalizing their wickedness. One writer called this "the clergyman's argument"— the kneejerk dismissal of skepticism as simply the product of sin. "Scepticism is a disease of the heart, engendered by evil passions, and strengthened and confirmed by viscous habits," as a journal in 1823 phrased the pulpit commonplace.[24]

The *Universalist Quarterly*'s 1856 effort to describe different modes of skepticism requiring different cures was an advance over the diagnoses of mental disease or the standard clergyman's argument. The *Quarterly* did attribute the swaggering skeptical infidelity of Tom Paine and other vocal freethinkers to sinful arrogance and dark desires for vice. The Paines of the world needed to turn inward and face the loathsomeness of their own sin, the article recommended. The lazy doubter who never got past the threshold of religious doctrine, however, was a different sort of skeptic requiring a different antidote. Such a person needed to realize that his Christian neighbor "makes no extravagant demand when he asks of him faith in the gospel and zeal for its furtherance": the sluggard was being called to "labor earnestly" for the good of his fellow men as well as himself. Finally, the anxiously obsessive skeptical inquirer was directed to the New Testament, which he should read without morbidly focusing on minor objections.[25]

Actual skeptics (rather than imagined or reformed ones) insisted, though, that their habits of thought were neither feckless nor fretful. THE SCEPTIC, Robert Dale

Owen, countered the charges that skepticism derived from or was characterized by laziness or irrationality. He himself had sought God "perseveringly" and examined religious questions repeatedly. But logic, language, ideas and experience—"every thing that informs or guides or enlightens us in human affairs or human discussions"—deserts us when we try to speculate about an infinite and eternal God and his supposed heaven, he wrote. The design argument, for example—the notion that the universe implies a God the way a watch implies a watchmaker—stretches analogy beyond the breaking point, abandoning reason for flights of the imagination. So "why should we madly persist to wander forth into trackless, endless darkness?" Since we cannot answer questions about the existence of God or the origins of the universe, "let us, in the name of modesty and common sense ... cease teasing each other to presumptuous decisions, be they positive or negative." To make God the cause of what we cannot otherwise explain merely gives our ignorance a grand title. The skeptic refuses to pretend to knowledge he does not have: "In default of evidence to warrant assertion, *I suspend judgment.*"[26]

The SCEPTIC, too, had only contempt for the notion that skepticism was connected to immorality. He called the root of the standard "clergyman's argument"—the idea that moral virtue depended upon orthodox religious belief—the "master-error of Intolerance." The assumption that skeptics recoiled from faith because they feared God's wrath for their sins on Judgment Day was a fantasy concocted by those who never talked to actual skeptics, doubters who instead doubted because of the "inconsistent mysteries" of religion itself. The SCEPTIC also turned the moral argument against his opponent. To sing along with Christian hymns to Omnipotent Goodness, he would have to close his eyes to war and misery, to the strong continually being allowed to oppress the weak, and to the "wrong and outrage that stalk in our day, through our own republic," determining "the fate of the enslaved African and of the hunted Indian." As for the "pseudo-sacred book" held up as the essential guide to ethics, he pointed to where the Bible commanded the execution of "witches," justified slavery, and endorsed genocide. Religious doubt was a virtue, not a vice.[27]

Several different modes of skepticism, then, were prevalent in American discussion and debate between the Revolution and the Civil War: skepticism as an initial posture of intellectual hesitation or an extended process of reasoning; as lazy doubting or obsessively indecisive inquiry; as a developmental stage or a constant companion in the progress toward knowledge; or as an expression of infirmity, disease, or sin. Religious believers had antidotes for all of them: scripture, the inner witness, and the faithful community.

ACKNOWLEDGMENTS

This book has taken a very long time, in part because I was the editor of the *William and Mary Quarterly* (2000–2013), and the project mostly had to simmer on the back burner during those years. The study was launched by a National Endowment for the Humanities summer grant in 1998, sustained by an NEH Faculty Fellowship for 2008–9, and completed with an American Council of Learned Societies Fellowship and a National Humanities Center Fellowship for 2016–17. Support from the Dean's Office and the History Department at the College of William and Mary also facilitated my research leaves. The book would not have been possible without the generous support of these institutions.

I have benefited from the assistance of many research librarians and archivists, and am especially indebted to the staffs of the American Antiquarian Society, Worcester, Massachusetts; the American Philosophical Society, Philadelphia, Pennsylvania; the Andover-Harvard Theological Library, Cambridge, Massachusetts; the Beinecke Rare Book and Manuscript Library, Yale University, New Haven, Connecticut; the Boston Public Library; the Caroliniana Library at the University of South Carolina at Columbia; the Connecticut State Library, Hartford, Connecticut; the Huntington Library, San Marino, California; the Indiana State Library, Indianapolis, Indiana; the Indiana University Archives, Bloomington, Indiana; the Library Company of Philadelphia; the Library of Congress, Washington, D.C.; the Massachusetts Historical Society, Boston, Massachusetts; the Missouri History Museum, St. Louis, Missouri; the National Humanities Center, Durham, North Carolina; the New-York Historical Society, New York City; the O'Neill Library and the Theology and Ministry Library at Boston College, Chestnut Hill, Massachusetts; the Peabody Institute Library, Danvers, Massachusetts; the Presbyterian Historical Society, Philadelphia, Pennsylvania; the Rhode Island Historical Society, Providence; the South Carolina Historical Society, Charleston; the Special Collections Research Center, Swem Library, College of William and Mary, Williamsburg, Virginia; the State Historical

Society of Missouri, Columbia, Missouri; the Sterling Memorial Library, Manuscripts and Archives, Yale University, New Haven, Connecticut; the University of Notre Dame Archives, University of Notre Dame, Notre Dame, Indiana; and the Virginia State Library, Richmond, Virginia. I'm also very grateful to Joe and Martin Dieu for access to their Kelso manuscripts.

Earlier versions of material in chapters 1 and 10 and some paragraphs in the introduction and chapter 3 appeared in "Deist Monster: On Religious Common Sense in the Wake of the American Revolution," *Journal of American History* 95, 1 (June 2008): 43-68; "Skepticism and American Faith: Infidels, Converts, and Religious Doubt in the Early Nineteenth Century," *Journal of the Early Republic* 22, 3 (Fall 2002): 465–508; "Skepticism and Faith: The Early Republic," *Common-place* 9, 2 (Jan. 2009), http://www.common-place.org/vol-09/no-02/grasso/; and "The Boundaries of Toleration and Tolerance: Religious Infidelity in the Early American Republic," in Chris Beneke and Christopher S. Grenda, eds., *The First Prejudice: Religious Tolerance and Intolerance in Early America* (Philadelphia: University of Pennsylvania Press, 2011). I'm grateful for the work of the editors and referees on those publications, and for the publishers' permission to present revised versions here. Thanks also to Tom Baker, Peter Mancall, Sophia Rosenfeld, Rixey Ruffin, and Leigh Schmidt, who read early versions of "Deist Monster," and to Scott Casper, Peter Field, Catherine Kaplan, Andrew Lewis, and Jonathan Sassi, who did the same for my *JER* article.

Over the years I have presented pieces of this project at various conferences and workshops. Thanks to the commentators and audience members who offered helpful feedback at the following: American Antiquarian Society Seminar (2001); American Historical Association Annual Meeting (2001); Society for the History of the Early American Republic Annual Meeting (2005); Omohundro Institute Annual Conference (2006); Organization of American Historians Annual Meeting (2007, 2015); Rocky Mountain Seminar, University of Utah (2007); Society for United States Intellectual History Annual Conference (2016); Triangle Early American History Seminar (2017); Huntington-USC Early Modern Studies Institute Seminar (2017).

I'm grateful to Karen Halttunen, Sue Juster, Peter Mancall, Roy Ritchie, and Leigh Schmidt, who in a variety of ways have supported this project and its author. Thanks, too, to John Demos, who read several chapters and offered crucial advice and encouragement late in the process. The National Humanities Center in Durham, North Carolina, was a wonderful place to finish this book; special thanks to Josh Rivkin, P.P.P., for helping to make my time there fun as well as productive.

Peter Thuesen, Mark Valeri, and an anonymous reader for OUP offered generous and insightful readings of a long manuscript. Susan Ferber and Joellyn Ausanka at OUP have been helpful in a thousand ways. Thanks to India Cooper for the copyediting and Christopher Cannon Jones for the index.

I am, of course, indebted to all the rich scholarship that I enjoyed learning from while researching and pondering this topic. As always, I'd also like to thank inspiring teachers, especially Kate Burgess, Mark Heidmann, Charlotte Wing, Jon Butler, and Harry Stout.

My deepest debts are to Karin Wulf, who had faith in this project even in those moments when I had some doubts.

NOTES

Introduction

1. The series in the *Free Enquirer* was subsequently republished I have used Origen Bacheler and Robert Dale Owen, *Discussion on the Existence of God and the Authenticity of the Bible, between Origen Bacheler and Robert Dale Owen*, 2nd ed. (New York, 1833), 2:183–84, 316, 146–47, 159–60. The first American edition was published in 1832; five London editions were published by 1855.
2. Ezra Stiles, *The United States Elevated to Glory and Honor* (New Haven, Conn., 1783), 85.
3. John R. Kelso, "Auto-Biography," in "John R. Kelso's Complete Works in Manuscript," Huntington Library, San Marino, Calif., 702.
4. James Turner, *Without God, without Creed* (1985) treats the pre–Civil War period as a kind of extended prologue to the emergence after 1865 of "unbelief" in God as a viable alternative for a small group of thinkers; his focus in the earlier period is on how Christian apologists themselves unwittingly helped build the foundation of later agnosticism. Richard H. Popkin's half century of scholarship—most recently *The History of Scepticism from Savonarola to Bayle* (2003)—is an essential philosophical foundation. Also helpful is Franklin L. Baumer's *Religion and the Rise of Scepticism* (1960); it too deals with European intellectuals and not America or "nonintellectual groups."
5. William Smyth Babock, "Journal," Babock Papers; [William A. Alcott], *My Progress in Error, and Recovery to Truth; or, A Tour through Universalism, Unitarianism, and Skepticism* (Boston, 1842).
6. [Alice Hayes Mellen], *The Female Skeptic; or, Faith Triumphant* (New York, 1859), 244, 436.
7. Bacheler and Owen, *Discussion* 1:176, 163.
8. On Tocqueville and skepticism, see Mitchell, "Tocqueville's Flight from Doubt and His Search for Certainty," in Van Der Zande and Popkin, eds., *The Skeptical Tradition around 1800* (1998), esp. 271–72; on Tocqueville and religion, see Kahan, *Tocqueville, Democracy, and Religion* (2015). For older visions of American culture emerging from Puritanism, see esp. Miller, *The New England Mind* (1954) and *Errand into the Wilderness* (1956); Bercovitch, *The Puritan Origins of the American Self* (1975) and *American Jeremiad* (1979); and Arne, "Anxieties of Influence" (1997). For the democratization thesis, see Hatch, *The Democratization of American Christianity* (1989). For Christianization in the early Republic, see Butler, *Awash in a Sea of Faith* (1990); for it deriving from a free market of religion after disestablishment, see Stark and Fink, *The Churching of America, 1776–1990* (1992). For the synthesis, see Noll, *America's God* (2002).
9. Popular neo-atheist books: Harris, *The End of Faith* (2004); Dawkins, *The God Delusion* (2006); Dennett, *Breaking the Spell* (2006); Hitchens, *God Is Not Great* (2007); see also Hecht, *Doubt: A History* (2003) and Jacoby, *Freethinkers* (2004). Gallup polls of Americans show the percentage choosing a religious preference of "none" doubling from 7 to 14 from 1992 to 2012;

58 percent continued to find religion "very important" in their own lives in 2012, as in 1992, but the percentage calling it "not very important" rose from 12 to 19. See http://www.gallup.com/poll/1690/religion.aspx; see also 2015 data from the Pew Research Center, http://www.pewresearch.org/fact-tank/2015/11/11/religious-nones-are-not-only-growing-theyre-becoming-more-secular/. For a discussion of recent work on secularity, secularism, and secularization, some of it inspired by or responding to Taylor, *A Secular Age* (2007), see Grasso, "The Religious and the Secular in the Early American Republic" (2016).

10. As Fisher has argued in "Evangelicals and Unevangelicals" (2016), "evangelical" is "a polemical, contested, and constructed term" with meanings that have varied historically (187). Some scholars have recently abandoned it as a descriptive term, but I think it remains useful, at least for the period of this study. By the early nineteenth century, it became, as Fisher argues, a "more fully self-conscious and intentional" term of self-identification claimed particularly (though not exclusively) by Protestants who focused on emotional conversion experiences, fervent Biblicism, and a commitment to evangelization, revivals, and missions (196). That is how I use the term in this book.

11. On the freethinkers' debate over adopting the term "infidel," see *The Meteor of Light, Containing the Minutes of the Proceedings of the Infidel Convention, Held in the City of New York, May 4th, 5th and 6th, 1845* (Boston, 1845). The standard monographs on American deism remain Koch, *Republican Religion* (1933) and Morais, *Deism in Eighteenth Century America* (1934), and on infidels, Post, *Popular Freethought in America, 1825–1850* (1943). See also Walters, *Rational Infidels* (1992); Walters, "Introduction," in Walters, ed., *The American Deists* (1992) and Marty, *The Infidel* (1961).

12. Orestes A. Brownson, *Charles Elwood, or the Infidel Converted* (1840), in *The Works of Orestes A. Brownson* (1966), 4:315; "Infidelity," *Christian Register* 8, 29 (July 18, 1829): 114; "Scepticism and Infidelity," *Christian Secretary* 2, 29 (Oct. 4, 1839): 2–3; M. Stuart, "The Evidences of the Genuineness of the Gospels, by Andrews Norton," *American Biblical Repository* 11, 30 (April 1, 1838): 265–343; Gardner Jones, "Infidelity—Its Consequences!" *Catholic Telegraph* 3, 31 (June 27, 1834): 244–46; "Natural History of Enthusiasm," *Spirit of the Pilgrims* 3, 5 (May 1830): 256–79, esp. 277; "Progress of Skepticism," *Christian Advocate and Journal* 38, 12 (March 19, 1863): 89; "Dr. Bellows on 'The Suspense of Faith,'" *New Englander* 17, 28 (Nov. 1859): 968–79; "The Scepticism of Science," *Biblical Repertory and Princeton Review* 35, 1 (Jan. 1863): 43–75, esp. 47.

13. Bacheler and Owen, *Discussion* 2:18, 1:187.

14. [Sceptic], "To the Editors of the Free Enquirer," *Free Enquirer* 2, 28 (May 8, 1830): 222–23, esp. 222. For contemporary philosophical argument debating these issues, see, for example, Schellenberg, *The Wisdom to Doubt* (2007) and Moser, *The Elusive God* (2008). Moser's "Religious Skepticism," in Greco, ed., *The Oxford Handbook of Skepticism* (2008), a brief against religious skepticism from a Christian perspective, summarizes the main arguments of *Elusive God*.

15. Noah Webster, *An American Dictionary of the English Language* (New York, 1829), 687.

16. "Religion," *Encyclopedia Britannica* (Edinburgh, 1823), 17:696–713, esp. 696.

17. Harriet Martineau, *Society in America* (1837), quoted in "Miss Martineau on America," *Christian Review* 2, 8 (Dec. 1, 1837): 584–96, esp. 593. On the changing definition of "religion" in the eighteenth and nineteenth centuries, see Harrison, *"Religion" and the Religious in the English Enlightenment* (1990) and Stroumsa, *A New Science* (2010), esp. 5–6. See also Smith, "Religion, Religions, Religious," in Taylor, ed., *Critical Terms for Religious Studies* (1998). On the older theological and newer comparative definitions blurring in nineteenth-century America, see Taves, *Fits, Trances and Visions* (1999), 6–7, 348–51, and Fluhman, *"A Peculiar People"* (2012), esp. 14–20.

18. "Miss Martineau on America," 584–96, esp. 593.

19. [No title], *Prospect* 1, 42 (Sept. 22, 1804): 330 ("a complex idea"); "Has the State a Religion?" *American Review: A Whig Journal of Politics, Literature, Art, and Science* 3, 3 (March 1846): 273–89, esp. 273.

20. "Religion," *Encyclopedia Britannica* (Edinburgh, 1823), 17:696; see also "Faith and Religion," *Gospel Herald* 2, 50 (March 30, 1822): 399–400: "FAITH is the *cause* and RELIGION the *consequence*" (399). Eller, "What Is Atheism?" in Zuckerman, ed., *Atheism and Secularity*, vol. 1

(2010), esp. 10. See also Lightman, *The Origins of Agnosticism* (1987) and Buckley, *At the Origins of Modern Atheism* (1987).
21. Bacheler and Owen, *Discussion* 1:v; 2:vi; 1:10, 13.
22. Robert Owen and Alexander Campbell, *Debate on the Evidences of Christianity* (Bethany, Va., 1829); William W. Sleigh, *The New-York Discussion, between Dr. Sleigh, in Defence of Divine Revelation, and the Delegates of the Tammany Hall Infidels* (New York, 1836); "Christianity Victorious," *Baltimore Gazette and Daily Advertiser*, Nov. 3, 1835, 2. See also Holifield, "Theology as Entertainment: Oral Debate in American Religion" (1998).
23. Bacheler and Owen, *Discussion* 2:v.
24. On the dialogical self, see Hermans and Hermans-Konopka, *Dialogical Self Theory* (2010). See also Hermans and Gieser, eds., *Handbook of Dialogical Self Theory* (2011); Marková, "On 'the Inner Alter' in Dialogue" (2006); Van Meijl, "Culture and Identity in Anthropology" (2008); Joerchel, "Cultural Processes within Dialogical Self Theory" (2013); Hermans and Kempen, *The Dialogical Self* (1993).
25. Bacheler and Owen, *Discussion* 2:vi.
26. "Skepticism or Superstition," *American Quarterly Church Review, and Ecclesiastical Register* 11, 2 (July 1858): 276–87, esp. 285, 278, 281.
27. John Wood, *A Full Exposition of the Clintonian Faction, and the Society of the Columbian Illuminati* (Newark, N.J., 1802), 56; "The Effects of Scepticism in the Last Moments of Life," *Theological Magazine; or, Synopsis of Modern Religious Sentiment* 3, 3 (March–May 1798): 186–92, esp. 187. On the continued arguments with Paine, see "Rennell on Scepticism, No. 4," *Religious and Literary Repository* 1, 8 (April 22, 1820): 123–24; "Tom Paine-ism," rpt. from *Buffalo Spectator, Christian Secretary* 16, 17 (May 6, 1837): 368; J. C., "Causes of Scepticism," *Universalist Watchman* 16, 6 (Aug. 24, 1844), 42; J. J., "Remarks on, and Reply," *Universalist Watchman* 16, 19 (Nov. 23, 1844): 146; Clio, "Infidelity, No. III," *Christian Register* 24, 36 (Sept. 6, 1845): 1.
28. "Efforts of Infidelity," *Episcopal Watchman* 3, 39 (Dec. 12, 1829): 309–10; review of "Report of the Arguments of the Attorney of the Commonwealth at the Trial of Abner Kneeland... and a Speech Delivered before the Municipal Court of the City of Boston, in Defence of Abner Kneeland," *Christian Examiner and General Review* 17, 1 (Sept. 1834), 23–43; "Atheism in New-England," *New-England Magazine*, Dec. 1834, 500–509; "Snakes in the Grass! Mark Them!!" *Christian Advocate and Journal* 19, 40 (May 14, 1845): 159; C. L., "Modern Skepticism," *Independent* 5, 240 (July 7, 1853): 1; and see "Infidelity: Its Erroneous Principles of Reasoning," *New Englander* 12, 47 (Aug. 1854): 341–62, and R. E., "Bayne's Christian Life," *Christian Examiner and Religious Miscellany* 59, 3 (Nov. 1855): 438–59.
29. W. H. C. [William Henry Channing], "The Skepticism of the Present Age; Being a Translation of One of the Lectures of M. Jouffroy, in his *Cours de Droit Naturel*," *Christian Examiner and General Review* 25, 2 (Nov. 1838): 137–57; "Preachers and Preaching," *Christian Inquirer* 7, 27 (April 9, 1853): 1–2, esp. 1; C. L., "Modern Skepticism," *Independent* 5, 240 (July 7, 1853): 1. See also "Skepticism," *Albion* 37, 47 (Nov. 19, 1859): 554; "Modern Skepticism and Its Refutation," *Christian Review* 100 (April 1, 1860): 307–34; "Review 6," *Methodist Quarterly Review* 14 (July 1862): 522–25; C. K. W., "Abstract of a Discourse, Delivered by Rev. David A. Wasson,... 'The Relation of Theodore Parker to Hume, Voltaire, and the Skeptics of the Eighteenth Century,'" *Liberator* 34, 15 (April 8, 1864): 60; Henry Darling, "Difficulties of Revelation," *American Presbyterian and Theological Review* 2, 8 (Oct. 1864): 636–52.
30. "Scepticism Becoming Fashionable," *New World: A Weekly Family Journal* 9, 11 (Sept. 14, 1844): 337.

Part One

1. Origen Bacheler and Robert Dale Owen, *Discussion on the Existence of God and the Authenticity of the Bible, between Origen Bacheler and Robert Dale Owen*, 2nd ed. (New York, 1833), 2:151–52, 137, 163.
2. Historians sometimes cast the Revolution broadly as a long cultural transformation with its roots in the 1730s and its full flowering in the Jacksonian democracy of the 1830s. Scholars,

too, sometimes define religion broadly as the devotion to things deemed "sacred," or to "ultimate concerns." For critiques of "ultimate concerns" (Paul Tillich) and the "sacred" (Émile Durkheim), see Frankenberry and Penner, *Language, Truth, and Religious Belief* (1999); see also Taves, *Religious Experience Reconsidered* (2009); on conceptualizing the question of the relationship of religion and the American Revolution, see Wilson, "Religion and Revolution in American History" (1993).

3. [Sceptic], "To the Editors of the Free Enquirer," *Free Enquirer* 2, 28 (May 8, 1830): 222–23, quotation on 222 ("what [was] taught in the churches"). For the denominational statistics, see Butler, *Awash in a Sea of Faith* (1990), 270; and Fink and Stark, *Churching of America*, 28, and see 56. On the movement away from Calvinism, see Thuesen, *Predestination* (2009), esp. 100–135.

4. The democratization thesis holds that when the state no longer establishes a particular form of worship, a free market of religious competition is created in which the successful competitors will be those who get the most popular support. Therefore, it should be no surprise that the most successful denominations—the Methodists and the Baptists—were those who appealed most directly to the common sense of common people. These evangelical churches passionately proclaimed a simple message of salvation. By highlighting religious life as a choice made by individuals, the Methodists and other early national evangelicals imbibed and put into practice the populist, individualist ethos of the Revolution itself. What resulted, according to this interpretation, set a template for popular religious life in the United States through subsequent generations. A more recent interpretive argument turns the democratization thesis on its head, though still agreeing that the Revolution was a powerful catalyst for religious change. The Revolution, in this view, was a successful assault upon traditional political authority (monarchy and aristocracy) that caused Americans to doubt authority in all realms and relations—the authority of fathers, husbands, masters, clergymen, and even God. After any utopian political hopes were dashed by the bitter factionalism of the Federalist era, Americans, with nostalgic longing for their lost king, turned back to the comforting hierarchical authorities of religion. Both the democratization thesis and its nostalgic-monarchical inversion, however, assume an oversimplified and holistic understanding of culture. In the first, an asymmetry between the elitist, hierarchical churches and the new democratic order is thought to create a cognitive dissonance that was resolved by the democratization of Christianity. In the second, through the iron logic of analogy, rebelling against King George entailed a challenge to authority of all sorts, and only the reassertion of the kingship of God and the power of His church—the intensified Christianization of American culture—could make all the messy uncertainties of political conflict in a democracy less of an existential threat. Both overestimate how difficult it was for a man to play the powerful patriarch at home, consider himself a citizen among equals at a town meeting, and submit himself as a powerless sinner to religious authority in church. See Hatch, *The Democratization of American Christianity* (1989) and Porterfield, *Conceived in Doubt* (2012). For a model of "culture" as contradictory, only loosely integrated, weakly bounded, and thinly coherent, see Sewell, "Concept(s) of Culture" (1999); for this model applied to early American religion, see Scully, *Religion and the Making of Nat Turner's Virginia* (2008).

Chapter 1

1. *Connecticut Courant*, Dec. 17, 1782; John Marsh, *The Great Sin and Danger of Striving with God* (Hartford, Conn., [1783]), 17. The story about Allen cursing the moral cowardice of the Hartford printers is in the unsigned introduction to the 1836 edition of *Reason the Only Oracle of Man* (New York); the author, probably John Fellows, claims to have heard it from Allen himself. Fitzgerald discussed the Beadle case as an inspiration for Charles Brockden Brown's *Wieland* in "Wieland's Crime: A Source and Analogue Study of the Foremost Novel of the Father of American Literature" (1980), chap. 5, as did Samuels in "*Wieland*: Alien and Infidel" (1990), 58–59. The literature on Brown's novel is extensive, but there has been little scholarly work on Beadle. Halttunen, in *Murder Most Foul* (1998), 51–56, 138–39, discusses the Beadle narratives as an early example of American gothic literature. Cohen also examines the case briefly in "Homicidal Compulsion and the Conditions of Freedom" (1995). Smart's "Life of

William Beadle," a 1989 Princeton senior thesis, discusses the case and gathers together Beadle's writings.
2. Ethan Allen, *Reason the Only Oracle of Man* (Bennington, Vt., 1784 [actually, 1785]); [Josiah Sherman], *A Sermon to Swine* (Litchfield, Conn., [1787?]), reprinted with a longer preface as *Oracles of Reason, as Formed by the Deists, Are Husks for Deistical and Heathen Swine* (Litchfield, Conn., [1787?]). Scholars have not devoted much attention to Allen's book, complaining that it was poorly written, lacked originality, and did not really reflect popular sentiments in late eighteenth-century Vermont. But see Walters, *Rational Infidels*, 84–114; Bellesiles, *Revolutionary Outlaws* (1993), 217–44; Madden and Madden, "Ethan Allen, His Philosophical Side" (1999); and Stewart, *Nature's God* (2014). On Allen more generally, see also Pell, *Ethan Allen* (1929); Jellison, *Ethan Allen* (1969); and Randall, *Ethan Allen* (2011).
3. For a brief overview of deism, see Lund, "Deism," in Kors, ed., *Encyclopedia of the Enlightenment* (2003). Two good studies of English deism are Sullivan, *John Toland and the Deist Controversy* (1982) and Herrick, *The Radical Rhetoric of the English Deists* (1997). In studies of America, deism has rarely been seen as a powerful force. In Hutson, *Forgotten Features of the Founding* (2003) and Hutson, ed., *Religion and the New Republic* (2000), for example, deism does not merit an index reference. For a recent argument for deism's importance, see Stewart, *Nature's God*. For deism as a historiographical myth, see Barnett, *The Enlightenment and Religion* (2003).
4. [John Murray], *Bath-Kol: A Voice from the Wilderness* (Boston, 1783), 165; Ezra Stiles, *The United States Elevated to Glory and Honor* (New Haven, Conn., 1783). "Bath kol" is a biblical term meaning "divine voice," first appearing in Daniel 4:31.
5. Henry Pattillo, *Sermons* (Wilmington, N.C., 1788), 200. On the rhetorical use of common sense in the eighteenth century, see especially Rosenfeld, *Common Sense* (2011). For the reception of Scottish Common Sense philosophy in America (particularly the sentimentalist ethics of Francis Hutcheson [1694–1746] and the realist epistemology of Thomas Reid [1710–96] and its relation to American Protestant theology in the eighteenth and nineteenth centuries) see Noll, *America's God*, chap. 6; see also Meyer, *The Instructed Conscience* (1972). On the stylistic features of common sense as a font of wisdom, see Geertz, "Common Sense as a Cultural System" (1975). See also Rescher, *Common Sense* (2005) and van Holthoon and Olson, eds., *Common Sense* (2005). Unlike Common Sense philosophers like Hutcheson who stressed the sufficiency of a moral sense common to all mankind, antideist writers in the 1780s insisted it was commonsensically obvious that common sense alone, without being grounded in the scriptures, was a grossly inadequate foundation for society.
6. Currier, *History of Newburyport, Massachusetts, 1764–1905* (1906), 1:265–66, 413n1; Weis, *The Colonial Clergy and the Colonial Churches of New England* (1936), 148; see also Coffin, *The History of Newbury, Newburyport, and West Newbury, from 1635 to 1845* (1845).
7. [Murray], *Bath Kol*, 87, ix, 99, references to Philip Dormer Stanhope, 4th Earl of Chesterfield (1694–1773) and Thomas Chubb (1679–1746). Which of Chubb's publications Murray intended is not clear; the mention of Chesterfield is surely to reference the *Letters*, first published in London in 1774.
8. Nathaniel Whitaker, *An Antidote against Toryism* (Newbury-Port, [Mass.], 1777); Whitaker, *The Reward of Toryism* (Newbury-Port, [Mass.], 1783), preface; John Murray, *Nehemiah, or the Struggle for Liberty Never in Vain* (Newbury, Mass., 1779), 21, 43–44. See also Nathaniel Niles, *Two Discourses on Liberty* (Newbury-Port, [Mass.], 1774); Peter Powers, *Jesus Christ the True King and Head of Government* (Newbury-Port, [Mass.], 1778); Abraham Keteltas, *God Arising and Pleading His People's Cause* (Newbury-Port, [Mass.], 1777). The clerical stress on communalism and the ethic of stewardship (see, for, example Niles, *Two Discourses*, 15n: "We and all we have belong to the community") differed considerably from the social contract theory and emphasis on the individual's limited surrender of alienable rights invoked by Newburyport's Theophilus Parsons in the famous *Result of the Convention of Delegates Holden at Ipswich in the County of Essex* (Newbury-Port, [Mass.], 1778).
9. On the "black regiment," see Gura, "The Role of the 'Black Regiment'" (1988). On preaching in the Revolutionary era, see Hatch, *The Sacred Cause of Liberty* (1977); Endy, "Just War, Holy War, and Millennialism" (1985); Stout, *The New England Soul* (1986); Weber, *Rhetoric and History in Revolutionary New England* (1988); Griffin, *Revolution and Religion* (1994); Byrd, *Sacred Scripture, Sacred War* (2013); McBride, *Pulpit and Nation* (2016); and Mailer, *John*

Witherspoon's American Revolution (2017). On Dissent, see Bridenbaugh, *Mitre and Sceptre* (1962); Clark, *The Language of Liberty, 1660–1832* (1994); and Bonomi, *Under the Cope of Heaven* (1986). On millennialism, see Davidson, *The Logic of Millennial Thought* (1977); and Bloch, *Visionary Republic* (1985). On virtue, see Kloppenberg, "The Virtues of Liberalism: Christianity, Republicanism, and Ethics in Early American Political Discourse" (1987); Bloch, "The Gendered Meanings of Virtue in Revolutionary America" (1987); Withington, *Toward a More Perfect Union* (1991); and Wood, *The Radicalism of the American Revolution* (1992), 213–25. For a broader range of Christian opinion in the era, see Noll, *Christians and the American Revolution* (2006). On religion and the American Revolution generally, contrast Stewart, *Nature's God* to Kidd, *God of Liberty* (2010).

10. [Murray], *Bath Kol*, 79. The story about Whitefield's relics is in Butler, *Awash in a Sea of Faith*, 188.
11. [Murray], *Bath Kol*, 67–68, 349, and see 338. On "Salvation" Murray in Newburyport, see Currier, *History of Newburyport* 2:457–60.
12. [Murray], *Bath Kol*, 97, 98, and see 101–2. Pyrrho (c. 360–270 BCE); Thomas Hobbes (1588–1679); John Toland (1679–1722); Anthony Ashley Cooper, 3rd Earl of Shaftesbury (1671–1713); Henry St. John Bolingbroke (1678–1751); David Hume (1711–76); John Locke (1632–1704). Murray probably drew his summary from John Leland, *A View of the Principal Deistic Writers* (London, 1757).
13. The problem of assurance, of not being able to determine whether one is to be saved or damned, which Max Weber famously saw as the anxious engine producing the industrious spirit of capitalism, often led, despite the valorization of "faith alone," to a stress on belief and morality anyway. If anxious Christians could not woo Christ or beckon grace, they could at least assent to the Gospel truth and try to walk the path of righteousness.
14. On the movement away from the "national covenant," see Grasso, *A Speaking Aristocracy* (1999), 22–143, and Noll, *America's God* (2002), 31–50. Language that can seem ambiguous has led to historiographical confusion about this topic.
15. Whitaker, *An Antidote against Toryism*, 21–23; Whitaker, *The Reward of Toryism*, preface. The alliance with French Catholics, whom many of the same clerical voices had decried two decades earlier as minions of the Anti-Christ, also troubled the notion of an American nation as a single moral community. See Hanson, *Necessary Virtue* (1998).
16. John Murray, *Jerubbaal; or, Tyranny's Grove Destroyed, and the Altar of Liberty Finished* (Newbury-Port, Mass., 1801), 59, 72.
17. Thomas Jefferson, *Notes on the State of Virginia* (Philadelphia, 1788), 169; [Murray], *Bath-Kol*, x.
18. [Murray], *Bath-Kol*, 165–66.
19. Ethan Allen to James Caldwell, Feb. 7, 1785, in *Ethan Allen and His Kin: Correspondence, 1772–1819*, ed. John. J. Duffy (Hanover, N.H., 1998), 1:169; Ethan Allen to Stephen R. Bradley, Sept. 7, 1785, 1:182. On the debate about how much of *Reason the Only Oracle* was Young's work rather than Allen's, see Bellesiles, "Works of Historical Faith" (1989). On Thomas Young, see Aldridge, "Natural Religion and Deism in America before Ethan Allen and Thomas Paine" (1997). However, Young was defending deism in signed letters to newspapers more than two years before the public dispute Aldridge discusses. See Thomas Young, "To the Reverend George Whitefield," *Massachusetts Spy*, Aug. 16–18, 1770; his untitled letter in the *Boston Evening Post*, Aug. 24, 1770; and his letter "To the Public," *Massachusetts Spy*, Aug. 28–30, 1770.
20. Allen, *Reason the Only Oracle*, preface; Allen to St. John de Crèvecoeur, March 2, 1786, *Correspondence* 1:191.
21. Ethan Allen, *A Narrative of Colonel Ethan Allen's Captivity* (Philadelphia, 1779), 4, 44.
22. Allen, *Narrative*, [3]; Allen, *Reason the Only Oracle*, 104–5.
23. Allen, *Reason the Only Oracle*, 210, 227–29, 203, 471, 424, 95, and see 198. In something of a Cartesian moment, he made the *cogito* the essence of humanity, quoting an Indian who, when asked what his soul was, answered, "It is my think." Allen seems especially sensitive to the problem of communication. John Pell, in his introduction to an edition of Allen's *Reason the Only Oracle* (New York, 1940), vi, records a story about Allen pacing back and forth in frustration as he dictated the text, yelling at the college student taking dictation, and in the preface

Allen confesses to the difficulties that he, as a man "deficient in education," had "particularly in matters of composition" (unpaginated).

24. Ethan Allen, "An Essay on the Universal Plentitude of Being and on the Nature and Immortality of the Human Soul and Its Agency. Proposed as an Appendix, to a System of Moral Philosophy, lately Published at Bennington, entitled Oracles of Reason," first published in the *Historical Magazine* (April, May, June, July 1873) and reprinted in Pell's 1940 publication of *Reason the Only Oracle*. In *Reason* Allen argued that our notions of right and wrong are discovered by reasoning as we examine works of nature and the consequences of things. But in the appendix he insisted that conscience is intuitive. Either way, as surely as we know that we have a body and a mind, we also know that we are morally accountable free agents. Allen also altered his view of the soul, in the appendix considering it as a substance.
25. Allen, *Reason the Only Oracle*, 49, 25.
26. Allen, *Reason the Only Oracle*, 315 (and see appendix, 43); ibid., appendix, 44, 43, 41; ibid., 334; Allen, *Narrative*, 34.
27. Allen, *Reason the Only Oracle*, 468; ibid., appendix, 46; ibid., 471, 468, preface; Allen, *Narrative*, 44, 15. On the Continental tradition of good sense (*bon sens*) used to criticize the falsehoods of commonly held opinions, see Rosenfeld, *Common Sense*.
28. Allen, *Reason the Only Oracle*, 413; Allen, *Narrative*, 44.
29. Allen, *Narrative*, 35, 43, 39, 35–36, 43, 39, 44. Allen would neither say that the corrupt system makes monsters of men who were naturally good nor that it simply unleashed the sinful impulses that all corrupted men had since Adam's fall. Human beings are imperfect creatures, neither angels nor devils.
30. Allen, *Narrative*, 10, 11, 15, 21, 22, 26, 44, esp. [2].
31. Allen, *Narrative*, 15–16, 31, 32, 35.
32. Allen, *Narrative*, 17–18, 24, 26. He accepted the custom that allowed officers to receive the lion's share of charity given by some Irish merchants: he enjoyed fine clothing, good wine, chocolate, and fat turkeys, while the privates got tea and sugar (18); he did not question wartime conventions that allowed officers to be paroled—that is, to move about freely in the occupied city upon the promise that they would not run away—and kept common soldiers confined. On fewer occasions does he refer to the whole group of prisoners as an egalitarian "common-wealth" or a "republic" (23, 25). Herman Melville's Allen in *Israel Potter* (1855) continually insists that he is a gentleman and a Christian; Allen actually claimed the first title and not the second, and most Britons would not have granted him either.
33. Allen, *Narrative*, 17, 20, 22.
34. Allen, *Narrative*, 14, 15, 29, 11, 18.
35. [Timothy Dwight], *The Triumph of Infidelity* ([Hartford, Conn.?], 1788), 23; [Lemuel Hopkins], "On Ethan Allen's Oracles of Reason," *American Mercury*, July 24, 1786; "A Correction of those Lines on Allen's Oracles of Reason in N. 107," ibid., Aug. 21, 1786; "From the Vermont Journal: Messieurs Printers, The following is said to be a genuine copy of a letter from Mr. Woolston, of London, to General Ethan Allen," London, Jan. 4, 1788, printed in the *Norwich Packet*, July 3, 1788.
36. Allen, *Reason the Only Oracle*, 472, and see 469; advertisement for Sherman's *Sermon to Swine*, *New Haven Gazette and Connecticut Magazine* 2, 9 (April 19, 1787): 71; [Sherman], *Oracles of Reason...Are Husks*, iii; [Sherman], *Sermon to Swine*, 38, 21 [*sic*, 22]. Sherman, in *Oracles of Reason...Are Husks*, iv, directed deists, who apparently missed the Bible's self-evident divinity because they lacked common sense, to Soame Jenyns, Esq., *A View of the Internal Evidence of the Christian Religion* (London, 1776).
37. Allen, *Reason the Only Oracle*, 395, 396, 414; [Sherman], *Sermon to Swine*, 20.
38. [Sherman], *Sermon to Swine*, 20, 18. On the New Divinity view of atonement, see Guelzo, *Edwards on the Will* (1989), 129–35; the comment by the colleague (John Smalley) is on 131. See also Valeri, *Law and Providence in Joseph Bellamy's New England* (1994), 123–25.
39. [Sherman], *Sermon to Swine*, 19–20. Actually, Allen's brother Levi had been a Patriot recruiter; Ethan accused him of treason in 1779, and Levi became a quartermaster for the British army in South Carolina. See Duffy's introduction to *Ethan Allen and His Kin: Correspondence* 1:xxxiii.

40. [Stephen Mix Mitchell], *A Narrative of the Life of William Beadle* (Hartford, Conn., 1783) included extracts from John Marsh's 1783 funeral sermon for the Beadle family, *The Great Sin and Danger of Striving with God*. The narrative was also published as "A Letter, from a Gentleman in Wethersfield to His Friend," appended to Marsh's sermon. The narrative was republished in an edition with "A True Account of the House on the Morning after the Dreadful Catastrophe," almost certainly written by Dr. Joseph Farnsworth (Bennington, Vt., 1794). Mitchell's *Narrative* was published again by Alden Spooner (Windsor, Vt., 1795), by an unknown publisher in Greenfield, Mass. (1805), and in a German translation, *William Beadles Lebens-Beschreibung* (Ephrata, Pa., 1796). Extracts from Marsh and Mitchell were published in Timothy Alden, *A Collection of American Epitaphs and Inscriptions* (New York, 1812-14), 4:154-59. Quotations: [Mitchell], *Narrative* (1783), 10, 11; Marsh, *Great Sin and Danger*, 19. The description of Mitchell steadying himself is in [Farnsworth], "A True Account," in [Mitchell], *Narrative* (1794), 38; James Dana, *Men's Sins Not Chargeable on God, but on Themselves. A Discourse Delivered at Wallingford, December 22, 1782. Occasioned by the Tragical Exit of William Beadle, His Wife, and Four Children, at Wethersfield* (New Haven, Conn., [1783]), 20.
41. *Connecticut Courant*, Dec. 17, 1782.
42. The first article was reprinted in the *Massachusets Spy*, Dec. 19, 1782; *Independent Chronicle*, Dec. 19, 1782; *Salem Gazette*, Dec. 19, 1782; *Connecticut Gazette*, Dec. 20, 1782; *Pennsylvania Evening Post*, Dec. 21, 1782; *Pennsylvania Packet*, Dec. 21, 1782; *New York Gazette*, Dec. 30, 1782; *New-Jersey Gazette*, Jan. 1, 1783; *Independent Gazetter*, Jan, 4, 1783; *Providence Gazette and Country Journal*, Jan. 4, 1783; *Virginia Gazette, or American Advertiser*, Jan. 18, 1783. The article was also printed as a broadside in Providence, R.I., by B. Wheeler, Jan. 1, 1783, and with a poem by Ezekiel Russell in Boston (undated, but apparently within weeks of the crime). For "A letter from a Gentleman in Wethersfield" and "The Will of William Beadle," see *Continental Journal*, Jan. 16, 1783.
43. Letter from "A humble Professor of Christianity," *Connecticut Gazette*, Jan. 3, 1783, rpt. in *Boston Gazette*, Jan. 20, 1783, and *Connecticut Journal*, Jan. 23, 1783; "A Friend to Justice," *Connecticut Courant*, Jan. 21, 1783. The account of the burial is by Colonel Thomas Belden of Wethersfield, in Dwight, *Travels*, 166, and see [Mitchell], *Narrative* (1783), 12.
44. *Massachusets Spy*, Feb. 13, 1783.
45. Dana, *Men's Sins*, 21, advertised as "Just Published" in *Connecticut Journal*, March 6, 1783; Marsh, *Great Sin and Danger*, 23, advertised as "Just Published" in *Connecticut Courant*, May 20, 1783.
46. Marsh, *Great Sin and Danger*, 24, 26; George Beckwith, *An Attempt to Shew and Maintain, the Wisdom* (Norwich, [Conn.], 1783), reference to Beadle on 22. On Beckwith, see Dexter, *Biographical Sketches of the Graduates of Yale College* (1885), vol. 1. On Marsh, see Shipton, *Sibley's Harvard Graduates* (1970), 15:73-78. On Dana, see Shipton, *Harvard Graduates*, 13:305-22 (the "heretick" comment, attributed to Jonathan Edwards Jr., is on 316); and Guelzo, "From Calvinist Metaphysics to Republican Theory" (1995). Marsh also implied a link between Beadle's fatalism and Edwardsean and New Divinity teachings (23). This link was explicit in a letter signed "A Friend to Pure Scriptural Orthodoxy" in the *Continental Journal*, June 26, 1783, and in Israel Holly, *Old Divinity Preferable to Modern Novelty* (Litchfield, Conn., 1795), 32.
47. See Timothy Dwight, *The Nature and Danger of Infidel Philosophy* (New Haven, Conn., 1798), 35, 66-68, 83.
48. Dwight, *Triumph of Infidelity*, lines 585-603. Lines 585-88 allude to the last supper of oysters that Beadle prepared for his family (cf. [Mitchell], *Narrative* [1783], 8). The poem continues: "There ****** grinn'd, his conscience sear'd anew, / And scarcely wish'd the doctrine false or true" (589-90). The asterisks correspond to the number of letters in Beadle's name (a pattern Dwight uses throughout the poem). Line 590 seems to refer to another passage from Beadle's papers that was quoted in Marsh, *Great Sin and Danger*, 20-21, about Beadle's uncertainly over whether or not Christianity was true. Dwight then alluded to the murder: "Scarce smil'd, himself secure from God to know, / So poor the triumph over so weak a foe" (592). Previous studies of Dwight's *Triumph* do not mention the Beadle connection.

49. Timothy Dwight, Letter XIX, *Travels in New England and New York* (Cambridge, Mass., 1969; orig. pub. 1821–22), 1:167. In *The Nature and Danger of Infidel Philosophy* Dwight argued that "the true character of all men may be certainly known by their opinions," and "no man is better than the moral opinions, which he holds, will make him, if drawn out into his life and practice" (39). All men's actions spring from their volitions, and their volitions are in accord with "the prevailing dictates of the understanding" (44). But opinions are more an effect (of a sinful heart) than a cause (of sinful actions). "Singular and Melancholy Delusion," *Cincinnati Mirror, and Western Gazette of Literature, Science, and the Arts*, Dec. 22, 1832, 52, an account of the Beadle tragedy, misreads the tombstone inscription's characterization of Beadle as an "Infuriated" rather than "Infatuated" man.

50. "A humble Professor of Christianity," *Connecticut Gazette*, Jan, 3, 1783, points to his giving up the Bible, pride, and the devil; "Benevolens," *Connecticut Courant*, Jan. 14, 1783, described the tragedy as the "natural fruit of infidelity"; "A Friend to Justice," *Connecticut Courant*, Jan. 14, 1783; "A Letter to a Friend," *Connecticut Gazette*, Jan, 27, 1783, mentions despair, depravity and the Devil, but denies the connection to Universalism; "A Friend to Common Sense," *Independent Chronicle*, Jan. 16, 1783, points to Beadle's denial of the doctrine of future punishment; "A Friend to Moderation," *Independent Chronicle*, March 20, 1783, called him an atheist; "A Friend to Truth," *Massachusetts Spy*, Feb. 6, 1783, referred to the devil and corrupt principles; "An Essay on Self Murder," ibid., blamed passions of the heart and Satanic suggestions. Writers seemed less sure about the locus of public moral authority that ought to respond to the tragedy. Some considered it a Wethersfield matter, others looked to the state legislature, and at least one believed that the issue needed to come before the Continental Congress.

51. Letter from "A Friend to Common Sense," *Independent Chronicle*, Jan. 16, 1783; Letter from "A Friend to Moderation and Free Inquiry," ibid., March 20, 1783. Anti-Universalist writers would continue to use Beadle as a bogeyman for decades. See John Kelly, *Solemn and Important Reasons against Becoming a Universalist* (Haverhill, Mass., 1815), 20; and Bell, "Do Not Despair" (2006), 341 (on references to Beadle in the anti-Universalist literature of the 1820s).

52. [Mitchell], *Narrative* (1783), 6, 16.

53. [Mitchel], *Narrative* (1783), 15n, 16; Marsh, *Great Sin and Danger*, 23.

54. [Mitchell], *Narrative* (1783), 10–11. The elaborated version is in Stiles and Adams, *The History of Ancient Wethersfield* (1904), 700, which interpolates the quoted phrase into the passage from Mitchell's *Narrative*. The tree inscription is in the *Albany Bouquet and Literary Spectator*, June 13, 1835, 38.

55. [Mitchell], *Narrative* (1783), 16. Ezra Stiles, *Literary Diary of Ezra Stiles*, ed. Franklin Bowditch Dexter (New York, 1901), 3:49–54, contains Stiles's first mention of the murder (entry for Dec. 12, 1782), receiving the packet of Beadle's writings (Dec. 25), and his extracts (Jan. 7, 1783). Dexter prints only a portion of Stiles's extracts. All quotations below are from the manuscript version of the Literary Diary (microfilm edition), labeled "Extracts from Mr Beadles Letters," with page numbers (172–89) referring to the manuscript. I have spelled out what Stiles abbreviated and have not reproduced underlines, which may not have been in Beadle's original papers (no longer extant).

56. "Extracts from Mr Beadles Letters," 173, 183, 184, 183–84, 185, 177.

57. "Extracts from Mr Beadles Letters," 180.

58. "Extracts from Mr Beadles Letters," 182, 181, 179. Sir William Temple (1628–99), *Miscellanies, in Four Essays* (Glasgow, 1761); see esp. 53, 58 (Ezra Stiles, in *United States Elevated*, labeled Temple a "learned deist" [83]). Michel de Montaigne (1533–92), *The Complete Essays*, trans. and ed. M. A. Screech (London, 1991); see esp. "An Apology for Raymond Sebond," 489–683. It is not clear which editions of Temple and Montaigne Beadle owned.

59. Montaigne, *Complete Essays*, 552, 653; "Extracts from Mr Beadles Letters," 181, 183, 176, 177, 182. Beadle's reference to Shakespeare (misquoting from *Hamlet* about "the stings and arrows of outrageous fortune") was from a part of the "First Letter to Col. Chester" that Stiles did not copy, but it is in Marsh, *Great Sin and Danger*, 22.

60. "Extracts from Mr Beadles Letters," 187. The line missing from this passage in Stiles's transcript, about Beadle's narrow circumstances, is supplied by Marsh, *Great Sin and Danger*, 22.

61. [Mitchell], *Narrative* (1783), [5], 6; Beadle's "Advertisement Addressed to the Ladies," *Connecticut Courant*, Feb. 13, 1775; Stiles's commentary in "Extracts from Mr Beadles Letters," 180; "Extracts from Mr Beadles Letters," 184. Beadle announced his "new Plan" when he first opened his Wethersfield store in 1773 (*Connecticut Courant*, May 4, 1773): "To prevent all Distinctions, and the Difficulties and Inconveniences that attend the common Practice of trusting, he is determined not to trust at all, not even a Shilling to any person whatsoever.— As he is a Stranger in this Place, and consequently free from all Connections, he hopes this Resolution will give no Offence, and begs the favour of those who may become his Customers to return the Compliment. He also hopes that all persons who are convinced of the Utility of Business being done in this Method, (considered either as a public or private Advantage) will favour him with their Countenance and Custom." Some of Beadle's later newspaper ads were similarly chatty but more despairing. An ad describing nails of various sizes, including "some that look large enough to be Grand-Fathers" of the others, concluded, "I wonder whether this advertisement will do any GOOD?" (*Connecticut Courant*, March 20, 1775); another ad for cloth and spices promised to sell other items "so Cheap that I cannot afford to Pay the Printer for telling you their Names; therefore would be glad you would Please to come & Buy them without my Advertising them at large" (*Connecticut Courant*, May 8, 1775).

62. "Extracts from Mr Beadles Letters," 177, 179, 174, 174–75, 175. James Thomson, "Summer," in *The Seasons, viz. Spring, Summer, Autumn, Winter. And a Hymn* (London, [1760?]). Dr. Farnsworth, in "A True Account of the House on the Morning after the Dreadful Catastrophe," first printed in the 1794 edition of Mitchell's *Narrative*, 40, concluded that Beadle's main problem had been an irrational fear of poverty. In the early nineteenth century, Timothy Dwight scoffed that Beadle "died worth three hundred pounds sterling. The farmers in Connecticut were, at an average, probably not worth more at the same period" (*Travels* 1:168). Smart, in "A Life of William Beadle," 141–47, reproduces the tax abstracts from the First Society of Wethersfield (Wethersfield Tax Abstracts Collection, 1772–83, Connecticut State Library, Hartford, Conn.), and notes that from 1773 to 1781, Beadle fell from 79th of 322 (75th percentile) to 213th of 339 (39th percentile). See also Beadle Estate Inventory, 26 March 1783, Estates of Deceased Persons, Connecticut State Library, Hartford.

63. "Extracts from Mr Beadles Letters," 176, 179.

64. "Extracts from Mr Beadles Letters," 185, 175, 174, 178. The "hand in bringing" quotation, 178, is actually about his wife: because, unlike with the children, he did not have a hand in bringing her into the world he had no right to help her exit it.

65. Beadle quoted in Marsh, *Great Sin and Danger*, 19; "Extracts from Mr Beadles Letters," 178, 186; [Mitchell], *Narrative* (1783), 13; Stiles, *Literary Diary* 3:53 (Jan. 7, 1783).

66. "Extracts from Mr Beadles Letters," 188, 174, 182.

67. "Extracts from Mr Beadles Letters," 181, 187.

68. Stiles, *United States Elevated*, 85. On Stiles's religious and intellectual development, see Grasso, *A Speaking Aristocracy*, chap. 5, and Morgan, *The Gentle Puritan* (1962).

69. Stiles, *United States Elevated*, 76, 80, 78, 83. He mentions Beadle again on 86. John Wilmot, 2nd Earl of Rochester (1647–80), and Philip Dormer Stanhope, 4th Earl of Chesterfield (1694–1773).

70. Stiles, *United States Elevated*, 72, 70, 74. Stiles wrote that "it is greatly to be wished for that these principles of our common christianity, might be found in general reception among *all the churches* of these states": belief in God as the Trinity; the scriptures as divinely inspired; the divinity and atonement of Jesus Christ; virtue as the conformity to divine law; holiness as the love of God; salvation through free grace (74).

71. Curry, *The First Freedoms* (1986); see also Levy, *The Establishment Clause* (1994) and Gaustad, "Religious Tests, Constitutions, and 'Christian Nation,'" in Hoffman and Albert, eds., *Religion in a Revolutionary Age* (1994), 218–35. John Leland, *The Rights of Conscience Inalienable, and Therefore Religious Opinions Not Recognizable by Law* (New London, Conn., 1791), 18.

72. *Acts and Laws of His Majesty's English Colony of Connecticut* (New London, Conn., 1750), 69. The condemnation remained in place in 1796, now labeled "Atheism and Deism": *Acts and Laws of the State of Connecticut* (Hartford, Conn., 1796), 183. Zephaniah Swift, *A System of Laws of the State of Connecticut* (Windham, Conn., 1795–96), 1:320–25, esp. 323. Swift describes the prohibition as being against Unitarianism (denial of the Trinity) and apostasy

(denial of the truth of Christianity or of the divine inspiration of the scriptures), 321. Colonial Virginia had language almost identical to Connecticut's (*The Acts of Assembly, Now in Force, in the Colony of Virginia* [Williamsburg, Va., 1769], 26). The phrase "contumaciously reproaching" is from "An Act against Blasphemy," *Acts and Laws… of Massachusetts* (Boston, 1782), 150.
73. Stiles, *Literary Diary* 3:465 (June 28, 1792), 546 (Nov. 11, 1794), 172 (July 20, 1785), 345 (Feb. 27, 1789), 397 (June 22, 1790).
74. Stiles, *Literary Diary* 3:386–87 (March 27, 1790); Benjamin Franklin to Ezra Stiles, March 9, 1790, in Ziff, ed., *The Portable Benjamin Franklin* (New York, 2005), 468–70, and see Franklin to ———, Dec. 13, 1757, in *The Papers of Benjamin Franklin* (New Haven, Conn., 1959–), 7:293. "Extracts from Mr Beadles Letters," 185, 179; [Mitchell], *Narrative* (1783), 16.
75. Pattillo, *Sermons*, v; Letter from "Philologus," *Western Star*, Jan. 4, 1791.
76. "The Folly of Freethinking: An Anecdote," *Essex Journal*, March 9, 1785; "Preparation for Sunday/The Reasonableness of Christianity," *Massachusetts Centinel*, Jan. 15, 1785. "Deism" by "Hortentius" ran in the *New-Jersey Gazette*, June 12, 1786, the *New-Haven Gazette, and Connecticut Magazine*, June 22, 1786, and the *Massachusetts Centinel*, July 8, 1786; as "Thoughts on Deism, Ascribed to his excellency William Livingston, esq., governor of New Jersey," it was published in the *Federal Gazette, and Philadelphia Evening Post*, Dec. 29, 1788, the *New-Jersey Journal*, Dec. 31, 1788, and the *United States Chronicle*, April 16, 1789. "Definitions. From the 3d. volume of Dr. Jebb's works, lately published," ran in the *Massachusetts Centinel*, March 26, 1788, the *Litchfield Weekly Monitor*, April 14, 1788, the *United States Chronicle*, April 17, 1788, the *Massachusetts Spy*, May 22, 1788, and the *Vermont Journal*, June 16, 1788. John Jebb (1736–86) began the passage by defining an atheist as "a man who denies the existence, or the providence of God, and consequently is, for the most part, a profligate, both in principle and practice."

Chapter 2

1. On early Methodism, see esp. Baker, *From Wesley to Asbury* (1976); Hempton, *Methodism and Politics in British Society, 1750–1850* (1984); Richey, *Early American Methodism* (1991); Richey et al., eds., *Perspectives on American Methodism* (1993); Schneider, *The Way of the Cross Leads Home* (1993); Heyrman, *Southern Cross* (1997); Lyerly, *Methodism and the Southern Mind* (1998); Wigger, *Taking Heaven by Storm* (1998); Taves, *Fits, Trances, and Visions* (1999); Andrews, *The Methodists and Revolutionary America* (2000); Hatch and Wigger, eds., *Methodism and the Shaping of American Culture* (2001); Ruth, *A Little Heaven Below* (2000); Ruth, ed., *Early Methodist Life and Spirituality* (2005); Hempton, *Methodism: Empire of the Spirit* (2005); Mack, *Heart Religion in the British Enlightenment* (2008); Wigger, *American Saint* (2009); Williams, *Religion and Violence in Early American Methodism* (2010); Lawrence, *One Family under God* (2011); and Jones, "Methodism, Slavery, and Freedom in the Revolutionary Atlantic World" (2016).
2. "On Inanimate Devotions," *Observer* 6 (March 26, 1809): 46. Minter is briefly mentioned in the historiography of early American Methodism. See, for example, Heyrman, *Southern Cross*, 65, 132, 152; Lyerly, *Methodism and the Southern Mind*, 40, 41, 110; Wigger, *American Saint*, 6–7, 18, 134–37; Lawrence, *One Family under God*, 154. The fullest treatment previously is Lyerly, "A Tale of Two Patriarchs" (2003).
3. Jeremiah Minter, *A Brief Defence of the Bible of the Old and New Testament; Against Infidelity* (Richmond, Va., 1820), which included Minter, *Warning against Imposture in Religion: In a Concise Account of the Evil Life and Conduct of Francis Asbury* (Richmond, Va., 1820). (*Warning* has its own title pages, but the two tracts were bound together and numbered consecutively.) Jones is a major figure in the work of Lyerly: "Passion, Desire, and Ecstasy," in Clinton and Gillespie, eds., *The Devil's Lane* (1997); *Methodism and the Southern Mind* (1998); and "A Tale of Two Patriarchs" (2003). But Lyerly did not know of the existence of the journal of over 100,000 words (Sarah Anderson Jones Diary, Manuscripts and Rare Books Department, Swem Library, College of William and Mary, Williamsburg, Virginia — hereafter cited as "Journal," the term Jones used for it on the first page), because it had been previously misidentified as the diary of an anonymous Quaker. Jones is discussed, and some of her work (includ-

ing from her journal) is quoted, in Ruth, *Early Methodist Life*. Hartwig in "All in Raptures" (2007) sampled the journal and provided a brief overview. The first attempt to fully place Jones and all her extant writings in their historical context was Sandford, "Practicing Piety" (2004). I have, with gratitude, used Sandford's transcription of the journal.

4. For examples of early Methodist spirituality, see Lobody, "Lost in the Ocean of Love" (1990), which includes an edition of Garrettson's diaries, Nov. 1787–June 1793; Chilcote, ed., *Her Own Story* (2001); Ruth, *Early Methodist Life*, a collection and discussion of early American Methodism that includes several excerpts from Sarah Jones and a few from Jeremiah Minter; and Chilcote, ed., *Early Methodist Spirituality* (2007).

5. Goss, *Statistical History of the First Century of American Methodism* (1866), 41–75. Methodists liked to count, and the membership records Goss drew from, if not as precise as the tabulators liked to suggest, still reflect the remarkable growth of the movement in its early decades.

6. Hatch, "The Puzzle of American Methodism," in Hatch and Wigger, *Methodism and the Shaping of American Culture*, 23–40, esp. 38; Wigger, *Taking Heaven by Storm*, 5; Lyerly, *Methodism and the Southern Mind*, 118. Hatch's *Democratization of American Christianity*, stressing free choice and voluntary association, argued that a democratic ethos pervaded popular groups like the Methodists after the Revolution. A prominent critic of Hatch's thesis was Butler, in *Awash in a Sea of Faith*; Butler noted that the Methodists in particular were "almost ostentatiously hierarchal," with authority flowing from the top down (272–73). Porterfield in *Conceived in Doubt* (2012) stresses submission to hierarchical forms of authority in such groups, explaining their popularity as a nostalgia for stable order in the absence of monarchism. But see esp. Richey, *The Methodist Conference in America* (1996), 81: "Ideally the principled impulses that pulled in different directions remained in dynamic tension. Ideally authority (connection, superintendency, centrism, discipline, polity, conference, clergy) and freedom (Arminianism, populism, localism, initiative, pragmatism, fraternity, lay prerogatives) worked together for revival (conversion, holiness, testimony, education, concern for the neighbor)." Minter made the charge about sorcery in *Scripture Proofs of Sorcery, and Warning against Sorcerers* (Richmond, Va., 1814).

7. [Devereux Jarratt], *A Brief Narrative of the Revival of Religion in Virginia. In a Letter to a Friend* (London, 1778). On early Methodism in Virginia, see Sweet, *Virginia Methodism* (1955), 44–70, and Andrews, *The Methodists and Revolutionary America*, 32–44. See also William W. Bennett, *Memorials of Methodism in Virginia: From Its Introduction into the State, in the Year 1772, to the Year 1829* (Richmond, Va., 1871). On Methodism in Jones's Mecklenburg County, see Bracey, *Life by the Roaring Roanoke* (1977), 101–6.

8. [Jarratt], *A Brief Narrative*, 15, 29; Andrews, *The Methodists*, 61; Sweet, *Virginia Methodism*, 71.

9. Thomas Ware is quoted in George Coles, *Heroines of Methodism: or, Pen and Ink Sketches of the Mothers and Daughters of the Church* (New York, 1857), 165–66. See also John Lednum, *A History of the Rise of Methodism: Containing Sketches of Methodist Itinerant Preachers, from 1736 to 1785* (Philadelphia, 1859), 354. According to Elliott (comp.), *Marriage Records, 1765–1810: Mecklenburg County, Virginia* (1963), 187, Sarah's father, Thomas Anderson, came to the county as an overseer for Colonel William Byrd and owned 1,050 acres in 1764, putting him in the category of "large land owners" (190). See also Elliott (comp.), *Early Settlers: Mecklenburg County, Virginia*, vol. 1 (1983), 151, a list of tithables taken in St. James Parish, Lunenberg County, 1764 (St. James became Mecklenburg County in that year). Anderson's will, abstracted in Elliott (comp.), *Early Wills, 1765–1799: Mecklenburg County, Virginia* (1963; rpt. 1983), 9, dated Dec. 4, 1779, and recorded May 8, 1780, listed ten children, including Sarah. Tignal Jones and Sarah Anderson were married on Nov. 16, 1767 (Elliott, *Marriage Records*, 75). Tignal was listed as having forty slaves on a county census in 1782 (Elliott, *Early Settlers*, 215); Jeremiah Minter, who met him in the early 1790s, estimated that he had by that time "70 or 80" slaves (Sarah Jones, *Devout Letters; or, Letters Spiritual and Friendly. Written by Mrs. Sarah Jones. Corrected and Published by Jeremiah Minter* [Alexandria, Va., 1804], 7n.).

10. "Recollections of Dr. T. Hinde," *Methodist Magazine and Quarterly Review* 12, 1 (Jan. 1, 1830): 121–27, esp. 122–23; "A Sketch of the Life & Character of Dr. Thomas Hinde," *Western Journal of the Medical and Physical Sciences* 12 (March 1829): 625–34, esp. 629; and on Mary Hinde, see "Recollections of Mrs. Mary T. Hinde," *Methodist Magazine and Quarterly Review*

13, 1 (Jan. 1, 1831): 121–32. A Georgia deist also prevented his wife from attending church until he converted; see Owen, *The Sacred Flame of Love* (1998), 11. On family resistance to Methodist conversion, see Lobody, "Lost in the Ocean of Love," 64, and the C. L. Garrettson diary in ibid., 280, 298; "The Experience of Francis Pawson," in Chilcote, ed., *Her Own Story*, 94; and Chilcote, ed., *Early Methodist Spirituality*, 38, 72, 90, 104, 106. Heyrman, *Southern Cross*, 184–90, argues that Methodist literature exaggerated the trope of the angry patriarch; but see also Lyerly, "Enthusiasm, Possession, and Madness: Gender and the Opposition to Methodism in the South, 1770-1810," in Coryell et al., eds., *Beyond Image and Convention* (1998), 53–73; and Lawrence, *One Family under God*, chap. 2. On "Mothers in Israel," see Heyrman, *Southern Cross*, chap. 4; Wigger, *Taking Heaven by Storm*, chap. 7; and Schmidt, *Grace Sufficient* (1999), chap. 2.

11. Jones, *Devout Letters*, 87–88; Methodist Episcopal Church, *A Form of Discipline, for the Ministers, Preachers, and Members of the Methodist Episcopal Church in America* (New York, 1787), sec. XXII, "On Dress," 131 [*sic*, 31]. Ruth, in *Early Methodist Life*, 241, thinks that on the matter of dress "Sarah Jones's zeal ran beyond the normal Methodist standard."

12. Jones, *Devout Letters*, 1; Jones, Journal, March 24, 1792, April 1, 1792, April 9, 1792; James O'Kelly, *Essay on Negro-Slavery* (Philadelphia, 1789). On Methodists and slavery, see Mathews, *Slavery and Methodism* (1965) and Andrews, *The Methodists and Revolutionary America*, 125–32. For Methodist documents illustrating their various views on slavery, see Ruth, *Early Methodist Life*, 245–56.

13. "To the Honourable the General Assembly of Virginia, the Remonstrance and Petition of the [ ] Inhabitants of Mecklenburg County," Nov. 8, 1785, Box 160, Folder 13 [microfilm: "Virginia General Assembly, Legislative Petitions. Mecklenburg County, 1776–1818 Dec. 14," Reel 123], Virginia State Library, Richmond. The petition is signed by several Joneses, none of them Tignal. One Jones has an illegible first name, but even if it is "Tignal," it could be an unrelated neighbor in the same precinct of the same county (records usually distinguish the two Tignals by referring to Sarah's husband as "Tignal Sr." and the other as "Jr."). On this and the other county petitions, see Schmidt and Wilhelm, "Early Proslavery Petitions in Virginia" (1973).

14. Jones, *Devout Letters*, 7, 6. Some antislavery white Methodists left Virginia for Ohio: see Jones, "Methodism, Slavery, and Freedom in the Revolutionary Atlantic World," chap. 1.

15. Ruth, *Early Methodist Life*, 11. Ruth identifies "common elements in early American Methodist spirituality" as "emotionalism, ecstasy, rigorousness, exuberance, and evangelism" (16). Americans, compared with their British counterparts, "had a marked tendency to emphasize—perhaps even exaggerate—the interior, subjective aspect of religious experience and the strong emotions that often accompanied such experiences" (28). Jones, Journal, Oct. 31, May 13, April 30, Sept. 14, May 26, 1792.

16. Jones, Journal, April 1, 1792, May 24, June 11, June 18, 1792; ibid., Feb. 12, 1793; ibid., May 30, June 5, June 6, Feb. 28, 1792; Minter, editor's note in Jones, *Devout Letters*, 66. See also *Devout Letters*, 61, 43. Catherine Livingston Garrettson's diaries described a similarly assured state: see Lobody, "Lost in the Ocean of Love," 96, and the diary in ibid., 180, 197, 261, 283. On the yearning for more faith etc., cf. "An Account of Isabella Wilson," in Chilcote, ed., *Her Own Story*, 62; John Wesley's counsel to Hester Ann Rogers in Chilcote, ed., *Early Methodist Spirituality*, 110; and Hanna Ball to Ann Bolton, in ibid., 263. On unbelief, cf. Sarah Crosby in ibid., 83: "I was scarce ever tempted to doubt the divinity of Jesus Christ"; Jane Cooper in ibid., 89: "But still the stupidity and unbelief I felt caused me to mourn"; Hester Ann Rogers in ibid., 108: "unbelief greatly distressed me," and see 114 and 116; and William Keith, *The Experience of William Keith* (Utica, New York, 1806), 12: "I soon fell into darkness by reason of unbelief." After Calvinism and universalism, Keith briefly became a deist.

17. William Glendinning, *The Life of William Glendinning, Preacher of the Gospel* (Philadelphia, 1795), 11, 8, 12.

18. Glendinning, *Life*, 14. Heyrman, *Southern Cross*, features Glendinning in chap. 1 but focuses only on his diabolism.

19. Jones, Journal, June 7, Nov. 9, June 10, June 24, 1792; ibid., Jan. 8, 1793; ibid., April 19, 1792, and see also June 28, Sept. 22, Oct. 12, 1792. She actually calls her second volume "creation providence," but in practice, she focuses on God's providential kindness in the beauties of the

created world rather than pondering his providential intervention in history. Jones mentions her morning practice of applying scripture in *Devout Letters*, 17. She calls the Bible a "perfect and inffallible System of truth" and asserts that "wee gain more in reading [it] aright than wee could derive from the voluminous commentaries of the Learned" (Journal, June 7, 1792). Other than some glancing references to a few other authors (Seneca, Thomas Newton, Thomas Young), the Bible and John Wesley's works are the only printed books mentioned in the Journal. She suggests that "just reading Gods word" rather than reading for pleasure in "the regions of Science" kept her from dangers (Journal, Aug. 9, 1793). A rare example of biblical interpretation is in Journal, Dec. 29, 1792 (on Rev. 1:20). The sacred text did not contain all of divine knowledge. In reading Canticles she concluded that "the Spouse in canticles hath Not opened all. There is yet Something left which only the heart can utter and Immortality declare" (Journal, Nov. 17, 1792). Cf. C. L. Garrettson, in whose diaries "hundreds of scriptural references" are "sometimes quoted directly but more frequently slipped in so unconsciously and so subtly that they appear to be in her own words" (Lobody, "Lost in the Ocean of Love," 100). On scripture as a catalyst for experience for other women in early Methodism, see Chilcote, ed., *Her Own Story*, 40.

20. Jones, Journal, April 1, April 26, June 26, May 5, May 30, Aug. 7, 1792. On the use of the created world, cf. "The Diary of Bathsheba Hall," in Chilcote, ed., *Her Own Story*, 104; Chilcote, ed., *Early Methodist Spirituality*, 52–54; and C. L. Garrettson, Diary, in Lobody, "Lost in the Ocean of Love," 177, 223, 232, 233.

21. Jones, Journal, June 8, May 9, Sept. 16, Aug. 13, 1792; Jones, *Devout Letters*, 106; Jones, Journal, June 14, 1792. See also Journal, April 17, April 19, June 11, June 15, June 21, June 22, June 26, July 27, Sept. 13, Sept. 21, and Oct. 27, 1792. Ruth, *Early Methodist Life*, 162: "Sarah Jones could fall into rapture in almost any setting, triggered by almost any activity."

22. Jones, Journal, June 18, March 19, March 27, July 7, 1792. For assurances to her friends that her faith remained "solid," see Jones, *Devout Letters*, 51, 59, 93, 97, 99, 100, 143, and 154. On self-examination, cf. "Sarah Cooper to John Wesley," in Chilcote, ed., *Early Methodist Spirituality*, 266.

23. Jones, *Devout Letters*, 58, 101; Jones, Journal, Nov. 23, 1792; Jones, *Devout Letters*, 64; Jones, Journal, May 15, Aug. 14, 1792. See also Journal, June 5, Aug. 20, Sept. 8, 1792; and *Devout Letters*, 6, 23, 32, 60, 64. C. L. Garrettson, Diary, in Lobody, "Lost in the Ocean of Love," 138–298, usually envisions her relationship with God as with a master or father.

24. Jones, Journal, May 7, April 29, May 4, June 13, July 5, May 20, May 2, 1792. Jones uses the term "ecstasy" in thirty-nine entries over the seventeen and a half months covered by her journal. Lobody, "Lost in the Ocean of Love," 8, describes Garrettson's similar devotional practice as being informed by an "erotic theology" and "a spirituality of desire." Like Jones, Garrettson, too, felt "espoused to Jesus" and referenced the Song of Songs in her "ecstasy" (Diary, in ibid., 272–73, and see 288). Unlike Jones's, however, Garrettson's "mystical" experiences began when she was betrothed (to Freeborn Garrettson), intensified as her wedding day approached, and ceased after her wedding day (ibid., 132). On the erotic relationship with Jesus, see also Mary Langston's *Dying Testimony* in Chilcote, ed., *Her Own Story*, 220; Sarah Ryan in Chilcote, ed., *Early Methodist Spirituality*, 76; Mrs. Lefevre in ibid., 265; and Lucy Watson hymn in Ruth, *Early Methodist Life*, 59. See also Lyerly, "Passion, Desire, and Ecstasy." Ruth, *Early Methodist Life*, 36–37, describes Jones as "the most striking example" of the erotic quality of the relationship with Christ but concludes that "Jones's spirituality was not too far removed from the center of Methodism. It might be best characterized as a more intense form of something inherent in Methodist piety." On out-of-body experiences, see also Chilcote, ed., *Her Own Story*, 49, 58, 62.

25. Jones, Journal, Sept. 16, March 13, Sept. 18, Nov. 28, 1792. On the language of looking, cf. C. L. Garrettson in Lobody, "Lost in the Ocean of Love," 220, 267, 268, 285; Chilcote, ed., *Early Methodist Spirituality*, 77; and Ruth, *Early Methodist Life*, 147, 156–57. On the frequent use of and allusions to hymns in Methodist writing, see Chilcote, ed., *Her Own Story*, 68. Both Jones and Minter wrote hymns as well as quoted from others.

26. Jones, Journal, April 14, March 12, 1793. On Methodist ecstatic experiences and the supernatural, see Garrettson in Lobody, "Lost in the Ocean of Love," 267–77, 288–94; Ruth, *Early Methodist Life and Spirituality*, 146–86; Chilcote, ed., *Early Methodist Spirituality*, 44–45, 56,

82, 84, 90; Taves, *Fits, Trances, and Visions*, chap. 3; and Williams, *Religion and Violence*, esp. chap. 3.

27. Jones, *Devout Letters*, 38, 42, 96. Cf. William Jessop, Journal, quoted in Ruth, *A Little Heaven Below*, 117: "It seemed as if the Lord Jesus had come down & visibly stood in the midst of us"; Ruth cites this as an example of Methodists "resort[ing] to staggering theological claims" as "their language strained to capture the experience of God's presence in their private worship" (117). On the concern about saying too much, see also "Memoirs of Grace Bennet," in Chilcote, ed., *Her Own Story*, 76. In *Memoirs of the Life, Religious Experience, Ministerial Travels and Labours of Mrs. Zilpha Elaw, An American Female of Colour* (1846), in Andrews, ed. *Sisters of the Spirit* (1986), 49–160, Elaw, recalling an incident from about 1808, distinguished between seeing in the mind and a "supernatural appearance" (77). She saw a tall figure in a white robe, who stood with open arms, smiled, and then disappeared: "I might have tried to imagine, or persuade myself, perhaps, that it had been a vision presented merely to the eye of the mind; but, the beast of the stall [the cow she was milking] gave forth evidence to the reality of the heavenly appearance; for she turned her head and looked round as I did; and when she saw, she bowed her knees and cowered down upon the ground. I was overwhelmed with astonishment at the sight, but the thing was certain and beyond all doubt" (56–57).

28. Glendinning, *Life*, 40, 22, 23.

29. Glendinning, *Life*, 53, 58. Glendinning tellingly modifies the Wesley quotation from "their whole castle in the air (Deism, Atheism, Materialism) falls to the ground" to "Deism, Atheism, &c.") to stress his own two temptations. Glendinning had the excerpt published: John Wesley, *The Extraordinary Case of Elizabeth Hobson* (Philadelphia, 1792), esp. 4. Williams, *Religion and Violence*, 85, reads the response to Glendinning as "the first inklings of a church deeply ambivalent about Satan's power." But then Williams endorses Glendinning's own interpretation on 88: "Glendinning used his experience to challenge the church's authority, whereas Garrettson and Wesley did not." Williams does not note the direct link to the threat of deistic and atheistic skepticism in Glendinning's account. On Freeborn Garrettson's struggles with Satan, see 80–83.

30. Jones, Journal, Nov. 4, 1792. On fictive kin, see Lyerly, "A Tale of Two Patriarchs." Francis Asbury, *Journal of Rev. Francis Asbury* (New York, 1821), 2:76, mentions staying at Jones's house on June 9, 1790; Richard Whatcoat makes a similar reference for June 10, 1790. See Whatcoat, *To Go and Serve the Desolate Sheep of America*, ed. Rogal (2001). Chilcote calls the link between inner experience and communal practice a crucial element in Methodism: "Whenever the individual encounters the good news (*evangelion*) of God's love, she is drawn immediately into a community (*koinonia*), the purpose of which is service (*diakonia*) to others" (*Her Own Story*, 41). Chilcote defines spirituality itself as "a dialectic of movement inward and outward, of personal and social engagement" (*Early Methodist Spirituality*, 2). Thus, "for the women of early Methodism there could be no separation of their personal experience of God and devotion to Christ from their active role as agents of reconciliation and social transformation in the world" (31–32). Ruth better describes the relation of the personal and social as an ideal which in practice involved tension: "Original Wesleyan spirituality, at its best, 'combined inward faith with outward works, individual interiority with communal fellowship, the grace of god with the response of men (sic), spiritual experience with social involvement, ascetic intent with a purpose to actively love all men (sic).' The dynamic tensions of this 'Wesleyan' spirituality were transported to America with the early Methodist immigrants" (*Early Methodist Life*, 23).

31. Jones, *Devout Letters*, 104, 92, 87; Jones, Journal, Aug. 17, 1793. On journals, diaries, and spiritual autobiographies in Methodism, see Chilcote, ed., *Her Own Story*, 67–68, 96–98, 107–8; and Chilcote, ed., *Early Methodist Spirituality*, 61–62. See also Lobody, "Lost in the Ocean of Love," 15–19, 58, and cf. C. L. Garrettson's comments on the practice in ibid., 138, 191, 210, 242, 281, 284.

32. Jones, Journal, March 22, 1793; ibid., April 2, Aug. 13, 1792; ibid., Sept. 18, 1792; ibid., Jan. 24, May 20, 1793; Jones, *Devout Letters*, 21. On worldly company as a trial for the godly, cf. "Memoirs of Elizabeth Mortimer," in Chilcote, ed., *Her Own Story*, 107. John Wesley had advised Methodist women: "Put off the gentlewoman; You bear a higher character" (Chilcote, ed., *Early Methodist Spirituality*, 33).

33. Jeremiah Minter, *A Brief Account of the Religious Experience, Travels, Preaching, Persecutions from Evil Men, and God's Special Helps in the Faith and Life* (Washington, D.C., 1817), 1–13.
34. Jones, *Devout Letters*, 61, 79, 8, 32, 148, 18, 34, 11, 19, 16. On the effect reading his journal and letters had upon her, see also 7, 13, 15, and 41; on their agreement to pray while thinking of each other each night at ten o'clock (covenant prayer), see 7 and 51. On the image of the believer as suckling infant, cf. Chilcote, ed., *Early Methodist Spirituality*, 156. On loving friendship as "already experiencing something from heaven," see Ruth, *Early Methodist Life*, 136.
35. Jones, *Devout Letters*, 33, 24, 18, 33, 23, 33, 8, 24, 14, 24, 43, 18. There were, however, some female preachers in early Methodism. See Chilcote, ed., *Her Own Story*, 77; Chilcote, ed., *Early Methodist Spirituality*, 41; Ruth, *Early Methodist Life*, 203; and Brekus, *Strangers and Pilgrims* (1998).
36. Jones, *Devout Letters*, 51, 147. Minter describes the reaction to his becoming a eunuch in *Brief Account*, 13–27; on the request to change his name and the report of Asbury's statement about his motives, see Minter, *Warning against Imposture*, 85.
37. Jones, *Devout Letters*, 71, 58–59; Jones, Journal, June 25, 1792; Jones, *Devout Letters*, 129. See also her comments in a letter to Pemberton Smith, *Devout Letters*, 120.
38. Minter, *A Brief Account*, 19, 25; James O'Kelly, *A Vindication of the Author's Apology* (Raleigh, N.C., 1801), 61–62. For "Ecclesiastical Monarchy" see [3]; the blessings of liberty, 4; and an analogy to Caesar and the Roman Republic, 10. On O'Kelly, see Kilgore, *The James O'Kelly Schism in the Methodist Episcopal Church* (1963); Allen, "Religion and Politics: James O'Kelly's Republicanism versus Francis Asbury's Federalism" (2006) and "'Some Expectation of Being Promoted'" (2007); Georgian, "'That Unhappy Division'" (2012); and Jones, "Methodism, Slavery, and Freedom in the Revolutionary Atlantic World" (2016). British Methodism experienced a similar schism in the late 1790s: see Hempton, *Methodism and Politics*, 55–80; Chilcote, ed., *Her Own Story*, 99; and Chilcote, ed., *Early Methodist Spirituality*, 287, 360n134.
39. Glendinning, *Life*, 69, 71, 78, 79.
40. Kilgore, *The James O'Kelly Schism*, chap. 3, presents a good summary of both sides of the argument.
41. Jones, Journal, Jan. 4, Jan. 28, July 29, 1793; Jones, *Devout Letters*, 153. See also Journal, Feb. 18, Feb. 21, May 13, July 30, Aug. 10, Aug. 11, 1793.
42. Jones, Journal, March 29, May 1, June 21, July 10, June 29, July 1, 1792.
43. Jones, Journal, July 22, July 28, July 29, 1792.
44. Jones, Journal, July 21, July 14, 1792; ibid., March 14, March 15, May 11, Aug. 19, 1793. With the last quotation—"In prayer and in praises I still upward rise"—she was quoting from her own hymn, preserved in the Edward Dromgoole Papers, University of North Carolina Library, and printed in Ruth, *Early Methodist Life*, 141–42. On martial imagery in early Methodism, see Williams, *Religion and Violence in Early American Methodism*.
45. Jones, *Devout Letters*, 146, 153–54.
46. On gendered difference in conversion narratives, see Lyerly, "Passion, Desire, and Ecstasy." On the problem of projecting modern notions of self and agency into early modern materials, see Mack, *Visionary Women* (1992), 7, 88, 135–37; and Mack, "Religion, Feminism, and the Problem of Agency" (2003). On the importance of analytically distinguishing individualism, individuation, and individuality, see Wuthnow, *Meaning and Moral Order* (1987), 194–203. See also the provocative (if overstated) Shain, *The Myth of American Individualism* (1994).
47. Minter, *Brief Defence of the Bible*, 77n; Jones, *Devout Letters*, 30. See Ruth, *Early Methodist Life*, 69: "Although Methodist conversions were deeply personal, it would be wrong to consider them individualistic"; and Sanders, "The Sacraments of Early American Methodism," in Richey et al., eds., *Perspectives on American Methodism*, 77–92: Methodist conversion "put God at the center" of life rather than the self (79). See also Hester Ann Rogers to Mrs. Condy in Chilcote, ed., *Her Own Story*, 211: "We may be said thus to love him with a *pure heart* when proud *self* and great *I* are slain ... when *I will* and *I will not* is brought into subjection to the will of our heavenly Father." See also C. L. Garrettson in Lobody, "Lost in the Ocean of Love," 140; and Jane Cooper (92) and Hester Ann Rogers (109) in Chilcote, ed., *Early Methodist Spirituality*.
48. Glendinning, *Life*, 37, 39, 40, 46, 48. On Methodist theology, see Langford, *Exploring Methodism: Methodist Theology* (1998); on Methodist Arminian opposition to Calvinism, see Ruth, *Early Methodist Life*, 96–99.

49. Minter accused Asbury of "Tyranny" in *Warning against Imposture*, [75], 82, 83, 85.
50. Minter, *Brief Account*, 6, 7, 29, 47, 92, 101–2, 92, 14, 47, 42, 80, 105. For examples of Methodists seeing supernatural lights in the sky, see Ruth, *Early Methodist Life*, 182; on hearing voices, see Chilcote, ed., *Early Methodist Spirituality*, 82, 90, 242, and Ruth, *Early Methodist Life*, 74, 78–79; on visions of Christ, see Chilcote, ed., *Early Methodist Spirituality*, 56, 84, 239, and Ruth, *Early Methodist Life*, 178. C. L. Garrettson had a vision of Christ (seeing his wounded hands, feet, and side at Calvary) and a view of God—the latter confusing her because she had learned that God not embodied in Christ was an all-consuming fire, and that it was impossible to see him and live. "With my bodily Eye I saw nothing all was presented to my mind, and what I then saw, no pen or tongue can describe" (Garrettson in Lobody, "Lost in the Ocean of Love," 271). She discerned important differences in encountering the Father and the Son. Seeing Christ, believers felt his love like "a well of water springing up within us" (274); seeing the Father (in this way) was to encounter something "to be gazed at in astonishment and admiration" (274).
51. Minter, *Brief Account*, 23, 17, 82, 70, 70–71, 71, viii, 74; Minter, *Brief Defence of the Bible*, 75–76, 82. Minter wrote in *Brief Account* that he charged Asbury with witchcraft in the "public News" about "nine years before [Asbury's] death" in 1816, but I have not found any newspaper articles (70). He made the charge again in *Scripture Proofs of Sorcery, and Warning against Sorcerers* (Richmond, Va., 1814) and expanded it in *Warning against Imposture* (1820). Wigger's sympathetic biography of Asbury, *American Saint*, dismisses this as "nuttiness" (136), though Wesley, like many if not most other eighteenth-century Methodists, believed in witchcraft, and Asbury believed in Satanic harassment and possession; see Williams, *Religion and Violence*, chap. 3. Minter also reported seeing Asbury's ghost floating along a road a few days after the bishop's death (*Warning against Imposture*, 86); cf. C. L. Garrettson talking with the ghost of her niece in Lobody, "Lost in the Ocean of Love," 294.
52. Minter, *Brief Account*, [1], 33, 34.
53. Minter discusses his ordeal in *Brief Account*, 34–50, esp. 48.
54. Minter, *Brief Account*, 27, 27–28, 106. In ibid., Minter mentions his edition of Sarah Jones's *Devout Letters* (1804), 72, and his *Hymns and Spiritual Songs* (Baltimore, 1809), 81, 114; he also refers to other publications, which I have not been able to locate (some, like his biography of Jones, may be no longer extant): 50, 53, 55, 62, 72, 96. For example, he refers to "A fourfold Treatise on important divine subjects" (120), which, since he mentions an 1817 publication date, does not seem to be a reference to his *Four Sermons* (Baltimore, 1806). Minter liked to speak of *circulating* rather than *selling* the publications in his saddlebags, most of which he had written and published himself (*Brief Account*, xii). "Some of my mockers call me, for reproach, a pedlar; but this moves not my temper. I am a Missionary for Christ and his cause, sent, not of man, but of God; and my circulating so many books, is from a love to souls, and to circulate spiritual knowledge; tis not from the love of money. Had money been my object, I might have made abundantly more, with abundantly less trouble, and fatigue, and hardships, and more agreeable to the honor that cometh of men" (88–89). The copy of his *Brief Defence of the Bible* at the American Antiquarian Society, Worcester, Mass., has a back flyleaf inscription noting that on July 12, 1820, Edward Walker had purchased the book directly from Minter for seventy-five cents.
55. Minter, *Brief Account*, 8, 78. Contrast chap. 3, "The Circuit Rider among Frontier Folk," in Posey, *The Development of Methodism in the Old Southwest* (1933), 35–47.
56. Minter, *Brief Account*, 54–55, 83, 101, 94, 132. On the importance of Christian friendship, and of a Methodist's friendship with Jesus or God, see Chilcote, ed., *Early Methodist Spirituality*, 55–58; Ruth, *Early Methodist Life*, 33, 260, 263; and Caroline Matilda Thayer, *Religion Recommended to Youth in a Series of Letters* (New York, 1817), 31–32, 97. On Hammet, see Wigger, *American Saint*, 207–11.
57. Minter, *Brief Account*, 122, 83, 56, 53, 55, 75. Minter's approach seems little different, however, than that of the "zealous Methodist exhorter" who confronted Freeborn Garrettson before his conversion and told him he was heading to hell; see Garrettson in Ruth, *Early Methodist Life*, 77–78. Over the years in his hometown of Richmond, Minter was only allowed to preach a few times in the penitentiary and the poorhouse and once, when he managed with great difficulty to borrow the key to the building, in the Capitol (*Brief Account*, 59).

58. Minter, *Brief Account*, 112, 33, 98, 99, 58, 119, 111–12, 120.
59. Minter, *Brief Account*, 84, [iii], 81; Minter, *Brief Defence of the Bible*, [3].
60. Minter, *Brief Account*, 59, 117–18; *Brief Defence of the Bible*, 34. On the lack of much of a civic theology among Methodists before 1812, see Richey, *Early American Methodism*, 36–43; for its development after that point, see Williams, *Religion and Violence*, chap. 4.
61. Minter, *Brief Defence of the Bible*, 12, 35, 36.
62. Minter, *Brief Defence of the Bible*, 25, [3], 58, 32, 61, 69, 65, 41. Minter thought that the author of *A Blow at Priestcraft* might be Thomas Steel Cavender (7), but I have found no other record of this publication.
63. Minter, *Brief Defence of the Bible*, 84, 34.
64. Minter, *Brief Defence of the Bible*, 87; *Brief Account*, 77.
65. *Baltimore Patriot*, 34, 156, Dec. 31, 1829, [3]. The death notice misidentified him as a "Methodist Minister."

Chapter 3

1. Elihu Palmer, *An Enquiry into the Moral and Philosophical Improvement of the Human Species* (New York, 1797), 6, 25, 8, 9, 23; Elihu Palmer, *Posthumous Pieces* (London, 1824), 47, written ca. 1804–5. See also *Political Miscellany...III. Extracts from an Oration, delivered by Elihu Palmer, the 4th of July, 1793* (New York, 1793); Elihu Palmer, *The Political Happiness of Nations: An Oration, Delivered at the City of New York, in the Fourth of July* [New York? 1800?].
2. Elihu Palmer, *Principles of Nature; or, a Development of the Moral Causes of Happiness and Misery among the Human Species*, 3rd ed. ([New York?], 1806), 13, and see 234–35. I have used the third edition (the last in Palmer's lifetime, though apparently identical to the second edition (1802), which was revised and expanded from the first (1801).
3. Palmer, *Principles*, 240, 137, 139.
4. Palmer, *Political Happiness of Nations*, 18.
5. Thomas Paine, *The Age of Reason: Being an Investigation of True and Fabulous Theology* was published in two parts (1794, 1795), and a third part was published in 1806. On Palmer, see John Fellows, "Memoir of Mr. Palmer," in Palmer, *Posthumous Pieces*, [3]–10; Walters, "Elihu Palmer and the Religion of Nature: An Introductory Essay," in Walters, ed., *Elihu Palmer's "Principles of Nature"* (1990), 3–67; and Walters, *Rational Infidels*, 205–28. Matthew Stewart's provocative *Nature's God* (2014), 217, calls Palmer's *Principles of Nature* a "classic" work but, surprisingly, devotes no attention to it.
6. Palmer, *Principles*, 209, 59, 240, and see 207. The chapter discussing pure and simple deism remained the penultimate one, although the last chapter was new in the second and subsequent editions.
7. French, "Elihu Palmer, Radical Deist, Radical Republican" (1979), esp. 89; Fischer, "Vitalism in America" (2016). I am indebted to Fischer's essay, though I disagree with it, for helping to sharpen my own understanding of Palmer.
8. Palmer, *Principles*, 191, 242. In *Principles* he wrote of this understanding of matter as an "opinion" with pragmatic ethical and psychological consequences to recommend it; in a chapter for his next book, intended to be called *The Political World*, of which only four short chapters had been composed at his death, this opinion has hardened into "fact" (*Posthumous Pieces*, 15).
9. Palmer, *Principles*, 222n, 177. Palmer responded in this note in the second edition to a charge of atheism in a review of the first: "Article VIII, Principles of Nature...by Elihu Palmer," *American Review and Literary Journal* 1, 4 (Oct.–Dec. 1801), 448–54, esp. 452. He was also called an atheist in "Communication: Extracts from 'Principles of Nature'...No. 3," *New York Gazette*, Oct. 20, 1802, 2, and "The Booksellers Toast," *New York Herald*, Dec. 19, 1802, 2.
10. [Elihu Palmer], "Comments on the Sacred Writings," *Prospect* 1, 7 (Jan. 21, 1804): 49; 1, 10 (Feb. 11, 1804): 73; 1, 30 (June 30, 1804): 235.
11. [Palmer], "Comments on the Sacred Writings," *Prospect* 1, 50 (Nov. 17, 1804): 394. In *Temple of Reason*, *Christianity Unveiled* is attributed to [Nicolas-Antoine] Boulanger, although this has been considered to be a pseudonym for Paul Henri Thiry, baron d'Holbach.

12. [Palmer], "Comments on the Sacred Writings," *Prospect* 1, 48 (Nov. 2, 1804): 37; 1, 9 (Feb. 4, 1804), 65.
13. [Palmer], "Comments on the Sacred Writings," *Prospect* 2, 6 (Feb. 9, 1805): 41.
14. "A Demonstration of the Being and Attributes of God," *Temple of Reason* 1, 1 (Nov. 8, 1800): 2–5 and 1, 2 (Nov. 15, 1800), 9–10; Samuel Clarke, "On the Immortality of the Soul," *Temple of Reason* 1, 3 (Nov. 22, 1800): 24, and 1, 4 (Nov. 29, 1800), 27–29; [Palmer], "Comments on the Sacred Writings," *Prospect* 1, 49 (Nov. 10, 1804): 386, and 1, 33 (July 21, 1804): 257.
15. John Locke, "Enthusiasm," *Prospect* 2, 5 (Feb. 2, 1805): 39; David Hume, [No title], *Prospect* 2, 3 (Jan. 19, 1805): 18; "Religious Insanity," *Prospect* 2, 2 (Jan. 12, 1805): 12–13.
16. Editorial Headnote, "Profession of Faith of a Savoyard Curate, from Rosseau [^]," *Prospect* 1, 22 (May 5, 1804): 172.
17. Jean-Jacques Rousseau, "Profession of Faith of a Savoyard Curate," *Prospect* 1, 22 (May 5, 1804): 172, 173; 1, 42 (Sept. 22, 1804): 226.
18. Jean-Jacques Rousseau, "Profession of Faith of a Savoyard Curate," *Prospect* 1, 43 (Sept. 29, 1804): 343; 1, 50 (Nov. 17, 1804): 399.
19. On institutionalization, see Williams, *The Sociology of Culture* (1981); Wuthnow, *Meaning and Moral Order* (1987); Powell and DiMaggio, eds., *The New Institutionalism in Organizational Analysis* (1991); Bourdieu, *Language and Symbolic Power* (1991), esp. chap. 8, "Political Representation: Elements for a Theory of the Political Field"; Demerath et al., eds., *Sacred Companies* (1998); Davis et al., eds., *Social Movements and Organizational Theory* (2005); Emirbayer and Johnson, "Bourdieu and Organizational Analysis" (2008); Mohr and White, "How to Model an Institution" (2008); Colyvas and Jonsson, "Ubiquity and Legitimacy" (2011); Gorski, ed., *Bourdieu and Historical Analysis* (2013); and Wang, "Homology and Isomorphism" (2016).
20. On voluntary association in colonial Philadelphia, see Roney, *Governed by a Spirit of Opposition* (2014); for early republican Philadelphia, see Koschnik, *"Let a Common Interest Bind Us Together"* (2007); for Massachusetts, see Neem, *Creating a Nation of Joiners* (2008); for partisanship and culture in Connecticut during the 1790s, see Grasso, *A Speaking Aristocracy* (1999), chap. 8.
21. Koschnik, *"Let a Common Interest Bind Us Together,"* chaps. 1–2; Cotlar, *Tom Paine's America* (2011), chap. 5.
22. Curry, *First Freedoms* (1986); Levy, *The Establishment Clause* (1994); Green, *The Second Disestablishment* (2010); Sehat, *The Myth of American Religious Freedom* (2011); Buckley, *Establishing Religious Freedom* (2013); Gordon, "The First Disestablishment" (2014), esp. 317.
23. John Fitch, *The Autobiography of John Fitch*, ed. Frank D. Prager (Philadelphia, 1967), 132, 138, 139. See also Boyd, *Poor John Fitch, Inventor of the Steamboat* (1935); and Schlereth, "A Tale of Two Deists" (2008).
24. Fitch, *Autobiography*, 123, 132.
25. Fitch, *Autobiography*, 123, 124.
26. Fitch, *Autobiography*, 138, 139; "To the Friends of Liberal Sentiments," *Dunlap's American Daily Advertiser*, March 3, 1792, 3; *National Gazette*, March 21, 1792, 3; Elihu Palmer, "To the Public," *General Advertiser*, March 17, 1792, 3; Fellows, "Memoir," in Palmer, *Posthumous Pieces*, 6–7.
27. A. B., "For the Federal Gazette," *Federal Gazette*, March 19, 1792, 3; Fitch, *Autobiography*, 138. Palmer responded to A. B. in "For the Federal Gazette," *Federal Gazette*, March 22, 1792, 3.
28. Fellows, "Memoir," in Palmer, *Posthumous Pieces*, 6; Palmer, "To the Public," *Federal Gazette*, March 17, 1792, 3. On reason and piety in Universalism, see Bressler, *The Universalist Movement in America* (2001).
29. Miller, *The Larger Hope* (1979), 3–91; Marini, *Radical Sects of Revolutionary New England* (1982), 68–75, 83–99, 106–9, 122–27, 144. On Winchester and the Philadelphia Baptists-turned-Universalists, see Lindman, "'Bad Men and Angels from Hell'" (2011).
30. Miller, *Larger Hope*, xxvii; John Murray, *Some Hints Relative to the Forming of a Christian Church.... Concluding with a Character of a Consistent Universalist* (Boston, 1791), esp. 41–42. Marini, *Radical Sects*, stresses the persistence of chaotic diversity and how long denominational definition took.
31. Miller, *Larger Hope*, 86–87.

32. Miller, *Larger Hope*, 160; "Veritas contra Free Thinker," *Mirror*, April 3, 1795, 2; "For the Federal Mirror," *Mirror*, July 31, 1795, 4; "For the Maryland Herald," *Herald*, July 13, 1797, 2; "Comparison between Atheism and Universalism with Regard to Their Moral Tendency," *New York Missionary Magazine* 2, 1 (Jan. 1801): 57–59; "A Series of Letters from a Father to His Son," *Christian's Weekly Monitor* 2, 2 (Aug. 1, 1815): 53–60, esp. 53. See also Zadock, "To the Editor of the Balance," *Balance* 5, 31 (Aug. 5, 1806): 24, on Universalism causing a rise in suicides.
33. Fellows, "Memoir," in Palmer, *Posthumous Pieces*, 8. See also "Discourse of Thomas Paine at the Society of the Theophilanthropists," *Temple of Reason* 1 (Jan. 3, 1801): 68–70; [Elihu Palmer], *The Examiners Examined: Being a Defence of "The Age of Reason"* (New York, 1794).
34. "Principles of the Deistical Society of the State of New York," in Palmer, *Posthumous Pieces*, 11–12; "Public Instruction," *Temple of Reason* 1 (Dec. 27, 1800): 63; "To the Liberal Minded of All Professions," *Temple of Reason* 2 (Nov. 25, 1801): 367.
35. "The Theophilanthropists," *Temple of Reason* 1 (Dec. 13, 1800): 46; [Jean-Baptiste Chemin-Dupontès], *Manual of Theophilanthropes, or Adorers of God, and Friends of Men*, 2nd ed., trans. John Walker (London, 1797), 2; [Jean-Baptiste Chemin-Dupontès], *Manual of the Theophilanthropes* (Philadelphia, 1800); "A Discourse Delivered before the Theophilanthropic Society of Philadelphia," *Temple of Reason* 1 (May 27, 1801): 153–54, esp. 154; (June 3, 1802): 161–62; "For the American Daily Advertiser," *Poulson's American Daily Advertiser*, April 2, 1803, 2.
36. In the *Temple of Reason*: "Domestic, an Universal Insult to the Citizens of Philadelphia!" 1 (July 8, 1801): 207; "The Temple," 2 (April 17, 1802): 94, (May 8, 1802): 118; "The Temple," 2 (May 15, 1802): 124.
37. Formisano and Pickering, "The Christian Nation Debate and Witness Competency" (2009).
38. T. W., "Litchfield Decision," nos. 1–5, *Trumpet and Universalist Magazine* 1, 16 (Oct. 18, 1828): 61; 1, 18 (Nov. 1, 1828): 69; 1, 20 (Nov. 15, 1828): 77; 1, 22 (Nov. 29, 1828): 85; 1, 25 (Dec. 20, 1828): 97. J. A. B., "Qualifications of Witnesses: Ought Any Man to be Excluded from Bearing Witness, on the Ground of Religious Belief?" *Christian Review* 1, 4 (Dec. 1, 1836): 479–502, esp. 491.
39. On Denniston at Newburgh, see "Theistical Society," *Philadelphia Gazette*, Sept. 21, 1802, 2; and "Extract of a Letter from a Gentleman in Orange County," *Evening Post*, May 24, 1803, 3. On *Denniston v. Coles* and Gardner's decision, see "Interesting Decision," *Evening Post*, July 22, 1803, 2, an account reprinted in many papers, and Editor's Column, *Recorder of the Times*, Sept. 14, 1803. The Denniston-Coles feud was played out in the *Rights of Man* and the *Recorder of the Times* from the end of June through September 1804, and then somewhat less regularly through an issue of the *Recorder* published a day after Denniston's death (Dec. 14, 1803).
40. On the *Denniston v. Coles* appeal, see *Recorder of the Times*, Sept. 14, 1803; the fullest account of the arguments was published in the *Rights of Man* and reprinted as "From the Newburgh Rights of Man. Orange County Common Pleas," *American Citizen*, Sept. 23, Sept. 27, and Oct. 14, 1803, 2 of each issue. This account summarizes the argument from one of Denniston's lawyers (W. Ross), apparently using Ross's notes; the arguments from Coles's attorneys are inferred from Ross's response.

Chapter 4

1. [John Fellows], *Some Doubts Respecting the Death, Resurrection, and Ascension of Jesus Christ... to Which Are Added, Reasons for Scepticism in Religion, by John Hollis* (New York, 1797), a more accurately titled version of what was published the previous year as *The Character and Doctrines of Jesus Christ*; "An Abridgement of Barruel's Memoirs of Jacobinism," *Connecticut Courant*, Sept. 2, 1799, 2 ("This bookseller"); Walt Whitman, *Specimen Days* (Glasgow, 1883; orig. pub. 1882), 96; John Fellows, "Memoir of Mr. Palmer," in Elihu Palmer, *Posthumous Pieces* (London, 1824), 3–10; John Fellows, *An Exposition of the Mysteries, or Religious Dogmas and Customs, of the Ancient Egyptians, Pythagoreans, and Druids; Also, an Inquiry into the Origin, History, and Purport of Freemasonry* (New York, 1835). On Fellows, see Stevens, "John Fellows: A Minor Deist" (1956).

2. On the failure of deism, see Koch, *Republican Religion*, 239–99; Morais, *Deism in Eighteenth-Century America* (1934), chap. 6; Walters, *Rational Infidels* (1992), chap. 8; see also, on the failure of the Enlightenment as a religion, May, *Ideas, Faiths, and Feelings* (1983), esp. 155, 166; and May, *The Enlightenment in America* (1976), 325–34. For a different view of the late eighteenth-century activist deists and politics than the one presented here, see Schlereth, *Age of Infidels* (2013), chaps. 1–4.

3. James Lackington, *Memoirs of James Lackington* (Newburgh, N.Y., 1796), 174; Elihu Palmer, *Principles of Nature; or, A Development of the Moral Causes of Happiness and Misery among the Human Species*, 3rd ed. ([New York?], 1806), 69, 135; John Wood, *A Full Exposition of the Clintonian Faction, and the Society of the Columbian Illuminati* (Newark, N.J., 1802), 38.

4. Jedidiah Morse, *A Sermon, Delivered...May 9th, 1798* [National Fast] (Boston, 1798); Wood, *Full Exposition*. See also Morse's two subsequent Illuminati sermons: *A Sermon, Preached at Charlestown, November 29, 1798, on the Anniversary Thanksgiving in Massachusetts. With an Appendix...Exhibiting Proofs of the Early Existence, Progress, and Deleterious Effects of French Intrigue and Influence in the United States* (Boston, 1798); and *A Sermon, Exhibiting the Present Dangers, and Consequent Duties of the Citizens of the United States of America...April 25, 1799* [National Fast] (Charlestown, Mass., 1799). John Robison, *Proofs of a Conspiracy against All the Religions and Governments of Europe, Carried on in the Secret Meetings of Free Masons, Illuminati, and Reading Societies* (Philadelphia, 1798), 1st American ed., 3rd ed., orig. pub. 1797.

5. Morse, *A Sermon, Delivered...May 9th, 1798*, 23 (citing Robison, *Proofs of a Conspiracy*, 153), 22n; Jedidiah Morse, *A Sermon Delivered before the Grand Lodge of Free and Accepted Masons of the Commonwealth of Massachusetts* (Leominster, Mass., 1798), 20–22; Timothy Dwight, *The Duty of Americans, at the Present Crisis* (New Haven, Conn., 1798). The classic study is Stauffer, *New England and the Bavarian Illuminati* (1918); see also Hoffman, "Opinion, Illusion, and the Illusion of Opinion" (1993); Waterman, "The Bavarian Illuminati, the Early American Novel, and Histories of the Public Sphere" (2005); Wallace, "Threats of Illuminism" (2010); and Taylor, "British Conservatism, the Illuminati, and the Conspiracy Theory of the French Revolution" (2014).

6. *Constitutions of the Ancient and Honorable Fraternity of Free and Accepted Masons* (Worcester, Mass., 1798), 34; and see Thomas Smith Webb, *The Freemason's Monitor* (Albany, N.Y., 1797), 10, 22, 34, 49, 59, 83, 153, and Morais, *Deism*, 150–51; Dwight, *Duty of Americans*, 11, 12, 32n. On Freemasonry see esp. Bullock, *Revolutionary Brotherhood* (1996), Bullock, "Initiating the Enlightenment?" (1996), and Hackett, *That Religion in Which All Men Agree* (2014).

7. Stauffer, *New England and the Bavarian Illuminati*, 150–96; Augustin Barruel, *Memoirs Illustrating the History of Jacobinism* (Hartford, Conn., 1799), 1st American ed. of 2nd London ed. (the first volume appeared in French in 1797); Morse, *A Sermon, Exhibiting the Present Dangers*, 25–42. For a response, see, for example, *Demosthenes versus Cicero...Being a Suitable reply to the Anti-Masonic, Anti-Illuminati, Anti-Republican Reveries, in a Late Publication* (Baltimore, 1799). On the Christianization of Masonry and the defense of the order by the clergy, see Bullock, *Revolutionary Brotherhood*, 169–75; for the charge thrown back against the Federalist clergy, see [John Cosens Ogden], *A View of the New-England Illuminati* (Philadelphia, 1799).

8. Fellows, *Exposition of the Mysteries*, esp. 403–4, 249n ("mummery").

9. [Denis Driscoll], "Domestic," *Temple of Reason* 1 (April 22, 1801): 119; [Elihu Palmer], *The Examiners Examined: Being a Defence of "The Age of Reason"* (New York, 1794), 73.

10. Even when antideist writers tried to sidestep theological issues and attack deists on other grounds (not wanting to be seen as infringing upon the rights of conscience), the code words were there. The charge that public deism was "subversive of man's highest and most dear interests," for example, was code for the assumption that the Gospel offer of salvation through Christ was a public good that deserved political protection; *Goshen Repository*, Oct. 10, 1797, in Schlereth, *Age of Infidels*, 101 (quotation).

11. *General Remarks, on the Proceedings Lately Had in the Adjacent Country, Relative to Infidelity* (Newburgh, N.Y., 1798), quotations on 21, 10, 45. Wood, *Full Exposition*, compares deism to treason (30); Wood focuses on an allied group in New York City, but David Denniston and Elihu Palmer were leaders of both that and the Newburgh club (later called the Druids). See

also "A True Declaration of the Character and Principles of the Infidels in Orange County, and Especially those of Newburgh" by "A Countryman," *Recorder of the Times*, Aug. 3, 1803, which condemned what the author saw as the seeds of an anti-Christian political party, ready to "draw the sword" for power.

12. "Toleration," *Philadelphia Gazette*, Oct. 14, 1797; Mason Locke Weems, *The Philanthropist; or, A Good Twenty-Five Cents Worth of Love Powder, for the Honest Adamites and Jeffersonians* (Charleston, S.C., 1799), 25, 28; "On Provision by Law for the Support of Christian Institutions," *Christian Disciple and Theological Review* 2, 11 (Sept. 1, 1820): 368–72.

13. For "universal toleration" or "toleration, complete and perfect" as religious liberty, broadly construed, see Americanus, "Mr. Jefferson," *National Magazine* 2, 7 (Sept. 1, 1800): 226–335; and "Philadelphia, Sept. 9," *Carolina Gazette*, Sept. 25, 1800. Richard Price, *Observations on the Importance of the American Revolution, and the Means of Making It a Benefit to the World* (Boston, [1784]; orig. pub. London, 1784), 30; Thomas Paine, *The Rights of Man, Part One* (London, 1791; rpt. Philadelphia, 1791), 47; these passages from Price and Paine were excerpted in newspapers: see, for example, "Rights of Man," [Charleston, S.C.] *City Gazette*, June 28, 1791, 2, and "Extract from 'Observation on the Importance of the American Revolution' by Richard Price," *Republican Spy*, April 23, 1804, 4. On toasting, cf. [July Fourth Toasts in King's County], *Greenleaf's New York Journal*, July 15, 1795, 3; and "George-town, February 24" [President's Birthday Toasts], [Baltimore, Md.] *Federal Gazette*, Feb. 27, 1796, 3 (quotation); see also "Revolution Dinner. Crown and Anchor," *New-York Packet*, Sept. 15, 1791, 2.

14. "The President's Answer. To the Hebrew Congregation, in Newport, Rhode Island," [Boston, Mass.] *Herald of Freedom*, Sept. 7, 1790; William Linn, *Discourses on the Signs of the Times* (New York, 1794), 44; William Findley, *Observations on "The Two Sons of Oil"* (Pittsburgh, 1812), responding to Samuel B. Wylie, *The Two Sons of Oil; or, The Faithful Witness for Magistracy and Ministry* (Greensburg, Pa., 1803).

15. "Liberty—No. XLIX, Extract from a Sermon Delivered Aug. 20, 1812, by John Giles," [Philadelphia] *Herald of Gospel Liberty*, March 5, 1813; "Toleration—Liberality," *Evangelical and Literary Magazine and Missionary Chronicle* 4, 2 (Feb. 1821): 89–93, esp. 89; "Religious Toleration," *Christian Watchman* 13, 46 (Nov. 16, 1832): 182.

16. Thomas Jefferson, *Notes on the State of Virginia* (Philadelphia, 1788), 169; Wylie, *Two Sons of Oil*, 15, 40–41, esp. 40. For a sampling of the debate about Jefferson and religion, see "Philadelphia, Sep. 9," *Carolina Gazette*, Sept. 25, 1800; *A Vindication of the Religion of Mr. Jefferson and a Statement of his Services in the Cause of Religious Liberty. By a Friend to Real Religion* (Baltimore, Md., [1800]); [John M. Mason], *The Voice of Warning, to Christians, on the Ensuing Election of a President of the United States* (New York, 1800); [DeWitt Clinton], *A Vindication of Thomas Jefferson* (New York, 1800); "From the Bee: Advice to Federalists," *Constitutional Telegraph*, Feb. 21, 1801; "From the Boston Chronicle," *True American*, May 4, 1801. On Jefferson and religion, see Gaustad, *Sworn on the Altar of God* (1996). For another call for the United States to declare itself a Christian nation and restrict the rights of deists and other infidels, see "Indifference to Religion in the Administration of a Government a Great National Sin: Taggart's Fast Sermons," *Utica Christian Magazine* 1, 6 (Dec. 1, 1813): 229–36; 1, 7 (Jan. 1, 1814): 267–71; 1, 8 (Feb. 1, 1814): 310–14.

17. Wood, *Full Exposition*, 25. On the Newburgh Druid Society, see Ruttenber, *History of the Town of Newburgh* (1859), 88–89, 90; and Koch, *Republican Religion*, 114–29. On Wood's earlier career, see Durey, *Transatlantic Radicals* (1997), 160–63. "From the Palladium: Illuminism," *Evening Post*, Oct. 6, 1802, related the story about the cat baptism and dog communion, later resurrected in "Decline of Infidelity," *Newburgh* [N.Y.] *Witness*, rpt. in *Hampshire Gazette*, Feb. 5, 1823. Abner Cunningham, *Practical Infidelity Portrayed and the Judgments of God Made Manifest* (New York, 1836), 43–47, passed on stories about the bizarre deaths experienced by the deists. See also John Johnston, *The Autobiography and Ministerial Life of the Rev. John Johnston* (New York, 1856), 81–89. On the kin connections of the Newburgh deists, see Baker, "Speculations on the Genealogy of Deism in New York" (2008).

18. Wood, *Full Exposition*, 25, 26, 30.

19. Wood, *Full Exposition*, 34, 35.

20. Wood, *Full Exposition*, 33, 36, 46.

Notes to Pages 130–134

21. Extracts of Wood's *Full Exposition* ran in several papers in Sept. 1802, including New York's *Evening Post, Herald*, and *Spectator*, the Philadelphia *Gazette*, the Boston *Gazette*, the *Connecticut Courant*, and the Baltimore *Republican, or Anti-Democrat*. James Cheetham's four letters "For the Evening Post" appeared in that New York paper Sept. 15 (p. 3), 20 (p. 2), 24 (p. 2), and 30 (p. 2), 1802. Other commentary: William Carver, "To the Editors of the Evening Post," *Evening Post*, Sept. 18, 1802, 2; [George Baron affidavit], *Evening Post*, Sept. 21, 1802, and many other papers; "Deistical Society of New York," *Gazette*, Sept. 22, 1802, 2; "For the American Citizen, to John Wood," *American Citizen*, Sept. 18, 1802, 2; "Columbian Illuminati," *Boston Commercial Gazette*, Sept. 30, 1802, 2; [No title], *Salem Register*, Sept. 23, 1802, 3; "Attention!" *New York Gazette*, Sept. 27, 1802, 2; [Multiple articles], *Temple of Reason* 2 (Sept. 25, 1802): 246; ibid. (Oct. 2, 1802): 251; ibid. (Oct. 16, 1802): 268; "Philosophical Society, or Columbian Illuminati," *Evening Post*, Oct. 5, 1802, 3, and Oct. 9, 1802, 2; John Wood, "For the Evening Post," ibid., Oct. 16, 1802, 2; [No title—on John Wood], *American Citizen*, Oct. 26, 1802, 2, and Nov. 3, 1802, 2; Lucius, "For the Sun: Consolatory Letter to Aristocrats," *Sun*, Nov. 20, 1802, 2.

22. "Philosophical Society, or Columbian Illuminati," *Evening Post*, Oct. 5, 1802, 3 ("the zealous"); "Constitution of the Theistical Society," *Temple of Reason* 2 (Sept. 25, 1802): 246; "Illuminism," ibid. (Oct. 16, 1802): 268 (Deistical Society principles); "Wood's Exposition of the Clintonian Faction," ibid. (Oct. 2, 1802): 252 ("a silly kind"); "Wood's Exposition of the Clintonian Faction," ibid. (Sept. 25, 1802): 246 ("wooden headed"); "From the *Virginia Gazette*," *Baltimore Republican, or Anti-Democrat*, Nov. 17, 1802, 2 ("infidels").

23. See the notice of the *Temple of Truth* in the *Gazette of the United States*, Aug. 4, 1801, 3. John Hargrove and J. B. Colvin are listed as editors, but most of the work was done by Hargrove. Walters, *Rational Infidels*, 10 ("an orthodox antidote"). On Wood's claim, see *Full Exposition*, 47. Wood alleges that the deists had tried to persuade Donald Fraser, who had written against Paine, to start a Christian paper to oppose the *Temple of Reason*, and suggested the "Temple of Christ" and the "Temple of Truth" as possible names, but Fraser smelled a rat and declined. Wood does not mention Hargrove and the actual *Temple of Truth*.

24. I have used the volume of collected issues (Aug. to Oct. 1801) subsequently published as John Hargrove, *The Temple of Truth; or, A Vindication of Various Passages and Doctrines of the Holy Scriptures: Lately Impeached in a Deistical Publication* (Baltimore, 1801): v, 2, 3, 35, 74, 36, 159, 128, 175, 100, 98. William Richards, *Reflections on French Atheism and on English Christianity*, 3rd ed. (Philadelphia, 1796), 24 ("a Paine"). The author's point was that corrupt Christianity was even worse than the abominations of Paineite deism or Swedenborgianism.

25. Palmer, *Posthumous Pieces*, 20, and see 14; Hargrove, *Temple of Truth*, v, 82.

26. James Wilmer, *A Sermon on the Doctrine of the New-Jerusalem Church, Being the First Promulgated within the United States of America* (Baltimore, 1792); James Wilmer, *Consolation: Being a Replication to Thomas Paine, and Others, on Theologics* (Philadelphia, 1794); "Rev. John Hargrove," *New Jerusalem Magazine* 14, 12 (1841): 485–91, a biographical sketch composed from Hargrove's autobiographical notes. On Robert Carter's Swedenborgianism and involvement with the Baltimore church, see Block, *The New Church in the New World* (1932), 83–90; and Zwelling, "Robert Carter's Journey" (1986).

27. "Rev. John Hargrove," *New Jerusalem Magazine*, 487, 488.

28. John Wesley, "Thoughts on the Writings of Baron Swedenborg," [orig. written 1782], *Methodist Magazine*, Feb. 1797, 73–76; March 1797, 120–23, esp. 120; April 1797, 158–60, esp. 160; May 1797, 211–18; June 1791, 261–65, esp. 265; July 1797, 302–7, esp. 307; Barruel, *Memoirs Illustrating the History of Jacobinism*, 82–95, esp. 85; *An Investigation of the Doctrine of Baron Swedenborg or of the Church Called New Jerusalem, in Two Letters, Addressed to the Rev. Mr. H—, by an Inhabitant of Baltimore County* (Baltimore, 1799), 43.

29. Robert Hindmarsh, *The Rise and Progress of the New Jerusalem Church in England, America, and Other Parts* (London, 1861), esp. 301; "Rev. John Hargrove," *New Jerusalem Magazine*, 487. The 1784 public address of the London Theosophical Society disavowing any intention to spark sectarian controversy declared not that a divine revelation was given unto Emanuel Swedenborg but only the group's fundamental principles: that Jesus was God, and that saving faith had to include good works as well as belief (Hindmarsh, *Rise and Progress of the New Jerusalem Church*, 24–25). Similarly, in America, early advocates did not hide Swedenborg's

supernaturalism; they just did not emphasize it. See Philip Morin Freneau, *A Compendious View and Brief Defence of the Peculiar and Leading Doctrines of the New Jerusalem Church* (Baltimore, 1798). Later in life Hargrove would be the president of a New Church Convention that voted down a proposal to publish an abridgement of Swedenborg's *True Christian Religion* with just the "abstract truths" and excluding the accounts of the seer's "heavenly and spiritual communications" (Hindmarsh, *Rise and Progress of the New Jerusalem Church*, 301). That decision was made, though, at a more confident and mature stage in the New Church's institutional development.

30. Hindmarsh, *Rise and Progress of the New Jerusalem Church*, 27, 273, 380.
31. Hindmarsh, *Rise and Progress of the New Jerusalem Church*, chaps. 4 and 5.
32. "Extract of a letter from the Rev. James Wilmer, of Baltimore, to Mr. Robert Hindmarsh, of London...April 23, 1792" and "Extract of a letter from the Society at Baltimore, to the Society at London...April 25, 1792," in Hindmarsh, *Rise and Progress of the New Jerusalem Church*, 152–54, esp. 152; "Copy of a Letter from Mr. Christian Kramer of Baltimore, directed to Robert Hindmarsh...April 10, 1792," in ibid., 150–52, esp. 151. Wilmer did not fail to mention that he had studied at Christ Church, Oxford and had been ordained by the bishop of London, but now he had cast his "everlasting all" for the New Jerusalem Church (ibid., 153), though he would renounce Swedenborgianism and return to the Episcopalians in 1799.
33. Hindmarsh, *Rise and Progress of the New Jerusalem Church*, 167, 168, appendix; "Domestic," *Temple of Reason* 1 (April 22, 1801): 119; John Hargrove, "To the Ministers and Members of the New Jerusalem Church in Great Britain (Baltimore, 1814)," in Hindmarsh, *Rise and Progress of the New Jerusalem Church*, 219–21, esp. 220; "Rev. John Hargrove," *New Jerusalem Magazine*, 491. On the salaries of Baltimore clergymen, see Bilhartz, *Urban Religion and the Second Great Awakening* (1986), 41–44. Hargrove's title was spelled "Register" in the press accounts.
34. Hindmarsh, *Rise and Progress of the New Jerusalem Church*, 127, 351, 155–56.
35. *Laws of Maryland* (Annapolis, Md., 1803), chap. 111; *A Short Reply to Mr. Burk and Guy, with Some Ripe Fruit for a Friend to Truth* (Baltimore, [1804]), 6; *A Copy of the Incorporated Constitution of the New Jerusalem Church, in the City of Baltimore* (Baltimore, 1804). Hargrove, however, responded to the challenge to his clerical identity by invoking not "the office of the Chancellor of Maryland" but his 1798 ordination by a clergyman licensed in Britain: see [John Hargrove], *The War Dance, No War Whoop, No. 2* ([Baltimore, 1804]), 16.
36. *Minutes of the Common Council of the City of New York*, 2 (New York, 1917), 359 and note (June 26, 1797), and see Koch, *Republican Religion*, 81.
37. Hindmarsh, *Rise and Progress of the New Jerusalem Church*, 142, 289, 276.
38. "An Address to George Washington, Esq., from the Members of the New Church at Baltimore," Jan. 22, 1793, and George Washington, "To the Members of the New Church at Baltimore," in Hindmarsh, *Rise and Progress of the New Jerusalem Church*, 154–55. For the publication of the items, taken from the *Maryland Journal*, see *Dunlap's Daily Advertiser*, Feb. 9, 1793, 3; *Diary*, Feb. 13, 1793, 2; *Norwich Packet*, Feb. 28, 1792, 2. For Washington's response, see also "From George Washington to the Members of the New Jerusalem Church of Baltimore, 27 January 1793," *Founders Online*, National Archives, last modified July 12, 2016, http://founders.archives.gov/documents/Washington/05-12-02-0027. Original source: *The Papers of George Washington, Presidential Series*, vol. 12, *16 January 1793–31 May 1793*, ed. Christine Sternberg Patrick and John C. Pinheiro (Charlottesville, 2005), 52–53.
39. "Address to Thomas Jefferson, Esq., President of the United States of America, Baltimore, March 4, 1801" and "The President's Answer, Washington, 11 March, 1801," in Hindmarsh, *Rise and Progress of the New Jerusalem Church*, 180–81. The "Address" and "Answer" were published in several newspapers: see, for example, *Federal Gazette*, March 14, 1801, 3, and *Mirror of the Times*, March 21, 1801, 2. Thomas Jefferson, "Letter to the Danbury Baptists," Jan. 1, 1802, Library of Congress, https://www.loc.gov/loc/lcib/9806/danpre.html.
40. "Domestic," *Temple of Reason* 1 (Sept. 23, 1801): 295; Hargrove, *Temple of Truth*, 147.
41. John Hargrove, [Letter to the Editor], [New York] *Morning Chronicle*, Dec. 1, 1802, 2; John Hargrove, [Letter to Robert Hindmarsh], in Hindmarsh, *Rise and Progress of the New Jerusalem Church*, 181.

42. Hindmarsh, *Rise and Progress of the New Jerusalem Church*, 181, 188, 220; John Hargrove, *The Substance of a Sermon, on the Leading Doctrines of the New Jerusalem Church, delivered on the 26th of Dec., 1802, before the President of the United States and Several Members of Congress* ([Baltimore,], 1803); Hargrove, *A Sermon, on the Second Coming of Christ… Delivered the 25th of Dec., 1804, before Both Houses of Congress* ([Baltimore], 1805); Hargrove, "To Harmodius," *Baltimore Patriot* (August 3, 1818), esp. 2; Hargrove, *A Sermon, Delivered before the City of Baltimore* [Public Thanksgiving] (Baltimore, 1814); Hargrove, "Benevolence: The Substance of a Sermon: Delivered before Temple Lodge, No. 26," *Freemason's Magazine* 2, 1 (Oct. 1, 1811): 6–16; "Managers of the Bible Society of Baltimore," *Federal Republican*, Nov. 16, 1810, 2; "Rev. John Hargrove," *New Jerusalem Magazine*, 491; "Remarks on Communications," *New Church Herald and Monthly Repository* 9 (Nov. 1856): 600. When he resumed his correspondence with his British New Church brethren after the war, Hargrove merely nodded in passing to the recent, unfortunate, "unhappy differences between our two Governments" (Hindmarsh, *Rise and Progress of the New Jerusalem Church*, 219).
43. Cotlar, *Tom Paine's America* (2011), 11; James Cheetham, *Life of Thomas Paine* (New York, 1809), 179, and see 186–87 and 209–10; Elihu Palmer to Thomas Jefferson, Sept. 1, 1802, Thomas Jefferson Papers, ser. 1, General Correspondence, 1651–1827, Library of Congress, http://www.loc.gov/collections/thomas-jefferson-papers, and see Fischer, "Vitalism in America" (2016), 501. On Cheetham, see Durey, *Transatlantic Radicals*, 270–73; Lasher, "James Cheetham" (1965), esp. 170–82; and Smith, "The Art of Printing Shall Endure" (2007), chap. 2. On Driscoll, see Koch, *Republican Religion*, 104–5; see also Schlereth, *Age of Infidels*, 115–25. Cheetham had been the only New York City editor willing to run ads for the *Temple of Reason* (see *Temple of Reason*, March 13, 1802, 55).
44. Hindmarsh, *Rise and Progress of the New Jerusalem Church*, 187, 266, 274, 307. In 1817, the first conference counted seventeen organized societies and a total of approx. 360 members in nine states. Membership grew as follows (Block, *New Church in the New World*, 171–73):

	Societies	Ordained Ministers	Members
1820	12	8	230
1830	28	16	500
1840	26	20	850
1850	54	32	1,450
1860	64	42	2,550

45. S. Noble, "Address to the Seventeenth General Conference," in Hindmarsh, *Rise and Progress of the New Jerusalem Church*, 428; Hindmarsh, paraphrasing a June 22, 1817, letter from William Schlatter of Philadelphia, ibid., 285; Editor of the *American New Church Repository*, quoted in ibid., 307–8; ibid., 336.
46. "A Letter from a Theophilanthropist to a Prudent Deist," *Temple of Reason* 2 (March 27, 1802): 67–68 and 2 (April 3, 1802): 75–76; 2 (Oct. 2, 1802): 255; 3 (Nov. 20, 1802): 303; 3 (Nov. 27, 1802): 311 ("A Rich Deist"); Fellows, "Memoir," in Palmer, *Posthumous Pieces*, 9.
47. Fellows, "Memoir," in Palmer, *Posthumous Pieces*, 9; Fellows, *Exposition of the Mysteries*, 402. On an American edition of Paine's theological writings falsely indicating its place of publication as London because American publishers were afraid of repercussions, see John Fellows to Thomas Jefferson, October 3, 1825, Library of Congress, https://www.loc.gov/item/mtjbib025537.
48. Jarena Lee, *Religious Experience and Journal of Mrs. Jarena Lee* (Philadelphia, 1849), 15, 15, 17. An earlier, shorter edition was published as *The Life and Experience of Jerena Lee* in 1836 and is the text published in the modern edition in Andrews, ed., *Sisters of the Spirit* (1986), 25–48. On Allen, see Newman, *Freedom's Prophet* (2008). On female preaching, see Brekus, *Strangers and Pilgrims* (1998).

49. On the black Methodist exodus from St. George's Church, see Newman, *Freedom's Prophet*, 63–70; on their efforts to secure their legal rights to church property, see Gordon, "The African Supplement" (2015). On Northern black churches and community building, see Smith, *Climbing Jacob's Ladder* (1988); Gravely, "The Rise of African Churches in America" in Fulop and Raboteau, eds., *African-American Religion* (1977); Raboteau, *Canaan Land* (2001), chap. 2; and Ernest, *A Nation within a Nation* (2011), esp. chap. 3.
50. Lee, *Religious Experience*, 15.
51. Absalom Jones et al., "Address of the Representatives of the African Church...to the Friends of Liberty and Religion in the City of Philadelphia," in Benjamin Rush, *Extract of a Letter from Dr. Benjamin Rush of Philadelphia, to Granville Sharp* (London, 1792), 6–7: "A majority of them are ignorant unknown to any religious society, and while the few who worship God, are the scattered and unconnected appendages of most of the religious societies in the City"; the Philadelphia black community as a whole—"the attraction and relationship which are established among the Africans and their descendants"—was constituted "by the sameness of colour, by a nearly equal and general deficiency of education, by total ignorance, or only humble attainments in religion, and by the line drawn by custom, as well as nature between them and white people." "Domestic Assistant," [Richmond, Va.] *Southern Churchman*, Feb. 13, 1835, 4; Henry Walton Bibb, "Narrative of the Life and Adventures of Henry Bibb" (1849), in Bland, ed., *African American Slave Narratives: An Anthology* (Westport, Conn., 2001), 2:357–58; Henry "Box" Brown, "Narrative of Henry Box Brown, Who Escaped from Slavery Enclosed in a Box 3 Feet Long and 2 Wide" (1849), in ibid., 454; James W. C. Pennington, "The Fugitive Blacksmith; or, Events in the History of James W. C. Pennington, Pastor of a Presbyterian Church, New York" (1849), in ibid., 575.
52. Bibb in Bland, ed., *African American Slave Narratives*, 358; Charles A. Raymond, "The Religious Life of the Negro Slave" [pt. 2], *Harper's New Monthly Magazine*, Oct. 1863, 676.
53. Nash, *Forging Freedom* (1988), 181; Glaude, *Exodus!* (2000), 20; Fountain, *Slavery, Civil War, and Salvation* (2010), 2; Raboteau, *Slave Religion* (1978). For a discussion of the scholarship since Raboteau's landmark study, see Frey, "The Visible Church" (2008). See esp. Sobel, *Trablin' On* (1979); Frey and Wood, *Come Shouting to Zion* (1998); and Young, *Rituals of Resistance* (2007). Raboteau's classic study did note that "many slaves cared not at all about church, revival meetings, or prayer services.... Not all slaves took solace in religion. Some slaves would not accept belief in a supposedly just God who could will or permit slavery" (*Slave Religion*, 225, 313).
54. Fountain, *Slavery, Civil War, and Salvation*, 65, 68, 69. Others suggesting that the power and pervasiveness of Christianity may have been exaggerated are Kolchin, *American Slavery* (1993), Gomez, *Exchanging Our Country Marks* (1998), and Diouf, *Servants of Allah* (1998). On conjure, see Chireau, "Conjure and Christianity in the Nineteenth Century" (1997); Chireau, *Black Magic* (2003); White, "The Gold Diggers of 1833" (2014). On humanism and freethinking, see Jones, "Religious Humanism" in Pinn, ed., *By These Hands* (2001), esp. the section entitled "The Invisibility of Black Humanism: Causal Factors"; Pinn, *Why, Lord?* (1995), chap. 6; Pinn, *Varieties of African American Religious Experience* (1998), chap. 4; and Cameron, *Black Freethinkers* (forthcoming 2019). (I am indebted to Professor Cameron for sharing a draft of his second chapter, "Slavery and the Origins of Black Freethought").
55. Charles Colcock Jones, *The Religious Instruction of the Negroes in the United States* (Savannah, Ga., 1842), 127. On Jones see Clark, "Jones, Charles Colcock"; and Clark, *Wrestlin' Jacob* (2000), 10.
56. Daniel Payne, "Daniel Payne's Protestation of Slavery" [1839], in Pinn, ed., *By These Hands*, 123–30, esp. 128, 129. For other slaves denouncing the hypocrisy of Christian slaveholders, see Fountain, *Slavery, Civil War, and Salvation*, a study of four thousand slave narratives. On Frederick Douglass and religion, see esp. Williamson, *The Narrative Life* (2002).
57. John Jea, "The Life, History, and Unparalleled Sufferings of John Jea, the African Preacher" (c. 1815), in Graham Russell Hodges, ed., *Black Itinerants of the Gospel: The Narratives of John Jea and George White* (New York, 2002), 90–95; "Conversion of a Kentucky Slave," *Boston Recorder*, March 17, 1826, 42; Bibb in Bland, *African American Slave Narratives*, 358; Douglass

in Raboteau, *Slave Religion*, 314; John Dixon Long, *Pictures of Slavery in Church and State*, 3rd ed. (Philadelphia, 1857), 126.
58. William W. Patton, *Slavery and Infidelity; or, Slavery in the Church Insures Infidelity in the World* (Cincinnati, Ohio, 1856), 45; an earlier effort was William W. Patton, *Slavery—The Bible—Infidelity: An Attempt to Prove That Pro-slavery Interpretations of the Bible are Productive of Infidelity* (Hartford, Conn., 1846). One main character in *Uncle Tom's Cabin*, the escaped slave George Harris, while not a purveyor of "subversive atheism," as one modern reader would have it, can certainly be called a religious skeptic. See McCann, "'We Have Many Uncle Toms'" (2004/2005), esp. 168.
59. Patton, *Slavery and Infidelity*, 54, 55. Winch, *The Elite of Our People* (2000), 6n6, 31 (churches): "African-American churchgoers had their choice of sixteen churches by 1841—Episcopal, Methodist, African Methodist Episcopal (AME), Lutheran, Presbyterian, and Baptist. Only the AME was an independent black denomination. The other congregations enjoyed varying degrees of autonomy within a predominantly white hierarchy." Grubbs, "Riots (1830s and 1840s)."
60. Lee, *Religious Experience*, 15.
61. "Conversion of a Kentucky Slave"; Jea in Hodges, ed., *Black Itinerants*, 96. Jones, "Religious Humanism," 29–35, drawing from Cone, *The Spiritual and the Blues* (1972), discusses "secular spirituals." See also Brown, "Negro Folk Expression," in Pinn, ed., *By These Hands*, 103–22, esp. 105; and Levine, "Slave Songs and Slave Consciousness," in Hareven, ed., *Anonymous Americans* (1971).
62. Lee, *Religious Experiences*, 59, 19.
63. William Graham, *A View of Ecclesiastical Establishments in Europe*, 2nd ed. ([Windham, Conn.], 1808), 245; "I Don't Care," *Hampshire Gazette*, April 11, 1832, 1; "Extract of a Letter from the Rev. Andrew S. Morrison," *Boston Recorder*, Sept. 26, 1818, 166; "Death Bed of an Unbeliever," *Farmer's Cabinet*, Feb. 13, 1830, 1; David Simpson, *A Plea for Religion and the Sacred Writings: Addressed to the Disciples of Thomas Paine* (Baltimore, 1807), xiv. On Gallio connected to negligent moral authority, see also Ebenezer Smith, *A Defence of Ebenezer Smith, against the Poison of the Cruelty of the Baptist Church* ([Amherst, N.H.], 1804), title page, 71, 77, [86]; "The Corrector, No. 3," *Connecticut Herald*, Sept. 2, 1806, 1; John Willson, *A Fair and Impartial Testimony, Essayed in the Name of…the Church of Scotland* (Pittsburgh, 1808), 197; Gilbert M'Master, *The Duty of Nations* [Thanksgiving sermon] (Ballston-Spa, N.Y., 1810), 7; [Anon.], *The Evils of the Work Now Prevailing in the United States of America under the Name of a Revival of Religion* (Washington, Pa., 1804), 50. On "Gallio-like" as personal indifference to one's salvation or to religion in general, see also George Burder, *Village Sermons* (Boston, 1807), 2:183; *An Important Case Argued; in Four Dialogues, between Dr. Opium, Mr. Gallio, and Discipulus* (Boston, 1810); William Harris, *A Sermon* (New York, 1810), 23; John Wesley, *Explanatory Notes upon the New Testament* (New York, 1812; orig. U.S. pub. 1791]), 2:337; Donald M'Leod, *A Sermon, Preached in the Presbyterian Church* (Charleston, S.C., 1812), 52; George Stanley Faber, *A Practical Treatise on the Ordinary Operations of the Holy Spirit* (New York, 1814), 80: *The Good Old Way; or, The Religion of Our Forefathers* (Annapolis, Md., 1816), 17; Richard D. Hall, *A Humble Attempt to Promote the Salvation of the Rising Generation* (Philadelphia, 1818), 19; Samuel Taggart, *A Farewell Sermon* (Greenfield, Mass., 1819), 19.
64. "Mr. Hill's Election Sermon," *American Mercury*, May 26, 1829, 1; Price, *Observations on the Importance of the American Revolution* ([Boston], 1812; orig. pub. 1784), 13. On the link to Madison, see Themistius, *Madison and Religion: or, A Warning to the People of the United States of America* (Philadelphia, 1811), preface and 77; William Parkinson, *A Sermon* [Fast Day] (New York, 1812), 18n–19n. For other pro-Gallio sentiments, see Daniel Merrill, *Balaam Disappointed: A Thanksgiving Sermon* (Concord, N.H., 1815), 21; Elias Smith, *A Discourse…Thanksgiving Day* (Danville, Vt., 1815), 38; [Shakers], *An Address to the State of Ohio* (Lebanon, Ohio, 1818), 6–7. Richard Stack, in *Lectures on the Acts of the Apostles* (Annapolis, Md., 1815), 223–25, praised Gallio for distinguishing between opinions that "affect the peace and happiness of society" and "merely points of faith" that do not, but criticized him for not punishing those who beat the Jewish leader.

Part Two

1. Origen Bacheler and Robert Dale Owen, *Discussion on the Existence of God and the Authenticity of the Bible, between Origen Bacheler and Robert Dale Owen*, 2nd ed. (New York, 1833), 2:63–64, 69, 347.
2. Immanuel Kant, "An Answer to the Question: What Is Enlightenment?" in Schmidt, ed., *What Is Enlightenment?* (1997), esp. 58. See also Fleischacker, *What Is Enlightenment?* (2013). Scholars and critics continue to argue about what has come to be called "the Enlightenment": a set of ideas about knowledge, or habits of knowing, or aspirations for putting knowledge to work, that became a characteristic of the modernizing West. Most studies place it in the long eighteenth century, though sometimes they push its beginnings a century or more earlier. Scholars have found, instead of a unitary Enlightenment project, complex and contradictory strands of thought and practice that defy simple summary. Some historians have stressed that in different national contexts, optimism about human reason or about natural knowledge improving society had quite different social, political, and religious origins and effects. In France, for example, enlightened philosophes grew hostile to Christianity, but in Scotland much enlightened thought developed within the church. Henry F. May's *The Enlightenment in America* (1976) defined it as consisting of all those who believed that "we understand nature and man best through the use of our natural faculties," combined with the sense that their own age was "more enlightened than the past." It excludes, therefore, all "who think that the surest guide for human beings is revelation, tradition, or illumination." The Enlightenment in America, in this view, existed in dialectical tension with Protestantism, the latter serving variously as "matrix, rival, ally, [or] enemy" (xiii, xiv). More recent histories have focused on the social practices that cultivated enlightenment, and historians have peered into salons, clubs, coffeehouses, and Masonic societies, and have mapped the republic of letters and the circulation of print. A recent discussion of the American context is Winterer, *American Enlightenments* (2016). On the Enlightenment generally, important studies include Gay, *The Enlightenment* (2 vols., 1966–69); Porter and Teich, eds., *The Enlightenment in National Context* (1981); Pocock, *Barbarism and Religion*, vol. 1, *The Enlightenments of Edward Gibbon* (1999); Israel, *Radical Enlightenment* (2001); Israel, *Enlightenment Contested* (2006); and Israel, *Democratic Enlightenment* (2011). For recent historiographical overviews, see O'Brien, "The Return of the Enlightenment" (2010); Conrad, "Enlightenment in Global History" (2012); and Dixon, "Henry F. May and the Revival of the American Enlightenment" (2014). For discussions of postmodernism and the Enlightenment, see Baker and Reill, eds., *What's Left of Enlightenment?* (2001); and Wilson, "Postmodernism and the Enlightenment," in Fitzpatrick et al., eds., *The Enlightenment World* (2004).
3. [Stephen Cullen Carpenter], *Memoirs of the Honorable Thomas Jefferson, Secretary of State, Vice-President and President of the United States of America* (New York, 1809), 1:4.
4. [Carpenter], *Memoirs* 1:5; 2:94, 95. The relationship between "the Enlightenment" and "religion" is especially fraught since neither is a stable and coherent concept in contemporary scholarship. But see Byrne, *Religion and the Enlightenment* (1996); Barnett, *The Enlightenment and Religion* (2003); Sheehan, "Enlightenment, Religion, and the Enigma of Secularization" (2003); and Sorkin, *The Religious Enlightenment* (2008).
5. For "enlightened and Christian," or, less frequently, "Christian and enlightened" in speeches, sermons, essays, editorials, advertisements, and other sources, see, for example, "Extract from the North Carolina Act Respecting Slaves," *Columbian Centinel*, March 31, 1792, 22; "For the Federal Gazette," *Federal Gazette*, Jan. 7, 1801, 3; "We Believe Gen. Hamilton Could Not Avoid Meeting Col. Burr," *Albany Gazette*, Aug. 30, 1804, 3; [Advertisement—book on capital punishment], *Public Advertiser*, Feb. 23, 1811, 3; James Fishbeck, *The Philosophy of the Human Mind in Respect to Religion* (Lexington, Ky., 1813), 295; Whitney Griswold, *Sermon Delivered January 1st, 1811* (Cooperstown, N.Y., 1815), 12; "An Oration: On the Moral History of the United States," *Adviser, or, Vermont Evangelical Magazine* 7, 1 (Jan.–Feb. 1815): 41–49, esp. 46; Bible Society of Union College, "Constitution," *Columbian Magazine* 1 (May 1, 1815): 278–82, esp. 279; A Friend to His Country, *The Reformer* (New York, 1816), 198; "Christian Mirror and Theological Repository," *Commercial Advertiser*, Jan. 10, 1817, 2; "Town Hall Meeting: Foreign Missions," *Hampshire Gazette*, Sept. 16, 1817, 3; Nathan Parker, *A Sermon Preached at*

Concord (Concord, [N. H.], 1819), 23; Religious Tract Society of Baltimore, *Third Annual Report* (Baltimore, 1819), 12; Louisiana State Senate, *Journal* (New Orleans, 1819), 17; "Pacifick Policy," *Rhode Island American*, May 19, 1820, 2.

6. For the claim that human nature, despite being marred by sin, was "possessed of faculties capable of being exalted to the highest pitch of knowledge and refinement," see John Bartlett, *A Discourse on the Subject of Animation* (Boston, 1792), 6. For the argument that this knowledge and refinement was not just possessed by an educated elite but had been broadly diffused through society, mostly by the dissemination of print, to elevate the character of the common people, see Jonathan Jackson, *Thoughts upon the Political Situation of the United States of America* (Worcester, Mass., 1788), 103. Appeals to the enlightened age became a rhetorical weapon as denominations competed for power and authority. Some writers thought that the achievements of the enlightened age would purify Christianity—that is, finally extinguish the forms and practices championed by their misguided opponents. The Unitarian Enos Hitchcock insisted that religion, just like science, could only flourish in the soil of liberty, by which he meant "an independent spirit of inquiry, free from the shackles of superstition, the wild-fire of enthusiasm, or the terror of bigotry"—language that in some quarters could be interpreted as saying that Catholics, New Lights, and doctrinaire Calvinists were un-American as well as unenlightened (*A Discourse Delivered at the Ordination of the Rev. Abel Flint* [Hartford, Conn., 1791], 16). In 1799, John Clarke was thankful that he lived in an enlightened age with rational ideas of the Lord's Supper rather than absurdities about the real presence or transubstantiation (*Sermons* [Boston, 1799], 443). Catholic missionary John Thayer conceded progress in science, politics, art, and philosophy, but said that the "science of religion" needed the authority of the Catholic Church. See *Controversy between the Rev. John Thayer, Catholic Missionary, of Boston, and the Rev. George Leslie* ([Newburyport, Mass.? 1793]), 94–95. Some writers tried to shield only particular aspects of religious faith from the solvent of enlightened inquiry. Hannah Moore, writing on female education, was happy that her age had banished dreams, ghosts, and witches, but she wanted to protect belief in the power of Satan. In a 1796 funeral sermon, however, John Newton urged that the enlightened age's spirit of inquiry, which endeavored "to trace every fact to its proper and adequate cause," should be brought more fully to bear upon the phenomena of religious experience. Others applauded improvements in knowledge and manners but decried a declension of piety—what the evangelical biographer Erasmus Middleton called "the spiritual darkness of our *present enlightened age.*" See Hannah Moore, *Strictures on the Modern System of Female Education* (Philadelphia, 1800), 201; John Newton, *A Monument to the Praise of the Lord's Goodness* (Philadelphia, 1796), vi; and Erasmus Middleton, *Evangelical Biography* (Philadelphia, 1798), 4.

7. The literature on the public sphere since the publication of Habermas, *The Structural Transformation of the Public Sphere* (1962, trans. 1989) is large, but see esp. Calhoun, ed., *Habermas and the Public Sphere* (1992) and Martin, "Between Consensus and Conflict" (2005).

8. Thomas Cooper featured extracts from Ely on the "Christian party in politics" as evidence to show the "plans and schemes of the orthodox clergy of the Presbyterian denomination in particular, to acquire a sectarian influence over the political government of the Country and all seminaries of education" in *The Case of Thomas Cooper, M.D., President of the South Carolina College*, 2nd ed. (Columbia, S.C., 1832), appendix 1, [1]–3, 8–9.

Chapter 5

1. Thomas Jefferson to Joseph C. Cabell, March 1, 1819, Thomas Jefferson Papers, Series 1, General Correspondence, 1651–1827, Library of Congress, American Memory (hereafter LOC), https://www.loc.gov/resource/mtj1.051_0355_0358/?sp=1; Thomas Cooper, *Dr. Cooper's Defence before the Board of Trustees, from the Times and Gazette of December 14, 1832* ([Columbia, S.C., [1832]), 17.

2. On the tension between equal rights and unequal talents and virtues in Enlightenment thought, see Carson, "Differentiating a Republican Citizenry" (2002).

3. Thomas Cooper, *Tracts Ethical, Theological, and Political*, vol. 1 (Warrington, England, 1789), dedication, [iii]–vi, and preface, [vii]–xiv; Thomas Cooper, *A Reply to Mr. Burke's Invective*

against Mr. Cooper, and Mr. Watt, in the House of Commons on the 30th April, 1792 (Manchester, England, 1792), 10; Thomas Cooper, *Some Information respecting America* (London, 1794), 3; E. P. [Elizabeth Priestley] and Thomas Cooper, "On the Propriety and Expediency of Unlimited Enquiry," in Cooper, *Political Essays*, 2nd ed. (Philadelphia, 1800), 62–88 (Priestley wrote pt. 1 [62–70] and Cooper pt. 2 [71–88]). Cooper quotes Burke on 83 and references the Whiskey Rebellion on 84; these essays originally appeared in the *Northumberland Gazette*. On Cooper as cofounder of the Manchester Constitutional Society, see Chernock, *Men and the Making of Modern British Feminism* (2010), 139.
4. Elizabeth Priestley, in pt. 1 of "On the Propriety and Expediency of Unlimited Enquiry," in Cooper, *Political Essays*, wrote that if communication were suppressed people would cease to think (68). On the expectation of communication as a stimulation to mental labor, see Thomas Cooper, *A Treatise on the Law of Libel and the Liberty of the Press... as Applicable to Individuals and to Political and Ecclesiastical Bodies and Principles* (New York, 1830), 48. Cooper argued that there was no way to arrive at truth except by unlimited discussion in *Petition of Thomas Cooper, President of South Carolina College, Praying the Restoration of a Fine, with Interest, Incurred under the Sedition Law of 1798 for a Libel against the Then President of the United States* (Washington, D.C., 1825), 4. Thomas Cooper, *Lectures on the Elements of Political Economy*, 2nd ed. (Columbia, S.C., 1829), 21.
5. Cooper, *Lectures on the Elements of Political Economy*, 347; Cooper, "Propositions respecting the Foundation of Civil Government," delivered before the Manchester Society in 1787 and first published in the *Memoirs of the Literary and Philosophical Society of Manchester*, vol. 3 (Warrington, England, 1790), 481–509, esp. 509; republished in Cooper, *Political Arithmetic* ([Philadelphia? 1798], 21–40; and in Cooper, *Two Essays* (Columbia, S.C., 1826), 1–18, esp. 18.
6. On the Birmingham attacks, see Graham, "Revolutionary in Exile" (1995), 17. Cooper's praise of the U.S. Constitution appeared in *Some Information respecting America* (London, 1794), a promotional tract for a settlement along the Susquehanna River for like-minded English émigrés that he was planning with Priestley's son Joseph. The political backlash against Cooper had contributed to his bankruptcy, announced in November 1793 (Graham, "Revolutionary in Exile," 31). See also Malone, *The Public Life of Thomas Cooper* (1926), 34–72. Chernock, *Men and the Making of Modern British Feminism*, 139, identifies Cooper as a coeditor of the *Herald*.
7. Cooper reprinted his letter to the *Reading Weekly Advertiser*, Oct. 26, 1799, in Thomas Cooper, *An Account of the Trial of Thomas Cooper of Northumberland; on a Charge of Libel against the President of the United States* (Philadelphia, 1800), 4–7, esp. 6. Cooper served as editor of the *Northumberland Gazette* from April 20 to June 29, 1799, and wrote most of the political articles that appeared within it. These were republished in *Political Essays, Originally Inserted in the Northumberland Gazette, with Additions* (Northumberland, Pa., 1799), which included two essays that had been published separately as *Political Arithmetic* [Philadelphia, 1798]; a second edition was published as *Political Essays by Thomas Cooper, Esq., of Northumberland* (Philadelphia, 1800). One of the essays, Cooper's "Address to the Readers of the Northumberland Gazette," which was highly critical of Adams, was published in the Philadelphia *Aurora*, July 12, 1799. See Graham, "Revolutionary in Exile," 120–24, and Malone, *Public Life of Thomas Cooper*, 91–120. Jefferson wrote to Priestley in January 1800 that "yours and Mr. Cooper's pamphlets are the most precious gifts that can be made to us" (Thomas Jefferson to Joseph Priestley, Jan. 18, 1800, *The Papers of Thomas Jefferson Digital Edition*, ed. James P. McClure and J. Jefferson Looney [Charlottesville, Va., 2008–17]). For Adams on Cooper, see Timothy Pickering to John Adams, Aug. 1, 1799, and Adams to Pickering, Aug. 13, 1799, in Graham, "Revolutionary Exile," 123, citing Adams, *Works* 9:5–6, 13–14. The writ charged that Cooper, "being a person of a wicked and turbulent disposition, designing and intending to defame the President of the United States, and bring him into contempt and disrepute, and so excite against him the hatred of the good people of the United States,... wickedly and maliciously did write, print and publish a false, scandalous, and malicious writing against the said President" (Cooper, *Account of the Trial*, 7).
8. Cooper, *Account of the Trial*, 34, 49.

9. Cooper, *Account of the Trial*, 16, 15, 42nB, 19. Public donations, not Cooper himself, paid the fine (see Graham, "Revolutionary in Exile," 162n420); Cooper for the rest of his life sought reimbursement from Congress.
10. Cooper, *Account of the Trial*, 45nK, preface.
11. Cooper, *Account of the Trial*, 45nK, 18.
12. Cooper, *Account of the Trial*, 58, 64, 61.
13. Cooper, *Account of the Trial*, 16, 15, 38; [Thomas Cooper], *An Exposition of the Doctrines of Calvinism* (n.p., 1830), preface. Joseph Priestley complained about the isolation of Northumberland, too, when he moved there in 1794, lamenting its lack of a reliable postal service and regular communication with Philadelphia (see Graham, "Revolutionary in Exile," 7). See the publisher's note in [Thomas Cooper], *To Any Member of Congress* (n.p., 1831), about Cooper denying that anyone had even heard of the pamphlet in his neighborhood. Cooper also did not insist that in the public arena of print an argument had to be severed from the character of its author—that citizens, in the name of disinterested virtue, needed always to debate in the press behind pseudonyms like "Publius" and "Common Sense." He hailed the virtues of both public authorship and anonymous publication as it suited his purposes. At the sedition trial the prosecution charged that Cooper's cavalier declaration to a local justice of the peace that he had authored a handbill critical of Adams was "indecent" and "outrageous" (*Account of the Trial*, 43). Cooper responded incredulously: "Is it a crime that I do not shelter myself under anonymous signature? that what I do, I do openly?" (43nD). The identity and character of an author, Cooper wrote in another context, were important for readers to know if a publication purported to contain factual claims or be a true history of some event. Yet he also insisted on a citizen's right to address his countrymen anonymously, and did so frequently in his career. While boldly attaching his name to most of his political opinions, he was usually careful to leave his more frankly skeptical statements about religion unsigned (*To Any Member of Congress*, publisher's note).
14. Cooper, *Account of the Trial*, 51; Thomas Cooper, *The Scripture Doctrine of Materialism* (Philadelphia, 1823), 305; Cooper, *A Treatise on the Law of Libel and the Liberty of the Press*, 124.
15. Cooper, *Lectures on the Elements of Political Economy*, 28; Thomas Cooper, "Outline of the Association of Ideas," in Cooper, *Scripture Doctrine of Materialism*, 380, 385. See also Thomas Cooper, *An Introductory Lecture to a Course of Law* (Columbia, S.C., 1834), 6. On mystery and the Protestant (esp. Calvinist) clergy, see Cooper, *Scripture Doctrine of Materialism*, "Appendix to Clergy," 324; on the clergy's disinclination to debate, see Cooper's appendix in *On Irritation and Insanity... by F. J. V. Broussais*, trans. Thomas Cooper (Columbia, S.C., 1831): "When the gentlemen of the clerical profession shew such morbid irritability at the discussion of metaphysical or theological doctrines which they would fain persuade us are too sacred to be disputed, they give rise by so doing, to the strong suspicion that they themselves are not fully persuaded, that the doctrines they inculcate are clear of all doubt, and liable to no overthrow" [3].
16. Thomas Cooper, *On the Connection between Geology and the Pentateuch, in a letter to Professor Silliman* (Boston, 1833), 64. These comments were attached to one of the very works that reignited the controversy over his skeptical opinions and dragged him before the "court of ecclesiastical inquisition" at the South Carolina Statehouse in 1832 for violating a "clerical sedition law." See *Dr. Cooper's Defence before the Board of Trustees, from the Times and Gazette of December 14, 1832*, 2; Thomas Cooper, *The Case of Thomas Cooper... Submitted to the Legislature and the People of South Carolina, December 1831* (Columbia, S.C., 1831), 25.
17. Mott, *A History of American Magazines, 1741–1850* (1930), 119–335, esp. 120–21 (number of periodicals 1800–1825). On the encyclopedias see Arner, *Dobson's* Encyclopedia (1991); on Bradford's *New Cyclopaedia*, which reprinted and supplemented Abraham Rees's London publication (1802–20), see 173–79. See also Kronick, *A History of Scientific and Technical Periodicals* (1976); Yeo, "Reading Encyclopedias" (1991); Baatz, "'Squinting at Silliman'" (1991); Topham, "Scientific Publishing and the Reading of Science in Nineteenth-Century Britain" (2000); Werner, "Bringing Down Holy Science" (2000); Geoffrey Cantor et al., introduction to *Culture and Science in the Nineteenth-Century Media* (2004); Sher, *The Enlightenment and the Book* (2006), chap. 9; Loveland, "Unifying Knowledge and Dividing Disciplines" (2006);

Pethers, "'The Rage for Book-Making'" (2007); Yeo, "Lost Encyclopedias" (2007); Shields, "The Learned World," in Gross and Kelley, eds., *A History of the Book in America* 2 (2010); Tucker, "Newspapers and Periodicals," ibid.; and Lewis, *A Democracy of Facts* (2011).

18. *Emporium of Arts and Sciences*, ed. John Redman Coxe (Philadelphia) 1 (May–Oct. 1812), 2 (Nov. 1812–April 1813); n.s., ed. Thomas Cooper (Philadelphia) 1 (June–Oct. 1813), 2 (Dec, 1813–April 1814), 3 (June–Oct. 1814). Quotations: Coxe, "Prospectus," *Emporium* 1:vi–vii.

19. "Subscriber's Names," *Emporium* 2: appendix, [i]–iv. No lists of subscribers for subsequent volumes were published. The *Emporium*'s eleven hundred subscribers after its first year can be compared to other periodicals of the period: the *Port Folio*, the leading literary journal, claimed 2,000 subscribers in 1801; the *Massachusetts Baptist Missionary Magazine* (1803–16) grew from 1,000 to 4,000 by the latter date; the *Medical Repository* (1797–1824) sold fewer than 300 copies of each issue; the prestigious *North American Review* had only 500–600 subscribers after five years of operation in 1820 (Mott, *History of American Magazines*, 199–200, 251); 1,200 subscribers signed up for the *American Journal of Science* in 1818, but fewer than 400 paid (Baatz, "'Squinting at Silliman,'" 233).

20. Both Coxe and Cooper were listed as "conductors" on their respective title pages.

21. Coxe, "Notice," *Emporium* 2: appendix; Cooper, "Notice to Correspondents," *Emporium*, n.s., 1:182–83; Cooper, "Summary of the Rise and Progress of the Steam Engine," ibid., n.s., 2:378–85.

22. Cooper, "Geology," *Emporium*, n.s., 3:412–25, esp. 412, 415.

23. E. Bolling, "Political Economy: Vindication of Foreign Commerce," *Emporium*, n.s., 2:119–61; Cooper, "Notice to Correspondents," ibid., n.s., 1:341–45, 345; Cooper, "On Patents," ibid., n.s., 1:431–55, 455; Cooper, "Statistics," ibid., n.s., 3:276–81, 280; Cooper, "To Correspondents," n.s., 1, 504–6, 504; Cooper, "To Readers: Various Notices," ibid., n.s., 2:316–18, 316; Cooper, "Statistics: Of the Quantity of Land Necessary to Maintain a Working Horse," ibid., n.s., 3:280–81.

24. Cooper, "Notice to Correspondents," *Emporium*, n.s., 1:341–45, esp. 342.

25. Cooper, "Foreign Commerce," *Emporium*, n.s., 1:161–63, 161; Cooper, "Notice to Correspondents," ibid., n.s., 1:341–45, 342; Cooper, "Conditions," ibid., n.s., 1:11–14, 12; Cooper, "Prospectus," ibid., n.s., 1:1–10, esp. 4.

26. Cooper, "Conditions," *Emporium*, n.s., 1:11–14, esp. 13. Cooper republished his essay "Political Arithmetic" (previously published in 1799 and 1800) in ibid., n.s., 1:164–79.

27. Cooper, "Prospectus," *Emporium*, n.s., 1:7; and see esp. Cooper, "Political Arithmetic," ibid., n.s., 1:173–74.

28. Cooper, "Prospectus," 5, 9; Cooper, "Political Arithmetic."

29. Coxe, "Prospectus," *Emporium* 1:[iii]; Cooper, "Prospectus," *Emporium*, n.s., 1:5, 6; Cooper, "Summary of the Rise and Progress of the Steam Engine," 385.

30. Cooper, "Prospectus," 2.

31. Cooper, "Notice to Correspondents," *Emporium*, n.s., 1:341, 342; "Notices," ibid., n.s., 3:328.

32. Thomas Cooper, *Narrative of the Proceedings against Thomas Cooper, Esquire, President Judge of the Eighth District of Pennsylvania, on a Charge of Official Misconduct* (Lancaster, Pa., 1811), 6; Thomas Cooper, *The Institutes of Justinian with Notes* (Philadelphia, 1812); Cooper to James Henry Hammond, March 20, 1836: "In England I was and should still be a decided radical, altho' here I incline to the Conservatives" (Hammond Papers, Manuscript Division, Library of Congress, in Kilbride,"Slavery and Utilitarianism" [1993], esp. 472).

33. Maximilian LaBorde, *History of the South Carolina College* (Columbia, S.C., 1859), 166–68. Malone, in *The Public Life of Thomas Cooper*, argued that Cooper "adopted the traditional southern attitude toward the negro.... He went somewhat out of his way to express his conviction of the essential inferiority of the negro race. Presumably he had become less of a theorist and more a realist as he had grown older" (285). But this assessment misperceives the philosophical grounds of his earlier radicalism (linking it to Jeffersonian egalitarianism) and echoes (rather than explains) Cooper's later racism. The charge that Cooper's opinions changed with his "latitude"—his move to South Carolina—is mentioned in Himes, *Life and Times of Judge Thomas Cooper* (1918), 41, although in this instance in connection with Cooper's opinion on protecting domestic manufactures; Himes goes on to discuss Cooper's shift on slavery on 62–64. Davis, in an influential account in *The Problem of Slavery in the Age of Revolution* (1975), cites Cooper as a prime example of "a number of political radicals and revolutionaries from other societies" who

found "refuge by accommodating to southern norms": "Thomas Cooper, of Manchester, a radical democrat and outspoken opponent of Negro slavery, escaped Pitt's reign of terror and finally found haven in South Carolina, where he became a slaveowner, an antidemocrat, and an extreme racist. The only element in Cooper's world view that remained unchanged was his hostility to organized religion" (184–85). Chernock, in *Men and the Making of Modern British Feminism*, has Cooper renouncing his early radicalism in South Carolina; Hoffer, in *The Free Press Crisis of 1800* (2011), 111, argues that Cooper "changed his views [on slavery] dramatically when he went south." Newman, in "Thomas Cooper, 1759–1839" (1985), stresses the continuities of Cooper's "bourgeois individualism" despite the modifications prompted by his moves from Manchester to Pennsylvania to South Carolina; Kilbride, in "Slavery and Utilitarianism," sees Cooper through the prism of utilitarianism, which became especially pronounced in his last decade of life as he announced his affinity to Jeremy Bentham.

34. Cooper, *Tracts Ethical, Theological and Political* 1:174, [465], 372, 6; Cooper, *Institutes of Justinian*, 581. Chernock, *Men and the Making of Modern British Feminism*, 31, argues that the majority of British political radicals in the 1790s were Rational Dissenters, most identifying as Unitarians. The "standard account," articulated by Bishop Joseph Butler's *Analogy of Religion, Natural and Revealed, to the Constitution and Course of Nature* (1736), one of the most popular books of its kind in the eighteenth century, and Hartley's response to it, are described in Allen's *David Hartley on Human Nature* (1999), esp. 178–82.

35. Thomas Cooper, *Letters on the Slave Trade* (Manchester, England, 1787), 30, 31, 32; Thomas Cooper, *Supplement to Mr. Cooper's Letters on the Slave Trade* (Warrington, England, 1788), 24. See also Thomas Cooper, *Considerations on the Slave Trade; and the Consumption of West Indian Produce* (London, 1791). Chernock, *Men and the Making of Modern British Feminism*, 139, identifies Cooper as a committee member of the Society for the Purpose of Effecting the Abolition of the Slave Trade.

36. Cooper, *Letters*, 18; Cooper, *Supplement*, 48.

37. Cooper, *Letters*, 5, 28, 27; Cooper, *Supplement*, 49; Cooper, *Considerations*, 14–15.

38. Thomas Cooper, *Memoirs of Dr. Joseph Priestley, to the Year 1795, Written by Himself: With a Continuation, to the Time of His Decease, by His Son, Joseph Priestley: And Observations on His Writings, by Thomas Cooper, President Judge of the 4th District of Pennsylvania: and the Rev. William Christie* (Northumberland, Pa., 1806), 295–96. On Priestley noting Cooper's skepticism, see Graham, "Revolutionary in Exile," 85.

39. Cooper, *Memoirs of Priestley*, 371–72, 423, 344. On perfectibility, see Cooper to J. Watt Jr., Feb. 1, 1801, in Graham, "Revolutionary in Exile," 162: "I am not like that literary egotist Godwin a Champion for the perfectibility of the human race."

40. Thomas Cooper, "Propositions respecting the Foundation of Civil Government," *Memoirs of the Literary and Philosophical Society of Manchester*, vol. 3 (Warrington, England, 1790), 506, 509; Thomas Cooper, "Propositions respecting the Foundation of Civil Government," in *Two Essays, 1. On the Foundation of Civil Government; 2. On the Constitution of the United States* (Columbia, S.C., 1826), 8, [5]. The essay, first delivered to the Manchester Society in 1787, was published with some changes in Cooper, *Reply to Mr. Burke's Invective* (London, 1792); the 1792 version was published in Cooper, *Political Arithmetic* ([Philadelphia, 1798]). His essay established the proposition that the right of exercising political power was derived entirely from the consent of the people. He made the argument by setting up and then knocking down ten counterarguments attempting to root political authority elsewhere—in divine right, parental authority, conquest, the superior abilities of rulers, and so on. He then derived thirty-three "principal deductions" from that "grand maxim."

41. Cooper, "Propositions" (1790), 491.

42. Cooper, "Propositions" (1798), 35, 36; Cooper, *Institutes of Justinian*, 633. Arguing for Parliamentary reform in 1783, Cooper had supported universal suffrage, though he considered it a difficult question worthy of more discussion. See Thomas Cooper, *Lectures on the Elements of Political Economy*, 366.

43. Cooper, "Propositions" (1826), 16; Cooper *Lectures on the Elements of Political Economy*, 362–63.

44. Cooper, *Narrative of the Proceedings against Thomas Cooper*, 47, [3], 7, 6, 19, 27n, 5. The charge about Cooper being a political turncoat had first been raised publicly in disputes over the calling of a state constitutional convention in 1805 (see Malone, *Public Life of Thomas*

Cooper, chap. 6). Cooper was allied with the moderate Jeffersonian faction called the Tertium Quids, who opposed the more radical Philadelphia democrats and the rural radicals led by Governor Simon Snyder. On political battles and the courts in Pennsylvania in the era of Cooper's trial, see Ferguson, *Early Western Pennsylvania Politics* (1938), 176–259; Ellis, *Jeffersonian Crisis* (1971), 157–83; Keller, "Rural Politics and the Collapse of Pennsylvania Federalism" (1982); and Shankman, *Crucible of American Democracy* (2004).

45. Cooper, *Narrative*, 26.
46. Cooper, *Narrative*, 51; Cooper, *Institutes of Justinian*, 632; [Thomas Cooper], *Extract of a Letter to a Student at Law. July, 1815* [Philadelphia? 1815], 12–13.
47. Cooper, *Extract of a Letter*, 8; Cooper, *Narrative*.
48. Cooper, "Propositions" (1790), 491; Cooper, "Propositions" (1798), 27n, 28n. On Cooper's role in British feminism in the early 1790s, see Chernock, *Men and the Making of Modern British Feminism*, esp. 16, 21–23, 76, 112–13.
49. Cooper, *Institutes of Justinian*, 432; Cooper, "Propositions" (1826), 9.
50. [Thomas Cooper], "Slavery," *Southern Literary Journal and Magazine of Arts* 1, 3 (Nov. 1835): 188–93; T. C. [Thomas Cooper], "On Phrenology, Craniology, Organology," *Southern Literary Journal and Magazine of Arts* 1, 6 (Feb. 1836): 393–402, esp. 400.
51. Thomas Cooper to Mahlon Dickerson, March 16, 1826, in "Letters of Dr. Thomas Cooper, 1825–1832," *American Historical Review* 6, 4 (July 1901): 725–36, esp. 729; [Thomas Cooper], "Coloured Marriages," *Carolina Law Journal* 1, 1 (1831): 96, 103, orig. pub. as "Mixed Marriages," *Charleston Mercury*, Oct. 29, 1823.
52. For testimonials on his work as a physician, see [Thomas Cooper], *The Following Papers, Stated to have been Mislaid…Are Now Printed in Confirmation of Dr. Cooper's Claims as a Physician* [Philadelphia, 1818]. [Cooper], "Slavery," 193; Cooper, *Letters on the Slave Trade*, 30; [Cooper], "Coloured Marriages," 100. On free blacks in Philadelphia, see Nash, *Forging Freedom* (1988).
53. Thomas Cooper to James Watt Jr., April 4, 1796, Birmingham Reference Library, quoted in Graham, "Revolutionary in Exile," 87. On antislavery and the press, see Cotlar, *Tom Paine's America* (2011), 65–67.
54. Cooper, *Institutes of Justinian*, 413. Cooper advised liberty-loving English emigrants to avoid the slave South in *Some Information respecting America*, 3–4, 7, and 20. On his eagerness to purchase slaves, see Malone, *Public Life*, 284. Local and family lore passed down a story about how Cooper in South Carolina gave his slave Sancho an inscribed Bible and benevolently allowed him to attend his Methodist class meetings on Tuesday nights (Himes, *Life and Times*, 59). There were eight slaves in the Cooper household according to the 1830 Federal Census.
55. Thomas Cooper, *A Manual of Political Economy* (Washington, D.C., 1834), 103.
56. [John Holt Rice], "Review [of *Memoirs of Dr. Joseph Priestley.… and Observations on His Writings, by Thomas Cooper*]," *Virginia Evangelical and Literary Magazine* 3, 2 (Feb. 1820): 63–74, esp. 71–74.
57. Thomas Jefferson to John Holmes, April 22, 1820, LOC. On Cooper and the University of Virginia, see Malone, *Public Life*, 226–47; see also Patton, *Jefferson, Cabell and the University of Virginia* (1906), 68–74. Cooper, dissatisfied with his position (and the low pay) at Carlisle College, had resigned his position there in 1815. From 1816 to 1818 he taught chemistry and mineralogy at the University of Pennsylvania.
58. Thomas Cooper to Thomas Jefferson, Oct. 18, 1822, *Collections of the Massachusetts Historical Society*, 7th ser., 1 (Boston, 1900) (hereafter *CMHS*), 315; Cooper to Jefferson, Nov. 23, 1823, LOC.
59. Cooper to Jefferson, Oct. 18, 1822, *CMHS*, 315, 316–18.
60. Jefferson to Cooper, Nov. 2, 1822, LOC. For Franklin's similar opinion about the Presbyterians, see Buxbaum, *Benjamin Franklin and the Zealous Presbyterians* (1975) (thanks to Peter Thuesen for this reference).
61. Jefferson to Cooper, Nov. 2, 1822, LOC.
62. Cooper to Jefferson, April 15, 1825, LOC; Cooper to Jefferson, Nov. 20, 1822, LOC.
63. Cooper to Jefferson, Oct. 18, 1822, *CMHS*, 318.

Chapter 6

1. Thomas Cooper, *The Case of Thomas Cooper, M.D., President of the South Carolina College. Submitted to the Legislature and People of South Carolina, December, 1831*, 2nd ed. (Columbia, S.C., 1832), appendix 1, [1]-3, 8-9.
2. David Nelson, *The Cause and Cure of Infidelity: With an Account of the Author's Conversion* (New York, 1837). "Nelson on Infidelity," an announcement of the book's publication in the *New York Evangelist* 8, 1 (Jan. 1837): 3, predicted that the book would "save from the snares of scepticism, a vast number who have not known the shallowness of the reasoning by which infidelity is supported." I have used the second, corrected edition, *The Cause and Cure of Infidelity: Including a Notice of the Author's Unbelief, and the Means of his Rescue* (New York, 1841): see esp. the prologue. "Brief Sketch of the Author's Life," a disbound appendix (95–99) to an unknown edition of *Cause and Cure* included in the Nelson Papers reports that the book had sold nearly a hundred thousand copies. There is some useful information about Nelson in Richardson, "Dr. David Nelson and His Times" (1921).
3. Ezra Stiles Ely, *A Sermon Delivered by Ezra Stiles Ely on the First Sabbath after His Ordination* (Hartford, Conn., 1806); Zebulon Ely, *A Gospel Minister, Though Young, Should Be Respectable by His Example* (Hartford, Conn. 1806). For biographical information on Zebulon, see Dexter, *Biographical Sketches of the Graduates of Yale College* 4 (1907), 109–13; on Ezra, see ibid. 5 (1911), 647–51.
4. Ely's Second Street mansion is discussed in "The Rev. Dr. Ezra Stiles Ely" (1904); on the Pine Street Church and its velvet-trimmed pulpit, see Mackie, "The Presbyterian Churches of Old Philadelphia" (1953).
5. [Ezra Stiles Ely], *The Journal of the Stated Preacher to the Hospital and Almshouse in the City of New-York, for the Year of Our Lord 1811* (New York, 1812), 270; [Ezra Stiles Ely], *The Second Journal of the Stated Preacher to the Hospital and Almshouse in the City of New-York, for a Part of the Year of Our Lord 1813* (Philadelphia, 1815), 119, xi. "Let it not be thought, however," he wrote, "that half, or even a fourth part of the thousand people in this Institution [the Almshouse], are disposed to pay constant attention to the preaching of the Gospel"; and he lamented that of forty prostitutes, not more than four showed any concern for their immortal souls (*Journal* [1812], 80, 228). See also Rosenwaike, *Population History of New York City* (1972), 16, and Cray, *Paupers and Poor Relief in New York City* (1988), 100–119 (population, economy, and urban poor ca. 1810). The Almshouse population had risen from 976 to 1,217 between 1807 and 1811; a third of the residents were foreign born, 20 percent of the total being Irish (Cray, *Paupers and Poor Relief*, 118, 173–74). There were fifty-four churches and one synagogue in the city in 1811, Presbyterians and Episcopalians having the most with twelve each (Rosenwaike, *Population History*, 28). On the religious response to the city's social and moral challenges 1812–37, see Smith-Rosenberg, *Religion and the Rise of the American City* (1971), pt. 1.
6. Ely, *Journal*, 40, 41.
7. Ely, *Journal*, 40, 42, 43, 43–44.
8. Ely, *Journal*, 40. Ely was frustrated with another scoffer later in the journal. One ailing man who made the minister listen to his "deistical whisperings" claimed that he was ready to die and did not need the consolations of Ely's faith. Dodging questions about Jesus, the man said that he had always ignored all the nonsense about which Methodist, Presbyterian, and Episcopal clergymen argued. He asserted, too, that most churchgoers were hypocrites who gathered on the Sabbath to gossip, gawk, and parade about in their best clothing, while he had spent his Sundays "in a rational way," having a friendly smoke with his neighbors. Ely found all of this "much more than any good man would desire to hear" and greatly preferred talking with a "negro servant" who trembled with emotion while confessing his guilt before God (174).
9. Ely, *Journal*, 280, 287, 289.
10. Ely, *Journal*, 262–69, esp. 262.
11. Later American editions of the two-volume set of the Almshouse journals—Ely brought out a sixth edition in 1829—bore the London title, *Visits of Mercy*. [Ezra Stiles Ely], *William and Ellen: A Poem in Three Cantos; with Other Poetical Works of an American* (New York, 1811), xi.

His critic was the anonymous *St. Paul in America* [New York? 1811?], 8. Ezra Stiles Ely, *A Sermon for the Rich to Buy, That They May Benefit Themselves and the Poor* (New York, 1810), 7; [John Steele], *A History of Ecclesiastical Proceedings relative to the Third Presbyterian Church in Philadelphia, the Rev. Ezra Stiles Ely, and Several of the Judicatories of the Church with Which They Are Connected* (Philadelphia, 1814), 164. On the reception of the published journal, see Ely, *Second Journal*, x–xi, and [Steele], *History of Ecclesiastical Proceedings*, 26.
12. [Steele], *History of Ecclesiastical Proceedings*, 161, 19.
13. For a discussion of the broader theological and philosophical context, see Guelzo, *Edwards on the Will* (1989). See also Conforti, *Samuel Hopkins and the New Divinity Movement* (1981); Breitenbach, "Unregenerate Doings" (1982); Breitenbach, "The Consistent Calvinism of the New Divinity Movement" (1984); Sweeney, *Nathaniel Taylor, New Haven Theology, and the Legacy of Jonathan Edwards* (2003); Sweeney and Guelzo, eds., *The New England Theology* (2006); and Crisp and Sweeney, eds., *After Jonathan Edwards* (2012).
14. Ezra Stiles Ely, *A Contrast between Calvinism and Hopkinsianism* (New York, 1811), 196, 278. On the origins of the book, see [Steele], *History of Ecclesiastical Proceedings*, 160. For the Arminian response to *A Contrast*, see James Wilson, *Letters to the Rev. Ezra Stiles Ely, A.M.* (Boston, 1814), who remarks on "such a number of 'Isms,' industriously collected, and singularly arranged" [3]. On Gardiner Spring, see Spring, *Personal Reminiscences of the Life and Times of Gardiner Spring*, 2 vol. (New York, 1866); "The Life and Times of Gardiner Spring," *North American Review* 103, 212 (July 1866), 269–76, with mention of Ely on 271; Dexter, *Biographical Sketches of the Graduates of Yale College* 5 (1911), 791–801; and Hoyt, "The Religious Thought of Gardiner Spring with Particular Reference to His Doctrine of Sin and Salvation" (1962). Spring notes in *Personal Reminiscences* (1:103) that he and Ely had been college roommates for a few months; he calls the *Contrast* a "perversion" of Hopkinsianiam that was "utterly destitute of candor and honesty" and intended only to cause "mischief" (1:129).
15. See [Steele], *History of Ecclesiastical Proceedings*, esp. 160; Ely said that he "was sensible that the Trial was for his Ministerial Life or Death" (155). See also *The Complaint of the Commissioners of the Third Presbyterian Church in the City of Philadelphia, to the Rev'd Synod of Philadelphia* (Philadelphia, [1814]) and *Presbyterian Popery: Animadversions upon the Decision of the Last General Assembly of the Presbyterian Church: Respecting the Third Congregation, Philadelphia* (Philadelphia, 1814). Conflicts over Hopkinsianism divided the Young Men's Missionary Society of New York in 1816 and led to the formation of the rival New York Evangelical Missionary Society of Young Men. See *History of the Young Men's Missionary Society of New York, Containing a Correct Account of the Recent Controversy, respecting Hopkinsian Doctrines* (New York, 1817) and [Gardiner Spring], *A Brief View of Facts Which Gave Rise to the New York Evangelical Missionary Society* (New York, 1817).
16. [Ezra Stiles Ely], "Orthodoxy and Heterodoxy Explained," *Philadelphian* 6, 31 (July 30, 1830): 122; Ezra Stiles Ely, *Memoirs of the Rev. Zebulon Ely, A.M., of Lebanon, Connecticut* (Philadelphia, 1825).
17. Ely, *Memoirs*, 8, 17, 22–23: "O happy marriage! Methinks I have been with the Bridegroom of souls, and that he has taken me into some of the chambers of his delights: glory to God.... What a new world I am in!... My soul has been in a transport.... These are joys, which though they ravish the heart, do not satiate nor cloy. They are eternal delights, that ravish the soul in its inmost faculties." In his rapture, Zebulon turned to address his lover, Jesus: "I find no rest without thee, my beloved. Thou hast ravished my heart.... When thou art absent, behold my despondency. See me a feeble creature, languish and faint away. See the tumult of my breast, if thou dost frown: I tremble, I am astonished. Thy smiles chase away the gloom of my countenance, and dispel the darkness that hangs round my eyes. My brows are smoothed, and the principle of immortality sparkles in my soul. My affections glow at the thoughts of fruition, and then the endless duration of that fruition, raises my soul in a transport. Come my dear Jesus!" (25–26).
18. Ely, *Memoirs*, 36, 38, and see 42 (despair on June 4, 1820).
19. Ely, *Contrast*, 251.
20. Ezra Stiles Ely, *Ten Sermons on Faith* (Philadelphia, 1816); *Quarterly Theological Review* (Philadelphia, 1818–19), esp. 1:333–38, 447–53, 469–93, 518–40, 3–31, and particularly

"Review of Several American Writers on Moral Agency (2:45–87) and "Moral Agency" (2:333–78); *Conversations on the Science of the Human Mind* (Philadelphia, 1819); *A Synopsis of Didactic Theology* (Philadelphia, 1822); *Retrospective Theology; or, Opinions of the World of Spirits* (Philadelphia, 1825); [Ezra Stiles Ely], "Free Agency and Predestination," *Philadelphian* 6, 26 (June 25, 1830): 102–3. See also Ely articles in the *Philadelphian*: "New Haven Divinity," 6, 37 (Sept. 10, 1830): 145; "Faith Defined," 7, 34 (Aug. 19, 1831): 133; "Calvinistic Arminians and Arminian Calvinists," 7, 36 (Sept. 2, 1831): 143; "Hopkinsianism and Biblical Calvinism," 7, 36, (Sept. 2, 1831): 143; "Can a Sinner Change His Heart?—Remarks by the Editor," 8, 1 (Jan. 5, 1832): 6; "Human Ability—Remarks by the Editor," 8, 3 (Jan. 19, 1832): 9; "The Importance of the Means of Grace—Editor's Remarks," 8, 6 (Feb. 9, 1832): 22; "Friends Alarmed—Reply," 8, 3 (March 29, 1832): 50; "Grace—Reply to J. P. W.," 8, 15 (April 12, 1832): 57; "Reply to the Letters of the Rev. Robert Stuart of Kentucky, No. II," 8, 16 (April 19, 1832): 63; "Regeneration and the New Birth," 8, 31 (Aug. 2, 1832): 122–23; "Some Notice of the Sermon Entitled 'Regeneration not Wrought by Light' by the Rev. Edward D. Griffin,' 8, 34 (Aug. 23, 1832), 134; "Predestination and Election," 8, 42 (Oct. 1832), 166; "Human Power," 8, 50 (Dec. 13, 1832), 198.

21. Ely, *Contrast*, 30n. In 1819, Ely called Dwight's *Theology* (1818) the best system of divinity ever written in America (*Quarterly Theological Review* 2: 498), and he praised it again in "Taylorism and Fitchism," *Philadelphian* 7, 10 (March 4, 1831): 39. On Dwight, see esp. Grasso, *Speaking Aristocracy* (1999), 327–85, and Fitzmier, *New England's Moral Legislator* (1998). On intellectualism in moral philosophy, see Fiering, *Moral Philosophy at Seventeenth-Century Harvard* (1981), esp. 110–14, 196. On Puritan preparationism, Pettit's important *The Heart Prepared* (1966) has been superseded by subsequent scholarship, including Stoever, *"A Faire and Easie Way to Heaven"* (1978) and Charles R. Cohen, *God's Caress* (1986).

22. On the Massachusetts Society for Promoting Christian Knowledge and the relationship of moderate Calvinists and the New Divinity in New England reform, see Smith, "The Forming of a Modern American Denomination" (1962) and Nord, *Faith in Reading* (2004), 29–39. Ely was one of the American editors of the works of Thomas Reid; he mentions his (unsigned) contributions to *The Works of Thomas Reid, D.D., F.R.S., Edinburgh...with Notes, by the American Editors* (Charleston, S.C., 1813) in *Conversations on the Human Mind*, 144. Ely endorsed Reid's philosophy in *Quarterly Theological Review* 1:78 but noted in *Conversations* that Reid focused more on demolishing the old system of moral philosophy rather than building a new one (20). In *Conversations*, Ely himself disclaimed "all *metaphysics* but those of *common sense*" (preface).

23. See Nord, *Faith in Reading* and Brown, *The Word in the World* (2004). See also Nord, "Benevolent Books," in Gross and Kelley, eds., *A History of the Book in America*, vol. 2 (2010), esp. 230; Shantz, "Religious Tracts, Evangelical Reform, and the Market Revolution in Antebellum America" (1997), esp. 426; Kelley, "'Pen and Ink Communion'" (2011), esp. 561–62; Albaugh, *History and Annotated Bibliography of American Religious Periodicals and Newspapers*, vol. 1 (1994), esp. xii, xiv, xx.

24. Ezra Stiles Ely, "Religious Newspapers," *Philadelphian* 6, 3 (Jan. 15, 1830): 10; Ely, "Reply to the Preceding Address," *Philadelphian* 8, 37 (Sept. 13, 1832): 146–47. For agents, see "Agents for the Philadelphian," *Philadelphian* 7, 20 (May 13, 1831): 80; "Agents for the Presbyterian," *Presbyterian* 3, 3 (Feb. 29, 1832); "Agents for the Calvinist Magazine," *Calvinist Magazine* 2, 4 (Feb. 1830): [end page]. The first issue of the *Philadelphian* to list Ely on the masthead was 5, 48 (Nov. 27, 1829), but a "Notice" (190) identifies him as the "Future Editor"; his first editorial column, "The Duty of Christian Freemen," appeared in 5, 50 (Dec. 11, 1829): 198. There was some dispute in Ely's day and subsequently about the first weekly religious newspaper, but see Mott, *History of American Magazines*, 137: "The first of the tribe appears to have been the *Herald of Gospel Liberty*, founded by Elias Smith in Portsmouth, New Hampshire, in 1808....The *Herald* is not, however, the oldest religious weekly with a record of continuous publication. That distinction belongs to...'a Presbyterian Family Newspaper,' founded in Philadelphia in 1813 by John W. Scott under the name of the *Religious Remembrancer*."

25. "The Future Destinies of America, as Affected by the Doings of the Present Generation," *Philadelphian* 6, 46 (Nov. 11, 1830): 180, and 6, 47 (Nov. 18, 1830): 185; "Missionary Survey—Obstacles to the Diffusion of Christianity," *Philadelphian* 6, 40 (Oct. 1, 1830): 160.

26. Ezra Stiles Ely, "A Statistical Peace Offering," *Philadelphian* 6, 10 (March 5, 1830): 38, and "Reply to the Letters of the Rev. Robert Stuart, of Kentucky," *Philadelphian* 8, 15 (April 12, 1832): 59.
27. [Ezra Stiles Ely], "Gov. William Findlay of Pennsylvania, Inaugural Address," *Quarterly Theological Review* 1, 1 (Jan. 1818): 83–85, esp. 83, 84. See also Ely's review of "William Wirt's Life of Patrick Henry," ibid., 25–26, where Ely complained that although deism was not as fashionable as it was in the eighteenth century, in the early nineteenth public characters gave lip service to Christianity but lived without it. Ely, "The Duty of Christian Freemen to Elect Christian Rulers," *Philadelphian* 3, 29 (July 20, 1827): 1, and 3, 30 (July 27, 1827): 12–15. The sermon was published in pamphlet form (Philadelphia, 1828), and then again by the *Philadelphian* as an extra in November 1831. For a discussion of Beecher, Wayland, Ely, and others on ministers and politics, see West, *The Politics of Revelation and Reason* (1996), 126–34. For a standard New England election sermon of the previous generation, see Zebulon Ely, *The Wisdom and Duty of Magistrates: A Sermon Preached at the General Election, May 10th, 1804* (Hartford, Conn., 1804), esp. 31. For a discussion of New England preachers and politics in the previous century, see Grasso, *Speaking Aristocracy*, esp. 24–85. Carwardine's *Evangelicals and Politics in Antebellum America* (1997), though focused on the 1840s and '50s, has much to say about the 1820s and '30s as well.
28. I am quoting from the 1828 pamphlet version of the sermon: Ely, *Duty of Christian Freemen*, 4, 5, 6, 8; Ely, "The Duty of Christian Freemen," *Philadelphian* 5, 50 (Dec. 11, 1829): 198. On the call for an organizational meeting in New York, see Ely, [Response to Abner Hazeltine], *Philadelphian* 6, 2 (Jan. 1830): 6. See also Ely's *Philadelphian* commentary: [Response to Thomas Whittemore], 6, 4 (Jan. 22, 1830): 14; "The Christian Party in Politics," and "A Baptist Enemy to the Christian Party in Politics," 6, 13 (March 26, 1830): 50; "Test Oath for Office," 6, 31 (July 30, 1830): 123; "Church and State," 7, 40 (Sept. 30, 1831): 21; "Christian Freemen," 6, 3 (Jan. 15, 1830): 11; "First Letter to the Rev. Solomon Aiken," 6, 29 (July 16, 1830): 15; "Church and State," 6, 50 (Dec. 10, 1830): 199. See also Blau, "The Christian Party in Politics" (1946). Abolitionists who formed the Liberty Party (James G. Birney was their presidential candidate in 1840 and 1844) adopted the slogan "Vote as you pray and pray as you vote" (Howe, *What Hath God Wrought* [2007], 652).
29. Ely, *Duty of Christian Freemen*, 11, 13.
30. On Ely's support for Jackson, see the appendix in *Duty of Christian Freemen*, 30–32; "General Jackson's Religious Character," *Connecticut Herald* 25, 25 (March 18, 1828): [3]; and *Gen. Jackson and the Rev. Ezra Stiles Ely* [New York, 1828], an eight-page pamphlet. On his criticism of Adams, see Ezra Stiles Ely, "Discourse on the Christian Sabbath," a manuscript of a sermon delivered to his congregation on Sept. 28, 1828, Ely Papers, Record Group 317, Folder 3 (all references to the Ely Papers are to the microfilmed edition); and "Sunday Travelling," *New Hampshire Sentinel*, Feb. 27, 1829, [3]. On the Eaton affair, see Clark, "Margaret Eaton—(Peggy O'Neal)" (1942–43); Wood, "'One Woman So Dangerous to Public Morals'" (1997); Howe, *What Hath God Wrought*, 335–42. On Jackson as "Grand Seignor" and Ely as "Chief Mufti," see [untitled], *Rhode Island Republican*, July 24, 1828, [2].
31. "A Writer in the Boston Trumpet," *Vermont Gazette*, May 12, 1829, [2], and "Christian Party in Politics," *Columbian Register*, Feb. 27, 1830, [2]; Letter to the Editor from "A Rhode Islander," *Literary Cadet and Rhode-Island Statesman*, July 9, 1828, [2]; "Union of Church and State," *Universalist Magazine* 9, 17 (Oct. 13, 1827): 68.
32. Ely, *Duty of Christian Freemen* [1828], appendix, [15], and see Ely, "Church and State," *Philadelphian* 7, 40 (Sept. 30, 1831): 159; Ely, "Appendix—Defensive Publications," in "Duty of Christian Freemen," *Philadelphian*, extra issue (Nov. 1831): 15 ("the *union of the State and Infidelity*"); Samuel B. Wylie, "Pastoral Address," *Philadelphian* 8, 33 (Aug. 16, 1833): 129–30, endorsed by Ely in prefatory note.
33. Ely called Universalists "anti-Christians" in [Reply to Thomas Whittemore], *Philadelphian* 6, 4 (Jan. 22, 1830): 14; "Public Meeting in Philadelphia, in Favor of Sunday Mails," *Philadelphian* 6, 8 (Feb. 19, 1830): 30. See Anne Newport Royall, *Mrs. Royall's Pennsylvania; or, Travels Continued in the United States* (Washington, D.C., 1829), esp. 1:88–91, 231–32; and see Clapp, "'A Virago-Errant in Enchanted Armor?'" (2003); Dorsey, "Friends Becoming Enemies" (1998); Wyatt-Brown, "The Antimission Movement in the Jacksonian South" (1970); Wyatt-

Brown, "Prelude to Abolitionism" (1971); Nolt, "Becoming Ethnic Americans in the Early Republic" (2000). The votes for moderator of the Presbyterian Church's General Assembly are reported in the *New-York Spectator*, May 23, 1828, [1]: Ely received seventy-seven votes, New England's Lyman Beecher got forty-five, and John Holt Rice, Thomas Cooper's main antagonist in Virginia, got nine. [Resolution of the First Baptist Society in Portsmouth, New Hampshire], *New-Hampshire Gazette*, Aug. 18, 1829, [3] and reprinted under the headline "A Good Beginning" in the *New-Hampshire Patriot*, Aug. 24, 1829, [2].

34. The handbill and excerpts from Duncan's and Powel's speeches are in Ely, appendix in *Duty of Christian Freemen*, 15–32; see esp. 18, 20, 21, 23, 25. For the publication of the speeches in newspapers outside Pennsylvania, see, for example, "Mr. Powel's Speech," *Village Register*, April 10, 1828, [1], and [Sunday School Union], *Watch-Tower*, May 19, 1828, [4]. See also Willard Hall, *A Defence of the American Sunday School Union against the Charges of Its Opponents* (Philadelphia, 1828).

35. On Sabbatarianism, see Wyatt-Brown, "Prelude to Abolitionism"; Rohrer, "Sunday Mails and the Church-State Theme in Jacksonian America" (1987); John, "Taking Sabbatarianism Seriously" (1990); and West, *Politics of Revelation and Reason*, chap. 3.

36. "The Philadelphian," *Liberator* 3, 16 (April 20, 1833): 63; *New-Hampshire Sentinel*, Aug. 16, 1832, [2]; "The Clergy," *New-York Spectator*, Oct. 8, 1832, [3]; "More Seceders," *Portland* [Me.] *Advertiser*, Oct. 15, 1832, [4]; "Queer Notions," *Philadelphian* 8, 51 (Dec. 20, 1832): 22; "Dr. Ely and Jacksonism," *New-York Spectator*, Sept. 8, 1834, [4]. For Ely's view of the conservative (he would call it "High Church") Presbyterian reaction to the Barnes case and its purported connection to New Haven Theology, see "Reply to the Son of an Irishman," *Philadelphian* 8, 5 (Feb. 2, 1832): 18. Pope argues in "Albert Barnes, 'The Way of Salvation,' and Theological Controversy" (1979) that Barnes was actually closer to the Hopkinsianism Ely despised than to the New Haven Theology he tolerated. On the Presbyterian schism of 1837–38, see Smith, "The Role of the South in the Presbyterian Schism of 1837–38" (1960); Smith, "The Forming of a Modern American Denomination" (1962); MacCormac, "Missions and the Presbyterian Schism of 1837" (1963); and Doherty, "Social Bases for the Presbyterian Schism of 1837–1838" (1968). Ironically, Ely's old Hopkinsian antagonist from 1811, Gardiner Spring, would move in the opposite direction and align with the Old School (see Hoyt, "Religious Thought of Gardiner Spring," 72–76).

37. Lyman Beecher, "Political Atheism," lecture 3 in *Lectures on Scepticism* (Cincinnati, Ohio, 1835), lectures first delivered in Boston in 1830–31 and in Cincinnati in 1833; for an excerpt in the press, including a passage where Beecher defends Ely, see "Political Atheism," *Essex* [Mass.] *Gazette*, Jan. 26, 1831, [1], reprinted from the *Boston Courier*. Beecher, *A Plea for the West* (New York and Cincinnati, 1835); for an appreciative essay, see "Beecher's Plea for the West," *Quarterly Christian Spectator*, 7, 3 (Sept. 1, 1835): 481–504.

38. For Ely's views on the tendency of Hopkinsianism to lead to deism and atheistic fatalism, see Ely, *Contrast*, 255; Nelson, *Cause and Cure*, 11, 12, 10. For earlier notice of the spread of infidelity, see "Eulogium for Samuel Nelson, to the Editors of the *Calvinist Magazine*," *Calvinist Magazine* 12, 1 (Dec. 27, 1827): 355.

39. Nelson, *Cause and Cure*, 222, 222–23, 221. On Nelson, see his entries in Sprague, *Annals of the American Pulpit* 4 (1859): 677–88, and Malone, ed., *Dictionary of American Biography* 13:414–15. See also Richardson, "Dr. David Nelson and His Times" (1921).

40. Nelson, *Cause and Cure*, 226. Nelson argued that in his first disillusioning experience with an infidel author, a claim made in the text (about glass in Solomon's day) first contradicted Nelson's understanding of a historical fact, and then prompted him to do additional research (about the translation). The experience encapsulated, in short, his cure for infidel ignorance: supply historical knowledge and biblical literacy. In his case, however, there may have been more than just a clue on the page that pricked his memory and prompted him to pursue his own research, leading to his "cure." He may have had the criticism about cup and glass specifically and about Voltaire's entire approach more generally already laid out for him at the bottom of the same pages in the *Philosophical Dictionary*. It is impossible to know which edition of Voltaire's work Nelson read. But a New York edition of the *Philosophical Dictionary, for the Pocket*, published for I. Carnan, and sold by Berry, Rogers, and Berry (1792–95) republished the London 1765 English translation and included "Notes, Containing a Refutation of such

Passages as are in any way exceptionable in regard to Religion." The longest footnote accompanies Voltaire's article on Solomon and amounts to an 1,800-word essay criticizing the author's deism, his satirical style, and his "puerile" objections to the authorship of the Book of Proverbs. The commentary begins with what was Nelson's central example—the translation of the word "cup" as "glass" in Prov. 23:31. Nelson may have read this commentary when he first read Voltaire; he may have neglected to mention this in *Cause and Cure* because he wanted to stress the reader himself bringing historical knowledge and outside research to bear on the text. He would argue for the usefulness of scholarly commentary, but at the same time wanted to avoid seeming to rely too much upon it. Another edition of Voltaire's *Philosophical Dictionary, for the Pocket* (Catskill [N.Y.], 1796), did not contain the critical notes. It is possible that Nelson read this edition, its reprint in 1805, or another edition without the notes and simply focused on the same sentence in Voltaire, and the same translated word, to similarly criticize the entire book.

41. Nelson, *Cause and Cure*, 338.
42. Nelson, *Cause and Cure*, 248, 251, 253.
43. Nelson, *Cause and Cure*, 261. The first volume of the first edition of what became known as Scott's Family Bible was published as *The Holy Bible, Containing the Old and New Testaments, with Original Notes, and Practical Observations, by the Rev. Thomas Scott* (London, 1788). The first American edition, from the second London edition, was published in Philadelphia (1804–9). A single-volume Bible incorporating Scott's notes, which is probably what Nelson used, was *The Holy Bible, Containing the Old and New Testaments... and the Copious Marginal Reference of Scott's Family Bible* (New York, 1813). On the popularity of Scott's and other "study Bibles" in this period, see Holland, *Sacred Borders* (2011), 106.
44. Sprague, *Annals of the American Pulpit* 4:684; Nelson, *Cause and Cure*, 110, 188, [Young's prologue].
45. Nelson, *Cause and Cure*, 18, 41–42, 60, 131, 138, 186, 221. "Brief Sketch of the Author's Life," a disbound appendix (395–99) to an unknown edition of *Cause and Cure* included in the Nelson Papers, mentions his father-in-law. A Nelson sermon against infidelity converted another skeptical physician, and at Marion College Nelson then convinced him to become a missionary to the Sandwich Islands (Hawaii); see "Dr. Lafon's Sermon," *New York Evangelist* 7, 52 (Dec. 24, 1836): 206.
46. Nelson, *Cause and Cure*, 13, 164.
47. Nelson, *Cause and Cure*, 117, 61.
48. Nelson, *Cause and Cure*, 344, 99 (see also 16), 100.
49. Nelson, *Cause and Cure*, 47, 48.
50. Nelson, *Cause and Cure*, 109, 156. On Nelson's recommended reading list, see 10, 11, 133, and esp. 156–58.
51. Nelson, *Cause and Cure*, 119, 153. On the populist (Reformed literal) hermeneutic, see Noll, *America's God*, chap. 18.
52. Nelson, *Cause and Cure*, 324.
53. Nelson, *Cause and Cure*, 115, 160, 82–87; and see 238: "Is falsehood, black, ungainly falsehood, loved in place of truth? Only in matters of religion. The carnal mind loves darkness there, but in other things men prefer light."
54. Nelson, *Cause and Cure*, 151, 152, 234, 14, 21.
55. Nelson, *Cause and Cure*, 29, 107, 155.
56. Nelson, *Cause and Cure*, 98, and see 127, 337–38, 279, 292, 23.
57. Nelson, *Cause and Cure*, 164, 48, 184–85.
58. Nelson, *Cause and Cure*, 165, 185, 167, 168, 173.
59. Nelson, *Cause and Cure*, 262–63.

Chapter 7

1. Ezra Stiles Ely, "To the Moderator of the General Assembly of the Presbyterian Church convened in Pittsburgh May, 1836," April 25, 1835, Ely Papers, Folder 2.
2. The founding of Marion College and City is discussed in four articles by J. P. Rutter in the *Western Journal and Civilian*: "Origin of Marion College," 14, 3 (Aug. 1855): 165–69; "Origin

Notes to Pages 228–235   551

of Marion College [pt. 2]," 14, 4 (Sept. 1855): 244–50; "An Extract from a Forthcoming Work to be Entitled 'Twenty-Four Years' View of Palmyra and Marion County, in Missouri,'" 14, 5 (Oct. 1855): 316–23; and "The End and Removal of Marion College," 14, 6 (Nov. 1855): 416–18. See also [Holcombe], *History of Marion County, Missouri* (1884), 203–8, 226–48; Whitaker, "Marion College and Marion City" (1886), 798–807. There was a third member of the early planning group—Dr. David Clark—though it is unclear what he contributed besides enthusiasm, some fund-raising, and collateral for the initial loan.

3. Ely, in a piece from the *Philadelphian* reprinted in the *Christian Advocate and Journal* 9, 42 (June 12, 1835): 166, retells the story, and is the source for Muldrow's previous infidelity and quotation ("Why should I not do for Christ"). Nelson, Clark, and Muldrow published an explanation of their early financing, dated Oct. 29, 1834, in the *Missouri Republican*, reprinted in the *New York Evangelist* 5, 50 (Dec. 13, 1834): 198; Clark supplied an even fuller statement, signed by eleven trustees in November 1834, to the *Baltimore Gazette and Daily Advertiser*, Dec. 23, 1834, 2; one of the new trustees, William Potts, supplied a separate and corroborating financial account to the Philadelphia *National Gazette*, Dec. 25, 1834, 2. The Palmyra, Mo., *Courier* reported that fund-raising ambassadors were being sent out in the fall of 1834: David Nelson to the east, David Clark to the south, two other men to Kentucky, Virginia, Pennsylvania, and Ohio, and Muldrow to Boston and intermediate cities (rpt. in [No title], *Man* 3, 69 [Nov. 19, 1834]: 279). On Muldrow, see Rutter, "Origin of Marion College" (Aug. and Sept.), "Extract from a Forthcoming Work," and "End and Removal of Marion College"; Holcombe, *History of Marion County*, 205–8, 226–48; Whitaker, "Marion College and Marion City"; and Whitaker, "Forgotten Page of Missouri History" (1909).

4. Rutter, "Origins of Marion College" (Aug.), 168; [Ezra Stiles Ely], "Marion College, Missouri," *Christian Advocate and Journal* 9, 42 (June 12, 1835): 166, rpt. from *Philadelphian*.

5. [James Gallaher], "Marion College," *New York Evangelist* 5, 21 (May 24, 1834): 83. The Palmyra, Mo., *Courier* printed detailed charges against the Marion College promoters, which were widely reprinted in newspapers across the country. See "From the Palmyra Courier Oct. 17," *Western Examiner* 1, 21 (Nov. 11, 1834): 167–68; "Marion College, Mo.," *Man* 3, 69 (Nov. 19, 1834): 279; "Marion College, Mo.," *Workingman's Advocate*, Nov. 22, 1834, 2. David Clark defended the project against the "implacable enmity" of the *Courier's* editor in "Marion College," *Baltimore Gazette*, Dec. 23, 1834, 2; see also Wm. S. Potts, "To the Editor," *National Gazette*, Dec. 25, 1834, 2.

6. William Muldrow to [unknown], Dec. 16, 1835, in Holcombe, *History of Marion County*, 237n1; Rutter, "Extract," 318–19.

7. David Nelson, "Interesting Letter from Missouri," *Religious Intelligencer* 18, 7 (July 13, 1833): 110; see also *Western Luminary*, July 10, 1833, 3. [Ezra Stiles Ely], "Palmyra in Missouri," *Richmond Enquirer*, July 21, 1855, 4; Rutter, "Extract," 321; Ezra Stiles Ely, "Memorandum of Real Estate in Marion City deeded by ESE," "Ralls County Abstract of Real Estate Deeded to ESE," and "Ralls County Abstract of Real Estate Deeded by ESE," Ely Papers, Folder 4.

8. "Missionary. Fifteen Thousand Missionaries for Heathen Lands!" *New York Evangelist* 6, 50 (Dec. 12, 1835): 1.

9. "Marion City," *Daily Commercial Bulletin*, April 6, 1836, 2, rpt. from *Wheeling Gazette*.

10. [No title], *Daily Commercial Bulletin*, May 6, 1836, 2 (three feet); "Marion City," ibid., May 23, 1836, 2 (sixteen inches); "Marion City," ibid., May 25, 1836, 2 (two feet); cartoon described in Rutter, "Extract," 323, and Holcombe, *History of Marion County*, 242; "Marion City" (Proprietors' Handbill), in ibid., 242–43; Impartial Spectator, "To Wm. P. Clark, Esq.," *Daily Commercial Bulletin*, Sept. 16, 1836, 2.

11. "Case of Conscience," *Christian Register and Boston Observer* 14, 59 (Sept. 26, 1835): 234, rpt. from *Philadelphian*.

12. "Case of Conscience," *Christian Register and Boston Observer*, 14, 59 (Sept. 26, 1835): 234, rpt. from *Philadelphian*.

13. See, for example, "A Slaveholder," *Boston Recorder* 20, 40 (Oct. 2, 1835): 158. In "Rev. Dr. Ely a Slaveholder: The Reply," *New York Evangelist* 6, 40 (Oct. 3, 1835): 248, Joshua Leavitt wrote: "And you see how quickly the papers, which are trying to shield the consciences of the nation against the goodness of truth, take up the matter, and blazen it with capitals and exclamations, 'DR. ELY A SLAVEHOLDER!'"

14. E. S. Ely, "Reply to the Rev. Joshua Leavitt," *Philadelphian* (Nov. 19, 1835), rpt. in "Dr. Ely and His Slave," *New York Evangelist* 7, 1 (Jan. 2, 1836): 1, with "Remarks" by Joshua Leavitt.
15. Joshua Leavitt, "Remarks" in "Dr. Ely and His Slave," *New York Evangelist* 7, 1 (Jan. 2, 1836): 1.
16. Finnie, "The Antislavery Movement in the Upper South before 1840" (1969), esp. 336–37; McCandless, *A History of Missouri*, vol. 2, *1820–1860* (1972), 60–66; Holcombe, *History of Marion County*, 203–5; "Nelson, David," in Malone, ed., *Dictionary of American Biography* 13:415; "Synod of Missouri—Abolitionism," *Liberator* 6, 2 (Jan. 9, 1836): 1. David Nelson's "In Further Contrast: To the Presbyterians of Missouri Who Hold Slaves" was published in the *St. Louis Observer*, edited by Elijah P. Lovejoy, who would die defending a similar antislavery newspaper two years later in Illinois; Nelson's piece was republished in *New York Evangelist* 6, 33 (Aug. 15, 1835): 222, *Philanthropist* 1, 19 (May 6, 1836): 1, and other places. See also "Slavery: Letter from the Rev. David Nelson," *New York Evangelist* 6, 51 (Dec. 19, 1835): 284A (a different address, to his former congregation in Danville, Ky.), and "David Nelson's Address to the Presbyterians of East Tennessee, Kentucky and Missouri," *New York Evangelist* 7, 14 (April 2, 1836) and in *Philanthropist* 1, 19 (May 6, 1836): 1, and continued in *Philanthropist* 1, 20 (May 13, 1836): 1. Nelson's comments were excerpted and criticized in "The Harrow No. 3," *Western Examiner* 2, 43 (Nov. 19, 1835): 338. On Muldrow as Ambrose's owner, see Whitaker, "Marion College and Marion City," 800, and for Muldrow's antislavery sentiments, 802.
17. "Excitement in Missouri" [letter from A. C. Garratt, Quincy, Ill., May 21, 1836], *New York Evangelist* 7, 25 (June 18, 1836): 98, rpt. in *Liberator* 7, 28 (July 9, 1836): 112. See also "The Excitement in Missouri" [letter dated "Near Palmyra, May 27, 1836"], *Liberator* 6, 25 (June 18, 1836): 98, and Holcombe, *History of Marion County*, 203–5.
18. [A Letter from Marion City] [St. Louis] *Daily Commercial Bulletin*, May 27, 1836, said that the paper Nelson read was about abolition; a May 27 account printed with other items in "Excitement in Missouri," *Liberator* 6, 25 (June 18, 1836): 98 and in *New York Evangelist* 7, 25 (June 18, 1836): 98 said the paper was about an indemnity. Nelson's explanation is in "Dr. Nelson's Letter," *New York Evangelist* 7, 28 (July 9, 1836): 111. See also undated manuscript, which seems to be a longer draft of "Brief Sketch of the Author's Life," in Nelson Papers.
19. For the stabbing story and its immediate aftermath, see [A Letter from Marion City] [St. Louis] *Daily Commercial Bulletin*, May 27, 1836, 2; "Public Meeting," ibid., June 1, 1836, 2; [Little Rock] *Arkansas Gazette*, June 28, 1836; "Mobs in Missouri," *Essex Gazette*, June 18, 1836, 2; "The Excitement in Missouri: Public Meeting," *Boston Recorder* 21, 26 (June 24, 1836): 104; Holcombe, *History of Marion County*, 205–8; Whitaker, "Marion College and City," 804–6; and Richardson, "Dr. David Nelson and His Times," esp. 443 (account by Nelson's son). Nelson's comments are in "Dr. Nelson's Statement," *Liberator* 6, 33 (Aug. 13, 1836).
20. "Public Meeting," [St. Louis] *Daily Commercial Bulletin*, June 1, 1836, 2. Other college officers quickly published statements to correct falsehoods that had circulated about the college: Garratt and Williams were not students, the trunk of abolitionist tracts had never been on college grounds, no blacks had ever been enrolled, Muldrow was neither a professor nor a trustee, Nelson had not been publicly whipped, and the college had not been attacked and burned down by the posse. See "Marion College," *New York Spectator*, June 23, 1836, 1 (statement by college officer Daniel Clark); [Letter from Marion College president William S. Potts], *Arkansas Gazette*, July 5, 1836, orig. pub. in *Louisville City Gazette* and dated June 1, 1836.
21. "Marion City, Missouri," *Daily National Intelligencer*, Aug. 9, 1837; "Scenes and Incidents in the Far West," ibid., July 10, 1837. The Marion City fiasco provided material for Charles Dickens's *The Life and Adventures of Martin Chuzzlewit* (orig. pub. 1843–44): see Holcombe, *History of Marion County*, 244, and Mets, *The Companion to "Martin Chuzzlewit"* (2001), 249.
22. Ezra Stiles Ely, "Memoirs of His Own Life and Times" (typed transcript), Ely Papers, Folder 7, 53 (Muldrow testimony about the Bank of the U.S. loan), 3 (Hayes accusation that Ely was sheltering money from creditors), 87 (winding up with Barnes's slaves). References to this source will be to the paginated typescript; quotations have been checked against the unpaginated manuscript (Folder 6, precedes typescript on microfilm).

23. "Marriage Contract between Rev. E. S. Ely & Caroline T. Holmes," June 17, 1843, Ely Papers, Folder 5. According to the 1840 Federal Census, three years earlier Ely's household contained 6 slaves (1 male under age 10, 1 male ages 36–54, 2 females under 10, and 2 females ages 10–23) and 1 "free colored" male under age 10.
24. Rutter, "End and Removal of Marion College," 415–17. Rutter was the recorder for the Marion County Circuit Court when Ely filed his marriage contract with Caroline T. Holmes there in 1843 (see copy of the contract in Ely Papers); Ely, "Legal Papers regarding the Carswell Estate and Property in Missouri, 1836," Ely Papers, Folder 4; Ely, "Memoirs," 87 (what he owed to Marion City Co.).
25. Ely, "Memoirs," 3, 6, 10.
26. [Ezra Stiles Ely], To Mr. Ferguson, McIlvain & other Elders of the 3d Presbyterian Church in Philadelphia [1813–14], Ely Papers, Folder 2; Ely, "Memoirs," 23–24, 46.
27. Ely, "Memoirs," 37, 52.
28. Ely, "Memoirs," 40, 58–59, 9, 109.
29. Ely, "Memoirs," 12, 27, 55, 63. Ely's brother-in-law J. L. Hyde told Ely after the trial that the previous fall he had heard Hayes admit that the only reason he forced a trial before the presbytery was to lure Ely back to Missouri so Hayes could sue him in U.S. Circuit Court over some property ("Memoirs," 64).
30. Ely, "Memoirs," 65, 73, 70, 84, 74, 75.
31. Ely, "Memoirs," 90, 91, 92.
32. Ely, "Memoirs," 92; "The Late Ezra Stiles Ely, D.D.," *New York Evangelist* 32, 28 (July 11, 1861): 6.
33. [Ezra Stiles Ely], *The Journal of the Stated Preacher to the Hospital and Almshouse in the City of New-York, for the Year of Our Lord 1811* (New York, 1812), 33, 6, 146, and *The Second Journal of the Stated Preacher to the Hospital and Almshouse in the City of New-York, for a Part of the Year of Our Lord 1813* (Philadelphia, 1815), appendix 1. On the formalization of benevolent reform, see Wright, *The Transformation of Charity in Postrevolutionary New England* (1992).
34. [Ely], *Journal of the Stated Preacher*, 123. Nord, in *Faith in Reading* (2004), stresses the "noncommercial" or "anticommercial" character of religious publishing, but Brown, in *The Word in the World* (2004), argues for seeing how "evangelicals configured commerce as a religious instrument" (19).
35. David Nelson, "Marion College—Circular," *Philadelphian* 9, 10 (March 7, 1833): 35; "Scepticus," "The Tables Turned," and J. Keith, [Letter to the Editor], *Boston Investigator* 42 (Jan. 8, 1836); Ezra Stiles Ely, "Remarks by the Editor," *Philadelphian* 9, 10 (March 7, 1833): 38; R. P., "To the Editors," *Western Examiner* 2, 4 (Jan. 25, 1835), 27; Ezra Stiles Ely, "Second Letter to the Rev. Solomon Aiken of Vermont," *Philadelphian* 6, 30 (July 23, 1830): 117, and "Third Letter to the Rev. Solomon Aiken of Vermont," *Philadelphian* 6, 31 (July 30, 1830): 123. On the conspiracy theories of religious radicals and their antagonism to benevolent fund-raising, see Gribbin, "Antimasonry, Religious Radicalism, and the Paranoid Style of the 1820's" (1974). Contrary to what Ely said about benevolent societies and the print market, see Nord, "Benevolent Books," in Gross and Kelley, eds., *A History of the Book, in America*, vol. 2 (2010), 231: "By the end of the 1820s, the American Bible Society had built in New York a highly capitalized, technologically sophisticated printing operation that virtually monopolized the production of inexpensive Bibles in the United States."
36. By the 1830s both Ely and Nelson wanted to prevent theological divisions among Old and New School Presbyterians from causing a schism and urged evangelical unity in education, revivalism, and reform to combat common enemies. See *A Correspondence between Reverend David Nelson, M.D., and J. L. Wilson* (Cincinnati, 1834); and see Ely, "Orthodoxy and Heterodoxy Explained," *Philadelphian* 6, 31 (July 30, 1830): 122: "My mother has several times said to me, 'you have written a *Contrast*: I wish you would now write a *Harmony* to show how far all evangelical Christians really agree.'" For Nelson's treatise on "Wealth and Honor" and the Mission Institute, see "Brief Sketch of the Author's Life"; an undated manuscript that seems to be a longer draft of "Brief Sketch"; "Instances in Dr. Nelson's Life—Written by a Friend"; and Copy of a letter by Mrs. A[manda] F[rances] D[eaderick] Nelson dated March 1, 1852, all in Nelson Papers. On the Mission Institute, see also David Nelson, *An Appeal to the Church*

in Behalf of a Dying Race (New York, 1838), esp. 18–19. On Nelson's manner of dress and other eccentricities, see Sprague, *Annals of the American Pulpit* 4:682–87, esp. 682n.

37. "Brief Sketch of the Author's Life," 398, in Nelson Papers, says he wrote *Cause and Cure* in the summer of 1836; a longer, undated manuscript draft of or source for the "Sketch" in the same collection, quoting an account by one of Nelson's students, says he began writing it even as he hid from the mob in a hazel thicket in the days after the stabbing.

38. For the reference to urban infidels, see Nelson, *Cause and Cure*, 46: "Thousands who range the streets of our large cities, seem to be beyond remedy. Their furious hatred towards all that is meek or holy, prevents their listening to expostulation; and their ignorance renders them incapable of weighing argument, on almost any subject."

Chapter 8

1. George Bethune English, *The Grounds of Christianity Examined by Comparing the New Testament with the Old* (Boston, 1813), iii, xvi, xvii. For the Lithuanian rabbi (Rabbi Isaac Ben Abraham of Troki), see the introduction to Popkin, *Disputing Christianity* (2007) (the book itself is a reprint of English's *Grounds*).
2. Joseph S. Buckminster, *Sermons by the Late Joseph S. Buckminster*, 3rd ed. (Boston, 1821), 117 and see 123, 279–80, 130 (Buckminster died of an acute epileptic attack in 1812, age twenty-eight). [Andrews Norton], "*Nec Temere, Nec Timide*: A Defence of Liberal Christianity," *General Repository and Review* 1, 1 (Jan. 1, 1812): 1–25; Andrews Norton, "Letter to the Rev. Dr. Holmes at Cambridge," ibid. 3, 2 (April 1, 1813): 299–307; "Reply of the Rev. Dr. Holmes to the Preceding Letter," ibid., 312–15, esp. 312–13. On the liberals (Unitarians), see Wright, *The Beginnings of Unitarianism in America* (1955); Howe, *The Unitarian Conscience* (1988; orig. pub. 1970); Wright, ed., *American Unitarianism, 1805–1865* (1989); Wright, *The Unitarian Controversy* (1994).
3. On the Transcendentalists, see esp. Miller, ed., *The Transcendentalists* (1950) and Gura, *American Transcendentalism* (2007). On biblical criticism in nineteenth-century New England, see Brown, *The Rise of Biblical Criticism in America, 1800–1870* (1969); Gura, *The Wisdom of Words* (1981), chap. 1; Grosin, *Transcendentalist Hermeneutics* (1991); Hurth, *Between Faith and Unbelief* (2007). On the "higher criticism" of the Bible more broadly, see esp. Frei, *The Eclipse of Biblical Narrative* (1974); see also Cameron, *Biblical Higher Criticism and the Defense of Infallibilism in 19th Century Britain* (1987).
4. Paine's *Age of Reason* had also attacked Christianity using the prophecies.
5. English, *Grounds*, 78, 182, 165.
6. William Ellery Channing, *Two Sermons on Infidelity, Delivered October 14, 1813* (Boston, 1813), 28, 20, 30–31.
7. Samuel Cary, *Review of a Book Entitled, "The Grounds of Christianity Examined"* (Boston, 1813); [George Bethune English], *A Letter to the Reverend Mr. Cary, Containing Remarks upon His Review of the Grounds of Christianity Examined* (Boston, 1813), 12.
8. Edward Everett, *A Defence of Christianity, against the Work of George B. English* (Boston, 1814), 240, 241, 424.
9. Everett, *Defence*, 302, 243, 126, 239, 479; Cary, *Review*, 37.
10. "Review: *A Defence of Christianity*...by Edward Everett," *Christian Disciple* 2, 12 (Dec. 2, 1814): 369–74, esp. 372, 374, 373. "Professorship of Greek Literature in Harvard University," *North American Review* 1, 1 (May 1815): 127–30.
11. *A List of the Winners of Academic Distinctions in Harvard College* (Cambridge, Mass., 1907), 21; "Review: *A Defence of Christianity*," *Christian Disciple*, 371–72; [Andrews Norton], [Review of George Bethune English, *The Grounds of Christianity Examined*; Samuel Cary, *Review*; William Ellery Channing, *Two Sermons on Infidelity*; and George Bethune English, *A Letter to the Rev. Mr. Cary*], *General Repository and Review* 4, 2 (Oct. 1, 1813): 299–312, esp. 302, 312; English, *Letter to the Reverend Mr. Cary*, 8–9; Sharples, ed., *Records of the Church of Christ at Cambridge in New England, 1632–1830* (1906), 389–90, 392–94; U.S. Marine Corps., "List of Officers," *Lancaster Journal*, May 2, 1817, 3; Samuel Lorenzo Knapp, "George Bethune English," in Knapp, *American Biography*, pt. 6, *The Treasury of Knowledge* (New York, 1833), 92–98, rpt. in Popkin, *Disputing Christianity*, 233–46.

12. "Review," *Christian Disciple*, 371; "George B. English," *Essex Register*, July 6, 1822, 2; "English," *American Mercury*, July 22, 1822, 2; "George Bethune English," *Rhode-Island American*, Oct. 7, 1828, 1; English, *A Narrative of the Expedition to Dongola and Sennaar; under the Command of His Excellence Ismael Pasha, Undertaken by Order of His Highness Mehemmed Ali Pasha, Viceroy of Egypt* (London, 1822; Boston, 1823). For other discussions or mentions of English in the press, see *Alexandria Herald*, Feb. 5, 1819, 2; *Christian Messenger*, Feb. 10, 1819, 3; *Newburyport Herald*, Feb. 19, 1819, 1; *Franklin Monitor*, Feb. 20, 1819, 3; "George B. English," *Journal of Literature and Politics*, July 20, 1822, 1; "George B. English," *Village Register*, Aug. 2, 1822, 2; "Mr. George Bethune English," *Boston Commercial Gazette*, Nov. 18, 1822, 1; "The Apostate," *Alexandria Herald*, Nov. 25, 1822, 2; "George B. English's Narrative," *Haverhill Gazette*, March 1, 1823, 2; "The Jews," *Farmer's Cabinet*, May 15, 1824, 1; *Essex Register*, April 7, 1825, 2; "Mr. George B. English," *National Gazette*, May 10, 1828, 1; "George Bethune English," *Essex Gazette*, Oct. 4, 1828, 2; "George Bethune English," *Salem Gazette*, Oct. 7, 1828, 1. On English's career after leaving Massachusetts, see Heyrman, *American Apostles* (2015), 61–63, 147–48, 173–82, and 185–88.
13. "Review," *Christian Disciple*, 374; Edward Everett to Alexander Hill Everett, Gottingen, Jan. 5, 1816, Everett Papers, Box 1, Folder 2 (microfilm roll 1); see also Brown, *Rise of Biblical Criticism in America*, 40; and Hurth, *Between Faith and Unbelief*, 13.
14. Everett, Letter to A. H. Everett; George Bethune English, *Five Pebbles from the Brook: A Reply to "A Defence of Christianity" Written by Edward Everett* (Philadelphia, 1824). The errata page describes this book, which mostly just reiterated English's position, as being "written in little more than three weeks at Cairo, amidst the hurry and bustle of my preparations to accompany Ismael Pasha to the Upper Nile." On Everett's later career, see Frothingham, *Edward Everett, Orator and Statesman* (1925) and Varg, *Edward Everett* (1992).
15. On Bancroft, see Brown, *Rise of Biblical Criticism in America*, 43; on Bancroft and William Emerson, see Hurth, *Between Faith and Unbelief*, 6–13, and esp. Bosco and Myerson, *The Emerson Brothers* (2006), esp. chap. 2, "William in Germany." George Ticknor, too, was shocked to find Eichhorn challenging the historical reliability of the Gospels and treating Christ as a figure little different from Socrates (see Hurth, *Between Faith and Unbelief*, 10–11).
16. Andrews Norton, *The Evidences of the Genuineness of the Gospels* (Boston, 1837–44). On Norton and Stewart, see esp. Brown, *Rise of Biblical Criticism in America*, chaps. 2 and 3. Brown suggests that Thomas Carlyle dubbed Norton the "Unitarian Pope" (76); Grodzins, in *American Heretic* (2002), 83, says his students secretly called him that and "his Highness."
17. Andrews Norton, *A Discourse on the Latest Form of Infidelity* (Cambridge, Mass., 1839). For Norton on the Old Testament prophecies, see Grodzins, *American Heretic*, 48.
18. G[eorge] R[ipley], "The Rationale of Religious Enquiry," *Christian Examiner* 21, 2 (Nov. 1836): 225–54, esp. 225 ("degraded," "idea of infusing," "withered form"), 226 ("encrusted"), 227 ("hard to imagine"), 247 ("the fancies"), 250 ("fallacy"), 251 ("error"). On Ripley, see Crowe, *George Ripley* (1967), esp. chap. 5, "The Ripley-Norton Controversy."
19. Ripley, "Rationale of Religious Enquiry," 247, 250.
20. Andrews Norton, [Letter to the Editor], *Boston Daily Advertiser*, Nov. 5, 1836, rpt. in Meyerson, ed., *Transcendentalism* (2000), 161–62, esp. 162; Norton, *Discourse on the Latest Form of Infidelity*, 4–15.
21. George Ripley, "To Andrews Norton," *Boston Daily Advertiser*, Nov. 9, 1836, in Miller, ed., *The Transcendentalists*, 160–63, esp. 162 ("age of skepticism," "evidence of miracles"), 163 ("Locke"); [George Ripley], *"The Latest Form of Infidelity" Examined. A Letter to Mr. Andrews Norton* (Boston, 1839), 12, 35, 55.
22. George Ripley, *Discourses on the Philosophy of Religion, Addressed to Doubters Who Wish to Believe* (Boston, 1836), 11n, 35.
23. Norton, *Discourse on the Latest Form of Infidelity*, 8; Ripley, *"The Latest Form of Infidelity" Examined*, 106.
24. Norton, *Discourse on the Latest Form of Infidelity*, 33, 34, 54, 56–57.
25. Ripley, *"The Latest Form of Infidelity" Examined*, 107, 108, 112, 11.
26. Norton, *Discourse on the Latest Form of Infidelity*, 53. See also Andrews Norton, *Remarks on a Pamphlet Entitled "'The Latest Form of Infidelity' Examined* (Cambridge, Mass., 1839); A[ndrews] N[orton], introductory note, *Two Articles from the Princeton Review concerning the Transcendental Philosophy of the Germans* (Cambridge, Mass., 1840); George Ripley, *Defence of "'The Latest Form of Infidelity' Examined": A Second Letter to Mr. Andrews Norton* (Boston,

1840); George Ripley, *Defence of "'The Latest Form of Infidelity' Examined": A Third Letter to Mr. Andrews Norton* (Boston, 1840).
27. Levi Blodgett [Theodore Parker], *The Previous Question between Mr. Andrews Norton and His Alumni Moved and Handled in a Letter to All Those Gentlemen* (1840), in Meyerson, ed., *Transcendentalism*, 260–80; Theodore Parker, *Discourse on the Transient and the Permanent in Christianity* (Boston, 1841). On Parker, see esp. Grodzins, *American Heretic*.
28. Parker, *Transient and the Permanent*, 13, 15, 14, 14–15, 18.
29. Parker, *Transient and the Permanent*, 12.
30. J. H. Fairchild, Thos. Davis, and Z. B. C. Dunham, "The New Christianity," [Philadelphia] *North American*, June 18, 1841, an account summarizing and condemning Parker's sermon as preached, by three ministers, first published in the Baptist *Christian Watchman*; [Review of *A Discourse on the Transient and Permanent in Christianity*], *Monthly Miscellany of Religion and Letters* 5, 1 (July 1841): 45–47; "A Discourse on the Transient and Permanent in Christianity," *Christian Examiner and General Review* 31, 1 (Sept. 1841): 98–116, esp. 114; "A Review of the Rev. Mr. Parker's Discourse," *Oliver's Magazine* 1, 1 (Oct. 1841): 1–11, esp. 2, 8; "Mr. Parker's Discourse," *Christian Review* 7, 26 (June 1, 1842): 161–81, esp. 162–64; Theodore Parker, *A Discourse of Matters pertaining to Religion* (Boston, 1842); S. O., "Parker's Discourse," *Monthly Miscellany of Religion and Letters* 7, 3 (Sept. 1842): 144–51, esp. 149. See also "The South Boston Ordination Sermon," *Boston Courier*, June 17, 1841, 1; Theodore Parker, "A Letter to the Editors of the Register Touching Their Strictures on My Late Discourse," *Christian Register and Boston Observer* 20, 27 (July 3, 1841): 106; "Polemics," *Boston Courier*, July 12, 1841, 4; "Mr. Parker's Discourse," *Salem Gazette*, Aug. 17, 1841, 1; and Noah Porter Jr., "Transcendentalism," *American Biblical Repository* 9, 3 (July 1842): 195–218. The comparison of Paine and Parker would continue after the latter's death: see "Paine and Parker, No. 1," *Boston Recorder*, Sept. 20, 1860, 150.
31. James Walker, *Unitarianism Vindicated against the Charge of Skeptical Tendencies* (Boston, 1839), 20 ("latent and passive"); James Barr Walker, *Philosophy of Skepticism and Ultraism, Wherein the Opinions of the Rev. Theodore Parker and Other Writers Are Shown to be Inconsistent with Sound Reason and the Christian Religion* (New York and Cincinnati, 1857), 120.
32. [Richard Hildreth], *A Letter to Andrews Norton, on Miracles as the Foundation of Religious Faith* (Boston, 1840), 3, 24, 19. On Hildreth see Emerson, *Richard Hildreth* (1946); Pingel, *An American Utilitarian* (1948). A version of this paragraph also appeared in Grasso, "The Religious and the Secular in the Early Republic" (2016).
33. Richard Hildreth, *My Connection with the Atlas Newspaper; Including a Sketch of the History of the Armory Hall Party of 1838, and an Account of the Senatorial and Representative Elections in the City of Boston for the Year 1839* (Boston, 1839).
34. Richard Hildreth, trans., *Theory of Legislation by Jeremy Bentham: Translated from the French of Etienne Dumont* (London, 1864; orig. pub. Boston, 1840), iii, 18, 19. On Bentham, see Crimmins, *Secular Utilitarianism* (1990); McKown, *Behold the Antichrist* (2004); and Schofield, *Bentham* (2009).
35. Richard Hildreth to Caroline Weston, Georgetown, Demerara [Guyana, South America], Jan. 8, 1841, Caroline Weston Correspondence, Boston Public Library; and see Emerson, *Richard Hildreth*, 97–99.
36. Richard Hildreth, *Theory of Morals: An Inquiry concerning the Law of Moral Distinctions and the Variations and Contradictions of Ethical Codes* (Boston, 1844), esp. 48.
37. Hildreth, *Theory of Morals*, 111, 126, 127, 128n.
38. [Orestes Brownson], "Theory of Morals," *Brownson's Quarterly Review* 1, 3 (July 1844): 328–49, esp. 328; "Theory of Morals," *North American Review* 60, 127 (April 1845): 393–403, esp. 399; Richard Hildreth, *A Joint Letter to Orestes A. Brownson and the Editor of the North American Review* [1844], 20, 21.
39. Hildreth, *Theory of Morals*, 262; Hildreth, *Joint Letter*, 29.
40. Richard Hildreth, *Despotism in America; or, An Inquiry into the Nature and Results of the Slaveholding System in the United States* (Boston, 1840); Richard Hildreth, *The Slave: or Memoirs of Archy Moore* (Boston, 1836); Richard Hildreth, *Archy Moore, the White Slave; or, Memoirs of a Fugitive: With a New Introduction, Prepared for This Edition* (New York, 1856); "Can Any True Whig Vote for Richard Hildreth?" *Boston Courier*, Nov. 11, 1839, 1; Emerson, *Richard Hildreth*, 65–66, 130–31. The first three volumes of his *History of the United States*

(covering 1497–1798) were published in 1849; the second three (1788–1821), in 1851–52. See also [Richard Hildreth], *Native Americanism, Detected and Exposed* (Boston, 1845) and Richard Hildreth, *The Theory of Politics: An Inquiry into the Foundations of Governments and the Causes and Progress of Political Revolutions* (New York, 1853).

41. Theodore Parker, *Sermons of Theism, Atheism, and the Popular Theology* (Boston, 1853), esp. xxvi. On Parker's turn to abolitionism, see Grodzins, *American Heretic*, 333–40, 471–75, 498; on Hildreth, abolitionism, and Parker in the 1840s, see Emerson, *Richard Hildreth*, 128–32, and [Hildreth], "Has Slavery in the United States a Legal Basis?" *Massachusetts Quarterly Review* 1, 2 (March 1848): 145–67, and 1, 3 (June 1848): 273–93; "The Legality of American Slavery," *Massachusetts Quarterly Review* 1, 5 (Dec. 1848): 32–39.

42. [Richard Hildreth], "The Limping Philosopher, No. 2," *New-England Magazine* 1, 4 (Oct. 1831): 307–11, esp. 308, 310, 311; Richard Hildreth to Andrew Preston Peabody, Oct. 1, 1851, Collections of the Pennsylvania Historical Society, quoted in Emerson, *Richard Hildreth*, 121.

Part Three

1. Origen Bacheler and Robert Dale Owen, *Discussion on the Existence of God and the Authenticity of the Bible, between Origen Bacheler and Robert Dale Owen*, 2nd ed. (New York, 1833), 2:152, 29.
2. Kate, "Reform," *Lowell Offering* 5 (March 1845): 6–69, esp. 66; "Reform," *Mechanic's Advocate* 1, 25 (May 20, 1847): 1. On socioeconomic change in this period, see Sellers, *The Market Revolution* (1991); "A Symposium on Charles Sellers, *The Market Revolution*" (1992); Stokes and Conway, *The Market Revolution in America* (1996); and Larson, *The Market Revolution in America* (2010). For general discussions of antebellum reform, see esp. Walters, *American Reformers, 1815–1860* (1978); Abzug, *Cosmos Crumbling* (1994); Mintz, *Moralists and Modernizers* (1995); and Garvey, *Creating the Culture of Reform in Antebellum America* (2005). For comparisons to movements outside the United States, see Butler, *Critical Americans* (2007) and Calhoun, *The Roots of Radicalism* (2012).
3. The advertisement for the *Christian Reformer* by Charles Stearns of Boston is discussed in "Reform," *Trumpet and Universalist Magazine* 20, 19 (Oct. 23, 1847): 74.
4. "Reform," *Christian Register* 27, 19 (May 6, 1848): 74; G.W.M., "The Gospel as the Source of Reform Power," *Trumpet and Universalist Magazine* 20, 5 (June 3, 1848): 201.
5. W. H. C. [William Henry Channing], "The Skepticism of the Present Age; Being a Translation of One of the Lectures of M. Jouffroy, in his *Cours de Droit Naturel*," *Christian Examiner and General Review* 25, 2 (Nov. 1838): 137–57, esp. 140, 143, 146, 145. On the reception of Jouffroy's work, see O. A. Brownson, "*Cours de Droit Naturel*," *Christian Examiner and General Review* 22, 2 (May 1837): 181–217; "Jouffroy on Natural Law," *American Jurist and Law Magazine* 13, 35 (Oct. 1837): 11–36; "Channing's Translation of Jouffroy," *Dial: A Magazine for Literature, Philosophy, and Religion* 1, 1 (July 1840): 99–117; on the news that papers left at Jouffrey's death revealed how he had become a skeptical "infidel" after studying with Victor Cousin, see "The Philosopher Cousin, a Teacher of Infidelity," *Christian Reflector* 6, 12 (March 22, 1843): 46; on Brownson's later (post-Catholic conversion) change of heart about Jouffroy, see "*Cours de Droit Naturel*," *Brownson's Quarterly Review* 2, 1 (Jan. 1, 1845): 53–76.
6. "Reform," *American Magazine of Useful and Entertaining Knowledge* 3, 1 (Oct. 1836): 29; "Robert Owen and his Plans," *National Era* 1, 4 (Jan. 28, 1847): 2.

Chapter 9

1. *Evening Post*, quoted in Perkins and Wolfson, *Frances Wright, Free Enquirer* (1939), 232; and see Eckhardt, *Fanny Wright* (1984), 186–87. See also F. W. [Frances Wright, hereafter FW], "Answer to Vindicia," *Free Enquirer* (hereafter *FE*), ser. 2, vol. 1 (March 4, 1829): 151. On Wright generally see also Lane, *Frances Wright and the "Great Experiment"* (1972). On Wright and oratory, see Eastman, *A Nation of Speechifiers* (2009), chap. 6.
2. [William A. Alcott], *My Progress in Error and Recovery to Truth; or, A Tour through Universalism, Unitarianism, and Skepticism* (Boston, 1842). Short articles containing early versions of mate-

rial later incorporated into the book were published as "My Progress in Error," *Boston Recorder* 18, 11 (March 13, 1833): 41; 18, 12 (March 20, 1833): 45–46; 18, 13 (March 27, 1833): 49–50; 18, 14 (April 3, 1833): 33; 18, 15 (April 10, 1833): 37. For biography and bibliography, see "Dr. William A. Alcott," *American Journal of Education* 4, 12 (March 1858): 628–56; see also Orcutt, *History of the Town of Wolcott, Connecticut* (1874). The best discussion of Alcott is in Whorton, *Crusaders for Fitness* (1982), 49–60, 92–134. See also Whorton, "'Christian Physiology'" (1975); Smith-Rosenberg, "Sex as Symbol in Victorian Purity" (1978); Burbick, *Healing the Republic* (1994), 104–11; and Abzug, *Cosmos Crumbling* (1994), chap. 7. None of these authors mentions *My Progress in Error*. The only full-length study is Van Buren, "The Indispensable God of Health" (1977); this work contains useful insights and briefly references *My Progress in Error*, but its heavy-handed application of psychoanalytic theory distorts the relation of religion and reform in Alcott's works.

3. Rose in Doress-Worters, ed., *Mistress of Herself* (2007), 258. *Mistress of Herself*, a good collection of Rose's extant writings, contains, however, only Rose's first address to the Hartford Bible Convention in 1853. For a record of all her remarks there, see *Proceedings of the Hartford Bible Convention* (New York, 1854). On Rose, see Suhl, *Eloquent Crusader* (1970); Kolmerten, *The American Life of Ernestine L. Rose* (1999); and Anderson, *The Rabbi's Atheist Daughter* (2016).

4. FW, "Lecture III," *FE*, ser. 2, vol. 1 (April 15, 1829): 195; FW, "Progress of Principle," *FE*, ser. 2, vol. 2 (May 22, 1830): 238 (other quotations).

5. Post, *Popular Freethought in America, 1825–1850* (1943); Brown and Stein, *Freethought in the United States* (1978), chap. 2.

6. Robert Dale Owen [hereafter RDO], "New Lanark and New Harmony," *FE*, ser. 2, vol. 1 (June 10, 1829): 262; RDO, "Extracts from an Address," *FE*, ser. 2, vol. 1 (Sept. 2, 1829): 353. On Robert Owen and New Harmony, see esp. Bestor Jr., *Backwoods Utopias* (1950); Harrison, *Quest for a New Moral World* (1969); Carmony and Elliott, "New Harmony, Indiana" (1980); Bernard, Owen, and Maclure, "Irreconcilable Opinions" (1988); Kolmerten, *Women in Utopia* (1990); Pitzer, "The New Moral World of Robert Owen and New Harmony," in Pitzer and Boyer, eds., *America's Communal Utopias* (1997); Royle, *Robert Owen and the Commencement of the Millennium* (1998); Donnachie, *Robert Owen* (2000); Jennings, *Paradise Now* (2016), 79–148.

7. Frances Wright D'Arusmont, *Life, Letters, and Lectures, 1834/1844* (New York, 1972), v–vi. This volume reprints her *Course of Popular Lectures* (London, 1834), *Supplement Course of Lectures* (London, 1834), and *Biography, Notes, and Political Lectures* (New York, 1844); the short biography was written by Wright, in the third person.

8. On Wright and Nashoba, see Lane, *Frances Wright*, 22–30; Perkins and Wolfson, *Frances Wright*, 123–207 (on purchase, 141–42); and Eckhardt, *Fanny Wright*, 102–65.

9. "Frances Wright's Establishment," *Genius of Universal Emancipation* 1, 4 (July 28, 1827): 29–30 (James Richardson's letter of June 25, 1827, with extracts from his Nashoba log); see also Perkins and Wolfson, *Frances Wright*, 168.

10. FW, "Explanatory Notes, Respecting the Nature and Objects of the Institution of Nashoba," *New Harmony Gazette* 3, 16 (Jan. 30, 1828): 124–25; 3, 17 (Feb. 6, 1828): 132–33; 3, 18 (Feb. 13, 1828): 140–41, esp. 132, 133, 140. "Explanatory Notes" was also published in *Genius of Universal Emancipation* and the *Correspondent*. Owen's "Oration Containing Declaration of Mental Independence," *New Harmony Gazette* 1, 42 (July 12, 1826): 329–32, and in Gregory Claeys, ed., *Selected Works of Robert Owen*, vol. 2, *The Development of Socialism* (London, 1993), 48–55, had attacked the pernicious trinity that had long plagued mankind: private property, absurd religion, and a marriage doctrine that had resulted from both.

11. "Extract of a Letter to the Editor," *Western Luminary* 4, 37 (March 12, 1828): 292. See also "Philanthropy," *Philadelphia Album and Ladies' Literary Gazette* 2, 46 (April 16, 1828): 364; "Frances Wright's Establishment," *Genius of Universal Emancipation* 1, 7 (Aug. 18, 1827): 54. The failure of the Nashoba experiment was acknowledged in "Communication from the Trustees of Nashoba," *New Harmony Gazette* 3, 22 (March 26, 1828): 172.

12. FW, "An Address," *FE*, ser. 2, vol. 2 (Oct. 31, 1829): 1.

13. Wright D'Arusmont, *Life, Letters, and Lectures*, 40, 41; FW, "Address," *FE*, ser. 2, vol. 2 (Aug. 14, 1830): 330.

14. Wright D'Arusmont, *Life, Letters, and Lectures*, 49 ("MATTER"), 11. First published as *Course of Popular Lectures...with Three Addresses and a Reply to the Charges against the French Reformers of 1789* (New York, 1829).
15. Wright D'Arusmont, *Life, Letters, and Lectures*, 73, 74, 70.
16. Wright D'Arusmont, *Life, Letters, and Lectures*, 97; FW, "Of Religion and Irreligion as Distinct from Knowledge and Morality," *FE*, ser. 2, vol. 1 (July 1, 1829): 284. The commentary on the work of John Rawls is useful for thinking about religion and political liberalism. See esp. Fern, "Religious Belief in a Rawlsian Society" (1987); Weithman, "Rawlsian Liberalism and the Privatization of Religion" (1994); Dombrowski, *Rawls and Religion* (2001); Papastephanou, "The Implicit Assumptions of Dividing a Cake" (2004); Moran, "Religious Reasons and Political Argumentation" (2006); Martin, "Configured for Exclusion" (2007); Zackariasson, "A Critique of Foundationalist Conceptions of Comprehensive Doctrines in the Religion in Politics–Debate" (2009); Wagoner, "Deliberation, Reason, and Indigestion" (2010).
17. Wright D'Arusmont, *Life, Letters, and Lectures*, 67, 68, 144, 145.
18. RDO, "An Urgent Duty," *FE*, ser. 2, vol. 1 (July 8, 1829): 293; "Hall of Science: Continuation of the Debate," *FE*, ser. 2, vol. 2 (Sept. 11, 1830): 368 (debate on the evidence for the divine origin of Christianity).
19. RDO, "To the Editors of the Commercial Advertiser," *FE*, ser. 2, vol. 2 (Nov. 7, 1829): 15; FW quoted by RDO, "To S.," *FE*, ser. 2, vol. 1 (Sept. 9, 1829): 366; FW, "To the People of Pittsburgh," *FE*, ser. 2, vol. 2 (Dec. 26, 1829): 67; FW, "The New York Daily Sentinel," *FE*, ser. 2, vol. 2 (May 22, 1830): 239. (FW was being disingenuous about the *Sentinel*, however; RDO was secretly directing that political paper.) See also FW in her final address of June 1830: "Thus let us associate; not as Jews, not as Christians, not as Deists, not as believers, not as sceptics, not as poor, not as rich, not as artisans, not as merchants, not as lawyers, but as human beings, as fellow creatures, as American citizens, pledged to protect each other's rights—to advance each other's happiness!" FW, "Address," *FE*, ser. 2, vol. 2 (July 31, 1830): 315.
20. On the question of skepticism as sectarianism: Tullus, "A Stumbling Block," *FE*, ser. 2, vol. 2 (Dec. 26, 1829): 68; "RDO, "The Free Enquirer," *FE*, ser. 2, vol. 2 (April 10, 1830): 191–92. Not atheism: RDO, "To Mr. R. in Reply," *FE*, ser. 2, vol. 2 (Jan. 9. 1830): 86; RDO, "To Menzes Rayner," *FE*, ser. 2, vol. 2 (Feb. 6, 1830): 119–20; RDO, "Evidences of Christianity," *FE*, ser. 2, vol. 2 (March 13,1830): 153. RDO calls himself a sceptic: RDO, "Demerit of Unbelief," *FE*, 2, 2 (Aug. 28, 1830): 352. Contrast L. S. Everett, *An Exposure of the Principles of the "Free Inquirers"* (Boston, 1831), 26: "He who does not believe in God, is an *unbeliever*; there is no such thing as neutrality in this case. Skepticism is not the word to be applied to these persons—*they are Infidels.*"
21. "Communications": S. to RDO, *FE*, ser. 2, vol. 1 (Sept. 9, 1829): 363; RDO, "The Spiritual Steeple," *FE*, ser. 2, vol. 2, (Nov. 14, 1829): 22.
22. Wright D'Arusmont, "Opening Address to the Hall of Science" and "Address to Young Mechanics," in *Life, Letters, and Lectures*, 142, 198–99 (quotations); FW, "Editorial: To the Intelligent among the Working Classes; and Generally, to All Honest Reformers," *FE*, ser. 2, vol. 2 (Dec. 5, 1829): 46.
23. FW, "Editorial: To the Intelligent among the Working Classes, 47; Matthew Carey et al., "Situation of the Working Classes, and More Especially of Seamstresses and Others, in Philadelphia," *FE*, ser. 2, vol. 1 (May 6, 1829): 217–18.
24. RDO, "Extracts from an Address," *FE*, ser. 2, vol. 1 (Sept. 2, 1829): 355; FW, "An Address on the State of the Public Mind," *FE*, ser. 2, vol. 2 (July 31, 1830): 313.
25. On the Workingmen's movement in New York City, see Wilentz, *Chants Democratic* (1984).
26. Henry Guyon, quoted in Wilentz, *Chants Democratic*, 208; RDO, "Things Temporal and Spiritual," *FE*, ser. 2, vol. 2 (June 19, 1830): 272. See also "Political Movements of the People," *FE*, ser. 2, vol. 2 (March 20, 1830): 161–64; "Origin of the Workingmen's Party," *FE*, ser. 2, vol. 2 (May 8, 1830): 220–21; RDO, "The Approaching Struggle," *FE*, ser. 2, vol. 3 (Oct. 30, 1830): 8; and RDO, "The Elections," *FE*, ser. 2, vol. 3 (Nov. 13, 1830): 24.
27. FW, "Parting Address as Delivered in the Bowery Theatre, to the People of New York, in June, 1830," *FE*, ser. 2, vol. 2 (Aug. 28, 1830): 347; RDO, "Inroads of Superstition, Calling for Continued Exertions by Freedom's Friends," *FE*, ser. 2, vol. 4 (Nov. 12, 1831): 23; RDO, *An Address on the Influence of the Clerical Profession, as Delivered in the Hall of Science, New York*

(New York, 1833). Owen also published a notable (in many circles at the time, notorious) seventy-two-page pamphlet advocating birth control: *Moral Physiology; or, A Brief and Plain Treatise on the Population Question* (1830).
28. Perkins and Wolfson, *Frances Wright*, 310; Leopold, *Robert Dale Owen* (1940), 111.
29. On Graham, see esp. Nissenbaum, *Sex, Diet, and Debility in Jacksonian America* (1980); see also Tompkins, "Sylvester Graham's Imperial Dietetics" (2009).
30. [William A. Alcott], *Confessions of a School Master* (Andover, Mass., 1839); [William A. Alcott], *Forty Years in the Wilderness of Pills and Powders; or, The Cogitations of an Aged Physician* (Boston, 1859). Alcott intended *Forty Years* to be published anonymously like *Confessions* and *My Progress and Error*, but he died as the book was about to go to press, and the published version, though still lacking his name on the title page, has his portrait as its frontispiece.
31. Smith-Rosenberg, "Sex as Symbol," S220.
32. Alcott, *Confessions of a School Master*, 121 ("parental"). Van Buren, "The Indispensable God of Health," (over)emphasizes the tension between Alcott and his father. Alcott, in *Familiar Letters to Young Men on Various Subjects* (Buffalo, N.Y., 1850) 290, described skeptics as anxious and fretful: skeptics "are the last men to trust, or be trusted. Doubting and distrusting heaven, they doubt and distrust every thing else. They are timid, fearful, irresolute and capricious. They are fretful, moreover, beyond other men. There is fretfulness enough every where; but it grows in richest profusion in the hot-bed of practical skepticism."
33. Alcott, *My Progress in Error*, 17, 11, 14; *Forty Years*, 1–2. The Revolutionary War veteran goes unnamed in *My Progress*, but I am assuming this is the same friend of the family, Sergeant K., mentioned in *Forty Years* (58). Sergeant K. also seems to be fictionalized as "Capt. Simonds" in Alcott, *The Mother in the Family; or, Sayings and Doings at Rose Hill Cottage* (Boston, 1838) chap. 14. On William Alcott's letters with his cousin Bronson, see *The Letters of A. Bronson Alcott*, ed. Herrnstadt (1969), 3–5, 9–12, 75–77; "Eighty-Six Letters of A. Bronson Alcott (Part One)," *Studies in the American Renaissance* (1979): 239–308, esp. 264, 267–71. On the relationship between the two cousins, see esp. Dahlstrand, *Amos Bronson Alcott* (1982). For a detailed account of the two churches in Wolcott, see Orcutt, *History of the Town of Wolcott*.
34. Alcott, *My Progress in Error*, 14, 15.
35. Alcott, *Confessions of a School Master*, esp. 177. On education reform in New England before Horace Mann in 1837, see Gordon, "Patriots and Christians" (1978).
36. Alcott, *Confessions of a School Master*, 232; Alcott, *My Progress in Error*, 21; William A. Alcott, *Charles Hartland, the Village Missionary* (Boston, 1839).
37. Alcott, *My Progress in Error*, 230, 11–12. On Alcott joining the Congregational society, see also Orcutt, *History of the Town of Wolcott*, 271.
38. Alcott, *My Progress in Error*, 135, 118, 36, 68, 52, 88–89n. On the Fall as allegory, see also [Alcott], "My Progress in Error," *Boston Recorder* 18, 15 (April 3, 1833): 33.
39. Alcott, *My Progress in Error*, 130–31.
40. Alcott, *Forty Years in the Wilderness*. On tobacco, see also Alcott, *The Use of Tobacco: Its Physical, Intellectual, and Moral Effects on the Human System*, 3rd ed. (Boston, 1848). On poisonous beverages, see also Alcott, *Tea and Coffee* (Boston, 1839). On diet, see also Alcott, *Vegetable Diet, as Sanctioned by Medical Men* (Boston, 1838). On masturbation (the "solitary vice"), see Alcott, *The Young Man's Guide*, 2nd ed. (Boston, 1834), 306–14.
41. Alcott, *Forty Years in the Wilderness*, 72, 73, 74, 75.
42. Alcott, *Forty Years in the Wilderness*, 77.
43. Alcott, *My Progress in Error*, 61, 62, 69.
44. Alcott, *My Progress in Error*, 150, 151, 157, 149.
45. Alcott, *My Progress in Error*, 120, 117, 132.
46. Alcott, *My Progress in Error*, 121, 148.
47. Alcott, *My Progress in Error*, 159.
48. Alcott, *My Progress in Error*, 166, 163–64.
49. Alcott, *My Progress in Error*, 167–68.
50. Alcott, *My Progress in Error*, 168, 166, 169.
51. Alcott, *My Progress in Error*, 169, 170; Thomas Chalmers, *The Evidence and Authority of the Christian Revelation* (Hartford, Conn., 1816; orig. pub. Edinburgh, 1814).
52. Alcott, *My Progress in Error*, 172.

53. Alcott, *Confessions of a School Master*, 235: William A. Alcott, *An Address Delivered before the American Physiological Society* (Boston, 1837), 21–22. On Alcott on slavery, see also "A Chapter for Parents," *Moral Reformer and Teacher on the Human Constitution* 1 (March 1835): 77. In *The Young Husband*, 6th ed. (Boston, 1842), 102–3, Alcott argues that reform efforts from the perspective of "perverted" or unredeemed nature begin by trying to work on the masses and then move down the scale to communities, and then to individual families. "But Christianity... reverses this order, and sets everything right." On health reform as a social and political panacea, see Burbick, *Healing the Republic*, 111: "The body becomes the means to discover social laws and to create social order. Its 'constitution' is quite literally what will preserve the union."
54. William A. Alcott, *Essay on the Construction of School-Houses* (Boston, 1832). On the sale of *The Young Man's Guide* freeing Alcott from debt, see "Dr. William A. Alcott," 651.
55. On the book trade, see esp. Green, "The Rise of Book Publishing," in Kelley and Gross, eds., *A History of the Book in America*, vol. 2 (2010); Zboray and Zboray, "The Boston Book Trades, 1789–1850" in Wright and Viens, eds., *Entrepreneurs* (1997); Casper, introduction to Casper et al., eds., *The History of the Book in America*, vol. 3 (2007). On reading in the countryside, see Gilmore, *Reading Becomes a Necessity of Life* (1989). On the middle class, see esp. Ryan, *Cradle of the Middle Class* (1981); Halttunen, *Confidence Men and Painted Women* (1982); and Blumin, *The Emergence of the Middle Class* (1989). See also Bledstein, introduction to Bledstein and Johnston, eds., *The Middling Sorts* (2001); Applegate, "Henry Ward Beecher and the 'Great Middle Class,'" in ibid.; López and Weinstein, introduction to López and Weinstein, eds., *The Making of the Middle Class* (2012); Gunn, "Between Modernity and Backwardness," in ibid.
56. Alcott, *The Young Man's Guide*, 248; *The Young Husband*, 248; *Gift Book for Young Men* (New York, 1856) 4. See also Alcott, preface to *Home-Book of Life and Health* (Boston, 1858), for comments on his middle style. His *Living on Small Means: A Cheap Manual on Health and Economy* (Boston), written in the panic year of 1837, was directed toward "the poorer and middling classes of society" (137). On the American Physiological Society, see Nissenbaum, *Sex, Diet, and Debility*, 144. On hybrid provincial sociability, see Kelly, "'Well Bred Country People'" (1999). On the limits of middle-class sensibility in rural New England in the same period, see Hansen, *A Very Social Time* (1994).
57. William A. Alcott, *The Young Woman's Guide to Excellence* (Boston, 1840), 97. On Alcott joining Beecher's former church in May 1833, see *The Articles of Faith and Covenant of the Bowdoin Street Church, Boston, Massachusetts* (Boston, 1837), 40. Alcott may have heard Beecher preach in Wolcott years before (1814) on "the insidious influence of infidel philosophy" (see Orcutt, *History of the Town of Wolcott*, 86). On Catharine Beecher, see Sklar, *Catharine Beecher* (1973).
58. William A. Alcott, "The Past and the Future," in Alcott, ed., *Moral Reformer and Teacher on the Human Constitution* (Feb. 1836): 37–45, esp. 38 and 41; William A. Alcott, *The Young House-Keeper* (Boston, 1838), 3. On the importance of the family, see also Alcott, *The Moral Philosophy of Courtship and Marriage* (Boston, 1857), 15. On political argument as a waste of time, see also Alcott, "Prevention," in Alcott, ed., *Teacher of Health, and the Laws of the Human Constitution* (March 1843): 83–85.
59. William A. Alcott, *The Laws of Health* (Boston, 1856). Van Buren, "The Indispensable God of Health," 165, describes Alcott as advocating only a "graceless moralism."
60. On the limits of the analogy between the two sets of laws, see Alcott, *My Progress in Error*, 184–85; on the lack of atonement for violations of the physical law, see Alcott, *Laws of Health*, 11. Although he wrote that Christ would not atone for violations of physical laws, the two realms were not unrelated: "We believe that man's body, as the habitation of the immortal spirit, is included in the great work of redemption; and until his body is trained as it should be—until physical education is conducted on the strict principles of anatomy and physiology—man cannot be in the fullest sense redeemed or happy." William A. Alcott, "Advertisement," in Alcott, ed., *The Library of Health and Teacher on the Human Constitution* (Boston, 1837): 10–11.
61. Alcott, *My Progress in Error*, 198. On hygiene and health as means to promote the ultimate end of moral and spiritual advancement, see also Alcott, "Physical Education," *Teacher of Health, and the Laws of the Human Constitution*, n.s., 1, 1 (Jan. 1843): [9].

62. Alcott, *My Progress in Error*, 180, 204. On Alcott and the devil, see also Alcott, *The Story of Ananias and Sapphira* (New York, 1845), 57, where he argues that those who deny that the devil is a person by the same logic could deny that the deity was one, and they also set aside the teachings of the scriptures.
63. Alcott, *Forty Years in the Wilderness*, 74; Alcott, *My Progress in Error*, 203. On his opium addiction, see *Forty Years*, 194. The mountaintop scene fits Abzug's interpretation of Alcott as "Mosaic lawgiver" (*Cosmos Crumbling*, 172); Wharton, in *Crusaders for Fitness*, 54, calls the mountaintop scene "garishly melodramatic." On Alcott on independence and dependence, see also "July and Independence," *Moral Reformer and Teacher on the Human Constitution*, July 1835, 197–98, 201; "On Mobs," ibid., Oct. 1835, 314; "Levelling," ibid., Nov. 1835, 331; and Alcott, *Familiar Letters*, 45–60.
64. Alcott, *My Progress in Error*, 30, 31, 197, 200–201, 203, 303–4. Alcott may have also seen a covenant renewal; the Rev. Erastus Scranton's journal describes one occurring at a conference meeting of the town's Congregational church in early May 1828 (Orcutt, *History of the Town of Wolcott*, 104–8). Van Buren, "The Indispensable God of Health," 160, thinks that Alcott's conversion to body reform (marked by his mountaintop declaration) and his conversion to Christianity happened at the same time, but textual evidence indicates that the former occurred about 1826 and the later about 1832.
65. William A. Alcott, *Travels of Our Savior* (Boston, 1840), 138, 286. On his recommended (in) frequency of marital sexual intercourse, see Alcott, *The Physiology of Marriage* (Boston, 1856), 114–28. Alcott focused on moral practice, not the inner experience of faith, but not to devalue the latter. In his *Life of Robert Morrison, the First Protestant Missionary to China* (New York, 1856), 15, he merely notes that his subject had a conversion experience and moves on, rather than choosing to dwell on the (admittedly formulaic) account in his source material, [Eliza A. Morrison, comp.], *The Life and Labours of Robert Morrison, D.D.* (London, 1839), 3–5. In his Sunday school literature, Alcott often inserted lessons on manners and hygiene into his Bible stories. See, for example, *The First Foreign Mission; or, Journey of Paul and Barnabas* (Boston, 1834); *The Young Missionary: Exemplified in the Life of Timothy* (Boston, 1837); and *Jesus at Nain; or, The Widow's Son Raised* (Boston, 1839). On the self-regulation of small things in "the formation of virtuous, and even of holy character," see Alcott, *The Young Mother*, 2nd ed. (Boston, 1836), 23.
66. Alcott, *My Progress in Error*, 231, 221.
67. Alcott, *Familiar Letters to Young Men*, 112; Alcott, *My Progress in Error*, 211, 230–31.
68. "Editor's Table," *Harper's New Monthly Magazine* 7, 39 (August 1853): [415]–18. On *Harper's* and nationalism, see Lilly, "The National Archive" (2005).
69. "A Review of Harper's Editorial," *New York Reformer*, rpt. in *Liberator* (Sept. 9, 1853): 144.
70. "Anti-Bible Convention," *Gospel Banner*, rpt. in *Liberator* 23, 24 (June 17, 1853): 96; "The Anti-Bible Convention at Hartford, Conn.," *New York Tribune*, rpt. in *Daily Scioto Gazette*, June 8, 1853, 2; Antelope, "Letter from New York," *Daily Picayune*, June 11, 1853, 1 ("There is not a person"); "The Convention of Infidels," *New York Times*, June 7, 1853, 4 ("wildest rant"). The *New York Herald* in particular was practiced at mocking and attacking reformers' conventions; see Kolmerten, *American Life of Ernestine L. Rose*, 81, 100, 114.
71. *New York Herald*, "Anti-Bible Convention," rpt. in *Liberator* 23, 24 (June 17, 1853): 96; "The Convention of Infidels," *New York Times*, June 7, 1853, 4; "Anti-Bible Convention," *New York Observer*, rpt. in *Liberator* (June 17, 1853): 96. On the call for participants, see "The Bible Convention," *Liberator* 23, 21 (May 27, 1853): 93; *Daily Ohio Statesman*, April 16, 1853, 3; A. J. Davis, "The Hartford Bible Convention," *Hartford Times*, rpt. in *Liberator* (June 1, 1853): 2. For the text of the call and the list of endorsers, see *Proceedings of the Hartford Bible Convention*, [9]–12, esp. [9]–10. One signer each was from Missouri, Alabama, and Vermont. Thirty-one women signed; thirty-five signers used initials rather than first or middle names, so their gender is unknown.
72. See esp. Delp, "A Spiritualist in Connecticut" (1980). On Spiritualism, see Braude, *Radical Spirits* (1989); Carroll, *Spiritualism in Antebellum America* (1997); Cox, *Body and Soul* (2003); and McGarry, *Ghosts of Futures Past* (2008).
73. "Spirit Rappings," *Litchfield Republican*, June 9, 1853, 2; *Proceedings of the Hartford Bible Convention*, 21. See also "Anti-Bible Convention," *Constitution*, June 15, 1853, 2: "The men

who head this infidel movement are the leaders of the spirit rapping delusion in this part of the country." The published *Proceedings* that appeared in 1854, however, might have reinforced the false impression of Spiritualists dominating the convention conversation: the book was distributed by a firm, Partridge & Brittan, that published Spiritualist works, it carried ads for some of them, and it featured an appendix in which alleged spirits, through the medium C. Hammond, made some vague comments in response to the convention.

74. "The Anti-Bible Convention at Hartford, Conn.," *New York Tribune*, rpt. in [Chillicothe, Ohio] *Daily Scioto Gazette*, June 8, 1853, 3; "The Hartford Ismite Convention," *New York Herald*, rpt. in *Liberator* (June 17, 1853): 96; *Proceedings of the Hartford Convention*, 27.
75. *Proceedings of the Hartford Convention*, 153, 187, 298. Garrison became very interested in Spiritualism; Rose considered it nonsense. See Kolmerten, *American Life of Ernestine L. Rose*, 154–55.
76. "Anti-Bible Convention," *Portsmouth Journal*, rpt. in *Liberator* 23, 24 (June 17, 1853): 96; "Anti-Bible Convention," *Hartford Courant*, rpt. in *Liberator* 23, 24 (June 17, 1853): 96; "The Bible Convention," *Liberator* 23, 23 (June 10, 1853): 90.
77. *Proceedings of the Hartford Convention*, 339, 171. On Garrison's religious change, see Van Deburg, "William Lloyd Garrison and the 'Pro-Slavery Priesthood'" (1975).
78. *Proceedings of the Hartford Convention*, 178; see also 180, 351–55, and "The Bible Convention at Hartford," *Liberator* 23, 24 (June 17, 1853): 95. On press silence, see also "Anti-Bible Convention," *New York Evangelist* 24, 23 (June 9, 1853): 91: "Silence was the most fitting and considerate treatment they could receive"; Antelope, "Letter from New York," *Daily Picayune*, June 11, 1853, 1: "And why, I ask, should the respectable newspaper press of the United States countenance them by even the slightest mention in their respective journals? If such fanatical meetings, women's conventions and like assemblages, where only blasphemy and ridicule of the laws of God and man is uttered, were never alluded to in the least by the press, such meetings would soon receive their quietus."
79. "Anti-Bible Convention," *Constitution*, June 15, 1853, 2; "The Bible Convention," *Republican Farmer*, June 14, 1853, 2; "Anti-Bible Convention," *Hartford Courant*, rpt. in *Liberator* 23, 24 (June 17, 1853): 96.
80. *Proceedings of the Hartford Convention*, 268.
81. *Proceedings of the Hartford Convention*, 268. The convention recorder, Andrew J. Graham, tried to record the event "phonographically"—that is, creating a transcript that preserved the sounds in the hall: the audience response as well as the speaker's words (*Proceedings*, title page). The correspondent for the *New York Herald* also attempted this for portions of Rose's speeches and for a few other moments in the convention ("The Hartford Ismite Convention," *New York Herald*, rpt. in *Liberator* [June 17, 1853]: 96). Rose described the crowd of 1,600 in her letter to the editor, *Hartford Courant*, June 29, 1853, in Doress-Worters, ed., *Mistress of Herself*, 145–46.
82. *Proceedings of the Hartford Convention*, 269.
83. *Proceedings of the Hartford Convention*, 270.
84. *Proceedings of the Hartford Convention*, 270, 271; "Hartford Ismite Convention."
85. *Proceedings of the Hartford Convention*, 272. Rose discussed themes she would develop further in *A Defense of Atheism, Being a Lecture Delivered in Mercantile Hall, Boston, April 10, 1861* (Boston, 1861). As a child, Rose had studied what Christians called the Old Testament in Hebrew, with her father.
86. *Proceedings of the Hartford Convention*, 273.
87. *Proceedings of the Hartford Convention*, 274; "Hartford Ismite Convention."
88. *Proceedings of the Hartford Convention*, 274, 275.
89. "Hartford Ismite Convention," and see *Proceedings of the Hartford Convention*, 275.
90. *Proceedings of the Hartford Convention*, 277, 278; "Hartford Ismite Convention."
91. *Proceedings of the Hartford Convention*, 279; "Hartford Ismite Convention."
92. *Proceedings of the Hartford Convention*, 305, 306.
93. *Proceedings of the Hartford Convention*, 319, 320, 321.
94. *Proceedings of the Hartford Convention*, 321, 322, 323, 324, 333.
95. *Proceedings of the Hartford Convention*, 331, 337, 338.
96. *Proceedings of the Hartford Convention*, 369, 370; "Hartford Ismite Convention."

Chapter 10

1. John Barton Derby, *Political Reminiscences, Including a Sketch of the Origin and History of the "Statesman Party" of Boston* (Boston, 1835), 98, 143; "Lectures on Catholicism: Its Influence on Republican Institutions," *Christian Watchman* 11, 52 (Dec. 24, 1830): 206 (discussion of Beecher's four lectures); Lyman Beecher, *Lectures on Scepticism, Delivered in Park Street Church, Boston, and in the Second Presbyterian Church, Cincinnati* (Cincinnati, 1835) (lectures first delivered 1831); Patkus, "A Community in Transition" (1997), 44–45 (population figures); Rev. Dr. O'Flaherty, "Sunday Evening Catholic Lecture," *Jesuit* 2, 22 (Jan. 29, 1831): 173–75, esp. 173. On the Catholic response to Beecher in the *Jesuit*, see also [No title], 2, 18 (Jan. 1, 1831): 141; "Dialogue VI," ibid., 143; "The Catholic Lectures," 2, 21 (Jan. 22, 1831): 164–65, and Patkus, "Community in Transition," 231.
2. On Brownson, see Schlesinger, *Orestes A. Brownson* (1963; orig. pub. 1939), still a fine study of Brownson's radical period; Gilmore, "Orestes Brownson and New England Religious Culture, 1803–1827" (1971); Gilhooley, *Contradiction and Dilemma* (1972); Ryan, *Orestes A. Brownson* (1976); Griffioen, *Orestes Brownson and the Problem of Revelation* (2003); Carey, *Orestes A. Brownson* (2004); Hughes, *Becoming Brownson* (2016). Butler's *In Search of the American Spirit* (1992) applauds Brownson's later religious and political conservatism. Brownson's early works (to 1844) are available in Patrick W. Carey, ed., *The Early Works of Orestes A. Brownson*, 7 vols. (Milwaukee, 2000–2007); citations here, however, are to the original publications or to the earlier collected *Works*.
3. Brownson himself had trouble characterizing these works. See Brownson, *Charles Elwood, or the Infidel Converted*, in *The Works of Orestes A. Brownson* (New York, 1966; orig. pub. Detroit, 1884), 4:xx; Brownson, *The Spirit-Rapper: An Autobiography*, in *Works* 9:1–234; *The Convert; or, Leaves from My Experience*, in *Works* 5:1–200, esp. 3. These narratives differ from autobiography because their primary aim is not to reveal the self or tell a life story but to illustrate the quest for truth or knowledge and to justify beliefs before the court of reason. They also differ from religious conversion narratives. However linked to spiritual experience, the stories Brownson tells focus more upon providing a rational warrant for a new view of the world as it unfolds than upon pious testimonies about God's gracious acts.
4. Schmitt, "Socializing Epistemology," in Schmitt, ed., *Socializing Epistemology* (1994), 1: "Social epistemology is the conceptual and normative study of the relevance of social relations, roles, interests, and institutions to knowledge. Thus it differs from the sociology of knowledge, which is an empirical study of the contingent social conditions or causes of knowledge or of what passes for knowledge in a society, a study initiated by Karl Mannheim." See also Fuller, *Social Epistemology* (1988); Goldman, "Innovation and Change in the Production of Knowledge" (1995); Kögler, "Alienation as Epistemological Source" (1997); Kögler, "Reconceptualizing Reflexive Sociology" (1997); "Special Issue on Real Knowing: Situating Social Epistemology" (1998); Goldman, *Knowledge in a Social World* (1999).
5. As Bratt has argued, the decade from 1835 to 1845 "is less distinguished by the radical extension of evangelicalism's logic than as the launching ground of new departures." See Bratt, "The Reorientation of American Protestantism, 1835–1845" (1998), esp. 52–53. Alienation from one's taken-for-granted views of the world can lead to a critical reflexivity, where one does not merely question previously held values and goals but analyzes how they are socially generated and personally internalized. See Kögler, "Alienation as Epistemological Source" and "Reconceptualizing Reflexive Sociology."
6. Joshua V. Himes's *Views of the Prophecies and Prophetic Chronology, Selected from the Manuscripts of William Miller, with a Memoir of His Life* (Boston, 1842) and Sylvester Bliss's *Memoirs of William Miller, Generally Known as a Lecturer on the Prophecies, and the Second Coming of Christ* (Boston, 1853) both used Miller's own writings to portray the man and the movement from an Adventist perspective. Kneeland's autobiographical reflections usually appeared as brief editorial asides or in his prefaces to longer works, with two main exceptions: the first was when he played up an early bout of religious skepticism for the sake of *A Series of Letters, in Defence of Divine Revelation* (Boston, 1820), written with Hosea Ballou; the second was when he became a symbolic figure—the persecuted free inquirer—in publications about his blasphemy trials. See Abner Kneeland, *Speech of Abner Kneeland Delivered before the Supreme*

Court of the City of Boston, in His Own Defence, on an Indictment for Blasphemy (Boston, 1834); Kneeland, *Speech of Abner Kneeland, Delivered before the Full Bench of Judges of the Supreme Court, in His Own Defence, for the Alleged Crime of Blasphemy* (Boston, 1836); and Kneeland, *A Review of the Trial, Conviction, and Final Imprisonment in the Common Jail of the County of Suffolk, of Abner Kneeland, for the Alleged Crime of Blasphemy* (Boston, 1838); see also "Abner Kneeland versus Abner Kneeland," *Boston Investigator*, Dec. 21 and 28, 1832. Mann's private journal recorded personal doubt and despair about the realm of the spirit but passionate commitment to what he understood as natural moral laws; his speeches and reports promoted a generic public Christianity while removing what critics considered to be the essence of Christianity from the public sphere. Horace Mann, "Journal, 1837–1843," Mann Papers; Mann, *Lectures and Annual Reports on Education* [1837–38] (Cambridge, Mass., 1867); Mann, *Annual Report of the Board of Education* (Washington, D.C., 1839–48). Brownson, in *Charles Elwood*, in *Works* 4:315, wrote, "There is not much open skepticism, not much avowed infidelity, but there is a vast amount of concealed doubt, and untold difficulty."

7. Brownson, *Convert*, 9; *Charles Elwood*, chap. 1. Gilmore, "Orestes Brownson," argues that Brownson's early religious experience was considerably more complex than the outline given in *The Convert* would indicate.
8. On Miller and Millerism, see Dick, *William Miller and the Advent Crisis* (1994; orig. pub. 1930); Numbers and Butler, eds., *The Disappointed* (1987); Doan, *The Miller Heresy, Millennialism, and American Culture* (1987); Knight, *Millennial Fever and the End of the World* (1993); Rowe, *God's Strange Work* (2008).
9. In Himes, *Views*, 8. Other benefactors were Judge James Witherell and Alexander Cruikshanks. Poultney, Vermont, had a population of 1,700–1,900 when Miller lived there; the Library Association had been organized in 1790, and the Masons' Morning Star Lodge No. 27 was established prior to 1800. During the War of 1812, the town split into two factions, with Democrats meeting at the Eagle Tavern, and Federalists at the Rising Sun Tavern. See Joslin, Frisbie, and Ruggles, *A History of the Town of Poultney, Vermont* (1875) and Latham, *Poultney* (1961).
10. William Miller, quoted in Himes, *Views*, 10; Miller, Letter to Lucy Miller, Oct. 28, 1814, in Bliss, *Memoirs*, 54.
11. Bliss, *Memoirs*, 68, and see 46–58 and Himes, *Views*, 10–11.
12. Miller, "An Address to the Believers in the Second Advent Near, Scattered Abroad," in Himes, *Views*, 55 ("with the *Bible alone*"); see also Miller, "Rules of Scriptural Interpretation," in ibid., 24, Miller, *Evidence from Scripture and History of the Second Coming of Christ, about the Year 1843* (Troy, N.Y., 1838), viii, Miller, "Unfinished Compendium of Beliefs, Sept. 5, 1822," in Bliss, *Memoirs*, 77–80, "Synopsis of Mr. Miller's Religious Views," in Himes, *Views*, 32–35; Miller, Letters to Elder Hendryx, May 26 and Oct. 1, 1832, and April 10, 1833, in Bliss, *Memoirs*, 101 ("not well indoctrinated," "you must preach *Bible*"), 107–8 ("O may the Bible").
13. Miller, "Rules of Interpretation," in Himes, *Views*, [20]–23.
14. Miller, Letter to Elder Hendryx, Jan. 25, 1832, in Bliss, *Memoirs*, 100; Miller in Himes, *Views*, 176; Miller, in ibid., 12: "Infidelity in many cases has been made to yield her iron grasp on the mind of many an individual. Deism has yielded to the truth of God's word, and many men of strong minds have acknowledged that the scriptures must be of divine origin." The report from Maine is in Bliss, *Memoirs*, 16, and see also 125–28. In "An Address to the Believers in the Second Advent Near, Scattered Abroad," in Himes, *Views*, 59, Miller noted that one of the effects of his new doctrine was that "the sceptic, the deist, [and] the Universalist" were made to feel the Spirit's power. In "Lecture on What Is Truth?" in Himes, *Views*, 114, Miller boasted of the triumph over deism, and in "Lecture XVIII," in ibid., 271, he wrote that the radicalism of Robert Owen and Frances Wright was a sign that the end was near. See also the report of deists converting in Palmer, Massachusetts, in Bliss, *Memoirs*, 164.
15. Miller, in Bliss, *Memoirs*, 207, and see also 248, where Miller, writing after his predicted date for the world's end had passed, pointed to the infidels converted to God as evidence of the good work of his ministry; Miller, "Apology and Defence," dictated July 1845, in ibid., 327. Seven hundred to fourteen hundred infidels would be approximately 12–24 percent of the six thousand conversions Miller claimed to have witnessed.
16. Miller, in Bliss, *Memoirs*, 139.

17. Bliss, *Memoirs*, 288, 294; William Miller, Address in the *Advent Herald*, Sept. 9, 1846, in ibid., 350; Miller, Letter to Brethren, Dec. 3, 1844, in ibid., 281.
18. Brownson, *Convert*, 9–20.
19. Brownson, *Convert*, 11–12. Brownson exaggerated the "espionage," though New York Presbyterians in the 1820s did try to discipline themselves and their communities. See Johnson, *Shopkeeper's Millennium* (1978) and Johnson, *Islands of Holiness* (1989), chaps. 7 and 9. Brownson also alluded to the effort to discipline the nation in similar ways in 1827 with the campaign to stop the mail on Sunday and Ezra Stiles Ely's call for a Christian politics. See also Brownson, "The Princeton Review and the Convert," *Brownson's Quarterly Review* [hereafter *BrQR*] (April 1858), in *Works* 5:200–40.
20. Brownson often discussed Protestant sectarianism but had little to say specifically about the Millerites and Adventists. His review of Alpheus Crosby's *The Second Advent* (Boston, 1850) reads, in toto: "We have not read this book: we broke down before we had got beyond half a dozen pages" (*BrQR* 4, 2 [April 1, 1850]: 271).
21. Brownson, *Convert*, 24.
22. "Note from the Publisher," *Gospel Advocate* 7, 22 (Nov. 14, 1829): 355, 369; the comment about honesty is in "Orestes A. Brownson," *Gospel Advocate* 7, 25 (Dec. 12, 1829): 396. Isaac B. Pierce's letters to Brownson, July 25, 1834, May 26, 1835, and Dec. 19, 1839, illustrate another Universalist clergyman wishing he could supplement his income—and free himself from weekly preaching—by becoming an editor of a journal (Brownson Papers). On religion and politics in the 1820s, see West, *The Politics of Revelation and Reason* (1996), chaps. 2 and 3.
23. The best study of Kneeland is French, "The Trials of Abner Kneeland" (1971). See also Gallaher, "Abner Kneeland—Pantheist" (1939); Bonney, "The Salubria Story" (1975), on Kneeland's last years in Iowa; French, "Liberation from Man and God in Boston" (1980); and Burkholder, "Emerson, Kneeland, and the Divinity School Address" (1986).
24. Hosea Ballou and Abner Kneeland, *A Series of Letters, in Defence of Divine Revelation: In Reply to Rev. Abner Kneeland's Serious Inquiry into the Authenticity of the Same* (Boston, 1820), 161; Peter Niles, *The Writings of Peter Niles, Who Put a Period to His Own Life with the Discharge of His Gun* (Walpole, N.H.: Printed for Abner Kneeland, 1811).
25. Ballou and Kneeland, *Series of Letters*, 84–96.
26. Kneeland, *A Review of the Evidences of Christianity: In a Series of Lectures Delivered in Broadway Hall, New-York, August, 1829*, 6th ed. (Boston, 1831?), 7. On the Prince Street Congregational Church, see French, "Trials of Abner Kneeland," 46–51; Philo-Veritas [Thomas Cooper], "On Historical Evidence," *Correspondent*, May 2, 9, 1829; "Evidences of Christianity," *Correspondent*, June 6, 13, 20, 27, July 4, 11, 18, 1829.
27. Abner Kneeland, ed., "Preface, by the Publisher of this American Edition," in *A Philosophical Dictionary, from the French of M. de Voltaire: With Additional Notes, Both Critical and Argumentative, by Abner Kneeland* (Boston, [1836]), li. On churches and church establishment in Boston and Massachusetts generally, see Rose, "Social Sources of Denominationalism Reconsidered" (1986);Wright, "Institutional Reconstruction in the Unitarian Controversy" in Wright, ed., *American Unitarianism* (1989); and Field, *The Crisis of the Standing Order* (1998). On Boston, see esp. Rich, "'A Wilderness of Whigs'" (1971); Cayton, "Who Were the Evangelicals?" (1997); Dodd, "The Working Classes and the Temperance Movement in Antebellum Boston" (1978); Pease and Pease, *The Web of Progress* (1985); Roth, "Did Class Matter in American Politics?" (1998) (includes an analysis of class and voting in 1830s Boston); Tomlins, "Criminal Conspiracy and Early Labor Combinations" (1987); Knights, *The Plain People of Boston, 1830–1860* (1971); Formisano, *The Transformation of Political Culture* (1983); Formisano, "Boston, 1800–1840," in Formisano and Burns, eds., *Boston, 1700–1980* (1984); Crocker, *The Magic of the Many* (1999).
28. Kneeland wrote that "a great portion" of his subscribers were workingmen (*Investigator*, April 27, 1832). Kneeland's office in the early 1830s was right above the Workingmen's Reading Room, and the Free Enquirers and mechanics both used Julien Hall for their meetings. The *Investigator* supported workers' rights, denounced monopolies and imprisonment for debt, and called for tax and electoral reforms that would benefit the working class (see, for example, *Investigator*, April 23 and Oct. 21, 1831). The paper also featured a regular "Workingmen's Department" that carried news of labor organizing outside Boston. When the *Workingmen's*

Advocate failed, Kneeland sent out the *Investigator* to the *Advocate's* subscribers (*Investigator*, Sept. 30 and Oct. 7, 1831). Leaders of the Workingmen's Party, however, tried to distance the movement from the taint of infidelity. At an 1832 Boston convention, they had a clergyman open the meeting with a prayer and severed ties to New York Workingmen because of links to Robert Dale Owen and other infidels. See French, "Trials of Abner Kneeland," 122–26; and Formisano, *Transformation of Political Culture*, 222–43.

29. Robert Landis, in *Infidelity Exposed, and Its Charges against Christianity Repelled* (Philadelphia, 1836), iv, noted that many advised silence; English physician W. W. Sleigh's *Christian's Defensive Dictionary* (Philadelphia, 1837) was careful to refute objections without exhibiting the objections themselves; George Coles, *The Antidote; or, Revelation Defended, and Infidelity Repulsed: In a Course of Lectures* (Hartford, Conn., 1836) followed a similar tactic. Sleigh, however, challenged infidels to a series of public debates, published as *The New-York Discussion, between Dr. Sleigh, in Defence of Divine Revelation; and the Delegates of the Tammany Hall Infidels, and Others, In Defense of Infidelity* (New York, 1836). See also J. H. Fairchild, *The Gospel Defended against Infidels* (Boston, 1833), 18; Elihu W. Baldwin, *The Young Freethinker Reclaimed* (Philadelphia, [1838]); *Christianity and Infidelity Contrasted* (Philadelphia, [1832]); Andrew Fuller, *Three Queries to the Rejecters of Christianity* (New York, [1832]); Ebenezer Porter, *The Presumption of Skeptical and Careless Contemners of Religion* (Andover, Mass., 1829); and William Gibbons, *An Exposition of Modern Skepticism* (Wilmington, Del., [1829]). On the diffusion of infidel philosophy since the French Revolution, see John Morison, *Counsels to Young Men on Modern Infidelity, and the Evidences of Christianity* (Boston, 1834), 15, and Benjamin Godwin, *Lectures on the Atheistic Controversy*, 1st American ed. (Boston, 1835), 8. *The Conversion of an Infidel, Being the Confession and Exhortation of an Old Man, Who Wishes Well to His Fellow Mortals, Near the Close of His Life*, (Enfield, Mass., 1830) blamed the clergy; [R. J. Cleveland], *A Dialogue on Some of the Causes of Infidelity* (Boston, 1828) indicted Calvinism; [Stephen C. Phillips], *Practical Infidelity Considered in Reference to the Present Times* (Boston, 1830) implicated commerce; Cyrus Pitt Grosvenor, *Infidelity: Some of Its Modern Features* (Boston, 1829), 10 (Wright); Derby, *Political Reminiscences*. See also Peter G. Obert, in *Obert's System of Nature* (New York, 1837), 12, which argued that the proliferation of contending sects had caused people to doubt them all.

30. Beecher, *Lectures on Scepticism*, 86. Beecher began his lectures by discussing the different paths to the knowledge of truth: self-consciousness, intuition, the senses, and evidence (testimony or deduction). He then defined skepticism as "a state of mind in which these constitutional grounds of certainty fail to produce confidence" (11).

31. Beecher, *Lectures on Scepticism*, 77, 93.

32. Derby, *Political Reminiscences*, 144: "It is said that 2000 have been present [at Kneeland's Sunday lectures] at once! And, monstrous to relate, a considerable proportion of the assemblage *were females*, not the abandoned and reckless, but respectable and educated females!" Bernard Whitman's letter to Brownson, Dec. 26, 1833, solicited essays on infidelity and the Workingmen's movement; Channing's letter, Jan. 11, 1834, and Ripley's, March 26, 1834, also discussed Brownson's ministry to the working class; Henry Channing's of Dec, 27, 1836, criticized Brownson for his leveling spirit and for the sympathy he still showed infidels (Brownson Papers). On "evangelical" Unitarianism, see Rose, *Transcendentalism as a Social Movement* (1981), chap. 1.

33. "Questions to the Editor," *Boston Reformer*, Aug. 12, 1836; Brownson, *A Discourse on the Wants of the Times* (Boston, 1836), 9–10.

34. The debate was announced in the *Investigator*, May 24, 1837, and ran for seven successive weeks in that paper from April 7 through May 19, concluding with final notes and remarks on May 26. It also ran in the *Boston Weekly Reformer* and the *Ohio Watchman*. For other commentary on Brownson and his philosophy in the *Investigator*, see Kneeland on Brownson's "Cousin's Philosophy," Oct. 14, 1836; Kneeland on Brownson's "New Views," Dec. 9, 1836; criticism of Cousin's attempt to refute Hume, and "The Present State of Unitarianism," an essay dealing with epistemology from the *Boston Recorder*, with Kneeland's commentary, Jan. 20, 1837; "Transcendentalism," Feb. 3, 1837; [J. Foster], "Essay on the Uniformity of Causation," a series beginning Nov. 3, 1837; Kneeland recommending Brownson's "Tendency of Modern Civilization" and *Boston Quarterly Review* to workingmen, May 4, 1838; "Philosophy and

Common Sense," Mar. 9, 1838; "Orestes A. Brownson," Sept. 7, 1838; on Cousin, Brownson, and Emerson, Sept. 21, 1838; "The Eclectic Philosophy," Jan. 25, 1839.
35. Brownson, editing the Ithaca. N.Y., *Philanthropist* in 1831, wrote, "This paper [the *Boston Investigator*] professes to advocate the principles of the workingmen. So far I approve it. But I regret to see it connected with the cause of any particular religious, or irreligious, theory. Scepticism will not go down in this country. It is opposed to all the prejudices of the people and Mr. Kneeland will find that his cause will rather retard than advance the moral and political reform he wishes to effect" (quoted in *Boston Investigator*, May 21, 1831). In *Discourse on the Wants of the Times*, Brownson argued that Christianity was essential to reform.
36. [Lucius M. Sargent], *I Am Afraid There Is a God! Founded on Fact* (Boston, 1833). The story about Kneeland throwing the Bible circulated as a rumor. Kneeland angrily confronted Sargent at a public meeting and denied it. Sargent got his revenge by initiating the blasphemy trial against Kneeland. See also Eliza Lee Cabot Follen, *The Skeptic* (Boston and Cambridge, Mass., 1835); Mary Anna Fox, *George Allen, the Only Son: By a Young Lady of Boston* (Boston, 1835); [Cleveland], *Dialogue on Some of the Causes of Infidelity*. George Ripley published a translation of William Martin Leberecht de Wette's *Theodore; or, The Skeptic's Conversion* (Boston, 1841), a philosophical novel much closer in spirit to *Charles Elwood*. The translator's preface mentions *Charles Elwood* as one of the half dozen or so original theological works in America.
37. Brownson, *Charles Elwood*, 242–46.
38. George Thompson, in a letter to Brownson on July 26, 1839, described a personal experience similar to Elwood's; Anne C. Lynch's of April 18, 1840, praised the book and said it reflected her experience with doubt and faith; Isaac Pierce, who had also struggled with materialism, said in his letter of August 14, 1841, that he had read the book several times; James Kennard Jr.'s of September 8, 1843, said *Elwood* and a Brownson article had "opened my eyes" (Brownson Papers).
39. Pamphlets and court documents related to the case have been reprinted in Levy, ed., *Blasphemy in Massachusetts* (New York, 1973). Kneeland's objectionable sentence, originally in a letter to the editor of the Universalist *Trumpet*, is in Kneeland, *An Introduction to the Defence*, in Levy, *Blasphemy*, 37. Just as Kneeland argued that the signifier "God" did not have a fixed referent that a statute could protect, he believed it should have been obvious to Unitarians and Trinitarians that the same could be said of the Bible. Defending himself in his third trial, he introduced two Bibles as evidence, to show the New Testament misquoting the Old, theologians mistranslating "girl" as "virgin," and Unitarians italicizing passages to signal dubious authenticity (*Speech of Abner Kneeland Delivered before the Supreme Court*, 7–11, in Levy, *Blasphemy*, 317–21).
40. "Law Case," *Religious Remembrancer* 6, 13 (Nov. 21, 1818): 51–52.
41. "The People against Ruggles: Judgment Affirmed," *Christian Visitant* 1, 25 (Nov. 18, 1815): 193–95. On blasphemy cases and the common law, see Banner, "When Christianity Was Part of the Common Law" (1998) and Gordon, "Blasphemy and the Law of Religious Liberty in Nineteenth-Century America" (2000). Banner persuasively argues that the common law argument made little difference to the legal logic deciding the cases, but he fails to see the political power of such discussions outside the courtroom. Gordon exaggerates in the other direction, however, when she claims that blasphemy jurisprudence "elevated legists into enforcers of Christian doctrine," became "a proven mechanism for the management of religious dissent," and vanquished deists and freethinkers (702, 707, 699).
42. [Samuel Parker], *Report of the Arguments of the Attorney of the Commonwealth at the Trials of Abner Kneeland, for Blasphemy, in the Municipal and Supreme Courts, in Boston, January and May, 1834* (Boston, 1834), 12, 16, in Levy, *Blasphemy*, 188, 192; Judge Peter Thacher, "Charge to the Jury in the Trial of Abner Kneeland on an Indictment of Blasphemy," Jan. 1834, in ibid., 284. Kneeland, in *A Review of the Trial, Conviction, and Final Imprisonment*, 112, in ibid., 572, noted that Judge Thacher, allegedly so sympathetic to the poor, had a few years before bitterly denounced workers who attempted to unionize for a ten-hour workday. On Wilde's comments, see Kneeland, *Review*, 92, in Levy, *Blasphemy*, 552; and [David Henshaw], *A Review of the Prosecution against Abner Kneeland: By a Cosmopolite* (Boston, 1835), 10, in Levy, *Blasphemy*, 352.
43. In early 1837, Kneeland had discovered that his publisher, J. Q. Adams, had embezzled $7,000 and incurred another $3,000 in debt. When the economy collapsed, Kneeland still published

three thousand copies of the *Investigator* each week, but subscription payments slowed to a trickle (*Investigator*, June 16, 1837; French, "Trials of Abner Kneeland," 225). Martin Moore's *Boston Revival, 1842* (Boston, 1842), 82–89, gleefully told of a handful of Boston freethinkers who, after Kneeland's departure, converted to Christianity, and of one who leapt to his death from a fourth-floor window, thinking the devil was after him.

44. "Scepticism," *Investigator*, May 7, 1831: "We are sceptic therefore rather in a theological, than a philosophical sense." "Principles of Free Enquirers," *Investigator*, Nov. 3, 1837. Kneeland quickly added, a week later, that he was willing to give up any of these principles or replace them with better ones upon good evidence. They were, therefore, pragmatic, falsifiable conjectures rather than articles of dogmatic faith. See also Kneeland's broadside, *Abner Kneeland's Code of Morals, Philosophical Creed, and Declaration of Character* [Boston, 1833].
45. David Hall, in the introduction to Hall, ed., *Lived Religion in America* (1997), describes the study of "lived religion" as the effort to study "religion as practiced" and "the everyday thinking and doing of lay men and women"([vii]). One might similarly call for studies of "lived philosophy" and even "lived irreligion."
46. Derby, *Political Reminiscences*, 143; [Henshaw], *Review of the Prosecution against Abner Kneeland*, in Levy, *Blasphemy*, 343–418. On complaints about the *Investigator*'s political bias, and Kneeland's response, see "Letter from 'Theon,' Oak Grove, Christian Co., Ky.," Oct. 28, 1836; Editorial column, Nov. 4, 1836; "Extract from a letter from Donaldsville, Louisiana," Jan. 6, 1837; and "Free Enquiry—Politics," April 7 and Aug. 4, 1837.
47. Kneeland, *An Oration, Delivered July 4, 1826* (New York, 1826), 23; "Prospectus," *Investigator*, April 2, 1831; letter from "Lorenzo" on the relation to Garrison's *Liberator*, and Kneeland on Johnson, *Investigator*, Sept. 23, 1831; Kneeland on inflammatory abolitionist rhetoric, *Investigator*, Feb. 3, 1837; Kneeland denies he is an abolitionist, *Investigator*, April 27, 1837; slavery quotation, "Abolitionists," *Investigator*, April 7, 1837.
48. On Mann, see Mann, *Life of Horace Mann* (1865); Tharp, *Until Victory* (1953); Culver, *Horace Mann and Religion in the Massachusetts Public Schools* (1969); and Messerli, *Horace Mann* (1971). Messerli notes that Mann exaggerated his family's penury.
49. Mann, *Life*, 14; Messerli, *Horace Mann*, 20, 169–75; Mann, "Journal, 1837–1843," June 15, 1837; April 22, 1838; April 21, 1839; Aug. 9, 1840. Years later, Mary Peabody remembered meeting Mann and described him as a man who mourned without hope, and even made her question the virtue of God ("Mary [Peabody] Mann's Estimate of Horace Mann, 1860–1880," Mann Papers).
50. E[lizabeth] Peabody to Orestes Brownson, July 6, 1839, Brownson Papers; Mann, "Journal," July 31, 1841; Horace Mann to Mr. Craig, Jan. 1856, in Mann, *Life*, 480; Mann, "Journal," June 30, 1837: "*Faith* is the only sustainer. I have faith in the improvability of the race—in their accelerating improvability"; Horace Mann to George Combe, March 25, 1839, in Mann, *Life*, 113; Mann, "Journal," Sept. 15, 1837.
51. Mann, "Journal," 3–4, 153.
52. George Combe, *The Constitution of Man Considered in Relation to External Objects: A Facsimile Reproduction with an Introduction by Eric T. Carlson, M.D.* (Delmar, N.Y., 1974), which reproduces the third American edition (Boston, 1834; 1st ed. 1828). Carlson estimates that by midcentury, Combe had sold three hundred thousand copies of this work. See also Combe, "On Secular Education," *Westminster Review*, July 1852, in Reeder, ed., *Educating Our Masters* (1980).
53. *Common School Journal* 1, 1 (Nov. 1838), 14; *New York Observer*, Oct. 20, 1838, quoted in Culver, *Horace Mann and Religion*, 87.
54. Brownson, "Pretensions of Phrenology," *Boston Quarterly Review* [hereafter *BQR*] 2, 2 (April 1839), in *Works* 9:235–54. Brownson also noted that the shape of Abner Kneeland's head seemed to refute the phrenological notion that people with a large region of causality would display a strong veneration for God. Kneeland discusses his phrenological exam in "Phrenology," *Investigator*, June 30, 1837.
55. Orestes Brownson, "Review of the Second Annual Report of the Board of Education, Together with the Second Annual Report of the Secretary of the Board," *BQR* 2, 4 (Oct. 1839), 393–434; "Remarks on the Seventh Annual Report of the Hon. Horace Mann, Secretary of the Board of Education," *BrQR* 1, 4 (Oct. 1844), 547: "We regard his [Mann's] whole theory of

education as founded in error.... Mr. Mann knows nothing of the philosophy of education, for he knows nothing of the philosophy of human nature, and nothing of Christian morals and theology. His theory is derived from German quacks, and can only rear up a generation of infidels." See also Lasch, *The Revolt of the Elites and the Betrayal of Democracy* (1995), 141–60. Mann to Howe, July 21, 1839, quoted in Culver, *Horace Mann and Religion*, 127.

56. Brownson, "The Laboring Classes," *BQR* 3, 3 (July 1840), 358–94; Brownson, "Charles Elwood Reviewed," *BQR* (April 1842), in *Works* 4:316–61; Brownson, *Convert*, 144. See also "Schmucker's Psychology," *Democratic Review*, Oct. 1842, in *Works* 1:19–57; "Synthetic Philosophy," *Democratic Review*, Dec. 1842, Jan. and March 1843, in *Works* 1:58–129; "The Philosophy of History," *Democratic Review*, May and June 1843, in *Works* 4:361–423; "Kant's Critique of Pure Reason," *BrQR* (1844), in *Works* 1:130–213; "Liberalism and Catholicity," *BrQR*, July 1846, in *Works* 5:476–527; "Hume's Philosophical Works," *BrQR* 3, 4 (Oct. 1855): 445–72; "Graty on the Knowledge of God," *BrQR* (1855), in *Works* 1:324–61; "Primitive Elements of Thought," *BrQR* (Jan. 1859), in *Works* 1:408–37.

57. Brownson, "Charles Elwood Revisited," *BQR*, April 1842, in *Works* 4:337. Brownson, who in the 1830s had championed the "minority rights" of slaveholders and workingmen, showed more concern for the former by the early 1840s. Brownson was baptized and confirmed in the Roman Catholic Church on October 22, 1844, and remained a Catholic until his death in 1876.

58. Brownson, *Convert*, 17, 47, 135, 170–71, 175. See also Brownson, "Schmucker's Psychology," in *Works* 1:19–57; "Synthetic Philosophy," in *Works* 1:58–129; "Kant's Critique of Pure Reason," in *Works* 1:130–213; "Liberalism and Catholicity," *BrQR* (July 1846), in *Works*, 1: 446–527.

59. Brownson had written on this subject years earlier in his review of Chauncy Townsend's *Facts of Mesmerism, or Animal Magnetism* (Boston, 1841), *BQR*, Oct. 1841, 521–22. Anne Lynch's letters to him (Sept. 29, 1840; June 2, 27, Nov. 4, Dec. 13, 1841; June 12, 1842) discuss animal magnetism (Brownson Papers). Kneeland called an article claiming that animal magnetism "sweeps away the *Kneeland Doctrine* entirely" utter nonsense (*Investigator*, Jan. 20, 1837).

60. Brownson, *Spirit-Rapper*, 29, 44, 55.

61. Brownson, *Spirit-Rapper*, 228.

62. Brownson, *Spirit-Rapper*, [1], 97, 142.

63. Brownson, "An A Priori Autobiography," *BrQR*, Jan. 1850, in *Works* 1:214–52, a review of [William B. Greene], *Remarks on the Science of History: Followed by an A Priori Autobiography* (Boston, 1849); Brownson, "Bancroft's History of the United States," *BrQR*, Oct. 1852, in *Works* 19:382–418, esp. 385. At the end of his own later attempt to make both theological and historical sense out of the Protestant Reformation, "Essays Theological, Philosophical, and Historical, on the Reformation in the Sixteenth Century" [1862], in *Works* 12:514–607, he reversed the argument he made in his review of Bancroft and contended that true history writing must be informed by true philosophy and religion. Still, he concluded that only God could discern the whole logical pattern, and implied that any neat thesis about historical change has to ignore innumerable complexities of the interwoven "political, economical, commercial, and industrial, and religious and theological" causes (607).

Chapter 11

1. Maxwell Pierson Gaddis, *The Conversion of a Skeptic: A Member of the Bar* (Cincinnati, 1858), 96.
2. John Scarlett, *The Life and Experience of a Converted Infidel* (New York, 1854; orig. pub. 1853), 91–96, esp. 91. A fair amount of the material later in his autobiography was serialized in twenty-eight "Christian Experience" columns in the *Christian Advocate and Journal* between March 1 and December 20, 1849. As an eighty-year-old, Scarlett published another version of his autobiography, in verse: *Almond: A True Story in Five Parts* (Orange, N.J., 1883).
3. John Bayley, *Confessions of a Converted Infidel: With Lights and Shades of Itinerant Life, and Miscellaneous Sketches*, 3rd ed. (New York, 1856; orig. pub. 1854), 31, 38, 39.
4. Gaddis, *Conversion of a Skeptic*, 153.
5. Noll, introduction to Noll, ed., *God and Mammon* (2001), esp. 8; Samuel Harris, *Zaccheus; or, The Scriptural Plan of Benevolence* (New York, [ca. 1850]), 38, 39; see also Hudnut-Beumler, *In Pursuit of the Almighty's Dollar* (2007), 26, and see chap. 1. On the theme of piety aiding

economic prosperity, see also Pointer, "Philadelphia Presbyterians, Capitalism, and the Morality of Economic Success" in Noll, ed., *God and Mammon*. For Protestant criticism of the materialism and an overemphasis on secular progress, which they linked to infidel political economy and philosophy, see Hanley, *Beyond a Christian Commonwealth* (1994), chap. 4.
6. On British Protestant laissez-faire political economy, see Hilton, *The Age of Atonement* (1988); Berg, "Progress and Providence in Early Nineteenth-Century Political Economy" (1990); and Waterman, *Revolution, Economics and Religion* (1991). On Wayland, see Francis Wayland, *The Elements of Political Economy* (New York, 1837), esp. v (the relation of political economy and moral philosophy), 125–28 (government poor relief a bad idea), 141–49 (protective tariffs a bad idea); Dorfman, *The Economic Mind in American Civilization, 1606–1865* (1966; orig. pub. 1946), 2:758–70; and Wauzzinski, *Between God and Gold* (1993), 138–50.
7. On the combination of economic individualism and moral paternalism, see Hilton, *Age of Atonement*, and Waterman, *Revolution, Economics and Religion*. On other ways capitalism and Protestantism intersected, see Thomas, *Revivalism and Cultural Change* (1989) and Moore, *Selling God* (1994). Noll, "Protestant Reasoning about Money and the Economy, 1790–1860," in Noll, ed., *God and Mammon*, has argued that most American Protestant commentators accepted commercial society and repeated traditional scruples about greed; see also Carwardine, "Charles Sellers's 'Antinomians' and 'Arminians': Methodists and the Market Revolution" in ibid., 75–98. Davenport's intellectual history, *Friends of the Unrighteous Mammon* (2008) focuses on a small group of writers who tried to engage the issue in more sophisticated ways. Those he calls "clerical economists" attempted to reconcile Adam Smith's free market with Christianity, seeing Smith's "invisible hand" as the hand of God. Davenport's "pastoral moralists" tried to help individuals balance capitalist self-interest and Christian selflessness. "Contrarians" attacked the ethical failures of secular society's new economic order. Davenport's "clerical economists" include Baptist Francis Wayland, Episcopalian John McVickar, and Unitarian Francis Bowen; his "pastoral moralists" include Unitarian Orville Dewey and Congregationalist Leonard Bacon; his "contrarians" are the Presbyterian industrialist Stephen Colwell and Orestes Brownson before his conversion to Catholicism.
8. For an "ideological map" of the range of opinion in Britain in the 1820s, see Waterman, *Revolution, Economics and Religion*, 201; on Alban de Villeneuve-Bargemont, *Économie politique chrétienne* (Paris, 1834), see ibid., 12. On Emerson, the Transcendentalists, and political economy, see Sklansky, *The Soul's Economy* (2002), chap. 2; see also Newfield, *The Emerson Effect* (1996) and Dolan, *Emerson's Liberalism* (2009). John Hughes, *A Lecture on the Importance of a Christian Basis for the Science of Political Economy, and Its Applications to the Affairs of Life* (New York, [1844]). On Clay's American System and internal improvements more generally, see Larson, *Internal Improvement* (2001).
9. [Stephen Colwell], *New Themes for the Protestant Clergy: Creeds without Charity, Theology without Humanity, and Protestantism without Christianity* (Philadelphia, 1851), 124, 183. On the theme of morality and profit-seeking in newspapers, magazines, and popular literature, see Ratner, Kaufman, and Teeter, *Paradoxes of Prosperity* (2009).
10. [Samuel Austin Allibone], *New Themes Condemned; or, Thirty Opinions on "New Themes" and its "Reviewer"* (Philadelphia, 1853), 35, 38, 10, 5; and for various quoted writers linking *New Themes* to religious infidelity, see also 35n, 71, 74n, 95, 97, 102, 103, 109. [Colwell], *New Themes*, 303, 150–51, 259, 266, 302–5, 359–66. See also Stephen Colwell, "Preface to the Second Edition," *New Themes for the Protestant Clergy*, 2d ed. rev. (Philadelphia, 1852); and *Charity and the Clergy: Being a Review by a Protestant Clergyman of the "New Themes" Controversy* (Philadelphia, 1853), which supports Colwell. On Colwell, see Henry Charles Carey, *A Memoir of Stephen Colwell* (Philadelphia, 1871) and Davenport, *Friends of the Unrighteous Mammon*, 109–22; on Colwell as an economic thinker, see Dorfman, *Economic Mind* 2:809–25.
11. The classic study of the moral meaning of economic change for the middling classes is Johnson, *A Shopkeeper's Millennium* (1978), but see important revisions of Johnson in Ryan, *Cradle of the Middle Class* (1981), Johnson, *Islands of Holiness* (1989), and Corrigan, *Business of the Heart* (2002). On freethought and the labor movement, see Dorfman, *Economic Mind* 2: chap. 24; Wilentz, *Chants Democratic* (1984); and Lazerow, *Religion and the Working Class in Antebellum America* (1995), chap. 2.
12. On religion and the working class, see Lazerow, *Religion and the Working Class* and Sutton, *Journeymen for Jesus* (1998). On not confusing labor spokesmen for "the mind of antebellum

labor" as a whole (the phrase in in Lazerow, title of pt. 3), see Rockman, *Scraping By* (2009). On religion of the enslaved, see esp. Raboteau, *Slave Religion* (1978).
13. Gaddis, *Conversion of a Skeptic*, 23.
14. Gaddis, *Conversion of a Skeptic*, 36, 50.
15. Gaddis, *Conversion of a Skeptic*, 36, 48, 38, 46–47.
16. Gaddis, *Conversion of a Skeptic*, 78.
17. He does admit that the death of both Thomas Jefferson and John Adams on July 4, 1776, the fiftieth anniversary of the signing of the Declaration, suggests the hand of Providence (55–56).
18. Gaddis, *Conversion of a Skeptic*, 201, 43, 62–63, 74.
19. Gaddis, *Conversion of a Skeptic*, 62–63.
20. Bayley, *Confessions*, 281–84.
21. Gaddis, *Conversion of a Skeptic*, 140, 70, 75–76.
22. Gaddis, *Conversion of a Skeptic*, 92, 93, 94.
23. Gaddis, *Conversion of a Skeptic*, 153, 151.
24. Gaddis, *Conversion of a Skeptic*, 131, 130.
25. Gaddis, *Conversion of a Skeptic*, 131, 185.
26. Gaddis, *Conversion of a Skeptic*, 296–98, 102.
27. Gaddis, *Conversion of a Skeptic*, 246, 168.
28. Gaddis, *Conversion of a Skeptic*, 150, 145, 146.
29. Gaddis, *Conversion of a Skeptic*, 236–37.
30. Gaddis, *Conversion of a Skeptic*, 165, 167, 307, 160, 163–64.
31. Gaddis, *Conversion of a Skeptic*, 177, 295.
32. Scarlett: *Life and Experience*, 53; "Christian Experience [No. 1]," *Christian Advocate and Journal* 24, 9 (March 1, 1849): 33.
33. Scarlett, *Life and Experience*, 15.
34. Scarlett, *Life and Experience*, 42.
35. Scarlett: *Life and Experience*, 47, 44 (and in *Almond* [1883], 105, he adds Abner Kneeland to the list of influential infidel writers), 36; "The Methodist Quarterly Review," *Christian Advocate and Journal* 22, 3 (Jan. 29, 1847): 11.
36. Scarlett, *Life and Experience*, 48–52, esp. 51.
37. Scarlett, *Life and Experience*, 62; "Christian Experience [No. 1]." For commentary on the comet, see "The Comet," *Atkinson's Saturday Evening Post*, Oct. 15, 1831, 1–2; "The Safety of God's People," *Christian Advocate and Journal* 6, 25 (Feb. 17, 1832): 97; "The Cholera and the Comet," *Trumpet and Universalist Magazine* 4, 47 (May 19, 1832): 187; "The Comets of 1832," *Ariel* 6, 1 (April 28, 1832): 14; and "Tract on Comets," *Journal of the Franklin Institute* 10, 5 (Nov. 1, 1832): 315–21.
38. Scarlett, "Christian Experience No. IV," *Christian Advocate and Journal* 24, 13 (March 29, 1849): 49.
39. Scarlett: *Life and Experience*, 66–68; "Christian Experience No. III," *Christian Advocate and Journal* 24, 12 (March 22, 1849): 48; "Christian Experience No. II," ibid. 24, 11 (March 15, 1849): 11.
40. Scarlett, "Christian Experience No. V," *Christian Advocate and Journal* 24, 14 (April 5, 1849): 53.
41. Scarlett: *Life and Experience*, 85–88; "Christian Experience No. VII," *Christian Advocate and Journal* 14, 17 (April 26, 1849): 68.
42. Scarlett: *Life and Experience*, 88–96; "Christian Experience No. VIII," *Christian Advocate and Journal* 24, 19 (May 10, 1849): 73; "Christian Experience No. IX," ibid. 24, 21 (May 24, 1849): 81; "Christian Experience No. X," ibid. 24, 22 (May 31, 1849): 85; *Almond*, 59.
43. Scarlett: "Saving Faith," *Christian Advocate and Journal* 25, 16 (April 18, 1850): 61; "Christian Experience No. XXII," ibid. 24, 43 (Oct. 25, 1849): 169.
44. Scarlett: *Life and Experience*, 105–7; "Christian Experience No. VIII," *Christian Advocate and Journal* 24, 27 (July 5, 1849): 108.
45. Scarlett: *Life and Experience*, 187; "Christian Experience No. XXVIII," *Christian Advocate and Journal* 24, 52 (Dec. 27, 1849): 205; "Christian Experience No. XXVII," ibid. 24, 51 (Dec. 20, 1849): 201.
46. Scarlett: "Christian Experience No. XX," *Christian Advocate and Journal*, 24, 39 (Sept. 27, 1849): 153; "Christian Experience No. XVI," ibid. 24, 33 (Aug. 16, 1849): 129; *Life and Experience*, 177, 197, 199–200, 202, 208, 210, 213.

47. Scarlett: *Life and Experience,* 125; "Christian Experience No. XX," *Christian Advocate and Journal* 24, 39 (Sept. 27, 1849): 153; "Christian Experience No. XXI," ibid. 24, 42 (Oct. 18, 1849): 165.
48. On the Moral Philanthropists, see Post, *Popular Freethought in America* (1943), esp. 76–97. Scarlett describes his visits to Tammany Hall in *Life and Experience,* chap. 7, and "Christian Experience" nos. XXI–XXV.
49. Scarlett: "Christian Experience No. XXIV," *Christian Advocate and Journal* 24, 19 (May 10, 1849): 180; "Christian Experience No. XX," ibid. 24, 39 (Sept. 27, 1849): 153; "Christian Experience No. XXI," ibid. 24, 42 (Oct. 18, 1849): 165.
50. Scarlett, "Christian Experience No. XXI," *Christian Advocate and Journal* 24, 42 (Oct. 18, 1849): 165.
51. Scarlett: "Christian Experience No. XXII," *Christian Advocate and Journal* 24, 43 (Oct. 25, 1849): 165; *Life and Experience,* 80; "Christian Experience No. XXIII," *Christian Advocate and Journal* 24, 44 (Nov. 1, 1849): 173.
52. Scarlett, "Christian Experience No. XXIV," *Christian Advocate and Journal* 24, 19 (May 10, 1849): 180.
53. Scarlett, "Christian Experience No. XXV," *Christian Advocate and Journal,* 24, 46 (Nov. 15, 1849): 184.
54. Scarlett: *Life and Experience,* 146, and see variation in "Christian Experience No. XXV," *Christian Advocate and Journal* 24, 46 (Nov. 15, 1849): 184; "Christian Experience No. XXIV," *Christian Advocate and Journal* 24, 45 (May 10, 1849): 180.
55. Scarlett, "Christian Experience No. XXVIII," *Christian Advocate and Journal* 24, 52 (Dec. 27, 1849): 205, and see *Life and Experiences,* 185.
56. Bayley, *Confessions,* 15–17, esp. 15.
57. Bayley, *Confessions,* 11–12, esp. 11.
58. Bayley, *Confessions,* 14, 15.
59. Bayley, *Confessions,* 19, 21.
60. Bayley, *Confessions,* 21, 22, 22–23, 264–65.
61. Bayley, *Confessions,* 22, and see 31.
62. Bayley, *Confessions,* 26, 27, 29.
63. Bayley, *Confessions,* 30, 31, 40, 41.
64. Bayley, *Confessions,* 50, 51, 227.
65. Bayley, *Confessions,* 228, 229.
66. Bayley, *Confessions,* 103, 106–7, 106n.
67. Bayley, *Confessions,* 125, 126, 127.
68. Bayley, *Confessions,* 128.
69. Bayley, *Confessions,* 128–29.

Part Four

1. Origen Bacheler and Robert Dale Owen, *Discussion on the Existence of God and the Authenticity of the Bible, between Origen Bacheler and Robert Dale Owen,* 2nd ed. (New York, 1833), 2:17–18, 24.
2. Weed and von Hekring, introduction to Weed and von Hekring, eds., *Civil Religion in Political Thought* (2010), 3, 10. See also Beiner, *Civil Religion* (2010) and Babik, "Nazism as a Secular Religion" (2006). Civil religion has an ancient pedigree (Augustine commented on Roman uses); it was given particular prominence in Rousseau's *Social Contract* and revived by scholars and commentators in the second half of the twentieth century, especially with Bellah, "Civil Religion in America" (1967). For applications and criticism of the concept after Bellah, see Richey and Jones, eds., *American Civil Religion* (1974); Wilson, *Public Religion in American Culture* (1979); Bellah and Hammond, *Varieties of Civil Religion* (1980); Gehrig, "The American Civil Religion Debate" (1981); Demerath and Williams, "Civil Religion in an Uncivil Society" (1985); Stackhouse, "Civil Religion, Political Theology, and Public Theology" (2004); and Kao and Copulsky, "The Pledge of Allegiance and the Meanings and Limits of Civil Religion" (2007). Bellah himself would abandon the term: see *Beyond Belief* (1991). On the continuing use of the term for antebellum and Civil War materials, see Smith, *Daniel Webster and the Oratory of Civil Religion* (2005) and Stout, *Upon the Altar of the Nation* (2006), xvii–xxii.

Chapter 12

1. Dr. Cooper's *Defence before the Board of Trustees, from the Times and Gazette of December 14, 1832* ([Columbia, S.C.], 1832), 2. For an example of a Presbyterian joining the attack on Cooper in 1832, see Samuel P. Pressley, *Letters to Thomas Cooper, M.D., President of the South Carolina College*. ([Newberry, S.C.?], 1832). On Presbyterian complaints about Cooper at Carlisle College, see Himes, *Life and Times of Judge Thomas Cooper* (1918), 31; on his appearance, see ibid., 68. See also Cooper to Thomas Jefferson, Nov. 8, 1813, *Collections of the Massachusetts Historical Society*, 7th ser., 1 (Boston: 1900), 185: "I am looked at with great suspicion and distrust by a body of parsons who form a large part of the trustees of this college [Carlisle]."
2. Benjamin M. Palmer, *The Life and Letters of James Henley Thornwell* (Richmond, Va., 1875), 1–117. See also Farmer, *The Metaphysical Confederacy* (1986) and O'Brien, *Conjectures of Order* (2004), esp. vol. 2, chap. 19.
3. Francis Lieber, "On Political Hermeneutics, or Political Interpretation and Construction," *American Jurist and Law Magazine* 13, 35 (Oct. 1837): 37–101. O'Brien, *Conjectures of Order* 2:818: "Though John C. Calhoun became the political champion of what Thomas Cooper called the 'South Carolina Doctrines,' Cooper himself had defined them in a series of pamphlets from 1823 onwards, and offered its accessible summation in 1836."
4. O'Brien, *Conjectures of Order* 2:959: "Ministers were consistently the most energetic proponents of slavery; the matter was dialectically useful, for not only did the Bible help to sanction slavery, but proslavery helped to legitimate an expansive evangelicalism once suspect for its radical tendencies. But each paid a price for the alliance. Proslavery was obliged to put on a reforming and humane face...and argue that slavery, being Christian, was helping to ameliorate the human condition, slave and free. But religion had to become increasingly literalist about biblical exegesis, for it was inerrancy that the Bible seemed most serviceable to the proslavery cause." However, the price was cheap on both sides: literalism merely accented a core tendency among Southern evangelicals, and a humane and reforming slavery was mostly a rhetorical façade. See esp. Snay, *Gospel of Disunion* (1993); Daly, *When Slavery Was Called Freedom* (2002).
5. Hollis, *University of South Carolina*, vol. 1, *South Carolina College* (1951), 3–64, 75–76, 99. On the consolidation of lowcountry and upcountry (called backcountry before 1790) elite, see Klein, *Unification of a Slave State* (1990).
6. Thomas Cooper, *Address to the Graduates of the South Carolina College, December, 1821* (Columbia, S.C., 1821), 3–4.
7. Cooper, *Address to the Graduates*, 12, 13; Thomas Cooper to Thomas Jefferson, April 19, 1818, *Collections of the MHS*, 7th ser. (Boston, Mass., 1900), 270. A writer in a Presbyterian weekly sarcastically quoted from Cooper's 1821 *Address* to support a theological seminary. See "Dr. Cooper on Theological Education," *Charleston Observer*, April 16, 1831.
8. Malone, *The Public Life of Thomas Cooper, 1783–1829* (1926), 26; Gov. Thomas Bennet, "Message No. 1," *Southern Chronicle*, Dec. 4, 1822; Thomas Cooper to Thomas Jefferson, May 6, 1823, Thomas Jefferson Papers, Library of Congress (hereafter LOC). The arguments of the letters in the Columbia *Telescope* on April 9 and 15 are rehearsed and answered in William K. Clowney, *Reply to the Goats of Columbia, in the State of South Carolina* (Columbia, S.C., 1823). See also *City Gazette*, "To 'One of the Goats,'" May 7, 1823; *Southern Chronicle*, May 14, 1823 (excerpt from Clowney, with editor's approving introduction); *Religious Miscellany* 1, 19 (May 30, 1823): 300, which names Cooper and his "friends" as being behind the original publication; and "The Wrath of Men Praising God," *Christian Repository* 2, 84 (Nov. 14, 1823): 334, a report claiming that the "Goat's" attack increased rather than dampened the work of the American Bible Society in South Carolina.
9. William Johnson, "To the City Gazette," *City Gazette*, April 12, 1823. Johnson had published a two-volume biography of Revolutionary War general Nathanael Greene. On Johnson and the church, see Ford, *Deliver Us from Evil* (2009), 150.
10. [Letter from Thomas Cooper], *City Gazette*, April 19, 1823, rpt. from *Telescope*; Cooper to Jefferson, LOC, Nov. 23, 1823; Cooper, *The Scripture Doctrine of Materialism* (Philadelphia, 1823).

11. [Gov. John Lide Wilson], "Governor's Message No. 1," *Southern Chronicle*, Dec. 3, 1823.
12. Editor of *National Gazette* quoted in "College of South Carolina," *Religious Intelligencer* 8, 29 (Dec. 20, 1823): 458–59; "University of South Carolina," ibid. 7, 42 (March 15, 1823): 671; "South Carolina College," *Columbian Star*, March 8, 1823; "South Carolina College," *New Hampshire Observer*, July 14, 1823; *Boston Recorder*, quoted and countered in ["The College of Columbia, S.C."], *Vermont Gazette*, June 3, 1823; "Fanaticism," *New-England Galaxy and United States Literary Advertiser*, Jan. 9, 1824, 1; [No title], *Boston Commercial Gazette*, April 15, 1824, 2, rpt. from *Charleston Courier*. On Holley versus the Presbyterians at Transylvania University, see Hix, "The Conflict between Presbyterianism and Freethought in the South, 1776–1838" (1937), 112–19.
13. Cooper to Jefferson, Dec. 27, 1823, LOC.
14. [Thomas Cooper], *Extract of a Letter to a Student at Law, July, 1815* (Philadelphia? 1815), 4 (quotation), and see *Dr. Cooper's Defence*, 12; Thomas Cooper, "On the Constitution of the United States," in *Two Essays* (Columbia, S.C., 1826), 25; [Thomas Cooper], *Consolidation: An Account of Parties in the United States, from the Convention of 1787, to the Present Period* (Columbia, S.C., 1824).
15. Cooper, "On the Constitution," 45; Thomas Cooper, "Speech of Thomas Cooper," *Niles' Weekly Register*, Sept. 8, 1827, 28–32, esp. 32.
16. *Baltimore Patriot*, Sept. 21, 1830; "For the City Gazette to the Voters of the Parishes of St. Philips and St. Michaels," *City Gazette*, Sept. 9, 1830. On public toasts praising and denouncing Cooper for his political opinions, see Malone, *Public Life*, 349. For the significance of his role, see Sinha, *The Counterrevolution of Slavery* (2000), 17: "The notion that the tariffs were a northern conspiracy to destroy the South became the peculiar contribution of the Cooper-led Columbia junto to the general opposition against the revenue policy of Congress."
17. Thomas Cooper, *On the Connection between Geology and the Pentateuch, in a Letter to Professor Silliman* (Boston, 1833), preface, 46, 16, 44. Cooper also draws from the work of Benedict Spinoza; Richard Simon; Constantin François de Chassebœuf, comte de Volney; and *The Fabrication of the Pentateuch Proved, by the Anachronisms Contained in Those Books* (New York, 1829). See also Robert Means, *Considerations respecting the Pentateuch, with Special Reference to a Pamphlet Entitled "The Connexion between Geology and the Pentateuch" by Thomas Cooper, M.D.* (Columbia, S.C., 1834). On Silliman, see Brown, *Benjamin Silliman* (1989).
18. Philo-Veritas [Thomas Cooper], essays in *Correspondent*: "On the Authenticity of the Scripture Books," 2, 5 (Aug. 25, 1827): 68–71; "Philo-Veritas," 2, 12 (Oct. 13, 1827): 188–90; "The Epistle to the Hebrews," 5, 6 (Feb. 28, 1829): 81–83; "Free Discussion," 5, 10 (March 28, 1829): 145–48; "Evidences of Christianity," 5, 14 (April 25, 1829): 209–13; "On Historical Evidence," 5, 15 (May 2, 1829): 225–32; "On Historical Evidence, Continued," 5, 16 (May 9, 1829): 241–46; "Evidences of Christianity," 5, 20 (June 6, 1829): 305–15; "Evidences of Christianity," 5, 21 (June 13, 1829): 321–24; "Philo-Veritas," 6, 22 (June 20, 1829): 337–46; "Evidences of Christianity: Account of the Ancient Fathers, Continued," 5, 23 (June 27, 1829): 353–58; "Evidences of Christianity: Account of the Ancient Fathers, Continued," 5, 24 (July 4, 1829): 369–74; "Evidences of Christianity: Account of the Ancient Fathers, Continued," 5, 25 (July 11, 1829): 385–91; "Evidences of Christianity, Concluded," 5, 26 (July 18, 1829): 401–6. Quotation: "Evidences," April 25, 209.
19. "Evidences," April 25, 211. See Ehrman, *Forgery and Counterforgery* (2013).
20. "Evidences," May 2, 229; July 18, 405.
21. "Evidences," June 13, 322; March 28, 145, 147; April 29, 209; July 11, 390. On the clerical manipulation of women, see "Evidences," April 25, 212; May 9, 245.
22. "Evidences," July 11, 388, 389; July 18, 404, 405. Even his twentieth-century biographers were unaware of Cooper's *Correspondent* essays. The contents of the essays make Cooper's authorship obvious to anyone familiar with Cooper's writing, so apparently the *Correspondent* did not circulate in South Carolina, although newspapers there did note the periodical's existence as a scandalous publication attacking the Bible. Cooper acknowledged authorship in a letter to Thomas Hertell, posthumously published in *Thomas Hertell's Epistolary Correspondence with Dr. Thomas Cooper, of Columbia, (S.C.) during His Last Sickness, on the Subjects of Human Life, Death, &c., in the years 1838, 1839* (New York, 1845). In marginalia on the last page (252) in his copy of William Howitt, *A Popular History of Priestcraft in All Ages and Nations* (London

and New York, 1833), Cooper Papers, Cooper summarized his critique of the common idea of God: "A man who doubts about a *'moral Governor of the Universe'* is by common consent of all the Clergy, an Atheist. I wd humbly ask, whether Kingcraft, Priestcraft, enormous wealth in a few, and abject poverty in the many—whether War, plague & famine, are among the instruments necessary to the moral government of the Universe? Either he can & does prevent vise & misery; or, he can, and does not; Or, he would if he cd, but cannot."

23. On the United States not being a Christian country, Cooper referred to the First Amendment, to Jefferson's argument that American law did not incorporate Christianity as part of the common law, and to the Adams administration's letter to the dey of Algiers, which explicitly denied it. [Thomas Cooper], *To Any Member of Congress: By a Layman* ([Columbia, S.C.], 1831; orig. pub. 1829), 15, 10. The exchange of letters between Cooper and Blair, originally published in the *Camden Journal* in January and February 1831, was republished in *Niles' Weekly Register,* April 30, 1831, 154–56, esp. 154, 155. On Blair, see Kirkland and Kennedy, *Historic Camden* (1905–26), 2: 92–98. Blair committed suicide in 1834.

24. [Thomas Cooper], *An Exposition of the Doctrines of Calvinism* (n.p., 1830); F. J. V. Broussais, *On Irritation and Insanity... Translated by Thomas Cooper, M.D.: To Which Are Added Two Tracts on Materialism, and an Outline of the Association of Ideas* (Columbia, S.C., 1831). Censor, *An Appeal to the State* ([n.p., 1831]). Censor denied that he was a clergyman and claimed to share Cooper's states'-rights politics. See also *An Appeal to the State by Censor, Continued* (Columbia, S.C., 1831). [Samuel P. Pressley], *Letters to Thomas Cooper, M.D., President of the South Carolina College* ([Newberry, S.C.?], 1832). The *Charleston Observer* noticed *To Any Member of Congress* in its March 19, 1831, issue, and criticized Cooper with various articles weekly through April 16. On June 11, the *Observer* approvingly summarized Censor's *Appeal* (commenting again on it Nov. 19). The first series of eight "Letters to Thomas Cooper, M.D." ran from June 25 to Aug. 31; the second series of eight, by Pressley, were published March 3–April 7, 1832. See also in the *Observer* "Extracts from Dr. Cooper's Works," July 9, 1831; "Dr. Cooper on Materialism," July 30, 1831; "For the Christian Observer," by "A Brief Remarker," Aug. 31, 1831; "Dr. Cooper's Case," Feb. 11, 1832; and "Materialism," March 24, 1832.

25. "Atheism and Disunion," *Norwich* [Conn.] *Courier,* March 26, 1831, quoting from the *Lynchburg Virginian*. Pro-Cooper: *Reply to Censor; or, An Appeal to the Good Sense of the People of South Carolina, by Justice* (Columbia, S.C., [1831]); *An Appeal to the People of South Carolina by Wesley* (Columbia, S.C., [1831]).

26. Pressly ran for Congress in 1834 and was soundly defeated by the States' Rights candidate ("Election Returns—Abbeville," *Southern Patriot,* Oct. 21, 1834). The standard accounts of the Pressly resolution (Malone, *Public Life,* 350, and Hollis, *University of South Carolina* 1:109) do not mention his Presbyterian connection, for which see Lathan, *History of the Associate Reformed Synod of the South* (1882), 349; Meriwether, *History of Higher Education in South Carolina* (1889), 89; *Handbook of South Carolina* (1908), 216. Pressly was probably kin to the Rev. Samuel P. Pressley, who published *Letters* against Cooper in 1832 (there are variant spellings of both men's last names in the records). Both may have been descended from Scots-Irish brothers who emigrated to South Carolina in the 1730s, but the genealogy is uncertain. On Samuel, see Carwile, *Reminiscences of Newberry* (1890), 258–64. For Petigru's speech, see *Daily National Journal,* Dec. 24, 1831; it is praised in the *City Gazette,* Dec. 9, 1831.

27. Thomas Cooper, *The Case of Thomas Cooper, M.D., President of the South-Carolina College; Submitted to the Legislature and the People of South Carolina, December, 1831* (Columbia, S.C., [1831]), vi, 9.

28. Cooper, *Case of Thomas Cooper,* [iii]; in the second edition (Columbia, S.C., 1832), a fourteen-page appendix contains evidence of "Plans and schemes of the orthodox Clergy of the Presbyterian denomination" (appendix 1, [1]).

29. *Dr. Cooper's Defence,* 2. Hollis, *University of South Carolina* 1:113, notes how Cooper's hearing was "sandwiched between these stirring occasions" and suggests that the public may have had a hard time paying attention to it because of the excitement and confusion over Nullification. But press attention and the crowded hall suggest otherwise. No figure was more identified with Nullification than Cooper; the hearing was part of, not a distraction from, the Nullification battle.

30. G. W. Featherstonhaugh, *Excursions through the Slave States* (New York, 1844), 155–57, in Freehling, ed., *The Nullification Era* (1967), 192–93.
31. Cooper in *Hertell's Epistolary Correspondence with Dr. Thomas Cooper*, 36 [sic, 28]; on Cooper's revision of the *Correspondent* essays and projected work on Christian history (the papers were scattered with the sale of his library in January 1839 and were never published), see 11, 23.
32. Prominent Presbyterian arguments can be found in the pages of the *Charleston Observer*. See, for example, "South-Carolina College," July 25, 1835; "Messrs. John G. Brown, N. Herbemont, Albert Moore Smith, James M. Taylor, and Theodore Stark" [Letter to the Editor], Aug. 15, 1835; "A Graduate of the South Carolina College," Aug. 15, 1835; "The South Carolina College," Aug. 29, 1835; "The South Carolina College," Sept. 5, 1835; "Another Suggestion" [Editorial], Sept. 19, 1835; "The South Carolina College," Sept. 19, 1835; "Appeal in Behalf of the South Carolina College," Sept. 19, 1835; "Appeal Continued," Sept. 26, 1835; Letter to the Editor from "Several Presbyterians," Sept. 26, 1835; "The South Carolina College" [Editorial], Oct. 3, 1835; "The College," Oct. 17, 1835; "What Constitutes a Religious Man," Oct. 17, 1835; and "The South Carolina College," Dec. 5, 1835. The fuller story of the dispute can be found in Hollis, *University of South Carolina* 1:119–28.
33. Robert Y. Hayne et al., *Appeal in Behalf of South Carolina College* (Charleston, S.C., 1835), a twenty-page pamphlet, excerpted in the *Charleston Observer*, Sept. 19, 26, 1835; [Benjamin Gildersleeve], "The South Carolina College" [Editorial], ibid., Oct. 3, 1835; "What Constitutes a Religious Man," ibid., Oct. 17, 1835. Gildersleeve was joined in the continuing campaign against the college by the Rev. Richard S. Gladney of Columbia, who directed both the *Southern Christian Herald* and the *Columbia Times and Gazette*, and the Rev. S. P. Pressley, by this time a professor at the College of Georgia; see John G. Brown et al., *True Motives Exposed for the Attacks upon South Carolina College* ([Charleston, S.C.], 1835).
34. "The South Carolina College," *Charleston Observer*, Aug. 29, 1835; [Gildersleeve], "The South Carolina College," [Editorial], ibid., Oct. 3, 1835.
35. See Hollis, *University of South Carolina* 1:119–26; see, for, example "South Carolina College," *Southern Patriot*, Oct. 6, 1835, 2.
36. Thomas Cooper, *A Treatise on the Law of Libel and the Liberty of the Press . . . as Applicable to Individuals and to Political and Ecclesiastical Bodies and Principles* (New York, 1830), 133; [Abner A. Porter], "North and South," *Southern Presbyterian Review* 3, 3 (Jan. 1850): 338–81, esp. 378.
37. *Abstract of the Returns of the Fifth Census* (Washington, D.C., 1832), 21–22; Ford, *Origins of Southern Radicalism* (1988), 32–33 (population), 28 (Presbyterians and camp meetings); Thompson, *Presbyterians in the South*, vol. 1, *1607–1861* (1963), 175; A. W. Leland, *A Discourse at the Annual Examination of the Students in the Theological Seminary* (Columbia, S.C., 1839), [3]; McCurry, *Masters of Small Worlds* (1995), 152 (lowcountry revivals). The Synod of South Carolina and Georgia in 1829 recorded 73 ministers, 128 churches, and 8,560 communicants; see George Howe, *History of the Presbyterian Church in South Carolina* (Columbia, S.C., 1883), 2:429. Howe notes that had the membership of the Congregationalist and Independent churches, who at that time were still in union with the Presbyterians, been counted, the number of communicants would have been over ten thousand—still hardly an overwhelming figure.
38. *Population of the United States in 1860 Compiled from the Original Returns of the Eighth Census* (Washington, D.C., 1864), 451; on the population of South Carolina 1820–60, see also Sinha, *Counterrevolution of Slavery*, 12; Ford, *Origins of Southern Radicalism*, 44; McCurry, *Masters of Small Worlds*, 46; and Thompson, *Presbyterians in the South* 1:413 (emigration), 433 (denominational comparison).
39. Howe, *History of the Presbyterian Church in South Carolina* 1:414; Robinson, *Columbia Theological Seminary and the Southern Presbyterian Church* (1931), 28, 11. The quoted phrase is from a retrospective statement of founding intentions endorsed by the seminary's Board of Trustees in 1841, but it reflects sentiments expressed by I. K. Douglas for the committee directing the relocation in 1829.
40. John Holt Rice in William Maxwell, *A Memoir of the Rev. John H. Rice, D.D.* (Philadelphia, 1835), 330; George Howe, *An Address Delivered at Columbia, (S.C.) March 28, 1832* (Charleston, S.C., 1832), 6, 7, 24, 20. See Also Thomas Smyth, "Assurance—Witness of the Spirit—and Call to the Ministry," *Southern Presbyterian Review* (hereafter *SPR*) 2, 1 (June

1848): 99–132, esp. 110–11: "We *savingly* believe in the Scriptures, not because of any private voice, whisper, or suggestion from the Spirit, separate from the written word, suggesting to our mind that they are the word of God. Such an internal testimony would be delusive, as it has ever proved to be, and would itself stand in need of testimony—it would imply as many distinct reasons for believing as there are believers, and it would imply that no one is under obligation to believe the Scriptures unless he has received this internal testimony."

41. W. C. Dana, *A Reasonable Answer to a Skeptic* (Columbia, S.C., 1858), 3, 4, also published in *SPR* 11, 3 (Oct. 1858): 386–401; E. A. Nesbit, "Presbyterian Preaching at the South," *SPR* 13, 1 (April 1860): 102–22, quotation on 113. See also B. M. Palmer, "A Plea for Doctrine as the Instrument of Sanctification," *SPR* 3, 1 (July 1849): 32–53, which argues for the importance of preaching doctrine to counter the "latent skepticism" of those in the pews who had received biblical tenets "upon trust, an heir-loom from their fathers," but were too lazy to investigate them (33); "Pulpit Oratory: By a Georgia Pastor," *SPR* 14, 2 (July 1861): 275–96; and James Woodrow, "Inaugural Address of the Rev. James Woodrow, PhD., Perkins Professor, Theological Seminary, Columbia, S.C.," *SPR* 14, 4 (Jan. 1862): 505–30, which argues that clergymen need to be better informed about natural science in order to answer infidels.

42. James Henley Thornwell, "The Office of Reason in Regard to Revelation," *SPR* 1, 1 (June 1847): 1–34, 2 ("infidels," "speaks," "demands"), 7 ("particularly in modern"). See also Thomas Smyth, "Assurance—Witness of the Spirit—and Call to the Ministry," *SPR*, 2, 1 (June 1848): 99–132, esp. 111: "We savingly believe the Scriptures, therefore, to be the word of God, solely because of that evidence they give of the authority, veracity, wisdom and holiness of God, by which they were dictated. The *capacity* to discern this *evidence* is given by the Holy Spirit, but the evidence itself in is the Scriptures, and while the Holy Ghost is the author of that spiritual capacity by which we perceive and appreciate the evidence, it is the evidence and not the capacity which gives us the assurance of faith."

43. Thornwell, "The Office of Reason," 14, 19.

44. Thomas Smyth, *Claims of the Presbyterian Church*, Tracts on Presbyterianism No. 1 (Charleston, S.C., 1840), 14.

45. Thomas Smyth, "Argument for Church-Boards," in James Henley Thornwell, *Collected Writings*, ed. John B. Adger and John L. Girardeau (Richmond, Va., 1873), vol. 4, appendix A, 595.

46. Thornwell, "The Argument for Church-Boards Answered," in *Collected Writings* 4:183, 190. Although Thornwell lost the argument about boards in 1841, when the Presbyterian Church of the Confederate States was organized in 1861, it made no provision for them. See Westerkamp, "James Henley Thornwell, Pro-Slavery Spokesman with a Calvinist Faith" (1986), 54.

47. [Benjamin M. Palmer], "[Synopsis of and Commentary upon] The Minutes of the General Assembly of the Presbyterian Church in the U.S.A. (1859)," *SPR* 12, 3 (Oct. 1959): 513–603, esp. 594, 596. See also "The General Assembly of 1860," *SPR* 13, 2 (July 1860): 352–417; James H. Thornwell, "The Princeton Review and Presbyterianism," *SPR* 13, 4 (Jan. 1861): 757–810; and "Northern and Southern Views of the Church," *SPR* 16, 4 (March 1866): 384–411. See Maddex, "From Theocracy to Spirituality" (1976). Thornwell's "new theory," however, was not for a "church silenced on social questions" but for a church silenced without biblical mandate, and it was not hastily devised by Thornwell in 1859, as Maddex suggests (441). Maddex does persuasively show that "it was not in the Confederacy but in the border slave states of the Union that the 'spirituality of the church' idea flourished during the War" (446); it took hold more generally for Southern Presbyterians after the Confederate defeat. In contrast, Smith, "Slavery, Secession, and Southern Protestant Shifts on the Authority of the State" (1994) argues that antebellum Southern Presbyterians and Methodists understood religion and politics as separate spheres, though this started to break down with the Nullification Crisis and dissolved by the 1850s. See also Maddex, "Proslavery Millennialism" (1979) and Kellison, "Toward Humanitarian Ends?" (2002).

48. [Thornwell], "Memoir of Dr. Henry," *Southern Quarterly Review* 1, 1 (April 1856): 1–101; [Garrison], "Thomas Paine," *Liberator*, 15, 45 (Nov. 1845): 186.

49. J. C. Coit, *The Substance of a Discourse Delivered upon the Occasion of the "Semi-Centenary Celebration," on the Second Sabbath in December, 1839* (Columbia, S.C., 1840), title page, 28, 29, 13, 55.

50. Benjamin M. Palmer, *Warrant and Nature of Public Worship* (Columbia, S.C., 1853), 31.

51. Thomas Smyth, *Ecclesiastical Republicanism; or, The Republicanism, Liberality, and Catholicity of Presbytery, in Contrast with Prelacy and Popery* (Boston, 1843), 23. See also Thomas Smyth, "Presbyterianism—The Revolution, the Declaration, and the Constitution," *SPR* 1, 4 (March 1847): 33–79.
52. Smyth, *Ecclesiastical Republicanism*, 181, 191, 203, 75, 207.
53. Thornwell, "The Ruling Elder: Being a Review of Two Speeches of Dr. Breckinridge," in *Collected Writings* 4:101.
54. Thomas Smyth to Dr. J. B. Adger, Sept. 12, 1833, in Smyth, *Autobiographical Notes, Letters and Reflections*, ed. Louisa Cheves Stoney (Charleston, S.C., 1914), 106; Jasper Adams, "The Relation of Christianity to Civil Government in the United States," *Observer*, Nov. 30, 1833. Gildersleeve, criticized in the *Mercury* for not taking a public stand on the tariff, defended himself in an *Observer* column on November 23, 1833; he praised Adams's sermon on November 30 and ran extracts on December 7 and 14 as well. Adams's sermon has been republished in an elaborate and admiring modern scholarly edition: Dreisbach, ed., *Religion and Politics in the Early Republic* (1996).
55. Thomas Smyth, *The Unity of the Human Races Proved to Be the Doctrine of Scripture, Reason, and Science* (New York, 1850), esp. 143; see also 109, 112, 125, 305; on Smyth's library, see Smyth, *Autobiographical Notes*, 270. On Bachman's debates with Nott and Agassiz, 1847–56, see Stephens, *Science, Race, and Religion in the American South* (2000), 165–211.
56. Thornwell, *Collected Writings* 1:54n; 4:542. Thornwell discussed the slave's natural yearnings of the soul in *A Review of the Rev. J. B. Adger's Sermon on the Religious Instruction of the Colored Population* (Charleston, S.C., 1847), 12, reprinted from the *Southern Presbyterian Review*, and the infidelity of polygenesis in *The Rights and Duties of Masters* (Charleston, S.C., 1850), 10–11. See also James Henley Thornwell, "National Sins: A Fast-Day Sermon: Preached in the Presbyterian Church, Columbia, S.C., Wednesday, 21 November 1860," *SPR* 13, 4 (Nov. 1861): 649–88. On the debates over polygenesis, see Horsman, *Josiah Nott of Mobile* (1987) and Stephens, *Science, Race, and Religion in the American South*, esp. chap. 9 and 10.
57. "Review of Josiah C. Nott, Two Lectures," *SPR* 3, 2 (Oct. 1849): 335–35, esp. 335; "Review of Nott's Two Lectures," *SPR* 3, 3 (Jan. 1850): 426–90, esp. 449, 468, 471; George Howe, "Unity of the Race," *SPR* 3, 1 (July 1849): 124–68; Howe, "Ethnography," *SPR* 3, 2 (Oct. 1849): 233–58; A. A. Porter, "The Unity of the Human Race," *SPR* 4, 3 (Jan. 1851): 357–80, esp. 361.
58. "Ancient and Scripture Chronology," *SPR*: 4, 3 (Jan. 1851): 398–426, esp. 398; John B. Adger, "The Credibility and Plenary Inspiration of the Scriptures," *SPR* 5, 1 (July 1851): 73–92, esp. 73; "Review of George Morton, Types of Mankind," *SPR* 8, 2 (Oct. 1854): 302; John B. Adger, "The Plenary Inspiration of the Scriptures," *SPR* 3, 4 (April 1851): 460–98, esp. 460.
59. Smyth, *Unity of the Human Races*, 104, 14, 346 (approvingly quoting Arnold Henry Guyot on the providentially assigned labors of the inferior and superior nations); Thornwell, *Rights and Duties of Masters*, 15. "The Mark of Cain and the Curse of Ham," *SPR* 3, 4 (Jan. 1850): 415–26, an unsigned article, argued that explanations positing blackness as a mark of God's curse make little sense. It cannot be the mark of Cain, for his descendants were destroyed in the Flood. And the descendants of Ham through Canaan were said to populate the Middle East and North Africa, none of whose peoples resemble sub-Saharan Africans. The group ethnologists labeled "Caucasians" included peoples traditionally held to descend from Japeth, Shem, and Ham as well. In any case, the notion of complexion as God's mark did not explain red and yellow people. S. J. P. Anderson, "The Unity of the Human Race," *SPR* 5, 4 (April 1852): 572–601, uses horses to illustrate variety within species (576), though somewhat differently than here. Carrigan, "In Defense of the Social Order" (2000), a useful contrast of antebellum and postbellum attitudes, nonetheless confuses Thornwell's position. Insisting that blacks and whites were members of the same human "race" (biological and moral species) did not mean that he denied blacks' "racial" inferiority—the social and intellectual inferiority of this racial variety. Smyth, too, wrote of different "races" (varieties) and one race (human species). Noll, *The Civil War as a Theological Crisis* (2006), points to two main components of the theological crisis involving the Bible and slavery as "an inability to act on biblical teaching about the full humanity of all people, regardless of race; and a confusion about principles of interpretation between what was in the Bible and what was in the common sense of the culture" (74). The proslavery Christians discussed here, however, endorsed the "full humanity" of Africans; they

simply denied, with powerful scriptural support, that the Bible's notion of "full humanity" entailed the sort of social and political (as opposed to religious) rights that their abolitionist opponents, from a modern progressive perspective, presumed. Nor were they confusedly unaware when they had to shift from biblical exegesis to extrabiblical argument. Instead, they confused a projection of their own racial prejudices with historical and empirical evidence. Irons, *The Origins of Proslavery Christianity* (2008), follows Noll here and writes of a "faulty scriptural hermeneutic" (16).

60. [John B. Adger], *The Christian Doctrine of Human Rights and of Slavery* (Columbia, S.C., 1849), orig. pub. in *SPR* 2, 4 (March 1849): 569–86; J. H. Thornwell, *Report on the Subject of Slavery* (Columbia, S.C., 1852), 10; Smyth, *Unity of the Human Races*, 330.

61. Clark, "Jones, Charles Colcock" *ANB Online*; Charles Colcock Jones, "The Religious Instruction of Negroes," *Observer*, Sept. 19, 1835; [Charles Colcock Jones], "Instruction of Negroes," *Charleston Observer*, Feb. 4, 1832. On Jones, see also Clarke, *Wrestlin' Jacob* (2000; orig. pub. 1979), 10.

62. For the 1833 incident, see "Columbia and the Missionary," *Observer*, Sept. 14 and 28, 1833. For the 1847 incident, see John B. Adger, *My Life and Times, 1810–1899* (Richmond, Va., 1899), 164–78; Clarke retells the story in *Wrestlin' Jacob*, 144–51. Clarke describes the appearance and location of Charleston's houses of worship circa 1845 on 87–91 ("city full of churches," 88): St. Michael's (Episcopal), French Huguenot, St. Philip's (Episcopal), First (Scots) Presbyterian, Circular Congregational, Unitarian, Cumberland (Methodist), Trinity (Methodist), Bethel (Methodist), St. Mary's (Roman Catholic), Second Presbyterian, First Baptist, Wentworth St. (Baptist), Morris St. (Baptist), St. John's (Lutheran), and Beth Elohim Synagogue; see also 114–15.

63. Smyth, *Unity of the Human Races*, 337, 332.

64. Richard Furman, *Rev. Dr. Richard Furman's Exposition of the Views of the Baptists, Relative to the Colored Population of the United States, in a Communication to the Governor of South-Carolina* (Charleston, S.C., 1823), 10, 18; George Howe, "The Baptism of Servants," *SPR* 1, 1 (June, 1847): 63–102, esp. 65; R. S. Gladney, "The Downfall of the Union," *SPR* 16,1 (July 1863): 39–54; E. T. Baird, "The Religious Instruction of Our Colored Population," *SPR* 12, 2 (July 1859): 346–61, esp. 351; "Report of a Conference by the Presbytery of Charleston, on the Subject of 'The Organization, Instruction, and Discipline of the Coloured People,'" *SPR* 3, 1 (July 1854): 1–17, esp. 3, 4. Dierksheide, "Missionaries, Evangelical Identity, and the Religious Ecology of Early Nineteenth-Century South Carolina and the British Caribbean" (2006) contrasts a South Carolina evangelical paternalism with slave-owning antievangelicalism in the British Caribbean.

65. "A Slave Marriage Law," *SPR* 16, 2 (Oct. 1863): 145–62, esp. 145, 155. The *Confederate Baptist*, a weekly newspaper published in Columbia from October 1862 to January 1865, complained that "in the course of time, the patriarchal has been superseded by the praedial relation; and the owners of slaves have come to regard them, not as members of the family—dependents, for whose moral and spiritual welfare they are responsible—but as mere instruments in the accumulation of wealth and of the facilities of sensual gratification" (quoted in Kellison, "Toward Humanitarian Ends?" 220–21). Thornwell, Smyth, and Adger, too, insisted on a moral relation and not just a "praedial" one, but that moral relation need not be cast as familial.

66. J. H. Thornwell, "The Relation of the Church to Slavery," in *Collected Writings* 4:396; John B. Adger, *The Religious Instruction of the Colored Population* (Charleston, S.C., 1847), 6; [J. H. Thornwell], "[Review of] The Religious Instruction of the Colored Population: A Sermon Preached by John B. Adger," *SPR* 1, 2 (Sept. 1847): 137–52, esp. 137; Thornwell, *Rights and Duties of Masters*, 48. Thompson, *Presbyterians in the South* 1:210, quoting from the synod's minutes of 1831: "That in the discharge of this duty [preaching to blacks], we separate entirely the civil and religious condition of this people; and while we devote ourselves to the improvement of the latter, we disclaim all interference with the former."

67. Clarke, "An Experiment in Paternalism" (1975), esp. 234–35, and Clarke, *Wrestlin' Jacob*, 103, 155–58. On Presbyterian "embarrassment" over slave marriages, see "Report of a Conference by the Presbytery of Charleston, on the Subject of 'The Organization, Instruction, and Discipline of the Coloured People,'" *SPR* 8, 1 (July 1854): 1–17, esp. 15–16. Freehling, in "James Henley Thornwell's Mysterious Antislavery Moment" (1991), argues that Thornwell "loathed slaveholders" for breaking up slave families, but Freehling cites an *SPR* article

attributed to George Howe (390). Instead, Thornwell minimized this flaw in the Southern slave system: "He who would condemn the institution as essentially and inherently evil, because it sometimes incidentally involves the disruption of family-ties, would condemn the whole texture of society in the non-slaveholding States, where the separation of parents and children, of husbands and wives, is often a matter of stern necessity" ("The Relation of the Church to Slavery," in *Collected Writings* 4:381–97, esp. 391; originally written and submitted to the synod in 1847).

68. J. Leighton Wilson, "Report of the Committee on the Religious Instruction of the Colored People," *SPR* 16, 2 (Oct. 1863): 191–98, esp. 194; Smyth, *Autobiographical Notes*, 324, 342, 643, 665. On Cooper and Sancho, see Himes, *Life and Times of Judge Thomas Cooper*, 59.

69. McCurry, *Masters of Small Worlds*, 197, 209–10.

70. James A. Lyon, "Slavery, and the Duties Growing Out of the Relation," *SPR* 16, 1 (July 1863): 1–37, esp. 21; "Report of a Conference by Presbytery, on the Subject of 'The Organization, Instruction And Discipline Of The Colored People,'" *SPR* 8, 1 (July, 1854): 1–17. On black leadership in Charleston's churches, see Clarke, *Wrestlin' Jacob*, 118–21.

71. Charles Colcock Jones, *The Religious Instruction of the Negroes in the United States* (Savannah, Ga., 1842), 127. About 4,000 to 5,000 black Charlestonians were Methodist communicants, and perhaps 2,000 were Baptists (Clarke, *Wrestlin' Jacob*, 114–15). See also Thompson, *Presbyterians in the South* 1:443: "At the outbreak of the Civil War approximately 200,000 Negroes held membership in the Methodist churches of the South; and the Baptists were probably more numerous still. Southern Old School presbyteries reported less than 8,000 Negro communicants; South Carolina led with 3,244; North Carolina followed with 1,774; in Virginia there were only 754; Georgia and Florida, with a slave population of 500,000, had only 577." Letter from Anonymous Black Presbyterian to Thomas Smyth, July 8, 1871, in Smyth, *Autobiographical Notes*, 694–96.

72. O'Brien, *Conjectures of Order* 2:1109 (on Miles); E. A. Nesbit, "Presbyterian Preaching at the South," *SPR* 13, 1 (April 1860): 102–22, esp. 113–14, 115; Smyth, *Unity of the Human Races*, 335; Thornwell, *Rights and Duties of Masters*, 14.

73. John B. Adger, "The Revival of the Slave Trade," *SPR* 11, 1 (April 1858): 100–35, esp. 133. For articles in the Charleston *Mercury*, see, for example, the series beginning with "The South and the African Slave Trade, No. 1," July 24, 1858. A *Mercury* correspondent responded to the Episcopal critics in "African Immigration and the Southern Episcopalian," April 8, 1858; "The African Slave Trade—Is It to Be Reopened" was reprinted from the *Southern Episcopalian* in the *Mercury*, Aug. 9, 1859. For a thorough discussion of the movement to reopen the African slave trade, see Sinha, *Counterrevolution of Slavery*, 125–86.

74. [Edward B. Bryan], *Notice of the Rev. John B. Adger's Article on the Slave Trade* (Charleston, S.C., 1858), 28, 16, 8, 4. For Bryan's authorship, see Adger's untitled review, *SPR* 11, 3 (Oct. 1858), 500–502.

75. [Bryan], *Notice*, 26, 22, 5, 4. See also "African Immigration and the Southern Episcopalian," *Mercury*, April 8, 1858: "We think the editor has failed to give us any direct Scripture authority for his denunciation of the trade; implication is dangerous ground for him to occupy."

76. On the separate "orbits" of religion and politics, see John H. Rice, "The Princeton Review on the State of the Country," *SPR* 14, 1 (April 1861): 1–44, esp. 3, and "Address of the Presbyterian Church in the Confederate States of America to All the Churches of Jesus Christ throughout the Earth," ibid., 531–50, esp. 534. John B. Adger, in "Explanatory Note," ibid., 502–4, confessed that secession and the creation of the Confederacy had clouded the whole question: "It is, indeed, difficult to say, in every case, where, precisely, Church power ends, and the power of the State begins.... When a new Government is set up, *de facto*, and Christian men have to judge whether they ought to obey it or to adhere to their old allegiance, we must acknowledge that the Word of God does not enable any Church court to give them light in their doubts and darkness." The scriptures command obedience to the lawful ruler, but we cannot always easily tell who that is. "Here the moral question depends on a political one; and that political one is not determined by the Word, and, therefore, it is not the Church that can point out to the honest but doubting subject where his allegiance is due" (503). See also James A. Lyon, "Religion and Politics," *SPR* 15, 4 (Oct. 1862): 569–610.

77. James H. Thornwell, "National Sins: A Fast Day Sermon," *SPR* 13, 4 (Jan. 1861): 649–88, esp. 650, 651, 653.

78. Thornwell, "National Sins," 656, 657–58, 649, 666, 670.
79. "The Petition of the General Assembly of the Presbyterian Church in the Confederate States of America, Now Met and Sitting in the City of Augusta, in the State of Georgia, to the Congress of the Confederate States of America," in Thornwell, *Collected Writings* 4:553, 554. The Constitution of the C.S.A. was adopted March 11, 1861; representatives of forty-seven Southern presbyteries met in Augusta, Georgia, on December 4, 1861, to form the Presbyterian Church of the C.S.A. On Thornwell authoring and then withdrawing the petition because it faced vigorous opposition by some and there was no time for a full discussion, see Palmer, *Life and Letters of James Henley Thornwell*, 507. The reference to God, the explicit acknowledgment of slaveholders' rights, and the stronger safeguards for states' rights were the major changes from the U.S. Constitution.
80. "Petition of the General Assembly...to the Congress of the C.S.A.," 552, 553, 554, 556.
81. "The General Assembly of Columbia," *SPR* 16, 1 (July 1863): 102–19, esp. 102; Thomas E. Peck, "Church and State," *SPR* 16, 2 (Oct. 1863): 121–44, esp. 135, 129.
82. Thornwell, "National Sins," 688; Thomas Smyth to Dr. Jacobus, Dec. 31, 1860, in Smyth, *Autobiographical Notes*, 568; Thomas Smyth, *The Battle of Fort Sumter: Its Mystery and Miracle: God's Mastery and Mercy* (Columbia, S.C., 1861), [3], 4, 22.
83. "The Southern Cross," *Camden Confederate*, Oct. 10, 1862. On these other themes, see, for example, "Interesting Religious News from the Soldiers," ibid., Nov. 1, 1861; "The Attempted Invasion of Our State," ibid., Nov. 15, 1861; "Day of Fasting, Humiliation and Prayer," ibid., Feb. 21, 1862; "Put Reliance on God," *Charleston Daily Courier*, Feb. 21, 1862; "The Call to Prayer," ibid., Feb. 21, 1862; "The Allotments of Providence," *Charleston Courier, Tri-Weekly*, Feb. 27, 1862; "National Merits and Demerits," ibid., Feb. 27, 1862; "A Useful Lesson," ibid., April 10, 1862; "Delusions," ibid., May 1, 1862; "Our Cause," *Camden Confederate*, June 20, 1862; "To All Christians of the Southern Confederacy," *Charleston Courier, Tri-Weekly*, July 31, 1862; "Day of Thanksgiving" (Proclamation by Pres. Jefferson Davis), ibid., Sept. 9, 1862; "God in the War," ibid., Dec. 11, 1862; "The Crisis and Our Duty," ibid., Jan. 10, 1863; "The Obligations Involved in Our Cause," ibid., Jan. 27, 1863; "A Short Sermon" [Editorial] and "Reconstruction: A Short Sermon to the People," ibid., Feb. 17, 1863; "How to Observe the Coming Fast," *Camden Confederate*, Aug. 14, 1863; "Our Private Soldiers," *Daily South Carolinian*, April 2, 1864; "A Lady in Whose Heart Burns the Holy Patriotism," ibid., Jan. 12, 1865.
84. Editorial, *Daily Richmond Examiner*, Aug. 6, 1863. See Stout and Grasso, "Civil War, Religion, and Communications" in Miller, Stout, and Wilson, eds., *Religion and the American Civil War* (1998). See also Stout, *Upon the Altar of the Nation* (2006), esp. 134–35, 256–58.

Chapter 13

1. John R. Kelso, "Auto-biography," in "John R. Kelso's Complete Works in Manuscript," Huntington Library, San Marino, Calif., 708. The twelve Civil War chapters from this source have been published in Grasso, ed., *Bloody Engagements* (2017), but citations here are to the manuscript.
2. George S. Phillips, *The American Republic and Human Liberty Foreshadowed in Scripture* (Cincinnati, 1864). "Biographical Note," Phillips Papers: "From May 1863 to July 1864, he served as chaplain of the 49th Regiment of Ohio. With his regiment, he was in the Chickamauga (Ga.) Campaign, including the battle of Chickamauga (Sept. 19–20), the siege of Chattanooga, Tenn. (Sept. 24–Nov. 23), the Chattanooga-Ringgold Campaign (Nov. 23–27); the Atlanta Campaign, including the battle of Resaca (May 14–15); advance on Dallas (May 22–25), and battles about Dallas, New Hope Church and Allatoona Hills (May 25–June 5); the operations about Marietta and Kennesaw Mountain (June 10–July 2). In June 1864, Phillips was at a hospital, although he was able to follow the regiment then fighting about Marietta and Kennesaw Mountains. In July 1864, Phillips resigned for reasons of disability." On Union chaplains, see Armstrong, *For Courageous Fighting and Confident Dying* (1998) and Brinsfield et al., eds., *Faith in the Fight* (2003).
3. Kelso, "Auto-Biography," 711, 712.
4. McPherson, *For Cause and Comrades* (1997), 99 ("abstract and intangible" but "nonetheless just as real" as its Southern counterpart "and as deeply felt"). See also Moorhead, *American*

Apocalypse (1978); Miller, Stout, and Wilson, eds., *Religion and the American Civil War* (1998); Woodworth, *While God Is Marching On* (2001), good archival work, but the author's own version of conservative evangelicalism seems to be taken as normative; Noll, *America's God*, pt. 5; Sandow, "The Limits of Northern Patriotism" (2003); Stout, *Upon the Altar of the Nation* (2006); Noll, *The Civil War as a Theological Crisis* (2006); Miller, *Both Prayed to the Same God* (2007); Rolfs, *No Peace for the Wicked* (2009); and Rable, *God's Almost Chosen Peoples* (2010).

5. Phillips Papers; Phillips Collection.
6. Phillips, *American Republic*, 156. Cf. the Rev. Samuel Harris of Maine, who in an 1861 Fourth of July oration argued that American nationality was based not on ethnicity, geography, or history but on an idea: "It is the embodiment of our great American idea [of universal justice and individual freedom] into our institutions which constitutes us a nation," quoted in Moorhead, *American Apocalypse*, 129.
7. Clebsch, *From Sacred to Profane America* (1968), 184–97, compares Bushnell and Phillips, but Clebsch's own interpretation is itself too Bushnellian; see also Jones, *The Sectional Crisis and Northern Methodism* (1979), 162–63. On the organic unity of the nation, see also Vinton, *The Christian Idea of Civil Government* (1861): "The people of these United States, under the Federal Constitution, are ONE NATION organic, corporate, divinely established," quoted in Paludan, "Religion and the Civil War," in Miller et al., eds., *Religion and the American Civil War*, esp. 22; and Fredrickson, "The Coming of the Lord" in ibid., 110–30, esp. 117.
8. On the tension between republican universalism and the idea that free institutions were best suited to Anglo-Saxons, see Horsman, *Race and Manifest Destiny* (1981). On the assimilation of different ethnicities into the American nation, see the Rev. William R. Williams's 1862 "Address to the American Baptist Home Missionary Society," quoted in Moorhead, *American Apocalypse*, 166.
9. Phillips, *American Republic*, 31. As Byrd writes about the American Revolution in *Sacred Scripture, Sacred War* (2013), 177n23, the "parallel between America and Israel was important, but most ministers were careful not to call America the equal of Israel or the direct fulfillment of Israel." Much of the literature on America as "God's New Israel" misses the important distinction, pointed out by Holifield in *Era of Persuasion* (1989), 44–48, between typological arguments (prophetic fulfillments of scripture) and the uses of biblical analogies, models, and metaphors. Shalev, *American Zion* (2013) for example, blurs the difference between type and metaphor as he opposes both to an ontological relation (American Indians as actual, biological descendants of the Lost Tribes of Israel)—see esp. 119–20, 150. Guyatt, in *Providence and the Invention of the United States* (2007), 6, usefully distinguishes three kinds of national providentialism (God controlling the historical events of a people): "judicial" (God rewards and punishes nations according to their virtues and vices, but without any necessary connection to a grand plan for humanity); "historical" (God's judgments also operate according to a special role he has assigned particular nations in history, though these are not linked to any specific scriptural prophecies); and "apocalyptic" (the special nations are linked to specific prophecies, usually in connection to the coming millennial age—the thousand years of Christ's reign on earth). Historians have frequently mistaken "judicial" or "historical" providentialist language for apocalyptic claims that America is the Redeemer Nation; Guyatt on 106–7 is right to caution that historians frequently find evidence of "millennialism" only by employing weak, vague, or overly broad definitions of it (Byrd, *Sacred Scripture*, 223, agrees). The same can be said for those who see the ghost of the Puritan national covenant constantly haunting later American history. Phillips, however, was unambiguously employing typology, invoking the national covenant, and voicing apocalyptic providentialism.
10. Phillips, *American Republic*, 82, 84, 173.
11. See Moorhead, *American Apocalypse*. In chap. 2, Moorhead reviews the work of others who made prophetic calculations similar to Phillips's but concludes that "most Protestants, especially the theologically sophisticated, maintained a healthy skepticism toward efforts to achieve a precise calibration of particular prophecies with the events of the Civil War" (62) even as they affirmed the same general meaning of the conflict.
12. Jones, *Sectional Crisis and Northern Methodism*, 147: "There was an almost automatic tendency [among northern Methodist writers] to articulate correspondence between the birth, growth, and destiny of the Republic and the birth, growth, and mission of the Methodist Episcopal Church." New England writers made a similar case for the Puritans, and their views were more successfully incorporated into the national mythology.

13. Carwardine, *Evangelicals and Politics in Antebellum America*, 60, and see chap. 2.
14. George S. Phillips to D. J. Phillips (June 12, 1840), Phillips Papers.
15. Phillips, "Books Read during the Conference Year commencing 1841," in "The Life and Travels of Rev. G. S. Phillips, Preacher in the M. E. Church, Sept. 1 A.D. 1841" (his diary, Sept. 1, 1841—Aug 13, 1842), unpaginated; a similar record of twenty-one books read the following year in "Journal for 1842–1843," Phillips Papers, unpaginated, includes Abner Cunningham's colorful denunciation of deists and freethinkers, *Practical Infidelity Portrayed and the Judgments of God Made Manifest* (1836). Phillips, "Cause and Cure of Unbelief" (sermon outline). in "Journal of G. S. Phillips" (journal, sermons, commonplace book, Sept. 19, 1843—June 1, 1847), unpaginated; outline of a sermon on Heb. 2:3, in "Life and Travels," unpaginated; sermon [outline] on Luke 14:16, Kenton, Ohio, Dec. 21, 1843, in "Journal," unpaginated; sermon [outline] on John 4:24, Kenton, Ohio, Jan. 20, [1844], in "Journal," unpaginated; "Journal," Dec. 12, 1842.
16. Elizabeth Kauffman to George S. Phillips, Feb. 23, 1843; Kauffman to Phillips, June 27, 1843; Phillips to Luke Johnson, March 1842; Phillips, "Knowledge Is Power," undated lecture in "Journal" (1843–47); Phillips, "Journal," June 3, 1845 (blaming demagogues). All in Phillips Papers.
17. Phillips, Diaries (vol. 1, Dec. 1851–Jan. 1854; vol. 2, Feb. 1854–March 1855), Phillips Collection, entry for Dec. 29, 1851. On the early relations of Northern and Southern Methodists in California, see William Taylor, *California Life Illustrated* (New York, 1861), 156–57.
18. Anthony, *Fifty Years of Methodism* (1901), 10. See also Frankiel, *California's Spiritual Frontiers* (1988), chap. 1.
19. William Taylor, *Seven Years' Street Preaching in San Francisco, California: Embracing Incidents, Triumphant Death Scenes, Etc.*, ed. W. P. Strickland (New York, 1857), 58; Taylor, *California Life*, 104, and see 317, 324–28.
20. Taylor, *California Life*, 189.
21. Maffly-Kipp, *Religion and Society in Frontier California* (1994), 151; Taylor, *California Life*, 158, 54, 17; Taylor, *Seven Years' Street Preaching*, 343. Other denominations: according to one count, in late 1849 there were 7 churches in San Francisco—2 Presbyterian and 1 each for the Methodists, Roman Catholics, Episcopalians, and Baptists; by 1854 there were 22 ("The Contrast," [San Francisco] *Alta California*, Sept. 1, 1854). Another account has 30 churches in the city, with Methodists leading the list with 4, and notes the addition of a Congregationalist, a Swedenborgian, and a Welsh congregation ("Churches in San Francisco," [San Francisco] *Daily Placer Times and Transcript*, Jan. 14, 1853). Sacramento in 1856 had 2 each for Methodists, Baptists, and Episcopalians and single congregations of Presbyterians, Roman Catholics, Congregationalists, Chinese, and Germans ("Churches," [Sacramento] *Daily Democratic State Journal*, May 5, 1856). A report about Stockton boasted that although the town had only been founded in 1850, by 1861, with a population of 4,000, it had 13 houses of worship with seating for 5,000–6,000: Episcopal, Northern Methodist, Southern Methodist, German Methodist, Presbyterian, Baptist, Roman Catholic, Christian, Cumberland Presbyterian, 2 African churches, and a synagogue ("A City of Churches," *San Francisco Bulletin*, Aug. 3, 1861). In 1860, 118 of the 293 churches in the state were Methodist (Maffly-Kipp, *Religion and Society in Frontier California*, 6).
22. Phillips, Diaries, Phillips Collection, April 6, May 3, Aug. 3, 1854, Oct. 17, 1862; Taylor, *California Life*, 204.
23. Editorial, *California Christian Advocate*, May 18, 1853.
24. [Untitled—meeting of liberals], *California Christian Advocate*, Feb. 17, 1853; "Unitarian Development," ibid., May 18, 1853; "The Confession of a Deist," ibid., March 9, 1853.
25. Martin Clock Briggs, [Washington Birthday Address to the Sons of Temperance], *California Christian Advocate*, March 9, 1853.
26. On Briggs, see Foote, *Pen Pictures from the Garden of the World* (888), 286–87. On the libel suit, see "Christian Libelers," *Daily Placer Times and Transcript*, Dec. 18, 1854; for Phillips's reaction, see Phillips, Diary, vol. 2, Phillips Collection, entry for Dec. 22, 1854. [Methodist Episcopal Church South Conference, Sacramento], *San Joaquin Republican*, Nov. 15, 1856. On the *Advocate*'s name change, see Anthony, *Fifty Years of Methodism*, 77. On clergymen and the topic of slavery, see Maffly-Kipp, *Religion and Society*, 92: "By the mid-1850s ... the subject of slavery was all but taboo in California pulpits."
27. George S. Phillips to Elizabeth Kauffman, Jan. 6, 1843, Phillips Papers.

28. Kauffman to Phillips, Jan. 14, 1843, Phillips Papers.
29. Phillips to Kauffman, Feb. 4, 1843; Kauffman to Phillips, Feb. 23, 1843, Phillips Papers.
30. Phillips to Kauffman, March 19, 1843; Kauffman to Phillips, March 24, 1843, Phillips Papers.
31. Kauffman to Phillips, June 1, 1843; Phillips to Kauffman, June 13, 1843; Kauffman to Phillips, June 27, 1843, Phillips Papers.
32. Phillips to Kauffman, June 19, 1843, Phillips Papers.
33. Phillips to Kauffman, July 13, 1843, Phillips Papers.
34. Phillips to Kauffman, July 13, 1843, Phillips Papers.
35. Kauffman to Phillips, July 27, 1843, Phillips Papers.
36. Phillips to Kauffman, Aug. 10, 1843; Kauffman to Phillips, Oct. 13, 1843, Phillips Papers. They were married on September 19, 1843.
37. Many decades later, a California friend, Mrs. Otis Gibson, providing a capsule biography of Elizabeth to a Methodist historian, suggested a sharper rebellion against parental authority. Elizabeth, she wrote, "was converted in a Methodist meeting. Her wealthy father was greatly distressed. When she united with the despised Church he turned her out from her home of luxury and ease. Some good Methodist sister gave her a home, and she began teaching for a living. She soon married George S. Phillips.... After Dr. Phillips's death [in Ohio in 1865], she returned to San Francisco and lived with her daughter, Mrs. Austin Moore. Then she became interested in the Chinese, and began teaching in the Sunday-school and trying in every way to bring them to a saving knowledge of the truth" (quoted in Anthony, *Fifty Years of Methodism*, 298). In 1870, Elizabeth Phillips was also the president of the Women's Missionary Society of the Pacific Coast (297).
38. Phillips, *American Republic*, 12, 157.
39. Phillips, *American Republic*, 12; Maffly-Kipp, *Religion and Society*, 5–6, 92.
40. Taylor, *Seven Years' Street Preaching*, 294, 300, 296.
41. Taylor, *Seven Years' Street Preaching*, 345, 346.
42. Phillips, *American Republic*, 156, 155. On the links of the personal and the political, see Ackerman, "The Personal Is Political" (2002) and Bougher, "The Case for Metaphor in Political Reasoning and Cognition" (2012). On "The Nation as Human Writ Large" in Northern Methodist Civil War preaching, see Jones, *Sectional Crisis and Northern Methodism*, 61, 155–58. Schaff in Clebsch, *From Sacred to Profane*, 197. On the Emancipation Proclamation and the Northern opinion, see Frederickson, "The Coming of the Lord," 118; Stout, *Upon the Altar of the Nation*, 169; Rolfs, *No Peace for the Wicked*, chap. 8; and Rable, *God's Almost Chosen Peoples*, 224–27.
43. John R. Kelso, preface to "The Devil's Defense," in "Works," 64, 65. This work was published, but no copies seem to have survived.
44. Kelso, "Deity Analyzed," in "Works," 280, 346, 276, 284. I have used Kelso's manuscript copy, but this work was published: John R. Kelso, *Deity Analyzed: In Six Lectures* (New York, 1890).
45. Kelso, "Deity Analyzed," in "Works," 273, 336, 310.
46. Kelso, Preface to "The Devil's Defense," in "Works," 64; "Auto-Biography," in "Works," 684, 685.
47. Kelso, Preface to "The Devil's Defense," in "Works," 64.
48. Kelso, "Auto-Biography," in "Works," 687.
49. Kelso, "Auto-Biography," in "Works," 687.
50. Kelso, "Auto-Biography," in "Works," 692, 693, 694, 695.
51. Kelso, "Auto-Biography," in "Works," 696.
52. Kelso, "Auto-Biography," in "Works," 696, 697.
53. Kelso, "Auto-Biography," in "Works," 697, 698.
54. Kelso, "Auto-Biography," in "Works," 698.
55. Kelso, "Auto-Biography," in "Works," 699.
56. Kelso, "Auto-Biography," in "Works," 701.
57. Kelso, "Auto-Biography," in "Works," 700, 701, 704.
58. Kelso, "Auto-Biography," in "Works," 701.
59. Kelso, "Auto-Biography," in "Works," 702.
60. Kelso, "Auto-Biography," in "Works," 702. On Caples, see W. S. Woodard, *Annals of Methodism in Missouri* (Columbia, Mo., 1893), 163.
61. Kelso, "Auto-Biography," in "Works," 703.
62. Kelso, "Auto-Biography," in "Works," 707.

63. Kelso, "Auto-Biography," in "Works," 709, 708.
64. Kelso, "Auto-Biography," in "Works," 697, 709. Kelso did not know that the man, William Phillips, was indeed an abolitionist; when he returned to his home in Leavenworth, Kansas, he was gunned down on his veranda by another proslavery mob, but not before killing two of his assailants. On Phillips, see Trexler, *Slavery in Missouri* (1914), 198–99, and Grimsted, *American Mobbing* (1998), 250.
65. Kelso, "Auto-Biography," in "Works," 709, 710.
66. Kelso, "Auto-Biography," in "Works," 710, 709.
67. Kelso, "Auto-Biography," in "Works," 710, 711.
68. Kelso, "Auto-Biography," in "Works," 710, 711.
69. Kelso, "Auto-Biography," in "Works," 711.
70. Kelso, "Auto-Biography," in "Works," 712.
71. Kelso served as a captain and then a major in the Dallas County Home Guards (July–Sept. 1861), as a private (to make a point about selflessness) in the 24th Missouri Infantry Regiment (Oct. 1861–April 1862), as a first lieutenant in the 14th Missouri Calvary (April 1862–March 1863), and as lieutenant and then captain in the 8th Missouri State Militia Cavalry (March 1863–April 1865, promoted to captain March 1864, and then to brevet colonel a month before being mustered out). See Kelso, "Auto-Biography," in "Works," 712, 718–19, 756, 800. See also Grasso, introduction to *Bloody Engagements*.
72. Britton, *The Civil War on the Border*, vol. 2 (1899), 208, 207, 72–73, 201–2; Kelso, "Speech Delivered at Walnut Grove, Mo., Sept. 18, 1865," in "Works," 10–27, esp. 18.
73. Kelso, "Auto-Biography," in "Works," 772, 676.
74. Kelso, "Speech Delivered at Mt. Vernon, Mo., April 23, 1864," in "Works," 1–9, esp. 1.
75. Kelso, "Speech" (Walnut Grove, 1865), in "Works," 10, 13; "Speech" (Mt. Vernon, 1864), in "Works," 3.
76. Kelso, "Speech" (Mt. Vernon, 1864), in "Works," 7; "Speech" (Walnut Grove, 1865), in "Works," 24, 22. See also "Reconstruction: A Speech Delivered in the House of Representatives, Washington, D.C., Feb. 7, 1866," in "Works," 28–41.
77. Kelso, "Speech" (Mt. Vernon, 1864), in "Works," 7; "Speech" (Walnut Grove, 1865), in "Works," 27, 22.
78. Kelso, "Auto-Biography," in "Works," 737.
79. Kelso, "Deity Analyzed," in "Works," 292–93; "Speech" (Walnut Grove, 1865), in "Works," 19, 14, 11; "Speech" (Mt. Vernon, 1864), in "Works," 6, 1.
80. Kelso, "Deity Analyzed," in "Works," 282.
81. On religion and the soldiers, especially those who fought for the Union, see the sources in note 4. At the Battle of Chickamauga (Sept. 19–20, 1863), the Union lost about sixteen thousand men (dead, wounded, or missing) and the Confederates about twenty thousand (McPherson, *Battle Cry of Freedom* [1988], 672–75; Cozzens, *This Terrible Sound* [1992], 534). Phillips, who came under fire when the enemy shelled the hospital, wrote to Elizabeth after the battle: "The privilege of being present at that battle I feel was more than a compensation for all I have suffered in the war thus far." See G. S. Phillips to E. Phillips, after Sept. 23, 1863, and Sept. 29, 1863 (Phillips Papers). Union commander William Rosecrans, who had earlier in life converted from religious skepticism, was a pious military man who supported the work of his chaplains and made it a policy to never fight on the Sabbath. After he disastrously fled the field of battle at Chickamauga and was removed from command, the *New York Times* speculated that he had been paralyzed by his overreliance on God. See Rable, *God's Almost Chosen Peoples*, 139, and Shattuck, *A Shield and a Hiding Place* (1987), 77–79.
82. John R. Kelso, *Government Analyzed* (Longmont, Colo., 1892), 47, 48, 487, 49.

Epilogue

1. James Smith, *The Christian's Defence, Containing a Fair Statement, and Impartial Examination of the Leading Objections Urged by Infidels against the Antiquity, Genuineness, Credibility, and Inspiration of the Holy Scriptures* (Cincinnati, 1843), x; "[Review of] *The Christian's Defence*," *Biblical Repertory and Princeton Review* 16, 4 (Oct. 1844): 498–507, esp. 503; Charles G.

Olmsted, *The Bible, Its Own Refutation* (Louisville, Ky., 1836). On Olmsted, see Dexter, *Biographical Sketches of the Graduates of Yale College* 6:273–74. On Smith, see Smith, "The Pilgrimage of James Smith" (1988). On the debate, see Smith, "Frontier Ecumenism" (1989).
2. James Smith in a letter to William Bishop, quoted in Barton, *The Soul of Abraham Lincoln* (1920), 162–63. On Smith and Lincoln, see Havlik, "Abraham Lincoln and the Reverend Dr. James Smith" (1999).
3. William Rounseville Alger, *A Critical History of the Doctrine of a Future Life* (Philadelphia, 1864), 644, 610, 615.
4. Alger, *Critical History*, 637, 645. Here the Unitarian Alger inverted the famous image of the Calvinist Jonathan Edwards: rather than a soul dangling precariously over the pit of hell, suspended, for the moment, only by the unmerited act of a sovereign God, the spider escapes despair with a leap of faith.
5. William Taylor, *Seven Years' Street Preaching in San Francisco, California: Embracing Incidents, Triumphant Death Scenes, Etc.*, ed. W. P. Strickland (New York, 1857), 350–94; [William A. Alcott], *My Progress in Error, and Recovery to Truth; or, A Tour through Universalism, Unitarianism, and Skepticism* (Boston, 1842), 141; William A. Alcott, *Life of Peter the Apostle* (Boston, 1830), 44–47; 288–89; David Nelson, *The Cause and Cure of Infidelity: Including a Notice of the Author's Unbelief, and the Means of his Rescue* (New York, 1841; orig. pub. 1837), 264–76. Examples of Christian criticism of infidel deaths: David Parsons, "To the Editors," *Connecticut Evangelical Magazine* 1, 9 (March 1801): 347–52 (local Ethan Allen fan); D. B., "On the Infidelities of Mr. Gibbon," *Beauties of the Evangelical Magazine* 1 (Jan. 1, 1802): 459–61; "The Recantation of Monsieur Voltaire, a Celebrated Deist, in Favour of Christianity," *Christian Cabinet* 1, 2 (Jan. 1, 1802): 16–18; "Remarks on the Accounts of the Deaths of David Hume, Esqr. and Samuel Finley, D.D.," *Christian's Magazine* 1, 4 (Jan. 4, 1806): 419–36; "Death of Thomas Paine," *Vehicle* 1, 2 (Aug. 1, 1814): 72–76; "A Shocking Death!" *Recorder and Telegraph* 10, 25 (June 17, 1825): 97–98 (frantic infidel); "Lord Byron in a Storm at Sea," *Philadelphia Recorder* 2, 98 (Feb. 12, 1825): 342 (contrasts Byron to Shelley); "Conversations between a Christian and an Infidel Physician," *Christian Secretary* 13, 23 (June 21, 1834): 90; "Pious Frauds," *Boston Investigator* 15, 51 (April 29, 1846): 3 (Abner Kneeland); "The Skeptic's Daughter," *New York Evangelist* 28, 35 (Aug. 27, 1857): 278 (Ethan Allen). Examples of skeptics' response: Origen Bacheler and Robert Dale Owen, *Discussion on the Existence of God and the Authenticity of the Bible, between Origen Bacheler and Robert Dale Owen*, 2nd ed. (New York, 1833), 1:90; Aristedes, "Death-Bed Repentance of Liberals," *Correspondent* 5, 13 (April 18, 1829): 193–97 and 5, 14 (April 25, 1829): 213–15; *Thomas Hertell's Epistolary Correspondence with Dr. Thomas Cooper of Columbia, S.C., during His Last Sickness*, excerpted and commented on in *Boston Investigator* 15, 22 (Oct. 8, 1845): 1; "Death-Bed Experiences," *Boston Investigator* 16, 50 (April 21, 1847): 2 (tranquilizing effects of disease); "Death-Bed Recantations of Infidelity," *Boston Investigator* 39, 49 (March 28, 1860): 1 (heroic death of an atheist). On the "good death," see Faust, *This Republic of Suffering* (2008). See also Farrell, *Inventing the American Way of Death* (1980).
6. "Review: *A Defence of Christianity against the Work of George B. English*," *Christian Disciple* 2, 12 (Dec. 2, 1814): 369–74; "Review," *Western Monthly Review* 3, 8 (Feb. 1830): 427 (on Wright and Owen); "Report of the Arguments of the Attorney of the Commonwealth at the trial of Abner Kneeland," *Christian Examiner* 17, 1 (Sept. 1834): 23; "Review of 'The Eclipse of Faith' by Henry Rogers," *North American Review* 77, 60 (July 1853): 60–70; "The Eclipse of Faith," *Christian Review* 18, 71 (Jan 1., 1853): 59–84; [Alice Hayes Mellen], *The Female Skeptic; or, Faith Triumphant* (New York, 1859), 425–31.
7. Robert Hare, *Experimental Investigation of the Spirit Manifestations* (New York, 1855), 247; Robert Hare, "On Spiritualism," n.d., Hare Papers. On Hare, see also Hazen, *The Village Enlightenment in America* (2000), 65–112; Cox, "Vox Populi" (2003), esp. 259–72; and Kneeland, "Robert Hare" (2008). Smith's *Life of Robert Hare* (1917), the single full-length biography, devotes only three pages to his Spiritualism (482–84).
8. Hare, *Experimental Investigation*, 87; Hare, "On Spiritualism," Hare Papers; B[enjamin] Silliman to Robert Hare, May 1857, Hare Papers.
9. Robert Dale Owen, *Footfalls on the Boundary of Another World* (Philadelphia, 1860); "Opinions of Robert Dale Owen," *Boston Investigator*, Feb. 29, 1860, 1. On Owen, see Robert

Dale Owen Correspondence, Owen Family Papers; Robert Dale Owen Correspondence and Robert Dale Owen Collection; and Leopold, *Robert Dale Owen*.
10. Robert Dale Owen, *The Debatable Land between This World and the Next* (New York, 1872), 158, 26, 159; Robert Dale Owen, "What after Death?" *Boston Investigator*, Jan. 31, 1872, 1.
11. John R. Kelso, "The Autobiography of John R. Kelso" (privately held manuscript), 11:46, 14:54; John R. Kelso, *Spiritualism Sustained in Five Lectures* (New York, 1886), 157, 227–28.
12. Alger, *Critical History*, 52, 643, 642. For doubting Thomas, see John 20:25; for the man seeking help, Mark 9:24.
13. On Lincoln's religion, see esp. Guelzo, *Abraham Lincoln* (1999) and Winger, *Lincoln, Religion, and Romantic Cultural Politics* (2003). See also Wolf, *Lincoln's Religion* (1970; orig. pub. 1959); Endy, "Abraham Lincoln and American Civil Religion" (1975); Carwardine, "Lincoln, Evangelical Religion, and American Political Culture in the Era of the Civil War" (1997); Parillo, "Lincoln's Calvinist Transformation" (2000); and Calhoun and Morel, "Abraham Lincoln's Religion" (2012). On the debate over Lincoln's character generally, see Peterson, *Lincoln in American Memory* (1994); on the debate over his religious character, see Noll, "Lincoln's God" (2004). On Lincoln and Spiritualism, see George, "Some Lincoln Spiritualist Acquaintances" (2011).
14. Noll, "Lincoln's God." On Herndon, see Donald, *Lincoln's Herndon* (1948).
15. Abraham Lincoln, "Handbill Replying to Charges of Infidelity," in Roy P. Basler, ed., *The Collected Works of Abraham Lincoln* (New Brunswick, N.J., 1953), 1:383, http://quod.lib.umich.edu/l/lincoln/.
16. On Lincoln's "covenant" with God concerning the Emancipation Proclamation, see Guelzo, *Abraham Lincoln*, 338–43. On special Providence and superstition, see Abraham Lincoln to Joshua F. Speed, July 4, 1842, in *Collected Works* 1:289.
17. Abraham Lincoln, "Address Delivered at the Dedication of the Cemetery at Gettysburg," in *Collected Works* 7:23.
18. Abraham Lincoln, "Second Inaugural Address," in *Collected Works* 8:332–33. William Henry Herndon published an interview with Mary Todd Lincoln, who said her husband "was not a technical Christian": see Herndon, *Mrs. Lincoln's Denial and What She Says* (Springfield, Ill., 1874), broadside, Alfred Whital Stern Collection of Lincolniana, Library of Congress, https://www.loc.gov/item/scsm000585/. Herndon's notes from this interview have been published in Wilson and Davis, eds., *Herndon's Informants* (1998). Herndon recorded Mrs. Lincoln as saying that "Mr. Lincoln had no hope and faith in the usual acceptation of those words: he never joined a Church: he was a religious man always, I think: he first thought— I say think—about this subject when Willie died—never before. [H]e felt religious More than Ever about the time he went to Gettysburg: he was not a technical Christian: he read the bible a good deal about 1864" (360).
19. Borden, "The Christian Amendment" (1979), esp. 160 ("the Lord Jesus Christ"), from the National Reform Association's proposed amendment; Fisher and Mourtada-Sabbah, "Adopting 'In God We Trust' as the U.S. National Motto" (2002). The lawyer, political orator, and Civil War veteran Robert G. Ingersoll would draw popular attention to the resurgence of religious skepticism; on Ingersoll, see Larson, *American Infidel* (1962) and Jacoby, *The Great Agnostic* (2013). For the argument that "the faith of ordinary people appeared little shaken," see Rable, *God's Almost Chosen Peoples* (2010), 395. For the later nineteenth century, see esp. Turner, *Without God, without Creed* (1985), pt. 2; Croce, *Science and Religion in the Era of William James*, vol. 1 (1995); and Schmidt, *Village Atheists* (2016).

Appendix

1. The contextualized history of concepts (or what the Germans call *Begriffsgeschichte*) is a more systematic and elaborate version of what is being attempted in this appendix. See Sheehan, "*Begriffsgeschichte*: Theory and Practice" (1978); Richter, "*Begriffsgeschichte* and the History of Ideas" (1987); Richter, *The History of Political and Social Concepts* (1995); and Koselleck, *The Practice of Conceptual History* (2002).
2. Origen Bacheler and Robert Dale Owen, *Discussion on the Existence of God and the Authenticity of the Bible, between Origen Bacheler and Robert Dale Owen*, 2nd ed. (New York, 1833), 2:143, 1:49.

3. Rotenstreich, *On Faith* (1998), 5; Heb. 11:1; "Foundations of Faith: One of a Course of Lectures on the Evidences on the Evidences of Christianity, Lately Delivered before the Young Men of Boston," *Christian Examiner and General Review,* Sept. 1834, 1–14; for a skeptic's response to this verse, see "On Faith: A Discourse by the Lady of Isis," *Free Enquirer* 5, 20 (March 9, 1833): 156–59.
4. William R. Williams, "The Elements of Evangelical Faith," *Christian Watchman,* July 11, 1834, 1–2.
5. [George Park Fisher], "The Conflict with Skepticism: First Article—The Questions at Issue," *New Englander* 23, 86 (Jan. 1864): 113–32.
6. "Science and Skepticism," *Christian Advocate and Journal* 38, 39 (Sept. 24, 1863): 305; "Conversion of Two Physicians from Skepticism," *Religious Intelligencer* 17, 46 (April 13, 1833): 732–33, esp. 733; R. E., "Letter from a Believer to a Skeptic," *Monthly Miscellany of Religion and Letters* 7, 5 (Nov. 1842): 258–63, esp. 261.
7. "The Sceptic," *Weekly Messenger,* March 20, 1844, 1.
8. Timothy Dwight, *A Discourse, on the Genuineness and Authenticity of the New-Testament* (New York, 1794); Gardner Jones, "Infidelity the Offspring of Protestancy," *United States Catholic Miscellany* 13, 45 (May 10, 1834): 355–56.
9. William C. Brownlee, "The Authenticity and Genuineness of the Bible, and the Madness of Infidelity," *American National Preacher* 10, 5 (Oct. 1835): 257–63; See also review of George Rawlison, *The Historical Evidences of the Scripture Records Stated Anew,* in *Danville Quarterly Review* 1, 2 (June 1861): 354–57, and D. S., "Scepticism," *Evangelical Magazine and Gospel Advocate* 16, 2 (Jan. 10, 1845): 14.
10. "Is Protestantism Responsible for Modern Unbelief?" *New Englander* 16, 61 (Feb. 1858): 1–26; C. H. F., "Our Duties in Respect to the Skepticism of the Age," *Universalist Quarterly and General Review* 5 (July 1848), 232–47; Jones, "Infidelity the Offspring of Protestancy."
11. M. K., "Romanizing Tendencies," *Mercersburg Quarterly Review* 5, 3 (Oct. 1853): 615–39, esp. 625. Arguing that Protestant interpretive differences were often exaggerated, one writer noted that American politicians in opposing parties similarly argued over the language and details of the Constitution, but all stood by that document as the foundation of their beloved republic. See Bernard Whitman, "A Letter to Unbelievers," *Western Messenger* 3, 5 (June 1837): 732–44.
12. M. K., "Romanizing Tendencies," 636.
13. "Familiar Dialogues on the Holy Scriptures, No. IV," *Friends' Intelligencer* 10, 48 (Feb. 18, 1854): 757–59, esp. 757; "Natural History of Enthusiasm," *Spirit of the Pilgrims* 3, 5 (May 1830): 256–79, esp. 268; P. P., "Modern Scepticism: Some of Its Causes and Cures," *Home Magazine* 3, 5 (May 1854): 359–61, esp. 360; C. A. B., "Modern Scepticism," *Christian Examiner and Religious Miscellany* 49, 3 (Nov. 1850): 317–41, esp. 341. Clericus's appeal to the authority of learned men was a familiar device; apologists liked to line up Christian geniuses like John Locke or Isaac Newton against any team of skeptics an opponent could field. Fewer, however, would go as far as the essayist in 1840 who argued that society was the bearer of beliefs about God, Providence, duty, and immortality across history, while individuals contributed to and drew from this common reservoir of faith "to a great degree" unconsciously. See R. E., "The Argument from Universal Belief," *Monthly Miscellany of Religion and Letters* 3, 2 (Aug. 1840): 61–66, esp. 65. Such a view would seem to shove God and the individual aside and make faith into something that could be called a social construction.
14. S. P., "Liberal Preacher for March, MDCCCXXX," *Christian Register,* April 3, 1830, 1; "Letters to the Methodists," *Zion's Herald,* Dec. 22, 1824, 1; "John Wesley on the 'Witness of the Spirit,'" *Quarterly Christian Spectator* 8, 3 (Sept. 1, 1836): 353–68.
15. L. P. Hickok, "Philosophy and Theology in Conflict," *American Presbyterian and Theological Review* 2 (April 1863): 204–32; and see "Psychology and Skepticism," *American Theological Review* 15 (July 1862): 391–415, a review of Hickok's *Rational Psychology.*
16. "Modern Scepticism and Its Refutation," *Christian Review* 24, 100 (April 1, 1860): 307–34, esp. 5; "Review of the Argument in Support of Natural Religion," *Christian Examiner and General Review* 19, 2 (Nov. 1835): 137–62; Richard W. Dickinson, "On the Origin of Our Idea Respecting God," *Literary and Theological Review* 2, 8 (Dec. 1835): 541–77; C. A. B., "Modern Skepticism" *Christian Examiner and Religious Miscellany* 49, 3 (Nov. 1850): 317–42; "The Eclipse of Faith," *North American Review* 77, 160 (July 1853): 60–80, esp. 70.
17. Bachler and Owen, *Discussion,* 1:14, 20, 37, 18.

18. Kurtz, *The New Skepticism* (1992), 21; "A Sketch of the History of Philosophy...Modern Sceptics," *Christian's, Scholar's, and Farmer's Magazine* 2, 6 (Feb./March 1791): 682–84; R. D., "Of Religion," *New Harmony Gazette* 3, 27 (April 30, 1828): 214–15, esp. 214, and see "Prossimo," *Free Enquirer* 1, 6 (Dec. 3, 1828): 43–44; "Scepticism of the Times," *Christian Observer* 39, 7 (Feb. 16, 1860): 26, and see "The Skeptic," *Boston Recorder* 30, 16 (April 17, 1845): 61.

19. "Scepticism," *Albion: A Journal of News, Politics and Literature* 37, 47 (Nov. 19, 1859): 554; "Are Great Minds Prone to Skepticism?" *New-England Magazine*, Aug. 1835, 87–96.

20. "Scepticism," *Albion: A Journal of News, Politics, and Literature* (Nov. 19, 1859): 554; "Psychology and Skepticism," *American Theological Review* (July 1862): 391–414, esp. 406; "The Tendency of Scientific Men to Skepticism," *Methodist Quarterly Review* 14 (Oct. 1862): 1–19, esp. 6. As a healthy sign, see "Dr. Milnor: From Memoirs by Rev. Dr. Stone," *Episcopal Recorder* 26, 44 (Jan. 13, 1849): 173; "The Present Form of Infidelity," *Christian Register* 29, 34 (Aug. 24, 1850): 134; and "The Eclipse of Faith," *North American Review* (July 1853): 60–80, esp. 4.

21. M. G., "Skepticism: Its Causes; Its Cure," *Universalist Quarterly and General Review* 13 (Jan. 1856): 42–58, esp. 50; "The Art of Doubting," *Christian Secretary* 11, 10 (March 24, 1832): 38; O. W. White, "Soul-Contracting Power of Skepticism," *Christian Advocate and Journal* 24, 7 (Feb. 15, 1849): 25. On hesitating skeptics, see also R. E., "Letter from a Believer to a Skeptic," *Monthly Miscellany of Religion and Letters* 7, 5 (Nov. 1842): 258–63, and T. T. S., "Believing Doubt," *Monthly Religious Magazine and Independent Journal* 21, 2 (Feb. 1859): 103–12.

22. T., "The Eclipse of Faith," *Christian Review* 18, 71 (Jan 1, 1853): 59–84, esp. 79; "Scepticism," *Albion: A Journal of News, Politics, and Literature* 37, 47 (Nov. 19, 1859): 554; J. K., "Toleration," *Knickerbocker* 21, 5 (May 1843): 429–32; "Family Reading," *Christian Advocate and Journal* 36, 45 (Nov. 7, 1861), 358; "Characters," *Philadelphia Repository and Weekly Register* 2, 27 (May 15, 1802): 213–14, esp. 214; William A. Alcott, "Letters to Young Men, XVII: On Religion and Skepticism," *New York Evangelist*, Feb. 8, 1849, 1; M. G., "Skepticism: Its Causes; Its Cure," *Universalist Quarterly and General Review* (Jan. 1856): 42–58, 51, 52.

23. "The Experience of a Converted Skeptic," *New York Evangelist*, April 28, 1853, 1; [Alcott], "My Progress in Error," *Boston Recorder* 18, 13 (March 27, 1833): 49–50; "The Evidences of Christianity," *Methodist Magazine and Quarterly Review* 14, 1 (Jan. 1, 1832): 191–99, and see also A. B. G., "The Utilitarian: Atheism," *Evangelical Magazine and Gospel Advocate* 7, 30 (July 23, 1836): 237–39; "Infidelity: Its Erroneous Principles of Reasoning," *New Englander* 12, 47 (Aug. 1854): 341–62; O. A. B. [Orestes A. Brownson], "Introduction to the History of Philosophy," *Christian Examiner and General Review* 21, 1 (Sept. 1836): 33–64; W. S. Grayson, "Mental Philosophy," *Southern Literary Messenger* 21, 5 (May 1855): 296–73, and see also "The Scepticism of Science," *Biblical Repertory and Princeton Review* 35, 1 (Jan. 1863), 43–75, and "The Conflict with Skepticism and Unbelief: Third Article," *New Englander* 23, 88 (July 1864): 401–53; "Faith the Way of Life," *Christian Watchman*, June 12, 1846, 1.

24. On Kneeland, see chap. 10; "Blasphemy—Atheism—Prosecution," *Evangelical Magazine and Gospel Advocate* 5, 16 (April 19, 1834): 125–26; on infidelity as a disease of the mind, see "Rennell on Scepticism, No. 2," *Religious and Literary Repository* 1, 6 (March 25, 1820), 85–88; on infidelity as the result of an undeveloped moral nature, see "Review of the Argument in Support of Natural Religion," *Christian Examiner and General Review* 19, 2 (Nov. 1835): 137–62; on doubt as a reflex mental habit, see "Credulity and Incredulity," *Evangelical and Gospel Advocate* 3, 18 (May 5, 1832): 139–40; on calls for pity or kindness, see "Review of Duties of Christians toward Deists," *Christian Disciple and Theological Review* 3, 15 (May 1, 1821): 202–9, and C. S., "Skepticism," *Evangelical Magazine and Gospel Advocate* 4, 23 (June 8, 1833): 180–81; "Are Great Minds Prone to Skepticism?" *New-England Magazine* (Aug. 1835): 87–96; Orestes A. Brownson, *Charles Elwood; or, The Infidel Converted* (1840), in *Works* 4; for "the clergyman's argument," see "The Tendency of Scientific Men to Skepticism," *Methodist Quarterly Review* (Oct. 1862): 1–19, quotation on 6; F. W., "Remarks on Infidelity," *Washington Theological Repertory* 4, 6 (Jan. 1823): 163–64, esp. 164. See also T., "The Eclipse of Faith," *Christian Review* (Jan. 1, 1853): 59–84; Joseph P. Tuttle, "Skepticism and Faith," *New York Evangelist*, Feb. 3, 1853, 1; R. W. Dickinson, "Infidelity: Its Aspects, Causes, and Agencies," *Theological and Literary Journal* 6, 4 (April 1854): 620–39.

25. M. G., "Skepticism: Its Causes; Its Cure," *Universalist Quarterly and General Review* (Jan. 1856): 42–58, esp. 57. Three months after publication of this *Quarterly* essay a short narrative appeared in the *New York Observer* that seemed to illustrate the three skeptical types. The author first recalled a village raconteur from the turn of the century who read his Paine, joked about religion in the tavern, and died a sinner. Fifty years later, the Paineite's former friends were all moral men who gave lip service to Christianity, but none had progressed beyond superficial doubts to convert and join a church. A final anecdote concerned an anxious skeptic who desperately sought faith in later life but died before he could settle his convictions. All these skeptics had failed to read the Bible properly, examine their own minds and hearts candidly, and join the Christian community. See W., "What a Sceptic Did," *New York Observer and Chronicle,* April 17, 1856, 1.
26. Bacheler and Owen, *Discussion* 1:73, 60, 64, 93. See also "Prossimo," *Free Enquirer* (Dec. 3, 1828): 43, and R. D. O. [Robert Dale Owen], "On the Coldness and Heartlessness of Scepticism," *Free Enquirer* 1, 13 (Jan. 21, 1829): 102.
27. Bacheler and Owen, *Discussion* 1:60, 67.

REFERENCES

I. Archival Sources

Babock, William Smyth. William Smyth Babcock Papers, 1757, 1788–1839, American Antiquarian Society, Worcester, Mass.
Brownson, Orestes A. Orestes Augustus Brownson Papers. University of Notre Dame Archives, University of Notre Dame, Notre Dame, Ind. Microfilm.
Cooper, Thomas. Thomas Cooper Papers. South Caroliniana Library, University of South Carolina, Columbia, S.C.
Ely, Ezra Stiles. Ezra Stiles Ely Papers. Presbyterian Historical Society, Philadelphia, Pa. Microfilm.
Everett, Edward. Edward Everett Papers. Massachusetts Historical Society, Boston, Mass. Microfilm.
Hare, Robert. Robert Hare Papers. American Philosophical Society, Philadelphia, Pa.
Hildreth, Richard. Caroline Weston Correspondence. Boston Public Library, Boston, Mass.
Jones, Sarah Anderson. Sarah Anderson Jones Diary. Special Collections Research Center, Swem Library, College of William and Mary, Williamsburg, Va.
Kelso, John R. "The Autobiography of John R. Kelso." Privately held manuscript.
Kelso, John R. "John R. Kelso's Complete Works in Manuscript." Huntington Library, San Marino, Calif.
Mann, Horace. Horace Mann Papers. Massachusetts Historical Society, Boston, Mass. Microfilm.
Nelson, David. David Nelson Papers, Record Group 411. Presbyterian Historical Society, Philadelphia, Pa. Microfilm.
Owen, Robert Dale. Robert Dale Owen Correspondence, Owen Family Papers. Indiana University Archives, Bloomington, Ind.
Owen, Robert Dale. Robert Dale Owen Correspondence and Robert Dale Owen Collection. Indiana State Library, Indianapolis, Ind.
Phillips, George S. George S. Phillips Collection, California State Library, Sacramento, Calif.
Phillips, George S. George S. Phillips Papers. Huntington Library, San Marino, Calif.
Stiles, Ezra. Ezra Stiles Papers. General Collection, Beinecke Rare Book and Manuscript Library, Yale University. Microfilm.
Virginia General Assembly. Legislative Petitions. Mecklenburg County, 1776–1818. Virginia State Library, Richmond, Va.

II. Newspapers and Periodicals

Advent Herald. Boston, Mass., 1846–1848.
Adviser, or, Vermont Evangelical Magazine. Middlebury, Vt., 1809–1815.

Albany Bouquet and Literary Spectator. Albany, N.Y., 1835.
Albany Gazette. Albany, N.Y., 1788–1821.
Albion: A Journal of News, Politics and Literature. New York, 1822–1876.
Alexandria Herald. Alexandria, Va., 1811–1825.
American. Providence, R.I., 1799–1781.
American Biblical Repository. New York, N.Y., 1837–1838.
American Citizen. New York, N.Y., 1800–1810.
American Journal of Education. Boston. Mass., 1826–1830.
American Jurist and Law Magazine. Boston, Mass., 1829–1843.
American Magazine of Useful and Entertaining Knowledge. Boston. Mass., 1834–1837.
American Mercury. Hartford, Conn., 1784–1829.
American National Preacher. New York, N.Y., 1827–1857.
American New Church Repository. Philadelphia, Pa., 1817–1818.
American Presbyterian and Theological Review. New York, N.Y., 1863–1868.
American Quarterly Church Review, and Ecclesiastical Register. New York, N.Y., 1863–1870.
American Review: A Whig Journal of Politics, Literature, Art, and Science. New York, N.Y., 1845–1847.
American Review and Literary Journal. New York, N.Y., 1801–1802.
American Theological Review. New York, N.Y., 1859–1862.
Ariel. Philadelphia, Pa., 1827–1832.
Arkansas Gazette. Arkansas Post, Ark. Ter., 1819–1839.
Atkinson's Saturday Evening Post. Philadelphia, Pa., 1831–1839.
Balance. Hudson, N.Y., 1801–1808.
Baltimore Gazette and Daily Advertiser. Baltimore, Md., 1826–1838.
Baltimore Patriot. Baltimore, Md., 1812–1834.
Baltimore Republican, or Anti-Democrat. Baltimore, Md., 1802–1804.
Beauties of the Evangelical Magazine. Philadelphia, Pa., 1802–1803.
Biblical Repertory and Princeton Review. New York, N.Y., 1837–1871.
Boston Commercial Gazette. Boston, Mass., 1800–1826.
Boston Courier. Boston, Mass., 1795.
Boston Daily Advertiser. Boston, Mass., 1796–1797.
Boston Evening Post. Boston, Mass., 1781–1784.
Boston Investigator. Boston, Mass., 1831–1904.
Boston Quarterly Review. Boston, Mass., 1838–1842.
Boston Recorder. Boston, Mass., 1817–1824; 1830–1849.
Brownson's Quarterly Review. Boston, Mass., 1844–1875.
California Christian Advocate. San Francisco, Calif., 1851–1932.
Calvinist Magazine. Rogersville, Tenn., 1827–1850.
Camden Confederate. Camden, S.C., 1861–1865.
Carolina Gazette. Charleston, S.C., 1798–1840.
Carolina Law Journal. Columbia, S.C., 1830–1831.
Catholic Telegraph. Cincinnati, Ohio, 1831–1846.
Charleston Courier. Charleston, S.C., 1803–1820.
Charleston Mercury. Charleston, S.C., 1854–1859.
Charleston Observer. Charleston, S.C., 1827–1845.
Christian Advocate and Journal. Chicago, Ill., 1827–1828.
Christian Cabinet. Philadelphia, Pa., 1802.
Christian Disciple and Theological Review. Boston, Mass., 1819–1823.
Christian Examiner and General Review. New York, N.Y., 1829–1844.
Christian Examiner and Religious Miscellany. New York, N.Y., 1844–1857.
Christian Inquirer. New York, N.Y., 1846–1864.
Christian Messenger. Baltimore, Md., 1817–1819.
Christian Observer. Boston, Mass., 1802–1842.
Christian Reflector. Boston, Mass., 1838–1848.

Christian Register. Boston, Mass., 1821–1835.
Christian Register and Boston Observer. Boston, Mass., 1835–1843.
Christian Repository. Woodstock, Vt., 1820–1825.
Christian Review. Boston, Mass., 1836–1863.
Christian's, Scholar's, and Farmer's Magazine. Elizabethtown, N.J., 1789–1791.
Christian Secretary. Hartford, Conn., 1822–1889.
Christian Visitant. Albany, N.Y., 1815–1816.
Christian Watchman. Boston, Mass., 1819–1848.
Christian's Magazine. New York, N.Y., 1806.
Christian's Weekly Monitor. Sangerfield, N.Y., 1814–1818.
Cincinnati Mirror, and Western Gazette of Literature, Science, and the Arts. Cincinnati, Ohio, 1831–1836.
City Gazette. Charleston, S.C., 1787–1833.
Columbian Centinel. Boston, Mass., 1804–1840.
Columbian Magazine. Hudson, N.Y., 1815–1816.
Columbian Register. New Haven, Conn., 1813–1876.
Columbian Star. Washington, D.C., 1822–1829.
Commercial Advertiser. New York, N.Y., 1797–1820.
Common School Journal. Boston, Mass., 1838–1852.
Connecticut Courant. Hartford, Conn., 1764–1850.
Connecticut Evangelical Magazine. Hartford, Conn., 1800–1807.
Connecticut Gazette. New London, Conn., 1763–1844.
Connecticut Herald. New Haven, Conn., 1803–1889.
Constitution. Middletown, Conn., 1841–1879.
Constitutional Telegraph. Boston, Mass., 1799–1802.
Continental Journal. Boston, Mass., 1776–1787.
Correspondent. New York, N.Y., 1827–1829.
Daily Commercial Bulletin. St. Louis, Mo., 1835–1838.
Daily Democratic State Journal. Sacramento, Calif., 1853–1858.
Daily National Intelligencer. Washington, D.C., 1800–1869.
Daily National Journal. Washington, D.C., 1824–1831.
Daily Ohio Statesman. Columbus, Ohio, 1837–1852.
Daily Picayune. New Orleans, La., 1837–1900.
Daily Placer Times and Transcript. San Francisco, Calif., 1852–1855.
Daily Scioto Gazette. Chillicothe, Ohio, 1832–1857.
Daily South Carolinian. Columbia, S.C., 1849–1867.
Danville Quarterly Review. Danville, Ky., 1861–1864.
Democratic Review. Washington, D.C., 1837–1851.
The Dial: A Magazine for Literature, Philosophy, and Religion. Boston, Mass., 1840–1844.
Diary. New York, N.Y., 1792–1797.
Dunlap's American Daily Advertiser. Philadelphia, Pa., 1791–1795.
Emporium of Arts and Sciences. Philadelphia, Pa., 1812–1814.
Episcopal Recorder. Philadelphia, Pa., 1831–1851.
Episcopal Watchman. Hartford, Conn., 1827–1833.
Essex Gazette. Salem, Mass., 1768–1775.
Essex Journal. Newburyport, Mass., 1784–1794.
Essex Register. Salem, Mass., 1807–1827.
Evangelical and Literary Magazine and Missionary Chronicle. Richmond, Va., 1821.
Evangelical Magazine and Gospel Advocate. Utica, N.Y., 1830–1848.
Evening Post. New York, 1801–1821.
Farmer's Cabinet. Amherst, N. H., 1802–1879.
Federal Gazette. Baltimore, Md., 1796–1801.
Federal Gazette, and Philadelphia Evening Post. Philadelphia, Pa., 1788–1793.

Federal Republican. Baltimore, Md., 1803–1804.
Franklin Monitor. Charlestown, Mass., 1819–1820.
Free Enquirer. New Harmony, Ind.; New York, N.Y., 1828–1835.
Freemason's Magazine. Philadelphia, Pa., 1811–1812.
Friends' Intelligencer. Philadelphia, Pa., 1853–1910.
Gazette of the United States. Philadelphia, Pa., 1789–1790.
General Advertiser. Philadelphia, Pa., 1790–1794.
General Repository and Review. Cambridge, Mass., 1812–1813.
Genius of Universal Emancipation. Mt. Pleasant, Ohio, 1821–1839.
Gospel Advocate. Buffalo, N.Y., 1827–1829.
Gospel Herald. New York, N.Y., 1820–1829.
Greenleaf's New York Journal. New York, N.Y., 1794–1800.
Harper's New Monthly Magazine. New York, N.Y., 1850–1900.
Haverhill Gazette. Haverhill, Mass., 1823–1841.
Herald. Hagerstown, Md., 1797–1820.
Hampshire Gazette. Northampton, Mass., 1820–1916.
Herald of Freedom. Boston, Mass., 1788–1791.
Herald of Gospel Liberty. Philadelphia, Pa., 1808–1816.
Home Magazine. Philadelphia, Pa., 1852–1856.
Independent. New York, N.Y., 1848–1921.
Independent Chronicle. Boston, Mass., 1776–1817.
Independent Gazetter. Philadelphia, Pa., 1753–1796.
The Jesuit. Boston, Mass., 1829–1831, 1833–1834.
Journal of the Franklin Institute. Tarrytown, N.Y., 1829-
Knickerbocker. New York, N.Y., 1833–1862.
Lancaster Journal. Lancaster, Pa., 1810–1818.
Liberator. Boston, Mass., 1831–1865.
Litchfield Republican. Litchfield, Conn., 1819–1822.
Literary Cadet and Rhode-Island Statesman. Providence, R.I., 1826–1829.
Literary and Theological Review. New York, N.Y., 1834–1839.
Lowell Offering. Lowell, Mass., 1840–1845.
The Man. New York, N.Y., 1834.
Massachusetts Centinel. Boston, Mass., 1784–1790.
Massachusetts Quarterly Review. Boston, Mass., 1847–1850.
Massachusetts Spy. Boston, Mass., 1770–1775.
Mechanic's Advocate. Albany, N.Y., 1846–1848.
Mercersburg Quarterly Review. Lancaster, Pa., 1849–1856.
Methodist Magazine and Quarterly Review. New York, N.Y., 1830–1840.
Methodist Quarterly Review. New York, N.Y., 1841–1844.
Mirror. Concord, N.H., 1792–1799.
Mirror of the Times. Wilmington, Del., 1800–1806.
Missouri Republican. St. Louis, Mo. 1841–1888.
Monthly Miscellany of Religion and Letters. Boston, Mass., 1839–1843.
Monthly Religious Magazine and Independent Journal. Boston, Mass., 1856–1861.
Moral Reformer and Teacher on the Human Constitution. Boston, Mass., 1835–1836.
Morning Chronicle. New York, N.Y., 1802–1807.
National Era. Washington, D.C., 1847–1860.
National Gazette. Philadelphia. Pa., 1820–1841.
National Magazine. Washington, D.C., 1801–1802.
New Church Herald and Monthly Repository. Philadelphia, Pa., 1856.
New-England Galaxy and United States Literary Advertiser. Boston, Mass., 1830–1836.
New-England Magazine. Boston, Mass., 1831–1835.
New Englander. New Haven, Conn., 1843–1885.

New-Hampshire Gazette. Portsmouth, N.H., 1756–1851.
New Hampshire Observer. Concord, N.H., 1822–1826.
New-Hampshire Patriot. Concord, N.H., 1809–1890.
New-Hampshire Sentinel. Keene, N.H., 1799–1891.
New Harmony Gazette. New Harmony, Ind., 1825–1828.
New Haven Gazette and Connecticut Magazine. New Haven, Conn. 1786–1789.
New-Jersey Gazette. Burlington, N.J., 1777–1778.
New Jerusalem Magazine. London, 1790.
New Jerusalem Magazine. Boston, Mass., 1827–1893.
New York Gazette. Albany, N.Y., 1788–1821.
New York Evangelist. New York, N.Y., 1830–1902.
New York Herald. New York, N.Y., 1794–1797.
New York Missionary Magazine. New York, N.Y., 1800–1803.
New-York Packet. New York, N.Y., 1783–1792.
New-York Spectator. New York, N.Y., 1797–1842.
New York Tribune. New York, N.Y., 1859–1899.
New World: A Weekly Family Journal. New York, N.Y., 1840–1845.
Newburyport Herald. Newburyport, Mass., 1797–1833.
Niles Weekly Register. Baltimore, Md., 1814–1837.
North American. Philadelphia, Pa., 1832–1835.
North American Review. Boston, Mass., 1841–1940.
Northumberland Gazette. Sunbury, Pa., 1792–1801.
Norwich Courier. Norwich, Conn., 1796–1833.
Norwich Packet. Norwich, Conn., 1773–1802.
Oliver's Magazine. Boston, Mass., 1841.
Pennsylvania Evening Post. Philadelphia, Pa., 1775–1784.
Pennsylvania Packet. Philadelphia, Pa., 1771–1790.
Philadelphia Album and Ladies Literary Gazette. Philadelphia, Pa., 1827–1830.
Philadelphia Recorder. Philadelphia, Pa., 1823–1831.
Philadelphia Repository and Weekly Register. Philadelphia, Pa., 1800–1805.
Philadelphian. Philadelphia, Pa., 1825–1836.
Philanthropist. Cincinnati, Ohio, 1836–1843.
Portland Advertiser. Portland, Maine, 1824–1832.
Portsmouth Journal of Literature and Politics. Portsmouth, N. H., 1821–1859.
Poulson's American Daily Advertiser. Philadelphia, Pa., 1800–1820.
Presbyterian. Philadelphia, Pa., 1821–1822.
Prospect. New York, N.Y., 1803–1805.
Providence Gazette and Country Journal. Providence, R.I., 1782–1825.
Public Advertiser. New York, N.Y., 1807–1813.
Quarterly Christian Spectator. New Haven, Conn., 1829–1838.
Quarterly Theological Review. Philadelphia, Pa., 1818–1819.
Reading Weekly Advertiser. Reading, Pa., 1796–1797.
Recorder and Telegraph. Boston, Mass., 1825.
Recorder of the Times. Newburgh, N.Y., 1803–1806.
Reformer. Philadelphia, Pa., 1820–1831.
Religious Intelligencer. New Haven, Conn., 1816–1837.
Religious and Literary Repository. Annapolis, Md., 1820.
Religious Miscellany. Carlisle, Pa., 1823–1824.
Religious Remembrancer. Philadelphia, Pa., 1813–1823.
Republican Farmer. Bridgeport, Conn., 1810–1876.
Republican Spy. Springfield, Mass., 1803–1804.
Rhode Island American. Providence, R.I., 1808–1809.
Rhode Island Republican. Newport, R.I., 1801–1803.

Richmond Enquirer. Richmond, Va., 1804–1863.
Richmond Examiner. Richmond, Va., 1861–1866.
Salem Gazette. Salem, Mass., 1781–1785, 1790–1849.
Salem Register. Salem, Mass., 1802–1807.
San Francisco Bulletin. San Francisco, Calif., 1855–1891.
San Joaquin Republican. Stockton, Calif., 1855–1860.
Southern Chronicle. Camden, S.C., 1822–1825.
Southern Churchman. Richmond, Va., 1835–1952.
Southern Literary Messenger. Richmond, Va., 1834–1845.
Southern Patriot. Charleston, S.C., 1831–1848.
Southern Presbyterian Review. Columbia, S.C., 1847–1885.
Southern Quarterly Review. New Orleans, La., 1842–1857.
Spirit of the Pilgrims. Boston, Mass., 1833.
Sun. Dover, N.H, 1795–1818.
Teacher of Health, and the Laws of the Human Constitution. Boston, Mass., 1843.
Telescope. Columbia, S.C., 1815–1839.
Temple of Reason. New York, N.Y., Nov. 8, 1800–Feb. 7, 1801; Philadelphia, Pa., April 22, 1801–Feb. 19, 1803.
Temple of Truth. Baltimore, Md., 1801.
Theological Magazine, or Synopsis of Modern Religious Sentiment. New York, N.Y., 1795–1799.
True American, Trenton, N.J., 1801–1818.
Trumpet and Universalist Magazine. Boston, Mass., 1828–1851.
United States Catholic Miscellany. Charleston, S.C., 1822–1835.
United States Chronicle. Providence, R.I., 1784–1804.
Universalist Magazine. Boston, Mass., 1819–1828.
Universalist Quarterly and General Review. Boston, Mass., 1844–1891.
Universalist Watchman. Woodstock, Vt., 1831–1847.
Utica Christian Magazine. Utica, N.Y., 1813–1816.
The Vehicle. Morrisville, N.Y., 1811–1812.
Vermont Gazette. Bennington, Vt., 1783–1850.
Village Register. Dedham, Mass., 1820–1829.
Virginia Evangelical and Literary Magazine. Richmond, Va., 1818–1820.
Virginia Gazette, or American Advertiser. Williamsburg, Va., 1781–1786.
Washington Theological Repertory. Washington, D.C., 1819–1828.
Watch-Tower. Cooperstown, N.Y., 1814–1831.
Weekly Messenger. Chambersburg, Pa., 1841–1844.
Western Examiner. St. Louis, Mo., 1833–1835.
Western Journal of the Medical and Physical Sciences. Cincinnati, Ohio, 1828–1838.
Western Luminary. Lexington, Ky., 1824–1834.
Western Messenger. Cincinnati, Ohio, 1835–1841.
Western Star. Stockbridge, Mass., 1789–1806.
Wheeling Gazette. Wheeling, Va., 1824–1842.
Workingman's Advocate. New York, N.Y., 1829–1836, 1844–1845.
Zion's Herald. Boston, Mass., 1823–1841.

III. Other Cited Primary Published Sources

Abstract of the Returns of the Fifth Census. Washington, D.C., 1832.
Acts of Assembly, Now in Force, in the Colony of Virginia. Williamsburg, Va., 1769.
Acts and Laws... of Massachusetts. Boston, 1782.
Acts and Laws of His Majesty's English Colony of Connecticut. New London, Conn., 1750.
Acts and Laws of the State of Connecticut. Hartford, Conn., 1796.

Adams, Jasper. *Religion and Politics in the Early Republic: Jasper Adams and the Church-State Debate.* Ed. Daniel L. Dreisbach. Lexington, Ky., 1996. Modern ed. of Adams, "The Relation of Christianity to Civil Government in the United States" (1833).
Adams, John. *The Works of John Adams.* 10 vols. Boston, 1850–56.
[Adger, John B.] *The Christian Doctrine of Human Rights and of Slavery.* Columbia, S.C., 1849.
Adger, John B. *My Life and Times, 1810–1899.* Richmond, Va., 1899.
Adger, John B. *The Religious Instruction of the Colored Population.* Charleston, S.C., 1847.
Alcott, A. Bronson. "Eighty-Six Letters of A. Bronson Alcott (Part One)." Ed. Frederick Wagner. *Studies in the American Renaissance* (1979): 239–308.
Alcott, A. Bronson. *The Letters of A. Bronson Alcott.* Ed. Richard L. Herrnstadt. Ames, Ia., 1969.
Alcott, William A. *An Address Delivered before the American Physiological Society.* Boston, 1837.
Alcott, William A. *Charles Hartland, the Village Missionary.* Boston, 1839.
[Alcott, William A.]. *Confessions of a School Master.* Andover, Mass., 1839.
Alcott, William A. *Essay on the Construction of School-Houses.* Boston, 1832.
Alcott, William A. *Familiar Letters to Young Men on Various Subjects.* Buffalo, N.Y., 1850.
Alcott, William A. *The First Foreign Mission; or, Journey of Paul and Barnabas.* Boston, 1834.
[Alcott, William A.]. *Forty Years in the Wilderness of Pills and Powders; or, The Cogitations of an Aged Physician.* Boston, 1859.
Alcott, William A. *Gift Book for Young Men.* New York, 1856.
Alcott, William A. *Home-Book of Life and Health.* Boston, 1858.
Alcott, William A. *Jesus at Nain; or, The Widow's Son Raised.* Boston, 1839.
Alcott, William A. *The Laws of Health.* Boston, 1856.
Alcott, William A. *Life of Peter the Apostle.* Boston, 1836.
Alcott, William A. *Life of Robert Morrison, the First Protestant Missionary to China.* New York, 1856.
Alcott, William A. *Living on Small Means: A Cheap Manual on Health and Economy.* Boston, 1837.
Alcott, William A. *The Moral Philosophy of Courtship and Marriage.* Boston, 1857.
Alcott, William A. *The Mother in Her Family; or, Sayings and Doings at Rose Hill Cottage.* Boston, 1838.
[Alcott, William A.]. *My Progress in Error, and Recovery to Truth; or, A Tour through Universalism, Unitarianism, and Skepticism.* Boston, 1842.
Alcott, William A. *The Physiology of Marriage.* Boston, 1856.
Alcott, William A. *The Story of Ananias and Sapphira.* New York, 1845.
Alcott, William A. *Tea and Coffee.* Boston, 1839.
Alcott, William A. *Travels of Our Savior.* Boston, 1840.
Alcott, William A. *The Use of Tobacco: Its Physical, Intellectual, and Moral Effects on the Human System.* 3rd ed. Boston, 1848.
Alcott, William A. *Vegetable Diet, as Sanctioned by Medical Men.* Boston, 1838.
Alcott, William A. *The Young House-Keeper.* Boston, 1838.
Alcott, William A. *The Young Husband.* 6th ed. Boston, 1842.
Alcott, William A. *The Young Man's Guide.* 2nd ed. Boston, 1834.
Alcott, William A. *The Young Missionary: Exemplified in the Life of Timothy.* Boston, 1837.
Alcott, William A. *The Young Mother.* 2nd ed. Boston, 1836.
Alcott, William A. *The Young Woman's Guide to Excellence.* Boston, 1840.
Alden, Timothy. *A Collection of American Epitaphs and Inscriptions.* 5 vols. New York, 1812–14.
Alger, William Rounseville. *A Critical History of the Doctrine of a Future Life.* Philadelphia, 1864.
Allen, Ethan. *Ethan Allen and His Kin: Correspondence, 1772–1819.* Ed. John. J. Duffy. 2 vols. Hanover, N. H., 1998.
Allen, Ethan. *A Narrative of Colonel Ethan Allen's Captivity.* Philadelphia, 1779.
Allen, Ethan. *Reason the Only Oracle of Man.* Bennington, Vt., 1784 [actually, 1785].
Allen, Ethan. *Reason the Only Oracle of Man.* New York, 1836.
Allen, Ethan. *Reason the Only Oracle of Man.* Ed. John Pell. New York, 1940.
[Allibone, Samuel Austin]. *New Themes Condemned; or, Thirty Opinions on "New Themes" and Its "Reviewer."* Philadelphia, 1853.

Andrews, William L. ed. *Sisters of the Spirit: Three Black Women's Autobiographies of the Nineteenth Century*. Bloomington, Ind., 1986.
An Appeal to the People of South Carolina by Wesley. Columbia, S.C., [1831].
The Articles of Faith and Covenant of the Bowdoin Street Church, Boston, Massachusetts. Boston, 1837.
Asbury, Francis. *Journal of Rev. Francis Asbury*. 3 vols. New York, 1821.
Bacheler, Origen, and Robert Dale Owen. *Discussion on the Existence of God and the Authenticity of the Bible, between Origen Bacheler and Robert Dale Owen*. 2nd ed. 2 vols. New York, 1833.
Baldwin, Elihu W. *The Young Freethinker Reclaimed*. Philadelphia, [1838].
Ballou, Hosea, and Abner Kneeland. *A Series of Letters, in Defence of Divine Revelation: In Reply to Rev. Abner Kneeland's Serious Inquiry into the Authenticity of the Same*. Boston, 1820.
Barruel, Augustin. *Memoirs illustrating the History of Jacobinism*. 4 vols. Hartford, Conn., 1799; orig. pub. 1797.
Bartlett, John. *A Discourse on the Subject of Animation*. Boston, 1792.
Bayley, John. *Confessions of a Converted Infidel: With Lights and Shades of Itinerant Life, and Miscellaneous Sketches*. 3rd ed. New York, 1856; orig. pub. 1854.
Beckwith, George. *An Attempt to Shew and Maintain, the Wisdom*. Norwich, [Conn.], 1783.
Beecher, Lyman. *Lectures on Scepticism, Delivered in Park Street Church, Boston, and in the Second Presbyterian Church, Cincinnati*. Cincinnati, 1835.
Beecher, Lyman. *A Plea for the West*. New York and Cincinnati, 1835.
Bennett, William W. *Memorials of Methodism in Virginia: From Its Introduction into the State, in the Year 1772, to the Year 1829*. Richmond, Va., 1871.
Bibb, Henry Walton. "Narrative of the Life and Adventures of Henry Bibb" (1849). In Sterling Lecater Bland Jr., ed., *African American Slave Narratives: An Anthology* 2:357–58. Westport, Conn., 2001.
Bliss, Sylvester. *Memoirs of William Miller, Generally Known as a Lecturer on the Prophecies, and the Second Coming of Christ*. Boston, 1853.
Brown, Henry "Box." "Narrative of Henry Box Brown, Who Escaped from Slavery Enclosed in a Box 3 Feet Long and 2 Wide" (1849). In Sterling Lecater Bland Jr., ed., *African American Slave Narratives: An Anthology* 2:454. Westport, Conn., 2001.
Brown, John G., et al. *True Motives Exposed for the Attacks upon South Carolina College* [Charleston, S.C.], 1835.
Brownson, Orestes A. *Charles Elwood; or, The Infidel Converted* (1840), in *Works* 4.
Brownson, Orestes A. *The Convert; or, Leaves from My Experience* (1857), in *Works* 5.
Brownson, Orestes A. *A Discourse on the Wants of the Times*. Boston, 1836.
Brownson, Orestes A. *The Spirit-Rapper: An Autobiography* (1854), in *Works* 9.
Brownson, Orestes A. *The Works of Orestes A. Brownson*. 20 vols. New York, 1966; orig. pub. 1882–1907.
[Bryan, Edward B.] *Notice of the Rev. John B. Adger's Article on the Slave Trade*. Charleston, S.C., 1858.
Buckminster, Joseph S. *Sermons by the Late Joseph S. Buckminster*. 3rd ed. Boston, 1821.
Burder, George. *Village Sermons*. 3 vols. Boston, 1807.
[Carpenter, Stephen Cullen]. *Memoirs of the Honorable Thomas Jefferson, Secretary of State, Vice-President and President of the United States of America*. 2 vols. New York, 1809.
Cary, Samuel. *Review of a Book Entitled, "The Grounds of Christianity Examined."* Boston, 1813.
Censor. *An Appeal to the State*. [Columbia, S.C.], 1831.
Censor. *An Appeal to the State by Censor, Continued*. Columbia, S.C., 1831.
Chalmers, Thomas. *The Evidence and Authority of the Christian Revelation*. Hartford, Conn., 1816; orig. pub. Edinburgh, 1814.
Channing, William Ellery. *Two Sermons on Infidelity, Delivered October 14, 1813*. Boston, 1813.
Charity and the Clergy: Being a Review by a Protestant Clergyman of the "New Themes" Controversy. Philadelphia, 1853.
Cheetham, James. *Life of Thomas Paine*. New York, 1809.
[Chemin-Dupontès, Jean-Baptiste]. *Manual of the Theophilanthropes*. Philadelphia, 1800.

[Chemin-Dupontès, Jean-Baptiste]. *Manual of Theophilanthropes, or Adorers of God, and Friends of Men.* 2nd ed. Trans. John Walker. London, 1797.
Chilcote, Paul Wesley, ed. *Early Methodist Spirituality: Selected Women's Writings.* Nashville, Tenn., 2007.
Chilcote, Paul Wesley, ed. *Her Own Story: Autobiographical Portraits of Early Methodist Women.* Nashville, Tenn., 2001.
Christianity and Infidelity Contrasted. Philadelphia, [1832].
Clarke, John. *Sermons.* [Boston, 1799].
[Cleveland, R. J.]. *A Dialogue on Some of the Causes of Infidelity.* Boston, 1828.
[Clinton, DeWitt]. *A Vindication of Thomas Jefferson.* New York, 1800.
Clowney, William K. *Reply to the Goats of Columbia, in the State of South Carolina.* Columbia, S.C., 1823.
Coit, J. C. *The Substance of a Discourse Delivered upon the Occasion of the "Semi-Centenary Celebration," on the Second Sabbath in December, 1839.* Columbia, S.C., 1840.
Coles, George. *The Antidote; or, Revelation Defended, and Infidelity Repulsed: In a Course of Lectures.* Hartford, Conn., 1836.
Coles, George. *Heroines of Methodism: Or, Pen and Ink Sketches of the Mothers and Daughters of the Church.* New York, 1857.
[Colwell, Stephen]. *New Themes for the Protestant Clergy: Creeds without Charity, Theology without Humanity, and Protestantism without Christianity.* Philadelphia, 1851.
Colwell, Stephen. "Preface to the Second Edition." *New Themes for the Protestant Clergy.* 2nd ed. rev. Philadelphia, 1852.
Combe, George. *The Constitution of Man Considered in Relation to External Objects: A Facsimile Reproduction with an Introduction by Eric T. Carlson, M.D.* Delmar, N.Y., 1974; orig. pub. 1828.
Combe, George. "On Secular Education." *Westminster Review,* July 1852. In David A. Reeder, ed., *Educating Our Masters,* 43–68. Leicester, England, 1980.
A Compendious View and Brief Defence of the Peculiar and Leading Doctrines of the New Jerusalem Church. Baltimore, 1798.
The Complaint of the Commissioners of the Third Presbyterian Church in the City of Philadelphia, to the Rev'd Synod of Philadelphia. Philadelphia, [1814].
Constitutions of the Ancient and Honorable Fraternity of Free and Accepted Masons. Worcester, Mass., 1798.
The Conversion of an Infidel, Being the Confession and Exhortation of an Old Man, Who Wishes Well to His Fellow Mortals, Near the Close of His Life. Enfield, Mass., 1830.
A Copy of the Incorporated Constitution of the New Jerusalem Church, in the City of Baltimore. Baltimore, 1804.
Cooper, Thomas. *Address to the Graduates of the South Carolina College, December, 1821.* Columbia, S.C., 1821.
Cooper, Thomas. *An Account of the Trial of Thomas Cooper of Northumberland; on a Charge of Libel against the President of the United States.* Philadelphia, 1800.
Cooper, Thomas. *The Case of Thomas Cooper, M.D., President of the South Carolina College.* 2nd ed. Columbia, S.C., 1832.
Cooper, Thomas. *The Case of Thomas Cooper, M.D., President of the South-Carolina College: Submitted to the Legislature and the People of South Carolina, December, 1831.* Columbia, S.C., 1831.
[Cooper, Thomas]. "Coloured Marriages." *Carolina Law Journal* 1, 1 (1831): 96–103.
Cooper, Thomas. *Considerations on the Slave Trade; and the Consumption of West Indian Produce.* London, 1791.
[Cooper, Thomas]. *Consolidation: An Account of Parties in the United States, from the Convention of 1787, to the Present Period.* Columbia, S.C., 1824.
Cooper, Thomas. *Dr. Cooper's Defence before the Board of Trustees, from the Times and Gazette of December 14, 1832.* [Columbia, S.C., 1832].
Cooper, Thomas. *Two Essays: 1. On the Foundation of Civil Government; 2. On the Constitution of the United States.* Columbia, S.C., 1826.

[Cooper, Thomas]. *Extract of a Letter to a Student at Law, July, 1815.* [Philadelphia? 1815].
[Cooper, Thomas]. *An Exposition of the Doctrines of Calvinism.* N.p., 1830.
[Cooper, Thomas]. *The Following Papers, Stated to Have Been Mislaid...Are Now Printed in Confirmation of Dr. Cooper's Claims as a Physician.* [Philadelphia, 1818].
Cooper, Thomas. *The Institutes of Justinian with Notes.* Philadelphia, 1812.
Cooper, Thomas. *An Introductory Lecture to a Course of Law.* Columbia, S.C., 1834.
Cooper, Thomas. *Lectures on the Elements of Political Economy.* 2nd ed. Columbia, S.C., 1829.
Cooper, Thomas. "Letters of Dr. Thomas Cooper, 1825–1832." *American Historical Review* 6, 4 (July 1901): 725–36.
Cooper, Thomas. *Letters on the Slave Trade.* Manchester, England, 1787.
Cooper, Thomas. Letter to Thomas Jefferson, Oct. 18, 1822. *Collections of the Massachusetts Historical Society,* 7th ser., 1 (Boston, 1900): 315.
Cooper, Thomas. *A Manual of Political Economy.* Washington, D.C., 1834.
Cooper, Thomas. *Memoirs of Dr. Joseph Priestley, to the Year 1795, Written by Himself: With a Continuation, to the Time of His Decease, by His Son, Joseph Priestley: And Observations on His Writings, by Thomas Cooper, President Judge of the 4th District of Pennsylvania: and the Rev. William Christie.* Northumberland, Pa., 1806.
Cooper, Thomas. *Narrative of the Proceedings against Thomas Cooper, Esquire, President Judge of the Eighth District of Pennsylvania, on a Charge of Official Misconduct.* Lancaster, Pa., 1811.
Cooper, Thomas, trans. *On Irritation and Insanity...by F. J. V. Broussais, Translated by Thomas Cooper, M.D.: To Which Are Added Two Tracts on Materialism, and an Outline of the Association of Ideas.* Columbia, S.C., 1831.
[Cooper, Thomas]. "On Phrenology, Craniology, Organology." *Southern Literary Journal and Magazine of Arts* 1, 6 (Feb. 1836): 393–402.
Cooper, Thomas. *On the Connection between Geology and the Pentateuch, in a Letter to Professor Silliman.* Boston, 1833.
Cooper, Thomas. "On the Foundation of Civil Government." In *Memoirs of the Literary and Philosophical Society of Manchester* 3:481–509. Warrington, England, 1790.
Cooper, Thomas. *Petition of Thomas Cooper, President of South Carolina College, Praying the Restoration of a Fine, with Interest, Incurred under the Sedition Law of 1798 for a Libel against the Then President of the United States.* Washington, D.C., 1825.
Cooper, Thomas. *Political Arithmetic.* [Philadelphia?], 1798.
Cooper, Thomas. *Political Essays by Thomas Cooper, Esq., of Northumberland.* 2nd ed. Philadelphia, 1800.
Cooper, Thomas. *Political Essays, Originally Inserted in the Northumberland Gazette, with Additions.* Northumberland, Pa., 1799.
Cooper, Thomas. "Propositions respecting the Foundation of Civil Government." In *Memoirs of the Literary and Philosophical Society of Manchester.* Vol. 3. Warrington, England, 1790.
Cooper, Thomas. *A Reply to Mr. Burke's Invective against Mr. Cooper, and Mr. Watt, in the House of Commons on the 30th April, 1792.* Manchester, England, 1792.
Cooper, Thomas. *The Scripture Doctrine of Materialism.* Philadelphia, 1823.
[Cooper, Thomas?]. "Slavery." *Southern Literary Journal and Magazine of Arts* 1, 3 (Nov. 1835): 188–93.
Cooper, Thomas. *Some Information respecting America.* London, 1794.
Cooper, Thomas. *Supplement to Mr. Cooper's Letters on the Slave Trade.* Warrington, England, 1788.
[Cooper, Thomas]. *To Any Member of Congress: By a Layman.* [Columbia, S.C.], 1831; orig. pub. 1829.
Cooper, Thomas. *Tracts Ethical, Theological, and Political.* Vol. 1. Warrington, England, 1789.
Cooper, Thomas. *A Treatise on the Law of Libel and the Liberty of the Press...as Applicable to Individuals and to Political and Ecclesiastical Bodies and Principles.* New York, 1830.
Cooper, Thomas, and E. P. [Elizabeth Priestley]. "On the Propriety and Expediency of Unlimited Enquiry." In Cooper, *Political Essays* (1800).
Cunningham, Abner. *Practical Infidelity Portrayed and the Judgments of God Made Manifest.* New York, 1836.

Dana, James. *Men's Sins Not Chargeable on God, but on Themselves. A Discourse Delivered at Wallingford, December 22, 1782. Occasioned by the Tragical Exit of William Beadle, His Wife, and Four Children, at Wethersfield.* New Haven, Conn., [1783].

Dana, W. C. *A Reasonable Answer to a Skeptic.* Columbia, S.C., 1858.

Demosthenes versus Cicero...Being a Suitable reply to the Anti-Masonic, Anti-Illuminati, Anti-Republican Reveries, in a Late Publication. Baltimore, 1799.

Derby, John Barton. *Political Reminiscences, Including a Sketch of the Origin and History of the "Statesman Party" of Boston.* Boston, 1835.

de Wette, William Martin Leberecht. *Theodore; or, The Skeptic's Conversion.* Trans. George Ripley. Boston, 1841.

Dwight, Timothy. *A Discourse, on the Genuineness and Authenticity of the New-Testament.* New York, 1794.

Dwight, Timothy. *The Duty of Americans, at the Present Crisis.* New Haven, Conn., 1798.

Dwight, Timothy. *The Nature and Danger of Infidel Philosophy.* New Haven, Conn., 1798.

Dwight, Timothy. *Travels in New England and New York.* 4. Vols. Cambridge, Mass., 1969; orig. pub. 1821-22.

[Dwight, Timothy]. *The Triumph of Infidelity.* [Hartford, Conn.?], 1788.

"Editors Table." *Harper's New Monthly Magazine* 7, 39 (Aug. 1853): [415]-18.

Elaw, Zilpha. *Memoirs of the Life, Religious Experience, Ministerial Travels and Labours of Mrs. Zilpha Elaw, An American Female of Colour* (1846). In William L. Andrews, ed., *Sisters of the Spirit: Three Black Women's Autobiographies of the Nineteenth Century*, 49-160. Bloomington, Ind., 1986.

Elliott, Katharine (comp.). *Early Settlers: Mecklenburg County, Virginia.* Vol. 1. South Hill, Va., 1983; orig. pub. 1964.

Elliott, Katharine B. (comp.). *Early Wills, 1765-1799: Mecklenburg County, Virginia.* South Hill, Va., 1983; orig. pub. 1963.

Elliott, Katharine B. (comp.). *Marriage Records, 1765-1810: Mecklenburg County, Virginia.* South Hill, Va., 1963.

Ely, Ezra Stiles. *A Contrast between Calvinism and Hopkinsianism.* New York, 1811.

Ely, Ezra Stiles. *Conversations on the Science of the Human Mind.* Philadelphia, 1819.

Ely, Ezra Stiles. *The Duty of Christian Freeman to Elect Christian Rulers.* Philadelphia, 1828.

Ely, Zebulon. *A Gospel Minister, Though Young, Should Be Respectable by His Example* Hartford, Conn. 1806.

[Ely, Ezra Stiles]. *The Journal of the Stated Preacher to the Hospital and Almshouse in the City of New-York, for the Year of Our Lord 1811.* New York, 1812.

Ely, Ezra Stiles. *Memoirs of the Rev. Zebulon Ely, A.M., of Lebanon, Connecticut.* Philadelphia, 1825.

Ely, Ezra Stiles. *Retrospective Theology; or, Opinions of the World of Spirits.* Philadelphia, 1825.

[Ely, Ezra Stiles]. *The Second Journal of the Stated Preacher to the Hospital and Almshouse in the City of New-York, for a Part of the Year of Our Lord 1813.* Philadelphia, 1815.

Ely, Ezra Stiles. *A Sermon Delivered by Ezra Stiles Ely on the First Sabbath after His Ordination.* Hartford, Conn., 1806.

Ely, Ezra Stiles. *A Synopsis of Didactic Theology.* Philadelphia, 1822.

Ely, Ezra Stiles. *A Sermon for the Rich to Buy, That They May Benefit Themselves and the Poor.* New York, 1810.

[Ely, Ezra Stiles]. *William and Ellen: A Poem in Three Cantos; with Other Poetical Works of an American.* New York, 1811.

Ely, Ezra Stiles. *Ten Sermons on Faith.* Philadelphia, 1816.

Ely, Zebulon. *The Wisdom and Duty of Magistrates: A Sermon Preached at the General Election, May 10th, 1804.* Hartford, Conn., 1804.

English, George Bethune. *The Grounds of Christianity Examined by Comparing the New Testament with the Old.* Boston, 1813.

[English, George Bethune]. *A Letter to the Reverend Mr. Cary, Containing Remarks upon His Review of the Grounds of Christianity Examined.* Boston, 1813.

English, George Bethune. *A Narrative of the Expedition to Dongola and Sennaar; under the Command of His Excellence Ismael Pasha, Undertaken by Order of His Highness Mehemmed Ali Pasha, Viceroy of Egypt*. London, 1822; Boston, 1823.

English, George Bethune. *Five Pebbles from the Brook: A Reply to "A Defence of Christianity" Written by Edward Everett*. Philadelphia, 1824.

Everett, Edward. *A Defence of Christianity, against the Work of George B. English*. Boston, 1814.

Everett, L. S. *An Exposure of the Principles of the "Free Inquirers."* Boston, 1831.

The Evils of the Work Now Prevailing in the United States of America Under the Name of a Revival of Religion. Washington, Pa., 1804.

Faber, George Stanley. *A Practical Treatise on the Ordinary Operations of the Holy Spirit*. New York, 1814.

Fairchild, J. H. *The Gospel Defended against Infidels*. Boston, 1833.

Featherstonhaugh, G. W. *Excursions through the Slave States*. New York, 1844. In William W. Freehling, ed., *The Nullification Era: A Documentary Record*, 192–93. New York, 1967.

Fellows, John. *An Exposition of the Mysteries, or Religious Dogmas and Customs, of the Ancient Egyptians, Pythagoreans, and Druids; Also, an Inquiry into the Origin, History, and Purport of Freemasonry*. New York, 1835.

Fellows, John. Letter to Thomas Jefferson, October 3, 1825. Thomas Jefferson Papers. Library of Congress, Manuscript Division. https://www.loc.gov/item/mtjbib025537/.

[Fellows, John]. *Some Doubts respecting the Death, Resurrection, and Ascension of Jesus Christ...to Which Are Added, Reasons for Scepticism in Religion, by John Hollis*. New York, 1797.

Findley, William. *Observations on "The Two Sons of Oil."* Pittsburgh, 1812.

Fishbeck, James. *The Philosophy of the Human Mind in Respect to Religion*. Lexington, Ky., 1813.

Fitch, John. *The Autobiography of John Fitch*. Ed. Frank D. Prager. Philadelphia, 1967.

Follen, Eliza Lee Cabot. *The Skeptic*. Boston and Cambridge, Mass., 1835.

Fox, Mary Anna. *George Allen, the Only Son: By a Young Lady of Boston*. Boston, 1835.

Franklin, Benjamin. *The Papers of Benjamin Franklin*. 41 vols. to date. New Haven, Conn., 1959–.

Franklin, Benjamin. *The Portable Benjamin Franklin*. Ed. Larzer Ziff. New York, 2005.

Freneau, Philip Morin. *A Compendious View and Brief Defence of the Peculiar and Leading Doctrines of the New Jerusalem Church*. Baltimore, 1798.

Fuller, Andrew. *Three Queries to the Rejecters of Christianity*. New York, [1832].

Furman, Richard. *Rev. Dr. Richard Furman's Exposition of the Views of the Baptists, Relative to the Colored Population of the United States, in a Communication to the Governor of South-Carolina*. Charleston, S.C., 1823.

Gaddis, Maxwell Pierson. *The Conversion of a Skeptic: A Member of the Bar*. Cincinnati, 1858.

Gen. Jackson and the Rev. Ezra Stiles Ely. [New York, 1828].

General Remarks, on the Proceedings Lately Had in the Adjacent Country, Relative to Infidelity. Newburgh, N.Y., 1798.

Gibbons, William. *An Exposition of Modern Skepticism*. Wilmington, Del., [1829].

Glendinning, William. *The Life of William Glendinning, Preacher of the Gospel*. Philadelphia, 1795.

Godwin, Benjamin. *Lectures on the Atheistic Controversy*. 1st American ed. Boston, 1835.

The Good Old Way; or, The Religion of Our Forefathers. Annapolis, Md., 1816.

Goss, Charles Chaucer. *Statistical History of the First Century of American Methodism*. New York, 1866.

Graham, William. *A View of Ecclesiastical Establishments in Europe*. 2nd ed. [Windham, Conn.], 1808.

Griswold, Whitney. *Sermon Delivered January 1st, 1811*. Cooperstown, N.Y., 1815.

Grosvenor, Cyrus Pitt. *Infidelity: Some of Its Modern Features*. Boston, 1829.

Hall, Richard D. *A Humble Attempt to Promote the Salvation of the Rising Generation*. Philadelphia, 1818.

Hall, Willard. *A Defence of the American Sunday School Union against the Charges of Its Opponents*. Philadelphia, 1828.

Hare, Robert. *Experimental Investigation of the Spirit Manifestations*. New York, 1855.

Hargrove, John. *A Sermon, Delivered before the City of Baltimore* [Public Thanksgiving]. Baltimore, 1814.

Hargrove, John. *A Sermon, on the Second Coming of Christ...Delivered the 25th of Dec., 1804, before Both Houses of Congress*. [Baltimore], 1805.

Hargrove, John. *The Substance of a Sermon, on the Leading Doctrines of the New Jerusalem Church, Delivered on the 26th of Dec., 1802, before the President of the United States and Several Members of Congress.* [Baltimore], 1803.

Hargrove, John. *The Temple of Truth; or, A Vindication of Various Passages and Doctrines of the Holy Scriptures: Lately Impeached in a Deistical Publication.* Baltimore, 1801.

[Hargrove, John]. *The War Dance, No War Whoop, No. 2.* [Baltimore, 1804].

Harris, Samuel. *Zaccheus; or, The Scriptural Plan of Benevolence.* New York, [ca. 1850].

Harris, William. *A Sermon.* New York, 1810.

[Henshaw, David]. *A Review of the Prosecution against Abner Kneeland: By a Cosmopolite* Boston, 1835.

Herndon, William Henry. *Mrs. Lincoln's Denial, and What She Says.* Broadside. Springfield, Ill., 1874. Alfred Whital Stern Collection of Lincolniana, Library of Congress. http://www.loc.gov/item/scsm000585.

Hertell, Thomas. *Thomas Hertell's Epistolary Correspondence with Dr. Thomas Cooper, of Columbia, (S.C.) during His Last Sickness, on the Subjects of Human Life, Death, & C. In the years 1838, 1839.* New York, 1845.

Hildreth, Richard. *Archy Moore, the White Slave; or, Memoirs of a Fugitive: With a New Introduction, Prepared for This Edition.* New York, 1856.

Hildreth, Richard. *Despotism in America; or, An Inquiry into the Nature and Results of the Slaveholding System in the United States.* Boston, 1840.

Hildreth, Richard. *History of the United States.* 6 vols. New York, 1849; 1851–1852.

Hildreth, Richard. *A Joint Letter to Orestes A. Brownson and the Editor of the North American Review.* [N.p., 1844].

[Hildreth, Richard]. *A Letter to Andrews Norton, on Miracles as the Foundation of Religious Faith.* Boston, 1840.

Hildreth, Richard. *My Connection with the Atlas Newspaper; Including a Sketch of the History of the Armory Hall Party of 1838, and an Account of the Senatorial and Representative Elections in the City of Boston for the Year 1839.* Boston, 1839.

[Hildreth, Richard]. *Native Americanism, Detected and Exposed.* Boston, 1845.

Hildreth, Richard. *The Slave: or Memoirs of Archy Moore.* Boston, 1836.

Hildreth, Richard, trans. *Theory of Legislation by Jeremy Bentham. Translated from the French of Etienne Dumont.* London, 1864; orig. pub. Boston, 1840.

Hildreth, Richard. *Theory of Morals: An Inquiry Concerning the Law of Moral Distinctions and the Variations and Contradictions of Ethical Codes.* Boston, 1844.

Hildreth, Richard. *The Theory of Politics: An Inquiry into the Foundations of Governments and the Causes and Progress of Political Revolutions.* New York, 1853.

Himes, Joshua V. *Views of the Prophecies and Prophetic Chronology, Selected from the Manuscripts of William Miller, with a Memoir of His Life.* Boston, 1842.

Hindmarsh, Robert. *The Rise and Progress of the New Jerusalem Church in England, America, and Other Parts.* London, 1861.

History of the Young Men's Missionary Society of New York, Containing a Correct Account of the Recent Controversy, respecting Hopkinsian Doctrines. New York, 1817.

Hitchcock, Enos. *A Discourse Delivered at the Ordination of the Rev. Abel Flint.* [Hartford, Conn., 1791].

Holly, Israel. *Old Divinity Preferable to Modern Novelty.* Litchfield, Conn., 1795.

The Holy Bible, Containing the Old and New Testaments.... and the Copious Marginal Reference of Scott's Family Bible. New York, 1813.

Howe, George. *An Address Delivered at Columbia, (S.C.) March 28, 1832.* Charleston, S.C., 1832.

Howe, George. *History of the Presbyterian Church in South Carolina.* 2 vols. Columbia, S.C., 1883.

Hughes, John. *A Lecture on the Importance of a Christian Basis for the Science of Political Economy, and Its Applications to the Affairs of Life.* New York, [1844].

An Important Case Argued; in Four Dialogues, between Dr. Opium, Mr. Gallio, and Discipulus. Boston, 1810.

An Investigation of the Doctrine of Baron Swedenborg or of the Church Called New Jerusalem, in Two Letters, Addressed to the Rev. Mr. H—, by an Inhabitant of Baltimore County. Baltimore, 1799.

Jackson, Jonathan. *Thoughts upon the Political Situation of the United States of America.* Worcester, Mass., 1788.
[Jarratt, Devereux]. *A Brief Narrative of the Revival of Religion in Virginia. In a Letter to a Friend.* London, 1778.
Jea, John. "The Life, History, and Unparalleled Sufferings of John Jea, the African Preacher" (c. 1815). In Graham Russell Hodges, ed., *Black Itinerants of the Gospel: The Narratives of John Jea and George White.* New York, 2002.
Jefferson, Thomas. *Notes on the State of Virginia.* Philadelphia, 1788.
Jefferson, Thomas. *The Papers of Thomas Jefferson Digital Edition.* Ed. James P. McClure and J. Jefferson Looney. Charlottesville, Va., 2008–17. http://rotunda.upress.virginia.edu/founders/TSJN.html.
Jefferson, Thomas. Thomas Jefferson Papers, 1606–1827. Library of Congress, Manuscript Division. https://www.loc.gov/collections/thomas-jefferson-papers/.
Jenyns, Soame. *A View of the Internal Evidence of the Christian Religion.* London, 1776.
Johnston, John. *The Autobiography and Ministerial Life of the Rev. John Johnston.* New York, 1856.
Jones, Absalom, et al. "Address of the Representatives of the African Church...to the Friends of Liberty and Religion in the City of Philadelphia." In Benjamin Rush, *Extract of a Letter from Dr. Benjamin Rush of Philadelphia, to Granville Sharp.* London, 1792.
Jones, Charles Colcock. *The Religious Instruction of the Negroes in the United States.* Savannah, Ga., 1842.
Jones, Sarah. *Devout Letters; or, Letters Spiritual and Friendly. Written by Mrs. Sarah Jones. Corrected and Published by Jeremiah Minter.* [Alexandria, Va., 1804].
Kant, Immanuel. "An Answer to the Question: What Is Enlightenment?" In James Schmidt, ed., *What Is Enlightenment? Eighteenth-Century Answers and Twentieth-Century Questions,* 58–64. Berkeley, Calif., 1997.
Keith, William. *The Experience of William Keith.* Utica, New York, 1806.
Kelly, John. *Solemn and Important Reasons against Becoming a Universalist.* Haverhill, Mass. 1815.
Kelso, John R. *Deity Analyzed: In Six Lectures.* New York, 1890.
Kelso, John R. *Government Analyzed.* Longmont, Colo., 1892.
Kelso, John R. *Spiritualism Sustained in Five Lectures.* New York, 1886.
Keteltas, Abraham. *God Arising and Pleading His People's Cause.* Newbury-Port, [Mass.], 1777.
Kneeland, Abner. *Abner Kneeland's Code of Morals, Philosophical Creed, and Declaration of Character.* [Boston, 1833].
Kneeland, Abner. *An Oration, Delivered July 4, 1826.* New York, 1826.
Kneeland, Abner, ed. *A Philosophical Dictionary, from the French of M. de Voltaire: With Additional Notes, Both Critical and Argumentative, by Abner Kneeland.* Boston, [1836].
Kneeland, Abner. *A Review of the Evidences of Christianity: In a Series of Lectures Delivered in Broadway Hall, New-York, August, 1829.* 6th ed. Boston, [1831?].
Kneeland, Abner. *A Review of the Trial, Conviction, and Final Imprisonment in the Common Jail of the County of Suffolk, of Abner Kneeland, for the Alleged Crime of Blasphemy* Boston, 1838.
Kneeland, Abner. *Speech of Abner Kneeland Delivered Before the Supreme Court of the City of Boston, in His Own Defence, on an Indictment for Blasphemy.* Boston, 1834.
Kneeland, Abner. *Speech of Abner Kneeland, Delivered before the Full Bench of Judges of the Supreme Court, in His Own Defence, for the Alleged Crime of Blasphemy.* Boston, 1836.
LaBorde, Maximilian. *History of the South Carolina College.* Columbia, S.C., 1859.
Lackington, James. *Memoirs of James Lackington.* Newburgh, N.Y., 1796.
Landis, Robert. *Infidelity Exposed, and Its Charges against Christianity Repelled.* Philadelphia, 1836.
Laws of Maryland. Annapolis, Md., 1803.
Lednum, John. *A History of the Rise of Methodism: Containing Sketches of Methodist Itinerant Preachers, from 1736 to 1785.* Philadelphia, 1859.
Lee, Jarena. *Religious Experience and Journal of Mrs. Jarena Lee.* Philadelphia, 1849.
Leland, A. W. *A Discourse at the Annual Examination of the Students in the Theological Seminary.* Columbia, S.C., 1839.
Leland, John. *The Rights of Conscience Inalienable, and Therefore Religious Opinions Not Recognizable by Law.* New London, Conn., 1791.

Levy, Leonard, ed. *Blasphemy in Massachusetts: Freedom of Conscience and the Abner Kneeland Case*. New York, 1973.
"The Life and Times of Gardiner Spring." *North American Review* 103, 212 (July 1866): 269–76.
Lincoln, Abraham. *The Collected Works of Abraham Lincoln*. Ed. Roy P. Basler. 8 vols. New Brunswick, N.J., 1953, http://quod.lib.umich.edu/l/lincoln/.
Linn, William. *Discourses on the Signs of the Times*. New York, 1794.
Long, John Dixon. *Pictures of Slavery in Church and State*. 3rd ed. Philadelphia, 1857.
Louisiana State Senate. *Journal*. New Orleans, 1819.
Mann, Horace. *Annual Report of the Board of Education*. Washington, D.C., 1837–48.
Mann, Horace. *Lectures and Annual Reports on Education* (1837–38). Cambridge, Mass., 1867.
Mann, Mary. *Life of Horace Mann*. Vol. 1 of *Life and Works of Horace Mann*. 2nd ed. Boston, 1865.
Marsh, John. *The Great Sin and Danger of Striving with God*. Hartford, Conn., [1783].
[Mason, John M.], *The Voice of Warning, to Christians, on the Ensuing Election of a President of the United States*. New York, 1800.
Maxwell, William. *A Memoir of the Rev. John H. Rice, D. D.* Philadelphia, 1835.
Means, Robert. *Considerations respecting the Pentateuch, with Special Reference to a Pamphlet Entitled "The Connexion between Geology and the Pentateuch" by Thomas Cooper, M.D.* Columbia, S.C., 1834.
[Mellen, Alice Hayes]. *The Female Skeptic; or, Faith Triumphant*. New York, 1859.
Melville, Herman. *Israel Potter: His Fifty Years of Exile*. New York, 1855.
Merrill, Daniel. *Balaam Disappointed: A Thanksgiving Sermon*. Concord, N.H., 1815.
The Meteor of Light, Containing the Minutes of the Proceedings of the Infidel Convention, Held in the City of New York, May 4th, 5th and 6th, 1845. Boston, 1845.
Methodist Episcopal Church. *A Form of Discipline, for the Ministers, Preachers, and Members of the Methodist Episcopal Church in America*. New York, 1787.
Middleton, Erasmus. *Evangelical Biography*. Philadelphia, 1798.
Miller, William. *Evidence from Scripture and History of the Second Coming of Christ, about the Year 1843*. Troy, N.Y., 1838.
Minutes of the Common Council of the City of New York. Vol. 2. New York, 1917.
Minter, Jeremiah. *A Brief Account of the Religious Experience, Travels, Preaching, Persecutions from Evil Men, and God's Special Helps in the Faith and Life*. Washington, D.C., 1817.
Minter, Jeremiah. *A Brief Defence of the Bible of the Old and New Testament; Against Infidelity*. Richmond, Va., 1820.
Minter, Jeremiah. *Scripture Proofs of Sorcery, and Warning against Sorcerers*. Richmond, Va., 1814.
Minter, Jeremiah. *Warning against Imposture in Religion: In a Concise Account of the Evil Life and Conduct of Francis Asbury*. Richmond, Va., 1820, pub. with *Brief Defence of the Bible*.
[Mitchell, Stephen Mix]. *A Narrative of the Life of William Beadle*. Hartford, Conn., 1783.
M'Leod, Donald. *A Sermon, Preached in the Presbyterian Church*. Charleston, S.C., 1812.
M'Master, Gilbert. *The Duty of Nations*. Ballston-Spa, N.Y., 1813.
Montaigne, Michel de. *The Complete Essays*. Trans. and ed. M. A. Screech. London, 1991.
Moore, Hannah. *Strictures on the Modern System of Female Education*. Philadelphia, 1800.
Moore, Martin. *Boston Revival, 1842*. Boston, 1842.
Morison, John. *Counsels to Young Men on Modern Infidelity, and the Evidences of Christianity*. Boston, 1834.
[Morrison, Eliza A.]. *The Life and Labours of Robert Morrison, D. D.* London, 1839.
Morse, Jedidiah. *A Sermon Delivered before the Grand Lodge of Free and Accepted Masons of the Commonwealth of Massachusetts*. Leominster, Mass., 1798.
Morse, Jedidiah. *A Sermon, Delivered... May 9th, 1798* [National Fast]. Boston, 1798.
Morse, Jedidiah. *A Sermon, Exhibiting the Present Dangers, and Consequent Duties of the Citizens of the United States of America... April 25, 1799* [National Fast]. Charlestown, Mass., 1799.
Morse, Jedidiah. *A Sermon, Preached at Charlestown, November 29, 1798, on the Anniversary Thanksgiving in Massachusetts. With an Appendix... Exhibiting Proofs of the Early Existence, Progress, and Deleterious Effects of French Intrigue and Influence in the United States*. Boston, 1798.
[Murray, John]. *Bath-Kol: A Voice from the Wilderness*. Boston, 1783.

Murray, John. *Jerubbaal; or, Tyranny's Grove Destroyed, and the Altar of Liberty Finished.* Newbury-Port, Mass., 1801.

Murray, John. *Nehemiah, or the Struggle for Liberty Never in Vain.* Newbury, Mass., 1779.

Murray, John. *Some Hints Relative to the Forming of a Christian Church.... Concluding with a Character of a Consistent Universalist.* Boston, 1791.

Myerson, Joel, ed. *Transcendentalism: A Reader.* New York, 2000.

Nelson, David. *An Appeal to the Church in Behalf of a Dying Race.* New York, 1838.

Nelson, David. *The Cause and Cure of Infidelity: Including a Notice of the Author's Unbelief, and the Means of his Rescue.* New York, 1841; orig. pub. 1837.

Nelson, David, and J. L. Wilson. *A Correspondence between Reverend David Nelson, M.D., and J. L. Wilson.* Cincinnati, 1834.

Newton, John. *A Monument to the Praise of the Lord's Goodness.* Philadelphia, 1796.

Niles, Nathaniel. *Two Discourses on Liberty.* Newbury-Port, [Mass.], 1774.

Niles, Peter. *The Writings of Peter Niles, Who Put a Period to His Own Life with the Discharge of His Gun.* Walpole, N.H., 1811.

Norton, Andrews. *A Discourse on the Latest Form of Infidelity.* Cambridge, Mass, 1839.

Norton, Andrews. *The Evidences of the Genuineness of the Gospels.* 3 vols. Boston, 1837–44.

N[orton], A[ndrews]. "Introductory Note." In *Two Articles from the Princeton Review Concerning the Transcendental Philosophy of the Germans.* Cambridge Mass., 1840.

Norton, Andrews. *Remarks on a Pamphlet Entitled "The Latest Form of Infidelity" Examined.* Cambridge, Mass., 1839.

Obert, Peter G. *Obert's System of Nature.* New York, 1837.

[Ogden, John Cosens]. *A View of the New-England Illuminati.* Philadelphia, 1799.

O'Kelly, James. *A Vindication of the Author's Apology.* Raleigh, N.C., 1801.

Olmsted, Charles G. *The Bible, Its Own Refutation.* Louisville, Ky., 1836.

"An Oration: On the Moral History of the United States." *Adviser, or, Vermont Evangelical Magazine* 7, 1 (Jan.–Feb. 1815): 41–49.

Owen, Robert. *Selected Works of Robert Owen.* Vol. 2, *The Development of Socialism.* Ed. Gregory Claeys, London, 1993.

Owen, Robert, and Alexander Campbell. *Debate on the Evidences of Christianity.* 2 vols. Bethany, Va., 1829.

Owen, Robert Dale. *An Address on the Influence of the Clerical Profession, as Delivered in the Hall of Science, New York.* New York, 1833.

Owen, Robert Dale. *The Debatable Land between This World and the Next.* New York, 1872.

Owen, Robert Dale. *Footfalls on the Boundary of Another World.* Philadelphia, 1860.

Owen, Robert Dale. *Moral Physiology; or, A Brief and Plain Treatise on the Population Question.* New York, 1831.

Paine, Thomas. *The Age of Reason: Being an Investigation of True and Fabulous Theology.* Parts 1 and 2. Paris, 1794, 1795.

Paine, Thomas. *The Rights of Man, Part One.* Philadelphia, 1791; orig. pub. London, 1791.

Palmer, Benjamin M. *The Life and Letters of James Henley Thornwell.* Richmond, Va., 1875.

Palmer, Benjamin M. *Warrant and Nature of Public Worship.* Columbia, S.C., 1853.

Palmer, Elihu. *An Enquiry into the Moral and Philosophical Improvement of the Human Species.* New York, 1797.

[Palmer, Elihu]. *The Examiners Examined: Being a Defence of "The Age of Reason."* New York, 1794.

Palmer, Elihu. *Extracts from an Oration, delivered by Elihu Palmer, the 4th of July, 1793.* In *Political Miscellany.* New York, 1793.

Palmer, Elihu. *The Political Happiness of Nations: An Oration, Delivered at the City of New York, in the Fourth of July.* [New York? 1800?].

Palmer, Elihu. *Posthumous Pieces.* London, 1824.

Palmer, Elihu. *Principles of Nature; or, A Development of the Moral Causes of Happiness and Misery among the Human Species.* 3rd ed. [New York?], 1806.

Palmer, Elihu. Letter to Thomas Jefferson, Sept. 1, 1802. Thomas Jefferson Papers. Ser. 1, General Correspondence, 1651–1827. Library of Congress. http://www.loc.gov/collections/thomas-jefferson-papers.

Parker, Nathan. *A Sermon Preached at Concord.* Concord, N.H., 1819.
[Parker, Samuel]. *Report of the Arguments of the Attorney of the Commonwealth at the Trials of Abner Kneeland, for Blasphemy, in the Municipal and Supreme Courts, in Boston, January and May, 1834.* Boston, 1834.
Parker, Theodore. *A Discourse of Matters pertaining to Religion.* Boston, 1842.
Parker, Theodore. *Discourse on the Transient and the Permanent in Christianity.* Boston, 1841.
Parker, Theodore. *Sermons of Theism, Atheism, and the Popular Theology.* Boston, 1853.
Parker, Theodore [Levi Blodgett, pseud.]. *The Previous Question between Mr. Andrews Norton and His Alumni Moved and Handled in a Letter to All Those Gentlemen* (1840). In Myerson, ed., *Transcendentalism*, 260–80.
Parkinson, William. *A Sermon* [Fast Day]. New York, 1812.
Parsons, Theolphilus. *Result of the Convention of Delegates Holden at Ipswich in the County of Essex.* Newbury-Port, [Mass.], 1778.
Pattillo, Henry. *Sermons.* Wilmington, N.C., 1788.
Patton, William W. *Slavery and Infidelity; or, Slavery in the Church Insures Infidelity in the World.* Cincinnati, Ohio, 1856.
Patton, William W. *Slavery—The Bible—Infidelity: An Attempt to Prove That Pro-slavery Interpretations of the Bible are Productive of Infidelity.* Hartford, Conn., 1846.
Payne, Daniel. "Daniel Payne's Protestation of Slavery" (1839). In Pinn, ed., *By these Hands*, 123–30.
Pennington, James W. C. "The Fugitive Blacksmith: or, Events in the History of James W. C. Pennington, Pastor of a Presbyterian Church, New York" (1849). In Sterling Lecater Bland, Jr., ed., *African American Slave Narratives: An Anthology* 2:541–98. Westport, Conn., 2001.
Phillips, George Shane. *The American Republic and Human Liberty Foreshadowed in Scripture.* Cincinnati, 1864.
[Phillips, Stephen C.]. *Practical Infidelity Considered in Reference to the Present Times.* Boston, 1830.
Population of the United States in 1860 Compiled from the Original Returns of the Eighth Census. Washington, D.C., 1864.
Porter, Ebenezer. *The Presumption of Skeptical and Careless Contemners of Religion.* Andover, Mass., 1829.
Powers, Peter. *Jesus Christ the True King and Head of Government.* Newbury-Port, [Mass.], 1778.
Presbyterian Popery: Animadversions upon the Decision of the Last General Assembly of the Presbyterian Church: Respecting the Third Congregation, Philadelphia. Philadelphia, 1814.
[Pressley, Samuel P.] *Letters to Thomas Cooper, M.D., President of the South Carolina College.* [Newberry, S.C.?], 1832.
Price, Richard. *Observations on the Importance of the American Revolution, and the Means of Making It a Benefit to the World.* Boston, [1784]; orig. pub. London, 1784.
Proceedings of the Hartford Bible Convention. New York, 1854.
Raymond, Charles A. "The Religious Life of the Negro Slave, [pt. 2]." *Harper's New Monthly Magazine,* Oct. 1863, 676–82.
Reply to Censor; or, An Appeal to the Good Sense of the People of South Carolina, by Justice. Columbia, S.C., [1831].
"Religion." *Encyclopedia Britannica* 17:696–713. Edinburgh, 1823.
Religious Tract Society of Baltimore. *Third Annual Report.* Baltimore, 1819.
[Rice, John Holt]. "Review [of *Memoirs of Dr. Joseph Priestley.... and Observations on His Writings, by Thomas Cooper*]." *Virginia Evangelical and Literary Magazine* 3, 2 (Feb. 1820): 63–74.
Richards, William. *Reflections on French Atheism and on English Christianity.* 3rd ed. Philadelphia, 1796.
Ripley, George. *Defence of "'The Latest Form of Infidelity' Examined": A Second Letter to Mr. Andrews Norton.* Boston, 1840.
Ripley, George. *Defence of "'The Latest Form of Infidelity' Examined": A Third Letter to Mr. Andrews Norton.* Boston, 1840.
Ripley, George. *Discourses on the Philosophy of Religion, Addressed to Doubters Who Wish to Believe.* Boston, 1836.

[Ripley, George]. *"The Latest Form of Infidelity" Examined: A Letter to Mr. Andrews Norton.* Boston, 1839.

Robison, John. *Proofs of a Conspiracy against All the Religions and Governments of Europe, Carried on in the Secret Meetings of Free Masons, Illuminati, and Reading Societies.* 1st American ed., 3rd ed. Philadelphia, 1798; orig. pub. 1797.

Rose, Ernestine. *A Defense of Atheism, Being a Lecture Delivered in Mercantile Hall, Boston, April 10, 1861.* Boston, 1861.

Rose, Ernestine. *Mistress of Herself: Speeches and Letters of Ernestine L. Rose, Early Women's Rights Leader.* Ed. Paula Doress-Worters. New York, 2007.

Royall, Anne Newport. *Mrs. Royall's Pennsylvania; or, Travels Continued in the United States.* 2 vols. Washington, D.C., 1829.

Rutter, J. P. "Origin of Marion College," "Origin of Marion College [pt. 2]," "An Extract from a Forthcoming Work to be Entitled 'Twenty-Four Years' View of Palmyra and Marion County, in Missouri,'" and "The End and Removal of Marion College." *Western Journal and Civilian* 14, 3 (Aug. 1855), 165–9; 14, 4 (Sept. 1855), 244–50; 14, 5 (Oct. 1855), 316–23; 14, 5, 14, 6 (Nov. 1855), 416–18.

[Sargent, Lucius M.]. *I Am Afraid There Is a God! Founded on Fact.* Boston, 1833.

Scarlett, John. *Almond: A True Story in Five Parts.* Orange, N.J., 1883.

Scarlett, John. *The Life and Experience of a Converted Infidel.* New York, 1854; orig. pub. 1853.

[Shakers]. *An Address to the State of Ohio.* Lebanon, Ohio, 1818.

Sharples, Stephen Paschall, ed. *Records of the Church of Christ at Cambridge in New England, 1632–1830.* Boston, 1906.

[Sherman, Josiah]. *Oracles of Reason, as Formed by the Deists, are Husks for Deistical and Heathen Swine.* Litchfield, Conn., [1787?].

[Sherman, Josiah]. *A Sermon to Swine.* Litchfield, Conn., [1787?]

A Short Reply to Mr. Burk and Guy, with Some Ripe Fruit for a Friend to Truth. Baltimore, [1804].

Simpson, David. *A Plea for Religion and the Sacred Writings: Addressed to the Disciples of Thomas Paine.* Baltimore, 1807.

Sleigh, William W. *The Christian's Defensive Dictionary.* Philadelphia, 1837.

Sleigh, William W. *The New-York Discussion, between Dr. Sleigh, in Defence of Divine Revelation, and the Delegates of the Tammany Hall Infidels, and Others, In Defense of Infidelity.* New York, 1836.

Smith, Ebenezer. *A Defence of Ebenezer Smith, against the Poison of the Cruelty of the Baptist Church.* [Amherst, N.H.], 1804.

Smith, Elias. *A Discourse... Thanksgiving Day.* Danville, Vt., 1815.

Smith, James. *The Christian's Defence, Containing a Fair Statement, and Impartial Examination of the Leading Objections Urged by Infidels against the Antiquity, Genuineness, Credibility, and Inspiration of the Holy Scriptures.* Cincinnati, 1843.

Smyth, Thomas. *Autobiographical Notes, Letters and Reflections.* Ed. Louisa Cheves Stoney. Charleston, S.C., 1914.

Smyth, Thomas. *The Battle of Fort Sumter: Its Mystery and Miracle: God's Mastery and Mercy.* Columbia, S.C., 1861.

Smyth, Thomas. *Claims of the Presbyterian Church.* Tracts on Presbyterianism, No. 1. Charleston, S.C., 1840.

Smyth, Thomas. *Ecclesiastical Republicanism; or, The Republicanism, Liberality, and Catholicity of Presbytery, in Contrast with Prelacy and Popery.* Boston, 1843.

Smyth, Thomas. *The Unity of the Human Races Proved to Be the Doctrine of Scripture, Reason, and Science.* New York, 1850.

[Spring, Gardiner]. *A Brief View of Facts Which Gave Rise to the New York Evangelical Missionary Society.* New York, 1817.

Spring, Gardiner. *Personal Reminiscences of the Life and Times of Gardiner Spring.* 2 vols. New York, 1866.

St. Paul in America. [New York? 1811?].

Stack, Richard. *Lectures on the Acts of the Apostles.* Annapolis, Md., 1815.

[Steele, John]. *A History of Ecclesiastical Proceedings relative to the Third Presbyterian Church in Philadelphia, the Rev. Ezra Stiles Ely, and Several of the Judicatories of the Church with Which They Are Connected*. Philadelphia, 1814.

Stiles, Ezra. *Literary Diary of Ezra Stiles*. Ed. Franklin Bowditch Dexter. 3 vols. New York, 1901.

Stiles, Ezra. *The United States Elevated to Glory and Honor*. New Haven, Conn., 1783.

Swift, Zephaniah. *A System of Laws of the State of Connecticut*. 2 vols. Windham, Conn., 1795–96.

Taggart, Samuel. *A Farewell Sermon*. Greenfield, Mass., 1819.

Taylor, William. *California Life Illustrated*. New York, 1861.

Taylor, William. *Seven Years' Street Preaching in San Francisco, California: Embracing Incidents, Triumphant Death Scenes, Etc*. Ed. W. P. Strickland. New York, 1857.

Temple, William. *Miscellanies, in Four Essays*. Glasgow, 1761.

Thayer, Caroline Matilda. *Religion Recommended to Youth in a Series of Letters*. New York, 1817.

Thayer, John. *Controversy between the Rev. John Thayer, Catholic Missionary, of Boston, and the Rev. George Leslie*. [Newburyport, Mass.? 1793].

Themistius. *Madison and Religion: or, A Warning to the People of the United States of America*. Philadelphia, 1811.

Thomson, James. "Summer." In *The Seasons, viz. Spring, Summer, Autumn, Winter. And a Hymn*. London, [1760?].

Thornwell, James Henley. *Collected Writings*. 4 vols. Ed. John B. Adger and John L. Girardeau. Richmond, Va., 1873.

Thornwell, James Henley. *Report on the Subject of Slavery*. Columbia, S.C., 1852.

Thornwell, James Henley. *A Review of the Rev. J. B. Adger's Sermon on the Religious Instruction of the Colored Population*. Charleston, S.C., 1847.

Thornwell, James Henley. *The Rights and Duties of Masters*. Charleston, S.C., 1850.

A Vindication of the Religion of Mr. Jefferson and a Statement of his Services in the Cause of Religious Liberty. By a Friend to Real Religion. Baltimore, [1800].

Voltaire [Arouet, François-Marie]. *Philosophical Dictionary, for the Pocket*. Catskill [N.Y.], 1796.

Voltaire [Arouet, François-Marie]. *Philosophical Dictionary, for the Pocket*. New York, 1792–95.

Walker, James. *Unitarianism Vindicated against the Charge of Skeptical Tendencies*. Boston, 1839.

Walker, James Barr. *Philosophy of Skepticism and Ultraism, Wherein the Opinions of the Rev. Theodore Parker and Other Writers Are Shown to be Inconsistent with Sound Reason and the Christian Religion*. New York and Cincinnati, 1857.

Washington, George. "From George Washington to the Members of the New Jerusalem Church of Baltimore, 27 January 1793." Founders Online, National Archives, last modified July 12, 2016, http://founders.archives.gov/documents/Washington/05-12-02-0027. [Original source: *The Papers of George Washington, Presidential Series*. Vol. 12, *16 January 1793–31 May 1793*, 52–53. Ed. Christine Sternberg Patrick and John C. Pinheiro. Charlottesville, Va., 2005.]

Wayland, Francis. *The Elements of Political Economy*. New York, 1837.

Webb, Thomas Smith. *The Freemason's Monitor*. Albany, N.Y., 1797.

Webster, Noah. *An American Dictionary of the English Language*. New York, 1829.

Weems, Mason Locke. *The Philanthropist; or, A Good Twenty-Five Cents Worth of Love Powder, for the Honest Adamites and Jeffersonians*. Charleston, S.C., 1799.

Wesley, John. *Explanatory Notes upon the New Testament*. 3 vols. New York, 1812; orig. pub. in U.S. 1791.

Wesley, John. *The Extraordinary Case of Elizabeth Hobson*. Philadelphia, 1792.

Whatcoat, Richard. *To Go and Serve the Desolate Sheep of America: The Diary/Journal of Bishop Richard Whatcoat, 1789–1800*. Ed. Samuel J. Rogal. Bethesda, Md., 2001.

Whitaker, Nathaniel. *An Antidote against Toryism*. Newbury-Port, [Mass.], 1777.

Whitaker, Nathaniel. *The Reward of Toryism*. Newbury-Port, [Mass.], 1783.

Whitman, Walt. *Specimen Days*. Glasgow, 1883; orig. pub. 1882.

Willson, John. *A Fair and Impartial Testimony, Essayed in the Name of…the Church of Scotland*. Pittsburgh, 1808.

Wilmer, James. *Consolation: Being a Replication to Thomas Paine, and Others, on Theologics* Philadelphia, 1794.
Wilmer, James. *A Sermon on the Doctrine of the New-Jerusalem Church, Being the First Promulgated within the United States of America.* Baltimore, 1792.
Wilson, James. *Letters to the Rev. Ezra Stiles Ely, A.M.* Boston, 1814.
Wood, John. *A Full Exposition of the Clintonian Faction, and the Society of the Columbian Illuminati.* Newark, N.J., 1802.
Wright, Frances. *Biography, Notes, and Political Lectures.* New York, 1844.
Wright, Frances. *Course of Popular Lectures... with Three Addresses and a Reply to the Charges against the French Reformers of 1789.* New York, 1829.
Wright, Frances. *Supplement Course of Lectures.* London, 1834.
Wright [D'Arusmont], Frances. *Life, Letters, and Lectures, 1834/1844.* New York, 1972.
Wylie, Samuel B. *The Two Sons of Oil; or, The Faithful Witness for Magistracy and Ministry.* Greensburg, Pa., 1803.

IV. Secondary Sources

Abzug, Robert H. *Cosmos Crumbling: American Reform and the Religious Imagination.* New York, 1994.
Ackerman, Susan. "The Personal Is Political: Covenantal and Affectionate Love... in the Hebrew Bible." *Vetus Testamentum* 52, fasc. 4 (Oct. 2002): 437–58.
Albaugh, Gaylord P. *History and Annotated Bibliography of American Religious Periodicals and Newspapers, Established from 1730 through 1830.* Vol. 1. Worcester, Mass., 1994.
Aldridge, A. Owen. "Natural Religion and Deism in America before Ethan Allen and Thomas Paine." *William and Mary Quarterly*, 3rd ser., 54, 4 (Oct. 1997): 835–48.
Allen, J. Timothy. "Religion and Politics: James O'Kelly's Republicanism versus Francis Asbury's Federalism." *Methodist History* 44, 3 (April 2006): 153–65.
Allen, J. Timothy. "'Some Expectation of Being Promoted': Ambition, Abolition, and the Reverend James O'Kelly." *North Carolina Historical Review* 84, 1 (Jan. 2007): 59–81.
Allen, Richard C. *David Hartley on Human Nature.* Albany, N.Y., 1999.
Anderson, Bonnie S. *The Rabbi's Atheist Daughter: Ernestine Rose, International Feminist Pioneer.* New York, 2016.
Andrews, Dee E. *The Methodists and Revolutionary America, 1760–1800: The Shaping of an Evangelical Culture.* Princeton, N.J., 1999.
Anthony, Charles Volney. *Fifty Years of Methodism: A History of the Methodist Episcopal Church within the Bounds of the California Annual Conference from 1847 to 1897.* San Francisco, 1901.
Applegate, Debby. "Henry Ward Beecher and the 'Great Middle Class': Mass Markets, Intimacy, and Middle-Class Identity." In Burton J. Bledstein and Robert D. Johnston, eds., *The Middling Sorts: Explorations in the History of the American Middle Class*, 107–24. New York, 2001.
Armstrong, Warren B. *For Courageous Fighting and Confident Dying: Union Chaplains in the Civil War.* Lawrence, Kans., 1998.
Arne, Delfs. "Anxieties of Influence: Perry Miller and Sacvan Bercovich." *New England Quarterly* 70, 4 (Dec. 1997): 601–14.
Arner, Robert D. *Dobson's Encyclopedia: The Publisher, Text, and Publication of America's First Britannica, 1789–1803.* Philadelphia, 1991.
Baatz, Simon. "'Squinting at Silliman': Scientific Periodicals in the Early American Republic, 1810–1833." *Isis* 82, 2 (June 1991): 223–44.
Babik, Milan. "Nazism as a Secular Religion." *History and Theory* 45, 3 (Oct. 2006): 375–96.
Baker, Frank. *From Wesley to Asbury: Studies in Early American Methodism.* Durham, N.C., 1976.
Baker, Keith Michael, and Peter Hanns Reill, eds. *What's Left of Enlightenment? A Postmodern Question.* Stanford, Calif., 2001.
Baker, Thomas N. "Speculations on the Genealogy of Deism in New York, 1700–1850." *New York History* 89, 1 (Winter 2008): 43–53.

Banner, Stuart. "When Christianity Was Part of the Common Law." *Law and History Review* 16, 1 (1998): 27–62.
Barnett, S. J. *The Enlightenment and Religion: The Myths of Modernity.* Manchester, England, 2003.
Barton, William E. *The Soul of Abraham Lincoln.* New York, 1920.
Baumer, Franklin L. *Religion and the Rise of Scepticism.* New York, 1960.
Beiner, Ronald. *Civil Religion: A Dialogue in the History of Political Philosophy.* Cambridge, 2010.
Bell, Richard James. "Do Not Despair: The Cultural Significance of Suicide in America." Ph.D. diss., Harvard University, 2006.
Bellah, Robert N. *Beyond Belief: Essays on Religion in a Post-Traditionalist World.* Berkeley, Calif., 1991.
Bellah, Robert N. "Civil Religion in America." *Daedalus* 96, 1 (Winter 1967): 1–21.
Bellah, Robert N., and Phillip E. Hammond. *Varieties of Civil Religion.* San Francisco, 1980.
Bellesiles, Michael A. *Revolutionary Outlaws: Ethan Allen and the Struggle for Independence on the Early American Frontier.* Charlottesville, Va., 1993.
Bellesiles, Michael A. "Works of Historical Faith: Or, Who Wrote *Reason the Only Oracle of Man?*" *Vermont History* 57 (1989): 69–83.
Bercovitch, Sacvan. *American Jeremiad.* Madison, Wisc., 1979.
Bercovitch, Sacvan. *The Puritan Origins of the American Self.* New Haven, Conn., 1975.
Berg, Maxine. "Progress and Providence in Early Nineteenth-Century Political Economy." *Social History* 15, 3 (Oct. 1990): 365–75.
Bernard, Paul R., Robert Owen, and William Maclure. "Irreconcilable Opinions: The Social and Educational Theories of Robert Owen and William Maclure." *Journal of the Early Republic* 8, 1 (1988): 21–44.
Bestor, Arthur Eugene, Jr. *Backwoods Utopias: The Sectarian and Owenite Phases of Communitarian Socialism in America, 1663–1829.* Philadelphia, 1950.
Bilhartz, Terry P. *Urban Religion and the Second Great Awakening: Church and Society in Early National Baltimore.* Rutherford, N.J., 1986.
Blau, Joseph L. "The Christian Party in Politics." *Journal of Religion* 2, 1 (Nov. 1946): 18–35.
Bledstein, Burton J. "Introduction: Storytellers to the Middle Class." In Bledstein and Robert D. Johnston, eds., *The Middling Sorts: Explorations in the History of the American Middle Class,* 1–25. New York, 2001.
Bloch, Ruth. *Visionary Republic: Millennial Themes in American Thought, 1756–1800.* New York, 1985.
Bloch, Ruth H. "The Gendered Meanings of Virtue in Revolutionary America." *Signs* 13, 1 (1987): 37–59.
Block, Marguerite Beck. *The New Church in the New World: A Study of Swedenborgianism in America.* New York, 1932.
Blumin, Stuart M. *The Emergence of the Middle Class: Social Experience in the American City, 1760–1900.* Cambridge, 1989.
Bonney, Margaret Atherton. "The Salubria Story." *Palimpsest* 56, 2 (1975): 34–45.
Bonomi, Patricia. *Under the Cope of Heaven: Religion, Society, and Politics in Colonial America.* New York, 1986.
Borden, Morton. "The Christian Amendment." *Civil War History* 25, 2 (June 1979): 156–67.
Bosco, Ronald A., and Joel Myerson. *The Emerson Brothers: A Fraternal Biography in Letters.* New York, 2006.
Bougher, Lori D. "The Case for Metaphor in Political Reasoning and Cognition." *Political Psychology* 33, 1 (Feb. 2012): 143–63.
Bourdieu, Pierre. *Language and Symbolic Power.* Cambridge, Mass., 1991.
Boyd, Thomas. *Poor John Fitch, Inventor of the Steamboat.* New York, 1935.
Bracey, Susan L. *Life by the Roaring Roanoke: A History of Mecklenburg Count, Virginia.* Mecklenburg, Va. 1977.
Bratt, James D. "The Reorientation of American Protestantism, 1835–1845." *Church History* 67, 1 (March 1998): 52–53.

Braude, Ann. *Radical Spirits: Spiritualism and Women's Rights in Nineteenth-Century America.* Boston, 1989.
Breitenbach, William. "The Consistent Calvinism of the New Divinity Movement." *William and Mary Quarterly,* 3rd ser., 41, 2 (April 1984): 241–64.
Breitenbach, William. "Unregenerate Doings: Selflessness and Selfishness in New Divinity Theology." *American Quarterly* 34, 5 (Winter 1982): 478–502.
Brekus, Catherine A. *Strangers and Pilgrims: Female Preaching in America, 1740–1845.* Chapel Hill, N.C., 1998.
Bressler, Ann Lee. *The Universalist Movement in America, 1770–1880.* New York, 2001.
Bridenbaugh, Carl. *Mitre and Sceptre: Transatlantic Faiths, Ideas, Personalities, and Politics, 1689–1775.* New York, 1962.
Brinsfield, John W., et al., eds. *Faith in the Fight: Civil War Chaplains.* Mechanicsburg, Pa., 2003.
Britton, Wiley. *The Civil War on the Border: A Narrative of Military Operations in Missouri, Kansas, Arkansas, and the Indian Territory, during the Years 1863–65, Based upon Official Reports and Observations of the Author.* 2 vols. New York, 1899.
Brown, Candy Gunther. *The Word in the World: Evangelical Writing, Publishing, and Reading in America, 1789–1880.* Chapel Hill, N.C., 2004.
Brown, Chandos Michael. *Benjamin Silliman: A Life in the Young Republic.* Princeton, N.J., 1989.
Brown, Jerry Wayne. *The Rise of Biblical Criticism in America, 1800–1870: The New England Scholars.* Middletown, Conn., 1969.
Brown, Marshall G., and Gordon Stein. *Freethought in the United States: A Descriptive Bibliography.* Westport, Conn., 1978.
Brown, Sterling. "Negro Folk Expression: Spirituals, Seculars, Ballads, and Work Songs." In Pinn, ed. *By These Hands,* 103–22.
Buckley, Michael J. *At the Origins of Modern Atheism.* New Haven, Conn., 1987.
Buckley, Thomas E. *Establishing Religious Freedom: Jefferson's Statute in Virginia.* Charlottesville, Va., 2013.
Bullock, Steven C. "Initiating the Enlightenment? Recent Scholarship on European Freemasonry." *Eighteenth-Century Life* 20, 1 (1996): 80–92.
Bullock, Steven C. *Revolutionary Brotherhood: Freemasonry and the Transformation of the American Social Order, 1730–1840.* Chapel Hill, N.C., 1996.
Burbick, Joan. *Healing the Republic: The Language of Health and the Culture of Nationalism in Nineteenth-Century America.* Cambridge, 1994.
Burkholder, Robert E. "Emerson, Kneeland, and the Divinity School Address." *American Literature* 58 (March 1986): 1–14.
Butler, Gregory S. *In Search of the American Spirit: The Political Thought of Orestes Brownson.* Carbondale, Ill., 1992.
Butler, Jon. *Awash in a Sea of Faith: Christianizing the American People.* Cambridge, Mass., 1990.
Butler, Leslie. *Critical Americans: Victorian Americans and Transatlantic Liberal Reform.* Chapel Hill, N.C., 2007.
Buxbaum, Melvin H. *Benjamin Franklin and the Zealous Presbyterians.* University Park, Pa., 1975.
Byrd, James P. *Sacred Scripture, Sacred War: The Bible and the American Revolution.* New York, 2013.
Byrne, James M. *Religion and the Enlightenment: From Descartes to Kant.* Louisville, Ky., 1996.
Calhoun, Craig, ed. *Habermas and the Public Sphere.* Cambridge, Mass., 1992.
Calhoun, Craig. *The Roots of Radicalism: Tradition, the Public Sphere, and Early Nineteenth-Century Social Movements.* Chicago, 2012.
Calhoun, Samuel W., and Lucas E. Morel. "Abraham Lincoln's Religion: The Case for His Ultimate Belief in a Personal, Sovereign God." *Journal of the Abraham Lincoln Association* 33, 1 (Winter 2012): 38–74.
Cameron, Christopher. *Black Freethinkers: African American Secularism, 1800–1975.* Evanston, Ill., forthcoming, 2019.
Cameron, Nigel M. de S. *Biblical Higher Criticism and the Defense of Infallibilism in 19th Century Britain.* Lewiston, N.Y., 1987.

Cantor, Geoffrey, et al. Introduction to Louise Henson et al., eds., *Culture and Science in the Nineteenth-Century Media*. Hants, England, 2004.
Carey, Henry Charles. *A Memoir of Stephen Colwell*. Philadelphia, 1871.
Carey, Patrick W. *Orestes A. Brownson: American Religious Weathervane*. Grand Rapids, Mich., 2004.
Carmony, Donald F., and Josephine Elliott. "New Harmony, Indiana: Robert Owen's Seedbed for Utopia." *Indiana Magazine of History* 76, 3 (Sept. 1980): 161–261.
Carrigan, William D. "In Defense of the Social Order: Racial Thought among Southern White Presbyterians in the Nineteenth Century." *American Nineteenth Century History* 1, 2 (Summer 2000): 31–52.
Carroll, Bret E. *Spiritualism in Antebellum America*. Bloomington, Ind., 1997.
Carson, John. "Differentiating a Republican Citizenry: Talents, Human Science, and Enlightenment Theories of Governance." *Osiris*, 2nd ser., 17 (2002): 74–103.
Carwardine, Richard J. "Charles Sellers's 'Antinomians' and 'Arminians': Methodists and the Market Revolution." In Noll, ed., *God and Mammon*, 75–98.
Carwardine, Richard J. *Evangelicals and Politics in Antebellum America*. Knoxville, Tenn., 1997.
Carwardine, Richard J. "Lincoln, Evangelical Religion, and American Political Culture in the Era of the Civil War." *Journal of the Abraham Lincoln Association* 18, 1 (Winter 1997): 27–55.
Carwile, John B. *Reminiscences of Newberry*. Charleston, S.C., 1890.
Casper, Scott E. Introduction to Casper et al., eds., *The History of the Book in America*. Vol. 3, *The Industrial Book, 1840–1880*, 1–39. Chapel Hill, N.C., 2007.
Cayton, Mary Kupiec. "Who Were the Evangelicals? Conservative and Liberal Identity in the Unitarian Controversy in Boston, 1804–1833." *Journal of Social History* 31, 1 (1997): 86–107.
Chernock, Arianne. *Men and the Making of Modern British Feminism*. Stanford, Calif., 2010.
Chireau, Yvonne. *Black Magic: Religion and the African American Conjuring Tradition*. Berkeley, Calif., 2003.
Chireau, Yvonne. "Conjure and Christianity in the Nineteenth Century: Religious Elements in African American Magic." *Religion and American Culture* 7, 2 (Summer 1997): 225–46.
Clapp, Elizabeth J. " 'A Virago-Errant in Enchanted Armor?' Anne Royall's 1829 Trial as a Common Scold." *Journal of the Early Republic* 23, 2 (Summer 2003): 207–32.
Clark, Allen C. "Margaret Eaton—(Peggy O'Neal)." *Records of the Columbia Historical Society* 44/45:1–33. Washington, D.C., 1942–43.
Clark, J. C. D. *The Language of Liberty, 1660–1832: Political Discourse and Social Dynamics in the Anglo-American World*. Cambridge, 1994.
Clarke, T. Erskine. "An Experiment in Paternalism: Presbyterians and Slaves in Charleston, South Carolina." *Journal of Presbyterian History* 53, 3 (Aug. 1975): 223–38.
Clarke, T. Erskine. "Jones, Charles Colcock." *American National Biography Online*, http://www.anb.org.
Clarke, T. Erskine. *Wrestlin' Jacob: A Portrait of Religion in Antebellum Georgia and the Carolina Low Country*. Tuscaloosa, Ala., 2000; orig. pub. 1979.
Clebsch, William A. *From Sacred to Profane America: The Role of Religion in American History*. New York, 1968.
Coffin, Joshua. *The History of Newbury, Newburyport, and West Newbury, from 1635 to 1845*. Boston, 1845.
Cohen, Charles R. *God's Caress: The Psychology of Puritan Religious Experience*. New York, 1986.
Cohen, Daniel A. "Homicidal Compulsion and the Conditions of Freedom: The Social and Psychological Origins of Familicide in America's Early Republic." *Journal of Social History* 28, 4 (Summer 1995): 725–64.
Colyvas, Jeannette A., and Stefan Jonsson. "Ubiquity and Legitimacy: Disentangling Diffusion and Institutionalization." *Sociological Theory* 29, 1 (March 2011): 27–53.
Conforti, Joseph A. *Samuel Hopkins and the New Divinity Movement: Calvinism, the Congregational Ministry, and Reform in New England between the Great Awakenings*. Grand Rapids, Mich., 1981.
Conrad, Sebastian. "Enlightenment in Global History: A Historiographical Critique." *American Historical Review* 117, 4 (Oct. 2012): 999–1027.

Corrigan, John. *Business of the Heart: Religion and Emotion in the Nineteenth Century*. Berkeley, Calif., 2002.
Cotlar, Seth. *Tom Paine's America: The Rise and Fall of Transatlantic Radicalism in the Early Republic*. Charlottesville, Va., 2011.
Cox, Robert S. *Body and Soul: A Sympathetic History of American Spiritualism*. Charlottesville, Va., 2003.
Cox, Robert S. "Vox Populi: Spiritualism and George Washington's Postmortem Career." *Early American Studies* 1, 1 (Spring 2003): 230–72.
Cozzens, Peter. *This Terrible Sound: The Battle of Chickamauga*. Urbana, Ill., 1992.
Cray, Robert E., Jr. *Paupers and Poor Relief in New York City and its Rural Environs, 1700–1830*. Philadelphia, 1988.
Crimmins, James E. *Secular Utilitarianism: Social Science and the Critique of Religion in the Thought of Jeremy Bentham*. Oxford, 1990.
Crisp, Oliver D., and Douglas A. Sweeney, eds. *After Jonathan Edwards: The Courses of the New England Theology*. New York, 2012.
Croce, Paul Jerome. *Science and Religion in the Era of William James*. Vol. 1, *Eclipse of Certainty, 1820–1880*. Chapel Hill, N.C., 1995.
Crocker, Matthew H. *The Magic of the Many: Josiah Quincy and the Rise of Mass Politics in Boston, 1800–1830*. Amherst, Mass., 1999.
Crowe, Charles. *George Ripley: Transcendentalist and Utopian Socialist*. Athens, Ga., 1967.
Culver, Raymond B. *Horace Mann and Religion in the Massachusetts Public Schools*. New York, 1969.
Currier, John J. *History of Newburyport, Massachusetts, 1764–1905*. 2 vols. Newburyport, Mass., 1906.
Curry, Thomas J. *The First Freedoms: Church and State in America to the Passage of the First Amendment*. New York, 1986.
Dahlstrand, Frederick C. *Amos Bronson Alcott: An Intellectual Biography*. Rutherford, N.J., 1982.
Daly, John Patrick. *When Slavery Was Called Freedom: Evangelicalism, Proslavery, and the Causes of the Civil War*. Lexington, Ky., 2002.
Davenport, Stewart. *Friends of the Unrighteous Mammon: Northern Christians and Market Capitalism, 1815–1860*. Chicago, 2008.
Davidson, James West. *The Logic of Millennial Thought: Eighteenth-Century New England*. New Haven, Conn., 1977.
Davis, David Brion. *The Problem of Slavery in the Age of Revolution, 1770–1823*. Ithaca, N.Y., 1975.
Davis, Gerald F., et al., eds. *Social Movements and Organizational Theory*. New York, 2005.
Dawkins, Richard. *The God Delusion*. Boston, 2006.
Delp, Robert W. "A Spiritualist in Connecticut: Andrew Jackson Davis, the Hartford Years, 1850–1854." *New England Quarterly* 53, 3 (Sept. 1980): 345–62.
Demerath, N. J., III, and Rhys H. Williams. "Civil Religion in an Uncivil Society." *Annals of the American Academy of Political and Social Science* 480 (July 1985): 154–66.
Demerath, N. J., et al., eds. *Sacred Companies: Organizational Aspects of Religion and Religious Aspects of Organization*. New York, 1998.
Dennett, Daniel C. *Breaking the Spell: Religion as a Natural Phenomenon*. New York, 2006.
Dexter, Franklin Bowditch. *Biographical Sketches of the Graduates of Yale College*. 6 vols. New York, 1885–1912.
Dick, Everett N. *William Miller and the Advent Crisis*. Berrien Springs, Mich., 1994; orig. pub. 1930.
Dierksheide, Christa. "Missionaries, Evangelical Identity, and the Religious Ecology of Early Nineteenth-Century South Carolina and the British Caribbean." *American Nineteenth Century History* 7, 1 (March 2006): 63–88.
Diouf, Sylviane A. *Servants of Allah: African Muslims Enslaved in the Americas*. New York, 1998.
Dixon, John M. "Henry F. May and the Revival of the American Enlightenment: Problems and Possibilities for Intellectual and Social History." *William and Mary Quarterly*, 3rd ser., 71, 2 (April 2014): 255–80.
Doan, Ruth Alden. *The Miller Heresy, Millennialism, and American Culture*. Philadelphia, 1987.

Dodd, Jill Siegel. "The Working Classes and the Temperance Movement in Ante-bellum Boston." *Labor History* 19, 4 (1978): 510–31.
Dolan, Neal. *Emerson's Liberalism*. Madison, Wisc., 2009.
Dombrowski, Daniel A. *Rawls and Religion: The Case for Political Liberalism*. Albany, N.Y., 2001.
Donald, David. *Lincoln's Herndon*. New York, 1948.
Donnachie, Ian. *Robert Owen: Owen of New Lanark and New Harmony*. East Lothian, Scotland, 2000.
Doherty, Robert W. "Social Bases for the Presbyterian Schism of 1837–1838: The Philadelphia Case." *Journal of Social History* 2, 1 (Autumn 1968): 69–79.
Dorfman, Joseph. *The Economic Mind in American Civilization, 1606–1865*. 2 vols. New York, 1966; orig. pub. 1946.
Dorsey, Bruce. "Friends Becoming Enemies: Philadelphia Benevolence and the Neglected Era of American Quaker History." *Journal of the Early Republic* 18, 3 (Autumn 1998): 395–428.
"Dr. William A. Alcott." *American Journal of Education* 4, 12 (March 1858): 628–56.
Durey, Michael. *Transatlantic Radicals and the Early American Republic*. Lawrence, Kans., 1997.
Eastman, Carolyn. *A Nation of Speechifiers: Making an American Public after the Revolution*. Chicago, 2009.
Eckhardt, Celia Morris. *Fanny Wright: Rebel in America*. Cambridge, Mass., 1984.
Ehrman, Bart D. *Forgery and Counterforgery: The Use of Literary Deceit in Early Christian Polemics*. New York, 2013.
Eller, Jack David. "What Is Atheism?" In Paul Zuckerman, ed., *Atheism and Secularity*. Vol. 1, *Issues, Concepts, and Definitions*, [1]–18. Santa Barbara, Calif., 2010.
Ellis, Richard E. *The Jeffersonian Crisis: Courts and Politics in the Young Republic*. New York, 1971.
Emerson, Donald E. *Richard Hildreth*. Johns Hopkins University Studies in Historical and Political Science, ser. 64, no. 2. Baltimore, 1946.
Emirbayer, Mustafa, and Victoria Johnson. "Bourdieu and Organizational Analysis." *Theory and Society* 37, 1 (Feb. 2008): 1–44.
Endy, Melvin B., Jr. "Abraham Lincoln and American Civil Religion: A Reinterpretation." *Church History* 44, 2 (June 1975): 229–41.
Endy, Melvin B., Jr. "Just War, Holy War, and Millennialism." *William and Mary Quarterly*, 3rd ser., 42, 1 (Jan. 1985): 3–25.
Ernest, John. *A Nation within a Nation: Organizing African-American Communities before the Civil War*. Chicago, 2011.
Farmer, James Oscar, Jr. *The Metaphysical Confederacy: James Henley Thornwell and the Synthesis of Southern Values*. Macon, Ga., 1986.
Farrell, James J. *Inventing the American Way of Death, 1830–1920*. Philadelphia, 1980.
Faust, Drew Gilpin. *This Republic of Suffering: Death and the American Civil War*. New York, 2008.
Ferguson, Russell J. *Early Western Pennsylvania Politics*. [Pittsburgh], 1938.
Fern, Richard L. "Religious Belief in a Rawlsian Society." *Journal of Religious Ethics* 15, 1 (Spring 1987): 33–58.
Field, Peter S. *The Crisis of the Standing Order: Clerical Intellectuals and Cultural Authority in Massachusetts, 1780–1833*. Amherst, Mass., 1998.
Fiering, Norman. *Moral Philosophy at Seventeenth-Century Harvard: A Discipline in Transition*. Chapel Hill, N.C., 1981.
Finnie, Gordon E. "The Antislavery Movement in the Upper South before 1840." *Journal of Southern History* 35, 3 (Aug. 1969): 319–42.
Fischer, Kirsten. "Vitalism in America: Elihu Palmer's Radical Religion in the Early Republic." *William and Mary Quarterly*, 3rd ser., 73, 3 (July 2016): 501–30.
Fisher, Linford D. "Evangelicals and Unevangelicals: The Contested History of a Word, 1500–1950." *Religion and American Culture* 26, 2 (July 2016): 184–226.
Fisher, Louis, and Nada Mourtada-Sabbah. "Adopting 'In God We Trust' as the U.S. National Motto." *Journal of Church and State* 44, 4 (autumn 2002): 671–92.
Fitzgerald, Neil King. "Wieland's Crime: A Source and Analogue Study of the Foremost Novel of the Father of American Literature." Ph.D. diss., Brown University, 1980.

Fitzmier, John R. *New England's Moral Legislator: Timothy Dwight, 1752–1817*. Bloomington, Ind., 1998.
Fleischacker, Samuel. *What Is Enlightenment?* London, 2013.
Fluhman, J. Spencer. *"A Peculiar People": Anti-Mormonism and the Making of Religion in Nineteenth-Century America*. Chapel Hill, N.C., 2012.
Foote, Horace S. *Pen Pictures from the Garden of the World; or, Santa Clara County, California*. Chicago, 1888.
Ford, Lacy K. *Origins of Southern Radicalism: The South Carolina Upcountry, 1800–1860*. New York, 1988.
Ford, Lacy K. *Deliver Us from Evil: The Slavery Question in the Old South*. New York, 2009.
Formisano, Ronald P. "Boston, 1800–1840: From Deferential-Participant to Party Politics." In Formisano and Constance K. Burns, eds., *Boston, 1700–1980: The Evolution of Urban Politics*, 29–57. Westport, Conn., 1984.
Formisano, Ronald P. *The Transformation of Political Culture: Massachusetts Parties, 1790s–1840s*. New York, 1983.
Formisano, Ronald P., and Stephen Pickering. "The Christian Nation Debate and Witness Competency." *Journal of the Early Republic* 29 (Summer 2009): 219–48.
Fountain, Daniel L. *Slavery, Civil War, and Salvation: African American Slaves and Christianity, 1830–1870*. Baton Rouge, La., 2010.
Frankenberry, Nancy K., and Hans H. Penner. *Language, Truth, and Religious Belief: Studies in Twentieth-Century Theory and Method in Religion*. Atlanta, Ga., 1999.
Frankiel, Sandra Sizer. *California's Spiritual Frontiers: Religious Alternatives in Anglo-Protestantism, 1850–1910*. Berkeley, Calif., 1988.
Fredrickson, George M. "The Coming of the Lord: The Northern Protestant Clergy and the Civil War Crisis." In Miller et al., eds., *Religion and the American Civil War*, 110–30.
Freehling, William W. "James Henley Thornwell's Mysterious Antislavery Moment." *Journal of Southern History* 57, 3 (Aug. 1991): 383–406.
Frei, Hans W. *The Eclipse of Biblical Narrative: A Study in Eighteenth and Nineteenth Century Hermeneutics*. New Haven, Conn., 1974.
French, Roderick S. "Elihu Palmer, Radical Deist, Radical Republican: A Reconsideration of American Free Thought." *Studies in Eighteenth-Century Culture* 8 (1979): 87–108.
French, Roderick S. "Liberation from Man and God in Boston: Abner Kneeland's Free-Thought Campaign, 1830–1839." *American Quarterly* 32 (1980): 202–21.
French, Roderick S. "The Trials of Abner Kneeland: A Study in the Rejection of Democratic Secular Humanism." Ph.D. diss., George Washington University, 1971.
Frey, Sylvia R. "The Visible Church: Historiography of African Religion since Raboteau." *Slavery and Abolition* 29, 1 (March 2008): 83–110.
Frey, Sylvia R., and Betty Wood. *Come Shouting to Zion: African American Protestantism in the American South and British Caribbean to 1830*. Chapel Hill, N.C., 1998.
Frothingham, Paul Revere. *Edward Everett, Orator and Statesman*. Boston, 1925.
Fuller, Steve. *Social Epistemology*. Bloomington and Indianapolis, 1988.
Gallaher, Ruth A. "Abner Kneeland—Pantheist." *Palimpsest* 10, 7 (1939): 209–25.
Garvey, T. Gregory. *Creating the Culture of Reform in Antebellum America*. Athens, Ga., 2005.
Gaustad, Edwin S. "Religious Tests, Constitutions, and 'Christian Nation.'" In Ronald Hoffman and Peter J. Albert, eds., *Religion in a Revolutionary Age*, 218–35. Charlottesville, Va., 1994.
Gaustad, Edwin S. *Sworn on the Altar of God: A Religious Biography of Thomas Jefferson*. Grand Rapids, Mich., 1996.
Gay, Peter. *The Enlightenment: An Interpretation*. Vol. 1, *The Rise of Modern Paganism*. New York, 1966. Vol. 2, *The Science of Freedom*. New York, 1969.
Geertz, Clifford. "Common Sense as a Cultural System." *Antioch Review* 33, 1 (Spring 1975): 5–26.
Gehrig, Gail. "The American Civil Religion Debate: A Source for Theory Construction." *Journal for the Scientific Study of Religion* 20, 1 (March 1981): 51–63.

George, Joseph, Jr. "Some Lincoln Spiritualist Acquaintances." *Lincoln Herald* 113, 3 (Fall 2011): 162–205.
Georgian, Elizabeth A. "'That Unhappy Division': Reconsidering the Causes and Significance of the O'Kelly Schism in the Methodist Episcopal Church." *Virginia Magazine of History and Biography* 120, 3 (2012): 210–35.
Gilhooley, Leonard. *Contradiction and Dilemma: Orestes Brownson and the American Idea*. New York, 1972.
Gilmore, William J. "Orestes Brownson and New England Religious Culture, 1803–1827." Ph.D. diss., University of Virginia, 1971.
Gilmore, William J. *Reading Becomes a Necessity of Life: Material and Cultural Life in Rural New England, 1780–1835*. Knoxville, Tenn., 1989.
Glaude, Eddie S., Jr. *Exodus! Religion, Race, and Nation in Early Nineteenth-Century Black America*. Chicago, 2000.
Goldman, Alvin. *Knowledge in a Social World*. Oxford, 1999.
Goldman, Harvey. "Innovation and Change in the Production of Knowledge." *Social Epistemology: A Journal of Knowledge, Culture and Policy* 9, 3 (July–Sept. 1995): 211–32.
Gomez, Michael A. *Exchanging Our Country Marks: The Transformation of African Identities in the Colonial and Antebellum South*. Chapel Hill, N.C., 1998.
Gordon, Mary McDougall. "Patriots and Christians: A Reassessment of Nineteenth-Century School Reformers." *Journal of Social History* 11, 4 (Summer 1978): 554–73.
Gordon, Sarah Barringer. "The African Supplement: Religion, Race, and Corporate Law in Early National America." *William and Mary Quarterly*, 3rd ser., 72, 3 (July 2015): 385–422.
Gordon, Sarah Barringer. "Blasphemy and the Law of Religious Liberty in Nineteenth-Century America." *American Quarterly* 52, 4 (2000): 682–719.
Gordon, Sarah Barringer. "The First Disestablishment: Limits on Church Power and Property before the Civil War." *University of Pennsylvania Law Review* 162 (2014): 307–72.
Gorski, Philip S., ed. *Bourdieu and Historical Analysis*. Durham, N.C., 2013.
Graham, Jenny. "Revolutionary in Exile: The Emigration of Joseph Priestley to America, 1794–1804." *Transactions of the American Philosophical Society*, n.s., 85, no. 2 (1995).
Grasso, Christopher, ed. *Bloody Engagements: John R. Kelso's Civil War*. New Haven, Conn., 2017.
Grasso, Christopher. "The Religious and the Secular in the Early American Republic." *Journal of the Early Republic* 36 (Summer 2016): 359–88.
Grasso, Christopher. *A Speaking Aristocracy: Transforming Public Discourse in Eighteenth-Century Connecticut*. Chapel Hill, N.C., 1999.
Gravely, Will B. "The Rise of African Churches in America (1786–1822): Re-examining the Contexts." In Timothy E. Fulop and Albert J. Raboteau, eds., *African-American Religion: Interpretive Essays in History and Culture*, 133–51. New York, 1997.
Greco, John, ed. *The Oxford Handbook of Skepticism*. New York, 2008.
Green, James N. "The Rise of Book Publishing." In Kelley and Gross, eds., *A History of the Book in America* 2:75–127.
Green, Steven K. *The Second Disestablishment: Church and State in Nineteenth-Century America*. New York, 2010.
Gribbin, William. "Antimasonry, Religious Radicalism, and the Paranoid Style of the 1820s." *History Teacher* 7, 2 (Feb. 1974): 239–54.
Griffin, Keith L. *Revolution and Religion: American Revolutionary War and the Reformed Clergy*. New York, 1994.
Griffioen, Arie J. *Orestes Brownson and the Problem of Revelation*. New York, 2003.
Grimsted, David. *American Mobbing, 1828–1861: Toward Civil War*. New York, 1998.
Grodzins, Dean. *American Heretic: Theodore Parker and Transcendentalism*. Chapel Hill, N.C., 2002.
Grosin, Richard. *Transcendentalist Hermeneutics: Institutional Authority and the Higher Criticism of the Bible*. Durham, N.C., 1991.

Gross, Robert A., and Mary Kelley, eds. *A History of the Book in America*. Vol. 2, *An Extensive Republic: Print, Culture, and Society in the New Nation, 1790–1840*. Chapel Hill, N.C., 2010.

Grubbs, Patrick. "Riots (1830s and 1840s)." *The Encyclopedia of Greater Philadelphia*. http://www.philadelphiaencyclopedia.org.

Guelzo, Allen C. *Abraham Lincoln: Redeemer President*. Grand Rapids, Mich., 1999.

Guelzo, Allen C. *Edwards on the Will: A Century of American Theological Debate*. Middletown, Conn., 1989.

Guelzo, Allen C. "From Calvinist Metaphysics to Republican Theory: Jonathan Edwards and James Dana on Freedom of the Will." *Journal of the History of Ideas* 56, 3 (July 1995): 399–418.

Gunn, Simon. "Between Modernity and Backwardness: The Case of the English Middle Class." In López and Weinstein, eds., *Making of the Middle Class*, 58–74.

Gura, Philip F. *The Wisdom of Words: Language, Theology, and Literature in the New England Renaissance*. Middletown, Conn., 1981.

Gura, Philip F. "The Role of the '*Black Regiment*': Religion and the American Revolution." *New England Quarterly* 61, 3 (1988): 439–54.

Gura, Philip F. *American Transcendentalism: A History*. New York, 2007.

Guyatt, Nicholas. *Providence and the Invention of the United States, 1607–1876*. New York, 2007.

Habermas, Jürgen. *The Structural Transformation of the Public Sphere: An Inquiry into a Category of Bourgeois Society*. Trans. Thomas Burger with Frederick Lawrence. Cambridge, Mass., 1989; orig. pub. 1962.

Hackett, David G. *That Religion in Which All Men Agree: Freemasonry in American Culture*. Berkeley, Calif., 2014.

Hall, David D. Introduction to Hall, ed., *Lived Religion in America: Toward a History of Practice*. Princeton, N.J., 1997.

Halttunen, Karen. *Confidence Men and Painted Women: A Study of Middle-Class Culture in America, 1830–1870*. New Haven, Conn., 1982.

Halttunen, Karen. *Murder Most Foul: The Killer and the American Gothic Imagination*. Cambridge, Mass., 1998.

Handbook of South Carolina: Resources, Institutions and Industries of the State. 2nd ed. Columbia, S.C., 1908.

Hanley, Mark Y. *Beyond a Christian Commonwealth: The Protestant Quarrel with the American Republic, 1830–1860*. Chapel Hill, N.C., 1994.

Hansen, Karen V. *A Very Social Time: Crafting Community in Antebellum New England*. Berkeley, Calif., 1994.

Hanson, Charles P. *Necessary Virtue: The Pragmatic Origins of Religious Liberty in New England*. Charlottesville, Va., 1998.

Harris, Sam. *The End of Faith: Religion, Terror, and the Future of Reason*. New York, 2004.

Harrison, J. F. C. *Quest for a New Moral World: Robert Owen and the Owenites in Britain and America*. New York, 1969.

Harrison, Peter. *"Religion" and the Religious in the English Enlightenment*. Cambridge, 1990.

Hartwig, Rhonda D. "All in Raptures: The Spirituality of Sarah Anderson Jones." *Methodist History* 45, 3 (April 2007): 166–79.

Hatch, Nathan O. *The Democratization of American Christianity*. New Haven, Conn., 1989.

Hatch, Nathan O. *The Sacred Cause of Liberty*. New Haven, Conn., 1977.

Hatch, Nathan O., and John H. Wigger, eds. *Methodism and the Shaping of American Culture*. Nashville, Tenn., 2001.

Havlik, Robert J. "Abraham Lincoln and the Reverend Dr. James Smith: Lincoln's Presbyterian Experience in Springfield." *Journal of the Illinois State Historical Society* 92, 3 (Autumn 1999): 222–37.

Hazen, Craig James. *The Village Enlightenment in America: Popular Religion and Science in the Nineteenth Century*. Urbana, Ill., 2000.

Hecht, Jennifer Michael. *Doubt: A History*. New York, 2003.

Hempton, David. *Methodism and Politics in British Society, 1750–1850*. London, 1984.

Hempton, David. *Methodism: Empire of the Spirit.* New Haven, Conn., 2005.
Hermans, Hubert J. M., and Thorsten Gieser, eds. *Handbook of Dialogical Self Theory.* New York, 2011.
Hermans, Hubert J. M., and Agnieszka Hermans-Konopka. *Dialogical Self Theory: Positioning and Counter-Positioning in a Globalizing Society.* New York, 2010.
Hermans, Hubert J. M., and Harry J. G. Kempen. *The Dialogical Self: Meaning as Movement.* San Diego, Calif., 1993.
Herrick, James A. *The Radical Rhetoric of the English Deists.* Columbia, S.C., 1997.
Heyrman, Christine Leigh. *American Apostles: When Evangelicals Entered the World of Islam.* New York, 2015.
Heyrman, Christine Leigh. *Southern Cross; The Beginnings of the Bible Belt.* Chapel Hill, N.C., 1997.
Hilton, Boyd. *The Age of Atonement: The Influence of Evangelicalism on Social and Economic Thought, 1795–1865.* Oxford, 1988.
Himes, Charles Francis. *Life and Times of Judge Thomas Cooper: Jurist, Scientist, Educator, Author, Publicist.* Carlisle, Pa., 1918.
Hitchens, Christopher. *God Is Not Great: How Religion Poisons Everything.* New York, 2007.
Hix, Clarence Eugene. "The Conflict between Presbyterianism and Freethought in the South, 1776–1838." Ph.D. diss., University of Chicago, 1937.
Hoffer, Peter Charles. *The Free Press Crisis of 1800: Thomas Cooper's Trial for Seditious Libel.* Lawrence, Kans., 2011.
Hoffman, Amos. "Opinion, Illusion, and the Illusion of Opinion: Barruel's Theory of Conspiracy." *Eighteenth-Century Studies* 27, 1 (Autumn 1993): 27–60.
[Holcombe, Return Ira]. *History of Marion County, Missouri.* St. Louis, Mo., 1884.
Holifield, E. Brooks. *Era of Persuasion: American Thought and Culture, 1521–1680.* Boston, 1989.
E. Brooks Holifield. "Theology as Entertainment: Oral Debate in American Religion." *Church History* 67, 3 (Sept. 1998): 499–520.
Holland, David F. *Sacred Borders: Continuing Revelations and Canonical Restraint in Early America.* New York, 2011.
Hollis, Daniel Walker. *University of South Carolina.* Vol. 1, *South Carolina College.* Columbia, S.C., 1951.
Horsman, Reginald. *Josiah Nott of Mobile: Southerner, Physician, and Racial Theorist.* Baton Rouge, La., 1987.
Horsman, Reginald. *Race and Manifest Destiny: The Origins of American Racial Anglo-Saxonism.* Cambridge, Mass., 1981.
Howe, Daniel Walker. *The Unitarian Conscience: Harvard Moral Philosophy, 1805–1861.* Middletown, Conn., 1988; orig. pub. 1970.
Howe, Daniel Walker. *What Hath God Wrought: The Transformation of America, 1815–1848.* New York, 2007.
Hoyt, William Russell, III. "The Religious Thought of Gardiner Spring with Particular Reference to His Doctrine of Sin and Salvation." Ph.D. diss., Duke University, 1962.
Hudnut-Beumler, James. *In Pursuit of the Almighty's Dollar: A History of Money and American Protestantism.* Chapel Hill, N.C., 2007.
Hughes, Lynn Gordon. *Becoming Brownson: The Early Life of Orestes A. Brownson.* Providence, R.I., 2016.
Hurth, Elisabeth. *Between Faith and Unbelief: American Transcendentalists and the Challenge of Atheism.* Leiden, 2007.
Hutson, James. *Forgotten Features of the Founding: The Recovery of Religious Themes in the Early American Republic.* Lanham, Md., 2003.
Hutson, James, ed. *Religion and the New Republic: Faith in the Founding of America.* Lanham, Md., 2000.
Irons, Charles F. *The Origins of Proslavery Christianity: White and Black Evangelicals in Colonial and Antebellum Virginia.* Chapel Hill, N.C., 2008.
Israel, Jonathan I. *Democratic Enlightenment: Philosophy, Revolution, and Human Rights, 1750–1790.* New York, 2011.

Israel, Jonathan I. *Enlightenment Contested: Philosophy, Modernity, and the Emancipation of Man, 1670–1752.* New York, 2006.
Israel, Jonathan I. *Radical Enlightenment: Philosophy and the Making of Modernity, 1650–1750.* New York, 2001.
Jacoby, Susan. *Freethinkers: A History of American Secularism.* New York, 2004.
Jacoby, Susan. *The Great Agnostic: Robert Ingersoll and American Freethought.* New Haven, Conn., 2013.
Jellison, Charles A. *Ethan Allen: Frontier Rebel.* Syracuse, N.Y., 1969.
Jennings, Chris. *Paradise Now: The Story of American Utopianism.* New York, 2016.
Joerchel, Amrei C. "Cultural Processes within Dialogical Self Theory: A Socio-Cultural Perspective of Collective Voices and Social Language." *International Journal for Dialogical Science* 7, 1 (Spring 2013): 137–55.
John, Richard R. "Taking Sabbatarianism Seriously: The Postal System, the Sabbath, and the Transformation of American Political Culture." *Journal of the Early Republic* 10, 4 (Winter 1990): 517–67.
Johnson, Curtis D. *Islands of Holiness: Rural Religion in Upstate New York, 1790–1860.* Ithaca, N.Y., 1989.
Johnson, Paul E. *A Shopkeeper's Millennium: Society and Revivals in Rochester, New York, 1815–1837.* New York, 1978.
Jones, Christopher Cannon. "Methodism, Slavery, and Freedom in the Revolutionary Atlantic World." Ph.D. diss., College of William and Mary, 2016.
Jones, Donald G. *The Sectional Crisis and Northern Methodism: A Study in Piety, Political Ethics and Civil Religion.* Metuchen, N.J. 1979.
Jones, William R. "Religious Humanism: Its Problems and Prospects in Black Religion and Culture." In Pinn, ed., *By These Hands,* 25–54.
Joslin, J., B. Frisbie, and F. Ruggles. *A History of the Town of Poultney, Vermont.* Poultney, Vt., 1875.
Kahan, Alan S. *Tocqueville, Democracy, and Religion.* New York, 2015.
Kao, Grace Y., and Jerome E. Copulsky. "The Pledge of Allegiance and the Meanings and Limits of Civil Religion." *Journal of the American Academy of Religion* 75, 1 (March 2007): 121–44.
Keller, Kenneth W. "Rural Politics and the Collapse of Pennsylvania Federalism." *Transactions of the American Philosophical Society,* n.s., 72, 6 (1982): 1–73.
Kelley, Mary. "'Pen and Ink Communion': Evangelical Reading and Writing in Antebellum America." *New England Quarterly* 84, 4 (Dec. 2011): 555–87.
Kellison, Kimberly R. "Toward Humanitarian Ends? Protestants and Slave Reform in South Carolina, 1830–1865." *South Carolina Historical Magazine* 103, 3 (July 2002): 210–25.
Kelly, Catherine E. "'Well Bred Country People': Sociability, Social Networks, and the Creation of a Provincial Middle Class, 1820–1860." *Journal of the Early Republic* 19, 3 (Autumn 1999): 451–79.
Kennedy, Robert MacMillan. *Historic Camden.* 2 vols. Columbia, S.C., 1905–26.
Kidd, Thomas S. *God of Liberty: A Religious History of the American Revolution.* New York, 2010.
Kilbride, Daniel. "Slavery and Utilitarianism: Thomas Cooper and the Mind of the Old South." *Journal of Southern History* 59, 3 (Aug. 1993): 469–86.
Kilgore, Charles Franklin. *The James O'Kelly Schism in the Methodist Episcopal Church.* Mexico, 1963.
Klein, Rachel N. *Unification of a Slave State: The Rise of the Planter Class in the South Carolina Backcountry.* Chapel Hill, N.C., 1990.
Kloppenberg, James T. "The Virtues of Liberalism: Christianity, Republicanism, and Ethics in Early American Political Discourse." *Journal of American History* 74, 1 (June 1987): 9–33.
Kneeland, Timothy W. "Robert Hare: Politics, Science, and Spiritualism in the Early Republic." *Pennsylvania Magazine of History and Biography* 132, 3 (July 2008): 245–60.
Knight, George R. *Millennial Fever and the End of the World: A Study of Millerite Adventism.* Boise, Id., 1993.
Knights, Peter R. *The Plain People of Boston, 1830–1860: A Study in City Growth.* New York, 1971.

Koch, G. Adolf. *Republican Religion: The American Revolution and the Cult of Reason.* New York, 1933.
Kögler, Hans-Herbert. "Alienation as Epistemological Source: Reflexivity and Social Background after Mannheim and Bourdieu." *Social Epistemology* 11, 2 (April–June 1997): 141–64.
Kögler, Hans-Herbert. "Reconceptualizing Reflexive Sociology: A Reply." *Social Epistemology* 11, 2 (April–June 1997): 223–50.
Kolchin, Peter. *American Slavery, 1619–1877.* New York, 1993.
Kolmerten, Carol A. *The American Life of Ernestine L. Rose.* Syracuse, N.Y., 1999.
Kolmerten, Carol A. *Women in Utopia: The Ideology of Gender in the American Owenite Communities.* Bloomington, Ind., 1990.
Koschnik, Albrecht. *"Let a Common Interest Bind Us Together": Associations, Partisanship, and Culture in Philadelphia, 1775–1840.* Charlottesville, Va., 2007.
Koselleck, Reinhart. *The Practice of Conceptual History: Timing History, Spacing Concepts.* Stanford, Calif., 2002.
Kronick, David A. *A History of Scientific and Technical Periodicals: The Origins and Development of the Scientific and Technical Press, 1665–1790.* Metuchen, N.J., 1976.
Kurtz, Paul. *The New Skepticism: Inquiry and Reliable Knowledge.* Buffalo, N.Y., 1992.
Lane, Margaret. *Frances Wright and the "Great Experiment."* Totowa, N.J., 1972.
Langford, Thomas A. *Exploring Methodism: Methodist Theology.* Peterborough, Great Britain, 1998.
Larson, John Lauritz. *Internal Improvement: National Public Works and the Promise of Popular Government in the Early United States.* Chapel Hill, N.C., 2001.
Larson, John Lauritz. *The Market Revolution in America: Liberty, Ambition, and the Eclipse of the Common Good.* Cambridge, 2010.
Larson, Orvin. *American Infidel: Robert G. Ingersoll.* New York, 1962.
Lasch, Christopher. *The Revolt of the Elites and the Betrayal of Democracy.* New York and London, 1995.
Lasher, Lawrence M. "James Cheetham: Journalist and Muckraker." Ph.D. diss., University of Maryland, 1965.
Latham, Alison Rees. *Poultney: A Chronicle of Yesterday.* Poultney, Vt., 1961.
Lathan, Robert. *History of the Associate Reformed Synod of the South.* [Harrisburg, Pa., 1882].
Lawrence, Anna M. *One Family under God: Love, Belonging, and Authority in Early Transatlantic Methodism.* Philadelphia, 2011.
Lazerow, Jama. *Religion and the Working Class in Antebellum America.* Washington, D.C., 1995.
Leopold, Richard William. *Robert Dale Owen: A Biography.* Cambridge, Mass., 1940.
Levine, Lawrence W. "Slave Songs and Slave Consciousness: An Exploration in Neglected Sources." In Tamara K. Hareven, ed., *Anonymous Americans: Explorations in Nineteenth-Century Social History*, 99–130. Englewood Cliffs, N.J., 1971.
Levy, Leonard W. *The Establishment Clause: Religion and the First Amendment.* 2nd ed. Chapel Hill, N.C., 1994.
Lewis, Andrew J. *A Democracy of Facts: Natural History in the Early Republic.* Philadelphia, 2011.
Lightman, Bernard. *The Origins of Agnosticism: Victorian Unbelief and the Limits of Knowledge.* Baltimore, 1987.
Lilly, Thomas. "The National Archive: *Harper's New Monthly Magazine* and the Civic Responsibilities of a Commercial Literary Periodical, 1850–1853." *American Periodicals* 15, 2 (2005): 142–62.
Lindman, Janet Moore. "'Bad Men and Angels from Hell': The Discourse of Universalism in Early National Philadelphia." *Journal of the Early Republic* 31, 2 (Summer 2011): 259–82.
A List of the Winners of Academic Distinctions in Harvard College. Cambridge, Mass., 1907.
Lobody, Diane Helen. "Lost in the Ocean of Love: The Mystical Writings of Catherine Livingston Garrettson." Ph.D. diss., Drew University, 1990.
López, A. Ricardo, with Barbara Weinstein. "Introduction: We Shall Be All: Toward a Transnational History of the Middle Class." In López and Weinstein, eds., *The Making of the Middle Class: Towards a Transnational History*, 1–25. Durham, N.C., 2012.

Loveland, Jeff. "Unifying Knowledge and Dividing Disciplines: The Development of Treatises in the *Encyclopedia Britannica*." *Book History* 9 (2006): 57–87.
Lund, Roger D. "Deism." In Alan Charles Kors, ed. *Encyclopedia of the Enlightenment* 1:335–40. New York, 2003.
Lyerly, Cynthia Lynn. "Enthusiasm, Possession, and Madness: Gender and the Opposition to Methodism in the South, 1770–1810." In Janet L. Coryell et al., eds., *Beyond Image and Convention: Explorations in Southern Women's History*, 53–73. Columbia, Mo., 1998.
Lyerly, Cynthia Lynn. *Methodism and the Southern Mind, 1710–1810*. New York, 1998.
Lyerly, Cynthia Lynn. "Passion, Desire, and Ecstasy: The Experimental Religion of Southern Methodist Women, 1770–1810." In Catherine Clinton and Michelle Gillespie, eds., *The Devil's Lane: Sex and Race in the Early South*, 168–86. New York, 1997,.
Lyerly, Cynthia Lynn. "A Tale of Two Patriarchs: or How a Eunuch and a Wife Created a Family in the Church." *Journal of Family History* 28 (Oct. 2003): 490–509.
MacCormac, Earl R. "Missions and the Presbyterian Schism of 1837." *Church History* 32, 1 (March 1963): 32–45.
Mack, Phyllis. *Heart Religion in the British Enlightenment: Gender and Emotion in Early Methodism*. Cambridge, 2008.
Mack, Phyllis. "Religion, Feminism, and the Problem of Agency: Reflections in Eighteenth-Century Quakerism." *Signs* 29, 1 (Autumn 2003): 149–77.
Mack, Phyllis. *Visionary Women: Ecstatic Prophecy in Seventeenth-Century England*. Berkeley, Calif., 1992.
Mackie, Alexander. "The Presbyterian Churches of Old Philadelphia." *Transactions of the American Philosophical Society*, n.s., 43, 1 (1953): 217–29.
Madden, Edward H., and Marian C. Madden. "Ethan Allen, His Philosophical Side." *Transactions of the Charles S. Peirce Society* 35, 2 (1999): 270–83.
Maddex, Jack P., Jr. "From Theocracy to Spirituality: The Southern Presbyterian Reversal on Church and State." *Journal of Presbyterian History* 54 (Winter 1976): 438–57.
Maddex, Jack P., Jr. "Proslavery Millennialism: Social Eschatology in Antebellum Southern Calvinism." *American Quarterly* 31, 1 (Spring 1979): 46–62.
Maffly-Kipp, Laurie F. *Religion and Society in Frontier California*. New Haven, Conn., 1994.
Mailer, Gideon. *John Witherspoon's American Revolution*. Chapel Hill, N.C., 2017.
Malone, Dumas. *The Public Life of Thomas Cooper, 1783–1839*. New Haven, Conn., 1926.
Marini, Stephen. *Radical Sects of Revolutionary New England*. Cambridge, Mass., 1982.
Marková, Ivana. "On 'the Inner Alter' in Dialogue." *International Journal for Dialogical Science* 1, 1 (Spring 2006): 124–48.
Martin, Craig. "Configured for Exclusion: Characterizations of Religion in Liberal Political Philosophy." *Method and Theory in the Study of Religion* 19 (2007): 38–57.
Martin, Robert W. T. "Between Consensus and Conflict: Habermas, Postmodern Agonism and the Early American Public Sphere." *Polity* 37, 3 (July 2005): 365–88.
Marty, Martin E. *The Infidel: Freethought in American Religion*. Cleveland, Ohio, 1961.
Mathews, Donald G. *Slavery and Methodism: A Chapter in American Morality, 1780–1845*. Princeton, N.J., 1965.
May, Henry F. *The Enlightenment in America*. New York, 1976.
May, Henry F. *Ideas, Faiths, and Feelings: Essays on American Intellectual and Religious History, 1952–1982*. New York, 1983.
McBride, Spencer W. *Pulpit and Nation: Clergymen and the Politics of Revolutionary America*. Charlottesville, Va., 2016.
McCandless, Perry. *A History of Missouri*. Vol. 2, *1820–1860*. Columbia, Mo., 1972.
McCann, Sharon. "'We Have Many Uncle Toms': Looking at *Uncle Tom's Cabin*." *Irish Journal for American Studies* 13/14 (2004/2005): 167–85.
McCurry, Stephanie. *Masters of Small Worlds: Yeoman Households, Gender Relations, and the Political Culture of the Antebellum South Carolina Low Country*. New York, 1995.
McGarry, Molly. *Ghosts of Futures Past: Spiritualism and the Cultural Politics of Nineteenth-Century America*. Berkeley, Calif., 2008.

McKown, Delos B. *Behold the Antichrist: Bentham on Religion*. Amherst, N.Y., 2004.
McPherson, James M. *Battle Cry of Freedom: The Civil War Era*. New York, 1988.
McPherson, James M. *For Cause and Comrades: Why Men Fought in the Civil War*. New York, 1997.
Meriwether, Colyer. *History of Higher Education in South Carolina*. Washington, D.C., 1889.
Messerli, Jonathan. *Horace Mann: A Biography*. New York, 1971.
Mets, Nancy Acock. *The Companion to "Martin Chuzzlewit."* Westport, Conn., 2001.
Meyer, D. H. *The Instructed Conscience: The Shaping of the American National Ethic*. Philadelphia, 1972.
Miller, Perry. *Errand into the Wilderness*. Cambridge, Mass., 1956.
Miller, Perry. *The New England Mind: From Colony to Province*. Cambridge, Mass., 1954.
Miller, Perry, ed. *The Transcendentalists: An Anthology*. Cambridge, Mass., 1950.
Miller, Randall M., Harry S. Stout, and Charles Reagan Wilson, eds. *Religion and the American Civil War*. New York, 1998.
Miller, Robert J. *Both Prayed to the Same God: Religion and Faith in the American Civil War*. Lanham, Md., 2007.
Miller, Russell E. *The Larger Hope: The First Century of the Universalist Church in America, 1770–1870*. Boston, 1979.
Mintz, Steven. *Moralists and Modernizers: America's Pre–Civil War Reformers*. Baltimore, 1995.
Mitchell, Harvey. "Tocqueville's Flight from Doubt and His Search for Certainty: Skepticism in a Democratic Age." In Johan Van Der Zande and Richard H. Popkin, eds., *The Skeptical Tradition around 1800: Skepticism in Philosophy, Science, and Society*, 261–79. Dordrecht, Netherlands, 1998.
Mohr, John W., and Harrison C. White. "How to Model an Institution." *Theory and Society* 37, 5 (Oct. 2008): 485–512.
Moore, R. Laurence. *Selling God: American Religion in the Marketplace of Culture*. New York, 1994.
Moorhead, James H. *American Apocalypse: Yankee Protestants and the Civil War, 1860–1869*. New Haven, Conn., 1978.
Morais, Herbert M. *Deism in Eighteenth-Century America*. New York, 1934.
Moran, Jon. "Religious Reasons and Political Argumentation." *Journal of Religious Ethics* 34, 3 (Sept. 2006): 421–37.
Morgan, Edmund S. *The Gentle Puritan: A Life of Ezra Stiles, 1727–1795*. New Haven, Conn., 1962.
Moser, Paul K. *The Elusive God: Reorienting Religious Epistemology*. New York, 2008.
Mott, Frank Luther. *A History of American Magazines, 1741–1850*. New York, 1930.
Nash, Gary B. *Forging Freedom: The Formation of Philadelphia's Black Community, 1720–1840*. Cambridge, Mass., 1988.
Neem, Johann N. *Creating a Nation of Joiners: Democracy and Society in Early National Massachusetts*. Cambridge, Mass., 2008.
"Nelson, David." In Dumas Malone, ed., *Dictionary of American Biography* 13:414–15. New York, 1934.
Newfield, Christopher. *The Emerson Effect: Individualism and Submission in America*. Chicago, 1996.
Newman, Richard S. *Freedom's Prophet: Bishop Richard Allen, the AME Church, and the Black Founding Fathers*. New York, 2008.
Newman, Stephen L. "Thomas Cooper, 1759–1839: The Political Odyssey of a Bourgeois Ideologue." *Southern Studies* 24 (Fall 1985): 295–305.
Nissenbaum, Stephen. *Sex, Diet, and Debility in Jacksonian America: Sylvester Graham and Health Reform*. Westport, Conn., 1980.
Noll, Mark A. *America's God: From Jonathan Edwards to Abraham Lincoln*. New York, 2002.
Noll, Mark A. *Christians and the American Revolution*. 2nd ed. Vancouver, 2006.
Noll, Mark A. *The Civil War as a Theological Crisis*. Chapel Hill, N.C., 2006.
Noll, Mark A., ed. *God and Mammon: Protestants, Money, and the Market, 1790–1860*. New York, 2001.
Noll, Mark A. "Lincoln's God." *Journal of Presbyterian History*, 82, 2 (Summer 2004): 77–88.
Noll, Mark A. "Protestant Reasoning about Money and the Economy, 1790–1860." In Noll, ed., *God and Mammon*, 265–94.
Nolt, Steven M. "Becoming Ethnic Americans in the Early Republic: Pennsylvania German Reaction to Evangelical Protestant Reformism." *Journal of the Early Republic* 20, 3 (Fall 2000): 423–46.

Nord, David Paul. "Benevolent Books: Printing, Religion, and Reform." In Gross and Kelley, eds., *A History of the Book in America* 2:221–46.
Nord, David Paul. *Faith in Reading: Religious Publishing and the Birth of Mass Media in America.* New York, 2004.
Numbers, Ronald L., and Jonathan M. Butler, eds. *The Disappointed: Millerism and Millenarianism in the Nineteenth Century.* Bloomington and Indianapolis, 1987.
O'Brien, Karen. "The Return of the Enlightenment." *American Historical Review* 115, 5 (Dec., 2010): 1426–35.
O'Brien, Michael. *Conjectures of Order: Intellectual Life and the American South, 1810–1860.* 2 vols. Chapel Hill, N.C., 2004.
Orcutt, Samuel. *History of the Town of Wolcott, Connecticut.* Waterbury, Conn., 1874.
Owen, Christopher H. *The Sacred Flame of Love: Methodism and Society in Nineteenth-Century Georgia.* Athens, Ga., 1998.
Paludan, Phillip Shaw. "Religion and the Civil War." In Miller et al., eds., *Religion and the American Civil War,* 21–40.
Papastephanou, Marianna. "The Implicit Assumptions of Dividing a Cake: Political or Comprehensive?" *Human Studies* 27 (2004): 307–34.
Parillo, Nicholas. "Lincoln's Calvinist Transformation: Emancipation and War." *Civil War History* 46, 3 (2000): 227–53.
Patkus, Ronald D. "A Community in Transition: Boston Catholics, 1815–1845." Ph.D. diss., Boston College, 1997.
Patton, John S. *Jefferson, Cabell and the University of Virginia.* New York, 1906.
Pease, William H., and Jane H. Pease. *The Web of Progress: Private Values and Public Styles in Boston and Charleston, 1828–1843.* New York, 1985.
Pell, John. *Ethan Allen.* London, 1929.
Perkins, A. J. G., and Theresa Wolfson. *Frances Wright, Free Enquirer: The Study of a Temperament.* New York, 1939.
Peterson, Merrill D. *Lincoln in American Memory.* New York, 1994.
Pethers, Matthew. "'The Rage for Book-Making': Textual Overproduction and the Crisis of Knowledge in the Early Republic." *Early American Literature* 42, 3 (2007): 573–609.
Pettit, Norman. *The Heart Prepared: Grace and Conversion in Puritan Spiritual Life.* New Haven, Conn., 1966.
Pingel, Martha M. *An American Utilitarian: Richard Hildreth as a Philosopher.* New York, 1948.
Pinn, Anthony B., ed. *By These Hands: A Documentary History of African American Humanism.* New York, 2001.
Pinn, Anthony B. *Varieties of African American Religious Experience.* Minneapolis, 1998.
Pinn, Anthony B. *Why, Lord? Suffering and Evil in Black Theology.* New York, 1995.
Pitzer, Donald E. "The New Moral World of Robert Owen and New Harmony." In Pitzer and Paul S. Boyer, eds., *America's Communal Utopias,* 88–134. Chapel Hill, N.C., 1997.
Pocock, J. G. A. *Barbarism and Religion.* Vol. 1, *The Enlightenments of Edward Gibbon, 1737–1764.* Cambridge, 1999.
Pointer, Richard W. "Philadelphia Presbyterians, Capitalism, and the Morality of Economic Success." In Noll, ed., *God and Mammon,* 171–91.
Pope, Earl A. "Albert Barnes, 'The Way of Salvation,' and Theological Controversy." *Journal of Presbyterian History* 51, 1 (Jan. 1979): 20–54.
Popkin, Richard H. *Disputing Christianity: The 400-Year-Old Debate over Rabbi Isaac Ben Abraham of Troki's Classic Arguments.* Amherst, N.Y., 2007.
Popkin, Richard H. *The History of Scepticism from Savonarola to Bayle.* New York, 2003.
Porter, Roy S., and Mikuláš Teich, eds. *The Enlightenment in National Context.* Cambridge, 1981.
Porterfield, Amanda. *Conceived in Doubt: Religion and Politics in the New American Nation.* Chicago, 2012.
Posey, Walter Brownlow. *The Development of Methodism in the Old Southwest, 1783–1824.* Tuscaloosa, Ala., 1933.
Post, Albert. *Popular Freethought in America, 1825–1850.* New York, 1943.

Powell, Walter W., and Paul J. DiMaggio, eds. *The New Institutionalism in Organizational Analysis.* Chicago, 1991.
Rable, George C. *God's Almost Chosen Peoples: A Religious History of the American Civil War.* Chapel Hill, N.C., 2010.
Raboteau, Albert J. *Canaan Land: A Religious History of African Americans.* New York, 2001.
Raboteau, Albert J. *Slave Religion: The "Invisible Institution" in the Antebellum South.* New York, 1978.
Randall, Willard Sterne. *Ethan Allen: His Life and Times.* New York, 2011.
Ratner, Lorman A., Paula T. Kaufman, and Dwight L. Teeter Jr. *Paradoxes of Prosperity: Wealth-Seeking versus Christian Values in Pre–Civil War America.* Urbana, Ill., 2009.
Rescher, Nicholas. *Common-Sense: A New Look at an Old Philosophical Tradition.* Milwaukee, Wisc., 2005.
"The Rev. Dr. Ezra Stiles Ely." *Journal of the Presbyterian Historical Society* 2, 6 (Sept. 1904): 321–24.
Rich, Robert. "'A Wilderness of Whigs': The Wealthy Men of Boston." *Journal of Social History* 4, 3 (1971): 263–76.
Richardson, William A., Jr. "Dr. David Nelson and His Times." *Journal of the Illinois State Historical Society* 13, 4 (Jan. 1921): 433–63.
Richey, Russell E. *Early American Methodism.* Bloomington, Ind., 1991.
Richey, Russell E., and Donald G. Jones, eds. *American Civil Religion.* New York, 1974.
Richey, Russell E., et al., eds. *Perspectives on American Methodism: Interpretive Essays.* Nashville, Tenn., 1993.
Richter, Melvin. "*Begriffsgeschichte* and the History of Ideas." *Journal of the History of Ideas* 48, 2 (April–June 1987), 247–63.
Richter, Melvin. *The History of Political and Social Concepts: A Critical Introduction.* New York, 1995.
Robinson, William Childs. *Columbia Theological Seminary and the Southern Presbyterian Church: A Study in Church History, Presbyterian Polity, Missionary Enterprise, and Religious Thought.* [Decatur, Ga.], 1931.
Rockman, Seth. *Scraping By: Wage Labor, Slavery, and Survival in Early Baltimore.* Baltimore, 2009.
Rohrer, James R. "Sunday Mails and the Church-State Theme in Jacksonian America." *Journal of the Early Republic* 17 1 (Spring 1987): 57–74.
Rolfs, David. *No Peace for the Wicked: Northern Protestant Soldiers and the American Civil War.* Knoxville, Tenn., 2009.
Roney, Jessica Choppin. *Governed by a Spirit of Opposition: The Origins of American Political Practice in Colonial Philadelphia.* Baltimore, 2014.
Rose, Anne C. "Social Sources of Denominationalism Reconsidered: Post-Revolutionary Boston as a Case Study." *American Quarterly* 38 (1986): 243–64.
Rose, Anne C. *Transcendentalism as a Social Movement, 1830–1850.* New Haven, 1981.
Rosenfeld, Sophia. *Common Sense: A Political History.* Cambridge, Mass., 2011.
Rosenwaike, Ira. *Population History of New York City.* Syracuse, N.Y., 1972.
Rotenstreich, Nathan. *On Faith.* Chicago, 1998.
Roth, Randolph. "Did Class Matter in American Politics? The Importance of Exploratory Data Analysis (EDA)." *Historical Methods* 31, 1 (1998): 5–25.
Rowe, David L. *God's Strange Work: William Miller and the End of the World.* Grand Rapids, Mich., 2008.
Royle, Edward. *Robert Owen and the Commencement of the Millennium: A Study of the Harmony Community.* Manchester, England, 1998.
Ruth, Lester. *Early Methodist Life and Spirituality: A Reader.* Nashville, Tenn., 2005.
Ruth, Lester. *A Little Heaven Below: Worship at Early Methodist Quarterly Meetings.* Nashville, Tenn., 2000.
Ruttenber, E. M. *History of the Town of Newburgh.* Newburgh, N.Y., 1859.
Ryan, Mary P. *Cradle of the Middle Class: The Family in Oneida County, New York, 1790–1865.* Cambridge, 1981.
Ryan, Thomas R. *Orestes A. Brownson: A Definitive Biography.* Huntington, Ind., 1976.
Samuels, Shirley. "*Wieland*: Alien and Infidel." *Early American Literature* 25, 1 (Spring 1990): 46–66.

Sandford, Chad. "Practicing Piety: Sarah Jones and Methodism in 1790s Virginia." M.A. thesis, College of William and Mary, 2004.
Sandow, Robert M. "The Limits of Northern Patriotism: Early Civil War Mobilization in Pennsylvania." *Pennsylvania History* 70, 2 (Spring 2003): 175–203.
Schellenberg, J. L. *The Wisdom to Doubt: A Justification of Religious Skepticism.* Ithaca, N.Y., 2007.
Schlereth, Eric. *An Age of Infidels: The Politics of Religious Controversy in the Early United States.* Philadelphia, 2013.
Schlereth, Eric. "A Tale of Two Deists: John Fitch, Elihu Palmer, and the Boundary of Tolerable Religious Expression in Early National Philadelphia." *Pennsylvania Magazine of History and Biography* 132, 1 (Jan. 2008): 5–31.
Schlesinger, Arthur M., Jr. *Orestes A. Brownson: A Pilgrim's Progress.* New York, 1963; orig. pub. 1939.
Schmidt, Fredrika Teute, and Barbara Ripel Wilhelm. "Early Proslavery Petitions in Virginia." *William and Mary Quarterly* 3rd ser., 30, 1 (Jan. 1973): 133–46.
Schmidt, Jean Miller. *Grace Sufficient: A History of Women in American Methodism, 1760–1939.* Nashville, Tenn., 1999.
Schmitt, Frederick F. "Socializing Epistemology: An Introduction through Two Sample Issues." In Schmitt, ed., *Socializing Epistemology: The Social Dimensions of Knowledge,* 1–28. Lanham, Md., 1994.
Schmidt, Leigh Eric. *Village Atheists: How America's Unbelievers Made Their Way in a Godly Nation.* Princeton, N.J., 2016.
Schneider, A. Gregory. *The Way of the Cross Leads Home: The Domestication of American Methodism.* Bloomington, Ind., 1993.
Schofield, Philip. *Bentham: A Guide for the Perplexed.* London, 2009.
Scully, Randolph Ferguson. *Religion and the Making of Nat Turner's Virginia: Baptist Community and Conflict, 1740–1840.* Charlottesville, Va., 2008.
Sehat, David. *The Myth of American Religious Freedom.* New York, 2011.
Sellers, Charles. *The Market Revolution: Jacksonian America, 1815–1846.* New York, 1991.
Sewell, William E., Jr. "The Concept(s) of Culture." In Victoria E. Bonnell and Lynn Hunt, eds., *Beyond the Cultural Turn: New Directions in the Study of Society and Culture,* 35–61. Berkeley, Calif., 1999.
Shain, Barry Alan. *The Myth of American Individualism: The Protestant Origins of American Political Thought.* Princeton, 1994.
Shalev, Eran. *American Zion: The Old Testament as a Political Text from the Revolution to the Civil War.* New Haven, Conn., 2013.
Shankman, Andrew. *Crucible of American Democracy: The Struggle to Fuse Egalitarianism and Capitalism in Jeffersonian Pennsylvania.* Lawrence, Kans., 2004.
Shantz, Mark S. "Religious Tracts, Evangelical Reform, and the Market Revolution in Antebellum America." *Journal of the Early Republic* 17, 3 (Autumn 1997): 425–66.
Shattuck, Gardiner H., Jr. *A Shield and a Hiding Place: The Religious Life of the Civil War Armies.* Macon, Ga., 1987.
Sheehan, James J. "*Begriffsgeschichte*: Theory and Practice." *Journal of Modern History* 50, 2 (June 1978): 312–19.
Sheehan, Jonathan. "Enlightenment, Religion, and the Enigma of Secularization: A Review Essay." *American Historical Review* 108, 4 (2003): 1061–80.
Sher, Richard B. *The Enlightenment and the Book: Scottish Authors and Their Publishers in Eighteenth-Century Britain, Ireland, and America.* Chicago, 2006.
Shields, David S. "The Learned World." In Gross and Kelley, eds., *A History of the Book in America* 2:247–65.
Shipton, Clifford K. *Sibley's Harvard Graduates.* 17 vols. Boston, 1873–1970.
Sinha, Manisha. *The Counterrevolution of Slavery: Politics and Ideology in Antebellum South Carolina.* Chapel Hill, N.C., 2000.
Sklansky, Jeffrey P. *The Soul's Economy: Market Society and Selfhood in American Thought, 1820–1920.* Chapel Hill, N.C., 2002.

Sklar, Kathryn Kish. *Catharine Beecher: A Study in American Domesticity.* New Haven, Conn., 1973.
Smart, James R. "A Life of William Beadle." Senior thesis, Princeton University, 1989.
Smith, Craig R. *Daniel Webster and the Oratory of Civil Religion.* Columbia, Mo., 2005.
Smith, Edgar Fahs. *The Life of Robert Hare, and American Chemist (1781–1858).* Philadelphia, 1917.
Smith, Edward D. *Climbing Jacob's Ladder: The Rise of Black Churches in Eastern American Cities, 1740–1877.* Washington, D.C., 1988.
Smith, Elwyn A. "The Forming of a Modern American Denomination." *Church History* 31, 1 (March 1962): 74–99.
Smith, Elwyn A. "The Role of the South in the Presbyterian Schism of 1837–38." *Church History* 29, 1 (March 1960): 44–63.
Smith, James D., III. "Frontier Ecumenism: The Olmsted-Smith Debate of Christian Evidences." *Journal of Mississippi History* 51, 2 (May 1989): 133–39.
Smith, James D., III. "The Pilgrimage of James Smith (1798–1871): Scottish Infidel, Southern Evangelist, and Lincoln's Springfield Pastor." *American Presbyterians* 66, 3 (Fall 1988): 147–56.
Smith, Jonathan Z. "Religion, Religions, Religious." In Mark C. Taylor, ed., *Critical Terms for Religious Studies.* Chicago, 1998, 269–84.
Smith, R. Drew. "Slavery, Secession, and Southern Protestant Shifts on the Authority of the State." *Journal of Church and State* 36, 2 (1994): 261–76.
Smith, Steven C. "'The Art of Printing Shall Endure': Journalism, Community, and Identity in New York City, 1800–1810." M.A. thesis, University of Missouri-Columbia, 2007.
Smith-Rosenberg, Carroll. *Religion and the Rise of the American City: The New York City Mission Movement, 1812–1870.* Ithaca, N.Y., 1971.
Smith-Rosenberg, Carroll. "Sex as Symbol in Victorian Purity: An Ethnohistorical Analysis of Jacksonian America." *American Journal of Sociology* 84, Supplement (1978): S212–47.
Snay, Mitchell. *Gospel of Disunion: Religion and Separatism in the Antebellum South.* Chapel Hill, N.C., 1993.
Sobel, Mechal. *Trablin' On: The Slave Journey to an Afro-Baptist Faith.* Princeton, N.J., 1979.
Sorkin, David Jan. *The Religious Enlightenment: Protestants, Jews, and Catholics from London to Vienna.* Princeton, N.J., 2008.
"Special Issue on Real Knowing: Situating Social Epistemology." *Social Epistemology* 12, 3 (July–Sept. 1998).
Sprague, William. *Annals of the American Pulpit.* Vol. 4. New York, 1859.
Stackhouse, Max L. "Civil Religion, Political Theology, and Public Theology: What's the Difference?" *Political Theology* 5, 3 (July 2004): 275–93.
Stark, Rodney, and Roger Fink. *The Churching of America, 1776–1990: Winners and Losers in Our Religious Economy.* New Brunswick, N.J., 1992.
Stauffer, Vernon. *New England and the Bavarian Illuminati.* New York, 1918.
Stephens, Lester D. *Science, Race, and Religion in the American South: John Bachman and the Charleston Circle of Naturalists, 1815–1895.* Chapel Hill, N.C., 2000.
Stevens, George L. "John Fellows: A Minor Deist." M.A. thesis, University of Maryland, 1956.
Stewart, Matthew. *Nature's God: The Heretical Origins of the American Republic.* New York, 2014.
Stiles, Henry R., and Sherman W. Adams. *The History of Ancient Wethersfield, Connecticut.* New York, 1904.
Stoever, William K. B. *"A Faire and Easie Way to Heaven": Covenant Theology and Antinomianism in Early Massachusetts.* Middletown, Conn., 1978.
Stokes, Melvyn and Stephen Conway, eds. *The Market Revolution in America: Social, Political, And Religious Expressions, 1800–1880.* Charlottesville, Va., 1996.
Stout, Harry S. *The New England Soul: Preaching and Religious Culture in Colonial New England.* New York, 1986.
Stout, Harry S. *Upon the Altar of the Nation: A Moral History of the Civil War.* New York, 2006.
Stout, Harry S., and Christopher Grasso. "Civil War, Religion, and Communications: The Case of Richmond." In Miller et al., eds., *Religion and the American Civil War,* 313–59.
Stroumsa, Guy G. *A New Science: The Discovery of Religion in the Age of Reason.* Cambridge, Mass., 2010.

Suhl, Yuri. *Eloquent Crusader: Ernestine Rose.* New York, 1970.
Sullivan, Robert E. *John Toland and the Deist Controversy: A Study in Adaptations.* Cambridge, Mass., 1982.
Sutton, William R. *Journeymen for Jesus: Evangelical Artisans Confront Capitalism in Jacksonian Baltimore.* University Park, Pa., 1998.
Sweeney, Douglas A. *Nathaniel Taylor, New Haven Theology, and the Legacy of Jonathan Edwards.* New York, 2003.
Sweeney, Douglas A., and Allen C. Guelzo, eds. *The New England Theology: From Jonathan Edwards to Edwards Amasa Park.* Grand Rapids, Mich., 2006.
Sweet, William Warren. *Virginia Methodism: A History.* Richmond, Va., 1955.
"A Symposium on Charles Sellers, *The Market Revolution: Jacksonian America, 1815–1846.*" *Journal of the Early Republic* 12, 4 (Winter 1992): 445–76.
Taves, Ann. *Fits, Trances and Visions: Experiencing Religion and Explaining Experience from Wesley to James.* Princeton, N.J., 1999.
Taves, Ann. *Religious Experience Reconsidered: A Building-Block Approach to the Study of Religion and Other Special Things.* Princeton, N.J., 2009.
Taylor, Charles. *A Secular Age.* Cambridge, Mass., 2007.
Taylor, Michael. "British Conservatism, the Illuminati, and the Conspiracy Theory of the French Revolution, 1797–1802." *Eighteenth-Century Studies* 47, 3 (Spring 2014): 293–312.
Tharp, Louise Hall. *Until Victory: Horace Mann and Mary Peabody.* Boston, 1953.
Thomas, George M. *Revivalism and Cultural Change: Christianity, Nation Building, and the Market in the Nineteenth-Century United States.* Chicago, 1989.
Thompson, Ernest Trice. *Presbyterians in the South.* Vol. 1, *1607–1861.* Richmond, Va., 1963.
Thuesen, Peter J. *Predestination: The American Career of a Contentious Doctrine.* New York, 2009.
Tomlins, Christopher L. "Criminal Conspiracy and Early Labor Combinations: Massachusetts, 1824–1840." *Labor History* 28, 3 (1987): 370–85.
Tompkins, Kyla Wazana. "Sylvester Graham's Imperial Dietetics." *Gastronomica* 9, 1 (Winter 2009): 50–60.
Topham, Jonathan R. "Scientific Publishing and the Reading of Science in Nineteenth-Century Britain: A Historiographical Survey and Guide to Sources." *Studies in the History and Philosophy of Science* 31, 4 (2000): 559–612.
Trexler, Harrison Anthony. *Slavery in Missouri, 1804–1865.* Baltimore, 1914.
Tucker, Andie. "Newspapers and Periodicals." In Gross and Kelley, eds., *A History of the Book in America* 2:389–408.
Turner, James. *Without God, without Creed: The Origins of Unbelief in America.* Baltimore, 1985.
Valeri, Mark. *Law and Providence in Joseph Bellamy's New England: The Origins of the New Divinity in Revolutionary America.* New York, 1994.
Van Buren, Martin Cornelius. "The Indispensable God of Health: A Study of Republican Hygiene and the Ideology of William Alcott." Ph.D. diss., UCLA, 1977.
Van Deburg, William L. "William Lloyd Garrison and the 'Pro-Slavery Priesthood': The Changing Beliefs of an Evangelical Reformer, 1830–1840." *Journal of the American Academy of Religion* 43, 2 (June 1975): 224–37.
van Holthoon, Fritz, and David R. Olson, eds. *Common Sense: The Foundations for Social Science.* Lanham, Md., 2005.
van Meijl, Toon. "Culture and Identity in Anthropology: Reflections on 'Unity' and 'Uncertainty' in the Dialogical Self." *International Journal for Dialogical Science* 3, 1 (Fall 2008): 165–90.
Varg, Paul A. *Edward Everett: The Intellectual in the Turmoil of Politics.* Selinsgrove, Pa., 1992.
Vinton, Francis. *The Christian Idea of Civil Government.* New York, 1861.
Wagoner, Zandra. "Deliberation, Reason, and Indigestion: Response to Daniel Dombrowski's *Rawls and Religion: The Case for Political Liberalism.*" *American Journal of Theology and Philosophy* 31, 3 (Sept. 2010): 179–95.
Wallace, Mark C. "Threats of Illuminism: Eighteenth-Century Scottish Masonic Conspiracy Theories." *History Scotland* 10, 3 (May/June 2010): 20–24.

Walters, Kerry S. "Elihu Palmer and the Religion of Nature: An Introductory Essay." In Walters, ed., *Elihu Palmer's "Principles of Nature": Text and Commentary*. Wolfeboro, N.H., 1990, 3–67.

Walters, Kerry S. Introduction to Walters, ed., *The American Deists: Voices of Reason and Dissent in the Early Republic*. Lawrence, Kans., 1992.

Walters, Kerry S. *Rational Infidels: The American Deists*. Durango, Colo., 1992.

Walters, Ronald. *American Reformers, 1815–1860*. New York, 1978.

Wang, Yingyao. "Homology and Isomorphism: Bourdieu in Conversation with New Institutionalism." *British Journal of Sociology*, 67, 2 (June 2016): 348–70.

Waterman, A. M. C. *Revolution, Economics and Religion: Christian Political Economy, 1798–1833.* Cambridge, 1991.

Waterman, Bryan. "The Bavarian Illuminati, the Early American Novel, and Histories of the Public Sphere." *William and Mary Quarterly*, 3rd ser., 62, 1 (June 2005): 9–30.

Wauzzinski, Robert A. *Between God and Gold: Protestant Evangelicalism and the Industrial Revolution, 1820–1914*. Rutherford, N.J., 1993.

Weber, Donald. *Rhetoric and History in Revolutionary New England*. New York, 1988.

Weed, Ronald, and John von Hekring. Introduction to Weed and von Hekring, eds., *Civil Religion in Political Thought: Its Perennial Questions and Enduring Relevance in North America*. Washington, D.C., 2010.

Weis, Frederick Lewis. *The Colonial Clergy and the Colonial Churches of New England*. Lancaster, Mass., 1936.

Weithman, Paul J. "Rawlsian Liberalism and the Privatization of Religion: Three Theological Objections Considered." *Journal of Religious Ethics* 22, 1 (Spring 1994): 3–28.

Werner, James V. "Bringing Down Holy Science: The *North American Review* and Jacksonian Scientific Inquiry." *American Periodicals* 10 (2000): 27–42.

West, John G., Jr. *The Politics of Revelation and Reason: Religion and Civic Life in the New Nation*. Lawrence, Kans., 1996.

Westerkamp, Marilyn J. "James Henley Thornwell, Pro-Slavery Spokesman with a Calvinist Faith." *South Carolina Historical Magazine* 87, 1 (Jan. 1986): 49–64.

Whitaker, Albert P. "A Forgotten Page of Missouri History." *Kansas City Star*, June 13, 1909, 1.

Whitaker, Albert P. "Marion College and Marion City—Missouri Enterprises of Fifty Years Ago." *Magazine of Western History* 4, 6 (Oct. 1886): 798–807.

White, Shane. "The Gold Diggers of 1833: African American Dreams, Fortune-Telling, Treasure-Seeking, and Policy in Antebellum New York City." *Journal of Social History* 47, 3 (Spring 2014): 673–95.

Whorton, James C. "'Christian Physiology': William Alcott's Prescription for the Millennium," *Bulletin of the History of Medicine* 49, 4 (Winter 1975): 466–81.

Whorton, James C. *Crusaders for Fitness: The History of American Health Reformers*. Princeton, N.J., 1982.

Wigger, John H. *American Saint: Francis Asbury and the Methodists*. New York, 2009.

Wigger, John H. *Taking Heaven by Storm: Methodism and the Rise of Popular Christianity in America*. New York, 1998.

Wilentz, Sean. *Chants Democratic: New York City and the Rise of the American Working Class, 1788–1850*. New York, 1984.

Williams, Jeffrey. *Religion and Violence in Early American Methodism: Taking the Kingdom by Force*. Bloomington, Ind., 2010.

Williams, Raymond. *The Sociology of Culture*. New York, 1981.

Williamson, Scott C. *The Narrative Life: The Moral and Religious Thought of Frederick Douglass*. Macon, Ga., 2002.

Wilson, Douglas L., and Rodney O. Davis, eds. *Herndon's Informants: Letters, Interviews, and Statements about Abraham Lincoln*. Urbana, Ill., 1998.

Wilson, John F. *Public Religion in American Culture*. Philadelphia, 1979.

Wilson, John F. "Religion and Revolution in American History." *Journal of Interdisciplinary History* 23, 3 (Winter 1993): 597–614.

Wilson, Susan. "Postmodernism and the Enlightenment." In Martin Fitzpatrick et al., eds., *The Enlightenment World*, 648–59. London, 2004.

Winch, Julie. *The Elite of Our People: Joseph Willson's Sketches of Black Upper-Class Life in Antebellum Philadelphia*. University Park, Pa., 2000.

Winger, Stewart. *Lincoln, Religion, and Romantic Cultural Politics*. DeKalb, Ill., 2003.

Winterer, Caroline. *American Enlightenments: Pursuing Happiness in the Age of Reason*. New Haven, Conn., 2016.

Withington, Ann Fairfax. *Toward a More Perfect Union: Virtue and the Formation of American Republics*. New York, 1991.

Wolf, William J. *Lincoln's Religion*. Philadelphia, 1970; orig. pub. 1959.

Wood, Gordon S. *The Radicalism of the American Revolution*. New York, 1992.

Wood, Kirsten E. "'One Woman So Dangerous to Public Morals': Gender and Power in the Eaton Affair." *Journal of the Early Republic* 17, 2 (Summer 1997): 237–75.

Woodard, W. S. *Annals of Methodism in Missouri*. Columbia, Mo., 1893.

Woodworth, Steven E. *While God Is Marching On: The Religious World of Civil War Soldiers*. Lawrence, Kans., 2001.

Wright, Conrad. *The Beginnings of Unitarianism in America*. Boston, 1955.

Wright, Conrad. "Institutional Reconstruction in the Unitarian Controversy." In Conrad Edick Wright, ed., *American Unitarianism, 1805–1865*, 3–29.

Wright, Conrad. *The Unitarian Controversy: Essays on American Unitarian History*. Boston, 1994.

Wright, Conrad Edick, ed. *American Unitarianism, 1805–1865*. Boston, 1989.

Wright, Conrad Edick. *The Transformation of Charity in Postrevolutionary New England*. Boston, 1992.

Wuthnow, Robert. *Meaning and Moral Order: Explorations in Cultural Analysis*. Berkeley, Calif., 1987.

Wyatt-Brown, Bertram. "The Antimission Movement in the Jacksonian South: A Study in Regional Folk Culture." *Journal of Southern History* 36, 4 (Nov. 1970): 501–29.

Wyatt-Brown, Bertram. "Prelude to Abolitionism: Sabbatarian Politics and the Rise of the Second Party System." *Journal of American History* 58, 2 (Sept. 1971): 316–41.

Yeo, Richard. "Lost Encyclopedias: Before and after the Enlightenment." *Book History* 10 (2007): 47–68.

Yeo, Richard. "Reading Encyclopedias: Science and the Organization of Knowledge in British Dictionaries of Arts and Sciences, 1730–1850." *Isis* 82, 1 (March 1991): 24–49.

Young, Jason R. *Rituals of Resistance: African Atlantic Religion in Kongo and the Lowcountry South in the Era of Slavery*. Baton Rouge, La., 2007.

Zackariasson, Ulf. "A Critique of Foundationalist Conceptions of Comprehensive Doctrines in the Religion in Politics–Debate." *International Journal of Philosophy and Religion* 65 (2009): 11–28.

Zboray, Ronald J., and Mary Saracino Zboray. "The Boston Book Trades, 1789–1850: A Statistical and Geographical Analysis." In Conrad Edick Wright and Katheryn P. Viens, eds., *Entrepreneurs: The Boston Business Community, 1700–1850*, 211–68. Boston, 1997.

Zwelling, Shomer S. "Robert Carter's Journey: From Colonial Patriarch to New Nation Mystic." *American Quarterly* 38, 4 (Dec. 1986): 613–36.

INDEX

Abbott, Jacob, 384
Adams, James H., 435
Adams, Jasper, 425, 579n54
Adams, John, 128, 159, 163–65, 540n7, 541n13, 572n17, 576n23
Adams, John Quincy, 211, 256, 292, 548n30, 568n43
Adger, John B., 426–27, 429, 431, 434–36, 580n65, 581n76
Adventism, 278, 313–15, 320, 327, 331–33, 564n6, 565n14, 566n20. *See also* Miller, William
African Americans, 87, 119, 186–88, 236–37, 351, 427, 536n51
  and independent black churches, 119, 144–45, 147, 149, 151, 537n59
  religious skepticism among, 119–20, 144–51, 536n53
  See also African Methodist Episcopal Church (AME); slavery
African Methodist Episcopal Church (AME), 22, 99, 119–20, 144–45, 148–49, 537n59
Agassiz, Louis, 425–26
Age of Reason (Paine), 6, 94, 114, 120, 135, 198, 217, 267, 372, 382, 528n5, 554n4
  reactions to, 14, 22, 100, 362
Alcott, Amos Bronson, 269, 296
Alcott, William Andrus, 296–98, 483, 560n30, 561n56
  conversion to Christianity, 303–4, 562nn64–65
  and health reform, 277, 279–80, 293–296, 299–301, 304–10, 313, 483, 561n53, 562n65
  and religious skepticism, 280, 296, 298–99, 302–3, 307–8, 310, 503, 560n32, 562n62
Alger, William Rounseville, 482–83, 486–87, 587n4
Alien and Sedition Acts, 123, 156, 159, 163, 405

Allen, Ethan, 47, 53, 61–62, 101, 328, 483, 516–17n23, 517n29
  and deism, 21, 25–27, 33–43, 63–64, 296, 514n1, 517n24
  and religious skepticism, 2–4
  in the Revolutionary War, 2, 21, 25, 33, 35, 38–39, 517n32, 517n39
Allen, Levi, 517n39
Allen, Richard, 144, 149
Ambrose (enslaved man), 234–36, 240, 243, 247
American Association for the Advancement of Science, 485
American Bible Society, 206, 301, 553n35
American Physiological Society, 305
American Republic and Human Liberty Foreshadowed in Scripture, The (Phillips), 395, 441–44, 452–52, 457
American Revolution, 1–2, 103, 107, 146, 221, 283, 306, 388–89, 482, 513–14n2
  and American religion, 4–5, 19–21, 25–33, 58–61, 64, 67–68, 97, 202–3, 421, 443–45, 514n4, 583n9
  and deism, 25–27, 30–32, 38–43, 58–61, 64, 99, 124, 444
  and millennialism, 32
  and nationalism, 32, 58, 443–45
  and religious liberty, 31, 60–61, 97, 108–9, 125–26, 439
  and slavery, 70
American Society for the Dissemination of the Doctrines of the New Jerusalem Church, 141
American Sunday School Union, 213, 228
American Tract Society, 206, 218, 226
Anderson, Thomas, 522n9
Andover Theological Seminary, 250, 257–58
Anglicans, 29, 67–68, 180, 365, 382, 399. *See also* Church of England
Anti-Masonic Party, 121

Antinomians, 49, 58
Appleseed, Johnny. *See* Chapman, John
Arianism, 98, 180–81, 201
Arminianism, 47, 49, 98, 195, 200–201, 204, 206, 214, 522n6
   and Calvinism, 88, 98, 195, 214–15
   Methodist, 88, 195, 200
Arnold, Benedict, 472
Articles of Confederation, 21
Asbury, Francis, 69–70, 73, 78–79
   criticisms of, 83–84, 89, 91–96
   and James O'Kelly, 82–83
   and Jeremiah Minter, 66, 82–83, 89, 91–96, 522n6, 526n36, 527n51
   and slavery, 69–70, 89
atheism, 16, 22, 30, 106, 178, 181, 201, 225, 311, 316, 327, 356, 434, 446, 483–84, 521n76, 575–76n22
   and the Civil War, 436, 438–40
   and deism, 8, 15, 21, 32, 45–49, 52, 63, 73, 78, 101, 114–17, 121, 127, 134, 142, 208, 368, 520n72
   and enslaved African Americans, 148
   and freethought, 279, 289–90
   and French Revolution, 14, 94, 409
   John Kelso and, 475–76, 486
   and materialism, 26–27, 101, 178, 189, 261, 403, 525n29
   and religious freedom, 126–27, 192, 342
   and Transcendentalism, 265, 272
   and Unitarianism, 251, 253, 258, 271
   and Universalism, 30, 48–49, 114–15, 117

Bacheler, Origen, 1, 5, 8, 11, 289, 293, 483, 485, 511n1
Bachman, John, 425
Bacon, Francis, 267, 269, 348
Bacon, Leonard, 571n7
Baird, E.T., 430
Baker, Daniel, 415
Baldwin, Charles R., 368–69
   conversion of, 278, 357, 359, 363, 366–67, 370
   and religious skepticism, 364–66, 368, 373, 389–90
Baldwin, Cornelius, 368, 373
Baldwin, Cyrus, 367
Baldwin, Elizabeth, 357, 366
Baldwin, Mary Jane, 369
Ballou, Adin, 302
Ballou, Hosea, 335, 564n6
Bancroft, George, 257, 273, 570n63
Bank of the United States, 214, 232, 239, 241, 244
Baptists, 81, 191, 212, 252, 266–67, 287, 334, 338, 399, 494, 498, 584n21
   and Adventism, 324, 327–31

African-American, 537n59, 581n71
   Freewill, 4, 16, 20, 195, 200
   growth of, 20, 22, 208, 399, 415–16, 514n4
   and politics, 23, 209–11, 445
   and religious liberty, 29, 61, 138, 289
   and slavery, 314, 430, 432–33
   Southern, 31, 207, 325, 399, 430, 432, 580n62, 581n71
   and Universalism, 109–12, 323
Barclay, Mag. *See* Mellen, Alice Hayes
Barker, Joseph, 313, 322
Barlow, Joel, 118
Barnes, Abram, 240–41, 243, 552n22
Barnes, Albert, 214–15, 549n36
Barnes, Suzie, 469
Baron, George, 128, 130, 135
Barruel, Abbé Augustin, 123, 128, 134, *Bath Kol* (Murray), 26–30, 515n4
Bavarian Illuminati. *See* Illuminati
Bayley, John, 278, 358–59, 363, 365, 381–90
Beadle, Ansell, 43
Beadle, Elizabeth, 43
Beadle, Lydia (daughter), 44
Beadle, Lydia (mother), 44, 51
Beadle, Mary, 44
Beadle, William, 21, 25–26, 33, 43–58, 62–64, 519n50
Beattie, James, 372
Beckwith, George, 46
Beecher, Catharine, 306
Beecher, Lyman, 205, 209, 213, 215, 306, 323–24, 337–39, 548–49n33, 561n57, 567n30
Bellamy, Joseph, 42
Bennett, Thomas, 402
Bentham, Jeremy, 158, 269–71, 283, 360, 542–43n33
Benton, Thomas Hart, 475
Bibb, Henry, 146, 148
Bible
   Bible societies, 7, 22, 136, 140, 206, 301, 565n35
   and common sense, 13, 15, 27, 32, 64, 103, 253, 329–30, 419
   evangelical practices of piety and, 73–74
   higher criticism and, 3, 7, 102–5, 159, 252, 256–58, 264–65, 334–35, 338, 406–8, 416–17, 425–26
Bible Society of Baltimore, 140
Biddle, Nicholas, 239
Blackstone, William, 116
Blair, James, 409, 576n23
Bolingbroke, Henry St John, 30, 59, 99, 315, 419, 516n12
Bollman, Dr. E., 171
Bonnet, Charles, 374

Book of Mormon, 418–19, 496. *See also* Mormonism
Bosley, John, 237–38, 248
Boston Investigator, 331, 337, 341, 345, 568n35
Bowen, Francis, 571n7
Bowman, Jane, 240, 243
Briggs, Martin Clock, 451
Brittan, Samuel B., 313–14, 562–63n73
Brook Farm, 296
Broussai, F.J.V., 410
Brown, Charles Brockden, 168, 514n1
Brown, Henry "Box," 146
Brown, John, 273
Brownlee, William C., 496
Brownson, Orestes, 269, 330–31, 504, 564n3, 565n7, 566nn19–20, 570n59, 570n63
    conversion to Catholicism, 278, 324, 326, 332, 346, 351, 354–56, 570n57, 571n7
    conversion to Protestantism, 278, 324, 326–27, 332
    debate with Abner Kneeland, 339–41, 568n35, 569n54
    and religious skepticism, 7, 277–78, 301, 324–28, 332, 339–41, 348–56, 564–65n6, 567n32, 568n38
    and Spiritualism, 353–54
    and Universalism, 332–34,
Brown University, 360
Bryan, Edward B., 435–36
Buckminster, Joseph, 250, 254, 554n2
Buddhism, 484
Buonaparte, George, 240, 243
Burgoyne, John, 38
Burke, Edmund, 159, 161–62, 372, 539–40n3
Burr, Aaron, 120, 128
Burr, Thaddeus, 53
Burt (enslaved man), 432
Burtt, John, 207
Bushnell, Horace, 443, 445
Butler, Joseph, 384, 543n34
Byrd, William, 522n9
Byron, Lord, 372, 382, 485

Calhoun, John C., 351, 406, 411, 435, 574n3
California Christian Advocate, 447, 450–51
Calvin, John, 42, 98, 486, 496
Calvinism, 35, 46–47, 63, 166, 180, 194–96, 235, 498–99
    Abraham Lincoln and, 488–89
    and Arminianism, 88, 98, 195, 214–15
    and Christian Enlightenment, 200–207
    movement away from, 20
    and politics, 28–31, 120, 215
    and religious skepticism, 15, 135, 326–27, 332–35, 338, 346–48

    and Unitarianism, 157, 191, 205, 250, 404, 408–9, 439, 520–21n72, 539n6, 587n4
    and Universalism, 7–8, 29–30, 47, 201, 210–12, 519n51, 523n16
    See also Congregationalists; Presbyterians; Trinitarians
Calvinist Magazine, 207, 227, 229
Campbell, Alexander, 12, 288, 447, 465
Campbellites. *See* Disciples of Christ
capitalism, 337, 381, 516n13
    and Christianity, 6, 67, 228–29, 359–362, 390, 516n13, 553n35, 571n7
    and moral reform, 247, 295
    and socialism, 283, 285, 291, 390
Caples, William Goss, 468
Carey, Mathew, 291
Carlile, Robert, 301, 382–83
Carlisle (Dickinson) College, 167, 188, 397, 544n57, 574n1
Carpenter, Stephen Cullen, 154–55
Carswell, Margaret, 239
Carter, Robert, 133
Carver, William, 128–29
Cary, Samuel, 253–57, 260
Case of Thomas Cooper, M.D., The (Cooper), 411–12, 539n8, 576n28
Cater, Richard B., 424
Catholics, 10, 54, 100, 123, 130, 158, 197, 210, 229, 271–72, 361, 439, 457, 485, 516n15
    and anti-Catholicism, 91, 98, 208–9, 218, 223, 337, 386, 423, 446–47, 487, 539n6
    debates with Protestants, 155, 167, 495–97
    immigration and expansion of, in early America, 208, 323, 325, 388
    Orestes Brownson and, 278, 324, 326, 332, 346, 351, 354–56, 570n57, 571n7
    and religious skepticism, 16, 215, 223, 252, 289
    and religious toleration, 29, 109, 290, 323
Catto, Thomas, 433
Cause and Cure of Infidelity (Nelson), 156, 194, 217–18, 225–28, 238, 248–49, 313, 483, 545n2, 549–50n40, 550n45
Centre College, 219
Chalmers, Thomas, 303, 360–61
Channing, William Ellery, 251, 253, 339, 567n32
Channing, William Henry, 276, 567n32
Chapman, John, 134
Charles Elwood; or, The Infidel Convert (Brownson), 324, 327–28, 332, 341, 350–51, 354, 568n36, 568n38
Charleston Literary and Philosophical Society, 425
Chase, Samuel, 163–66
Chauncy, Charles, 47
Cheetham, James, 129, 140, 535n43
Chester, John, 45, 52–55, 58, 62, 519n59

Chesterfield, Lord Philip, 28, 60, 515n7, 520n69
Childs, John Wesley, 384
Christian Disciple (Boston), 255–56
Chubb, Thomas 28, 515n7
church and state, 3, 26, 97, 107–8, 117, 125, 136, 138, 151, 211–15, 228, 301, 344, 351, 361, 394
  in the Confederate States of America, 438, 440
  in England, 383
  establishment and disestablishment, 20, 60–61, 109, 112–13, 116–17, 125–17, 136, 142, 190–91, 209–10, 214, 338, 341, 343–44, 394, 399, 422–23, 438–39, 514n4
  separation of, 17, 117, 213, 343, 351, 411, 423–24, 436–38
  and state constitutions, 21, 60–61, 343
  in U.S. Constitution, 411, 383
  See also nationalism; religious liberty; religious toleration
Church of England, 20, 65, 136, 362. *See also* Anglicans; Episcopalians
Cicero, 220, 367
civil religion, 17, 138, 344, 350, 393–94, 573n2
  Northern, 395, 478–79
  Southern, 394, 399
  See also nationalism
Civil War, 1, 64, 67, 146–47, 505, 583n11
  and civil religion, 395, 442, 478–79, 490–91
  and death, 482–83, 586n81
  and John Kelso, 469–79, 486
  and nationalism, 442–45, 451–52, 457–58, 473–76, 478–79
  and race, 476–77
  as religious conflict, 436–40, 442–43, 579–80n59
  and religious schism, 421
  and religious skepticism, 3, 442, 459–60, 472, 475–76, 479, 482, 486, 488–91, 511n4, 588n19
  and slavery, 433–34, 439–40, 441, 451–52, 465, 469–70, 473–76, 479, 579–80n59
Clark, David, 228, 230, 550–51nn2–3, 551n5
Clarke, John, 539n6
Clarke and Erskine Theological Seminary, 410
Clay, Henry, 214, 237, 292, 475
Clinton, DeWitt, 128–30
Clinton, George, 128
Clintonians, 120, 127–28, 140, 143
Clowney, William K., 402
Coit, J.C., 422
Coke, Thomas, 70, 73, 78–79, 82
Coles, Dennis, 116, 530nn39–40
College of Charleston, 425
College of Georgia, 577n33
Collins, Anthony, 254
colonization, 207, 214, 236–37, 285, 297, 429, 475
  proposals for, to Haiti, 283–284
  proposals for, to Mexico, 474
  See also Liberia; slavery
Columbia Theological Seminary, 428, 577n39
Colvin, J.B., 533n23
Colwell, Stephen, 362, 571n7
Combe, George, 348–49, 352, 383
Committee of 50, 292
common school movement, 294, 347–50. *See also* education reform; Mann, Horace
common sense, 26–27, 63, 333, 340, 547n22
  and critiques of religion, 13, 37, 41–42, 48–49, 65, 103, 421, 425, 460–62, 467, 476–77
  religious, 2, 5, 13, 15, 26, 32, 64, 193, 206, 253–54, 341, 354, 514n4, 579–80n59
  religious critiques of, 220–21, 419
  Scottish philosophy of, 64, 167, 206, 325, 425, 515
Condillac, Étienne Bonnot de, 261
Condorcet, Marquis de, 118, 360, 426
Confederate States of America, 415–16, 470–74, 476, 581n76
  civil religion and, 393–94, 399, 440
  constitution of, 436, 438–39, 582n79
  and nationalism, 393, 440, 441, 443
Confessions of a Converted Infidel (Bayley), 359, 385–86
Congregationalists, 29, 202, 208, 210, 266, 296, 298, 327, 346, 352, 402, 498, 562n64
  and growth of evangelical churches, 20, 22–23, 577n37
  and religious skepticism, 148, 157, 250, 337–38, 484
  and religious tolerance, 60, 112–13
  and Unitarianism, 157, 205, 250, 258, 337
  See also Calvinism; Trinitarians
Connecticut Courant (Hartford), 25, 44, 118, 533n21
Conservation Club. *See* Charleston Literary and Philosophical Society
Constant, Benjamin, 340
constitution
  Confederate, 438–39, 582n79
  France, 126
  Pennsylvania, 109, 342, 543–44n44
  South Carolina, 399, 402–3, 412, 437
  state, 21, 28, 60–61, 108–9, 116, 125–26, 342–44
  U.S. (*see* U.S. Constitution)
Contrast Between Calvinism and Hopkinsianism (Ely), 200–201, 546n14
Convert, The (Brownson), 324, 327, 332, 350, 354, 564n3, 565n7, 566n19
Cooper, Thomas, 193, 301, 439, 539–40n3, 540n6, 543–44n44, 576n29
  and Carlisle College, 167, 188, 544n57

as editor of the *Emporium of the Arts and Sciences*, 168–76, 540n7, 542n20
and Joseph Priestley, 161–62, 178, 180–81, 335, 402, 404, 540nn6–7, 541n13
political philosophy of, 162, 164–67, 170–76, 177–88, 395, 397–400, 402, 404–13, 422–24, 426, 540n4, 541n13, 543n40, 543n42, 574n3, 576n23
and religious skepticism, 156, 180–81, 189–92, 212, 281, 336, 395, 397–413, 415–18, 420–22, 425, 428–29, 432, 440, 483, 539n8, 541n16, 575n17, 575–76n22, 576n24
sedition trial of, 156, 159, 163–66, 183–84, 540n7, 541n9
and slavery, 160–61, 177–80, 186–88, 395, 404–6, 409, 423, 428–29, 431–32, 542–43n33, 544n54
and South Carolina College, 159, 177, 188, 190, 212, 395, 397–416
and Thomas Jefferson, 155–56, 159, 188–92, 401–2, 404, 540n7
and the University of Virginia, 189
views on women, 185–86
Cousin, Victor, 340, 350, 557n5, 567n34
Coxe, John Redman, 168–74
Crèvecoeur, Hector St. John de, 33
Crosby, Alpheus, 566n20
Cruikshanks, Alexander, 565n9
Curtiss v. Strong (1809), 116

d'Alembert, Jean-Baptiste le Rond, 353, 426
Dana, James, 44, 46–47, 52
Dana, W.C., 417
Daniel, John Moncure, 440
Dartmouth College, 100
Darwin, Erasmus, 181
Davis, Andrew Jackson, 281, 312–15, 317
Davis, Jefferson, 440
Deaderick, David, 219
Declaration of Independence, 27, 68, 363, 443, 445, 496, 572n17
  Frances Wright and, 283, 290
  and individual rights, 117, 182, 321, 442, 444, 475, 477
  and religious freedom, 116–17
Deistical Society of New York City, 100, 114, 129–30, 143
deism
  and atheism, 8, 15, 21, 32, 45–49, 52, 63, 73, 78, 101, 114–17, 121, 127, 134, 142, 208, 368, 520n72
  Elihu Palmer and, 22–23, 97, 99–106, 109–12, 114–17, 118–21, 124, 129, 131, 135, 137, 143, 313, 531–32n11

Ethan Allen and, 21, 25–27, 33–43, 63–64, 296, 514n1, 517n24
and Freemasons, 120–30, 142–43, 328, 356
and the New Jerusalem (Swedenborgian) Church, 130–43
organized, 22–23, 97–99, 107–12, 118–20, 124, 127, 130–31, 137, 142–43
and religious liberty, 26–27, 32, 61, 64, 125–28
Thomas Jefferson and, 6, 8, 23, 32, 127, 140, 155
Thomas Paine and, 6, 14, 22–23, 99–100, 114, 117, 135, 140, 143–44, 266, 281, 296, 480
and Universalism, 22, 27–28, 30, 32–33, 48–49, 98–99, 106–17, 142–43, 147, 433
William Beadle and, 21, 25–26, 33, 43–58, 62–64
Democracy in America (Tocqueville), 5, 107, 272
Democratic Party, 214, 323–24, 345–46, 350, 361, 372, 445, 485, 513–14n2
  and Workingmen's movement, 292–93
Democratic-Republican Party. *See* Republican Party (Jefferson)
Democratic-Republican Societies, 108, 120–21
Denniston, David, 116–17, 127, 129, 140, 143, 530n39, 531n11
Derby, John Barton, 323–24, 337, 345
Descartes, René, 58, 105, 351, 501
de Wette, William Martin Leberecht, 427, 568n36
Dewey, Orville, 571n7
d'Holbach, Baron, 99, 271, 281, 301, 528n11
Dickens, Charles, 372, 552n21
Dickinson College. *See* Carlisle (Dickinson) College
Diderot, Denis, 353
Disciples of Christ, 12, 212, 327, 447, 449
Discourse on the Wants of the Times (Brownson), 339, 341, 568n35
Discussion on the Existence of God and the Authenticity of the Bible between the Christian and the Skeptic (Bacheler and Owen), 293, 511n1
Ditchet, John, 378
Divinity School Address (Emerson), 259, 265
Dobson, Thomas, 168
Doubleday, Ulysses F., 334
Douglas, I.K., 576n39
Douglas, Stephen, 475
Douglass, Frederick, 148
Driscoll, Denis, 100, 103–4, 124, 130–31, 139–40
Dumont, Etienne, 269
Duncan, Stephen, 213
Dunlap, Andrew, 345
Dutch Reformed Church, 126, 210

Duty of Christian Freemen to Elect Christian Rulers (Ely), 209–10, 547n24
Dwight, Timothy, 41, 202, 205, 547n21
  and religious skepticism, 47–48, 122–24, 496, 518n48, 519n49, 520n62

Eaton, John Henry, 211
Eaton, Margaret, 211
Eclipse of Faith; or, A Visit to a Religious Skeptic, The (Rogers), 484
Edward (enslaved man), 432
Edwards, Jonathan, 42, 47, 200–203
Edwards, W.B., 472
education reform, 219, 277, 280, 290–97, 303–6, 309, 324, 345–50, 356, 401, 411, 416, 447, 457
Eichhorn, Johann Gottfried, 256–58, 406, 426, 555n15
Elaw, Ziplha, 525n27
elections and voting, 164, 288, 291–93, 398, 405, 442, 454
  and Christianity, 2–3, 22–23, 62, 209–10, 528n48
  presidential, of 1800, 14, 20, 108, 120, 123, 127, 138, 140, 155, 176–77, 188
  presidential, of 1832, 214
  presidential, of 1840, 324, 445, 548n28
  presidential, of 1860, 437, 439, 459
  and property requirements, 182–83, 185, 428
  and religious skepticism, 22–23, 209, 292
Ely, Ezra Stiles, 245–49, 545n5, 546nn14–15, 547n22, 547n24, 548–49n33
  and enlightened Christian agency, 194–96, 200–209, 215, 226, 553n36
  and Marion College, 215, 226, 227–36, 238–45, 553n29
  and religious skepticism, 197–200, 545n8, 548n27
  and slavery, 195, 228–29, 234–36, 238, 240, 243, 249, 551n13
  views on Christianity and politics, 156, 193–94, 209–10, 286, 290, 411, 539n8, 566n19
Ely, Zebulon, 195–96, 202–4, 546n17
Emancipation Proclamation, 443, 459, 489.
  See also Civil War; Lincoln, Abraham; slavery
Embargo Act of 1807, 196
Emerson, Ralph Waldo, 157, 257, 259–60, 264–65, 269, 340, 361
Emerson, William, 257
Emmons, Nathaniel, 346–47
Emporium of the Arts and Sciences (Philadelphia), 168–76
encyclopedias, 9, 168, 360
English, George Bethune, 157, 250–58, 260, 264, 273, 484, 555n14
Enlightenment, 6, 97, 153–58, 167–68, 538n2

Christian, 125, 131, 157, 194–96, 204, 207–8, 215, 228–29, 249, 254–55
  and skepticism, 53, 154–58, 193, 251, 262, 353–54, 462
Episcopalians, 20, 23, 133, 191, 210, 290, 367, 372, 408, 419, 446, 480, 534n32, 571n7, 584n21
  in New York City, 20, 545n5
  and religious skepticism, 13, 16, 296, 362, 364–65, 372, 485, 545n8
  and slavery, 429, 433, 435–36, 581n73, 581n75
  in the South, 415, 429, 581n73
  See also Anglicans; Church of England
evangelicals, 5–6, 16, 21, 31, 64, 88, 99, 156, 373, 512n10, 564n5
  African American, 145–46, 151
  conversion narratives, 358–39, 364–65
  and disestablishment, 61
  growth of, in early republic, 20, 67, 194–95, 208, 415, 514n4
  and nationalism, 440, 444
  and the market economy, 361, 388, 553n34
  and politics, 190, 209, 211, 301, 424, 445–46
  and print culture, 195–96, 206–9, 226, 228, 232, 246, 553n34
  and reform, 193, 205, 207–8, 212, 215, 232, 249, 278, 304, 310, 359, 553n36
  and religious experience, 65–67, 80, 84, 105, 158, 191, 205, 297–98, 415, 497–98
  and religious skepticism, 150–51, 310, 327, 338, 358–59, 390
  and slavery, 228–29, 315, 432–34, 440, 574n4
  and women, 191, 432–33
  See also Baptists; Methodists; revivals
Evening Post (New York City), 129, 279
Everett, Edward, 253–57
Ewald, Henrich, 426–27

faith. *See* skepticism, and faith
Farnsworth, Joseph, 45, 518n40, 520n62
Federalist Party, 8, 22, 122–27, 155–56, 405, 514n4, 565n9
  and the Alien and Sedition Acts, 123, 163–65, 183–84
  clergy, 120, 122–23
  and the election of 1800, 14, 108, 120, 123, 127, 138, 140
Fellows, John, 111–14, 118–19, 123–24, 143–44, 514n1
Female Skeptic; or, Faith Triumphant, The (Mellen), 3–4, 484
Fenwick, Joseph, 323
Fielding, Henry, 271
Findley, William, 126
Fisher, George Park, 495
Fitch, John, 109–11, 114

Flower, George, 284
Forty Years in the Wilderness of Pills and Powders (Alcott), 295, 299–300, 308, 560n30, 560n32
Founding Fathers, 6, 442, 444
Fourier, Charles, 302
Fowler, L.N., 295
Fowler, O.S., 295
Fox, Ann, 312, 352
Fox, Catherine, 312, 352
Fox, Margaret, 312, 352
Franklin, Benjamin, 6, 62, 107, 217, 296, 342, 444, 482, 485, 544n60
Fraser, Donald, 533n23
Free Enquirer (New York City), 1, 8, 280–81, 285–86, 288, 290–91, 293, 336, 485, 511n1
Freemasonry, 14, 22, 99, 110, 118, 140, 298, 538n2
   and deism, 120–30, 142–43, 328, 356
Free Press Association, 281, 378
freethinkers, 6–8, 215, 224, 247–48, 261, 270, 272, 382–83, 386, 490–91
   Abner Kneeland and, 212, 277, 301, 331, 334–39, 344–45, 351, 356, 504, 567n32, 569n44
   African-American, 147–49
   Christian critiques of, 1, 12, 301–3, 309–10, 323, 355–56, 394, 425, 482–85, 584n15
   Frances Wright and, 212, 279–80, 281, 286–93, 310, 334, 336–38, 362, 378, 484–85, 559n19
   John Kelso and, 461–62, 468, 476–77
   and labor movement, 14, 280–82, 339, 345, 350, 362, 370, 566n28
   and reform, 6
   and religious liberty, 116, 127, 568n41
   Robert Dale Owen and, 212, 279–80, 281, 286–93, 310, 334, 336–38, 362, 378, 484–85, 504–5, 559n19, 566–67n28
   and Universalism, 333–45
   William Alcott and, 301–3, 309–10
   See also infidel(s); Society of Free Enquirers
French Revolution, 19, 94, 108, 124, 159, 283, 360, 516n15
   and American Republicanism, 8, 22, 108, 154
   and deism, 99, 116, 127, 137
   Reign of Terror, 14, 108, 154
   and religion, 14, 19, 21–22, 95, 97, 110, 120, 123, 126, 136, 143, 409
Friendly Association, 107
Fries, John, 164
Fugitive Slave Act (1850), 273, 315
Fulton, Robert, 247
Furman, Richard, 430

Gaddis, Maxwell Pierson, 363, 367–68, 370, 389, 446
Galileo, 105

Gallaher, James, 229–30, 241
Gallio, 149–51, 537n64
Gardner, George, 116–17, 530n39
Garratt, A.C., 236–37, 552n20
Garrettson, Catherine Livingston, 522n4, 523n16, 523–24n19, 524nn23–24, 527nn50–51
Garrettson, Freeborn, 78–79, 524n24, 525n29, 527n57
Garrison, William Lloyd, 281, 312, 322, 569n47
   and abolitionism, 314–15, 345–46
   critique of religion, 314–15, 317, 345, 421
   and Spiritualism, 563n75
gender, 182, 279–80, 291, 304, 346
   and evangelical religious experience, 87, 203
   and religious skepticism, 4
General Union for Promoting the Observance of the Christian Sabbath, 213
George III, 35, 39, 514n4
German idealism, 157, 325
German Reformed Church, 212, 458
Germany, 3, 13, 123, 255–57, 261, 325, 448
Gesenius, Wilhelm, 426
Gibbon, Edward, 220, 224, 266, 344, 483
Gibson, Mrs. Otis, 585n37
Gildersleeve, Benjamin, 413–14, 424, 577n33, 579n54
Gladney, Richard S., 577n33
Glendinning, William, 66, 73, 78–79, 83–84, 87–89, 91, 525n29
Godwin, William, 301, 303, 352, 360, 362, 543n39
Gold Rush, 275, 442, 448–50, 469
Goodwin, George, 25
Goss, Charles Chaucer, 67
Göttingen University, 256–57
Graham, Andrew J., 563n81
Graham, Sylvester, 294–95
"Great Awakening," 29, 58. *See also* revivals
Great Britain, 13, 43–44, 70, 80, 159, 162, 174–75, 177, 220, 360–61, 381, 411, 431
   and the American Revolution, 19, 27–28, 33, 68
   immigrants from, to America, 278, 280–81, 358, 378, 383–84, 386
   New Jerusalem (Swedenborgian) Church in, 134–137, 534n35
   religious skepticism in, 29, 37, 215, 301, 383
   Universalism in, 112
   and the War of 1812, 20, 170
Great Sin and Danger (Marsh), 47–48, 518n40, 518n48, 519n60
Greeley, Horace, 361, 386
Greene, Nathanael, 402, 574n9
Green Mountain Boys, 25, 33
Grosvenor, Cyrus Pitt, 338
Grounds of Christianity Examined (English), 157, 250–58, 484

Haiti, 187, 284
Hall, Julien, 566n28
Hall of Science, 281, 287–88, 290–91, 293
Hamilton, Alexander, 108, 405
Hammet, William, 93
Hammond, C., 562–63n73
Hammond, James Henry, 177
Hare, Robert, 484–86
Hargrove, John, 130–42, 533n23,
  533–34n29, 535n42
Harper's New Monthly Magazine, 310–11
Harris, Samuel, 583n6
Harrison, William Henry, 446
Hartford Bible Convention, 281, 310–22,
  562n71, 562–63n73, 563n78, 563n81
Hartley, David, 178, 543n34
Harvard College, 47, 157, 250–51, 254–58, 264,
  269, 425–26
Hayes, Henry H., 241–44, 552n22, 553n29
health reform, 4, 277, 279–80, 293–96,
  299–301, 304–10, 313, 483, 561n53,
  561n60, 562n65
Henry, Patrick, 69
Henshaw, David, 345
Herbert, Edward, of Cherbury, 30, 419
Herndon, William, 487, 588n18
Hertell, Thomas, 575n22
Hickok, Laurens P., 499
Hildreth, Richard 158, 251, 264, 267–73,
  556–57n40
Himes, Joshua, 331, 542n33
Hinde, Thomas, 69
Hindmarsh, Robert, 135–37, 139, 141
Hindus, 116, 223
Hitchcock, Enos, 539n6
Hobbes, Thomas, 30, 261, 451, 516n12
Hobson, Elizabeth, 78
Hodge, Charles, 421
Holland, Josiah, 487
Holley, Horace, 404
Holmes, Caroline Thompson, 240, 553n24
Holyoake, George Jacob, 11
Hopkins, Lemuel, 41
Hopkins, Samuel, 201, 203–5
Hopkins, Stephen, 62
Hopkinsians, 201–5, 215, 546nn14–15,
  549n36, 549n38
Horace, 220
Houston, George, 281, 378
Howe, George, 416–17, 426, 430,
  577n37, 580–81n67
Howe, Samuel Gridley, 350
Howe, William, 39
Hudson, Barzillai, 25
Hughes, John, 361
Hume, David, 105, 224, 328, 340, 351, 483
  and deism, 30, 59, 180, 266
  mother of, 198
  and religious skepticism, 94–95, 99, 271, 344,
  356, 364, 368, 372, 417, 419
  and Transcendentalists, 266, 271
  and Unitarians, 303
Hutcheson, Francis, 499, 515n5
Huxley, Thomas Henry, 11

Illuminati, 120–23, 127–30, 140
infidel(s), 6–7, 16, 47, 95–96, 137, 208, 215,
  272, 299, 342, 407–9, 411, 501–2,
  559n20
  abolitionists as, 345
  Abraham Lincoln as, 488
  as atheists, 404
  and ignorance, 156, 195–97, 219–20, 504,
  545n2, 549n40, 554n38
  and insanity, 199, 312
  and materialism, 360
  Northerners as, 434, 439–40
  and radical politics, 120–22, 130
  and reform, 341
  rejection of, as label, 115, 224, 288–89,
  345, 566–67n28
  and religious toleration, 121, 125, 438,
  532n16
  and slavery, 148–49
  and Thomas Jefferson, 139–40, 155
  Transcendentalists as, 251, 258, 261, 265
Inner Temple, 161
Isabel (enslaved woman), 284

Jackson, Andrew, 210–11, 214, 284, 342,
  412–13, 475, 485
Jackson, Claiborne F., 470
Jackson, James, 385
Jackson, Rachel, 211
Jackson, Stonewall, 438
Jacobin Clubs, 108, 159, 161
Jacobs, J.A., 146
Jane (enslaved woman), 240, 243
Jarratt, Devereux, 68
Jea, John, 148, 150
Jebb, John, 63, 521n76
Jefferson, Thomas, 14, 101, 154, 159, 170, 184,
  301, 342, 572n17
  charges of religious infidelity, 139–40,
  154–55
  Christian supporters of, 155, 444
  and the Declaration of Independence,
  182, 443–45
  and deism, 6, 8, 23, 32, 127, 140, 155
  and election of 1800, 20, 108, 120, 127,
  138, 140, 188
  letter to Danbury Baptists, 138

and religious liberty, 23, 32, 61, 127, 181, 439, 576n23
and slavery, 190, 284, 475
and Thomas Cooper, 155–56, 159, 188–92, 401–2, 404, 540n7
Jennings, Robert L., 301
Jesuits, 123, 191
Jews, 9, 104, 126, 150–51, 209, 217, 256, 288, 352, 417, 435, 457
critiques of Christianity, 250–54
Jewish scriptures, 252, 312, 319
and religious liberty, 61, 288, 438
Johnson, Richard M., 214, 345–46
Johnson, William, 187, 402, 574n9
Jones, Charles Colcock, 147–48, 428–29, 431, 433–34
Jones, Gardner, 497
Jones, Sarah Anderson, 21, 92–93, 203, 365, 456, 522n4, 527n54
conversion of, 68
and Jeremiah Minter, 21, 66, 77, 80–83, 85, 86–87, 94, 96, 526n34
journal, 75–76, 79–80, 521–22n3
personal piety of, 66–67, 71–78, 79–82, 85–86, 523n11, 523–24n19, 524n21, 524n24, 526n44
and sanctification, 71–72, 75
and slavery, 69–71, 85, 89
struggle with doubt, 73, 85
and Tignal Jones, 66, 68–69, 79, 81, 86, 89, 522n9
and visions, 77–78
Jones, Tignal, 79, 81–82, 86
conversion of, 89
and slavery, 68–71, 522n9, 523n13
Jouffroy, Théodore, 15, 276–77
Journal of the Stated Preacher to the Hospital and Almshouse in the City of New-York (Ely), 196–200, 545n5

Kant, Immanuel, 153, 260, 350–51
Kauffman, Elizabeth. *See* Phillips, Elizabeth Kauffman
Keef, Sergeant, 38
Kelso, Adelia. *See* Moore, Adelia
Kelso, Florella, 465
Kelso, John Russell, 3, 395, 441
and atheism, 475, 478–79, 486
and civil religion, 395, 478
Methodist preacher, 441, 459–60, 465–66
and nationalism, 441–42, 472, 473–75, 477–79
and religious skepticism, 441, 459–62, 467–68, 475–79
schoolteacher, 395, 441
and slavery, 464–65, 469–70, 473–75, 586n64

and Spiritualism, 486
Union soldier, 395, 441–42, 459, 472, 586n71
Kennard, James Jr., 568n38
Kent, James, 343–44
Kneeland, Abner, 204, 383, 483, 570n59, 572n35
blasphemy trials of, 277, 323, 341–44, 350, 484, 564n6, 568n36, 568n39
and common sense philosophy, 340
debate with Orestes Brownson, 339–41, 568n35
as editor of the *Boston Investigator*, 331, 337, 341, 345, 356, 564n6, 568–69n43
and freethought movement, 212, 277, 301, 334–39, 344–45, 351, 356, 504, 567n32, 569n44
and phrenology, 569n54
and reform, 325–26, 337, 346
renunciation of Christianity, 323, 342, 348
and slavery, 345–46
and the Society of Free Enquirers, 337, 339, 341
and the workingmen's movement, 566–67n28
Koran, 418–19, 496. *See also* Muslims
Kramer, Christian, 135

LaBorde, Maximilian, 177
labor movement, 276–77, 291–92, 361–63, 370–71
and freethinkers, 14, 339, 345, 350
See also Workingmen's Party
Lackington, James, 119
Lafayette, Marquis de, 283, 285
Lectures on the Element of Political Economy (Cooper), 183, 543n42
Lectures on Scepticism (Beecher), 323, 338–39, 549n37, 567n30
Lee, Jarena, 144–46, 149–51, 535n48
Lee, Mother Ann, 335
Leland, A.W., 415
Leland, John, 61, 516n12
Liberia, 429
Liberty Party, 548n28
Library Company of Philadelphia, 107
Lieber, Francis, 398, 413
Life and Experience of a Converted Infidel, The (Scarlett), 359, 377–78, 570n2
Lincoln, Abraham, 482, 484
election of, 437, 439, 459
religious views of, 4, 478, 482, 487–90, 588n18
and slavery, 443, 459, 475
Lincoln, Eddie, 487
Lincoln, Mary Todd, 482, 588n18
Lincoln, Willie, 487
Linn, William, 126

Livingston, Edward, 130
Livingston, William, 63, 120
Locke, John, 30, 99, 105, 260–61, 267–69, 499, 516n12, 589n13
Lolotte, Josephine, 284
London Theosophical Society, 134, 533n29
Long, John Dixon, 148
Longinus, 220
Loring, Joshua, 38
Lovejoy, Elijah P., 236, 552n16
Luther, Martin, 98, 320, 496
Lutherans, 148, 208, 212, 425, 497, 537n59, 580n62
Lynch, Anne C., 568n38, 570n59
Lyon, Matthew, 327–28

Madison, James, 61, 151, 170, 184, 284, 405
Malthus, Thomas, 360, 362
Manchester Constitutional Society, 161–62, 184
Manchester Literary and Philosophical Society, 161, 186
Mann, Horace, 277, 324–26, 346–51, 355–36, 564–65n6, 569nn48–49, 569–70n55
Margaret (enslaved woman), 240, 243
Marion City, Missouri, 156, 195, 227, 230, 232, 239–45, 247–48, 552n21
  flooding of, 233–34, 236, 239,
  and the Panic of 1837, 239–40
Marion College, 156, 194, 241, 550–51n2
  and Christian Enlightenment, 194–95, 227–29, 232–33, 235, 245, 247–48
  and missionaries, 232, 237, 550n45
  and slavery, 234–37, 238, 240, 242–43, 248
Marsh, John, 25, 44, 46–49, 51, 518n40, 518n46, 518n48, 519n60
Martineau, James, 259–60
Masons. *See* Freemasonry
Massachusetts Society for Promoting Christian Knowledge, 205
Mather, Cotton, 483
Mather, Ralph, 133
Mathews, John, 433
Matilda (enslaved woman), 240, 243
McClaskey, John, 93
McClellan, Samuel, 239–40, 245
McConnell, John, 471
McDowell, Ephraim, 215
McGrath, A.G., 429
McVickar, John, 571n7
Mellen, Alice Hayes, 3–4
Memoirs of Dr. Joseph Priestley (Cooper), 189, 402, 404
Memoirs Illustrating the History of Jacobinism (Barruel), 123, 134

Memoirs of the Rev. Zebulon Ely (Ely), 202, 546n17
Methodist Episcopal Church, 73, 86, 89, 93, 96, 143, 446–47
  Discipline, 69–70
Methodist Episcopal Church, South, 386, 416, 451, 465, 467
Methodists, 110, 118, 180, 191, 197, 207, 210, 212, 266, 388, 441, 447, 485, 488, 585n37
  African-American, 22, 99, 119, 144–46, 149, 151, 537n59, 581n71
  and American nationalism, 445
  beginnings in America, 68
  in California, 447–52, 457–59, 584n21
  Christmas Conference (1784),
  and church hierarchy, 67, 514n4
  communal character of, 67, 79–81, 85–86, 88–89, 379, 390, 525n30
  and the democratization thesis, 67, 88, 514n4, 522n6
  growth in early republic, 20–21, 65, 67–68, 91, 96, 195, 208, 399, 415–16, 522n5
  itinerant preachers, 67, 79, 92, 455, 465
  and nationalism, 442–46, 456–59, 477, 528n60, 583n12
  and New Jerusalem (Swedenborgian) Church, 133, 135
  and religious authority, 21, 65, 67, 87–89, 200, 498
  and religious experience, 65–66, 71–78, 87, 192, 203, 252, 327, 365–381, 384, 452–56, 462, 495, 523n15, 524n24, 525n27
  and religious skepticism, 14, 16, 22–23, 66, 71–73, 78–79, 89, 133, 278, 357–59, 365–381, 384–86, 389–91, 418, 459–60, 467–68, 475, 502–3,
  and sanctification, 71–73, 395, 454–56
  schism within, 83–84, 91, 93, 325, 447, 526n38
  and slavery, 69–71, 85, 88–89, 325, 385–86, 415, 432, 447, 451–52, 523n14, 544n54
  and understanding of the self, 67, 87–89, 200, 526n47
  views of faith, 73–74
  See also African Methodist Episcopal Church (AME); Asbury, Francis; evangelicals; Jones, Sarah; Methodist Episcopal Church; Minter, Jeremiah; slavery; Wesley, John
Middleton, Erasmus, 539n6
Miles, John Warley, 434
Miles, Mary Ann Ely Carswell, 240, 244–45
Miles, Thomas J., 240, 245
Mill, John Stuart, 360
millennialism, 31–32, 207, 280, 307, 360, 442, 445, 474, 482, 583n9
Miller, William, 278, 325–26, 356, 565n9, 566n20

and the Bible, 329–32, 356, 565n14
conversion to Christianity from skepticism, 324, 326–29, 332, 351–52
predictions regarding Christ's Second Coming, 324, 330–32, 333, 565n15
and the War of 1812, 328–29
Millerites, 16, 333, 355, 5564n6, 566n20
Minter, Anthony, 91–92
Minter, Jeremiah, 21, 86, 522n9, 528n62
castration of, 66, 82, 90, 526n36
conversion of, 80–81, 90
and Francis Asbury, 66, 82–83, 89, 91–92, 522n6, 526n36, 527n51
as independent preacher, 66, 93–96, 527n54, 527n57
personal piety of, 66–67, 90–91, 524n25
publications of, 66, 92, 94–96, 520n3, 527n54
and religious skepticism, 66, 94–96
and Sarah Anderson Jones, 21, 66, 77, 80–83, 85, 86–87, 92–94, 96, 526n34
visions, 90
Mirabeau, 301, 353
missionaries, 190, 297, 301, 408, 442, 527n54
in California, 442, 447–48, 457, 585n37
Catholic, 539n6
and Christian Enlightenment, 232, 280
and deism, 22
and Marion College, 232, 237, 550n45
New Jerusalem (Swedenborgian) Church, 133–34
to skeptics, 227
to slaves, 147–48, 429, 433–34
Missouri Compromise, 190
Mitchell, Stephen Mix, 43, 49, 51–52, 55, 57–58, 62, 520n62
Monroe, James, 170, 284
Montague, James, 40
Montaigne, Michel de, 53–54, 501, 519n58
Moore, Adelia, 463–68
Moore, Hannah, 539n6
Moore, L.W., 466–67
Moore, Martin, 568–69n43
Mormons, 9, 218, 267, 326, 418–19, 461, 484, 496. *See also* Book of Mormon
Morse, Jedidiah, 120–24, 205, 251,
Morton, Samuel George, 426
Muldrow, William, 227–30, 232–33, 236–43, 248, 551n3, 552n20, 552n22
Murray, John ("Damnation"), 26–33, 37, 47, 515n7, 516n12
Murray, John ("Salvation"), 27, 29, 112–13
Murray, Robert C, 342–43
Muslims, 9, 91, 116, 127, 217, 223, 267, 457, 496. *See also* Koran
My Progress in Error (Alcott), 295, 297, 308–9, 557–58n2, 560n33

Napoleon, 154, 331
Narrative of Colonel Ethan Allen's Captivity (Allen), 33–35, 37–39, 516n29, 516n32
Nashoba, Tennessee, 277, 279, 282–85
National Intelligencer (Washington, D.C.), 134, 239
nationalism, 32, 38, 273, 310, 364, 405–6, 420, 478–79
Christian, 393–94, 442, 444–45, 451, 456
Confederate, 393, 440
and Methodism, 442–46, 477, 528n60, 583n12
and Puritanism, 445
secular, 395, 442, 477
and the War of 1812, 20
See also civil religion
Native Americans, 107, 207, 443, 446, 449, 505, 583n9
Nelson, David, 207, 313, 483, 545n2, 550n43, 553n36
and Marion College, 156, 194–95, 227–30, 232, 236–38, 247–49, 550n45, 551n3, 552n20
and religious skepticism, 156, 194–95, 215–226, 228, 549–50n40, 550n45, 554n37
and slavery, 195, 228–29, 236–37
New Divinity, 42, 47, 200–203, 205, 518n46, 547n22
New England Antislavery Association, 272
New France, 29
New Harmony, Indiana, 277, 279–80, 282–83, 285, 301, 501
New Lights, 31, 47, 539n6. *See also* evangelicals
New Jerusalem (Swedenborgian) Church, 22, 99, 118, 120, 533–34n29, 534n32, 535n44
and deism, 130–43
New Themes for the Protestant Clergy (Colwell), 361
Newton, Isaac, 99, 222, 267, 269, 484–85, 589n13
Newton, John, 539n6
New York City Almshouse and Hospital, 196, 245
New York Evangelical Missionary Society of Young Men, 546n15
Nicholas, Cyrus, 229
Nisbet, E.A., 417, 434
North, Frederick (Lord), 40
Norton, Andrews, 157, 251, 255–56, 258–67, 269, 271, 555n16
Notes on the State of Virginia (Jefferson), 32, 127, 139, 181
Nott, Josiah, 425–26
Nullification Crisis, 395, 397, 403, 406, 410–12, 415, 424, 432, 576n29, 578n47
Nullification Party, 395, 397

Offen, Benjamin, 281, 293, 378–80
O'Flaherty, Thomas J., 323

O'Kelly, James, 70, 82–85
Olmsted, Charles G., 480
Owen, Isaac, 448
Owen, Robert, 12, 204, 214, 288, 301–2, 360, 484, 565n14
    and New Harmony, Indiana, 280, 282–83, 285, 301
Owen, Robert Dale, 16, 301, 304, 323, 483–86, 504–5, 559n19
    debate with Origen Bacheler, 1, 5, 8, 12, 293, 483, 485, 511n1
    and the *Free Enquirer*, 1, 8, 280–81, 285–86, 288, 290–91, 293, 336, 485, 511n1
    and freethought, 212, 279–80, 281, 286–93, 310, 334, 336–38, 362, 378, 484–85, 504–5, 559n19, 566–67n28
    and Nashoba, Tennessee, 277, 279, 281–85
    and New Harmony, Indiana, 277, 279–80, 281–83, 285, 301
    and Spiritualism, 17, 485–86
    See also freethinkers; Nashoba, Tennessee; New Harmony, Indiana; socialism; Wright, Frances
Oxford University, 161, 186, 534n32

Paine, Thomas, 95–96, 118, 132, 194, 214, 224, 250, 301, 315, 356, 421, 484, 535n47, 556n30, 591n25
    and *The Age of Reason*, 6, 94, 114, 120, 135, 198, 217, 267, 362, 372, 382, 528n5, 554n4
    and *Common Sense*, 489
    criticism of, 66, 95–96, 99, 121, 133, 137, 140, 143, 328–29, 362, 368, 426, 451, 483, 504
    and deism, 6, 14, 22–23, 99–100, 114, 117, 135, 140, 143–44, 266, 281, 296, 480
    and the French Revolution, 14, 99, 126, 129, 137
    and religious liberty, 117, 125–26
    and *The Rights of Man*, 126
Paley, William, 303–4, 351, 360, 382
Palmer, Benjamin M., 422, 578n41
Palmer, Elihu, 98, 128–30, 132, 137, 139–40, 372, 382, 484
    on the American and French Revolutions, 97
    criticism of, 22, 111, 137, 489, 528n9
    and deism, 22–23, 97, 99–106, 109–12, 114–17, 118–21, 124, 129, 131, 135, 137, 143, 313, 531–32n11
    publications of, 100, 102, 143, 528n8
    and slavery, 119
    and Universalism, 109–12, 115–17
Panic of 1819, 275
Panic of 1837, 233, 239, 326, 344, 381
Paris Society of Theophilanthropists, 114
Parker, Samuel, 344
Parker, Theodore, 251, 254, 264–67, 271–73, 499
Parsons, Jonathan, 31
partialism, 16
Pattillo, Henry, 27, 63
Patton, William W., 148–49
Payne, Daniel, 148
Peabody, Mary, 569n49
Peck, George, 454
Peck, Thomas E., 439
Pelagians, 88
Pennington, James W.C., 146
People of New York v. Ruggles (1811), 343
perfectionism, 16, 204, 273
Petigru, James L., 410
Philadelphian, 206–7, 209–12, 214, 228, 234, 246, 547n24, 548n27
Philadelphia Theophilanthropic Society, 114–15
Phillips, Elizabeth Kauffman, 442
    in California, 447, 449, 451, 585n37
    and George Shane Phillips, 395, 452–56, 459, 585nn36–37
Phillips, George Shane, 582n2, 583n11, 586n81
    in California, 447–52
    and Elizabeth Kauffman Phillips, 395, 452–56, 459, 585nn36–37
    and nationalism, 395, 441–46, 456–59, 477–78, 582n9
    and religious skepticism, 446
    and slavery, 451–52, 459
phrenology, 186, 295, 348–50, 352, 504, 569n54
physiology, 178, 186, 280, 294, 299, 305, 320, 349, 561n60
Pierce, Isaac B., 566n22, 568n38
Pillsbury, Parker, 313, 317
Pinckney, Charles Cotesworth, 424
Pinfold, Charles, 49
Pitman, Charles, 373–74
Pleasant Ridge College, 469
polytheism, 32, 123
Pope, Alexander, 54, 372, 382,
Porter, Abner A. 414, 426
Potts, William S., 238–39, 551n3
Powel, John Hare, 213, 549n34
Pratt, Edwin G., 230
Presbyterian Church of the Confederate States, 578n46
Presbyterians, 20, 23, 27–29, 81, 180, 189, 196, 199, 332–33, 418–19, 547n24
    African-American, 149, 537n59
    criticism of, 130, 156, 190–92, 332–33, 544n60
    divisions among, 47, 201–2, 205–6, 214–15, 325, 420–22, 553–54n36, 582n79
    growth and decline of, 208, 210, 415–16, 545n5, 577n37

and Marion College, 156, 227–29, 232, 236–39, 241, 244, 247–49
in New England, 28–29, 47
and politics, 193, 210–13, 227, 399, 411, 413–16, 422–25, 436–40, 539n8
and religious skepticism, 418, 426–27, 436, 480
and religious toleration, 126–27, 193–94, 210–11, 403–4, 438–40
and Slavery, 146–47, 236–39, 395, 398–99, 415, 425–36, 439–40, 578n47
in South Carolina, 190, 397–99, 402–4, 410–11, 413–16, 580n62
Presbyterian Theological Seminary, 398, 416
Pressley, Samuel P., 410, 576n26, 577n33
Pressly, John M., 410, 576n26
Price, Richard, 126, 151
Priestley, Elizabeth, 161, 540n4
Priestley, Joseph, 118, 137, 335
and Thomas Cooper, 161–62, 178, 180–81, 335, 402, 404, 540nn6–7, 541n13
Princeton University, 421
Principles of Nature (Palmer), 97, 100, 102, 105, 128, 140, 372
prison reform, 207, 377, 566n28
Proofs of a Conspiracy against all the Religions and Governments of Europe (Robison), 120, 129
Prospect (New York City), 100–102, 104–5, 114, 143
Puritans, 2, 5, 17, 28, 42, 298, 337, 352
and American nationalism, 443–45, 583n9, 583n12
descendants of, 157, 352
and liberty, 29, 423
See also Calvinism; Congregationalists
Purser, George, 378

Quakers, 107, 110, 180, 252, 298, 353, 498
Hicksite, 212, 352
and religious toleration, 29, 112, 117
Quebec Act, 39

Rapp, George, 282–83
Rawle, William, 164–65
Raymond, Charles A., 146
Reason the Only Oracle of Man (Allen), 2, 21, 25, 33–38, 62, 514n1, 515n2, 516–17n23, 517n24
critiques of, 25–26, 41–42
Redrick (enslaved man), 284
reform. *See* education reform; evangelicals; health reform; labor movement; prison reform; slavery; women's rights movement
Reformation, 97–98, 259, 351, 354, 416–17, 496, 570n63
reformed theology. *See* Calvinism

Reid, Thomas, 340, 351, 515n5, 547n22
Reign of Terror. *See* French Revolution, Reign of Terror
religion
definitions of, 8–11, 20, 513–14n2
institutionalization of, 97–151
See also church and state; civil religion; religious liberty
religious liberty, 23, 96, 112, 117, 191, 210–11, 383, 411
and the American Revolution, 31
and civil liberty, 28, 60, 193, 406
in the Confederate constitution, 438–39
and deism, 26–27, 32, 61, 64, 125–28
and religious skepticism, 21, 121, 125–28, 181, 191, 356, 404
and religious toleration, 31–32, 125–26
and the separation of church and state, 342–43, 399, 403–4
Reply to Mr. Burke's Invective (Cooper), 161, 543n40
Republicanism, 8, 98, 100, 130, 423–24
Republican Methodist Church, 83–84, 91
Republican Party (Jefferson), 159, 163, 176–77, 543–44n44, 565n9
and Christian Enlightenment, 155–56
debates with Federalists, 22, 108, 120–21
and deism, 22–23, 140, 327–28
and religious freedom, 126
See also Democratic-Republican Societies; Jefferson, Thomas
Republican Party (Lincoln), 465
revivals, 5–7, 143, 190, 212, 293, 325, 394, 445, 453, 457, 512n10
army camp, 478
eighteenth century, 29, 31
and enthusiasm, 20, 105, 497
Methodist, 68, 85–86, 91–92, 96, 357, 384, 446, 462, 465, 522n6
and millennialism, 207, 331, 347, 482
and nationalism, 32, 482
and nullification, 415, 424, 432
and reform, 7, 14, 200, 214–15, 226–27, 236, 248, 286, 304, 553n36
Rhett, Robert Barnwell, 424
Rice, John Holt, 189, 416, 548–49n33
Richardson, James, 284
Ripley, George, 157, 259–65, 269, 339, 568n36
Roberts, William, 447–48
Robespierre, Maximilien, 22, 159. *See also* French Revolution, Reign of Terror
Robison, John, 120–23, 128–29
Rogers, Henry, 484
Rogers, Hester Ann, 523n16, 524n47
Roland, 301
Romantics, 3, 157, 361, 372, 483
Root, Daniel H., 468

Rose, Ernestine, 280, 312, 314, 378, 489, 563n75
  critique of the Bible and patriarchy, 277, 279, 281, 315–322, 563n85
Rose, William E., 280
Rosecrans, William, 586n81
Rousseau, Jean-Jacques, 94, 99, 105, 270, 368, 426, 573n2
Royall, Anne, 212
Rutter, J.P., 553n24
Ryan, Thomas, 431

Sabbatarianism, 109, 128, 193, 207, 212–14, 233, 286, 290
  and Anti-Sabbatarians, 212, 214
  legislative efforts, 334, 409, 566n19
  and the post office, 228, 409, 566n19
Sabellianism, 201
Sancho, Ignatius, 187
Sancho (enslaved man), 432, 544n54
Sargent, Lucius M., 341, 568n36
Satterlee, Samuel, 183
Saybrook Platform, 60
Scarlett, David (brother), 374
Scarlett, David (uncle), 373
Scarlett, John, 278, 370–81, 382, 570n2, 572n35
  conversion of, 357–58, 376, 379, 390
  economic prospects of, 363, 371, 373–74, 390
  and religious skepticism, 359, 363, 374, 377–79, 389–90
  sanctification, 376
Scarlett, Mary, 373
Schaff, Philip, 458
Schlatter, William, 142
Schleiermacher, Friedrich, 260, 265
Scott, John W., 206, 547n24
Scott, Thomas, 218, 550n43
Scott's Family Bible (Scott), 194, 218, 550n43
Scranton, Erastus, 562n64
Scripture Doctrine of Materialism, The (Cooper), 403
"Second Great Awakening," 5. *See also* reform; revivals
secularization/secularism, 5–6, 11, 346, 356, 485, 491, 511–12n9
Seneca, 150, 374, 523–24n19
Shaftesbury, Third Earl of (Anthony Ashley Cooper), 30, 180, 516n12
Shakers, 208, 252, 302, 335
Shakespeare, William, 54, 426, 519n59
Shays's Rebellion, 41
Shelley, Percy Bysshe, 372, 382, 483
Sherman, Josiah, 25–26, 41–43, 517n36
Silliman, Benjamin, 406–7, 485
Simpson, David, 151
skepticism and faith, 1–8, 10–17, 53, 195, 351, 354, 356, 480, 483, 488, 491, 493–96

Skidmore, Thomas, 292, 362
slavery, 6, 160–61, 192, 195, 198, 304, 345, 358–59, 363, 387–88, 390
  and antislavery, 5, 17, 22, 70–71, 85, 89, 104, 119, 160, 187–88, 205, 214, 228, 236–37, 269, 272–73, 276, 313–15, 345, 383, 421, 443, 446–47, 451–52, 464–65, 474, 523n14
  and the Civil War, 394–95, 415–16, 433–34, 439–40, 441, 443, 451–52, 465, 469–70, 473–76, 479, 482, 490, 579–80n59
  and colonization, 207, 214, 236–47, 283–85, 297, 429, 474–75
  and Marion College, 234–40, 242–43, 248
  Methodism and, 68–71, 80, 85, 88–89, 325, 385–86, 388, 415, 432, 447, 451–52, 523n14, 544n54, 581n71
  and missions to slaves, 147–48, 385–86, 415, 429, 433–34
  and Nashoba, Tennessee, 283–86
  and the Nullification Crisis, 395, 397, 403, 406, 410–12, 415, 424, 432, 576n29, 578n47
  Presbyterianism and, 147–48, 236–39, 325, 395, 398–99, 415, 425–36, 439–40, 578n47, 581n71
  and proslavery, 3, 5, 17, 70–71, 142, 148–49, 160, 186, 195, 228, 236, 239, 272, 345–46, 361, 394–95, 397–99, 421, 427, 430–36, 440, 443, 574n4, 579–80n59, 580–81n67, 586n64
  and race, 177–80, 186–88, 351, 542–43n33, 579n56, 579–80n59
  and religious skepticism among the enslaved, 146–51, 536n53
  and sectional division, 190, 325, 394–95, 405, 443, 469–70
  and the slave trade, 178–80, 188, 388, 434–46
  See also African Americans; names of enslaved individuals
Sleigh, William, 12, 567n29
Smith, Adam, 172, 360, 571n7
Smith, Elias, 547n24
Smith, James, 480, 481, 488
Smith, Joseph, 496. *See also* Book of Mormon; Mormons
Smyth, Margaret, 432
Smyth, Samuel, 432
Smyth, Thomas, 419–21, 423–24, 434, 439
  and race, 425, 427, 434, 579n56
  and slavery, 398, 421, 423, 425, 427–30, 432, 580n65
Snyder, Mima, 465–67
Snyder, Simon, 184, 543–44n44
socialism, 352, 382–83, 386
  and religious skepticism, 324, 332, 334, 362, 388, 434
  and Robert Dale Owen, 280, 283, 334, 360, 390–91

Society for Christian Union and Progress, 339
Society for Supporting the Gospel among the Poor in the City of New York, 246
Society for the Purpose of Effecting the Abolition of the Slave Trade, 178
Society of Free Enquirers, 337, 339, 341–42, 345, 566n28
Society of Moral Philanthropists, 293, 378, 383
Society of Universal Baptists, 112
Socinianism, 98, 201, 209–11
Some Doubts Respecting the Death, Resurrection, and Ascension of Jesus Christ (Fellows), 118
Sons of Temperance, 451
South Carolina College, 212, 413–14, 426, 436
 and Thomas Cooper, 159, 177, 188, 190, 212, 395, 397–402, 416
Southcote, Johanna, 408
Southern Presbyterian Review, 414, 418, 426, 430, 435–36
Spencer, Eliza, 240, 243
Spencer, Jesse, 240
Spencer, Matilda, 240, 243
Spencer, William, 79, 82–83
Spinoza, Benedict, 265, 575n17
Spirit-Rapper, The (Brownson), 324, 352–55, 564n3
Spiritualism, 16–17, 326, 346, 355, 562–63n73, 563n75, 587n7
 at the Hartford Bible Convention, 281, 312–15
 and religious skepticism, 484–86, 488
 and *The Spirit-Rapper*, 352–55
Spring, Gardiner, 201–2, 546n14, 549n36
Spring, Samuel, 201
Stack, Richard, 537n64
states' rights, 397, 400, 405–6, 412, 576n24
 and the Confederate Constitution, 582n79
 and religion, 406, 410, 440
 and slavery, 394, 415
 and white supremacy, 394, 415
States' Rights Party, 400, 576n26
Stewart, Dugald, 425
Stiles, Ezra, 2–4, 7, 13, 58–62, 202, 519n59, 520n70
 and religious skepticism, 2–4, 7, 13, 47, 58–62
 and William Beadle, 52, 55, 61
Stillman, William, 313
Storrs, George, 313–14, 322
Stowe, Harriett Beecher, 148, 272
Strauss, David, 258, 267, 271, 427
St. Simon, Henri de, 302
Stuart, Moses, 257–58
Swedenborg, Emanuel, 131–35, 137, 312, 533–34n29
Swedenborgians. *See* New Jerusalem (Swedenborgian) Church
Swift, Zephaniah, 61, 520–21n72
Symonds, Thomas, 39–40

Tammany Hall, 108, 281, 292–93, 378–80, 383
Taylor, Nathaniel William, 214
Taylor, Robert, 301, 382–83
Taylor, William, 448–50, 457–59, 483
temperance, 193, 233, 235, 269, 276, 320, 341, 373–74, 383, 446–49, 451
 and Christian Enlightenment, 207, 228, 301, 334, 457
Temple, William, 53–54, 519n58
Temple of Reason (New York City; Philadelphia), 100, 102–4, 114–15, 118, 129–30, 139–40, 142, 528n11, 533n23, 535n43
Temple of Truth (Baltimore), 118, 130–33, 139, 533n23
Tertium Quids, 543–44n44
Thayer, John, 539n6
Theistical Society of New York, 128–30
Theory of Legislation (Bentham), 269
Théroigne de Méricourt, Anne-Josèphe, 186
Thomas, Isaiah, 46
Thomson, James, 54, 56, 58
Thornwell, James Henley, 424, 578nn46–47
 and the Bible, 418–21, 425, 436–37
 and church and state, 418–21, 436–39
 conversion of, 398
 and race, 425–27, 579n59
 and religious skepticism, 418–19, 425, 434
 and slavery, 425–29, 431–32, 434, 579n59, 580n65, 580–81n67
 and Thomas Cooper, 397–98, 421
Tocqueville, Alexis de, 5, 107, 272
Toland, John, 30, 516n12
Toleration Acts (Great Britain), 136
Tracts Ethical, Theological, and Political (Cooper), 161, 180
Transcendental Club, 259
Transcendentalists, 3, 258, 259–73, 296, 324, 340, 350, 352, 361, 499
 debates with Trinitarians and Unitarians, 157–58, 251, 259–60, 264–67
 as "infidels," 157
Transylvania University, 404
Trinitarians, 4, 61, 131, 257, 304, 332, 342, 439, 568n39
 debates with Unitarians, 16, 181, 250, 252, 264, 337, 339
 and Transcendentalists, 264, 266–67
Trinity College, 314
Triumph of Infidelity (Dwight), 41, 47, 518n48
Turner, Elisha M., 313, 320–21
Turner, Nat, 428
Two Lectures on the Connection between the Biblical and Physical History of Man (Nott), 426
Two Sermons on Infidelity (Channing), 253

Uncle Tom's Cabin (Stowe), 148, 272, 537n58
Union army, 395, 475, 478

Union College, 499
Union Fire Company, 107
Union Theological Seminary, 439
Unitarians, 110, 137, 143, 158, 162, 200, 255, 278, 298, 301–3, 349, 352, 498–99, 571n7
    debates with Trinitarians, 16, 157, 191, 205, 250, 263–64, 337–39, 366, 404, 408, 439, 520–21n72, 539n6, 587n4
    at Harvard, 157, 255, 258
    and religious skepticism, 178, 181, 192, 210, 212, 250–52, 258, 267, 271, 295, 302–3, 309–10, 338, 342, 568n39
    Thomas Jefferson's prediction regarding, 191–92
    and Transcendentalists, 157, 251, 258–64, 266–67, 271–72, 324
Universal Church, 109, 111, 115
Universalists, 16, 64, 276, 278, 311, 330–31, 345, 523n16
    Abner Kneeland and, 323, 334–35, 342, 345
    and Calvinists, 7–8, 29–30, 47, 201, 210–12, 519n51
    and deism, 22, 27–28, 30, 32–33, 48–49, 98–99, 106–17, 142–43, 147, 433
    Orestes Brownson and, 278, 324, 327, 332, 333–34, 352, 366
    and religious liberty, 143, 211–12
    William Alcott and, 295–96, 298, 301–2, 309
Universal Society, 109–11
University of Glasgow, 283
University of Pennsylvania, 168, 484, 544n57
University of Virginia, 189, 397
U.S. Constitution, 83, 108, 162, 194, 363–64, 404–6, 411, 420, 583n7, 589n11
    and the Bible, 395, 397–98
    as a Christian document, 14, 193–94, 444–45
    First Amendment, 10, 20, 61, 117, 128, 212, 344, 383, 576n23
    and religious freedom, 126–28, 164, 209–12, 344, 383, 409, 411, 423
    and slavery, 398, 405–6, 435, 444, 474–76, 582n79
utilitarianism, 186, 345, 360, 427, 542–43n33
    Frances Wright and, 283, 286
    Richard Hildreth and, 158, 251, 264, 269–71

Vale, Gilbert, 378
vegetarianism, 280, 294, 300. *See also* health reform
Vesey, Denmark, 187, 402, 428–29
Views of Society and Manners in America (Wright), 279, 283
Vigilance Committee, 272, 457
Villeneuve-Bargemont, Alban de, 361
Virgil, 220, 363
Virginia and Kentucky Resolutions Act, 405

Virginia Statute for Religious Freedom, 23, 61, 117, 439
Volney, Comte de, 94–95, 118, 194, 217–18, 344, 372, 382, 480, 575n17
Voltaire, 47, 99, 118, 199, 224, 261, 315, 353, 368, 382, 426, 483
    and Abner Kneeland, 337, 341, 344,
    and David Nelson, 194, 217–18, 549–50n40
    and Jeremiah Minter, 94–95
    and Richard Hildreth, 268, 270
    and William Alcott, 301, 303
    and William Miller, 328
voodoo (vodun), 147

Walker, Edward, 527n54
Walker, James (Trinitarian), 267
Walker, James (Unitarian), 267
Walker, Thomas, 162
Ware, Thomas, 68
War of 1812, 20, 140–41, 172, 194, 216, 329, 371, 405, 565n9
Washington, George, 22, 39, 108, 138, 318, 374, 376, 441, 475, 485
    and freemasonry, 121, 123
    memory of, 62, 363–64, 444, 451, 472
    and religious liberty, 126
    and religious skepticism, 19
Washington College, 215
Watson, Richard, 382
Wayland, Francis, 209, 360–61, 571n7
Wealth of Nations (Smith), 172, 360
Weber, Max, 516n13
Webster, Daniel, 443, 475
Weishaupt, Adam, 123
Weld, Theodore Dwight, 236
Wesley, Charles, 79
Wesley, John, 74, 79, 84, 119, 445, 524–25n19, 525n32
    critiques of Emmanuel Swedenborg, 133
    and slavery, 69, 459
    and supernaturalism, 78, 527n51
    theology of, 65, 76, 88, 366, 455, 525n29
Westminster Confession of Faith, 206, 398, 409–10
Wheatley, Phillis, 187
Whig Party, 8, 29, 214, 269, 324, 345, 350, 361, 445–46, 488
Whiskey Rebellion, 108, 161, 164
Whitaker, Nathaniel, 28, 30–31
Whitby, Richeson, 284
Whitefield, George, 29, 331, 367
white supremacy, 161, 177, 394, 415, 429
Whitman, Walt, 118
Whittelsey, Chauncy, 52
Wilde, Samuel, 344
Wilkes, Peter, 441, 470–72
Wilkinson, Jemima, 408

Williams, Susannah, 69, 80
Williams, William R., 494–95
Wilmer, James J., 133, 135, 534n32
Wilson, John Lyde, 403
Winchester, Elhanan, 112
Witherell, James, 565n9
Wollstonecraft, Mary, 186, 291, 301, 306, 352
Women's Missionary Society of the Pacific Coast, 585n37
women's rights movement, 186, 277, 279, 281, 312, 316–17, 320–21, 352
Wood, John, 120–21, 127–30, 531n11, 533n23
Woodbridge, William C., 304–5
Woodward, S.B., 295
Workingmen's movement, 8, 324, 337, 340, 344, 370, 566–67n28, 568n35, 570n57
  and the Workingmen's Party, 287–88, 292–93, 337, 339
Wright, Camilla, 283–84
Wright, Frances, 214, 277, 301–2, 304, 306, 313, 323, 352, 558n7, 565n14
  and freethought, 212, 279–80, 281, 286–93, 310, 334, 336–38, 362, 378, 484–85, 559n19
  and Nashoba, Tennessee, 277, 279, 281–85
  and New Harmony, Indiana, 277, 279–80, 281–83, 285, 301
  proposal to privatize religion, 286–87, 290
  and slavery, 283–86
  See also freethinkers; Nashoba, Tennessee; New Harmony, Indiana; Owen, Robert Dale
Wright, Henry C., 313
Wright, Theodore S., 149
Wright, Uriel, 237–38
Wylie, Samuel B., 126–27

Yale College, 4, 26, 59, 122, 195, 201–2, 250–51, 299, 406, 480, 485
Young, John C., 219
Young, Thomas, 33, 516n19
Young Man's Guide (Alcott), 294, 305
Young Men's Missionary Society of New York, 546n15